5
F
G
H
J
K
BUCKTON MOOR
Micklehurst
Overgreen
Intake Cott.
Micklehurst Brook
HUDDERSFIELD RD.
HUDDERSFIELD ROAD
MOOR EDGE ROAD
CASTLE LANE
Buckton Castle
Buckton Vale Quarry
Castle Clough
Staly Brook
Castle Farm
Heyheads
HEYHEADS NEW RD.
B6175
Pav.
Ckt. Grd.
Carr
Moorgate
STALYBRIDGE COUNTRY PARK
Near Harehill Clough
Reservoir
Cowbury Dale
Carr Brook
Iron Tongue
Clough
Reservoirs
Buckton Grange
Buckton Vale
Buckton Vale Prim. Sch.
Carrbrook
BEACONSFIELD TER.
OAK VILLAS
LONG ROW
SOUTH VW.
CALICO
PRINTERS DR.
Shire Clough Farm
SLATEPIT MOOR
Fold Farm
THE FOLD
Winterhill Farm
Lwr. Little Bank Farm
Higher Littlebank Farm
SWINESHAW MOOR
Wicken Spring
Wicken Spring Clough
TURF PITS
Stalybridge
SK15
Harridge Hall
Hill Top
Millbrook Prim. Sch.
St. Raphael's Catholic Prim. Sch.
Resr.
Higher Hydegreen
Harridge Pike
Lwr. Hyde Green Fm.
Heritage House
SUN GREEN
Cooper Farm
HARRIDGE
Dry Clough
Higher Swineshaw Reservoir
Oakwood
Cote Farm
Millbrook
Brushes
BRUSHES ROAD
BRUSHES
Brushes Reservoir
Walkerwood Reservoir
Swineshaw Brook
Lower Swineshaw Reservoir
STALYBRIDGE COUNTRY PARK
Cock Wood
COCK KNARR
Range Ho.
Reservoir
PACK SADDLE
Flaxfield
WILD BANK
11
HOLLINGWORTHHALL MOOR
1
2
3
4
5
6
7
98
99
400
02
01
400
99

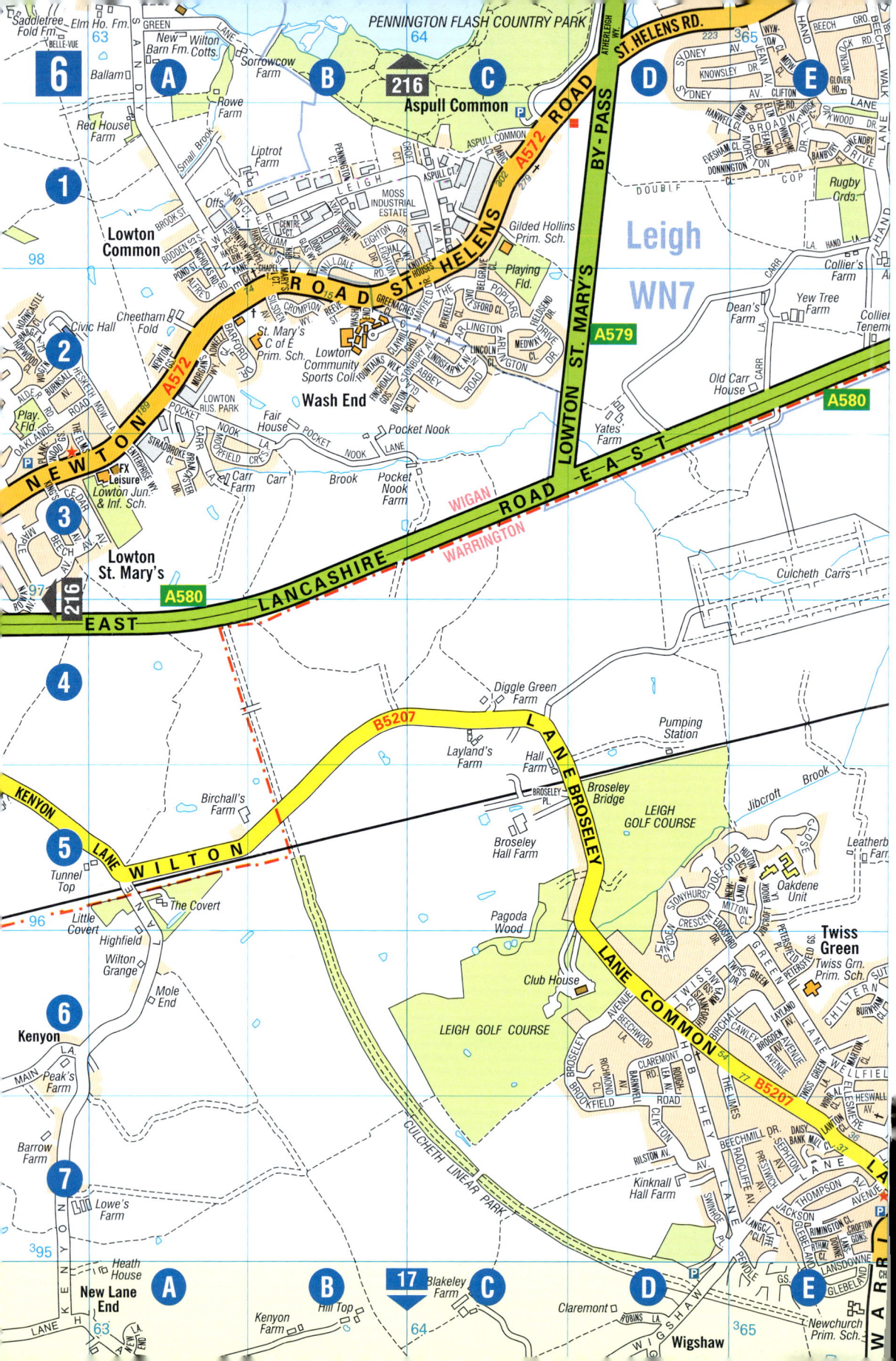
6
PENNINGTON FLASH COUNTRY PARK
216
Aspull Common
ST. HELENS RD.
Saddletree Fold Fm.
Elm Ho. Fm.
New Barn Fm.
Wilton Cotts.
Sorrowcow Farm
Ballam
Rowe Farm
Red House Farm
Liptrot Farm
Lowton Common
MOSS INDUSTRIAL ESTATE
Gilded Hollins Prim. Sch.
Playing Fld.
Leigh
WN7
Rugby Grds.
Collier's Farm
Yew Tree Farm
Dean's Farm
Old Carr House
Cheetham Fold
Civic Hall
St. Mary's C of E Prim. Sch.
Lowton Community Sports Coll.
Wash End
LOWTON BUS. PARK
Fair House
Pocket Nook
Yates' Farm
Carr Farm
Carr
Brook
Pocket Nook Farm
FX Leisure
Lowton Jun. & Inf. Sch.
Lowton St. Mary's
WIGAN
WARRINGTON
EAST LANCASHIRE ROAD
A580
A572
A579
LOWTON ST. MARY'S BY-PASS
NEWTON ROAD
ST. HELENS ROAD
Culcheth Carrs
Diggle Green Farm
Pumping Station
Layland's Farm
Hall Farm
Broseley Bridge
B5207
BROSELEY LANE
WILTON LANE
KENYON LANE
Birchall's Farm
Broseley Hall Farm
LEIGH GOLF COURSE
Jibcroft Brook
Oakdene Unit
Leatherbarrow Farm
Tunnel Top
The Covert
Little Covert
Highfield
Wilton Grange
Mole End
Pagoda Wood
Club House
Twiss Green
Twiss Grn. Prim. Sch.
COMMON LANE
Kenyon
Peak's Farm
Barrow Farm
Lowe's Farm
CULCHETH LINEAR PARK
Kinknall Hall Farm
Heath House
New Lane End
Kenyon Farm
Hill Top
Blakeley Farm
17
Claremont
Wigshaw
Newchurch Prim. Sch.
WIGSHAW LANE
A B C D E
1 2 3 4 5 6 7
63 64 365
98 97 96 395

A-Z CHESHIRE

CONTENTS

REFERENCE

Motorway	**M6**
Primary Route	**A55**
Under Construction	
Proposed	
A Road	**A5104**
B Road	**B5129**
Dual Carriageway	
One-way Street	
Traffic flow on A Roads is also indicated by a heavy line on the driver's left.	
Restricted Access	
Pedestrianized Road	
Track / Footpath	
Residential Walkway	
Railway	Station / Level Crossing / Tunnel
Metrolink (LRT)	
The boarding of Metrolink trams at stops may be limited to a single direction, indicated by the arrow.	
Built-up Area	BUNCE ST.
National Boundary	+ + +
Local Authority Boundary	
National Park Boundary	
Posttown Boundary	
Postcode Boundary (within Posttown)	
Map Continuation	22 Large Scale Centres 212 Road Map Pages 216

Airport	✈
Car Park (Selected)	P
Church or Chapel	†
City Wall (Large Scale only)	
Cycleway (Selected)	
Fire Station	■
Hospital	H
House Numbers (A & B Roads only)	13 8
Information Centre	i
National Grid Reference	³25
Park & Ride	Sealand Road P+
Police Station	▲
Post Office	★
Toilet: without facilities for the Disabled with facilities for the Disabled	▽ ▽
Safety Camera with Speed Limit Fixed cameras and long term road works cameras Symbols do not indicate camera direction	30
Viewpoint	※ ☀
Educational Establishment	
Hospital or Healthcare Building	
Industrial Building	
Leisure or Recreational Facility	
Place of Interest	
Public Building	
Shopping Centre or Market	
Other Selected Buildings	

SCALE

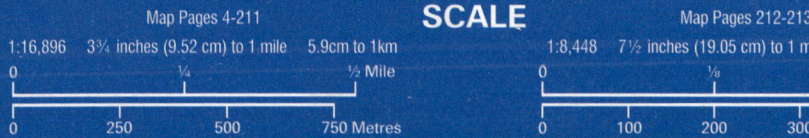

Map Pages 4-211	Map Pages 212-213
1:16,896 3¾ inches (9.52 cm) to 1 mile 5.9cm to 1km	1:8,448 7½ inches (19.05 cm) to 1 mile 11.8cm to 1km

Map Pages 4-211: 0 — ¼ — ½ Mile ; 0 — 250 — 500 — 750 Metres

Map Pages 212-213: 0 — ⅛ — ¼ Mile ; 0 — 100 — 200 — 300 — 400 Metres

Copyright of Geographers' A-Z Map Company Limited

Fairfield Road, Borough Green, Sevenoaks, Kent TN15 8PP
Telephone: 01732 781000 (Enquiries & Trade Sales)
01732 783422 (Retail Sales)
www.a-zmaps.co.uk
Copyright © Geographers' A-Z Map Co. Ltd.
EDITION 1   2009

OS Ordnance Survey® This product includes mapping data licensed from Ordnance Survey® with the permission of the Controller of Her Majesty's Stationery Office.
© Crown Copyright 2006. All rights reserved. Licence number 100017302
Safety camera information supplied by GPSWorld.com
Speed Camera Location Database Copyright 2008 © PocketGPSWorld.com

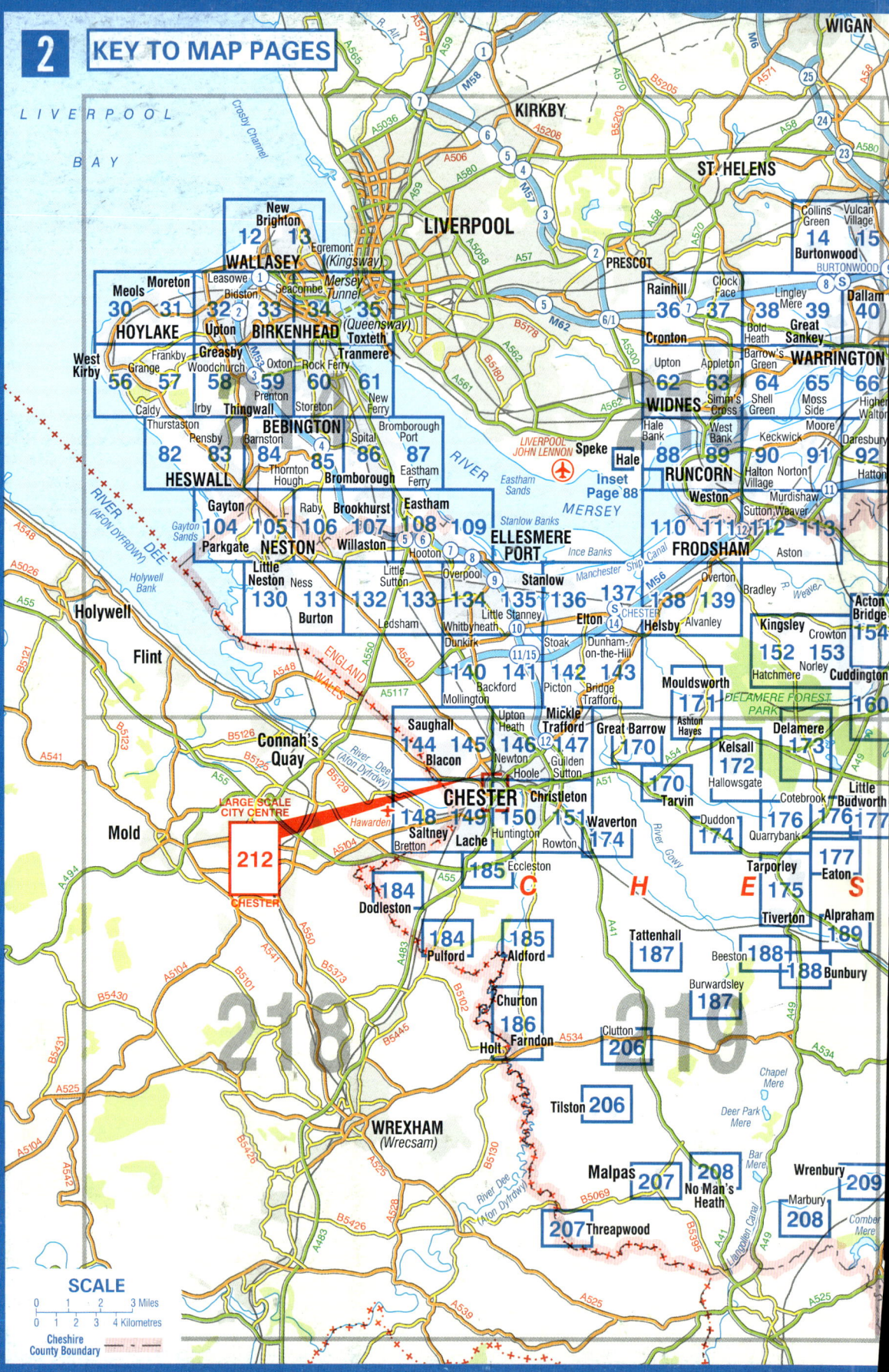

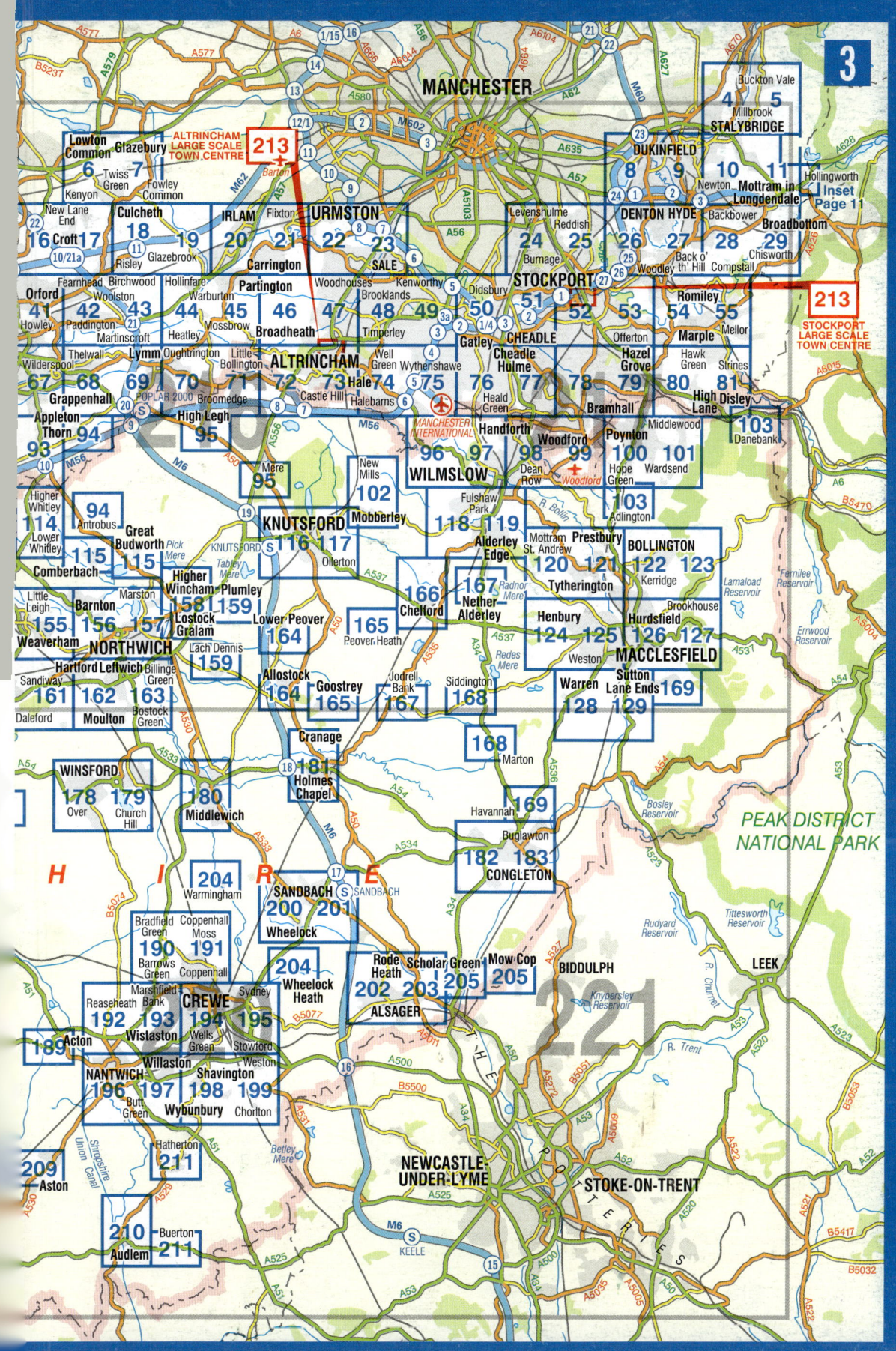
MANCHESTER
ALTRINCHAM LARGE SCALE TOWN CENTRE
213
Barton
Lowton Common
Glazebury
6
7
Twiss Green
Fowley Common
Kenyon
Buckton Vale
4
5
Millbrook
STALYBRIDGE
DUKINFIELD
8
9
10
11
Newton
Mottram in Longdendale
Hollingworth
Inset Page 11
New Lane End
Culcheth
IRLAM
Flixton
URMSTON
16
Croft
17
18
19
20
21
22
23
Risley
Glazebrook
Carrington
SALE
Levenshulme
Reddish
24
25
Burnage
DENTON
HYDE
Backbower
26
27
28
29
Broadbottom
Back o' th' Hill
Woodley
Compstall
Chisworth
Fearnhead
Birchwood
Hollinfare
Partington
Woodhouses
Kenworthy
Didsbury
STOCKPORT
Romiley
213
STOCKPORT LARGE SCALE TOWN CENTRE
Orford
41
Woolston
42
43
Warburton
44
45
46
47
Brooklands
48
49
50
51
52
53
54
55
Howley
Paddington
Martinscroft
Heatley
Mossbrow
Broadheath
Timperley
Gatley
CHEADLE
Offerton
Marple
Mellor
Thelwall
Lymm
Oughtrington
Little Bollington
ALTRINCHAM
Well Green
Wythenshawe
Cheadle Hulme
Hazel Grove
Hawk Green
Strines
Wilderspool
67
68
69
70
71
72
73
Hale
74
75
76
77
78
79
80
81
Grappenhall
POPLAR 2000
Broomedge
Castle Hill
Halebarns
Heald Green
Bramhall
High Lane
Disley
Appleton Thorn
94
High Legh
95
MANCHESTER INTERNATIONAL
Handforth
Woodford
Poynton
Middlewood
103
Danebank
93
96
97
98
99
100
101
WILMSLOW
Dean Row
Woodford
Hope Green
Wardsend
Mere
95
New Mills
102
Higher Whitley
94
114
Antrobus
Lower Whitley
Great Budworth
Pick Mere
KNUTSFORD
116
117
Mobberley
Fulshaw Park
118
119
R. Bollin
103
Adlington
Alderley Edge
Mottram St. Andrew
Prestbury
BOLLINGTON
120
121
122
123
Kerridge
Lamaload Reservoir
Fernilee Reservoir
115
115
Comberbach
Tabley Mere
Ollerton
Higher Wincham
Plumley
166
Chelford
167
Nether Alderley
Radnor Mere
Tytherington
Brookhouse
Little Leigh
Barnton
Marston
158
159
Lostock Gralam
155
156
157
Weaverham
NORTHWICH
Lower Peover
164
165
Peover Heath
Henbury
124
125
Hurdsfield
126
127
Weston
MACCLESFIELD
Erwood Reservoir
Redes Mere
Lach Dennis
159
Hartford
Leftwich
Billinge Green
Sandiway
161
162
163
Dalefood
Moulton
Bostock Green
Allostock
164
Goostrey
165
Jodrell Bank
167
Siddington
168
Warren
128
Sutton
Lane Ends
129
169
Cranage
181
Holmes Chapel
168
Marton
WINSFORD
178
179
Over
Church Hill
180
Middlewich
Havannah
169
Buglawton
182
183
CONGLETON
Bosley Reservoir
PEAK DISTRICT NATIONAL PARK
H
I
R
E
204
Warmingham
SANDBACH
200
201
Wheelock
SANDBACH
Bradfield Green
Coppenhall Moss
190
191
Barrows Green
Coppenhall
204
Wheelock Heath
Rode Heath
202
203
Scholar Green
205
Mow Cop
205
ALSAGER
BIDDULPH
Rudyard Reservoir
Tittesworth Reservoir
LEEK
R. Churnet
Knypersley Reservoir
221
Reaseheath
Marshfield Bank
192
193
Wistaston
CREWE
194
195
Sydney
Wells Green
Stowford
189
Acton
NANTWICH
Willaston
196
197
Butt Green
Shavington
198
199
Weston
Wybunbury
Chorlton
R. Trent
209
Aston
Hatherton
211
Shropshire Union Canal
Betley Mere
NEWCASTLE-UNDER-LYME
STOKE-ON-TRENT
THE POTTERIES
210
Audlem
Buerton
211
KEELE
M6
M56
M60
M62
M602
A6
A34
A50
A51
A52
A53
A54
A56
A57
A62
A500
A520
A523
A527
A529
A530
A533
A534
A535
A536
A537
A556
A577
A579
A580
A626
A627
A628
A635
A666
A670
A5005
A5009
A5035
A5051
A5103
A6015
A6104
B5032
B5051
B5053
B5074
B5077
B5237
B5417
B5470
B5500
1
2
3
4
5
6
7
8
9
10
11
12/1
13
14
15
16
17
18
19
20
21
22
23
24
25
26
27
1/15
10/21a
3a
1/4

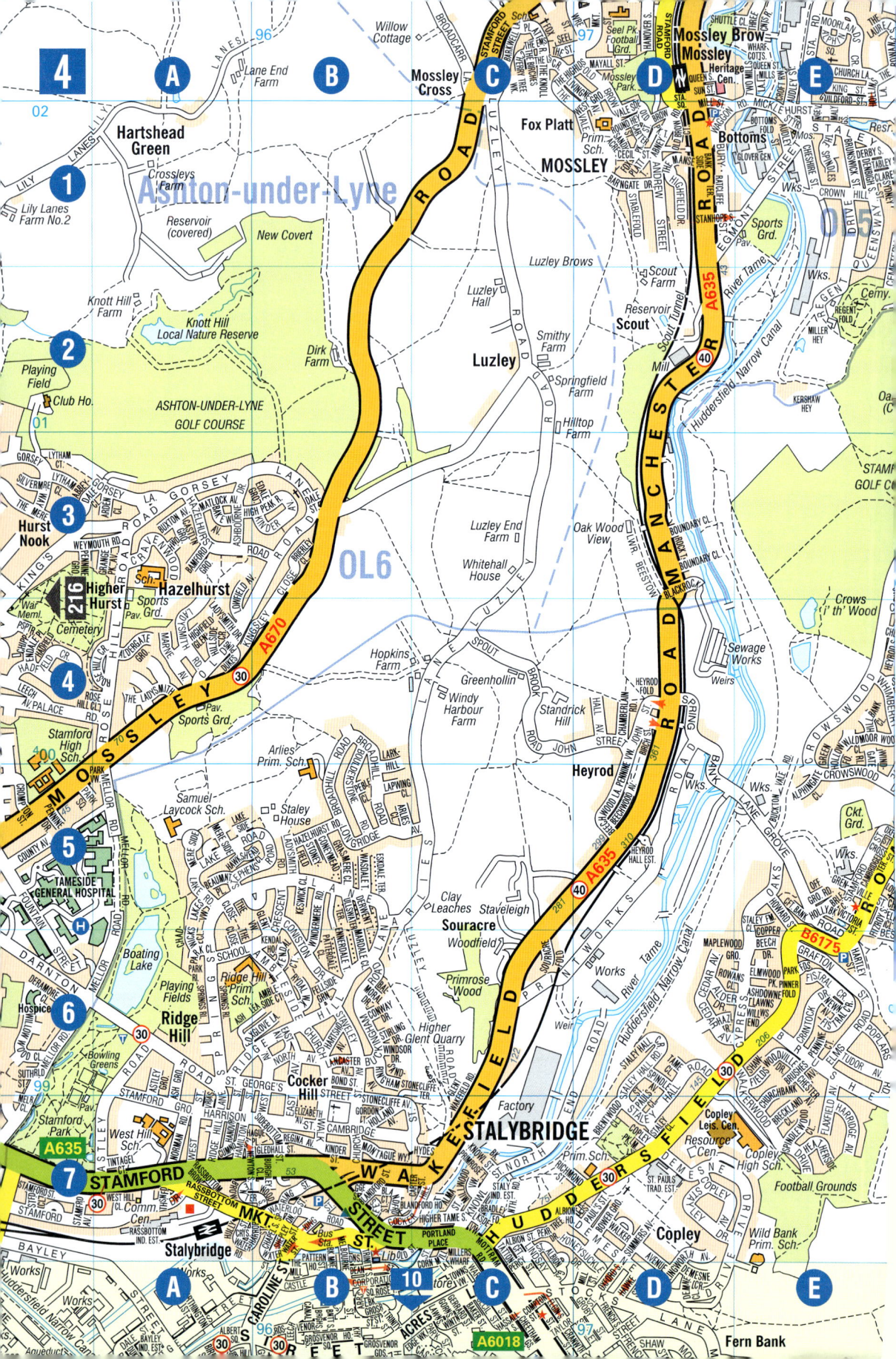
Ashton-under-Lyne
Hartshead Green
Crossleys Farm
Lily Lanes Farm No.2
Lane End Farm
Willow Cottage
Mossley Cross
Fox Platt
MOSSLEY
Mossley Brow
Mossley
Heritage Cen.
Bottoms
Reservoir (covered)
New Covert
Knott Hill Farm
Knott Hill Local Nature Reserve
Dirk Farm
Playing Field
Club Ho.
ASHTON-UNDER-LYNE GOLF COURSE
Luzley Brows
Luzley Hall
Smithy Farm
Luzley
Springfield Farm
Hilltop Farm
Scout Farm
Reservoir
Scout
Scout Tunnel
Huddersfield Narrow Canal
River Tame
Hurst Nook
Hazelhurst
Higher Hurst
Sports Grd.
Cemetery
War Meml.
OL6
OL5
Luzley End Farm
Whitehall House
Oak Wood View
Crows i' th' Wood
Sewage Works
Weirs
Hopkins Farm
Greenhollin
Windy Harbour Farm
Standrick Hill
Heyrod
Stamford High Sch.
Arlies Prim. Sch.
Samuel Laycock Sch.
Staley House
TAMESIDE GENERAL HOSPITAL
Boating Lake
Playing Fields
Ridge Hill
Ridge Hill Prim. Sch.
Hospice
Bowling Greens
Clay Leaches
Staveleigh
Souracre
Woodfield
Primrose Wood
Higher Glent Quarry
Cocker Hill
Stamford Park
West Hill Sch.
Factory
STALYBRIDGE
Stalybridge
Copley
Copley Leis. Cen.
Copley High Sch.
Football Grounds
Wild Bank Prim. Sch.
Fern Bank
Ckt. Grd.
MOSSLEY ROAD
MANCHESTER ROAD
WAKEFIELD ROAD
HUDDERSFIELD ROAD
STAMFORD STREET
MKT. STREET
A670
A635
A6018
B6175
216
10

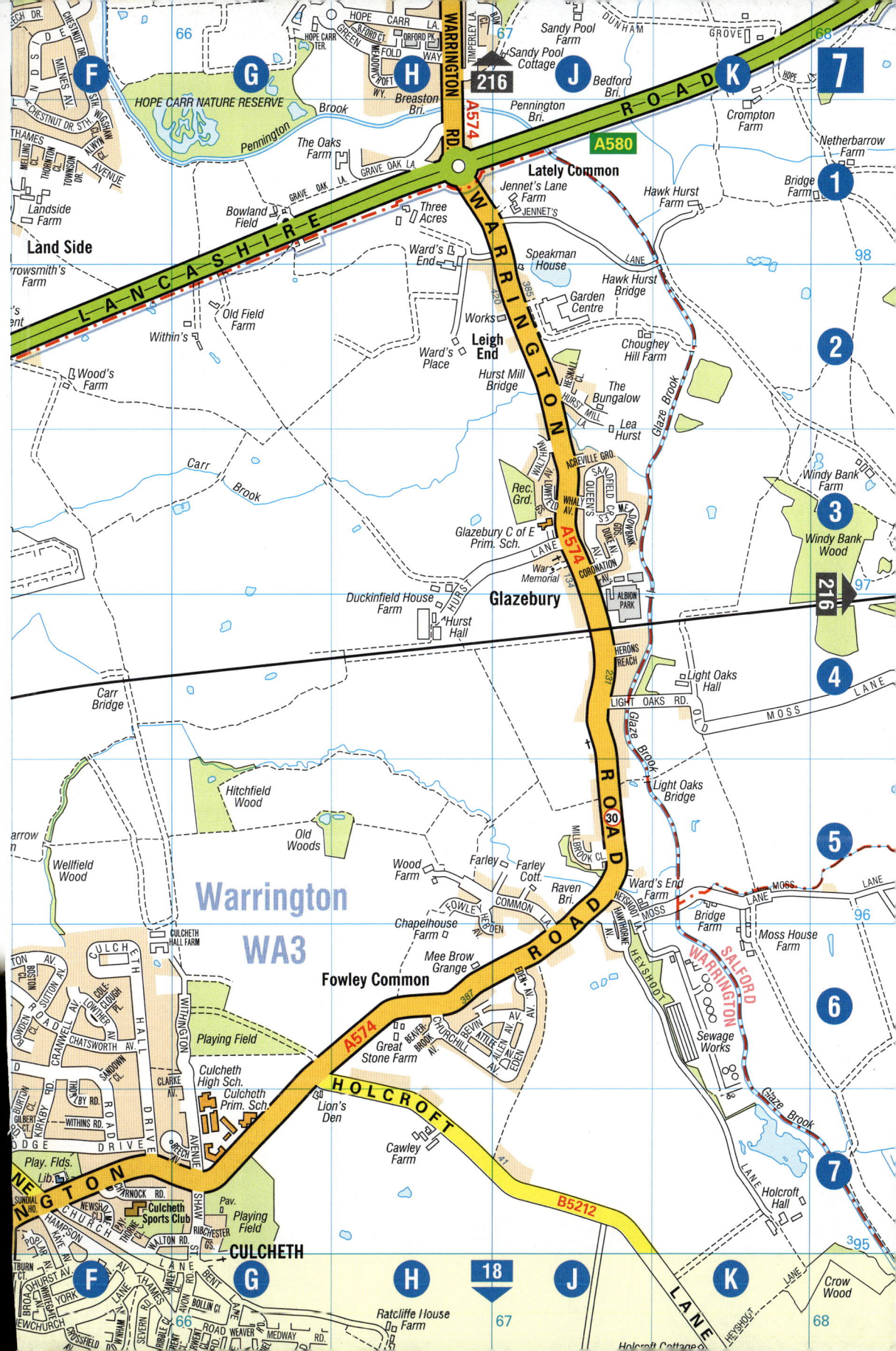

7
HOPE CARR LA.
HOPE CARR NATURE RESERVE
Pennington Brook
Breaston Bri.
WARRINGTON RD.
A574
216
Sandy Pool Farm
Sandy Pool Cottage
Bedford Bri.
Pennington Bri.
LANCASHIRE ROAD
A580
Crompton Farm
Netherbarrow Farm
Bridge Farm
The Oaks Farm
GRAVE OAK LA.
Lately Common
Jennet's Lane Farm
JENNET'S LANE
Hawk Hurst Farm
Bowland Field
Three Acres
Landside Farm
Land Side
Ward's End
Speakman House
Hawk Hurst Bridge
Garden Centre
Old Field Farm
Withins
Works
Leigh End
Ward's Place
Choughey Hill Farm
Wood's Farm
Hurst Mill Bridge
The Bungalow
Lea Hurst
Glaze Brook
Carr Brook
Rec. Grd.
Glazebury C of E Prim. Sch.
War Memorial
Windy Bank Farm
Windy Bank Wood
Duckinfield House Farm
HURST LANE
Hurst Hall
Glazebury
ALBION PARK
HERONS REACH
Light Oaks Hall
LIGHT OAKS RD.
OLD MOSS LANE
Carr Bridge
Hitchfield Wood
Light Oaks Bridge
Old Woods
Wellfield Wood
WARRINGTON ROAD
30
MILLBROOK CL.
Wood Farm
Farley
Farley Cott.
Raven Bri.
Ward's End Farm
Warrington WA3
FOWLEY COMMON LA.
Chapelhouse Farm
MOSS LANE
Bridge Farm
Moss House Farm
SALFORD
WARRINGTON
CULCHETH HALL FARM
Mee Brow Grange
Fowley Common
HEYSHOOT LA.
Sewage Works
Playing Field
Great Stone Farm
Culcheth High Sch.
Culcheth Prim. Sch.
HOLCROFT LANE
B5212
Lion's Den
Cawley Farm
Holcroft Hall
Culcheth Sports Club
Playing Field
Play. Flds.
Lib.
CULCHETH
WARRINGTON ROAD
CHURCH LANE
Ratcliffe House Farm
Crow Wood
Holcroft Cottages
18

A
B
C
D
E
1
2
3
4
5
6
7
217
26
91
92
95
96
97
98
M60
M60 MOTORWAY
M67
M67 MOTORWAY
A635
A6140
A662
A6017
A57
B6390
B6169
Junc. 23
Junction 24
Junc. 1
ASHTON RD.
DROYLSDEN RD.
MANCHESTER ROAD
MANCHESTER RD.
AUDENSHAW ROAD
LORD SHELDON WY.
MOSS WAY
GUIDE LANE
DENTON RD.
STOCKPORT ROAD
ASHTON ROAD
HYDE RD.
SHEPLEY
CORNHILL LANE
KINGS ROAD
THOMPSON LANE
MANCHESTER ROAD NORTH
MANCHESTER ROAD SOUTH
CORPORATION ROAD
DROYLSDEN
Droylsden FC
Lees Park
Aldwyn Prim. Sch.
Garden Centre
Police HQ
Factory
SNIPE RETAIL PARK
Ryecroft Hall
Playing Fields
Fairfield
Ashton Canal
Club House
Audenshaw
Manchester
Ashton-under-Lyne
Oxford Pk. Spts. Cen.
Guide Bridge
Hooley Hill
King George's Playing Field
Poplar St. Prim. Sch.
Audenshaw Sch.
AUDENSHAW RESERVOIRS
No.1
No.2
No.3
FAIRFIELD GOLF COURSE
DENTON GOLF COURSE
Audenshaw Lodge
Lodge Farm
The Barn
Dodgeleach Brook
Reservoir (covered)
Denton
Valve Ho.
ARROW TRADING ESTATE
Hawthorns Sch.
Cricket Grd.
Russell Scott Prim. Sch.
Egerton Pk. Arts College
CROWN POINT NORTH SHOPPING PARK
Superstore
Esporta Health & Fitness
TAMESIDE BUSINESS DEVELOPMENT CEN.
Swim. Pool
CROWN POINT SOUTH INDUSTRIAL PARK
Playing Fields
DENTON
Denton West End Prim. Sch.
Dane Bank
The City
St. Thomas More
Works
Audenshaw Cemy.
War Meml.
Sports Grd.
Rec. Grd.

DUKINFIELD
ASHTON-UNDER-LYNE
Dukinfield SK16
Newton Wood
Flowery Field
HYDE
Hyde SK14
Guide Bridge
Dukinfield Hall
Dukinfield Cemetery
Dukinfield Crematorium
Tame Valley
Dukinfield Park
Playing Fields
Cricket Ground
TAMESIDE PARK INDUSTRIAL ESTATE
Warehouse
Ravensfield Prim. Sch.
Sewage Works
Peak Forest Canal
Jet Amber Fields
Dunkirk Farm
Dunkirk Wood
Broomstair Farm
Football Grd.
Kingston Nursery
Junction 2
M67
M67 MOTORWAY
Junc. 3
MANCHESTER ROAD
CLARK WAY
MOTTRAM RD.
A57
A627
B6170
B6175
B6169
B6445
B6431
KING STREET
VICTORIA RD.
DUKINFIELD ROAD
ASHTON RD.
CHEETHAM HILL
BIRCH LANE
FOUNDRY ST.
OXFORD RD.
HIGH ST.
PARK ROAD
CLARENCE ROAD
ASTLEY ST.
ASHTON
Hyde North
Hyde Central
Hyde Park
Hyde Tech. Sch.
Yew Prim. Sch.
Cromwell High School
Astley High Sch.
Oakdale School & Acorn Nursery
St. Mary's Catholic Prim. Sch.
All Saints Catholic Coll.
Dukinfield Swim. Pool
Blocksages Playing Fields
Bayley Hall
Linden Rd. Prim. Sch.
Oakfield Prim. Sch.
Flowery Field Prim. Sch.
Clarke's Bridge
Hyde United FC (Ewen Fields)
Hyde Leisure Pool
Godley
Newton
Stamford
Alphabet Zoo
Superstore
Depot
River Tame
Huddersfield Narrow Canal
Johnson Brook
F
G
H
J
K
1
2
3
4
5
6
7
217
27
10

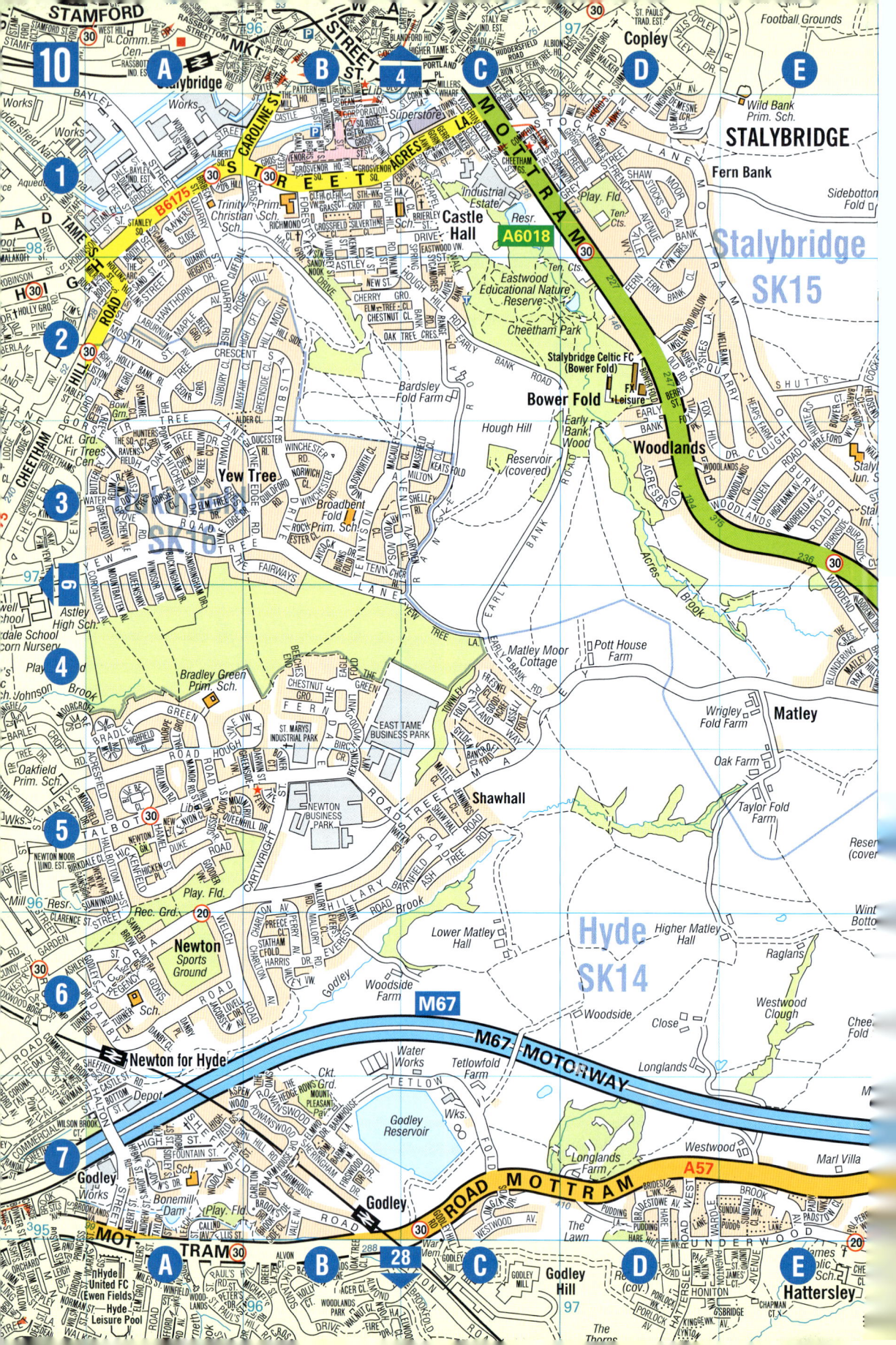
STAMFORD
Stalybridge
STALYBRIDGE
Copley
Football Grounds
Wild Bank Prim. Sch.
Fern Bank
Sidebottom Fold
Stalybridge SK15
MKT ST.
W STREET
STREET
MOTTRAM
MOTTRAM
A6018
B6175
Castle Hall
Industrial Estate
Superstore
Trinity Christian Sch.
Prim. Sch.
Eastwood Educational Nature Reserve
Cheetham Park
Stalybridge Celtic FC (Bower Fold)
Bower Fold
Woodlands
Hough Hill
Bardsley Fold Farm
Reservoir (covered)
Early Bank Wood
Yew Tree
Oakfield
Dukinfield SK16
Broadbent Fold Prim. Sch.
Astley High Sch.
Bradley Green Prim. Sch.
ST. MARYS INDUSTRIAL PARK
EAST TAME BUSINESS PARK
NEWTON BUSINESS PARK
Matley Moor Cottage
Pott House Farm
Wrigley Fold Farm
Matley
Oak Farm
Taylor Fold Farm
Shawhall
Lower Matley Hall
Higher Matley Hall
Hyde SK14
Woodside Farm
Woodside
Westwood Clough
Close
Longlands
Raglans
Newton Sports Ground
Play. Fld.
Rec. Grd.
Newton for Hyde
M67
M67 MOTORWAY
Water Works
Tetlowfold Farm
Godley Reservoir
Ckt. Grd.
Longlands Farm
Westwood
Marl Villa
A57
MOTTRAM ROAD
Godley
Bonemill Dam
Godley Hill
The Lawn
Hattersley
Hyde United FC (Ewen Fields)
Hyde Leisure Pool
UNDERWOOD
A B C D E
1 2 3 4 5 6 7
4
28
9

11
INSET
5
29
F
G
H
J
K
1
2
3
4
5
6
7
WILD BANK
HOLLINGWORTHHALL MOOR
Range Ho.
Reservoir
Flaxfield
Cockers Farm
Reservoir (covered)
Shawmoor
Ashtonhill Cross
Ivy Cottage
Shaw Moor
Gallows Clough
Hobson Moor
Mottram Rise
Nailors
Gallowsclough Farm
Hardtimes Farm
Thorncliffe Farm
Thorncliffe
Thorncliffe Hall
Meadowbank Farm
Lumb Farm
Bardsley Gate
Roe Cross
Dewsnap Farm
Golden Springs Farm
Lower Roe Cross
Mottram Old Hall
Playing Field
Longdendale Community Language College
Ckt. Grd.
Burial Grd.
Ingledene
Old Mill Farm
Harrop Edge
Paddock Farm
Silver Springs Farm
Bates
Albion Mill
Vale Farm
Resr.
Nettle Hall Farm
Hollingworth Prim. Sch.
Robin Hood Farm
Woolley Bridge
Mottram Moor Farm
Tara Brook Farm
Mottram in Longdendale
Mainsgrass
Grange Farm
Cemetery
Carr House
Longdendale Rec. Cen.
Playing Fields
Arundale Prim. Sch.
Mottram C of E Prim. Sch.
Warhill
Targeton Hill
Mudd
Mudd Farm
Pear Tree Farm
The Hague
Melandra Cottage
Melandra
River Etherow
ROE CROSS ROAD
A6018
A57
A560
B6174
MOTTRAM MOOR
MOTTRAM RD.
BACK MOOR
HYDE RD.
STOCKPORT RD.
MKT. ST.
ASHWORTH LANE
(Proposed)
Widowscroft Farm
Arnfield Reservoir
Filter Beds
Water Treatment Plant
Tintwistle C of E Prim. Sch.
Sewage Works
Football Grds.
Meadowbank Farm
Hyde SK14
Millbrook House
Millbrook Bridge
Hollingworth Manor Farm
Etherow Lodge
HIGH PEAK
TAMESIDE
River Etherow
ROSSINGTON PARK
Works
HADFIELD
Glossop SK13
Hollingworth
Weir
Prim. Sch.
ETHEROW IND. EST.
Ware-house
Home Farm
Woolley Bridge
Tara Brook Farm
A628
MANCHESTER ROAD
MARKET STREET
WOOLEY LA.
WOOLLEY BRI.

LIVERPOOL BAY
MOCKBEGGAR
Breakwater
KING'S PDE.
COASTAL DR.
Sailing Club
Miniature Golf Course
BAY VIEW DRIVE
NORTH WIRRAL COASTAL PARK
HARRISON RD.
HARRISON DR.
Warren Golf Course
HARRISON PARK
Tennis Courts
Bowling Greens
Wallasey Grove Rd.
Club House
WALLASEY GOLF COURSE
NORTH BAYSWATER ROAD
CH45
WALLASEY VILLAGE
B5427
St. Mary's Catholic College
Wallasey Vill.
GREEN LANE
Market Gardens
Stables
TELEGRAPH LANE
WALLASEY APPROACH
A551
A554
Club House
LEASOWE GOLF COURSE
LEASOWE ROAD
Our Lady of Lourdes Catholic Prim. Sch.
Solar Campus
Playing Fields
Playing Field
WALLASEY
Football Ground
Sports Ground
RSPCA Animal Cen.
The Mosslands School
The Wallacre Recreation Ground
Leasowe
Castleway Prim. Sch.
Wirral CH46
Leasowe Nurs. Sch.
Leasowe Millennium Cen.
A5139
KINGSWAY
Leasowe Rec. Cen.
Junction 1 M53
M53
Wallasey School
32
33
214

F
G
H
J
K
1
2
3
4
5
6
7
ROCK CHANNEL
Rock Lighthouse
Fort Perch Rock
Perch Rock
Breakwater
Marine Lake
W H A R F
RIVER MERSEY
SEFTON
WIRRAL
PARADE
A554
MARINE PROMENADE
New Brighton
NEW BRIGHTON
VICTORIA RD.
ROWSON ST.
ST. GEORGE'S PK.
Tower Grounds
TOWER PROMENADE
MAGAZINES PROMENADE
Comm. Cen.
Vale Park
ST. JAMES
Res. (cov.)
SEA BANK ROAD
RAKE LANE
B5143
Earlston Gardens
CEMETERY
Lib.
Ellerai Pk. Sch.
Mount Prim. Sch.
Captain's Pit
Club House
Prim. Sch.
Cricket Grd.
Wallasey
Tennis Courts
Superstore
The Oldershaw School
Liscard
Belvidere Rec. Ground
The Delph Rec. Grd.
Liscard Prim. Sch.
MANOR ROAD
B5142
YMCA
Egremont
KING ST.
ST. BRIGHTON
WALLASEY ROAD
A551
LISCARD VILLAGE
LISCARD
CH44
Cricket Ground
Play-ground
CENTRAL PARK
Liscard Hall
VICTORIA CENTRAL HOSPITAL
MILL LA.
A5088
BRECK
The Breck
B5145
ST. HILARY BROW
Prim. Sch.
33
34
214
93
92
94
95
30
31
32

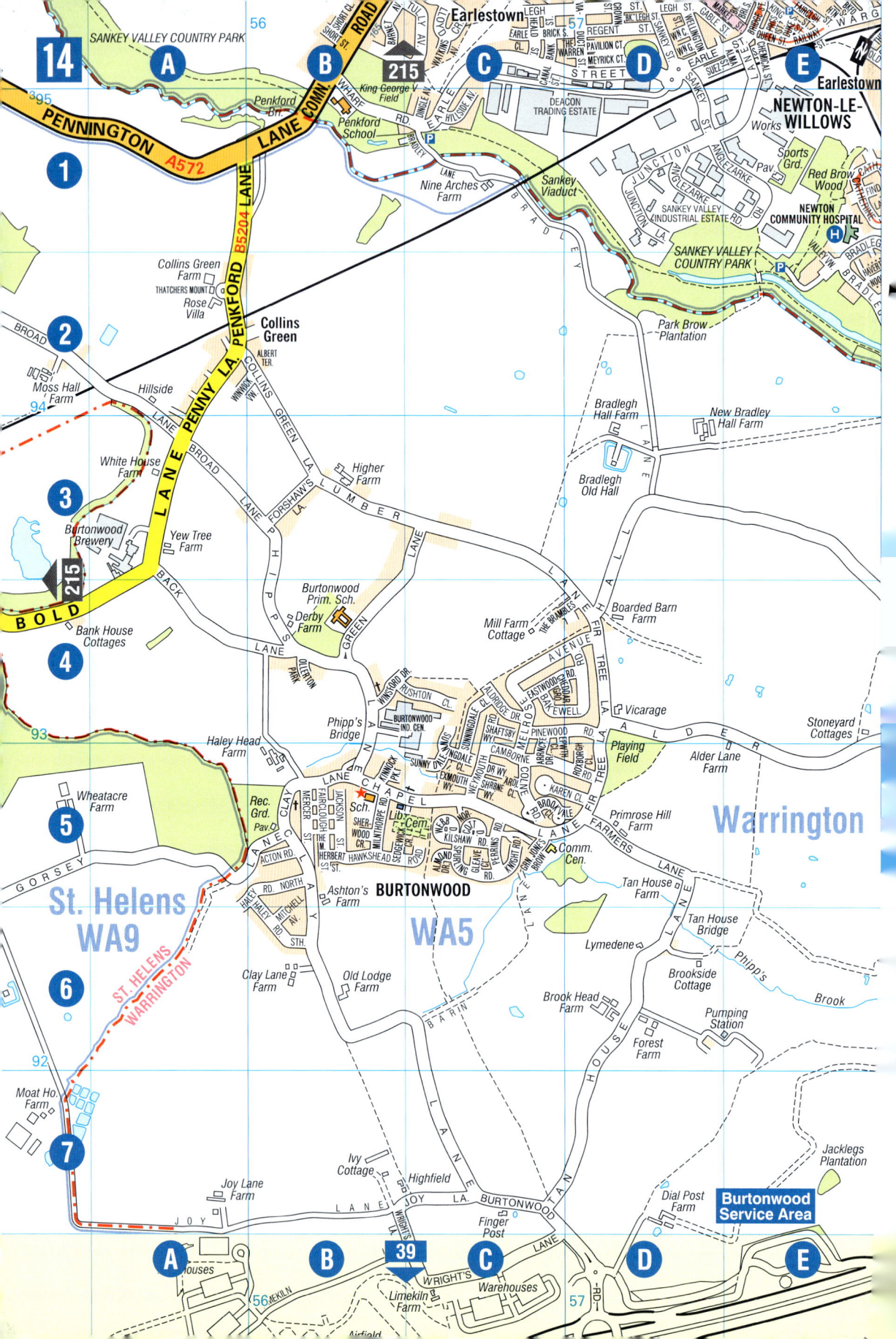
14
SANKEY VALLEY COUNTRY PARK
Earlestown
NEWTON-LE-WILLOWS
PENNINGTON LANE
A572
PENKFORD LANE
B5204
Penkford School
King George V Field
DEACON TRADING ESTATE
Nine Arches Farm
Sankey Viaduct
SANKEY VALLEY INDUSTRIAL ESTATE
NEWTON COMMUNITY HOSPITAL
Red Brow Wood
Sports Grd.
SANKEY VALLEY COUNTRY PARK
Park Brow Plantation
Collins Green Farm
Rose Villa
Collins Green
Moss Hall Farm
Hillside
Bradlegh Hall Farm
New Bradley Hall Farm
Bradlegh Old Hall
White House Farm
Higher Farm
Burtonwood Brewery
Yew Tree Farm
215
BOLD
Bank House Cottages
Burtonwood Prim. Sch.
Derby Farm
Mill Farm Cottage
Boarded Barn Farm
Vicarage
Phipp's Bridge
BURTONWOOD IND. CEN.
Haley Head Farm
Stoneyard Cottages
Alder Lane Farm
Playing Field
Wheatacre Farm
Rec. Grd.
Primrose Hill Farm
Warrington
Comm. Cen.
BURTONWOOD
Ashton's Farm
Tan House Farm
Tan House Bridge
St. Helens WA9
WA5
Lymedene
Clay Lane Farm
Old Lodge Farm
Brookside Cottage
ST. HELENS WARRINGTON
Brook Head Farm
Phipp's Brook
Pumping Station
Forest Farm
Moat Ho. Farm
Ivy Cottage
Highfield
Jacklegs Plantation
Joy Lane Farm
Dial Post Farm
Burtonwood Service Area
Finger Post
39
Limekiln Farm
Warehouses

Newton-le-Willows
WA12
WA2
Wargrave
Vulcan Village
Red Bank
WINWICK
Winwick Green
Hermitage Green
Bloody Stone
Newton Park Farm
Red Bank Community Home
Cemetery
Sports Grd.
Football Ground
Vulcan Gym
Prim. Sch.
Wargrave House Sch.
VULCAN INDUSTRIAL ESTATE
New Hey Farm
Cop Holt Wood
Cop Holt Farm
Hermitage Farm
Reeves House
The Orchard
Wood Head
Old Hey Wood
Sankey Brook
Sankey Canal
SANKEY VALLEY COUNTRY PARK
Hall Lane Farm
Winwick Junction
Club Ho.
Red House Farm
Alder Root Farm
ALDER ROOT GOLF COURSE
Alder Root Wood
Play. Fld.
Asps Wood
Reservoir (cov.)
Clayton's House Farm
Lower Alder Root Farm
HOLLINS PARK HOSPITAL
Causey Cottages
Causey West Bri.
Causey Bridge
Causeway Bridges Farm
Coney Grove Woods
Garden of Remembrance
Delph Farm
Delph Farm Cottage
Superstore
Junc. 9
M62 MOTORWAY
M62
M6 MOTORWAY
M6
Warehouses
QUAY BUS. CEN.
THE QUAY CENTRE
WINWICK QUAY
GEMINI BUSINESS PARK
ROYAL LONDON BUS. PK.
SANKEY VALLEY PARK
Superstores
Superstore
Depot
Winwick
ST. HELENS
WARRINGTON
A49
A573
A579
215
16
40
F G H J K
1 2 3 4 5 6 7

216
Parkside Farm
Moss Pits
Kenyon Hall
Green Bank
Kenylo Bridge
STONE PIT LANE
SANDY BROW
Sandy Bank Farm
Turret Hall
Rock House
WIGAN
ST. HELENS
BARROW LANE
PARKSIDE RD.
A573
M6
A579
Oven Back Cottage
Oven Back Farm
Wood Head
WARRINGTON
ST. HELENS
WINWICK LANE
Brook
Cockshot
The Orchard
PARKSIDE ROAD
Rough Farm
Hill Crest
Mains Pits
Hermitage Green
Junction 22
Island Plantation
Warrington
LINK ROAD
HIGHFIELD LANE
M6 MOTORWAY
Southworth Hall
Highfields
Cockshot Farm
Smithy Brow
SMITHY LANE
Cockshot Bridge
DAM LANE
15
Reservoir (cov.)
WINWICK
SOUTHWORTH LANE
The Lodge
Myddleton Hall
Stone House Farm
Arbury Cotts.
Myddleton Hall Farm
DELPH LANE
WATERWORKS
ST. OSWALDS CL.
Coppice Pit
Sandsfields Cottage
GOLBORNE
NEWTON
Sch.
Winwick Leis. Cen.
Arbury
WA2
Arbury Farm
Mainfield
WINWICK
A579
Pumping Station
Gorsey Brow
Spa Well House
Junction 10 M62
Bowling Greens
A49
Spa Brook
Midhops Farm
Delph Park Nursing Home
Arbury Pits
M62 MOTORWAY
Houghton Green
Peel Hall
M62
Birch Tree Farm
Junction 9
Bowl. Grn.
BIRCH AV.
Peel Cottage
Bowling Green Farm
POPLARS AVENUE
Radley Plantation
BALLATER DR.
ENFIELD
Cinnamon Brow
Radley Fm.
41
Radley Common
Hall Comm. Cen.
St. Andrew's C of E Prim. Sch.
Peel Hall Park
WINWICK RD.

17
WA3
Croft Heath
CROFT
Little Town
Wigshaw
New Lane End
Eaves Brow
Locking Stumps
Birchwood Park
Risley
BIRCHWOOD
M62 MOTORWAY
M6 MOTORWAY
Junc. 21a (M6)
A574
WARRINGTON ROAD
HMP RISLEY
BIRCHWOOD GOLF COURSE
Croft Golf Centre
St. Lewis Catholic Primary Sch.
Croft Primary School
Newchurch Prim. Sch.
Locking Stumps Prim. Sch.
Birchwood High Sch.
TRIDENT BUSINESS PARK
TAYLOR BUSINESS PARK
POULTON PARK GOLF COURSE
7
18
42

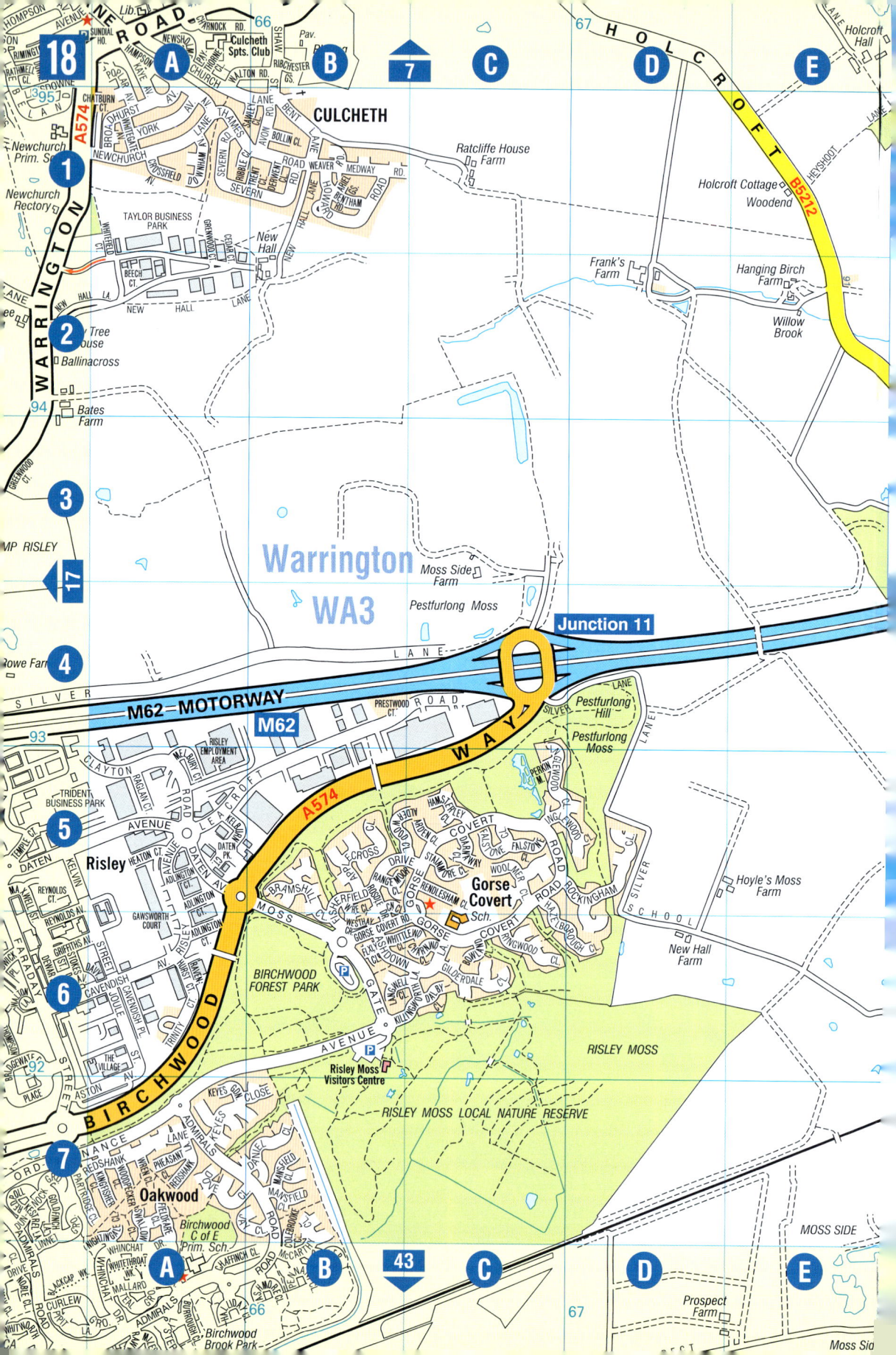

CULCHETH
Culcheth Spts. Club
Ratcliffe House Farm
HOLCROFT LANE
B5212
Holcroft Hall
Holcroft Cottage
Woodend
HEYSHOOT LANE
Newchurch Prim. Sch.
Newchurch Rectory
TAYLOR BUSINESS PARK
New Hall
NEW HALL LANE
Frank's Farm
Hanging Birch Farm
Willow Brook
WARRINGTON ROAD
A574
Ballinacross
Bates Farm
Warrington
WA3
Moss Side Farm
Pestfurlong Moss
Junction 11
M62 MOTORWAY
M62
SILVER LANE
RISLEY EMPLOYMENT AREA
TRIDENT BUSINESS PARK
Pestfurlong Hill
Pestfurlong Moss
BIRCHWOOD WAY
Risley
Gorse Covert
Sch.
BIRCHWOOD FOREST PARK
Hoyle's Moss Farm
New Hall Farm
SILVER SCHOOL LANE
RISLEY MOSS
Risley Moss Visitors Centre
RISLEY MOSS LOCAL NATURE RESERVE
Oakwood
Birchwood C of E Prim. Sch.
MOSS SIDE
Prospect Farm
Birchwood Brook Park
7
17
43

19
216
20
44
LITTLE WOOLDEN MOSS
IRLAM MOSS
Hollin Wood
Pigeon Wood
Crow Wood
Little Woolden Moss Drain
Birch Covert
Ringing Pits Farm
Gable End Farm
Mosshall Farm
Birch Tree Farm
Brackley Farm
Woodland Farm
Boundary Drain
Little Woolden Hall
Hope Cottage Farm
Plant Cottage Farm
Prospect Grange
GREAT WOOLDEN MOSS
Hole Mill Farm
Glaze Brook
Keeper's Cottage
Great Woolden Wood
M62 MOTORWAY
M62
CADISHEAD MOSS
Nook Farm
Woolden View Farm
Aikin Knowles's Bridge
Manchester M44
Rose Bank Farm
Tudor Rose Cottage
Great Woolden Hall Farm
Ryefield Farm
WOOLDEN ROAD
MOSS ROAD
GLAZEBROOK LANE
B5212
Nursery
Lower Stanley Bank Farm
HOLCROFT MOSS NATURE RESERVE
Ash Farm
NEW MOSS WOOD
Higher Stanley Bank Farm
Ellesmere Farm
GLAZEBROOK MOSS
Bridge House Farm
SALFORD
WARRINGTON
Glazebrook East Junction
Glazebrook
Brush Farm
School
Rec. Grd.
Milverton Farm
DAM LANE
MOSS LANE
Omrod Farm
Rose Cottage
HEAD DAM
BANK LANE
STREET
CARLTON WY.
VETCH CL.
Fairfield Rd.
Sewage Works
Fit City Cadishead
Rec. Grd.
Ivy Cottage
Bridge Farm
Birchley
Townley Brow Farm
Hollingreave Farm
Moss Hall Farm
Lea Brook Farm
Mount Pleasant Farm
GLAZEBROOK LA.
A57
LIVERPOOL RD.
LIVERPOOL ROAD
CADISHEAD WY.
CADISHEAD WAY CIR.
MANCHESTER SHIP CANAL
Barn End Farm
Ash Tree Farm
Grave Yard
LANE
BEDFORD GRO.
DURHAM GRO.
HERTFORD GRO.
OXFORD GRO.
PEMBROKE GRO.
FLINT GRO.
BUCKINGHAM RD.
SUSSEX
LORDS ST.
ENTICOTT RD.
KENT RD.
MELVILLE RD.
BERKSHIRE DR.
DORSET RD.
SOMERSET CL.
NORFOLK CL.
PURLEY DR.
HILTON DR.
LANCASTER RD.
DEVON RD.
DERBY CL.
CUMBERLAND AV.
DUDLEY RD.
LINCOLN AV.
KITCHENER AV.
HAIG AV.
VICTORY RD.
GRAHAM CR.
BYNG AV.
WOODBINE AV.
YORK RD.
F G H J K
1 2 3 4 5 6 7
69
370
395
94
93
92

20
216
19
45
M62
MOTORWAY
M44
A57
B5320
B5311
B5466
B5471
A6144
Hope Cottage Farm
Westholme
Hephzibah
Woodstock Farm
Plant Cottage Farm
Jenny Green
Springfield Farm
IRLAM
Worsley View
Prospect Grange
CADISHEAD MOSS
Rose Farm
Tudor Rose Cottage
CHAT MOSS
Lower Irlam
Astley Road Farm
Irlam & Cadishead Community High School
Lower Stanley Bank Farm
Higher Stanley Bank Farm
Nursery
Bridge House Farm
Irlam
Sports Ground
Fit City Irlam
Prince's Park
Irlam Prim. Sch.
Grave Yd.
River Irwell (Old Course)
Irlam Locks
THE LOCKS
FAIRHILLS ROAD
LIVERPOOL ROAD
Works
Superstore
Linear Park
Weir
Depot
Carrington Wharf
NORTHBANK INDUSTRIAL PARK
EXCALIBUR WAY
Depots
IRLAM WHARF
Wharf
Sewage Works
GILCHRIST ESTATE
OMEGA CIRCLE
BRINELL DRIVE
CADISHEAD WAY
SALFORD
TRAFFORD
Landing Stages
Partington Coal Basin
Petrol Storage Depot
CADISHEAD
Rec. Grd.
Fit City Cadishead
Hall
COMMON
MANCHESTER ROAD
PARTINGTON
Gas Works
Gas Holders
MANCHESTER SHIP CANAL
STATION COTTS.
BROADWAY
PARTINGTON SHOP. CEN.
WARBURTON LANE
Prim. Sch.
HEATH

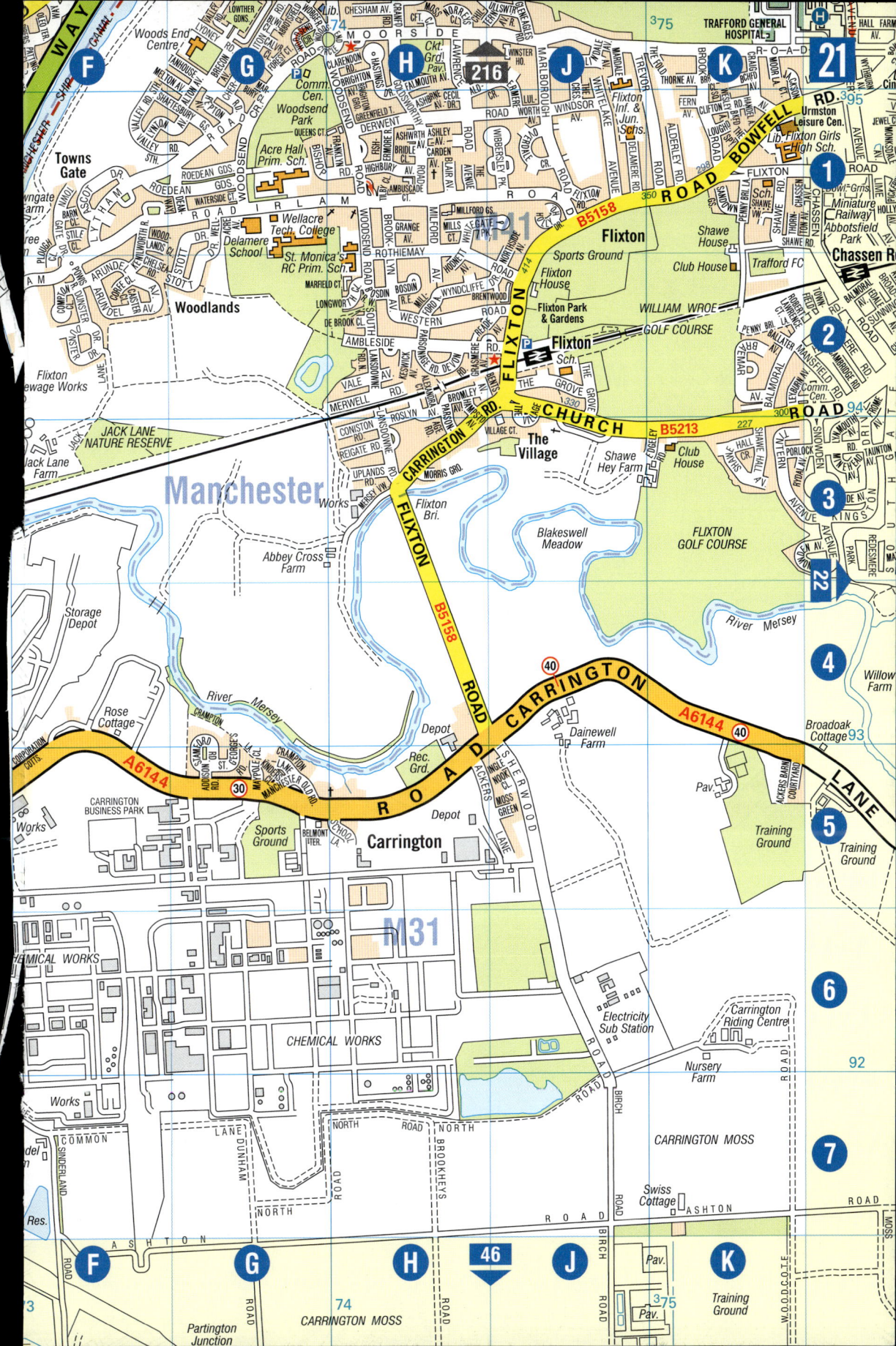
21
TRAFFORD GENERAL HOSPITAL
Urmston Leisure Cen.
Flixton Girls High Sch.
Woods End Centre
Woodsend Park
Acre Hall Prim. Sch.
Towns Gate
Wellacre Tech. College
Delamere School
St. Monica's RC Prim. Sch.
Woodlands
Flixton Inf. & Jun. Schs.
Flixton
Sports Ground
Flixton House
Flixton Park & Gardens
WILLIAM WROE GOLF COURSE
Shawe House
Club House
Trafford FC
Chassen Park
Abbotsfield Park
Miniature Railway
Flixton Sewage Works
JACK LANE NATURE RESERVE
Jack Lane Farm
Manchester
The Village
Shawe Hey Farm
Club House
Flixton Bri.
Abbey Cross Farm
Blakeswell Meadow
FLIXTON GOLF COURSE
River Mersey
Storage Depot
Rose Cottage
Dainewell Farm
Willow Farm
Broadoak Cottage
Depot
Rec. Grd.
CARRINGTON BUSINESS PARK
Works
Sports Ground
Carrington
Training Ground
CHEMICAL WORKS
Electricity Sub Station
Carrington Riding Centre
Nursery Farm
CARRINGTON MOSS
Swiss Cottage
Res.
Partington Junction
Pav.
FLIXTON ROAD
BOWFELL ROAD
CHURCH ROAD
CARRINGTON ROAD
CARRINGTON LANE
ASHTON ROAD
B5158
B5213
A6144
M41
M31
216
22
46
F
G
H
J
K
1
2
3
4
5
6
7

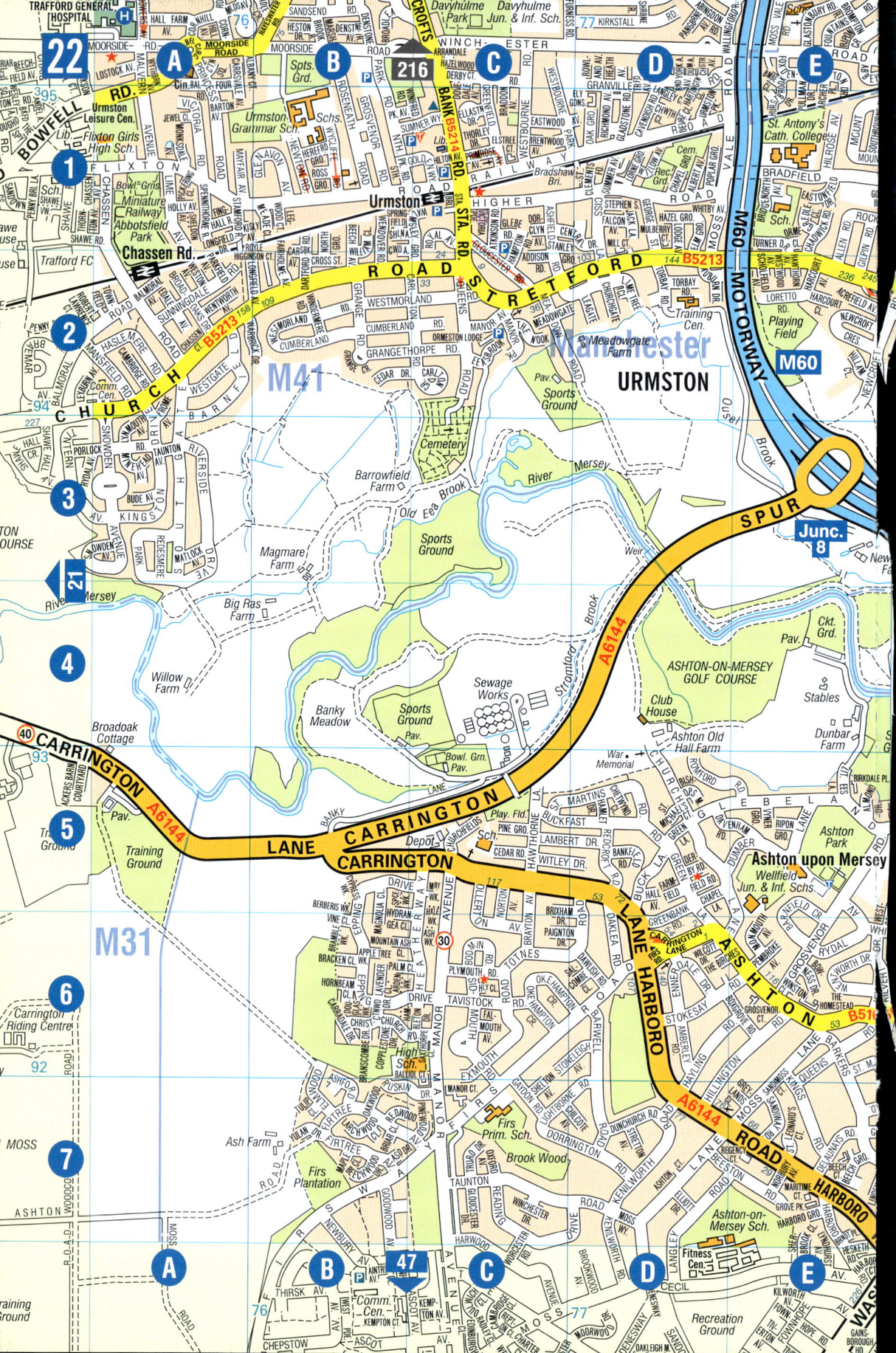

22
TRAFFORD GENERAL HOSPITAL
MOORSIDE ROAD
Urmston Leisure Cen.
Flixton Girls High Sch.
Urmston Grammar Sch.
Davyhulme Park
Davyhulme Jun. & Inf. Sch.
WINCHESTER RD.
216
St. Antony's Cath. College
BRADFIELD
Bowl. Grn.
Miniature Railway
Abbotsfield Park
Chassen Rd.
Trafford FC
Urmston
FLIXTON ROAD
HIGHER ROAD
STRETFORD ROAD
CHURCH ROAD
B5213
B5214
M41
Manchester
URMSTON
M60 MOTORWAY
M60
SPUR
Junc. 8
Cemetery
Barrowfield Farm
Old Eea Brook
River Mersey
Sports Ground
Magmare Farm
Big Ras Farm
Willow Farm
Weir
Stromford Brook
A6144
Sewage Works
Banky Meadow
Broadoak Cottage
CARRINGTON LANE
Training Ground
ASHTON-ON-MERSEY GOLF COURSE
Club House
Ashton Old Hall Farm
Stables
Dunbar Farm
Ckt. Grd.
Pav.
War Memorial
Ashton Park
Ashton upon Mersey
Wellfield Jun. & Inf. Schs.
ASHTON LANE
HARBORO ROAD
M31
Carrington Riding Centre
Ash Farm
Firs Plantation
Firs Prim. Sch.
Brook Wood
High Sch.
Ashton-on-Mersey Sch.
Fitness Cen.
Recreation Ground
Comm. Cen.
47
21
ASHTON
MOSS
1
2
3
4
5
6
7
A
B
C
D
E

216
217
48
Humphrey Pk.
Lostock College
Moss Park Inf. & Jun. Schs.
Playing Field
Victoria Park
Schools
A56
Longford Park Sch.
URMSTON LANE
B5213
KINGSWAY
EDGE LANE
CHESTER RD.
BARTON ROAD
A5181
A5145
ARNDALE SHOPPING CENTRE
Stretford
Stretford Cemetery
Stretford Grammar Sch.
STRETFORD
Playing Fields
Turn Moss
Cricket Ground
M32
St. Matthew's C of E Prim. Sch.
MANOR IND. ESTATE
Cut Hole Bridge
Eye Platt New Bridge
Bridgewater Canal
Mosley Acre Farm
Barfoot Bridge
BROAD EES DOLE LOCAL NATURE RESERVE
MANCHESTER
TRAFFORD
M21
CHORLTON EES NATURE RESERVE
Ivy Green
Ousel Brook
Junction 7
Nursery
New Manor Farm
Sewage Works
BRADLEY LANE
Crossford Bri.
Crossford Bridge Sports Ground
SALE WATER PARK
M60 MOTORWAY
River Mersey
A56
CROSS STREET
Gasholder
White's Bri.
DANE ROAD
Trafford Water Sports Cen.
M60
Junc. 6
Nature Reserve
Mersey Valley Visitor Cen.
Dane Rd.
Priory Gdns.
Bowling Green
B5397
SALE
Cricket Grd.
Recreation Ground
Atkinson Court
Superstore
Arts Cen.
Leis. Cen.
Worthington Park
Moorlands Jun. Sch.
OLD HALL RD.
A6144
WYTHENSHAWE RD.
SIBSON RD.
NORTHENDEN ROAD
B5166
Playing Field
Sale Cemy.
MARSLAND ROAD
Walkden Gdns.
NORTHENDEN
A6144

24
A
B
C
D
E
1
2
3
4
5
6
7
217
51
DICKENSON ROAD
A6010
A34
BIRCHFIELDS ROAD
STOCKPORT ROAD
A6
WILMSLOW ROAD
KINGSWAY
SLADE LANE
A5079
MOSELEY ROAD
B5093
ALBERT RD.
BROOM LANE
Platt Hall
PLATT FIELDS PK.
Manchester High Sch. for Girls
Fallowfield
Birchfields Park
Manchester Grammar Sch.
Manchester Metropolitan University (Hollings Campus)
Playing Fields
Tennis Courts
Halls of Res.
Armitage Sports Cen.
Manchester University Athletics Ground
Rushford Park
Coston Park
Levenshulme
Levenshulme Swim. Pool
Crowcroft Park
Cricket Grd.
Superstore
Burnage Park
Alma Park
Levenshulme High Sch.
Cringle Fields Park
Mauldeth Rd.
Ladybarn Park
Ladybarn
Ladybarn Prim. Sch.
Manchester
Works
Factory
ERRWOOD PARK WORKS
DISCOVERY PARK
Peel Moat
Peel Moat Sports Centre
Heaton School
Heaton Moor Pk.
HEATON MOOR GOLF COURSE
Camellia House
Club House
Mauldeth Hall
Heaton Moor
Bowling & Tennis Club
Burnage High Sch.
Green End
Burnage
FOG LANE PARK
Bowling Greens
Priestnall Rec. Cen.
Priestnall School
Tithe Barn Prim. Sch.
Playing Fields
M13
M14
M19
M20

25
Ryder Brow
Melland Playing Field
Sports Grd.
Melland High Sch.
Works
Reservoir
Fir Tree Prim. School
North Reddish
Reddish Nth.
North Reddish Park
Recreation Ground
Playing Fields
Dane Bank Prim. Sch.
Dane Bank
Cricket Ground
Houldsworth Golf Course
Highfield House
Highfield Country Park
Reddish
Club House
Reddish Green
Houldsworth Park
Reddish Leis. Cen.
Reddish Sth.
Superstore
SK5
Mid Reddish
Reddish Vale Sports Centre (NW Regional Basketball Centre)
Reddish Vale Technology College
Reddish Vale Farm
Reddish Vale
Reddish Vale Nature Reserve
Reddish Vale Visitor Cen.
Kennels
Woodhouse Farm
Hollow Cottage
Reddish Vale Golf Course
South Cliff Cotts.
Club House
Heaton Chapel
Broadstone Hall Prim. Sch.
Hurstfield Industrial Estate
Vauxhall Industrial Estate
Depot
St. Mary's C of E Prim. Sch.
South Reddish
Willow Grove Cemetery
Greg Street Industrial Estate
Whitehill Industrial Estate
Bamford Business Park
Whitehill Prim. Sch.
South Reddish Pk.
Picnic Area
Woodhall Fields
Tiviot Dale
Lancashire Hill
St. Anne's RC High School
Bankfield Trading Estate
St. Paul's C of E Prim. Sch.
Gorton Road
Reddish Road
Broadstone Road
Manchester Road
Longford Road West
Tiviot Way
B6167
B5169
B6178
A626
A6
M60
217
52
26
F G H J K
1 2 3 4 5 6 7

26
A
B
C
D
E
1
2
3
4
5
6
7
DENTON
8
25
53
Esporta Health & Fitness
TAMESIDE BUSINESS DEVELOPMENT CEN.
PARKWAY
ORBITAL 24
ALLIANCE IND. EST.
Works
The City
Play. Fld.
St. Thomas More RC College
STOCKPORT
A6017 RD.
ROAD
WINDMILL LANE
M60
Wks.
OAKDEN DR.
FIELDING INDUSTRIAL CENTRE
Greswell Prim. Sch.
Comm. Cen.
Manchester
M34
Denton Wood
Hyde Hall
Horse Close Wood
ROSS LAVE LANE
M60 MOTORWAY
Corrie Prim. Sch.
Holt Wood
Mid Reddish
Reddish Vale Nature Reserve
River Tame
TAMESIDE
STOCKPORT
Sewage Works
Hulme's Wood
Denton Cemetery
Hardy Wood
Nursery
Reddish Vale Visitor Cen.
REDDISH VALE COUNTRY PARK
Arden Hall
Arden Crest
Horse Shoe Farm
Beight Bridge
Millhill Farm
Tame Valley Prim. Sch.
Castle Hill
Bakery
Works
BLACKBERRY
Hollow Cottage
Lapwing Cen.
Castle Hill High Sch.
Brinnington
Westmorland Prim. Sch.
BREDBURY PARK INDUSTRIAL ESTATE
Stockport
CASTLE HILL PARK
REDDISH VALE GOLF COURSE
Youth Cen.
Comm. Cen.
Rec. Grd.
Brinnington Park
Brinnington
LINGARD
ASHTON
A6017
Refuse Works
Junction 25
M60
St. Bernadette's RC Prim. Sch.
ASHTON A560 RD.
Superstores
STOCKPORT RD. WEST
STOCKPORT ROAD
Bredbury
Crookilley Wood
Arden Park
Junction 26
St. Paul's C of E Prim. Sch.
M60 MOTORWAY
CROOKILLEY A560 WY.
Portwood Playing Fields
Welkin Mill
BREDBURY
Arden Prim. Sch.
HIGHER

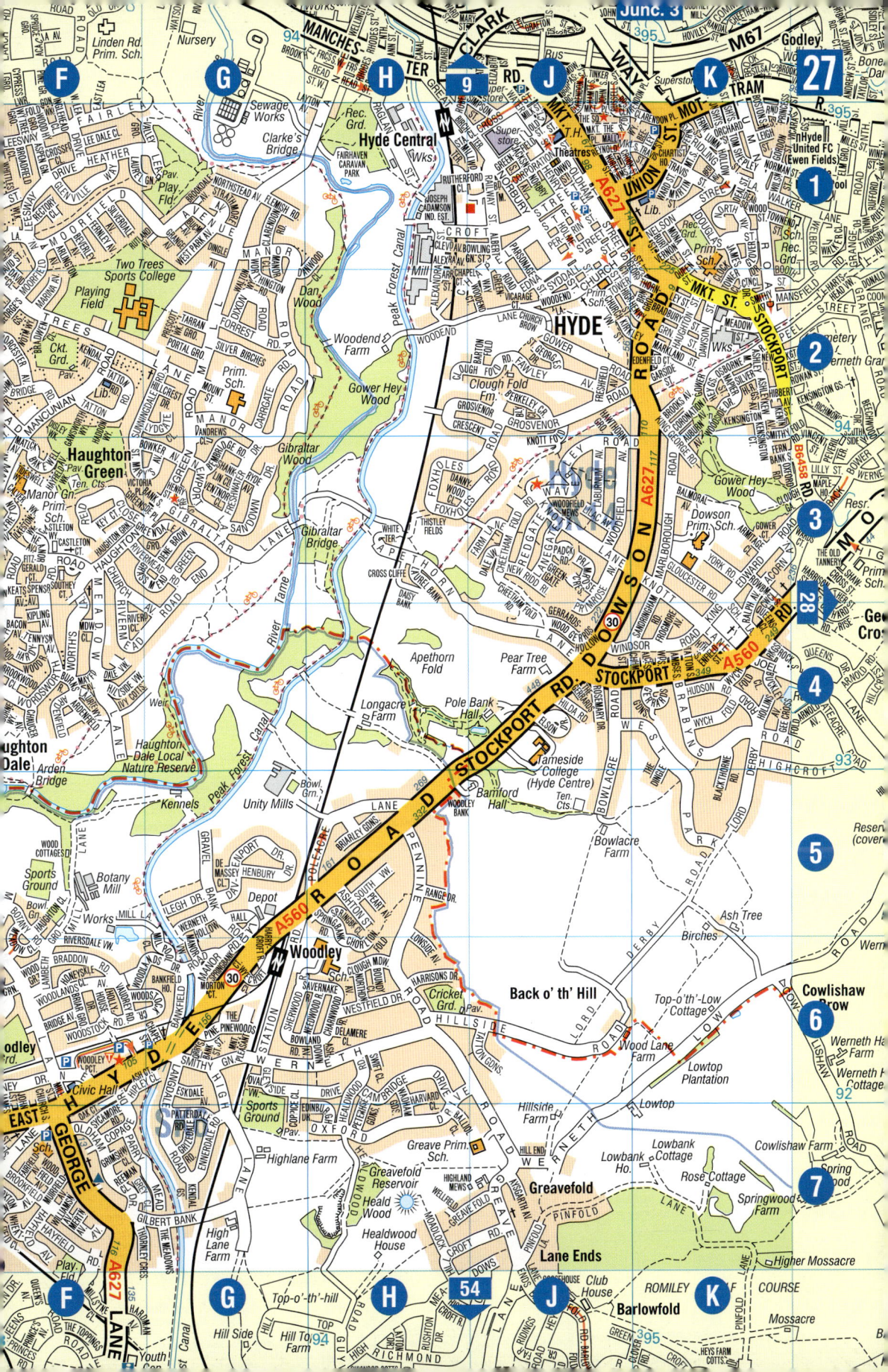

Junc. 3
M67
Godley
CLARK WAY
MANCHESTER RD.
MKT. ST.
UNION ST.
MOTTRAM
9
F
G
H
J
K
Nursery
Linden Rd. Prim. Sch.
Sewage Works
Clarke's Bridge
River Tame
Rec. Grd.
Hyde Central
Wks.
FAIRHAVEN CARAVAN PARK
Theatres
Super store
Lib.
Hyde United FC (Ewen Fields)
Pool
1
Two Trees Sports College
Playing Field
Pav.
Play. Fld.
Peak Forest Canal
Dan Wood
Woodend Farm
HYDE
Prim. Sch.
Mill
Wks.
Cemetery
Werneth Grange
2
Ckt. Grd.
Lib.
Gower Hey Wood
Clough Fold Fm.
Haughton Green
Ten. Cts.
Manor Gn. Prim. Sch.
Gibraltar Wood
Gibraltar Bridge
B6458
Gower Hey Wood
Dowson Prim. Sch.
Resr.
3
A627
DOWSON ROAD
THE OLD TANNERY
Prim. Sch.
28
Apethorn Fold
Pear Tree Farm
A560
STOCKPORT RD.
4
Longacre Farm
Pole Bank Hall
Weir
Haughton Dale Local Nature Reserve
Haughton Dale
Arden Bridge
Kennels
Unity Mills
Bowl. Grn.
Tameside College (Hyde Centre)
Bamford Hall
Ten. Cts.
93
Bowlacre Farm
5
Sports Ground
Botany Mill
Works
Depot
Woodley
Ash Tree
Birches
Back o' th' Hill
Top-o'th'-Low Cottage
Cowlishaw Brow
6
Werneth Hall Farm
Werneth Cottage
Wood Lane Farm
Lowtop Plantation
Cricket Grd.
Pav.
Godley Grd.
Civic Hall
Sports Ground
Hillside Farm
Lowtop
92
Greave Prim. Sch.
Highlane Farm
Lowbank Ho.
Lowbank Cottage
Rose Cottage
Cowlishaw Farm
Spring Wood
7
Greavefold Reservoir
Heald Wood
Greavefold
Springwood Farm
Healdwood House
High Lane Farm
Lane Ends
Higher Mossacre
Club House
Top-o'-th'-hill
54
ROMILEY GOLF COURSE
Barlowfold
Hill Side
Hill Top Farm
Mossacre
Youth Cen.
Canal

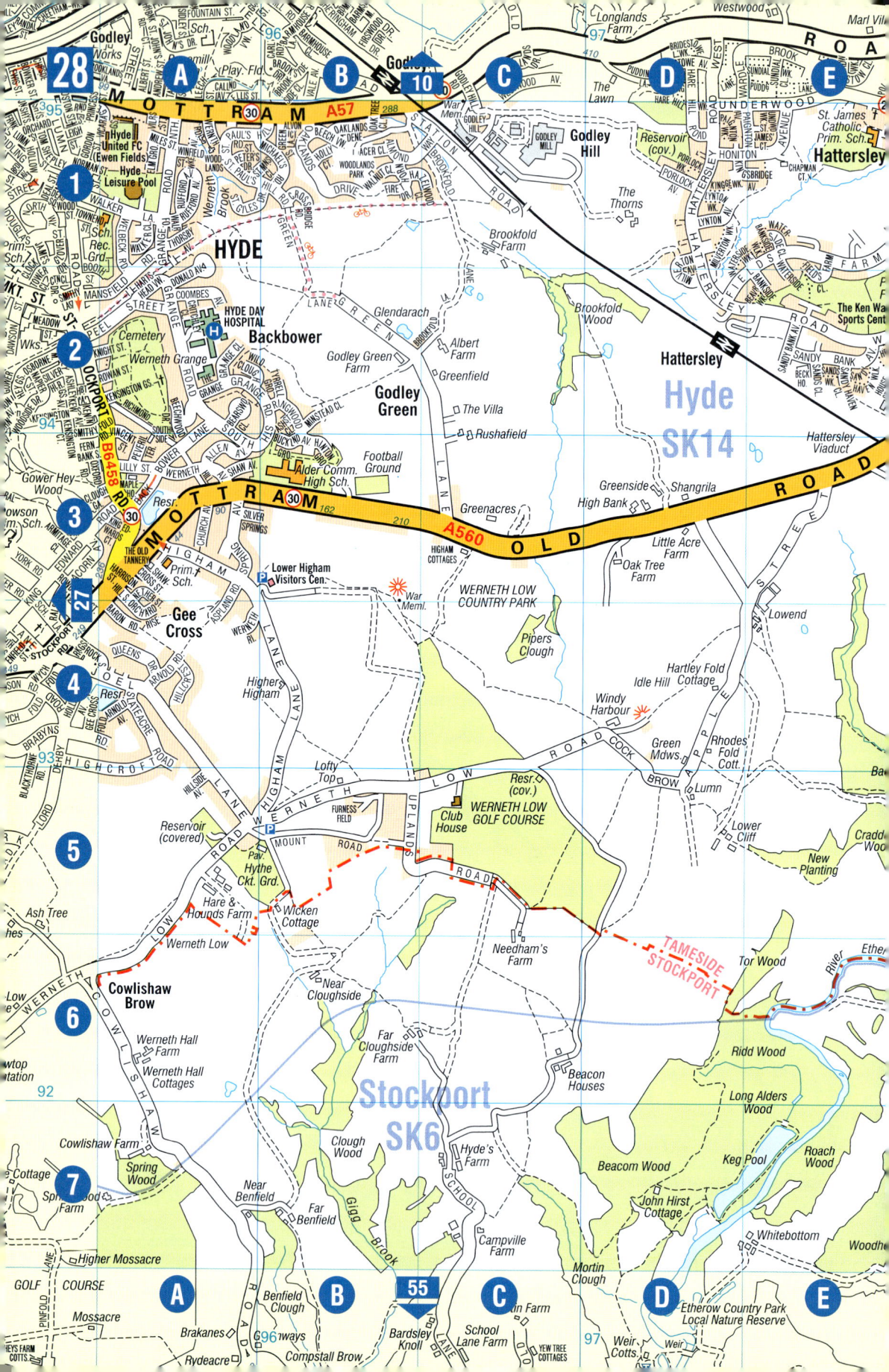
28
10
27
55
A
B
C
D
E
1
2
3
4
5
6
7
MOTTRAM A57
MOTTRAM A560 OLD ROAD
B6458
Godley
Godley Hill
Hattersley
HYDE
Backbower
Godley Green
Gee Cross
Hyde SK14
Stockport SK6
Hyde United FC (Ewen Fields)
Hyde Leisure Pool
HYDE DAY HOSPITAL
Cemetery
Werneth Grange
Alder Comm. High Sch.
Football Ground
Lower Higham Visitors Cen.
WERNETH LOW COUNTRY PARK
WERNETH LOW GOLF COURSE
Club House
Brookfold Farm
Brookfold Wood
Glendarach
Albert Farm
Greenfield
The Villa
Rushafield
Godley Green Farm
Greenacres
Greenside
High Bank
Shangrila
Little Acre Farm
Oak Tree Farm
Hattersley Viaduct
Lowend
Hartley Fold Cottage
Idle Hill
Windy Harbour
Green Mdws.
Rhodes Fold Cott.
Lumn
Lower Cliff
New Planting
Pipers Clough
Higher Higham
Lofty Top
Resr. (cov.)
Reservoir (covered)
Hythe Ckt. Grd.
Hare & Hounds Farm
Wicken Cottage
Werneth Low
Cowlishaw Brow
Werneth Hall Farm
Werneth Hall Cottages
Near Cloughside
Far Cloughside Farm
Needham's Farm
Beacon Houses
TAMESIDE
STOCKPORT
Tor Wood
Ridd Wood
Long Alders Wood
Keg Pool
Roach Wood
Beacom Wood
John Hirst Cottage
Whitebottom
Mortin Clough
Etherow Country Park Local Nature Reserve
Campville Farm
Hyde's Farm
Clough Wood
Gigg Brook
Near Benfield
Far Benfield
Benfield Clough
Cowlishaw Farm
Spring Wood
Higher Mossacre
Mossacre
GOLF COURSE
Brakanes
Rydeacre
Compstall Brow
Bardsley Knoll
School Lane Farm
Weir Cotts.
The Lawn
The Thorns
Longlands Farm
Reservoir (cov.)
St. James Catholic Prim. Sch.
The Ken Ward Sports Cent
Gower Hey Wood
Ash Tree
Lower Higham
War Meml.
HIGHAM COTTAGES
THE OLD TANNERY
FURNESS FIELD
MOUNT ROAD
WERNETH LOW ROAD
COCK BROW
APPLE STREET
HIGHCROFT ROAD
HATTERSLEY ROAD
STATION ROAD

Broadbottom
Charlesworth
Chisworth
Glossop
SK13
Hodgefold
Lymefield
Woodseats
Holehouse
Higher Chisworth
Mudd
The Hague
Bankwood
Bankwood Gate
Lee Head
Higher Gamesley
Warhill
11
River Etherow
Great Wood Local Nature Reserve
Tom Wood
Chew Wood
Robin Wood
Bot Wood
Great Wood
HIGH PEAK
TAMESIDE
A560
A626
A57
B6174
STOCKPORT ROAD
MARPLE ROAD
GLOSSOP ROAD
ASHWORTH
Sandy Lane Farm
Lymefield Visitor Cen.
Broadbottom C of E Prim. Sch.
Charlesworth Prim. Sch.
Mottram C of E Prim. Sch.
Arundale Prim. Sch.
Gymnastics Cen.
Holehouse Mill
Kinderlee Mill
The Golf Pavilion
Poultry Houses
Sewage Works
Moorside Farm
Intakes Farm
Thornbank
Sunnyside
Living Waters
Bench Wells
Meadowbank Farm
Hillfields
Lower Stirrup Farm
Higher Stirrup Farm
Boar Steps
Boarfold Farm
Botham's Hall
Botham's Hall Farm
Leylands Farm
Hodge House
Hodge Cottage
Warrastfold Bridge
Sylvandale Farm
Far Woodseats
Rosegrove Cottage
The Bungalow
Rarewood House
Woodseats Farm
Charlesworth Stud
Hunters Gate
Woodside
Maryville
Woodseat Chase
Fields Farm
Moat Hall
Sandy Oak Farm
Robinwood Farm
Melandra Cottage
Pear Tree Farm
Lower Mudd Farm
Parsonage Farm
Parsonage Fields Farm
Home Farm
Brown Road Farm
Hague
Resr. (cov.)
Bankwood Mill
Bankwood Cottage
Lymefield Farm
Camp Site
Hollow Cottage
Clough End
Hurstclough
Highgate Farm
Fold Fm.
Hilltop Farm
Oakwood Farm
High Ash Barn
Brick Houses
Cricket Grd.
Rec. Grd.
Play. Fld.
F
G
H
J
K
1
2
3
4
5
6
7
92
93
94
95
99
400

30
A
B
C
D
E
21
22
91
390
89
88
1
2
3
4
5
6
7
LIVERPOOL BAY
EAST HOYLE BANK
HOYLAKE
Meols Parade Gardens
Promenade
Ten. Cts.
Bowling Greens
Model Boating Pond
Comm. Cen.
Queens Park
Hoylake Cott.
Kingsmead School
Play. Flds.
Meols
Lifeboat Sta.
Lib.
Sch.
Manor Road
Football Ground
Rec. Ground
The Bungalow
Bowl. Grn.
CARR LANE IND. EST.
Hoylake
Play. Fld.
Sports Ground
New Hall Farm
Club House
Club House
HOYLAKE GOLF COURSE
ROYAL LIVERPOOL GOLF COURSE
Hilbre Point
STANLEY
MEOLS DRIVE
A540
A553
MARKET ST.
BIRKENHEAD
NORTH PARADE
DRUMMOND
The Birket
CARR
56
Waste Site
Playing Field
Football
RED ROCKS MARSH

31
F
G
H
J
K
24
325
EMBANKMENT
Leasowe Common
Pasture Farm
Leasowe Lighthouse
Caravan Site
The Birket
WALLASEY
Greenacres
North Wirral Coastal Park
Lingham Farm
Eve-a-lyn Farm
Parkfield House
PARK LANE CARAVAN SITE
WIRRAL BEACH CARAVAN PARK
Parkfields
Coastguard Station
Brook
Sewage Pumping Station
Refuse Tip
Arrowe
Moreton Golf Centre
Great Meols Prim. Sch.
Great Meols
Sewage Works
CH47
CH46
Meols
Lingham Prim. Sch.
Running Track
Lingham Park
Works
Refuse Tip
Clay Pit
Carr Hall Farm
Fornalls Bridge
A553
ROAD
HOYLAKE
Wirral
Carr Farm
Green Gates Farm
Playing Field
Foxfield Sch.
Saughall Massie
Nursery
Diamond Farm
Barnacre
Prospect Farm
The Heyes
B5192
CH48
Oldfield Court
Oldfield Manor Farm
Three Lanes End Farm
MASSIE
Three Lanes End
CH49
Greasby Brook
Arrow Brook
Rake House Farm
Long Rake Farm
SAUGHALL
57
32
1
2
3
4
5
6
7
Day Cen.

WALLASEY EMBANKMENT
Moreton Common
LEASOWE ROAD
A551
Leasowe
Castleway Prim.
Leasowe Common
Leasowe Lighthouse
Pasture Farm
The Birket
Ditton Lane Nature Area
Rugby Football Grounds
Reeds Bri.
Wallasey School
Leasowe Rec. Cen.
Comm. Cen.
Leasowe Prim. Sch.
Running Track
Playing Fields
Moreton Golf Centre
Pasture Rd. Bri.
Play. Field
Bowl. Grn.
Play. Fld.
Works
Moreton
Leasowe
PASTURE ROAD
Eastway Prim. Sch.
Clare Mount School
FENDER
A553
Fender Farm
Lingham Prim. Sch.
Running Track
CH46
Foxfield Sch.
HOYLAKE ROAD
Christ Church C of E Prim. Sch.
Wirral
Recreation Ground
Junction 2
M53
M53-MOTORWAY
UPTON ROAD
MORETON ROAD
The Fender
Greenfield
Arrowe Brook
Diamond Farm
SAUGHALL MASSIE ROAD
B5192
Day Cen.
Playground
Comm. Centre
CH49
Overchurch Jun. & Inf. Schools
Hayfield School
Nursery
Warwick Hey Rec. Grd.
Upton Hall School
St. Joseph's Catholic Prim. Sch.
UPTON
UPTON BY-PASS
A5027
Cricket Ground
OLD GREASBY ROAD
B5139
ARROWE PK. R.
M53-MOTORWAY
M53
Arrowe Brook
GREASBY ROAD
Upton Bridge
Cemy.
BY-PASS
A B C D E
1 2 3 4 5 6 7
12
31
58
26
27

33
12
13
59
34
F
G
H
J
K
1
2
3
4
5
6
7
29
330
390
89
88
Junction 1
M53 MOTORWAY
M53
KINGSWAY
TUNNEL ROAD
DOCKS LINK
DOCK ROAD
POULTON ROAD
A554
A5139
A5088
A5145
B5145
A5058
A5030
A553
A5027
B5151
CENTRAL HOSPITAL
Wallasey
Weatherhead High School
The Wallace Recreation Ground
BIDSTON MOSS NATURE RESERVE
The Stargazer
Bidston Moss Nature Reserve
BIDSTON GOLF COURSE
Club House
JUNCTION ONE RETAIL PARK
BIDSTON INDUSTRIAL ESTATE
Bidston
Dee Junction
BIDSTON LINK ROAD
Poulton Bridge
Warehouses
Refuse Incinerator
Lewis's Quay
Poulton Quay
Birkenhead
Superstore
Wirral Tennis and Sports Centre
Tennis Courts
Sports Ground
VALLEY ROAD BUSINESS PARK
Model Yacht Lake
CH41
BRIDGE ROAD
Works
Cheshire's Quay
Graving Dock No.3
Gillbrook Basin
Gas Holders
GALLAGHER IND. EST.
UVECO BUS. CEN.
Birkenhead Nth.
BEAUFORT ROAD
WALLASEY BRIDGE ROAD
HOYLAKE ROAD
LAIRD STREET
BOUNDARY ROAD
BIDSTON ROAD
PARK ROAD
Bus Depot
The Observatory Sch.
Bidston Hall
Church Fm.
Bidston Observatory
BIDSTON HILL
Hillside Farm
Kennels
Recreation Ground
Silver Birch Wood
Bidston Windmill
Park Wood
Beechwood
Manor Grn.
Taylor's Wood
Tam O'Shanter Urban Farm
Rec. Ground
Flaybrick Hill Cemetery
Cricket Ground
Birkenhead Sixth Form Coll.
Claughton
Rugby Grd.
Manor Prim. Sch.
Club House
THE WIRRAL LADIES GOLF COURSE
Prenton
CH43
Rec. Grd.
Sports Grd.
Hillside Prim. Sch.
St. Anselm's Coll. Sports Ground
St. Anselm's College
Convent
Birkenhead High Sch.
Tennis Courts
Play Field
Prep. Sch.
Play. Fld.
Noctorum
LC McAllister
Hosp.

34
A
B
C
D
E
1
2
3
4
5
6
7
13
33
60
LISCARD
A5088
A551
BRIGHTON ST.
SEACOMBE
Town Hall
Guinea Gap Baths & Rec. Cen.
WALLASEY
VICTORIA CENTRAL HOSPITAL
Cricket Ground
Play-ground
Football Ground
CENTRAL PARK
Bowling Greens
Park Prim. Sch.
Oxton Rd. Playing Fields
POULTON ROAD
B5145
BOROUGH RD.
OXTON RD.
GORSEY LA.
WHEATLAND RD.
CHURCH ST.
PROMENADE
KINGSWAY (ME
Comm. Cen.
Seacombe Ship Ferry (Foot) Terminal
Floating Stage
Bus Sta.
Sewage Works
Neighbourhood Resource Cen.
Play Field
Nurs. Sch.
Prim. Sch.
Victoria Park
Poulton
Gas Holders
KINGSWAY
TUNNEL
APP.
GORSEDALE ROAD
Toll Booths
NEW STAY BUSINESS CENTRE
WIRRAL BUSINESS CEN.
Works
Cheshire's Quay
WEST FLOAT IND. EST.
UVECO BUS. CEN.
DOCK ROAD
Seacombe
KELVIN RD.
B5145
BIRKENHEAD RD.
A554
Alfred Pier Head
Birkenhead to Wallasey (Foot Ferry) 10 minu
Dock Masters Office
Alfred Lock
Alfred Dock
Bascule Bridge
Twelve Quays Ferry Terminal
A5139
WEST FLOAT
Sheds
Gillbrook Basin
Cavendish Wharf
Duke St. Wharf
EAST FLOAT
EAST FLOAT QUAY
Vittoria Wharf
Vittoria Dock
MORTAR MILL QUAY
FOUR BRIDGES
TOWER RD.
A554
DUKE ST. BRIDGE
DUKE ST.
A5027
A5030
BEAUFORT RD.
CORPORATION RD.
CLEVELAND ST.
B5146
LAIRD ST.
PARK ROAD NORTH
A5027
Birkenhead Pk.
Rugby Grd.
Tennis Courts
Egerton Dock
Morpeth Dock
Egerton Bri.
Sewage Works
Birkenhead Transport Mus.
CANNING ST.
STREET
A5030
Transport Mus.
Hamilton Sq.
Birkenhead
CONWAY ST.
A553
WATSON ST.
Conway Pk.
BIRKENHEAD PARK
Cricket Ground
Pavilion
Sports Grd.
Playing Fields
Park High School
PARK DRIVE
St. Anselm's College
GROSVENOR
Convent
High Sch.
EXMOUTH ST.
A5029
Bingo
Bus Sta.
THE PYRAMIDS SHOP. CEN.
CHESTER ST.
BOROUGH ROAD
A552
WHETSTONE LA.
Clifton Park
B5148
Birkenhead Central
Gas Holders
ROCK RETAIL PARK
NEW CHESTER ROAD
A41
Art Gall. & Mus.
Green Lane
Hosp.
Birkenhead Priory
The Priory
Shipb Engineer

35
F
G
H
J
K
214
A59
Kingsway
Waterloo Rd.
Great Howard Rd.
Vauxhall Rd.
Scotland Rd.
Leeds Street
A565
A5053
A5036
Princes Half Tide Dock
Princes Jetty
Liverpool to: Douglas (Isle of Man) 2hrs. 30mins. (Fast Ferry)
Liverpool to Wallasey (Seacombe Foot Ferry) 7-8 minutes
LIVERPOOL
Birkenhead to: Belfast 8 hrs. Dublin 8 hrs.
Ship Ferry (Foot) Terminal
Queensway (Mersey Tunnel - Toll)
Mersey Railway Tunnel
Liverpool to Birkenhead (Woodside Foot Ferry) 7-8 minutes
BIRKENHEAD
Monk's Ferry
Graving Dock
Graving Docks
River Mersey
Liverpool
Wirral
Museum of Liverpool (under construction due open 2011)
Canning Graving Docks
Canning Half Tide Dock
Tate Liverpool
Albert Dock
The Beatles Story
Duke's Dock
Salthouse Dock
Wapping Basin
Wapping Dock
Echo Arena
BT Convention Cen.
Queen's Wapping Bridge
Gala Leo Casino
Queen's Dock
Customs & Excise
Merseysport
Coburg Dock (Marina)
Brunswick Dock (Marina)
HMS Eaglet
Brunswick Enterprise Cen.
Moorfields
Lime St.
Central
Liverpool John Moores Uni.
Liverpool Cathedral
Huskisson Mon.
A562
Strand St.
Wapping
Park La.
Jamaica St.
St. James St.
Parliament St.
Up. Parliament St.
Sefton St.
Great George St.
Berry St.
Renshaw St.
London Rd.
Pembroke Pl.
Islington
Hunter Street
Hanover St.
Duke St.
Park Rd.
Toxteth
Brunswick
Lifestyles Pk. Rd.
1
2
3
4
5
6
7
61
34
35

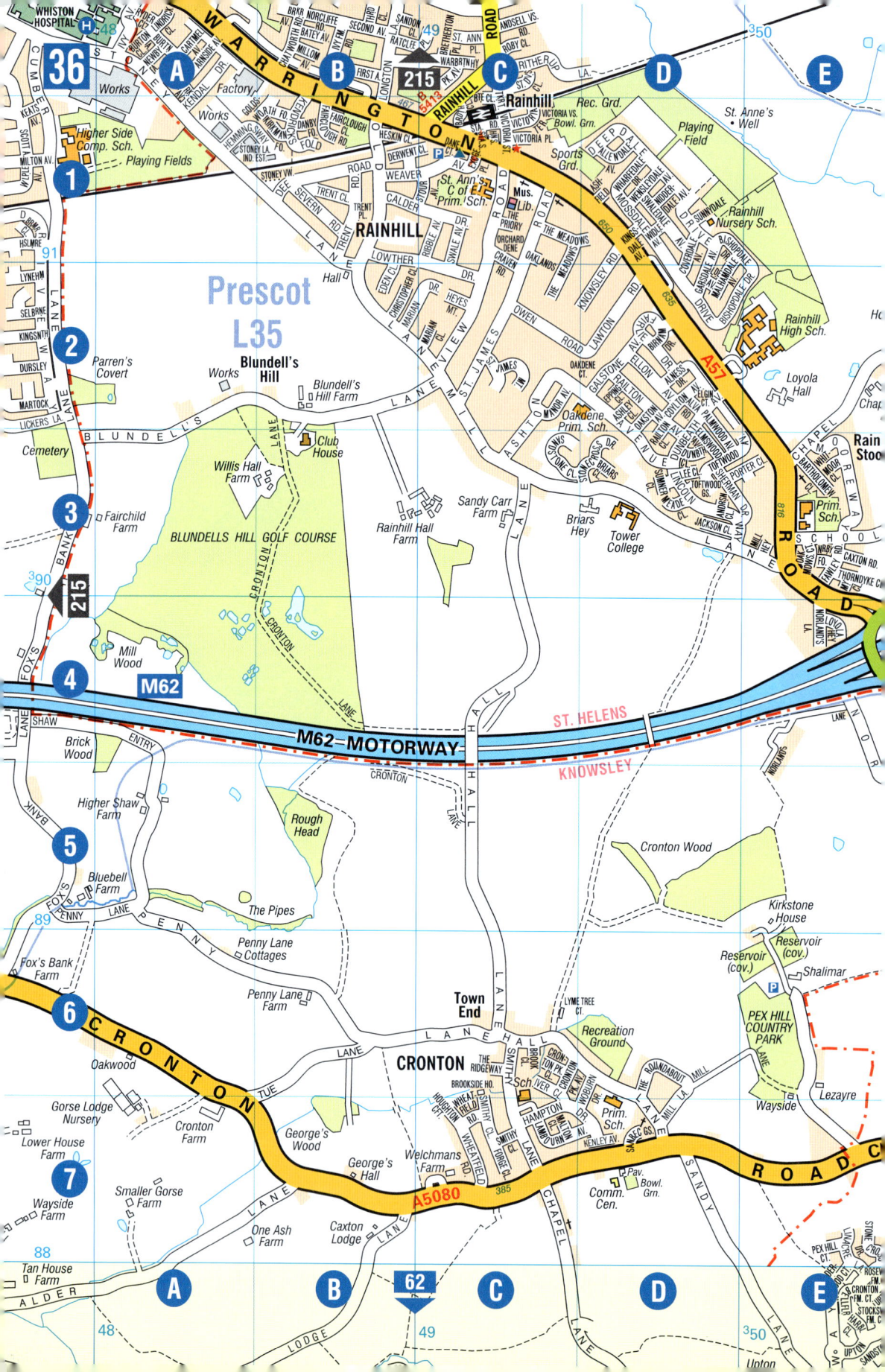
36
A
B
C
D
E
1
2
3
4
5
6
7
215
62
WHISTON HOSPITAL
Works
Factory
Higher Side Comp. Sch.
Playing Fields
WARRINGTON
RAINHILL ROAD
Rainhill
Rec. Grd.
Playing Field
St. Anne's Well
Sports Grd.
St. Ann's C of E Prim. Sch.
Mus. Lib.
RAINHILL
Rainhill Nursery Sch.
Rainhill High Sch.
Loyola Hall
Prescot
L35
Blundell's Hill
Blundell's Hill Farm
Parren's Covert
Cemetery
BLUNDELL'S LANE
Club House
Willis Hall Farm
Oakdene Prim. Sch.
Fairchild Farm
BLUNDELLS HILL GOLF COURSE
Rainhill Hall Farm
Sandy Carr Farm
Briars Hey
Tower College
Prim. Sch.
ROAD
A57
Mill Wood
M62
M62 MOTORWAY
ST. HELENS
KNOWSLEY
Brick Wood
Higher Shaw Farm
Rough Head
Cronton Wood
Bluebell Farm
The Pipes
Kirkstone House
Reservoir (cov.)
Shalimar
Penny Lane Cottages
Fox's Bank Farm
Penny Lane Farm
Town End
Recreation Ground
PEX HILL COUNTRY PARK
CRONTON
Oakwood
Gorse Lodge Nursery
Cronton Farm
George's Wood
Sch.
Prim. Sch.
Wayside
Lezayre
Lower House Farm
George's Hall
Welchmans Farm
Comm. Cen.
Pav.
Bowl. Grn.
A5080
ROAD
Wayside Farm
Smaller Gorse Farm
One Ash Farm
Caxton Lodge
Tan House Farm
ALDER
LODGE
CHAPEL LANE
SANDY LANE
48
49
350
88
89
90
91

St. Helens
WA9
Widnes
WA8
Micklehead Green
Sutton Manor
Clock Face
Bold Heath
Lunts Heath
M62 MOTORWAY
M62
Junction 7
WARRINGTON ROAD
WATKINSON WAY
JUBITS LANE
WILMERE LANE
LUNT'S HEATH ROAD
CLOCK FACE ROAD
DERBY ROAD
ST. HELENS LINKWAY
A570
A57
A557
A569
A5080
B5419
LEA GREEN BUSINESS PARK
LEA GREEN INDUSTRIAL ESTATE
King George's Field
Union Bank Farm
Upper Bank Farm Cottage
Tibb's Cross Farm
Old Brook Hall Farm
Bold Bridge Cottages
Willowbank Farm
Harefield Farm
Rainhill Place Farm
Wilmere House
Wilmere Park
Fairview House
Playing Fields
Pavilion
Cranshaw Hall
Glebe Farm
Garden Centre
Mill Green Farm
Mill Green Cottage
Barnside
Lunt's Bridge Farm
Nursery Farm
Bridge Farm
Model Farm
Union Bridge Farm
Sutton Side Farm
Sutton Road Farm
Yew Tree Farm
Wood's House Farm
Brookhouse Bridge
Micklehead Green Farm
ST. HELENS
HALTON
Farnworth C of E Prim. Sch.
BOLD IND. EST.
215
38
63

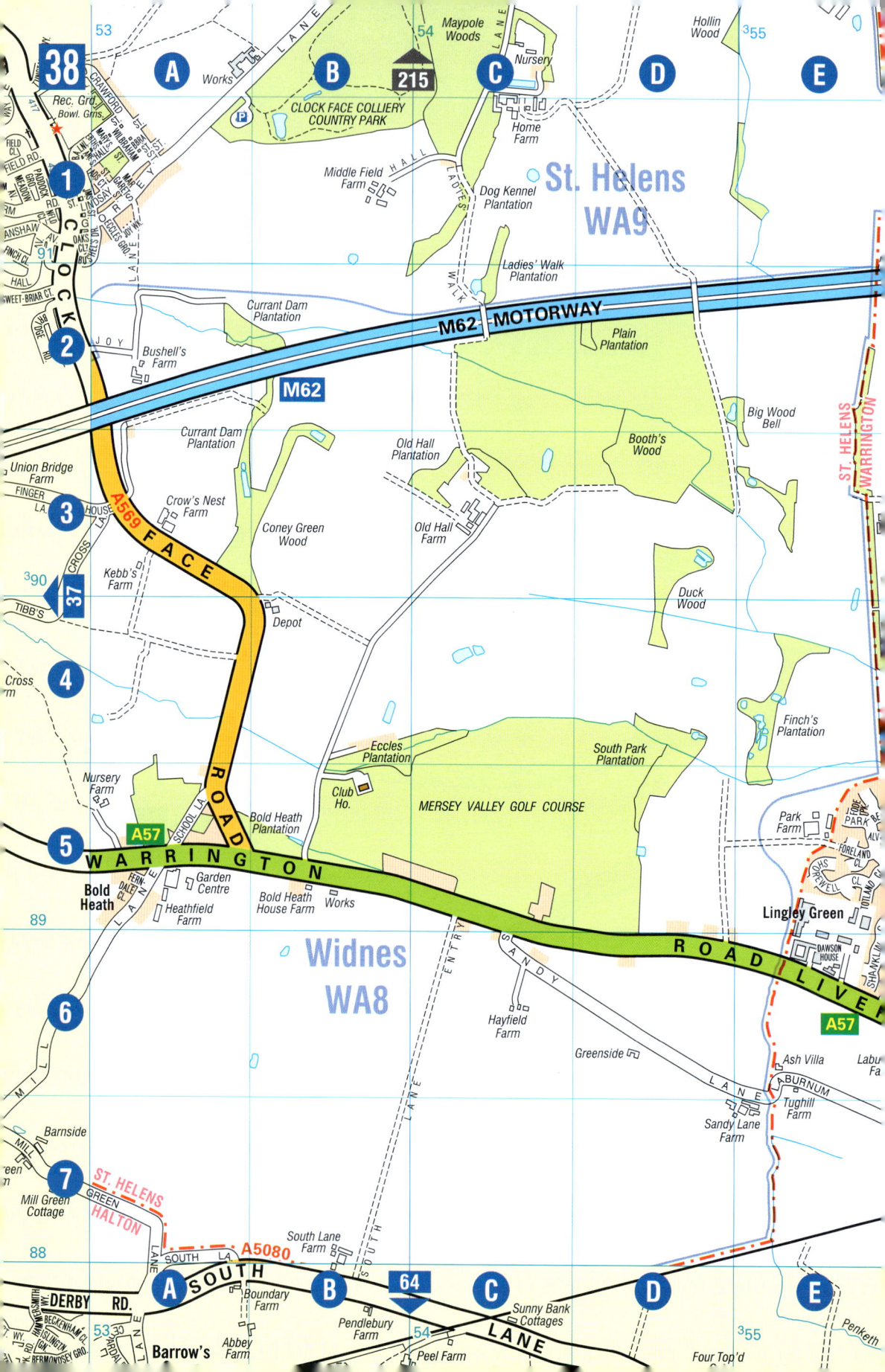
38
53
54
215
Maypole Woods
Nursery
Hollin Wood
355
A
B
C
D
E
Works
CLOCK FACE COLLIERY COUNTRY PARK
Rec. Grd.
Bowl. Grns.
CRAWFORD
Home Farm
Middle Field Farm
HALL
LADIES
Dog Kennel Plantation
St. Helens WA9
1
LINDSAY ST.
PADDOCK RD.
MEADOW
FIELD RD.
FIELD CL.
ANSHAW
FINCH CL.
HALL
SWEET-BRIAR CT.
OAKS CL.
ECCLES GRO.
JOY WK.
LANE
91
CLOCK
Ladies' Walk Plantation
WALK
Currant Dam Plantation
M62 MOTORWAY
JOY
Bushell's Farm
2
Plain Plantation
M62
Big Wood Bell
Currant Dam Plantation
Old Hall Plantation
Booth's Wood
ST. HELENS
WARRINGTON
Union Bridge Farm
FINGER LA.
3
HOUSE LA.
A569
FACE
Crow's Nest Farm
Coney Green Wood
Old Hall Farm
CROSS
Kebb's Farm
390
37
TIBB'S
Depot
Duck Wood
4
Cross
Finch's Plantation
Eccles Plantation
South Park Plantation
ROAD
Nursery Farm
Club Ho.
MERSEY VALLEY GOLF COURSE
Park Farm
A57
SCHOOL LA.
Bold Heath Plantation
5
WARRINGTON
FORELAND CL.
Bold Heath
FERNDALE CL.
LANE
Garden Centre
Heathfield Farm
Bold Heath House Farm
Works
Lingley Green
89
ENTRY
DAWSON HOUSE
ROAD
LIVER
Widnes WA8
SANDY
6
Hayfield Farm
A57
Greenside
Ash Villa
LANE
LABURNUM
Tughill Farm
MILL
Sandy Lane Farm
Barnside
MILL
7
ST. HELENS
HALTON
GREEN
Mill Green Cottage
South Lane Farm
SOUTH
88
LANE
SOUTH LA.
A5080
SOUTH
A
B
64
C
D
E
DERBY RD.
Boundary Farm
Sunny Bank Cottages
Pendlebury Farm
LANE
53
54
355
Penketh
Abbey Farm
Barrow's
Peel Farm
Four Top'd

Warrington
WA5
Burtonwood Service Area
M62 MOTORWAY
M62
Junction 8
Kingswood
Westbrook
Lingley Mere
LINGLEY MERE BUSINESS PARK
Sorting Office
Airfield (disused)
Warehouses
Limekiln Farm
Joy Lane Farm
Ivy Cottage
Highfield
Dial Post Farm
Jacklegs Plantation
GEMINI BUSINESS PARK
INTERNATIONAL BUSINESS CEN.
Mary Ann Meadows Plantation
Mary Ann Meadows
Cherry Tree Farm
Whittle Wood
Great Sankey Leisure Cen.
Great Sankey High Sch.
Barrow Hall Prim. Sch.
All Weather Pitch
Whittle Brook
Brow Farm
Chapelford Urban Village
Great Sankey
Reservoirs
Sankey (for Penketh)
Penketh High Sch.
Great Sankey Prim. Sch.
Heathside
Sports Grd.
Halton's Bri.
SANKEY WAY
A57
A562
PENKETH RD.
ORION BOULEVARD
LINGLEY GREEN AVENUE
WHITTLE AVENUE
BURTONWOOD ROAD
LIVERPOOL ROAD
STOCKS LANE
14
65
40
F
G
H
J
K
1
2
3
4
5
6
7
56
57
58

M62 MOTORWAY
CROMWELL AVENUE
A574
Callands
Westbrook
WESTBROOK WAY
Dallam
Winwick Quay
Bewsey
Old Hall
Gulliver's World Theme Park
Burtonwood Heritage Attraction
SANKEY VALLEY PARK
Sankey Brook
St. Helens Canal
WARRINGTON HOSPITAL
SANKEY WAY
A57
LIVERPOOL RD.
A5061
MIDLAND
Warrington Bank Quay
Sankey Bridges
WARRINGTON
WA5
Little Moss Wood
Big Wood
Twenty Acre Wood
Ladies Walk Wood
Bog Wood
Twig Wood
Bewsey Lock
Bewsey Old Hall
St. Gregory's Catholic High School
The Peace Centre
Sacred Heart Cath. Prim. Sch.
David Lloyd Leisure
Sports Ground
Playing Field
Depot
Works
Superstore
Warehouses
GEMINI BUSINESS PARK
ALBAN RETAIL PARK
WARRINGTON CENTRAL TRADING ESTATE
St. Rocco's Hospice
Council Offs.
Dallam Prim. Sch.
A49
15
39
66

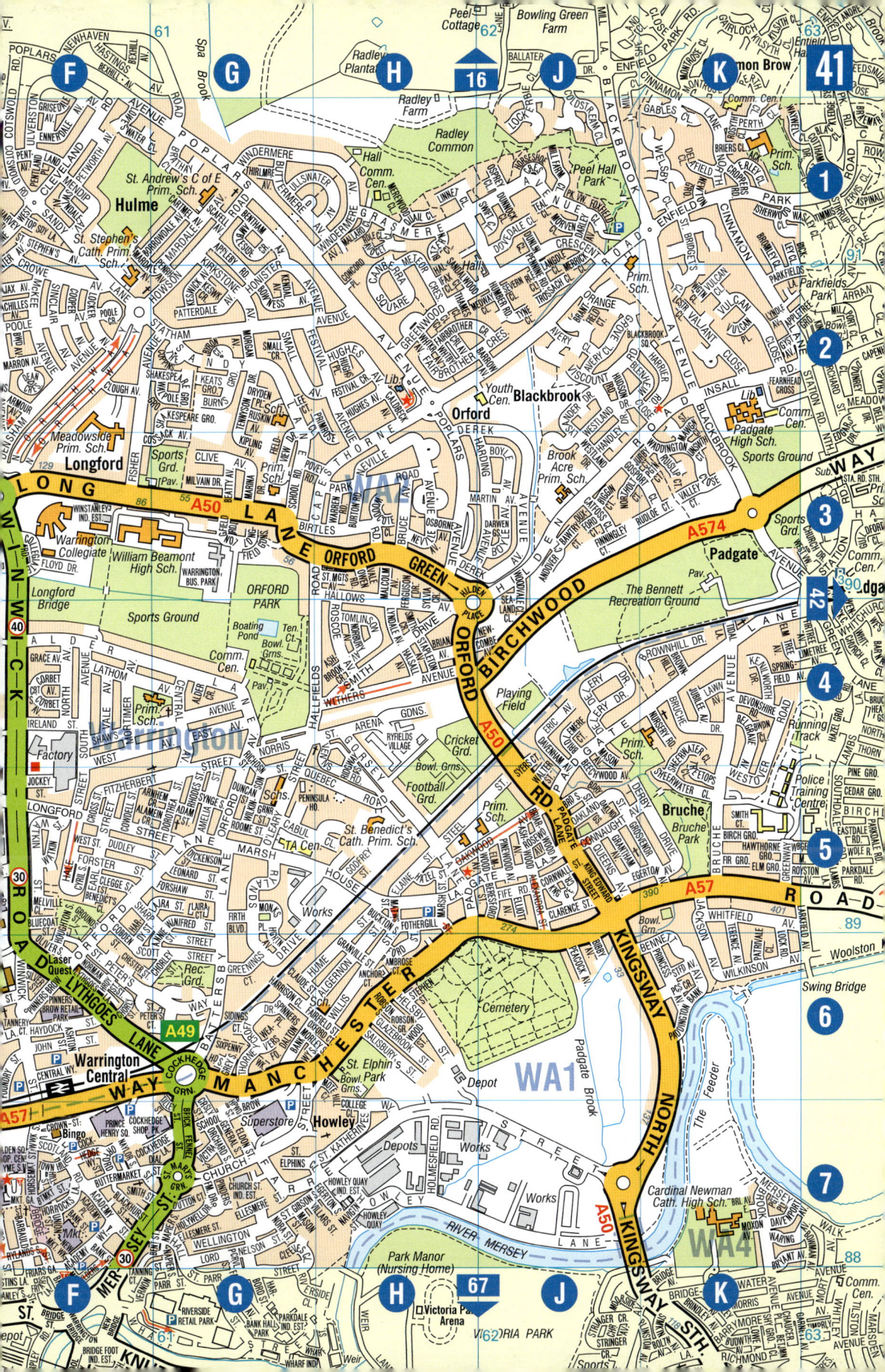

41
16
67
42
F
G
H
J
K
1
2
3
4
5
6
7
61
62
63
88
89
90
91
Peel Cottage
Bowling Green Farm
Radley Plantation
Radley Farm
Radley Common
Peel Hall Park
Hulme
St. Andrew's C of E Prim. Sch.
St. Stephen's Cath. Prim. Sch.
Longford
Meadowside Prim. Sch.
Orford
Blackbrook
Youth Cen.
Padgate High Sch.
Sports Ground
Padgate
Brook Acre Prim. Sch.
LONG LANE
ORFORD GREEN
BIRCHWOOD WAY
A50
A574
A57
A49
WA2
WA1
WA4
Warrington Collegiate
William Beamont High Sch.
Longford Bridge
ORFORD PARK
Boating Pond
The Bennett Recreation Ground
Playing Field
Warrington
Cricket Grd.
Football Grd.
Bruche
Bruche Park
Police Training Centre
Running Track
St. Benedict's Cath. Prim. Sch.
Cemetery
Padgate Brook
St. Elphin's Park
Depot
Howley
Superstore
Warrington Central
CENTRAL WAY
MANCHESTER ROAD
LYTHGOES LANE
WINWICK ROAD
KINGSWAY NORTH
KINGSWAY STH.
Swing Bridge
Woolston
The Feeder
Cardinal Newman Cath. High Sch.
RIVER MERSEY
Park Manor (Nursing Home)
Victoria Park Arena
VICTORIA PARK
Riverside Retail Park
Bingo
Mkt.
Works
Depots

42
A
B
C
D
E
17
64
65
M6
Club House
Playing Field
BIRCHWOOD GOLF COURSE
University of Chester (Padgate Campus)
BIRCHWOOD
Birchwood High Sch.
Birchwood Leisure & Tennis Complex
Playing Field
YMCA
Birchwood Shopping Centre
Birchwood
Fearnhead
Longbarn Park
A574
Warrington
Moss Lane Farm
B5210
M6 MOTORWAY
Padgate High Sch.
Sports Ground
Longbarn Prim. Sch.
Warehouses
Grange
Factory
Padgate
41
WOOLSTON PARK
Playing Fields
WOOLSTON
WA1
WA2
Green Lane School
Running Track
Police Training Centre
Paddington
Woolston High Sch.
Woolston Prim. Sch.
Woolston Leisure Cen.
A57
MANCHESTER
Woolston New Cut
Swing Bridge
Grey Mist
RIVER MERSEY
Woolston Weir
THE EYES
WA4
Morris Brook
68
Works
Thelwall Ferry (Foot)
88
89
90
91
1
2
3
4
5
6
7

Oakwood
Birchwood C of E Prim. Sch.
Birchwood Brook Park
WA3
WOOLSTON MOSS
MARTINCROFT MOSS
Moss Farm
Moss End Croft
Marshall's Farm
Moss Brow Cottages
New Moss Farm
Moss Side Farm
Nurseries
Junction 21
M6 MOTORWAY
M6
B5210
AVENUE
GRANGE
Martinscroft
ROAD
MANCHESTER
A57
Brookside Farm
Moss Side Farm
The Oaks
Lynbrook
Green Valley Farm
Woodside Farm
Swithen Hill Wood
Butchersfield Canal
BUTCHERSFIELD
Butchersfield Bight
Bollin Point
Rixton Junction
RIVER MERSEY
THELWALL EYE
THELWALL VIADUCT
MANCHESTER SHIP CANAL
LYMM GOLF COURSE
Lymm
WA13
Club House
Sow Brook
Whitbarrow Farm
Pump House
Playing Fld.
Prospect Farm
PROSPECT LANE
Moss Side Farm No. 2
Barn End Farm
Woodend Farm
Woodend Cottage
WOODEND LANE
The Bungalow
Top End Farm
Down's Covert
RIXTON MOSS
Moss Head
Rixton Firs
Tomfield Wood
BUSH LANE
HOLLY
Moss Farm
Green Alley Farm
BROOK LANE
JUNIPER
STATHAM LANE
Thelwall Brook
18
44
69
F G H J K
1 2 3 4 5 6 7
66 67 68
88 89 90 91

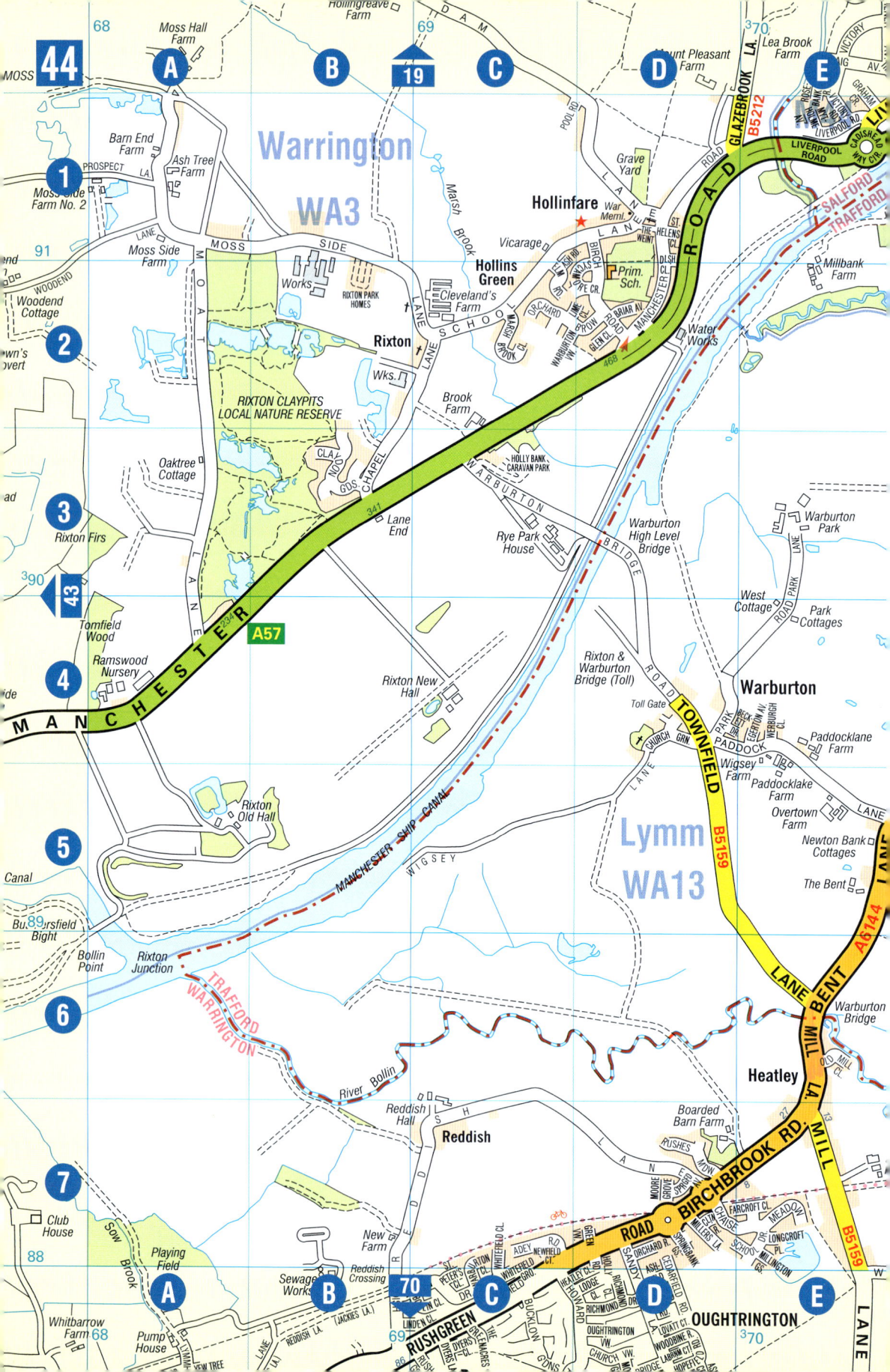
Warrington
WA3
Lymm
WA13
Moss Hall Farm
Hollingreave Farm
Mount Pleasant Farm
Lea Brook Farm
Barn End Farm
Ash Tree Farm
PROSPECT LA.
Moss Side Farm No. 2
Moss Side Farm
MOSS SIDE
MOAT LANE
WOODEND
Woodend Cottage
Works
RIXTON PARK HOMES
Cleveland's Farm
Rixton
SCHOOL LANE
Wks.
RIXTON CLAYPITS LOCAL NATURE RESERVE
Oaktree Cottage
CHAPEL LANE
Lane End
Brook Farm
HOLLY BANK CARAVAN PARK
WARBURTON BRIDGE
Rye Park House
Hollinfare
War Memi.
Vicarage
Hollins Green
Prim. Sch.
Grave Yard
POOL RD.
GLAZEBROOK LA.
B5212
LIVERPOOL ROAD
CADISHEAD WAY CIR.
MANCHESTER ROAD
A57
Water Works
Millbank Farm
SALFORD
TRAFFORD
Warburton High Level Bridge
Warburton Park
West Cottage
Park Cottages
PARK ROAD
PARK LANE
Rixton & Warburton Bridge (Toll)
Toll Gate
Warburton
CHURCH GRN.
TOWNFIELD
PADDOCK
Wigsey Farm
Paddocklane Farm
Paddocklake Farm
Overtown Farm
Newton Bank Cottages
The Bent
B5159
A6144
LANE
Rixton Firs
Tomfield Wood
Ramswood Nursery
Rixton New Hall
Rixton Old Hall
MANCHESTER SHIP CANAL
WIGSEY
Canal
Butterfield Bight
Bollin Point
Rixton Junction
TRAFFORD
WARRINGTON
River Bollin
Warburton Bridge
Heatley
BENT
MILL LA.
OLD MILL CL.
Reddish Hall
Reddish
REDDISH LANE
Boarded Barn Farm
RUSHES MDW.
MOORE GROVE
BIRCHBROOK RD.
ROAD
FARCROFT CL.
MEADOW DR.
LONGCROFT PL.
MILLINGTON GS.
SCHOOL
MILLERS LA.
SPRINGBANK
CEDARFIELD RD.
ORCHARD R.
SANDY
HOLLY
RICHMOND DR.
HEATLEY CL.
LODGE
HOWARD
BUCKLOW G'DNS
OUGHTRINGTON
OUGHTRINGTON VW.
CHURCH VW.
LOVATT CT.
WOODBINE R.
RUSHGREEN
LINDEN CL.
JACKIES LA.
REDDISH LA.
New Farm
Reddish Crossing
Sewage Works
Club House
Sow Brook
Playing Field
Whitbarrow Farm
Pump House
LYMM
YEW TREE
WHITEFIELD
ADEY RD.
NEWFIELD CT.
GREEN VW.
Rixton Firs
19
43
70
68
69
370
91
90
89
88

Works
Gas Holders
Gas Works
Res.
PARTINGTON
Manchester Ship Canal
A57
A6144
B5160
Partington Leisure Cen.
Broadoak School
Playing Fields
Recreation Ground
Coroners Wood
Broadoak Wood
Youth Cen.
Prim. Sch.
Sch.
Lib.
Partington Shop. Cen.
Red Brook
Brook Ho.
Broad Oak Farm
Covershaw Bridge
Sinderland Brook
Weir
Townsend Farm
Lands End Farm
Pear Tree Cottage
Birch Cottage
Birch Farm
Mosslane Farm
Lighthouse Farm
Heathlands Farm
Midlands Farm
Poultry Houses
Moss Wood
Jack Hey Gate Farm
Roughlands Cottage
Moss Hall Farm
Longridge Farm
Caldwell Brook
Villa Farm
Mossbrow
Moss Brow Farm
School House
Yewtree Farm
Warburton Nurseries
Moss Cottage
Petershouse Farm
Orchardhouse Farm
Reed House Farm
Matchington Farm
Silver Birches
Lane End Cottage
Holly Cottage
Box Edge
Carr Green
Higher Carr Green Farm
Wittenspithall Cottages
Bridge Farm
Carr Green House
Gatehouse Farm
Boundary Farm
Park View
Smithy Cottage
Warburton Bridge
Station House
Fox Covert
River Bollin
Lower Carr Green Farm
Holly Bank
The Hollies
Dunham Woodhouses
Ash Farm
Barns Lane Farm
Manor House Farm
Little Heatley
Bollin Cottages
Agden View
Dunham Underbridge
Whiteoak Wood
WARBURTON LANE
DUNHAM ROAD
PADDOCK LA.
STATION ROAD
WOODHOUSE LANE
MOSS LANE
SINDERLAND LANE
CARRGREEN LANE
GORSEY LANE
SAWPIT STREET
HENSHALL LANE
BACK LANE
BARNS LANE
HEATH FARM LANE
MOSS VIEW ROAD
BROADWAY
CROSS LANE EAST
CROSS LA. WEST
RED BROOK RD.
LOCK LANE
OAK ROAD
MANCHESTER NEW RD.
CHAPEL LANE
CENTRAL ROAD
RUSSELL RD.
20
71
46
F G H J K
1 2 3 4 5 6 7

Manchester
M31
CARRINGTON MOSS
Partington Junction
Sinderland Green
Altrincham Crematorium
Garden of Rest
Lawn Cemetery
Redhouse Farm Maize Maze
DARK LANE NATURE RESERVE
Brookheyes Farm
Hogswood Covert
Brookheys Covert
Birchouse Farm
Birchmoss Covert
Sewage Works
Woodcote Farm
Training Ground
Swiss Cottage
Pav.
Res.
Townsend Farm
Boxtree Cottages
Yewtree House
Green Lane Farm
Henshall Farm
Sinderland House Farm
Redhouse Farm
Whitehouse Farm
Red House Cottages
Pear Tree Farm
Blackbrow Farm
Black Moss Farm
Black Moss Covert
Dairyhouse Farm
Higher House
Brookfield Cottage
Four Cottages
Brook Cottage
Silver Birches
Raingill Cottages
Red Beech Farm
Park View
Grovehouse Farm
Cinderland Crossing
Seamons Moss Bridge
Playing Field
Oldfield Brow Prim. Sch.
Dunham Sch. Bri.
Dunham Massey
Little Heath Farm
WA14
Oldfield Brow
Whiteoaks Wood
Canal
Dunhamtown Bridge
Dunham Underbridge
Dunham Town
Club House
DUNHAM FOREST GOLF COURSE
Caldwell Brook
Sinderland Brook
ASHTON ROAD
SINDERLAND ROAD
SINDERLAND LANE
FARM LANE
DARK LANE
BROOKHEYS ROAD
BIRCH ROAD
WOODCOTE ROAD
RED HOUSE LANE
HENSHALL LANE
SCHOOL LANE
WHITEHOUSE LANE
BLACK MOSS ROAD
DAIRYHOUSE LANE
SEAMONS RD.
BACK LANE
OLDFIELD LANE
TAYLOR RD.
WEST AV.
GREENWAY
STAMFORD
ST. MARK'S RD.
HILLCROFT
BRADGATE
FOXHILL
WOODLEIGH
HILLSRISE
LITTLE HEATH LA.
COW LA.
AEGEAN RD.
PACIFIC
CASPIAN RD.
ATLANTIC
SYCAMORE AV.
THE CRESCENT
ASH AV.
STOKOE AV.
TALMAN GRO.
ARDEN PL.
CRES.
ALSTONE DR.
A B C D E
1 2 3 4 5 6 7
21 45 72
73 74 375 88 89 90 91

47
F
G
H
J
K
1
2
3
4
5
6
7
22
48
73
213
Woodhouses
West Timperley
Broadheath
ALTRINCHAM
Timperley
Navigation Rd.
Altrincham
Sale
M33
WA15
A56
A560
B5165
B5164
MANCHESTER ROAD
WASHWAY ROAD
PARK ROAD
STOCKPORT RD.
WOODLANDS RD.
HARBORO WY.
Firs Plantation
Ashton-on-Mersey Sch.
Recreation Ground
Walton Park Leis. Cen.
Miniature Railway
Walton Rd. Park
Woodheys Prim. Sch.
Woodheys Park
Woodheys Clough
Trafford College
Sports Ground
Timperley Brook
Bridgewater Canal
ALTRINCHAM RETAIL PARK
LYON IND. ESTATE
STAG IND. ESTATE
CEDAR TECHNOLOGY CENTRE
Playing Field
John Leigh Park
Navigation Rec. Grd.
St. Hugh's Cath. Prim. Sch.
Wellington School
Willows Prim. Sch.
Timperley Cricket, Hockey, Tennis & Lacrosse Club
St. Vincent Catholic Jun. & Inf. Schs.
ALTRINCHAM GOLF COURSE
Blessed Thomas Holford Catholic College
Grammar Schs.
Altrincham Leis. Cen.
Newton Park
Smith's Bri.
Brook
DUNHAM

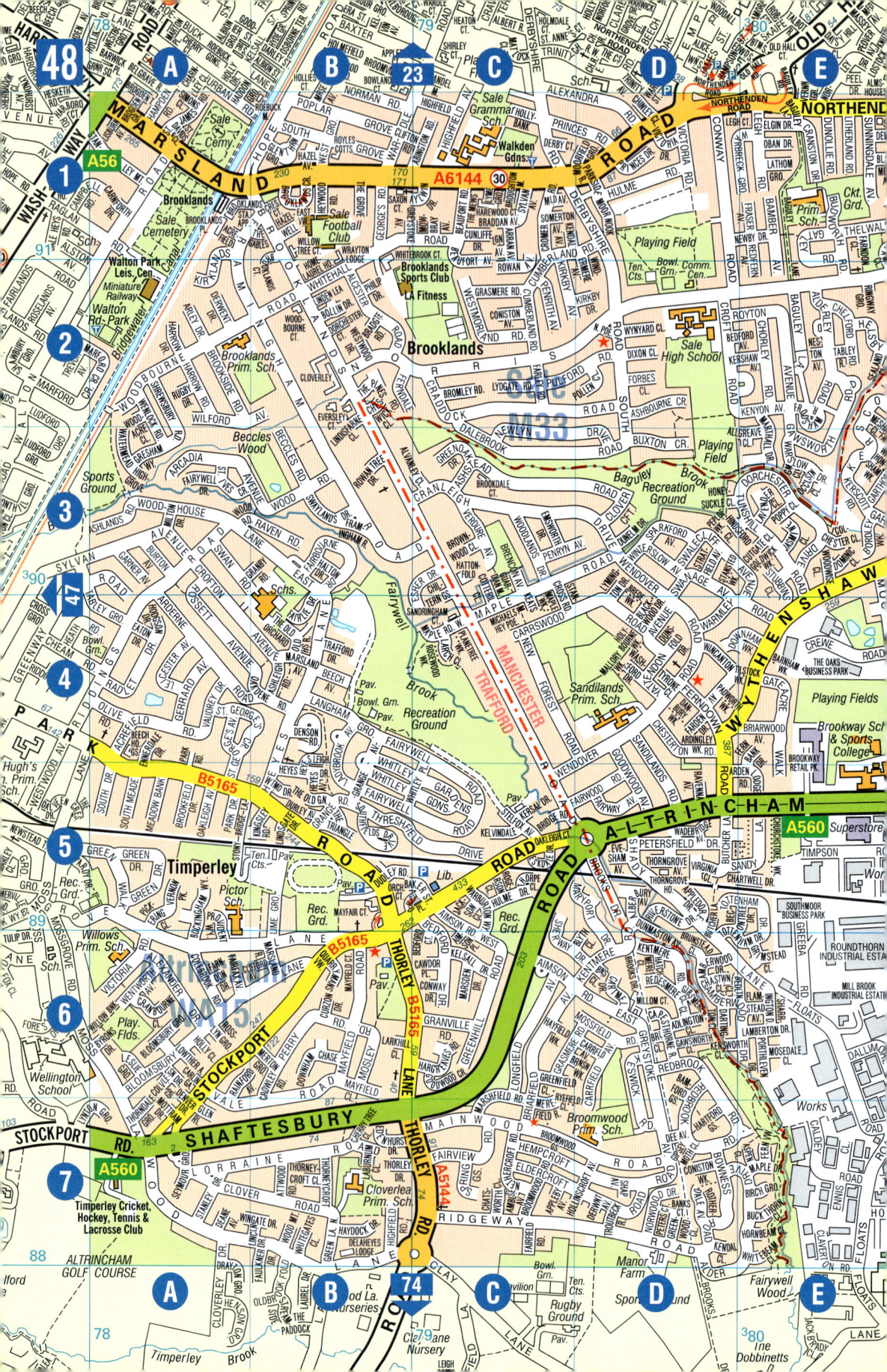
A
B
C
D
E
1
2
3
4
5
6
7
23
47
74
MARSLAND ROAD
A6144
A56
NORTHENDEN ROAD
NORTHENDEN
Brooklands
Sale Cemetery
Sale Football Club
Brooklands Sports Club
LA Fitness
Walton Park Leis. Cen.
Miniature Railway
Walton Rd. Park
Bridgewater Canal
Sale Grammar Sch.
Walkden Gdns.
Playing Field
Sale High School
Brooklands Prim. Sch.
Beccles Wood
Sports Ground
Sale
M33
Baguley Brook
Baguley Recreation Ground
Fairywell Brook
Recreation Ground
MANCHESTER
TRAFFORD
Sandilands Prim. Sch.
WYTHENSHAW
Playing Fields
Brookway Sch & Sports College
THE OAKS BUSINESS PARK
ALTRINCHAM
A560
Superstore
B5165
ROAD
Timperley
Pictor Sch.
Rec. Grd.
Lib.
Willows Prim. Sch.
Altrincham
WA15
Play. Flds.
Wellington School
STOCKPORT
SHAFTESBURY
THORLEY LANE
A5144
B5165
Broomwood Prim. Sch.
Cloverlea Prim. Sch.
Timperley Cricket, Hockey, Tennis & Lacrosse Club
ALTRINCHAM GOLF COURSE
Timperley Brook
RIDGEWAY
Manor Farm
Fairywell Wood
Rugby Ground
SOUTHMOOR BUSINESS PARK
ROUNDTHORN INDUSTRIAL ESTA
MILL BROOK INDUSTRIAL ESTATE
Works
FLOATS
Dobbinetts

49
SALE GOLF COURSE
Shevington Farm
Riding Centre
Riding School
The Bottoms
Electricity Sub. Sta.
217
CHORLTON WATER PARK
Mersey Bank Open Space
Parkway Playing Fields
A5103
PRINCESS ROAD
Kenworthy Wood
Mersey Bank Play. Flds.
Playing Fields
M60
University of Manchester Wythenshawe Sports Ground
Oak Farm Bungalow
Pavilion
Junction 5
NORTHENDEN GOLF COURSE
Club House
M60-MOTORWAY
Kenworthy
Piper Hill High Sch.
SALE ROAD
B5166
Button Lane Prim. Sch.
Rack Ho. Prim. Sch.
City College Manchester (Northern Campus)
PARKWAY
Northenden
Manchester
B5167
PALATINE ROAD
Nan Nook Wood
Northern Moor
Miniature Golf Course
Fir Coppice
Wythenshawe Park Running Track
Mere Wood
Tennis Courts
Bowling Greens
Wythenshawe Hall
The Big Round
WYTHENSHAWE PARK
The Horticultural Centre in Wythenshawe Park
Wythenshawe Community Farm
Garden
Baguley Brook
Royal Oak Rec. Grd.
Playing Fields
Baguley
A560
Gib Lane Wood
Junction 3a
M22
SHARSTON INDUSTRIAL AREA
Round Wood
ALTRINCHAM RD.
M23
Princes Spinney
Junction 2
Junction 3
Blackcarr Wood
Baguley Park
M56
Benchill Prim. Sch.
M56-MOTORWAY
Rodger's Park
WYTHENSHAWE HOSPITAL
Benchill
Newall Green Prim. Sch.
75
F
G
H
J
K
1
2
3
4
5
6
7
50

50
A
B
C
D
E
1
2
3
4
5
6
7
217
76
49
Fielden Park
Mersey Bank Open Space
NORTHENDEN GOLF COURSE
The Hollies Sports Grd.
Nazarene Theological College
Club House
Northenden Bridge
WITHINGTON GOLF COURSE
Sports Ground
Club House
Simon Playing Field
Playing Fields
Didsbury
Manchester Met. Univ. (Didsbury Campus)
Didsbury Sports Cen.
Francis Ho. Hospice
Cricket Grd.
East Didsbury
Fletcher Moss Botanical Gardens
Didsbury Park
River Mersey
DIDSBURY GOLF COURSE
Manchester
TOWERS BUSINESS PARK
Millgate Farm
Old Bedians RUFC
Playing Fields
MANCHESTER
STOCKPORT
Bridge Farm
Junction 4 (M60)
Junction 3
DIDSBURY GOLF COURSE
Sharston
SHARSTON INDUSTRIAL AREA
Refuse Treatment Plant
Rec. Ground
Junction 1 (M56)
Cycle Track
M60
M60 MOTORWAY
M56
M56 MOTORWAY
A34
A5145
A560
B5167
B5166
B5168
B5093
BARLOW MOOR ROAD
WILMSLOW RD.
KINGSWAY
PALATINE RD.
ROYLE GREEN RD.
LONGLEY LANE
SHARSTON RD.
ALTRINCHAM ROAD
NORTHENDEN ROAD
GATLEY ROAD
STYAL ROAD
PARK ROAD
SCHOOL LANE
STENNER LANE
MILLGATE LA.
PARRS WOOD ROAD
SHARSTON GREEN BUSINESS PARK
Gymnastic Cen.
Gatley
GATLEY
Gatley Prim. Sch.
Gatley Hill
Stonepail
Youth Cen.
HOLLYHEDGE PARK
HOLLYHEDGE
Scholes Park
The Kingsway Lower School
The Kingsway Upper Sch.
Patterdale Sports Ground
Prim. Sch.
Rec. Grd.
M20
M22

24
52
77
F
G
H
J
K
1
2
3
4
5
6
7
Burnage
Heaton Moor
Heaton Mersey
Norris Hill
Norris Bank
East Didsbury
Cheadle Heath
CHEADLE
Superstore
Playing Field
Priestnall Rec. Cen.
Priestnall School
Thornfield Park
Heatons Sports Club
Heaton Mersey Common
Cranford Golf Range
Cricket Grd.
Freshfield Nursy Sch.
Didsbury Rd. Prim. Sch.
Heaton Mersey Pk.
Play. Fields
Bowl. Grn.
Mersey Vale Prim. Sch.
Powerleague Soccer Cen.
Parrs Wood Sports Centre
Parrs Wood High School
Recreation Ground
Rugby Ground
HEATON MERSEY INDUSTRIAL ESTATE
The Bungalow
Reservoir
Vale Road Farm
River Mersey
Weir
Cheadle Bridge
Cheadlewood
Sewage Works
Junction 2
M60
M60 MOTORWAY
Abney Court
Abney Hall
Abney Hall Park
Offices
Cheadle Lane Bridge
Cemetery
THE ALEXANDRA BMI HOSPITAL
Playing Field
Cheadle Heath Prim. School
Superstores
Works
Sports Ground
MACKENZIE INDUSTRIAL PARK
Sports Field
Avondale Rec. Cen.
Diamond Jubilee Rec. Grd.
Cheadle Town FC (Park Rd. Stadium)
Cemetery
Rec. Grd.
Public Open Space
LAWNHURST TRADING ESTATE
EUROPA BUSINESS PARK
Ladybridge Prim. Sch.
Adswood Park
Brookfields Park
Cheadle Target Fitness Cen.
Club House
CHEADLE GOLF COURSE
DIDSBURY RD.
A5145
STOCKPORT RD.
A560
EDGELEY RD.
B5465
MANCHESTER RD.
B5095
WILMSLOW RD.
A5149
KINGSWAY
A34
MOORSIDE RD.
B5169
STOCKPORT
HIGH ST.
SK3
SK4
Stockport

52
A
B
C
D
E
1
2
3
4
5
6
7
88
89
90
25
51
78
213
Manchester Rd.
Wellington Rd. North
Wellington Rd. Sth.
Lancashire Hill
Tiviot Way
A626
M60
Junction 27
M60 Motorway
Crookilley Way
St. Marys Way
Stockport
Heaton Norris
Bowerfold Open Space
Heatons Sports Club
Didsbury Rd.
A5145
Travis Brow
Kings Rd.
Junc. 1
Chestergate
Brinksway
King's Valley
A560
Edgeley
Edgeley Rd.
Mercian Way
B5465
Alexandra Park
Stockport County FC & Sale Sharks RUFC (Edgeley Park)
Shaw Heath
Hempshaw La.
Stockport Cemetery & Crematorium
Buxton Rd.
Bramhall Lane
A5102
Heaviley
Adswood
Europa Business Park
Orion Business Park
Cale Green
War Meml. Cricket Grd.
Davenport
Adswood Park Bowl. Grn.
Hollywood Park
Avondale High Sch.
Avondale Rec. Cen.
Hospice
Bridge Hall Prim. Sch.
Sports Ground
Superstore
Rec. Grd.
Gala Bingo
The Old Rectory
Hillcrest Gram. Sch.
Fish Ponds
SK1
SK2
SK3
SK4
SK5
SK8
A6
30

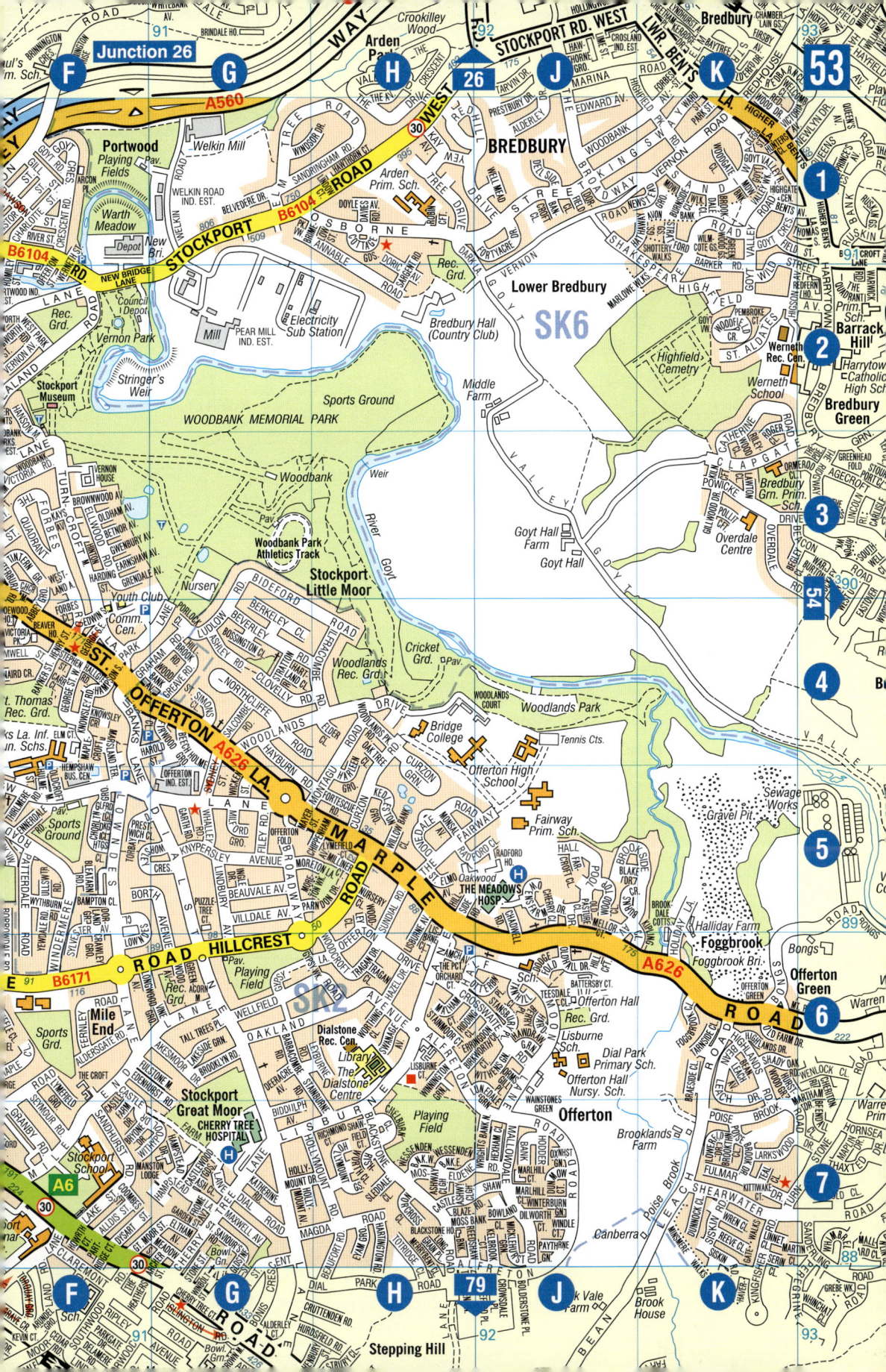

53
Junction 26
Bredbury
BREDBURY
Arden Park
Crookilley Wood
STOCKPORT RD. WEST
LWR. BENTS LA.
HIGHER BENTS LA.
Portwood Playing Fields
Welkin Mill
WELKIN ROAD IND. EST.
Warth Meadow
Depot
New Bri.
A560
B6104
STOCKPORT ROAD
NEW BRIDGE LANE
Arden Prim. Sch.
OSBORNE ROAD
Rec. Grd.
Lower Bredbury
SK6
Bredbury Hall (Country Club)
Electricity Sub Station
PEAR MILL IND. EST.
Mill
Council Depot
Vernon Park
Stringer's Weir
Stockport Museum
Sports Ground
WOODBANK MEMORIAL PARK
Woodbank
Weir
River Goyt
Middle Farm
GOYT VALLEY
Highfield Cemetery
Werneth School
Werneth Rec. Cen.
Barrack Hill
Harrytown Catholic High Sch.
Bredbury Green
Bredbury Grn. Prim. Sch.
Overdale Centre
Goyt Hall Farm
Goyt Hall
Woodbank Park Athletics Track
Stockport Little Moor
Nursery
Youth Club
Comm. Cen.
Cricket Grd.
Woodlands Rec. Grd.
Woodlands Park
Bridge College
Tennis Cts.
Offerton High School
Sewage Works
Gravel Pit
Fairway Prim. Sch.
Oakwood
THE MEADOWS HOSP.
ST. OFFERTON LA.
A626
MARPLE ROAD
HILLCREST ROAD
B6171
Sports Ground
Playing Field
SK2
Mile End
Sports Grd.
Dialstone Rec. Cen.
Library
The Dialstone Centre
Offerton Hall Rec. Grd.
Lisburne Sch.
Dial Park Primary Sch.
Offerton Hall Nursy. Sch.
Offerton
Brooklands Farm
Halliday Farm
Foggbrook
Foggbrook Bri.
Offerton Green
Warren
Stockport Great Moor
CHERRY TREE HOSPITAL
Stockport School
A6
Playing Field
Canberra
Poise Brook
Brook House
Stepping Hill
54
79
1
2
3
4
5
6
7
F
G
H
J
K

A
B
C
D
E
1
2
3
4
5
6
7
27
53
80
93
94
395
91
390
89
88
Greavefold
Reservoir
Heald Wood
Top-o'-th'-hill
Hill Side
Hill Top Farm
Barlowfold
ROMILEY GOLF
Club House
Youth Cen.
Peak Forest Canal
Fitness Centre
Romiley
Romiley Prim. Sch.
STOCKPORT
B6104
RD.
COMPSTALL
Rec. Ground
Tangshutt Fields
ROMILEY
Mills
Barrack Hill
Harrytown Catholic High Sch.
Werneth School
Bredbury Green
Hatherlow
Tang
Hyde Bank Farm
Hydebank Tunnel
Kirk Wood
Chadkirk Farm
Chadkirk Chapel
Oakwood Hall
River Wood
Lower Dale Farm
Marple Dale Farm
Peak Forest Canal
Overdale Centre
Bredbury Grn. Prim. Sch.
OTTERSPOOL
CHADKIRK COUNTRY ESTATE
River Goyt
Weir
Stockport
Marple Dale
Recreation Ground
Bunkers Hill
Ford
Rose Leigh
Chadkirk
Turncliff Wood
Marple Dale Hall
Ley Hey Park
Otterspool Bridge
CHADKIRK BUS. PK.
Garden Cen.
Playing Fields
Gravel Pit
Waterside Farm
Sewage Works
Valley Cottage
Marple Hall School
The Dale Prim. Sch.
Rose Hill Prim. Sch.
The Lodge
Bongs
Offerton Green
Nabwood
Warren Lodge
Nab Wood
Nab Wood Farm
Lower Danbank Farm
Warren Wood
MARPLE
A626
DOOLEY
A627
LANE
STOCKPORT
ROAD
Marple Brook
Rose Hill Marple
MARPLE
Danbank Bri.
High Trees
Higher Danbank Farm
Yew Tree Farm
Warren Wood Prim. Sch.
SK2
Westwood Trading Estate
Marple Wood
Peacefield Prim. Sch.
Club House
Torkington
Pav.
Playing Field
Wood Farm
Brook
The Hollow
STOCKPORT GOLF COURSE
Torkington Wood
OFFERTON
GEORGE
LANE
HIGHER
BENTS
BARRACK HILL
HATHERLOW
SCHOOL BROW
ROAD
A6017

55
28
81
217
F
G
H
J
K
1
2
3
4
5
6
7
96
97
98
91
90
89
88
Wood
Near Benfield
Far Benfield
Gigg Brook
Mossacre
John Hirst Cottage
Whitebottom
Woodheys
Mortin Clough
Etherow Country Park Local Nature Reserve
Benfield Clough
Mortin Farm
School Lane Farm
Bardsley Knoll
Brakanes
Greenways
Compstall Brow
Rydeacre House
Gothic Farm
Weir Cotts.
Ernocroft Wood
Compstall
The Mount
Rabbit Warren
Ernocroft
ETHEROW COUNTRY PARK
Priory Cottage
Compstall Brow
Compstall Hall
Fordsdale
Redbrow Wood
River Etherow
Cherry Tree
Visitor Cen.
Reservoir
Cowhey Farm
Bowling Green
Sewage Works
Lower Ernocraft Farm
Compstall Bri.
Cricket Grd.
The Lodes
Reservoirs
Hillside Farm
Lower Watermeetings Farm
Watermeetings Cottage
River Goyt
Cote Green
SK6
Lane Ends
Sun Hill
Iron Bridge
Aqueduct House
BRABYNS PARK
Bottomlocks House
Play. Field
Broadstone
Brabyns Pk. Rec. Cen.
Rec. Grd.
Pickerings
The Cottage
Marple Wharf Junction
Lime Fold
Mill Brow
Brabyns Wood
Ludworth Prim. Sch.
Marple Locks
Vale Cottage
Greenhill
St. Martins Cott.
Prim. Sch.
Burial Grd.
Prep. Sch.
Marple
Marple Bridge
Primrose Mill
Blackberry Hall
Mill Pond
Brabyn's Sch.
Heathy Bank
Tanpit Cottage
Townscliffe Farm
Old Vicarage
Memorial Park
Mills
Goyt House
Cataract Bridge
Knowle Farm
Mellor Parish Centre
Knowle House
Mellor Prim. Sch.
The Drive
Rec. Grd.
Sports Ground
Mellor Sports Club
Knowle Wood
Mellor
Marple Pool
Sixth Form College
All Saints C of E Prim. Sch.
Bottom's Bri.
Res.
Damsteads Farm
Tarden
Bottom's Hall
Brick Bridge
Linnet Clough
Club House
Whetmorhurst
Roman Lakes
MELLOR & TOWNSCLIFFE
A626
B6104
B6101
COMPSTALL ROAD
GLOSSOP ROAD
LOWER FOLD
BRABYNS BROW
STATION ROAD
STOCKPORT RD.
STRINES ROAD
ARKWRIGHT ROAD
LAKES ROAD
OLD ROAD
MILL LANE
CLEMENT
TOWNSCLIFFE LANE
LONGHURST
FERNWOOD
HOLLINS
KNOWLE ROAD
GIBB LANE

ROYAL LIVERPOOL
GOLF COURSE
HOYLAKE
GOLF COURSE
30
CH47
RED ROCKS MARSH
NATURE RESERVE
Playing Field
Hockey Pitch
Football Ground
Waste Site
Gilroy Nature Park
Newton B
WEST KIRBY
Wirral Sailing Club
West Kirby Marine Lake
Victoria Gdns.
Coronation Gdns.
Tanskey Rocks
Tell's Tower
Lime Wharf
Cubbins Green
Caldy Blacks
RIVER DEE
CALDY HILL
Grange Hill
Grange
Cemetery
Ashton Park
Calday Swim. Pool
Black Horse Hill Jun. & Inf. School
West Kirby Grammar Sch.
MEOLS DRIVE
GRANGE ROAD
BANKS ROAD
SANDY LANE
CALDY ROAD
COLUMN ROAD
BLACK HORSE HILL
SAUGHALL
A540
B5141
B5139
B5192
B5140
GREENBANK
GILROY ROAD
THORSWAY
KING'S DRIVE
CROFT DRIVE WEST
SHORE ROAD
214

F
G
H
J
K
1
2
3
4
5
6
7
31
82
58
Oldfield Manor Farm
Three Lanes End Farm
Three Lanes End
ROAD
PUMP
Greasby Brook
Arrow Brook
Rake House Farm
Long Rake Farm
MASSIE
B5192
OLDFIELD
LANE
CARR
Newton Hall Farm
China Plate Farm
CHINA FARM LANE
Larton
Larton Hey Farm
FRANKBY STILES
Nursery
Greasby Bri.
War Memorial
Football Ground
Manor Ho. Farm
Yew Tree Farm
Bay Tree Farm
B5139
Royden Hall
Bowling Green
Frankby
CH48
CH49
Hillcroft Poultry Farm
Newton
Newton Brook
Wirral
HILL BARK RD.
Cemetery
Royden Manor
Birch House
BIRCH HEYS
Torpenhow
B5140
HILL
Nurseries
IRBYSIDE RD.
FERNDALE AV.
BARK ROAD
ROYDEN PARK
Frankby Mere
Model Railway Centre
Hill Bark
Roodee Mere
Hill Bark Farm House
Quarry Farm
SANDY LA. NORTH
NORTH SANDY LANE
Irby Hill
Irby Hill Farm
Cricket Ground
Redstones Farm
Green Gates
ARROWE BROOK LANE
MILL LANE
Greasby Junior School
Primary Sch.
Greasby Inf. Sch.
MONTGOMERY
TELEGRAPH
ROAD
A540
THURSTASTON COMMON
LOCAL NATURE RESERVE
Playing Fields
Tennis Court
Bowl. Grn.
Poultry Houses
Stapledon Wood
EAST FARM MEWS
PIKES HEY RD.
Pavilion
Paton Field (Sports Ground)
Hockey Pitch
Playing Field
Thurstaston Hill
Thur's Stone
Benty Farm
Strowan
Thurstaston Common Recreation Ground
Hillside Farm
SCHOOL LANE
Dawpool C of E Prim. School
DAWPOOL COTTAGES
THURSTASTON ROAD
Greasby Brook
SANDY LANE
CH61
THORSTONE DR.
HEATHBANK AVENUE
HILLVIEW ROAD
MARTIN CLOSE
Irby Heath
Playing Fields
Club House
CALDY GOLF COURSE
Thurstaston
Dawpool
DAWPOOL FARM
Hill F.
IRBY
Irby Hall
Irby Farm
LONG HEY ROAD
EAST ROAD
LINKS HEY ROAD
GRANGE CROSS HEY
GRANGE CROSS LANE
NEWTON PARK ROAD
SPRINGFIELD AVENUE
FRANKBY ROAD
GREASBY ROAD
GREASBY DRIVE
THORNS DRIVE
MILES LA.
HALL
LLOYD
FERGUSON AV.
HARVEY AV.
BARKER LA.
DANEFIELD RD.
ALLANGATE CL.
STROUD
BROMSGROVE
Lib.
Comm. Cen.
MANOR CT.
LANE
24
25
85
86
87
88

32
57
83
A
B
C
D
E
1
2
3
4
5
6
7
UPTON
FRANKBY
Greasby
Arrowe Hill
Thingwall
Irby Heath
IRBY
CH49
CH61
Wirral
M53
A5027
A551
B5139
B5138
GREASBY ROAD
UPTON ROAD
UPTON BY-PASS
ARROWE PARK RD.
ARROWE PARK ROAD
ARROWE BROOK ROAD
ARROWE BROOK LANE
ARROWE LANE
LIMBO LANE
THINGWALL ROAD
BARNSTON ROAD
Arrowe Brook
Upton Bridge
Superstore
Factories
CHAMPIONS BUS. PARK
ARROWE COMMERCIAL PARK
Playing Fields
Gorse Covert
Fish Pond
Nicholson's Plantation
ARROWE PARK HOSPITAL
ARROWE COUNTRY PARK
Cricket Ground
Card Plantation
Robinson's Plantation
ARROWE PARK GOLF COURSE
Landican Cemetery and Crematorium
Miniature Golf Course
Tennis Courts
Bowling Greens
Day Care Centre
Club Ho.
Pavilion
Greasby Coronation Park
Bowling Greens Ten. Cts.
Brookdale Prim. Sch.
Greenhouse Farm
Arrowe Brook Farm
Arrowe Bridge
Greasby Copse
Our Lady of Pity Catholic Prim. Sch.
Greasby Junior School
Greasby Inf. Sch.
Green Gates
Redstones Farm
Irby Hill Farm
Limbo Lane Plantation
Neilson's Plantation
Tophouse Farm
Nursery
Irby Prim. Sch.
Play. Field
Playing Fields
Harrock Wood
Irby Hall
Thingwall Prim. Sch.
Stanley Sch.
Thingwall Rec. Cen.
Arrowe Hill Prim. Sch.
Res. (cov.)

F
G
H
J
K
33
1
2
3
4
5
6
7
60
84
Noctorum
Oxton
Prenton
CH43
CH42
CH63
Woodchurch
Landican
Storeton
Prenton
M53 MOTORWAY
M53
A552
B5151
Junction 3
TALBOT RD.
Hillside Prim. Sch.
St. Anselm's Coll. Sports Ground
Woodchurch Sports Barn
Comm. Cen.
Running Track
Woodchurch Leisure Cen.
Fender Prim. Sch.
Woodchurch High Sch. Engineering College
Playing Field
Subway
St. Michael & All Angels Catholic Prim. Sch.
Superstore
Ridgeway High School
Townfield Prim. School
Townfield Centre
Mere Hall
LC McAllester Memorial Field
TA Centre
Cricket Grd.
Recreation Ground
Oxton St. Saviour's C of E Prim. Sch.
Recreation Ground
Sports Ground
Prenton Prim. Sch.
Walker Park
Total Fitness
Prenton Way Bus. Units
North Cheshire Trading Estate
Prenton Dell
Old Rockferrians Rugby Ground
PRENTON GOLF COURSE
Cow Hey Covert
Stanley Wood
Prenton Brook
Home Farm
Old Hall Farm
Caravan Park
Grange Farm
Little Storeton
Storeton Hall Farm
Murrayfield Spire Hospital
Lower Heath Wood
Sewage Works
Storeton Brickfields
The Arno

34
59
85
A
B
C
D
E
1
2
3
4
5
6
7
Birkenhead Central
Clifton Park
Green Lane
Oxton
Devonshire Park
TRANMERE
VICTORIA PARK
Rock Ferry
Tranmere Rovers FC (Prenton Park)
Tranmere Rec. Cen.
Mersey Park
Lairdside Maritime Cen.
Walker Park
Club House
Marsh Hey Covert
Ethel's Covert
Storeton Hill
Little Storeton
Storeton
Grange Farm
Storeton Hall Farm
Storeton House Farm
Haven Cottage
The Cottage
CH63
CH43
CH42
Woodhey
Higher Bebington
Playing Field
BEBINGTON
Town Lane Infant School
Higher Bebington Recreation Ground
Bebington High Sports College
Bebington Cemetery
The Oval Sports Centre
The Oval
Ski Slope
Running Track
Games Courts
St. John's Catholic & Inf. Sch.
Dacre Hill
Rock Ferry High Sch.
Prenton High Sch.
Youth Centre
Tennis Courts
Bowling Green
Art Gall. & Mus.
ST. CATHERINE'S HOSP.
Cricket Ground
A552
A41
B5148
B5149
B5151
B5150
WOODCHURCH ROAD
SINGLETON AV.
BOROUGH ROAD
CHURCH ROAD
BEBINGTON ROAD
BEDFORD AV.
BEDFORD ROAD
OLD CHESTER ROAD
NEW CHESTER ROAD
STORETON ROAD
MOUNT ROAD
TOWN LANE
KINGS LANE
CAUSEWAY
STANLEY AVENUE
MARSH LANE
HIGHER BEBINGTON ROAD
VILLAGE ROAD

F
G
H
J
K
35
34
Toxteth
Brunswick
Liverpool
L3
Lifestyles Park Rd.
SEFTON
A5036
ST.
Brunswick Bus. Pk.
Studio
Glacier Building
Harrington
Riverside
Greens Health & Fitness
Ellerman Rd.
Rec. Grd.
88
87
86
85
1
2
3
4
5
6
7
214
LIVERPOOL
WIRRAL
RIVER
MERSEY
Tranmere Beach
Floating Stage
Pier
OIL TERMINAL
Rock Ferry Pier
Rock Ferry
A41
ROCK FERRY BY-PASS
B5136
CHESTER ROAD
NEW FERRY BY-PASS
ESPLANADE
New Ferry Park
Tennis Courts
Football Grd.
Bus Depot
Play. Field
CH62
Sewage Works
New Ferry Play. Fld.
Refuse Tip
Warehouse
Depot
Factory
Bebington
Lady Lever Art Gall.
Mus
Prim. Sch.
Port Sunlight Driving Range
Golf Course
Bromborough Pool
Depots
Pavilion
Cricket Ground
Mayer Park
Council Offices
Lower Bebington
Ormerod Gdns.
War Meml.
86
Refuse Tip
NEW CHESTER ROAD

62
CRONTON RD.
A5080
36
88
A
B
C
D
E
1
2
3
4
5
6
7
Wayside
Smaller Gorse Farm
One Ash Farm
ALDER LANE
STOCKSWELL ROAD
Stockswell Farm
Stock's Well House
LODGE LANE
CHAPEL LANE
SANDY LANE
Comm. Cen.
Bowl. Grn.
KNOWSLEY
HALTON
Holly Farm
Rugby Ground
Upton Lodge
Upton Ho.
Upton Rocks
Widnes WA8
Upton
Prim. Sch.
GREEN ROAD
CHERRY
Comm. Cen.
St. Basils Catholic Prim. Sch.
PRESCOT RD.
Prescot Road Playing Fields
QUEENSBURY WAY
CORNERHOUSE
HEATHFIELD PK.
Plumptons Farm
The Bungalow
215
NETHERLEY ROAD
B5178
Hough Green
Recreation Ground
Recreation Grd.
Widnes RUFC
Bowl. Grn.
Club
Hough Green
Sch.
The Bankfield School
Playing Fields
Tennis Cts.
LIVERPOOL ROAD
Ball o' Ditton
Sch.
Tennis Cts.
Club Ho.
Rec. Grd.
Ashley Sch.
Chestnut Lodge School
Play. Fld.
Comm. Cen.
Sch.
King George's Park
Tray Ash Cottage
Tray Ashes Farm
Tennis Cts.
Pav.
Bowl. Grn.
Hough Green Pk.
Schools
Offs.
Lib.
ROYAL AVENUE
DITCHFIELD RD.
CORONATION
Lower House
Pav.
Bowling Greens
Our Lady of Perpetual Succour Catholic Primary Sch.
30
Ditton
Clincton Wood
EVERITE ROAD INDUSTRIAL ESTATE
Factory
Works
EXPRESS IND. EST.
Prim. Sch.
Club House
ST. MICHAEL'S GOLF COURSE
Subway
SPEKE ROAD
A562
70
ST. MICHAEL'S IND. EST.
MARSHGATE
FIELDGATE
Ditton Brook
Steward's Brook
Lovel's Hall (site of)
Works
Depot
DITTON ROAD
Mill
Depot
Works
Mills
GOLDEN TRIANGLE IND. EST.
Works
Linner Farm
Halebank Rec. Grd.
CLAPGATE CRES.
FOUNDRY LA.
Ditton Brook
MATHIESON ROAD
The Marsh
WEST BANK DOCK ESTATE
48
49
350
385
87
86

FARNWORTH
WIDNES
Lunts Heath
Crow Wood
Appleton
Kingsway
Simm's Cross
Halton View
Moss Bank
Lugsdale
Woodend
Farnworth C of E Prim. Sch.
Widnes Crematorium
Cemetery
Widnes
Birchfield Nursery Sch.
Playing Fields
Saints Peter & Paul Catholic College
Wade Deacon High Sch.
Recreation Grd.
Victoria Park
Fairfield High School
Playing Field
Moorfield Prim. Sch.
Youth Cen.
The Bongs
Crow Wood Pk.
Crow Wood Health Pk.
Green Oaks Shop. Cen.
Superstore
Kingsway Leisure Cen.
Riverside Coll. Halton
Town Hall
Widnes Vikings RLFC (Halton Stadium)
Leigh Recreation Ground
Council Depot
Gala Bingo
The Barkin Centre
Widnes Trade Park
Bowers Business Park
Bowers Park Ind. Est.
Kingfisher Bus. Pk.
Heron Bus. Pk.
Carter House Br.
St. Helen's Canal (disused)
Widnes Warth
Iron Br.
Spike Island
Catalyst Science Discovery Cen.
River Mersey
Runcorn Sands
Mill Green Farm
Mill Green Cottage
Bold Industrial Estate
DERBY ROAD
A5080
A557
WATKINSON WAY
BIRCHFIELD ROAD
B5419
KINGSWAY
LEIGH AVENUE
B5178
DEACON RD.
ALBERT RD.
HALTON VIEW RD.
WARRINGTON RD.
FERRY ROAD
A562
FIDDLERS
WIDNES BY-PASS
ASHLEY WY. W.
ASHLEY WY.
EASTERN
NEW MERSEY CROSSING (Proposed)
QUEENS WAY
A533
MOOR LA.
MILTON AVENUE
LOCKETT ROAD
APPLETON
F G H J K
1 2 3 4 5 6 7
37
64
89
51 52 53
85 86 87 88

64
38
90
63
Barrow's Green
Sunnybank Woodland Park
Boundary Farm
Pendlebury Farm
Abbey Farm
Peel Farm
Sunny Bank Cottages
ST. HELENS
WARRINGTON
Four Top'd Oak
Brook Farm
Doe Green
A5080
FARNWORTH
SOUTH LANE
DERBY RD.
Whitfields Cross
Widnes WA8
Moorfield Prim. Sch.
Youth Cen.
Rec. Grd.
Fowl Farm
MOWCROFT LANE
Laburnum Cottage
Clock Lane Farm
Cuerdley Cross
Rosetree Farm
Cross Lane Farm
WIDNES ROAD
A562
DAN'S RD.
Crow Wood Health Pk.
Playing Fields
Marsh End Farm
Cooling Towers
Fiddlers Ferry Power Station
WA5
Shell Green
Works
Wks.
Prim. Sch.
Halton View
FIDDLERS FERRY RD.
Taylor's Crossing
Moss Bank
Works
St. Helens Canal (New Cut)
Hempstones Point
WIGG ISLAND
Runcorn WA7
RIVER
Cuerdley Marsh
Round Chevaral
Landing Stage
Runcorn Sands
Astmoor Salt Marsh

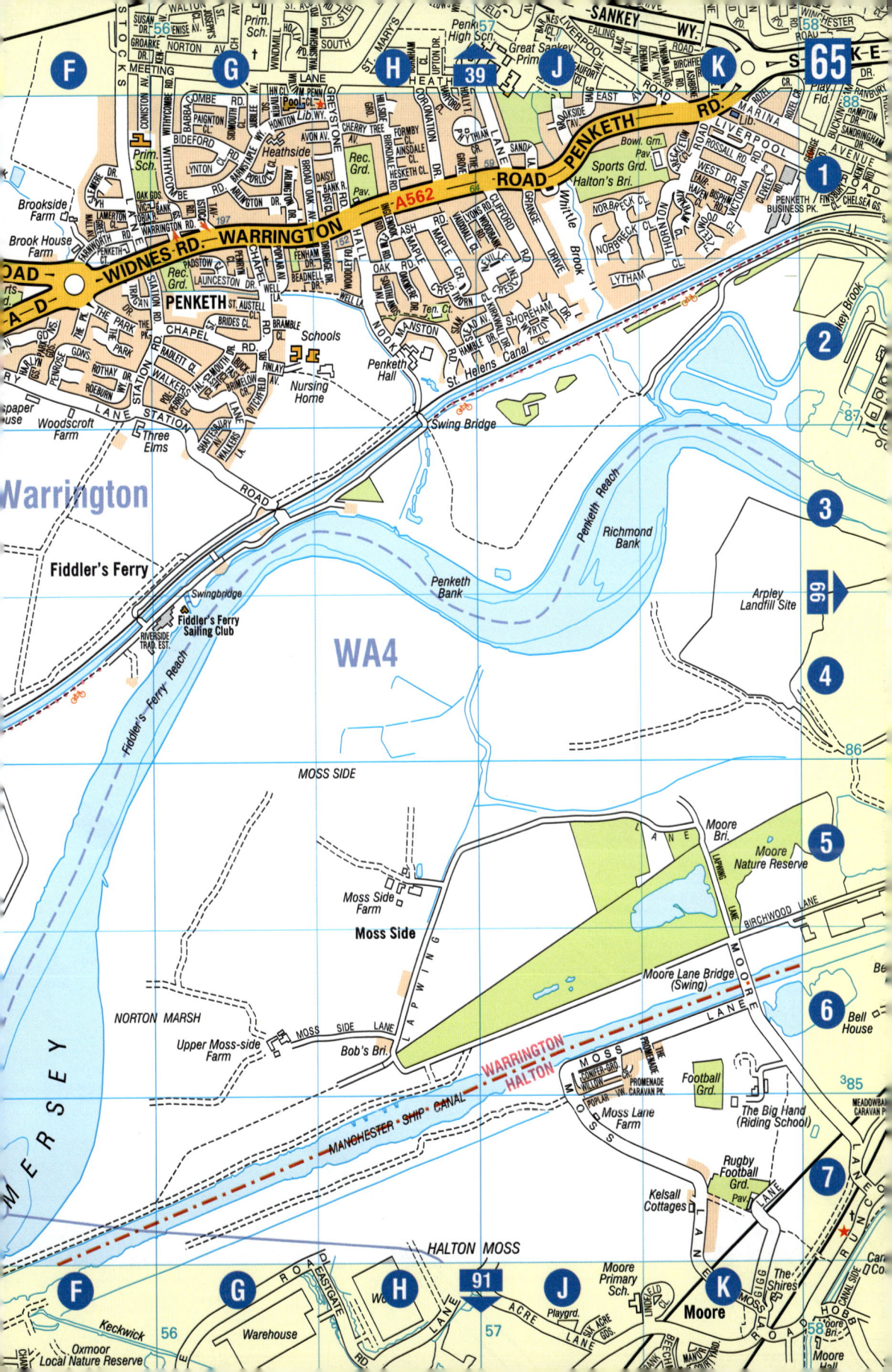
Warrington
WA4
PENKETH
Fiddler's Ferry
Fiddler's Ferry Sailing Club
Moss Side
MOSS SIDE
NORTON MARSH
HALTON MOSS
Moore
MERSEY
MANCHESTER SHIP CANAL
St. Helens Canal
WARRINGTON
HALTON
Penketh Reach
Fiddler's Ferry Reach
Penketh Bank
Richmond Bank
Arpley Landfill Site
Moore Nature Reserve
Moore Bri.
Moore Lane Bridge (Swing)
Bob's Bri.
Swing Bridge
Swingbridge
Moss Side Farm
Upper Moss-side Farm
Moss Lane Farm
Kelsall Cottages
The Big Hand (Riding School)
Bell House
Rugby Football Grd.
Football Grd.
Penketh Hall
Nursing Home
Schools
Woodscroft Farm
Three Elms
Brookside Farm
Brook House Farm
Sports Grd.
Halton's Bri.
Penketh High Sch.
Great Sankey Prim.
Heathside
Oxmoor Local Nature Reserve
Keckwick
Warehouse
Moore Primary Sch.
The Shires
WARRINGTON RD.
WIDNES RD.
PENKETH RD.
SANKEY WY.
A562
LAPWING LANE
MOSS SIDE LANE
MOORE LANE
BIRCHWOOD LANE
ACRE LANE
MOSS LANE
RUNCORN RD.
39
91
99
F G H J K
1 2 3 4 5 6 7
56 57 58
88 87 86 385

66
SANKEY
A57
40
WAY
LIVERPOOL RD.
Sankey Valley Park
David Lloyd Leisure
The Peace Centre
Sacred Heart Cath. Prim. Sch.
Superstore
Coun. Offs.
Sankey Bridges
St. Helens Canal
Evelyn St. Prim. Sch.
Rec. Grd.
Warrington Bank Quay
Bank Quay Works
WARRINGTON
WILSON PATTEN
A5061
Penketh Business Pk.
Sankey Bridges Ind. Est.
Sankey Mill Bri.
Gatewarth Ind. Est.
Bank Quay Trading Est.
Speedkarting
RSPCA Centre
WA5
WA1
Sankey Brook
Sewage Works
RIVER MERSEY
Arpley Meadows
A5060
Works
Centre Park
DriveTime (Golf Driving Range)
Bank Quay Reach
Tanks
65
Landfill Site
Runcorn & Latchford Canal
Moss Wood
Walton New Junction
Walton Old Junction
Morley Common
CHESTER RD.
Walnut Tree Farm
Lower Walton
Warrington
Birch Wood
Acton Grange Viaduct
Moore Nature Reserve
Warehouses
MANCHESTER SHIP CANAL
BIRCHWOOD LANE
Mill Lane Cotts.
Sewage Works
Grange Mill House
Grange Green Manor
Higher Walton
Walton
Walton Lea Crematorium
Warrington Sports Club
Church Park
Bellhouse Farm
Bell House
WARRINGTON
HALTON
Acton Grange Junction
Cockfight Cottages
A56
CHESTER NEW RD.
WALTON LEA RD.
Walton Hall Heritage Cen.
Walton Hall Gardens & Children's Zoo
Club House
Walton Hall
Bowl. Grns.
The Big Hand (Riding School)
Meadowbank Caravan Pk.
Porch-house Farm
Higher Walton Bridge
Thomason's Bri.
Canal Farm
Bridgewater Canal
Acton Grange Bridge
WALTON HALL GOLF COURSE
Rugby Football Grd.
The Shires
Canal Side Cottages
Rowswood Cottage
Woodlands
92
CHESTER ROAD
Rowswood Farm
The Kennels
New Plantation
Park House
Appleton Reservoir
Moore Hall
Uplands

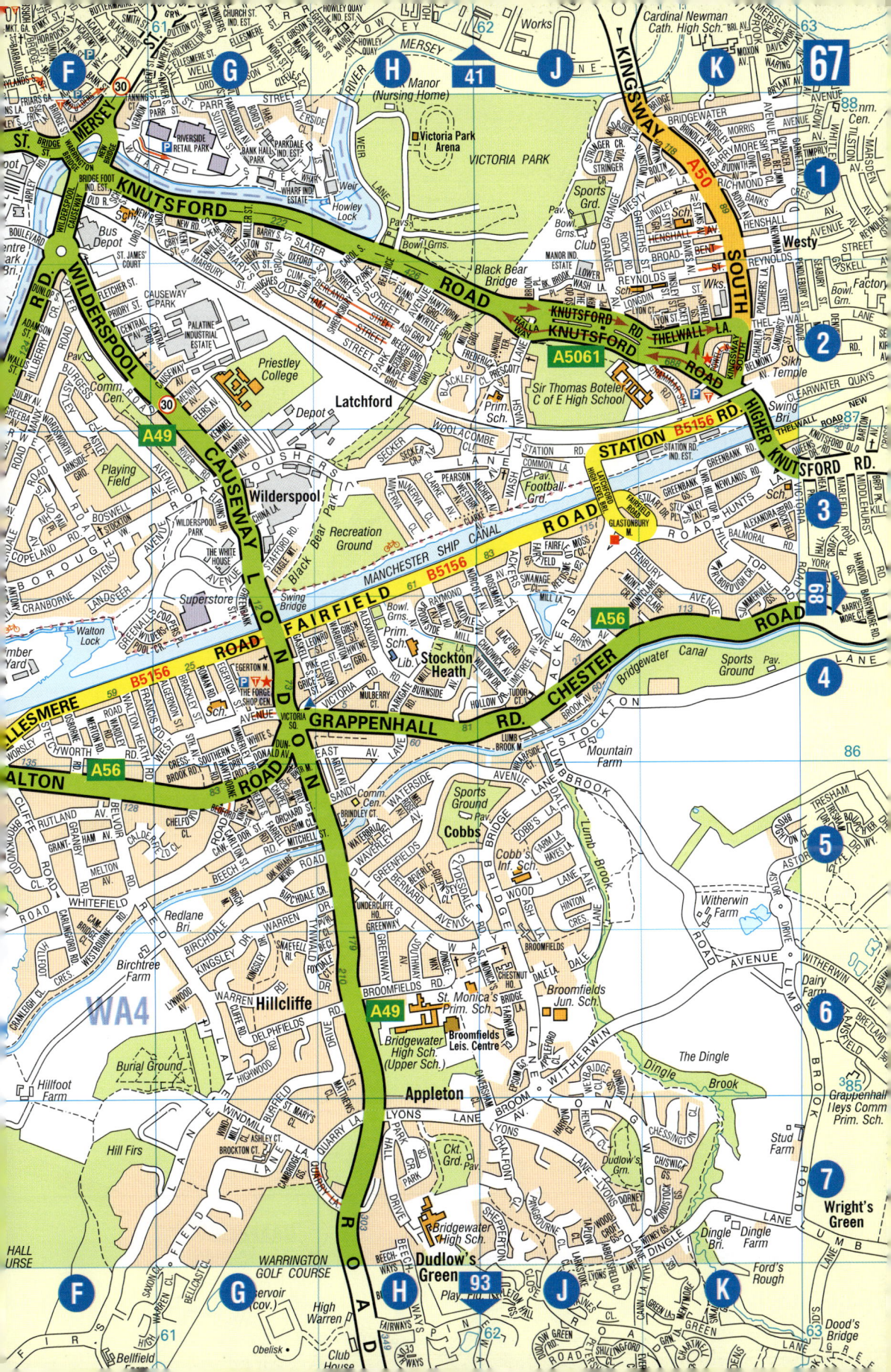

Victoria Park
Latchford
Wilderspool
Stockton Heath
Westy
Cobbs
Hillcliffe
Appleton
Dudlow's Green
Wright's Green
WA4
Knutsford Road
Wilderspool Causeway
London Road
Grappenhall Rd.
Chester Road
Fairfield Road
Station Rd.
Higher Knutsford Rd.
Kingsway South
Manchester Ship Canal
Bridgewater Canal
Priestley College
Sir Thomas Boteler C of E High School
Bridgewater High Sch. (Upper Sch.)
Broomfields Leis. Centre
Bridgewater High Sch.
Warrington Golf Course
Hill Firs
The Dingle
Redlane Bri.
Birchtree Farm
Burial Ground
Mountain Farm
Witherwin Farm
Stud Farm
Dingle Farm
Ford's Rough
Dood's Bridge
Walton Lock
Recreation Ground
Playing Field
Superstore
Black Bear Bridge
Swing Bri.
A49
A50
A56
A5061
B5156
41
93
68

41
93
68

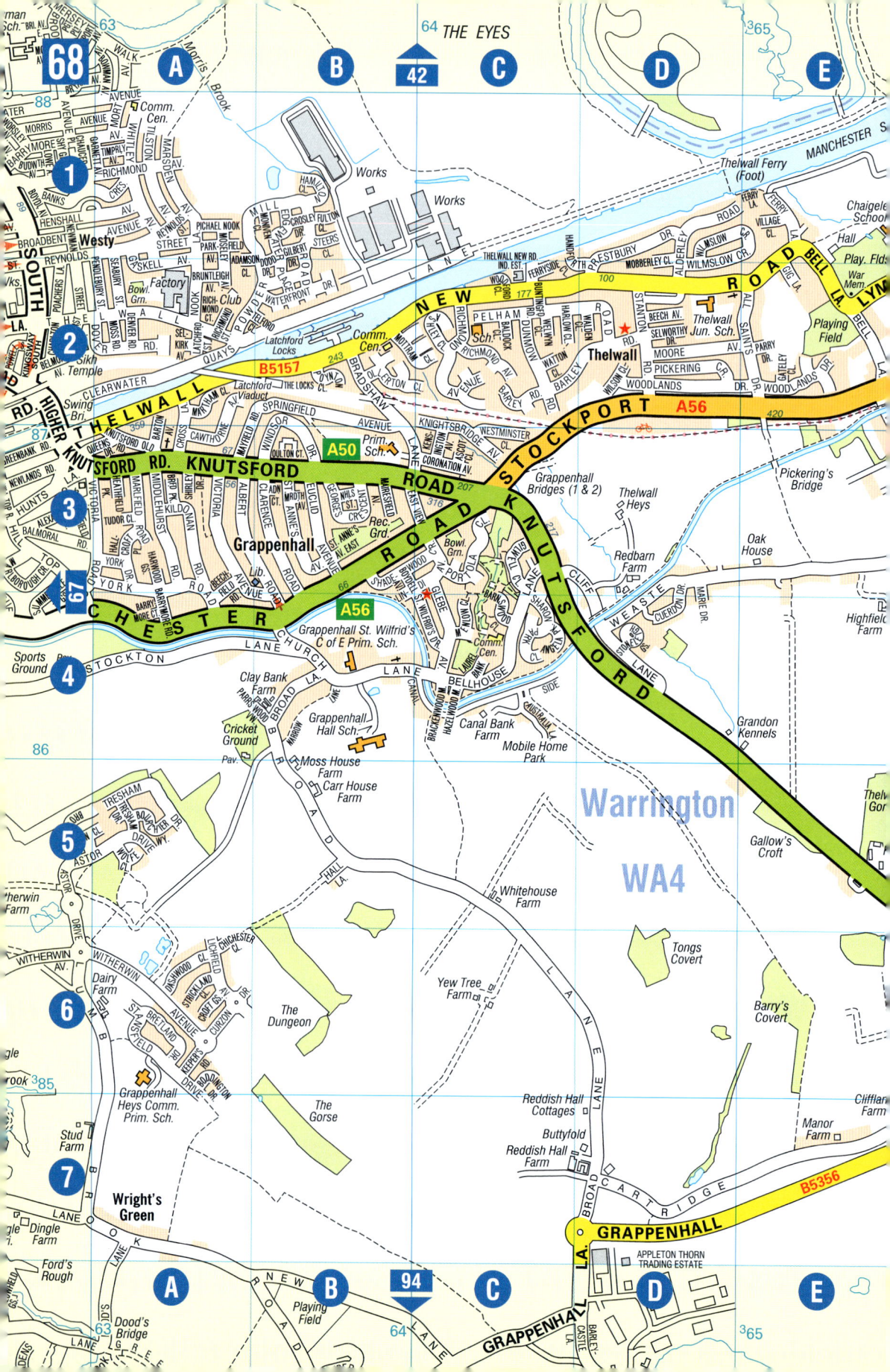
THE EYES
42
Works
MANCHESTER SHIP CANAL
Thelwall Ferry (Foot)
Chaigeley School
Play. Flds
War Mem.
Playing Field
Westy
Comm. Cen.
Factory
Club
Latchford Locks
Comm. Cen.
Thelwall
Thelwall Jun. Sch.
B5157
NEW ROAD
THELWALL
Latchford Viaduct
Swing Bri.
Sikh Temple
STOCKPORT
A56
A50
Prim. Sch.
KNUTSFORD ROAD
Grappenhall Bridges (1 & 2)
Thelwall Heys
Pickering's Bridge
Oak House
Redbarn Farm
Highfield Farm
Grappenhall
Rec. Grd.
Bowl. Grn.
Lib.
CHESTER ROAD
A56
Grappenhall St. Wilfrid's C of E Prim. Sch.
Comm. Cen.
Sports Ground
STOCKTON LANE
CHURCH LANE
Clay Bank Farm
Cricket Ground
Pav.
Grappenhall Hall Sch.
Canal Bank Farm
Mobile Home Park
Grandon Kennels
Moss House Farm
Carr House Farm
Warrington
WA4
Gallow's Croft
Whitehouse Farm
Dairy Farm
Tongs Covert
Yew Tree Farm
The Dungeon
Barry's Covert
Grappenhall Heys Comm. Prim. Sch.
The Gorse
Reddish Hall Cottages
Buttyfold
Reddish Hall Farm
Manor Farm
Stud Farm
Wright's Green
Dingle Farm
Ford's Rough
Dood's Bridge
Playing Field
CARTRIDGE LANE
GRAPPENHALL LANE
B5356
APPLETON THORN TRADING ESTATE
GRAPPENHALL LA.
NEW ROAD
94
67
A B C D E
1 2 3 4 5 6 7
63 64 365
88 87 86 385

69
43
70
216
F
G
H
J
K
1
2
3
4
5
6
7
Lymm
WA13
WA16
Knutsford
Statham
LYMM
Primrose Hill
CANAL
Thelwall Brook
Bridgewater Canal
THELWALL VIADUCT
STATHAM
Statham Pools
Club House
Whitbarrow Farm
Pump House
Pool Farm
Playing Fld.
Statham Lodge
Nursery
Woodacre Farm
WHITBARROW ROAD
WHITESANDS
Statham Prim. Sch.
Statham Lodge Riding Centre
Thelwall Bridge
Beech Farm
Home Farm
B5157
ROAD
CAMSLEY
WARRINGTON
Depot
A56
LANE
BOOTH'S
HILL
RD.
EAGLE BROW
CHURCH
A6144
Ridgway Grundy Meml. Park
Barsbank Aqueduct
LYMMINGTON AV.
CANAL BANK
ALBANY
AVENUE
BROOK RD.
DANE BANK
Lib.
Tennis Courts
Lymm Bri.
Lymm Dam
Reservoir
Rugby Ground
Ditchfield's Bri.
Camsley House Farm
WYCHWOOD AV.
HARDY ROAD
Cherry Tree Prim. Sch.
HIGHFIELD DR.
HILL TOP RD.
Cherrylane Farm
LADY HUNTS FIELD CL.
ACRE CLOSE
OAKLANDS DR.
Massey Hall School
Works
MASSEY BROOK LA.
WEASTE LANE
Weaste Lane Farm
Nursing Home
Masseybrook Farm
CINDER LANE
Nursery
Booth's Hill Farm
Higher House Farm
Ruloe
Res.
Tanners Pool
THE AVENUE
LAKESIDE ROAD
Crosfield Bridge
Bradley Brook
The Red House
M6
M6 MOTORWAY
Massey Brook
B5158
CHERRY LANE
Cherry Hall Farm
The Bongs
Scholars Bri.
The Gorse
Long Shoots
Oxheys Farm
A50
Junction 20 (M6)
ROAD
Howshoots
CLIFF LA.
Poplar Park
Redbank Bridge
WARRINGTON
CHESHIRE EAST
CLIFF LANE
Bradley View
Bradley Hall Cottages
Bradley Hall
Poplar 2000 Service Area
Broad Heyes Cotts.
Broad Heyes Farm
Oakdene
Manor Fm.
Ivyhouse Farm
Brookhouse Farm
Holly Farm
WITHERS LANE
M56
M56 MOTORWAY
Junction 9 (M56)
The Pheasantries
HEATH LA.
Bradley Gorse
Greenacres
Jones's Covert
Big
Swortons

70
A
B
C
D
E
1
2
3
4
5
6
7
44
69
95
68
69
370
88
87
86
385
Playing Field
Sewage Works
New Farm
Reddish Crossing
Whitbarrow Farm
Pump House
Sow Brook
OUGHTRINGTON
Rushgreen
Oughtrington Prim. Sch.
RUSHGREEN
NEW RD.
A6144
WHITEFIELD
ROAD
BIRCHBROOK
SANDY
HOWARD
B5159
LANE
Nursery
Bridgewater Canal
Lloyd Bri.
Grantham's Bridge
Lower Helsdale Wood
Helsdale Wood
Sports Ground
Pav.
Ckt. Grd.
Lymm Leisure Cen.
Lymm High School
Cotebrook
Lymm
WA13
Newhay's Plantation
LYMM
Ravenbank Prim. Sch.
Play. Fld.
SUTCH
STREET
BROW
EAGLE
CHURCH
A56
HIGHER
RD.
Lymm Bri.
Lymm Dam
Tennis Courts
THE CROSS
Lib.
Water Tower
Rugby Ground
Reservoir
Crosfield Bridge
Crouchley Hall Farm
CROUCHLEY HALL MEWS
FOXLEY HALL M.
Wildersmoor Farm
Model Farm
Ashlea Farm
Willow Pool Nurseries
Broomedge
Wildersmoor Hall Farm
WHITELEGGS LA.
WOODSIDE LA.
Field House
Top Farm
Yewtree Farm
Crouchley Cottage
Kaylane Brook
Nurseries
Dorkensville
Brook Cottage
Kaylane Farm
Deansgreen Hall
Deansgreen
The Bongs
Mag Brook
Gorse
Silent Valley Cottages
Willow Bed
Cornheys Cottage
Cornheys
WARRINGTON
CHESHIRE EAST
The Howlers
BEECHTREE
LANE
Old Farm
Redoak
Great Oak Farm
M56
M56-MOTORWAY
Long Shoots
Big Wood
Moss's Strip
Hey Wood
Beech Tree Farm
Depot
Diamond Cottages
Knutsford
WA16
Mowpenbrow Farm
Heywood Court
Sewage Works
Walnut Farm
Westlane Farm
Crossroads Farm
Abbey Cotts.
Mowpen Farm
MOWPEN
BROW
CRABTREE
HIGH LEGH
WEST LANE
Little Oaks
The Pheasantries
A50
Swarton Heath
Bearspaw Farmhouse
Crabtree Farm
HIGH LEGH
Rose Cottage

71
45
72
95
216
Dunham Woodhouses
Little Bollington
Altrincham
WA14
Arthill
Booth Bank
TRAFFORD
CHESHIRE EAST
WOODHOUSE
B5160
A56
M56 MOTORWAY
M56
AGDEN BROW
LYMM ROAD
STATION RD
Bridgewater Canal
River Bollin
Agden Brook
Wet Gate Farm
Little Heatley
Heatley Heath Farm
Gailey Wood
Spring Farm
Rose Cottages
Woolstencroft Farm
Agden Bridge Farm
Agden Bridge
The Smithy
Agdenlane Farm
Agden Brook Farm
Hollybank House
Broomedge Farm
Agden Park
Little Bollington C of E Prim. Sch.
Yewtree Farm
Four Winds
The Gables
Strathyre
Arthill Farm
Reddy Lane Cottage
Old Chapel House
The Paddock
Arthill Heath Farm
Agden Hall
Agden Hall Farm
Agden Ho.
Woodiers Farm
Hawthorn Cottage
Agden Cottage Thatch
Crackling Farm
Moss Lane Farm
Endfield Farm
Endfield Farm Caravan Pk.
Lime Tree Cott.
Abbey Leys Farm
Peacock Lodge
Broad Oak Farm
Whyte Cottage
Middlemoss Farm
Booth Bank Farm
Booth Bank Cotts.
Booth Bank Farm
Booth Bank House
Booth Bank Cottage
Stonedelph Farm
Thowlerlane Farm
Ivyhouse Farm
Little Moss Farm
Five Acres
Moss House Farm
Millington Hall
Keldan
Rushy-pits Covert
Grey's Gorse
Stamford Farm
Model Farm
New Cotts.
Bollington Hall Farm
Hillcroft
Ivy Lodge
Ash Farm
Aqueduct
Bollington Mill
Brickkiln Nursery Wood
Sewage Works
Sewage Works Cottage
Agden View
Bollin Cottages
Yewtree Farm
Manor Ho. Farm
Barns Lane Farm
Ash Farm
High Legh Park Golf Course
Wet Gate Lane Farm
Burford Lane Farm
Broomedge Nurseries
The Meadows
Dunham Underbridge
Whiteoak Wood
Bridgewater
Three O
F G H J K
1 2 3 4 5 6 7
71 72 73
85 86 87 88

Dunham Massey
Little Heath
Oldfield Brow
46
Bridgewater Canal
Dunhamtown Bridge
Dunham Town
Dunham Underbridge
WOODHOUSE LANE
B5160
SMITHY LA.
CHARCOAL LANE
Brickkiln Nursery Wood
North Park
Big Tree Cottages
Dunham Massey
Fish Pond
Forest Edge
Club House
DUNHAM FOREST GOLF COURSE
DUNHAM NEW PARK
Reservoir (covered)
Dunham Massey Sawmill
MAIN DRIVE
DUNHAM HOUSE
Levenot
Parklands
Langham Grove
Old Man Pool
Fish Pond
New Covert
DUNHAM PARK (Deer Park)
BOLLINGTON MILL
Ash Farm
Bollington Hall Farm
Hillcroft
Little Bollington
River Bollin
Headsman's Covert
Pitstead Covert
Altrincham
Redmoor Covert
Scout Camp
Dunham Massey Lodge
Home Farm
Stamford Cottage
FARM WALK
71
New Cotts.
New Farm
Paddock Covert
TRAFFORD
CHESHIRE EAST
BOW GREEN
B5161
A56
Sutt's Hollow
The Paddocks
Tipping's Bank
Watlingford
Bowgreen
LYMM ROAD
Ivy Bank
WA14
DUNHAM ROAD
M56
Castle Hill
The Meadows
The Old House
Spodegreen Farm
Brook Farm
The Dell
The Pastures
Brook Cottage
Bowdon View
Grey's Gorse
A556
Yarwood Heath Farm
Poolbank Farm
Bowgreen Farm
Hanging Bank Covert
Sewage Works
Yarwoodheath Covert
M56 MOTORWAY
Hope Cottage
Rushy-pits Covert
Junction 8
Junction 7
Trafford Bank Covert
Cherrytree Farm
Hancock's Banks
Mereside Farm
Mereside Cottage
Gale Bog
Newhall Cottages
Bowden View Farm
Mere Covert
Covert Cottage
Newhall Farm
Keldan
Three Oaks
Millington
Harpers Bank Wood
216
ROSTHERNE MERE
Mere Covert
Birkin House
CHESTER ROAD
CHERRY TREE LANE
TOM LANE
MILLINGTON LANE

ALTRINCHAM
Hale Moss
Hale
BOWDON
Rosehill
Ashley Heath
Ashley
WA15
ALTRINCHAM GOLF COURSE
Hockey, Tennis & Lacrosse Club
Timperley Bridge
Club House
Driving Range
St. Vincent Catholic Jun. & Inf. Schs.
Blessed Thomas Holford Catholic College
Play. Flds.
Altrincham Leisure Cen.
Ice Rink
Superstore
Cinema
Stamford Park
Altrincham FC (Moss Lane Ground)
Cemetery
Altrincham Grammar School for Girls
Altrincham Grammar Sch. for Boys
Playing Fields
Bowdon Cricket, Hockey & Squash Club
Bowdon C of E Prim. Sch.
Bollin Prim. Sch.
Convent
Football Grd.
Ckt. Grd.
Cricket Grd.
Grammar Schs.
Prim. Sch.
Adult Ed. Cen.
Prep. Sch.
Rec. Grd.
Lawns Comm. Cen.
Priory Farm
Priory House Farm
Vicarage Gorse Covert
Fish House Plantation
River Bollin
Ashley Mill
Riverside
Coppice Farm
Ashley Bridge
Sewage Wks.
Bankhall Farm
Nursery
Club House
Jackson's Bank
Dairyhouse Farm
Ashley Hall
The Rookery
Ryecroft Covert
M56 MOTORWAY
M56
Tanyard Farm
Midways
Cricket Grd.
Birkin Brook
STAMFORD NEW RD.
HALE ROAD
A538
ASHLEY RD.
B5161
B5162
B5357
LANGHAM
SOUTH DOWNS ROAD
PARK ROAD
BROOMFIELD LA.
ASHLEY ROAD
CASTLE MILL LANE
BANKHALL
A56
47
213
74
216
76
77
78
88
87
86
85
F
G
H
J
K
1
2
3
4
5
6
7

Hockey, Tennis & Lacrosse Club
Cloverlea Prim. Sch.
RIDGEWAY
Manor Farm
Fairywell Wood
ALTRINCHAM GOLF COURSE
Wood La. Nurseries
Clay Lane Nursery
Bowl. Grn.
Pavilion
Ten. Cts.
Rugby Ground
Sports Ground
Timperley Brook
Delaheys Farm
The Dobbinetts
Roundthorn
MANCHESTER
TRAFFORD
Holly Tree Cottage
Holly Tree Farm
Altrincham FC (Moss Lane Ground)
Altrincham College of Arts
Hale Moss
Duncalf Farm
Grove Park
Rec. Grd.
Clay House
THORLEY
A5144
ROAD
DELAHAYS RD.
Latham Hall Farm
Ash Farm
Well Green
Cemetery
Altrincham
Well Green Prim. Sch.
Davenport Green
HALE
B5162
PARK ROAD
HALE ROAD
A538
WA15
Davenport Green Hall
Ten. Ct.
Rec. Grd.
Oaklands Court
Syn.
RINGWAY GOLF COURSE
Humphrey's Wood
Davenport Wood
St. Ambrose College
Club House
St. Ambrose Prep. Sch.
THE SQUARE
Halebarns
Flaxhigh Covert
Cricket Ground
Elmridge Prim. Sch.
Club House
ALTRINCHAM PRIORY HOSPITAL
Graythwaite
Tomfield Bank
M56
Hotel
HALE GOLF COURSE
Warburton Green
Junction 6
Rec. Grd.
Jackson's Bank
CHESHIRE EAST
M56 MOTORWAY
216
Keepers Cottage
Oak Cottages
Halebank Farm
Tanyard Farm
Lower Thornsgreen Farm
Halebank Cottage
SUNBANK

49
Benchill
Newall Green
Newall Green Prim. Sch.
St. Paul's Catholic High Sch.
Manch. Coll. Newall Green High Sch.
Playing Field
Junction 4
M56
MOTORWAY
WYTHENSHAWE
Parklands Sports Cen.
Parklands High Sch.
Haveley Hey Prim. Sch.
Peter's Spinney
Kirkup Gdns.
Forum Leis. Cen.
The Forum Cen.
MARKET PLACE
Adult Learning Cen.
Gala Bingo
Offices
The Willows Prim. Sch.
Park Wood
Little Wood
Junction 5
Woodhouse Park
Sports Cen.
Painswick Park
Ringway Prim. Sch.
Hotel
Airport Long Term Car Park
TERMINAL 2
Manchester Airport
MANCHESTER INTERNATIONAL AIRPORT
World Freight Centre
TERMINAL 1
Pier C
Pier B
Pier A
TERMINAL 3
M90
Warehouses
Aircraft Hangars
Ringway
A538
WILMSLOW RD.
Moss Lane Farm
Moss Farm
Cloughbarn Farm
WYTHENSHAWE HOSPITAL
Fairywell Brook
MANCHESTER BUS. PARK
RINGWAY ROAD WEST
76
96
F G H J K
1 2 3 4 5 6 7
81 82 83
84 85 86 87 88

76
A
B
C
D
E
50
97
75
1
2
3
4
5
6
7
83
84
385
88
87
86
Youth Cen.
HOLLYHEDGE PARK
Gatley Hill
Scholes Park Track (Athletics Ground)
Scholes Park
Sports Ground
The Kingsway Lower School
The Kingsway Upper Sch.
Ten. Cts.
Tennis Cts.
Prim. Sch.
Crossacres Prim. Sch.
Ashgate Sch.
Dark Lane Bri.
M22
Park Wood
GATLEY GOLF COURSE
Lum Head Prim. Sch.
Club House
Peel Hall Prim. Sch.
Peel Hall
Peel Hall Play Park
Lumhead Wood
Adult Learning Cen.
Gala Bingo
Office
Sch.
High Grove Farm
North Cheshire Jewish Prim. Sch.
Rose Vale Park
Ash Wood
Hatchetts Wood
Little Wood
Big Wood
Chamber Hall
St. Ann's Hospice
CHEADLE ROYAL HOSPITAL
Prospect Vale Prim. Sch.
CONCORD BUS. PARK
ATLAS BUSINESS PARK
Sports Ground
Daisy Bank Farm
MOSS NOOK INDUSTRIAL AREA
RINGWAY TRADING ESTATE
Manchester
Heald Green
Lib.
Recreation Ground
Hall
Play Fld.
Moss Nook
GREENCOURTS BUS. CEN.
MANCHESTER INTERNATIONAL BUSINESS CENTRE
MANCHESTER BUS. PARK
Shadow Moss Farm
M90
Wood Farm
Bolshaw Prim. Sch.
Outwood Farm
Wilmslow
SK9
Boundary Farm
STOCKPORT
CHESHIRE EAST
MANCHESTER
Yew Tree Farm
Bolshaw Farm
Bowling Green
Beech Farm
Moss Lane Farm
Driving Range
Club House
STYAL GOLF COURSE
STYAL ROAD
B5166
HOLLIN LA.
KINGSWAY
A34
WEST RINGWAY
CROSSACRES
BROWN LANE
FINNEY LANE
OUTWOOD ROAD
BOLSHAW ROAD
SHADOWMOSS ROAD
SIMONSWAY
CORNISHWAY
PEEL HALL ROAD
ETCHELLS ROAD
MOSS LANE

77
F
G
H
J
K
51
1
2
3
4
5
6
7
78
98
Cheadle
SK8
CHEADLE HULME
Cheadle Hulme
Brookfields Park
Micker Brook
Cheadle Pools & Target Fitness Cen.
Club House
The Village Leis. Club
CHEADLE GOLF COURSE
CHEADLE RD.
A5149
Lady Barn House Sch. & Inscape Ho. Sch.
Miniature Golf Course
Bruntwood Hall
BRUNTWOOD PARK
Cheadle and Marple Sixth Form College
Cycle Track
Playing Field
Cheadle Park
Recreation Ground
Lacrosse Ground
Cricket Ground
Orrishmere Prim. Sch.
Queens Rd. Prim. Sch.
Lady Bridge
Ladybridge Farm
Ladybridge Prim. Sch.
Adswood Park
Ramillies Hall Sch.
Superstore
A34
ETCHELLS ROAD
KINGSWAY
WILMSLOW RD.
B5358
Cheadle Catholic Jun. & Inf. Sch.
Bruntwood Prim. Sch.
Ryecroft Park Sports Club
Bradshaw Hall Prim. Sch.
Greenbank School
Grammar School
Cheadle Hulme School
Tennis Courts
Pavilion
Playing Fields
Smithy Green
HULME HALL ROAD
B5095
STATION RD.
ALBERT RD.
CHURCH RD.
RAVENOAK RD.
ACK LANE
Chads Thtre.
Lib.
Hesketh Pk.
Oak Mdw.
Cheadle Hulme High Sch.
Cheadle Hulme Rec. Cen.
Youth Club
Rec. Ground
Thorn Grove Prim. Sch.
St. James Catholic High School
Football Grd.
Griffin Lodge
Outwood House
The South Gate Cen.
Royal School for the Deaf and Communication Disorders
Gill Bent Farm
Stanley Green
Gillbent
STANLEY ROAD
B5094
Stanley Hall Farm
A555
MANCHESTER AIRPORT EASTERN LINK ROAD
STANLEY GREEN INDUSTRIAL ESTATE
STANLEY GREEN RETAIL PARK
GROVE LANE
ACRE LANE
Lower Bent Farm
Manchester Rugby Club (Grove Park)
Football Ground
Depot
Playing Field
Hotel

78
A
B
C
D
E
1
2
3
4
5
6
7
52
77
99
Davenport
Davenport Park
Orion Business Park
Adswood Lane
Cheadle
SK8
SK3
Adswood Brick & Tile Works
Depot
Playing Fields
Lady Brook
Ladybridge Farm
Tenement Lane
Sports Ground
Cricket Grd.
Play Field
Nevill Road Jun. & Inf. Schs.
Stockport
Playing Field
Ramillies Hall School
Lane End Prim. Sch.
Bramhall Pk. Tennis Club
Bramhall Park
Bramall Hall
Lodge
Bowl. Grn.
Ten. Cts.
Bramhall Green
Bramhall Bri.
Bridge Lane
A5143
A5102
South Park Road
Bramhall Lane South
Womanscroft Bridge
Davenport Rugby Club & Ground
The White House
Wall Bank Farm
Buddhist Cen.
Club House
Bramhall Park
Bramall Park Golf Course
Carr Wood Park
Bramhall Lane Lawn Tennis Club
Bramhall High School
Bramhall Recreation Centre
Prim. Sch.
Pownall Green
Dairyground
Ravenoak Rd.
Ack Lane West
A5149
Ack Lane East
Hursthead Jun. & Inf. Schools
Kitt's Moss
Cheadle Hulme Rec. Cen.
B5094
Moss Lane
Acre Lane
Bramhall
BRAMHALL
Bramhall Golf Course
Club House
Moss Hey Prim. Sch.
Valley Sch.
Syddal
Woodford Road
Depot

Stockport School
Woodsmoor
Woods Moor
Stepping Hill
STEPPING HILL HOSPITAL
Gt. Moor Park
Works
Bramhall Moor
Hazel Grove
HAZEL GROVE
Superstore
Brook Vale Farm
Brook House
Canberra
Reservoir
Factory
TORKINGTON ROAD
A627
Torkington Park
The Secret Garden
Playing Field
BUXTON ROAD
A6
LONDON ROAD
MACCLESFIELD ROAD
A523
LONDON ROAD NORTH
DEAN LANE
A5143
Norbury Moor
Denbigh Farm
Hazel Grove High School
Moorfield Primary School
Hazel Grove Rec. Cen.
Dingle Farm
Norbury House Farm
Football Grd.
Norbury Hall Prim. Sch.
Norbury Hall
Norbury Bri.
Brookside Miniature Railway & Museum
Garden Cen.
Long Plantation
Towers Farm
Serpentine Wood
Sewage Works
Millbank
Millhill Bri.
Norbury Brook
Ladybrook Nursery
Mill Hill Farm
Barlowfold
Barlowfold Farm
Poynton Lake
Poynton Brook
Poynton Park
Park House Farm
Hill Green Farm
Birch Hall
Phillip's Bridge
CHESHIRE EAST
STOCKPORT
SK2
SK7
SK12
BRAMHALL MOOR INDUSTRIAL ESTATE
SCHOOL STREET INDUSTRIAL ESTATE
NEWBY ROAD IND. EST.
Cricket Ground
Rec. Ground
53
80
100
F
G
H
J
K
1
2
3
4
5
6
7

54
101
79
A B C D E
1 2 3 4 5 6 7
SK2
SK7
SK12
Stockport
Torkington
Windlehurst
Middlewood
STOCKPORT GOLF COURSE
MARPLE GOLF COURSE
HAZEL GROVE GOLF COURSE
Torkington Wood
Marple Wood
Hawk Green
OFFERTON ROAD
A627
BUXTON ROAD
A6
TORKINGTON ROAD
TORKINGTON LANE
THREAPHURST LANE
WINDLEHURST ROAD
MIDDLEWOOD ROAD
Club House
The Hollow
Poise Bridge
Reservoir
Manor Cottages
White House
The Willows
Holly Farm
Springfield Farm
Broadoak
Moat
Hazelbank
Hazel Knoll Farm
Torkington Manor
Brookside Farm
Torkington Prim. Sch.
Ochreley Brook
Greenclough Farm
Holly Cottages
Oak Cott.
Higher Farm
Clough House Farm
The Ash
Moult Wood
Higherfold Farm
Golf Course Cotts.
Dean Fold
Threaphurst Farm
Oakfield Farm
Brook Farm
Disley Tunnel
Ox Hey
Oxhey Farm
Oak Tree Farm
Reservoir (covered)
Shores Farm
Station Farm
Playing Fields
Norbury Hollow
Shady Nook
Parkgate Farm
Lower Fold Cotts.
Marsden House
Cricket Ground
Middlewood House
Middle Wood
Long Plantation
Serpentine Wood
Park Pit Plantation
Park Pit Cottages
Norbury Hollow Caravan Site
Correction Farm
New House Farm
Woodside Tennis Club
Macclesfield Canal
Bollinhurst Brook
Jackson's Brickworks Local Nature Reserve
Prince's Wood
Pool House Farm
Wood Farm
Playing Field
War Meml.
High Prim.
Brook Prim.

SK6
SK22
SK12
High Peak
Strines
Woodend
Turf Lea
HIGH LANE
DISLEY
Mellor & Townscliffe Golf Course
Disley Golf Course
Windybottom Wood
Stanleyhall Wood
Roman Lakes Leisure Park
Peak Forest Canal
River Goyt
Strines Road
B6101
Buxton Road
A6
Disley Tunnel
Stockport
Cheshire East
Wybersley Water Treatment Works
Jacksonsedge Quarry (disused)
Disleybank Wood
Disley Paper Mill
Lyme Park Country Park
Higher Banks
Whetmorhurst
Eccles Bridge
No Limits Fitness Cen.
Barnsfold
Windlehurst School
Broadhurst's Bridge
Hunters Park Farm
Lomber Hey Farm
Grange Farm
Beeston Park Farm
Ridge End Fold Farm
Lea Cote Farm
Swingbridge
Aqueduct
Greenhills
Littlewoodend
Dove House Farm
Wybersley Hall
Stanley Hall
Club House
Widowhurst
Hagg Bank Farm
Higgin's Clough
Roach-hey Wood
Haycroft
Whitecroft House
Whitecroft Farm
Greenclough Farm
Greenclough Cottage
Windybottom Farm
Marple Packhorse Bri.
Strawberry Hill
Barlow Wood
Floodgates Cottage
Sewage Works
The Grange
Lower Ridge Farm
Victoria Cottage
Brae Side
Hill Top Farm
War Memorial
Brick Bridge
All Saints C of E Prim. Sch.
Linnet Clough
Club House
Bull Hill Farm
Cross Gates
The Station
Primrose Bank
Lower Cliffe
Hague Bar Prim. Sch.
Lower Haguefold
Woodend Fold
Mill Ponds
Coppiceside Farm
Brookside Farm
Main Lodge
Lyme Gate Cott.
The Homestead
Homestead Farm
Sports Field
Disley
55
217
103

23 A B 57 C D 325 E

Irby Heath

THE STEEPLE
BADGER'S
MEREW
ATHERLEIGH
MEADOWGATE
Links Bridge
CALDY GOLF COURSE
Club House

SCHOOL LANE
Dawpool C of E Prim. School

CH48

TELEGRAPH

THURSTASTON

Thurstaston
Dawpool
Hill Farm

DAWPOOL FARM

CHURCH LANE
Rectory

Thurstaston Hall
Camping Site

Hall Farm

A540

84
Dee Sailing Club
Nature Reserve

Copperfields

1

Caravan Park

WIRRAL

Lee Farm

2

Caravan Park

P
P
Wirral Country Park Visitor Centre

DAWPOOL   BANK

COUNTRY

The Dungeon

3

83
Dungeon Bridge

PARK

Oldfield Farm

4

PIPERS

THE AKBAR

R I V E R

Heswall Fields

FERNS CL
BROMFIELD
REDSTON

5

82
White House

BROAD

D E E

6

DEESIDE RD
TARGET
ROAD

Playing Field

Holid Can

Sewage Works

Caravan Park

THE MOORINGS

B A
Slipwa

7

381

A B 214 C D E

23 24 325

F
G
H
J
K
58
104
84
1
2
3
4
5
6
7
26
27
28
CH61
CH60
Wirral
IRBY
Irby Farm
Harrock Wood
Thingwall
Thingwall Rec. Cen.
Crosshill Reservoir (cov.)
Res. (cov.)
Riding Centre
Gills Lane Farm
Pensby
Pensby High School for Boys
Pensby High School for Girls
Pensby Pk. Prim. Sch.
Catholic Prim. Sch.
Pensby Jun. & Inf. Schs.
Pensby Hall
Pensby Wood
Sports Ground
Comm. Cen.
Day Cen.
Cemetery
Prenton Brook
Beech Farm
Bank Fa
Barnston
Carnsdale Farm
Pensby House Farm
Poll Hill
Reservoir (covered)
Heswall Primary School
Whitfield Common
Tennis Courts
Cleaver Heath Nature Reserve
Dale Farm
Heswall Dales Nature Reserve
The Dales
The Cave
Adult Train. Cen.
Puddy Dale
Superstore
Bus Sta.
Lib.
Putt. Grn.
Prim. Sch.
Park
HESWALL
The Beacons
Dee Farm
Gayton Hole
Gayton
Gayton Prim. Sch.
Lwr. Vill.
TELEGRAPH ROAD
PENSBY ROAD
BARNSTON ROAD
CHESTER RD.
GILLS LANE
WHITFIELD LANE
A540
A551
B5138

Thingwall
Murrayfield Spire Hospital
Lower Heath Wood
Sewage Works
Cross Hill
Crosshill Reservoir
Football Ground
Youth Centre
Riding Centre
Storeton Brickfields
Station Road
Storeton Lane
M53 Motorway
New Hey Covert
New Hey Triangle
Rake Hey Covert
CH61
Wirral
Ley Farm
Beech Farm
Bank Farm
Barnston
Manor Farm
Carnsdale Farm
Greenheys Cottages
Lady Farm
Brimstage Hall Courtyard
Melite Cottage
Fairfield
The Brooklet
Fairfield Lodge
Whitehouse Farm
White House
Whitehouse Lane
Westwood Hall
Cloverley
Dunster House
Lake Lodge
A5137
A551
Barnston Road
Brimstage Road
Heswall
Lane End Farm
Willow Bank House
CH60
Manor Wood
Thornton Manor
Talbot Avenue
Manor Road
Westmead
Hesketh Grange
Thornton Hough
Barnston Prim. Sch.
Football Ground
Gayton
A540
Chester Rd.
Play Field
New Hall Farm
Lodge Farm
Rec. Grd.
Pav.

59
83
105

BEBINGTON
Bebington High Sports College
Higher Bebington Recreation Ground
Storeton Hall Farm
Storeton House Farm
Haven Cottage
The Cottage
Hillside Farm
Brook Cottage
Storeton Hill
Wishing Gate
Hillside Cottage
Club House
Brackenwood Park
BRACKENWOOD GOLF COURSE
Wirral Grammar Sch. for Girls
Wirral Grammar Sch. for Boys
Playing Field
Benty Hey
Brimstage Plantation
Keepers Cottage
Umberstone Covert
Lower Umberstone Covert
Home Farm
M53
A5137
B5151
B5137
B5136
Junction 4
CH63
Claremont House
Poulton Royd
ST JOHN'S HOSPICE
CLATTERBRIDGE HOSPITAL
CLAIRE HO. CHILDREN'S HOSPICE
CLATTERBRIDGE CENTRE FOR ONCOLOGY
Clatter Bridge
Clatter Brook
Wirral Manor House
New Rocklands
Rocklands Farm
Thornton Grange
Rocklands Lodge
Rugby Football Grd.
Thornton Common
Rugby Football Ground
Club Ho.
Drinkwater Cottage
Willows Farm
Oakwood Farm
The Foxes
Brook Farm
Rose Bank
Bank Farm
Raby Mere
Strawberry Farm
Grove Cotts.
Playing Field
Pavilion
Graveyard
Three Stacks
Lancelyn Farm
Stanton Rd. Prim. Sch.
Recreation Ground
M53 MOTORWAY
THORNTON COMMON ROAD
CLATTERBRIDGE RD.
MOUNT ROAD
BRIMSTAGE ROAD
STANTON ROAD
60
106
86
84
83
82
81

86
61
107
85
A
B
C
D
E
1
2
3
4
5
6
7
Lower Bebington
Council Offices
Town Hall
Mayer Park
Ormerod Gdns.
Port Sunlight
Gladstone Theatre
Trafalgar
Research Centre
Works
Port Sunlight Driving Range
Golf Course
Refuse Tip
Bromborough Pool Bridge
Bromborough Pool
Cricket Ground
Sports Club
Sports Ground
HGV Test Centre
Warehouses
Factories
Factory
Depots
Depot
Bromborough Port
Wirral
Spital
Dibbinsdale Local Nature Reserve
Brotherton Park
Woods Lee Cottages
Woodslee Prim. Sch.
Stanton Rd. Prim. Sch.
Poulton Lancelyn Prim. Sch.
Poulton
CH63
CH62
The Vineyard Farm
Lancelyn Farm
Poulton Lancelyn
Bromborough Rake
BROMBOROUGH
Dibbinsdale Local Nature Reserve
Rose Cott.
Poulton Hall
Poulton Bridge
Raby Mere
Bank Farm
Clatter Brook
Wirral Education Centre
Playing Field
Mendell Prim. Sch.
Rec. Ground
Civic Hall
Bromborough
Wirral Leisure Park
Odeon Cinema
Gala Bingo
Fitness First
South Wirral Retail Park
Super-store
Croft Bus. Park
Tennis Courts
Club
M53 MOTORWAY
NEW CHESTER ROAD
A41
B5136
B5137
CHURCH ROAD
SPITAL ROAD
THE VILLAGE
BRIMSTAGE ROAD
BROMBOROUGH ROAD
DIBBINSDALE ROAD
POULTON HALL ROAD
THORNTON COMMON RD.
RABY MERE RD.
33
34
35
81
82
83
84

RIVER MERSEY
LIVERPOOL
WIRRAL
214
108
Works
Slack Wood
PLANTATION BUSINESS PARK
PLANTATION COURT
STADIUM CT.
WIRRAL INTERNATIONAL BUSINESS PARK
Oak Wood
Offices
Storage Depots
Job's Ferry
Playing Field
Eastham Ferry
Long Plantation
Playing Fields
EASTHAM COUNTRY PARK
Eastham Woods Country Park
Tennis Courts
The Warrens Farm
Eastham Woods
Pavilion
Mayfields Remembrance Park
Wirral Metropolitan College
Playing Field
Custom House
Eastham Locks
Tank Farm Club House
Dock
A41

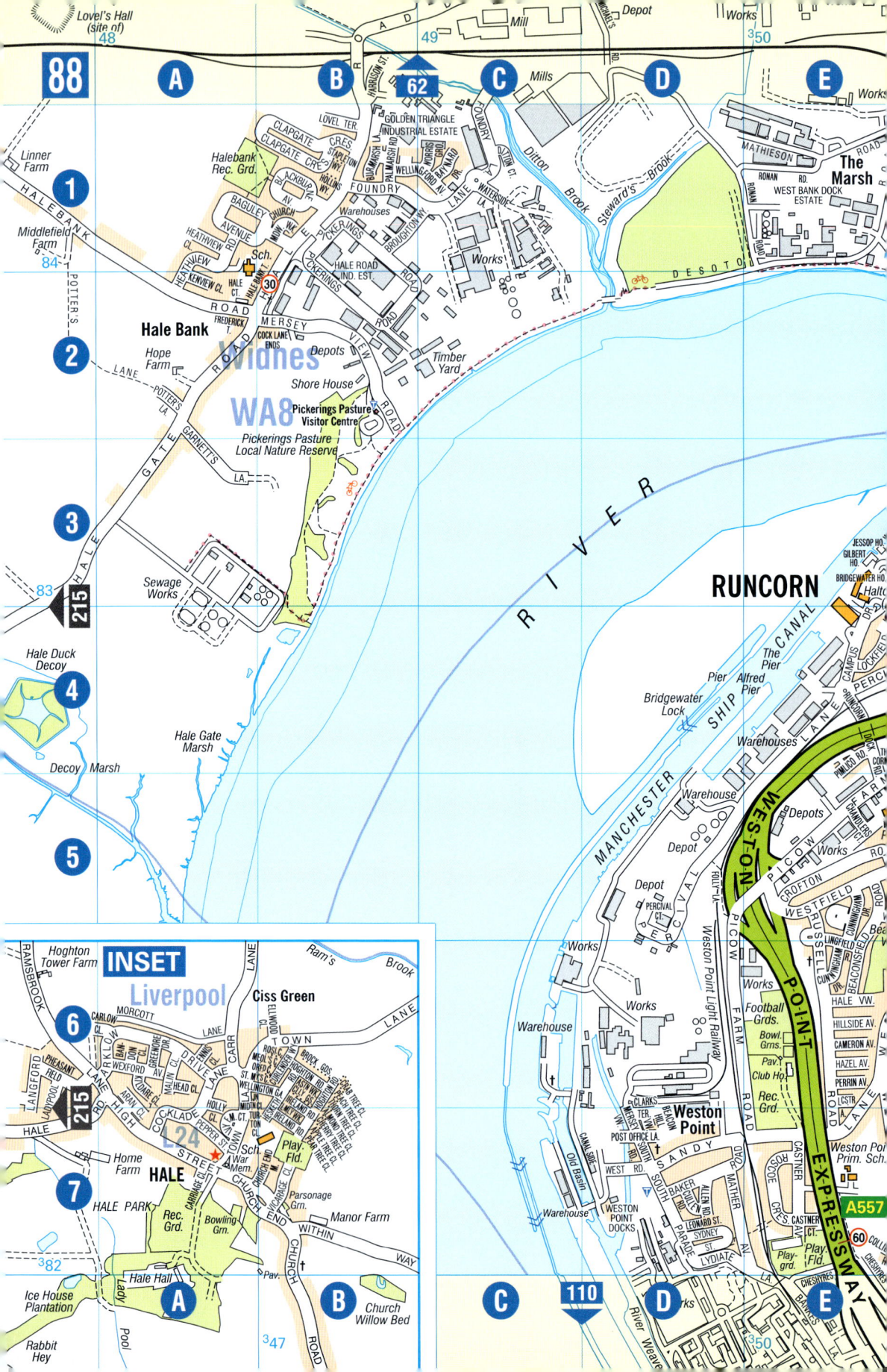
Hale Bank
Widnes
WA8
Pickerings Pasture Visitor Centre
Pickerings Pasture Local Nature Reserve
Sewage Works
Hale Duck Decoy
Hale Gate Marsh
Decoy Marsh
RIVER
RUNCORN
The Marsh
WEST BANK DOCK ESTATE
MANCHESTER SHIP CANAL
Bridgewater Lock
Weston Point
WESTON POINT EXPRESSWAY
A557
INSET
Liverpool
Ciss Green
HALE
L24
Hale Hall
Ice House Plantation
Rabbit Hey
Church Willow Bed
Manor Farm
Home Farm
Hoghton Tower Farm
62
110
215

89
F
G
H
J
K
63
111
1
2
3
4
5
6
7
51
52
53
84
83
82
81
Widnes Warth
Woodend
Iron Br.
SPIKE ISLAND
Spike Island Visitor Cen.
Catalyst
West Bank
West Bank Rec. Grd.
NEW MERSEY CROSSING (Proposed)
Runcorn Sands
MERSEY
QUEENSWAY
Silver Jubilee Bridge
A533
Runcorn Gap
Wigg Island Community Park Local Nature Reserve
Runcorn Old Quay Lock
Landing Stages
Old Quay Bridge (Swing)
MANCHESTER SHIP CANAL
EAST MOOR
BUSWAY
EXPRESSWAY
DARESBURY
HIGH ST.
BRIDGE ST.
HEATH ROAD
The Brindley
Bridgewater Canal
A557
Runcorn
Runcorn Cemetery
RUNCORN SPUR ROAD
B5155
Town Hall
Park
Grange Nursery Sch.
Playing Fields
Football Grd.
The Grange Jun. & Inf. Sch.
Grange Comp. Sch.
Stenhills
Works
CASTLE RISE
Halton Brook
Higher Runcorn
Beacon Hill
Cricket Grd.
Runcorn Hill Visitor Cen.
Runcorn Hill Local Nature Reserve
The Lake
Runcorn Heath
Playing Fields
Club House
Pewithall Primary Sch.
The Heath Specialist Technology College
Halton Junc.
Halton Lodge
St. Chad's Catholic High School
Comm. Cen.
Runcorn WA7
CENTRAL EXPRESSWAY
Woodside
YMCA

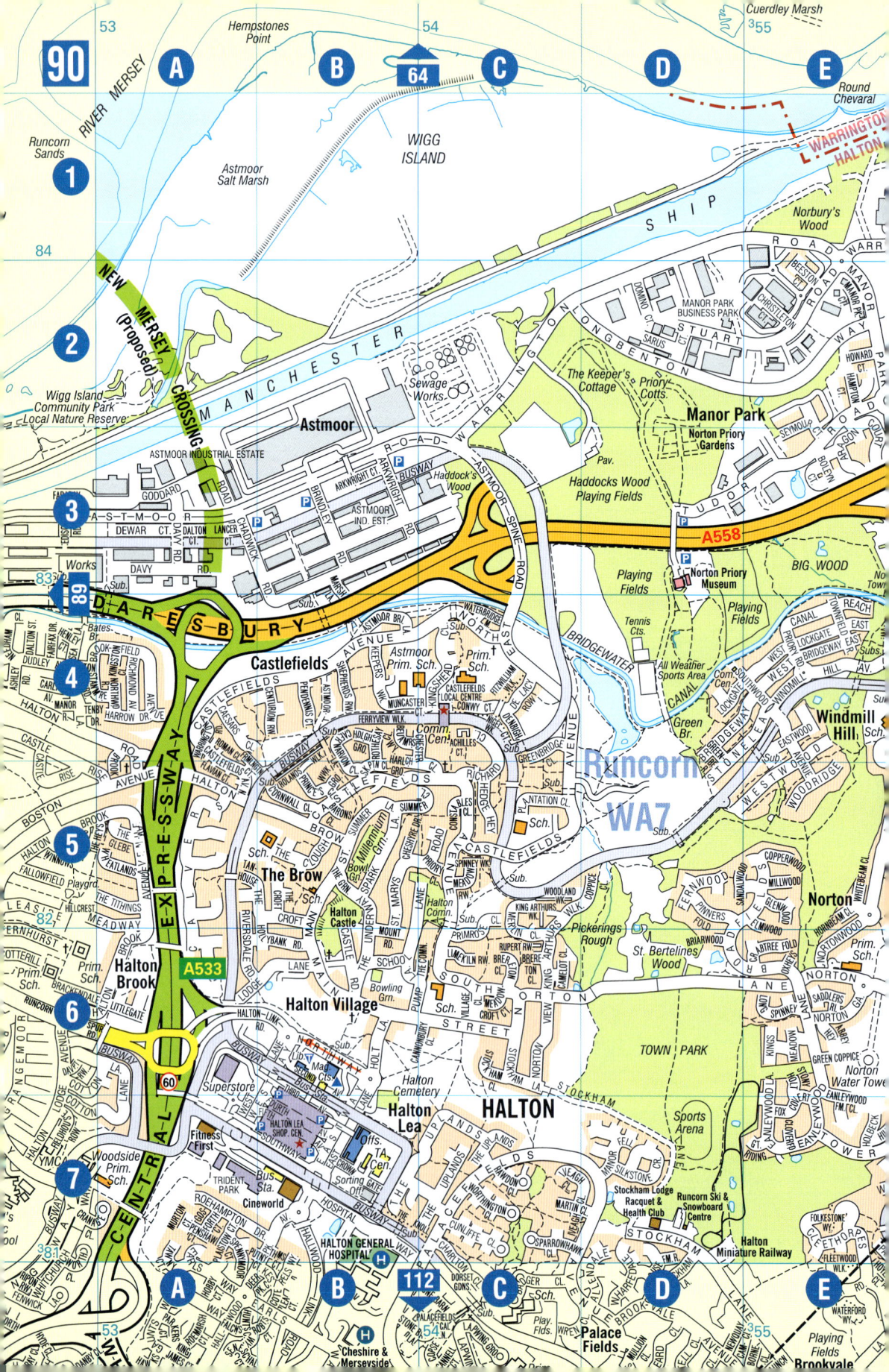

A
B
C
D
E
1
2
3
4
5
6
7
53
54
55
84
83
82
81
64
112
89
Cuerdley Marsh
Hempstones Point
Round Chevaral
RIVER MERSEY
Runcorn Sands
Astmoor Salt Marsh
WIGG ISLAND
WARRINGTON
HALTON
MANCHESTER SHIP CANAL
Norbury's Wood
NEW MERSEY CROSSING (Proposed)
Wigg Island Community Park Local Nature Reserve
Sewage Works
Astmoor
ASTMOOR INDUSTRIAL ESTATE
ASTMOOR IND. EST.
MANOR PARK BUSINESS PARK
The Keeper's Cottage
Priory Cotts.
Manor Park
Norton Priory Gardens
Haddock's Wood
Haddocks Wood Playing Fields
Pav.
A558
Norton Priory Museum
Playing Fields
BIG WOOD
Tennis Cts.
All Weather Sports Area
BRIDGEWATER CANAL
DARESBURY EXPRESSWAY
Castlefields
Astmoor Prim. Sch.
Prim. Sch.
CASTLEFIELDS LOCAL CENTRE
Comm. Cen.
Green Br.
Windmill Hill
Runcorn WA7
The Brow
Millennium Green
Halton Castle
Halton Comm.
Pickerings Rough
St. Bertelines Wood
Norton
Halton Brook
A533
Halton Village
Bowling Grn.
Superstore
HALTON LEA SHOP. CEN.
Halton Cemetery
Halton Lea
HALTON
TOWN PARK
Sports Arena
Norton Water Tower
Fitness First
Woodside Prim. Sch.
TRIDENT PARK
Bus Sta.
Cineworld
CENTRAL EXPRESSWAY
HALTON GENERAL HOSPITAL
Stockham Lodge Racquet & Health Club
Runcorn Ski & Snowboard Centre
Halton Miniature Railway
Cheshire & Merseyside
Palace Fields
Playing Fields
Brookvale

91
65
Halton Moss
Moore
Keckwick
Sandymoor
Daresbury
Warrington WA4
Daresbury Expressway
A558
A56
M56
Junction 11
Green Wood
Lodge Plantation
Oxmoor Local Nature Reserve
Oxmoor Wood
Dorchester Park Local Nature Reserve
Sandymoor Wood
Bog Wood
Pitts Heath
New Farm
Village Farm
Poplar Farm
Keckwick Bri.
Laboratory
Daresbury Science Park
Daresbury Firs
Keckwick Hill
Keckwick Hill Bridge
George Gleave's Bridge
Crow's Nest
Bridgewater Canal
Norton Town Br.
Borrow's Br.
Aqueduct
Red Brow
Daresbury Park
Slaughter's Rough
Newtonbank Farm
Little Manor Farm
Marina House
Preston Brook Marina
Dukes Wharf
Runcorn East
Catholic Prim. Sch.
Windmill Farm
Browside Farm
Hilltop Farm
Preston on the Hill
Preston Brook Br.
Moore Primary Sch.
Moorefield Br.
Cricket Grd.
Football Grd.
Kelsall Cottages
The Shires
Warehouse
Works
Depot
113
92

Football Grd.
Pav.
Farm
Acton Grange Bridge
66
WALTON HALL GOLF COURSE
Canal Side Cottages
The Shires
Moore Bri.
Moore Hall
Moore
Uplands
Rowswood Cottage
Rowswood Farm
Woodlands
The Kennels
The Cottage
New Plantation
Park House
Wood Cottage
Appleton Reservoir
The Elms Farm
The Elms Cottage
ROW'S WOOD
Bog Rough
A56
Outer Wood
CHESTER ROAD
Hatton Lodge
Cricket Grd.
Daresbury Lodge
DARESBURY EXPRESSWAY
DARESBURY SCIENCE PARK
Morts Wood
Bluecoat Farm
Hatton Cottage
COMMONSIDE BUSINESS CT.
Common Side Farm
Stables
Daresbury
Hall Lane Farm
Hatton Hall
DARESBURY LANE
B5356
Village Farm
Sch.
Greenside Farm
Daresbury Hall
Hatton
New House Farm
HALTON
WARRINGTON
Slaughter's Rough
Daresbury Farm
Keeper's Cottage
Owl's Nest Wood
Newtonbank Farm
Dairy Farm Cottages
M56 MOTORWAY
M56
Owl's Nest
Queastybirch Hall
Summer Lane Farm
Newton Gorse
Penkridge Lake Farm
Summer Lane Cottages
Little Manor Farm
Hallam Hall Farm
215
Black Jane
Black Jane Farm
Newton Ho.
Crowholt Farm
91

93
67
94
114
216
F
G
H
J
K
1
2
3
4
5
6
7
61
62
63
84
83
82
81
Dudlow's Green
Reservoir (cov.)
High Warren
Obelisk
Club House
WARRINGTON GOLF COURSE
Bellfield Farm
Dennow Cottage
Dennow Farm
Appleton Park
A49
Dingle Farm
Ford's Rough
Dood's Bridge
Dipping Brook
Pewterspear
Cann Lane Farm
Crosslands
Walnut-Tree Farm
Appleton Cross (rems. of)
Hillside Farm
Old Gorse
Warrington
WA4
Great Shepcroft Farm
Shepcroft Cottages
Little Shepcroft Farm
Pav.
Sports Ground
Stretton St. Matthew's C of E Prim. Sch.
Mosswood Hall
The Barns
Dorothy Farm
Road Side Farm
Hotel
Stretton
CHESHIRE SPIRE HOSPITAL
Oaktree Farm
Hatton Lame Farm
Whitegate Farm
New Farm
Fir Tree Farm
B5356
M56
Junction 10
M56 MOTORWAY
Tanyard Farm
Mossways
Tanner's Row Cotts.
Lower Stretton
Stretton Hall
Brookside Farm
Bradley Brook House
Pillmoss Farm
Lower Hall
Swallow Barns
Stretton House
A559
Walnut Tree Farm
Stockley Rough
Stockley Farm
WARRINGTON
CHESHIRE WEST and CHESTER
Bradley Brook
Cobbles
The Limes
Greenbank
Greenbank Farm
Spring View Cottage
The Woodlands
Firtree Farm
LONDON ROAD
LONDON RD.
TARPORLEY RD.
TARPORLEY ROAD
NORTHWICH ROAD
STRETTON LANE
DUDLOW GREEN
LONGWOOD ROAD
PEWTERSPEAR GREEN ROAD
SHEPCROFT LANE
HILLSIDE ROAD
WILLOW LA.
ROSEMOOR GDNS
DINGLE LANE
CANN LANE SOUTH
DISTRICT DISTRIBUTOR ROAD
WALNUT TREE LANE
MOSS HALL LANE
WELL LANE
COMMON LANE
HALL LANE
MOSS LANE
LIMES LANE
SCHOOL LANE
DARK LANE
STOCKLEY LA.
BIRCH TREE LA.
FOGG'S LA.
SPARK HALL CLOSE
FIR TREE CL.
SUMMIT CL.
OWENS CORNER

Wright's Green
Ford's Rough
Dood's Bridge
Dipping Brook
Greenlane Farm
APPLETON THORN
Playing Field
Warrington
WA4
B5356
GRAPPENHALL ROAD
STRETTON ROAD
APPLETON THORN TRADING ESTATE
Beehive Farm
Booth's Farm
Yewtree Farm
HM Young Offenders' Institution Thorn Cross
BARLEYCASTLE TRADING ESTATE
STRETTON GREEN DISTRIBUTION PARK
Oakleigh Lodge
Crosslands
Cross Farm
Walnut-Tree Farm
Hatton Farm
Appleton Cross (rems. of)
Appleton Thorn Prim. School
Nook Farm
RED GABLES
M56 MOTORWAY
AIRFIELD (Disused)
Burley Heyes Cottages
Burleyheyes
Burley House
Mosswood Hall
Sunnyside Farm
Antrobus Farm
Antrobus Hall
Moss Side Farm
Pools Platt Farm
Flash Farm
Nook House
Nook Bungalow
Ashwood Tree Farm
The Old Pump House
Brow Farm
Greenfield Farm
Potternell Farm
Orchard Farm
Hunters Moon
The White House
Nutmeg Farm
Manley Farm
Oakdale Farm
Keepers Cottage
Fosshey Stables
Shawbrook
ANTROBUS
Northwich
CW9
Firtree Farm
Grandsires Green
Foxley Brow Farm
Antrobus St. Marks C of E Prim. Sch.
Fox Farm
Well Farm
Frandley
Old Pole Farm
Frandley Brow Farm
Frandley Farm
The Folly
Deakin Yard
Morris Farm
Pole Farm
Belmont Dairy Farm
Thellow Heath Farm
NORTHWICH RD.
A559

68
93
216

HIGH LEGH
Knutsford
WA16
HIGH LEGH PARK GOLF COURSE
MERE
MERE GOLF & COUNTRY CLUB
THE MERE
Tatton Park Mansion
Tatton Dale
Gauntlet Birds of Prey Eagle and Vulture Park
A50
A556
B5159
A5034
WEST LANE
WARRINGTON ROAD
MANCHESTER RD.
CHESTER ROAD
MERESIDE ROAD
216
70
71

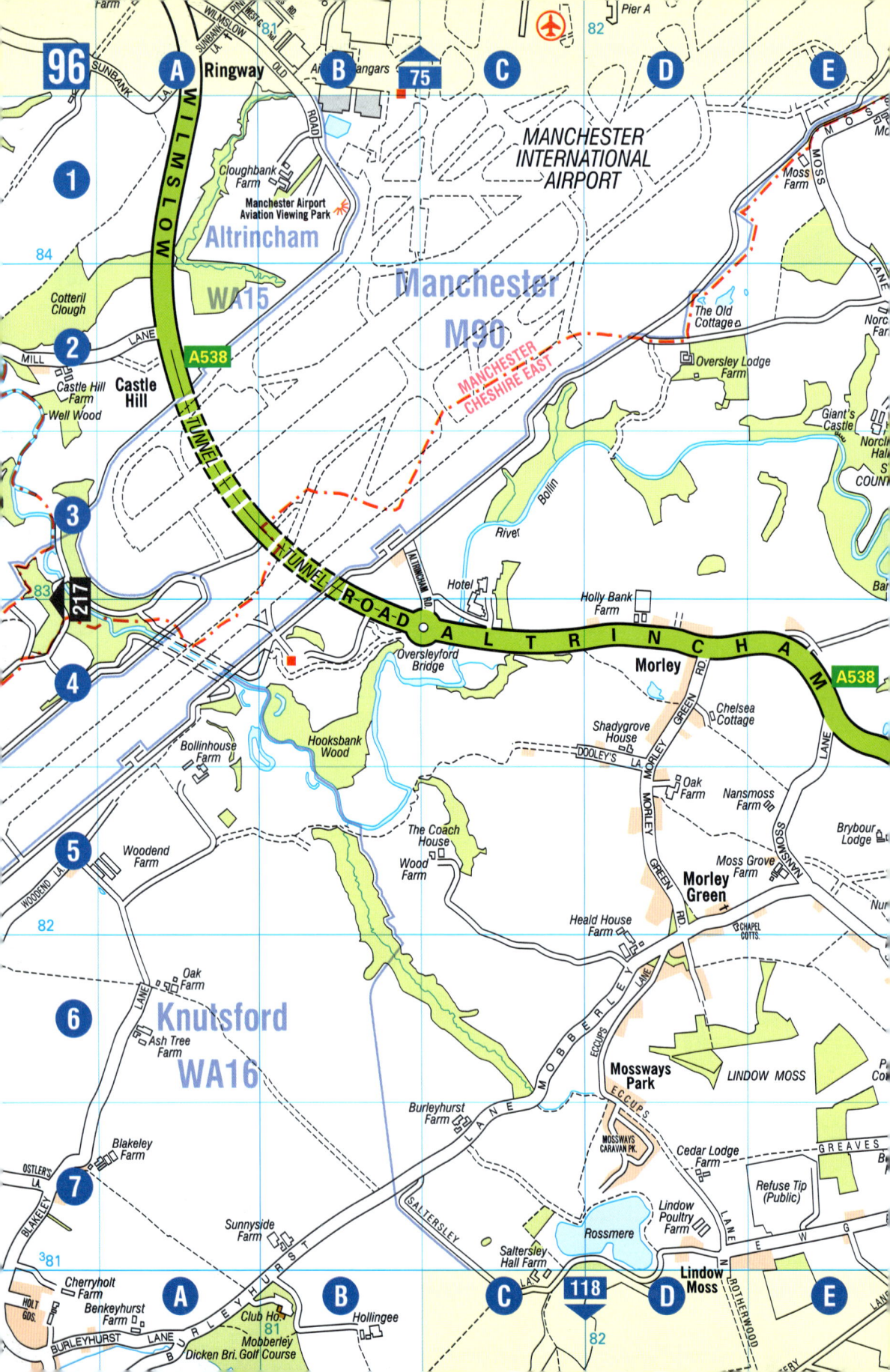

Ringway
WILMSLOW
Manchester Airport Aviation Viewing Park
Cloughbank Farm
Altrincham
WA15
Cotteril Clough
MILL LANE
Castle Hill Farm
Castle Hill
Well Wood
A538
TUNNEL
ROAD
ALTRINCHAM
MANCHESTER INTERNATIONAL AIRPORT
Manchester
M90
MANCHESTER
CHESHIRE EAST
75
217
118
Pier A
Moss Farm
MOSS LANE
The Old Cottage
Oversley Lodge Farm
Giant's Castle
River Bollin
Hotel
ALTRINCHAM RD.
Holly Bank Farm
Oversleyford Bridge
Morley
Chelsea Cottage
Shadygrove House
DOOLEY'S LA.
MORLEY GREEN RD.
Oak Farm
Nansmoss Farm
NANSMOSS LANE
Brybour Lodge
Moss Grove Farm
Morley Green
Heald House Farm
CHAPEL COTTS.
Hooksbank Wood
Bollinhouse Farm
The Coach House
Wood Farm
Woodend Farm
WOODEND LA.
Oak Farm
Knutsford
WA16
Ash Tree Farm
MOBBERLEY LANE
ECCUPS
Mossways Park
LINDOW MOSS
MOSSWAYS CARAVAN PK.
Burleyhurst Farm
Cedar Lodge Farm
GREAVES
Refuse Tip (Public)
Blakeley Farm
OSTLER'S LA.
BLAKELEY
Sunnyside Farm
SALTERSLEY LA.
Saltersley Hall Farm
Rossmere
Lindow Poultry Farm
Lindow Moss
ROTHERWOOD
NEWGATE
Cherryholt Farm
Benkeyhurst Farm
HOLT GDS.
BURLEYHURST LANE
Club Ho.
Mobberley
Dicken Bri. Golf Course
Hollingee
A B C D E
1 2 3 4 5 6 7
81 82 83 84

76
Boundary Farm
Beech Farm
Yew Tree Farm
Bolshaw Farm
Bowling Green
HOLLIN LANE
Driving Range
Club House
STYAL GOLF COURSE
The Grange
Lode Hill Farm
Styal House
Lode Hill
Woodend
HANDFORTH
Football Grd.
Cricket Grd.
Oak Farm
Styal Prim. Sch.
Styal
STATION ROAD
Highfield
Nursing Home
STYAL
Wilmslow
SK9
Kent House
Langley House
Cross Fm.
Styal Green
Sports Ground
QUARRY BANK ROAD
Weirs
Quarry Bank Mill
Res.
Norcliffe Farm
Oakwood Farm
Viaduct
Linney's Bridge
Gallops
Stables
Garden Centre
River Dean
Handforth Bridge
Weir
STYAL COUNTRY PARK
Transmitting Station
HMP STYAL
Finney Green
Stamford Lodge
Deadman's Clough
Sewage Works
Willow Ground Wood
Burned Hey Wood
Twinnies Bri.
Lacey Green Prim. Sch.
Lacey Green
Cemetery
Jim Evison Playing Field
Rugby Grd.
Pownall Hall Sch.
Pownall Hall Farm
River Bollin
Carr Wood
B5166
STYAL ROAD
Hill Top
A34
Wilmslow Park
THE CARRS
Pownall Park
Ten. Cts.
Bowl. Grn.
Miniature Golf Course
Play. Flds.
WILMSLOW
MANCHESTER RD.
BOLLIN LINK
WILMSLOW BY-PASS
Gorsey Bank Prim. Sch.
Carnival Field
Lindow Common Local Nature Reserve
Black Lake
A538
WATER LA.
ALDERLEY RD.
Wilmslow
Wilmslow Leis. Cen.
Cricket Grd.
119
Lib.
Superstore
Wilmslow High Sch.
Weir
F
G
H
J
K
1
2
3
4
5
6
7
98

STANLEY ROAD
Gill Bent Farm
Hotel
Stanley Hall Farm
STANLEY GREEN INDUSTRIAL ESTATE
77
GROVE
LANE
ACRE
Lower Bent Farm
Sports Ground
South Park
Manchester Rugby Club (Grove Park)
MANCHESTER AIRPORT EASTERN
A555
The Firs
Football Ground
Sports Grd.
CHESTER'S CROFT PARK HOME ESTATE
SPATH LANE EAST
Playing Field
STANLEY GRN. BUS. PARK
Depot
STANLEY GREEN IND. EST.
COMMERCIAL AV.
COUNTESS AV.
Redesmere Cen.
Government Buildings
Cheadle
SK8
Nursery
Prim. Sch.
GRANGEWAY
Ten. Cts.
Pav.
B5358
HANDFORTH DEAN
Superstores
Total Fitness
BY PASS
WILMSLOW ROAD
MERITON
SAGARS
SCHOOL
Lib
Youth Cen.
St. Benedict's Catholic Prim. Sch.
HANDFORTH
Handforth
Handforth Bridge
STATION RD.
DEAN ROAD
HALL ROAD
A34
Wilmslow
SK9
Kenn
Threewa Farm
River Dean
83
97
Garden Centre
Rec. Grd.
DEANWAY TRAD. EST.
DEANWAY TECH. CEN.
FINSBURY WAY
Blossoms Turkey Farm
BLOSSOMS
Grove-end Farm
Bollinfee Bri.
Hall Wood
Finney Green
MANCHESTER
HANDFORTH
Fitness Club
Cemetery
Dean Oaks Prim. Sch.
CHESHIRE EAST
STOCKPORT
Dean Farm
KING STREET
DEAN ROW ROAD
82
WILMSLOW-BY-PASS
Melville
Deanwater Bridge
WILMSLOW
MOSS TER.
Upton House
CROSS LANE
DEAN ROW RD.
WOODFORD RD.
Dean Row
Wilmslow Park
ADLINGTON ROAD
Recreation Ground
Hall
Brick Yard Farm
A5102
LEES LANE
Depot
Nurseries
Vicar Farm
Nursery
B5358
ADLINGTON
Weir
River
Bollin
Vardon Bri.
Hollies Farm
Nursery
119
217
Newton Farm
86
87
A
B
C
D
E
1
2
3
4
5
6
7

BRAMHALL GOLF COURSE
Club House
BRAMHALL
Depot
Distaff Farm
MOSS B5094 LANE
WOODFORD ROAD
LINK A555 ROAD
A5102
Moss Hey Prim. Sch.
Valley Sch.
Woodford Recreation Ground
Queensgate Prim. Sch.
MOOREND GOLF COURSE
Driving Range
Club House
Walnut-Tree Farm
CHESTER ROAD
A5149
Longfield Poultry Farm
Hawthorn Farm
Oaklea Farm
Long Acre
Side House
Meadow Farm
Nursery
Cornerstone House
Moor Farm
Peartree Cottage
Ckt. Grd.
Stockport
SK7
Cricket Ground
Hall
The Croft
Nursery
Woodford
Upper Swineseye Farm
Lostockhall Farm
SK12
Lostock Hall Prim. Sch.
Mast
Community Centre
Aircraft Factory
Homelea
Westgate
Boldmere
Hilltop Farm
Moss Wood
Cricket Grd.
A5102 ROAD CHESTER
Old Fold Farm
New Fold
Vicarage
Dellhaven
WOODFORD AERODROME
Old Hall Farm
AVRO GOLF COURSE
Club House
New Hall Farm
Aircraft Factory
Dairyhouse Wood
Pitch & Putt Course
Lumb Brook
Pitlane Farm
Lumb Farm
Macclesfield
SK10
Isles Wood
Bent Farm
Florence Farm
Yew Tree Farm
Dean Close Farm
WILMSLOW RD.
Water Treatment Plant

78
100
217

A
B
C
D
E
1
2
3
4
5
6
7
79
103
99
91
92
84
83
82
381
SK7
SK10
Macclesfield
Birch Hall
Hill Green Farm
Park House Farm
Poynton Brook
Phillip's Bridge
Poynton Lake
Poynton Park
Anglesey
Towers Cl.
Towers Drive
A523
A5149
Chester Road
London Road North
London Road South
London Road
Lower Park Road
Park Road
Woodford Road
Meadway
Distaff Road
Warren Rd.
Merton Rd.
Deva Cl.
Silk Mill
Spinners La.
Playing Field
Lower Park Prim. Sch.
Poynton
POYNTON
Hazelbadge Rd.
Wayside Dr.
Oakland Ct.
Milton Drive
Oak Grove
Burton Dr.
Vicarage La.
Dundrennan Cl.
Abbotsbury Cl.
Newstead Cl.
Neath Cl.
Hartland Cl.
Tintern Cl.
Buckfast Cl.
Covell Rd.
Tulworth Rd.
Whitby Cl.
Easby Cl.
Furness Cl.
Kirkstall Cl.
Bolton Cl.
Glastonbury
Tewkesbury Cl.
Lindisfarne
Malmesbury
Lambourn Cl.
Selby Cl.
Mayfair
South Park Drive
Warren Lea
Lakeside Dr.
Waters Reach
Millstone Cl.
Incline
Prince's Incline
Lady's Wood
Woodside Lane
Parklands Way
Beech Cres.
Oakfield Road
Lady's Cl.
Capenhurst Cl.
Charlecote Rd.
Moreton Dr.
Sulgrave Av.
Blenheim
Hardwick Rd.
Holker
Knole Av.
Ragley Cl.
Poynton Sports Club
Civic Hall
Lib.
Park Av.
Park Lane
School La.
School Cl.
Brecon Cl.
Play. Fld.
Woburn Cl.
Hockley Paddock
Cedarwood
Leigh Cl.
Bulkeley Rd.
George's Rd. W.
George's Rd. E.
George's Cl.
Bowl. Grn.
Vernon Primary Sch.
Granary
Birch Vale
Cedar Cl.
Holland Cl.
Willow Cl.
Brookside Cl.
Holly Rd.
Maple Av.
Chestnut Av.
Chestnut Dr.
Homelyme House
Hockley
Avenue
Alder Av.
Cherry Tree
Ash Rd.
Hazel Dr.
Elm Cl.
Clumber Rd.
Clumber Cl.
Stiperson
Ivy Rd.
Fir Road
Yewtree
Dickens Lane
Poynton Leisure Centre
Poynton High Sch. & Performing Arts Coll.
Playing Field
Gawsworth Cl.
Adlington
Siddington
Pickwick Rd.
Nickleby Rd.
Dombey Rd.
Varden Rd.
Bardell Cr.
Marley Rd.
St. Paul's Catholic Prim. Sch.
Adams Cl.
Bagstock Av.
Brownlow Cl.
Tapley Av.
Curzon Rd.
Barclay Rd.
Micawber
Fielding Av.
Dorrit Cl.
Graymarsh Dr.
Spring Rd.
Spenlow Cl.
Weller Av.
Weller Cl.
Hale Av.
Copperfield
Barnaby Rd.
Lawrence Pl.
Calder Pl.
Vernon Cl.
Midway
Ash Lodge
Fountain Cl.
Nursery Dr.
Abbey Ct.
Gloucester Rd.
Windsor Dr.
Balmoral Rd.
Buckingham Rd.
Queensway
Sandringham Dr.
Clifford Rd.
Brookfield
Wigwam Cl.
The Spinney
Grosvenor Dr.
Grosvenor Road
Glenfield Dr.
Darlington Dr.
Woolley Av.
Worth Ct.
Lostock Rd.
Coppice Ho.
Hope Grn. Wy.
Tern Dr.
Brent Cl.
Grebe Cl.
Swan Cl.
Widgeon Cres.
Mallard Cl.
Petrel Av.
Puffin Av.
Dunlin Cl.
Bittern Cl.
Heron Dr.
Gull Cres.
Snipe Cl.
Lostock Av.
Lostock Hall Rd.
Lostock Hall Prim. Sch.
Wigwam Wood
Nursery
Lostockhall Farm
Poynton Brook
Adlington Bus. Park
Adlington Industrial Estate
Adlington Rd.
First Avenue
Second Av.
Third Av.
Poynton Industrial Estate
Hope La.
Hope Lane
Hope Green
Hope Green Farm
Shirdfold Farm
Depot
Media Ho.
Europa House
Park
Candy La.
Street Lane
Streetlane Farm
Driving Range
Pitch & Putt Course
Sandholes Moss
Sandholes Farm
Marlfields House
Marlfields Hall
Gibson Wood
Red Brook
Sewage Works
Hope Lane Cottage
The Oaks
Brookside Farm
Clayton Greaves Farm
Adlington Manor
Oak Farm
Skellorngreen Farm
Skellorn Green
Skellorn Green Lane
Ash Tree Farm
Cawley Lane
Gorsewood Farm
Booth Green Farm
Pedleyhill Farm
Pedley
Boothgreen Farm
Booth Green
Walnut Tree Cottage
Roundy House
Sprink Farm
Wardsend Old Farm

Park Pit Plantation
Park Pit Cottages
Correction Farm
Tennis Club
Prim. Sch.
80
Bollinhurst
Brookside Farm
Bank Farm Riding Sch.
Jacksons' Brickworks Local Nature Reserve
POOL HOUSE RD.
Pool House Farm
Prince's Wood
Rabbit Burrow Farm
Middlewood
PRINCES WOOD RD.
Middlecale Cottage
Middlecale Wood
Ryles Wood
Beechfield
DAVENPORT GOLF COURSE
PRINCE ROAD
Middlecale Farm
Water Tower
HAWTHORNE GRO.
ST. ELMO PK.
CARLETON ROAD
Red Legg Farm
Club House
Stockport
DAVENPORT GOLF COURSE
Potters Clough
The Anson Engine Museum
The Gables Farm
Barlow House Farm
Petre Bank
Woodlands
MIDDLEWOOD
ANSON ROAD
Works
Platt Wood Cottages
Platt Wood
Newtown
SK12
LYME LANE
Marine Ville Mooring
Nelson Pit Visitor Cen.
HEPLEY RD.
TRAFALGAR AV.
TRAFALGAR CL.
NELSON AV.
NELSON CL.
COPPICE ROAD
Water Tower
Reservoir (covered)
Griffins Cottage
Platt Wood Farm
Springbank Farm
SHRIGLEY RD.
Play Fld.
Hilltop Farm
217
ROAD
Alma Cottages
Coppice Farm
Higher Poynton
ELM BEDS ROAD
SHELDON RD.
Elm Wood
Harestead Farm
Lynden
Kennels
High Lodge
Res. (cov.)
ELM BEDS CARAVAN PARK
Macclesfield Canal
Ben's Wood
Windgather
Poynton Coppice
Garden Cen.
COPPICE
Poynton Coppice
Throstlenest Farm
Hagg Farm
Brook Bank Farm
NARROW LA.
Yewtree Farm
Wood Lane End Farm
Green Farm
Wardsend
Wood Lane End
Woodhouse Farm
Holly Bank Farm
YEW TREE RD.
NORTH
Rams Clough
Knott
Welfield
Well Farm
Hase Bank
Noggin Farm
Mitchell Fold
Hase Bank Wood
Nelson Farm
WEST WOOD
MEADOWSIDE
Lyme View Marina
Poynton
Pursefield Wood
Fourlane Ends
SOUTH
Adlington Basin
Needygate
West Parkgate
Trugs i' th' Hole Farm
Redacre Hall Farm
PEAK DISTRICT NATIONAL PARK
Greenclose Farm
Clusc Hay
Simpson Lane Cottage
Brook
SIMPSON LA.
HILL WOOD LANE
SCHOOLFOLD
Eastwood End
Schoolfold
Woodend Farm
Lockgate Farm
EAST LANE
Oak Tree Cottage
SHRIGLEY
Eastwood End House
EASTWOOD END CARAVAN PARK
Higher House Farm
Jepsonclough Farm
East Woodend Farm
Highbarn Farm
Newfold Farm
Harrop Brow
Park Moor Cottage
Moorside
94
395
84
83
82
381
F
G
H
J
K
1
2
3
4
5
6
7

216
Blackshaw Heys Farm
Stock-in-Hey Farm
Breach House Farm
Kell House Farm
Brook House
Brookside Farm
Barnshaw Farm
Two Gates
Clay House
Yarwood House Farm
Parkside Farm
New Mills
Coldstream Cottages
MANCHESTER INTERNATIONAL AIRPORT
Manchester
M90
Sugar Brook
Owen House Farm
Mobberley
Barnfield
Bowl. Grn.
Key House Farm
Greenoaks Farm
Greenbank
Hobcroft House
Hobcroft Farm
Sunny Bank Farm
Orchard Lea
Wee Bridge Farm
Holly House
Kimbles
Hazelhurst Farm
Meadow Cottage
Willow House
Cinder Lane Farm
Knutsford
WA16
Smithlane Farm
Valewood Farm
Broad Oak Farm
Rathlin
Works
Mobberley Brook
Dairy Farm
Mobberley C of E Primary Scool
War Meml.
Sewage Works
Spring Gds.
Mobberley Hall Farm
Stubbs Farm
Cricket Ground
Sports Grd.
MOBBERLEY
Gorsey Brow
Hall
Mobberley Old Hall
BARCLAY HALL
Grove House
Town Lane Hall Farm
Park Farm
B5085
Town Lane Farm
Lodge
Dukenfield Hall
117
Grimsditch Farm
Dam Head Farm
Merry Fox
Pavement Lane Farm
Braebrooke
Gleavehouse Farm

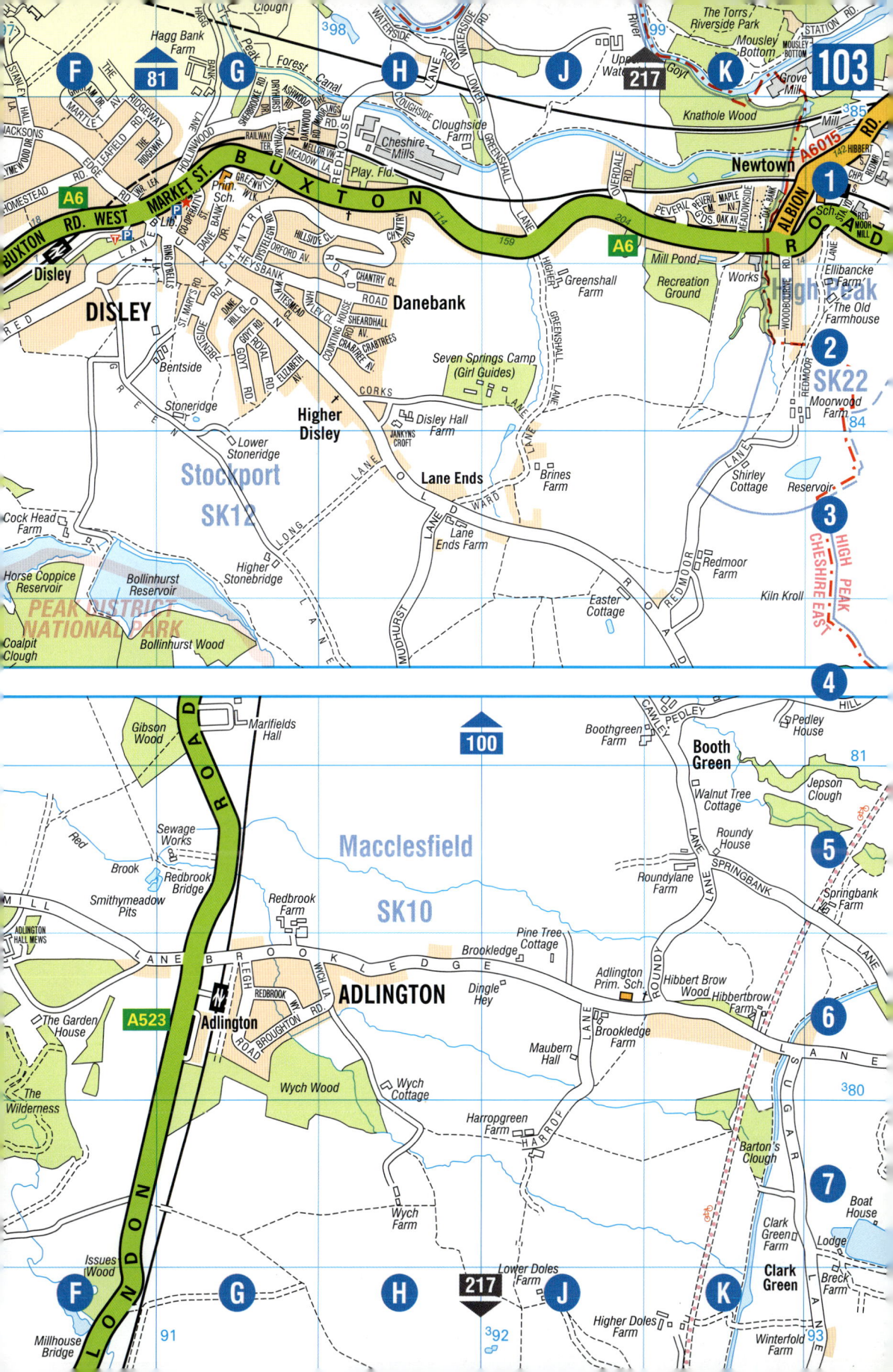

DISLEY
Disley
Danebank
Higher Disley
Lane Ends
Newtown
High Peak
Stockport
SK12
SK22
SK10
Macclesfield
ADLINGTON
Adlington
Booth Green
Clark Green
BUXTON RD. WEST
MARKET ST.
BUXTON ROAD
ALBION ROAD
A6
A6015
A523
LONDON ROAD
Cheshire Mills
Cloughside Farm
Play. Fld.
Prim. Sch.
Lib.
Recreation Ground
Mill Pond
Works
Greenshall Farm
Seven Springs Camp (Girl Guides)
Disley Hall Farm
Brines Farm
Lane Ends Farm
Bentside
Stoneridge
Lower Stoneridge
Higher Stonebridge
Cock Head Farm
Horse Coppice Reservoir
Bollinhurst Reservoir
PEAK DISTRICT NATIONAL PARK
Bollinhurst Wood
Coalpit Clough
Easter Cottage
Redmoor Farm
Kiln Kroll
Shirley Cottage
Reservoir
Moorwood Farm
Ellibancke Farm
The Old Farmhouse
Knathole Wood
The Torrs Riverside Park
Mousley Bottom
Grove Mill
River Goyt
Peak Forest Canal
Hagg Bank Farm
HIGH PEAK
CHESHIRE EAST
Gibson Wood
Marlfields Hall
Boothgreen Farm
Pedley House
Jepson Clough
Walnut Tree Cottage
Roundy House
Roundylane Farm
Springbank Farm
Sewage Works
Red Brook
Redbrook Bridge
Smithymeadow Pits
Redbrook Farm
Pine Tree Cottage
Adlington Prim. Sch.
Hibbert Brow Wood
Hibbertbrow Farm
Dingle Hey
Brookledge Farm
Maubern Hall
The Garden House
The Wilderness
Wych Wood
Wych Cottage
Harropgreen Farm
Barton's Clough
Wych Farm
Issues Wood
Millhouse Bridge
Lower Doles Farm
Higher Doles Farm
Clark Green Farm
Boat House
Lodge
Breck Farm
Winterfold Farm
BROOKLEDGE LANE
SPRINGBANK LANE
SUGAR LANE
HARROP
MILL LANE
F G H J K
1 2 3 4 5 6 7
81
100
217

104
83
214
HESWALL
Wirral
CH60
Gayton Hole
GAYTON SANDS
Gayton Prim. Sch.
Gayton Hall
Club House
Gayton Wood
HESWALL GOLF COURSE
Backwood Hall
The Lodge
Nursery
WIRRAL
CHESHIRE WEST and CHESTER
GAYTON SANDS NATURE RESERVE
RIVER DEE
B5135
THE PARADE
BOATHOUSE LA.
MARINE DR.
PARK WEST
DAVENPORT LA.
RECTORY CL.
MANNERS
SEABANK ROAD
RIVERBANK ROAD
STATION ROAD
RIVERBANK CL.
WOODBURN DR.
WESTWAY
MEADWAY
HINDERTON DR.
LONG LILLYFIELD
MEADOW LANE
GAYTON ROAD
GAYTON DRIVE
LAPWING RI.
VICTORIA AV.
STRATHEARN RD.
BEECHFIELD CL.
WALLRAKE
DAWSTONE ROAD
MOORLAND PK.
CHANTRY WLK.
BASKERVYLE ROAD
BASKERVYLE CL.
HOLMES RI.
THE KNAP
GAYTON LANE
GAYTON FARM RD.
GAYTON PARK
DEE PARK CL.
THE CRES.
LATCHFORD ROAD
ASH WY.
FIR WY.
CEDARWAY
LYNTON CL.
PORLOCK CL.
THORNTON CRES.
BEVERLEY DR.
COTTAGE LANE
COTTAGE DR. WEST
COTTAGE DR. EAST
NORTH PDE.
HAMILTON CL.
GREENWAY
TITHEBARN
BROOK HEY
BEVYL RD.
MEALOR'S WEINT
DEESIDE CT.
MOSTYN SQ.
SCHOOL LA.
The Beacons
A B C D E
1 2 3 4 5 6 7
26 27 81 80 79 78

Gayton
Barnston Prim. Sch.
Thornton Hough
Wirral
CH63
Neston
CH64
Parkgate
NESTON
Moorside
CHESTER HIGH ROAD
A540
NESTON ROAD
LIVERPOOL ROAD
B5136
B5135
B5134
HINDERTON ROAD
PARKGATE ROAD
STATION ROAD
RABY ROAD
UPPER RABY ROAD
PARK ROAD
LEIGHTON ROAD
WOOD LANE
RUNNELL
PARKGATE LANE
GAYTON LANE
Bridges House Farm
New Hall Farm
Crows Nest
NEW HALL MANOR
Lyndale Farm
The Runnell
West Point
Lone Acres
Leighton Hall Farm
Leighton House
Leighton Brow
Hydestyle House
Woodcote
Brook House
Windy Knowe
Ashfield Hall Farm
Ashfield Farm
Westwood Farm
Westwood Grange
Yew Tree Farm
Thornton Hall
Lodge Farm
Hesketh Grange
Hill Top Farm
Poultry Houses
Kennels & Cattery
Upland's Farm
Cherry Farm
Leawood
Five Ways Nurseries
The Red Farm
The Lodge
Hinderton Hall
The Grey House
Overdale Farm
Witchwood
Kennels
FIVEWAYS PARK
CLAYHILL LIGHT INDUSTRIAL PARK
Household Waste Site
Neston Recreation Centre
Neston High School
Cemetery
MAYFIELD GARDENS
Sports Ground
Parkgate Prim. Sch.
Cricket Grd.
Rec. Grd.
84
106
130

106
A
B
C
D
E
1
2
3
4
5
6
7
85
105
131
31
32
81
80
79
78
Thornton Common Rd.
B5136
Grange Rd.
Hill Top Farm
Crofts Bank Cottages
Thornton
St. George's Wy.
Church Rd.
Thornton House
THORNTON HOUGH
Pav.
Graveyard
Kennels
Sewage Works
Thornton Farm Cottages
Thornton Farm Coach House
Strawberry Farm
Groveside Cottages
Pear Tree Farm
Playing Field
Pavilion
Raby Vale
Raby Vale Cottage
Willows Farm
Oakwood Farm
The Foxes
Rose Bank
Brook Farm
Bank Farm
Raby Mere Road
Wirral
Three Stacks
M53
M53 MOTORWAY
Raby Hall Farm Blws.
Raby Hall Farm
Four Lanes End Farm
Four Lanes End
Mere Road
Raby
CH63
Willaston Road
B5151
Keeper's Cottage
Pear Tree Farm
White House Farm
Raby Road
Corner Farm
Grange Farm
The Green
The Cross Way
Willowbrow Road
Willowbrow Farm
Willow Lane
Hargrave
Hargrave Hall Farm
Hargrave Cottages
Benty Heath
Raby House Farm
Raby House
Poultry Houses
Kennels & Cattery
Upland's Farm
Cherry Farm
The Field House
Raby Road
Upper Raby
School Lane
Neston
CH64
The Red Farm
The Lodge
Hinderton Hall
Birkenhead Road
Greenwood Nurseries
Mill Cottages
Hinderton Grange
Fieldhead
Tower Cott.
Bluebell Lane
Quarry Road
Theakston
Hinderton
Chester
The Lydiate
Mill Lane
Mill Lane Farm
Poultry Houses
Two Oaks Farm
Recreation Ground
Meadow Cres.
White Gates Cl.
Whitegates
Meadow Cft.
Meadow Cl.
Willaston C of E Prim. Sch.
Hinderton Rd.
B5134
Overdale Farm
A540 High Road
Hall Road
B5133
Weatherstones Cottages
Hanns Hall
Windle Hill
Hanns Hall Farm
Cherry Cl.
Hanns
Lydiate Lane
Neston Road
Elm Rd.
Mill Grn.
Elm Grn.
Church Farm Ct.
Gordon
Broadlake
Mews Ct.
Willaston Grn. M.
The Courtyard
Ness Acre Lane
Poultry Houses
Poultry Houses
Mare Hall Lane
Windle Hill
Weatherstones Business Centre
Leahurst University of Liverpool Veterinary Field Station
Wood Park
Lees Lane
Damhead Lane
Hadlow La.
Buckley

Raby Mere
Bromborough
EASTHAM
Brookhurst
BROMBOROUGH GOLF COURSE
Eastham Rake
M53 MOTORWAY
WIRRAL
CHESHIRE WEST and CHESTER
Hooton
WILLASTON
Ellesmere Port
CH62
CH66
B5133
HOOTON ROAD
NEW CHESTER RD.
86
108
132

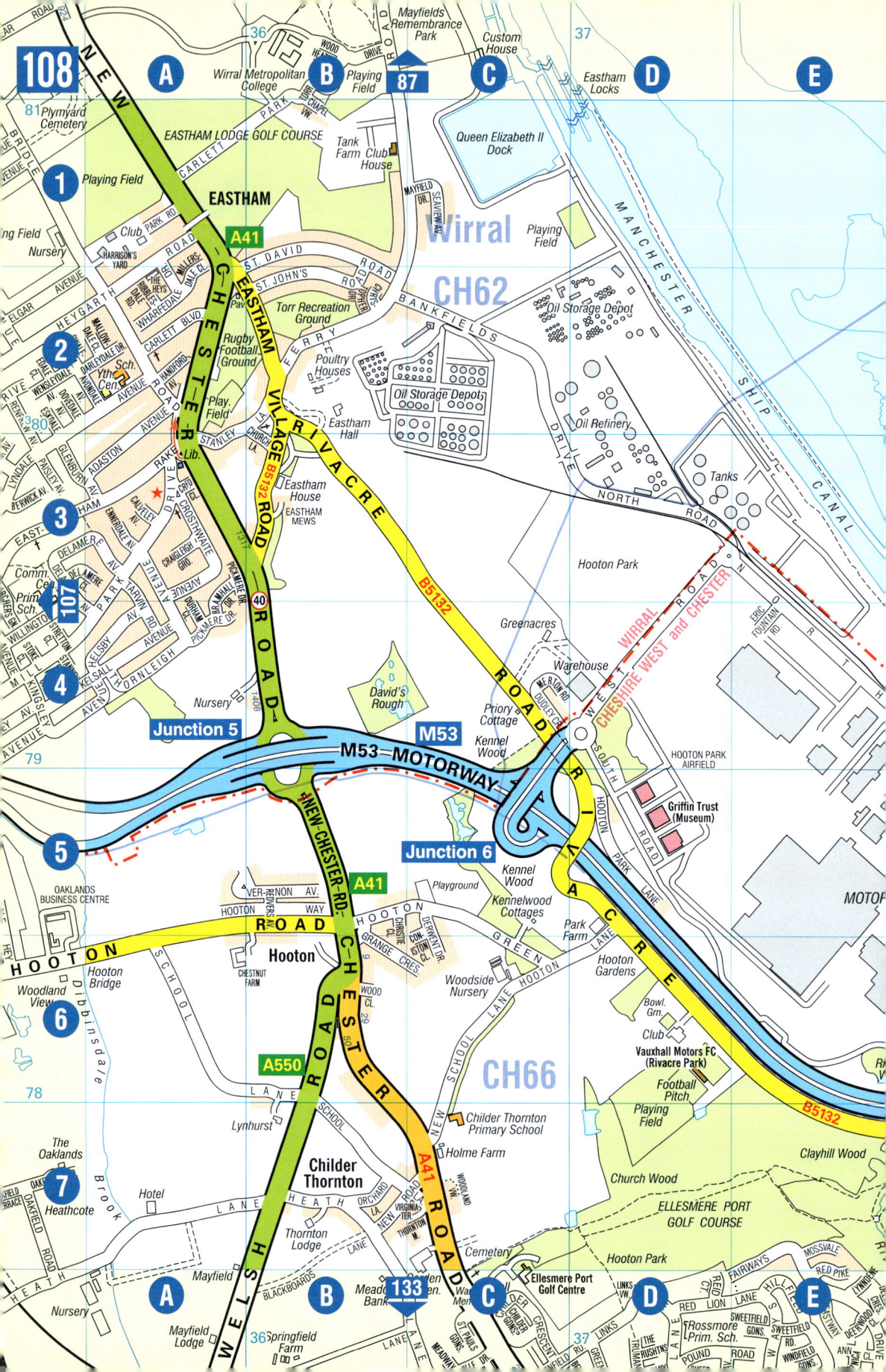

A
B
C
D
E
1
2
3
4
5
6
7
87
107
133
EASTHAM
Eastham Lodge Golf Course
Wirral Metropolitan College
Mayfields Remembrance Park
Custom House
Eastham Locks
Queen Elizabeth II Dock
Plymyard Cemetery
Playing Field
Tank Farm Club House
Wirral
CH62
Oil Storage Depot
Oil Refinery
Tanks
Manchester Ship Canal
Torr Recreation Ground
Rugby Football Ground
Poultry Houses
Eastham Hall
Eastham House
Eastham Mews
Hooton Park
Greenacres
Warehouse
Wirral
Cheshire West and Chester
David's Rough
Priory Cottage
Kennel Wood
Junction 5
M53
M53 Motorway
Junction 6
Hooton Park Airfield
Griffin Trust (Museum)
Oaklands Business Centre
Hooton
Hooton Bridge
Woodland View
Kennelwood Cottages
Park Farm
Hooton Gardens
Woodside Nursery
CH66
Vauxhall Motors FC (Rivacre Park)
Football Pitch
Playing Field
Childer Thornton Primary School
Holme Farm
Clayhill Wood
Church Wood
Ellesmere Port Golf Course
Childer Thornton
Thornton Lodge
Hooton Park
Ellesmere Port Golf Centre
The Oaklands
Heathcote
Hotel
Mayfield
Nursery
Mayfield Lodge
Springfield Farm
Rossmore Prim. Sch.
Dibbinsdale Brook
A41
A550
B5132
New Chester Road
Welsh Road
Rivacre Road
Eastham Village Road
Hooton Road
North Road
Bankfields Drive

RIVER MERSEY
Poole Hall Rocks
Booston Wood
Rivacre Brook
Mount Manisty
Poole Hall Sands
Ellesmere Port
Works
Power Station
MANCHESTER SHIP CANAL
CH65
Junction 7
M53
M53 MOTORWAY
Manchester Ship Canal Railway
Well Wood
Rivacre Valley Country Park
EVANS BUS. PK.
PIONEER PARK
POOLE HALL INDUSTRIAL ESTATE
NETHERPOOL ROAD
B5132
Junction 8
MERSEYTON RD.
NEW EXTENSION QUAY
PORTSIDE BUS. PK.
PORTSIDE INDUSTRIAL ESTATE
NORTH WALL TERMINAL
Depot
TELFORD'S QUAY
National Waterways
ROSSMORE ROAD EAST
B5463
ROTHER DRIVE BUSINESS PARK
ROSSMORE BUSINESS PARK
Rivacre Valley Prim. Sch.
HILLSIDE DRIVE

214
215
134

110
88
215
138
A
B
C
D
E
1
2
3
4
5
6
7
48
49
350
81
380
79
78
RIVER MERSEY
MANCHESTER SHIP CANAL
River Weaver Canal
Landing Stage
Weaver Sluices
Weaver
Weston Marsh Lock
Warehouse
WESTON POINT DOCKS
Works
Play-grd.
BAKER
CULLEN
ALLEN RD.
LEONARD ST.
SYDNEY ST.
PARADE
LYDIATE
CRES.
CASTNER AV.
CT.
CHESHYRES LA.
BANKES LA.
60
Frodsham Score
Refuse Tip
ALDER LANE
Frodsham Marsh Farm
BROOK
FRODSHAM MARSH
Jetty
CROSS LANE
LANE
HARE'S
STRAIGHT LENGTH
GRASSY LANE
LORDSHIP
ELTON LORDSHIP LA.
Lordship Marsh

111
89
112
139
F
G
H
J
K
1
2
3
4
5
6
7
51
52
53
81
80
79
78
Technology College
Halton Junc.
St. Chad's Catholic High Sch.
Reservoirs
Weston
Weston Prim. Sch.
RUNCORN GOLF COURSE
Cavendish Sch.
Cavendish Farm
Manor Farm
A557
A5126
POINT EXPRESSWAY
ROCKSAVAGE EXPRESSWAY
Bus Depot
Works
Power Station
Rocksavage
Clifton Hall
Rock Savage Grange
Clifton
Junction 12
Weaver Navigation
HALTON
CHESHIRE WEST and CHESTER
Lagoon
The Lum
RIVER WEAVER
Electricity Sub Station
M56
MOTORWAY
Frodsham WA6
Weaver Sailing Club
Frodsham Bri.
Saltworks Farm Playing Flds.
Frodsham Weaver Vale Prim. Sch.
Playground
Newtown
BRIDGE LANE
A56
B5152
Frodsham
Frodsham Leis. Cen.
Frodsham Sch.
Frodsham Prim. Sch.
Playing Field
Marsh Green Farm
Marsh Green
MILLBANK COTTAGES
Arts Cen.
Castle Park
FRODSHAM
MAIN STREET
HIGH STREET
CHURCH STREET
RED LANE
FURLONG LANE
CHESTER RD.
COW HEY LANE
CLIFTON LA.
CHOLMONDLEY ROAD
SUTTON CAUSEWAY
Bradley
Dig Lane Farm
The Paddock

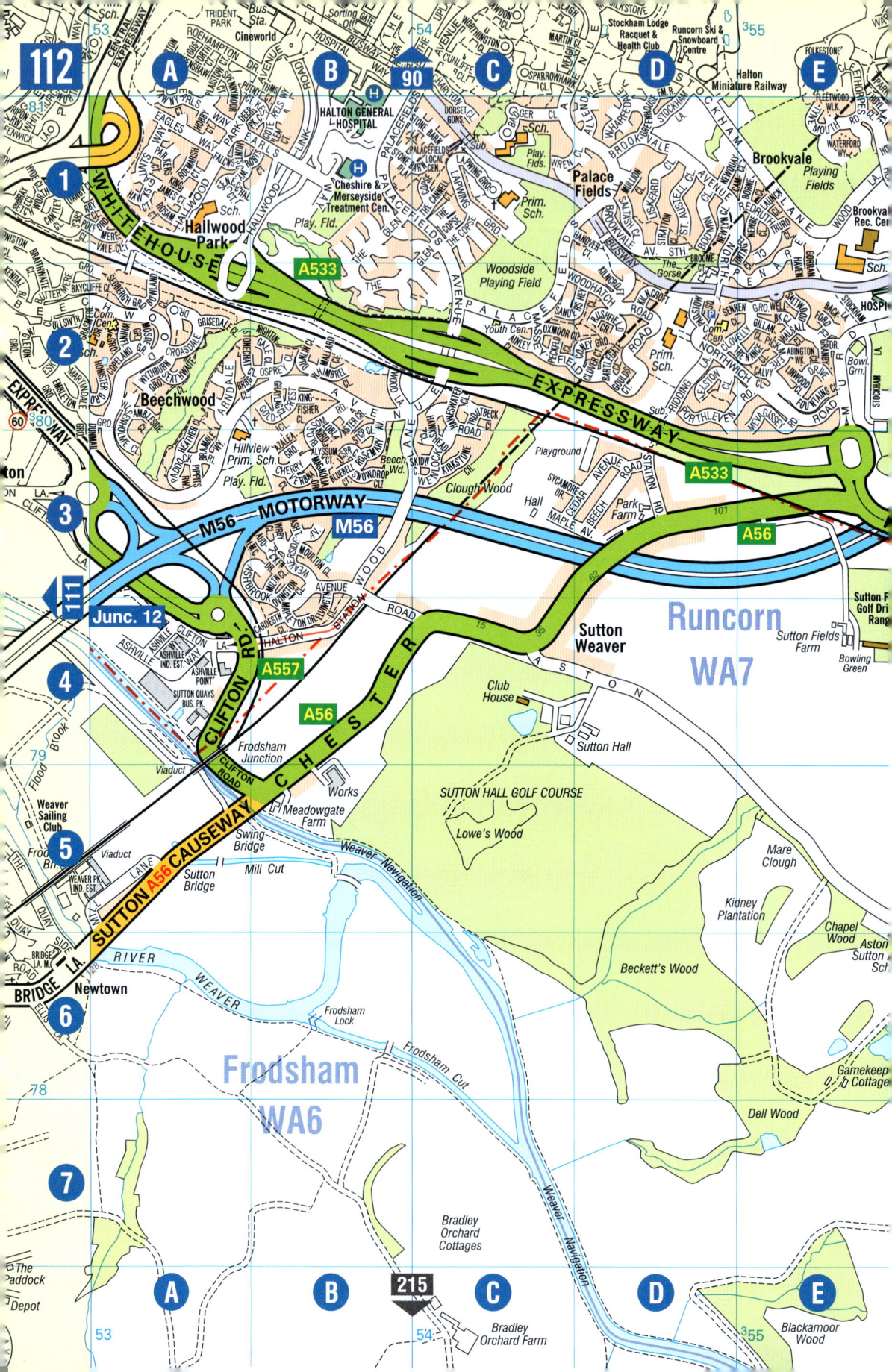

90
215
111
Runcorn WA7
Frodsham WA6
Halton General Hospital
Cheshire & Merseyside Treatment Cen.
Hallwood Park
Beechwood
Palace Fields
Brookvale
Brookvale Playing Fields
Woodside Playing Field
Halton Miniature Railway
Stockham Lodge Racquet & Health Club
Runcorn Ski & Snowboard Centre
Cineworld
Whitehouse Expressway
Expressway
M56 Motorway
Junc. 12
A533
A56
A557
Clifton Rd.
Chester Road
Sutton Causeway
Sutton Weaver
Sutton Hall
Sutton Hall Golf Course
Lowe's Wood
Mare Clough
Kidney Plantation
Chapel Wood
Beckett's Wood
Dell Wood
Gamekeeper's Cottage
Blackamoor Wood
Weaver Navigation
River Weaver
Frodsham Lock
Frodsham Cut
Mill Cut
Sutton Bridge
Swing Bridge
Meadowgate Farm
Frodsham Junction
Works
Viaduct
Weaver Sailing Club
Newtown
Bridge La.
Bradley Orchard Cottages
Bradley Orchard Farm
Sutton Fields Farm
Clough Wood
Hillview Prim. Sch.
Park Farm
Club House

Junction 11
Newton Gorse
Little Manor Farm
Railway Plantation
Aston Brook Marina
Catholic Prim. Sch.
Prim. Sch.
Sch.
Dukes Wharf
CANAL
91
ROAD
Windmill Farm
Browside Farm
LANE
A56
Hilltop Farm
SUMMER
Preston on the Hill
NEW
MANOR
ROAD
Preston Brook Br.
HILL TOP RD.
Murdishaw
Valley
Manor House Farm
Sumners Farm
Murdishaw
Moat
M56
MOTORWAY
BRINDLEY WHARF
West View
New Manor Farm
Dpt.
Preston Brook
Bridgewater
MURDISHAW WOOD
M56
CHESTER
ABBOTS BUS. PK.
NORTH
Canal
WHITEHOUSE INDUSTRIAL ESTATE
White House Farm
Brook
Keckwick
A56
Barker's Hollow
NORTHWICH
A533
Whitehouse
Humble Bee House
HOLLOW
Warrington
WA4
ROAD
ASTON FIELDS ROAD
Works
BUSWAY
HALTON
CHESHIRE WEST and CHESTER
WHITEHOUSE INDUSTRIAL ESTATE
Works
Rose Cott.
Dutton
Preston Brook Tunnel
HIGHER
Hall Cottage
LANE
Stretche's Gorse
Aston Heath Farm
Aston Heath
Aston Heath Cottage
ROAD
Union Farm
Union Farm
Tunnel End
Birdswood Farm
Dutton Stop Lock
A533
Bird's Wood
Trent & Mersey Canal
Smithy Cottages
War Meml.
ASTON
LANE
Aston
Aston Lodge
SPENDERS LA.
Longacre Wood
Dale Farm
Weaver View Cottages
Aston Lea
Grange House
Aston Grange
LODGE LA.
Parkside Cottage
Dutton Lodge Farm
Parkside Farm
Bankfield
Rye Grass Pipes
F
G
H
J
K
1
2
3
4
5
6
7
56
57
58
81
80
79
78
215
Old Moat Wood
Whittle's Corner
Dutton Park Farm

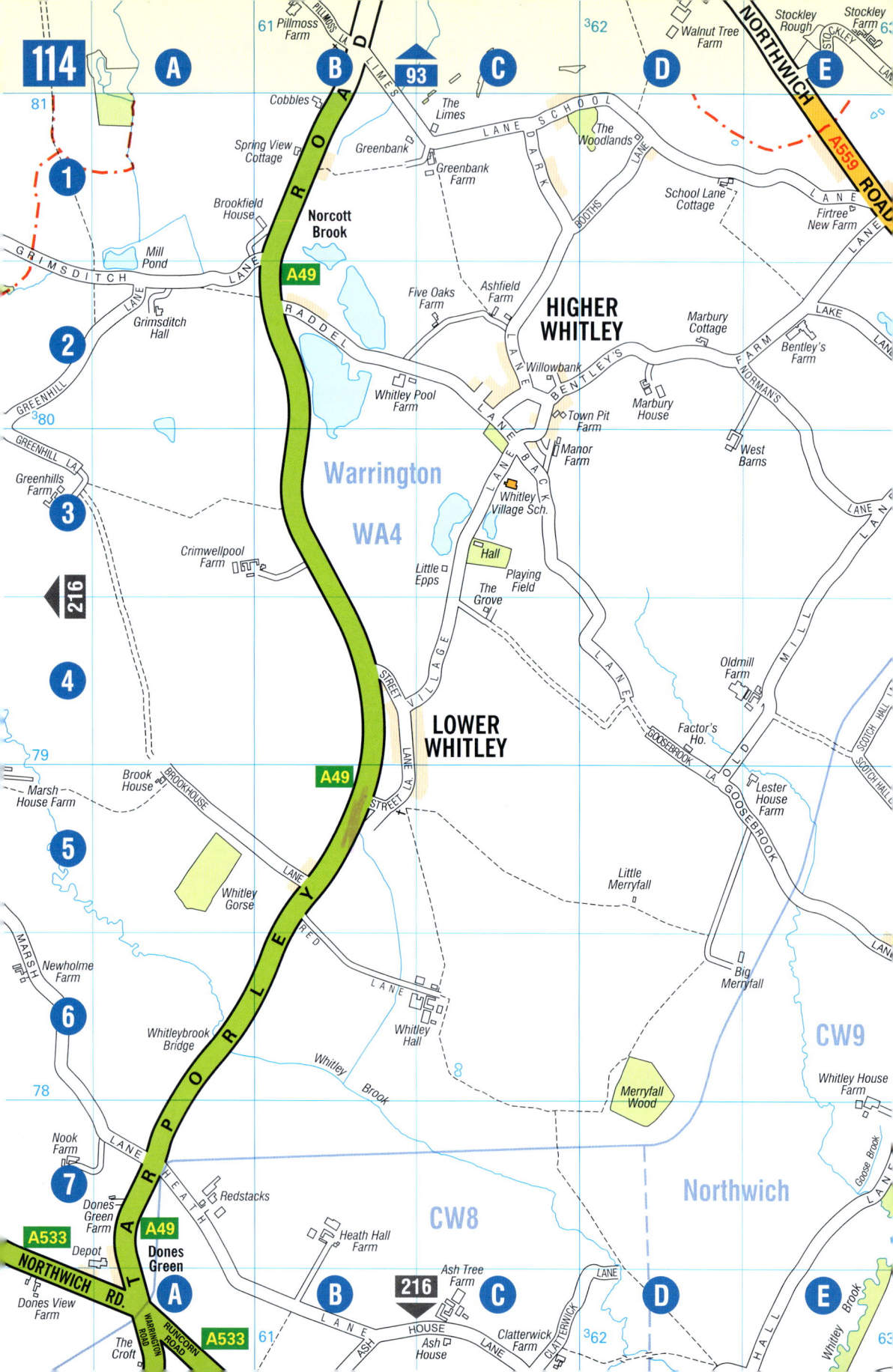
A
B
C
D
E
1
2
3
4
5
6
7
93
216
216
81
80
79
78
61
362
63
Pillmoss Farm
Pillmoss La.
Limes
Cobbles
The Limes
School Lane
Walnut Tree Farm
Northwich Road
A559
Stockley Rough
Stockley Farm
Stockley La.
Spring View Cottage
Greenbank
Greenbank Farm
The Woodlands
Dark Lane
Booths Lane
School Lane Cottage
Firtree New Farm
Brookfield House
Norcott Brook
Mill Pond
Grimsditch Lane
Grimsditch Hall
A49
Raddel Lane
Five Oaks Farm
Ashfield Farm
HIGHER WHITLEY
Marbury Cottage
Lake Lane
Bentley's Farm
Farm Lane
Bentley's Lane
Willowbank
Whitley Pool Farm
Town Pit Farm
Marbury House
Norman's Lane
West Barns
Greenhill Lane
Greenhill La.
Greenhills Farm
Manor Farm
Back Lane
Warrington
WA4
Whitley Village Sch.
Crimwellpool Farm
Hall
Little Epps
Playing Field
The Grove
Village Street
Oldmill Farm
Mill Lane
LOWER WHITLEY
Factor's Ho.
Goosebrook La.
Scotch Hall
Old Goosebrook
Lester House Farm
Brook House
Brookhouse Lane
Marsh House Farm
Street La.
Little Merryfall
Whitley Gorse
Red Lane
Marsh Lane
Newholme Farm
Big Merryfall
Whitley Hall
CW9
Whitleybrook Bridge
Whitley Brook
Merryfall Wood
Whitley House Farm
Goose Brook
Nook Farm
Heath Lane
Redstacks
Northwich
Tarporley Road
Dones Green Farm
CW8
A533
Heath Hall Farm
Depot
Dones Green
Ash Tree Farm
Northwich Rd.
Clatterwick Lane
Hall Lane
Dones View Farm
Warrington Road
Runcorn Road
House Lane
Ash Lane
Ash House
Clatterwick Farm
The Croft
Whitley Brook

Northwich
CW9
COMBERBACH
GREAT BUDWORTH
Higher Marston
Knutsford
WA16
NORTHWICH ROAD
MARSTON LANE
A559
B5075
BUDWORTH MERE
PICK MERE
MARBURY COUNTRY PARK
CHESHIRE EAST
CHESHIRE WEST and CHESTER
Sandiway Farm
Senna Green Farm
Claypit Wood
Fields Farm
Thellow Heath Farm
The Pole
Belmont Hall
Moat Covert
Cransley Sch.
Moat
Ladies Wood
Brownslow Farm
Cogshall Hall
Senna Lane Farm
Avenue Farm
Comberbach Prim. Sch.
Bogs Wood
Brook Farm
Brook House Farm
Ivy Lodge Farm
Playing Field
Marbury Home Farm
Reed Bed Nature Reserve
Kid Brook
Cogshall Brook
Aston Park
Aston Park House
Gravestones Farm
New Westage Farm
Dene House
Hield House
Pickmere Rough
Graveyard
Budworth Sailing Club
Lane-ends Farm
Leigh Farm
Whalebone Farm
Marston Hall
Forge Brook
Big Wood
227
216
158
BELOW
ABOVE

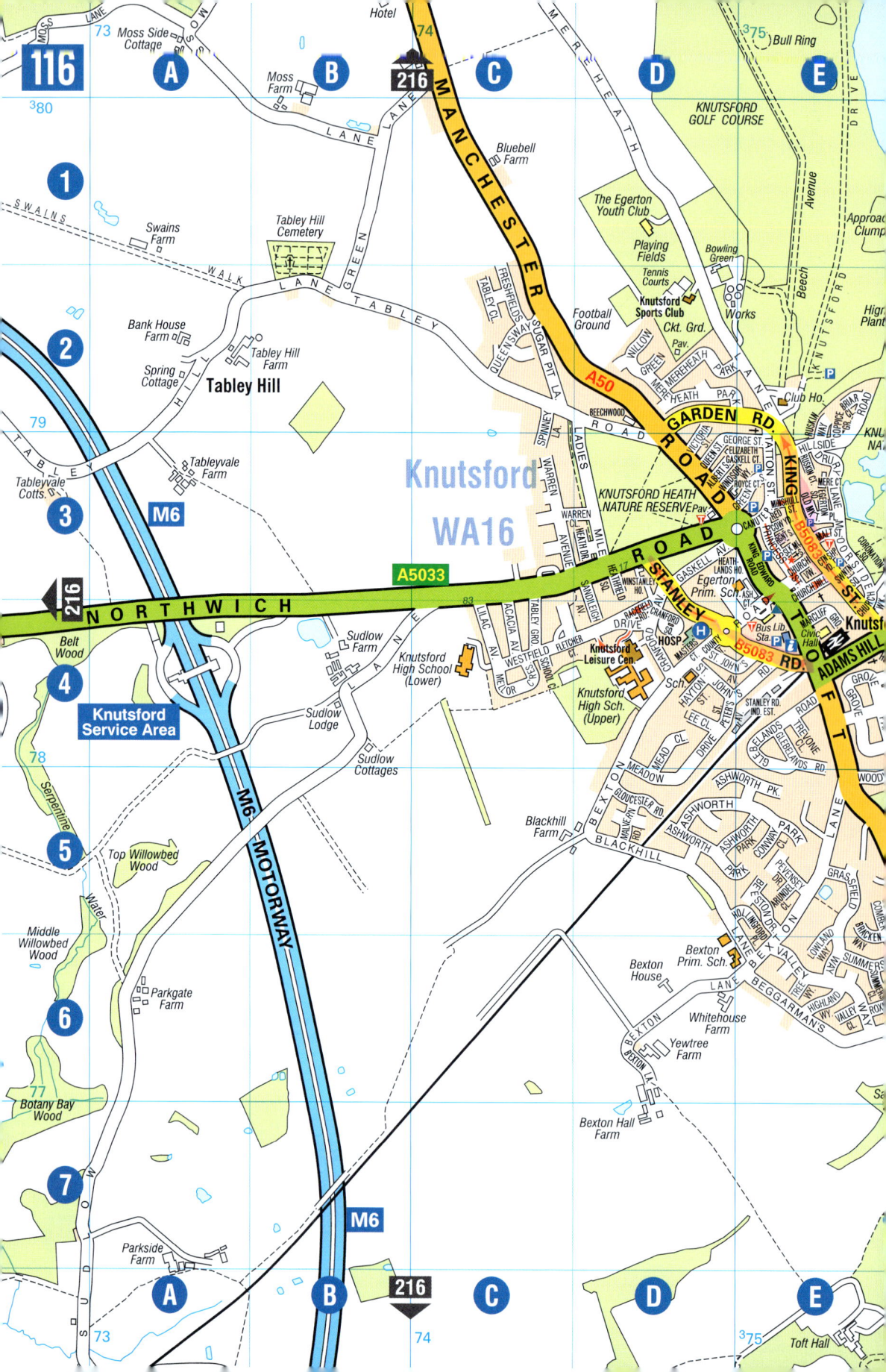
Knutsford
WA16
Tabley Hill
Moss Side Cottage
Moss Farm
Hotel
Bluebell Farm
Swains Farm
Tabley Hill Cemetery
Bank House Farm
Tabley Hill Farm
Spring Cottage
Tableyvale Farm
Tableyvale Cotts.
Belt Wood
Knutsford Service Area
Serpentine
Top Willowbed Wood
Middle Willowbed Wood
Parkgate Farm
Botany Bay Wood
Parkside Farm
Sudlow Farm
Sudlow Lodge
Sudlow Cottages
Knutsford High School (Lower)
Knutsford Leisure Cen.
Knutsford High Sch. (Upper)
Egerton Prim. Sch.
HOSP.
Blackhill Farm
Bexton House
Bexton Prim. Sch.
Whitehouse Farm
Yewtree Farm
Bexton Hall Farm
Toft Hall
Bull Ring
KNUTSFORD GOLF COURSE
The Egerton Youth Club
Playing Fields
Tennis Courts
Bowling Green
Knutsford Sports Club
Ckt. Grd.
Works
Football Ground
KNUTSFORD HEATH NATURE RESERVE
Club Ho.
Bus Sta.
Lib.
Civic Hall
Sch.
MANCHESTER ROAD
A50
NORTHWICH ROAD
A5033
M6
M6 MOTORWAY
GARDEN RD.
KING ST.
B5083
STANLEY ROAD
ADAMS HILL
TOFT ROAD
TABLEY LANE
GREEN LANE
MOSS LANE
MERE HEATH
SWAINS WALK
TABLEY HILL
TABLEY ROAD
SUDLOW LANE
BEXTON LANE
BLACKHILL LANE
BEGGARMAN'S LANE
ASHWORTH PARK
GLEBELANDS ROAD
GRASSFIELD WAY
Beech Avenue
KNUTSFORD
LADIES MILE
WARREN AVENUE
SUGAR PIT LA.
QUEENSWAY
FRESHFIELDS
TABLEY CL.
SPINNEY LA.
BEECHWOOD
WESTFIELD DRIVE
LILAC AV.
ACACIA AV.
TABLEY GRO.
FLETCHER CT.
MELFORD
HEATHFIELD SQ.
SANDILEIGH AV.
WINSTANLEY HO.
GASKELL AV.
HEATHLANDS HO.
KING EDWARD ROAD
CRANFORD SQ.
MASTERS CT.
COUNTY
ST. JOHN'S RD.
ST. JOHN'S AV.
ST. PETER'S
HAYTON ST.
LEE CL.
MEAD CL.
MEADOW DRIVE
GLOUCESTER RD.
MALVERN RD.
BEXTON
PARK LANE
MEREHEATH PARK
WILLOW GREEN
VICTORIA
QUEEN ST.
GEORGE ST.
ELIZABETH
GASKELL CT.
ALBERT ST.
WINDSOR WAY
ROYCE CT.
TATTON ST.
CANUTE SQ.
MINSHULL ST.
HILLSIDE
DRURY LANE
RUSKIN
BRIAR
COPPICE
MERE CT.
EGERTON
MOORSIDE
CHURCH HILL
MARCLIFF GRO.
TREVONE CL.
GLEBELANDS
STANLEY RD. IND. EST.
BEESTON DR.
HOLLINGFORD PL.
VALLEY
ARUNDEL CL.
PEVENSEY DR.
CONWAY
LOWLAND WAY
SUMMERS
HIGHLAND WY.
TREE WY.
VALLEY CL.
BRACKEN WAY
GROVE
216
116
A B C D E
1 2 3 4 5 6 7
73 74 375 380 79 78 77

117
216
102
216
216
F
G
H
J
K
1
2
3
4
5
6
7
76
77
78
79
80
MOBBERLEY
KNUTSFORD
Shaw Heath
Cross Town
Over Knutsford
Ollerton
TATTON MERE
Jetty
Tatton Mere Covert
Shawheath Plantation
Dog Wood
Parkgate Farm
PARKGATE TRADING ESTATE
Sewage Works
Oak Tree Farm
Rooks Wood
KNUTSFORD BUS. PK.
Dukenfield Hall
Works
Boothmill Bridge
LONGRIDGE TRADING ESTATE
Birkin
Waste Disposal Site
Pavement Lane Farm
St. John's Wood
St. John's Wood Sch.
Manor Pk. Sch.
Prim. Sch.
Play. Fld.
BOOTHS MERE
Boat House
Springwood Cottage
Springwood Farm
Pedley Brook
Brook
The Belt
Spring Wood
Booths Hall Farm
BOOTHS HALL
Moat
Hallside
Bowling Green
Cricket Ground
Booths Park
Brickhill Wood
Sanctuary Moor
THE HILL
Moseley Hall Farm
Moseley Hall
Ollerton Grange
Kerfield House
Nursery
Garthollerton
Windmill Wood
Oak Wood
Meadowland Farm
Hill Cottage
Sycamore Farm
Manor Farm
Sports Grd.
B5085
A537
A50
KNUTSFORD ROAD
TOWN LANE
MOBBERLEY ROAD
SHAW HEATH
BROOK ST.
CHELFORD ROAD
HOLMES CHAPEL RD.
PAVEMENT LANE
BROAD OAK LANE
LONGRIDGE
SEVEN SISTERS LANE
GOUGH'S LANE
LEYCESTER ROAD
PARKFIELD ROAD
MANOR PARK
HIGHER DOWNS
BEECHWOOD
WOODLANDS
THORNEYHOLME
MAYFIELD RD.
SPRINGFIELD RD.
RYECROFT
SMITH LANE
SUMMERFIELD RD.
MARTHALL LANE
MANOR LA.
SCHOOL LA.
OAKLANDS RD.
ASHDOWN RD.
CHAPEL RD.
BEECH CL.
WOOD'S CL.
CROFT
LEGH ROAD
LODGE RD.
PARKGATE
SPRINGWOOD AV.
HAIG RD.
HAIG CT.
MONTGOMERY CL.
WELLINGTON CL.
NORBURY CL.
CHALFONT CT.
ST. JOHN'S WOOD
FORESTER AV.
AUTUMN AV.
KENILWORTH AV.
BROOKDALE AV.
SOUTH DOWNS
CARR WOOD
WARWICK CL.
OVER PL.
TREE AV.
FIR
HALLSIDE PARK
ROCKFORD LODGE
MOULTON CL.
DELMAR RD.
LYNTON GRO.
SPARROW
AYLESBY CL.
PARKHILL CT.
GREENACRE CL.
RUTHERFORD DR.
LOVAT DR.
ASTLEY CL.
OAKLEIGH
ST. GEORGE'S CL.
LEYCESTER CL.
MOLLY POTTS CL.
Kenwood
BADGERS CFT.
TOWNFIELD RD.
MEADOW
SWEET RD.
BERNISDALE RD.
Oak Wood

118
A
B
C
D
E
1
2
3
4
5
6
7
96
217
166
81
80
79
78
82
83
Lindow Moss
Rossmere
Lindow Poultry Farm
Refuse Tip (Public)
Sandy Lea Poultry Farm
Lindow Common Local Nature Reserve
Black Lake
Saltersley Hall Farm
Hollingee
MOBBERLEY GOLF COURSE
Coppock House Farm
Sugar Brook
Lindow Manor Farm
Barlow House Farm
LINDOW COURT FARM CARAVAN PARK
Paddock Chase
Garden Centre
Green Hedges
Hetlee Farm
Maple Farm
Lime Cottage Farm
Yew Tree Farm
Rec. Grd.
Prim. Sch.
Thoresway
Ashdene Prim. Sch.
Five Acres
High Lee
The Yews
Knutsford WA16
Paddockhill
Rosemary Cottage
Edge View Farm
Whim Brook
Stables
Gore Lane Farm
Woodmoss Farm
Rush Cottage
Rose Cottage
Cottage Farm
Nursery
Edgeview Farm
Moss Meadow Farm
Kelsall House
Lindow End
Gorse House
Davenport House Farm
Row-of-Trees
Sunnybank Farm
Lindow Primary School
Cricket Grd.
Football Grd.
Club House
ALDERLEY EDGE GOLF COURSE
Davenport Green
Stockton Farm
Brookfield Bridge
Hole Farm
Brook House
Alderley Edge
Whitehall Brook
Oak Ridge Farm
Alderley Edge Water Works
Common Carr Farm
SK9
Pear Tree Farm
Foden House
Lindow End Farm
Pownall House Farm
Club House
Mobberley Brook
WILMSLOW GOLF COURSE
Foden House Farm
Lingards Farm
Grange House Farm
Alderley Edge Cemetery
The Ryleys Sch.
Old Chorley Hall
Tanyard Farm
Alderley Grange
Lammasfield
Oswald Farm
The Paddock
The Little Moss
Little Moss Farm
Abberley Hall
Sandpit Farm
Field's Farm
Springfield
Heathgate Farm
KNUTSFORD ROAD
BROOK ROAD
B5085
B5086
A535
RYLEYS ROAD
CHELFORD
ALDERLEY EDGE BY-PASS (Est. Comp.)
WARFORD ROAD
FODEN LANE
CARR LANE
GORE LANE
CLAY LANE
MOOR LANE
ROTHERWOOD ROAD
BATTERY LANE
PADDOCK LANE
PADDOCK HILL
NOAHS ARK LA.
EDGE VIEW
PROSPECT LA.
BESWICKS LA.
STRAWBERRY LANE
CHAPEL LANE
RACECOURSE
LINDOW LA.
GRAVEL LANE
ALTRINCHAM ROAD
WESTWARD RD.
GREEN LANE

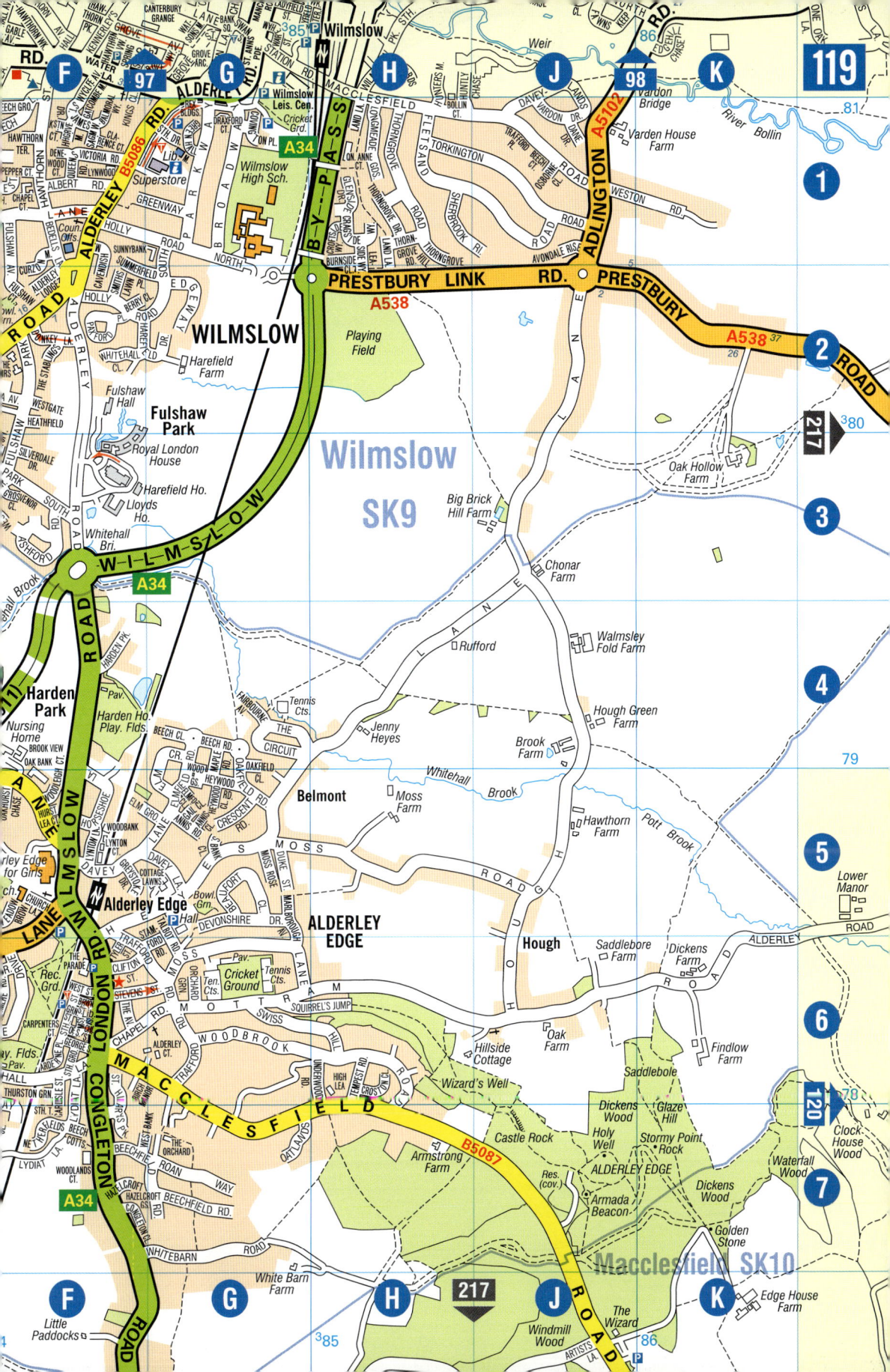
Wilmslow
WILMSLOW
Wilmslow
SK9
Fulshaw Park
Harden Park
Belmont
ALDERLEY EDGE
Alderley Edge
Hough
Macclesfield SK10
PRESTBURY LINK RD.
PRESTBURY ROAD
A538
A34
A5102
B5086
B5087
WILMSLOW ROAD
ADLINGTON ROAD
ALDERLEY ROAD
MACCLESFIELD ROAD
LONDON RD.
CONGLETON ROAD
MOTTRAM ROAD
MOSS ROAD
HOUGH LANE
WHITEBARN ROAD
Wilmslow High Sch.
Wilmslow Leis. Cen.
Playing Field
Harefield Farm
Fulshaw Hall
Royal London House
Harefield Ho.
Lloyds Ho.
Whitehall Bri.
Varden Bridge
Varden House Farm
River Bollin
Weir
Oak Hollow Farm
Big Brick Hill Farm
Chonar Farm
Rufford
Walmsley Fold Farm
Hough Green Farm
Brook Farm
Jenny Heyes
Moss Farm
Whitehall Brook
Hawthorn Farm
Pott Brook
Lower Manor
Saddlebore Farm
Dickens Farm
Findlow Farm
Oak Farm
Hillside Cottage
Wizard's Well
Saddlebole
Dickens Wood
Glaze Hill
Holy Well
Stormy Point Rock
Castle Rock
Armstrong Farm
Armada Beacon
Golden Stone
Waterfall Wood
Clock House Wood
Edge House Farm
The Wizard
Windmill Wood
White Barn Farm
Little Paddocks
Harden Ho. Play. Flds.
Nursing Home
Cricket Ground
Tennis Cts.
Superstore
Lib.
97
98
217
120
F G H J K
1 2 3 4 5 6 7
380
385
86
81
79
78

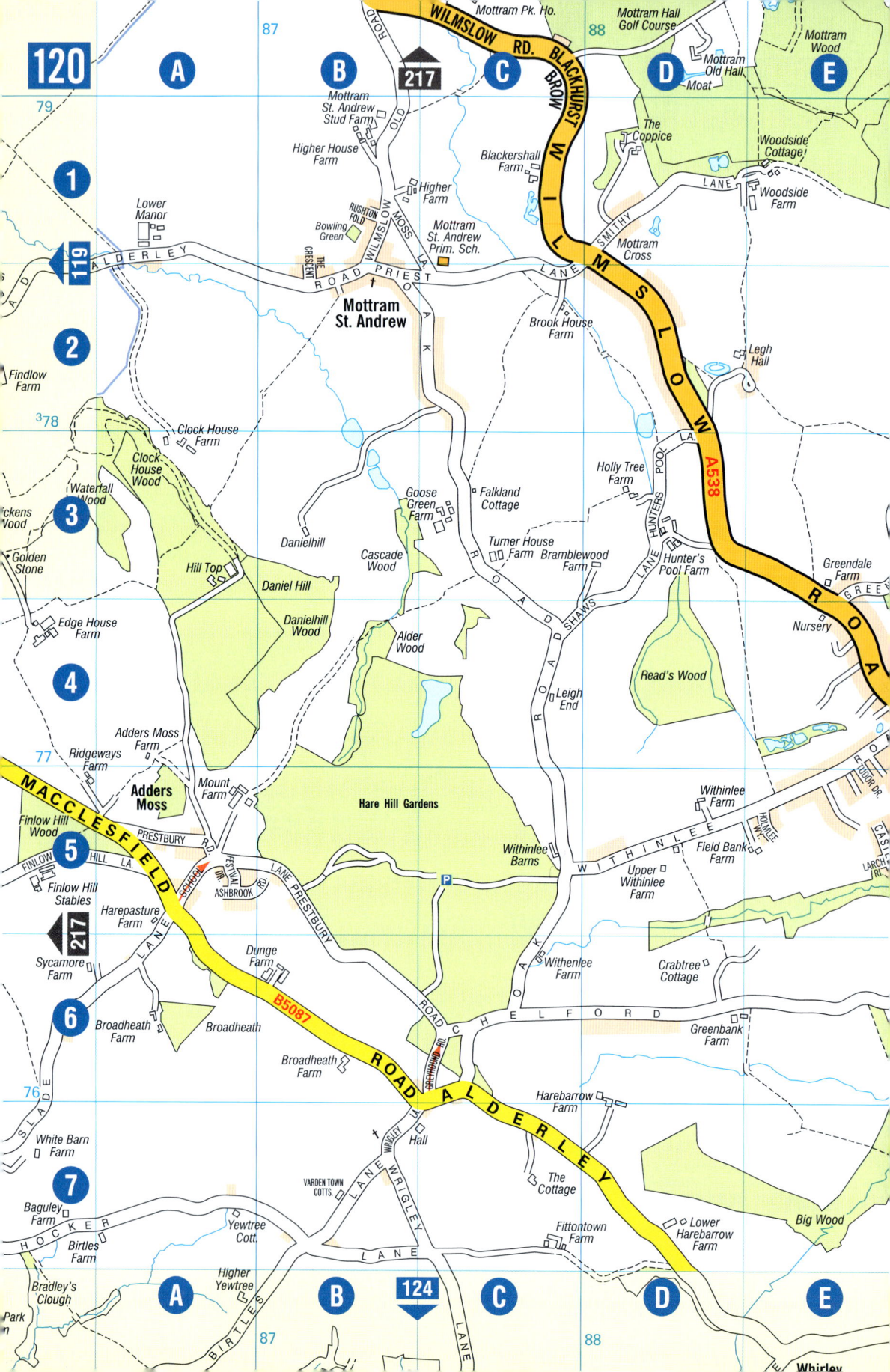

A
B
C
D
E
1
2
3
4
5
6
7
87
88
79
78
77
76
217
119
124
Mottram Pk. Ho.
WILMSLOW RD.
BLACKHURST BROW
Mottram Hall Golf Course
Mottram Wood
Mottram Old Hall
Moat
Mottram St. Andrew Stud Farm
Higher House Farm
Higher Farm
The Coppice
Woodside Cottage
Woodside Farm
Blackershall Farm
SMITHY LANE
Mottram Cross
Lower Manor
RUSHTON FOLD
Bowling Green
WILMSLOW
MOSS LA.
Mottram St. Andrew Prim. Sch.
THE CRESCENT
ALDERLEY ROAD
PRIEST LANE
Mottram St. Andrew
Brook House Farm
Legh Hall
Findlow Farm
Clock House Farm
Clock House Wood
Waterfall Wood
Golden Stone
Hill Top
Daniel Hill
Danielhill Wood
Danielhill
Goose Green Farm
Cascade Wood
Falkland Cottage
Turner House Farm
Bramblewood Farm
Holly Tree Farm
POOL LA.
HUNTERS LANE
Hunter's Pool Farm
A538
WILMSLOW ROAD
Greendale Farm
GREEN
Nursery
Edge House Farm
Alder Wood
OAK ROAD
SHAWS ROAD
Leigh End
Read's Wood
Adders Moss Farm
Ridgeways Farm
Adders Moss
Mount Farm
Hare Hill Gardens
Withinlee Farm
TUDOR DR.
MACCLESFIELD
Finlow Hill Wood
PRESTBURY RD.
FINLOW HILL LA.
FESTIVAL DR.
ASHBROOK RD.
SCHOOL
PRESTBURY LANE
Withinlee Barns
WITHINLEE
HOLMLEE WY.
Field Bank Farm
Upper Withinlee Farm
CASTLE
LARCH RI.
Finlow Hill Stables
Harepasture Farm
LANE
Sycamore Farm
Dunge Farm
Withenlee Farm
Crabtree Cottage
B5087
Broadheath Farm
Broadheath
CHELFORD ROAD
Greenbank Farm
GREYHOUND RD.
Broadheath Farm
ROAD
ALDERLEY
SLADE
Harebarrow Farm
White Barn Farm
WRIGLEY LA.
Hall
The Cottage
VARDEN TOWN COTTS.
WRIGLEY LANE
Baguley Farm
HOCKER
Yewtree Cott.
Birtles Farm
Fittontown Farm
Lower Harebarrow Farm
Big Wood
Bradley's Clough
Higher Yewtree
BIRTLES
LANE
Park
Whirley

Macclesfield
SK10
PRESTBURY
Prestbury
Bradley Mount
Butley Town
Tytherington
Millhouse Bridge
Adlington Farm
Mill House
New Mill House
Bonis Wood
Bonis Hall
The Lodge
Dod's Marsh
Higher Yewards Farm
Sewage Works
Plant House
Park House Farm
Woodend Farm
Spittle House
Cockshead
Weirs
Football Ground
Pav.
Club
Prestbury C of E Prim. Sch.
White Gables
Cricket Grd.
Vicarage
Library
Abbey Mill
Playing Field
Bridge End Farm
Sandyhead Farm
Whiteley Hey Farm
Lane-end Farm
Mount Farm
Hilltop
The Rookery
Flash Farm
Walnut Tree Farm
Manor Farm
Club House
Packsaddle Park
PRESTBURY GOLF COURSE
Prestbury Wood
THE TYTHERINGTON CLUB GOLF COURSE
Tytherington Wood
Dumber Wood
Walnut Tree Farm
Yew Tree Farm
Fallibroome Farm
Playing Field
Lane Ends Cottage
Upton Wood
Bollin Valley Riverside Park
River Bollin
River Dean
Prestbury Tunnel
Brook
BONIS HALL LANE
B5358
LONDON ROAD
A523
HOLEHOUSE LANE
PRESTBURY LANE
HEYBRIDGE LANE
A538
CASTLE HILL
THE VILLAGE
NEW ROAD
FLASH LA.
B5091
THE SILK RD.
LONDON RD.
MANCHESTER ROAD
DUMBAH LANE
BUTLEY LANES
PARK HOUSE DR.
LEGH ROAD
MEADOW DRIVE
BRIDGE END LA.
SUMMERHILL ROAD
MACCLESFIELD ROAD
COLLAR HOUSE DR.
DALE HEAD RD.
217
122
125

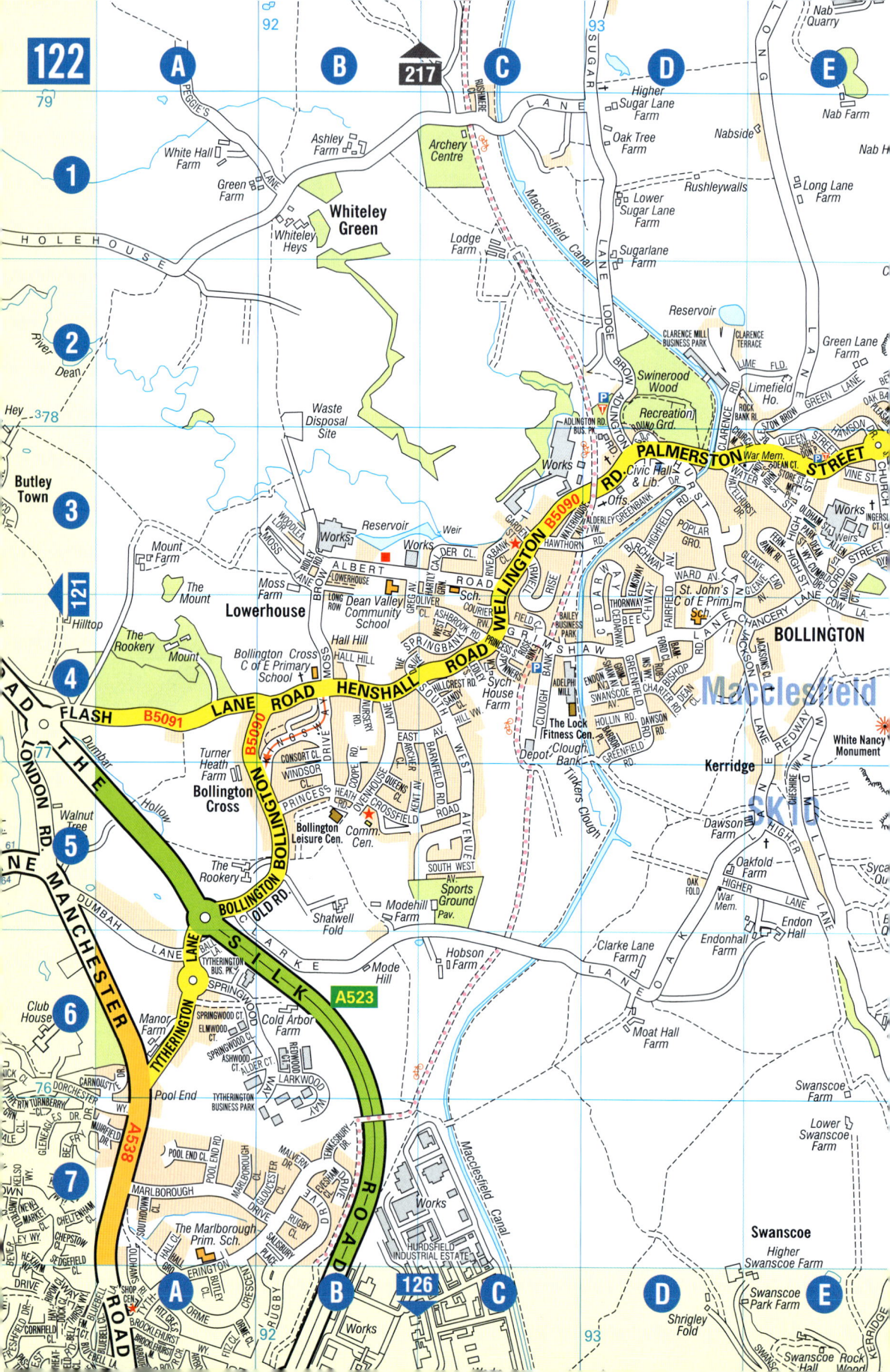
122
A
B
C
D
E
217
92
93
79
78
77
76
61
64
1
2
3
4
5
6
7
Nab Quarry
Nab Farm
Nabside
Sugar Lane
Higher Sugar Lane Farm
Oak Tree Farm
Rushmere
Archery Centre
Ashley Farm
White Hall Farm
Peggie's Lane
Green Farm
Whiteley Green
Whiteley Heys
Holehouse
Rushleywalls
Long Lane Farm
Lower Sugar Lane Farm
Sugarlane Farm
Lodge Farm
Macclesfield Canal
Reservoir
River Dean
Hey
Clarence Mill Business Park
Clarence Terrace
Green Lane Farm
Lime Fld.
Limefield Ho.
Green Lane
Swinerood Wood
Recreation Grd.
Waste Disposal Site
Butley Town
Adlington Rd. Bus. Pk.
Works
Civic Hall & Lib.
Offs.
Palmerston Rd.
Palmerston Street
War Mem.
Queen Street
Church St.
Vine St.
Woodlea
Moss Lane
Ridley
Reservoir
Weir
Albert Road
Lowerhouse
Mount Farm
The Mount
121
Moss Farm
Lowerhouse
Dean Valley Community School
Sch.
Courier
Wellington Road
B5090
Hawthorn Rd.
Greenbank
Poplar Gro.
Highfield Rd.
Ward Av.
St. John's C of E Prim. Sch.
Chancery Lane
Bollington
Hilltop
The Rookery
Mount
Hall Hill
Bollington Cross C of E Primary School
Henshall Road
Grimshaw Lane
Bailey Business Park
Sych House Farm
Adelphi Mill
Cedarway
Thornway
Beechway
Fairfield
Macclesfield
Flash Lane
B5091
Bollington Road
B5090
Turner Heath Farm
Bollington Cross
Consort Cl.
Windsor Cl.
Princess
Nursery Rd.
East Archer Cl.
Barnfield Rd.
West Avenue
Hill Vw.
The Lock Fitness Cen.
Clough Bank
Depot
Dawson Rd.
Greenfield Rd.
Kerridge
White Nancy Monument
SK10
The Silk Road
London Rd.
Dumbah Lane
Hollow
Walnut Tree
Bollington Leisure Cen.
Comm. Cen.
Crossfield
Road
South West Av.
Sports Ground
Pav.
Tinkers Clough
Dawson Farm
Higher Lane
Oakfold Farm
Oak Fold
War Mem.
Endon Hall
Endonhall Farm
Redway
Cheshire Vw.
The Rookery
Old Rd.
Shatwell Fold
Modehill Farm
Clarke Lane
Mode Hill
Hobson Farm
Clarke Lane Farm
Oak Lane
Manchester Road
Tytherington Lane
Tytherington Bus. Pk.
Springwood
A523
Club House
Manor Farm
Cold Arbor Farm
Larkwood Way
Moat Hall Farm
Swanscoe Farm
Lower Swanscoe Farm
Pool End
Tytherington Business Park
Dorchester
Turnberry Cl.
Gleneagles Dr.
Muirfield Dr.
A538
Pool End Cl.
Pool End Rd.
Marlborough
Gloucester Cl.
Malvern Dr.
Tewkesbury Dr.
Evesham
Rugby Cl.
Kelso Wy.
Newmarket
Cheltenham
Chepstow
Sedgefield
Hexham
Southdown Cl.
The Marlborough Prim. Sch.
Salisbury Place
Works
Hurdsfield Industrial Estate
Swanscoe
Higher Swanscoe Farm
Swanscoe Park Farm
Shrigley Fold
126
Works
Shop Cen.
Road
Brocklehurst
Butley
Orme
Crescent
Rugby
Bluebell
Cornfield Cl.
Swanscoe Hall
Rock Wood
Kerridge

Pott Shrigley
Pott Shrigley Church Sch.
Pott Hall Farm
Pott Hall
Jumber Clough
Andrews Knob
Brinks Farm Cottage
Wood
Pav.
Cricket Grd.
Engine Wood
Berristall Wood
Berristall Hall Farm
Sherrowbooth
Harrop Wood
Gausie Brow
Harrop Brook
Further Harrop Farm
Abattoir
Harrop Sowcar Farm
Hedgerow Farm
Heyshead Farm
Bower Clough
Bower Clough Farm
Swindelsgate Farm
PEAK DISTRICT NATIONAL PARK
Winterside Farm
Billingeside Farm
Mellow Clough
Mellow Brook
Harrop Fold Farm
Sowcar
Smithy Brow
Blaze
Billinge Hill
Billinge Quarries
Brown Ho.
New Hey Farm
Oakenbank Farm
Oaken Bank
Lima Farm
Billinge Head Farm
Works
Higher Ingersley Farm
Savio House
The Cottage
Dale View Farm
Withinlow Farm
Ingersley Clough
Ingersley Vale
Rainowlow Farm
Rainowlow
Gorseyknoll
Top o' th' Stones
Four Lane Ends Farm
Four Winds
Paddock Knoll Farm
Waulkmill Farm
Little Low
Big Low
Clough Pool
Back-of-the-Crofts
Clarke House
Wimberry Moss
Lower House Farm
Black Rock Farm
Saddle of Kerridge
Reservoir
Ginclough
Lower Brook Farm
Washpool
The Mill
Gin Clough Farm
Hough-hole Farm
Hayles Clough
Smithy Lane Farm
Jollycock Farm
Kerridge Hill
Rainow
Slack-oth-Moor
Cutlers Farm
Clews Head
Rainow Prim. Sch.
Tower Hill Farm
Tower Hill
Marksend Quarries
Thornsett Farm
The Oaks
River Dean
Lamaload Treatment Works
New Barn Farm
Brookhouse Farm
Brookhouse
Berristal Farm
Danebent Farm
Snipe House
Reservoir (covered)
Macclesfield Road
Church La.
Pike Road
Hill
Smith Lane
Sugar Lane
Oakenbank Lane
Jumper Lane
Kiskhill
Lamaload Rd.
Berristal La.
Berristal Lane
Hawkins Lane
Tower Hill
B5470
217
127

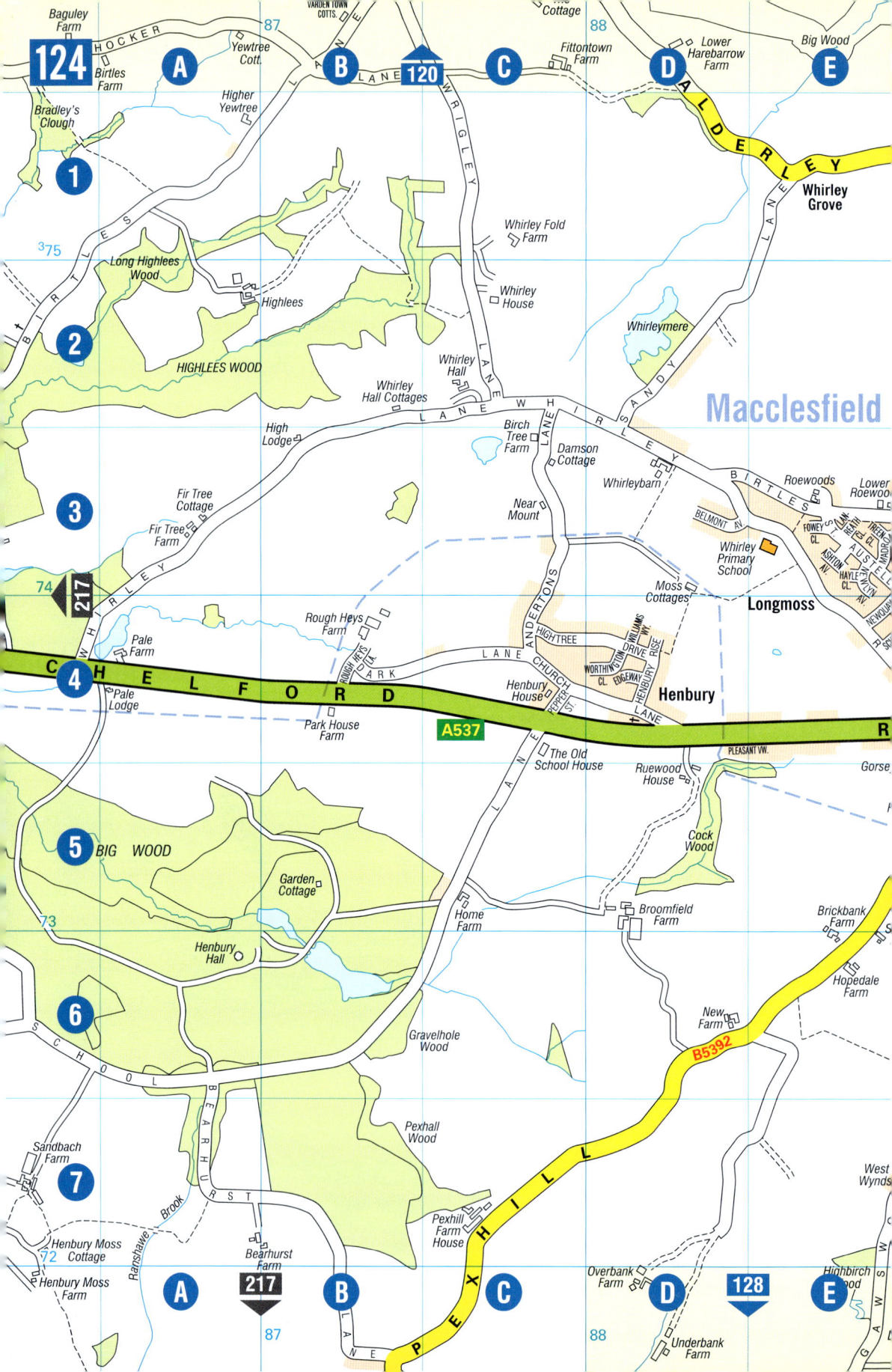
124
Baguley Farm
HOCKER LANE
Birtles Farm
Yewtree Cott.
Higher Yewtree
Bradley's Clough
VARDEN TOWN COTTS.
120
Cottage
Fittontown Farm
Lower Harebarrow Farm
Big Wood
ALDERLEY
Whirley Grove
WRIGLEY LANE
BIRTLES LANE
Long Highlees Wood
Highlees
HIGHLEES WOOD
Whirley Fold Farm
Whirley House
Whirleymere
Whirley Hall
Whirley Hall Cottages
WHIRLEY LANE
SANDY LANE
Macclesfield
High Lodge
Birch Tree Farm
Damson Cottage
Whirleybarn
BIRTLES
Roewoods
Lower Roewood
BELMONT AV.
FOWEY CL.
ASHTON AV.
HAYLE CL.
AUSTELL
NEWQUAY
Whirley Primary School
Longmoss
Fir Tree Cottage
Fir Tree Farm
Near Mount
ANDERTONS LANE
Moss Cottages
WHIRLEY
74
217
Rough Heys Farm
HIGHTREE
WILLIAMS WY.
DRIVE
RISE
WORTHINGTON CL.
EDGEWAY
HENBURY LANE
Pale Farm
ROUGH HEYS LA.
PARK LANE
CHURCH LANE
Henbury House
PEPPER ST.
Henbury
CHELFORD ROAD
Pale Lodge
Park House Farm
A537
The Old School House
PLEASANT VW.
Ruewood House
Gorse
BIG WOOD
Cock Wood
Garden Cottage
Home Farm
Broomfield Farm
Brickbank Farm
73
Henbury Hall
Hopedale Farm
New Farm
Gravelhole Wood
B5392
SCHOOL LANE
BEARHURST LANE
Pexhall Wood
Sandbach Farm
PEXHILL
Ranshawe Brook
Henbury Moss Cottage
72
Henbury Moss Farm
Bearhurst Farm
Pexhill Farm House
Overbank Farm
128
Highbirch Wood
West Wynds
GAWSWORTH
Underbank Farm
87
88
375
A B C D E
1 2 3 4 5 6 7

F
G
H
J
K
121
1
2
3
4
5
6
7
126
128
129
SK10
SK11
MACCLESFIELD
B5087
A537
A536
B5088
PRESTBURY ROAD
CHESTER ROAD
BROKEN CROSS
CUMBERLAND ST.
OXFORD ROAD
CONGLETON ROAD
PARK LANE
MANCHESTER ROAD
BEECH LANE
VICTORIA ROAD
CHURCHILL WAY
Dumber Wood
Walnut Tree Farm
Yew Tree Farm
Tytherington Wood
Fallibroome Farm
Playing Field
Lane Ends Cottage
Playing Fields
Upton Wood
Upton Hall
Upton Priory Sch.
Cricket Grd.
Weir
Bollin Valley Riverside Park
River Bollin
Macclesfield Riverside Park
Backlane Farm
Fallibroome High School
Running Track
Macclesfield Leisure Centre
Beech Hall Sch.
Tytherington High Sch
Cemetery
Macclesfield Crematorium
West Park
Mus.
Bowling Green
Superstore
Hospice
Priors Hill
MACCLESFIELD DISTRICT GENERAL HOSPITAL
Cricket Grd.
Millbrook Unit
REGENCY SPIRE HOSP.
The King's Sch.
Henbury High Sch.
Broken Cross
Broken Cross Comm. Sch.
Weston Rec. Grd.
Weston
Primary Sch.
Playing Fields
All Hallows Catholic Coll.
Macclesfield College
Council Offs.
Park Lane School
Play. Fld.
Ten.Ct.
Bandstand
SOUTH PARK
Ryle's Pk
Ivy Bank Pri. Sch.
St. Edward's Catholic Prim Sch.
Comm. Cen.
Tansy Moss Farm
Little Bailey Riddings Farm
Big Bailey Riddings Farm
Weston Park Nursing Home
Moss Lane
Depot
Playing Field
Playing Fields
Brownhills Farm
Macclesfield (Moss Rose)
Wood's Cut
390
375
91
73
72

126
A
B
C
D
E
1
2
3
4
5
6
7
122
125
129
169
92
93
74
73
72
SK10
MACCLESFIELD
Macclesfield
Hurdsfield
Higher Hurdsfield
Higherfence
Commonside
Swanscoe
Plungebrook
Bradley Smithy
Gurnett
SOUTH PARK
MACCLESFIELD COMMON
MACCLESFIELD GOLF COURSE
A538
A523
A537
B5470
B5181
MANCHESTER ROAD
THE SILK ROAD
RAINOW ROAD
HURDSFIELD ROAD
BUXTON ROAD
CHURCHILL WAY
BEECH LANE
HIBEL RD.
PARK LA.
MILL LA.
CROSS ST.
LONDON ROAD
BLAKELOW ROAD
OLD BUXTON ROAD
CLIFF LANE
BROCKLEHURST AVENUE
VICTORIA PARK
Macclesfield Canal
River Bollin
Tytherington High School
Marlborough Prim. Sch.
Hurdsfield Industrial Estate
Fence Avenue Industrial Estate
Silk Road Retail Pk.
Silk Road Bus. Pk.
Works
Depot
Superstore
Shores Clough
Shrigley Fold
Swanscoe Park Farm
Higher Swanscoe Farm
Swanscoe Hall
Rock Wood
Jenny's Farm
Doncasterhill Farm
Lower Marsh Farm
Shoresclough Farm
Dodgemore Well
Reservoir
Higherfold Farm
Lowerfold Farm
Cliffe Farm
Close House Farm
Mill Dam
Reservoir (covered)
Reservoirs
Homestead Farm
Lark Hall
Eddisbury Hall
Eddisbury Hill
Eddisbury Park Field
Eddisbury Farm
Leadbeaters Reservoir
Brae-side
Braedon
Karibu
Lower Blakelow Farm
Blakelow Gate
Higher Blakelow Farm
Middlehills Gate
Club House
Hollins Farm
Birch Knoll
Pyegreave Farm
Foden Bank Farm
Byrons Wood
Nursery
Sutton Bridge
Aqueduct
Knight's Pool
King George's Field
Boat Yard
Puss Bank Sch.
Playing Fields
St. Edward's Catholic Prim Sch.
Macclesfield Town FC (Moss Rose Ground)

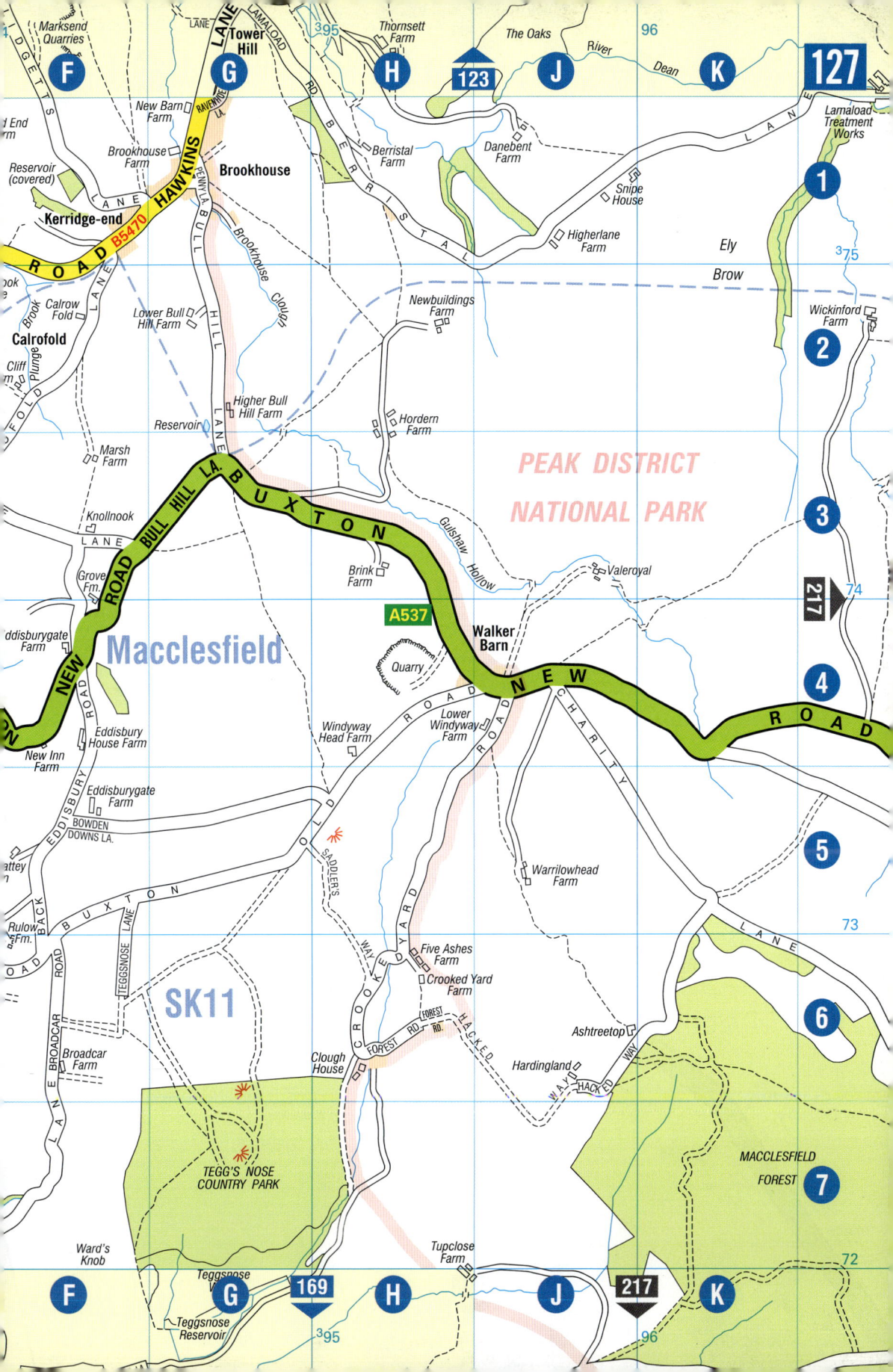

Marksend Quarries
Tower Hill
Thornsett Farm
The Oaks
River Dean
123
New Barn Farm
Brookhouse Farm
Brookhouse
Reservoir (covered)
Kerridge-end
B5470
HAWKINS LANE
ROAD
Berristal Farm
Danebent Farm
Snipe House
Higherlane Farm
Lamaload Treatment Works
LAMALOAD RD.
BERRISTAL LANE
Ely Brow
Calrow Fold
Calrofold
Lower Bull Hill Farm
Brookhouse Clough
Newbuildings Farm
Wickinford Farm
Higher Bull Hill Farm
Reservoir
Hordern Farm
Marsh Farm
PEAK DISTRICT NATIONAL PARK
Knollnook
BULL HILL LA.
BUXTON NEW ROAD
Gulshaw Hollow
Valeroyal
Grove Fm.
Brink Farm
217
A537
Walker Barn
Eddisburygate Farm
Macclesfield
Quarry
Eddisbury House Farm
Windyway Head Farm
Lower Windyway Farm
OLD ROAD
New Inn Farm
Eddisburygate Farm
BOWDEN DOWNS LA.
CHARITY LANE
SADDLER'S WAY
Warrilowhead Farm
Rulow Fm.
BACK EDDISBURY ROAD
BUXTON
TEGGSNOSE LANE
Five Ashes Farm
Crooked Yard Farm
SK11
CROOKED YARD ROAD
FOREST RD.
HACKED WAY
Ashtreetop
Broadcar Farm
BROADCAR LANE
Clough House
Hardingland
TEGG'S NOSE COUNTRY PARK
MACCLESFIELD FOREST
Ward's Knob
Tupclose Farm
Teggsnose Reservoir
169
217
F G H J K
1 2 3 4 5 6 7
395 96 375 74 73 72

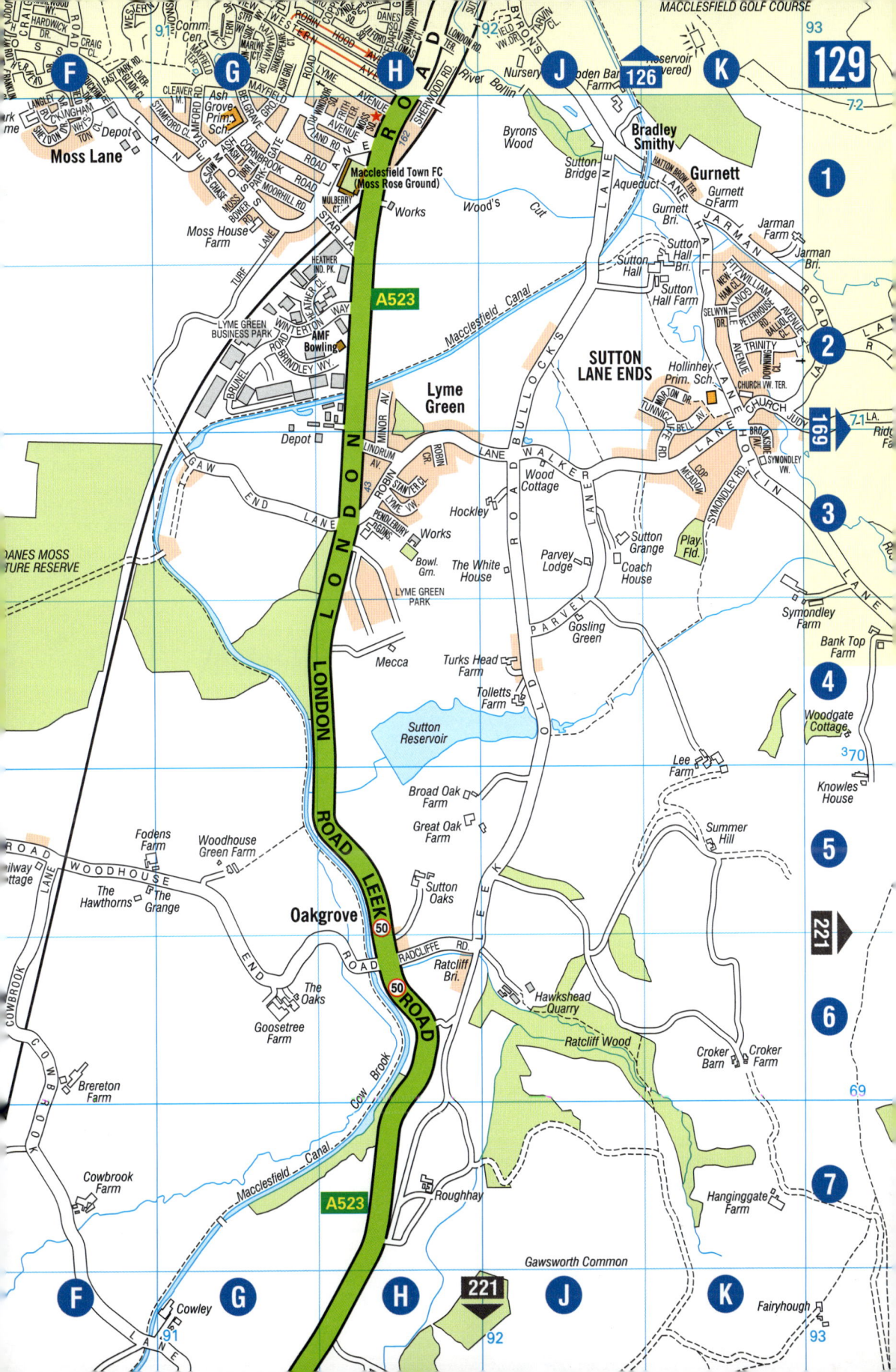

MACCLESFIELD GOLF COURSE
Moss Lane
Macclesfield Town FC (Moss Rose Ground)
Works
Moss House Farm
Heather Ind. Pk.
Lyme Green Business Park
AMF Bowling
A523
Macclesfield Canal
Lyme Green
Depot
Byrons Wood
Sutton Bridge
Aqueduct
Bradley Smithy
Gurnett
Gurnett Farm
Gurnett Bri.
Jarman Farm
Jarman Bri.
Sutton Hall
Sutton Hall Bri.
Sutton Hall Farm
SUTTON LANE ENDS
Hollinhey Prim. Sch.
Wood's Cut
River Bollin
Nursery
Reservoir (covered)
Hockley
Wood Cottage
Sutton Grange
Coach House
Parvey Lodge
The White House
Play. Fld.
Works
Bowl. Grn.
Lyme Green Park
Mecca
Gosling Green
Turks Head Farm
Tolletts Farm
Sutton Reservoir
Symondley Farm
Bank Top Farm
Woodgate Cottage
Lee Farm
Knowles House
Broad Oak Farm
Great Oak Farm
Summer Hill
Fodens Farm
Woodhouse Green Farm
The Hawthorns
The Grange
Sutton Oaks
Oakgrove
Ratcliff Bri.
The Oaks
Goosetree Farm
Hawkshead Quarry
Ratcliff Wood
Croker Barn
Croker Farm
Brereton Farm
Cow Brook
Cowbrook Farm
Roughhay
Hanginggate Farm
Gawsworth Common
Cowley
Fairyhough
DANES MOSS NATURE RESERVE
LONDON ROAD
LEEK ROAD
OLD BULLOCK'S ROAD
WALKER LANE
PARVEY LANE
GAW END LANE
WOODHOUSE END ROAD
RADCLIFFE RD.
COWBROOK LANE
HOLLIN LANE
JARMAN ROAD
HALL LANE
CHURCH LANE
TURF LANE
STAR LA.
126
169
221
F G H J K
1 2 3 4 5 6 7
91 92 93
72 71 70 69

130
105
214
A
B
C
D
E
1
2
3
4
5
6
7
28
29
330
77
76
375
74
NESTON
Moorside
Little Neston
Nesshölt
Neston CH64
Deeside CH5
DANGER AREA
Denhall Gutter
Sports Ground
Parkgate Road
Hinderton Road
B5134
Chester Road
High St.
Bridge St.
Station Road
Quay Lane
Burton Road
Bull Hill
Woodfall Lane
Marshlands Rd.
Greenfields
New Houses Lane
Denhall Lane
Station Lane
Neston Road
Sandy Lane
Bendee Road
Old Quay
Sewage Works
The Old Laundry
Kelvin
Gascott Cottages
Neston Prim. Sch.
Yth. Cen.
Comm. Cen.
Putt. Grn.
Stanney Fields
Lib.
Royal Shop. Arc.
Prim. Sch.
Woodfall Primary School
Quay Ho. Fm.
Denhall Quay
Brook Well
Snab Wood
Mast
Denhall House Farm
The Coach House
Denna Hall
Chapel Cottages
Station House
Burton Marsh Farm
Goldstraw Farm
Ness Botanic Gardens
Ness Gardens Visitor Centre
Witchwood

F
G
H
J
K
1
2
3
4
5
6
7
31
32
33
77
76
75
74
106
132
214
WILLASTON
Ness
Burton
CHESTER HIGH ROAD
A540
HADLOW ROAD
B5151
Poultry Houses
Windle Hill
HANNS HALL RD.
Hanns Hall Farm
Leahurst University of Liverpool Veterinary Field Station
WEATHERSTONES BUSINESS CENTRE
Wood Park
Wood Bank Farm
The White House
DAMHEAD LANE
Eyrefield Lodge
Leahurst
FERNYESS LANE
OAKTREE CT. BUSINESS CENTRE
Ness Wood
Shotwick Brook
Hilltop Farm
Mill House
Mill Farm
Errington's Plantation
Haddon Hall Farm
NEW HEY LANE
Willaston Grange
Hadlow Wood
Framley
New Hey Farm
Upholland
Nursery
Haddon Hall Farm
Haddon Hall Farm Cottage
Wirral Riding School
HADDON LANE
WOODEND LA.
Heath Farm
Friends Hall
Haddon Wood
The Birches
Fiddleston Farm
Dunstan Farm
Fiddleston Wood
DUNSTAN LANE
Hillcrest
Red Bank Farm
Greenacres
Fiddleston Plantation
Brackley
Fiddleston Lodge
Mudhouse Wood
MUDHOUSE LANE
WOOD LA.
WOOD LANE
HADDON LANE
Burton Wood
Windmill (disused)
Perrywood
VICARAGE LANE
Nursery
PRIESTWAY
Wildflower
MILL LANE
Graveyard
VILLAGE
Tennis Courts
Rec. Ground
Hall
THE RAKE
THE ROAD
Bath Wood
Manor Farm
Burton Manor College
PUDDINGTON LANE
Bishop Wilson C of E Primary School
Whitegates Farm
Clartie Cottage
Whitehouse

132

WILLASTON

A B 🏠107 C D E

33 ROAD 34 HEATH 35 Oakfield Terrace Oakfield Heat

GORDON MEWS OLD VICARAGE CL PEMBERTON CT Roseville Farm

ASHTREE FARM SMITHY Grange Picnic Site Heath Farm Nur

HADLOW LA TER OAK FARM CL Woodbank Farm The Grange

1 Museum Willaston Picnic Site LANE

HADLOW B5151 ROADFALENT NEW HEY LANE

77 Willaston Grange Leaswood Cottages Oaks Farm

2 Hadlow Wood Leaswood Farm

New Hey Farm Upholland

LANE The Oaks

3 *Neston* Jack's Wood The Oaks Cotts

76 131 *CH64* HALLWOOD DRIVE Ledsham Hall Farm

CHESTER A540 Hallwood Farm Woodlands Farm

4 Bentheath Covert Foxes Farm Inglewood Dairy Farm Cross Lanes Farm Ivy Fm

HIGH Garden Centre Hallwood Cottages

The Birches Badger's Rake House BADGERS RAKE

5 ROAD Badger's Rake Farm Badgersrake Covert A550 Quaint Farm

375 Heybridge House Badgersrake Farm

Brackley Mudhouse Wood LANE

MUDHOUSE Benty Heys Wood ROAD

6 PARKGATE Manor House Farm Cottages Aviary Farm

Manor House Farm The Cottage Daisy Bank Farm

The Craxton

7 Cross Plantation

Beechwood Heath Hey Works WELSH

Whitegates Farm Stocks Farm Welshgate

PUDDINGTON LANE Park Farm ROAD A540

74 PIPERS LANE Ferndale House **214** A550

33 Oaklands Farm Allsprings 34 A540 335 WALDEN DRIVE CHAP

Whitehouse Farm

A B C D E

Ellesmere Port
CH66
Chester
CH1
LITTLE SUTTON
Little Sutton
Great Sutton
Sutton Green
Ledsham
Capenhurst
CAPENHURST
ELLESMERE PORT GOLF COURSE
Ellesmere Port Golf Centre
A41
A550
B5463
108
134
214
Water Treatment Works
Works
CAPENHURST TECHNOLOGY PARK
Sutton Sports Centre
All Weather Sports Pitch
Ellesmere Port Specialist Sch. of Performing Arts
Capenhurst Grange Sch.
Parklands Prim. Sch.
Rossmore Prim. Sch.
St. Mary of the Angels Catholic Prim. Sch.
Little Sutton C of E Prim. Sch.
Sutton New Hall Cottages
Sutton New Hall Farm
Bank Farm
Grange Farm
Oak Leigh Farm
Thornton Hey Farm
Harefield Cottage
Springfield
Nursery
Court Farm
Home Farm
Hollybank Farm
Bailiff Cottage
Millhey Farm
Meadow Farm
Football Grd.
Fox Covert
Sports Grd.
Mayfield
Mayfield Lodge
Springfield Farm
Meadow Bank
Garden Cen.
Hotel
Playground
Rec. Grd.
Oakdene
Fairacre

134
A
B
C
D
E
1
2
3
4
5
6
7
109
133
140
38
39
40
77
76
75
74
Junction 8
M53 MOTORWAY
MERSEYTON RD.
DOCK
QUEEN
STATION
RIVACRE
HILLSIDE DRIVE
NETHERPOOL RD.
RIVACRE RD.
B5132
Rivacre Valley Prim. Sch.
Overpool
Cemetery
ROSSMORE RD. WEST
ROSSMORE ROAD
B5463
ROSSMORE ROAD EAST
ROTHER DRIVE BUSINESS PARK
Comm. Cen.
ROSSMORE BUSINESS PARK
ROSSMORE BUS. VILLAGE
ROSSMORE INDUSTRIAL ESTATE
JUNCTION EIGHT BUSINESS CENTRE
WESTMINSTER INDUSTRIAL PARK
ROSSMORE TRADING ESTATE
Big Shallacres
Playground
St. Mary of the Angels Catholic Prim. Sch.
Play. Field
Overpool
OVERPOOL ROAD
WESTENRA
ELLESMERE PORT
Ellesmere Port
Sutton Sports Centre
All Weather Sports Pitch
Ellesmere Port Specialist Sch. of Performing Arts
Play. Fld.
The Acorns Prim. & Nursery Sch.
Pooltown Jun. Sch.
West Cheshire Coll. (Ellesmere Port Campus)
REGENT STREET
THE BOULEVARD
SUTTON WAY
B5132
Playing Fields
Whitby
WHITBY ROAD
A5032
STANNEY LANE
Civic Hall
Coun. Offs.
Lib.
Bus Sta.
THE PORT ARCADES
Market
Bingo
Superstore
EPIC Leis. Cen.
TA Centre
Whitby Park
Whitby Hall
Great Sutton
Schs.
Playing Field
Ellesmere Port Catholic High Sch.
Hinderton Sch.
Playing Field
ELLESMERE PORT HOSP.
Capenhurst Grange Sch.
Meadow Prim. Sch.
Whitbyheath
Prim. Sch.
The Whitby High Sch.
Hockey Pitch
Sports & Social Club
Sports Grd.
Stanney Wood
STANNEY WOOD LOCAL NATURE RESERVE
Lobitos Sports Grd.
Cheshire Oaks High Sch.
Running Track
CHESTER ROAD
A41
A5032
Oakdene
Fairacre
SHOTWICK
HELSBY

RIVER MERSEY
215
F
G
H
J
K
Stanlow Point
Jetties
Club
Dock
MANCHESTER
SHIP
CANAL
Jetty
Landing Stages
Jetties
Dock
Powell's Bri.
Junction 9
M53
Works
Depot
SITES ROAD
INDIGO ROAD
CORRIDOR
RIVER GOWY
CH65
STANLOW
BRIDGES ROAD
CLOISTER WAY
Oil Terminal
Works
Stanlow Bridge
Gas Holders
Warehouse
Depot
Sch.
Wolverham
Play. Fld.
Comm. Cen.
Prim. Sch.
Club
Ellesmere Port Stadium
SHROPSHIRE UNION
NEWBRIDGE ROAD
ELM COURT
DEANS RD.
SHELLWAY ROAD
Weaver's Bri.
M53
All Weather Sports Area
The Stanney Grange Sports Complex
M53 MOTORWAY
STANNEY MILL
CANAL
Warehouses
Depot
Stanney Mill Bri.
Depot
OIL REFINERY
Thornton Brook
CHESHIRE OAKS OUTLET VILLAGE
COLISEUM SHOPPING & LEISURE PARK
Vue Cinema
Tenpin
David Lloyd Leisure
Blue Planet
Superstore
Wood Farm
Old Hall Farm
Lime Tree Farm
KINSEY RD.
B5132
SHOTWICK-HELSBY BY-PASS
A5117
Junction 10
M53
LITTLE STANNEY
Filter Beds
Pollution Control Works
Chester CH2
Mason's Bridge
Meadow Lane Bridge
Hill Farm
A5117
141
136
1
2
3
4
5
6
7
41
42
43
74
75
76
77

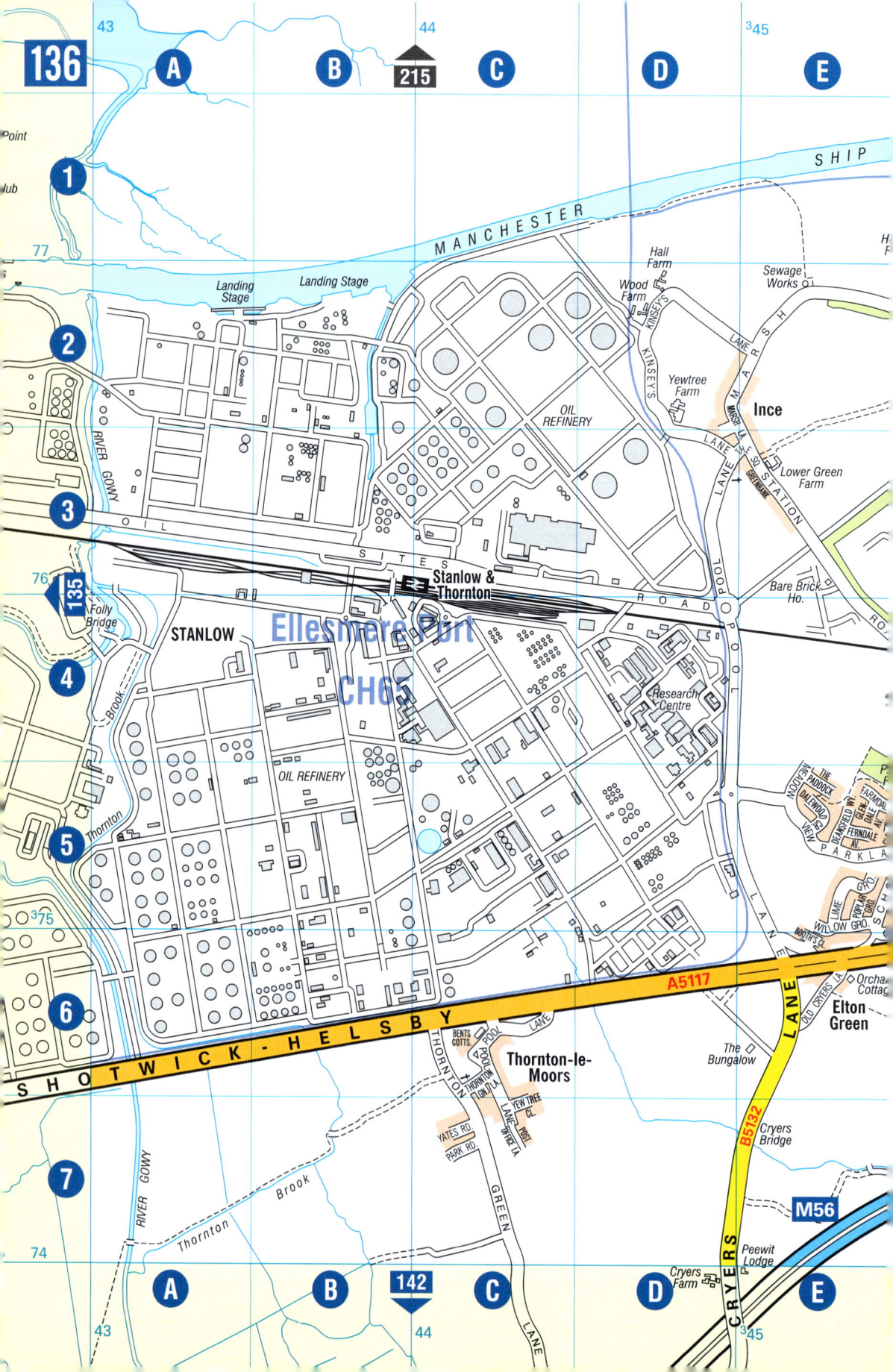
A
B
C
D
E
215
43
44
345
1
2
3
4
5
6
7
77
76
375
74
135
142
Point
lub
MANCHESTER SHIP
Landing Stage
Landing Stage
Hall Farm
Wood Farm
Sewage Works
KINSEY'S
Yewtree Farm
Ince
MARSH LANE
OIL REFINERY
Lower Green Farm
STATION
GREENBANK
SQ.
RIVER GOWY
OIL SITES ROAD
Stanlow & Thornton
Bare Brick Ho.
POOL LANE
Folly Bridge
STANLOW
Ellesmere Port
CH65
Research Centre
Brook
OIL REFINERY
Thornton
THE PADDOCK
MEADOW VIEW
DALEWOOD CR.
DEANSFIELD WY.
GLEN DALE
FARMDALE AV.
FERNDALE AV.
PARKLA
LIME GRO.
POPLAR GRO.
WILLOW GRO.
BOOTH'S CL.
A5117
Orchard Cottag
OLD CRYERS LA.
Elton Green
SHOTWICK-HELSBY
BENTS COTTS.
POOL LANE
Thornton-le-Moors
THORNTON GN.
THORNTON GN. LA.
YEW TREE CL.
POST OFFICE LA.
YATES RD.
PARK RD.
The Bungalow
B5132
Cryers Bridge
M56
RIVER GOWY
Thornton Brook
GREEN LANE
Peewit Lodge
Cryers Farm
CRYERS LANE

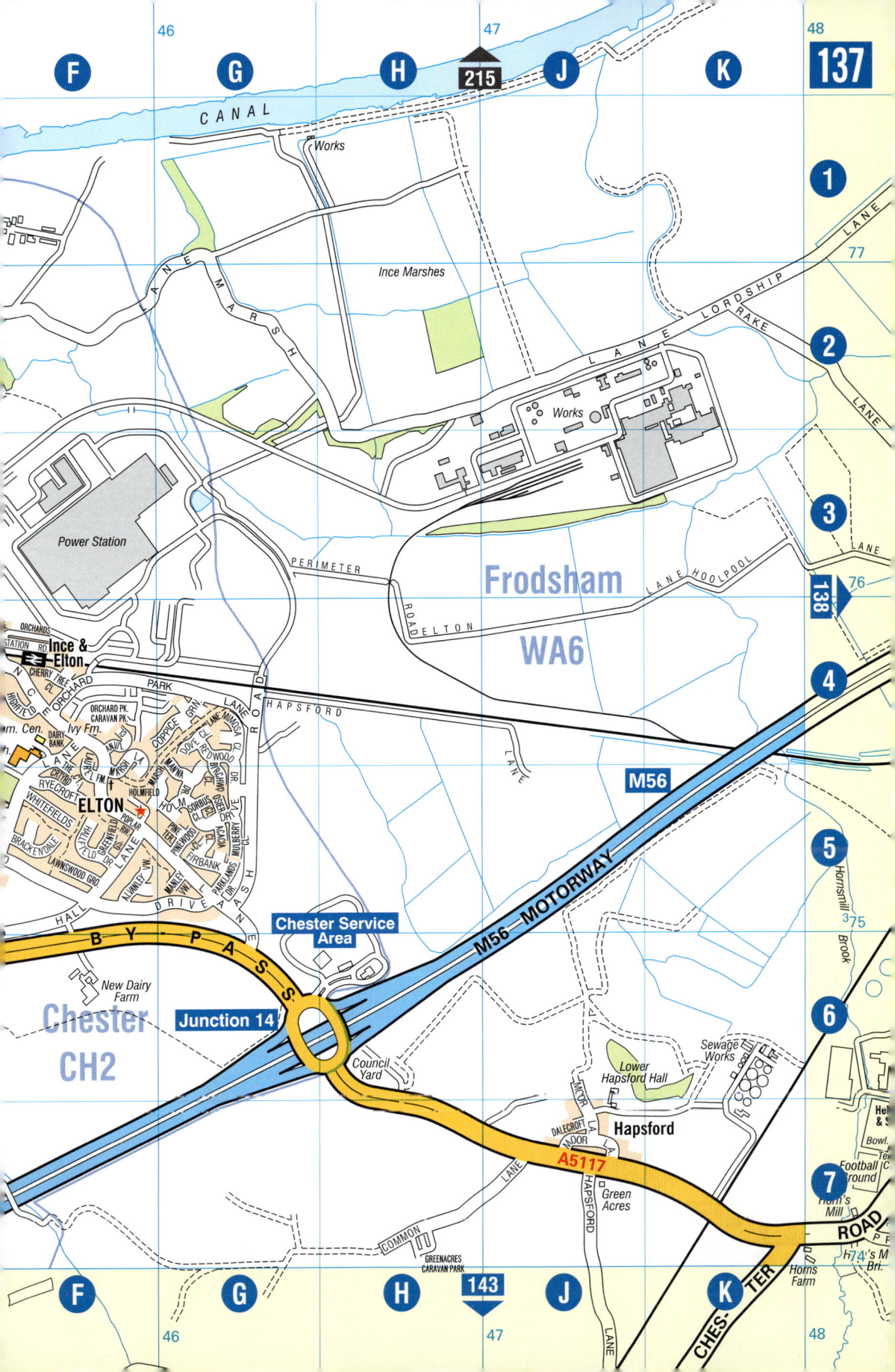

215
138
143
F
G
H
J
K
1
2
3
4
5
6
7
46
47
48
77
76
75
74
CANAL
Works
Ince Marshes
MARSH LANE
LORDSHIP LANE
RAKE LANE
Works
Power Station
PERIMETER
Frodsham
WA6
HOOLPOOL LANE
ELTON ROAD
Ince & Elton
ORCHARDS
STATION RD.
CHERRY TREE CL.
ORCHARD PARK
HAPSFORD LANE
ORCHARD PK. CARAVAN PK.
Ivy Fm.
DAIRY BANK
COPPICE GRN.
MIMOSA CL.
DOVE CL.
REDWOOD DR.
BIRCHWD. CL.
OSIER DRIVE
MANNA DR.
SORBUS CL.
ACACIA CL.
MULBERRY CL.
HOLMFIELD
RYECROFT
WHITEFIELDS
ELTON
MARSH LA.
POPLAR RW.
HALLFIELD DR.
BRACKENDALE
LAWNSWOOD GRO.
FIRBANK
PINEWOOD CL.
PARKLANDS DR.
MANLEY VW.
ALVANLEY VW.
HALL DRIVE
ASH LANE
M56
M56 MOTORWAY
Chester Service Area
BY-PASS
New Dairy Farm
Junction 14
Chester
CH2
Council Yard
Lower Hapsford Hall
Sewage Works
Hapsford
DALECROFT
MOOR LA.
A5117
HAPSFORD LANE
Green Acres
COMMON LANE
GREENACRES CARAVAN PARK
CHESTER ROAD
Horns Farm
Hornsmill Brook
Football Ground
Horn's Mill

Lordship Marsh
Helsby Marsh
M56
M56 MOTORWAY
Hill View Farm
Spring Farm
Meadow Farm
Helsby Junction
Helsby
HELSBY
Helsby Hill Fort
Hope Farm
Playing Field
Tennis Courts
Helsby High School
A56
CHESTER ROAD
Cemy.
Playing Field
Woodhouse
Oak Mount Farm
Harmers Lake Farm
Spring Hill
Firs Farm
Hillside Cottage
Helsby Quarry Woodland Pk.
Ivy Dene
Birch Cottage
Rock Farm
Ashfield
Walnut Tree Farm
Poplar Tree Farm
Greenbank Farm
Alvanley Primary School
Alvanley
Cricket Grd.
Commonside Farm
Teuthill Farm
Hillside Cottage
B5393
TARVIN RD.
FRODSHAM RD.
MANLEY ROAD
Mere's Edge Business Park
Sewage Works
Helsby Sports & Social Club
Bowl. Grn.
Tennis Cts.
Football Ground
Horn's Mill
Horns Mill Prim. Sch.
Horn's Mill Bri.
Horns Farm
Helsby Golf Course
Hornsmill Brook
Three Acres
Poultry Houses
Godscroft Hall
Haydan Mews
Chestnut Farm
Cromwell Court
Alvanley Hall
110
137
215

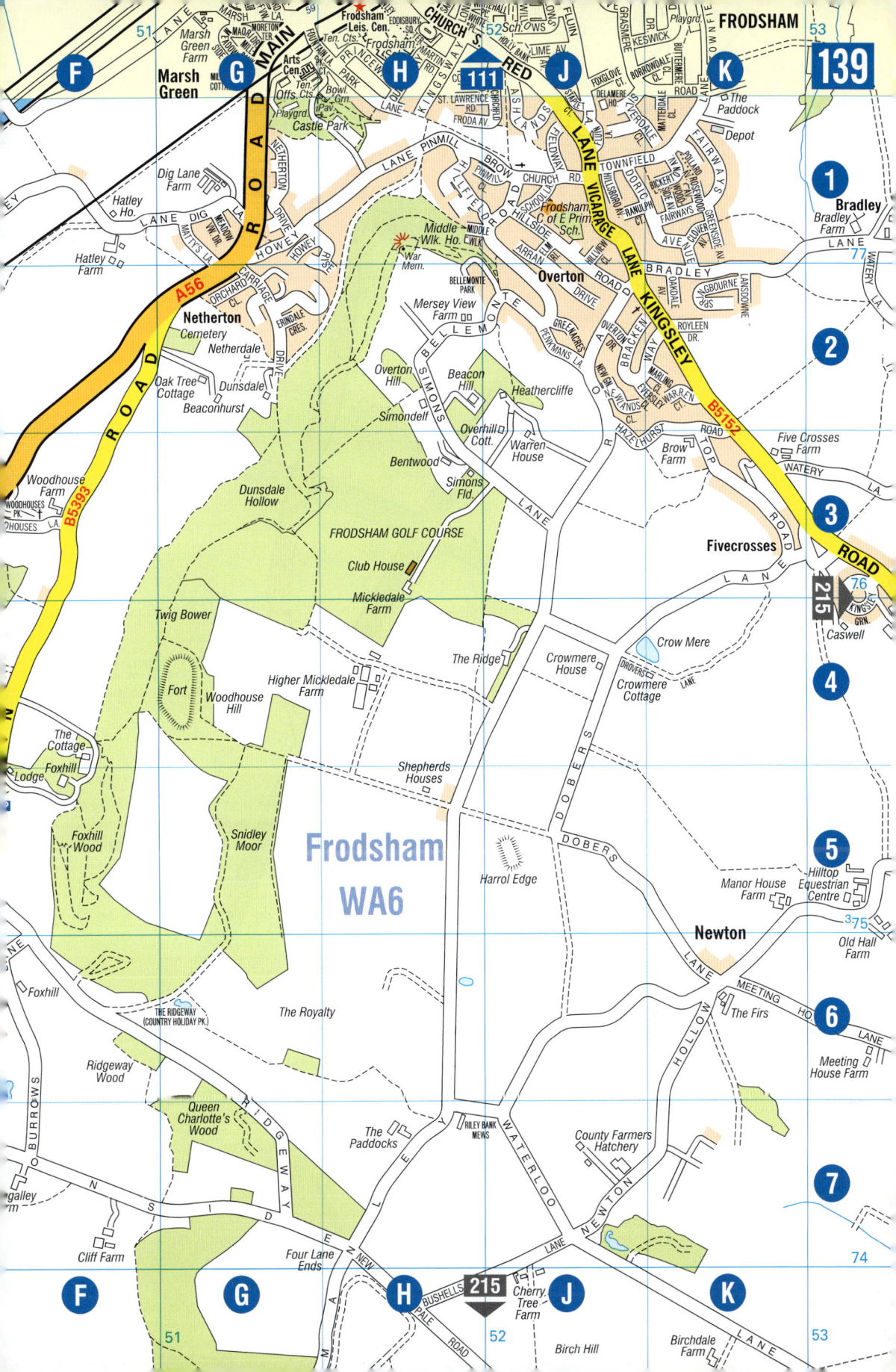

FRODSHAM
Marsh Green
Marsh Green Farm
Frodsham Leis. Cen.
Arts Cen.
Castle Park
Bowl. Grn.
Frodsham
CHURCH ST.
111
MAIN ROAD
A56
LANE VICARAGE LANE
KINGSLEY ROAD
B5152
B5393
Dig Lane Farm
Hatley Ho.
Hatley Farm
Netherton
Cemetery
Netherdale
Oak Tree Cottage
Dunsdale
Beaconhurst
Woodhouse Farm
Middle Wlk. Ho.
War Mem.
Bellemonte Park
Mersey View Farm
Overton
Frodsham C of E Prim. Sch.
Depot
The Paddock
Bradley
Bradley Farm
BRADLEY LANE
Overton Hill
Beacon Hill
Heathercliffe
Simondelf
Overhill Cott.
Warren House
Bentwood
Simons Fld.
Brow Farm
Five Crosses Farm
WATERY LA.
Fivecrosses
Dunsdale Hollow
FRODSHAM GOLF COURSE
Club House
Mickledale Farm
Twig Bower
Fort
Woodhouse Hill
Higher Mickledale Farm
The Ridge
Crowmere House
Crow Mere
Crowmere Cottage
Caswell
215
The Cottage
Foxhill
Lodge
Shepherds Houses
Foxhill Wood
Snidley Moor
Frodsham
WA6
Harrol Edge
Manor House Farm
Hilltop Equestrian Centre
Newton
Old Hall Farm
DOBERS LANE
MEETING HO. LANE
The Firs
Meeting House Farm
The Ridgeway (Country Holiday Pk.)
The Royalty
Ridgeway Wood
Queen Charlotte's Wood
RIDGEWAY
The Paddocks
Riley Bank Mews
WATERLOO
County Farmers Hatchery
HOLLOW
NEWTON LANE
BURROWS
Cliff Farm
Four Lane Ends
BUSHELLS
Cherry Tree Farm
PALE ROAD
Birch Hill
Birchdale Farm
F G H J K
1 2 3 4 5 6 7
51 52 53
77 76 75 74

134
145
214
CHESTER GATES INDUSTRIAL PARK
Ellesmere Port
CH66
CH1
Dunkirk
Backford
Lea by Backford
Mollington
Moston
Stanney Wood
Stanney Wood Local Nature Reserve
Sports & Social Club
Lobitos Sports Grd.
Applegold
Backford Cross
Heath Farm
Acres Farm
Heath Wood
Dunkirk Farm
Manor Farm
The Croft
Depot
DUNKIRK TRADING ESTATE
Fernlea
Acres Wood
Axes Farm
The Cottages
Gordon Lane Farm
Fairfield Farm House
Pump Farm
Thomas Farm
Mount Cottages
Rosscroft
Poplarhall
Reservoir
Lea Manor Farm
The Laurels
Wood Farm
Lee Manor Cotts.
The Spinney
Home Farm
HOSPICE
Backford Hall (Council Offs.)
School
Church Farm
Lea Hall Farm
Lea Hall
Old Barn
Tarla Yesil
Hall
Collinge Farm
Friars Park Cottages
Friars Park
Friars Park Farm
Grove Farm
St. Oswalds C of E Prim. Sch.
Leamoll
Lea Farm
Backford Bridge
Warren Farm
Willow Farm
Viaduct Wood
Moston Hall
Moston Hill Farm
Fish Ponds
Overwood Farm
TA Cen.
SHOTWICK-HELSBY BY-PASS
RING ROAD
CHESTER ROAD
WHITBY ROAD
LIVERPOOL ROAD
M56 MOTORWAY
A41
A5117
A5032
M56
GORDON LANE
CHURCH LANE
THE CHANNEL
STANNEY LANE
POPLAR HALL LANE
STATION ROAD
DEMAGE LANE
GROVE ROAD
TOWNFIELD LANE
WELL LANE
MOLLINGTON COURT
GYPSY LANE
CHORLTON LANE
BRIDLE LANE
COALPIT LANE

Junc. 10
135
Blue Planet
Old Hall Farm
Lime Tree Farm
LITTLE STANNEY
Hill Farm
A5117 BY-PASS
Filter Beds
Pollution Control Works
Mason's Bridge
Stoke Grange
Meadow Lane Bridge
M53
M53 MOTORWAY
Caravan Park
Church Farm
Dension's Bridge
Stoke Farm
CHURCH LA.
Vicarage
Stoak
HEATH LANE
HEATH LA.
M56
M56 MOTORWAY
Works
Stoke Bridge
CROUGHTON RD.
BUNBURY CL.
Picton Lane Bridge
The Laurels
Clover Cottage
Junction 11 (M53)
Junction 15 (M56)
Chester
Ashwood House Farm
Ashwood House
142
Grove Farm
The Dungeon
Croughton Bridge
Bridge Farm
WERVIN RD.
Middle Farm
Croughton
Ash Wood
Croughton Cottage
Top Farm
Lodge
CH2
CANAL
Kennel Farm
Chorltonlodge Farm
Chapel House Farm
ASHWOOD
Walnut Cottage
Wervin
Wervin Old Hall
WERVIN MOBILE HOME PARK
Chorlton Hall
Chorlton House
UNION
Rock Bank
Wervin New Hall
M53
SHROPSHIRE
RAKE LANE
LITTLE LANE
WERVIN ROAD
Woodside Farm
Ashton House
Henlleys
Caughall Bridge
CAUGHALL
Depot
Caughall Manor
BADGERS WLK.
Caughall Farm
Coach & Car Park
WERVIN
FOX COVERT LANE
GREEN LANE
Greenland
Upton (The Zoo)
CHESTER ZOO
ROAD
146
Mill Brook
F G H J K
1 2 3 4 5 6 7
41 42 43
74 73 72 71

Thornton Brook
River Gowy
136
Cryers Farm
Peewit Lodge
B5132
Thornton Green Cottage
Manor Lodge
Thornton Green Farm
Cross House Farm
M56
M56 MOTORWAY
Spring Farm
Field Farm
Hallsgreen La.
Sunny Bank
Hob
Mill
Heath Farm
Manor Farm
Chester
Cryers Lane
Inic Lane
141
Picton Lane
Brook
River Gowy
Hall Farm
Wimbolds Trafford
Trafford Hall
CH2
B5132
Park Farm
Sandfield Golf Course
Club House & Driving Range
The Gables
Hill Farm
Depot
Manor Farm
Lower Farm
Pear Tree Cottage
Picton Hall
Berry Cottage
Bridge Trafford Hall
Henlleys
Picton
Picton Valley
Picton Hall Farm
Hassalls La.
Sandfield Farm
Bridge Trafford
Chester Road
Trafford Bridge
Lane
Warrington Road
Trafford Mill
New House Farm
The Willows
Mill Farm
A56
Sewage Works
Meadow Farm
Ash Hey Farm
Hey Lane
The Grange
Green
147
Beech Farm
Ash
Lane
The Street
River

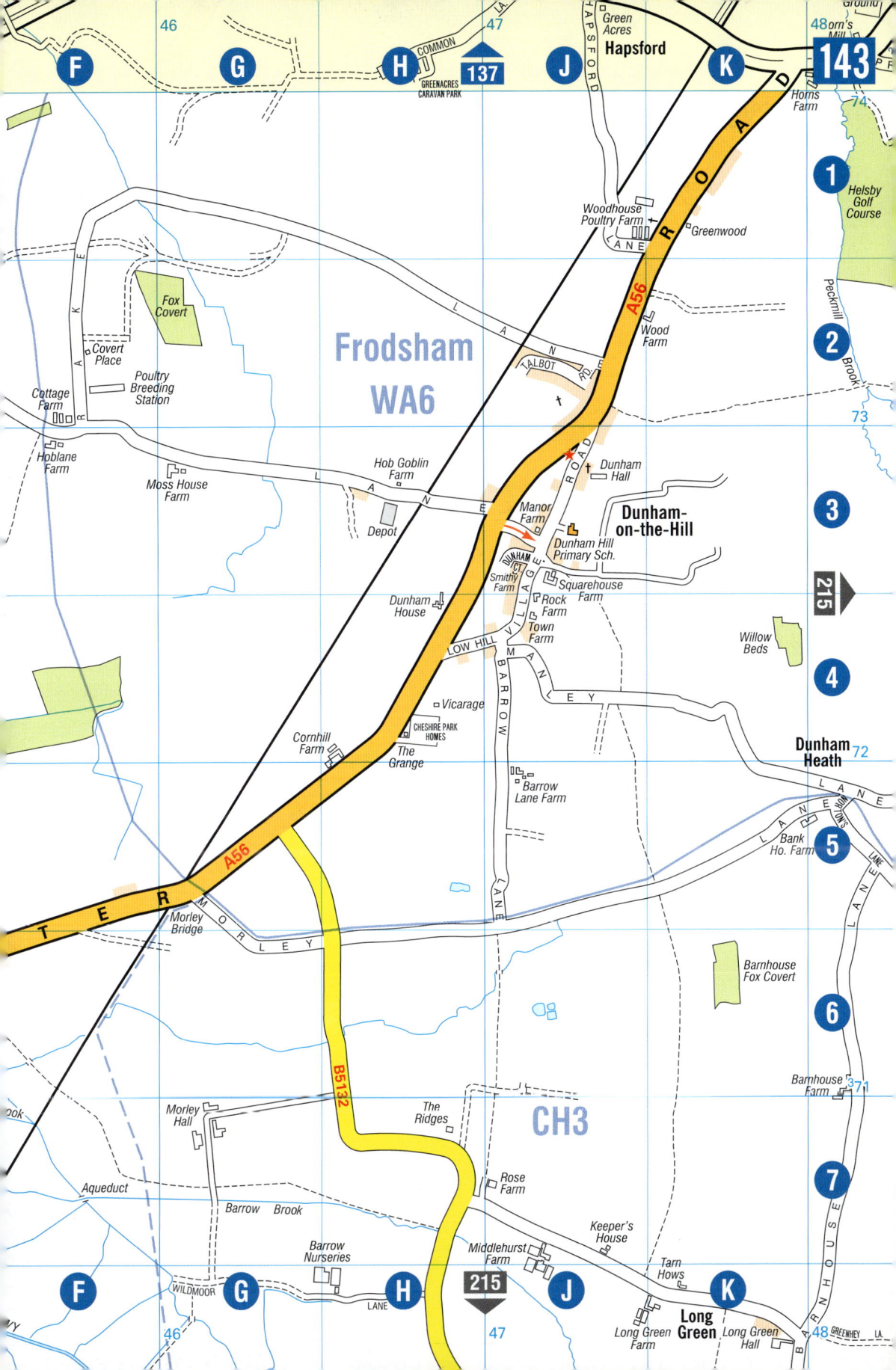
Frodsham
WA6
CH3
Hapsford
Green Acres
Dunham-on-the-Hill
Dunham Heath
Long Green
A56
B5132
CHESTER ROAD
137
215
Helsby Golf Course
Woodhouse Poultry Farm
Greenwood
Wood Farm
Fox Covert
Covert Place
Poultry Breeding Station
Cottage Farm
Hoblane Farm
Moss House Farm
Hob Goblin Farm
Depot
Manor Farm
Dunham Hall
Dunham Hill Primary Sch.
Smithy Farm
Squarehouse Farm
Rock Farm
Town Farm
Dunham House
Vicarage
CHESHIRE PARK HOMES
Cornhill Farm
The Grange
Barrow Lane Farm
Willow Beds
Bank Ho. Farm
Morley Bridge
Barnhouse Fox Covert
Barnhouse Farm
Morley Hall
The Ridges
Rose Farm
Aqueduct
Barrow Brook
Barrow Nurseries
Middlehurst Farm
Keeper's House
Tarn Hows
Long Green Farm
Long Green Hall
Horns Farm
Peckmill Brook
GREENACRES CARAVAN PARK
COMMON
TALBOT RD.
LOW HILL
MANLEY LANE
BARROW LANE
MORLEY LANE
WILDMOOR LANE
BARNHOUSE LANE
GREENHEY LA.
DUNHAM CT.
VILLAGE ROAD
HAPSFORD LANE
LAKE LANE

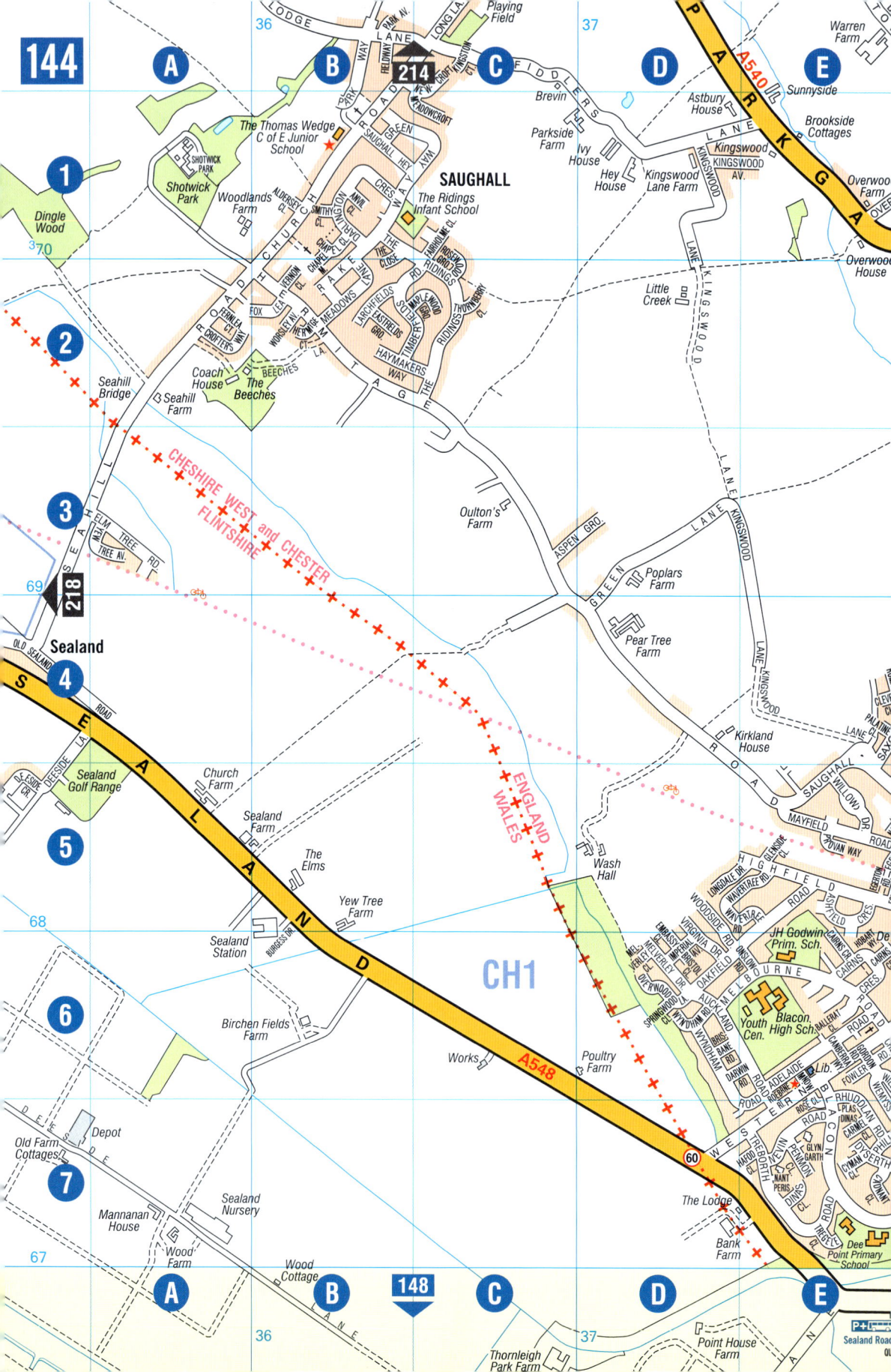
A
B
C
D
E
1
2
3
4
5
6
7
36
37
70
69
68
67
214
218
148
SAUGHALL
Sealand
CH1
A540
A548
PARKGATE
SEALAND ROAD
Playing Field
LODGE LANE
PARK AV.
LONG LA.
FIELDWAY
NEW CROFT
KINGSTON CT.
MEADOWCROFT
FIDDLERS
Brevin
Astbury House
Warren Farm
Sunnyside
Brookside Cottages
Parkside Farm
Ivy House
Hey House
Kingswood Lane Farm
Kingswood
KINGSWOOD AV.
Overwood Farm
Overwood House
The Thomas Wedge C of E Junior School
SHOTWICK PARK
Shotwick Park
Woodlands Farm
Dingle Wood
The Ridings Infant School
SAUGHALL HEY
GREEN WAY
CHURCH ROAD
ALDERSEY CL.
SMITHY CL.
DARLINGTON CRES.
ANVIL CL.
CHAPEL CL.
RAKE LANE
THE CLOSE
FAIRHOLME CL.
ROSEWOOD GRO.
RIDINGS
VERNON CL.
FOX LEA
HERMITAGE
MEADOWS
LARCHFIELDS
EASTFIELDS GRO.
TIMBERFIELDS RD.
MAPLEWOOD GRO.
THORNBERRY CL.
THE RIDINGS
HAYMAKERS WAY
FERNLEA CT.
CROFTERS WAY
WORSLEY AV.
BEECHES
Coach House
The Beeches
Seahill Bridge
Seahill Farm
Little Creek
KINGSWOOD LANE
CHESHIRE WEST and CHESTER
FLINTSHIRE
SEAHILL
ELM TREE RD.
YEW TREE AV.
Oulton's Farm
ASPEN GRO.
GREEN LANE
Poplars Farm
Pear Tree Farm
OLD SEALAND ROAD
ENGLAND
WALES
Kirkland House
SAUGHALL ROAD
WILLOW DR.
MAYFIELD ROAD
PROVAN WAY
GLENSIDE CL.
HIGHFIELD ROAD
LONGDALE DR.
WAVERTREE RD.
ASHFIELD CRES.
EGERTON RD.
DEESIDE LA.
DEESIDE GR.
Sealand Golf Range
Church Farm
Sealand Farm
The Elms
Wash Hall
Yew Tree Farm
Sealand Station
BURGESS DR.
WOODSIDE RD.
EMBASSY CL.
VIRGINIA DR.
IMPERIAL AV.
BRISTOL CL.
MELVERLEY CL.
MELVERLEY DR.
OVERWOOD LA.
SPRINGWOOD CL.
OAKFIELD
ONSLOW RD.
JH Godwin Prim. Sch.
CAIRNS CR.
MELBOURNE
CAIRNS CRES.
Blacon High Sch.
Youth Cen.
WYNDHAM RD.
AUCKLAND
BRISBANE RD.
BALLERAT CL.
CANBERRA
GORDON
ADELAIDE RD.
Lib.
DARWIN RD.
FOWLER
BLACON
RHUDDLAN RD.
ROSE CL.
PLAS DINAS
CARMEL
DYSERTH
Birchen Fields Farm
Works
Poultry Farm
WESTERN
60
TREBORTH
NEVIN CL.
PENMON CL.
GLYN GARTH
NANT PERIS CL.
DINAS CL.
CYMAN CL.
HAFOD CL.
The Lodge
Bank Farm
TREGELE CL.
Dee Point Primary School
Depot
Old Farm Cottages
DEESIDE
Mannanan House
Sealand Nursery
Wood Farm
Wood Cottage
LANE
Thornleigh Park Farm
Point House Farm
Sealand Road

Mollington
Willow Farm
Viaduct Wood
Moston Hall
Moston Hill Farm
140
Greenlands
A41
Moston
Upton (The Zoo)
Icehouse Plantation
Fish Ponds
The Dale
TA Cen.
Hillcrest
Moston Community Nature Reserve
Dodd's Wood
MOLLINGTON GRANGE GOLF COURSE
Club House
The Paddock
Crabwall Farm
Crabwall Hall
Crabwall Manor
Grange Cotts.
MOLLINGTON GRANGE BUSINESS PARK
Knolls Bridge
SHROPSHIRE UNION CANAL
A540
Chester
CH2
146
UPTON-BY-CHESTER GOLF COURSE
Mollington Canal Bridge
COUNTESS OF CHESTER HOSPITAL
A5116
Playing Field
BOWMERE HOSPITAL
COUNTESS OF CHESTER HEALTH PARK
St.John's Ambulance HQ
Bache
Bache Hall
St. Theresa's RC Prim. Sch.
The Arches Prim. Sch.
King George's Field
Chester & Ellesmere Port Divisional Police Headquarters
Cemetery
Chester Crematorium
Depot
COUNTESS WAY
Abbot's Meads
Blacon
Highfield Prim. Sch.
Glenesk
The Queens Lwr. Sch.
Total Fitness
Aqueduct
CHESTER
A5480
A540 PARKGATE ROAD
LIVERPOOL ROAD
University of Chester
212
Victoria Inf.Sch. Jun.Sch.
Blacon Common Nature Park
Cineworld Cinema
Tenpin
GREYHOUND RETAIL PARK
THE STADIUM IND. EST.
CHESTER RETAIL PARK
Finchett's Gutter
Playing Field
149
Works
Bus Depot
Northgate Arena Leisure Cen.
ST. OSWALD'S WY.
A548
Superstore
CHESTER WEST EMPLOYMENT
F
G
H
J
K
1
2
3
4
5
6
7
38
39
340
370
69
68
67
300
174

146
A
B
C
D
E
1
2
3
4
5
6
7
141
145
150
212
41
42
Caughall Farm
Park
Greenlands
Upton (The Zoo)
CHESTER ZOO
MOSTON
A41
Hillcrest
Moston Community Nature Reserve
LIVERPOOL RD.
Upton Heyes House
Demage Farm
OAKFIELD AV.
OAKFIELD DR.
ALWYN GDNS.
Acresfield Primary School
ACRES LANE
GREENACRES CT.
WERVIN ROAD
CAUGHALL ROAD
FOX COVERT LANE
Fox Covert
FOX COVERT LA.
M53–MOTORWAY
M53
Upton Heath
Water Tower
Upton Heath C of E Prim.Sch.
LONG LANE
ROAD
CH2
Rec. Grd.
DALESIDE
DEMAGE LA.
MEADOWSWAY
Headstart Day Nursery
Upton
Hall
Club House
GOLF COURSE
UPTON-BY-CHESTER GOLF COURSE
A5116
Dorin Park Sch.
Lib.
Playing Field
Youth Club
Mill View Prim. Sch.
Upton Westlea Prim. Sch.
ST. JAMES AV.
GLASTONBURY AV.
Upton-by-Chester High Sch.
Cheshire County Sports Club
THE COURTYARD
THE BEECHES
Upton Grange
Moat
Playing Field
Brookhirst Athletics Ground
Pav.
Field House
Oak Farm
MANNINGS LANE
GREENFIELD LA.
A41
Bache
LIVER-POOL
WAY
Newton
Playing Field
Newton House
NEWTON LANE
Woodfield Prim. Sch.
The Firs Sch.
HALL DR.
SHEPHERD'S LANE
WELL LANE
TOTLAND GRO.
Sports Ground
Youth Centre
Newton Prim. Sch.
KINGSWAY WEST
Flookersbrook
Coronation Playing Field
Bowls
ALEXANDRA CT.
RING ROAD
30
A56
Lib.
Hoole Alexandra Park
Hoole
Playing Field
Hoole C of E Prim. Sch.
HOOLE BRI.
HOOLE WAY
CHESTER
Brook La. Bri.
Depot
Northgate Arena Leisure Cen.
ST. OSWALD'S WY.
Comm. Cen. & YMCA
Play. Fld.
CHESTER ENTERPRISE CEN.
CHESTER
Works
Tower

Chester
MICKLE TRAFFORD
GUILDEN SUTTON
Hoole Bank
Hoole Village
Piper's Ash
Plemstall
Vicarscross
CH3
WARRINGTON ROAD
A56
A55
A41
A51
Junc. 12
142
151
219
Sewage Works
Meadow Farm
The Grange
Mill
Beech Farm
Bankfield Farm
Plemondestall Bridge
Cedars
Ivy Bank Farm
Picton Gorse
Picton Gorse Farm
Cemetery
Prim. Sch.
Hoole Bank Farm
Works
Trafford House Farm
Manor Fields
SILVERDALE PARK INDUSTRIAL ESTATE
Meadow Lea Farm
Oak Bank
Mayfield House
Nursery
The Croft
Old Hall
Park Farm
The Stables
The Hall
Lynton Lodge
Hoole Hall
Guilden Sutton C of E Prim. Sch.
Depot
Res. (cov.)
The Brambles
Belle Vue Farm
The Byatts
Hillview Farm
Polruan
Bellevue Wood
VICARS CROSS GOLF COURSE
Club House
Manor Farm
Play. Fld.
Youth Cen.
Oldfield Prim. Sch.
Lib.
Heath
Stamford Lodge
Littleton Hall
Chester UFC
PICTON LANE
SALTER'S LANE
STATION LANE
SCHOOL LANE
GUILDEN SUTTON LANE
BELLE VUE LANE
WICKER LANE
HARE LANE
TARVIN ROAD
STAMFORD LA.
PARK LA.
PLEMSTALL LANE
THE STREET
OAK BANK LANE
HEY LANE
RIVER GOWY
F
G
H
J
K
1
2
3
4
5
6
7
43
44
345
370
69
68
67

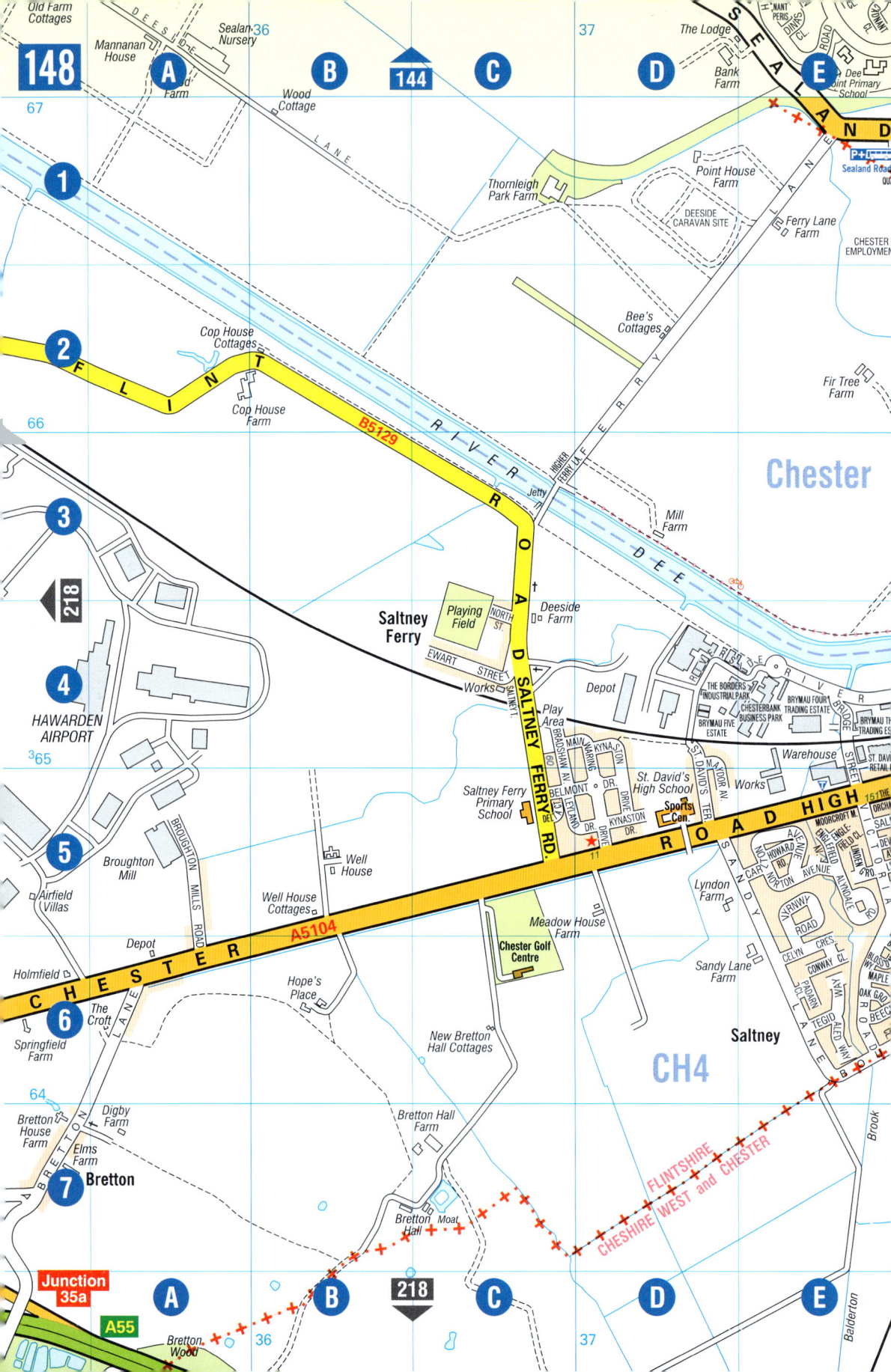
Old Farm Cottages
Mannanan House
Sealand Nursery
Wood Cottage
DEES IDE LANE
144
The Lodge
SEALAND ROAD
Bank Farm
Dee Point Primary School
Sealand Road
Thornleigh Park Farm
Point House Farm
DEESIDE CARAVAN SITE
Ferry Lane Farm
CHESTER EMPLOYMENT
Bee's Cottages
Cop House Cottages
FLINT ROAD
B5129
Cop House Farm
Fir Tree Farm
RIVER DEE
HIGHER FERRY LA.
FERRY LANE
Jetty
Chester
Mill Farm
218
Playing Field
Saltney Ferry
Deeside Farm
NORTH ST.
EWART STREET
Works
Depot
Play Area
HAWARDEN AIRPORT
THE BORDERS INDUSTRIAL PARK
CHESTERBANK BUSINESS PARK
BRYMAU FOUR TRADING ESTATE
BRYMAU FIVE ESTATE
RIVER BRIDGE
Warehouse
St. David's High School
Sports Cen.
Saltney Ferry Primary School
SALTNEY FERRY RD.
BRADSHAW AV.
MAIN
WARING
KYNASTON
BELMONT DR.
LEYLAND DR.
KYNASTON DRIVE
KYNASTON DR.
ST. DAVID'S TER.
MAYDOR AV.
Works
HIGH ROAD
Broughton Mill
BROUGHTON MILLS ROAD
Well House
Well House Cottages
Airfield Villas
Depot
Holmfield
CHESTER ROAD
A5104
Chester Golf Centre
Meadow House Farm
Lyndon Farm
SANDY LANE
HOWARD RD.
NORTON AVENUE
CARTON
MOORCROFT M.
ENGLEFIELD AV.
ENGLEFIELD CL.
LINDEN GRO.
ALYNDALE RD.
VYRNWY ROAD
CELYN CRES.
CONWAY CL.
PADARN CL.
TEGID WAY
ALED WAY
Sandy Lane Farm
MAPLE
OAK GRO.
BEECH
Hope's Place
The Croft
Springfield Farm
New Bretton Hall Cottages
Saltney
CH4
Bretton House Farm
Digby Farm
Elms Farm
BRETTON LANE
Bretton
Bretton Hall Farm
Bretton Hall
Moat
FLINTSHIRE
CHESHIRE WEST and CHESTER
Brook
Balderton
Junction 35a
A55
Bretton Wood
218
A B C D E
1 2 3 4 5 6 7
36 37
67 66 65 64

149
F
G
H
J
K
145
150
185
212
1
2
3
4
5
6
7
A548
A483
A5104
CH1
CHESTER
Blacon Common Nature Park
Cineworld Cinema
GREYHOUND RETAIL PARK
Tenpin
Playing Field
THE STADIUM IND. EST.
CHESTER RETAIL PARK
Works
Superstore
The Mulberry Centre
CHESTER WEST EMPLOYMENT PARK
SEALAND INDUSTRIAL ESTATE
CHESTER TRADE PK.
Sewage Works
Market
Chester City FC Saunders Honda Stadium)
Refuse Station
Border House Farm
Top Farm
Border House
ENGLAND
WALES
CHESTER GOLF COURSE
Club House
Gamon's Rough
Saltney Junction
Curzon Park
Chester Racecourse The Roodee
Grandstand
Pavilion
Water Tower
Water Tower Gds.
Cathedral
Chester History
The Castle
COUNTY HALL
Little Roodee
RIVER
DEE
Grosvenor Bridge
The Dingle
Cemy.
West Cheshire College
General Cemetery
Overleigh St. Mary's C E Primary Sch
The Catholic High School
GROSVENOR (CHESTER) NUFFIELD HOSPITAL
Dragons Health Club
Playing Fields
Play. Fld.
Ash Grove Farm
Water Treatment Works
Marlston Heyes Farm
The King's School
Tennis Courts
Fir Tree Farm
Moat Bungalow
CHESTER BUSINESS PARK
Bowling Greens
Westminster Sports Ground
WESTMINSTER PARK GOLF COURSE
Nursery
Comm. Cen.
St. Clare's Catholic Prim. Sch.
Lache Prim. Sch.
Lache
Playground
RIVERSIDE IND. EST.
BRYMAU ONE TRAD. EST.
BRYMAU TWO TRAD. EST.
SALTNEY BUS. CEN.
CHESTER ST.
HOUGH GREEN
GROSVENOR ROAD
NEW CRANE ST.
ST. MARTIN'S WAY
NICHOLAS ST.
ST. OSWALD'S WY.
CIRCULAR DRIVE
Victoria Inf.Sch. Jun.Sch.
Bus Depot
Arena Leisure Cen.

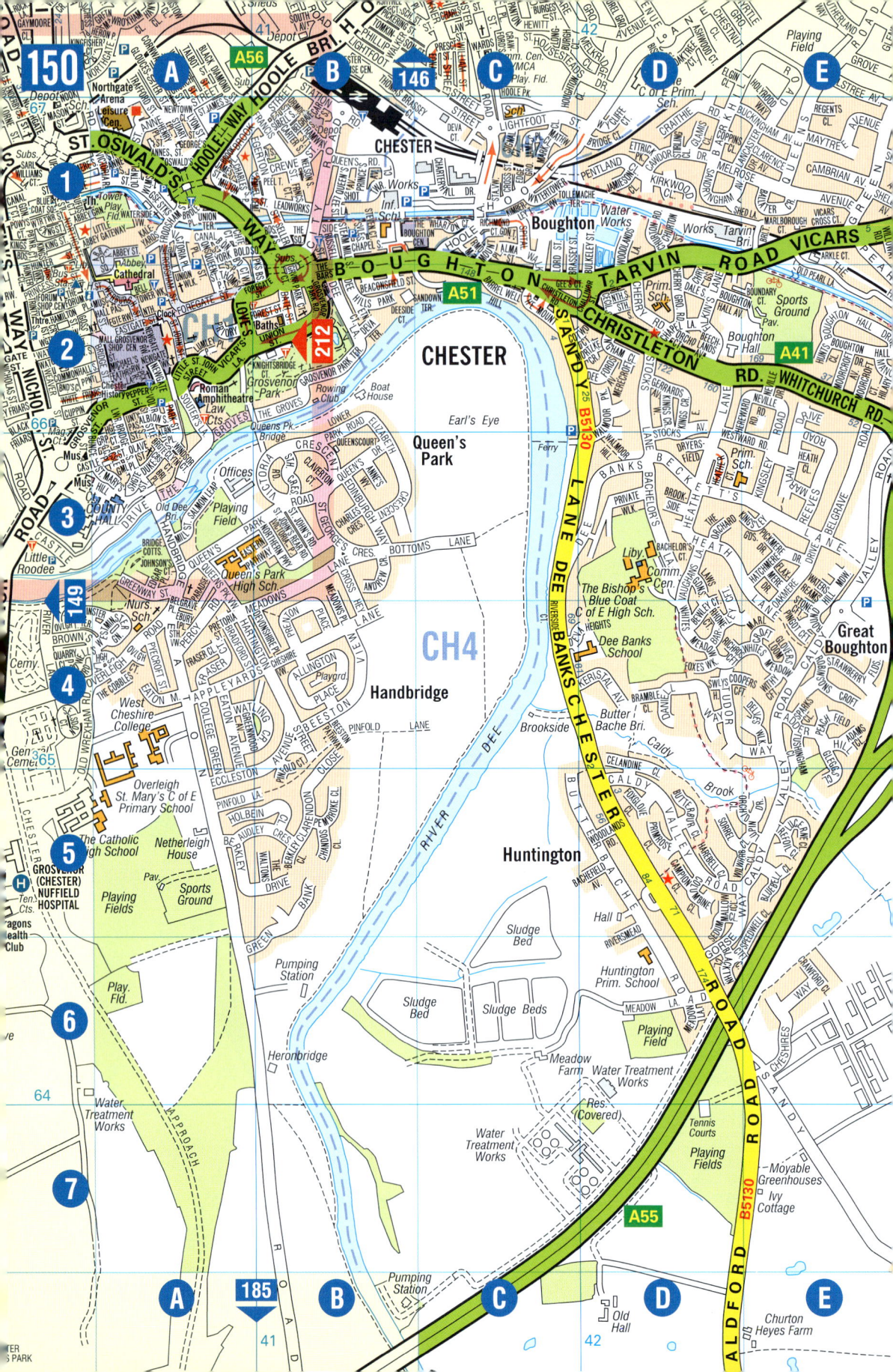
A
B
C
D
E
1
2
3
4
5
6
7
146
149
185
41
42
67
66
65
64
A56
A51
A41
A55
B5130
212
CHESTER
Northgate Arena Leisure Cen.
ST. OSWALD'S WAY
HOOLE WAY
HOOLE BRI.
Cathedral
BOUGHTON
TARVIN ROAD
VICARS CROSS
CHRISTLETON RD.
WHITCHURCH RD.
Boughton
Boughton Hall
Sports Ground
Roman Amphitheatre
Grosvenor Park
Rowing Club
Boat House
Earl's Eye
Queen's Park
COUNTY HALL
Little Roodee
GROSVENOR RD.
NICHOLAS ST.
Queen's Park High Sch.
Handbridge
CH4
RIVER DEE
Ferry
DEE BANKS
SANDY LANE
CHESTER ROAD
Prim. Sch.
Liby.
Comm. Cen.
The Bishop's Blue Coat C of E High Sch.
Dee Banks School
Great Boughton
Butter Bache Bri.
Brookside
Caldy Brook
CALDY VALLEY ROAD
Huntington
Huntington Prim. School
West Cheshire College
Overleigh St. Mary's C of E Primary School
The Catholic High School
Netherleigh House
Sports Ground
Playing Fields
Play. Fld.
GROSVENOR (CHESTER) NUFFIELD HOSPITAL
Gen. Cemetery
Cemy.
Pumping Station
Sludge Bed
Sludge Beds
Heronbridge
Meadow Farm
Water Treatment Works
Res. (Covered)
Tennis Courts
Playing Field
Playing Fields
Moyable Greenhouses
Ivy Cottage
ALDFORD ROAD
Old Hall
Churton Heyes Farm
APPROACH

151
147
219
174
Vicarscross
TARVIN ROAD
A51
A41
A55
RING ROAD
WHITCHURCH ROAD
Chester RUFC
Littleton Hall
Nursery
Manor House
Littleton
Five Oaks
Littleton Old Hall
Pitts Cottage
Playing Field
Football Ground
Pav.
Chester
Little Heath
CHRISTLETON
Christleton Lock
Christleton Hall (College of Law)
The Old Glass House
Boughton Heath
Abbot's Well
The Old Hall
Christleton Bridge
Christleton Primary School
Christleton High School
Christleton Sports Centre
Manor Farm
Parkfields Farm
Stamford Lodge
Heathfield
Club House
Stamford Hollows Farm
Birch Bank Farm
Birch Heath Farm
Bungalow Farm
Whitegate Farm
PEPPER STREET
BIRCH HEATH LANE
PLOUGH LANE
Rowton Bridge
Netherwood Touring Site
Riding Centre
Woodbank
Rowton Grange
Brook Lodge
Grange Farm
CH3
Brown Heath Farm
Nursery
Highfields
Brown Heath
The Drift
Rowton Moor
Works
Caldy Brook
SHROPSHIRE UNION CANAL
Gorse Hall New Farm
Gorse Hall Farm
Bridge Croft
Promisedland Farm
Holly Bank
Hall Farm Cottage
Rowton
Rowton Lane Farm
Moorfields
Elm Bank
Waverton Prim. Sch.
Play. Fld.
SAIGHTON CAMP
Claypits Farm
WAVERTON BUSINESS PARK
Portersheath Farm
RIDGES LANE
Black Dog Farm
BLACK DOG LANE
WAVERTON
Elm Cottage
The Old Smithy
Ridgeway Ho.
Ridgeway Farm
Heathcroft Farm
SAIGHTON LANE
QUARRY ROAD

Kingsley
Hollow Lane
B5153
B5152
Norley Road
Mill Lane
Clough Cotts.
Pike Lane
Pike House
Tan House Farm
Hillfoot La.
Ball La.
Marsh Green Farm
Abattoir
Westbrook Farm
Hall
Cemetery
Prim. Sch.
Cen.
Middle Lane
Playing Field
Clover Cottage
Depot
Depmore
Church Rw.
Westbrook Acres
Sch.
Comm. Cen.
Sunningdale
Roddy
Chapel La.
Chapel Av.
The Hurst
Chamber Brook La.
Meeting House Lane
Offal Pit Lane
Green Acres Farm
Castlehill House
Depmore Farm
KINGSLEY
Brookside
Highbank Road
Hunters Hill
Dodsley Dr.
Wigans Lake Fm.
Finney House
Dark Lane
Depot
Bowl. Grn.
Tennis Cts.
Top Road
Beech
Manse Fld. Rd.
Higher Heyes Dr.
Finney Farm
Ash Hill Farm
Guest Road
Beech Farm
Cooks Hill
Ravenslodge Farm
Millfield Farm
Mole End Cottage
Slack
Commonside
Waterloo Cottages
Waterloo Fm.
Crofton Lodge
Dodsley Farm
Hollins Farm
Waterloo
Norley Road
The Firs
Green Hedges
Castle Cob
Waterloo Road
Delamere Road
Dodgsleygate Farm
Foresthouse Farm
Nursery Park
New Pastures
Beech Lane
Haydan Lodge
Waterloo Gate
Frodsham
WA6
Brownmoss Farm
Greenslade Farm
Greenslade
Forestgate Farm
Forestgate Farm
Hondslough Farm
Hondslough Lane
Forest
Pinewood Farm
Black Nursery
Flaxmere Cottage
Moy Park Farm
Flaxmere
Hatch Mere Nature Reserve
Hatch Mere
Hatchmere Park
School Road
Fieldhouse Farm
Hatchmere
Blakemere Lane
Hunger Hill
Delamere Forest School
Ashton Road
Barnsbridge Gates
DELAMERE FOREST PARK
Blakemere Moss
DELAMERE FOREST
215
54
55
375
74
73
72

Green Bank Farm
Higher Hayes Farm
Kingsley Mill
Orchard Gate
Pear Tree Cottage
Mill Lane House Farm
Old Farm
Lane
Silvertrees
Crewood Common Road
Ball Lane
Rose Bank
Crowton Bridge
Brook House
October House
Cooksongreen
The Poplars
Back Lane
Gabriel Bank
Hilltop Farm
Sewage Works
Crowton Brook
Crowton Mill
Acton Brook
Pikenall Lane
Ainsworth Lane
Beech Ri.
Church Wk.
Kingsley Road
Meadows Ga.
Sch.
Comm. Cen.
Station Road
B5153
Crowton
Small Brook
Bent Lane
Bent Lane Farm
Big Wood
Darley Covert
Holly Bush Farm
Pingard's Lane
The Gorse
Northwich
CW8
Westwood
Stanneybrook Farm
Town Farm
Farm Lane
Norley Lane
Sandhole Lane
Sandhole Farm
Pingard's La.
Ruloe
Norley Bank
Gorse Cl.
Stanneybrook Cl.
Crowton Vw.
Foresters Cl.
School Bank
Marsh Lane
Town Road
Pytcheley Hollow
Hambletts Hollow
The Rookery
Crabmill La.
The Spinney
Norley
Hollow Lane
Bank
Dutton Lane
Woods Lane
Burges's Lane
Norley Bank Farm
Beechwood Farm
Home Fm. La.
The Home Farm
Sandycroft Farm
Office Lane
Pav.
Ten. Ct.
Hall
Maddocks Hill
West Vw. Rd.
Springfields
High Street
Hough La.
Norley C of E Prim. Sch.
Bratts Cottage
Yew Tree Ho.
Grove Farm
Finger Lane
Yearsley La.
Moss Farm
Moss Lane
Bratt's Lane
Camomile Lane
Hunt's Hill Wood
Finger Post Farm
Post Lane
Cheese Lane
Norley Road
Royalty Covert
Camomile Farm
Newpool Wood
Small Brook
Gallowsclough Lane
Harthill Bank
Hart Hill
Newpool Cottage
Newpool Farm
Gallowsclough Farm
Sweetbriar Hall
Fox Covert Lodge
Cuddington Lane
Stoneyford
Gill's Moss Wood
Town Moss
Delamere Manor
Cuddington Waste
Lower Fa
Westgate
Glade Ct.
The Spinney
The Coppice
The Dell
The Downs
The Burrows
Denehurst
Ten. Cts.
Park Wk.
The Uplands
Delamere Park
Ousel Nest
Westwood Way
Holl
Man Farm
215
154
160
F G H J K
1 2 3 4 5 6 7
56 57 58
375 74 73 72

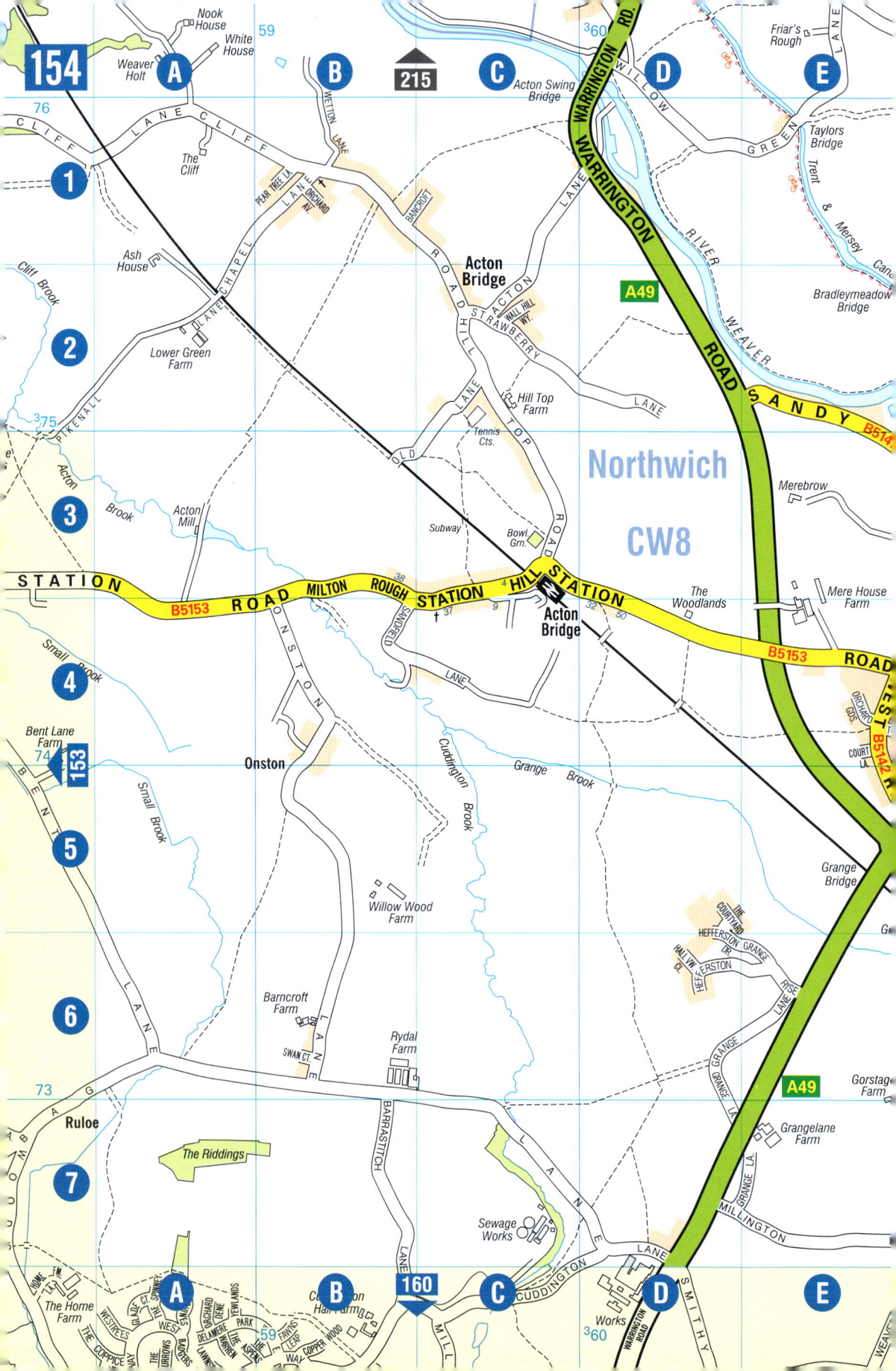

Nook House
White House
Weaver Holt
215
Acton Swing Bridge
WARRINGTON RD.
WILLOW
Friar's Rough
LANE
CLIFF LANE CLIFF
The Cliff
WETTON LANE
PEAR TREE LA.
ORCHARD AV.
BANCROFT
Taylors Bridge
Trent & Mersey Canal
GREEN
Ash House
CHAPEL LANE
ROAD HILL
Acton Bridge
ACTON
WALL HILL WY.
STRAWBERRY
RIVER WEAVER
WARRINGTON ROAD
A49
Bradleymeadow Bridge
Cliff Brook
Lower Green Farm
Hill Top Farm
LANE
SANDY
B5142
PIKENALL
OLD LANE
Tennis Cts.
TOP
Northwich
CW8
Acton Brook
Acton Mill
Subway
Bowl. Grn.
ROAD
Merebrow
STATION ROAD MILTON ROUGH STATION HILL STATION
B5153
SANDFIELD
Acton Bridge
The Woodlands
Mere House Farm
ROAD
Small Brook
LANE
ONSTON
WEST
ORCHARD GDS.
COURT LA.
Bent Lane Farm
153
Onston
Cuddington Brook
Grange Brook
Small Brook
BENT LANE
Grange Bridge
Willow Wood Farm
THE COURTYARD
HEFFERSTON GRANGE DR.
HALL VW. CL.
HEFFERSTON RISE
Barncroft Farm
Rydal Farm
SWAN CT.
LANE
GRANGE LANE
Ruloe
BARRASTITCH LANE
A49
Gorstage Farm
Grangelane Farm
The Riddings
GRANGE LA.
LANE
MILLINGTON
Sewage Works
CUDDINGTON LANE
160
HOME FM.
The Home Farm
THE COPPICE
WESTREES
GLADE CT.
THE SPINNEY
WEST WAY
THE BURROWS
BADGERS
ORCHARD
DELAMERE
DENE
WARREN
YEWLANDS
PARK
THE ASPENS
FAWNS LEAP
COPPER WOOD
Cuddington Hall Farm
MILL
Works
WARRINGTON ROAD
SMITHY

Little Leigh
Barnton
Weaverham
Gorstage
Hartfordbeach
Little Leigh Prim. Sch.
Church Farm
Brakeley Rough
Little Leigh Pond
Hawton Clough
Bradleymeadow Wood
Stoneheys Farm
Stone Leigh House Farm
Rosebank Farm
Cricket Field
Squash Ct.
Prim. Sch.
Rosebank Sch.
Lib.
Football Grd.
Saltersford Tunnel
Saltersford Locks
Barnton Tunnel
Ropery Farm
Sewage Works
Weaverham Wood Farm
Weir
River Weaver
Weaver Navigation
Barnton Cut
Owley Wood
Cricket Grd.
Wallerscote Comm. Sch.
Leis. Cen.
Play. Flds.
Prim. Sch.
Ten. Cts.
Weaverham High Sch.
The Russett Sch.
Beach Farm
Beach Hill Wood
Beech Hill Farm
Hartford Golf Club
Golf Driving Range
Back Wood
The Grange Jun. Sch.
Playing Fld.
Handford Brook
Gorstage House Farm
Gorstage Green Farm
Brook Farm
Hodgelane Farm
Brown Heath Farm
The Grange Sch.
Grange Park Rec. Grd.
Runcorn Road
A533
B5153
High St.
Northwich Road
Beach Rd.
Hodge Lane
Church Lane
Brakeley Lane
Stoneheyes Lane
Townfield Lane
Grange Av.
Wallerscote Rd.
Owley Wood Road
Forest St.
Gorstage Lane
Lime Av.
Walnut
Russet Rd.
Withens La.
Farm Road
Hill Way
Keeper's Lane
Meadow Lane
Avenue
Park Av.
Lydyett St.
Hough La.
216
161
156
62
63
74
73
75
76
F G H J K
1 2 3 4 5 6 7

156
216
155
162
A
B
C
D
E
1
2
3
4
5
6
7
BARNTON
Anderton
Marbury
MARBURY COUNTRY PARK
BIG WOOD
NORTHWICH
Winnington
Hartfordbeach
Greenbank
CW8
Claycroft Farm
Marbury Mill
Hopyards
Anderton Marina
Reservoir
Marbury Brook
Boat Yard
Uplands Farm
Bandshed Woodland
Cemetery
Visitor Centre
Anderton Boat Lift
Warehouses
ANDERTON NATURE PARK
Weaver Navigation
Cricket Field
Football Grd.
Play. Fld.
Works
Weir
Winnington Hall
Rec. Club
Bowl. Grn.
Ropery Farm
Tunnel
Wallerscote Works
Sewage Works
Winnington Sports Ground
AVENUE ENGINEERING PARK
Moss Farm Leisure Complex
Swimming Pool
Prim. Sch.
Football Grd.
Rugby Club
Golf Driving Range
Club Ho.
HARTFORD GOLF CLUB
Back Wood
Royalty Wood
The Grange Sch.
Mid Cheshire Coll.
St. Nicholas Catholic High Sch.
Greenbank Residential Sch.
St. Wilfrid's Catholic Prim. Sch.
Cloughwood
Hartford Manor Prim. Sch.
Victoria Infirmary
Verdin Pk.
Castle Hill
Timber Yard
Depot
Cinema
Coun. Offs.
Harlequin Theatre
The Salt Museum
Hunt's Locks
Leisure Cen.
All Weather Sports Area
Sir John Deane's Coll.
A533
A559
B5153
B5374
RUNCORN ROAD
WINNINGTON LANE
MOSS ROAD
CASTLE ROAD
CHESTER ROAD
WINNINGTON ST.
WATLING ST.
CHESTER WAY
LONDON ROAD
KINGSMEAD ROAD
WINNINGTON AVENUE
WALLERSCOTE ROAD
BEACH ROAD
HOUGH LANE
COGSHALL LANE
MARBURY LANE
MARBURY ROAD
SOOT HILL
NEW RD.
OLD RD.
LYDYETT LANE
BROADWAY
SOLVAY ROAD
MOSS LANE
CROMWELL ROAD
QUEENSGATE
NAVIGATION ROAD

216
163
158
Marston
Wincham
Northwich
CW9
Rudheath
Broken Cross
Higher Shurlach
Forge Pool
Trent & Mersey Canal
School Farm
Marston Church Hall
Cemetery
Manor Farm
Rose Farm Ct.
Bank Farm
Neumann's Flashes
Lion Salt Works
Works
Wincham Bus. Pk.
Keepers Wood
Garden Wood
Wincham Bri.
Northwich Victoria FC (Victoria Stadium)
Witton Albion FC (Wincham Park)
Depot
Wincham Brook
Witton Brook
Witton Mill Bridge
La Fitness Northwich
Worthington's Flash
Northwich Retail Pk.
Brickfield Bus. Cen.
Warehouse
Superstores
Superstore
Griffiths Park
Playing Field
Play. Fld.
Waste Lime Beds
Rudheath Leis. Cen.
High Sch.
Prim. Sch.
Distribution Centre
Vickers Way Park
River Dane
Manchester Way
Warrington Road
New Warrington Road
Ollershaw Lane
Marston Lane
Hall Lane
Church St.
Chapel Street
Wincham Lane
Manchester Road
Middlewich Road
Griffiths Road
King Street
Old Warrington Road
Shipbrook Road
Gadbrook Road
School Road Sth.
Pennys Lane
Cooke's Lane
A559
A530
A556
B5075
B5082
B5391

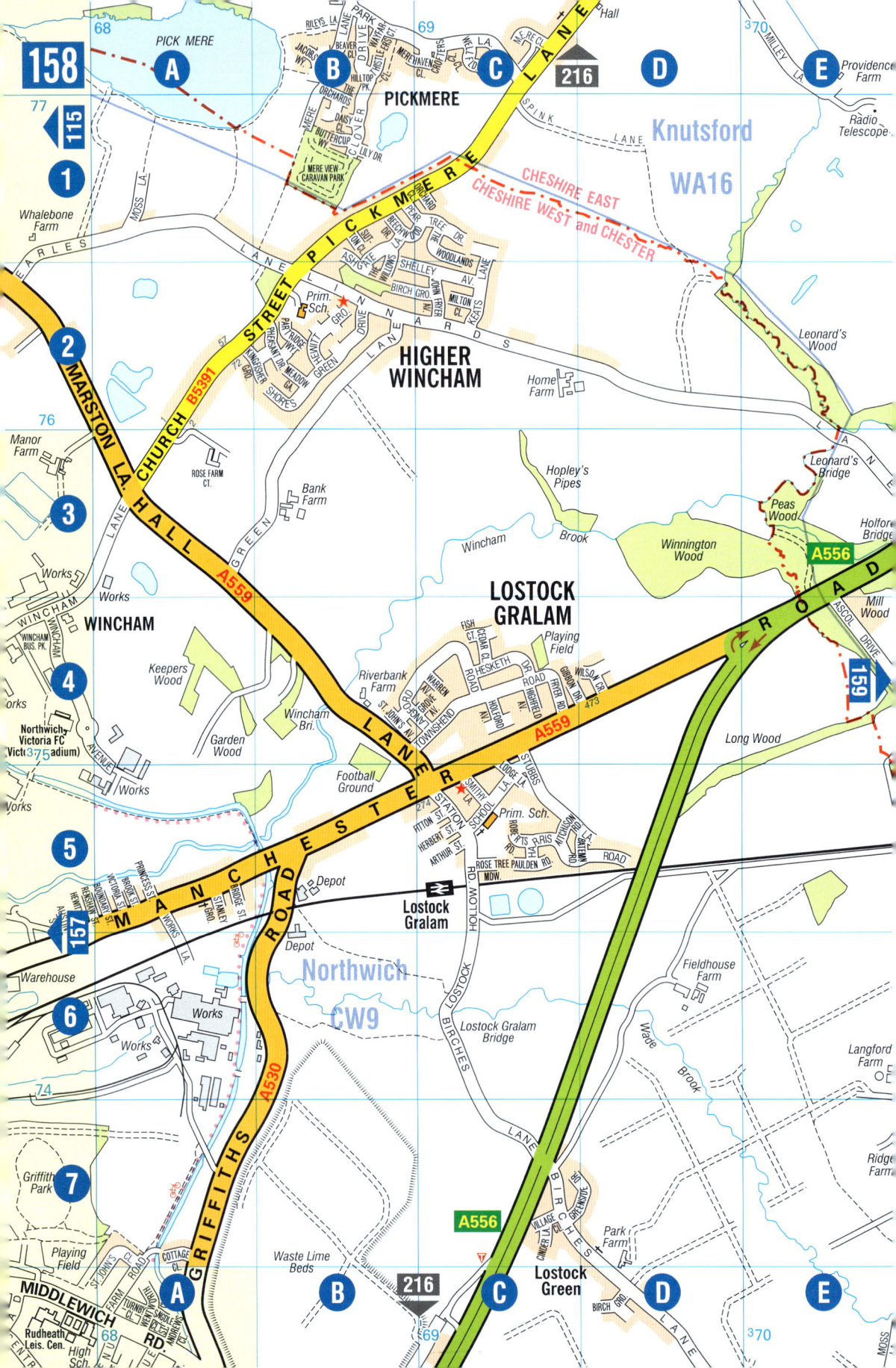
158
115
157
159
216
A
B
C
D
E
1
2
3
4
5
6
7
68
69
370
77
76
375
74
PICK MERE
PICKMERE
Knutsford
WA16
CHESHIRE EAST
CHESHIRE WEST and CHESTER
Providence Farm
Radio Telescope
Hall
MILLEY LA.
SPINK LANE
MERE VIEW CARAVAN PARK
RILEYS LA.
JACOBS WY.
BEAVER CL.
LANE PARK
DRIVE
WAYFAR
THISTLE CL.
MEREHAVEN CL.
CROFTERS CL.
WELLFIELD CL.
MERE CL.
HILLTOP PK.
THE ORCHARDS
DAISY CL.
CLOVER
BUTTERCUP WY.
LILY DR.
Whalebone Farm
MOSS LA.
EARLES LANE
CHURCH STREET PICKMERE LANE
B5391
ORCHARD
PEAR TREE DR.
THE WOODLANDS
BEECHWOOD DR.
THE WILLOWS
SHELLEY AV.
BIRCH GRO.
JOHN FRYER AV.
MILTON CL.
KEATS LANE
ASHGATE
SUTTON CL.
LINNARDS LANE
Prim. Sch.
HIGHER WINCHAM
Home Farm
Leonard's Wood
Leonard's Bridge
Peas Wood
PARTRIDGE WY.
PHEASANT DR.
KINGFISHER GRO.
MEADOW GA.
SHORES
HEWITT GRO.
GREEN DRIVE
Manor Farm
ROSE FARM CT.
Bank Farm
GREEN LANE
MARSTON LA.
HALL LANE
A559
Hopley's Pipes
Wincham Brook
Winnington Wood
Holford Bridge
A556
ROAD
ASCOL DRIVE
Mill Wood
LOSTOCK GRALAM
Playing Field
Works
WINCHAM
WINCHAM BUS. PK.
WINCHAM AVENUE
Keepers Wood
Northwich Victoria FC
Garden Wood
Wincham Bri.
Riverbank Farm
FISH CT.
CEDAR CL.
HESKETH DR.
ROAD
HIGHFIELD ROAD
FRYER RD.
GIBSON DR.
WILSON CR.
WARREN AV.
GROVE AV.
LANGFORD RD.
ST. JOHN'S AV.
TOWNSHEND
HOLFORD AV.
Long Wood
Football Ground
MANCHESTER ROAD
SMITHY LA.
STATION ROAD
SCHOOL LA.
LODGE LA.
STUBBS
FITTON ST.
HERBERT ST.
ARTHUR ST.
ROBERTS RD.
HARRIS RD.
AITCHISON RD.
BATEMAN LA.
ROSE TREE MDW.
PAULDEN RD.
ROAD
Depot
Lostock Gralam
HOLLOW
PRINCESS ST.
BROOK ST.
VICTORIA ST.
BOUNDARY ST.
RENSHAW ST.
HEWITT
STANLEY GRO.
BRIDGE ST.
WORKS LA.
Warehouse
Northwich
CW9
Fieldhouse Farm
Lostock Gralam Bridge
LOSTOCK BIRCHES LANE
Wade Brook
Langford Farm
Ridge Farm
A530
GRIFFITHS ROAD
Griffiths Park
Playing Field
Waste Lime Beds
Lostock Green
VILLAGE CL.
CINDER LA.
GREENSIDE DR.
Park Farm
BIRCH GRO.
LANE
ST. JOHN'S CL.
FARM ROAD
COTTAGE CL.
TURNBY
WENTWORTH
MIDDLEWICH RD.
ST. ANDREWS CL.
Rudheath Leis. Cen.
High Sch.
MOSS

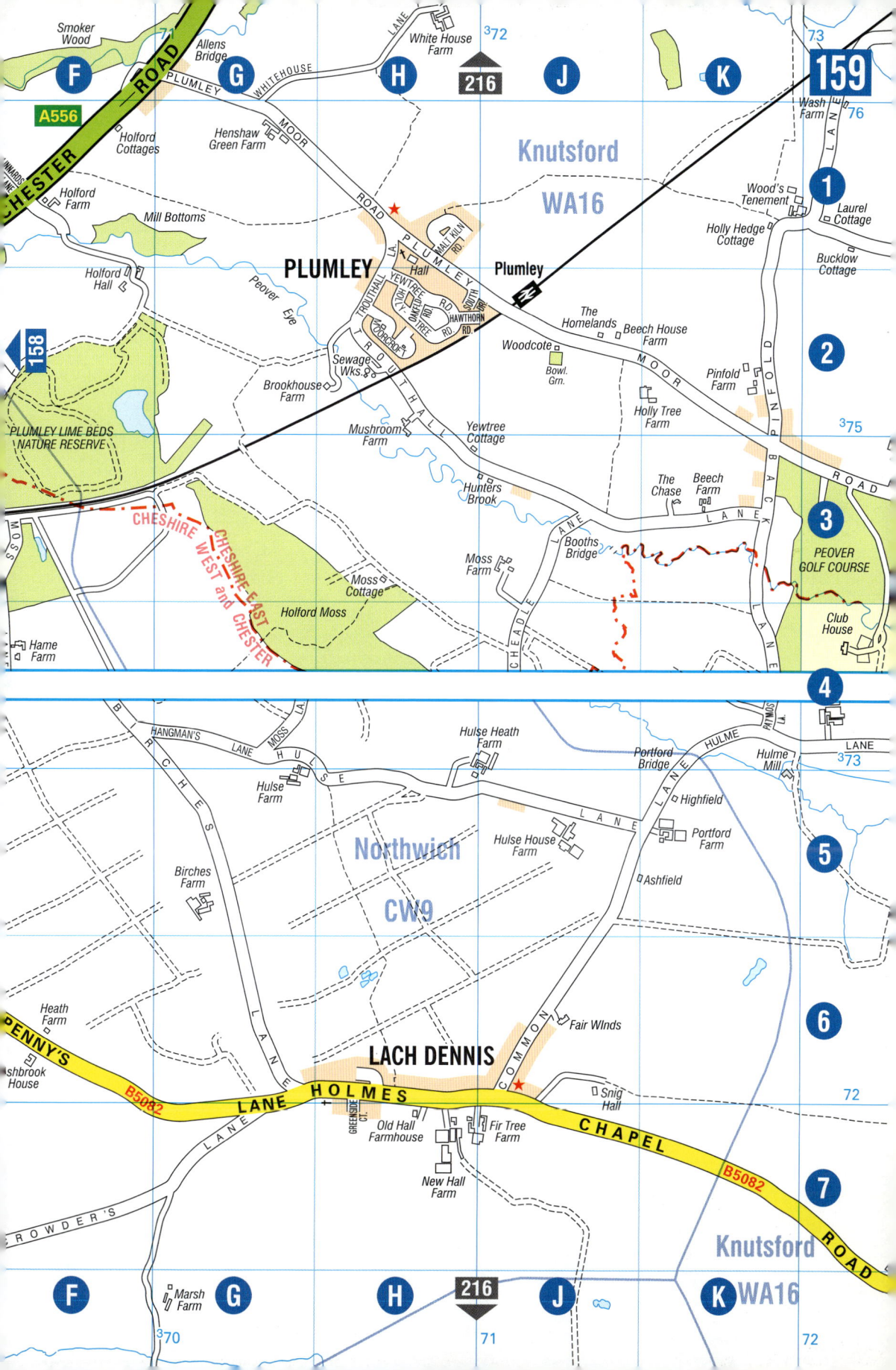
159
216
158
Smoker Wood
Allens Bridge
White House Farm
A556
CHESTER ROAD
PLUMLEY
WHITEHOUSE LANE
MOOR ROAD
Holford Cottages
Henshaw Green Farm
Knutsford
WA16
Holford Farm
Mill Bottoms
Holford Hall
PLUMLEY
Peover Eye
Hall
MALT KILN RD.
YEWTREE RD.
OAKFIELD RD.
HOLLY TREE RD.
SOUTH DR.
HAWTHORN RD.
MOORCROFT
TROUTHALL LA.
Plumley
Sewage Wks.
Brookhouse Farm
PLUMLEY LIME BEDS NATURE RESERVE
Mushroom Farm
Yewtree Cottage
Hunters Brook
Woodcote
Bowl. Grn.
The Homelands
Beech House Farm
Holly Tree Farm
Wash Farm
Wood's Tenement
Laurel Cottage
Holly Hedge Cottage
Bucklow Cottage
Pinfold Farm
PINFOLD LANE
BACK LANE
The Chase
Beech Farm
PEOVER GOLF COURSE
Club House
CHESHIRE
CHESHIRE WEST and CHESTER
CHESHIRE EAST
MOSS LANE
Moss Cottage
Holford Moss
Moss Farm
Booths Bridge
CHEADLE LANE
Hame Farm
BIRCHES LANE
HANGMAN'S LANE
MOSS LA.
HULSE LANE
Hulse Heath Farm
Hulse Farm
Portford Bridge
HULME LANE
PATMOS LA.
Hulme Mill
Highfield
Portford Farm
Hulse House Farm
Northwich
CW9
Birches Farm
Ashfield
Heath Farm
PENNY'S LANE
Ashbrook House
Fair Winds
LACH DENNIS
COMMON LANE
HOLMES CHAPEL ROAD
B5082
GREENSIDE CT.
Old Hall Farmhouse
Fir Tree Farm
Snig Hall
New Hall Farm
CROWDER'S LANE
Knutsford
WA16
Marsh Farm
F G H J K
1 2 3 4 5 6 7
370 71 372 73 72
376 375 373 72

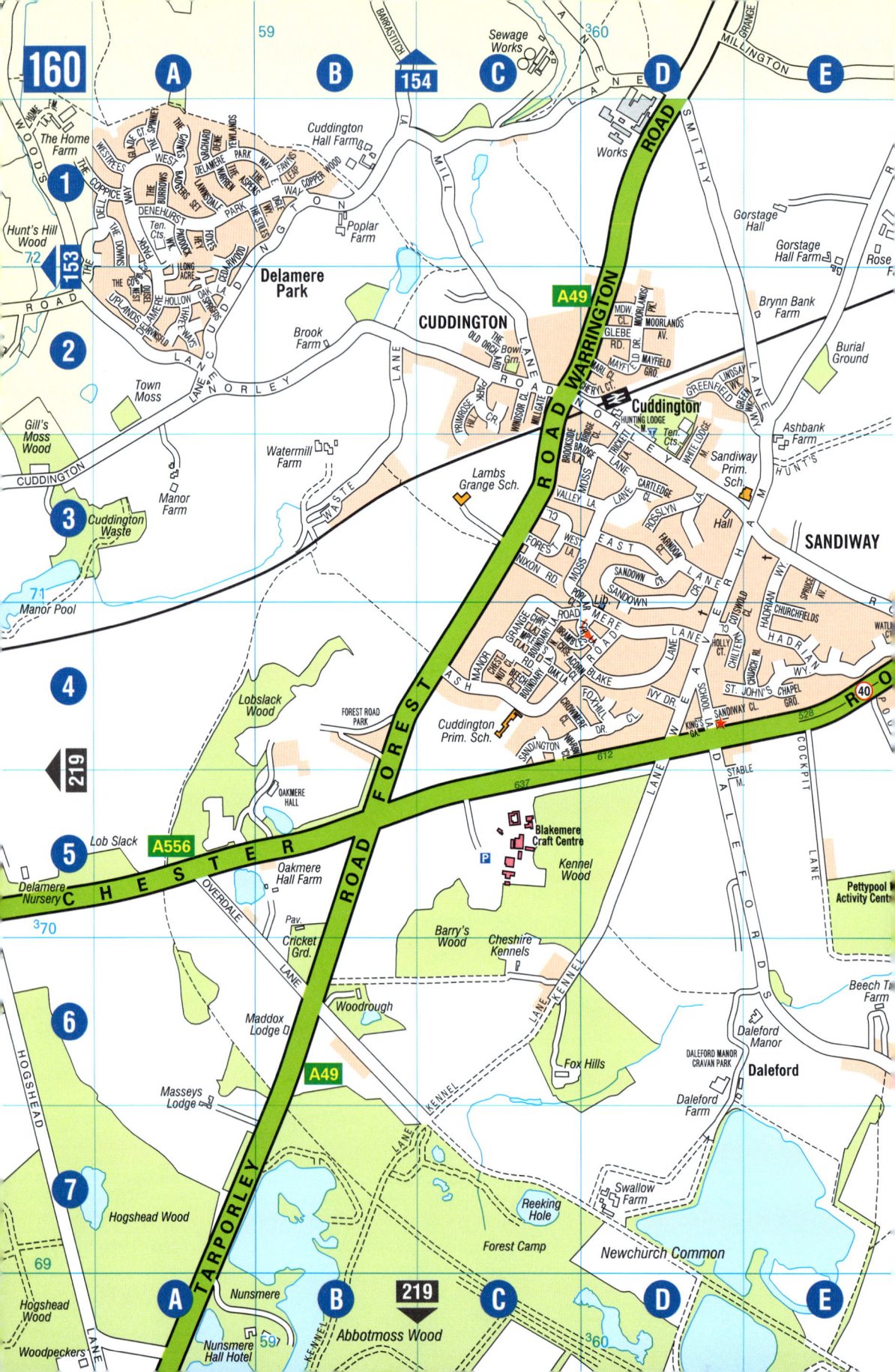

A
B
C
D
E
154
153
219
1
2
3
4
5
6
7
59
360
72
71
370
69
Sewage Works
Works
MILLINGTON
GRANGE
BARRASTITCH
The Home Farm
Cuddington Hall Farm
Poplar Farm
Delamere Park
Hunt's Hill Wood
WOOD'S ROAD
THE COPPICE
WESTREES
GLADE CT.
THE SPINNEY
THE CHINES
WEST WAY
ORCHARD DENE
YEWLANDS
DELAMERE WARREN
THE ASPENS
PARK WAY
FAWNS LEAP
COPPER WOOD
THE BURROWS
BADGERS SET
LAWNSDALE
DENEHURST PARK
PADDOCK
FOXES HEY
THE STILES
IVY DALE
DELL
THE DOWNS
Ten. Cts.
WK.
LONG ACRE
CEDARWOOD
HOLLOW
OAK SPINNEY
THREE WAYS
UPLANDS
DELAMERE
CUDDINGTON LANE
NORLEY LANE
Brook Farm
Town Moss
Gill's Moss Wood
CUDDINGTON
Manor Farm
Watermill Farm
Cuddington Waste
WASTE LANE
Manor Pool
MILL LANE
CUDDINGTON
A49
WARRINGTON ROAD
MDW. CL.
MOORLANDS PK.
MOORLANDS AV.
GLEBE RD.
MAYFIELD DR.
MAYFIELD GRO.
MARL CL.
CHERYL CT.
THE OLD ORCHARD
Bowl. Grn.
NORLEY ROAD
PRIMROSE HILL
PARK CR.
WINDSOR CL.
MILLGATE
Cuddington
HUNTING LODGE M.
Ten. Cts.
WHITE LODGE M.
GREENFIELD
LINDSAY WK.
GREEN WK.
SMITHY LANE
Gorstage Hall
Gorstage Hall Farm
Rose
Brynn Bank Farm
Burial Ground
Ashbank Farm
HUNT'S
Sandiway Prim. Sch.
Hall
SANDIWAY
Lambs Grange Sch.
BROOKSIDE
BRIDGE CL.
BRIDGE LA.
TRICKETT LA.
MOSS LANE
CARTLEDGE CL.
VALLEY LA.
ROSSLYN
FARNDON CL.
WEST LA.
FOREST CL.
NIXON RD.
EAST LANE
SANDOWN CR.
SANDOWN
Lib.
POPLAR CL.
MERE ROAD
WEAVERHAM LANE
CR.
COTSWOLD CL.
CHILTERN
HOLLY CT.
HADRIAN WY.
HADRIAN WY.
SPRUCE AV.
CHURCHFIELDS
CHURCH RI.
ST. JOHN'S
CHAPEL GRO.
GRANGE
MANOR
CHESTNUT CL.
BOUNDARY LA.
BECH CL.
OAK LA.
ACORN CL.
BLAKE LANE
FOXHILL
DR.
CL.
CROWMERE CL.
IVY DR.
SCHOOL LA.
SANDIWAY CL.
KING'S GA.
ASH ROAD
SANDINGTON
WHARTON CL.
40
528
612
637
FOREST ROAD PARK
Cuddington Prim. Sch.
Lobslack Wood
OAKMERE HALL
FOREST ROAD
STABLE M.
COCKPIT LANE
DALEFORDS
Pettypool Activity Centre
Lob Slack
A556
CHESTER ROAD
Delamere Nursery
Oakmere Hall Farm
OVERDALE LANE
Blakemere Craft Centre
P
Kennel Wood
Pav.
Cricket Grd.
Barry's Wood
Cheshire Kennels
KENNEL LANE
Beech Tree Farm
Daleford Manor
DALEFORD MANOR CRAVAN PARK
Daleford
Daleford Farm
Woodrough
Maddox Lodge
Fox Hills
HOGSHEAD
Masseys Lodge
A49
KENNEL
LANE
TARPORLEY ROAD
Hogshead Wood
Reeking Hole
Swallow Farm
Forest Camp
Newchurch Common
Nunsmere
Hogshead Wood
Woodpeckers
LANE
Nunsmere Hall Hotel
Abbotmoss Wood
KENNEL

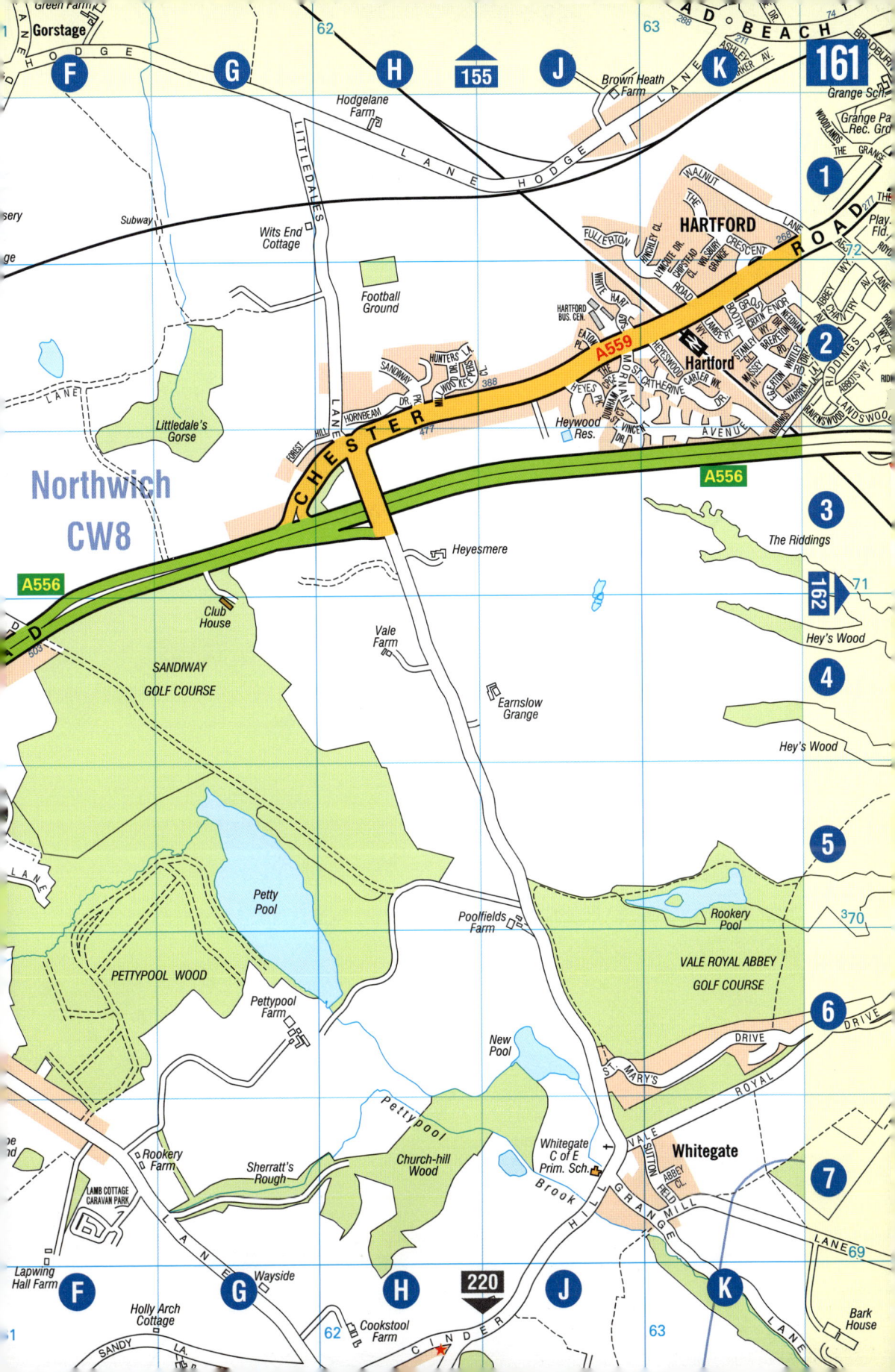
161
155
162
220
Gorstage
Hodgelane Farm
Brown Heath Farm
Wits End Cottage
Football Ground
HARTFORD
Hartford
Heywood Res.
Littledale's Gorse
Northwich
CW8
A556
A559
CHESTER ROAD
Heyesmere
The Riddings
Club House
Vale Farm
Hey's Wood
SANDIWAY GOLF COURSE
Earnslow Grange
Petty Pool
PETTYPOOL WOOD
Poolfields Farm
Rookery Pool
VALE ROYAL ABBEY GOLF COURSE
Pettypool Farm
New Pool
Rookery Farm
Sherratt's Rough
Church-hill Wood
Whitegate C of E Prim. Sch.
Whitegate
LAMB COTTAGE CARAVAN PARK
Lapwing Hall Farm
Wayside
Holly Arch Cottage
Cookstool Farm
Bark House
SANDY LA.
CINDER
Pettypool Brook
HILL
GRANGE MILL LANE
VALE ROYAL DRIVE
ST. MARY'S DRIVE
LITTLEDALES LANE
HODGE LANE
Subway

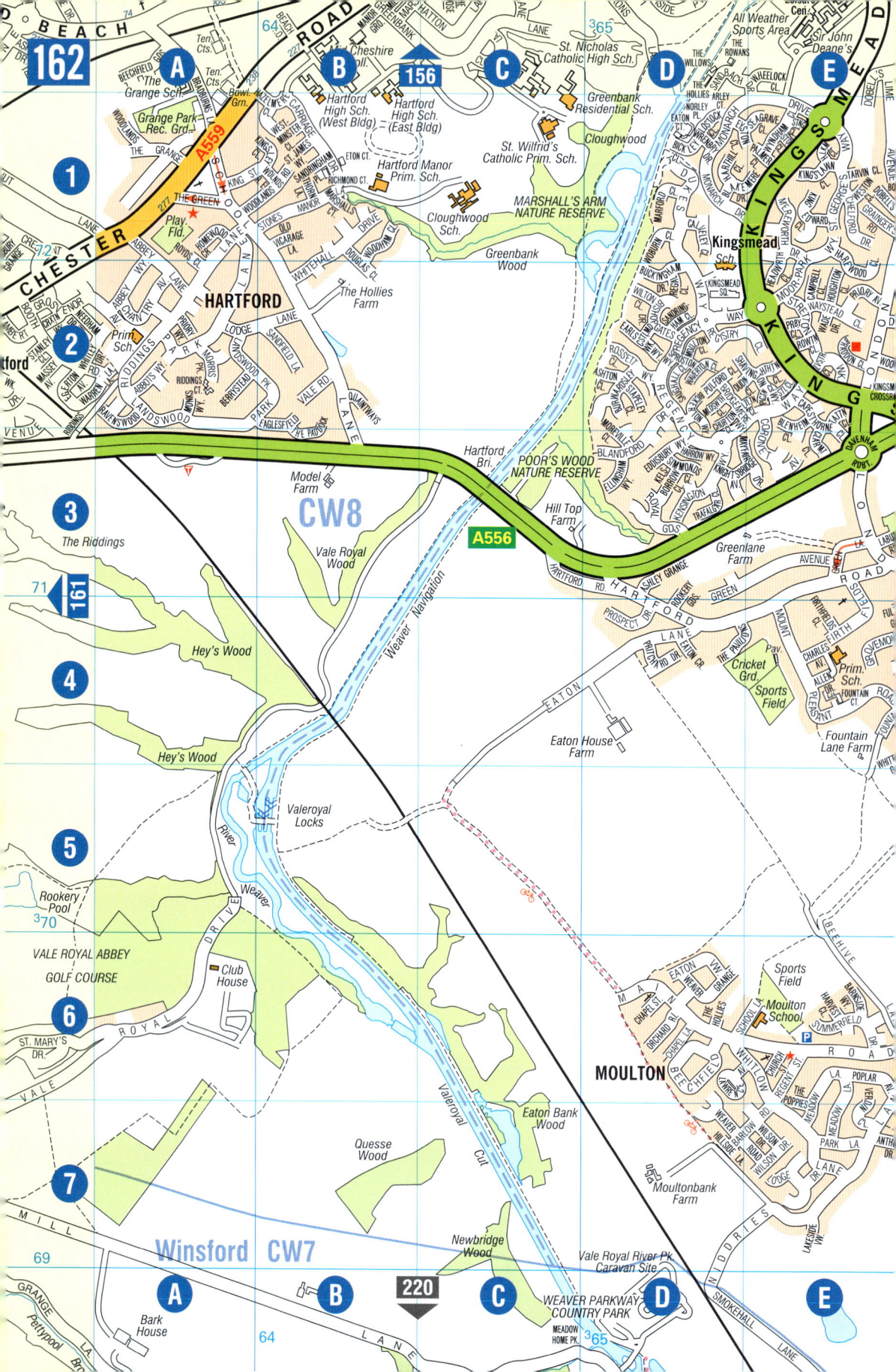

156
161
220
A
B
C
D
E
1
2
3
4
5
6
7
64
365
72
71
370
69
CHESTER ROAD
BEACH
A559
A556
HARTFORD
The Grange Sch.
Grange Park Rec. Grd.
Play. Fld.
Prim. Sch.
Mid Cheshire Coll.
Hartford High Sch. (West Bldg)
Hartford High Sch. (East Bldg)
Hartford Manor Prim. Sch.
Cloughwood Sch.
St. Nicholas Catholic High Sch.
Greenbank Residential Sch.
St. Wilfrid's Catholic Prim. Sch.
Cloughwood
MARSHALL'S ARM NATURE RESERVE
Greenbank Wood
The Hollies Farm
All Weather Sports Area
Sir John Deane's
Kingsmead
Kingsmead Sch.
KINGSMEAD
DAVENHAM RDBT.
Hartford Bri.
POOR'S WOOD NATURE RESERVE
Hill Top Farm
Model Farm
CW8
Vale Royal Wood
The Riddings
Hey's Wood
Weaver Navigation
Greenlane Farm
HARTFORD RD.
ASHLEY GRANGE
Cricket Grd.
Sports Field
Prim. Sch.
Fountain Lane Farm
EATON
Eaton House Farm
Valeroyal Locks
River Weaver
Rookery Pool
VALE ROYAL ABBEY GOLF COURSE
Club House
ROYAL
VALE
ST. MARY'S DR.
DRIVE
Valeroyal Cut
Eaton Bank Wood
Quesse Wood
MOULTON
Moulton School
Sports Field
Moultonbank Farm
Newbridge Wood
Vale Royal River Pk. Caravan Site
WEAVER PARKWAY COUNTRY PARK
MEADOW HOME PK.
Winsford CW7
MILL LANE
Bark House
GRANGE LA.
Pettypool
NIDDRIES
SMOKEHALL LANE

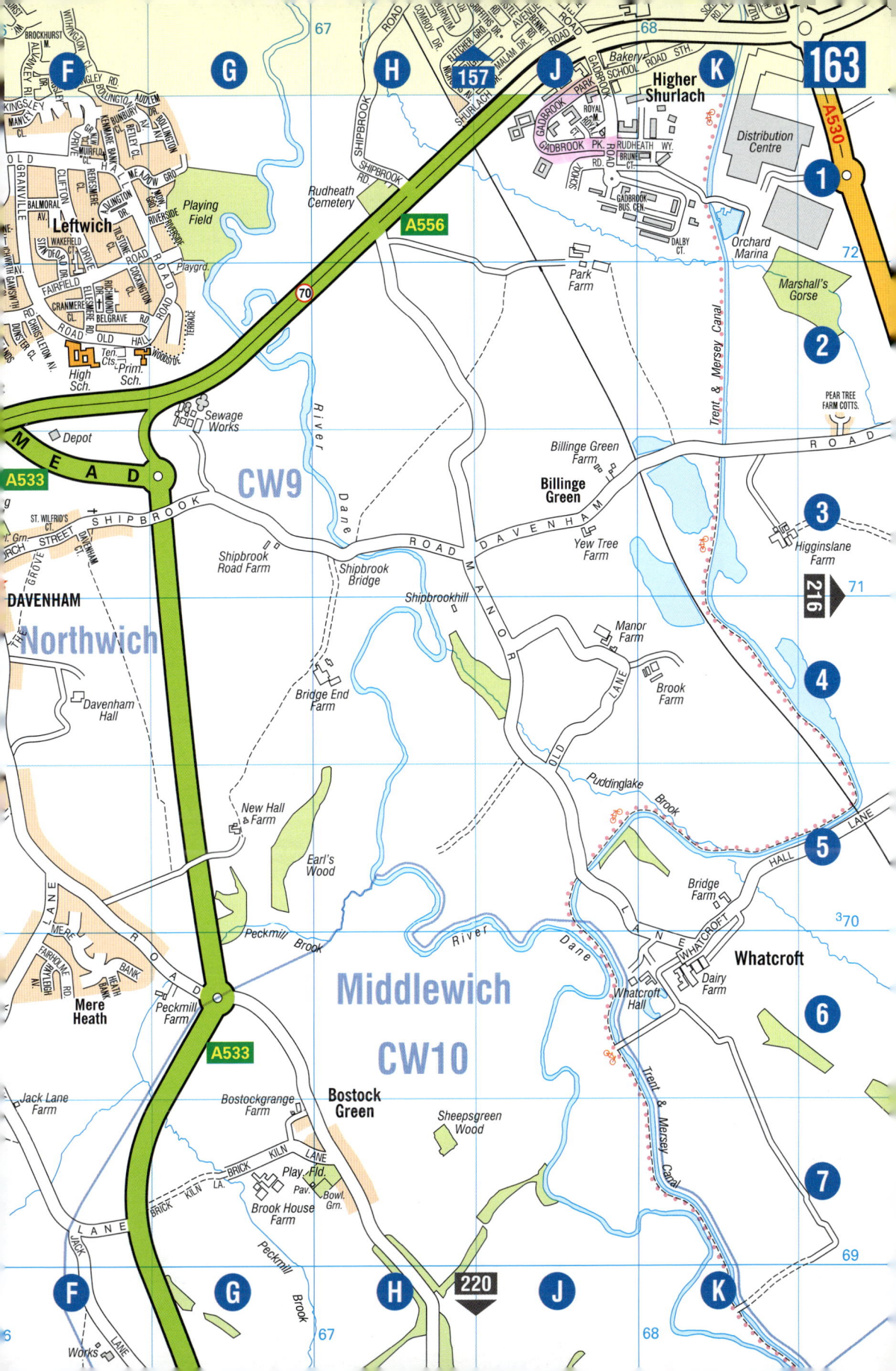
Higher Shurlach
Leftwich
Playing Field
Rudheath Cemetery
A556
A530
Distribution Centre
Orchard Marina
Marshall's Gorse
Park Farm
Sewage Works
Depot
A533
MEAD
CW9
SHIPBROOK ROAD
DAVENHAM ROAD
Billinge Green
Billinge Green Farm
Yew Tree Farm
Higginslane Farm
Shipbrook Road Farm
Shipbrook Bridge
Shipbrookhill
DAVENHAM
Northwich
Manor Farm
Brook Farm
Davenham Hall
Bridge End Farm
River Dane
Trent & Mersey Canal
Puddinglake Brook
New Hall Farm
Earl's Wood
Bridge Farm
Whatcroft
Dairy Farm
Whatcroft Hall
Peckmill Brook
Middlewich
CW10
Mere Heath
Peckmill Farm
Jack Lane Farm
Bostockgrange Farm
Bostock Green
Sheepsgreen Wood
Play. Fld.
Brook House Farm
BRICK KILN LANE
JACK LANE
Works
High Sch.
Prim. Sch.
PEAR TREE FARM COTTS.
MANOR
OLD LANE
WHATCROFT LANE
HALL LANE
GADBROOK PK.
GADBROOK BUS. CEN.
RUDHEATH WY.
SCHOOL ROAD STH.
Bakery
157
216
220

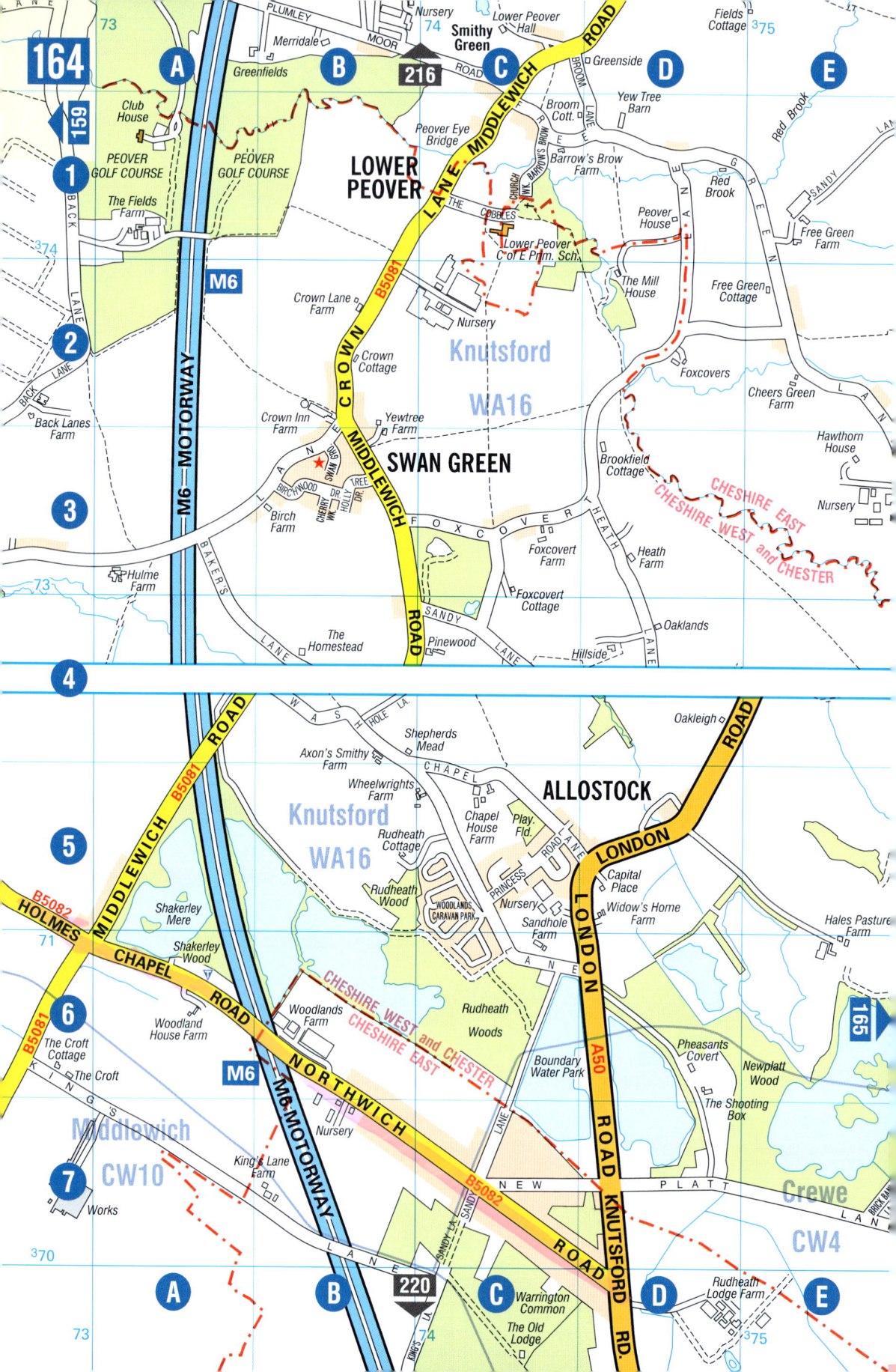
LOWER PEOVER
SWAN GREEN
ALLOSTOCK
Smithy Green
Knutsford
WA16
Middlewich
CW10
Crewe
CW4
M6 MOTORWAY
MIDDLEWICH LANE
CROWN LANE
MIDDLEWICH ROAD
LONDON ROAD
KNUTSFORD RD.
NORTHWICH ROAD
HOLMES CHAPEL ROAD
PLUMLEY MOOR ROAD
PEOVER GOLF COURSE
Club House
The Fields Farm
Back Lanes Farm
Hulme Farm
Greenfields
Merridale
Nursery
Lower Peover Hall
Greenside
Fields Cottage
Yew Tree Barn
Broom Cott.
Peover Eye Bridge
Barrow's Brow Farm
Red Brook
Peover House
Free Green Farm
Free Green Cottage
Lower Peover C of E Prim. Sch.
The Mill House
Crown Lane Farm
Crown Cottage
Foxcovers
Cheers Green Farm
Hawthorn House
Crown Inn Farm
Yewtree Farm
Brookfield Cottage
Nursery
Birch Farm
Foxcovert Farm
Heath Farm
Foxcovert Cottage
Oaklands
The Homestead
Pinewood
Hillside
CHESHIRE EAST
CHESHIRE WEST and CHESTER
Oakleigh
Shepherds Mead
Axon's Smithy Farm
Wheelwrights Farm
Chapel House Farm
Play. Fld.
Rudheath Cottage
Rudheath Wood
WOODLANDS CARAVAN PARK
Capital Place
Widow's Home Farm
Sandhole Farm
Hales Pasture Farm
Shakerley Mere
Shakerley Wood
Woodland House Farm
Woodlands Farm
Rudheath Woods
Boundary Water Park
Pheasants Covert
Newplatt Wood
The Shooting Box
The Croft Cottage
The Croft
King's Lane Farm
Works
Warrington Common
The Old Lodge
Rudheath Lodge Farm
B5081
B5082
A50
M6
216
220
159
165

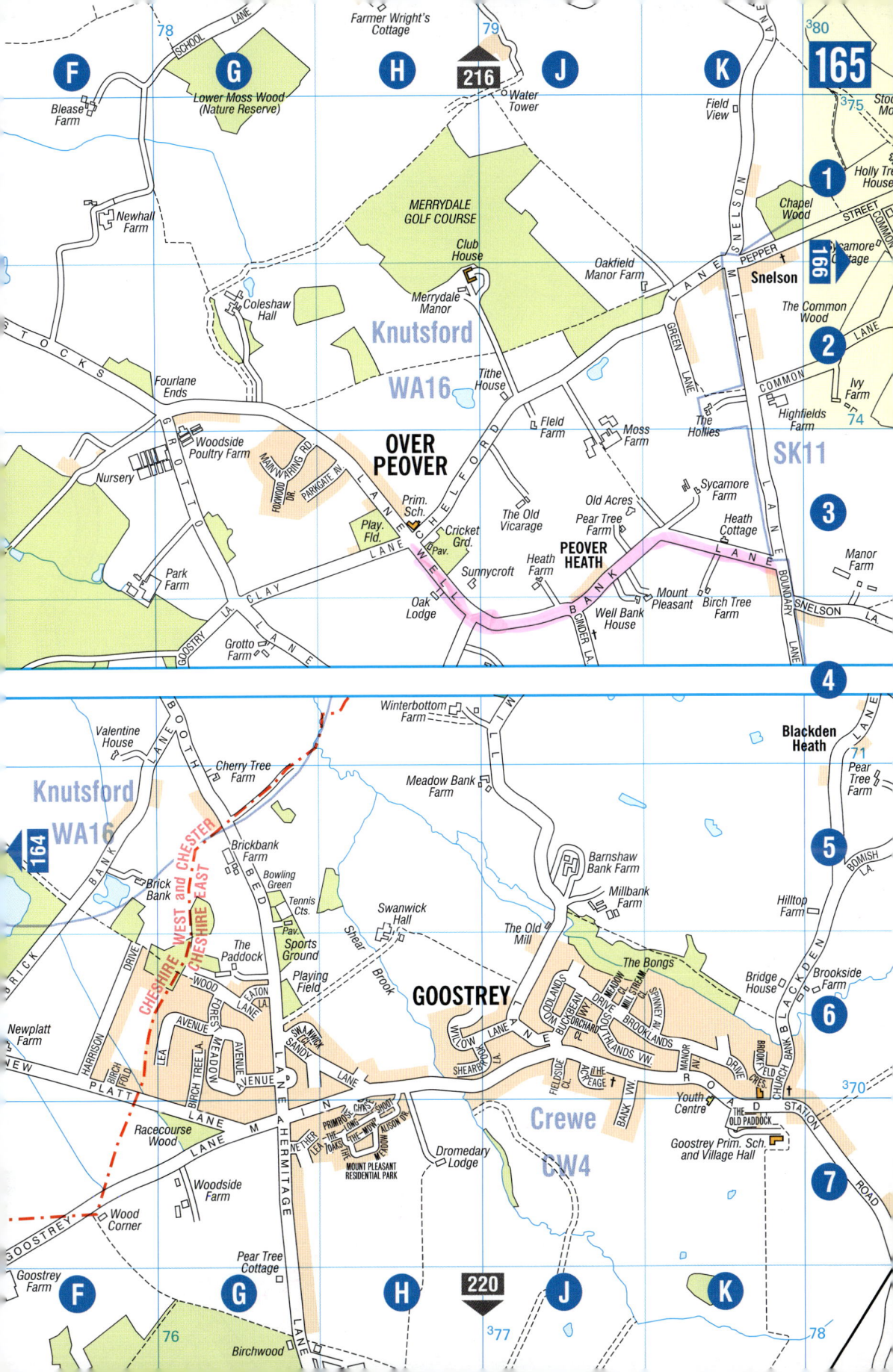
Farmer Wright's Cottage
Blease Farm
Lower Moss Wood (Nature Reserve)
School Lane
Water Tower
Field View
Newhall Farm
MERRYDALE GOLF COURSE
Club House
Merrydale Manor
Coleshaw Hall
Knutsford
WA16
Oakfield Manor Farm
Chapel Wood
Holly Tree House
Pepper Street
Sycamore Cottage
Snelson
The Common Wood
Common Lane
Ivy Farm
Highfields Farm
Stocks Lane
Fourlane Ends
Tithe House
Field Farm
Moss Farm
The Hollies
SK11
Woodside Poultry Farm
Nursery
Mainwaring Rd.
Foxwood Dr.
Parkgate Av.
OVER PEOVER
Prim. Sch.
Chelford
Play. Fld.
Cricket Grd.
Pav.
The Old Vicarage
Old Acres
Pear Tree Farm
Sycamore Farm
Heath Cottage
PEOVER HEATH
Manor Farm
Grotto Lane
Park Farm
Clay Lane
Well Lane
Sunnycroft
Heath Farm
Bank Lane
Mount Pleasant
Birch Tree Farm
Snelson La.
Boundary Lane
Oak Lodge
Well Bank House
Cinder La.
Goostrey La.
Grotto Farm
Green Lane
Mill Lane
Snelson Lane
Winterbottom Farm
Valentine House
Booth Bed Lane
Cherry Tree Farm
Blackden Heath
Pear Tree Farm
Meadow Bank Farm
Knutsford
WA16
Brickbank Farm
Bowling Green
Tennis Cts.
Barnshaw Bank Farm
Millbank Farm
Brick Bank
Swanwick Hall
Hilltop Farm
Bomish La.
CHESHIRE WEST and CHESTER
CHESHIRE EAST
The Old Mill
The Paddock
Pav.
Sports Ground
Shear Brook
The Bongs
Bridge House
Brookside Farm
Playing Field
GOOSTREY
Newplatt Farm
Harrison Drive
Wood Lane
Eaton La.
Avenue
Forest Lea
Meadow Avenue
Birch Tree La.
Swanwick Cl.
Sandy Lane
Willow Lane
Woodlands
Buckbean
Ivy
Orchard Cl.
Meadow Cl.
Mill Stream Cl.
Spinney Av.
Southlands Vw.
Brooklands
Manor Av.
Drive
Brookfield Cres.
Church Bank
Blackden Lane
Shearbrook La.
Fieldside Cl.
The Acreage
Bank Vw.
Youth Centre
The Old Paddock
Birch Fold
New Platt Lane
Main Road
Station Road
Racecourse Wood
Crewe
CW4
Goostrey Prim. Sch. and Village Hall
Nether Lea
Primrose Chase
The Oaks
The Long Shoot
The Mow
Alison Dr.
The Meadow
MOUNT PLEASANT RESIDENTIAL PARK
Dromedary Lodge
Woodside Farm
Hermitage Lane
Wood Corner
Goostrey Lane
Pear Tree Cottage
Goostrey Farm
Birchwood
F G H J K
1 2 3 4 5 6 7
78 79 380 375 74 71 370 76 377 78
216
166
164
220

217
118
216
165
217
A
B
C
D
E
1
2
3
4
5
6
7
Highgrove
Norbury Cottage
Heathgate Nursery
Heathgate Farm
The Little Moss
Little Moss Farm
Sandpit Farm
Brandons Poultry Farm
Playing Fields
Little Warford
Manor Farm
Warford Lodge
Ivy House
Pedley Brook Barn
Kell Green Hall
Enfield House
Oakside Cott.
Kell Green Farm
Ckt. Grd.
David Lewis National Epilepsy Centre
David Lewis School
Alderley Edge
SK9
Warford Hall
Jennings Farm
Baguley Fold
Oak Tree Farm
Homfield
Fairlea
Dale Hatton
Holly Tree Farm
Pinewood Farm
Beech Farm
Stelfox Hall Farm
SK10
Dog Hole Wood
Peckmill Bottoms
Sossmoss Wood
Sycamore Farm
Wyche Farm
Lomas's Bottoms
Macclesfield
Fir Tree Cottage
Corbishley Bri.
Peck Mill Farm
Marthall
Knutsford
WA16
Moat Hall
Pear Tree Farm
Marthall Mill
Wks.
Old Moat Hall
Firtree Farm
Brick Hills
Callwood's Moss
Line Pits
Roadside Farm
Roadside Ct.
CHELFORD
Long Meadow
A537
A535
Pedley Brook
Mere Hills Farm
Play. Fld.
Prim. Sch.
Cattle Market
SK11
Sunny Bank Farm
Bowling Green
Depot
Chelford
Stockin Moss
Holly Tree House
Chapel Wood
The Red House
Sycamore Cottage
Snelson
The Common Wood
Cinder Lane Farm
Pepper Trees
Heath Farm
Chelford Heath
Hall
Playing Field
Yewtree Farm
Bloor's Pits
CHELFORD ROUNDABOUT
Pav.
Cricket Grd.
Abbey Fm.
Willow Gaff
Chelford Bri. (North)
Manor Ho.
Church Cottages
Promontory Wood
War Mem.
Chelford Bri. (South)
Ivy Farm
Highfields Farm
Astle Cotts.
Kennel Bank
Peover Eye
Astle Hall
Astle Park
Chapel Wood
Heath Cottage
CHELFORD ROAD
KNUTSFORD ROAD
ALDERLEY ROAD
HOLMES CHAPEL RD.
PEPPER STREET
SNELSON LANE
MILL LANE
SANDLEBRIDGE LANE
KELL GREEN LANE
PINFOLD LANE
MILL LANE
ANCOATS LANE
ANCOATS ROAD
WARFORD LANE
MERRYMAN'S LANE
WARFORD HALL DR.
CARTER LANE
DIXON DRIVE
COMMON LANE
CINDER LA.
COMMON FARM LANE
PEOVER LANE
CONGLETON LANE
NURSERY LANE
SAND HOLE LA.
ENNERDALE CL.
ULLSWATER DR.
DERWENT WY.
BUTTERMERE DR.
CONISTON CL.
HEATHGATE COTTS.
SANDLEBRIDGE FARM
SANDLE BRIDGE RI.
WARFORD CR.
MILLBANK
DRUMBLE FLD.
HITCH
LOWES
BURNT ACRE
BARNCROFT
CHAPEL CT.
CHAPEL CFT.
HEYES DRIVE
WHEAT
CLAY
WOODLAND CL.
BROOMFIELD CL.
LANDS END
WOODFIN CT.
ELMSTEAD
ROBIN
OAK RD.
ASTLE CT.
STATION RD.
DIXON CT.
MERE CT.
GRGWD DR.

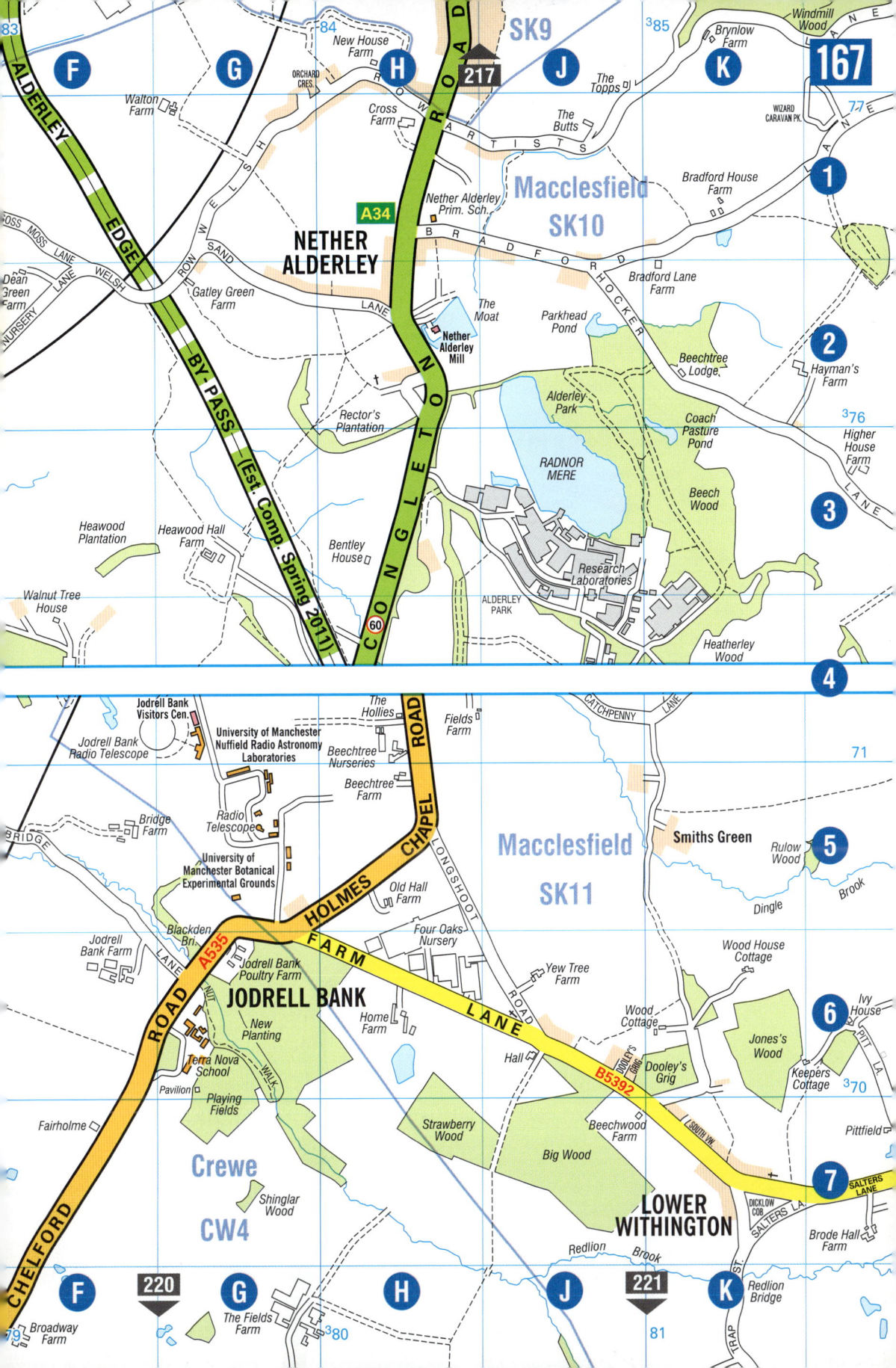

NETHER ALDERLEY
JODRELL BANK
LOWER WITHINGTON
Smiths Green
Macclesfield SK10
Macclesfield SK9
Macclesfield SK11
Crewe CW4
ALDERLEY EDGE BY-PASS (Est. Comp. Spring 2011)
CONGLETON ROAD
A34
A535
B5392
HOLMES CHAPEL ROAD
CHELFORD ROAD
FARM LANE
ARTISTS LANE
BRADFORD LANE
HOCKER LANE
WELSH ROW
SAND LANE
SOSS MOSS LANE
NURSERY LANE
CATCHPENNY LANE
LONGSHOOT ROAD
BLACKDEN LANE
SALTERS LANE
TRAP ST.
PITT LA.
SOUTH VW.
DOOLEY'S GRIG
NUT WALK
ORCHARD CRES.
WIZARD CARAVAN PK.
DICKLOW COB
ALDERLEY PARK
New House Farm
Walton Farm
Cross Farm
The Topps
The Butts
Brynlow Farm
Windmill Wood
Bradford House Farm
Nether Alderley Prim. Sch.
Gatley Green Farm
Dean Green Farm
Bradford Lane Farm
The Moat
Nether Alderley Mill
Parkhead Pond
Beechtree Lodge
Hayman's Farm
Alderley Park
Rector's Plantation
Coach Pasture Pond
Higher House Farm
RADNOR MERE
Beech Wood
Heawood Plantation
Heawood Hall Farm
Bentley House
Research Laboratories
Walnut Tree House
Heatherley Wood
Jodrell Bank Visitors Cen.
Jodrell Bank Radio Telescope
University of Manchester Nuffield Radio Astronomy Laboratories
The Hollies
Fields Farm
Beechtree Nurseries
Beechtree Farm
Bridge Farm
Radio Telescope
University of Manchester Botanical Experimental Grounds
Old Hall Farm
Rulow Wood
Dingle Brook
Four Oaks Nursery
Blackden Bri.
Jodrell Bank Farm
Jodrell Bank Poultry Farm
Yew Tree Farm
Wood House Cottage
Home Farm
New Planting
Wood Cottage
Jones's Wood
Ivy House
Hall
Dooley's Grig
Keepers Cottage
Terra Nova School
Pavilion
Playing Fields
Fairholme
Strawberry Wood
Beechwood Farm
Big Wood
Pittfield
Shinglar Wood
Brode Hall Farm
Redlion Brook
Redlion Bridge
The Fields Farm
Broadway Farm
F G H J K
1 2 3 4 5 6 7
217
220
221
83 84 385 77 376 71 370 79 380 81
60

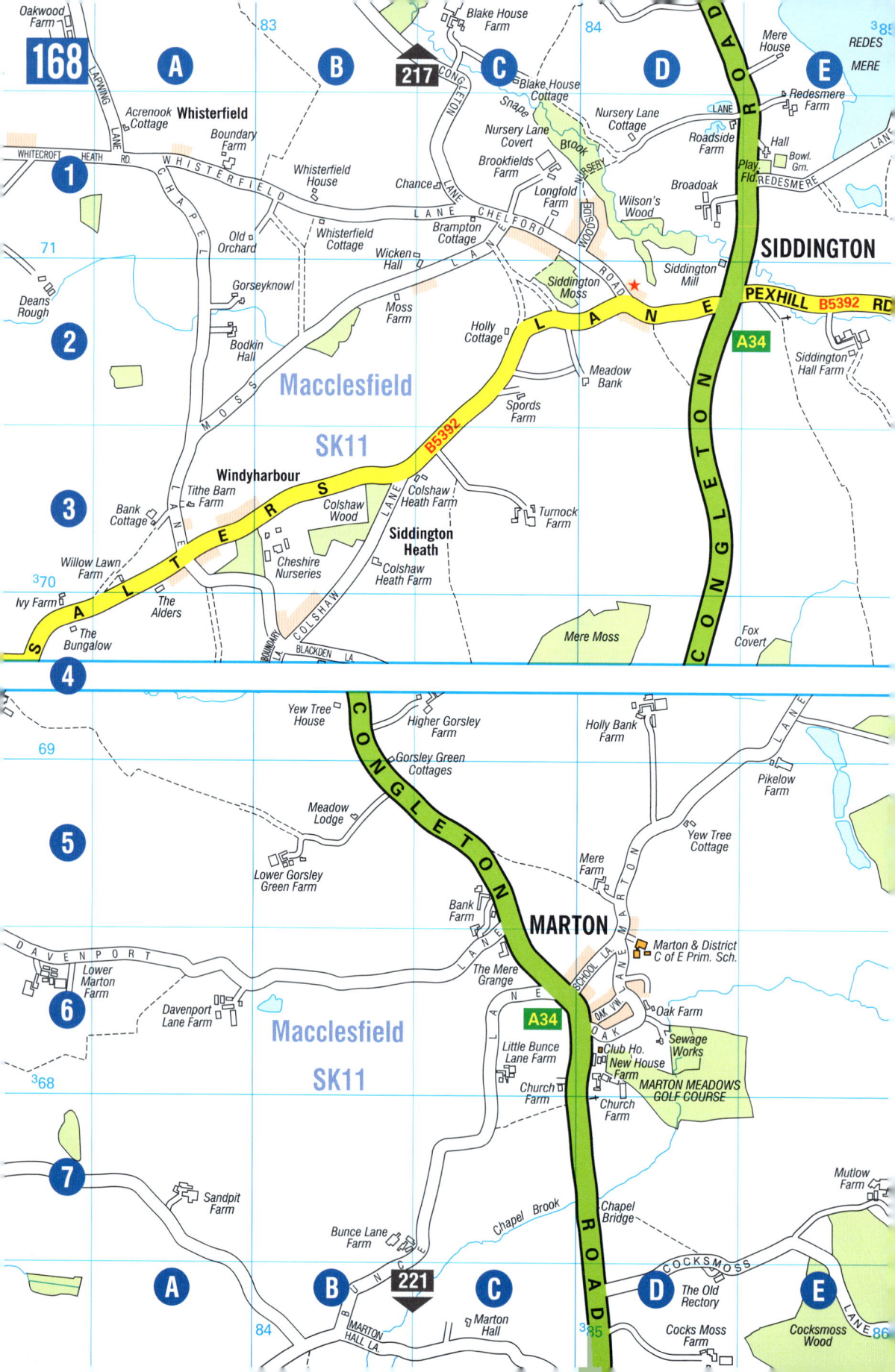
217
221
Whisterfield
SIDDINGTON
Windyharbour
Siddington Heath
MARTON
Macclesfield
SK11
Macclesfield
SK11
Oakwood Farm
Blake House Farm
Blake House Cottage
Mere House
REDES MERE
Redesmere Farm
Acrenook Cottage
Boundary Farm
Nursery Lane Cottage
Nursery Lane Covert
Roadside Farm
Hall
Bowl. Grn.
Play. Fld.
Brookfields Farm
Whisterfield House
Chance
Longfold Farm
Broadoak
Wilson's Wood
Old Orchard
Whisterfield Cottage
Brampton Cottage
Wicken Hall
Siddington Mill
Deans Rough
Gorseyknowl
Siddington Moss
Moss Farm
Holly Cottage
PEXHILL RD
B5392
A34
Siddington Hall Farm
Bodkin Hall
Meadow Bank
Spords Farm
Tithe Barn Farm
Colshaw Heath Farm
Turnock Farm
Bank Cottage
Colshaw Wood
Cheshire Nurseries
Colshaw Heath Farm
Willow Lawn Farm
Ivy Farm
The Alders
The Bungalow
Mere Moss
Fox Covert
SALTERS LANE
CONGLETON ROAD
WHITECROFT HEATH RD.
WHISTERFIELD LANE
LAPWING LANE
CHAPEL LANE
MOSS LANE
CONGLETON LANE
CHELFORD LANE
CHELFORD ROAD
WOODSIDE
NURSERY
Snape Brook
REDESMERE
COLSHAW
BOUNDARY LA.
BLACKDEN LA.
Yew Tree House
Higher Gorsley Farm
Holly Bank Farm
Gorsley Green Cottages
Pikelow Farm
Meadow Lodge
Yew Tree Cottage
Lower Gorsley Green Farm
Mere Farm
Bank Farm
Marton & District C of E Prim. Sch.
Lower Marton Farm
The Mere Grange
Oak Farm
Davenport Lane Farm
Little Bunce Lane Farm
Club Ho.
Sewage Works
New House Farm
MARTON MEADOWS GOLF COURSE
Church Farm
Church Farm
Sandpit Farm
Mutlow Farm
Chapel Bridge
Chapel Brook
Bunce Lane Farm
The Old Rectory
Marton Hall
Cocks Moss Farm
Cocksmoss Wood
DAVENPORT LANE
SCHOOL LA.
MARTON LANE
OAK VW.
OAK LANE
BUNCE LANE
COCKSMOSS LANE
MARTON HALL LA.
A B C D E
1 2 3 4 5 6 7
83 84 385 86
371 370 369 368

TEGG'S NOSE COUNTRY PARK
Birch Knoll
Ward's Knob
Tupclose Farm
Teggsnose Wood
Teggsnose Reservoir
LANGLEY
Playing Field
Factory
Bottoms Reservoir
Higher Ridgegate Farm
Sunnycroft
River Bollin
Weir
Highlow Farm
Clarke Lane Farm
Hollinhey Wood
Works
RIDGEGATE RESERVOIR
Reservoir
Macclesfield
SK11
Throstlenest
Greenbarn
Ridgehill Farm
Manor Farm
Ridgehill
Mosslea Farm
Hallycombs Farm
Rossendale Hall
Long Ridge
Backridges Farm
Wetton Way
Lees House Farm
Danes Farm
Rossendale Brook
Rossendale Wood
Lower Drove Hey Farm
Symondley Farm
Bank Top Farm
Ridge Hall
The Bungalow
Bollin Head House
Thickwithens
Big Plantation
White House Farm
Lane End Farm
Bank Farm
Old Brickbank Wood
Waggon Cottage
Smithy Farm
Bell Farm
Kennel Wood
Keeper's Cottage
EATON
Oakley
Hillmoor Farm
Quarry
A536
Hall
Yewtree Farm
Congleton
CW12
Rectory Cottage
Midway House Farm
A34
Tanhouse
River Dane
Cranberry Moss
Eaton Cottage Farm
Cave
Havannah
Weir
Moss Farm
Factory
Havannah Prim. Sch.
Lower Heath
Smithy Farm
Westlow Mere
Playing Field
Play. Fld.
Birch Moss Farm
CONGLETON RD.
MANCHESTER ROAD
MACCLESFIELD ROAD

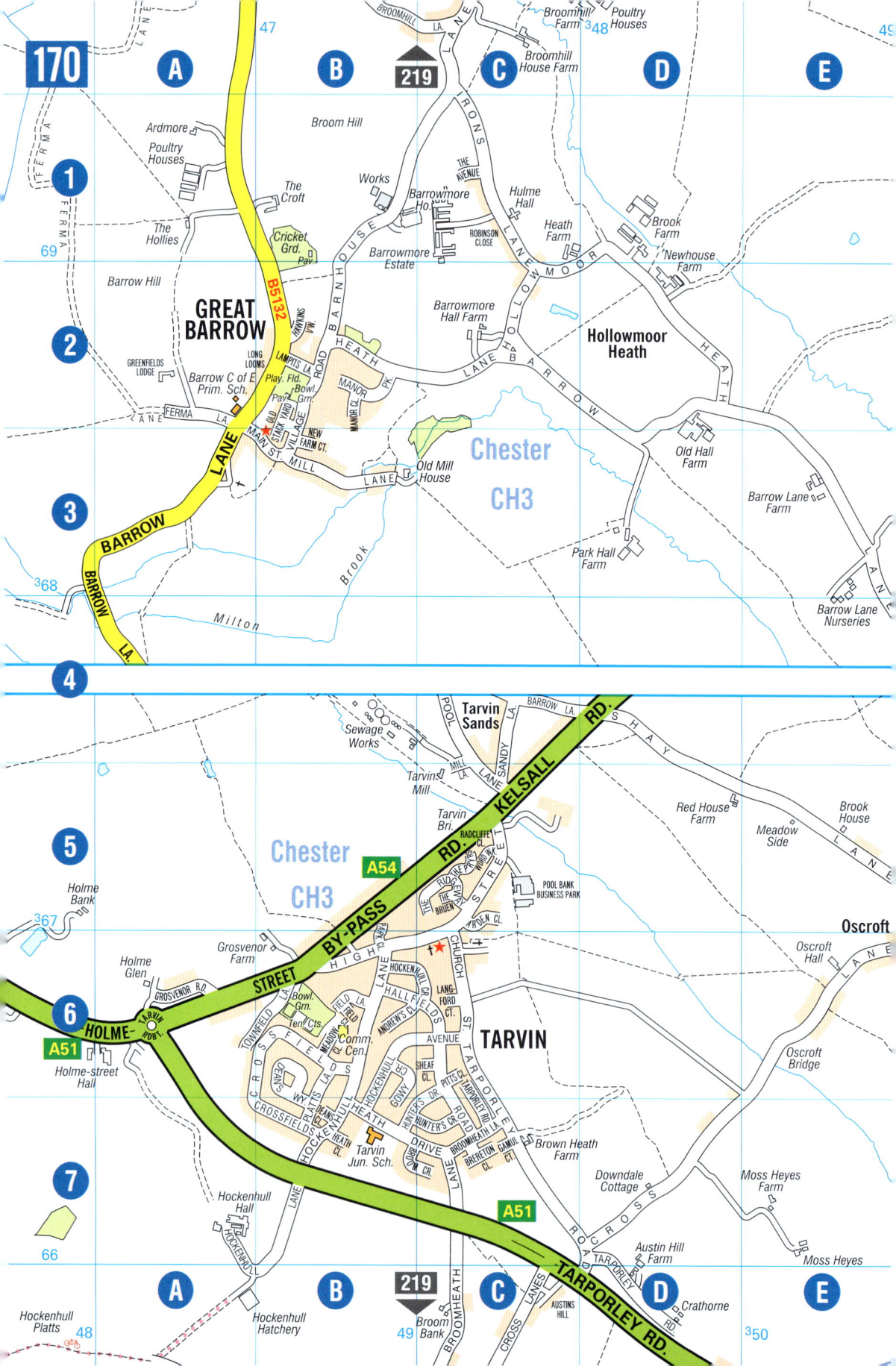

219
GREAT BARROW
Hollowmoor Heath
Chester CH3
Broom Hill
Ardmore
Poultry Houses
The Croft
The Hollies
Cricket Grd.
Barrow Hill
Works
Barrowmore Ho.
Barrowmore Estate
Robinson Close
The Avenue
Hulme Hall
Heath Farm
Brook Farm
Newhouse Farm
Broomhill Farm
Broomhill House Farm
Barrowmore Hall Farm
Greenfields Lodge
Barrow C of E Prim. Sch.
Long Looms
Hawkins Vw.
Lampits La.
Play. Fld.
Bowl. Grn.
Old Stack Yard
Village Road
New Farm Ct.
Manor Cl.
Manor Pk.
Main St.
Mill Lane
Old Mill House
Old Hall Farm
Barrow Lane Farm
Park Hall Farm
Barrow Lane Nurseries
Milton Brook
Barrow Lane
B5132
Broomhill La.
Irons Lane
Hollowmoor Heath Lane
Barnhouse Road
Heath Lane
Barrow Lane
Ferma Lane
TARVIN
Tarvin Sands
Sewage Works
Tarvins Mill
Tarvin Bri.
Chester CH3
Pool Lane
Mill La.
Sandy La.
Barrow La.
Shay Lane
Kelsall Rd.
By-Pass Rd.
A54
A51
Red House Farm
Meadow Side
Brook House
Pool Bank Business Park
Oscroft
Oscroft Hall
Oscroft Bridge
Holme Bank
Holme Glen
Grosvenor Farm
Grosvenor Rd.
Holme-street Hall
Holme Street
Tarvin Rdbt.
High St.
Church St.
Radcliffe Cl.
The Ridgeway
The Bruen
Arden Cl.
Langford Ct.
Hockenhull Cr.
Hallfields
Andrew's Cl.
Field La.
Meadow Cl.
Comm. Cen.
Ten. Cts.
Bowl. Grn.
Townfield La.
Crossfields
Deans Wy
Platts La.
Deans Cl.
Heath Cl.
Hockenhull Lane
Heath Drive
Avenue
Sheaf Cl.
Pitts Cl.
Gowy Cr.
Hunters Dr.
Hunter's Cr.
Tarporley Road
Tarporley Rd.
Broomheath La.
Brereton Cl.
Gamul Ct.
Brook Cr.
Tarvin Jun. Sch.
Brown Heath Farm
Downdale Cottage
Moss Heyes Farm
Moss Heyes
Austin Hill Farm
Austins Hill
Crathorne
Cross Road
Cross Lanes
Broomheath Lane
Broom Bank
Hockenhull Hall
Hockenhull Hatchery
Hockenhull Platts

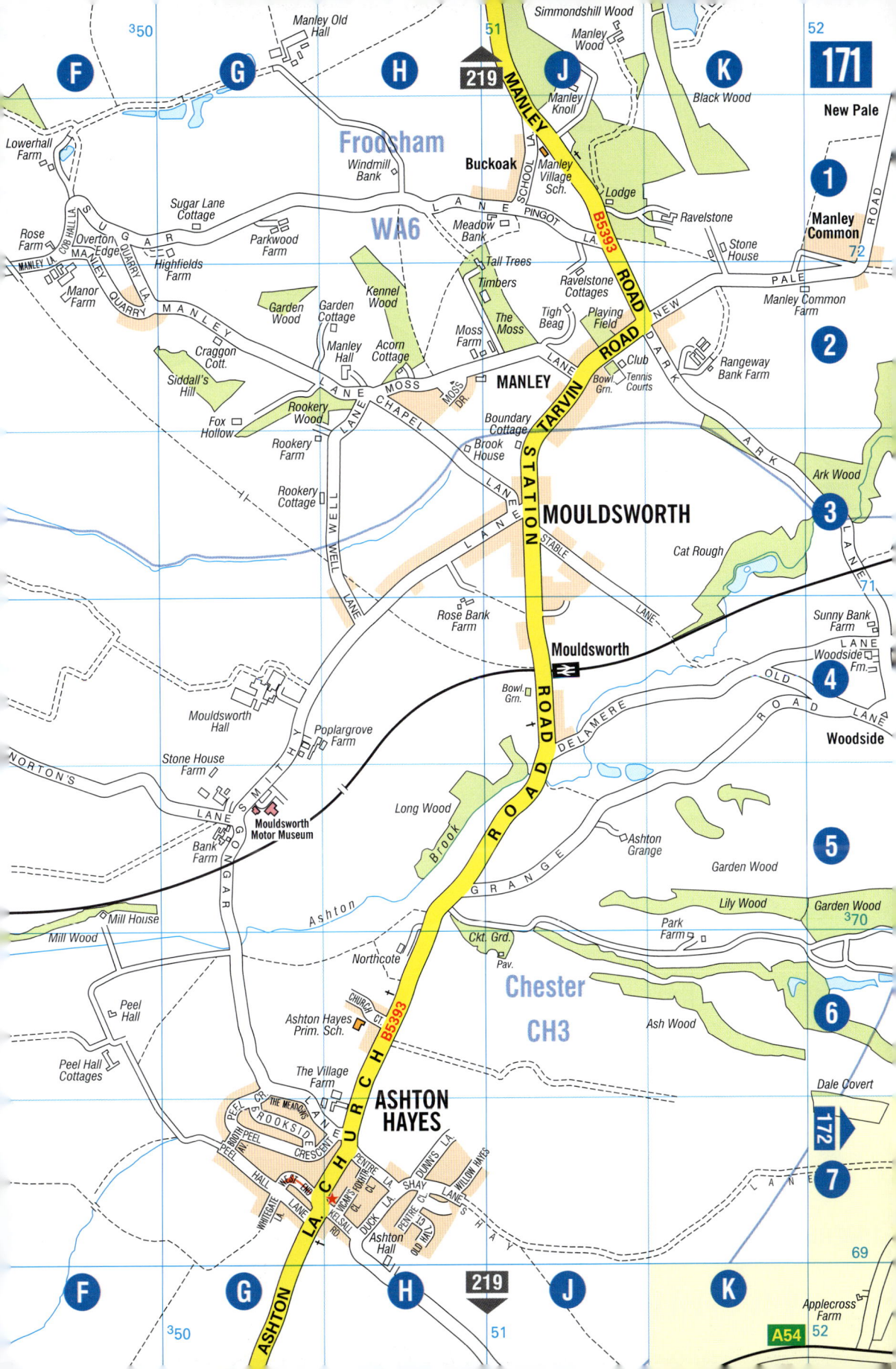
Frodsham
WA6
Buckoak
MANLEY
MOULDSWORTH
ASHTON HAYES
Chester
CH3
Manley Common
New Pale
Woodside
Mouldsworth
Manley Old Hall
Simmondshill Wood
Manley Wood
Manley Knoll
Black Wood
Lowerhall Farm
Windmill Bank
Manley Village Sch.
Lodge
Ravelstone
Sugar Lane Cottage
Parkwood Farm
Meadow Bank
Stone House
Rose Farm
Overton Edge
Highfields Farm
Tall Trees
Timbers
Ravelstone Cottages
Manley Common Farm
Manor Farm
Garden Wood
Garden Cottage
Kennel Wood
The Moss
Tigh Beag
Playing Field
Craggon Cott.
Moss Farm
Club
Bowl. Grn.
Tennis Courts
Rangeway Bank Farm
Siddall's Hill
Manley Hall
Acorn Cottage
Rookery Wood
Fox Hollow
Boundary Cottage
Rookery Farm
Brook House
Ark Wood
Rookery Cottage
Cat Rough
Rose Bank Farm
Sunny Bank Farm
Woodside Fm.
Mouldsworth Hall
Poplargrove Farm
Stone House Farm
Long Wood
Mouldsworth Motor Museum
Bank Farm
Ashton Grange
Garden Wood
Lily Wood
Mill House
Mill Wood
Ckt. Grd.
Pav.
Park Farm
Northcote
Peel Hall
Ashton Hayes Prim. Sch.
Ash Wood
Peel Hall Cottages
The Village Farm
Dale Covert
Ashton Hall
Applecross Farm
MANLEY ROAD
SCHOOL LA.
PINGOT LA.
SUGAR LANE
COB HALL LA.
MANLEY LA.
QUARRY LA.
MANLEY QUARRY
MANLEY LANE
MOSS LANE
MOSS DR.
CHAPEL LANE
NEW PALE
DARK LANE
ARK LANE
TARVIN ROAD
STATION ROAD
WELL LANE
STABLE LANE
OLD LANE
DELAMERE ROAD
NORTON'S LANE
SMITHY LANE
GONGAR LANE
GRANGE ROAD
Brook
Ashton
CHURCH CT.
CHURCH LA.
ASHTON LA.
PEEL CR.
THE MEADOWS
BROOKSIDE CRESCENT
BOOTH AV.
PEEL HALL LANE
WEST END
WHITEGATE LA.
VICAR'S CL.
FOXHILL CL.
PENTRE LA.
PENTRE CL.
KELSALL RD.
DUCK LA.
SHAY LANE
DUNN'S LA.
WILLOW HAYES
OLD HALL
B5393
A54
219
172
F G H J K
1 2 3 4 5 6 7
350 51 52 72 71 370 69

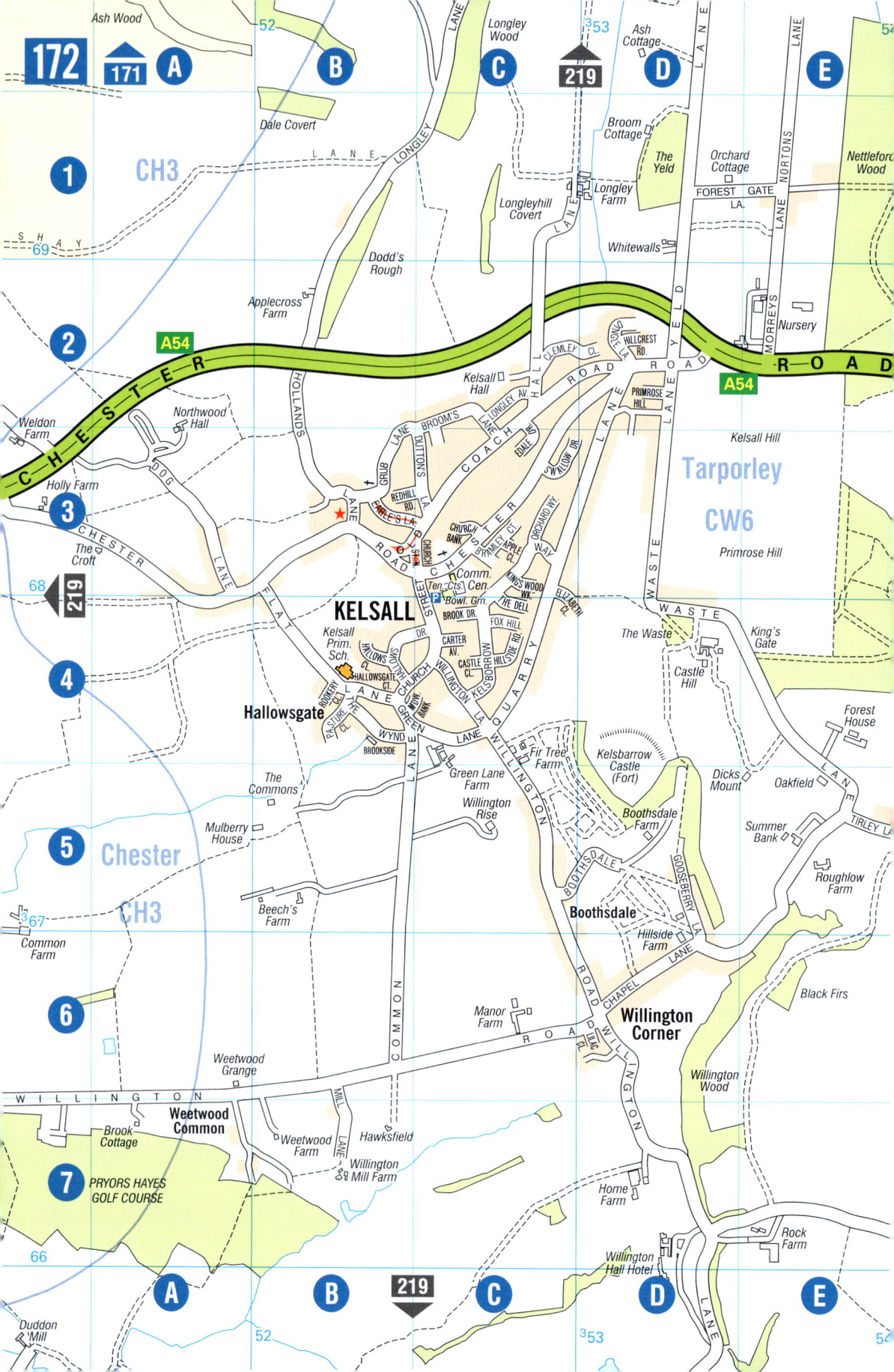

172
171
219
A
B
C
D
E
1
2
3
4
5
6
7
Ash Wood
Dale Covert
Longley Wood
Ash Cottage
Broom Cottage
The Yeld
Orchard Cottage
Nettleford Wood
CH3
LONGLEY LANE
SHAY LANE
Longleyhill Covert
Longley Farm
FOREST GATE LA.
NORTONS LANE
Whitewalls
Dodd's Rough
Applecross Farm
A54
CHESTER ROAD
MORREYS LANE
Nursery
HILLCREST RD.
DINGLE LA.
CLEMLEY CL.
Kelsall Hall
PRIMROSE HILL
YELD LANE
Weldon Farm
Northwood Hall
HOLLANDS
BROOM'S
LONGLEY AV.
HALL LANE
Kelsall Hill
Tarporley
CW6
Holly Farm
DOG LANE
GRUB LANE
DUTTON'S LA.
COACH ROAD
EDALE RD.
SWALLOW DR.
REDHILL RD.
EARLE'S LA.
The Croft
CHESTER ROAD
CHURCH BANK
BRAMLEY CT.
APPLE CL.
ORCHARD WY.
WAY
Primrose Hill
68
FLAT LANE
Comm. Cen.
Ten. Cts.
Bowl. Grn.
KINGSWOOD WK.
THE DELL
ELIZABETH CL.
WASTE LANE
KELSALL
BROOK DR.
FOX HILL
The Waste
King's Gate
Kelsall Prim. Sch.
CARTER AV.
HILLSIDE RD.
HALLOWS CL.
HALLOWSGATE CT.
CASTLE CL.
KELSBORROW
QUARRY LANE
Castle Hill
Hallowsgate
ROOKERY CL.
PASTURE CL.
THE WYND
BROOKSIDE
GREEN LANE
MDW. BANK
WILLINGTON LA.
Fir Tree Farm
Forest House
Kelsbarrow Castle (Fort)
Green Lane Farm
Dicks Mount
Oakfield
The Commons
Willington Rise
Boothsdale Farm
Mulberry House
TIRLEY LA.
Summer Bank
Chester
Roughlow Farm
BOOTHSDALE
GOOSEBERRY LA.
Beech's Farm
Boothsdale
67
Common Farm
CH3
Hillside Farm
CHAPEL LANE
Black Firs
COMMON LANE
Manor Farm
WILLINGTON ROAD
Willington Corner
LILAC CL.
Weetwood Grange
Willington Wood
Weetwood Common
Brook Cottage
Weetwood Farm
Hawksfield
MILL LANE
Willington Mill Farm
PRYORS HAYES GOLF COURSE
Home Farm
Rock Farm
66
Willington Hall Hotel
Duddon Mill
52
53
54

Windyhowe Farm
Dead Lake
215
DELAMERE FOREST TOURING PARK
Linmere-Moss Farm
Delamere
Hornby's Rough
DELAMERE FOREST GOLF COURSE
Long Ridge
Relicks Moss
Burnt Wood
Eddisbury Wood
STATION
GOLF
COURSE
ROAD
Club House
Works
Crown Farm Quarry
Stoneybutts Farm
FARM
Sand Quarry
B5152
FRITH AV.
Northwich
CW8
Station Farm
Oakmere
Eddisbury Hill
OLD PALE HEIGHTS
Eddisbury Hill Hill Fort
EDDISBURY HILL PARK
Hall Wood
Merrick's Hill
ROWAN CL.
DELAMERE GRO.
HILL
THE RIDGE
Delamere Lodge
Fourways Sand Quarry
A556
The Paddock
EDDISBURY
Eddisbury Hill Farm
Thieves Moss
Sewage Works
Brook Farm
STONEY
DELAMERE
ROAD
Moss Farm
Community Centre
Bowling Green
WASTE LA.
Bowyer's Waste
Rectory Farm
50
Works
CHRIMES DR.
MERE CR.
Waste Farm
WATLING DR.
LANE
Delamere C of E Prim. Sch.
CHESTER
ABBEY
A556
MIDDLEWICH
A54
Abbeywood Cottage
Nursery
Keeper's Cottage
Abbey Wood
Abbey Arms Wood
Tarporley
CW6
The Grange
Cherry Orchard Farm
LANE
ROAD
Works
Oak Tree Farm
CHESTER
Oak Mere
Water Farm
A54
Valley Farm
Harrow Hill
Blackbank Wood
FISHPOOL
Oakmere House
Pigwood Bungalows
ROAD
Fishpool Farm
B5152
Sandymere
Sandy Mere
Sandymere Plantation
Fishpool Lane Farm
OTTERSBANK MEWS
Tirley Hollow
219
ROAD
Quarry
Sandymere Nursery
Tirley End
A49
F
G
H
J
K
1
2
3
4
5
6
7
355
56
57
370
69
68
67

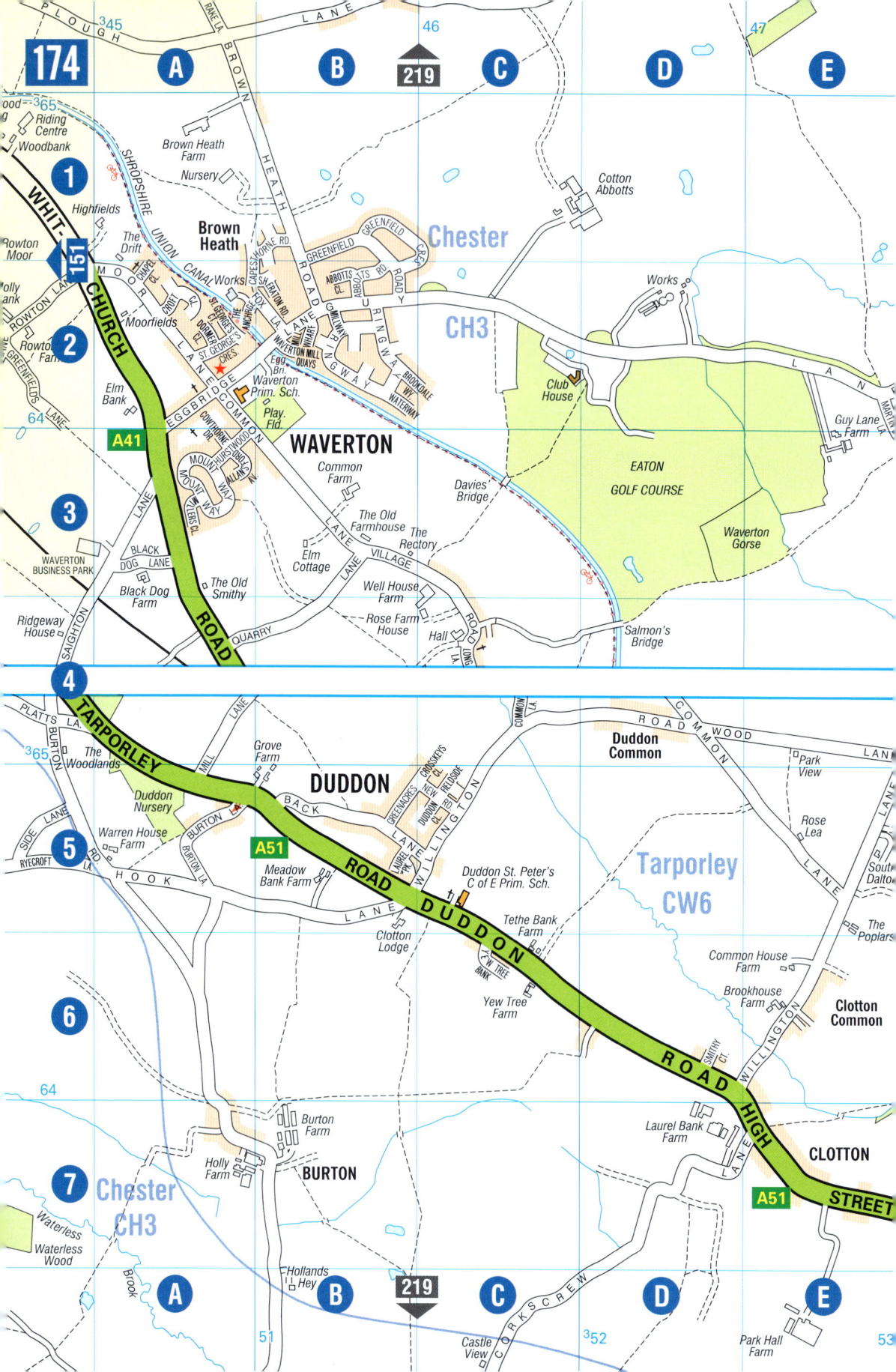

WAVERTON
Brown Heath
Chester
CH3
DUDDON
Duddon Common
Tarporley
CW6
Clotton Common
CLOTTON
BURTON
Chester
CH3
EATON GOLF COURSE
Waverton Gorse
Club House
Cotton Abbotts
Brown Heath Farm
Riding Centre
Woodbank
Highfields
Rowton Moor
The Drift
Moorfields
Elm Bank
Waverton Prim. Sch.
Play. Fld.
Common Farm
The Old Farmhouse
The Rectory
Elm Cottage
Well House Farm
Rose Farm House
Hall
Davies' Bridge
Salmon's Bridge
WAVERTON BUSINESS PARK
Black Dog Farm
The Old Smithy
Ridgeway House
Guy Lane Farm
Works
Nursery
SHROPSHIRE UNION CANAL
WHITCHURCH ROAD
A41
A51
TARPORLEY ROAD
DUDDON ROAD
HIGH STREET
Grove Farm
The Woodlands
Duddon Nursery
Warren House Farm
Meadow Bank Farm
Clotton Lodge
Duddon St. Peter's C of E Prim. Sch.
Tethe Bank Farm
Yew Tree Farm
Park View
Rose Lea
The Poplars
Common House Farm
Brookhouse Farm
Laurel Bank Farm
Burton Farm
Holly Farm
Waterless Wood
Waterless Brook
Hollands Hey
Castle View
Park Hall Farm
CORKSCREW
219
151

175
Ash Wood
Depot
Rode Street House
A51
A49
RODE STREET
Rode Street Forge
Ash Hill House
Heath Green Cott.
HEATH GRN.
UTKINTON
HEATH
219
Driving Range
TARPORLEY ROAD
GREEN
SAPLING
Works
LANE
Reservoir (covered)
Portal
COBBLERS
Salterswell House
MOSS
LANES
BACK
BACK
Cromwell Cottage
BURTON AV.
HEATHERWAYS
THE BLYTHINGS
WOODLANDS
Golf Academy
Arderne Golf Course
Club House
PORTAL GOLF COURSE
CROSS
177
63
Moss Cottage
LANE
TARPORLEY
HOSP.
Tennis Cts.
Tarporley C of E Prim. School
Bowling Green
COPPERFIELDS
RISE LANE
PORTAL BUSINESS PARK
FLAXYARDS
Comm. Cen.
Play. Fld.
CHURCHILL
DRIVE
ROAD
Arderne Home Farm
Poultry Farm
MEADOWFIELD
HONEY FLDS.
TARPORLEY BUS. CEN.
EATON
NANTWICH
Tarporley Community High School
Flaxyards Cottage
62
Redhill Farm
Birch Heath
Redhill Cottages
BIRCH
HEATH
Birch Heath Farm
Springfield Farm
LANE
Rhuddall Heath
ROAD
EATON
Tarporley
CW6
NANTWICH RD.
Four Lane Ends Farm
Sewage Works
Tiresford
CRIB
PUDDING
Ferney Lees
Four Lane Ends
Brook House
Field's Cottage
61
Town Fields
Laburnum Cottage
Daisybank
Heathfield
Tiverton Moss
HUXLEY
LANE
Hand Green
Holly Bank Farm
Drumber Castle Cottage
Fishpond Farm
The Gables
Pav.
Sports Ground
Sheenella Bank
The Old School
Simpson's Rough
LANE
Bank Farm
Foxey Wood
SHROPSHIRE UNION CANAL
Beeston Brook Bridge
Tiverton
360
Cattle Market
Beeston Bri.
54
355
56
F
G
H
J
K
1
2
3
4
5
6
7

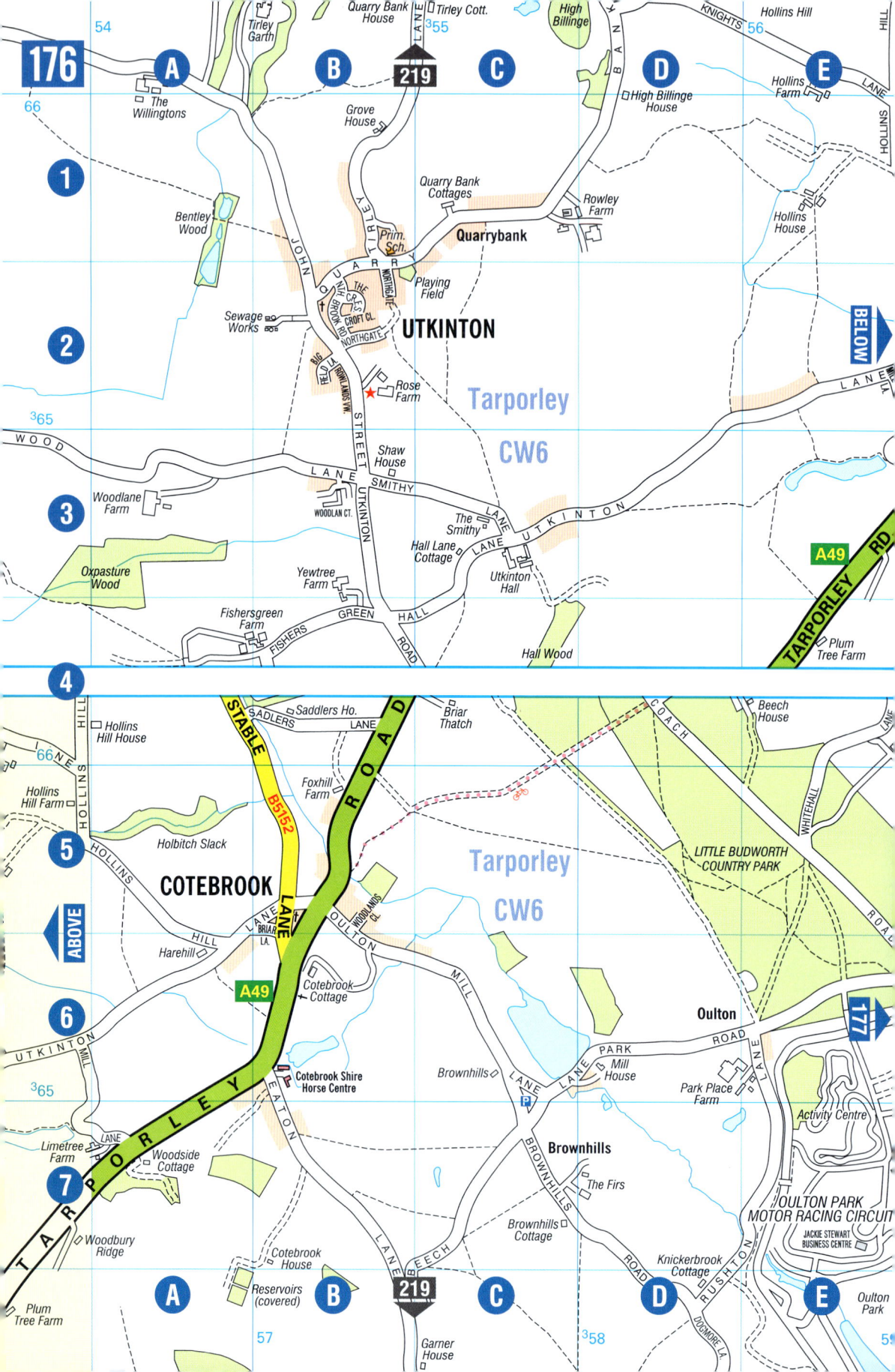
176
219
177
BELOW
ABOVE
UTKINTON
Quarrybank
Tarporley
CW6
COTEBROOK
Oulton
Brownhills
LITTLE BUDWORTH
COUNTRY PARK
OULTON PARK
MOTOR RACING CIRCUIT
JACKIE STEWART
BUSINESS CENTRE
Activity Centre
Oulton
Park
Tirley
Garth
Quarry Bank
House
Tirley Cott.
High
Billinge
Hollins Hill
The
Willingtons
Grove
House
High Billinge
House
Hollins
Farm
Quarry Bank
Cottages
Rowley
Farm
Bentley
Wood
Prim.
Sch.
Hollins
House
Playing
Field
Sewage
Works
Rose
Farm
Shaw
House
Woodlane
Farm
WOODLAN CT.
The
Smithy
Hall Lane
Cottage
Utkinton
Hall
Oxpasture
Wood
Yewtree
Farm
Fishersgreen
Farm
Hall Wood
Plum
Tree Farm
Saddlers Ho.
Briar
Thatch
Beech
House
Hollins
Hill House
Foxhill
Farm
Hollins
Hill Farm
Holbitch Slack
Harehill
Cotebrook
Cottage
Cotebrook Shire
Horse Centre
Brownhills
Mill
House
Park Place
Farm
Limetree
Farm
Woodside
Cottage
The Firs
Brownhills
Cottage
Woodbury
Ridge
Cotebrook
House
Knickerbrook
Cottage
Reservoirs
(covered)
Plum
Tree Farm
Garner
House
A49
B5152
TARPORLEY RD
TARPORLEY
KNIGHTS
WOOD LANE
SMITHY LANE
UTKINTON LANE
UTKINTON STREET
QUARRY
TIRLEY LANE
JOHN STREET
BANK
HOLLINS LANE
HILL
NORTHGATE
THE CRES.
CROFT CL.
NTH BROOK RD
BIG FIELD LA.
ROWLANDS VW.
FISHERS GREEN
HALL ROAD
STABLE LANE
SADLERS LANE
COACH ROAD
WHITEHALL
HOLLINS HILL
BRIAR LA.
WOODLANDS CL.
OULTON MILL LANE
PARK LANE
PARK ROAD
RUSHTON LANE
UTKINTON
MILL
EATON LANE
BEECH
BROWNHILLS ROAD
DOGMORE LA.
LANE
A B C D E
1 2 3 4 5 6 7
54 55 56 57 58
66 365

Beech House
Springfield
Coneygreaves Farm
Grange Bungalow
Meadow Holme
Poolhead Farm
WHITEHALL
219
220
Sandy Bank Farm
Mill House Farm
Budworth Pool
Old Hall
LITTLE BUDWORTH COUNTRY PARK
Pav.
Cricket Ground
Oulton
176
Tarporley
CW6
VICARAGE
Hall
Bowl. Grn.
YEW TREE CL.
TOWNSFIELD DR.
BOOTH AV.
ST. PETER'S
PINFOLD LA.
WELL LA.
MILL LANE
Lower Farm
LITTLE BUDWORTH
Park Place Farm
Activity Centre
OULTON PARK MOTOR RACING CIRCUIT
JACKIE STEWART BUSINESS CENTRE
Home Farm
Oulton House
Oulton Park
Hazelhurst Covert
Lower Farm
Darley Rough
Darley Hall
COACH ROAD
PARK ROAD
RUSHTON LANE
Red Beech Farm
Moss Hall Farm
MOSS HALL LA.
Rushton
KINGS LANE
Oulton Lake
Parkwall Farm
Pillarbox Farm
PORTAL GOLF COURSE
Bowl. Grn.
Chapel House
Ivy Cottage
Dogmore Cottages
DOGMORE
LIGHTFOOT LANE
EATON
Lower House Fm.
Works
SAPLING LANE
LOWER LA.
ELM TREE CT.
Eaton Primary Sch.
HICKHURST
WHALLEY
EDGEWELL LA.
Royal Farm
Hunt's Hill
Tarporley
CW6
175
PORTAL GOLF COURSE
ROYAL LANE
WINTERFORD
THE HALL
Boothouse Farm
MILL LANE
Winterford Farm
Winterford House
Oakfields Farm
Hillhouse Farm
PORTAL BUSINESS PARK
FLAXYARDS
EATON
Oxheys
OXHEYS LANE
LANE
219
F
G
H
J
K
1
2
3
4
5
6
7
59
360
61
66
365
364
63
57
358
59

Marton Sands
Marton Hall
Bradford Wood
Knights Grange Golf Course
Knights Grange Golf Course
Cricket Grd.
Club Ho.
Knights Grange Outdoor Complex
Salterswall
Marton View Farm
Westholme Farm
WINSFORD
Littler
Marton House Farm
A54
OAKMERE ROAD
CHESTER LANE
CHESTER LA.
The Verdin High Sch.
Play. Fld.
Play. Fld.
Playing Fields
Fire Brigade HQ
Coll.
Civic Hall
Lib.
Winsford Cross Shop. Cen.
Mkt.
Superstore
Rec. Grd.
Works
Nursing Home
Winsford Sports Complex
HIGH STREET
SWANLOW LANE
B5074
Over Sq.
Cheshire Police HQ
Lane End Farm
Woodford Park Ind. Est.
Over
Oaklands Sch.
Over Hall Prim. Sch.
Town Fields
Woodford Lodge High School
Hebden Green School
Hebden Green
Hebden Green Farm
Woodford Hall
Poolstead Brook
Playing Field
Church House Farm
Church Hill
Darnhall Prim. Sch.
Beech House
School Green
School Green Farm
Knobs Farm
Ash Brook
Pool Head Farm
Rookery Pool
Moors Lane Farm
220
A B C D E
1 2 3 4 5 6 7

Winsford
CW7
Wharton
Gravel
Way's Green
Winsford
Clive
Clive Green
PARK ROAD A5018
WHARTON ROAD
WHARTON RD.
CROOK LANE B5355
STATION RD.
MIDDLEWICH RD.
A54
BOSTOCK ROAD
Wharton Bri.
Factory
WINSFORD INDUSTRIAL ESTATE
PREMIER PARK
PINEAPPLE PARK
The Willowbeds
Works
Sewage Works
Verdin's Cut
Wharton Lodge Mills
WHARTON RETAIL PK.
NAT LANE BUS. PK.
NAT LANE RETAIL PK.
WHARTON (DONEFIELDS) IND. EST.
Weaver Parkway
Weaver Navigation
Superstore
NEW RD. BUS. CEN.
Sch.
Bowl. Grn.
Lib.
Willow Wood Prim.Sch.
Winsford Utd. FC (Barton Stadium)
Bowl. Grns.
Ten Cts.
Youth Cen.
Jun. Sch.
Town Park
Depot
Bowl. Green
Hospice
St. Chad's CE Prim. Sch.
Way's Green Farm
Nursing Home
Clive Hall Farm
Dairy House Farm
Rilshaw Farm
Clive Farm
Clive House
Double Wood
Mole House Farm
Pear Tree Farm
Clive Farm
Bottom Flash
LAKESIDE CARAVAN PARK
Winsford Flash Sailing Club
Weavergrove
Weaver Dairy House
Shaw's Wood
River Weaver
Fitwood Brook
Old Fields Farm
Swanlow House Farm
Badger Wood
Weaver Hall Farm
Weaver Hall
Wimboldsley Wood
Top Flash
WEAVER HALL LANE
NEW LANE
STOCKS HILL
RILSHAW LANE
CLIVEGREEN LANE
CLIVE LANE
CLIVE BACK LANE
GREEN LANE
WAY'S GREEN
COW LA.
MERE CT.
220
Clive
66

180
A
B
C
D
E
1
2
3
4
5
6
7
69
370
71
67
66
365
64
220
Croxton Hall Farm
Ravenscroft Hall Farm
Ravenscroft Hall
CROXTON LANE
KING STREET
Croxton Bridge
River Dane
Reservoir
Trent & Mersey Canal
Harbutt's Field
B5309
Kinderton Hall
B5081
BYLEY LA.
CENTURION WAY
A533
BOSTOCK RD.
Bostock House Farm
A54
Stanthorne Bridge
MIDDLEWICH RD.
CHESTER RD.
Stanthorne
Cricket Ground
Football Grd.
Cemy.
ST. MICHAEL'S WAY
HOLMES CHAPEL RD.
KING ST. TRADING ESTATE
MIDPOINT 18 MOTORWAY INDUSTRIAL ESTATE
Depot
Mill Farm
Stanthorne Mill House
Stanthorne Mill
River Wheelock
Nursy.
Town Bri.
Superstore
Lib.
Comm. Cen.
High Sch.
Leisure Centre
Middlewich
CW10
A530
Middlewich Primary Sch.
Newtonia
St. Mary's Catholic Prim. Sch.
Sewage Works
Sanderson's Brook
BROOKS LANE IND. EST.
BROOKS LANE INDUSTRIAL ESTATE
MIDDLEWICH
Shropshire Union Canal
Middlewich Branch
Wallange Bridge
Wallange Paddocks
Wallange Paddocks Farm
Works
Manor Park
LONG LANE
AVENUE
ST. ANNES AV.
KITFIELD AV.
LEWIN ST.
ST. BOOTH
Infant Sch.
Sch.
Warmingham CT.
Cledford Bri.
CLEDFORD LANE
Works
Norcroft Farm
New Gorse
Keepers Cottage
CHESHIRE EAST
CHESHIRE WEST and CHESTER
Sports Ground
Pav.
Old Gorse
Lea House Farm
NANTWICH RD.
NANTWICH ROAD
Sutton Hall Farm
Sutton Acres
Sutton Mill
River Wheelock
SUTTON LANE
CROSS LANE
Newfield Farm
COALPIT LANE
A530

Cranage
Crewe
CW4
HOLMES CHAPEL
Holmes Chapel
Middlewich
CW10
Sandbach
CW11
KNUTSFORD ROAD
TWEMLOW LANE
MIDDLEWICH ROAD
MACCLESFIELD ROAD
CHESTER ROAD
STATION ROAD
LONDON ROAD
DOG LANE
MARSH LA.
M6 MOTORWAY
BRERETON LANE
BROAD LANE
HERMITAGE LANE
BYLEY LANE
River Dane
Birchwood
Hermitage Turkey Farm
Rose Farm
Depot
Hall Farm Barns
Northbrook House
The Orchards
Peartree Farm
Willow Paddock
Barnfield
Hollins Farm
Hermitage Farm
Swan Farm
Cranage Manor Farm
Keepers Cottage
Cranage Cottage
Cranage Hall
Club
Bowling Grn.
Hermitage Thornes
Hermitage
Cranage Bridge
Hermitage Bridge
Saltersford Bri.
Playing Field
Play. Fld.
Sewage Works
Cranage Mill
Dane Bank Fm.
Dane Bank Bungalow
Graveyard
Playground
Equestrian Training Centre
Cotton Wood
Cotton Hall
Cotton Lodge
Hermitage Prim. Sch.
Saltersford Farm
Victoria Mills
Factory
Depot
Holmes Chapel Prim. Sch.
Holmes Chapel Bus. Cen.
Manor Lane Farm
Primrose Hall
Holmes Chapel Leisure Centre
Tennis Courts
Holmes Chapel Comprehensive School
Cricket Field
Sports Grd.
Bowls
Works
Hill Farm
Primrose Farm
Dunkirk Farm
Allan Brook Farm
Park Ho. Lodge
Court House Farm
Liby.
CHESHIRE EAST
CHESHIRE WEST and CHESTER
A50
A54
A535
B5308
M6
220

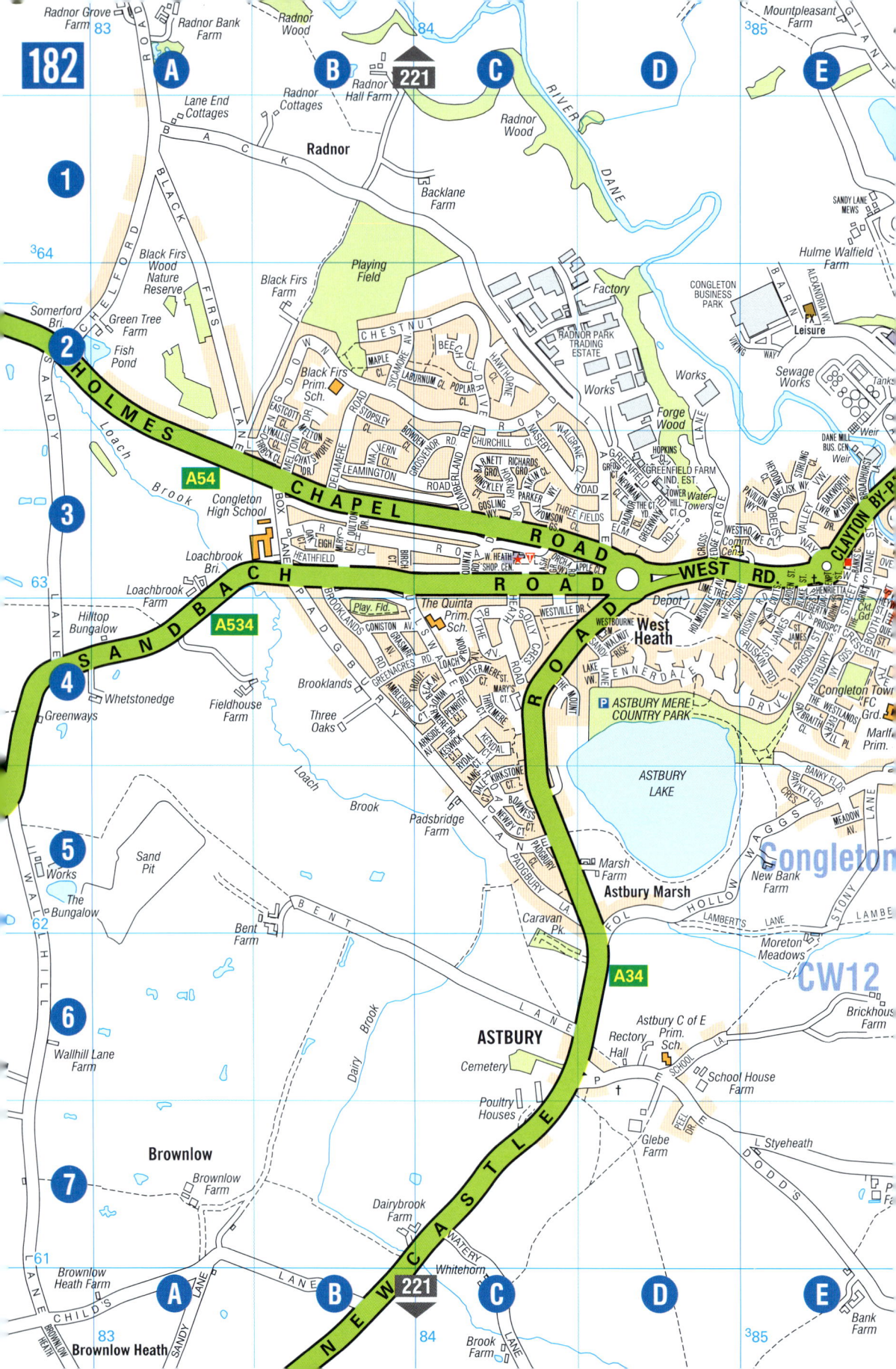
221
Radnor Grove Farm
Radnor Bank Farm
Radnor Wood
Radnor Hall Farm
Radnor Cottages
Lane End Cottages
Radnor
Radnor Wood
River Dane
Mountpleasant Farm
Backlane Farm
Back Lane
Black Firs Lane
Chelford Road
Black Firs Wood Nature Reserve
Playing Field
Black Firs Farm
Somerford Bri.
Green Tree Farm
Fish Pond
Sandy Lane
Holmes Chapel Road
A54
Congleton High School
Black Firs Prim. Sch.
Chestnut Dr.
Beech Cl.
Hawthorne Cl.
Maple Cl.
Sycamore Av.
Laburnum Cl.
Poplar Cl.
Stopsley Cl.
Malvern Cl.
Bowden Cl.
Grosvenor Rd.
Leamington Road
Delamere Rd.
Churchill Cl.
Cumberland Rd.
Naseby Road
Walgrane Cl.
Factory
Radnor Park Trading Estate
Works
Forge Wood
Congleton Business Park
Hulme Walfield Farm
Sandy Lane Mews
Leisure
Sewage Works
Viking Way
Barn Rd.
Alexandria Wy.
Hopkins Cl.
Greenfield Farm Ind. Est.
Forge Lane
Water Towers
Three Fields Cl.
Weir
Dane Mill Bus. Cen.
Clayton By-Pass
Loach Brook
Loachbrook Bri.
Loachbrook Farm
Sandbach Road
A534
Box Lane
Heathfield
W. Heath Shop. Cen.
West Rd.
Depot
Play. Fld.
The Quinta Prim. Sch.
Brooklands
Coniston Av.
Grasmere Av.
Greenacres Rd.
Padgbury Lane
Heath Road
Solly Cres.
Westville Dr.
Westbourne
West Heath
Ennerdale Drive
Astbury Mere Country Park
Astbury Lake
Congleton Town FC Grd.
Hilltop Bungalow
Whetstonedge
Greenways
Fieldhouse Farm
Three Oaks
Padsbridge Farm
Sand Pit
Works
The Bungalow
Wallhill Lane
Bent Farm
Bent Lane
Caravan Pk.
Marsh Farm
Astbury Marsh
Fol Hollow
Waggs Road
Congleton
New Bank Farm
Lamberts Lane
Moreton Meadows
CW12
Stony Lane
A34
Brickhouse Farm
Astbury
Rectory Hall
Astbury C of E Prim. Sch.
School Lane
School House Farm
Cemetery
Poultry Houses
Glebe Farm
Peel Dr.
Styeheath
Dodd's Lane
Dairy Brook
Wallhill Lane Farm
Brownlow
Brownlow Farm
Dairybrook Farm
Newcastle Road
Watery Lane
Whitehorn
Brownlow Heath Farm
Child's Lane
Sandy Lane
Brownlow Heath
Brook Farm
Bank Farm
83
84
385
364
63
62
61

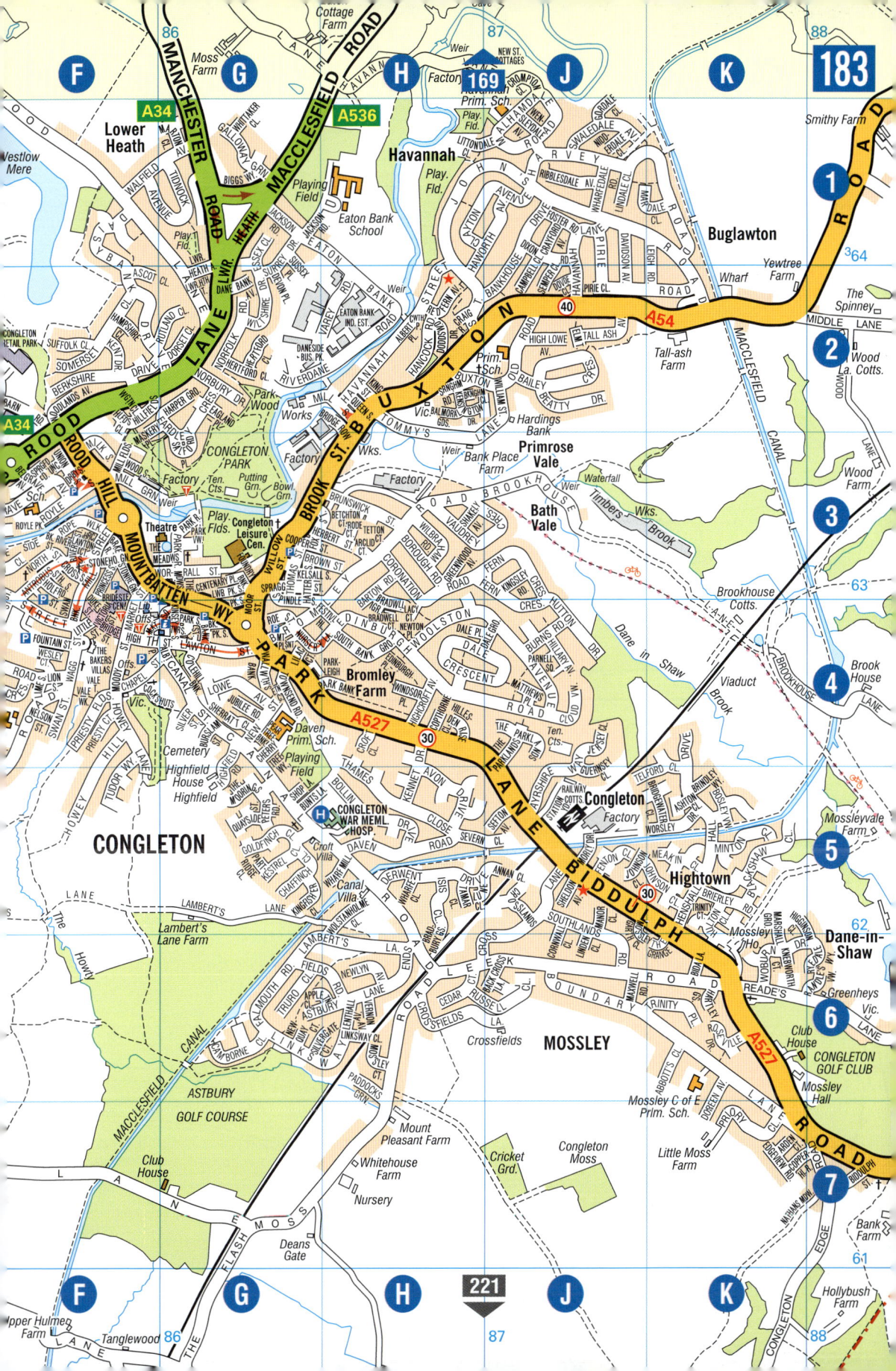
183
F
G
H
J
K
169
221
86
87
88
1
2
3
4
5
6
7
64
63
62
61
A34
A536
A54
A527
MANCHESTER ROAD
MACCLESFIELD ROAD
LOWER HEATH
LANE
ROOD HILL
MOUNTBATTEN WY.
PARK LANE
BIDDULPH ROAD
BUXTON ROAD
BROOK ST.
Lower Heath
Westlow Mere
Moss Farm
Cottage Farm
Havannah
Havannah Prim. Sch.
Play. Fld.
Playing Field
Eaton Bank School
Eaton Bank Ind. Est.
Daneside Bus. Pk.
Congleton Retail Park
Congleton Park
Park Wood
Putting Grn.
Bowl. Grn.
Ten. Cts.
Theatre
Congleton Leisure Cen.
Play. Flds.
Factory
Works
Wks.
Weir
Buglawton
Wharf
Yewtree Farm
Smithy Farm
The Spinney
Middle Lane
Wood La. Cotts.
Tall-ash Farm
Hardings Bank
Primrose Vale
Bank Place Farm
Bath Vale
Waterfall
Timbers Brook
Wood Farm
Brookhouse Cotts.
Brook House
Dane in Shaw Brook
Viaduct
Macclesfield Canal
Bromley Farm
Daven Prim. Sch.
Playing Field
Cemetery
Highfield House
Highfield
CONGLETON
Congleton War Meml. Hosp.
Croft Villa
Canal Villa
Congleton
Hightown
Mossleyvale Farm
Dane-in-Shaw
Greenheys
Club House
CONGLETON GOLF CLUB
Mossley Hall
MOSSLEY
Crossfields
Mossley C of E Prim. Sch.
Little Moss Farm
Congleton Moss
Cricket Grd.
Mount Pleasant Farm
Whitehouse Farm
Nursery
Lambert's Lane Farm
ASTBURY GOLF COURSE
Club House
Deans Gate
Flash Moss
Upper Hulme Farm
Tanglewood
Bank Farm
Hollybush Farm
Congleton Edge

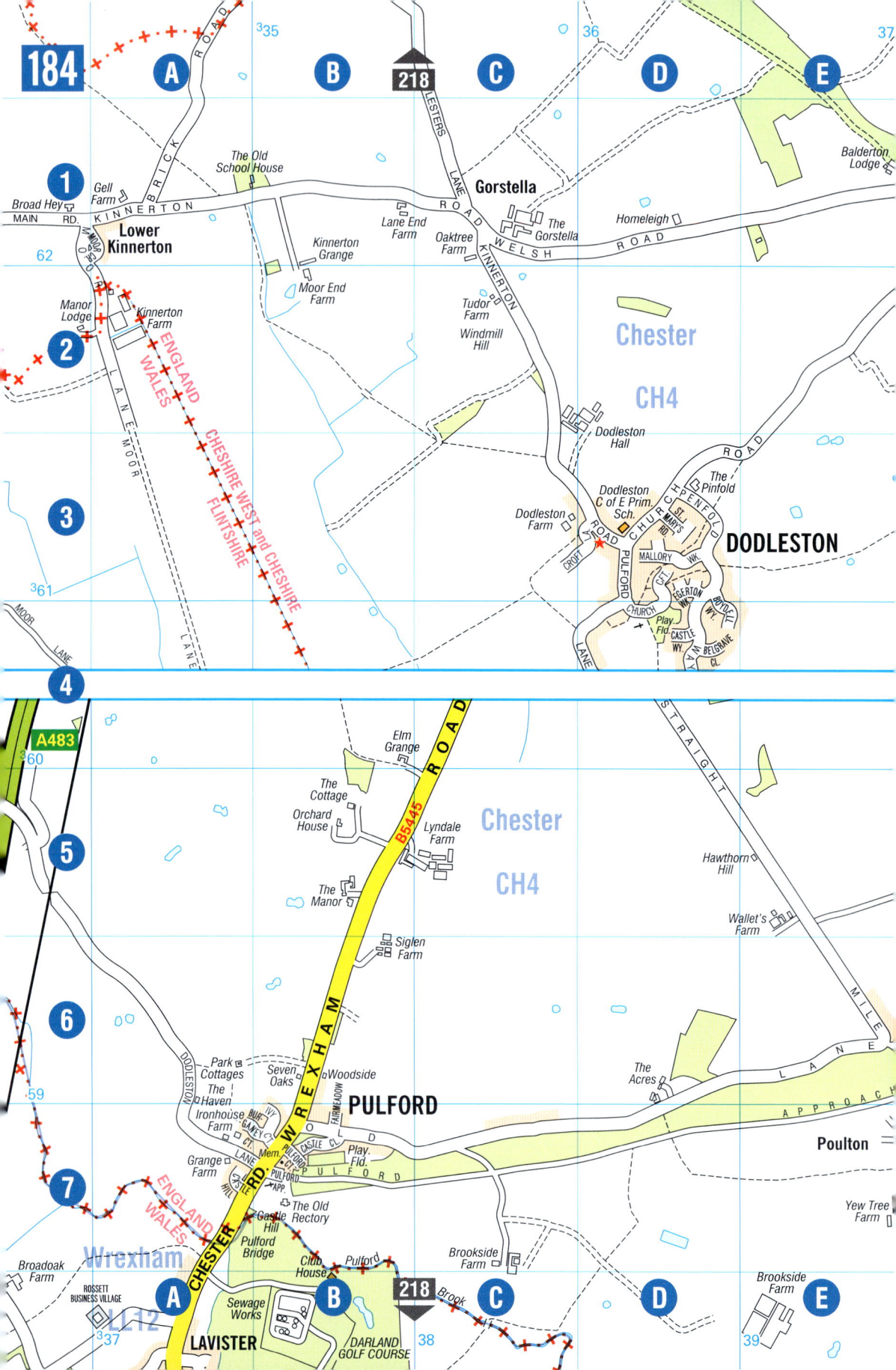
218
Lower Kinnerton
Gorstella
Chester
CH4
DODLESTON
Dodleston Hall
The Pinfold
Dodleston C of E Prim. Sch.
Dodleston Farm
Broad Hey
Gell Farm
Manor Lodge
Kinnerton Farm
The Old School House
Kinnerton Grange
Moor End Farm
Lane End Farm
Oaktree Farm
The Gorstella
Homeleigh
Balderton Lodge
Tudor Farm
Windmill Hill
ENGLAND
WALES
CHESHIRE WEST and CHESHIRE
FLINTSHIRE
MAIN RD.
KINNERTON ROAD
BRICK ROAD
LESTERS LANE
KINNERTON ROAD
WELSH ROAD
MOOR LANE
PULFORD ROAD
CHURCH ROAD
PENFOLD
ST. MARY'S RD.
MALLORY WK.
CROFT
EGERTON WK.
BOYDELL WY.
CASTLE WY.
BELGRAVE CL.
Play. Fld.
A483
B5445
WREXHAM ROAD
CHESTER RD.
Elm Grange
The Cottage
Orchard House
Lyndale Farm
The Manor
Siglen Farm
Hawthorn Hill
Wallet's Farm
STRAIGHT MILE
LANE
APPROACH
Poulton
The Acres
PULFORD
Park Cottages
Seven Oaks
Woodside
The Haven
Ironhouse Farm
Grange Farm
The Old Rectory
Castle Hill
Pulford Bridge
Club House
Pulford Brook
Sewage Works
DARLAND GOLF COURSE
Brookside Farm
Yew Tree Farm
Broadoak Farm
ROSSETT BUSINESS VILLAGE
Wrexham
LL12
LAVISTER
DODLESTON LANE
OLD PULFORD LANE
FAIRMEADOW
CASTLE CL.
PULFORD CT.
PULFORD APP.
Mem.
CASTLE HILL
IVY CT.
GANEY CT.
BUF.
35 36 37 38 39
62 61 60 59

218

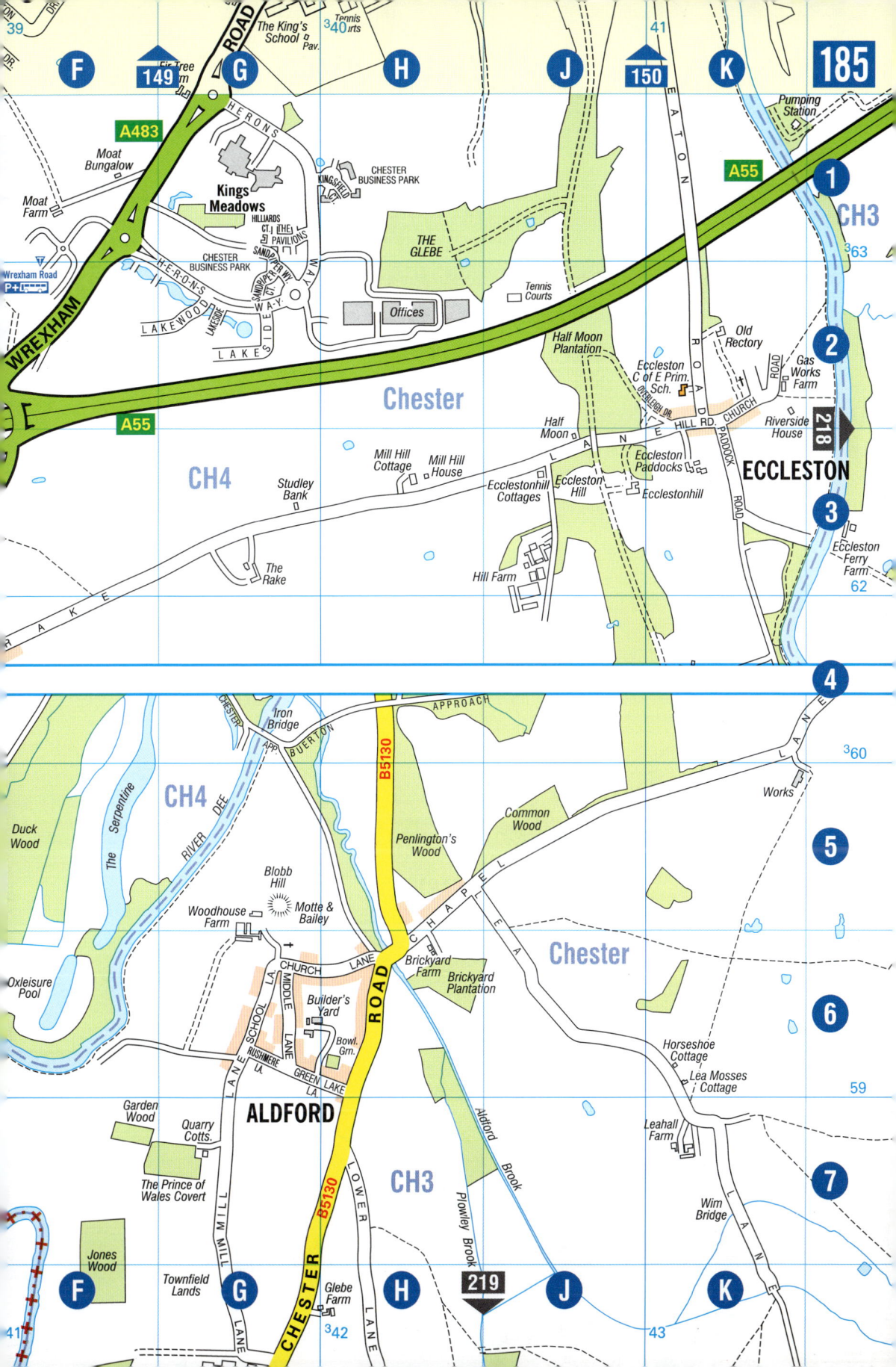

The King's School
Pav.
Tennis Courts
Fir Tree Farm
149
150
F
G
H
J
K
A483
A55
HERONS WAY
Moat Bungalow
Moat Farm
Kings Meadows
CHESTER BUSINESS PARK
KINGSHEAD CT.
HILLIARDS CT.
THE PAVILIONS
SANDPIPER WY.
SANDPIPER CT.
LAKEWOOD
LAKESIDE
LAKE SIDE
Wrexham Road P+R
WREXHAM ROAD
THE GLEBE
Tennis Courts
Offices
EATON ROAD
Pumping Station
CH3
Old Rectory
Half Moon Plantation
Eccleston C of E Prim. Sch.
OVERLEIGH DR.
Gas Works Farm
ROAD
CHURCH RD.
HILL RD.
Riverside House
218
Chester
Half Moon
LANE
Mill Hill Cottage
Mill Hill House
Ecclestonhill Cottages
Eccleston Hill
Eccleston Paddocks
Ecclestonhill
PADDOCK ROAD
ECCLESTON
CH4
Studley Bank
The Rake
RAKE LANE
Hill Farm
Eccleston Ferry Farm
363
62
41
339
340
Iron Bridge
CHESTER APP.
BUERTON APPROACH
B5130
360
Duck Wood
The Serpentine
RIVER DEE
Works
Common Wood
Penlington's Wood
Blobb Hill
Motte & Bailey
Woodhouse Farm
CHAPEL LANE
Chester
CHURCH LANE
MIDDLE LANE
SCHOOL LA.
Brickyard Farm
Brickyard Plantation
Oxleisure Pool
Builder's Yard
Bowl. Grn.
ROAD
RUSHMERE LA.
GREEN LAKE LA.
Horseshoe Cottage
Lea Mosses Cottage
59
ALDFORD
Garden Wood
Quarry Cotts.
Leahall Farm
CH3
Aldford Brook
The Prince of Wales Covert
MILL LANE
LOWER LANE
Plowley Brook
Wim Bridge
LANE
Jones Wood
Townfield Lands
CHESTER ROAD
Glebe Farm
219
342
43
41
1
2
3
4
5
6
7

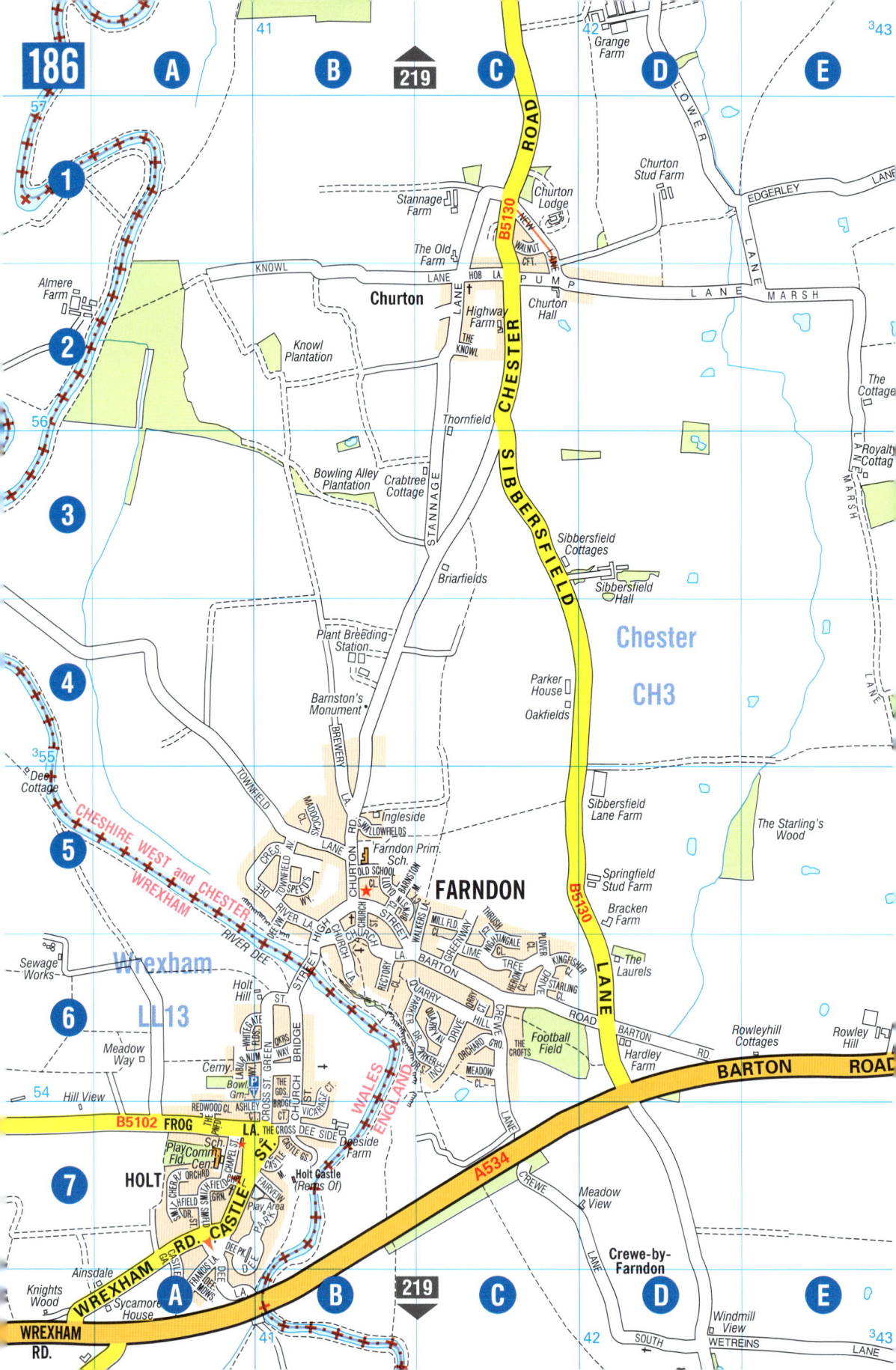

A
B
C
D
E
219
41
42
343
57
56
355
54
1
2
3
4
5
6
7
Grange Farm
LOWER
CHESTER ROAD
Stannage Farm
Churton Lodge
Churton Stud Farm
EDGERLEY LANE
B5130
NEW LANE
WALNUT CFT.
The Old Farm
KNOWL LANE
HOB LA.
PUMP LANE
MARSH
Almere Farm
Churton
Highway Farm
THE KNOWL
Churton Hall
Knowl Plantation
The Cottage
Thornfield
Royalty Cottage
MARSH LANE
Bowling Alley Plantation
Crabtree Cottage
STANNAGE
SIBBERSFIELD LANE
Sibbersfield Cottages
Briarfields
Sibbersfield Hall
Chester
CH3
Plant Breeding Station
Parker House
Oakfields
Barnston's Monument
BREWERY LA.
Dee Cottage
TOWNFIELD
Sibbersfield Lane Farm
CHESHIRE WEST and CHESTER
WREXHAM
MADDOCKS CL.
Ingleside
SWALLOWFIELDS
The Starling's Wood
LANE
CHURTON RD.
Farndon Prim. Sch.
CRES.
TOWNFIELD AV.
SPEEDS WY.
OLD SCHOOL CL.
LLOYD CL.
BARNSTON M.
FARNDON
Springfield Stud Farm
DEE VW.
RIVER LA.
HIGH STREET
CHURCH ST.
CHURCH LA.
STREET
WALKERS LA.
MILL FLD. CL.
GREENWAY
THRUSH CL.
NIGHTINGALE CL.
PLOVER DRIVE
Bracken Farm
RIVER DEE
LIME TREE
HERON CL.
KINGFISHER CL.
STARLING CL.
The Laurels
Sewage Works
Wrexham
LL13
Holt Hill
RECTORY CL.
BARTON ROAD
QUARRY AV.
QUARRY CT.
PARKER DR.
CREWE HILL GRO.
THE CROFTS
Football Field
BARTON RD.
Rowleyhill Cottages
Rowley Hill
Meadow Way
WHITEGATE FLDS.
OKRS WAY
BRIDGE
WALES
ENGLAND
INCE
ORCHARD
MEADOW CL.
Hardley Farm
BARTON ROAD
Cemy.
LABURNUM CT.
Bowl. Grn.
CROSS ST.
GREEN
THE GDS.
CHURCH ST.
VICARAGE CT.
Hill View
REDWOOD CL.
ASHLEY CT.
BRIDGE CT.
B5102 FROG LA.
THE CROSS
DEE SIDE
CASTLE GS.
Deeside Farm
Sch.
Play Fld.
Comm. Cen.
CHAPEL ST.
CASTLE ST.
CASTLE M.
Holt Castle (Rems Of)
A534
CREWE
Meadow View
HOLT
ORCHRD
SMITHFIELD
GRN.
FAIRVIEW
Play Area
PARK
WREXHAM RD.
CASTLE ST.
DEE PK.
DEE
LANE
Crewe-by-Farndon
Ainsdale
Knights Wood
Sycamore House
FRANCIS LA.
DEE MDWS.
LA.
WREXHAM RD.
Windmill View
SOUTH
WETREINS LANE

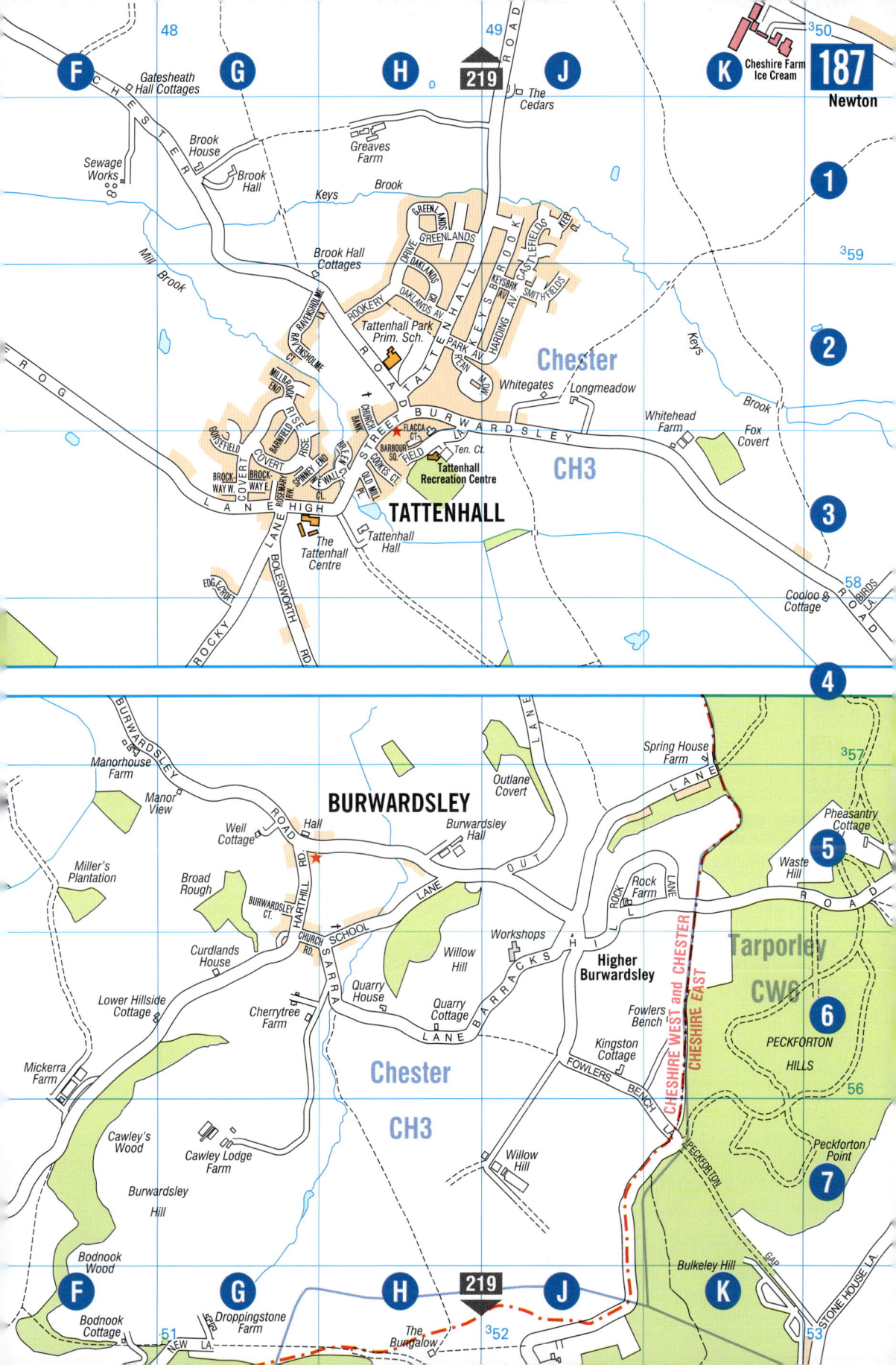
Gatesheath Hall Cottages
Brook House
Brook Hall
Sewage Works
Greaves Farm
The Cedars
Cheshire Farm Ice Cream
Keys Brook
Mill Brook
Brook Hall Cottages
Tattenhall Park Prim. Sch.
Chester
Whitegates
Longmeadow
Whitehead Farm
Fox Covert
Tattenhall Recreation Centre
CH3
TATTENHALL
The Tattenhall Centre
Tattenhall Hall
Cooloo Cottage
BURWARDSLEY
Manorhouse Farm
Manor View
Spring House Farm
Outlane Covert
Well Cottage
Hall
Burwardsley Hall
Pheasantry Cottage
Miller's Plantation
Broad Rough
Waste Hill
Rock Farm
Tarporley
CW6
Curdlands House
Willow Hill
Workshops
Higher Burwardsley
Lower Hillside Cottage
Quarry House
Quarry Cottage
Cherrytree Farm
Fowlers Bench
Kingston Cottage
PECKFORTON HILLS
Mickerra Farm
CHESHIRE WEST and CHESTER
CHESHIRE EAST
Cawley's Wood
Cawley Lodge Farm
Burwardsley Hill
Peckforton Point
Bodnook Wood
Bulkeley Hill
Bodnook Cottage
Droppingstone Farm
The Bungalow
219

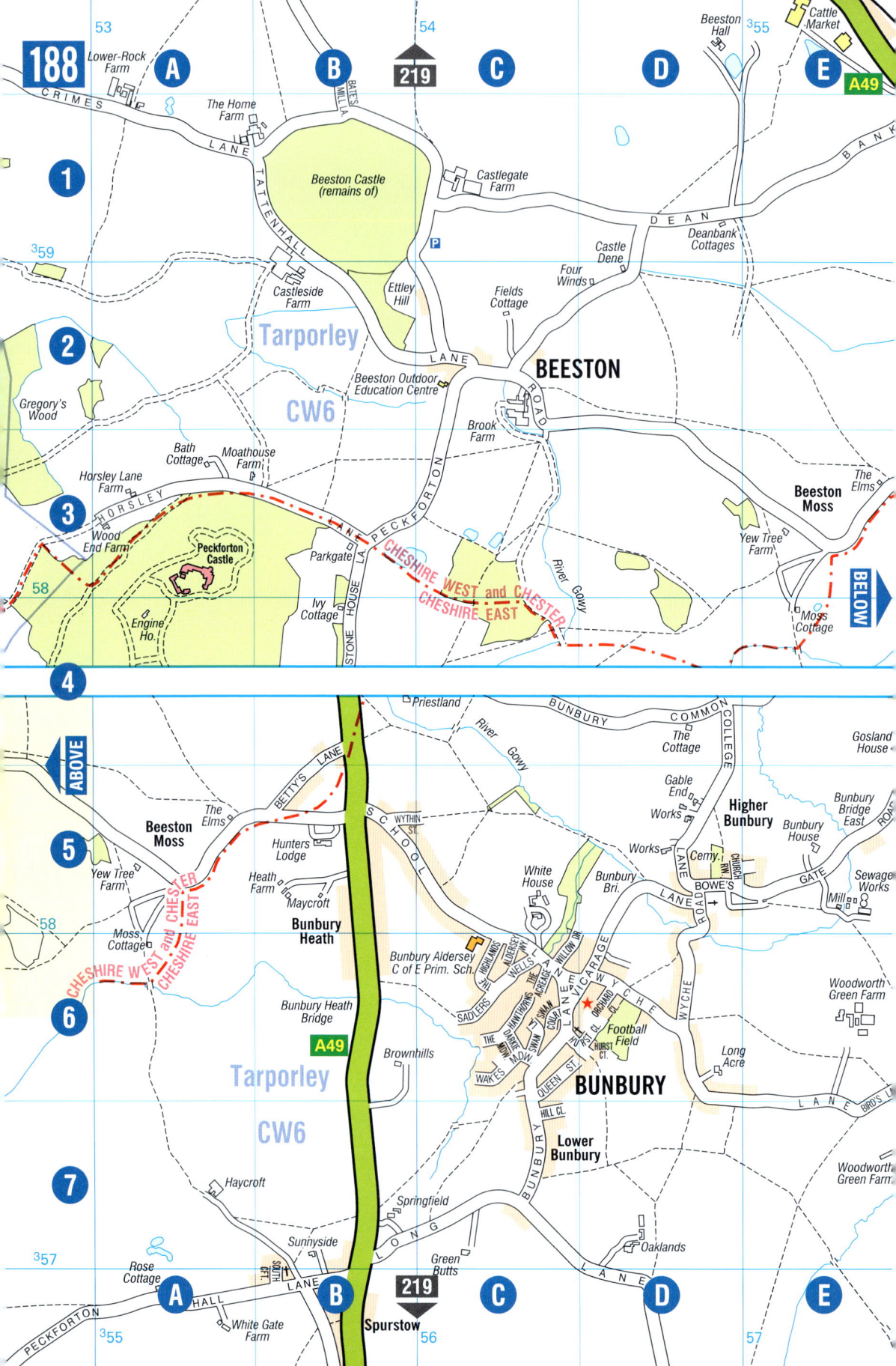

219
A49
Lower-Rock Farm
Crimes Lane
The Home Farm
Bates Mill La.
Beeston Castle (remains of)
Castlegate Farm
Beeston Hall
Cattle Market
Bank
Dean
Deanbank Cottages
Castle Dene
Four Winds
Tattenhall
Castleside Farm
Ettley Hill
Fields Cottage
Tarporley
Lane
BEESTON
Gregory's Wood
Beeston Outdoor Education Centre
CW6
Road
Brook Farm
Bath Cottage
Moathouse Farm
Horsley Lane Farm
Horsley
Peckforton
Beeston Moss
The Elms
Wood End Farm
Peckforton Castle
Parkgate
Cheshire West and Chester
Cheshire East
Yew Tree Farm
58
Engine Ho.
Ivy Cottage
Stone House La.
River Gowy
Moss Cottage
Below
Priestland
Bunbury Common
College
Above
River Gowy
The Cottage
Gosland House
Betty's Lane
Gable End
Works
Higher Bunbury
Bunbury Bridge East
Bunbury House
The Elms
Beeston Moss
School
Wythin St.
Hunters Lodge
Works
White House
Bunbury Bri.
Cemy.
Church Rw.
Bowe's
Gate
Sewage Works
Mill
Yew Tree Farm
Heath Farm
Maycroft
Lane
Road
Moss Cottage
Bunbury Heath
Bunbury Aldersey C of E Prim. Sch.
The Highlands
Aldersey Wy.
Wells
The Acreage
Willow Dr.
Vicarage
Wyche
Orchard Cl.
Cheshire West and Chester
Cheshire East
Sadlers
Hawthorns
Swan Court
Wyche
Woodworth Green Farm
Bunbury Heath Bridge
A49
The Mdw.
Darkie Mdw.
Swan
Pst. Cl.
Hurst Ct.
Football Field
Brownhills
Long Acre
Tarporley
Wakes
Queen St.
BUNBURY
Lane
Bird's L
Hill Cl.
CW6
Lower Bunbury
Bunbury
7
Haycroft
Springfield
Woodworth Green Farm
Long
Sunnyside
Oaklands
Rose Cottage
South Cft.
Lane
Green Butts
Lane
Hall
219
Peckforton
White Gate Farm
Spurstow

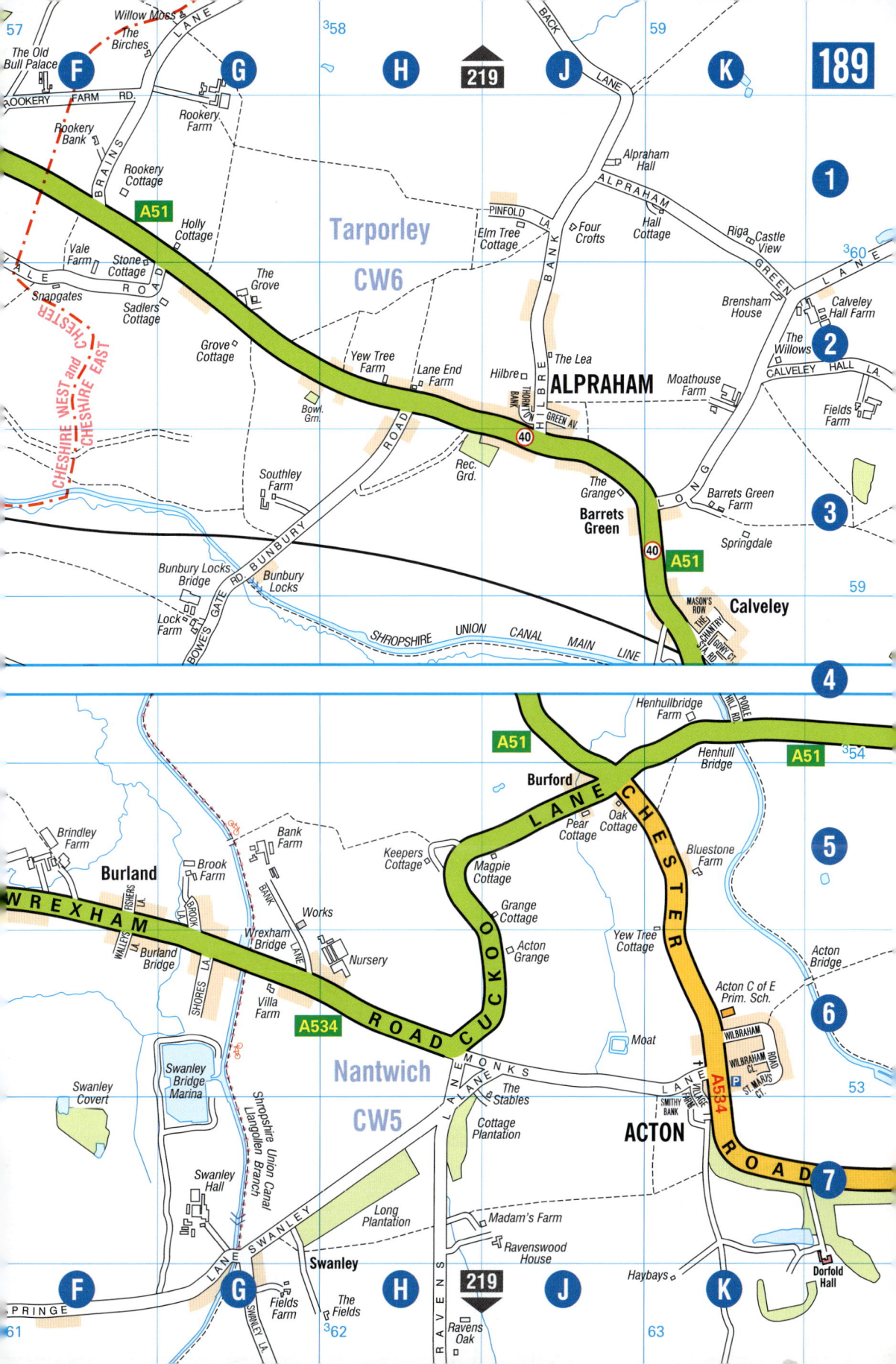

Willow Moss
The Birches
The Old Bull Palace
Rookery Farm Rd.
Rookery Farm
Rookery Bank
Brains Lane
Rookery Cottage
A51
Holly Cottage
Tarporley
CW6
Vale Farm
Stone Cottage
Vale Road
Snapgates
Sadlers Cottage
The Grove
Grove Cottage
Cheshire West and Chester
Cheshire East
Yew Tree Farm
Lane End Farm
Bowl. Grn.
Road
Rec. Grd.
Pinfold La.
Elm Tree Cottage
Back Lane
Alpraham Hall
Alpraham Green
Hall Cottage
Four Crofts
Riga
Castle View
Calveley Hall Farm
Brensham House
The Willows
Calveley Hall La.
Moathouse Farm
Fields Farm
Bank
The Lea
Hilbre
Hilbre Bank
Thornton Bank
Green Av.
ALPRAHAM
40
The Grange
Barrets Green
Long Lane
Barrets Green Farm
Springdale
Southley Farm
Bunbury Rd.
Bunbury Locks Bridge
Bunbury Locks
Lock Farm
Bowe's Gate Rd.
Shropshire Union Canal Main Line
Mason's Row
The Chantry
Sta. Rd
Gowy Ct.
Calveley
219
Henhullbridge Farm
Poole Hill Rd.
Henhull Bridge
Burford
Cuckoo Lane
Pear Cottage
Oak Cottage
Chester Road
Bluestone Farm
Keepers Cottage
Magpie Cottage
Grange Cottage
Acton Grange
Yew Tree Cottage
Acton Bridge
Acton C of E Prim. Sch.
Moat
Wilbraham Road
Wilbraham Cl.
St. Marys Ct.
Brindley Farm
Burland
Brook Farm
Brook La.
Fishers La.
Wrexham Road
Walleys La.
Burland Bridge
Shores La.
Bank Farm
Bank Lane
Works
Nursery
Wrexham Bridge
Villa Farm
A534
Swanley Bridge Marina
Swanley Covert
Nantwich
CW5
Monks Lane
The Stables
Cottage Plantation
Smithy Bank
Village
ACTON
Shropshire Union Canal Llangollen Branch
Swanley Hall
Swanley Lane
Long Plantation
Madam's Farm
Ravenswood House
Ravens Lane
Swanley
Haybays
Dorfold Hall
Spring Lane
Swanley La.
Fields Farm
The Fields
Ravens Oak

220
193
Eardswick Hall Bridge
Eardswick House
Eardswick Hall
R. Weaver
Beech Wood
Old Hoolgrave
Eardswick Bridge
Minshull Hall Court
Minshull Hall
Minshull Vernon
A530
Hoolgrave Bridge
Nantwich
CW5
Shropshire Union Canal
Middlewich Branch
EARDSWICK LANE
High Farm
Hoolgrave Cottage
Bradfield House
Prescott's Bridge
Bradfield Green
Hoolgrave Manor
Bradfield Green Farm
MOSS
Crewe
War Mem.
WEST VIEW
Minshulls Nursery
FLOWERS
CW1
Red Hall Cottages
B5076
Burial Ground
The Lodge
The Barn
Leighton Lodge
Red Hall
Treatment Centre
LEIGHTON HOSPITAL
Red Hall Wood
THE SOUTH CHESHIRE PRIVATE HOSPITAL
Barrow Green
LANE
SMITHY
Leighton
Mile House
Brayne Hall Farm
River Weaver
Leighton Grange
MIDDLEWICH RD.
Leighton Prim. Sch
Nursing Home
Holly Tree Cottage
The Willows
Leighton Hall Farm
Sewage Works
Brassey Bank Bridge
MIDDLEWICH ROAD
Leighton Brook
Leighton
A530
Waste Disposal Site
Works
Council Depot
PYM'S LANE
BADGER
Bridge Farm
Oakleigh Farm
MOTOR WORKS
SUNNYBANK ROAD
Field Farm
Green Paddocks Farm
CHRISTLETON AV.
NEW ROAD
MINSHULL NEW ROAD
DARLINGTON AV.

191
220
194
Sandbach CW11
Warmingham Moss
Lane Ends
Coppenhall Moss
Coppenhall
Maw Green
Ridding Farm
Stocia Farm
Moss Fields Farm
Moss Field House
Hall Lane Cottage
The Meadows
Fields Farm
Moss Lane Farm
Moss Farm
Moss Cottage
Lane Ends Farm
Moss End Farm
Bottoms Farm
Spring Farm Business Centre
Spring Farm
Springfield Cottage
White House
High Dean
Newstead Farm
Moss Side Fm.
Oaktree Farm
Coppenhall House Farm
Moss Bridge Farm
Bridge Farm
Moss Bridge
Ash Cottage
Rose Cottage
Woodbine Cottage
Holly Tree Farm
Groby Farm
Race Farm
Acton House
Ironstile Farm
Stoneley Farm
Foden Farm
Works
Sandon House Farm
Monks Coppenhall Primary School
Maw Green Farm
Cattle Arch Farm
Sydney Bri.
Sir William Stanier Sch.
Leis. Cen.
Playing Fields
Crewe Crematorium & Cemetery
Oakfield Prim. & Nurs. Sch.
The Leighton Cen.
Underwood Ind. Est.
Prim. Sch.
Play Fld.
Depot
Cemy.
Brooklands Flats
B5076
Road North St.
Middlewich St.
Warmingham Road
Groby Road
Moss Lane
Drury Lane
Hall Lane
Broughton Road
Stoneley Road
Remer Street
Maw Green Rd.
Sydney Road
Badger Avenue
Holland Street
West Street

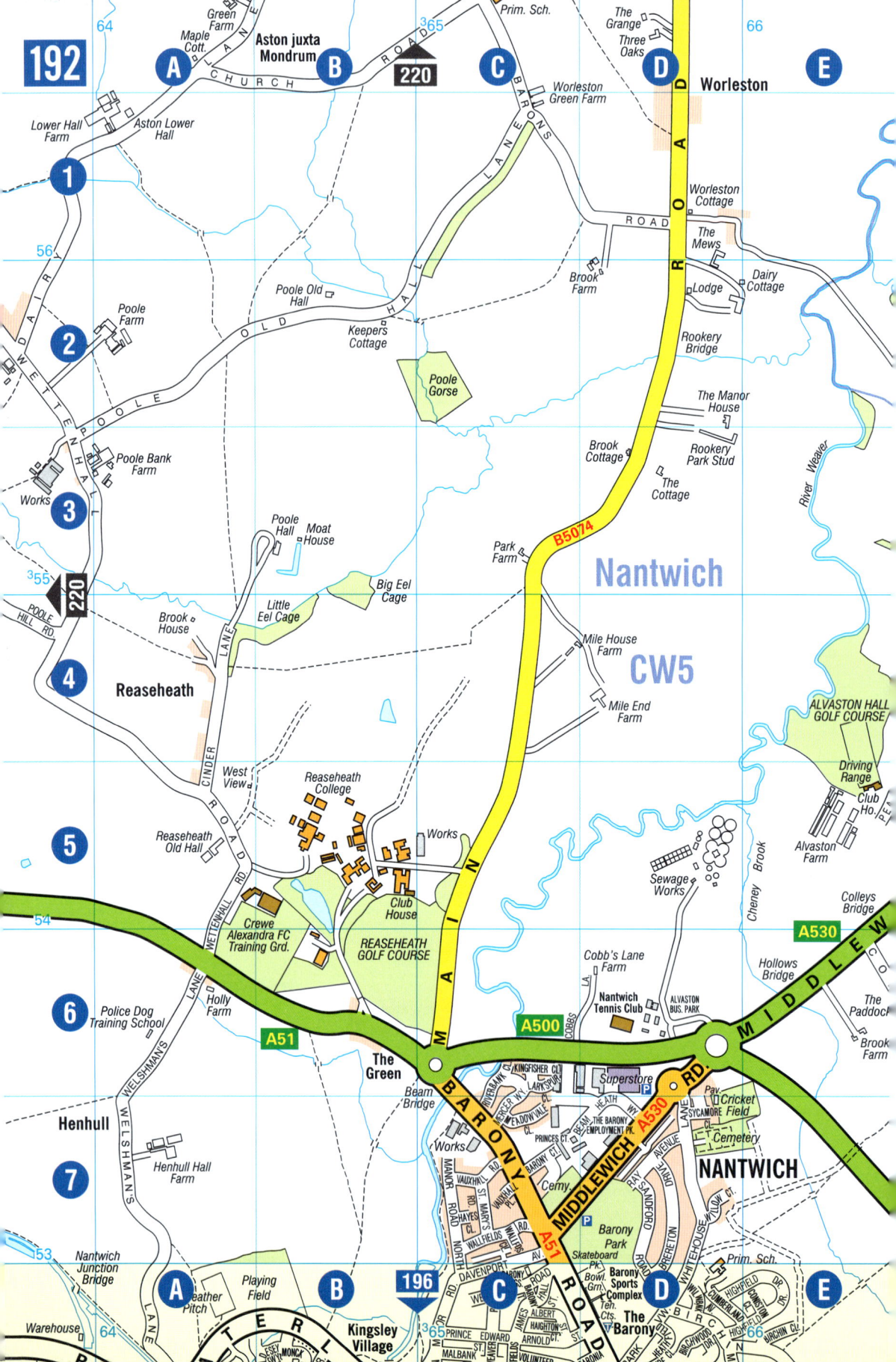

Aston juxta Mondrum
Worleston
Reaseheath
Henhull
Nantwich
CW5
NANTWICH
Green Farm
Maple Cott.
Prim. Sch.
The Grange
Three Oaks
Lower Hall Farm
Aston Lower Hall
Worleston Green Farm
Worleston Cottage
The Mews
Dairy Cottage
Lodge
Brook Farm
Poole Old Hall
Poole Farm
Keepers Cottage
Rookery Bridge
Poole Gorse
The Manor House
Rookery Park Stud
Brook Cottage
The Cottage
Poole Bank Farm
Works
Poole Hall
Moat House
Park Farm
Big Eel Cage
Little Eel Cage
Brook House
Mile House Farm
Mile End Farm
ALVASTON HALL GOLF COURSE
Driving Range
Club Ho.
Alvaston Farm
West View
Reaseheath College
Reaseheath Old Hall
Works
Sewage Works
Cheney Brook
Colleys Bridge
Club House
Crewe Alexandra FC Training Grd.
REASEHEATH GOLF COURSE
Cobb's Lane Farm
Nantwich Tennis Club
ALVASTON BUS. PARK
Hollows Bridge
The Paddock
Brook Farm
Holly Farm
Police Dog Training School
The Green
Beam Bridge
Superstore
Cricket Field
Cemetery
Henhull Hall Farm
Works
Cemy.
Barony Park
Skateboard Pk.
Bowl Grn.
Barony Sports Complex
Ten. Cts.
The Barony
Prim. Sch.
Nantwich Junction Bridge
Feather Pitch
Playing Field
Warehouse
Kingsley Village
River Weaver
CHURCH ROAD
BARONS LANE
ROAD
LANE
DAIRY
WETTENHALL
POOLE OLD HALL LANE
POOLE HILL RD.
CINDER LANE
CINDER ROAD
WETTENHALL RD.
WELSHMAN'S LANE
MAIN ROAD
B5074
BARONY ROAD
MIDDLEWICH RD.
A51
A500
A530
COBBS LA.
KINGFISHER CL.
LARKSPUR
RIVERBANK CL.
MERCER WY.
MEADOWVALE CL.
HEATH WY.
BEAM
PRINCES CT.
THE BARONY EMPLOYMENT PK.
BARONY CT.
SYCAMORE CL.
RAY AVENUE
SANDFORD DRIVE
BRERETON ROAD
WHITEHOUSE LANE
WILLOW CT.
MANOR ROAD
VAUXHALL RD.
VAUXHALL PL.
ST. MARY'S RD.
HAYES CL.
WALLFIELDS
WALTON
NORTH RD.
DAVENPORT AV.
BARONY HALL ROAD
JAMES
ALBERT ST.
HAIGHTON CT.
ARNOLD ST.
PRINCE EDWARD ST.
MALBANK
VOLUNTEER
CUMBERLAND PL.
HIGHFIELD DR.
CONISTON DR.
BIRCHWOOD DR.
BIRCHIN CL.
64
65
66
56
55
54
53
A
B
C
D
E
1
2
3
4
5
6
7

220
220
196

190
194
197
Crewe
CW1
CW2
Marshfield Bank
Wistaston
Wells Green
MIDDLEWICH ROAD
A530
COPPENHALL LANE WEST STREET
A532
A534
A500
CREWE ROAD
MOTOR WORKS
Sports Field
Works
Hall
Comm. Cen.
Fitness First Crewe
King George V Playing Fields
QUEEN'S PARK
War Mem.
Bowl. Grn.
Club House
QUEEN'S PARK GOLF COURSE
Tipkinder Park
Old Gorse Covert
Old Covert
Rec. Grd.
Rookerybank Covert
Prim. Sch.
Play Fld.
THE PRECINCT
Wistaston Hall Bridge
Wistaston Hall
Sports Ground
Sch.
Depot
HUNTSBANK BUSINESS PARK
Smithy House Farm
Broughton Farm
Ropegreen Bridge
Bridge Farm
Field Farm
Green Paddocks Farm
Wood Cottage
Wood Farm
Thorpe Cottage
QUANTUM MARSHFIELD BANK PARK
Marshfield Bank Farm
Buckley Mill Farm
Buckley Mill Stables
Valley Brook
Marshfield Bridge
Wistaston Brook
Garthmyl
Handforth House
Eriskay
West End
Keeper's Cottage
Nurseries
Red Hall
Reusands

191
193
198
A
B
C
D
E
1
2
3
4
5
6
7
69
370
71
56
55
54
53
CREWE
CW2
Crewe Crematorium & Cemetery
Rosedale Manor
Sir William Stanier Sch.
Leis. Cen.
Playing Field
Cumberland Sports Centre
Play. Fld.
Rec. Grd.
Works
Hall
Football Grd.
Superstore
Victoria Centre
Market Centre
Bus Sta.
Leisure Pk.
Apollo Cin.
Swim Pool
Tipkinder Park
Timber Yard
Station House
Depot
Grand Junction Retail Park
Manchester Bri.
Macon Industrial Park
The Railway Age
Warehouse
Sports Cen.
Crewe Alexandra FC (Alexandra Stadium)
Weston Centre
YMCA
Kings Grove Sch.
Gainsborough Prim. & Nurs. Sch.
South Cheshire College
St. Thomas More Catholic High Sch.
Ruskin Sports College
Pebble Brook Prim. Sch.
Manor Way Cen.
Wistaston Mill
Gresty Brook
Wells Green
Springbank
Greenbank Farm
Basford Hall Sorting Sidings
Broughton Farm
Ropegreen Bridge
Alexandra Centre
WEST ST.
DUNWOODY WAY
EARLE ST.
VERNON WAY
MIDDLEWICH ST.
MACON WAY
EDLESTON RD
MILL STREET
NANTWICH ROAD
GRESTY ROAD
SOUTH ST.
WESTON
CREWE ROAD
ROPE LANE
A532
A5019
A5078
A534
A530
B5076
B5071

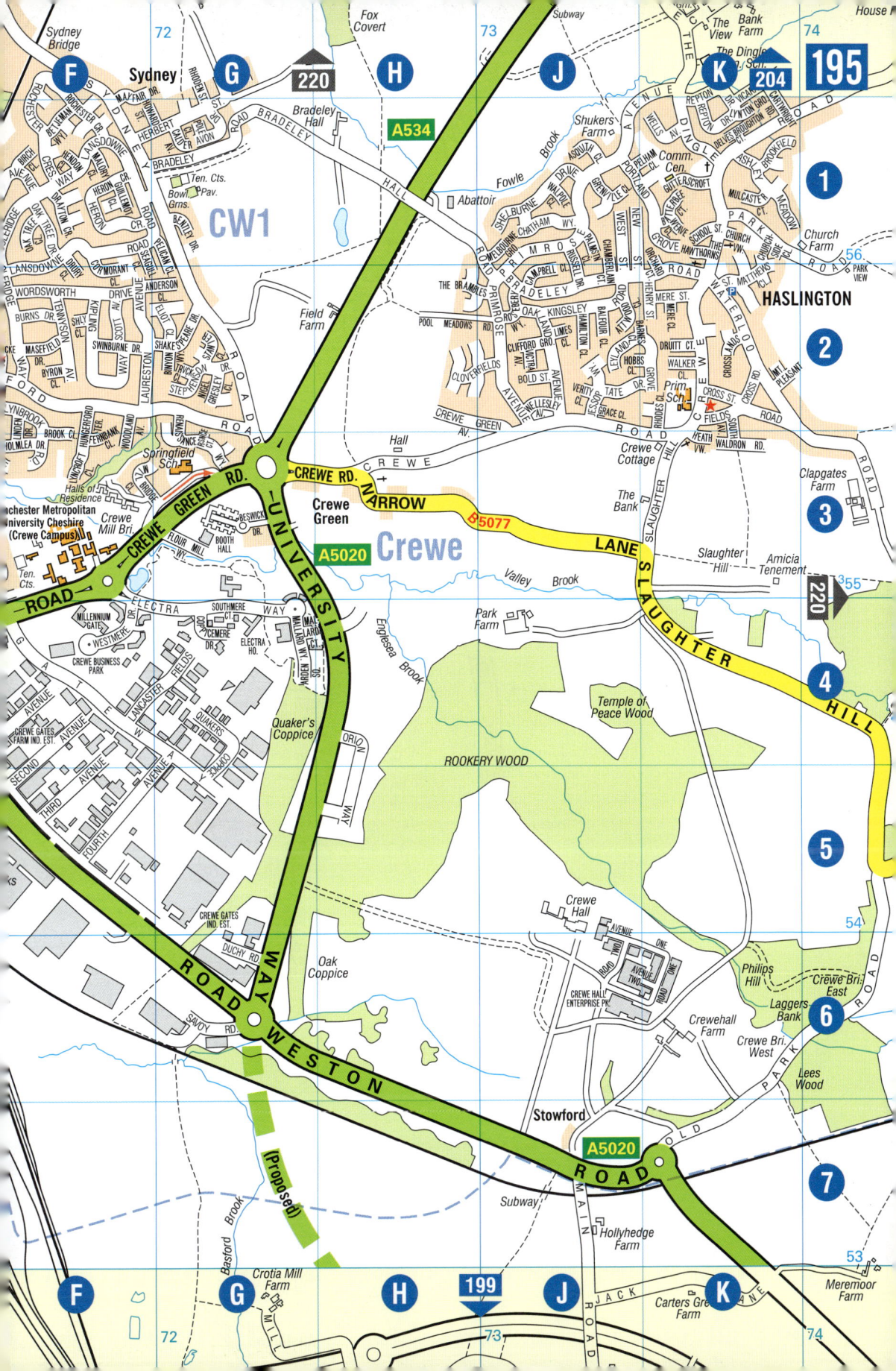

195
Sydney Bridge
Sydney
Fox Covert
220
204
Subway
The View
Bank Farm
The Dingle
House
A534
A5020
B5077
CW1
Crewe
Crewe Green
HASLINGTON
Bradeley Hall
Shukers Farm
Fowle Brook
Abattoir
Comm. Cen.
Church Farm
Field Farm
Hall
Crewe Cottage
The Bank
Clapgates Farm
Slaughter Hill
Amicia Tenement
Valley Brook
Park Farm
Englesea Brook
Temple of Peace Wood
ROOKERY WOOD
Quaker's Coppice
Springfield Sch.
Halls of Residence
Manchester Metropolitan University Cheshire (Crewe Campus)
Crewe Mill Bri.
Ten. Cts.
Bowl. Grns.
Pav.
BOOTH HALL
MILLENNIUM GATE
CREWE BUSINESS PARK
CREWE GATES FARM IND. EST.
CREWE GATES IND. EST.
ELECTRA HO.
Crewe Hall
CREWE HALL ENTERPRISE PK.
Oak Coppice
Philips Hill
Crewe Bri. East
Laggers Bank
Crewehall Farm
Crewe Bri. West
Lees Wood
Stowford
Subway
Hollyhedge Farm
Basford Brook
(Proposed)
Crotia Mill Farm
Carters Green Farm
Meremoor Farm
199
CREWE GREEN RD.
CREWE ROAD
UNIVERSITY WAY
CREWE RD.
NARROW LANE
SLAUGHTER HILL
WESTON ROAD
OLD PARK ROAD
MAIN ROAD
JACK LANE
BRADELEY HALL ROAD
SYDNEY ROAD
CREWE ROAD
WATERLOO ROAD
PRIMROSE AVENUE
THE DINGLE
CHURCH ROAD
F
G
H
J
K
1
2
3
4
5
6
7
72
73
74
56
55
54
53

192
220
NANTWICH
Nantwich
Nantwich Junction Bridge
All Weather Pitch
Playing Field
Kingsley Village
Swim. Pool
Barony Park
Skateboard Pk.
Bowl. Grn.
Barony Sports Complex
Ten. Cts.
The Barony
Cemy.
Prim. Sch.
Sch.
Millfields Prim. Sch.
The Belt
Wks.
Lib.
Bus. Sta.
Civic Hall
Mus.
Thtre.
Superstore
Football Ground
Regents Theological College
Marsh Lane House
Park Lodge
Marsh Lane Bridge
Fields Farm
Brookfield Park
Nantwich Lake
Edleston House Farm
Shropshire Union Canal Main Branch
Brine Leas High Sch.
Weaver Prim. Sch.
Stapeley Water Gardens
The Maylands
Shrewbridge House
Edleston Bridge
Bridge Farm
Elliott's Wood
The Willow Farm
Church House
Church House Farm
New Dairy House Farm
Brook House Farm
Stapeley Broad Lane C of E Prim. Sch.
River Weaver
Sewage Works
Baddington House
Batherton Hall
Baddington Bank Farm
Old Hall Austerson
Austerson
Ashtree Farm
CHESTER RD.
WATERLODE
A534
BEAM STREET
A51 ROAD
MILLSTONE LA.
CREWE
LONDON ROAD
A51
STATION ROAD
HOSPITAL ST.
WELLINGTON RD.
A530
PARK RD.
AUDLEM ROAD
A529
PETER DESTAPLEIGH
A5301
BROAD LANE
SHREWBRIDGE LANE
SHREWBRIDGE RD.
BADDINGTON LANE
COOLE LANE
MARSH LANE
QUEEN'S DRIVE
MILLFIELDS
WELSH ROW
BARONY
MIDDLEWICH

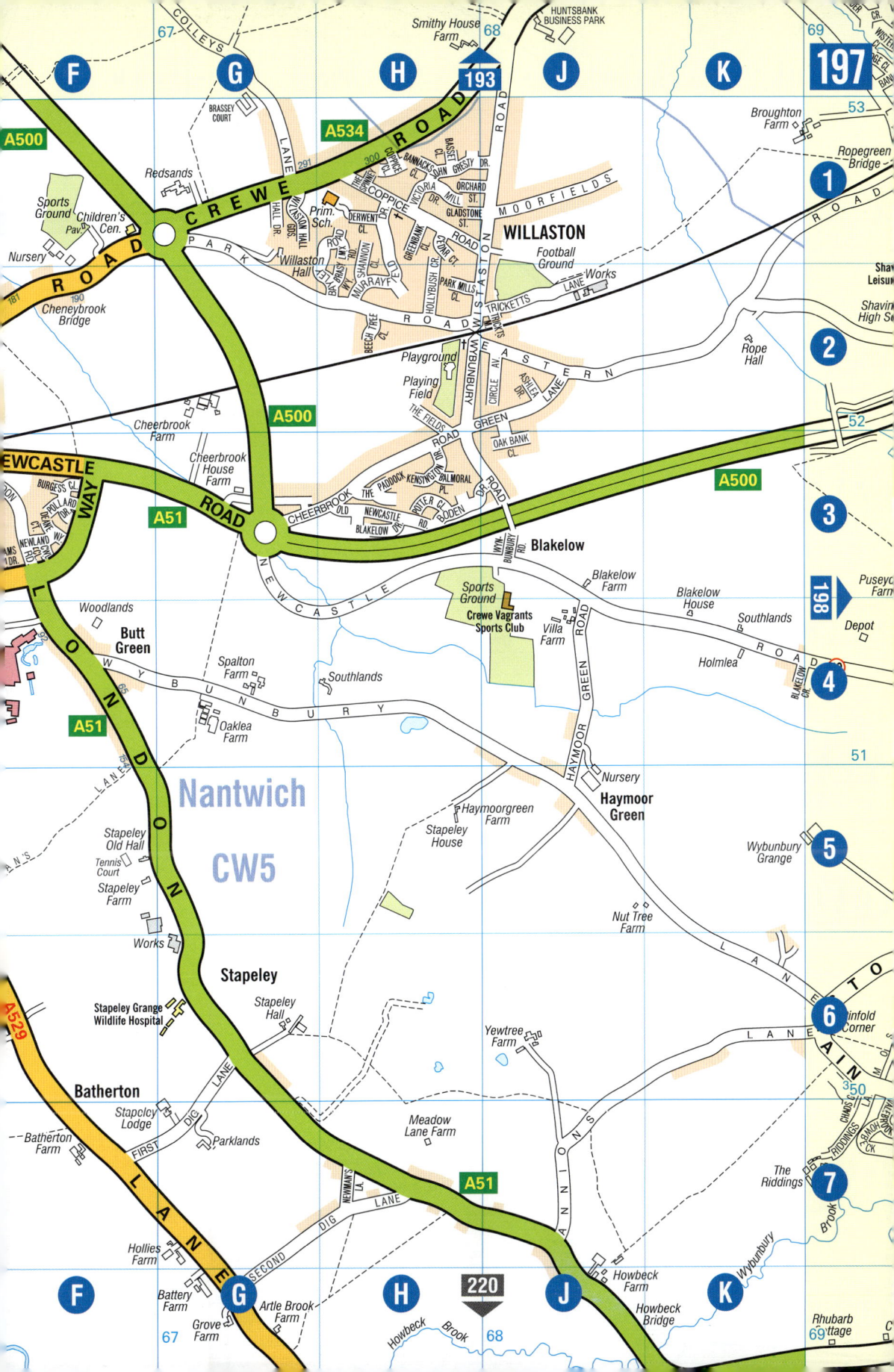

197

F   G   H   193   J   K

67   COLLEYS   68   69

Smithy House Farm

HUNTSBANK BUSINESS PARK

Broughton Farm

53

BRASSEY COURT

A534

CREWE ROAD

Ropegreen Bridge

ROAD

1

A500

Redsands

Children's Cen.

Willaston Hall

WILLASTON

MOORFIELDS

Sha Leisu

Shavin High S

Sports Ground

Pav.

Nursery

Prim. Sch.

Football Ground

Works

Rope Hall

2

Cheneybrook Bridge

ROAD

CREWE

PARK

52

A500

Cheerbrook Farm

Playground

Playing Field

A500

3

Cheerbrook House Farm

NEWCASTLE WAY

A51

ROAD

NEWCASTLE

CHEERBROOK OLD

NEWCASTLE BLAKELOW RD.

Blakelow

198

Puseyd Farm

ROAD

A500

BURGESS CL.

Woodlands

Butt Green

Spalton Farm

Southlands

Sports Ground

Crewe Vagrants Sports Club

Villa Farm

Blakelow Farm

Blakelow House

Southlands

Holmlea

Depot

4

BLAKELOW CR.

51

A51

Oaklea Farm

WYBUNBURY

HAYMOOR

GREEN

ROAD

Nantwich

Nursery

Haymoor Green

CW5

Stapeley Old Hall

Tennis Court

Stapeley Farm

Haymoorgreen Farm

Stapeley House

Wybunbury Grange

5

Works

Nut Tree Farm

LANE

Stapeley

Stapeley Hall

Yewtree Farm

6

TO

infold Corner

LANE

350

A529

Stapeley Grange Wildlife Hospital

Batherton

Stapeley Lodge

FIRST DIG

Parklands

Meadow Lane Farm

NEWMAN'S

The Riddings

7

CK

RIDDINGS

LANE

LONDON

A51

NANIONS

Brook

Batherton Farm

Hollies Farm

Battery Farm

Grove Farm

SECOND DIG

NEWMAN'S LA.

Artle Brook Farm

220

Howbeck Brook

Howbeck Farm

Wybunbury Brook

Howbeck Bridge

Rhubarb ottage

F   G   H   J   K

67   68   69

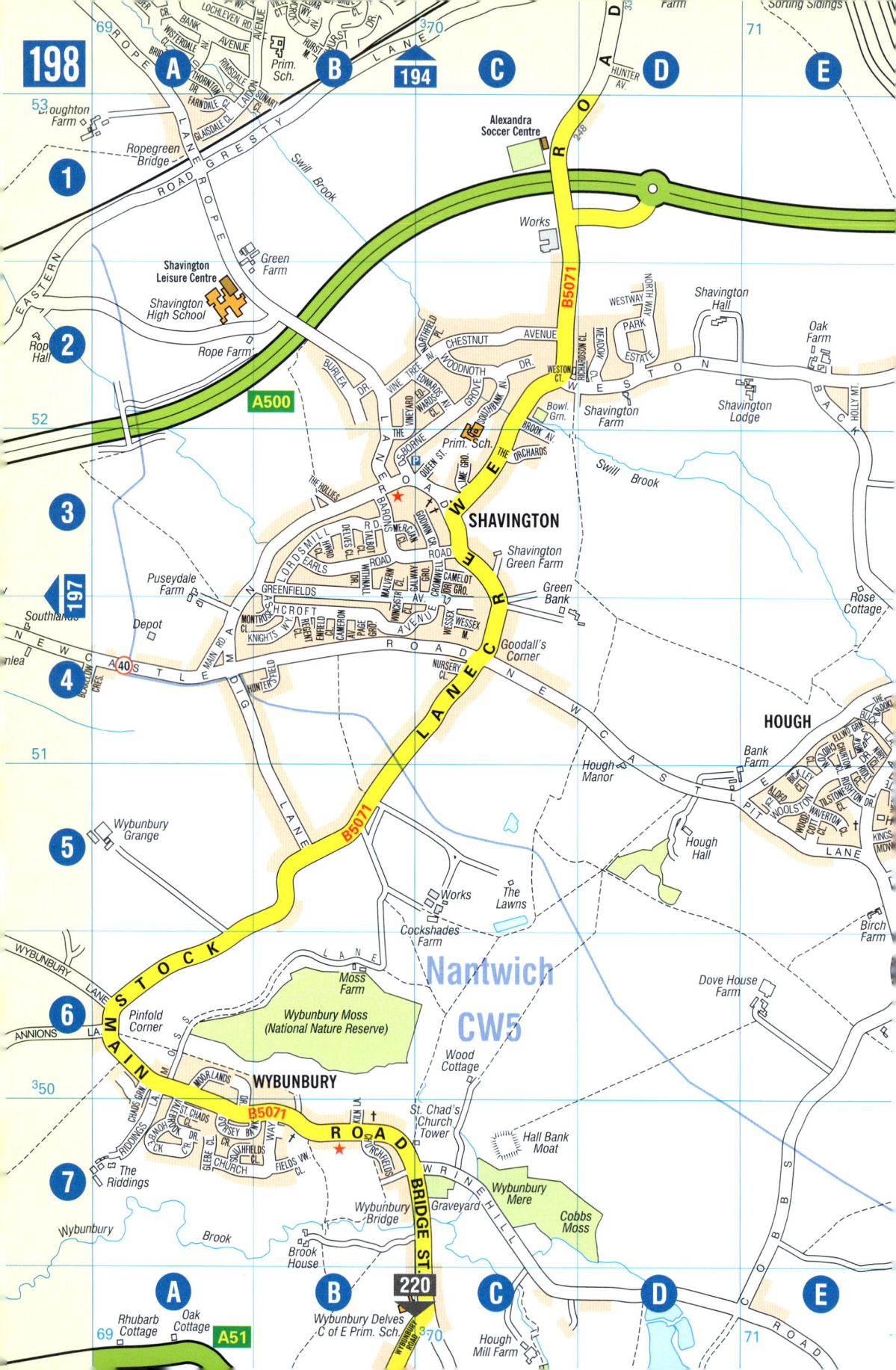

194
197
220
A
B
C
D
E
1
2
3
4
5
6
7
69
370
71
53
52
51
350
Broughton Farm
Ropegreen Bridge
ROPE LANE
GRESTY ROAD
LOCHLEVEN RD
BANK
WISTERDALE AV.
AVENUE
THORNTON DR.
RIMSDALE CL.
FARNDALE CL.
GLAISDALE CL.
LAIDON CL.
SUNART CL.
Prim. Sch.
HUNTER AV.
Swill Brook
Alexandra Soccer Centre
Works
EASTERN
Shavington Leisure Centre
Shavington High School
Green Farm
Rope Hall
Rope Farm
A500
B5071
WESTWAY
NORTH WAY
PARK ESTATE
Shavington Hall
Oak Farm
CHESTNUT AVENUE
NORTHFIELD PL.
WOODNOTH DR.
VINE TREE AV.
BURLEA DR.
EDWARDS AV.
GROVE AV.
SOUTHBANK AV.
RICHARDSON CL.
MEADOW CL.
WESTON CT.
WESTON
Shavington Farm
Shavington Lodge
BACK
HOLLY MT.
Bowl. Grn.
BROOK AV.
THE ORCHARDS
THE VINEYARD
OSBORNE
QUEEN ST.
LIME GRO.
Prim. Sch.
Swill Brook
THE HOLLIES
SHAVINGTON
BARONS RD.
MERCIAN CT.
GODWIN CR.
Shavington Green Farm
Green Bank
LORDSMILL
DELVES CL.
TALBOT CL.
EARLS ROAD
WITHNALL DR.
MALVERN CL.
GALWAY GRO.
CROMWELL DR.
CAMELOT GRO.
GREENFIELDS
ASHCROFT
MONTROSE CL.
KNIGHTS WY.
REGENT CL.
ENFIELD CL.
CAMERON AV.
PAGE GRO.
WINCHESTER CL.
AVENUE
WESSEX CL.
WESSEX M.
Puseydale Farm
Depot
Southlands
NEWCASTLE ROAD
40
MAIN RD.
BUCKLOW CRES.
HUNTERSFIELD
NURSERY CL.
Goodall's Corner
WESTON LANE
Rose Cottage
HOUGH
Bank Farm
Hough Manor
NEWCASTLE
PIT LANE
WOOLSTON
TILSTONE
WAVERTON CL.
CHURTON
RUSHTON DR.
KINGS MDW
Hough Hall
DIG LANE
Wybunbury Grange
Works
The Lawns
Cockshades Farm
Birch Farm
Dove House Farm
STOCK LANE
WYBUNBURY LANE
Moss Farm
Nantwich CW5
Pinfold Corner
ANNIONS LA.
Wybunbury Moss (National Nature Reserve)
MAIN ROAD
MOSS LA.
Wood Cottage
WYBUNBURY
MOORLANDS
ST. CHADS
GORSEY BANK
CHADS GRN
RIDDINGS
GLEBE CL.
SOUTHFIELDS CL.
CHURCH
FIELDS VW. CL.
KILN LA.
CHURCHFIELDS
St. Chad's Church Tower
Hall Bank Moat
The Riddings
Wybunbury Bridge
Graveyard
WRINEHILL
Wybunbury Mere
Cobbs Moss
BRIDGE ST.
Wybunbury Brook
Brook House
COBBS
ROAD
Rhubarb Cottage
Oak Cottage
A51
Wybunbury Delves C of E Prim. Sch.
WYBUNBURY ROAD
Hough Mill Farm

F
G
H
J
K
195
72
73
74
Subway
Hollyhedge Farm
Crotia Mill Farm
Basford Brook
Carters Green Farm
JACK LANE
Meremoor Farm
53
A5020
A500
1
Heath Farm
Ashleigh
WHITES LANE
Red Lion Farm
Larch Farm
LARCH AV.
Basford Hall Bridge
Brook House
CEMETERY
Cemy.
FOUR WAYS
FERNDALE CL.
SPINNEY DR.
WESTMERE CL.
MILL BECK
CLOSE
WESTON
SMITHY LA.
Yew Tree Farm
2
Basford
MERE CT.
ROAD
POPPY CL.
WEST AV.
EAST AV.
CROTIA AV.
MERE
FAIRVIEW AV.
MEADOW AV.
Basford Hall Junction
Weston Village Primary Sch.
Casey Bridge
Sutch Farm
220
52
Crewe
SNAPE LANE
A531
3
CW2
Cricket Ground
Weston Hall
Meadowside
CASEY LANE
Basford Dairy Store
MAIN ROAD
PETERSFIELD WY.
DELAMERE CL.
HEATON WY.
HADLEY DR.
GRGE DR. CL.
PASTURES DR.
PARKLANDS
GOLDEN DR.
HILLWAY
WICKHAM CT.
CHESTERTON
GORSTYHILL GOLF COURSE
Club House
ABBEY PARK
4
40
Chorlton Bank Farm
Heath Farm
HAVERHILL CL.
RYBURN CL.
KINGSWOOD AV.
OAKDALE CL.
CHALFONT CRES.
EDENBRIDGE CL.
ABBEYDALE CL.
WOODLANDS DR.
SYROLE
LITTLE LAKES
51
WYCHWOOD PARK GOLF COURSE
Club House
Hotel
5
Mere Gutter
SPRINGWATER DR.
ASHBOURNE
BRACKENWOOD M.
CRES.
FAIRHAVEN
CHILTERN CL.
HENLEY RD.
WESTWOOD CL.
KINGSWOOD CL.
SPRINGWATER DR.
DRIVE
SANDFORD
RICHMOND CL.
REDBOURNE DR.
Chorlton
WYCHWOOD
The Hollies Farm
Yew Tree Farm
CHORLTON LANE
KENDAL WY.
ST. CLEMENTS CL.
FRESHWATER
6
Field Farm
Dairy Farm
Lane End Farm
350
Fishery
7
HAMPSTEAD DR.
DRIVE
FERNDOWN WY.
Ellesmere Farm
WAYBUTT LANE
LANE

200
A
B
C
D
E
1
2
3
4
5
6
7
220
Crow Nest Bridge
Hollybank Farm
Crows Nest Farm
Townend Barn
The Swallows
Marshgreen Farm
Brickfield Cottages
Cricket Ground
Elm Tree Farm
Plex Flash
Trent & Mersey Canal
Moston House Farm
Works
Sandbach
ELWORTH
Holly Tree Farm
The Moat (Nature Reserve)
Cherry Farm
Ivy House Farm
Primary School
Prim. Sch.
SANDBACH GOLF COURSE
Play. Fld.
Sandbach High School & Sixth Form College
Sandbach Leis. Cen.
Club House
Coun. Offs.
Mag. Ct.
Sandbach School
Saxon Pl.
Pav.
Watchlane Flash (Nature Reserve)
Elton
Warehouse
Depots
Ettiley Heath
Rookery Bri.
Yeowood Farm
Big Hind Heath Farm
Sandbach
CW11
Wheelock Prim. Sch.
Elton Flashes (Nature Reserve)
Sewage Wks.
River Wheelock
Sports Ground
Mill
WHEELOCK
Brook Farm
Fields Farm
Crewe
CW1
Lane Ends Farm
Wks.
Hooter Hall Farm
Hooterhall
Lakemoor Country Park
New House Farm
Wheelock Hall Farm
BOOTH LA.
LONDON ROAD
MIDDLEWICH ROAD
A533
B5079
SALT LINE WAY
HIND HEATH ROAD
STATION RD.
A534
ABBEYFIELDS
73
74
375
62
61
360
59

SANDBACH
Sandbach Heath
Cold Moss Heath
Betchton Heath
Malkin's Bank
Hassall Green
Junction 17
Sandbach Service Area
M6
M6 MOTORWAY
A534
A533
A5022
220
CONGLETON ROAD
OLD MILL ROAD
THE HILL
NEWCASTLE RD.
OLD MILL RD.
Rugby Football Ground
Club Ho.
Three Ways Farm
Offley Prim. Sch.
Park House
Offley Wood
Depot
Sandbach Park
Ten. Cts.
Lib.
War Mem.
Cemetery
Football Grd.
Play. Fld.
Fields Farm
Houndings Lane Farm
The Hazles
Oldhouse Farm
Vicarage Farm
Boults Green Farm
Boults Green Cotts.
The Cross
The Grove
Drumber Farm
Manor Ho. Fm.
Betchton Villas Caravan Park
Pear Tree Farm
Manor House
Moor Ho. Farm
Cottage Farm
Gravel Bank Farm
Ivy Cottage Farm
Arclid Cottage Farm
Reynold's Farm
Heath Farm
Oak Farm
Brookside Hall
Brook-side Cotts.
Bowling Green
Sports Field
Far Arclid Bridge
Old Hall
Brick-house Farm
St. John's C of E Prim. Sch.
Woody Fields Farm
Malkin's Bank Farm
Factory
Club House
MALKINS BANK GOLF COURSE
Trent & Mersey Canal
Fountain Cottages
Jubilee Villas
Bank Farm
Hassall House Farm
Sun Cottage
Station Ho.
Bracken Lea Garth
Cross Bank Farm
The Fields Playing Field
Smithy Farm
Canal-side Farm
F
G
H
J
K
1
2
3
4
5
6
7
76
77
78
59
60
61
62

Station Ho.
Lwr. Roughwood Mill
Mill Terrace
Hillside
Roughwood Cottages
Roughwood
The Potters Barn
Roughwood Farm
220
Higher Roughwood Mill House
Bank Farm
Chellshill
Aqueduct
Roughwood Br.
Day Green Ho.
Day Green
Sandbach
Holly Tree Farm
Day Green Fm.
Roughwood Hill Farm
Chellshill Bridge
Thurlwood Farm
Hassall Pool
Daygreen Farm
CW11
Cresswell Farm
M6 MOTORWAY
Betchton Farm
Bottomless Mere
Sewage Works
Bostock Ho.
M6
Lawton Heath End
Whartons Pool Farm
Bridge Farm
Sandon Ho.
Heath End
Dunnock's Fold Farm
ALSAGER
Sports Ground
Playgrd.
Manchester Metropolitan University (Alsager Campus)
Castle Farm
Rose Villa
Manor Farm
Wilbraham Wood Playing Fields
Wyechila Kennels
The Common
Lady Farm Bungalow
Roseheyes
Moss End Farm
Sunnyside Farm
Emberton Hall Play. Fld.
Alsager Leisure Cen.
Holly Bank
Yew Tree Farm
Halls of Residence
Sports Ground
Alsager Comp. Sch.
Coronation Gardens
The Mere
Orchard Cottage
Northolme Gardens
Civic Cen. Coun. Offs.
Ashfields
Cranberry Prim. Sch.
Intone Fitness Cen.
Works
New Milton Ho.
Oak Lodge
Cranberry Moss
Jane Maddock Homes
Playing Field
WHITE MOSS
Weir
Mill Pond
Mill House
Home Farm
Brookhouse Farm
Lane-ends Farm
Alsager Hall
The Hall
Works
Bankhouse Farm
White Moss
Radway Green Fm.
Radway Green
BUTTERTON LA.
CREWE ROAD
B5077
B5078
SANDBACH ROAD NORTH
BETCHTON LANE
CHELLS HILL
HASSALL ROAD
ROUGHWOOD LANE
DUNNOCKSFOLD ROAD
CHURCH ROAD
LAWTON ROAD

Thurlwood
RODE HEATH
Lawton Heath
Stoke-on-Trent
ST7
Lawton-gate
Church Lawton
Alsager
Hardings Wood
Lunt Moss
RODE POOL
Rode Hall & Gardens
KNUTSFORD ROAD
LIVERPOOL ROAD
LINLEY LANE
TRENT & MERSEY CANAL
CHESHIRE EAST
NEWCASTLE-UNDER-LYME
ALSAGER GOLF & COUNTRY CLUB
Whartons Pool Plantation
Lawton Mere
Slum Wood
Stone Cliff Wood
Rye Low
Fish Pond
The Round Tower
Summer House Plantation
Bratt's Wood
Big Barr
Prize Plantation
Coronation Planting
Moss Wood
Church Lawton Prim. Sch.
Excalibur Prim. Sch.
NELSON INDUSTRIAL ESTATE
221
205

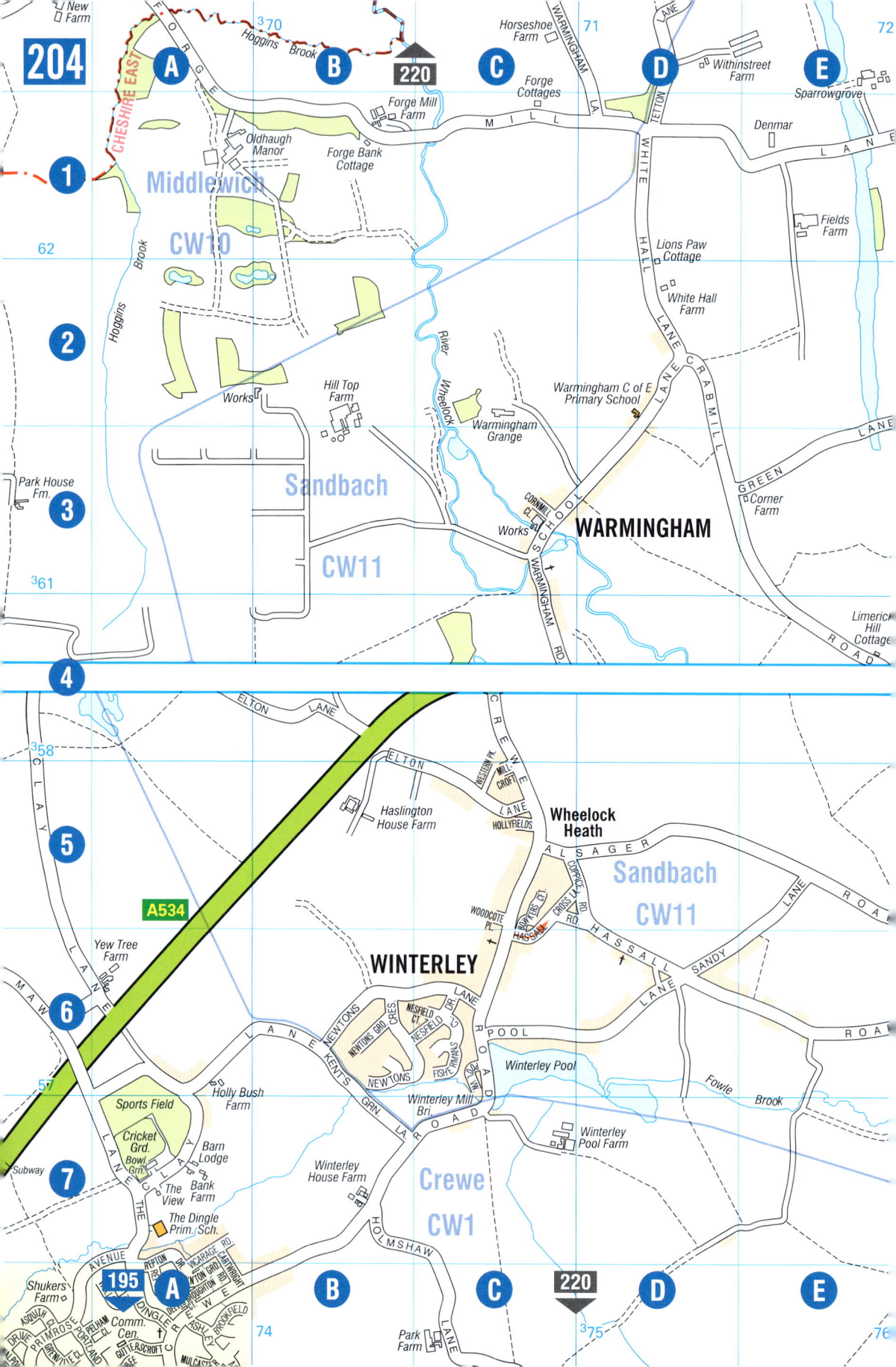

New Farm
Hoggins Brook
220
Horseshoe Farm
WARMINGHAM LA.
LANE
Withinstreet Farm
Sparrowgrove
A
B
C
D
E
Forge Cottages
Forge Mill Farm
FORGE
MILL
TETTON
Denmar
LANE
CHESHIRE EAST
Oldhaugh Manor
Forge Bank Cottage
1
Middlewich
CW10
WHITE HALL LANE
Fields Farm
Lions Paw Cottage
Hoggins Brook
White Hall Farm
2
River Wheelock
CRABMILL LANE
Hill Top Farm
Works
Warmingham C of E Primary School
LANE
Warmingham Grange
Park House Fm.
3
Sandbach
GREEN LANE
Corner Farm
CORNMILL CL.
Works
SCHOOL
WARMINGHAM
CW11
WARMINGHAM RD.
Limerick Hill Cottage
ROAD
4
ELTON LANE
CREWE
CLAY
ELTON
WESTERN PK.
MILL CROFT
Haslington House Farm
LANE
HOLLYFIELDS
Wheelock Heath
5
ALSAGER ROAD
COPPICE RD.
Sandbach
CW11
A534
WOODCOTE PL.
BOWYERS CFT.
CROSS LA.
HASSALL RD.
HASSALL
LANE
Yew Tree Farm
WINTERLEY
SANDY LANE
LANE
MAW
LANE
6
NEWTONS
NESFIELD CT.
NESFIELD
DR.
POOL
ROAD
NEWTONS GRO.
CRES.
NEWTONS
FISHERMANS
MILL CL.
ROAD
Winterley Pool
Fowle Brook
Holly Bush Farm
Sports Field
KENTS GRN. LA.
Winterley Mill Bri.
ROAD
Winterley Pool Farm
Cricket Grd.
Bowl Grn.
Barn Lodge
Subway
7
CLAY
The View
Bank Farm
Winterley House Farm
Crewe
CW1
THE
The Dingle Prim. Sch.
AVENUE
HOLMSHAW
REPTON
DR.
VICARAGE RD.
CARTWRIGHT RD.
195
Shukers Farm
DELVES BROUGHTON GRO.
CREWE
DINGLE
BROOKFIELD
ASHLEY
Comm. Cen.
PELHAM CL.
PORTLAND
PRIMROSE
ASQUITH CL.
GUTTERSCROFT
MULCASTER
Park Farm
LANE
220
B
C
D
E
A
370
71
72
62
361
358
57
74
375
76

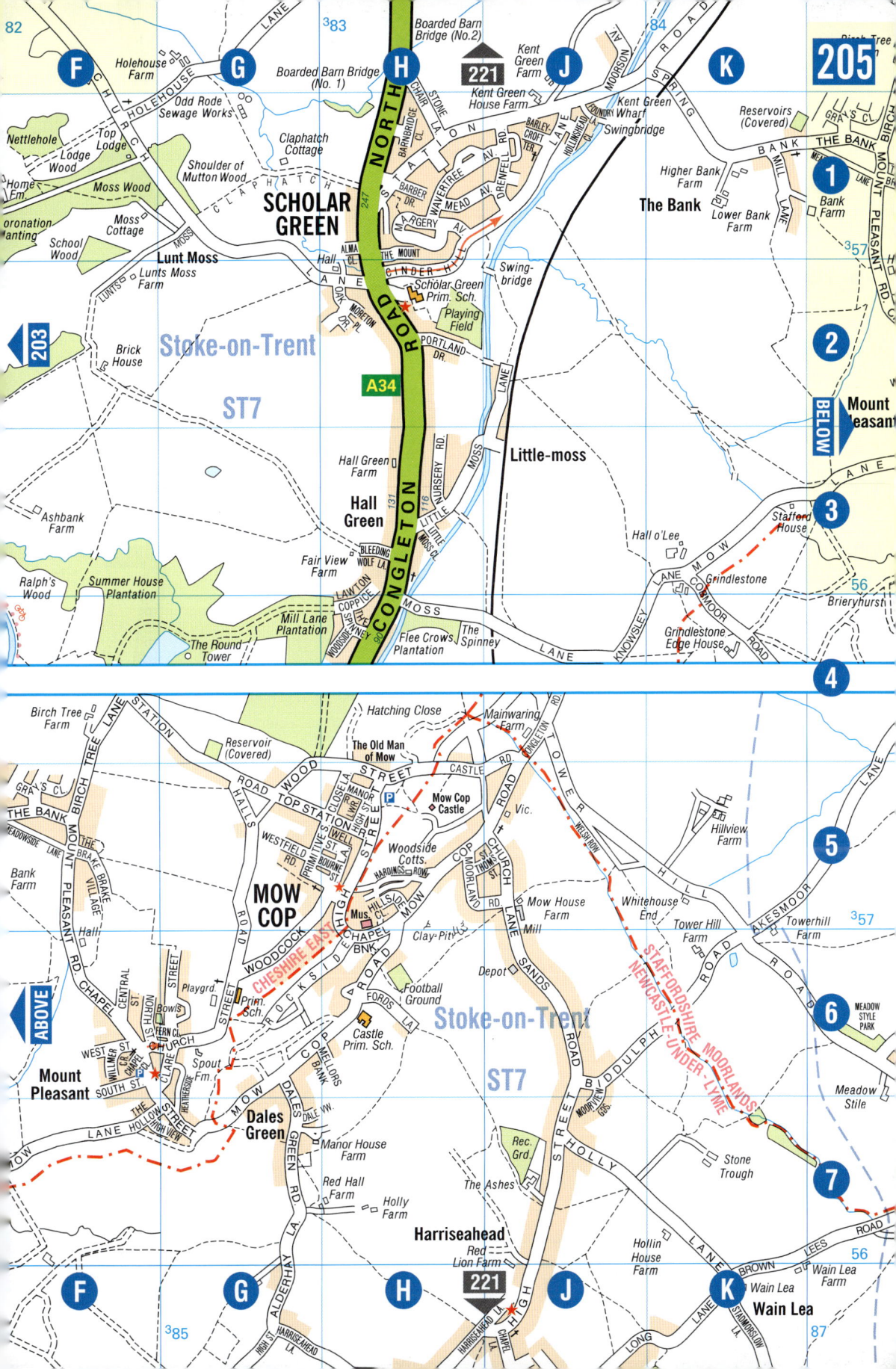

SCHOLAR GREEN
Stoke-on-Trent
ST7
Hall Green
Little-moss
The Bank
Lunt Moss
MOW COP
Mount Pleasant
Dales Green
Harriseahead
Wain Lea
A34
NORTH ROAD
CONGLETON
221
203
BELOW
ABOVE
Mount Pleasant
Holehouse Farm
Odd Rode Sewage Works
Boarded Barn Bridge (No.2)
Boarded Barn Bridge (No. 1)
Kent Green Farm
Kent Green House Farm
Kent Green Wharf
Swingbridge
Reservoirs (Covered)
Higher Bank Farm
Lower Bank Farm
Bank Farm
Nettlehole
Top Lodge
Lodge Wood
Moss Wood
Claphatch Cottage
Shoulder of Mutton Wood
Moss Cottage
School Wood
Lunts Moss Farm
Scholar Green Prim. Sch.
Playing Field
Swing-bridge
Brick House
Hall Green Farm
Ashbank Farm
Fair View Farm
Ralph's Wood
Summer House Plantation
Mill Lane Plantation
The Round Tower
Flee Crows Plantation
The Spinney
Hall o'Lee
Stafford House
Grindlestone
Grindlestone Edge House
Brieryhurst
Birch Tree Farm
Hatching Close
Mainwaring Farm
Reservoir (Covered)
The Old Man of Mow
Mow Cop Castle
Woodside Cotts.
Hillview Farm
Mow House Farm
Whitehouse End
Tower Hill Farm
Towerhill Farm
Meadow Style Park
Meadow Stile
Mus.
Clay Pit
Football Ground
Castle Prim. Sch.
Prim. Sch.
Playgrd.
Bowls
Spout Fm.
Depot
Mill
Vic.
CHESHIRE EAST
STAFFORDSHIRE MOORLANDS
NEWCASTLE-UNDER-LYME
Manor House Farm
Red Hall Farm
Holly Farm
Rec. Grd.
The Ashes
Stone Trough
Red Lion Farm
Hollin House Farm
Wain Lea Farm

CLUTTON
BROXTON ROAD
WHITCHURCH ROAD
BARNHILL RD
A534
A41
Broxton
Charity Farm
Pool Plantation
Huntsman Cottage
Smithy House
Clutton Hall Farm
Shawgreen Pit
Clutton Hill
Park House
Carden Hall
The Birches
Round Hill
CARDEN PARK GOLF COURSE
Club House
Carden Park Hotel
Cliff
French Bank
Moor Gorse
Cliffe Bank
Chester
CH3
Malpas
SY14
Holywell Farm
Holywell Brook
Fields Farm
Vilna House Farm
BROXTON HALL MEWS
Walker's Wood
Broxton Wood
Oak Farm
219
Stone House
Carden Brook
Hook's Brook
Tilston Ford Bridge
Little Tilston Bridge
Isle Farm
Keeper's Cottage
Hobb Hill
Hobb Hill Farm
Bank Farm
TILSTON
Old Hall Farm
Tilston Parochial C of E Prim. Sch.
Tilston Lodge
Ford
LOWCROSS
The Oaks
Lowcross Hill
Lowcross Hill Fm.
Churtoncroft
Play. Fld.
Yewtree Farm
LANE GRANGE
Littlehill
Flags Cottages
Church Farm
Rectory Cottage
CHURCH LANE
The Oaklands
Lowcross Gorse
Lowcross Farm
Lowcross Mill Farm
Hawthorn House
SCAR

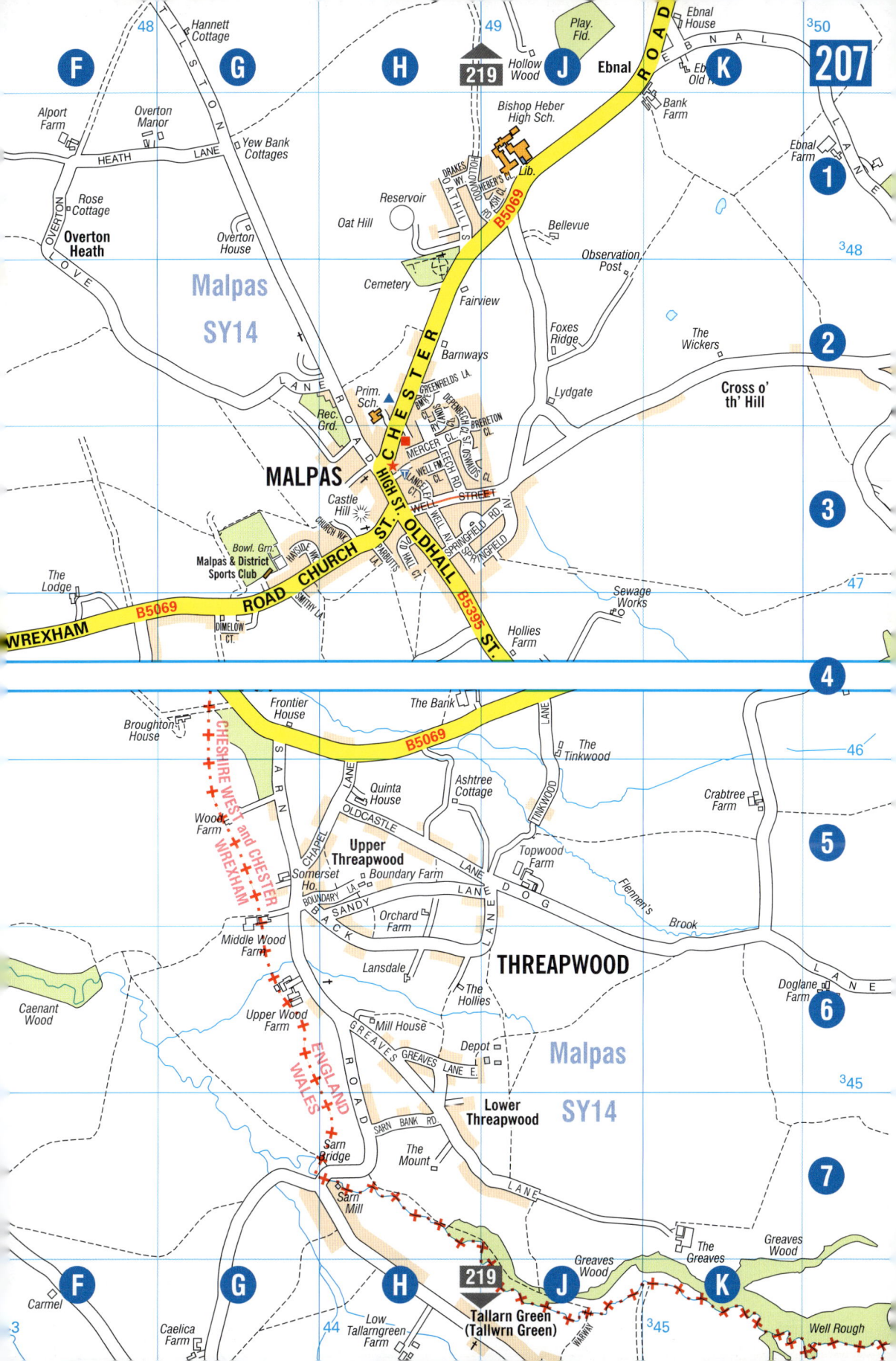

Malpas
SY14
MALPAS
Overton Heath
Ebnal
Cross o' th' Hill
Upper Threapwood
THREAPWOOD
Lower Threapwood
Tallarn Green (Tallwrn Green)
CHESHIRE WEST and CHESTER
WREXHAM
ENGLAND
WALES
CHESTER ROAD
HIGH ST.
CHURCH ST.
OLDHALL ST.
WREXHAM ROAD
B5069
B5395
219
Hannett Cottage
Alport Farm
Overton Manor
Yew Bank Cottages
HEATH LANE
TILSTON ROAD
OVERTON LOVE LANE
Rose Cottage
Overton House
Bishop Heber High Sch.
Lib.
Reservoir
Oat Hill
Cemetery
Fairview
Bellevue
Observation Post
Foxes Ridge
Barnways
The Wickers
Lydgate
Prim. Sch.
Rec. Grd.
Castle Hill
Bowl. Grn.
Malpas & District Sports Club
The Lodge
Dimelow Ct.
Smithy La.
Parbutts La.
Old Hall Ct.
Well Street
Sewage Works
Hollies Farm
Ebnal House
EBNAL LANE
Bank Farm
Ebnal Farm
Hollow Wood
Play. Fld.
Frontier House
Broughton House
The Bank
The Tinkwood
TINKWOOD LANE
Quinta House
Ashtree Cottage
Crabtree Farm
Wood Farm
OLDCASTLE LANE
CHAPEL LANE
Topwood Farm
Somerset Ho.
Boundary Farm
Boundary La.
SANDY LANE
DOG LANE
Flennen's Brook
Orchard Farm
BACK LANE
Middle Wood Farm
Lansdale
The Hollies
Caenant Wood
Upper Wood Farm
Mill House
GREAVES LANE
Greaves Lane E.
Depot
SARN ROAD
Sarn Bank Rd.
The Mount
Sarn Bridge
Sarn Mill
The Greaves
Greaves Wood
Doglane Farm
Well Rough
Carmel
Caelica Farm
Low Tallarngreen Farm
F
G
H
J
K
1
2
3
4
5
6
7
48
49
350
348
47
46
345
44

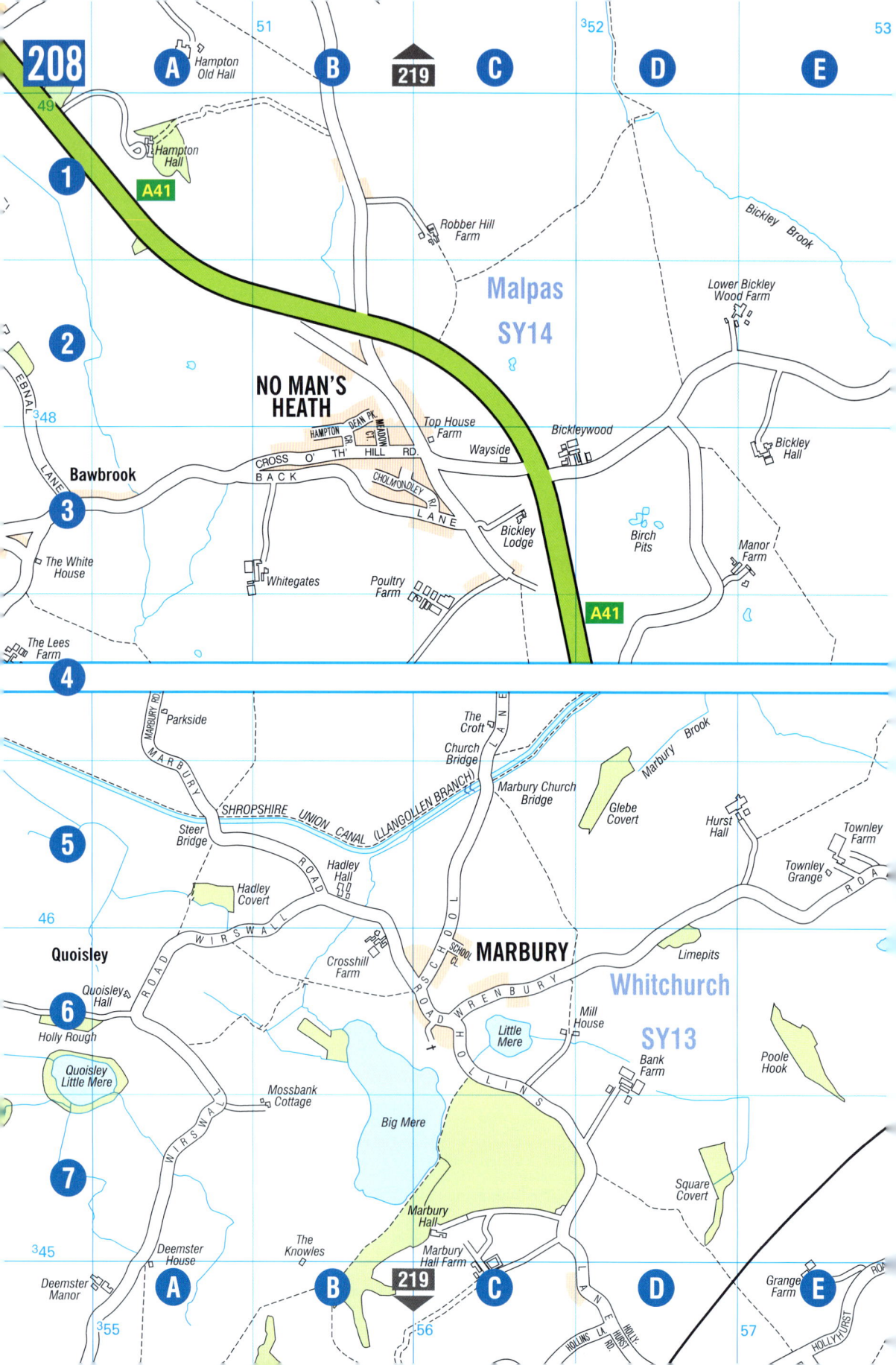

A   B   219   C   D   E

51   352   53

49

1

Hampton Old Hall

Hampton Hall

A41

Robber Hill Farm

Malpas

SY14

Bickley Brook

Lower Bickley Wood Farm

2

348

Bickleywood

Bickley Hall

NO MAN'S HEATH

Top House Farm

Wayside

HAMPTON DEAN PK. MEADOW CT. CR.

HILL RD.

Bawbrook

CROSS O' TH'

BACK

CHOLMONDELEY

LANE

3

EBNAL LANE

The White House

Whitegates

Poultry Farm

Bickley Lodge

Birch Pits

Manor Farm

A41

The Lees Farm

4

MARBURY RD.

Parkside

The Croft

Church Bridge

LANE

Marbury Brook

MARBURY

Glebe Covert

Hurst Hall

Townley Farm

5

MARBURY ROAD

Steer Bridge

SHROPSHIRE UNION CANAL (LLANGOLLEN BRANCH)

Marbury Church Bridge

Townley Grange

ROAD

46

Hadley Covert

Hadley Hall

WIRSWALL ROAD

HOLLINS ROAD

SCHOOL CL.

MARBURY

Limepits

Quoisley

Crosshill Farm

WRENBURY

Whitchurch

SY13

6

Quoisley Hall

Mill House

Bank Farm

Poole Hook

Holly Rough

Little Mere

Quoisley Little Mere

Mossbank Cottage

Big Mere

7

WIRSWALL ROAD

Square Covert

345

Deemster House

The Knowles

Marbury Hall

Deemster Manor

Marbury Hall Farm

Grange Farm

A   B   219   C   D   E

355   56   57

HOLLINS LA.   HURST RD.   LANE   HOLLY RD.   HOLLYHURST

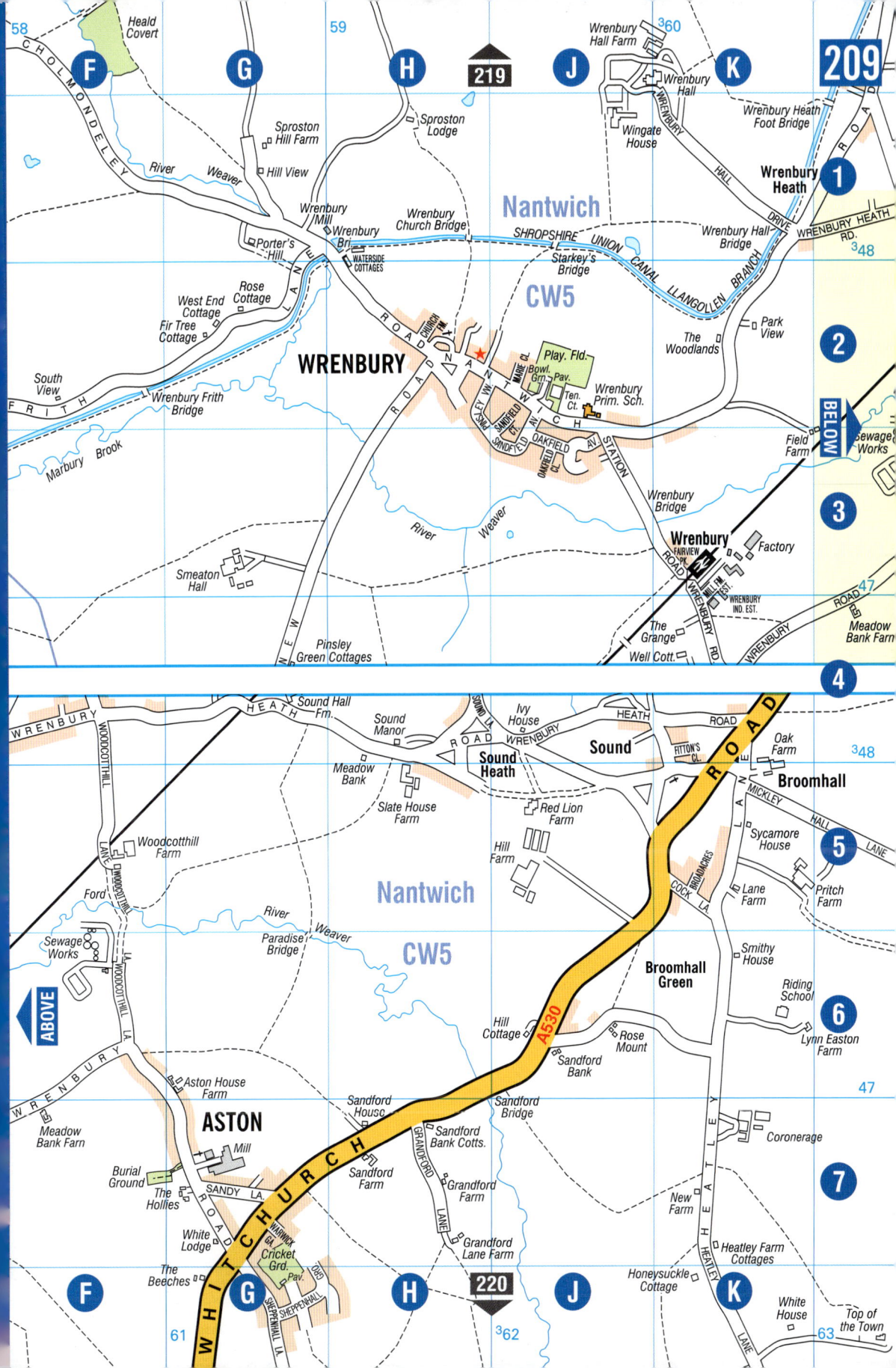

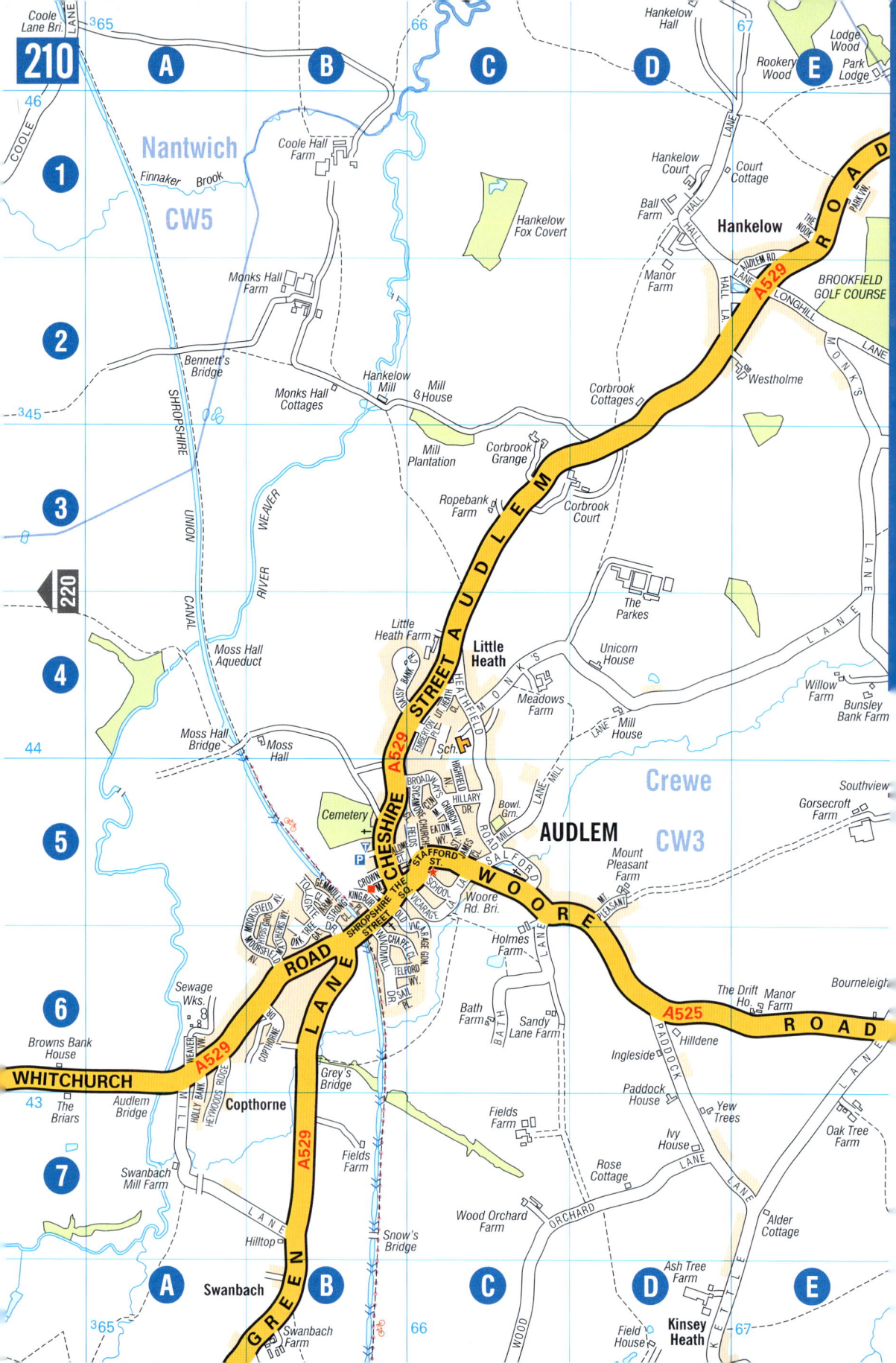

Coole Lane Bri.
LANE
365
66
67
A
B
C
D
E
46
COOLE
1
2
3
4
5
6
7
Nantwich
CW5
Finnaker Brook
Coole Hall Farm
Hankelow Hall
Lodge Wood
Rookery Wood
Park Lodge
Hankelow Court
Court Cottage
Ball Farm
Hankelow
HALL
Manor Farm
AUDLEM RD.
HALL LA.
LONGHILL LANE
BROOKFIELD GOLF COURSE
THE NOOK
PARK VW.
ROAD
A529
Hankelow Fox Covert
Monks Hall Farm
Bennett's Bridge
Monks Hall Cottages
Hankelow Mill
Mill House
Westholme
MONK'S
Corbrook Cottages
345
Mill Plantation
Corbrook Grange
Ropebank Farm
Corbrook Court
SHROPSHIRE
UNION
CANAL
RIVER
WEAVER
220
AUDLEM
STREET
The Parkes
LANE
Little Heath Farm
Little Heath
Unicorn House
Moss Hall Aqueduct
DAISY BANK CR.
EMBERTON PL.
LIT. HEATH CL.
HEATHFIELD
Meadows Farm
Willow Farm
Bunsley Bank Farm
Mill House
Moss Hall Bridge
Moss Hall
44
Sch.
Crewe
CW3
CHESHIRE
BROADWAYS
SYCAMORE
CHURCH
HIGHFIELD AV.
HILLARY DR.
CHURCH VW.
EATON WY.
ST. JAMES CL.
FIELDS
Bowl. Grn.
MILL LANE
Southview
Gorsecroft Farm
Cemetery
Mount Pleasant Farm
STAFFORD ST.
SALFORD
CROWN
THE SQ.
KINGBUR
GEMMELL CL.
TOLLGATE DR.
ARMSTRONG CL.
SCHOOL LA.
VICARAGE LA.
Woore Rd. Bri.
WOORE
MT. PLEASANT
MOORSFIELD AV.
MATTHEWS WY.
OAK TREE GA.
SHROPSHIRE STREET
OLD
VICARAGE GDN.
CHAPEL CL.
WINDMILL DR.
TELFORD WY.
SAIL PL.
Holmes Farm
ROAD
Sewage Wks.
Bath Farm
BATH
Sandy Lane Farm
The Drift Ho.
Manor Farm
Bourneleigh
A525
Hilldene
PADDOCK
Browns Bank House
WEAVER VW.
WHITCHURCH
Ingleside
HOLLY BANK
HEYWOODS RIDGE
COPTHORNE
Grey's Bridge
43
The Briars
Audlem Bridge
Copthorne
Paddock House
Yew Trees
Fields Farm
Ivy House
Oak Tree Farm
Swanbach Mill Farm
Fields Farm
Rose Cottage
GREEN
Wood Orchard Farm
ORCHARD
Alder Cottage
Hilltop
Snow's Bridge
Ash Tree Farm
Swanbach
KETTLE
Swanbach Farm
Field House
WOOD
Kinsey Heath

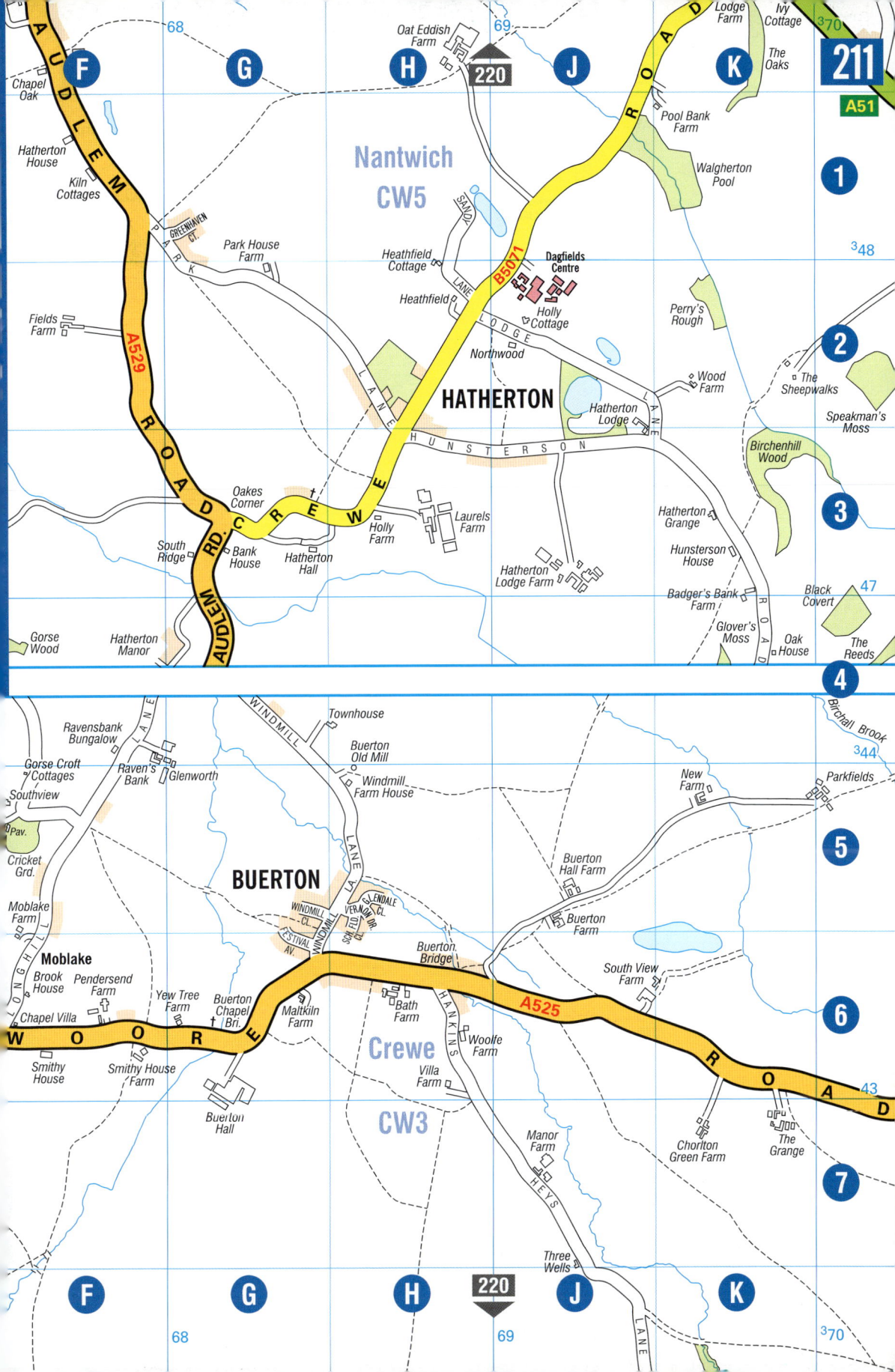

A51
Nantwich
CW5
HATHERTON
BUERTON
Moblake
Crewe
CW3
AUDLEM ROAD
A529
CREWE ROAD
B5071
WOORE ROAD
A525
PARK LANE
SANDY LANE
LODGE LANE
HUNSTERSON
WINDMILL LANE
HANKINS HEYS LANE
LONGHILL LANE
Chapel Oak
Hatherton House
Kiln Cottages
Greenhaven Ct.
Park House Farm
Heathfield Cottage
Heathfield
Dagfields Centre
Holly Cottage
Northwood
Oat Eddish Farm
Lodge Farm
Ivy Cottage
The Oaks
Pool Bank Farm
Walgherton Pool
Perry's Rough
The Sheepwalks
Speakman's Moss
Wood Farm
Hatherton Lodge
Birchenhill Wood
Fields Farm
Oakes Corner
South Ridge
Bank House
Hatherton Hall
Holly Farm
Laurels Farm
Hatherton Grange
Hunsterson House
Hatherton Lodge Farm
Badger's Bank Farm
Black Covert
Glover's Moss
Oak House
The Reeds
Gorse Wood
Hatherton Manor
Ravensbank Bungalow
Townhouse
Buerton Old Mill
Windmill Farm House
Birchall Brook
Gorse Croft Cottages
Raven's Bank
Glenworth
Southview
Pav.
Cricket Grd.
New Farm
Parkfields
Moblake Farm
Buerton Hall Farm
Buerton Farm
Windmill Cl.
Festival Av.
Sch. Fld. Cl.
Vernon Dr.
Glendale Cl.
Buerton Bridge
South View Farm
Brook House
Pendersend Farm
Yew Tree Farm
Buerton Chapel Bri.
Maltkiln Farm
Bath Farm
Chapel Villa
Smithy House
Smithy House Farm
Buerton Hall
Woolfe Farm
Villa Farm
Manor Farm
Chorlton Green Farm
The Grange
Three Wells
220
F G H J K
1 2 3 4 5 6 7
68 69 370 348 347 344 343

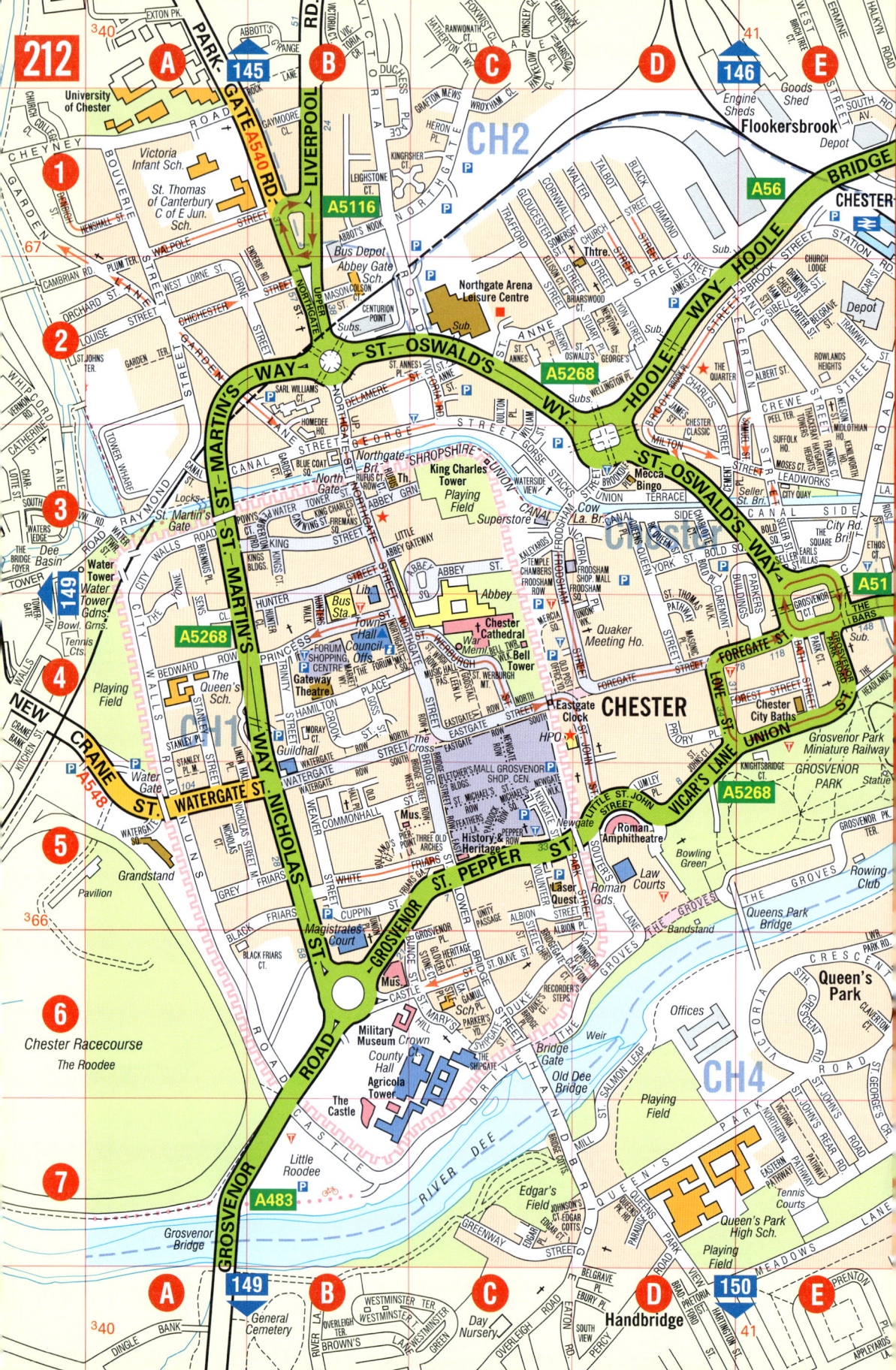

145
146
149
150
A
B
C
D
E
1
2
3
4
5
6
7
University of Chester
Victoria Infant Sch.
St. Thomas of Canterbury C of E Jun. Sch.
CH2
CH1
CH4
Flookersbrook
Goods Shed
Engine Sheds
Depot
CHESTER
A56
A5116
A540
A5268
A51
A548
A483
Bus Depot
Abbey Gate Sch.
Northgate Arena Leisure Centre
Thtre.
Centurion Point
The Quarter
King Charles Tower
Playing Field
Superstore
Mecca Bingo
Chester Classic
Leadworks
City Rd. Bri.
Water Tower
Water Tower Gdns.
Bowl. Grns.
Tennis Cts.
Dee Basin
The Bridge Foyer
Abbey
Chester Cathedral
War Meml.
Bell Tower
Town Hall
Council Offs.
Forum Shopping Centre
Gateway Theatre
The Queen's Sch.
Guildhall
Water Gate
Eastgate Clock
HPO
Chester City Baths
Quaker Meeting Ho.
Grosvenor Park Miniature Railway
Grosvenor Park
Roman Amphitheatre
Bowling Green
Law Courts
Roman Gdns.
Laser Quest
History & Heritage
Mus.
Magistrates' Court
Grandstand
Pavilion
Chester Racecourse
The Roodee
Military Museum
County Hall
Agricola Tower
The Castle
Crown Ct.
Little Roodee
Bridge Gate
Old Dee Bridge
Weir
Offices
Bandstand
Queens Park Bridge
Rowing Club
Queen's Park
Playing Field
Queen's Park High Sch.
Tennis Courts
Edgar's Field
Grosvenor Bridge
River Dee
General Cemetery
Day Nursery
Handbridge
St. Oswald's Way
St. Martin's Way
Nicholas St.
Grosvenor Road
Grosvenor St.
Pepper St.
Vicar's Lane
Little St. John Street
Foregate St.
Union St.
Hoole Way
Liverpool Rd.
Parkgate Rd.
Watergate St.
Crane St.
New Crane St.
Northgate Street
Eastgate
Frodsham Street
Bridge Street
Lower Bridge Street
Castle Drive
Queen's Park Road
The Groves
Canal Street
George Street
Garden Lane
City Road
Brook Street
Meadows Lane
Victoria Crescent
Union Terrace

ALTRINCHAM
Altrincham
WA14
WA15
Altrincham C of E Prim.Sch.
Loreto Grammar School
North Cestrian Grammar Sch.
Loreto Prep. Sch.
ALTRINCHAM GENERAL HOSP.
Altrincham Leisure Cen.
Altrincham
Silver Blades Ice Rink
Depot
Superstore
Gareth's Bridge
Apollo Cinema
Total Fitness
The Club Theatre
STAMFORD PARK
Catholic College
DUNHAM ROAD
STAMFORD NEW ROAD
WOODLANDS ROAD
CHURCH ST.
RAILWAY ST.
ASHLEY RD.
MOSS LANE
GROBY ROAD
HEATON NORRIS
STOCKPORT
Stockport
SK4
SK3
SK1
M60 MOTORWAY
WELLINGTON ROAD NORTH
KNIGHTSBRIDGE
GREAT PORTWOOD ST.
EGERTON STREET
TRAVIS BROW
CHESTERGATE
WELLINGTON
Recreation Ground
Kingsgate Playing Field
Portway House
Stockport Viaduct
Bus Station
Bus Depot
Hat Works
Stockport Garrick Theatre
Grand Central Pools
Stockport Megabowl
Cineworld Cinema
Town Hall
Council Offices
Mag. Court
Leisure Cen.
Market Hall
St. Joseph's Catholic Prim. Sch.
THE PEEL CENTRE
Gas Holders
Gala Bingo
The Old Rectory
Hollywood Pk. Combined Nursy. Cen.
Hollywood Park
Bowling Greens
Pavilion
River Mersey
River Goyt
Stockport

214 **A**

L I V E R P O O L

B A Y

Liverpool to:
Dublin 7hrs. 30mins.

Liverpool to:
Douglas 2hrs. 30mins.
(Fast Ferry)

Birkenhead to:
Belfast 8hrs.
Douglas 4hrs. 15mins.
(Seasonal)
Dublin 8hrs.

Hightown
Lady Green
Ince Blundell
MAGHULL
A59
B5193
Homer Green
Lunt
Sefton
Little Crosby
A5207
B5422
Netherton
Thornton
Great Crosby
B
Buckley Hill
Waddi
CROSBY
LITHERLAND
Aintree
Waterloo
A5036
A5038
Aintree
Seaforth Dock
Orrell
A506
Fazaker
Seaforth
Kirkdale
A59
A580
BOOTLE
Walton
Anfield
Norri
Gree
Fort Perch Rock
New Brighton
F.C.
WALLASEY
Liscard
A554-5
Everton
A580
Egremont
A57
Old Swan
TOLL
(Kingsway)
Mersey
Tunnel
A5047
Seacombe
Leasowe
Bidston
Moreton
Wave
Red Rocks Marsh
Meols
A553
Upton
(Queensway)
TOLL
Toxteth
Sefton Park
HOYLAKE
B5192
Greasby
BIRKENHEAD
Priory
Mossle
Hill
Hilbre Island
B5139
Newton
Woodchurch
Oxton
Tranmere
Dingle
A561
Aigburt
Hilbre Islands
Grange
Frankby
Arrowe
Prenton
Rock Ferry
Otterspool
Grass
WEST KIRBY
B5140
Irby
Storeton
Lady Lever Gallery
Caldy
M53
Thingwall
New Ferry
Thurstaston
Pensby
Barnston
BEBINGTON
Port Sunlight
R
Brimstage
HESWALL
A5137
Spital
A41
Bromborough
Eastham Woods
Thornton Hough
B5137
Brookhurst
Eastham
Gayton
Raby
B5136
Eastham Ferry
Gayton Sands
B5135
Windle Hill
B5133
Hooton
Parkgate
B5132
Childer Thornton
Overpool
Willaston
Little Sutton
C H E S H
NESTON
Little Neston
A540
Ledsham
Great Sutton
A41
Whitb
Ness
B5463
Burton
Botanic Garden
Puddington
Capenhurst
Woodbank
A550
ENGLAND
WALES
DANGER AREA
Shotwick Hall
Shotwick
A41
Mollington
Mostyn Quay
Mostyn
Rhewl-Mostyn
Glan-y-don
A548
Whitford
(Chwitffordd)
A5026
Greenfield
(Maes-glas)
Basingwerk Abbey
Whelston
A548
A494
Saughall
Garden City
Sealand
B
Gorsedd
Carmel
Pantasaph
Greenfield
Holywell Bank
A550
Blacon
A5
Brynford
Babell
Holywell
(Treffynnon)
Bagillt
Shotton
Higher Shotton
A548
Dolphin
Basingwerk Castle
Flint
(Y Fflint)
Queensferry
218
A550
Lixwm
Pentre Halkyn
Halkyn
(Helygain)
Oakenholt
A548
CHESTER
Ysceifiog
Tirnewydd
B5123
Flint Mountain
Kelsterton
CONNAH'S QUAY
B5126
Sandycroft
A548
Nannerch
FLINTSHIRE
Rhosesmor
A
Northop
B5125
Northop Hall
Shotton
Hawarden
Moel Famau
Rhydymwyn
A55
Soughton
(Sychdyn)
Alltami
Ewloe
A541
A5

215
KIRKBY
ST. HELENS
HAYDOCK
ASHTON IN-MAKERFIELD
GOLBORNE
LEIGH
PRESCOT
HUYTON
NEWTON-LE-WILLOWS
WARRINGTON
VERPOOL
WIDNES
RUNCORN
ELLESMERE PORT
FRODSHAM
Helsby
NORTHWI
Weaverham
Rainford
Billinge
Knowsley
Eccleston
Rainhill
Whiston
Cronton
Halewood
Woolton
Allerton
Childwall
Speke
Hale
Burtonwood
Winwick
Orford
Great Sankey
Penketh
Grappenhall
Appleton Thorn
Stretton
Daresbury
Keckwick
Norton
Halton
Weston
Murdishaw
Preston Brook
Sutton Weaver
Aston
Kingsley
Crowton
Acton Bridge
Comberbach
Cuddington
Sandiway
Hartford
Delamere
Kelsall
Tarvin
Mouldsworth
Manley
Alvanley
Dunham-on-the-Hill
Hapsford
Elton
Stanlow
Ince
Mickle Trafford
Bridge Trafford
Great Barrow
Guilden Sutton
Hoole
Upton
Littleton
LIVERPOOL JOHN LENNON
MERSEY
Manchester Ship Canal
DELAMERE FOREST PARK
Gulliver's World
Haydock Park
Knowsley Safari Park
BURTONWOOD
CHESTER
M6
M56
M57
M58
M62
M54
A49
A56
A57
A58
A570
A580
A562
A561
A557
A533
A556
A54
A51
A50
A579
A5300
B5201
219
216

216
Platt Bridge
Hindley Green
ATHERTON
Little Hulton
Walkden
WORSLEY
SWINTON
Pendlebu
Tyldesley
Astley
Westleigh
Bamfurlong
Abram
Bickershaw
Land Gate
Downall Green
Bryn
Simm's Lane End
ASHTON-IN-MAKERFIELD
Garswood
Haydock Park
LEIGH
Bedford
Blackmoor
Boothstown
Colliery
Canal
Bridgewater Park
ECCLES
GOLBORNE
Lowton
Pennington Flash
Pennington
Lowton Common
Glazebury
A580
Chat Moss
M62
Barton
Swing Aqdct.
HAYDOCK
Canal
Twiss Green
Fowley Common
Davyhulme
Earlestown
Lane Head
Kenyon
New Lane End
URMSTON
NEWTON-LE-WILLOWS
Collins Green
Vulcan Village
Culcheth
Flixton
Croft
Irlam
Mersey
Ashton upon Mersey
Burtonwood
BURTONWOOD
Winwick
Glazebrook
Cadishead
Carrington
Dainewell Woods
SALE
Risley
Risley Moss
Birchwood
Hollinfare
Rixton Claypits
Partington
Dark Lane
Woodhouses
M62
Fearnhead
Orford
Gulliver's World
WARRINGTON
Woolston
Paddington
Bridge TOLL
Mossbrow
Broadheath
Timperley
Brooklands
Warburton
Heatley
Great Sankey
Martinscroft
Oughtrington
Dunham Woodhouses
Bridgewater Canal
Dunham Town
ALTRINCHAM
Penketh
Howley
Lymm
Little Bollington
Dunham Massey
Bowdon
Hale
Cuerdley Cross
Thelwall
Wilderspool
Moore
Lower Walton
Higher Walton
Grappenhall
POPLAR 2000
Broomedge
Halebarns
Manchester Ship Canal
Stockton Heath
M56
Appleton Thorn
Sworton Heath
High Legh
Ashley
Keckwick
Daresbury
Stretton
Rostherne
Bucklow Hill
Norton
Hatton
Farm
Tatton Park
Old Hall
Mere
Stockley Farm
Arley
Arley Hall
Murdishaw
Higher Whitley
Tatton Park
Heritage
Preston on the Hill
Preston Brook
Antrobus
Bate Heath
Mobberley
Sutton Weaver
Dutton
Frandley
Lower Whitley
Cross Town
Aston
Great Budworth
Pick Mere
KNUTSFORD
Comberbach
A537
CHESHIRE WEST
Pickmere
Tabley Mere
Tabley House
Ollerton
Acton Bridge
Marbury
Lion Salt Works
Higher Wincham
Plumley
Anderton
Boat Lift
Marston
Wincham
Little Leigh
Barnton
Winnington
Crowton
Lostock Gralam
Plumley
Lime Beds
Smithy Green
Over Peover
Kingsley
NORTHWICH
Lostock Green
Lower Peover
Commonside
Weaverham
Rudheath
Swan Green
Peover Hall
& CHESTER
Salt
Norley
Leftwich
DELAMERE FOREST PARK
Cuddington
Hartford
Higher Shurlach
Lach Dennis
Jodrell Bank Observatory
Blackden Heath
Sandiway
Marshall's Arm
Davenham
Allostock
Lovell Radio Telescope
Goostrey
Jodrell Bank
Oakmere
Mere Heath
Puddinglake
Delamere
Moulton
Bostock Green
Byley
Twemlow Green
Whitegate
Foxwist Green
Meadowbank
Cranage
Cheshire Herbs
Trent & Mersey Canal
Sproston Green
Salterswall
Wharton
Swettenham
Sandlow Green
Little Budworth Common
Over
Stanthorne
Middlewich
Holmes Chapel
215
220

217
MANCHESTER
Crumpsall
Charlestown
Blackley
Broughton Park
Cheetham Hill
Harpurhey
Newton Heath
Woodhouses
FAILSWORTH
Hollinwood
Bardsley
Daisy Nook
Hurst
Mossley
Castle
Dove Stone Resr.
Chew Resr.
Tower
ASHTON-UNDER-LYNE
Buckton Vale
Millbrook
Stalybridge
Stamford Park
Swineshaw Resr.
Brook
STALYBRIDGE
Tintwistle
Arnfield
Swallows Wood
Hadfield
Clayton
DROYLSDEN
DUKINFIELD
Gorton
Audenshaw
Newton
Mottram in Longdendale
Hollingworth
Hulme
Moss Side
Rusholme
Old Trafford
STRETFORD
Levenshulme
Reddish
DENTON
HYDE
Hattersley
Gamesley
Higher Dinting
Old Glossop
GLOSSOP
Chorlton-cum-Hardy
Fallowfield
Withington
Burnage
Heaton Moor
Haughton Green
Gee Cross
Broadbottom
Chisworth
Charlesworth
Long Clough
Chunal
Woodley
Etherow
Compstall
Lee Head
Didsbury
Bredbury
Romiley
STOCKPORT
Offerton
Lock Flight
Mellor
Rowarth
Little Hayfield
Marple
Broadhurst Edge Wood
Thornsett
Birch Vale
Hayfield
Benchill
Gatley
CHEADLE
Cheadle Hulme
Hazel Grove
Hawk Green
Strines
New Mills
Low Leighton
Wythenshawe
Heald Green
Bramhall
High Lane
Disley
Newtown
Min. Rlwy.
Higher Poynton
Poynton
Danebank
Furness Vale
MANCHESTER INTERNATIONAL
Handforth
Styal
Styal NT
Quarry Bank Mill
Chinley
Morley
Woodford
Hope Green
Wardsend
Lyme Park
Bridgemont
Whaley Bridge
Whitehough
Buxworth
Lower Crossings
WILMSLOW
Dean Row
Adlington Hall
Skellorn Green
Booth Green
Bow Stones
Adlington
Kettleshulme
Taxal
Horwich End
Tunstead Milton
Cockyard
Combs Resr.
Combs
Knolls Green
Hough
Mottram St. Andrew
Pott Shrigley
Dunge Valley
Goyt Forest
Fernilee
Fernilee Resr.
Alderley Edge
Prestbury
BOLLINGTON
Nether Alderley
Radnor Mere
Bradley Mount
Kerridge
White Nancy Mon.
Higher Hurdsfield
Rainow
Jenkin Chapel
Lamaload Resr.
Chelford
Open spring 2011
Tytherington
West Park
Hurdsfield
Silk
Errwood Resr.
Errwood Hall Ruins
Pavilion Gardens
Longmoss
Henbury
Monk's Heath
Capesthorne Hall
Broken Cross
Weston
MACCLESFIELD
Shining Tor
Goyt's Moss
BUXTON
Burbage
Cat & Fiddle Inn
Redes Mere
Whisterfield
Withington Green
Siddington
Windyharbour
Warren
Moss Lane
Tegg's Nose
Langley
Sutton Lane Ends
Mount Farm Ponds
Macclesfield Forest
Trentabank Reservoir
Canholes
Lower Withington
Highlane
221
Oakgrove
Wildboarclough
Gawsworth Hall
Marton
Gleadsmoss
Rodeheath
North Rode
Blaze Farm
Allgreave
Flash
Axe Edge
Newsbank
The Quinta
Wincle
Bosley
M60
M67
A6
A34
A523
A537
A536
A54
A53
A538
A56
A576
A627
A635
A6010
A57
A5103
A628
A6018
B6105
A6015
A624
A626
A5143
A5149
A5102
B5091
B5470
A5004
B5392
B5086
B5087
B6062
B5470
Chapel
Buxton

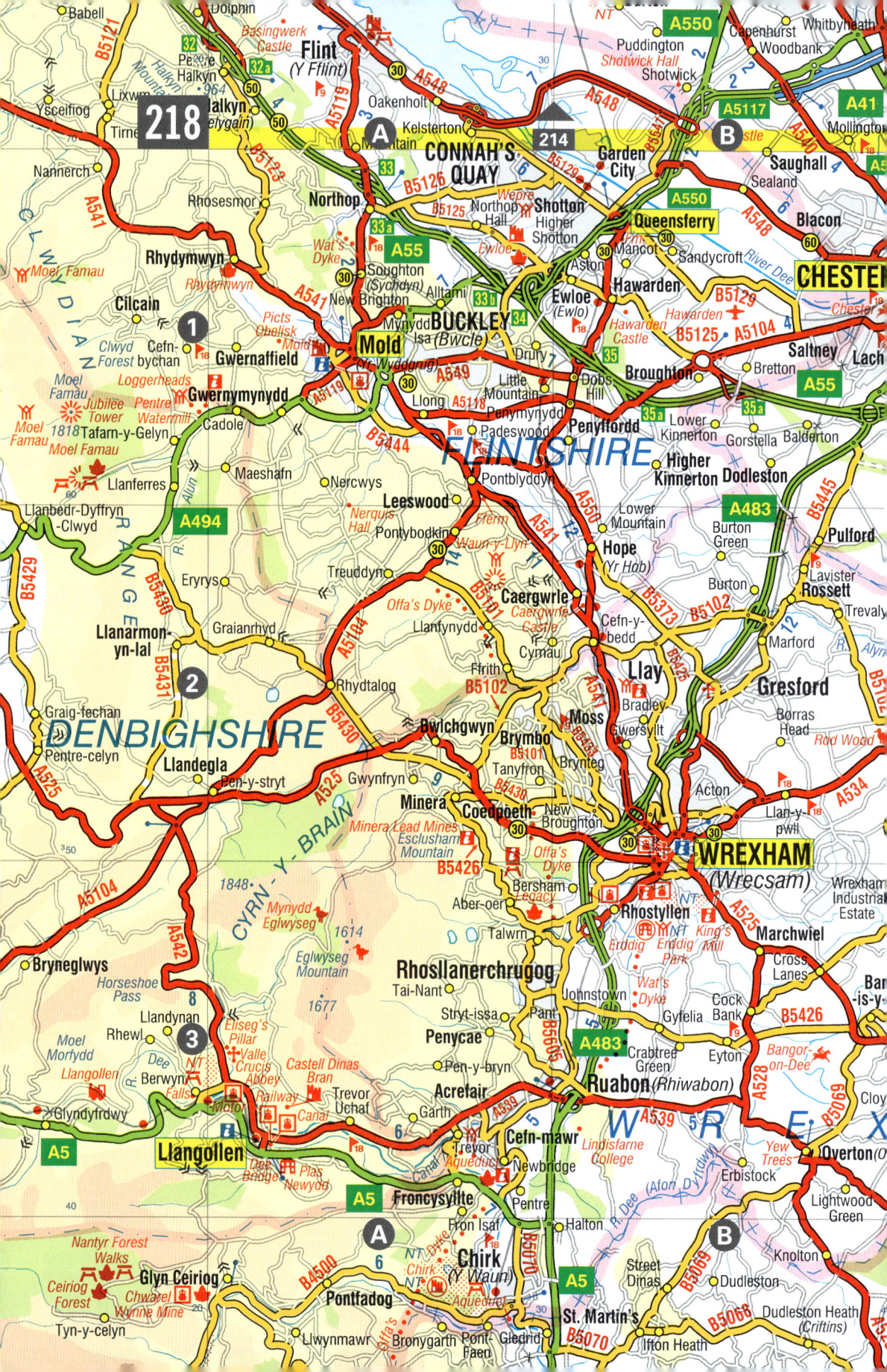
Flint
(Y Fflint)
CONNAH'S QUAY
Mold
(Yr Wyddgrug)
BUCKLEY
(Bwcle)
FLINTSHIRE
DENBIGHSHIRE
CHESTER
WREXHAM
(Wrecsam)
Llangollen
Chirk
(Y Waun)
Ruabon (Rhiwabon)
Queensferry
Garden City
Shotton
Hawarden
Broughton
Saltney
Holywell
Northop
Rhydymwyn
Cilcain
Gwernaffield
Gwernymynydd
Llanferres
Llanarmon-yn-Ial
Llandegla
Bwlchgwyn
Coedpoeth
Minera
Brymbo
Caergwrle
Hope
(Yr Hob)
Llay
Gresford
Rossett
Pulford
Dodleston
Penyffordd
Rhosllanerchrugog
Penycae
Acrefair
Cefn-mawr
Froncysyllte
Glyn Ceiriog
Pontfadog
St. Martin's
Overton
Marchwiel
Rhostyllen
Bryneglwys
CYRN - Y - BRAIN
CLWYDIAN RANGE
Moel Famau
Offa's Dyke
Erddig
Chirk Castle
Valle Crucis Abbey
Castell Dinas Bran
Horseshoe Pass
Nantyr Forest Walks
Ceiriog Forest
A55
A5
A483
A494
A541
A525
A5104
A542
A539
A548
A550
A549

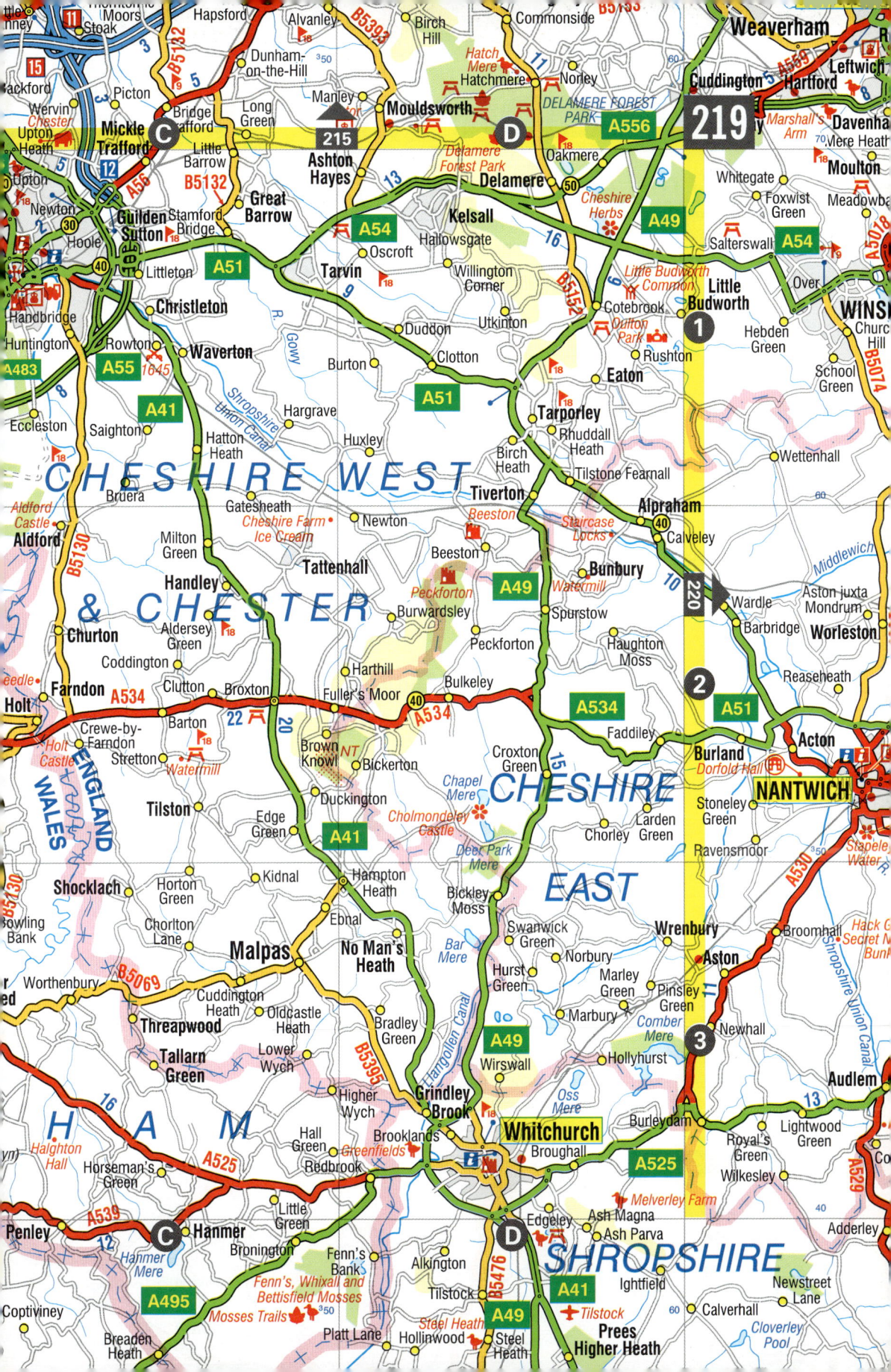
219
215
220
Weaverham
Cuddington
Hartford
Leftwich
Davenham
Marshall's Arm
Mere Heath
Moulton
Whitegate
Foxwist Green
Meadowbank
Salterswall
Over
WINSFORD
Little Budworth
Little Budworth Common
Oulton Park
Cotebrook
Rushton
Hebden Green
School Green
Eaton
Wettenhall
Commonside
Norley
Hatch Mere
Hatchmere
DELAMERE FOREST PARK
Oakmere
Delamere
Delamere Forest Park
Cheshire Herbs
Kelsall
Hallowsgate
Willington Corner
Utkinton
Mouldsworth
Manley
Birch Hill
Alvanley
Hapsford
Dunham-on-the-Hill
Ashton Hayes
Moors
Stoak
Picton
Wervin
Chester
Upton Heath
Upton
Mickle Trafford
Bridge Trafford
Long Green
Little Barrow
Great Barrow
Newton
Hoole
Guilden Sutton
Stamford Bridge
Littleton
Oscroft
Tarvin
Duddon
Clotton
Burton
Christleton
Handbridge
Huntington
Rowton
Waverton
1645
Eccleston
Saighton
Hatton Heath
Hargrave
Huxley
Shropshire Union Canal
R. Gowy
Tarporley
Rhuddall Heath
Birch Heath
Tilstone Fearnall
Tiverton
Alpraham
Calveley
Staircase Locks
Beeston
Beeston
CHESHIRE WEST
& CHESTER
Bruera
Gatesheath
Cheshire Farm Ice Cream
Newton
Aldford Castle
Aldford
Milton Green
Tattenhall
Handley
Bunbury
Watermill
Peckforton
Burwardsley
Peckforton
Spurstow
Haughton Moss
Wardle
Barbridge
Aston juxta Mondrum
Worleston
Middlewich
Reaseheath
Churton
Aldersey Green
Coddington
Clutton
Broxton
Harthill
Fuller's Moor
Bulkeley
Farndon
Holt
Barton
Crewe-by-Farndon
Stretton
Holt Castle
Watermill
Brown Knowl
NT
Bickerton
Croxton Green
Faddiley
Burland
Dorfold Hall
Acton
NANTWICH
Chapel Mere
CHESHIRE
Cholmondeley Castle
Duckington
Edge Green
Tilston
ENGLAND
WALES
Stoneley Green
Chorley
Larden Green
Ravensmoor
Stapeley Water
Deer Park Mere
EAST
Shocklach
Horton Green
Kidnal
Hampton Heath
Bickley Moss
Bowling Bank
Chorlton Lane
Ebnal
Malpas
No Man's Heath
Swanwick Green
Norbury
Wrenbury
Broomhall
Aston
Hack Green Secret Nuclear Bunker
Bar Mere
Hurst Green
Marley Green
Pinsley Green
Worthenbury
Cuddington Heath
Oldcastle Heath
Threapwood
Bradley Green
Marbury
Comber Mere
Newhall
Shropshire Union Canal
Llangollen Canal
Wirswall
Hollyhurst
Audlem
Tallarn Green
Lower Wych
Higher Wych
Grindley Brook
Oss Mere
Whitchurch
Burleydam
Lightwood Green
Royal's Green
Halghton Hall
Hall Green
Brooklands
Greenfields
Redbrook
Broughall
Wilkesley
Horseman's Green
Melverley Farm
Little Green
Edgeley
Ash Magna
Ash Parva
Adderley
Penley
Hanmer
Hanmer Mere
Bronington
Fenn's Bank
Alkington
SHROPSHIRE
Fenn's, Whixall and Bettisfield Mosses
Mosses Trails
Tilstock
Ightfield
Newstreet Lane
Calverhall
Cloverley Pool
Coptiviney
Breaden Heath
Platt Lane
Hollinwood
Steel Heath
Steel Heath
Prees Higher Heath
A556
A54
A49
A51
A55
A41
A483
A534
A525
A539
A495
A530
A529
A5018
B5074
B5132
B5393
B5152
B5130
B5069
B5395
B5476

CHESHIRE WEST
& CHESTER
CHESHIRE
SHROPSHIRE
216
219
M6
Commonside
Weaverham
Rudheath
Lostock Green
Lower Peover
Swan Green
Heat
Peover Hall
Norley
Cuddington
Hartford
Leftwich
Salt
Higher Shurlach
Lach Dennis
B5082
Blackden Heath
Jodrell Bank
DELAMERE PARK
Sandiway
A556
Davenham
A533
Puddinglake
Allostock
Goostrey
Lovell Radio Telescope
Oakmere
Whitegate
Moulton
Bostock Green
A530
Byley
B5081
Twemlow Green
Delamere
Foxwist Green
Meadowbank
Cranage
Cheshire Herbs
A49
Salterswall
A5018
B5355
Wharton
B5309
Sproston Green
Swettenham
Sandlow Green
Little Budworth Common
Little Budworth
A54
Over
WINSFORD
Stanthorne
Middlewich
Holmes Chapel
B5152
Cotebrook
Oulton Park
Hebden Green
Church Hill
Quarrybank
Brereton Heath
Rushton
Eaton
School Green
A533
Bradwall Green
Dukes Oak
Brereton Green
Tarporley
Rhuddall Heath
Occlestone Green
Arclid
Birch Heath
Wettenhall
B5074
Branch
Moston Green
Elworth
Arclid Green
Tilstone Fearnall
Warmingham
R. Wheelock
Ettiley Heath
Crosses
Tiverton
Alpraham
Church Minshull
SANDBACH
Staircase Locks
Calveley
Bradfield Green
Sandbach Flashes
Wheelock
Bunbury
Watermill
Coppenhall Moss
A534
Wheelock Heath
Hassall Green
Middlewich
Aston juxta Mondrum
A530
Maw Green
Winterley
Hassall
Spurstow
Wardle
Coppenhall
B5078
Barbridge
Worleston
A532
Sydney
Haslington
Haughton Moss
A51
Reaseheath
CREWE
Oakhanger
Alsager
A5020
Faddiley
Wells Green
B5077
Radway Green
A534
Wistaston
Croxton Green
Burland
Acton
Dorfold Hall
Willaston
A500
Larden Green
Rlwy. Age
Weston
Barthomley
Chapel Mere
NANTWICH
Stoneley Green
Shavington
Englesea-brook
Audley
Chorley
Butt Green
Hough
B5500
Ravensmoor
B5071
Chorlton
Stapeley Water
Stapeley
Wybunbury
Balterley
Bickley Moss
A530
R. Weaver
A529
Walgherton
Black Firs & Cranberry Bog
Betley
Swanwick Green
Wrenbury
Broomhall
Hack Green Secret Nuclear Bunker
Betley Mere
Norbury
Aston
Hatherton
Blakenhall
Wrinehill
Hurst Green
Marley Green
Shropshire Union Canal
Doddington Castle
A51
Madeley Heath
Pinsley Green
Marbury
Bridgemere
Checkley
A531
A49
Newhall
Hankelow
A525
Madeley
Wirswall
Hollyhurst
Bridgemere Garden World
Audlem
Buerton
Oss Mere
Lock Flight
Onneley
Whitchurch
Burleydam
Lightwood Green
Kinsey Heath
Woore
Broughall
Royal's Green
Coxbank
Pipe Gate
Aston
A525
Wilkesley
A529
Melverley Farm
Bearstone
Willoughbridge
Dorothy Clive
Edgeley
Ash Magna
Ash Parva
Adderley
Norton in Hales
Blackbrook
B5476
Ightfield
Devil's Ring & Finger
Winnington
A41
Ridgwardine
Ashley Heath
A53
Maer
A49
Tilstock
Newstreet Lane
Calverhall
Mucklestone
Prees Higher Heath
Steel Heath
Cloverley Pool
Betton
B5415
Ashley

221
217
Monk's Heath
A34
A537
Broken Cross
Weston
Silk
MACCLESFIELD
A537
Shining Tor
BUXTON
Burbage
Buxton
Goyt's Moss
Cat & Fiddle Inn
A54
Canholes
Capesthorne Hall
Redes Mere
Whisterfield
Withington Green
Siddington
B5392
Warren
Moss Lane
Mount Farm Ponds
Tegg's Nose
Langley
Sutton Lane Ends
Macclesfield Forest
Trentabank Reservoir
Windyharbour
Gawsworth
Oakgrove
Lower Withington
Highlane
Gawsworth Hall
A523
Wildboarclough
A53
Axe Edge
Gleadsmoss
Marton
A536
Blaze Farm
The Quinta
Mill
Rodeheath
Flash
Allgreave
Newsbank
North Rode
A54
A34
Hulme Walfield
Eaton
Bosley
Bosley Resr.
Wincle
PEAK DISTRICT
NATIONAL PARK
Lud's Church
Black Brook
Morridge Top
A54
Aqueduct
Danebridge
CONGLETON
Havannah
Key Green
R. Dane
A534
Buglawton
The Cloud
NT
Timbersbrook
Rushton Spencer
Heaton
Astbury Mere
Brookhouse Green
Mossley
Hightown
Astbury
DANGER AREA
Brownlow
Newtown
Ryecroft Gate
Meerbrook
Upper Hulme
Brownlow Heath
Macclesfield Canal
Marsh Green
Poolfold
Rudyard Resr.
A523
A53
Fourlanes End
A34
Little Moreton Hall
Limekiln Wood
Old Man of Mow
Gillow Heath
Biddulph Grange
Tittesworth Resr.
Upper Elkstone
Biddulph Moor
Rudyard
James Brindley
Thorncliffe
Mow Cop
Folly NT
Mount Pleasant
The Bank
A527
BIDDULPH
Horton
B5331
Poolend
LEEK
Scholar Green
Church Lawton
Gratton
Rudyard Lake Steam Railway
R. Churnet
Mixon
Hall Green
Harriseahead
Newchapel
Knypersley
Blackwood Hill
Greenway Bank
Dunwood
Ladderedge
Longsdon
Birchall
Bradnop
Onecote
Morridge Side
Hardings Wood
KIDSGROVE
Brindley Ford
Knypersley Resr.
Endon Bank
A53
A523
A50
A5011
Packmoor
Brown Edge
Ridgeway
Horse Bridge
Leekbrook
Craft Workshop
Dunkirk
Talke
Goldenhill
Norton Green
Endon
Stanley
Flint Mill
Churnet Valley
Coombes Valley
A34
Tunstall
B5051
Cheddleton
Stockton Brook
Basford Green
Blackbrook
Wedgwood's Monument
Red Street
A527
Ford Green Hall
Norton in the Moors
Bagnall
A520
STAFFORDSHIRE
B5053
A5272
Crackley
Water Park
Ceramica
A53
Baddeley Green
Light Oaks
Ipstones
Caldon Canal
B5500
Halmer End
Chesterton
Burslem
Milton
A5009
Abbey Hulton
Wetley Rocks
Froghall Wharf
A52
B5367
Apedale
Wolstanton
Hanley
Northwood
Bucknall
A52
Consall
Consall Nature Park
Hazles
Alsagers Bank
A34
Washerwall
Cellarhead
A522
Froghall
Silverdale
Borough
Werrington
Kingsley
Whiston
STOKE-ON-TRENT
Foxfield Steam Railway
Kingsley Holt
Whiston Eaves
B5044
A5272
Hulme
Park Hall
Weston Coyney
Roughcote
A521
A522
Oakamoor
NEWCASTLE-UNDER-LYME
A52
Stoke-upon-Trent
Fenton
Hawksmoor NT
Cheadle
Godleybrook
Dilhorne
KEELE
Seabridge
Clayton
Cookshill
Gladstone Pottery
Brookhouses
Lightwood
Threapwood
Caverswall Railway
Meir
Blythe Bridge
Longton
Boundary
Rakeway
B5032
A500
A53
Hanford
Blurton
B5038
Forsbrook
Freehay
Butterton
Trentham
Lightwood
Huntley
Mobberley
A5035
A5005
Blythe Marsh
Draycott in the Moors
Acton
Hem Heath & Newstead Woods
Whitmore
Hanchurch
Trentham Monkey Forest
Meir Heath
B5029
Winnothdale
Upper Tean
A34
Wedgwood
Rough Close
Cresswell
Lower Tean
Beech
Beech Caves
A520
Fulford
Saverley Green
Checkley
Chapel Chorlton
A51
A519
M6
Tittensor
Barlaston NT
B5066
Crossgate
Mossgate
R. Tean
R. Blithe
Fole
Knenhall
Downs Bank
Moddershall
Upper Leigh
A50
A522

INDEX

Including Streets, Places & Areas, Industrial Estates,
Selected Flats & Walkways, Junction Names & Service Areas, Stations and Places of Interest.

HOW TO USE THIS INDEX

1. Each street name is followed by its Postcode District, then by its Locality abbreviation(s) and then by its map reference; e.g. **Abbey Rd.** CH48: W Kir . . . .3C **56** is in the CH48 Postcode District and the West Kirby Locality and is to be found in square 3C on page **56**. The page number is shown in bold type.

2. A strict alphabetical order is followed in which Av., Rd., St., etc. (though abbreviated) are read in full and as part of the street name;
e.g. **Ash Wood Pk.** appears after **Ashwood La.** but before **Ashwood Rd.**

3. Streets and a selection of flats and walkways too small to be shown on street map pages **4-211**, appear in the index with the thoroughfare to which it is connected shown in brackets;
e.g. **Abbey Ct.** SK1: Stoc . . . . 4F **53** (off Abbey Gro.)

4. Addresses that are in more than one part are referred to as not continuous.

5. Places and areas are shown in the index in BLUE TYPE and the map reference is to the actual map square in which the town centre or area is located and not to the place name shown on the map. Map references for entries that appear on street map pages **4-213** are shown first, with references to road map pages **214-221** shown in brackets;
e.g. **ALDERLEY EDGE** . . . .6F **119 (3C 217)**

6. An example of a selected place of interest is **Anson Engine Mus., The** 2H **101**

7. An example of a station is **Acton Bridge Station (Rail)** . . . . 3C **154**. Included are Rail **(Rail)**, Metro **(Metro)** and **Park & Ride**.
e.g. **Boughton Heath (Park & Ride)** 3F **151**

8. Junction names and Service Areas are shown in the index in BOLD CAPITAL TYPE; e.g. **BURTONWOOD SERVICE AREA** 1K **39**

9. Map references for entries that appear on large scale pages **212 & 213** are shown first, with small scale map references shown in brackets; e.g. **Abbey Grn.** CH1: Ches . . . .3B **212 (1K 149)**

GENERAL ABBREVIATIONS

All. : Alley	**Ct.** : Court	**Intl.** : International	**Prom.** : Promenade
App. : Approach	**Cres.** : Crescent	**Junc.** : Junction	**Res.** : Residential
Arc. : Arcade	**Cft.** : Croft	**La.** : Lane	**Ri.** : Rise
Av. : Avenue	**Dr.** : Drive	**Lit.** : Little	**Rd.** : Road
Bk. : Back	**E.** : East	**Lwr.** : Lower	**Rdbt.** : Roundabout
Blvd. : Boulevard	**Ent.** : Enterprise	**Mnr.** : Manor	**Shop.** : Shopping
Bri. : Bridge	**Est.** : Estate	**Mans.** : Mansions	**Sth.** : South
Bldg. : Building	**Fld.** : Field	**Mkt.** : Market	**Sq.** : Square
Bldgs. : Buildings	**Flds.** : Fields	**Mdw.** : Meadow	**Sta.** : Station
Bungs. : Bungalows	**Gdn.** : Garden	**Mdws.** : Meadows	**St.** : Street
Bus. : Business	**Gdns.** : Gardens	**M.** : Mews	**Ter.** : Terrace
C'way. : Causeway	**Gth.** : Garth	**Mt.** : Mount	**Twr.** : Tower
Cen. : Centre	**Ga.** : Gate	**Mus.** : Museum	**Trad.** : Trading
Circ. : Circle	**Gt.** : Great	**Nth.** : North	**Up.** : Upper
Cl. : Close	**Grn.** : Green	**No.** : Number	**Va.** : Vale
Coll. : College	**Gro.** : Grove	**Pde.** : Parade	**Vw.** : View
Comn. : Common	**Hgts.** : Heights	**Pk.** : Park	**Vs.** : Villas
Cnr. : Corner	**Ho.** : House	**Pas.** : Passage	**Vis.** : Visitors
Cott. : Cottage	**Ho's.** : Houses	**Pav.** : Pavilion	**Wlk.** : Walk
Cotts. : Cottages	**Ind.** : Industrial	**Pl.** : Place	**W.** : West
	Info. : Information	**Pct.** : Precinct	**Yd.** : Yard

LOCALITY ABBREVIATIONS

Act : **Acton**	**Brad** : **Bradwall**	**Comp** : **Compstall**	**Gre** : **Greasby**
Act B : **Acton Bridge**	**Bram** : **Bramhall**	**Cong** : **Congleton**	**Gt Bar** : **Great Barrow**
Adl : **Adlington**	**Bred** : **Bredbury**	**Coo P** : **Coole Pilate**	**Gt Bou** : **Great Boughton**
Ald E : **Alderley Edge**	**Bre G** : **Brereton Green**	**Cote** : **Cotebrook**	**Gt Bud** : **Great Budworth**
Ald : **Aldford**	**Bret** : **Bretton**	**Cot E** : **Cotton Edmunds**	**Gt San** : **Great Sankey**
All : **Allostock**	**Bri T** : **Bridge Trafford**	**Cran** : **Cranage**	**Gt Sut** : **Great Sutton**
Alp : **Alpraham**	**Brim** : **Brimstage**	**Crewe** : **Crewe**	**Guil S** : **Guilden Sutton**
Als : **Alsager**	**B'tom** : **Broadbottom**	**Cre F** : **Crewe-by-Farndon**	**H Grn** : **Hack Green**
Alt : **Altrincham**	**B'ath** : **Broadheath**	**Cre G** : **Crewe Green**	**Had** : **Hadfield**
Alv : **Alvanley**	**Brom** : **Bromborough**	**Croft** : **Croft**	**Hale** : **Hale**
And : **Anderton**	**B'vale** : **Brookvale**	**Cron** : **Cronton**	**Hal B** : **Hale Bank**
Ant : **Antrobus**	**B'hall** : **Broomhall**	**Crou** : **Croughton**	**H'rns** : **Halebarns**
App : **Appleton**	**Brou** : **Broughton**	**Crow** : **Crowton**	**Halt** : **Halton**
App T : **Appleton Thorn**	**Bro L** : **Brown Lees**	**Cudd** : **Cuddington**	**Hand** : **Handforth**
Arc : **Arclid**	**Bro** : **Brownlow**	**Cuer** : **Cuerdley**	**Hank** : **Hankelow**
Arl : **Arley**	**Brox** : **Broxton**	**Cul** : **Culcheth**	**Haps** : **Hapsford**
Ash : **Ashley**	**Bru** : **Bruera**	**Dare** : **Daresbury**	**Harg** : **Hargrave**
Ash H : **Ashton Hayes**	**Bud H** : **Budworth Heath**	**Darn** : **Darnhall**	**Harr** : **Harriseahead**
Ash L : **Ashton-under-Lyne**	**Bue** : **Buerton**	**Dave** : **Davenham**	**H'ord** : **Hartford**
Astb : **Astbury**	**Bun** : **Bunbury**	**Dela** : **Delamere**	**Hart** : **Harthill**
Astm : **Astmoor**	**Burl** : **Burland**	**Den** : **Denton**	**Hasl** : **Haslington**
Ast : **Aston**	**Burt** : **Burton**	**Dis** : **Disley**	**Hass** : **Hassall**
Ast B : **Aston by Budworth**	**B'ood** : **Burtonwood**	**Dod** : **Dodleston**	**Ha Grn** : **Hassall Green**
Ast M : **Aston juxta Mondrum**	**Burw** : **Burwardsley**	**Droy** : **Droylsden**	**Hath** : **Hatherton**
Aude : **Audenshaw**	**Byl** : **Byley**	**Dud** : **Duddon**	**Hat** : **Hattersley**
Audl : **Audlem**	**Cad** : **Cadishead**	**Duk** : **Dukinfield**	**H'ton** : **Hatton**
Aus : **Austerson**	**Cald** : **Caldy**	**Dun M** : **Dunham Massey**	**Hav** : **Havannah**
Bac : **Backford**	**Call** : **Callands**	**Dun H** : **Dunham-on-the-Hill**	**H Gro** : **Hazel Grove**
B'ley : **Baddiley**	**Calv** : **Calveley**	**Dun** : **Dunkirk**	**He Grn** : **Heald Green**
B'ton : **Baddington**	**Cap** : **Capenhurst**	**Dutt** : **Dutton**	**Hel** : **Helsby**
Bald : **Balderton**	**Carrb** : **Carrbrook**	**East** : **Eastham**	**Henb** : **Henbury**
Balt : **Balterley**	**Carri** : **Carrington**	**Eat** : **Eaton**	**Henh** : **Henhull**
Barns : **Barnston**	**Cast** : **Castlefields**	**Ebnal** : **Ebnal**	**Hes** : **Heswall**
Barnt : **Barnton**	**Cau** : **Caughall**	**Ecc** : **Eccleston**	**Hey** : **Heyrod**
Bas : **Basford**	**Char** : **Charlesworth**	**Edle** : **Edleston**	**H Beb** : **Higher Bebington**
Bath : **Batherton**	**Chea** : **Cheadle**	**Ell P** : **Ellesmere Port**	**H Kin** : **Higher Kinnerton**
Beb : **Bebington**	**Chea H** : **Cheadle Hulme**	**Elt** : **Elton**	**H Wal** : **Higher Walton**
Beec : **Beechwood**	**Chel** : **Chelford**	**Elw** : **Elworth**	**H Whi** : **Higher Whitley**
Bees : **Beeston**	**Ches** : **Chester**	**Eng B** : **Englesea Brook**	**H Lan** : **High Lane**
Bet : **Betchton**	**Chil T** : **Childer Thornton**	**Ett H** : **Ettiley Heath**	**H Leg** : **High Legh**
Bet H : **Betchton Heath**	**Chis** : **Chisworth**	**Farn** : **Farndon**	**H'rth** : **Hollingworth**
Bid : **Bidston**	**Chor** : **Chorlton**	**Fear** : **Fearnhead**	**H'rst** : **Hollyhurst**
Bil G : **Billinge Green**	**Chor B** : **Chorlton-by-Backford**	**Fran** : **Frankby**	**H Cha** : **Holmes Chapel**
Birc : **Birchwood**	**Chor H** : **Chorlton-cum-Hardy**	**Frod** : **Frodsham**	**Holt** : **Holt**
Birk : **Birkenhead**	**Chri** : **Christleton**	**Gam** : **Gamesley**	**Hoo** : **Hoofield**
Blac : **Blacon**	**Chu L** : **Church Lawton**	**Gat** : **Gatley**	**Hoo V** : **Hoole Village**
Blak : **Blakelow**	**Chu** : **Churton**	**Gaw** : **Gawsworth**	**H'ton** : **Hooton**
Blet : **Bletchley**	**Clau** : **Claughton**	**Gil H** : **Gillow Heath**	**Hou** : **Hough**
Bold : **Bold**	**Clif** : **Clifton**	**G'ook** : **Glazebrook**	**Hoy** : **Hoylake**
Bold H : **Bold Heath**	**Clo F** : **Clock Face**	**G'ury** : **Glazebury**	**Hul W** : **Hulme Walfield**
Boll : **Bollington**	**Clot** : **Clotton**	**Gol** : **Golborne**	**Huns** : **Hunsterson**
Bos : **Bostock**	**Clut** : **Clutton**	**Goo** : **Goostrey**	**Hunt** : **Huntington**
Bow : **Bowdon**	**Col G** : **Collins Green**	**Gor** : **Gorstage**	**Hyde** : **Hyde**
Bra G : **Bradfield Green**	**Comb** : **Comberbach**	**Grap** : **Grappenhall**	**Ince** : **Ince**

Locality Abbreviations

Irby : Irby
Irlam : Irlam
Kel : Kelsall
Ker : Kerridge
Kidn : Kidnal
Kids : Kidsgrove
K'ley : Kingsley
K'ood : Kingswood
Kin H : Kinsey Heath
Knut : Knutsford
Lac D : Lach Dennis
Lang : Langley
Lea B : Lea-by-Backford
Leas : Leasowe
Leds : Ledsham
Leigh : Leigh
L'ton : Leighton
L Bar : Little Barrow
L Bol : Little Bollington
L Bud : Little Budworth
L Lei : Little Leigh
L Nes : Little Neston
L Sta : Little Stanney
L Sut : Little Sutton
Lit : Littleton
Liv : Liverpool
Los Gra : Lostock Gralam
Los Grn : Lostock Green
Lwr K : Lower Kinnerton
Lwr P : Lower Peover
Lwr S : Lower Stretton
L Whi : Lower Whitley
L Wit : Lower Withington
Low : Lowton
L Grn : Lyme Green
Lymm : Lymm
Mac : Macclesfield
Mac F : Macclesfield Forest
Mal B : Malkin's Bank
Mal : Malpas
Manc : Manchester
Man A : Manchester Airport
Manl : Manley
Man C : Manley Common
Man P : Manor Park
Marb : Marbury
Marl : Marlston-cum-Lache
Mar : Marple
Mar B : Marple Bridge
Mars : Marston
M'all : Marthall
Mart : Marton
Mat : Matley
Mea : Meadowbank
Mel : Mellor
Meols : Meols
Mere : Mere
Mic T : Mickle Trafford
Mid : Middlewich
M'ook : Millbrook
M'ton : Millington
Min V : Minshull Vernon
Mob : Mobberley

Mol : Mollington
Moo : Moore
More : Moreton
Moss : Mossley
Most : Moston
Mot : Mottram
Mot A : Mottram St Andrew
Mould : Mouldsworth
Moult : Moulton
Mow C : Mow Cop
Murd : Murdishaw
Nant : Nantwich
Ness : Ness
Nest : Neston
N Ald : Nether Alderley
N Bri : New Brighton
N Fer : New Ferry
N Mil : New Mills
New : Newton
New T : Newton by Tattenhall
New W : Newton-le-Willows
Noc : Nocturum
No H : No Man's Heath
Nor : Norbury
Nor B : Norcott Brook
Norl : Norley
N'den : Northenden
Nth R : North Rode
N'ich : Northwich
Nort : Norton
O'ger : Oakhanger
Oak : Oakmere
Oldc : Oldcastle Heath
Old H : Old Hall
Oll : Ollerton
Osc : Oscroft
Oul : Oulton
O Ald : Over Alderley
O Peo : Over Peover
O Tab : Over Tabley
O Hea : Overton Heath
Oxt : Oxton
Padd : Paddington
Padg : Padgate
Pal F : Palace Fields
Park : Parkgate
Part : Partington
Peck : Peckforton
Penk : Penketh
Pens : Pensby
Pick : Pickmere
Pict : Picton
Plum : Plumley
Poole : Poole
P Sun : Port Sunlight
P Shr : Pott Shrigley
Pou : Poulton
Poy : Poynton
Pren : Prenton
Pres : Prestbury
Pre B : Preston Brook
Pre H : Preston on the Hill
Pud : Puddington

Pul : Pulford
Quo : Quoisley
Raby : Raby
Rab M : Raby Mere
R Grn : Radway Green
R'ill : Rainhill
R'ow : Rainow
Rav : Ravensmoor
Rea : Reaseheath
R Hea : Rhuddal Heath
Ring : Ringway
Ris : Risley
Rix : Rixton
R Fer : Rock Ferry
Rod H : Rode Heath
Rom : Romiley
Roo : Rookery
Ross : Rossett
Rost : Rostherne
Row : Rowton
Rud : Rudheath
Run : Runcorn
Rus : Rushton
Sai : Saighton
St H : St Helens
Sale : Sale
Salt : Saltney
Salt F : Saltney Ferry
S'ach : Sandbach
S'way : Sandiway
Sau : Saughall
Sch G : Scholar Green
Sea : Sealand
Shar : Sharston
Shav : Shavington
Sidd : Siddington
Snel : Snelson
Som : Somerford
Sou : Sound
Spit : Spital
Spr G : Sproston Green
Spur : Spurstow
Stal : Stalybridge
Stan : Stanthorne
Stap : Stapeley
Stoak : Stoak
Stoc : Stockport
Stoc H : Stockton Heath
Store : Storeton
S'ord : Stretford
Stre : Stretton
Stri : Strines
Styal : Styal
Sut E : Sutton Lane Ends
Sut M : Sutton Manor
Sut W : Sutton Weaver
Tab : Tabley
Talk : Talke
T Grn : Tallarn Green
Tarp : Tarporley
Tar : Tarvin
Tar S : Tarvin Sands
Tatt : Tattenhall

Thel : Thelwall
Thin : Thingwall
Tho H : Thornton Hough
Tho M : Thornton-le-Moors
Thr : Threapwood
Thur : Thurstaston
Til : Tilstone Fearnall
Tils : Tilston
Timp : Timperley
Tint : Tintwistle
Tive : Tiverton
Tran : Tranmere
Upt : Upton
Urm : Urmston
Utk : Utkinton
Walg : Walgherton
Wal B : Walker Barn
Wall : Wallasey
Wal H : Wall Hill
Walt : Walton
Warb : Warburton
Warm : Warmingham
Warr : Warrington
Wave : Waverton
Weav : Weaverham
Wee C : Weetwood Common
Wer : Wervin
W Kir : West Kirby
W Tim : West Timperley
W'ook : Westbrook
West : Weston
Wes P : Weston Point
Westy : Westy
What : Whatcroft
Whe : Wheelock
Whis : Whiston
Whit : Whitby
W'ate : Whitegate
W Grn : Whiteley Green
Wid : Widnes
W'ston : Willaston
W'gton : Willington
Wilm : Wilmslow
Wim : Wimboldsley
Wim T : Wimbolds Trafford
Winc : Wincham
Win H : Windmill Hill
Winn : Winnington
Wins : Winsford
Wint : Winterley
Winw : Winwick
Wis : Wistaston
Woodb : Woodbank
Woodc : Woodchurch
Woodf : Woodford
W'ley : Woodley
W'ood : Woolstanwood
Wool : Woolston
Worl : Worleston
Wren : Wrenbury
Wyb : Wybunbury
Wyth : Wythenshawe

A

A41 Expressway CH42: Tran 2E 60
Abberley Hall SK9: Ald E 7C 118
Abbey Cl. CH41: Birk 7E 34
  CW7: Wins 6E 178
  CW8: W'ate 7K 161
  M32: S'ord 1E 22
  SK14: Mot 7G 11
  WA3: Croft 3F 17
  WA8: Wid 5C 62
  WA8: Bow 4E 72
Abbey Ct. *SK1: Stoc* 4F 53
  (off Abbey Gro.)
  SK12: Poy 3C 100
Abbeydale Cl. CW2: West 5J 199
  OL6: Ash L 3A 4
  SK8: Chea H 6G 77
Abbeyfield Cl. SK3: Stoc 6C 52
Abbeyfield Ho.
  CH65: Whit 5C 134
Abbeyfields CW2: Wis 6H 193
Abbeyfields WA7: S'ach 4D 200
Abbey Gdns. SK14: Mot 7G 11
Abbey Grn. CH1: Ches 3B 212 (1K 149)
Abbey Gro. SK1: Stoc 4F 53
  SK14: Mot 7G 11
Abbey Hey WA7: Nort 6E 90
ABBEY HULTON 3D 221
Abbey La. CH8: Dela, Oak 4H 173
  CW8: H'ord 1A 162
Abbey Mill SK10: Pres 5H 121
Abbey Pk. Way CW2: West 4K 199
Abbey Pl. CW1: Crewe 7J 191
Abbey Rd. CH48: W Kir 3C 56
  CW11: S'ach 3C 200
  M33: Sale 5F 23
  SK8: Chea 7J 51
  SK10: Mac 2J 125
  WA3: Low 2C 6
  WA8: Wid 5B 62
Abbey Sq. CH1: Ches 3C 212 (1A 150)
Abbey St. CH1: Ches 3C 212 (1A 150)
  CH41: Birk 7E 34
Abbey Way CW8: H'ord 2A 162
Abbot Cl. CH43: Bid 6F 33

Abbotsbury Cl. CW2: Wis 6B 194
  SK12: Poy 1C 100
Abbots Bus. Pk. WA7: Pre B 2G 113
Abbots Cl. M33: Sale 6J 23
  SK10: Mac 2J 125
Abbots Ct. CH2: Ches 6K 145
  M33: Sale 6J 23
Abbots Dr. CH2: Ches 6K 145
  CH63: Beb 1K 85
Abbotsfield CH41: Urm 1G 21
  WA4: App 7J 67
Abbotsford Gro. WA14: Timp 4J 47
Abbotsford St. CH44: Wall 2D 34
Abbot's Grange
  CH2: Ches 1B 212 (7K 145)
Abbots Hall Av. WA9: Clo F 1K 37
Abbots Knoll CH1: Ches 6K 145
Abbotsleigh Av. M23: Wyth 4F 49
Abbotsleigh Dr. SK7: Bram 3D 78
Abbots Mere Cl. CW8: S'way 4C 160
  (off Sandington Dr.)
Abbots M. CH65: Ell P 2D 134
Abbot's Nook CH2: Ches 1B 212 (7K 145)
Abbots Pk. CH1: Ches 6K 145
Abbots Quay CH41: Birk 6F 35
Abbot's Ter. CH1: Ches 5J 145
Abbots Way CH48: W Kir 2D 56
  CH64: Nest 6H 105
  CW8: H'ord 2A 162
Abbotts Cl. CH3: Wave 2B 174
  CW12: Cong 6K 183
  WA7: Run 6G 89
Abbotts Rd. CH3: Wave 2B 174
Abbotts Way CW7: Wins 2B 178
Aber Av. SK2: Stoc 1G 79
Aberdare Cl. M40: Call 3C 40
Aberdeen Cres. SK3: Stoc 4B 52
Aberdeen Gro. SK3: Stoc 4B 52
Aberdeen St. CH41: Birk 5B 34
Aberdeen Wlk. *SK10: Mac* 1G 125
  (off Berwick Cl.)
Aberfeldy Cl. CW4: H Cha 5H 181
Aberford Av. CH45: Wall 6E 12

Aberford Rd. M23: Wyth 7G 49
Abergele Rd. M14: Manc 3B 24
Abergele St. SK2: Stoc 7E 52
ABER-OER 3A 218
Aber Rd. SK8: Chea 6J 51
Abersoch Av. M14: Manc 3B 24
Abingdon Av. WA1: Wool 5E 42
Abingdon Cl. SK11: Mac 4G 125
Abingdon Cres. CH4: Ches 5G 149
Abingdon Rd. CH49: Gre 2J 57
  M41: Urm 1D 22
  SK5: Stoc 4J 25
  SK7: Bram 3C 78
Abington Cl. CW1: Crewe 7G 191
Abington Rd. M33: Sale 1C 48
Abington Wlk. WA7: B'vale 2E 112
Abney Grange OL5: Moss 1F 5
Abney Rd. OL5: Moss 1D 4
  SK4: Stoc 6F 25
Abney Steps *OL5: Moss* 1D 4
  (off Manchester Rd.)
ABRAM 1A 16
Abstone Cl. WA1: Wool 5C 42
Acacia Av. M34: Den 7F 9
  SK8: Chea H 3J 77
  SK9: Wilm 2E 118
  WA1: Wool 4D 42
  WA8: Wid 2H 63
  WA15: Hale 2K 73
  WA16: Knut 4C 116
Acacia Cl. CH2: Elt 5G 137
  CH49: Gre 3K 57
Acacia Cres. CW1: Crewe 7K 191
Acacia Dr. CH66: Gt Sut 7B 134
  CW11: S'ach 2C 200
  WA15: Hale 2K 73
Acacia Gro. CH44: Wall 2D 34
  CH48: W Kir 3B 56
  SK5: Stoc 7J 25
  WA7: Run 6J 89
Acacias *M41: Urm* 1D 22
  (off Granville Rd.)
Academy Pl. WA1: Warr 7F 41
Academy St. WA1: Warr 7F 41
Academy Way WA1: Warr 7F 41
Acer Av. CW1: Crewe 6K 191
Acer St. SK14: Hyde 1B 28

Achilles Av. WA2: Warr 2F 41
Achilles Ct. WA7: Cast 4C 90
Ackerley Cl. WA2: Fear 1K 41
Ackers Barn Courtyard
  M31: Carri 5K 21
Ackers La. M31: Carri 5H 21
  WA4: Stoc H 3J 67
Ackersley Ct. SK8: Chea H 5A 78
Ackers Rd. CH49: Woodc 3F 59
  WA4: Stoc H 4J 67
Ack La. E. SK7: Bram 6A 78
Ack La. W. SK8: Chea H 5K 77
Ackworth Dr. M23: Wyth 6G 49
Acland Rd. CH44: Wall 7H 13
Acorn Av. SK8: Chea 7G 51
  SK14: Hyde 3K 27
  (not continuous)
Acorn Bank Cl. CW2: Wis 7B 194
Acorn Bus. Pk.
  SK4: Stoc 6F 213 (3B 52)
Acorn Cl. CH63: H Beb 7C 60
  CW7: Wins 4H 179
  CW8: Cudd 4C 160
  M19: Manc 3C 24
  WA9: Clo F 1J 37
Acorn Ct. CH2: Upt 2B 146
  L8: Liv 6K 35
Acorn Dr. CH65: Whit 7D 134
Acorn Ho. *M22: Shar* 6A 50
  (off Altrincham Rd.)
Acorn Ho., The
  SK15: M'ook 5E 4
  (off Bramble Ct.)
Acorn M. SK2: Stoc 6G 53
Acorns, The CH7: Upt 2B 146
Acorn St. WA12: New W 1F 15
Acreage, The CW4: Goo 6J 165
  CW6: Bun 6C 188
ACREFAIR 3A 218
Acrefield M33: Sale 1A 48
Acrefield Av. M41: Urm 2E 22
  SK4: Stoc 7E 24
Acrefield Ct. CH42: Tran 4A 60
Acrefield Rd. CH42: Tran 4A 60
  WA8: Wid 4B 62
Acregate *M41: Urm* 1K 21
  (off Penny Bri. La.)

Acre La.—Alexandra Rd.

Acre La. CH60: Hes 5A 84
CH62: Brom 7C 86
CH63: Brom 7C 86
SK8: Chea H 1E 98
Acre Rd. CH66: Gt Sut 3K 133
Acresbrook SK15: Stal 3D 10
Acres Ct. M22: Wyth 1K 75
Acres Cres. WA6: K'ley 1C 152
Acresfield Av. M34: Aude 1B 8
Acresfield Rd. SK14: Hyde 5A 10
WA15: Timp 4A 48
Acres Fold Av. M22: Wyth 2A 76
Acres La. CH2: Upt 1C 146
SK15: Stal 1C 10
Acres Rd. CH47: Meols 5G 31
CH63: Beb 7E 60
SK8: Gat 7C 50
Acre St. M34: Den 7D 8
Acreville Gro. WA3: G'ury 3J 7
Acreville Rd. CH63: Beb 1K 85
ACTON
CW5 6K 189 (2A 220)
LL12 2B 218
ST5 3C 221
Acton Av. WA4: App 3H 93
ACTON BRIDGE 2C 154 (3D 215)
Acton Bridge Station (Rail) 3C 154
Acton La. CH46: More 5K 31
CW8: Act B 2C 154
Acton Pl. SK11: Mac 4G 125
Acton Rd. CH42: R Fer 4F 61
CW2: Crewe 1H 193
WA5: B'ood 5B 14
Actonville Av. M22: Wyth 2K 75
Acton Way ST7: Chu L 3E 202
Acuba Gro. CH42: Tran 1D 60
Adam Av. CH66: Gt Sut 4J 133
(not continuous)
Adam Cl. CH66: Gt Sut 4K 133
SK8: Chea H 1K 77
Adams Cl. SK12: Poy 4D 100
WA12: New W 1G 15
Adams Hill WA16: Knut 4E 116
Adamson Cl. WA4: Westy 2A 68
Adamson Ct. WA4: Grap 3B 68
Adamson Gdns. M20: Manc 1B 50
Adamson Ho. WA7: Run 3E 88
Adamson St. SK16: Duk 4H 9
WA4: Warr 2F 67
Adam St. WA2: Warr 5G 41
Adaston Av. CH62: East 3A 108
Adcroft St. SK1: Stoc 5D 52
(not continuous)
Addenbrook Cl. CH43: Bid 6F 33
Adder Hill CH3: Gt Bou 4E 150
ADDERLEY 3A 220
Adderley Cl. WA7: Run 5J 89
ADDERS MOSS 5A 120
Addingham Av. WA8: Wid 6C 62
Addington St. CH44: Wall 1C 34
Addison Cl. CW2: Wis 6K 193
Addison Grange M33: Sale 1C 48
(off Princes Rd.)
Addison Rd. M31: Carri 5G 21
M32: S'ord 1G 23
M41: Urm 2C 22
WA15: Hale 3J 73
Addison Sq. WA8: Wid 4G 63
Addison St. L3: Liv 1J 35
Addison Way L3: Liv 1J 35
Adelaide Ct. WA8: Wid 6G 63
Adelaide Rd. CH1: Blac 6E 144
CH42: Tran 1B 60
SK3: Stoc 4A 52
SK7: Bram 7D 78
Adelaide St. CH44: Wall 1A 34
CW1: Crewe 1C 194
SK10: Mac 3B 126
Adela Rd. WA7: Run 4F 89
Adelphi Mill SK10: Boll 4C 122
Adelphi St. CH41: Birk 6D 34
Adey Rd. WA13: Lymm 7C 44
Adfalent La. CH64: W'ston 1A 132
Adler Way L3: Liv 2K 61
ADLINGTON 6G 103 (2D 217)
Adlington Bus. Pk. SK10: Adl 4B 100
Adlington Cl. SK12: Poy 4E 100
WA15: Timp 6D 48
Adlington Ct. WA3: Ris 5A 18
(not continuous)
Adlington Dr. CW9: N'ich 1F 163
CW11: S'ach 2G 201
Adlington Hall M. SK10: Adl 5F 103
Adlington Ho. L3: Liv 1J 35
(off Henry Edward St.)
Adlington Ind. Est. SK10: Adl 5B 100
Adlington Pk. SK10: Adl 5B 100
Adlington Rd. CW2: Crewe 3K 193
SK9: Wilm 1J 119
SK10: Boll 2D 122
WA7: Win H 4F 91
Adlington Rd. Bus. Pk. SK10: Boll 2C 122
Adlington Station (Rail) 6G 103
Adlington St. L3: Liv 1J 35
(off Fontenoy St.)
SK10: Mac 4K 125
Adlington Wlk. SK1: Stoc 5H 213 (3C 52)
Adlington Way M34: Den 2F 27
(off Two Trees La.)
Admirals Rd. WA3: Birc 7K 17
Admirals Sq. WA3: Birc 1F 43
Adria Rd. M20: Manc 1E 50
Adshall Rd. SK8: Chea 7J 51
Adshead Cl. M22: Wyth 2H 75
Adshead Ct. SK10: Boll 3E 122
ADSWOOD 6B 52
Adswood Gro. SK3: Stoc 6B 52
Adswood Ind. Est. SK3: Stoc 6B 52
Adswood La. E. SK2: Stoc 6D 52
Adswood La. W. SK3: Stoc 6D 52
Adswood Old Hall Rd. SK8: Chea H 1B 78
Adswood Old Rd. SK3: Stoc 6C 52
Adswood Rd. SK3: Stoc 7B 52
SK8: Chea H 1A 78
Adswood Ter. SK3: Stoc 6C 52
Adwell Cl. WA3: Low 2A 6
Aegean Rd. WA14: B'ath 6E 46
Afton WA8: Wid 3A 62
Agden Brow WA13: Lymm 5F 71
Agden Brow Pk. WA13: Lymm 4F 71
Agden La. WA13: H Leg, Lymm 5F 71
(not continuous)
WA14: M'ton 5F 71
Agden Pk. La. WA13: Lymm 5F 71
Agecroft Rd. CW9: N'ich 6H 157
SK6: Rom 3A 54
Agnes Gro. CH44: Wall 6J 13
Agnes Rd. CH42: Tran 2D 60
Agnes St. M19: Manc 1D 24
WA9: Clo F 1J 37
Agricola Tower 6B 212
AIGBURTH 2B 214
Aigburth Gro. CH46: More 4A 32
SK5: Stoc 1H 25
Ailsa Rd. CH45: Wall 6G 13
Aimson Pl. WA15: Timp 6C 48
Aimson Rd. E. WA15: Timp 6C 48
Aimson Rd. W. WA15: Timp 5C 48
Ainley Cl. WA7: B'vale 2C 112
Ainley Rd. M22: Wyth 2K 75
Ainley Wood SK16: Duk 3J 9
Ainscough Rd. WA3: Birc 1E 42
Ainsdale Cl. CH61: Thin 1J 83
CH63: Brom 2H 107
SK7: Bram 6E 78
WA5: Penk 1H 65
Ainsdale Dr. M33: Sale 2J 47
SK8: He Grn 4D 76
Ainsdale Gro. SK5: Stoc 3J 25
Ainsford Rd. M20: Manc 6A 24
Ainsworth Av. CH46: More 5K 31
Ainsworth Cl. M34: Den 7A 8
Ainsworth La. CW8: Crow 1J 153
Ainsworth Rd. CW8: Weav 4H 155
Ainsworth St. L3: Liv 3K 35
AINTREE 1B 214
Aintree Av. M33: Sale 1G 47
Aintree Cl. CH46: Leas 1C 32
SK7: H Gro 3K 79
Aintree Gro. CH66: Gt Sut 5K 133
SK3: Stoc 6C 52
Airdale Cl. CH43: Bid 6F 33
Airdrie Cl. CH62: East 4J 107
Aire WA8: Wid 3B 62
Aire Cl. CH65: Ell P 1C 134
Airedale Cl. SK8: Chea 6E 50
WA5: Gt San 5H 39
Airedale Ct. WA14: Alt 1K 213
Aire Pl. CW7: Wins 3J 179
(off Trent Av.)
Airlie Rd. CH47: Hoy 6C 30
Aitchison Rd. CW9: Los Gra 5C 158
Aitken St. M19: Manc 2F 25
Ajax Av. WA2: Warr 2F 41
Akbar, The CH60: Hes 4E 82
Akesmoor Dr. SK2: Stoc 6G 53
Akesmoor La. ST8: Gil H, Mow C 5K 205
Alabama Way CH41: Birk 6E 34
Alamein Cres. WA2: Warr 5F 41
Alamein Dr. CW7: Wins 4E 178
SK6: Rom 2E 54
Alamein Rd. CH2: Most 1J 145
CW8: Barnt 1J 155
Alandale Av. M34: Aude 3D 8
Alandale Rd. SK3: Stoc 5A 52
Alan Dr. SK6: Mar 6E 54
WA15: Hale 5A 74
Alan Rd. M20: Manc 5A 24
SK4: Stoc 1J 51
Alan St. CW9: N'ich 5G 157
Alastair Cres. CH43: Pren 4J 59
Alban Retail Pk. WA2: Warr 2E 40
Alban St. CW1: Crewe 1C 194
Albany, The L3: Liv 2H 35
(off Old Hall St.)
Albany Ct. M33: Sale 6H 23
M41: Urm 1A 22
Albany Cres. WA13: Lymm 1K 69
Albany Gdns. CH66: L Sut 1J 133
Albany Gro. WA13: Lymm 1J 69
Albany Rd. CH42: R Fer 3D 60
SK7: Bram 2H 99
SK9: Wilm 2E 118
WA13: Lymm 2J 69
Albany Ter. WA7: Run 4G 89
Albany Way SK14: Hat 1F 29
Albemarle Rd. CH44: Wall 1C 34
Alberbury Av. WA15: Timp 5D 48
Alberta St. SK1: Stoc 7K 213 (4D 52)
Albert Av. M41: Urm 1D 22
SK16: Duk 4H 9
Albert Cl. SK8: Chea H 3J 77
Albert Ct. WA14: Alt 3H 213 (1H 73)
Albert Dock L3: Liv 4H 35
Albert Dr. CH64: Nest 7G 105
WA5: Gt San 6F 39
Albert Hill St. M20: Manc 1D 50
Albert Pl. CW9: N'ich 5G 157
CW12: Cong 4G 183
(Canal St.)
CW12: Cong 2H 183
(Havannah St.)
SK11: Mac 4A 126
WA14: Alt 1H 213 (7H 47)
Albert Rd. CH42: Tran 1B 60
CH47: Hoy 6C 30
CH48: W Kir 4B 56
M19: Manc 2C 24
M33: Sale 7H 23
SK4: Stoc 1J 51
SK8: Chea H 3J 77
SK9: Wilm 1F 119
SK10: Boll 3B 122
SK14: Hyde 1J 27
WA4: Grap 3A 68
WA8: Wid 5H 63
WA14: Alt 3H 213 (1H 73)
WA15: Hale 2J 73
Albert Rd. E. WA15: Hale 2J 73
Albert Row WA6: Frod 6H 111
Albert Sq. SK15: Stal 1A 10
WA8: Wid 5H 63
WA14: Bow 2G 73
Albert St. CH1: Ches 2E 212 (1B 150)
CH45: N Bri 2J 13
CW1: Crewe 1C 194
CW5: Nant 1C 196
M34: Den 7E 8
M43: Droy 1A 8
M44: Cad 5B 20
SK3: Stoc 7F 213 (3B 52)
SK7: H Gro 2H 79
SK11: Mac 4K 125
SK14: Hyde 7A 10
WA7: Run 4G 89
WA16: Knut 3D 116
Albert Ter. SK1: Stoc 6J 213
WA5: Col G 2B 14
Albert Wlk. OL7: Ash L 1F 9
Albinson Wlk. M31: Part 1J 45
Albion Cl. SK4: Stoc 1C 52
Albion Gdns. SK15: Stal 7C 4
Albion Gro. M33: Sale 7F 23
Albion Ho. SK15: Stal 7C 4
Albion M. CH1: Ches 5C 212
Albion Pk. WA3: G'ury 4J 7
Albion Pl. CH1: Ches 5C 212 (2A 150)
CH45: N Bri 3H 13
SK7: H Gro 2H 79
Albion Rd. CW9: N'ich 4F 157
M14: Manc 2A 24
SK22: N Mil 1K 103
Albion St. CH1: Ches 5C 212 (2A 150)
CH41: Birk 6E 34
(not continuous)
CH45: N Bri 3G 13
CW2: Crewe 3A 194
M33: Sale 7G 23
SK15: Stal 7C 4
Albright Rd. WA8: Wid 7A 62
Albury Cl. WA5: Warr 5D 40
Albury Dr. M19: Manc 2F 51
Alcester Av. SK3: Stoc 5H 51
Alcester Rd. M33: Sale 2B 48
SK8: Gat 1D 76
Alcock St. WA7: Run 3G 89
Alconbury Cl. WA5: Gt San 6A 40
Alconbury Ct. M43: Droy 2A 8
(off Florence St.)
Alcott Pl. WA2: Winw 5K 15
Aldelyme Ct. CW3: Audl 5B 210
Alden Wlk. SK4: Stoc 4G 25
Alder Av. SK12: Poy 3E 100
WA8: Wid 2G 63
Alderbank Rd. WA5: Gt San 6J 39
Alder Cl. SK8: He Grn 5F 77
SK13: Had 3K 11
SK16: Duk 2B 10
Alder Ct. SK10: Boll 6A 122
Alder Cres. WA2: Warr 4G 41
Aldercroft Av. M22: Wyth 3J 75
Alderdale Cl. SK4: Stoc 7D 24
Alderdale Dr. SK4: Stoc 6D 24
SK6: H Lan 6E 80
Alderdale Gro. SK9: Wilm 2D 118
Alderdale Rd. SK8: Chea H 1A 78
Alder Dr. CH66: Gt Sut 7B 134
CW1: Crewe 6E 190
SK15: Stal 6D 4
WA15: Timp 1D 74
Alder Edge M21: Chor H 2K 23
(off Alderford Rd.)
Alderfield Ho. M21: Chor H 2K 23
Alderfield Rd. M21: Chor H 2K 23
Aldergate Gro. OL6: Ash L 4A 4
Alder Gro. CH2: Ches 6E 146
M32: S'ord 1K 23
M34: Den 7F 9
SK3: Stoc 4A 52
Alderhay La. ST7: Roo 7G 205
Alder Hgts. SK1: Stoc 2F 53
Alder La. WA2: Warr 4F 41
WA5: B'ood 4D 14
WA6: Frod 4D 110
WA8: Cron 1A 62
Alderley Av. CH41: Birk 5J 33
Alderley Cl. CW11: S'ach 2H 201
SK7: H Gro 5K 79
SK12: Poy 4E 100
Alderley Ct. SK2: Stoc 1G 79
SK9: Ald E 6G 119
Alderley Dr. SK6: Bred 1J 53
ALDERLEY EDGE 6F 119 (3C 217)
Alderley Edge 7J 119
Alderley Edge By-Pass SK9: Ald E 7D 118
SK10: N Ald 1F 167
Alderley Edge Station (Rail) 5F 119
Alderley Lodge SK9: Wilm 2F 119
Alderley Pk. SK10: N Ald 4J 167
Alderley Pl. CH1: Blac 4F 145
Alderley Rd. CH44: Wall 1A 34
CH47: Hoy 5C 30
CW8: Winn 5C 156
M33: Sale 2E 48
M41: Urm 1K 21
SK5: Stoc 6J 25
SK9: Ald E 6K 119
SK9: Wilm 2F 119
SK10: Mot A 6K 119
SK10: O Ald, Pres 6C 120
SK11: Chel 6D 166
WA4: Thel 2D 68
Alderley Ter. SK16: Duk 1G 9
Alderley Vw. SK10: Boll 3D 122
Alderley Wlk. SK11: Mac 5B 126
(off Bank St.)
Alderley Way SK3: Stoc 1C 78
Aldermere Cres. M41: Urm 1H 21
Alderney Cl. CH65: Ell P 7E 134
SK11: Mac 4G 125
Alderney Ho. CH2: Ches 6E 146
Alder Rd. CH63: H Beb 2H 85
CW8: Weav 5G 155
SK8: Chea 7G 51
WA1: Wool 5D 42
WA3: Low 2A 6
Alder Root La. WA2: Winw 4G 15
Aldersey Cl. CH1: Sau 1B 144
WA7: Win H 5F 91
ALDERSEY GREEN 2C 219
Aldersey Rd. CW2: Crewe 3K 193
Aldersey St. L3: Liv 1J 35
Aldersey Way CW6: Bun 6C 188
Aldersgate CH42: R Fer 3E 60
Aldersgate Av. WA7: Murd 7F 91
Aldersgate Rd. SK2: Stoc 6F 53
SK8: Chea H 1F 99
Alders Grn. Av. SK6: H Lan 6F 81
Alders Rd. M22: Wyth 7J 49
SK12: Dis 6G 81
Alder St. WA12: New W 1F 15
Alders Way SK10: Pres 5G 121
Alderton Gro. CW7: Wins 1G 179
Alderue Av. M22: Wyth 6K 49
Alderwood Av. SK4: Stoc 3J 51
Alderwood Ct. WA8: Wid 1E 62
Aldewood Cl. WA3: Birc 5C 18
Aldfield Rd. M23: Wyth 3F 49
ALDFORD 6G 185 (2C 219)
Aldford Cl. CH43: Oxt 3H 59
CH63: Brom 1G 107
CW2: Hou 5E 198
M20: Manc 1E 50
Aldford Pl. SK9: Ald E 5E 118
Aldford Rd. CH2: Upt 3C 146
CH3: Hunt 7D 150
Aldford Way CW7: Wins 2C 178
Aldgate CH65: Ell P 3C 134
Aldington Dr. CW10: Mid 7D 180
Aldridge Dr. WA5: B'ood 4C 14
Aldwick Av. M20: Manc 1E 50
Aldwinians Cl. M34: Aude 5D 8
Aldworth Gro. M33: Sale 1H 47
Aldwyn Cl. M34: Aude 5D 8
Aldwyn Cres. SK7: H Gro 3G 79
Aldwyn Pk. Rd. M34: Aude 2B 8
Aled Way CH4: Salt 6E 148
Alexander Ct. CH3: Ches 2B 150
(off Dee La.)
Alexander Dr. CH61: Pens 3G 83
WA8: Wid 5D 62
WA15: Timp 6A 48
Alexander Pk. OL6: Ash L 1J 9
Alexanders Jazz Theatre 3B 212 (1K 149)
Alexandra, The M14: Manc 3A 24
Alexandra Av. SK14: Hyde 1H 27
Alexandra Cl. SK3: Stoc 6A 52
Alexandra Ct. CH2: Ches 6D 146
CH45: N Bri 3G 13
(off Alexandra Rd.)
M31: Part 1H 45
(off Bailey La.)
M41: Urm 2H 21
Alexandra Dr. CH42: R Fer 4D 60
M19: Manc 4C 24
Alexandra Gro. M44: Irlam 3C 20
WA7: Run 5J 89
Alexandra Ind. Est. WA8: Wid 6F 63
Alexandra M. WA6: Frod 6H 111
Alexandra Pl. CW1: Crewe 1B 194
Alexandra Rd. CH43: Oxt 7B 34
CH45: N Bri 3G 13
CH48: W Kir 4B 56
CW10: Mid 6D 180
M33: Sale 1C 48
M34: Den 6F 9
SK4: Stoc 1A 52
WA4: Grap 3K 67

Alexandra Rd.—Appleton M.

Alexandra Rd. WA4: Stoc H 4H 67
Alexandra Soccer Cen. 1C 198
Alexandra Sq. *CW7: Wins* 4B 178
(off Southwark Pl.)
Alexandra St. CH65: Ell P 1E 134
CW7: Wins 3D 178
SK14: Hyde 2H 27
WA1: Warr 5J 41
WA8: Wid 6G 63
Alexandra Ter. M19: Manc 2D 24
Alexandria Dr. OL7: Ash L 1D 8
Alexandria Stadium 4D 194
Alexandria Way
CW12: Cong 2E 182
Alford Ct. *CW9: N'ich* 1D 162
(off Harthill Cl.)
Alforde St. WA8: Wid 6G 63
(not continuous)
Alford Rd. SK4: Stoc 5E 24
Alfred Cl. WA8: Wid 5H 63
Alfred M. L1: Liv 5K 35
Alfred Morris Ct. *M23: Wyth* 2G 49
(off Fellpark Rd.)
Alfred Rd. CH43: Oxt 7B 34
CH44: Wall 3D 34
WA3: Low 2A 6
Alfred St. CW8: N'ich 7D 156
M44: Cad 5B 20
(off Dean Rd.)
SK14: Hyde 7H 9
WA8: Wid 5H 63
Alfreton Av. M34: Den 3F 27
Alfreton Rd. SK2: Stoc 6H 53
Alfriston Dr. M23: Wyth 2G 49
Algernon St. WA1: Warr 6H 41
WA4: Stoc H 4G 67
WA7: Run 3F 89
Algreave Rd. SK3: Stoc 4J 51
Alice Ct. WA8: Wid 2G 89
Alice St. M33: Sale 7J 23
SK14: Hyde 4K 27
Alison Av. CH42: R Fer 2E 60
Alison Ct. SK4: Stoc 7E 24
Alison Dr. CW4: Goo 7H 165
SK10: Mac 3C 126
Alistair Dr. CH63: Brom 2H 107
ALKINGTON 3D 219
Allandale WA14: Alt 1F 73
Allandale Rd. M19: Manc 2C 24
Allangate Cl. CH49: Gre 3K 57
Allans Cl. CH64: Nest 2C 130
Allansford Av. CH3: Wave 3A 174
Allans Mdw. CH64: Nest 2C 130
Allanson Rd. M22: N'den 3A 50
Allcard St. WA5: Warr 5D 40
Allcot Av. CH42: Tran 3C 60
Alldis St. SK2: Stoc 7F 53
Allen Av. SK14: Hyde 3A 28
WA3: Cul 6J 7
Allenby Rd. M44: Cad 7A 20
Allendale WA7: Pal F 1D 112
Allendale Av. L35: R'ill 1D 36
Allen Dr. CW9: Dave 4E 162
Allen Hall M14: Manc 1A 24
Allen Pl. CW1: Crewe 1B 194
Allen Rd. M41: Urm 1E 22
WA7: Wes P 7D 88
Allen St. SK10: Boll 3E 122
SK11: Mac 5B 126
WA2: Warr 6E 40
Allerdean Wlk. SK4: Stoc 1H 51
ALLERTON 2C 215
Allerton Gro. CH42: Tran 2D 60
Allerton Rd. CH42: Tran 2C 60
CH45: Wall 5G 13
WA8: Wid 4H 63
ALLGREAVE 1D 221
Allgreave Cl. CW10: Mid 6C 180
M33: Sale 3E 48
Alliance Ind. Est. M34: Den 7C 8
Allington Pl. CH4: Ches 4B 150
Allman Cl. CW1: Crewe 6E 190
Allonby Cl. CH43: Noc 1H 59
ALLOSTOCK 5C 164 (3B 216)
Allotment Rd. M44: Cad 5A 20
Allport La. CH62: Brom 6D 86
(not continuous)
Allport Rd. CH62: Brom 1H 107
CH63: Brom 1H 107
Allports, The CH62: Brom 7D 86
All Saints Ct. *M32: S'ord* 1G 23
(off Manor Rd.)
All Saints Dr. WA4: Thel 2E 68
All Saints' Rd. SK4: Stoc 7G 25
ALLTAMI 1A 218
Allysum Ct. WA7: Beec 3B 112
Alma Av. CW1: Crewe 7H 191
Alma Cl. SK11: Mac 5H 125
ST7: Sch G 1H 205
Alma La. SK9: Wilm 1F 119
ALMA PARK 3E 24
Alma Rd. M19: Manc 3D 24
M33: Sale 2J 47
SK4: Stoc 6E 24
SK7: H Gro 5A 80
Alma St. CH3: Ches 1C 150
CH41: Birk 6D 34
CH62: N Fer 6F 61
SK15: Stal 7C 4
WA12: New W 1E 14
Alma Works SK16: Duk 1G 9
Almer Dr. WA5: Gt San 7A 40
Almond Av. CW1: Crewe 7J 191
WA7: Run 6J 89
Almond Cl. SK3: Stoc 4A 52
Almond Ct. *SK16: Duk* 1H 9
(off Combermere St.)
Almond Dr. M33: Sale 5E 22
WA5: B'ood 5C 14
Almond Gro. CW8: Weav 6H 155
WA1: Padd 5B 42
WA8: Wid 5D 62
Almond Pl. CH46: More 4C 32
Almond Tree Cl. L24: Hale 7B 88
Almond Tree Rd. SK8: Chea H 4J 77
Almond Wlk. *M31: Part* 1F 45
(off Wood La.)
Almond Way CH49: Gre 3K 57
SK14: Hyde 1B 28
Almshouses M33: Sale 7K 23
Alness Dr. L35: R'ill 2D 36
Alnwick Dr. CH46: More 4J 31
CH65: Ell P 6F 135
Alpass Av. WA5: Warr 4E 40
Alphabet Zoo Adventure Play Cen. 1G 9
Alpha Ct. M34: Den 7B 8
Alpha Ct. Ind. Est. M34: Den 7B 8
Alpha Dr. CH42: R Fer 4F 61
Alphagate Dr. M34: Den 7B 8
Alpha Rd. M32: S'ord 1H 23
Alphingate Cl. SK15: Carrb 5E 4
Alphin Sq. OL5: Moss 1E 4
Alpine Rd. SK1: Stoc 2E 52
(not continuous)
ALPRAHAM 2J 189 (2D 219)
Alpraham Cres. CH2: Upt 3B 146
Alpraham Grn. CW6: Alp 1J 189
Alric Wlk. M22: Wyth 5A 76
ALSAGER 5E 202 (2B 220)
Alsager Leisure Cen. 5C 202
Alsager Rd.
CW11: Hass, Wint 5D 204 & 1A 202
ALSAGERS BANK 3C 221
Alsager Station (Rail) 6F 203
Alstead Av. WA15: Hale 2A 74
Alston Av. M32: S'ord 1G 23
M33: Sale 1K 47
Alston Cl. CH62: Brom 5C 86
SK7: H Gro 4E 78
Alstone Dr. WA14: Alt 6E 46
Alstone Rd. SK4: Stoc 5F 25
Alston Gdns. M19: Manc 6C 24
Alt WA8: Wid 3B 62
Altair Av. M22: Wyth 4K 75
Altcar Dr. CH46: More 5A 32
Altcar Gro. SK5: Stoc 1H 25
Altcar Wlk. M22: Wyth 3J 75
Althorn Wlk. M23: Wyth 7G 49
Althorp St. L8: Liv 2K 61
Alton Av. M41: Urm 1G 21
Alton Dr. SK10: Mac 2C 126
Alton Rd. CH43: Oxt 7K 33
SK9: Wilm 6G 97
Alton St. CW2: Crewe 3K 193
ALTRINCHAM 1J 213 (2B 216)
Altrincham Crematorium
WA14: Dun M 4B 46
Altrincham FC 1K 73
Altrincham Garrick Playhouse 6K 47
Altrincham Leisure Cen. 2K 213 (1J 73)
Altrincham Retail Pk. WA14: B'ath 5G 47
Altrincham Rd. M22: Shar 5J 49
(not continuous)
M23: Wyth 5D 48
SK8: Gat 6B 50
SK9: Styal 2E 96
SK9: Styal, Wilm 3B 96
Altrincham Station (Rail & Metro)
2K 213 (1J 73)
Alt Wlk. CW7: Wins 2H 179
Alumbrook Av. CW4: H Cha 4J 181
Alum Ct. CW4: H Cha 5J 181
Alun Cres. CH4: Ches 5H 149
Alundale Rd. CW7: Wins 1D 178
ALVANLEY 7D 138 (3C 215)
Alvanley Cl. M33: Sale 3B 48
Alvanley Cres. SK3: Stoc 6A 52
Alvanley Dr. WA6: Hel 6C 138
Alvanley Ind. Est.
SK6: Bred 7E 26
Alvanley Pk. WA6: Alv 6E 138
Alvanley Pl. CH43: Oxt 6B 34
Alvanley Ri. CW9: N'ich 7F 157
Alvanley Rd. CH66: Gt Sut 4A 134
WA6: Hel 5C 138
Alvanley Ter. WA6: Frod 7H 111
Alvanley Vw. CH2: Elt 5F 137
Alvanley Way *CH66: Gt Sut* 4A 134
(off Gawsworth Rd.)
Alva Rd. L35: R'ill 2D 36
Alvaston Av. SK4: Stoc 1K 51
Alvaston Bus. Pk. CW5: Nant 6D 192
Alvaston Rd. CW5: Nant 2D 196
Alvaston Wlk. CW2: Crewe 4K 193
Alvega Cl. CH62: N Fer 6H 61
Alveley Av. M20: Manc 6A 24
Alverstone Av. CH41: Birk 5J 33
Alverstone Cl. WA5: Gt San 5E 38
Alverstone Rd. CH44: Wall 1C 34
Alverton Cl. WA8: Wid 5D 62
Alveston Cl. SK10: Mac 3G 125
Alveston Dr. SK9: Wilm 6K 97
Alvingham Cl. CW9: N'ich 5G 157
Alvington Gro. SK7: H Gro 4E 78
Alvon Ct. SK14: Hyde 1B 28
Alwen St. CH41: Birk 3J 33
Alwinton Av. SK4: Stoc 1G 51
Alwyn Ct. WN7: Leigh 1F 7
Alwyn Gdns. CH2: Upt 2B 146
CH46: More 4C 32
Alyndale Rd. CH4: Salt 5E 148
Alyn Rd. CH2: Mic T 1J 147
Ambassador Pl.
WA15: Alt 1K 213 (7J 47)
Amber Gdns. *SK16: Duk* 2G 9
(off Railway St.)
Amberleigh Cl.
WA4: App T 3B 94
Amberley Av. CH46: More 5K 31
Amberley Cl. CH46: More 5K 31
Amberley Dr. M23: Wyth 1G 75
M44: Irlam 2D 20
WA15: H'rns 5B 74
Amberley Rd. M33: Sale 6D 22
SK11: Mac 6H 125
Amberwood Dr. M23: Wyth 6D 48
Ambleside CH2: Ches 4C 146
SK15: Stal 6B 4
Ambleside Av. CH46: More 4A 32
WA15: Timp 7C 48
Ambleside Cl. CH61: Thin 7D 58
CH62: Brom 7E 86
CW2: Crewe 4J 193
CW7: Wins 1D 178
SK11: Mac 6G 125
WA7: Beec 2A 112
Ambleside Ct. CW12: Cong 4B 182
SK8: Chea 7E 50
SK15: Stal 6B 4
Ambleside Cres. WA2: Warr 1G 41
Ambleside Rd. CH65: Ell P 6E 134
M41: Urm 2H 21
SK5: Stoc 5J 25
Ambrose Ct. *M22: N'den* 3K 49
(off Kenworthy La.)
WA1: Warr 6H 41
Ambrose Dr. M20: Manc 1A 50
Ambrose St. SK14: Hyde 4K 27
Ambuscade Cl. CW1: Crewe 1E 194
Ambuscade Ct. M41: Urm 1H 21
Amelia Cl. WA8: Wid 1H 63
Amelia St. *SK14: Hyde* 1K 27
(off Lumn Hollow)
WA2: Warr 5G 41
Amelia St. W. M34: Den 6E 8
Amersham Cl. SK10: Mac 1K 125
Amersham Pl. M19: Manc 5D 24
Amery Gro. CH42: Tran 3B 60
Amesbury Gro. SK5: Stoc 6J 25
AMF Bowling
Macclesfield 2H 129
Amherst Rd. M14: Manc 4A 24
M20: Manc 4A 24
Amidian Ct. *CH44: Wall* 1A 34
(off Poulton Rd.)
Amlwch Av. SK2: Stoc 6H 53
Amy St. CW2: Crewe 3C 194
Anchorage, The CH3: Wave 2A 174
CH64: Park 1A 130
L3: Liv 6J 35
WA13: Lymm 2K 69
Anchorage Rd. M41: Urm 2F 23
Anchor Cl. M19: Manc 2F 25
WA7: Murd 1F 113
Anchor Ct. SK9: Wilm 6J 97
WA1: Warr 6H 41
Anchor Courtyard *L3: Liv* 4H 35
(off Gower St.)
Ancoats La. SK9: Ald E 1A 166
Ancoats Rd. SK9: Ald E 1B 166
Anderson Cl. CH61: Irby 7D 58
CW1: Crewe 2F 195
L35: R'ill 3D 36
WA2: Padg 2B 42
Anderson Ct. CH62: Brom 1J 107
Anderson St. SK10: Mac 4K 125
Anderson Trad. Est. *WA8: Wid* 7G 63
(off Croft St.)
ANDERTON 2C 156 (3A 216)
Anderton Boat Lift 2C 156
Anderton Boat Lift Vis Cen. 2C 156
Anderton Grange CW9: N'ich 6E 156
Anderton Nature Pk. 2D 156
Andertons La. SK10: Henb 4C 124
SK11: Henb 4C 124
Anderton Way SK9: Hand 3A 98
Andover Cl. WA2: Padg 3J 41
Andrew Cl. WA8: Wid 5C 62
Andrew Cres. CH4: Ches 3B 150
Andrew Gro. SK10: Mac 5D 126
SK16: Duk 2J 9
Andrew Ho. *L8: Liv* 5K 35
(off Birley Ct.)
SK4: Stoc 7E 24
Andrew La. SK6: H Lan 4E 80
Andrews Bldgs. *OL5: Moss* 1F 5
(off Bk. Micklehurst Rd.)
Andrews Cl. CH3: Tar 6B 170
M34: Den 2G 27
Andrew St. OL5: Moss 1D 4
SK4: Stoc 5F 213 (2B 52)
SK6: Comp 2G 55
SK14: Hyde 7A 10
Andrew's Wlk. CH60: Hes 6K 83
Anerley Rd. M20: Manc 1D 50
ANFIELD 1B 214
Anfield Rd. M33: Sale 6H 23
SK8: Chea H 3H 77
Angel Cl. SK16: Duk 2G 9
Angelina Cl. CW11: Elw 2B 200
Angel St. M34: Den 6F 9
SK7: H Gro 2H 79
Angier Gro. M34: Den 7E 8
Anglers Rest M44: Cad 6B 20
Anglesea Av. SK2: Stoc 6D 52
Anglesea Way L8: Liv 1K 61
Anglesey Cl. CH65: Ell P 7E 134
Anglesey Dr. SK12: Poy 7J 79
Anglesey Gro. SK8: Chea 6J 51
Anglesey Rd. CH44: Wall 6H 13
CH48: W Kir 1B 56
Anglesey Water SK12: Poy 7J 79
Angleside Av. M19: Manc 7B 24
Anglezarke Rd. WA12: New W 1D 14
Anglian Ct. *L8: Liv* 5K 35
(off Blair St.)
Angus Gro. CW10: Mid 2D 180
Angus Rd. CH63: Brom 1H 107
Angus Wlk. SK10: Mac 2G 125
Annable Rd. M43: Droy 1A 8
M44: Irlam 3C 20
SK6: Bred 1H 53
Annan Cl. CW12: Cong 5J 183
Annan St. M34: Den 6E 8
Ann Cl. CH66: L Sut 1K 133
Annesley Rd. CH44: Wall 1B 34
Anne St. SK16: Duk 2J 9
WA9: Clo F 1K 37
Anne's Way CH4: Ches 3B 150
Annie St. WA2: Warr 6G 41
Annions La. CW5: Stap, Wyb 7J 197
Annis Cl. SK9: Ald E 5G 119
Annis Rd. SK9: Ald E 5G 119
Ann St. CW9: N'ich 4J 157
M34: Den 7D 8
OL7: Ash L 2E 8
SK5: Stoc 7H 25
SK14: Hyde 7H 9
WA7: Run 3H 89
Ann St. W. WA8: Wid 6H 63
Anscot Av. CH63: Beb 7E 60
Ansdell Rd. SK5: Stoc 2K 25
WA8: Wid 3H 63
Ansdell Vs. Rd. L35: R'ill 1C 36
Ansley Gro. SK4: Stoc 1K 51
Anson Cl. SK7: Bram 1J 99
Anson Engine Mus., The 2H 101
Anson Rd. M34: Den 1K 25
SK9: Wilm 5B 98
SK12: Poy 2G 101
Anson St. L3: Liv 2K 35
Anstey Cl. CH46: More 3J 31
Anthony Dr. CW9: Moult 7E 162
Anthony's Way CH60: Hes 7J 83
Anthorn Cl. CH43: Noc 1G 59
Antons Rd. CH61: Pens 1J 83
Antony Rd. WA4: Warr 3F 67
Antrim Cl. M19: Manc 2F 51
Antrim Dr. CH66: Gt Sut 6B 134
Antrim Rd. WA2: Warr 2E 40
ANTROBUS 6B 94 (3A 216)
Antrobus St. CW12: Cong 3F 183
Anvil Cl. CH1: Sau 1B 144
CH2: Elt 4F 137
CW11: Whe 6D 200
Anzacs, The CH62: P Sun 7H 61
Apethorn La. SK14: Hyde 3H 27
Apex Ct. CH62: Brom 5E 86
Apollo Cinema
Altrincham 3J 213 (1H 73)
Crewe 3D 194
Apollo Ct. *CH44: Wall* 6K 13
(off Rudgrave Sq.)
Appin Rd. CH41: Birk 7D 34
Apple Blossom Gro. M44: Cad 7A 20
Appleby Av. M12: Manc 1D 24
SK14: Hyde 5H 9
WA15: Timp 7C 48
Appleby Cl. SK3: Stoc 7B 52
SK11: Mac 7G 125
WA8: Wid 5C 62
Appleby Cres. WA16: Mob 6B 102
Appleby Gro. CH62: Brom 1J 107
Appleby Lodge M14: Manc 1A 24
Appleby Rd. SK8: Gat 1D 76
WA2: Warr 1G 41
Appleby Wlk. WA8: Wid 5C 62
Apple Cl. CW12: Cong 3D 182
Applecross Cl. WA3: Birc 5B 18
Appledale Dr. CH66: Whit 1C 140
Appledore Dr. M23: Wyth 5D 48
Applefield CW8: N'ich 6C 156
Appleford Av. M23: Wyth 1G 75
Appleford Cl. WA4: App 6J 67
Apple Gth. CH46: More 6K 31
Apple Mkt. St. CW9: N'ich 5E 156
Apple St. SK14: Hyde 4D 28
APPLETON
WA4 6H 67
WA8 3H 63 (2D 215)
Appleton Cl. CW12: Cong 6G 183
Appleton Ct. M33: Sale 7G 23
Appleton Dr. CH49: Gre 2B 58
CH65: Whit 5B 134
Appleton Gro. M33: Sale 2J 47
Appleton Hall Gdns. WA4: App 1J 93
Appleton M. *WA13: Lymm* 1J 69
(off Oldfield Rd.)

Appleton Pk.—Ash Gro.

APPLETON PARK 2H 93
Appleton Rd. CH2: Upt 4B 146
SK4: Stoc 5G 25
WA8: Wid 4H 63
WA15: Hale 4J 73
Appleton St. CW8: Winn 4C 156
WA8: Wid 7H 63
APPLETON THORN 2B 94 (2A 216)
Appleton Thorn Trad. Est.
WA4: App T 7D 68
Appleton Village WA8: Wid 4G 63
Appleton Wlk. SK9: Wilm 5A 98
(off Colshaw Dr.)
Apple Tree Cl. L24: Hale 7B 88
Apple Tree Gro. CH66: Gt Sut 1B 140
Appletree Gro. WA2: Fear 2K 41
Apple Tree Wlk. M33: Sale 6B 22
Appleyards La. CH4: Ches 7E 212 (4A 150)
Apprentice La. SK9: Styal 3G 97
April Ri. SK10: Mac 3H 125
Apsley Av. CH45: Wall 5H 13
Apsley Cl. WA14: Bow 4F 73
Apsley Gro. CH63: Beb 7F 61
WA14: Bow 4F 73
Apsley Pl. OL6: Ash L 1F 9
Apsley Rd. CH62: N Fer 5G 61
M34: Den 6E 8
Apsley Side OL5: Moss 1D 4
(off Abney Rd.)
Apsley St. SK1: Stoc 6K 213 (3D 52)
Aqueduct Bus. Pk. SK6: Mar 4F 55
Aragon Ct. WA7: Man P 3E 90
Aragon Grn. CH1: Blac 4F 145
Aragon Way SK6: Mar 6E 54
Aran Cl. L24: Hale 6A 88
Arbor Av. M19: Manc 4C 24
Arbor Dr. M19: Manc 4C 24
Arborn Dr. CH49: Upt 6D 32
Arbour Cl. CW9: N'ich 5H 157
SK10: Mac 1A 126
Arbour Ct. SK6: Mar 7E 54
Arbour Cres. SK10: Mac 1A 126
Arbour M. SK10: Mac 1A 126
Arbournay St. SK10: Mac 3B 126
Arbury Av. SK3: Stoc 5J 51
Arbury La. WA2: Winw 5B 16
Arcade, The CH65: Ell P 3C 134
SK5: Stoc 6B 26
SK15: Stal 2A 10
Arcadia Av. M33: Sale 3A 48
Arcadia Sports Cen. 2D 24
Archbishop Warlock Ct.
L3: Liv 1H 35
Archer Av. WA4: Warr 3J 67
Archer Cl. SK10: Boll 4B 122
Archer Pl. M32: S'ord 1E 22
Archers Ct. CH49: Woodc 3D 58
(off Childwall Grn.)
Archers Cft. CH62: Brom 5D 86
Archers Grn. CH62: East 3K 107
Archers Grn. Rd. WA5: W'ook 1J 39
Archer St. SK2: Stoc 7G 53
Archers Way CH1: Ches 1H 149
CH49: Woodc 3D 58
CH66: Gt Sut 7A 134
Arch Vw. Cres. L1: Liv 4K 35
Archway Wlk. WA12: New W 1H 15
ARCLID 1B 220
Arclid Cl. SK9: Wilm 4B 98
Arclid Ct. CW12: Cong 3H 183
ARCLID GREEN 1B 220
Arcon Pl. SK1: Stoc 1F 53
WA14: Alt 6E 46
Arden WA8: Wid 3A 62
Ardenbrook Ri. SK10: Pres 5G 121
Arden Bldgs. SK3: Stoc 4C 52
(off Thomson St.)
Arden Bus. Cen. SK6: Bred 5D 26
Arden Cl. CH3: Tar 5C 170
OL6: Ash L 3A 4
SK8: He Grn 6E 76
WA3: Birc 5C 18
Arden Ct. CW12: Cong 7K 183
SK7: Bram 4B 78
Arden Dr. CH64: Nest 2C 130
Ardenfield M34: Den 4F 27
Ardenfield Dr. M22: Wyth 2A 76
Arden Lodge Rd. M23: Wyth 5E 48
ARDEN PARK 1H 53
Arden Rd. SK6: Bred 4D 26
Ardens Mdw. CW6: Tarp 4H 175
Arden Sq. CW1: Crewe 4G 195
(not continuous)
Arden Wlk. M33: Sale 6B 22
Arderne Av. CW2: Crewe 4K 193
Arderne Cl. CH63: Spit 4B 86
Arderne Ho. CH2: Upt 3C 146
Arderne Pl. SK9: Ald E 6F 119
Arderne Rd. WA15: Timp 4A 48
Ardern Fld. St. SK1: Stoc 5D 52
Ardern Gro. SK1: Stoc 4D 52
Ardern Lea WA6: Alv 7D 138
Ardern Wlk. SK1: Stoc 6H 213
Ardingley Wlk. M23: Wyth 4D 48
Ardleigh Cl. CW1: Crewe 5E 190
Ardmore Wlk. M22: Wyth 3A 76
Arena Gdns. WA2: Warr 4H 41
Argosy Dr. M90: Man A 6F 75
Argyle St. CH41: Birk 6D 34
L1: Liv 4J 35
M43: Droy 1A 8
SK7: H Gro 3J 79
Argyle St. Sth. CH41: Birk 7D 34
Argyll Av. CH4: Ches 4H 149
CH62: East 3J 107
M32: S'ord 1G 23
Argyll Cl. SK10: Mac 3H 125
Argyll Rd. SK8: Chea 7H 51
Ariel Gdns. WA3: Cul 1B 18
Arizona Cres. WA5: Gt San 5K 39
Arkenshaw Rd. WA3: Croft 3F 17
Arkenstone Cl. WA8: Wid 3C 62
Arkle Av. SK9: Hand 2B 98
Arkle Ct. CH3: Ches 1E 150
Arkle Rd. CH43: Bid 4J 33
Arklow Dr. L24: Hale 6A 88
Ark Royal Way CH41: Tran 1E 60
Ark St. M19: Manc 1D 24
Arkwood Cl. CH62: Spit 3C 86
Arkwright Cl. CW7: Wins 4B 178
Arkwright Ct. WA7: Astm 3B 90
Arkwright Dr. SK6: Mar 6G 55
Arkwright Rd. SK6: Mar 5G 55
WA7: Astm 3B 90
ARLEY 2A 216
Arley Av. WA4: Stoc H 5H 67
Arley Cl. CH2: Upt 4C 146
CH43: Bid 6F 33
SK11: Mac 5H 125
SK16: Duk 4J 9
ST7: Als 6D 202
WA14: W Tim 4H 47
Arley Ct. CW9: N'ich 1D 162
Arley Dr. M33: Sale 2A 48
WA8: Wid 3A 62
Arley End WA16: H Leg 2H 95
Arley Gro. SK3: Stoc 1B 78
WA13: Lymm 3C 70
Arley Ho. M23: Wyth 1G 75
Arleymere Cl. SK8: Chea H 2H 77
Arley Pl. CW2: Wis 6A 194
Arley Rd. CW9: N'ich 5H 157
WA4: App T 2B 94
Arley Wlk. CW11: Ett H 4B 200
Arley Way M34: Den 2F 27
(off Two Trees La.)
Arlies Cl. SK15: Stal 5B 4
Arlies La. SK15: Stal 5C 4
Arlington Av. M34: Den 1F 27
Arlington Cl. CW2: Wis 6C 194
Arlington Ct. CH43: Oxt 7J 33
Arlington Cres. SK9: Wilm 2D 118
Arlington Dr. SK2: Stoc 2E 78
SK11: Mac 5H 125
SK12: Poy 3C 100
WA5: Penk 1G 65
WN7: Leigh 2C 6
Arlington Rd. CH45: Wall 5E 12
M32: S'ord 1G 23
SK8: Chea 1E 76
Arlington Way SK9: Wilm 2D 118
Arliss Av. M19: Manc 3D 24
Armadale Cl. SK3: Stoc 7C 52
Armadale Rd. SK16: Duk 2H 9
Armentieres Sq. SK15: Stal 1B 10
Armentieres Way SK15: Stal 1B 10
(off Melbourne St.)
Armistead Way CW4: Cran 2G 181
Armitage Cl. SK14: Hyde 3K 27
Armitage Rd. WA14: Alt 3J 213 (2H 73)
Armitage Sports Cen. 2B 24
Armitstead Rd. CW11: Whe 5D 200
Armitt St. SK11: Mac 5K 125
Armour Av. WA2: Warr 2F 41
Armoury Ct. M. SK11: Mac 6K 125
(off Crompton Rd.)
Armoury St. SK3: Stoc 4C 52
Armoury Towers SK11: Mac 6J 125
(off Barracks Sq.)
Armstrong Cl. CW3: Audl 5B 210
WA3: Birc 7J 17
Armstrong Quay L3: Liv 2K 61
Armthorpe Dr. CH66: L Sut 3H 133
Arncliffe Dr. M23: Wyth 2G 75
WA5: B'ood 5C 14
Arndale WA7: Beec 2A 112
Arndale Shop. Cen. M32: S'ord 2H 23
Arne Cl. SK2: Stoc 7A 54
Arnesby Av. M33: Sale 6K 23
Arnfield Rd. M20: Manc 5A 24
SK3: Stoc 7B 52
Arnhem Cres. WA2: Warr 5G 41
Arno Ct. CH43: Oxt 2A 60
Arnold Av. SK14: Hyde 4A 28
Arnold Cl. SK16: Duk 3B 10
Arnold Pl. WA8: Wid 6C 62
Arnold Rd. SK14: Hyde 4A 28
Arnold St. CH45: Wall 6H 13
CW5: Nant 1C 196
SK3: Stoc 5C 52
WA1: Warr 6H 41
(off Manchester Rd.)
Arnolds Yd. WA14: Alt 1J 213 (7H 47)
Arnold Wlk. M34: Den 4F 27
(off Wordsworth Rd.)
Arno Rd. CH43: Oxt 2A 60
Arnot Way CH63: H Beb 7C 60
Arnside Av. CW12: Cong 4C 182
L35: R'ill 1A 36
SK4: Stoc 5G 25
SK7: H Gro 3G 79
Arnside Cl. CW7: Wins 2E 178
SK6: H Lan 5E 80
SK8: Gat 1D 76
Arnside Dr. SK14: Hyde 6H 9
Arnside Gro. M33: Sale 5G 23
WA4: Warr 3F 67
Arnside Rd. CH43: Oxt 1K 59
CH45: Wall 6H 13
Arosa Ct. M20: Manc 4A 24
ARPLEY MEADOWS 2F 67
Arpley Rd. WA1: Warr 1F 67
Arpley St. WA1: Warr 7E 40
Arradon Ct. CH2: Upt 5B 146
Arrad St. L7: Liv 4K 35
Arran Av. CH65: Ell P 7E 134
M32: S'ord 1F 23
M33: Sale 1C 48
Arran Cl. CW2: Crewe 3H 193
CW4: H Cha 5J 181
WA2: Fear 2A 42
Arran Ct. SK8: Chea H 3J 77
(off Vaudrey Dr.)
Arrandale Ct. M41: Urm 1C 22
Arran Dr. WA6: Frod 1J 139
Arran Rd. SK16: Duk 3H 9
Arras Gro. M34: Den 1J 25
Arreton Sq. M14: Manc 1A 24
(off Rusholme Gro.)
Arrivals Way M90: Man A 6H 75
Arrowcroft Rd. CH3: Guil S 5J 147
Arrowe Av. CH46: More 5A 32
Arrowe Brook La. CH49: Gre 4A 58
Arrowe Brook Rd. CH49: Woodc 3C 58
Arrowe Commercial Pk. CH49: Upt 2C 58
Arrowe Country Pk. 4C 58
Arrowe Ct. CH49: Woodc 3D 58
(off Childwall Grn.)
ARROWE HILL 2C 58
Arrowe Pk. Rd.
CH49: Upt, Woodc 1D 58
Arrowe Rd. CH49: Gre 2A 58
Arrowe Side CH49: Gre 1B 58
Arrowscroft Way SK14: H'rth 2J 11
Arrowsmith Dr. ST7: Als 6C 202
Arrow Trad. Est. M34: Aude 5C 8
ARTHILL 5K 71
Arthill La. WA14: L Bol 5K 71
Arthog Dr. WA15: Hale 5K 73
Arthog Rd. M20: Manc 1E 50
WA15: Hale 5K 73
Art House Sq. L1: Liv 4K 35
(off Fleet St.)
Arthur Av. CH65: Ell P 3E 134
(not continuous)
Arthur St. CH1: Ches 1H 149
CH41: Birk 5B 34
(not continuous)
CW2: Crewe 4D 194
CW9: Los Gra 5C 158
SK5: Stoc 4H 25
(not continuous)
SK14: Hyde 2H 27
WA2: Warr 6E 40
WA7: Run 4G 89
Arthur Ter. SK5: Stoc 4H 25
(off Arthur St.)
Artillery Pl. M22: Wyth 1B 76
Artists La. SK10: N Ald .....1H 167 & 7J 119
Artle Rd. CW2: Crewe 6C 194
Arundale Cl. SK14: Mot 7G 11
Arundale Gro. SK14: Mot 7G 11
Arundel Av. CH45: Wall 5F 13
M41: Urm 2F 21
SK7: H Gro 5H 79
Arundel Cl. CH61: Pens 1G 83
CW2: Wis 6J 193
SK10: Mac 2C 126
SK15: Carrb 3G 5
WA15: Hale 4C 74
WA16: Knut 5E 116
Arundel Ct. CH65: Ell P 5G 135
Arundel Gro. SK2: Stoc 1F 79
Arundell Cl. WA5: B'ood 5C 14
Arundel Rd. SK8: Chea H 7J 77
Asbury Rd. CH45: Wall 5D 12
Ascol Dr. WA16: Plum 4E 158
Ascot Av. M33: Sale 1G 47
WA7: Run 1H 111
Ascot Cl. CW12: Cong 2F 183
SK10: Mac 1K 125
WA1: Wool 5E 42
WA4: Grap 3C 68
Ascot Dr. CH63: Beb 1K 85
CH66: Gt Sut 5K 133
M41: Urm 1F 21
SK7: H Gro 3A 80
Ascot Gro. CH63: Beb 1K 85
Ascot Ho. CH1: Ches 1J 149
Ascot Pde. M19: Manc 5C 24
Ash Av. M44: Cad 6A 20
SK8: Chea 7G 51
WA12: New W 1F 15
WA14: Alt 7E 46
Ash Bank CH3: Guil S 6F 147
Ashbank CW9: Rud 6J 157
Ashberry Cl. SK9: Wilm 6A 98
Ashberry Dr. WA4: App T 1B 94
Ashbourne Av. M41: Urm 1H 21
SK8: Chea 6H 51
WA7: Run 1H 111
Ashbourne Cl. CH66: Gt Sut 1A 140
Ashbourne Cres. M33: Sale 2D 48
Ashbourne Dr. CW2: West 5J 199
OL6: Ash L 3A 4
SK6: H Lan 7E 80
Ashbourne M. SK10: Mac 4G 125
Ashbourne Rd. M34: Den 1D 26
SK7: H Gro 5K 79
WA5: Gt San 7K 39
Ashbrook Av. M34: Den 7A 8
WA7: Sut W 3A 112
Ashbrook Cl. M34: Den 7A 8
SK8: He Grn 4D 76
Ashbrook Cres. WA2: Warr 4H 41
Ashbrook Dr. SK10: Pres 5H 121
Ashbrook Farm Cl. SK5: Stoc 1J 25
Ashbrook La. SK5: Stoc 1J 25
Ashbrook Office Pk. M22: Wyth 5C 76
Ashbrook Rd. SK10: Boll 4C 122
SK10: O Ald 5A 120
Ashbrook Ter. CH63: Beb 7F 61
Ashburn Av. M19: Manc 6C 24
Ashburne Hall M14: Manc 2A 24
Ashburn Gro. SK4: Stoc 1B 52
Ashburnham Way L3: Liv 1K 35
Ashburn Rd. SK4: Stoc 1A 52
Ashburton Av. CH43: Clau 6J 33
Ashburton Cl. SK14: Hat 1F 29
Ashburton Rd. CH43: Clau 6H 33
CH44: Wall 7H 13
CH48: W Kir 2C 56
SK3: Stoc 1C 78
Ashbury Cl. WA7: Win H 4F 91
Ashby Av. M19: Manc 7B 24
Ashby Cl. CH46: More 3J 31
Ashby Dr. CW11: Ett H 4A 200
Ashby Pl. CH2: Ches 7B 146
Ash Cl. CH66: Gt Sut 7B 134
CW4: H Cha 3K 181
CW6: Tarp 2J 175
SK2: Stoc 7G 53
SK14: Mot 6H 11
SY14: Mal 1J 207
Ashcott Av. M22: Wyth 1K 75
Ash Ct. SK4: Stoc 1K 51
SK6: W'ley 6F 27
WA16: Knut 3E 116
Ashcroft Av. CW2: Shav 4B 198
Ashcroft Cl. SK9: Wilm 2E 118
Ashcroft Dr. CH61: Hes 3H 83
Ashcroft Ho. WA14: Alt 2J 213
Ashcroft Rd. WA13: Lymm 1D 70
Ashdale Cl. SK5: Stoc 6J 25
ST7: Als 4D 202
Ashdale Dr. M20: Manc 6A 24
SK8: He Grn 3D 76
Ashdale Pk. CH49: Gre 2J 57
Ashdene Rd. M20: Manc 5A 24
SK4: Stoc 2F 51
SK9: Wilm 2E 118
Ashdown Av. SK6: W'ley 6H 27
Ashdown Cl. SK8: Chea H 7J 77
Ashdown Cres. WA9: Clo F 1J 37
Ashdown Dr. CH49: Gre 3K 57
Ashdowne Lawns SK15: Stal 6E 4
Ashdown La. WA3: Birc 6B 18
Ashdown Rd. SK4: Stoc 1A 52
WA16: Oll 7K 117
Ashenhurst Rd. ST7: Als 6G 203
Asher Ct. WA4: App T 2D 94
Ashes Cl. SK15: Stal 2D 10
Ashes La. SK15: Stal 2D 10
Ashfield L35: R'ill 1D 36
M34: Den 5F 9
Ashfield Cl. WA13: Lymm 1D 70
Ashfield Cres. CH1: Blac 5E 144
CH62: Brom 6D 86
SK8: Chea 6F 51
Ashfield Dr. SK10: Mac 2H 125
Ashfield Gdns. WA4: Westy 2K 67
Ashfield Gro. M44: Irlam 5B 20
SK3: Stoc 1D 78
SK6: Mar B 3H 55
Ashfield Ho. CH64: Nest 7H 105
(off Churchill Way)
Ashfield Lodge M20: Manc 2B 50
SK3: Stoc 1D 78
Ashfield Rd. CH62: Brom 6C 86
CH65: Ell P 3E 134
M33: Sale 6G 23
M41: Urm 1C 22
SK3: Stoc 1D 78
SK8: Chea 6F 51
(not continuous)
WA15: Alt 4K 213 (2J 73)
Ashfield Rd. Nth. CH65: Ell P 3E 134
Ashfield St. CW10: Mid 4D 180
Ashford M33: Sale 7B 22
Ashford Av. SK5: Stoc 1J 25
Ashford Cl. SK9: Hand 2K 97
Ashford Ct. SK5: Stoc 1J 25
(off Ashford Av.)
Ashford Dr. WA4: App 3J 93
Ashford Rd. CH41: Birk 1B 60
CH47: Meols 4D 30
SK4: Stoc 5G 25
SK9: Wilm 3F 119
Ashford Way WA8: Wid 4K 63
Ashgate Av. M22: Wyth 1A 76
Ashgate La. CW9: Winc 1B 158
Ash Gro. CH4: Ches 6J 149
CH45: N Bri 4J 13
CH66: L Sut 2J 133
CW5: Nant 3C 196
CW7: Wins 4E 178
CW8: Weav 6H 155
CW10: Mid 5D 180

Aviator Way—Bankside Cl.

Aviator Way M22: Wyth 5J 75
Aviemore Dr. WA2: Fear 1A 42
Avocet Cl. WA2: Warr 1H 41
Avocet Dr. CW7: Wins 6E 178
WA14: B'ath 4F 47
Avon WA8: Wid 3A 62
Avon Av. WA5: Penk 1G 65
Avon Bank SK6: Bred 1K 53
Avon Cl. CH64: Nest 2C 130
SK6: Mar 7E 54
SK10: Mac 2H 125
Avon Ct. ST7: Als 4D 202
Avondale CH65: Whit 5D 134
Avondale Av. CH46: More 3C 32
CH62: East 2A 108
SK7: H Gro 3K 79
Avondale Cres. M41: Urm 1B 22
Avondale Dr. WA8: Wid 4B 62
Avondale Ind. Est. SK3: Stoc 5K 51
Avondale Lodge *M33: Sale* 1B 48
(off Whitehill Rd.)
Avondale Recreation Cen. 5K 51
Avondale Ri. SK9: Wilm 1J 119
Avondale Rd. CH47: Hoy 5C 30
SK3: Stoc 5K 51
SK7: H Gro 3K 79
Avon Dr. CW1: Crewe 1G 195
CW12: Cong 5H 183
Avon Gdns. M19: Manc 5D 24
Avonlea Cl. CH4: Ches 7F 149
Avonlea Dr. M19: Manc 5B 24
Avonlea Rd. M33: Sale 3H 47
Avon Rd. M19: Manc 5C 24
SK8: He Grn 6D 76
WA3: Cul 1B 18
WA15: Hale 5J 73
Avonside Way SK11: Mac 7K 125
Avon St. CH41: Birk 3J 33
SK3: Stoc 5C 52
Avon Wlk. CW7: Wins 2H 179
Avril Cl. SK5: Stoc 3J 25
Avro Way M90: Man A 6F 75
Awburn Rd. SK14: Hat 2F 29
Axholme Cl. CH61: Thin 1K 83
Axholme Rd. CH61: Thin 1J 83
Axminster Wlk. SK7: Bram 6C 78
Aycliffe Wlk. WA8: Wid 5C 62
Aylesbury Av. CH43: Oxt 3H 59
M34: Den 2E 26
Aylesbury Cl. CH66: Gt Sut 5J 133
SK10: Mac 1A 126
Aylesbury Rd. CH45: N Bri 4J 13
Aylesby Cl. WA16: Knut 4F 117
Aylesford Rd. M14: Manc 1A 24
Aylsham Cl. SK6: Bred 6E 26
WA8: Wid 1C 62
Aylsham Dr. CH49: Upt 5D 32
Aylwin Dr. M33: Sale 1C 48
Ayr Cl. SK7: H Gro 3A 80
Ayrshire Cl. CW10: Mid 2D 180
Ayrshire Way CW12: Cong 5J 183
Aysgarth Av. CW1: L'ton 4G 191
SK6: Rom 7J 27
SK8: Chea 6E 50
Aysgarth Cl. M33: Sale 1H 47
Aysgarth Rd. CH45: Wall 5F 13
Ayshford Cl. WA14: Alt 6F 47
Azalea Gro. WA7: Beec 3B 112

B

Babbacombe Rd. SK2: Stoc 6G 53
WA5: Penk 1G 65
BABELL 3A 214
Bache Av. CH2: Upt 5K 145
Bache Dr. CH2: Ches 4A 146
Bachefield Av. CH3: Hunt 5D 150
Bache Hall Ct. CH2: Ches 5K 145
Bache Hall Est. CH2: Ches 5K 145
Bachelor's Ct. CH3: Gt Bou 3D 150
Bachelor's La. CH3: Ches, Gt Bou 3D 150
Bache Station (Rail) 5A 146
Bk. Adcroft St. *SK1: Stoc* 5D 52
(off Adcroft St.)
Bk. Andrew St. *OL5: Moss* 1D 4
(off Fox Platt Ter.)
Bk. Berry St. *L1: Liv* 4K 35
(off Seel St.)
Bk. Bold St. *L1: Liv* 3J 35
(off Newington)
BACKBOWER 2K 27
Bk. Bower Fold *SK15: Stal* 2D 10
(off Bower Fold)
Bk. Bower La. SK14: Hyde 3A 28
Bk. Bridge St. WA12: New W 1E 14
Bk. Bridport St. *L3: Liv* 2K 35
(off Hotham St.)
Bk. Brook Pl. WA4: Westy 2J 67
Bk. Cambridge St. *OL7: Ash L* 1E 8
(off Bennett St.)
Bk. Canning St. L8: Liv 4K 35
Bk. Cecil St. *OL5: Moss* 1D 4
(off Park Ter.)
Bk. Chapel St. *M19: Manc* 2D 24
(off Bankley St.)
SK7: H Gro 2J 79
Bk. Colquitt St. L1: Liv 4K 35
Bk. Commutation Row *L3: Liv* 2K 35
(off London Rd.)
Bk. Crossland Ter. WA6: Hel 6B 138
Bk. Cross La. CW12: Cong 6J 183
Bk. Eddisbury Rd. SK11: Mac 5F 127
BACKFORD 5D 140 (3C 215)
Backford Cl. CH43: Oxt 2H 59
WA7: B'vale 2E 112
Backford Gdns. CH1: Bac 2B 140
Backford Rd. CH61: Irby 1F 83
Bk. Forshaw St. *WA2: Warr* 5G 41
(off Forshaw St.)
Bk. Grafton St. WA14: Alt 3J 213
Bk. Grosvenor St. SK15: Stal 1B 10
Bk. Hamel St. *SK14: Hyde* 5A 10
(off Hamel St.)
Bk. High St. WA7: Run 4G 89
Bk. Hope Pl. *L1: Liv* 4K 35
(off Pilgrim St.)
Bk. Huskisson St. L8: Liv 5K 35
Bk. Knight St. *L1: Liv* 4K 35
(off Berry St.)
Bk. Knowl St. SK15: Stal 7C 4
Backlands, The CW1: Crewe 7H 191
Back La. CW2: Shav 2E 198
CW6: Alp 1J 189
CW6: Dud 5B 174
CW8: Crow 2H 153
CW12: Cong, Som 1A 182
CW12: Eat 5H 169
SK13: Char 5K 29
SK14: Mot 7H 11
SY14: No H 3B 208
SY14: Thr 5H 207
WA4: H Whi 3C 114
WA5: Col G 4A 14
WA5: Cuer 3C 64
WA6: Alv 6C 138
WA14: Dun M 7K 45
WA14: M'ton 7H 71
WA16: Plum 3K 159
Back Lanes CW6: Tarp 2F 175
Bk. Leeds St. L3: Liv 1G 35
Bk. Legh St. WA12: New W 1D 14
Bk. Lime St. *L1: Liv* 3J 35
(off Elliot St.)
Bk. Maryland St. *L1: Liv* 4K 35
(off Baltimore St.)
Bk. Massie St. SK8: Chea 6F 51
Bk. Melbourne St. SK15: Stal 7B 4
Bk. Menai St. CH41: Birk 6B 34
Bk. Micklehurst Rd. OL5: Moss 1F 5
Back Moor SK14: Mot 6H 11
Back of Hoole La. *CH2: Ches* 1C 150
(off Hoole La.)
Bk. Oliver St. *CH41: Birk* 6D 34
(off Argyle St.)
BACK O' TH' HILL 6J 27
Bk. Paradise St. SK11: Mac 5K 125
Bk. Park St. CW12: Cong 4G 183
Bk. Percy St. *L8: Liv* 5K 35
(off Percy St.)
Bk. Pickop St. *L3: Liv* 2H 35
(off Vauxhall Rd.)
Bk. Price St. CH41: Birk 5C 34
Bk. Queen St.
CH1: Ches 3D 212 (1A 150)
Bk. Renshaw St. L1: Liv 3K 35
Bk. River St. CW12: Cong 3F 183
Back Seaview CH47: Hoy 5C 30
Bk. Seel St. L1: Liv 4J 35
Bk. Vernon St. *SK14: Hyde* 1K 27
(off Vernon St.)
Bk. Wall Ga. SK11: Mac 4A 126
Bk. Water St. SK1: Stoc 4K 213
Bacon Av. M34: Den 4F 27
Baddeley Cl. SK3: Stoc 7B 52
BADDELEY GREEN 2D 221
Baddington La. CW5: B'ton 7A 196
Baden Ct. CH48: W Kir 2B 56
Bader Cl. CH61: Pens 3G 83
Badger Av. CW1: Crewe 7E 190
Badger Bait CH64: L Nes 2D 130
Badger Cl. CW7: Wins 3B 178
SK6: Mar 2F 81
SK14: Hyde 6K 9
WA7: Pal F 1C 112
Badger Ho. SK10: Mac 2A 126
Badger Rd. SK10: Mac 2A 126
SK10: Pres 4H 121
WA14: W Tim 4G 47
Badgers Cl. CH3: Chri 4H 151
CH66: Gt Sut 1B 140
Badgers Cft. WA16: Mob 6B 102
Badgers Pk. CH64: L Nes 2D 130
Badgersrake La. CH66: Leds 5C 132
Badgers Set CH48: Cald 7E 56
CW8: Cudd 1A 160
Badgers Wlk. CH2: Cau 7G 141
M22: Wyth 4A 76
Badgers Wood CW2: Wis 6J 193
Badger Way CH43: Pren 5H 59
Baffin Cl. CH46: Leas 7A 12
BAGILLT 3A 214
Bag La. CW8: Crow, Cudd 6A 154
WA6: Norl 5J 153
Bagmere Cl. CW11: S'ach 2C 200
BAGNALL 2D 221
Bagnall Cl. WA5: Gt San 7A 40
Bagnall Ct. M22: N'den 4A 50
Bagnall Wlk. M22: N'den 4A 50
Bagot Av. WA5: Warr 4D 40
Bagshaw St. SK14: Hyde 5K 9
Bagstock Av. SK12: Poy 4D 100
BAGULEY 5F 49
Baguley Av. WA8: Hal B 1A 88
Baguley Cres. SK3: Stoc 6B 52
Baguley La. M33: Sale 1E 48
(not continuous)
Baguley Rd. M33: Sale 7K 23
Baguley St. M43: Droy 1A 8
Baildon Grn. *CH66: L Sut* 3H 133
(off Askrigg Av.)
Bailey Av. CH65: Ell P 2B 134
Bailey Bri. Cl. CH2: Ches 6A 146
Bailey Bus. Pk.
SK10: Boll 4C 122
Bailey Cl. CW1: Crewe 6H 191
Bailey Ct. ST7: Als 6F 203
Bailey Cres. CW11: S'ach 3H 201
CW12: Cong 2J 183
Bailey La. M31: Part 1H 45
M90: Man A 4H 75
Baileys Cl. WA8: Wid 7G 37
Bailey St. L1: Liv 4K 35
Bailey Wlk. WA14: Bow 5G 73
Bainbridge Av. WA3: Low 2A 6
Bainbridge Cres.
WA5: Gt San 4G 39
Baines Av. M44: Irlam 3C 20
Baker Cl. CW2: Crewe 4A 194
Baker Dr. CH66: Gt Sut 5A 134
Baker Rd. WA7: Wes P 7D 88
Bakers Ct. *CH3: Ches* 1B 150
(off Steam Mill St.)
CW7: Wins 2F 179
Bakersfield Pl. M33: Sale 7H 23
Baker's La. CW7: Wins 2F 179
WA16: All 3A 164
Baker St. SK4: Stoc 1C 52
SK11: Mac 5K 125
SK15: Stal 1C 10
WA15: Timp 5C 48
Bakers Villas, The
CW12: Cong 4F 183
Bakewell Av. M34: Den 3F 27
OL6: Ash L 3A 4
Bakewell Cl. CH66: Gt Sut 1A 140
Bakewell Rd. M32: S'ord 1F 23
SK7: H Gro 5J 79
WA5: B'ood 4C 14
Bakewell St. SK3: Stoc 4B 52
Bala Cl. WA5: Call 2C 40
Bala Gro. CH44: Wall 1K 33
BALDERTON 1B 218
Baldock Cl. WA4: Thel 2C 68
Baldock Rd. M20: Manc 1F 51
Baldwin Rd. M19: Manc 5C 24
BALDWIN'S GATE 3B 220
Balfour Cl. CW1: Hasl 2J 195
Balfour Gro. SK5: Stoc 3J 25
Balfour Rd. CH43: Oxt 7A 34
CH44: Wall 2K 33
M41: Urm 1A 22
WA14: B'ath 5H 47
Balfour St. WA7: Run 5F 89
Balham Cl. WA8: Wid 1G 63
Ballantyne Dr. CH43: Bid 3F 33
Ballantyne Pl. WA2: Winw 5K 15
Ballantyne Wlk. CH43: Bid 3F 33
Ballard Rd. CH48: W Kir 2F 57
Ballater Av. M41: Urm 2K 21
Ballater Cres. CH3: Ches 1E 150
Ballater Dr. WA2: Warr 7D 16
Ball Av. CH45: N Bri 3G 13
Ballerat Cl. CH1: Blac 6E 144
Ballerat St. M19: Manc 2D 24
Balliol Cl. CH43: Bid 3F 33
SK6: W'ley 7H 27
SK11: Sut E 2K 129
Balliol Ct. M33: Sale 6C 22
Ball La. SK10: Boll 6A 122
WA6: K'ley 1E 152 & 1G 153
BALL O' DITTON 4E 62
Ball Path WA8: Wid 4F 63
Ball Path Way WA8: Wid 4E 62
Ball's Rd. CH43: Oxt 1A 60
Balls Rd. E. CH41: Birk 7B 34
Ball Wlk. SK14: Hat 2G 29
Balmer Dr. M23: Wyth 1H 75
Balmoral Av.
CW2: Crewe 5B 194
CW9: N'ich 1F 163
M32: S'ord 1J 23
M34: Aude 3C 8
M41: Urm 2A 22
SK8: Chea H 3J 77
SK14: Hyde 3K 27
Balmoral Cl. CW7: Wins 1D 178
WA16: Knut 4F 117
Balmoral Ct. *OL7: Ash L* 1F 9
(off Victoria St.)
Balmoral Cres. SK10: Mac 2C 126
Balmoral Dr. CW4: H Cha 5H 181
M34: Den 7A 8
SK6: H Lan 6E 80
SK12: Poy 3C 100
SK15: Stal 6B 4
WA6: Hel 4B 138
WA14: Timp 4K 47
Balmoral Gdns.
CH43: Pren 4J 59
CH65: Ell P 5F 135
CW12: Cong 2H 183
Balmoral Gro. CH43: Noc 2G 59
SK7: H Gro 2K 79
Balmoral Pk. CH1: Ches 7J 145
Balmoral Pl. CW5: W'ston 3H 197
Balmoral Rd. CH45: N Bri 2J 13
M14: Manc 3A 24
M41: Urm 2K 21
SK4: Stoc 1J 51
WA4: Grap 3K 67
WA8: Wid 1F 63
WA15: Alt 2K 213 (1J 73)
Balmoral Way SK9: Wilm 1F 119
Balniel St. WA9: Clo F 1K 37
Balshaw Av. M44: Irlam 1C 20
Balshaw Ct. M44: Irlam 1D 20
BALTERLEY 2B 220
Baltic Rd. WA14: B'ath, Dun M 6E 46
Baltimore Gdns. WA5: Gt San 5A 40
Baltimore St. L1: Liv 4K 35
Bamber Av. M33: Sale 1E 48
Bamburgh Ct. CH65: Ell P 5G 135
Bamford Av. M34: Den 3E 26
Bamford Bus. Pk. SK4: Stoc 6H 25
Bamford Cl. SK8: He Grn 5F 77
SK10: Boll 4D 122
WA7: Run 7J 89
Bamford Gdns. WA15: Timp 6D 48
Bamford Gro. M20: Manc 1C 50
OL6: Ash L 3A 4
Bamford Rd. M20: Manc 1C 50
Bamford St. SK1: Stoc 7J 213 (4D 52)
SK10: Mac 3B 126
BAMFURLONG 1D 215
Bampton Cl. SK2: Stoc 5F 53
Bampton Rd. M22: Wyth 4K 75
Banastre Dr. WA12: New W 1J 15
Banbury Cl. SK10: Mac 2B 126
WN7: Leigh 1E 6
Banbury Dr. WA5: Gt San 1A 66
WA14: Timp 4J 47
Banbury Rd. M23: Wyth 7F 49
Banbury St. SK1: Stoc 7J 213 (3D 52)
Banbury Way CH43: Oxt 3H 59
Bancroft CW8: Act B 1B 154
Bancroft Av. SK8: Chea H 4J 77
Bancroft Cl. SK6: Bred 1J 53
Bancroft Ct. *WA15: Hale* 2A 74
(off Bancroft Rd.)
Bancroft Fold SK14: Hyde 5C 10
Bancroft Rd. WA8: Wid 3K 63
WA15: Hale 2A 74
Bandon Cl. L24: Hale 6A 88
Banff Av. CH63: East 2J 107
Bangor Cl. CH66: Gt Sut 2A 140
BANGOR-IS-Y-COED 3B 218
Bangor Rd. CH45: Wall 5D 12
SK8: Chea 6H 51
Bangor St. OL6: Ash L 1K 9
SK5: Stoc 7J 25
BANK, THE 5F 205 (2C 221)
Bank, The ST7: Sch G 5F 205
Bank Cl. CH2: Ches 5B 146
CH64: L Nes 2E 130
SK11: Mac 5B 126
Bank Dene CH42: R Fer 5F 61
Bankes La. WA7: Wes P 1E 110
(not continuous)
Bankfield SK14: Hyde 5J 9
Bankfield Av. CW2: Wis 7A 194
M44: Cad 6A 20
SK4: Stoc 2A 52
Bankfield Cotts. *SK6: W'ley* 6G 27
(off Woodlands Dr.)
Bankfield Ct. CH62: Brom 3F 87
Bankfield Ho. SK6: W'ley 6G 27
Bankfield Rd. M33: Sale 5D 22
SK6: W'ley 6G 27
SK8: Chea H 4H 77
WA8: Wid 4B 62
Bankfields Dr. CH62: East 2C 108
Bankfield St. SK5: Stoc 7H 25
Bankfield Trad. Est. SK5: Stoc 7H 25
Bank Gdns. WA5: Penk 1G 65
Bank Ga. SK14: B'tom 3H 29
Bankhall La. WA15: Hale 5J 73
Bank Hall Pk. WA1: Warr 1G 67
Bankhall Rd. SK4: Stoc 1J 51
Bank Hey CH64: L Nes 3D 130
Bank Ho. CW7: Wins 3D 178
Bankhouse Dr. CW12: Cong 2J 183
Bank Ho. La. WA6: Hel 4C 138
Banklands Cl. M44: Cad 6A 20
Bank La. CW5: Burl 5G 189
CW12: Nth R 4K 169
Bankley St. M19: Manc 2D 24
Bank M. WA6: Hel 4C 138
Bank Pl. Apartments *SK9: Wilm* 7J 97
(off Green La.)
BANK QUAY 1C 66
Bankquay Ct. M44: Irlam 2E 20
Bank Quay Trad. Est. WA1: Warr 1D 66
Bank Rd. SK6: Bred 1A 54
SK15: Carrb 4F 5
Banks, The CH45: Wall 4E 12
Bank's Av. CH47: Meols 4E 30
Banks Cl. CW12: Cong 3E 182
Banks Ct. WA15: Timp 7D 48
Banks Cres. WA4: Westy 1K 67
Bank Side OL5: Moss 1D 4
Bankside CW8: Weav 4F 155
SK14: Hat 2E 28
WA1: Warr 7D 40
WA7: Pre B 7G 91
WA15: H'rns 7D 74
Bankside Cl. SK6: Mar B 3J 55
SK9: Wilm 4A 98

Bankside Ct.—Beacon Pde.

Bankside Ct. SK4: Stoc 2J 51
ST7: Als 4F 203
Bankside Rd. CH42: R Fer 5E 60
M20: Manc 5D 50
Bankside Wlk. SK14: Hat 1E 28
Banks La. SK1: Stoc 4F 53
Bank Sq. SK9: Wilm 7J 97
Banks Rd. CH48: W Kir 3B 56
CH60: Hes 7E 82
Bank St. CH41: Birk 6D 34
CW12: Cong 4G 183
M33: Sale 6H 23
M34: Aude 4E 8
M34: Den 3G 27
OL7: Ash L 1G 9
SK6: W'ley 6G 27
SK8: Chea 6G 51
SK11: Mac 5B 126
SK14: B'tom 3H 29
SK14: Hyde 7J 9
WA1: Warr 7F 41
WA3: G'ook 6H 19
WA8: Wid 2G 89
WA12: New W 1C 14
Bank Top Cotts. *CW5: Nant 1D 196*
(off Birchin La.)
Bank Vw. CW4: Goo 7J 165
Bankville Rd. CH42: Tran 2D 60
BANKWOOD 2K 29
BANKWOOD GATE 3K 29
Banky Flds. CW12: Cong 5E 182
Banky Flds. Cres. CW12: Cong 5E 182
Banky La. M33: Sale 5B 22
Bannacks Cl. CW5: W'ston 1H 197
Bannerman Rd. M43: Droy 1A 8
Banning Cl. CH41: Birk 5C 34
Bannister Ct. CW7: Wins 5C 178
Bannister Dr. SK8: Chea H 3H 77
Bannister Gro. CW7: Wins 6C 178
Bannister St. SK1: Stoc 5D 52
Bann St. SK3: Stoc 7G 213 (4C 52)
Banstead Av. M22: N'den 5K 49
Barbara St. WA9: Clo F 1A 38
Barbauld St. WA1: Warr 7F 41
Barber Dr. ST7: Sch G 1H 205
Barberry Cl. CH46: More 4J 31
WA14: B'ath 5F 47
Barberry Wlk. *M31: Part 1H 45*
(off Wychelm Rd.)
Barber's La. CW8: N'ich 5D 156
CW9: Ant 6B 94
Barber St. SK11: Mac 6B 126
Barbondale Cl. WA5: Gt San 5H 39
Barbour Sq. CH3: Tatt 3H 187
BARBRIDGE 2A 220
Barcheston Rd. SK8: Chea 1E 76
Barcicroft Rd. M19: Manc 7B 24
SK4: Stoc 7B 24
Barcicroft Wlk. M19: Manc 7B 24
Barclay Hall WA16: Mob 6E 102
Barclay Rd. SK12: Poy 4D 100
Barcombe Cl. M32: S'ord 1E 22
Barcombe Rd. CH60: Hes 5B 84
Bardell Cres. SK12: Poy 4C 100
Bardon Rd. M23: Wyth 6F 49
Bardsea Av. M22: Wyth 4K 75
Bardsey Cl. CH65: Ell P 7E 134
BARDSLEY 1D 217
Bardsley Av. WA5: Warr 2D 40
Bardsley Cl. SK14: Hat 1F 29
BARDSLEY GATE 4F 11
Bardsley Ga. Av. SK15: Stal 4F 11
Bardsley St. SK4: Stoc 1B 52
Barfold Cl. SK2: Stoc 7A 54
Barford Cl. CH43: Bid 6E 32
WA5: W'ook 3K 39
Barford Dr. SK9: Wilm 5K 97
WA3: Low 2A 6
Barford Grange CH64: W'ston 7G 107
Barford Wlk. M23: Wyth 1H 75
Barham Ct. WA3: Ris 7J 17
Barington Dr. WA7: Murd 7G 91
Baristow Cl. CH2: Ches 1C 212 (7A 146)
Barker La. CH49: Gre 3K 57
(not continuous)
Barker Rd. CH61: Irby 7C 58
SK6: Bred 2K 53
Barkers Hollow Rd.
WA4: Dutt, Pre H 1J 113
Barkers La. M33: Sale 6E 22
Barker St. CW2: Crewe 5D 194
CW5: Nant 2C 196
Barkhill Rd. CH3: Ches 1D 150
Barkin Cen., The WA8: Wid 5J 63
Bark St. *CW12: Cong 4G 183*
(off Park St.)
Barkway Rd. M32: S'ord 1F 23
Barkwell La. OL5: Moss 1C 4
BARLASTON 3C 221
Barley Castle Cl. WA4: App T 3B 94
Barleycastle La. WA4: App T 1D 94
Barleycastle Trad. Est.
WA4: App T 2C 94
Barleycorn Cl. M33: Sale 1G 49
Barley Cft. CH3: Gt Bou 4D 150
SK8: Chea H 4H 77
ST7: Als 7F 203
Barleycroft SK13: Had 3K 11
Barley Cft. Rd. SK14: Hyde 4K 9
Barleycroft Ter. ST7: Sch G 1J 205
Barley Dr. SK7: Bram 6C 78
Barleyfield CH61: Pens 2G 83
Barley Mere Cl. WA12: New W 1F 15
Barleymow Cl. CH66: Gt Sut 6J 133
Barley Rd. WA4: Thel 2C 68
Barleywood Cl. CW2: Wis 6B 194
Barleywood Wlk. SK15: Stal 2E 10
Barlow Av. CH63: Beb 7F 61
Barlow Cres. SK6: Mar 1F 81
Barlow Dr. CW7: Wins 4A 178
BARLOWFOLD 1E 54
Barlow Fold SK6: Rom 1D 54
Barlow Fold Rd. SK5: Stoc 3J 25
SK6: Rom 1D 54
Barlow La. Nth. SK5: Stoc 3J 25
Barlow Moor Rd. M20: Manc 1B 50
Barlow Rd. CW9: Moult 7D 162
M19: Manc 2D 24
SK9: Wilm 5J 97
SK16: Duk 2J 9
WA14: B'ath 4F 47
Barlow's La. Sth. SK7: H Gro 2G 79
Barlow Wlk. *SK5: Stoc 3J 25*
(off Barlow La. Nth.)
Barlow Way CW11: S'ach 1E 200
Barlow Wood Dr. SK6: Mar 2H 81
Barmhouse Cl. SK14: Hyde 7B 10
Barmhouse La. SK14: Hyde 7B 10
(Carlton Rd.)
SK14: Hyde 7B 10
(Mt. Pleasant)
Barmhouse M. SK14: Hyde 7B 10
Barmouth Cl. WA5: Call 2C 40
Barmouth Rd. CH45: Wall 5D 12
Barnabas Av. CW1: Crewe 1K 193
Barnaby Chase CH3: Clut 1A 206
Barnaby Rd. SK12: Poy 4C 100
Barnack Cl. WA1: Padg 4A 42
Barnacre Av. M23: Wyth 2F 75
Barnacre Dr. CH64: Park 5E 104
Barnacre La. CH46: More 6J 31
Barnard Av. SK4: Stoc 2K 51
Barnard Cl. SK11: Mac 6G 125
Barnard Dr. CH65: Ell P 5G 135
Barnard Rd. CH43: Oxt 7A 34
Barnard St. WA5: Warr 2B 66
Barnato Cl. CW1: Crewe 6E 190
Barnbridge Cl. ST7: Sch G 1H 205
Barnbrook Cl. CW7: Wins 3B 178
Barn Cl. M41: Urm 1F 21
Barnclose Rd. M22: Wyth 4K 75
Barn Ct. *CH3: Clut 1B 206*
(off Lwr. Hall La.)
Barn Cft. WA6: Hel 4C 138
Barncroft CH61: Pens 3H 83
WA7: Nort 7F 91
Barncroft, The CH49: Gre 1A 58
Barncroft Cl. SK11: Chel 5C 166
Barncroft Gdns. M22: Wyth 7J 49
Barnes Av. SK4: Stoc 2J 51
WA2: Fear 2B 42
Barnes Cl. CH1: Blac 4G 145
CW1: Hasl 2K 195
WA5: Gt San 7J 39
WA8: Wid 3K 63
Barnes Grn. CH63: Spit 4A 86
Barnes Rd. WA8: Wid 3J 63
Barneston Rd. WA8: Wid 2A 64
Barnett Av. WA12: New W 1B 14
Barnett Gro. CW12: Cong 3C 182
Barnett St. SK11: Mac 5J 125
Barnett Wlk. *CW2: Crewe 6C 194*
(off Brookhouse Dr.)
Barnfield CH3: Tatt 3G 187
M41: Urm 2A 22
Barnfield Av. SK6: Rom 1D 54
WA7: Murd 2F 113
Barnfield Cl. CH47: Meols 3F 31
CH66: Gt Sut 6J 133
Barnfield Cres. M33: Sale 6E 22
Barnfield Rd. M19: Manc 7B 24
SK10: Boll 4C 122
SK14: Hyde 5C 10
WA1: Wool 5C 42
Barnfield Rd. E. SK3: Stoc 1D 78
Barnfield Rd. W. SK3: Stoc 1B 78
Barnfield St. M34: Den 6C 8
Barnfield Wlk. *WA15: Timp 7C 48*
(off Merefield Rd.)
Barngate Dr. OL5: Moss 1D 4
Barngate Rd. SK8: Gat 6C 50
Barn Gro. M34: Aude 3D 8
Barnham Wlk. M23: Wyth 4E 48
Barn Hey CH47: Hoy 7B 30
Barn Hey Cres. CH47: Meols 4G 31
Barnhill Rd. CH3: Brox 2E 206
Barnhouse La.
CH3: Gt Bar, L Bar 2B 170 & 7K 143
Barn La. WA5: B'ood 6C 14
Barn Mdw. CW8: Winn 4C 156
Barnmoore Cl. SY14: Mal 2H 207
Barn Rd. CW12: Cong 2E 182
Barnsdale Av. CH61: Thin 1K 83
Barnsfold Rd. SK6: Mar 2F 81
Barnside Way CW9: Moult 6E 162
SK10: Mac 1K 125
Barns La. WA13: Warb 6J 45
WA14: Dun M, Warb 7J 45
Barnsley St. SK1: Stoc 4F 53
Barns Pl. WA15: H'rns 5C 74
Barnstaple Way WA5: Penk 1G 65
Barnstead Av. M20: Manc 6A 24
BARNSTON 3A 84 (2A 214)
Barnston Av. CH65: Ell P 3B 134
Barnston Ct. CH2: Mic T 2J 147
CH3: Farn 5B 186
Barnston La. CH46: More 3B 32
Barnston M. CH3: Farn 5B 186
Barnston Rd. CH60: Hes 7K 83
CH61: Barns, Thin 7K 83
Barnston Towers Cl.
CH60: Hes 6A 84
Barn St. WA8: Wid 7G 63
Barnswood Cl. WA4: Grap 4C 68
BARNTON 2A 156 (3A 216)
Barnview Dr. M44: Irlam 2C 20
Barnwell Av. CH44: Wall 6H 13
WA3: Cul 6D 6
Barnwell Cl. CW2: Wis 6B 194
M34: Aude 5D 8
Barnwood CH66: L Sut 1F 133
Barnwood Rd. M23: Wyth 2G 75
Baron Cl. WA1: Wool 5D 42
Baronet M. WA4: Warr 4E 66
Baronet Rd. WA4: Warr 4E 66
Baron Grn. SK8: He Grn 6F 77
Baronia Pl. CW5: Nant 1D 196
Baron Rd. SK14: Hyde 4A 28
Barons Cl. WA7: Cast 5B 90
WA8: Wid 5C 62
Barons Ct. CH2: Ches 6K 145
SK9: Wilm 7J 97
(off Swan St.)
Barons Quay CW9: N'ich 4E 156
Barons Quay Rd. CW9: N'ich 4E 156
Barons Rd. CW2: Shav 3B 198
CW5: Ast M, Poole, Worl 1C 192
BARONY, THE 1D 196
Barony Bldgs. CW5: Nant 1C 196
Barony Ct. CW5: Nant 7C 192
Barony Employment Pk., The
CW5: Nant 7D 192
Barony Rd. CW5: Nant 7C 192
Barony Sports Complex 1D 196
Barony Ter. CW5: Nant 1C 196
Barony Way CH4: Ches 7F 149
BARRACK HILL 2A 54
Barrack Hill SK6: Rom 2A 54
Barrack Hill Cl. SK6: Bred 1A 54
Barracks La. CH3: Burw 6J 187
M33: Sale 5C 22
(off Banky La.)
SK10: Mac 4C 126
Barracks Sq. SK11: Mac 6J 125
Barrastitch La. CW8: Cudd 1B 160
Barratt Rd. ST7: Als 6G 203
Barrel Well Hill CH3: Ches 2C 150
Barren Gro. CH43: Oxt 1A 60
BARRETS GREEN 3J 189
Barrie Gro. CW1: Crewe 2E 194
Barrington Av. SK8: Chea H 4J 77
Barrington Cl. WA14: Alt 6H 47
Barrington Dr. CW10: Mid 5C 180
Barrington Rd. CH44: Wall 1B 34
WA14: Alt 1J 213 (6H 47)
Barrow Av. WA2: Warr 2J 41
Barrowfield Rd. M22: Wyth 3G 75
Barrow Hall La. WA5: Gt San 5G 39
Barrow La. CH3: Gt Bar 3A 170
CH3: Gt Bar, Tar S 2C 170 & 4C 170
WA2: Winw 1A 16
WA3: Croft 1A 16
WA6: Dun H 4J 143
WA15: Hale 6B 74
Barrow Mdw. SK8: Chea H 5G 77
BARROW NOOK 1C 215
Barrow's Brow WA16: Lwr P 1C 164
Barrows Cl. CW1: Crewe 5F 191
BARROWS GREEN
CW1 5E 190
WA8 1K 63 (2D 215)
Barrows Grn. La. WA8: Wid 3A 64
Barrow's Row WA8: Wid 1H 63
Barrule Av. SK7: H Gro 4J 79
Barrule Cl. WA4: App 6H 67
Barry Cl. CH65: Ell P 1E 140
Barrymore Av. WA4: Westy 1K 67
Barrymore Ct. WA4: Grap 4A 68
Barrymore Cres. CW9: Comb 2J 115
Barrymore Rd. CW8: Weav 4H 155
WA4: Grap 4A 68
WA7: Run 7H 89
Barrymore Way CH63: Brom 1G 107
Barry Ri. WA14: Bow 3E 72
Barry Rd. M23: Wyth 2H 49
SK5: Stoc 6J 25
Barry St. WA4: Warr 1G 67
Bars, The CH3: Ches 4E 212 (2B 150)
Barsbank Cl. WA13: Lymm 2J 69
Barsbank La. WA13: Lymm 2J 69
Barshaw Gdns. WA4: App 2J 93
Bartholomew Cl. L35: R'ill 3E 36
Bartholomew Way CH4: Ches 5K 149
BARTHOMLEY 2B 220
Barthomley Cres. CW2: Crewe 2H 193
Bartlegate Cl. WA7: B'vale 2D 112
Bartley Rd. M22: N'den 4J 49
BARTON 2C 219
Barton Av. M41: Urm 1A 22
WA4: Grap 3A 68
Barton Cl. CH47: Hoy 6A 30
SK9: Wilm 4A 98
WA7: Murd 7F 91
Barton Ct. CW7: Wins 3G 179
Barton Fold SK14: Hyde 2J 27
Barton Hey Dr. CH48: Cald 7D 56
Barton Rd. CH3: Farn 6C 186
(not continuous)
CH47: Hoy 6A 30
CW12: Cong 4H 183
M32: S'ord 1G 23
SK4: Stoc 3G 51
SK16: Duk 4H 9
Bartons Pl. CW9: N'ich 4G 157
Barton St. CH41: Birk 6B 34
(not continuous)
SK11: Mac 6K 125
Barwell Cl. SK5: Stoc 3J 25
Barwell Rd. M33: Sale 6D 22
Barwick Pl. M33: Sale 7F 23
Barwood Av. ST7: Chu L 4H 203
Barwoods Dr. CH4: Ches 6F 149
BASFORD 2G 199
BASFORD GREEN 2D 221
Basford Rd. CW2: Crewe 6D 194
Basford Way CW7: Wins 2C 178
Basil St. SK4: Stoc 1C 52
Baskervyle Cl. CH60: Hes 1D 104
Baskervyle Rd. CH60: Hes 1D 104
Basle Cl. SK7: Bram 1C 78
Baslow Av. M19: Manc 1F 25
Baslow Dr. SK7: H Gro 5K 79
SK8: He Grn 6E 76
Baslow Gro. SK5: Stoc 6J 25
Baslow Rd. M34: Den 3E 26
Basnett St. L1: Liv 3J 35
Bassendale Rd. CH62: Brom 4E 86
Bassenthwaite Av. CH43: Noc 7G 33
Basset Cl. CW5: W'ston 1H 197
Bass St. SK16: Duk 2G 9
BATE HEATH 3A 216
Bateman Cl. CW1: Crewe 2B 194
Bateman Rd. CW9: Los Gra 5D 158
Batemans Ct. CW2: Wis 6B 194
Batemill Cl. SK10: Mac 3G 125
Bates La. WA6: Hel 4D 138
Bates Mill La. CW6: Bees 1B 188
Bateson St. SK1: Stoc 2E 52
Bates St. SK16: Duk 2H 9
Batey Av. L35: R'ill 1B 36
Bath Cl. SK7: H Gro 3A 80
Bath Cres. SK8: Chea H 7K 77
BATHERTON 6F 197
Batherton Cl. WA8: Wid 6H 63
Batherton La. CW5: Bath, Nant 5D 196
Bath La. CW3: Audl 6C 210
Bath Pl. WA14: Alt 3H 73
Bath St. CH1: Ches 4E 212 (2B 150)
CH62: P Sun 1B 86
CW11: S'ach 3G 201
L3: Liv 2G 35
WA1: Warr 7E 40
WA14: Alt 3H 73
BATH VALE 3J 183
Bathwood Dr. CH64: L Nes 3C 130
Batley St. *OL5: Moss 1C 4*
(off Seel St.)
Batterbee Ct. CW1: Hasl 1K 195
Battersbay Gro. SK7: H Gro 3J 79
Battersby Ct. SK2: Stoc 6J 53
Battersby La. WA2: Warr 6G 41
Battersea Ct. WA8: Wid 2F 63
Battersea Rd. SK4: Stoc 3G 51
Battery La. SK9: Wilm 1C 118
WA1: Wool 5F 43
Baumville Dr. CH63: Spit 4K 85
BAWBROOK 3A 208
Bawtry Ct. WA2: Padg 3J 41
Baxter Cl. WA7: Murd 7F 91
(not continuous)
Baxter Gdns. M23: Wyth 5G 49
Baxter Rd. M33: Sale 7G 23
Baxter St. WA5: Warr 7C 40
Baycliffe WA13: Lymm 3A 70
Baycliffe Cl. WA7: Beec 2K 111
Baycroft Gro. M23: Wyth 3G 49
Bayley Cl. SK14: Hyde 5K 9
Bayleyfield SK14: Hyde 6J 9
Bayley Ind. Est. SK15: Stal 1A 10
Bayley Rd. CW5: W'ston 2H 197
Bayley St. SK15: Stal 1K 9
Baynard Dr. WA8: Hal B 1C 88
Bayswater Cl. WA7: Nort 2H 91
Bayswater Ct. CH45: Wall 5D 12
Bayswater Gdns. CH45: Wall 4D 12
Bayswater Rd. CH45: Wall 5D 12
Baytree Av. M34: Den 6F 9
Baytree Cl. CH66: Gt Sut 7B 134
Baytree Dr. SK6: Bred 7E 26
Baytree Rd. CH42: Tran 2D 60
CH48: Fran 3G 57
Bay Vw. Dr. CH45: Wall 4C 12
Bayvil Cl. WA7: Murd 7G 91
Bazley Rd. M22: N'den 3K 49
Beachcroft Rd. CH47: Meols 3F 31
Beach Gro. CH45: Wall 4J 13
CW8: H'ord 7B 156
Beach Rd. CH47: Hoy 6A 30
CW8: H'ord 7K 155
Beach Wlk. CH48: W Kir 5C 56
Beaconfold SK6: Comp 1H 55
Beacon Ct. CH60: Hes 6J 83
Beacon Dr. CH48: W Kir 3D 56
M23: Wyth 3G 75
Beaconfield Av. SK14: Hyde 1K 27
Beacon Hill Vw. WA7: Wes P 7D 88
Beacon La. CH60: Hes 6J 83
Beacon Pde. CH60: Hes 6J 83

Beacon Rd.—Bellflower Cl.

Beacon Rd. SK6: Rom 3A **54**
Beacons, The CH60: Hes 7J **83**
Beaconsfield M14: Manc 4A **24**
Beaconsfield Cl. CH42: Tran 2E **60**
Beaconsfield Cres. WA8: Wid 1G **63**
Beaconsfield Gro. WA8: Wid 1H **63**
Beaconsfield Rd. CH62: N Fer 6G **61**
WA7: Run 6E **88**
WA8: Wid 2H **63**
WA14: B'ath 5H **47**
Beaconsfield St. CH3: Ches 2B **150**
Beaconsfield Ter. SK15: Carrb 2G **5**
Beacon Vw. SK6: Mar 4F **55**
Beadnell Dr. WA5: Penk 2G **65**
Beaford Rd. M22: Wyth 5K **75**
Beagle Point CW7: Wins 3B **178**
Beagle Wlk. M22: Wyth 5A **76**
Beal Cl. SK4: Stoc 1F **51**
Beames Ho. *CW1: Crewe 2B 194*
(off Harrison Rd.)
Beam Heath Way CW5: Nant 7D **192**
Beaminster Av. SK4: Stoc 1H **51**
Beaminster Cl. SK4: Stoc 1H **51**
Beaminster Ct. *SK4: Stoc 1H 51*
(off Priestnall Rd.)
Beaminster Rd. SK4: Stoc 1H **51**
Beamish Cl. WA4: App 3H **93**
Beamont St. WA8: Wid 2G **89**
Beamsley Dr. M22: Wyth 3H **75**
Beam St. CW5: Nant 1C **196**
Bean Leach Av. SK2: Stoc 6K **53**
Bean Leach Dr. SK2: Stoc 6K **53**
Bean Leach Rd. SK2: Stoc 1J **79**
SK7: H Gro 1J **79**
Bearhurst La. SK11: Henb 7A **124**
BEARSTONE 3B **220**
Bearswood Cl. SK14: Hyde 2A **28**
Beasley Cl. CH66: Gt Sut 5K **133**
Beathwaite Dr. SK7: Bram 4A **78**
Beatles Story, The 4H **35**
Beatrice Av. CH63: H Beb 6D **60**
SK8: Chea H 3H **77**
Beatrice St. M34: Den 7D **8**
WA4: Warr 2H **67**
Beatty Av. WA2: Warr 3G **41**
Beatty Cl. CH48: Cald 7D **56**
Beatty Dr. CW12: Cong 2J **183**
Beatty Rd. CW5: Nant 3B **196**
Beaufort Av. M33: Sale 1C **48**
Beaufort Chase SK9: Wilm 5C **98**
Beaufort Cl. SK9: Ald E 5G **119**
SK14: Hat 1F **29**
WA5: Gt San 7J **39**
WA7: Run 7H **89**
WA8: Wid 5A **62**
Beaufort Dr. CH44: Wall 6E **12**
Beaufort Rd. CH41: Birk 3J **33**
M33: Sale 1C **48**
SK2: Stoc 1H **79**
SK14: Hat 1F **29**
Beaufort St. L8: Liv 6K **35**
(Brassey St.)
L8: Liv 6K **35**
(Hill St.)
L8: Liv 7K **35**
(Northumberland St.)
WA5: Warr 1C **66**
Beaufort Way *SK14: Hat 2F 29*
(off Beaufort Rd.)
Beaulieu WA15: Hale 3K **73**
Beaulieu Av. CW7: Wins 2G **179**
Beaumaris Ct. CH43: Oxt 7A **34**
Beaumaris Cres. SK7: H Gro 5G **79**
Beaumaris Dr. CH61: Thin 7E **58**
CH65: Ell P 6F **135**
Beaumaris Rd. CH45: Wall 5D **12**
Beaumaris Saltney Sports Cen. 5D **148**
Beaumaris Way WA7: Cast 4B **90**
Beaumont Cl. CH4: Salt 5F **149**
CW2: Wis 6K **193**
Beaumont Ct. *SK9: Hand 1K 97*
(off Clay La.)
WA4: Warr 3G 67
(off Elphins Dr.)
Beaumont Pl. SK15: Stal 5A **4**
Beau St. L3: Liv 1K **35**
Beauvale Av. SK2: Stoc 5G **53**
Beauworth Av. CH49: Gre 2K **57**
Beaverbrook Av. WA3: Cul 6H **7**
Beaver Cen., The CW9: N'ich 6E **156**
Beaver Cl. CH4: Salt 6F **149**
WA16: Pick 1B **158**
Beaver Ho. SK1: Stoc 4F **53**
Beaver Rd. M20: Manc 1D **50**
Beaver Wlk. SK14: Hat 2E **28**
Bebbington Cl. M33: Sale 1F **49**
BEBINGTON 2K **85** (2B **214**)
Bebington Rd. CH42: R Fer, Tran 3C **60**
CH62: N Fer 7F **61**
CH63: Beb 7F **61**
CH66: Gt Sut 4K **133**
Bebington Station (Rail) 6F **61**
Beccles Rd. M33: Sale 3B **48**
Becconsall Cl. CW1: Crewe 5F **191**
Becconsall Dr. CW1: Crewe 5F **191**
Bechers WA8: Wid 2B **62**
Beckenham Cl. WA8: Wid 1K **63**
Beckenham Gro. CW7: Wins 3B **178**
Beckenham Rd. CH45: N Bri 2H **13**
Beckett Dr. WA2: Winw 6K **15**
WA13: Warb 4E **44**
Beckett Gro. CH63: H Beb 6C **60**
Beckett's La. CH3: Ches, Gt Bou 3D **150**
Beckfield Rd. M23: Wyth 7G **49**
Beckford Cl. CW1: Crewe 5E **190**
Beck Ho. SK14: Hat 2E **28**
Beckside SK5: Stoc 2K **25**
Becks La. SK10: Mac 2F **125**
Beckton Gdns. M22: Wyth 2J **75**
Beckwith Ct. *CH41: Birk 4B 34*
(off Beckwith St.)
Beckwith St. CH41: Birk 4A **34**
L1: Liv 4J **35**
Beckwith St. E. CH41: Birk 5C **34**
Becontree Av. M34: Den 6F **9**
Becontree Dr. M23: Wyth 5D **48**
Bedells La. SK9: Wilm 1F **119**
BEDFORD 1A **216**
Bedford Av. CH42: R Fer 4D **60**
CH65: Whit 6C **134**
M33: Sale 2D **48**
SK14: Hyde 7K **9**
Bedford Av. E. CH65: Whit 6D **134**
Bedford Ct. CH42: R Fer 3E **60**
CW2: Crewe 5D **194**
WA15: Timp 6C **48**
Bedford Dr. CH42: R Fer 4C **60**
WA15: Timp 5C **48**
Bedford Gdns. CW2: Crewe 5C **194**
Bedford Gro. M44: Cad 5J **19**
ST7: Als 4C **202**
Bedford Pl. CH42: R Fer 3F **61**
CW2: Crewe 5C **194**
Bedford Ri. CW7: Wins 6D **178**
Bedford Rd. CH42: R Fer 3E **60**
CH45: Wall 5H **13**
SK11: Mac 5J **125**
Bedford Rd. E. CH42: R Fer 3F **61**
Bedford St. CW2: Crewe 5C **194**
SK5: Stoc 3H **25**
(not continuous)
WA4: Stoc H 5G **67**
Bedford Wlk. M34: Den 1E **26**
Bedlington Cl. M23: Wyth 6E **48**
Bedward Row CH1: Ches 4A **212** (2K **149**)
BEECH 3C **221**
Beech Av. CH49: Upt 6A **32**
CH61: Pens 2J **83**
M22: N'den 4K **49**
M32: S'ord 2K **23**
M34: Den 6C **8**
M41: Urm 1B **22**
SK3: Stoc 6D **52**
SK6: Mar 6D **54**
SK7: H Gro 3J **79**
SK8: Gat 1D **76**
ST7: Rod H 1G **203**
WA3: Cul 7G **7**
WA3: Low 3A **6**
WA4: Thel 2D **68**
WA5: Penk 2E **64**
WA6: Frod 7J **111**
WA15: Timp 4B **48**
WA16: Mob 4A **102**
Beech Bank SK10: Mac 2K **125**
Beech Cl. CW4: H Cha 3K **181**
CW8: Cudd 4C **160**
CW12: Cong 2C **182**
M31: Part 1H **45**
SK9: Ald E 4G **119**
WA12: New W 1F **15**
WA16: Oll 7K **117**
Beech Cotts. SK9: Ald E 7F **119**
WA4: Stre 4J **93**
Beech Ct. CH42: Tran 1C **60**
M21: Chor H 2K **23**
M33: Sale 7E **22**
SK9: Wilm 1J **119**
WA3: Ris 2A **18**
Beech Cres. SK12: Poy 2D **100**
Beechcroft Av. CW2: Wis 7B **194**
Beechcroft Dr. CH65: Whit 5D **134**
Beechcroft Rd. CH44: Wall 2B **34**
Beech Dr. CW2: Crewe 4J **193**
WA16: Knut 3G **117**
WN7: Leigh 1F **7**
Beeches, The CH2: Upt 4C **146**
CH42: R Fer 4F **61**
CH46: Leas 1B **32**
CH66: Gt Sut 4K **133**
CW5: Nant 2C **196**
M20: Manc 1B **50**
OL6: Ash L 1J 9
(off Crawford M.)
SK6: Rom 2B **54**
SK8: Chea H 4K **77**
WA6: Hel 4C **138**
WA8: Wid 1K 63
(off Hampton Ct. Way)
WA14: Bow 3G **73**
Beeches End SK14: Hyde 4B **10**
Beeches La. CH1: Sau 2B **144**
Beeches M., The M20: Manc 1B **50**
Beech Farm Dr. SK10: Mac 2A **126**
Beechfield CW9: Moult 6D **162**
SK9: Wilm 1F 119
(off Albert Rd.)
WA14: Alt 2G **73**
Beechfield Av. M41: Urm 1K **21**
SK9: Wilm 2D **118**
Beechfield Cl. CH60: Hes 7J **83**
M33: Sale 2K **47**
Beechfield Dr. CW10: Mid 2B **180**
Beechfield Gdns. CW8: H'ord 7A **156**
Beechfield M. SK14: Hyde 7B **10**
Beechfield Rd.
CH65: Ell P 3D **134**
SK3: Stoc 1D **78**
SK8: Chea H 5K **77**
SK9: Ald E 7F **119**
WA4: Grap 3A **68**
Beechfields CW7: Wins 4J **179**
Beech Gro. CH2: Ches 7D **146**
CH66: Whit 1C **140**
CW1: Crewe 1E **194**
CW7: Wins 5E **178**
CW8: Weav 5G **155**
CW11: S'ach 3H **201**
M14: Manc 4A **24**
M33: Sale 7E **22**
OL7: Ash L 1E **8**
SK9: Wilm 1F **119**
SK11: Mac 7B **126**
SK15: Stal 2A **10**
WA1: Padd 5A **42**
WA4: Warr 2H **67**
WA13: Lymm 3H **69**
WN7: Leigh 1E **6**
Beech Hall Dr. SK10: Mac 2K **125**
Beech Heyes Cl. CW8: Weav 5H **155**
Beech Heyes Dr. CW8: Weav 6H **155**
Beech Hey La. CH64: W'ston 6G **107**
Beech Hill WA16: Mob 6C **102**
Beech Holme Gro.
SK2: Stoc 4G **53**
Beech Ho. CH1: Ches 1F **149**
M20: Manc 1A **50**
M22: Shar 6A 50
(off Lauriston Cl.)
Beech Ho. Gdns.
WA15: Timp 4A **48**
Beechlands WA14: Alt 2F **73**
Beechlands Av. CH3: Ches 2D **150**
Beech La. CW6: Eat, Rus 7C **176**
CW8: Barnt 2K **155**
SK6: Rom 2C **54**
SK9: Wilm 1F **119**
SK10: Mac 3A **126**
WA6: K'ley 4E **152**
Beech Lawn WA14: Alt 2F **213** (1G **73**)
Beech M. SK2: Stoc 7E **52**
Beechmill Dr. WA3: Cul 7E **6**
Beechmore WA4: Moo 1K **91**
Beech Muir CH1: Blac 7F **145**
Beechpark Av. M22: N'den 5J **49**
Beech Range M19: Manc 2D **24**
Beech Ri. CW8: Crow 1J **153**
Beech Rd. CH42: Tran 1B **60**
CH60: Hes 6A **84**
CH63: H Beb 6E **60**
M33: Sale 7J **23**
SK2: Stoc 6D **52**
SK3: Stoc 6C **52**
SK6: H Lan 6F **81**
SK8: Chea H 4K **77**
SK9: Ald E 4G **119**
WA4: Stoc H 5G **67**
WA7: Run 6J **89**
WA7: Sut W 3D **112**
WA15: Hale 4K **213** (2J **73**)
WA16: Mob 2A **118**
Beech St. CW1: Crewe 2C **194**
CW10: Mid 3C **180**
SK14: Hyde 7J 9
(off John St.)
Beech Ter. WA8: Wid 2G **89**
Beech Tree Cl. CW5: W'ston 2H **197**
Beechtree Farm Cl. WA16: H Leg 6D **70**
Beechtree La. WA13: Lymm 6D **70**
Beechurst Rd. SK8: Chea H 7K **51**
Beech Vw. SK14: Hyde 1B **28**
Beech Vw. Rd. WA6: K'ley 2C **152**
Beech Vs. *M33: Sale 7J 23*
(off Carlyn Av.)
Beech Wlk. M32: S'ord 2H **23**
WN7: Leigh 1E **6**
Beechway CH2: Upt 4K **145**
CH63: Beb 3K **85**
SK6: H Lan 6F **81**
SK9: Wilm 2F **119**
SK10: Boll 4D **122**
Beechways WA4: App 7H **67**
Beechways Dr. CH64: Nest 1B **130**
BEECHWOOD
CH43 4F **33**
WA7 2A **112**
Beechwood WA14: Bow 4F **73**
WA16: Knut 2D **116**
(Garden Rd.)
WA16: Knut 3G **117**
(Higher Downs)
Beechwood Av. CH45: Wall 6E **12**
CW8: H'ord 7K **155**
SK5: Stoc 7J **25**
SK6: Rom 2C **54**
SK15: Hey 5D **4**
WA1: Padg 5J **41**
WA5: Gt San 7H **39**
WA7: Beec 1J **111**
Beechwood Cl. CW5: Nant 3E **196**
WA9: Clo F 1J **37**
Beechwood Ct. *CH49: Woodc 4E 58*
(off Childwall Grn.)
M20: Manc 1C **50**
SK10: Boll 6B 122
(off Alder Ct.)
Beechwood Dr. CH43: Bid 5F **33**
CH66: Gt Sut 7K **133**
CW9: Winc 1B **158**
CW12: Eat 5H **169**
M33: Sale 7B **22**
SK6: Mar 6G **55**
SK9: Wilm 6B **98**
SK14: Hyde 2A **28**
ST7: Als 5C **202**
Beechwood Gdns. *M14: Manc 3A 24*
(off Ladybarn La.)
Beechwood Gro. SK8: Chea H 5J **77**
Beechwood La. SK15: Hey 5D **4**
WA3: Cul 6D **6**
Beechwood M. SK10: Mac 2K **125**
Beechwood Recreation Cen. 5F **33**
Beechwood Rd. CH4: Salt 6E **148**
CH62: Brom 6C **86**
Beecroft Cl. WA5: Old H 3B **40**
Beehive La. CW9: Moult 6E **162**
Beeley St. SK14: Hyde 1K **27**
Beenham Cl. M33: Sale 1G **47**
BEESTON 2C **188** (2D **219**)
Beeston Av. WA15: Timp 6K **47**
Beeston Brow SK10: Boll 3E **122**
Beeston Castle (remains of) 1B **188**
Beeston Cl. CH43: Bid 6F **33**
CW4: H Cha 4G **181**
CW10: Mid 7D **180**
SK10: Boll 2F **123**
WA3: Birc 7H **17**
Beeston Ct. WA7: Man P 2E **90**
Beeston Dr. CH61: Pens 2H **83**
CW7: Wins 5D **178**
ST7: Als 6D **202**
WA16: Knut 5E **116**
Beeston Grn. CH66: Gt Sut 3A **134**
Beeston Gro. SK3: Stoc 7C **52**
BEESTON MOSS 5A **188**
Beeston Mt. SK10: Boll 2E **122**
Beeston Pathway
CH4: Ches 4B **150**
Beeston Rd. M33: Sale 7D **22**
SK9: Hand 1A **98**
Beeston St. CW8: N'ich 6D **156**
Beeston Ter. SK11: Mac 6F **125**
Beeston Vw. *CH4: Ches 4B 150*
(off Appleyards La.)
Beetham Plaza *L2: Liv 3H 35*
(off The Strand)
Beggarman's La. WA16: Knut 6E **116**
Begley Cl. SK6: Rom 3K **53**
Belcroft Cl. M22: N'den 4A **50**
Belfield Dr. CH43: Oxt 2A **60**
Belfield Ho. WA14: Bow 3G **73**
Belfield Rd. M20: Manc 1D **50**
SK5: Stoc 1J **25**
Belford Av. M34: Den 1K **25**
Belford Dr. CH46: More 4K **31**
Belford Rd. M32: S'ord 1J **23**
Belford Wlk. M23: Wyth 6G **49**
Belfry Cl. CH46: More 3J **31**
SK9: Wilm 6A **98**
Belfry Dr. SK10: Mac 7K **121**
Belgrave Av. CH4: Salt 5F **149**
CH44: Wall 7J **13**
CW12: Cong 3E **182**
SK6: Mar 6F **55**
ST7: Als 4E **202**
WA1: Padg 4K **41**
Belgrave Cl. CH4: Dod 4D **184**
WA8: Wid 2A **64**
WN7: Leigh 2C **6**
Belgrave Ct. *M34: Den 6C 8*
(off Belgrave St.)
Belgrave Cres. SK2: Stoc 1F **79**
Belgrave Dr. CH65: Ell P 3B **134**
Belgrave Pl. CH4: Ches 7D **212** (4A **150**)
Belgrave Rd. CH3: Gt Bou 3E **150**
CW2: Crewe 4B **194**
CW9: N'ich 2F **163**
M33: Sale 7F **23**
M44: Cad 6A **20**
SK11: Mac 1G **129**
WA14: Bow 2G **73**
Belgrave St. CH1: Ches 2E **212** (1B **150**)
CH44: Wall 6H **13**
M34: Den 6C **8**
Belgravia Ct. *CW8: H'ord 1B 162*
(off Sandringham Pl.)
WA8: Wid 2F **63**
Belgravia Gdns. WA15: Hale 5J **73**
Belgravia Ho. *WA14: Alt 2H 73*
(off Brown St.)
Bellard Dr. CH2: Ches 6D **146**
Bell Av. SK11: Sut E 2K **129**
Bellcast Cl. WA4: App 1G **93**
Belldale Cl. SK4: Stoc 2J **51**
Belldene Gro. CH61: Hes 4H **83**
Bellemonte Cotts. *WA6: Frod 1K 139*
(off Rosewood Av.)
Bellemonte Pk. WA6: Frod 2H **139**
Bellemonte Rd. WA6: Frod 2H **139**
Belleville Av. M22: Wyth 5A **76**
Belle-Vue WA3: Low 1A **6**
Belle Vue La. CH3: Guil S 5H **147**
Belle Vue Rd. CH44: Wall 2D **34**
Belle Vue Ter. CW11: S'ach 3F **201**
Bell Farm Ct. SK10: Mac 1K **125**
Bellfield Av. SK8: Chea H 4K **77**
Bellfield Cres. CH45: N Bri 3G **13**
Bellflower Cl. WA8: Wid 1E **62**

Birches, The—Blyth Cl.

Birches, The CH44: Wall 2D 34
CH64: Nest 5J 105
CW2: Crewe 6C 194
M33: Sale 6D 22
OL5: Moss 1C 4
Birches Cl. CH60: Hes 6J 83
Birches Cft. Dr. SK10: Mac 3G 125
Birches La.
CW9: Lac D, Los Grn 6C 158 & 4F 159
Birchfield CH46: More 5K 31
OL7: Ash L 2E 8
Birchfield Av. ST7: Rod H 2G 203
WA8: Wid 3G 63
Birchfield Cl. CH46: More 6K 31
Birchfield M. SK14: Hyde 1J 27
Birchfield Rd. SK3: Stoc 5J 51
WA5: Gt San 7K 39
WA8: Wid 7G 37
WA13: Lymm 1D 70
Birchfields WA15: Hale 4K 73
Birchfields Rd. M13: Manc 1B 24
M14: Manc 1B 24
Birchfield St. L3: Liv 1K 35
Birch Fold CW4: Goo 6F 165
Birch Gdns. CW11: S'ach 4G 201
Birchgate Cl. SK10: Mac 3F 125
Birch Gro. CH45: N Bri 4J 13
CH66: Whit 7C 134
CW9: Los Grn 7D 158
CW9: Winc 2B 158
M14: Manc 1A 24
M34: Aude 4E 8
M34: Den 7D 8
WA1: Padd 5K 41
WA4: Warr 2H 67
WA15: Timp 7E 48
WA16: Knut 3H 117
Birch Hall La. M13: Manc 1B 24
BIRCH HEATH 4G 175 (1D 219)
Birch Heath La. CH3: Chri 3H 151
Birch Heath Rd. CW6: Tarp 4G 175
Birch Heys CH48: Fran 4H 57
BIRCH HILL 3D 215
Birch Ho. CH1: Ches 5J 145
SK7: Bram 1H 99
Birchinall Cl. SK11: Mac 6H 125
Birchin Cl. CW5: Nant 1E 196
Birchin La. CW5: Nant 1D 196
Birch La. CW2: Hou 5F 199
CW10: Stan 2A 180
SK16: Duk 2J 9
(not continuous)
Birchlea WA15: Alt 1K 73
Birchmere CH60: Hes 4G 83
Birch Muir CH1: Blac 7F 145
Birchmuir Cl. CW1: Crewe 7G 191
Birch Polygon M14: Manc 1A 24
Birchridge Cl. CH62: Spit 4C 86
Birch Ri. CH2: Ches 4A 146
Birch Rd. CH4: Ches 6G 149
CH43: Oxt 2A 60
CH47: Meols 4F 31
CH63: Beb 2A 86
CW12: Cong 3B 182
M31: Carri 7J 21
M31: Part 1F 45
SK8: Gat 7C 50
SK12: Poy 4E 100
WA3: Rix 1D 44
WA7: Run 6H 89
WA8: Wid 2H 63
WA14: Dun M 7J 21
Birch St. M43: Droy 2A 8
OL7: Ash L 1D 8
SK15: Hey 4D 4
Birch Ter. SK14: Hyde 1H 27
Birch Tree Av. SK7: H Gro 4A 80
Birchtree Cl. WA14: Bow 4G 73
Birch Tree Ct. CH2: Ches 1E 212 (7B 146)
M22: Wyth 2K 75
Birch Tree Dr. M22: Wyth 2K 75
Birch Tree La. CW4: Goo 6G 165
ST7: Sch G 5F 205
WA4: H Whi 7K 93
BIRCH VALE 2D 217
Birchvale Cl. SK12: Poy 3D 100
Birchvale Dr. SK6: Rom 1D 54
Birchview Way CH43: Noc 7G 33
Birchway CH60: Hes 1F 105
SK6: H Lan 6F 81
SK7: Bram 6B 78
SK10: Boll 3D 122
SK10: Pres 5F 121
Birchways WA4: App 1J 93
BIRCHWOOD 1E 42 (1A 216)
Birchwood Av. CH41: Birk 5D 34
Birchwood Blvd. WA3: Birc 2D 42
Birchwood Cl. CH2: Elt 5G 137
CH41: Birk 5C 34
CH66: Gt Sut 7K 133
SK4: Stoc 3J 51
Birchwood Corporate Ind. Est.
WA2: Birc 2C 42
Birchwood Cres. SK14: Hyde 4B 10
Birchwood Dr. CW5: Nant 1D 196
SK9: Wilm 6A 98
WA16: Lwr P 3B 164
Birchwood La. WA4: Moo 5K 65
Birchwood Leisure & Tennis Complex 1D 42
Birchwood Office Pk. WA2: Fear 1B 42
Birchwood One Bus. Pk.
WA3: Birc 2E 42
BIRCHWOOD PARK 6K 17
Birchwood Pk. Av. WA3: Birc, Ris 6J 17
Birchwood Point Bus. Pk. WA3: Birc 1D 42
Birchwood Science Pk. WA3: Ris 5K 17
Birchwood Shop. Cen. WA3: Birc 1D 42
Birchwood Station (Rail) 2E 42
Birchwood Way SK16: Duk 4J 9
WA2: Birc 2C 42
WA2: Padg 4J 41
WA3: Birc 1C 42
Bird Hall Av. SK8: Chea H 1A 78
Birdhall Gro. M19: Manc 3D 24
Bird Hall La. SK3: Stoc 5K 51
Bird Hall Rd. SK8: Chea H 7K 51
Birdlip Dr. M23: Wyth 2G 75
Birds La. CH3: Tatt 3K 187
CW6: Bun 7E 188
CW6: Tarp 3J 175
Birdwell Dr. WA5: Gt San 7J 39
Birkdale Av. CH63: Brom 1H 107
Birkdale Cl. SK7: Bram 6E 78
SK10: Mac 7K 121
SK14: Hyde 5K 9
Birkdale Ct. CW9: N'ich 5G 157
Birkdale Dr. M33: Sale 2J 47
Birkdale Gdns. CW7: Wins 2B 178
Birkdale Gro. SK5: Stoc 6J 25
Birkdale Pl. M33: Sale 5E 22
Birkdale Rd. SK5: Stoc 6H 25
WA5: Penk 1H 65
WA8: Wid 7H 37
BIRKENHEAD 6E 34 (2B 214)
Birkenhead Central Station (Rail) 7D 34
Birkenhead North Station (Rail) 3J 33
Birkenhead Park Station (Rail) 4A 34
Birkenhead Priory 6E 34
Birkenhead Rd. CH44: Wall 3D 34
CH47: Hoy, Meols 4D 30
CH64: W'ston 5C 106
Birkenhead St. CW9: N'ich 5H 157
Birkenhead Transport Mus. 5E 34
Birket Av. CH46: Leas 1C 32
Birket Cl. CH46: Leas 1D 32
Birket Ho. CH41: Birk 5C 34
Birket Sq. CH46: Leas 1C 32
Birkett Av. CH65: Ell P 6E 134
Birkett Rd. CH42: R Fer 4D 60
CH48: W Kir 1C 56
Birkett St. L3: Liv 1K 35
Birkin Cl. WA16: Knut 1H 117
Birkworth Ct. SK2: Stoc 6H 53
Birley Cl. WA15: Timp 5K 47
Birley Ct. L8: Liv 5K 35
Birley Pk. M20: Manc 1B 50
Birling Dr. M23: Wyth 1H 75
Birnam Dr. L35: R'ill 2D 36
Birnam Rd. CH44: Wall 1C 34
Birstall Ct. WA7: Run 7K 89
Birstall Wlk. M23: Wyth 6G 49
Birtles, The M22: Wyth 2K 75
Birtles Av. SK5: Stoc 1J 25
Birtles Cl. CW11: S'ach 2G 201
SK8: Chea 7J 51
SK16: Duk 4H 9
Birtles La. SK10: O Ald 2A 124
Birtlespool Rd. SK8: Chea H 1H 77
Birtles Rd. SK10: Mac 3E 124
WA2: Warr 3G 41
Birtles Way *SK9: Hand 1A 98*
(off Sandiway Rd.)
Birtley Ct. WA8: Wid 4B 62
Birtwistle Rd. CW9: Rud 7J 157
Bisham Pk. WA7: Nort 3F 91
Bishopdale Cl. WA5: Gt San 5H 39
Bishopdale Dr. L35: R'ill 1D 36
Bishopgates Dr. CW9: N'ich 2D 162
Bishop Rd. CH44: Wall 2A 34
M41: Urm 1G 21
SK10: Boll 4D 122
Bishops Cl. SK8: Chea 7J 51
WA14: Bow 4F 73
Bishops Ct. CH43: Oxt 2A 60
WA2: Winw 7J 15
Bishopsfield Ct. *CH2: Ches 7C 146*
(off Derby Pl.)
Bishops Gdns. CH65: Ell P 3C 134
Bishopsgate CH2: Ches 7D 146
Bishop Sheppard Ct. L3: Liv 1H 35
Bishops M. M33: Sale 5D 22
Bishop St. CH2: Ches 7C 146
SK1: Stoc 3E 52
Bishops Wlk. *OL7: Ash L 1F 9*
(off Hertford St.)
Bishops Way WA8: Wid 2K 63
Bishops Wood CW5: Nant 4D 196
Bishopton Cl. M19: Manc 2F 25
Bishopton Dr. SK11: Mac 4G 125
Bisley Av. M23: Wyth 6F 49
Bisley St. CH45: Wall 6H 13
Bispham Av. SK5: Stoc 1J 25
Bispham Dr. CH47: Meols 5F 31
Bispham Ho. *L3: Liv 1J 35*
(off Lace St.)
Bispham Rd. WA5: Gt San 1K 65
Bittern Cl. SK12: Poy 3K 99
WA2: Warr 1H 41
WA7: Nort 6F 91
Bittern Gro. SK10: Mac 3H 125
Bixteth St. L3: Liv 2H 35
Blackacres Cl. CW11: S'ach 3D 200
Blackberry Cl. WA14: B'ath 4F 47
Blackberry La. SK5: Stoc 4A 26
Blackboards La. CH66: Chil T 1G 133
BLACKBROOK
TF9 3B 220
WA2 2J 41
WA11 1D 215
Blackbrook Av. WA2: Padg, Warr 7D 16
Blackbrook Cl. WA8: Wid 2C 62
Black Brook Rd. SK4: Stoc 4G 25
Blackbrook Sq. WA2: Padg 2J 41
Blackbrook Trad. Est. M19: Manc 4F 25
Blackburne Av. WA8: Hal B 1B 88
Blackburne Cl. WA2: Padg 2C 42
Blackburne Pl. L8: Liv 4K 35
Blackburne Ter. *L8: Liv 4K 35*
(off Blackburne Pl.)
Blackcap Wlk. WA3: Birc 1E 42
Blackcarr Rd. M23: Wyth 6H 49
Black Cat Ind. Est. WA8: Wid 7F 63
Blackcroft Av. CW8: Barnt 3K 155
BLACKDEN HEATH 4K 165 (3B 216)
Blackden La. CW4: Goo, H Cha 6K 165
SK11: Sidd 4B 168
Black Denton's Pl. WA8: Wid 4J 63
Blackden Wlk. SK9: Wilm 5A 98
Black Diamond St.
CH1: Ches 1D 212 (7A 146)
Black Dog La. CH3: Wave 3A 174
Blackdown Cl. CH66: L Sut 3G 133
Blackenhall Dr. WA5: Gt San 7K 39
Blackeys La. CH64: Nest 7H 105
Black Firs La. CW12: Som 1A 182
Black Firs Wood Nature Reserve 1A 182
Blackford Rd. M19: Manc 4E 24
Black Friars CH1: Ches 6A 212 (2K 149)
Black Friars Ct. CH1: Ches 6B 212
Blackheath Dr. CH46: Leas 1C 32
Blackheath La. WA7: Man P 2G 91
Blackhill La. WA16: Knut 5D 116
Black Horse Cl. CH48: W Kir 2D 56
Black Horse Hill CH48: W Kir 3D 56
Blackhurst Brow SK10: Mot A 1C 120
Blackhurst St. WA1: Warr 7F 41
Black La. SK10: Mac 3B 126
Blackledge Cl. WA2: Fear 1A 42
BLACKLEY 1C 217
Blackley Cl. SK10: Mac 7J 121
WA4: Warr 2H 67
Black Lion La. CH66: L Sut 2H 133
Black Lion Pas. SK1: Stoc 7K 213
BLACKMOOR 1A 216
Black Moss Rd. WA14: Dun M 5B 46
Blackpool St. CH41: Birk 7D 34
Black Rd. SK11: Mac 6B 126
Blackrock OL5: Moss 3D 4
Blackshaw Cl. CW12: Cong 5K 183
Blackshaw Dr. WA5: Gt San, W'ook 4K 39
Blackshaw La. SK9: Ald E 6E 118
Blackshaw St. SK3: Stoc 4C 52
SK11: Mac 5K 125
Blackstairs Rd. CH66: Ell P 1B 134
Blackstock St. L3: Liv 1H 35
Blackstone Ho. SK2: Stoc 7H 53
Blackstone Rd. SK2: Stoc 7H 53
Black St. SK11: Mac 6B 126
Blackthorn Av. M19: Manc 4D 24
Blackthorn Cl. CH3: Hunt 6D 150
CW2: Wis 6B 194
Blackthorne Av. CH66: Whit 1C 140
Blackthorne Cl. CH46: More 5C 32
Blackthorne Dr. M33: Sale 2H 47
Blackthorne Rd. SK14: Hyde 5K 27
Blackthorn Wlk. *M31: Part 2G 45*
(off Wood La.)
Blackwell Cl. CW10: Mid 6D 180
Blackwood Dr. M23: Wyth 4D 48
BLACKWOOD HILL 2D 221
BLACON 6E 144 (1B 218)
Blacon Av. CH1: Blac 5F 145
Blacon Common Nature Pk. 7F 145
Blacon Hall Rd. CH1: Blac 5G 145
Blacon Point Rd. CH1: Blac 7E 144
Bladen Cl. SK8: Chea H 1J 77
Bladon Cres. ST7: Als 4D 202
Blagg Av. CW5: Nant 3A 196
Blair Av. M41: Urm 1H 21
Blair Cl. M33: Sale 3G 47
SK7: H Gro 5G 79
Blair Ct. CH43: Clau 6A 34
Blair Dr. WA8: Wid 2B 62
Blairgowrie Dr. SK10: Mac 7J 121
Blair Pk. CH63: Spit 3B 86
Blair St. L8: Liv 5K 35
Blake Cl. CH1: Blac 4G 145
CW2: Wis 5K 193
Blakeden La. CW7: Wins 4A 178
Blake Dr. SK2: Stoc 5J 53
Blake La. CW8: S'way 4D 160
Blakeley Brow CH63: Rab M 1F 107
Blakeley Ct. CH63: Rab M 1F 107
Blakeley Dell CH63: Rab M 1G 107
Blakeley Dene CH63: Rab M 7B 86
Blakeley La. WA16: Mob 7A 96
Blakeley Rd. CH63: Rab M 7A 86
BLAKELOW 3J 197
Blakelow Bank SK11: Mac 6C 126
Blakelow Cl. CW10: Mid 5B 180
Blakelow Cres. CW5: Blak 4K 197
Blakelow Dr. CW5: W'ston 3H 197
Blakelow Gdns. SK11: Mac 6C 126
Blakelow Rd. SK11: Mac 6C 126
Blakemere Av. M33: Sale 1E 48
Blakemere Ct. CH65: Ell P 1E 134
Blakemere Craft Cen. 5C 160
Blakemere Dr. CW9: N'ich 1D 162
Blakemere La. WA6: Norl 7E 152
Blakemere Way
CW11: S'ach 1D 200
Blakeney Cl. CH49: Upt 5D 32
BLAKENHALL 3B 220
Blakenhall Way CH49: Upt 6A 32
Blake St. CW12: Cong 4E 182
Blakeswell Cl. M41: Urm 1G 21
Blandford Ct. SK15: Stal 7B 4
Blandford Dr. CW9: N'ich 3D 162
SK11: Mac 4G 125
Blandford Ho. SK15: Stal 7B 4
Blandford Rd. SK4: Stoc 2K 51
WA5: Gt San 7K 39
Blandford St. SK15: Stal 7B 4
Blankney, The CW5: Nant 3C 196
Blantyre St. WA7: Run 3F 89
Blaven Cl. SK3: Stoc 7D 52
Blaydon Wlk. CH43: Clau 6H 33
Blaze Hill SK10: R'ow 3G 123
Blaze Moss Bank SK2: Stoc 7H 53
Bleadale Cl. SK9: Wilm 4A 98
Bleak Hey Rd. M22: Wyth 3B 76
Bleasdale Cl. CH49: Upt 6B 32
Bleasdale Rd. CW1: L'ton 4G 191
M22: Wyth 3G 75
Bleatarn Rd. SK1: Stoc 5F 53
Bleeding Wolf La. ST7: Sch G 3H 205
Blenheim Cl. CW2: Wis 6J 193
CW9: N'ich 2E 162
SK9: Wilm 7A 98
SK12: Poy 2E 100
WA2: Padg 2J 41
WA14: Bow 3H 73
Blenheim Ct. ST7: Als 4E 202
Blenheim Gdns. CW7: Wins 5D 178
Blenheim Ho. CH1: Ches 7J 145
Blenheim Pk. CW11: Whe 5E 200
Blenheim Rd. CH44: Wall 6K 13
SK8: Chea H 3K 77
Blenheim Way SK10: Mac 3H 125
Bletchley Av. CH44: Wall 7F 13
Bletchley Rd. SK4: Stoc 3G 51
Blinco Rd. M41: Urm 2E 22
Blithedale Ct. *CH42: R Fer 4F 61*
(off The Hawthornes)
Blithfield Wlk. M34: Den 1D 26
Blocksage St. SK16: Duk 3J 9
Bloomfield Cl. SK8: Chea H 6G 77
Bloomsbury Ct. CH47: Hoy 6B 30
Bloomsbury Gro. WA15: Timp 6A 48
Bloomsbury La. WA15: Timp 6A 48
Bloomsbury Way WA8: Wid 2D 62
Bloom St. SK3: Stoc 4A 52
Blossom Hgts. CW8: N'ich 6C 156
Blossom Rd. M31: Part 2G 45
Blossoms Hey SK8: Chea H 4G 77
Blossoms Hey Wlk.
SK8: Chea H 4G 77
Blossoms La. SK7: Woodf 4D 98
Blossoms St. SK2: Stoc 6D 52
Blossom Way CH4: Salt 6E 148
Blount Cl. CW1: Crewe 2B 194
Bluebell Av. CH41: Birk 4J 33
Blue Bell Cl. SK14: Hyde 5A 10
Bluebell Cl. CH3: Hunt 5E 150
CW8: Winn 4D 156
SK10: Mac 1A 126
Bluebell Ct. WA7: Beec 3B 112
Bluebell Gro. SK8: Chea 1F 77
Bluebell La. CH64: Nest 6B 106
SK10: Mac 1K 125
Bluebell M. *SK10: Mac 1A 126*
(off Cavendish Cl.)
Bluebell Rd. WA5: Warr 1C 66
Bluebell Way SK9: Wilm 5K 97
ST7: Als 6C 202
Blueberry Rd. WA14: Bow 3E 72
Blue Bri. La. WA6: Hel 3C 138
Blue Chip Bus. Pk. WA14: B'ath 5G 47
Blue Coat Almshouses CH1: Ches 3B 212
Bluecoat Arts Cen. 3J 35
Bluecoat Chambers *L1: Liv 3J 35*
(off School La.)
Bluecoat Display Cen. *3J 35*
(off College La.)
Blue Coat Sq. CH1: Ches 3B 212 (1K 149)
Bluecoat St. WA2: Warr 5F 41
Bluefields St. L8: Liv 5K 35
Blue Hatch WA6: Frod 7J 111
Blue Planet 7F 135
Blue Ridge Cl. WA5: Gt San 5G 39
Bluestone Dr. SK4: Stoc 1G 51
Bluestone Rd. M34: Den 1K 25
Bluestone Ter. M34: Den 1K 25
Bluewood Dr. CH41: Birk 3G 33
Blundell Rd. WA8: Wid 5C 62
Blundells Dr. CH46: More 3B 32
BLUNDELL'S HILL 2B 36
Blundell's La. L35: R'ill 3A 36
Blundell St. L1: Liv 5J 35
Blundering La. SK15: Stal 4E 10
Blunstone Cl. CW2: Crewe 4A 194
BLURTON 3C 221
Blyth Av. M23: Wyth 2J 49
Blyth Cl. SK10: Mac 3F 125
WA7: Murd 2F 113
WA15: Timp 6D 48

Blythe Av.—Bracken Cl.

Blythe Av. CW12: Cong 4C 182
SK7: Bram 7A 78
WA8: Wid 1H 63
BLYTHE BRIDGE 3D 221
BLYTHE MARSH 3D 221
Blythe Pl. *CW7: Wins* *3J 179*
(off Trent Av.)
Blythings, The CW6: Tarp 1H 175
Blyth Rd. CH63: Brom 7C 86
Blyton Way M34: Den 3E 26
Boardman Cl. SK5: Stoc 7J 25
Boardmans Pl. CW9: N'ich 1E 162
Boarfold La. SK13: Chis 6F 29
Boathouse La. CH64: Park 5E 104
Boat La. M22: N'den 3A 50
M44: Irlam 1E 20
Boat La. Ct. M22: N'den 3A 50
Boatman's Wlk. OL7: Ash L 1F 9
Boat Stage WA13: Lymm 2A 70
Boat Wlk. WA4: Warr 4E 66
Boatyard, The M32: S'ord 1K 23
Bob's La. M44: Cad 7A 20
Boddens Hill Rd. SK4: Stoc 3J 51
Bodden St. WA3: Low 1A 6
WA9: Clo F 1K 37
Boddington Dr. WA4: Grap 6A 68
Boden Dr. CW5: W'ston 3H 197
Boden St. SK11: Mac 4A 126
Bodiam Ct. CH65: Ell P 6G 135
Bodmin Av. SK10: Mac 3F 125
Bodmin Cl. WA7: B'vale 1D 112
Bodmin Cres. SK5: Stoc 6A 26
Bodmin Dr. SK7: Bram 6C 78
Bodmin Rd. M33: Sale 6C 22
Bodmin Wlk. M23: Wyth 7G 49
Bodnant Cl. CW1: Crewe 5F 191
Boggard La. SK13: Char 5K 29
Bognor Rd. SK3: Stoc 1C 78
Bohemia Cotts. *SK15: Stal* *7C 4*
(off Cocker Hill)
Bolam Cl. M23: Wyth 3F 49
Boland Dr. M14: Manc 3A 24
Bolderstone Pl. SK2: Stoc 1J 79
Bolde Way CH63: Spit 5A 86
BOLD HEATH 5A 38 (2D 215)
Bold Ind. Est. WA8: Wid 7J 37
Bold La. WA5: Col G 4A 14
Bold Pl. CH1: Ches 3D 212 (1A 150)
L1: Liv 4K 35
Bold Sq. CH1: Ches 3D 212 (1A 150)
(not continuous)
Bold St. CW1: Hasl 2J 195
CW11: S'ach 3F 201
L1: Liv 3J 35
WA1: Warr 7E 40
WA7: Run 3H 89
WA8: Wid 6G 63
WA14: Alt 2H 73
Bolesworth Rd. CH2: Upt 4C 146
CH3: Tatt 3G 187
Boleyn Cl. CH1: Blac 4F 145
Boleyn Cl. WA7: Man P 3E 90
Bolland's Ct. CH1: Ches 5B 212 (2K 149)
Bollands Row *CW5: Nant* *2C 196*
(off Churche's Ct.)
Bolleyn Wood Ct. SK9: Wilm 5J 97
Bollin Av. CW7: Wins 2J 179
WA14: Bow 5F 73
Bollinbarn SK10: Mac 2J 125
Bollinbarn Dr. SK10: Mac 2H 125
Bollinbrook Rd. SK10: Mac 3H 125
Bollin Cl. CW7: Wins 2J 179
CW11: S'ach 2C 200
SK9: Wilm 6J 97
ST7: Als 6A 202
WA3: Cul 1B 18
WA13: Lymm 1C 70
Bollin Ct. *M33: Sale* *2B 48*
(off Bollin Dr.)
SK9: Wilm 1H 119
WA14: Bow 4F 73
Bollin Dr. CW12: Cong 5H 183
M33: Sale 2B 48
WA13: Lymm 1C 70
WA14: Timp 4J 47
Bollin Gro. SK10: Pres 4G 121
BOLLINGTON 3E 122 (3D 217)
Bollington Av. CW9: N'ich 7F 157
Bollington Cl. CH43: Oxt 2J 59
BOLLINGTON CROSS 5B 122
Bollington Leisure Cen. 5B 122
Bollington Mill WA14: L Bol 2A 72
Bollington Old Rd. SK10: Boll 5A 122
Bollington Rd. SK4: Stoc 6G 25
SK10: Boll 5B 122
Bollington St. OL7: Ash L 1F 9
Bollin Hill SK9: Wilm 6H 97
SK10: Pres 6H 121
Bollin Link SK9: Wilm 7J 97
Bollin M. SK10: Pres 4G 121
Bollin Sq. WA14: Bow 4F 73
Bollin Wlk. SK5: Stoc 6J 25
SK9: Wilm 7J 97
Bollin Way SK10: Pres 5H 121
Bollinway WA15: Hale 5A 74
Bollinwood Chase SK9: Wilm 7A 98
Bolshaw Cl. CW1: Crewe 6F 191
Bolshaw Farm La. SK8: He Grn 7E 76
Bolshaw Rd. SK8: He Grn 7D 76
Bolton Av. M19: Manc 2F 51
SK8: Chea H 7K 77
WA4: Westy 1K 67
Bolton Cl. SK12: Poy 2C 100
WA3: Low 2B 6
Bolton Rd. CH62: P Sun 1B 86
Bolton Rd. E. CH62: P Sun 7H 61
Bolton St. L3: Liv 3K 35
SK5: Stoc 4H 25
Bombay Rd. SK3: Stoc 5A 52
Bomish La. CW4: H Cha 5K 165
Bonar Cl. SK3: Stoc 4A 52
Bonar Rd. SK3: Stoc 4A 52
Boncarn Dr. M23: Wyth 1G 75
Bond Cl. WA5: Warr 1B 66
Bond St. CW8: Winn 4C 156
L3: Liv 1J 35
M34: Den 7E 8
SK11: Mac 6K 125
SK15: Stal 6B 4
Bongs Rd. SK2: Stoc 6K 53
Bonington Ri. SK6: Mar B 4H 55
Bonis Cres. SK2: Stoc 1G 79
Bonis Hall La. SK10: Pres 1G 121
Bonnyfields SK6: Rom 2B 54
Bonville Chase WA14: Alt 1E 72
Bonville Rd. WA14: Alt 7E 46
Booth Av. CH3: Ash H 7G 171
CW6: L Bud 2H 177
CW11: S'ach 3G 201
M14: Manc 4A 24
BOOTH BANK 6J 71
Boothbank La. WA14: M'ton 7J 71
Booth Bed La. CW4: Goo 5G 165
WA16: All 4G 165
Boothby St. SK2: Stoc 1G 79
SK10: Mac 4K 125
Booth Cl. SK15: Stal 1A 10
Boothcote M34: Aude 4C 8
Boothdale Dr. M34: Aude 3A 8
Boothfield Av. M22: Wyth 6K 49
Boothfield Dr. M22: Wyth 6K 49
Boothfield Rd. M22: Wyth 6J 49
Boothfields WA16: Knut 3G 117
BOOTH GREEN 7E 100 (2D 217)
Booth Hall CW1: Crewe 3G 195
Booth La. CW10: Mid, Most 4D 180
CW11: Most, S'ach 1A 200
Booth Rd. CW8: H'ord 2K 161
M33: Sale 5G 23
M34: Aude 3A 8
SK9: Wilm 5H 97
WA14: Alt 2F 213 (1G 73)
Booth's Cl. CH2: Elt 6E 136
BOOTHSDALE 5D 172
Boothsdale CW6: W'gton 5C 172
Booths Hall WA16: Knut 4H 117
Booths Hill Cl. WA13: Lymm 3K 69
Booth's Hill Rd. WA13: Lymm 2J 69
Booths La. WA4: H Whi 1D 114
WA13: Lymm 3H 69
Boothsmere Cl. CW11: S'ach 1D 200
BOOTHSTOWN 1B 216
Booth St. CW12: Cong 4E 182
M34: Den 5E 8
SK3: Stoc 5C 52
SK14: H'rth 5K 11
SK14: Hyde 2K 27
SK15: Stal 2A 10
WA5: Warr 1C 66
BOOTLE 1B 214
Border Rd. CH60: Hes 6K 83
Borders Ind. Pk., The
CH4: Salt 4D 148
Border Way CH3: Ches 2F 151
Bordley Wlk. M23: Wyth 3E 48
Bordon Rd. SK3: Stoc 5K 51
Borough Arc. SK14: Hyde 7J 9
Borough Pavement CH41: Birk 6D 34
Borough Pl. *CH41: Birk* *6D 34*
(off Grange Rd. E.)
Borough Rd. CH41: Birk 1B 60
CH42: R Fer, Tran 2B 60
CH44: Wall 1C 34
CW12: Cong 3H 183
WA15: Alt 3K 213 (1J 73)
Borough Rd. E. CH41: Birk 6D 34
CH44: Wall 2D 34
Borough St. SK15: Stal 1B 10
Borough Way CH44: Wall 2D 34
BORRAS HEAD 2B 218
Borron St. SK1: Stoc 2E 52
Borrowdale Av. SK8: Gat 1D 76
WA2: Warr 1G 41
Borrowdale Cl. CW2: Crewe 3J 193
WA6: Frod 7J 111
Borrowdale Cres. M20: Manc 1A 50
Borrowdale Rd. CH46: More 4A 32
CH63: Beb 2J 85
SK2: Stoc 5F 53
WA8: Wid 5C 62
Borrowdale Ter. *SK15: Stal* *5B 4*
(off Springs La.)
Borth Av. SK2: Stoc 5F 53
Borth Wlk. M23: Wyth 6F 49
Boscombe Dr. SK7: H Gro 3G 79
Boscombe St. SK5: Stoc 1J 25
Bosden Av. SK7: H Gro 2J 79
Bosden Cl. *SK1: Stoc* *4D 52*
(off Bosden Fold)
SK9: Hand 1A 98
Bosden Fold SK1: Stoc 4D 52
Bosden Fold Rd. SK7: H Gro 1J 79
Bosden Hall Rd. SK7: H Gro 2J 79
Bosdin Rd. E. M41: Urm 2H 21
Bosdin Rd. W. M41: Urm 2H 21
BOSLEY 1D 221
Bosley Cl. CW10: Mid 6C 180
SK9: Wilm 4A 98
Bosley Dr. SK12: Poy 3F 101
Bosley Rd. SK3: Stoc 4J 51
Bosley Vw. CW12: Cong 5K 183
Bossington Cl. SK2: Stoc 4G 53
BOSTOCK GREEN 7G 163 (1A 220)
Bostock Grn. CH65: Ell P 2B 134
Bostock Rd. CW7: Wins 1H 179
CW10: Bos, Stan 1K 179 & 2A 180
SK11: Mac 5F 125
SK14: B'tom 3H 29
Bostock St. WA5: Warr 6C 40
Boston Av. WA7: Run 6H 89
Boston Blvd. WA5: Gt San 5J 39
Boston Cl. SK7: Bram 6B 78
WA3: Cul 6F 7
Boston St. SK14: Hyde 1K 27
Boston Wlk. M34: Den 2F 27
Boswell Av. M34: Aude 1C 8
WA4: Warr 3F 67
Boswell Rd. CH43: Pren 4J 59
Bosworth Cl. CH63: Spit 4K 85
Botany Rd. SK6: W'ley 5F 27
Boteler Av. WA5: Warr 5D 40
Boteler Ct. *WA4: Warr* *3G 67*
(off Elphins Dr.)
Botley Cl. CH49: Upt 7A 32
BOTTOMS 1E 4
Bottoms Fold OL5: Moss 1E 4
Bottoms La. CH4: Ches 3B 150
Bottoms Mill Rd. SK6: Mar B 7H 55
Bottom St. SK14: Hyde 7A 10
BOUGHTON 2D 150
Boughton CH3: Ches 2B 150
Boughton Cen., The CH3: Ches 1C 150
Boughton Hall Av. CH3: Ches 2D 150
Boughton Hall Dr. CH3: Gt Bou 2E 150
Boughton Heath (Park & Ride) 3F 151
Boulder Dr. M23: Wyth 3G 75
Boulderstone Rd. SK15: Stal 4B 4
Boulevard, The CH65: Gt Sut 3B 134
SK7: H Gro 3J 79
SK14: H'rth 2J 11
Boulevard Bus. Pk. WA3: Birc 2D 42
Boulting Av. WA5: Warr 2D 40
Boulton Av. CH48: W Kir 1C 56
CH62: N Fer 5G 61
Boulton Cl. CW11: Mal B 6G 201
BOUNDARY 3D 221
Boundary Cl. OL5: Moss 3D 4
(not continuous)
SK6: W'ley 6H 27
Boundary Cotts. SK15: Carrb 2F 5
Boundary Ct. CH3: Ches 2E 150
SK4: Stoc 4D 24
SK8: Chea 7E 50
Boundary Grn. M34: Den 5D 8
Boundary Gro. M33: Sale 1F 49
Boundary La. CH4: Salt 6E 148
CH60: Hes 6J 83
CW12: Cong 6J 183
SK11: Sidd 4B 168
SY14: Thr 5G 207
WA16: O Peo 3K 165
Boundary La. Nth. CW8: Cudd 4C 160
Boundary La. Sth. CW8: Cudd 4C 160
Boundary Pk. CH64: Park 1B 130
Boundary Rd. CH43: Bid, Noc 3G 33
CH48: W Kir 5E 56
CH62: P Sun 6G 61
M23: Wyth 1F 75
SK8: Chea 6H 51
Boundary St. CW9: N'ich 3K 157
WA1: Warr 5J 41
Bourchier Way WA4: Grap 5A 68
Bourne Cl. CW8: Weav 6H 155
Bournelea Av. M19: Manc 5C 24
Bournemouth Cl. WA7: Murd 1F 113
Bourne St. SK4: Stoc 7H 25
SK9: Wilm 1E 118
ST7: Mow C 5H 205
Bournville Av. SK4: Stoc 7H 25
Bournville Gro. M19: Manc 2F 25
Bouverie St. CH1: Ches 1A 212 (7K 145)
Boverton Cl. WA5: Call 3C 40
Bovey Ct. *WA1: Warr* *1F 67*
(off St Austins La.)
Bowden Cl. CW12: Cong 3B 182
SK14: Hat 2F 29
WA3: Cul 6F 7
WN7: Leigh 1J 7
Bowden Cricket, Hockey & Squash Club
4G 73
Bowden Downs La. SK11: Mac 5F 127
Bowden Dr. CW9: N'ich 5H 157
Bowden La. SK6: Mar 5E 54
Bowden St. M34: Den 7D 8
SK7: H Gro 2J 79
Bowden Vw. La. WA16: Mere 4K 95
BOWDON 3F 73 (2B 216)
Bowdon Cl. WA1: Padg 4K 41
Bowdon Ho. SK3: Stoc 4C 52
Bowdon Ri. WA14: Bow 3H 73
Bowdon Rd. CH45: Wall 5G 13
WA14: Alt 4F 213 (2G 73)
Bowdon St. SK3: Stoc 4C 52
(not continuous)
Bowen Cl. SK7: Bram 1J 99
WA8: Wid 1D 62
Bowen Cooke Av. CW1: Crewe 7F 191
Bowen St. CW2: Crewe 3A 194
Bower Av. SK4: Stoc 1A 52
SK7: H Gro 4H 79
Bower Ct. SK14: Hyde 5B 10
Bower Cres. WA4: Stre 4H 93
Bowercup Fold SK15: Carrb 5F 5
Bowerfield Av. SK7: H Gro 5H 79
Bowerfield Cres. SK7: H Gro 5H 79
BOWER FOLD 2C 10
Bower Fold 2D 10
Bower Fold SK15: Stal 2D 10
Bowerfold La. SK4: Stoc 2A 52
(not continuous)
Bower Gdns. SK15: Stal 2E 10
Bower Gro. SK15: Stal 7D 4
Bower Ho. CH49: Upt 5C 32
Bower Rd. CH60: Hes 6A 84
WA15: Hale 4J 73
Bowers Av. M41: Urm 1A 22
Bowers Bus. Pk. WA8: Wid 6H 63
Bowers Pk. Ind. Est.
WA8: Wid 6J 63
Bowers Row CW5: Nant 2C 196
Bowers St. M14: Manc 4B 24
Bower St. SK5: Stoc 1J 25
WA8: Wid 4J 63
Bowery Av. SK8: Chea H 7H 77
Bowe's Ga. Rd.
CW6: Bun 5D 188 & 4G 189
Bowfell Circ. M41: Urm 1A 22
Bowfell Cl. CH62: East 4J 107
Bowfell Dr. SK6: H Lan 5E 80
Bowfell Rd. M41: Urm 1K 21
BOWGREEN 4E 72
Bowgreen Cl. CH43: Bid 5F 33
Bow Grn. M. WA14: Bow 3F 73
Bow Grn. Rd. WA14: Bow 4D 72
Bowker Av. M34: Den 3G 27
Bowkers Cft. CW11: Wint 5C 204
Bowker St. SK14: Hyde 7K 9
Bowlacre Rd. SK14: Hyde 5J 27
Bowland Av. WA9: Sut M 1H 37
Bowland Cl. CH62: Brom 5D 86
SK2: Stoc 7J 53
WA3: Birc 6C 18
WA7: Beec 2A 112
Bowland Ct. M33: Sale 7G 23
Bowland Cft. CW1: L'ton 4G 191
Bowland Ri. CW7: Wins 5C 178
Bowland Rd. M23: Wyth 6F 49
M34: Den 7A 8
SK6: W'ley 6G 27
Bow La. WA14: Bow 5E 72
Bowler St. M19: Manc 3E 24
Bowles Cl. CW11: S'ach 3E 200
Bowley Av. M22: Wyth 3G 75
Bowline Cl. CW11: Mal B 6H 201
BOWLING BANK 3B 218
Bowling Grn., The
M32: S'ord 1H 23
Bowling Grn. Ct. *CW5: Nant* *2C 196*
(off The Gullet)
CW8: Winn 4D 156
Bowling Grn. St. SK14: Hyde 1J 27
Bowman Av. WA4: Westy 7A 42
Bowmans, The SK10: Mac 3J 125
Bowmere Cl. CW6: Tarp 3J 175
Bowmere Dr. CW7: Wins 4D 178
Bowmere Rd. CW6: Tarp 3J 175
Bowmont Cl. SK8: Chea H 1J 77
Bowness Av. CH43: Pren 3K 59
CH63: Brom 2H 107
CW7: Wins 2E 178
M44: Cad 7A 20
SK4: Stoc 5H 25
SK8: Chea H 4K 77
WA2: Warr 2G 41
Bowness Cl. CW4: H Cha 4G 181
Bowness Ct. CW12: Cong 5C 182
Bowness Dr. M33: Sale 6E 22
Bowness Rd. CW2: Crewe 3H 193
WA15: Timp 7D 48
Bowood Ct. WA2: Winw 7K 15
Bowood St. L8: Liv 2K 61
Bowring Dr. CH64: Park 6E 104
Bowscale Cl. CH49: Upt 7B 32
Bow St. SK3: Stoc 4A 52
SK16: Duk 1H 9
Bow Vs. WA14: Bow 3F 73
Bowyer Av. CW5: Nant 1C 196
Boxgrove Cl. WA8: Wid 2H 63
Boxgrove Rd. M33: Sale 6E 22
Boxhill Dr. M23: Wyth 3G 49
Box La. CW12: Cong 3B 182
Boxmoor Cl. CH4: Ches 6H 149
Box Tree M. SK11: Mac 5H 125
Box Wlk. M31: Part 1G 45
Boyd Cl. CH46: Leas 1E 32
Boydell Av. WA4: Grap 3B 68
WA4: Westy 1K 67
Boydell Way CH4: Dod 4D 184
Boyd's Wlk. SK16: Duk 3H 9
Boyle Av. WA2: Warr 3J 41
Brabant Rd. SK8: Chea H 3K 77
Brabyns Av. SK6: Rom 1D 54
Brabyns Brow SK6: Mar 5G 55
Brabyns Pk. Recreation Cen. 4G 55
Brabyns Rd. SK14: Hyde 4K 27
Bracadale Dr. SK3: Stoc 7C 52
Bracken Cl. M33: Sale 6B 22
SK6: Mar B 5J 55

Bronte St.—Brunstath Cl.

Bronte St. L3: Liv 3K 35
BRONYGARTH 3A 218
Brookash Rd. M22: Wyth 5C 76
Brook Av. CW2: Shav 2C 198
M19: Manc 1E 24
SK4: Stoc 6G 25
WA4: Stoc H 4J 67
WA4: Westy 7K 41
WA15: Timp 6J 47
Brook Cl. CH44: Wall 6J 13
CW1: Crewe 3F 195
WA8: Cron 6C 36
WA15: Timp 6J 47
Brookcot Rd. M23: Wyth 5F 49
Brook Ct. *CH1: Ches 7J 145*
(off Whipcord La.)
CW11: S'ach 3F 201
Brookcroft Av. M22: Wyth 7K 49
Brookcroft Rd. M22: Wyth 7K 49
Brookdale WA8: Wid 2A 62
Brookdale Av. M34: Aude 3C 8
M34: Den 1G 27
SK6: Mar 1G 81
WA16: Knut 3G 117
Brookdale Av. Nth. CH49: Gre 1B 58
Brookdale Av. Sth. CH49: Gre 1B 58
Brookdale Cl. CH49: Gre 1B 58
SK6: Bred 1K 53
Brookdale Cotts. SK2: Stoc 5K 53
Brookdale Ct. M33: Sale 3C 48
Brookdale Pk. CW2: Crewe 3A 194
Brookdale Pl. CH1: Ches 3D 212 (1A 150)
Brookdale Ri. SK7: Bram 4D 78
Brookdale Rd. SK7: Bram 4D 78
SK8: Gat 7B 50
Brookdale Way CH3: Wave 2B 174
Brookdene Rd. M19: Manc 5B 24
Brook Dr. CW6: Kel 4C 172
SK6: Mar 1F 81
WA5: Gt San 7J 39
Brooke Av. CH2: Upt 2C 146
SK9: Hand 2A 98
Brooke Ct. SK9: Hand 3B 98
Brooke Dr. SK9: Hand 2A 98
Brooke Ho. *SK10: Mac 3G 125*
(off Priory Ct.)
Brooke Pk. SK9: Hand 2B 98
Brooke Way SK9: Hand 2A 98
Brook Farm Cl. M31: Part 3G 45
Brookfield CW1: Hasl 1K 195
Brookfield Av. M41: Urm 1K 21
SK1: Stoc 5E 52
SK6: Bred 7F 27
SK12: Poy 2B 100
WA7: Run 4K 89
WA15: Timp 4K 47
Brookfield Bus. Cen. SK8: Chea 7G 51
Brookfield Cl. CW6: Tarp 4J 175
SK1: Stoc 5E 52
WA13: Lymm 2K 69
Brookfield Cotts. *WA13: Lymm 2K 69*
(off Elm Tree Rd.)
Brookfield Ct. CW1: Crewe 1B 194
M19: Manc 3C 24
Brookfield Cres. CW4: Goo 6K 165
SK8: Chea 1F 77
Brookfield Dr. CH2: Ches 6B 146
CW4: H Cha 4H 181
ST7: Als 4D 202
WA15: Timp 5A 48
Brookfield Gdns. CH48: W Kir 3C 56
M22: Wyth 6J 49
Brookfield Gro. OL6: Ash L 1J 9
Brookfield Ho. SK8: Chea 1F 77
Brookfield La. SK11: Mac 5C 126
Brookfield Pk. CW5: Nant 3C 196
WA4: Grap 3A 68
Brookfield Rd. CH48: W Kir 3C 56
CW9: Comb 2J 115
SK8: Chea 7G 51
WA3: Cul 7D 6
WA13: Lymm 2K 69
Brookfield St. WA12: New W 1E 14
Brookfield Ter. SK7: H Gro 2K 79
Brookfold La. SK14: Hyde 1C 28
Brookfold Rd. SK4: Stoc 5G 25
Brook Furlong WA6: Frod 5E 110
Brook Gro. M44: Irlam 1D 20
Brookhead Dr. SK8: Chea 7J 51
Brook Hey CH64: Park 5E 104
Brookhey SK14: Hyde 7G 9
Brookheys Rd WA14: Dun M 2C 46
Brookheys Rd. M31: Carri 7H 21
(not continuous)
BROOKHOUSE 1G 127
Brook Ho. *M23: Wyth 5C 48*
(off Bridge Rd.)
Brookhouse Cl. SK10: Mac 3G 125
Brook Ho. Ct. WA13: Lymm 3K 69
Brookhouse Dr. CW2: Crewe 5C 194
BROOKHOUSE GREEN 1C 221
Brookhouse La. CW12: Cong 3J 183
(not continuous)
WA4: L Whi 5A 114
Brookhouse Rd. CW11: S'ach 3F 201
ST7: Als 6E 202
BROOKHOUSES 3D 221
BROOKHURST 2H 107 (2B 214)
Brookhurst Av. CH62: East 1H 107
CH63: Brom, East 1H 107
Brookhurst Cl. CH63: Brom 2H 107
Brookhurst Rd. CH63: Brom 1H 107
Brookland Av. CW2: Wis 6K 193
Brookland Cl. M44: Irlam 1C 20
Brookland Dr. CW11: S'ach 3H 201
Brookland Rd. CH41: Birk 7C 34
BROOKLANDS
M33 2B 48 (1B 216)
SY13 3D 219
Brooklands CH41: Birk 5C 34
CW1: Crewe 1C 194
Brooklands, The CW2: Hou 4E 198
Brooklands Av. M34: Den 1C 26
SK11: Mac 5J 125
Brooklands Cl. M34: Den 6C 8
SK4: Stoc 6G 25
Brooklands Ct. M33: Sale 2B 48
Brooklands Cres. M33: Sale 1B 48
Brooklands Dr. CW4: Goo 6J 165
CW9: N'ich 2F 163
Brooklands Flats CW1: Crewe 7G 191
Brooklands Gdns. CH64: Park 6F 105
Brooklands Gro. CW1: Crewe 7F 191
Brooklands Ho. *M33: Sale 1B 48*
(off Brooklands Rd.)
Brooklands M. SK11: Mac 5J 125
Brooklands Pk. WA8: Wid 3J 63
Brooklands Pl. M33: Sale 1A 48
Brooklands Rd. CH64: Park 6F 105
CW12: Cong 4B 182
M23: Wyth 4C 48
M33: Sale 1B 48
SK5: Stoc 1H 25
SK7: H Gro 4J 79
Brooklands Sports Club 2B 48
Brooklands Station (Metro) 1A 48
Brooklands Sta. App. M33: Sale 1A 48
Brookland St. WA1: Warr 5J 41
Brooklands Va. SK14: Hyde 7K 9
Brook La. CH2: Ches 7K 145
CH64: Park 5F 105
CW5: Burl 5G 189
CW9: N'ich 6J 157
SK9: Ald E 4D 118
WA3: Rix 4G 43
WA15: Timp 6J 47
WA16: Knut 4F 117
Brookledge La. SK10: Adl 6G 103
Brookleigh Rd. M20: Manc 5A 24
Brooklet Rd. CH60: Hes 6A 84
Brook Lodge SK8: Chea 1F 77
Brooklyn Av. M41: Urm 1H 21
Brooklyn Cres. SK8: Chea 7F 51
Brooklyn Dr. CH65: Gt Sut 3B 134
WA13: Lymm 1A 70
Brooklyn Pl. SK8: Chea 6F 51
Brooklyn Rd. SK2: Stoc 6G 53
SK8: Chea 7F 51
Brooklyn St. CW2: Crewe 4C 194
Brook Mdw. CH61: Irby 6B 58
Brookmere Cl. CW11: S'ach 1C 200
Brookmoore Ct. *CH2: Ches 6A 146*
(off Brook La.)
Brook Pl. CH1: Ches 2D 212 (1A 150)
WA4: Westy 2J 67
Brook Rd. CH66: Gt Sut 3K 133
CW6: Tarp 4J 175
M14: Manc 4A 24
M41: Urm 1K 21
SK4: Stoc 6F 25
SK8: Chea 6F 51
WA13: Lymm 1A 70
Brooks All. L1: Liv 3J 35
Brooks Av. SK7: H Gro 2H 79
SK14: Hyde 2K 27
Brooks Dr. SK8: Chea 3E 76
WA15: Hale, Timp 1D 74
WA15: H'rns 5D 74
WA15: Timp 5D 48
Brook Side CW8: Weav 4F 155
Brookside CH3: Ash H 7G 171
CH3: Gt Bou 3D 150
CW6: Kel 4B 172
CW8: Cudd 3C 160
M20: Manc 2B 50
WA6: K'ley 1D 152
Brookside Av. SK2: Stoc 5J 53
SK11: Sut E 3K 129
SK12: Poy 3D 100
WA4: Stoc H 4H 67
WA5: Gt San 1J 65
WA13: Lymm 1J 69
Brookside Cl. SK8: Chea 1F 77
SK14: Hyde 7B 10
Brookside Ct. M19: Manc 1D 24
SK10: Mac 3H 125
Brookside Cres. CH49: Upt 7A 32
Brookside Dr. CH49: Upt 7B 32
SK14: Hyde 7B 10
Brookside Grn. *CW2: Crewe 6C 194*
(off Artle Rd.)
Brookside La. SK6: H Lan 6E 80
Brookside Mill *SK11: Mac 5B 126*
(off Brook St.)
Brookside Miniature Railway 6K 79
Brookside Railway Mus. 6K 79
Brookside Rd. CW12: Cong 3F 183
M33: Sale 2A 48
SK8: Gat 6C 50
WA6: Frod 7G 111
Brookside Ter. CH2: Ches 7A 146
SK9: Ald E 4D 118
Brookside Vs. *SK8: Gat 6C 50*
(off Pendlebury Rd.)
Brooks La. CW10: Mid 3D 180
Brooks La. Ind. Est. CW10: Mid 3D 180
(not continuous)
Brooks St. SK1: Stoc 5D 52
Brook St. CH1: Ches 2D 212 (1A 150)
CH41: Birk 4B 34
CH62: P Sun 7F 61
CH64: Nest 7H 105
CW2: Crewe 3D 194
CW9: N'ich 3K 157
(Victoria St.)
CW9: N'ich 4F 157
(Witton St.)
CW12: Cong 3G 183
L3: Liv 2G 35
M33: Sale 6H 23
SK7: H Gro 3J 79
SK8: Chea 6H 51
SK11: Mac 5A 126
SK14: Hyde 7K 9
WA3: Low 1A 6
WA7: Run 4G 89
(not continuous)
WA8: Wid 5H 63
WA16: Knut 4F 117
Brook St. E. CH41: Birk 5D 34
Brook St. Ind. Est. *SK1: Stoc 5D 52*
(off Brook St.)
Brook St. W. OL6: Ash L 1F 9
Brook Ter. CH48: W Kir 3B 56
CW11: Whe 6E 200
WA7: Run 5A 90
Brookthorn Cl. SK2: Stoc 7K 53
Brookthorpe Av. M19: Manc 5B 24
Brookthorpe Cl. CH45: Wall 5J 13
BROOKVALE 2E 112
Brookvale Av. Nth. WA7: B'vale 1D 112
Brookvale Av. Sth. WA7: B'vale 1D 112
Brookvale Cl. WA5: B'ood 5C 14
Brookvale Recreation Cen. 1E 112
Brook Vw. SK9: Ald E 4F 119
Brookview Cl. CW2: Wis 6C 194
Brook Vs. ST7: Als 6F 203
Brook Wlk. CH61: Irby 6A 58
M34: Den 3E 26
Brook Way CW5: Nant 4C 196
CW8: H'ord 2A 162
(off Riddings La.)
WA5: Gt San 7J 39
WA15: Timp 5K 47
Brookway CH43: Pren 4H 59
CH45: Wall 6G 13
CH49: Gre 7B 32
Brookway Cl. M19: Manc 7B 24
Brookway Ct. M23: Wyth 5F 49
Brookway Retail Pk. M23: Wyth 4E 48
Brook Well CH64: L Nes 3C 130
Brookwood Av. M33: Sale 1J 47
Brookwood Cl. M34: Den 4F 27
WA4: Walt 5F 67
Broom Av. M19: Manc 3E 24
SK5: Stoc 5J 25
WA4: App 7J 67
Broom Cres. CH3: Tar 7B 170
Broomcroft Ho. M20: Manc 2D 50
Broome Ct. WA7: B'vale 1D 112
BROOMEDGE 4E 70 (2B 216)
Broomehouse Av. M44: Irlam 3B 20
Broomfield Cl. CH60: Hes 5E 82
CW7: Wins 4B 178
SK5: Stoc 5J 25
SK9: Wilm 6B 98
SK11: Chel 5C 166
Broomfield Ct. M20: Manc 1C 50
WA15: Hale 2J 73
(off Broomfield La.)
Broomfield Cres. SK2: Stoc 1E 78
Broomfield Dr. SK5: Stoc 5J 25
Broomfield La. WA15: Hale 3J 73
Broomfield Rd. SK4: Stoc 7F 25
Broomfields M34: Den 5F 9
WA4: App 6J 67
Broomfields Leisure Cen. 6H 67
Broomfields Rd. WA4: App 6H 67
Broomgrove La. M34: Den 6F 9
BROOMHALL 5K 209 (3A 220)
BROOMHALL GREEN 6K 209
Broomheath La. CH3: Tar 7C 170
Broom Hill CH43: Clau 5J 33
Broomhill Dr. SK7: Bram 4B 78
Broomhill La. CH3: L Bar 1B 170
Broomhurst Hall M20: Manc 2D 50
Broomlands CH60: Hes 6H 83
Broom La. M19: Manc 3E 24
WA16: Lwr P 1C 164
Broomleigh WA14: Alt 1F 213 (7G 47)
Broomleigh Cl. CH63: H Beb 1H 85
Broom Rd. M31: Part 2H 45
WA15: Hale 2J 73
Broomsfield La. CW8: Barnt 1J 155
Broom's La. CW6: Kel 2C 172
Broomstair Rd. M34: Aude 4E 8
Broom St. CW1: Crewe 1A 194
Broomville Av. M33: Sale 7G 23
Broomwood Gdns. WA15: Timp 7C 48
Broomwood Rd. WA15: Timp 7C 48
Broseley Av. CH62: Brom 5C 86
M20: Manc 1F 51
WA3: Cul 6D 6
Broseley La. WA3: Cul 5D 6
Broseley Pl. WA3: Cul 5C 6
Broster Av. CH46: More 4K 31
Broster Cl. CH46: More 4K 31
Brosters La. CH47: Meols 4E 30
Brotherton Cl. CH62: Brom 5C 86
BROUGHALL 3D 219
Brougham Av. CH41: Tran 1E 60
Brougham Rd. CH44: Wall 1C 34
Brough St. W. SK11: Mac 5J 125
BROUGHTON 1B 218
Broughton Av. CH48: W Kir 2B 56
Broughton Cl. WA4: Grap 5K 67
Broughton La. CW2: Wis 5K 193
Broughton M. M33: Sale 1C 48
Broughton Mills Rd. CH4: Bret 5A 148
BROUGHTON PARK 1C 217
Broughton Rd. CH44: Wall 1A 34
CW1: Crewe 4H 191
SK5: Stoc 7J 25
SK10: Adl 6G 103
Broughton Way WA8: Hal B 1B 88
Broughville Dr. M20: Manc 4E 50
BROW, THE 5B 90
Brow, The WA6: K'ley 1D 152
Brow La. CH60: Hes 7H 83
CW9: Ant 5C 94
Browmere Dr. M20: Manc 1B 50
WA3: Croft 4F 17
Brown Av. CW5: Nant 4D 196
ST7: Chu L 5H 203
BROWN EDGE 2D 221
BROWN HEATH 1B 174
Brown Heath Rd.
CH3: Chri, Wave 4K 151
Brownhill Dr. WA1: Padg 4K 41
BROWNHILLS 7C 176
Brownhills Rd. CW6: Rus 7C 176
Browning Av. CH42: R Fer 4E 60
WA8: Wid 5F 63
Browning Cl. CH1: Blac 4G 145
CW11: Ett H 4B 200
Browning Dr. CH65: Gt Sut 4B 134
WA2: Winw 5K 15
Browning Grn. *CH65: Gt Sut 4B 134*
(off Browning Dr.)
Browning Rd. CH45: Wall 6D 12
SK5: Stoc 2G 25
Browning St. CW1: Crewe 2C 194
Browning Way CW7: Wins 5A 178
BROWN KNOWL 2C 219
Brown La. SK8: He Grn 4C 76
Brownlea Av. SK16: Duk 3H 9
Brownlees Cl. CW2: Crewe 5A 194
Brown Lees Rd. ST7: Bro L, Harr 7K 205
Brownley Ct. M22: Wyth 7A 50
Brownley Ct. Rd. M22: Wyth 7K 49
Brownley Rd. M22: Shar, Wyth 6A 50
BROWNLOW 7A 182 (1C 221)
Brownlow Cl. SK12: Poy 4D 100
BROWNLOW HEATH 7A 182 (1C 221)
Brownlow Heath La. CW12: Bro 7A 182
Brownlow Hill L3: Liv 3K 35
Brownlow Rd. CH62: N Fer 6G 61
Brownlow St. L3: Liv 3K 35
Brown's La. CH4: Ches 7B 212 (4K 149)
SK9: Wilm 6B 98
(not continuous)
Brown St. CW12: Cong 3G 183
M34: Aude 5D 8
(off Denton Rd.)
SK1: Stoc 5H 213 (3C 52)
SK9: Ald E 6F 119
SK11: Mac 5K 125
WA8: Wid 6K 63
WA14: Alt 2H 73
Brownsville Rd. SK4: Stoc 6E 24
Brownville Gro. SK16: Duk 3K 9
Brownwood Av. SK1: Stoc 3F 53
Brownwood Cl. M33: Sale 3C 48
Brow Rd. CH43: Bid 3G 33
Brows Av. M23: Wyth 2G 49
Brow Side L5: Liv 1K 35
BROXTON 2E 206 (2C 219)
Broxton Av. CH43: Pren 3J 59
CH48: W Kir 2C 56
CW10: Mid 6D 180
Broxton Cl. WA8: Wid 2C 62
Broxton Hall M. CH3: Brox 2E 206
Broxton Rd. CH3: Brox, Clut 2A 206
CH45: Wall 5F 13
CH66: Ell P 3A 134
Bruce Av. WA2: Warr 3H 41
Bruce Cres. CH63: Brom 1H 107
Bruce Dr. CH66: Gt Sut 4J 133
BRUCHE 5J 41
Bruche Av. WA1: Padd, Padg 5K 41
Bruche Dr. WA1: Padg 4K 41
Bruche Heath Gdns. WA1: Padg 4A 42
Bruen, The CH3: Tar 5C 170
BRUERA 1C 219
Bruera Rd. CH65: Gt Sut 4B 134
Brundage Rd. M22: Wyth 3K 75
Brundrett Pl. M33: Sale 7E 22
Brundrett St. SK1: Stoc 4E 52
Brunel Cl. M32: S'ord 1K 23
Brunel Ct. CW9: Rud 1J 163
Brunel Rd. CH62: Brom 5F 87
SK11: L Grn 2G 129
Brunner Gro. CW5: Nant 2E 196
Brunner Pl. CW7: Wins 4B 178
Brunner Rd. WA8: Wid 5G 63
Brunsborough Cl. CH62: Brom 1H 107
Brunsfield Cl. CH46: More 5K 31
Brunstath Cl. CH60: Hes 5A 84

Brunstead Cl.—Buttermere Cl.

Brunstead Cl. M23: Wyth 6D 48
Brunswick WA7: Run 3G 89
Brunswick Bus. Pk. L3: Liv 7J 35
(not continuous)
Brunswick Ct. *CH41: Birk 5D 34*
(off Brunswick M.)
SK11: Mac 6A 126
(off Chapel St.)
Brunswick Cres.
CH66: Gt Sut 5A 134
Brunswick Ent. Cen. L3: Liv 7J 35
Brunswick Hill SK10: Mac 4A 126
Brunswick M. CH41: Birk 5D 34
Brunswick Rd. WA14: Alt 5H 47
Brunswick Station (Rail) 1K 61
Brunswick St. CW12: Cong 3H 183
L2: Liv 3H 35
L3: Liv 3G 35
M32: S'ord 3J 23
OL5: Moss 1E 4
SK10: Mac 4A 126
SK16: Duk 1H 9
Brunswick Ter. *SK10: Mac 4A 126*
(off Brunswick St.)
Brunswick Way L3: Liv 7J 35
Bruntleigh Av. WA4: Westy 2A 68
Brunton Rd. SK5: Stoc 5J 25
Bruntwood Av. SK8: He Grn 4C 76
Bruntwood Cotts.
SK8: Chea 3G 77
Bruntwood La. SK8: Chea 1G 77
SK8: He Grn 4G 77
Bruntwood Pk. 3F 77
BRUSHES 6E 4
Brushes SK15: Stal 6H 5
Brushes Av. SK15: Stal 6E 4
Brushes Rd. SK15: Stal 6E 4
Brussels Rd. SK3: Stoc 6B 52
Bruton Av. M32: S'ord 2G 23
Bryanston Rd. CH42: Tran 3K 59
Bryant Av. WA4: Westy 7K 41
Bryce Dr. CH62: Brom 3C 86
Bryce St. SK14: Hyde 6J 9
Bryce Wlk. CH62: Brom 2C 86
Brydges Rd. SK6: Mar 7E 54
Brymau Five Est. CH4: Salt 4D 148
Brymau Four Trad. Est. CH4: Salt 4E 148
Brymau One Trad. Est. CH4: Salt 4F 149
Brymau Three Trad. Est.
CH4: Salt 4E 148
Brymau Two Trad. Est. CH4: Salt 4F 149
BRYMBO 2A 218
BRYN 1D 215
Bryn Bank CH44: Wall 7J 13
Bryndale Gro. M33: Sale 3K 47
Brynden Av. M20: Manc 6A 24
Bryn Dr. SK5: Stoc 6J 25
BRYNEGLWYS 3A 218
BRYNFORD 3A 214
BRYN GATES 1D 215
Brynlow Dr. CW10: Mid 4B 180
Brynmore Dr. SK11: Mac 5C 126
Brynmoss Av. CH44: Wall 7F 13
Brynn St. WA8: Wid 5H 63
BRYNTEG 2B 218
Brynton Cl. SK10: Mac 3K 125
Brynton Rd. M13: Manc 1B 24
(not continuous)
SK10: Mac 3K 125
Bryone Dr. SK2: Stoc 7F 53
Bryony Cl. M22: Wyth 4J 75
Bryony Way CH42: R Fer 5E 60
Brythen St. L1: Liv 3J 35
BT Convention Cen. 5H 35
Buccleuch St. CH41: Birk 3J 33
Buchanan Cl. WA8: Wid 2F 63
Buchanan Rd. CH44: Wall 1C 34
Buchan Cl. WA5: Gt San 4K 39
Buchan Gro. CW2: Crewe 3B 194
Buckbean Way CW4: Goo 6J 165
Buckden Rd. SK4: Stoc 4G 25
Buckden Wlk. M23: Wyth 2F 49
Buckden Way *SK10: Mac 4K 125*
(off Longacre St.)
Buckfast Cl. SK8: Chea H 7K 77
SK10: Mac 2J 125
SK12: Poy 1C 100
WA5: Penk 2G 65
WA15: Hale 3B 74
Buckfast Ct. WA7: Nort 3G 91
Buckfast Rd. M33: Sale 5C 22
Buckfast Way CW10: Mid 3B 180
Buckhurst Rd. M19: Manc 2D 24
Buckingham Av. CH3: Ches 1E 150
CH43: Clau 5J 33
CH63: H Beb 6D 60
M34: Den 1G 27
WA8: Wid 1G 63
Buckingham Bingo
East Didsbury 3F 51
Buckingham Cl. CW2: Wis 6J 193
CW12: Cong 2H 183
Buckingham Dr. CW7: Wins 5D 178
CW9: N'ich 2D 162
SK11: Mac 7J 125
SK16: Duk 3A 10
WA5: Gt San 1A 66
WA16: Knut 4F 117
Buckingham Gdns.
CH65: Ell P 6F 135
Buckingham Gro. WA14: Timp 3K 47
Buckingham Ri. SK11: Mac 1F 129
Buckingham Rd. CH44: Wall 7F 13
M44: Cad 5K 19
SK4: Stoc 6E 24
(not continuous)
SK8: Chea H 3J 77
SK9: Wilm 1E 118
SK12: Poy 3C 100
SK15: Stal 6B 4
Buckingham Rd. W.
SK4: Stoc 7D 24
Buckingham St. SK2: Stoc 6E 52
Buckingham Way *SK2: Stoc 6D 52*
(off Windsor St.)
WA15: Timp 5A 48
Buckland Cl. WA8: Wid 6D 62
Buckland Dr. CH63: Spit 4K 85
Buckland Gro. SK14: Hyde 3B 28
Buck La. CW2: Hou 4E 198
M33: Sale 5D 22
BUCKLEY 1A 218
Buckley Bldgs. OL5: Moss 1F 5
Buckley Cl. CW10: Mid 4B 180
SK14: Hyde 4K 27
Buckley Ct. CH64: W'ston 7E 106
Buckley Dr. SK6: Rom 3A 54
BUCKLEY HILL 1B 214
Buckley La. CH64: W'ston 7E 106
Buckley St. M34: Aude 3C 8
SK5: Stoc 1H 25
SK11: Mac 5A 126
SK15: Stal 2A 10
WA2: Warr 6E 40
Bucklow Av. M31: Part 1H 45
WA16: Mob 6B 102
Bucklow Cl. SK14: Mot 2G 29
Bucklow Dr. M22: N'den 4A 50
Bucklow Gdns. WA13: Lymm 1C 70
BUCKLOW HILL 2B 216
Bucklow Vw. WA14: Bow 2E 72
Bucklow Wlk. *SK11: Mac 5B 126*
(off Bank St.)
BUCKNALL 3D 221
BUCKOAK 1J 171
Buckthorn Cl. WA15: Timp 7E 48
Buckton Dr. SK15: Carrb 4F 5
Buckton St. WA1: Warr 5H 41
BUCKTON VALE 3H 5 (1D 217)
Buckton Va. M. SK15: Carrb 2G 5
Buckton Va. Rd. SK15: Carrb 3F 5
SK15: M'ook 5E 4
Buckton Vw. SK15: Carrb 2G 5
Buckwood Cl. SK7: H Gro 2A 80
Bude Av. M41: Urm 3A 22
SK5: Stoc 6A 26
Bude Cl. CH43: Bid 6F 33
CW1: Crewe 5G 191
SK7: Bram 6D 78
ST7: Als 6C 202
Bude Ho. *CH43: Bid 6F 33*
(off Bude Cl.)
Bude Rd. WA8: Wid 3E 62
Bude Ter. SK16: Duk 1G 9
Bude Wlk. M23: Wyth 7H 49
Budworth Av. WA4: Westy 1K 67
WA8: Wid 3D 62
WA9: Sut M 1H 37
Budworth Cl. CH43: Oxt 1H 59
CW11: S'ach 2C 200
WA7: Run 7K 89
Budworth Ct. CH43: Oxt 7J 33
Budworth Gdns. M43: Droy 1A 8
Budworth La. CW9: Comb, Gt Bud 3J 115
Budworth Rd. CH43: Noc, Oxt 1H 59
CH66: Gt Sut 6A 134
CW9: Arl, Ast B 4J 115
M33: Sale 1E 48
Budworth Sailing Club 6G 115
Budworth Wlk. SK9: Wilm 5B 98
BUERTON 5H 211 (3A 220)
Buerton App. CH3: Ald 4G 185
Buerton Cl. CH43: Noc 1H 59
Buffoline Trad. Est. M19: Manc 2E 24
Buffs La. CH60: Hes 5K 83
Buggen La. CH64: Nest 7G 105
BUGLAWTON 1K 183 (1C 221)
Buildbase Way SK3: Stoc 6K 51
Buildwas Rd. CH64: Nest 5H 105
Bulford Av. M22: Wyth 3H 75
BULKELEY 2D 219
Bulkeley Bus. Cen. SK8: Chea 7H 51
Bulkeley Rd. CH44: Wall 1C 34
SK8: Chea 6G 51
SK9: Hand 3K 97
SK12: Poy 3D 100
Bulkeley St. CH3: Ches 1D 150
CW1: Crewe 3E 194
SK3: Stoc 4B 52
Buller Rd. M13: Manc 1C 24
Buller St. M43: Droy 2A 8
Bull Hill CH64: L Nes 2D 130
Bull-Hill-La. SK11: Mac 3G 127
Bull Hill La. SK10: R'ow 1G 127
Bullock's La. SK11: Sut E 2J 129
Bullock St. SK1: Stoc 5D 52
Bull Ring *CW9: N'ich 5E 156*
(off Watling St.)
Bull Ring, The
CW10: Mid 3C 180
Bullrush Dr. CH46: More 2D 32
Bulwer St. CH42: R Fer 3E 60
Bumper's La. CH1: Ches 3F 149
BUNBURY 6D 188 (2D 219)
Bunbury Cl. CH2: Stoak 2J 141
CW9: N'ich 1F 163
CW10: Mid 7D 180
Bunbury Comn. CW6: Bees, Bun 4C 188
Bunbury Ct. CW6: Tarp 3J 175
Bunbury Dr. WA7: Run 1J 111
Bunbury Grn. CH65: Ell P 6F 135
BUNBURY HEATH 5B 188
Bunbury La. CW6: Bun 7C 188
Bunbury Rd. CW6: Alp 3G 189
Bunce La. SK11: Mart 7B 168
Bunce St. CH1: Ches 6C 212 (3A 150)
Bungalow Rd.
WA12: New W 2H 15
Bungalows, The SK7: H Gro 1K 79
BUNKERS HILL 4A 54
Bunkers Hill SK6: Rom 3B 54
Bunkers Hill Rd. SK14: Hat 2F 29
Buntingford Rd. WA4: Thel 2C 68
Bunts La. CW12: Cong 5G 183
BURBAGE 3D 217
Burbage Rd. M23: Wyth 3G 75
Burbo Way CH45: Wall 3E 12
Burdale Wlk. M23: Wyth 3F 49
Burden Rd. CH46: More 4K 31
Burdett Av. CH63: Spit 4K 85
Burdett Cl. CH63: Spit 4A 86
Burdett Rd. CH45: Wall 6D 12
CH66: Gt Sut 6A 134
Burdon Av. M22: Wyth 2A 76
Burfield Dr. WA4: App 7G 67
BURFORD 5J 189
Burford Av. CH44: Wall 1J 33
SK7: Bram 1F 99
Burford Cl. SK9: Wilm 2D 118
Burford Cres. SK9: Wilm 2D 118
Burford Gro. M33: Sale 3J 47
Burford La. WA13: Lymm 2E 70
Burgamot La. CW9: Comb 2J 115
Burganey Ct. CH4: Pul 7A 184
Burgess Av. WA4: Warr 2F 67
Burgess Cl. CW5: Stap 3F 197
Burgess Dr. CH1: Sea 6B 144
Burgess La. WA6: Norl 6J 153
Burgess Pl. *CW8: N'ich 5D 156*
(off Ryders St.)
Burgess St. L3: Liv 2K 35
SK10: Mac 4C 126
Burges St. CH2: Ches 7C 146
Burghley Cl. SK15: Stal 7B 4
Burjen Way CW1: Crewe 7G 191
Burkitt St. SK14: Hyde 1K 27
BURLAND 5F 189 (2A 220)
Burland Cl. WA7: Run 5F 89
Burland Gro. CW7: Wins 2B 178
Burlea Cl. CW2: Crewe 1J 193
Burlea Dr. CW2: Shav 2B 198
Burleigh Cl. SK7: H Gro 4E 78
Burlescombe Cl. WA14: Alt 6F 47
Burley Ct. SK4: Stoc 2A 52
Burleyhurst La. SK9: Wilm 7A 96
WA16: Mob 7A 96
Burley La. WA4: App T 2C 94
Burlingham Av. CH48: W Kir 4E 56
Burlington Cl. SK4: Stoc 2G 51
Burlington Ct. WA14: Alt 1J 213 (7H 47)
Burlington Dr. SK3: Stoc 1D 78
Burlington Gdns. SK3: Stoc 1D 78
Burlington M. SK3: Stoc 1D 78
Burlington Rd. CH45: N Bri 2H 13
M20: Manc 4A 24
WA14: Alt 1J 213 (7H 47)
Burlington St. CH41: Birk 6D 34
L3: Liv 1H 35
Burmarsh La. WA8: Hal B 1B 88
BURNAGE 6B 24 (1C 217)
Burnage Av. M19: Manc 3C 24
WA9: Clo F 1J 37
Burnage Hall Rd. M19: Manc 4B 24
Burnage La. M19: Manc 2F 51
BURNAGE PARK 3C 24
Burnage Range M19: Manc 2D 24
Burnage Station (Rail) 7A 24
Burnbray Av. M19: Manc 5B 24
Burnby Wlk. M23: Wyth 3F 49
Burnell Cl. CW5: Nant 4D 196
Burnell Rd. CH65: Ell P 4G 135
Burnet Cl. WA2: Padg 2C 42
Burnfield Rd. M18: Manc 1G 25
Burnham Av. SK5: Stoc 2J 25
Burnham Cl. SK8: Chea H 3H 77
WA3: Cul 6E 6
WA5: Penk 7H 39
WA8: Wid 2C 62
Burnham Dr. M19: Manc 3C 24
Burnham Rd. CH4: Ches 5G 149
Burnley Av. CH46: More 4C 32
BURNLEYDAM 3A 220
Burnley Gro. CH46: More 3C 32
Burnley Rd. CH46: More 3C 32
Burnsall Av. WA3: Low 2A 6
Burnsall Dr. WA8: Wid 2C 62
Burnsall Wlk. M22: Wyth 3G 75
Burns Av. CH45: Wall 6G 13
SK8: Chea 6H 51
Burns Cl. CH66: Gt Sut 4A 134
ST7: Rod H 1F 203
Burns Cres. SK2: Stoc 5J 53
WA8: Wid 5F 63
Burns Dr. CW1: Crewe 2F 195
Burns Fold SK16: Duk 3B 10
Burns Gro. WA2: Warr 2G 41
Burnside SK13: Had 3K 11
SK15: Stal 3E 10
WA15: H'rns 6D 74
Burnside Av. CH44: Wall 2A 34
SK4: Stoc 5H 25
WA4: Stoc H 4H 67
Burnside Cl. SK6: Bred 1K 53
SK9: Wilm 1H 119
SK15: Stal 3E 10
Burnside Dr. M19: Manc 5B 24
Burnside Rd. CH44: Wall 2A 34
SK8: Gat 7C 50
Burnside Way CW8: Winn 4C 156
Burns Rd. CW12: Cong 4J 183
M34: Den 4F 27
WA9: Sut M 1G 37
Burns Way CH1: Blac 4F 145
Burnt Acre SK11: Chel 5D 166
Burran Rd. M22: Wyth 5K 75
Burrell Cl. CH42: Tran 4B 60
Burrell Ct. CH42: Tran 4B 60
Burrell Dr. CH46: More 5A 32
Burrell Rd. CH42: Tran 4B 60
Burrough Cl. WA3: Birc 1F 43
Burroughs Gdns. L3: Liv 1J 35
Burrows, The CW8: Cudd 1A 160
Burrows Hill CW8: H'ord 6A 156
Burrows La. WA6: Alv 7F 139
Burrwood Dr. SK3: Stoc 7B 52
Burslam St. CW12: Cong 4G 183
BURSLEM 3C 221
BURTON
CH64 7H 131 (3B 214)
CW6 7B 174 (1D 219)
LL12 2B 218
Burton Av. CH45: Wall 6E 12
CW6: Tarp 1H 175
L35: R'ill 1A 36
WA15: Timp 3A 48
Burton Cl. L1: Liv 4J 35
L35: R'ill 1A 36
WA3: Cul 7F 7
WA8: Wid 2F 63
Burton Dr. SK12: Poy 2C 100
BURTON GREEN 2B 218
Burton Grn. CH66: Gt Sut 4K 133
Burton Gro. CW1: L'ton 4G 191
Burton La. CW6: Dud 5A 174
Burton Rd. CH1: Blac 5F 145
CH64: L Nes, Ness 1C 130
CW6: Dud 4A 174
WA2: Warr 3H 41
Burton Sq. CW6: Tarp 2H 175
Burton St. SK4: Stoc 1C 52
Burton Wlk. *SK4: Stoc 1C 52*
(off Heskith St.)
BURTONWOOD 5B 14 (1D 215)
Burtonwood Heritage Attraction Cen., The 3B 40
Burtonwood Ind. Cen.
WA5: B'ood 4C 14
Burtonwood Rd.
WA5: B'ood, Gt San, W'ook 7C 14
BURTONWOOD SERVICE AREA 1K 39
BURWARDSLEY 5G 187 (2D 219)
Burwardsley Ct. CH3: Burw 5G 187
Burwardsley Rd. CH3: Burw 4F 187
CH3: Tatt 2H 187
Burwardsley Way CW9: N'ich 2D 162
Burwell Gro. M23: Wyth 5F 49
Bury St. OL5: Moss 1D 4
SK5: Stoc 1D 52
Busby's Cotts. CH45: N Bri 3H 13
Bushell Cl. CH64: Nest 1D 130
Bushell Ct. CH43: Oxt 1K 59
Bushell Rd. CH64: Nest 1D 130
Bushells La. WA6: K'ood 7H 139
Bushel's Dr. WA9: Clo F 1K 37
Bushey Dr. M23: Wyth 7G 49
Busheyfield Cl. SK14: Hyde 5J 9
Bushfield Wlk. *M23: Wyth 5E 48*
(off Sandy La.)
Bush Rd. CH3: Chri 4H 151
WA8: Wid 1F 89
Bush Way CH60: Hes 6F 83
Butcher La. M23: Wyth 5D 48
(not continuous)
Bute St. L5: Liv 1K 35
(not continuous)
Butler Ct. M32: S'ord 2J 23
Butler Way CW5: Nant 4C 196
Butley Cl. CW10: Mid 6C 180
SK10: Mac 1A 126
Butley Lanes SK10: Pres 1G 121
Butley St. SK7: H Gro 1J 79
BUTLEY TOWN 3K 121
Butterbache Rd. CH3: Hunt 5C 150
Butterbur Cl. CH3: Hunt 5D 150
Buttercup Cl. CH46: More 2D 32
WA5: Warr 2C 66
Buttercup Dr. SK3: Stoc 7B 52
Buttercup Way WA16: Pick 1B 158
Butterfield Cl. SK8: Chea H 4K 77
Butterley Cl. SK16: Duk 3A 10
Buttermarket St.
WA1: Warr 7F 41
(not continuous)
Buttermere Av. CH43: Noc 6F 33
CH65: Ell P 5E 134
M22: Wyth 3H 75
WA2: Warr 1G 41
Buttermere Cl. WA6: Frod 7K 111

Buttermere Ct.—Capesthorne Cl.

Buttermere Ct. CH41: Birk 7B 34
(off Penrith St.)
CW12: Cong 4C 182
Buttermere Cres. WA2: Warr 1G 41
(off Poplars Av.)
Buttermere Dr. CW1: L'ton 4G 191
SK9: Ald E 1B 166
WA15: H'rns 7D 74
Buttermere Gro. WA7: Beec 2K 111
Buttermere Rd. CW7: Wins 2D 178
M31: Part 1G 45
SK8: Gat 2D 76
Buttermere Ter. SK15: Stal 6B 4
(off Springs La.)
Buttermill Cl. M44: Irlam 1E 20
BUTTERTON 3C 221
Butterton Av. CH49: Upt 6A 32
Butterton La.
CW1: Crewe, O'ger, R Grn 7A 202
Buttery Ho. La. WA15: H'rns 3E 74
BUTT GREEN 4F 197 (2A 220)
Button La. M23: Wyth 2G 49
Button St. L2: Liv 3J 35
Butts, The ST7: Als 5E 202
Butts Grn. WA5: W'ook 1J 39
BUXTON 3D 217
Buxton Av. CW1: Crewe 2E 194
OL6: Ash L 3A 4
Buxton Cl. WA5: Gt San 4J 39
Buxton Ct. SK2: Stoc 6E 52
Buxton Cres. M33: Sale 3D 48
Buxton La. CH44: Wall 6E 12
SK6: Mar 7E 54
Buxton New Rd. SK11: Mac, Wal B 4E 126
(not continuous)
Buxton Old Rd. CW12: Cong 2H 183
SK11: Mac 5D 126
SK12: Dis 1G 103
Buxton Rd. CH42: R Fer 3F 61
CW12: Cong 2H 183
M32: S'ord 1F 23
SK2: Stoc 6E 52
SK6: H Lan 4K 79
SK7: H Gro 4K 79
SK10: Mac 4B 126
SK11: Mac 4B 126
SK12: Dis 1G 103
(Market St.)
SK12: Dis 4K 79
(Melford Rd.)
SK22: N Mil 1G 103
Buxton Rd. W. SK12: Dis 7G 81
Buxton St. SK7: H Gro 2H 79
SK8: Gat 7C 50
Buxton Ter. SK14: H'rth 1J 11
Buxton Way M34: Den 3E 26
BUXWORTH 2D 217
Buxworth Rd. WA14: W Tim 3G 47
BWCLE 1A 218
BWLCHGWYN 2A 218
Bye Pass, The CH3: Lit 1H 151
Byerley St. CH44: Wall 1C 34
Bye St. M34: Aude 3E 8
Byfield Rd. M22: Wyth 1J 75
Byland Av. SK8: Chea H 7K 77
Byland Cl. WA8: Wid 7J 37
Bylands Cl. SK12: Poy 2C 100
Bylands Fold SK16: Duk 4J 9
Byland Wlk. M22: Wyth 4K 75
BYLEY 1B 220
Byley La. CW4: Cran 2F 181
CW10: Mid 2E 180
Byley Way CW7: Wins 3C 178
Byng Av. M44: Cad 7A 20
By-Pass Rd. CH3: Tar 5B 170
Byre Cl. M33: Sale 1G 49
Byrne Av. CH42: R Fer 4E 60
Byrne Avenue Recreation Cen. 4E 60
Byroe Ct. WA14: Alt 6H 47
Byrom Av. M19: Manc 2F 25
Byrom Pde. M19: Manc 2F 25
Byrom St. L3: Liv 1J 35
WA14: Alt 2H 73
Byron Cl. CH1: Blac 4F 145
CH43: Pren 5J 59
CW1: Crewe 2F 195
CW10: Mid 7D 180
CW11: Ett H 3B 200
ST7: Rod H 1F 203
Byron Ct. WA2: Warr 2G 41
Byron Dr. SK8: Chea 6H 51
Byron Gro. SK5: Stoc 2H 25
Byron Rd. M32: S'ord 1K 23
M34: Den 3E 26
Byrons Dr. WA15: Timp 6A 48
Byron's La. SK11: Mac 6B 126
Byrons St. SK11: Mac 6A 126
Byron St. WA7: Run 5G 89
Byron Wlk. CW5: Nant 1B 196
Byron Way CW2: Wis 5K 193
Bythom Cl. CH3: Chri 4H 151

C

Cablehouse L2: Liv 2H 35
(off Cheapside)
Cable Rd. CH47: Hoy 5B 30
Cable Yd., The L2: Liv 2H 35
(off Cheapside)
Cabot Cl. WA5: Old H 3A 40
Cabot Pl. SK5: Stoc 7J 25
Cabul Cl. WA2: Warr 5G 41
CADISHEAD 6B 20 (1B 216)
Cadishead Way M44: Cad, Irlam 1F 45
Cadishead Way Circ. M44: Cad 1E 44
Cadnam Dr. M22: Wyth 2B 76
Cadnant Cl. CH1: Blac 7E 144
CADOLE 1A 218
Cadshaw Cl. WA3: Birc 6J 17
Caer Castell LL13: Holt 7A 186
(off Dee Pk.)
CAERGWRLE 2B 218
Caerleon Cl. CW7: Wins 4B 178
CAER-LLEON 4C 212 (2A 150)
Caer Llew LL13: Holt 6B 186
(off Quakers Way)
Caernarvon Av. CW7: Wins 5C 178
Caernarvon Cl. CH49: Upt 6D 32
WA7: Cast 4B 90
Caernarvon Ct. CH63: Beb 2K 85
CH65: Ell P 6F 135
Caernarvon Dr. SK7: H Gro 4G 79
Caernarvon Rd. CW2: Wis 6J 193
Caernarvon Way M34: Den 2E 26
Caerwys Gro. CH42: Tran 1D 60
Caesars Cl. WA7: Cast 4A 90
Cains Brewery 6K 35
Cairns Cres. CH1: Blac 6E 144
Cairo St. WA1: Warr 7F 41
Caister Cl. M41: Urm 2F 21
Caister Way CW7: Wins 5D 178
Caistor St. SK1: Stoc 1F 53
Caithness Cl. M23: Wyth 1G 75
Caithness Ct. WA7: Run 4H 89
Caithness Dr. CH45: Wall 5J 13
Caithness Gdns. CH43: Pren 4J 59
CaJoBaH Gallery 5E 34
Calamanco Way M44: Irlam 3D 20
Calamine St. SK11: Mac 6B 126
Calcot Wlk. M23: Wyth 6F 49
Calcutta Rd. SK3: Stoc 5A 52
Calday Grange Cl. CH48: W Kir 4E 56
Calday Swimming Pool 4E 56
Caldbeck Av. M33: Sale 6K 23
WA2: Warr 2H 41
Caldbeck Rd. CH62: Brom 4D 86
Calder Av. CH43: Pren 3K 59
CW1: Crewe 1G 195
M22: N'den 4K 49
M44: Irlam 2C 20
Calderbeck Way M22: Shar 6A 50
Calderbrook Ct. SK8: Chea H 1K 77
Calderbrook Dr. SK8: Chea H 1J 77
Calder Cl. SK5: Stoc 6K 25
SK10: Boll 3C 122
SK12: Poy 4C 100
WA8: Wid 2B 64
Calder Dr. L35: R'ill 1B 36
Calderfield Cl. WA4: Stoc H 5F 67
Calder Rd. CH63: H Beb 1H 85
Caldervale Av. M21: Chor H 1J 49
Calder Way CH66: Gt Sut 3J 133
Caldey Rd. M23: Wyth 7E 48
Caldicott Av. CH62: Brom 7D 86
Caldicott Cl. CW7: Wins 5D 178
Caldwell Av. WA5: Warr 2D 40
Caldwell Cl. CW5: Stap 3F 197
Caldwell Dr. CH49: Woodc 3E 58
Caldwell Rd. WA8: Wid 6G 63
Caldwell St. SK5: Stoc 2J 25
CALDY 6E 56 (2A 214)
Caldy Chase Dr. CH48: Cald 6E 56
Caldy Cl. CH2: Ches 5A 146
Caldy Ct. CH48: W Kir 4C 56
Caldy Dr. CH66: Gt Sut 4K 133
Caldy Pk. CH48: W Kir 5D 56
Caldy Rd. CH45: Wall 6H 13
CH48: Cald, W Kir 4C 56
SK9: Hand 3A 98
ST7: Als 5D 202
Caldy Valley Rd.
CH3: Hunt, Gt Bou 5D 150
Caldy Way CW7: Wins 3C 178
Caldy Wood CH48: Cald 6E 56
Caledonia St. L7: Liv 4K 35
CALE GREEN 6D 52
Cale Grn. SK2: Stoc 6D 52
Cale Grn. Ct. SK2: Stoc 6D 52
Cale St. SK2: Stoc 5D 52
Calgarth Av. WA5: Warr 4E 40
Calico Cres. SK15: Carrb 3G 5
California Cl. WA5: Gt San 4A 40
Calland Av. SK14: Hyde 7A 10
CALLANDS 2B 40
Callands Rd. WA5: Call 2A 40
Callender Gdns. WA6: Hel 6A 138
Callington Cl. SK14: Hat 1F 29
Callington Dr. SK14: Hat 1F 29
Callington Wlk. SK14: Hat 1F 29
(off Callington Dr.)
Calmington La. WA7: Nort 2H 91
Calne Cl. CH61: Irby 6A 58
Calne Wlk. M23: Wyth 7G 49
CALROFOLD 2F 127
Calrofold La. SK11: Mac 3F 127
Calstock Cl. WA5: Penk 2G 65
Calthorpe Way CH43: Noc 6G 33
Calvary Ct. SK3: Stoc 4B 52
Calve Cft. Rd. M22: Wyth 3A 76
CALVELEY 4K 189 (2D 219)
Calveley Av. CH62: East 3A 108
Calveley Cl. CH43: Oxt 2H 59
CW9: N'ich 1D 162
Calveley Hall La. CW6: Calv 2K 189
Calveley Rd. SK10: Mac 3G 125
Calveley Way CW7: Wins 3C 178
(off Abbotts Way)
Calver Cl. M41: Urm 1G 21
CALVERHALL 3A 220
Calverley Av. M19: Manc 4C 24
Calverley Cl. SK9: Wilm 6K 97
WA7: B'vale 2E 112
Calverley Rd. SK8: Chea 7J 51
Calver Pk. Rd. WA2: Winw 1D 40
Calver Rd. WA2: Winw 7J 15
Calvers WA7: Halt 5A 90
Calver Wlk. M34: Den 3F 27
SK8: Chea H 4G 77
Camberley Cl. SK7: Bram 6E 78
Camberwell Pk. Rd. WA8: Wid 1K 63
Camborne Av. SK10: Mac 4F 125
Camborne Cl. CW12: Cong 6G 183
WA7: B'vale 1E 112
Camborne Rd. WA5: B'ood 5C 14
Cambourne Rd. SK14: Hat 7F 11
Cambo Wlk. SK4: Stoc 1H 51
Cambrai Av. WA4: Warr 3G 67
Cambrian Av. CH3: Ches 1E 150
Cambrian Cl. CH46: More 5J 31
(off Cambrian Rd.)
CH66: L Sut 2G 133
Cambrian Ct. CH1: Ches 1J 149
Cambrian Rd. CH1: Ches 2A 212 (1J 149)
CH46: More 5K 31
SK3: Stoc 4A 52
Cambrian Vw. CH1: Ches 7J 145
(off Whipcord La.)
Cambrian Way CW7: Wins 4C 178
Cambridge Av. CW7: Wins 3B 178
SK9: Wilm 7G 97
SK11: Mac 5J 125
Cambridge Cl. M33: Sale 1H 47
WA4: Stoc H 5F 67
Cambridge Ct. CH65: Ell P 3E 134
(off Cambridge Rd.)
Cambridge Dr. SK6: W'ley 6H 27
Cambridge Gdns. WA4: App 7G 67
WA6: Hel 4D 138
Cambridge Rd. CH2: Ches 5C 146
CH42: Tran 3A 60
CH45: N Bri 4H 13
CH62: Brom 6E 86
CH65: Ell P 3E 134
M41: Urm 2A 22
SK4: Stoc 6F 25
SK8: Gat 6D 50
SK11: Mac 6J 125
WA15: Hale 3J 73
Cambridge St. OL7: Ash L 1E 8
SK2: Stoc 6E 52
SK15: Stal 7B 4
SK16: Duk 1H 9
WA7: Run 4J 89
WA8: Wid 6H 63
Cambridge Ter. SK2: Stoc 6E 52
(off Russell St.)
SK15: M'ook 5E 4
Camden Cl. CH49: Woodc 1E 58
Camden Ct. WA7: Nort 5F 91
Camden Pl. CH41: Birk 6D 34
Camden Rd. CH65: Ell P 3C 134
Camden St. CW1: Crewe 2D 194
(off Earle St.)
L3: Liv 2K 35
Camelot Gro. CW2: Shav 3C 198
Camelot Way WA7: Cast 6C 90
Cameron Av. CW2: Shav 4B 198
WA7: Run 6E 88
Cameron Ct. WA2: Winw 7K 15
Cameron Rd. CH46: Leas 1E 32
WA8: Wid 5G 63
Cammell Ct. CH43: Clau 6A 34
Camm St. CW2: Crewe 4D 194
Camomile La. CW8: Cudd 6K 153
Camomile Wlk. M31: Part 1H 45
(off Wychelm Rd.)
Campbell Av. WA7: Run 6G 89
Campbell Cl. CW1: Hasl 2J 195
CW9: N'ich 2E 162
CW12: Cong 2J 183
SK10: Mac 3H 125
Campbell Cres. WA5: Gt San 6H 39
Campbell Rd. M13: Manc 1C 24
M33: Sale 1K 47
Campbell Sq. L1: Liv 4J 35
(off Campbell St.)
Campbell St. L1: Liv 4J 35
SK5: Stoc 2J 25
Campbeltown Rd. CH41: Tran 1E 60
Campden Way SK9: Hand 2A 98
Camperdown St. CH41: Birk 6E 34
Campion Cl. CH3: Hunt 5D 150
WA3: Birc 7H 17
Campion Way M34: Den 3F 27
Camp Rd. WA5: Old H 3B 40
Campsey Ash WA8: Wid 1F 63
Campus Dr. WA7: Run 4E 88
Camrose Cl. WA7: Run 1J 111
Camsley La. WA13: Lymm 2G 69
Canaan WA3: Low 2C 6
WN7: Low 2C 6
Canada Blvd. L3: Liv 3G 35
Canada Cl. WA2: Fear 2A 42
Canada St. SK2: Stoc 6E 52
Canadian Av. CH2: Ches 6D 146
Canal Bank WA13: Lymm 2J 69
(Statham Av.)
WA13: Lymm 2B 70
(Thirlmere Dr.)
Canal Bri. Ent. Cen.
CH65: Ell P 2F 135
Canal Reach WA7: Win H 4E 90
Canal Rd. CW12: Cong 4G 183
WA14: Timp 5J 47
Canal Side
CH1: Ches 3D 212 (1A 150)
CW8: Barnt 3A 156
SK11: Mac 5C 126
WA4: Grap 4B 68
WA4: Moo 1A 92
WA7: Wes P 7D 88
Canalside CH65: Ell P 2F 135
SK15: Stal 1B 10
(off Melbourne St.)
Canalside Ind. Est.
CH65: Ell P 1G 135
Canal Side Wlk. OL7: Ash L 1G 9
Canal St. CH1: Ches 3A 212 (1K 149)
CW12: Cong 4G 183
M43: Droy 2A 8
SK1: Stoc 7K 213 (3D 52)
SK6: Mar 6G 55
SK10: Mac 5B 126
SK14: Hyde 7H 9
SK15: Stal 1B 10
WA7: Run 4H 89
WA12: New W 1C 14
Canal Ter. CW10: Mid 4D 180
Canal Vw. SK15: Stal 7C 4
(off Bk. Knowl St.)
WA13: Lymm 2K 69
Canal Wharf SK4: Stoc 1C 52
Canberra Av. WA2: Warr 1H 41
(off Canberra Sq.)
Canberra Rd. SK7: Bram 1H 99
Canberra Sq. WA2: Warr 2H 41
Canberra Way CH1: Blac 6E 144
Candelan Way WA16: H Leg 2H 95
Candleford Pl. SK2: Stoc 1J 79
Candleston Cl. WA5: Call 3C 40
Candy La. SK10: Adl 6B 100
Canford Cl. CW1: Crewe 5G 191
WA5: Gt San 6A 40
CANHOLES 3D 217
Canley Cl. SK1: Stoc 4D 52
Cannell Ct. CH64: W'ston 7F 107
WA7: Pal F 1C 112
Cannell St. WA5: Warr 1B 66
Canning Pl. L1: Liv 4H 35
Canning St. CH1: Ches 3B 212 (1K 149)
CH41: Birk 5D 34
L8: Liv 4K 35
SK4: Stoc 2C 52
Cann La. Nth. WA4: App 1J 93
Cann La. Sth. WA4: App 2J 93
Cannock Cl. CH66: Gt Sut 1A 140
Cannock Dr. SK4: Stoc 2J 51
Cannonbury Cl. WA7: Halt 6C 90
Cannon Hill CH43: Clau 6A 34
Cannon Mt. CH43: Clau 6A 34
Cannon St. CH65: Ell P 3C 134
SK14: H'rth 5K 11
WA9: Clo F 1J 37
Cannon Wlk. M34: Den 1D 26
Canon Dr. WA14: Bow 4F 73
Canons Rd. WA5: Gt San 6B 40
Canon St. WA7: Run 3G 89
Canterbury Cl. CH66: Gt Sut 1A 140
SK16: Duk 4J 9
Canterbury Grange SK9: Wilm 7J 97
Canterbury Pk. M20: Manc 1B 50
Canterbury Rd. CH1: Blac 5G 145
CH42: R Fer 4F 61
CH44: Wall 1B 34
SK1: Stoc 3F 53
WA8: Wid 6C 62
WA15: Hale 2C 74
Canterbury St. L3: Liv 1K 35
WA4: Warr 1G 67
Canterbury Way L3: Liv 1K 35
Cantley Cl. WA7: Beec 1K 111
Canton Pl. CW8: N'ich 6C 156
Canton St. SK11: Mac 6A 126
Canton Walks SK11: Mac 6A 126
Canute Pl. WA16: Knut 3E 116
Canute Sq. WA16: Knut 3E 116
(off Canute Pl.)
Capeland Cl. CH4: Salt 6F 149
Capel Way CW5: Nant 1B 196
CAPENHURST 7H 133 (3B 214)
Capenhurst Av. CW2: Crewe 3K 193
WA2: Fear 2A 42
Capenhurst Cl. M23: Wyth 1F 75
SK12: Poy 2E 100
Capenhurst Gdns. CH66: Gt Sut 7K 133
Capenhurst La. CH1: Cap 7H 133
CH65: Whit 5B 134
CH66: Gt Sut 7H 133
Capenhurst Station (Rail) 7J 133
Capenhurst Technology Pk.
CH1: Cap 7H 133
Capesthorne Cl. CW4: H Cha 4H 181
CW9: N'ich 2E 162
CW11: S'ach 2G 201
SK7: H Gro 5K 79
ST7: Als 6D 202
WA8: Wid 5E 62

Capesthorne Rd.—Cavendish Cl.

Capesthorne Rd. CH3: Chri 2A **174**
CW2: Crewe 4J **193**
SK6: H Lan 6E **80**
SK7: H Gro 5K **79**
SK9: Wilm 2D **118**
SK16: Duk 4J **9**
WA2: Warr 3H **41**
WA15: Timp 6D **48**
Capesthorne Wlk. M34: Den 1D **26**
Capesthorne Way SK11: Mac 5C **126**
Capital Ga. L3: Liv 2K **35**
Capitol Wlk. *CW12: Cong 4F 183*
(off High St.)
Capstone Dr. SK6: Mar 6E **54**
Captain Charles Jones Wlk.
CH44: Wall 6K 13
(off Webster Av.)
Captain Clarke Rd. SK14: Hyde 5G **9**
Capton Cl. SK7: Bram 3E **78**
Carberry Ct. SK8: Chea H 3J **77**
Carden Av. CW7: Wins 3C **178**
M41: Urm 1H **21**
Cardenbrook Gro. *SK9: Wilm 4A 98*
(off Rookerypool Cl.)
Carden Cl. WA3: Birc 7J **17**
Cardeston Cl. WA7: Sut W 4B **112**
Cardew Av. M22: Wyth 1B **76**
Cardiff Cl. CH66: Gt Sut 1A **140**
Cardiff Wlk. M34: Den 2E **26**
Cardigan Av. CH41: Birk 6C **34**
Cardigan Cl. SK11: Mac 4H **125**
WA5: Call 2B **40**
Cardigan Rd. CH45: N Bri 4H **13**
Cardus Cl. CH46: More 4J **31**
Cardus St. M19: Manc 2D **24**
Caremine Av. M19: Manc 1E **24**
Carey Av. CH63: H Beb 7C **60**
Carey St. WA8: Wid 4H **63**
Cargill Gro. CH42: R Fer 5G **61**
Carham Rd. CH47: Hoy 6D **30**
Carill Dr. M14: Manc 3A **24**
Carina Pk. WA5: W'ook 2K **39**
Carisbrook Av. M41: Urm 2B **22**
SK10: Mac 2B **126**
Carisbrook Dr. CW7: Wins 5D **178**
Carisbrooke Av. SK7: H Gro 4H **79**
Carisbrooke Cl. CH48: Cald 5D **56**
CW2: Wis 6J **193**
Carlaw Rd. CH42: Tran 3K **59**
Carleton Rd. SK12: Poy 2H **101**
Carlett Blvd. CH62: East 2A **108**
Carlett Pk. CH62: East 1A **108**
Carlin Ga. WA15: Timp 6A **48**
Carling Dr. M22: Wyth 3A **76**
Carlingford Cl. SK3: Stoc 7C **52**
Carlingford Rd. WA4: Stoc H 5F **67**
Carlisle Cl. CW7: Wins 3B **178**
SK6: Rom 3A **54**
SK11: Mac 7G **125**
WA16: Mob 6B **102**
Carlisle Dr. M44: Irlam 1D **20**
WA14: Timp 4J **47**
Carlisle M. CH43: Oxt 7B **34**
Carlisle Rd. CH1: Blac 5F **145**
Carlisle St. CW2: Crewe 4B **194**
SK3: Stoc 4C **52**
SK9: Ald E 6F **119**
WA4: Stoc H 5G **67**
Carlisle Way M34: Den 2E **26**
Carloon Rd. M23: Wyth 3H **49**
Carlow Cl. L24: Hale 6A **88**
Carlow Dr. M22: Wyth 3A **76**
Carlton Av. CH4: Salt 5E **148**
SK6: Rom 1D **54**
SK7: Bram 1G **99**
SK8: Chea H 2H **77**
SK9: Wilm 4K **97**
WA7: Run 4K **89**
Carlton Cl. CH2: Mic T 2H **147**
CH64: Park 5F **105**
Carlton Ct. WA15: Hale 4B **74**
Carlton Cres. CH66: Ell P 7G **109**
M41: Urm 2C **22**
SK1: Stoc 2E **52**
Carlton Dr. SK8: Gat 6C **50**
Carlton La. CH47: Meols 4D **30**
Carlton Mt. CH42: Tran 2D **60**
Carlton Pl. CH2: Ches 6D **146**
SK7: H Gro 4A **80**
Carlton Rd. CH42: Tran 1B **60**
CH45: N Bri 3H **13**
CH63: Beb 2B **86**
CW9: N'ich 6F **157**
M33: Sale 5F **23**
M41: Urm 2B **22**
SK4: Stoc 2J **51**
SK14: Hyde 7B **10**
WA13: Lymm 7D **44**
(not continuous)
WA15: Hale 4B **74**
Carlton St. L3: Liv 1G **35**
WA4: Stoc H 5G **67**
WA8: Wid 5G **63**
Carlton Ter. CH47: Meols 4D **30**
Carlton Way WA3: G'ook 6K **19**
Carlyle Cl. ST7: Rod H 1F **203**
Carlyle Cres. CH66: Gt Sut 4A **134**
Carlyn Av. M33: Sale 7J **23**
Carmarthen Cl. CW7: Wins 5D **178**
WA5: Call 2B **40**
Carmarthen Cres. L8: Liv 6J **35**
CARMEL 3A **214**
Carmel Cl. CH1: Blac 7E **144**
CH45: N Bri 3H **13**
WA5: Call 2C **40**
Carmel Ct. WA8: Wid 1H **63**
Carmenna Dr. SK7: Bram 6D **78**
Carmichael Av. CH49: Gre 3A **58**
Carmichael Cl. M31: Part 1G **45**
Carmichael St. SK3: Stoc 4B **52**
Carnaby Pl. WA5: Gt San 6K **39**
Carna Rd. SK5: Stoc 1H **25**
Carnarvon St. SK1: Stoc 4E **52**
Carnegie Av. M19: Manc 2E **24**
Carnegie Cl. M33: Sale 1H **47**
SK10: Mac 3G **125**
Carnforth Cl. CH41: Birk 7B **34**
Carnforth Dr. M33: Sale 1A **48**
Carnforth Rd. SK4: Stoc 5F **25**
SK8: Chea H 1A **78**
Carnoustie Cl. CH46: More 3J **31**
CW7: Wins 2B **178**
SK9: Wilm 6A **98**
Carnoustie Dr. SK8: He Grn 4E **76**
SK10: Mac 6K **121**
Carnsdale Rd. CH46: More 4C **32**
Carol Dr. CH60: Hes 6A **84**
Carolina Rd. WA5: Gt San 5K **39**
Caroline Ho. CH1: Blac 4F **145**
Caroline Pl. CH43: Oxt 7A **34**
Caroline St. M44: Irlam 3C **20**
SK3: Stoc 5B **52**
(not continuous)
SK15: Stal 1B **10**
WA8: Wid 6H **63**
Carol St. WA4: Warr 1H **67**
Carpenter Gro. WA2: Padg 3A **42**
Carpenters Ct. SK9: Ald E 6F **119**
Carpenter's La. CH48: W Kir 3C **56**
Carpenters Row L1: Liv 4J **35**
CARR 2G **5**
Carradale Dr. M33: Sale 6B **22**
Carr Bri. Rd. CH49: Woodc 1E **58**
CARRBROOK 3G **5**
Carrbrook Cl. SK15: Carrb 3F **5**
Carrbrook Cres. SK15: Carrb 3F **5**
Carrbrook Rd. SK15: Carrb 2G **5**
(not continuous)
Carr Brow SK6: H Lan 6G **81**
Carr Cl. SK1: Stoc 4F **53**
Carrfield SK14: Hyde 6J **9**
Carrfield Av. SK3: Stoc 1E **78**
WA15: Timp 6D **48**
Carr Ga. CH46: More 5J **31**
Carrgate Rd. M34: Den 2G **27**
CARR GREEN 6H **45**
Carrgreen Cl. M19: Manc 6C **24**
Carrgreen La. WA13: Warb 6G **45**
Carr Hey CH46: More 5J **31**
Carr Hey Cl. CH49: Woodc 3F **59**
Carr Ho. La. CH46: More 4J **31**
Carrhouse La.
SK14: Gam, H'rth 6K **11**
(not continuous)
Carriage Cl. L24: Hale 7A **88**
Carriage Dr. CW8: H'ord 1B **162**
WA6: Frod 2G **139**
Carriage Dr., The SK13: Had 3K **11**
Carriages, The WA14: Alt 2F **213** (1G **73**)
Carrick Dr. CH65: Whit 6D **134**
Carrick Gdns. M22: Wyth 1K **75**
Carrick Rd. CH4: Ches 3H **149**
Carrill Gro. M19: Manc 2D **24**
Carrill Gro. E. M19: Manc 2D **24**
CARRINGTON 5H **21** (1B **216**)
Carrington Barn SK6: Mar 4F **81**
Carrington Bus. Pk. M31: Carri 5F **21**
Carrington Cl. WA3: Birc 7H **17**
Carrington Fld. St. SK1: Stoc 5D **52**
Carrington La. M31: Carri 4J **21**
M33: Sale 4J **21**
Carrington Rd. CH45: Wall 5J **13**
M41: Urm 3H **21**
SK1: Stoc 1E **52**
Carrington Spur M33: Sale 5B **22**
M41: Urm 5B **22**
Carrington St. CH41: Birk 4K **33**
Carrington Way CW1: Crewe 5G **191**
Carr La. CH46: More 3H **31**
CH47: Hoy 6C **30**
CH47: Meols 3G **31**
CH48: W Kir 7E **30**
L24: Hale 6A **88**
SK9: Ald E 4C **118**
SK15: Carrb 2G **5**
WA3: Low 3A **6**
WN7: Leigh 2E **6**
Carr La. Ind. Est. CH47: Hoy 6D **30**
Carr Mill M. SK9: Wilm 5J **97**
Carrock Rd. CH62: Brom 4E **86**
Carroll Dr. CW2: Wis 6K **193**
Carrow Cl. CH46: More 5J **31**
Carr Ri. SK15: Carrb 2G **5**
Carr Rd. M44: Irlam 1E **20**
WA15: Hale 3B **74**
Carrs Av. SK8: Chea 6J **51**
Carrs Ct. SK9: Wilm 7J **97**
Carrsfield Rd. M22: Shar 6A **50**
Carrs Rd. SK8: Chea 6H **51**
Carrsvale Av. M41: Urm 1A **22**
Carrswood Rd. M23: Wyth 4C **48**
Carruthers St. L3: Liv 1H **35**
Carrwood WA15: H'rns 6B **74**
WA16: Knut 5G **117**
Carr Wood Av. SK7: Bram 5C **78**
Carrwood Rd. SK7: Bram 4B **78**
SK9: Wilm 5G **97**
Carsdale Rd. M22: Wyth 5A **76**
Carsgoe Rd. CH47: Hoy 6D **30**
Carson Rd. M19: Manc 3D **24**
Carstairs Av. SK2: Stoc 1E **78**
Carsthorne Rd.
CH47: Hoy 6D **30**
Car St. CH1: Ches 2E **212** (1B **150**)
Carter Av. CW6: Kel 4C **172**
Carter Cl. CW5: Nant 1B **196**
M34: Den 1E **26**
Carter La. SK11: Chel 5C **166**
Carter Pl. SK14: Hyde 5J **9**
Carters, The CH49: Gre 1K **57**
Carter St. CH1: Ches 2E **212** (1B **150**)
OL5: Moss 1D **4**
SK14: Hyde 5J **9**
SK15: Stal 7C **4**
Carterton Rd. CH47: Hoy 6D **30**
Cartier Cl. WA5: Old H 4A **40**
Cartlake Cl. CW5: Nant 2A **196**
Cartledge Cl. CW8: Cudd 3D **160**
Cartmel Av. SK4: Stoc 5G **25**
WA2: Warr 1G **41**
Cartmel Cl. CH41: Birk 7B **34**
CW4: H Cha 4G **181**
CW7: Wins 2E **178**
SK7: H Gro 2G **79**
SK8: Gat 2E **76**
SK10: Mac 2J **125**
Cartmel Dr. CH46: More 5B **32**
CH66: Gt Sut 6B **134**
L35: R'ill 1A **36**
WA15: Timp 6D **48**
Cartmell Cl. WA7: Run 1H **111**
Cartridge Cl. M22: Wyth 2B **76**
Cartridge La. WA4: Grap 7D **68**
Cartwright Rd. CW1: Hasl 1K **195**
Cartwright St. M34: Aude 4E **8**
SK14: Hyde 5B **10**
WA5: Warr 6C **40**
WA7: Run 4J **89**
Carver Av. CW4: Cran 1G **181**
Carver Cl. CW7: Wins 1H **179**
Carver Dr. SK6: Mar 7E **54**
Carver Rd. SK6: Mar 7E **54**
WA15: Hale 3J **73**
Carver St. L3: Liv 1K **35**
Carver Theatre 7F **55**
Caryl Gro. L8: Liv 1K **61**
Caryl St. L8: Liv 7J **35**
(Atterbury St.)
L8: Liv 7K **35**
(Park St.)
L8: Liv 6J **35**
(Stanhope St.)
Casablanca Health and Fitness Cen. . . . *1B 10*
(off Armentieres Sq.)
Cases St. L1: Liv 3J **35**
Casey La. CW2: Bas, Chor, Shav 4F **199**
Cashel Rd. CH41: Birk 2A **34**
Cashmere Rd. SK3: Stoc 5A **52**
Caspian Rd. WA14: B'ath 6E **46**
Casson St. CW1: Crewe 1B **194**
Castle, The 7B **212** (3K **149**)
Castle Av. M34: Den 1D **26**
Castle Bank CW8: N'ich 6D **156**
Castlebridge Ct. *CH42: R Fer 4E 60*
(off Old Chester Rd.)
Castle Cliff *CW8: N'ich 6D 156*
(off Castle St.)
Castle Cl. CH4: Pul 7B **184**
CH46: Leas 1D **32**
CW6: Kel 4C **172**
M43: Droy 1A **8**
Castle Cotts. SK15: Carrb 1G **5**
Castle Ct. CH48: W Kir 4C **56**
CW8: N'ich 6D **156**
Castlecroft Rd. CH4: Ches 6J **149**
Castle Dr. CH1: Ches 7B **212** (3K **149**)
CH60: Hes 6H **83**
CH65: Whit 5C **134**
Castle Farm Dr. SK2: Stoc 7F **53**
Castle Farm La. SK2: Stoc 6F **53**
CASTLEFIELDS 4C **90**
Castlefields CH3: Tatt 2J **187**
CH46: Leas 1C **32**
Castlefields Av. E. WA7: Cast 5C **90**
Castlefields Av. Nth. WA7: Cast 4A **90**
Castlefields Av. Sth.
WA7: Cast 5B **90**
Castlefields Local Cen.
WA7: Cast 4C **90**
Castleford Dr. SK10: Pres 5E **120**
Castleford Ri. CH46: Leas 1B **32**
Castle Gdns. LL13: Holt 7B **186**
Castle Ga. LL13: Holt 7A **186**
Castlegate SK10: Pres 5F **121**
Castlegate M. SK10: Pres 5G **121**
Castlegrange Cl. CH46: Leas 1B **32**
Castle Grn. WA5: W'ook 2K **39**
CASTLE HALL 1C **10**
Castle Hall Cl. SK15: Stal 1C **10**
Castle Hall Ct. SK15: Stal 1B **10**
Castle Hall Vw. SK15: Stal 1B **10**
Castleheath Cl. CH46: Leas 1B **32**
CASTLE HILL
SK6 . . . . . 4D **26**
WA14 . . . . . 5D **72**
WA15 . . . . . 2A **96**
Castle Hill CH4: Pul 7A **184**
L2: Liv 3H 35
(off Lwr. Castle St.)
SK6: Bred 4D **26**
SK10: Pres 4F **121**
Castle Hill Ct. SK10: Pres 4F **121**
Castlehill Ind. Pk. SK6: Bred 6E **26**
Castle Hill Pk. SK6: W'ley 5E **26**
Castle La. OL5: Moss, Stal 1F **5**
SK15: Carrb, Moss 1F **5**
Castlemead Wlk. CW9: N'ich 2D **162**
Castlemere Dr. CW1: Crewe 6H **191**
Castle M. LL13: Holt 7B **186**
Castle Mill La. WA15: Ash 7K **73**
Castle Pk. 1G **139**
Castle Pk. Arts Cen. 7G **111**
Castle Pl. CH1: Ches 6C **212** (3A **150**)
Castlerigg Cl. SK4: Stoc 4G **25**
Castle Ri. SK10: Pres 5G **121**
WA7: Run 4K **89**
Castle Rd. CH45: Wall 5G **13**
ST7: Mow C 5H **205**
WA7: Halt 6B **90**
Castle Shaw Rd. SK2: Stoc 7H **53**
Castle St. CH1: Ches 6B **212** (3K **149**)
CH41: Birk 6E **34**
CW1: Crewe 2C **194**
CW5: Nant 2C **196**
CW8: N'ich 5D **156**
L2: Liv 3H **35**
LL13: Holt 7A **186**
SK3: Stoc 5B **52**
SK11: Mac 4A **126**
SK14: Hyde 7A **10**
SK15: Stal 1B **10**
WA8: Wid 4K **63**
Castle St. Mall *SK11: Mac 4A 126*
(off Grosvenor Cen.)
Castle Ter. SK15: Carrb 2G **5**
Castleton Ct. M34: Den 3F **27**
Castleton Dr. SK6: H Lan 7F **81**
Castleton Gro. OL6: Ash L 3A **4**
Castleton Rd. SK7: H Gro 4J **79**
Castleton St. WA14: B'ath 5G **47**
Castleton Way M34: Den 3F **27**
Castletown Cl. SK10: Mac 7K **121**
Castle Wlk. *SK15: Stal 1B 10*
(off Crossfield Cl.)
Castle Way CH4: Dod 4D **184**
Castleway WA15: H'rns 6C **74**
Castleway Nth. CH46: Leas 7A **12**
Castleway Sth. CH46: Leas 1D **32**
Castlewood Gdns. SK2: Stoc 7G **53**
Castle Yd. SK1: Stoc 5J **213**
Castner Av. WA7: Wes P 7E **88**
Catalan Cl. CW7: Wins 3H **179**
Catalyst 1G **89**
Catalyst Trade Pk. WA8: Wid 7G **63**
Catchpenny La. SK11: L Wit 4J **167**
Catford Cl. WA8: Wid 3C **62**
Catford Rd. M23: Wyth 7F **49**
Catfoss Cl. WA2: Padg 3J **41**
Catharine St. L8: Liv 4K **35**
Cathcart Grn. *CH3: Guil S 5J 147*
(off Oaklands)
Cathcart St. CH41: Birk 5C **34**
Cathedral Cl. L1: Liv 5K **35**
SK16: Duk 4J **9**
Cathedral Ct. *L1: Liv 5K 35*
(off Gambier Ter.)
Cathedral Ga. L1: Liv 4K **35**
Cathedral Wlk. L3: Liv 3K **35**
Catherine Ho. SK4: Stoc 2H **51**
Catherine Rd. SK6: Rom 3K **53**
WA14: Bow 2G **73**
Catherine St. CH1: Ches 3A **212** (1J **149**)
CH41: Birk 6C **34**
CW2: Crewe 4D **194**
SK7: H Gro 1J **79**
SK11: Mac 4K **125**
SK14: Hyde 7J **9**
WA5: Warr 5D **40**
(not continuous)
WA8: Wid 6G **63**
Catherine St. E. M34: Den 7C **8**
Catherine St. W. M34: Den 7C **8**
Catherine Way
WA12: New W 1E **14**
Catterall Av. WA2: Warr 2H **41**
Catterick Av. M20: Manc 1E **50**
M33: Sale 2G **47**
Catterick Rd. M20: Manc 1E **50**
Catterwood Dr. SK6: Comp 2H **55**
Catterwood Rd. SK6: Comp 2H **55**
Caughall Rd. CH2: Cau 6G **141**
CH2: Upt 2B **146**
Caulfield Dr. CH49: Gre 2B **58**
Caunce Av. WA12: New W 2F **15**
Causeway, The
CH62: P Sun 1B **86**
WA14: Alt 2J **213** (1H **73**)
Causeway Av. WA4: Warr 2G **67**
Causeway Cl. CH62: P Sun 7G **61**
Causeway Ho. CH46: Leas 1B **32**
Causeway Pk. WA4: Warr 2G **67**
Cavalier Dr. CH1: Blac 4F **145**
Cavan Cl. SK3: Stoc 5H **51**
Cavell Dr. CH65: Whit 4C **134**
Cavendish Av. WA3: Ris 6K **17**
Cavendish Cl. CW7: Wins 4B **178**
SK10: Mac 1K **125**
WA5: Old H 5B **40**

Clifton Av.—Congleton Retail Pk.

Clifton Av. CH62: East 4K 107
CW2: Crewe 3B 194
M14: Manc 3A 24
SK8: He Grn 3C 76
WA3: Cul 7D 6
WA15: Alt 7J 47
Clifton Cl. WA1: Wool 5D 42
Clifton Ct. CH41: Birk 7C 34
SK4: Stoc 7D 24
WA7: Run 1H 111
Clifton Cres. CH41: Birk 6D 34
WA6: Frod 6J 111
Clifton Dr. CH1: Blac, Ches 7F 145
CW9: N'ich 1F 163
SK6: Mar 5E 54
SK8: Gat 7B 50
SK8: He Grn 3C 76
SK9: Wilm 3D 118
Clifton Gdns. CH65: Ell P 5E 134
Clifton Ga. *CH41: Birk 7D 34*
(off Clifton Rd.)
Clifton Gro. CH44: Wall 7K 13
L5: Liv 1K 35
Clifton La. WA7: Clif 3K 111
(not continuous)
Clifton Lodge SK2: Stoc 7E 52
CLIFTON PARK 7C 34
Clifton Pk. Rd. SK2: Stoc 7E 52
Clifton Rd. CH41: Birk 7C 34
CW11: Elw 2B 200
M33: Sale 1B 48
M41: Urm 1K 21
SK4: Stoc 1J 51
WA7: Run 7G 89
WA7: Sut W 4A 112
WN7: Leigh 1E 6
Clifton St. CW2: Crewe 3B 194
SK9: Ald E 6F 119
WA4: Warr 1G 67
Clifton Vs. CH1: Bac 1C 140
Cliftonville Rd. WA1: Wool 5C 42
Climax Works SK5: Stoc 1H 25
Clincton Cl. WA8: Wid 5A 62
Clincton Vw. WA8: Wid 5A 62
Clipper Vw. CH62: N Fer 5H 61
Cliston Wlk. SK7: H Gro 3E 78
Clitheroe Rd. CW8: Weav 4G 155
M13: Manc 1C 24
CLIVE 4K 179
Clive Av. WA2: Warr 3G 41
Clive Bk. La. CW7: Wins 5K 179
Cliveden Rd. CH4: Ches 7G 149
CLIVE GREEN 5K 179
Clivegreen La. CW7: Wins 4K 179
CW10: Stan 6A 180
Clive La. CW7: Wins 4K 179
Clive Lloyd Ct. M32: S'ord 1K 23
Clive Rd. CH43: Oxt 1B 60
CLOCK FACE 1K 37 (1D 215)
Clock Face Colliery Country Pk. 1B 38
Clock Face Rd. WA8: Bold H, Clo F 1K 37
WA9: Clo F 1K 37
Clock La. WA5: Cuer 2B 64
Clocktower, The *WA4: Warr 3G 67*
(off Elphins Dr.)
Clock Twr. Cl. SK14: Hyde 2K 27
Cloister Cl. SK16: Duk 4H 9
Cloister Rd. SK4: Stoc 2F 51
Cloisters, The M33: Sale 7J 23
SK8: Chea 7J 51
Cloister Way CH65: Ell P 3G 135
Clonners Fld. CW5: Stap 3D 196
Close, The CH1: Sau 1B 144
CH49: Gre 3A 58
CH61: Irby 7A 58
CH63: H Beb 4C 60
CW6: Tarp 2H 175
CW8: N'ich 7C 156
M34: Den 6C 8
SK6: Mar B 3H 55
SK15: Stal 5A 4
(not continuous)
ST7: Als 6B 202
WA12: New W 2H 15
WA14: Alt 1F 213 (7G 47)
Closeburn Av. CH60: Hes 1B 104
Close La. ST7: Als 4A 202
ST7: Mow C 5H 205
Clothorn Rd. M20: Manc 1D 50
CLOTTON 7E 174 (1D 219)
CLOTTON COMMON 6E 174
Cloudberry Wlk. M31: Part 1H 45
Cloud Vw. CW12: Cong 4J 183
Clough, The SK5: Stoc 5A 26
WA7: Halt 5B 90
Clough Av. M33: Sale 3H 47
SK6: Mar B 6J 55
SK9: Wilm 4J 97
WA2: Warr 2F 41
Clough Bank SK10: Boll 4C 122
Clough Ct. CW5: Nant 2A 196
Clough End Rd. SK14: Hat 2F 29
Clough Fold Rd. SK14: Hyde 2H 27
Clough Ga. SK14: Hyde 3K 27
Clough La. CW8: N'ich 7C 156
Clough Mdw. SK6: W'ley 6H 27
Clough Rd. CW7: Wins 3F 179
Cloughside SK6: Mar B 5J 55
SK12: Dis 1H 103
Clough Wlk. CW2: Crewe 6D 194
SK5: Stoc 5A 26
Clovelly Av. WA5: Gt San 5G 39
Clovelly Ct. CH49: Gre 2A 58
Clovelly Gro. WA7: B'vale 2D 112
Clovelly Rd. SK2: Stoc 4G 53
Clover Av. SK3: Stoc 7B 52
WA6: Frod 1K 139
Cloverbank Av. M19: Manc 7A 24
Clover Birches CH65: Ell P 2C 134
Clover Ct. WA7: B'vale 2D 112
Clover Cft. M33: Sale 3D 48
Cloverdale CW8: N'ich 6B 156
Cloverdale Rd. SK11: Mac 7H 125
Clover Dr. CH41: Birk 3H 33
CW7: Wins 1E 178
WA16: Pick 1B 158
Cloverfield WA7: Nort 7E 90
WA13: Lymm 1B 70
Cloverfield Gdns. CH66: L Sut 1K 133
Cloverfields CW1: Hasl 2H 195
Clover La. CH4: Ches 6G 149
Cloverley M33: Sale 2B 48
Cloverley Dr. WA15: Timp 1A 74
Clover Pl. CH4: Ches 6G 149
Clover Rd. SK6: Rom 1E 54
WA15: Timp 7A 48
Clowes Av. ST7: Als 6G 203
Clowes St. SK11: Mac 5J 125
(not continuous)
CLOY 3B 218
Club Theatre 4J 213 (2H 73)
Clumber Cl. SK12: Poy 3D 100
Clumber Rd. SK12: Poy 3D 100
Clutha Rd. SK3: Stoc 1D 78
CLUTTON 2B 206 (2C 219)
Clwyd Av. SK3: Stoc 5B 52
Clwyd St. CH41: Birk 6C 34
CH45: N Bri 4G 13
Clwyd Way CH66: L Sut 2G 133
Clyde Cres. CW7: Wins 3J 179
Clyde Gro. CW2: Crewe 3A 194
Clyde Rd. M20: Manc 1B 50
SK3: Stoc 5A 52
Clydesdale CH65: Whit 5D 134
Clydesdale Av. CW2: Crewe 3B 194
Clydesdale Rd. CH44: Wall 6K 13
CH47: Hoy 4C 30
WA4: App 5H 67
Clyde St. CH42: R Fer 3E 60
OL7: Ash L 2E 8
Clysbarton Ct. SK7: Bram 4B 78
Coach Rd. CH3: Brox 1E 206
CW6: L Bud 4D 176 & 1F 177
SK14: H'rth 5H 11
Coachway SK10: Pres 4H 121
Coadys Way WA8: Wid 3J 63
Coalbrookdale Rd. CH64: Nest 5J 105
Coalpit La. CH1: Dun, Lea B, Mol 4A 140
CW10: Stan 5A 180
SK11: Lang 1H 169
Coalport Dr. CW7: Wins 1G 179
Coal St. L3: Liv 2K 35
Coare St. SK10: Mac 3K 125
Coastal Dr. CH45: Wall 3D 12
(not continuous)
Coastal Point *CH46: Leas 1B 32*
(off Leasowe Rd.)
Coastguard La. CH64: Park 6E 104
Cobal Ct. SK2: Stoc 7E 52
WA6: Frod 7H 111
Cobbett's Way SK9: Wilm 3E 118
Cobblers Cross La. CW6: Tarp 1K 175
Cobbles, The CH4: Ches 4A 150
CW8: Cudd 2A 160
WA16: Lwr P 1C 164
COBBS 5H 67
Cobbs La. CW2: Hou 7E 198
CW5: Nant 6C 192
CW5: Wyb 7E 198
WA4: App 5J 67
Cobden Av. CH42: Tran 2E 60
Cobden Ct. CH42: Tran 2E 60
Cobden Pl. CH42: Tran 2E 60
Cobden St. WA2: Warr 5F 41
Cob Hall La. WA6: Manl 1F 171
Cob Hall Rd. M32: S'ord 2H 23
Cobham Rd. CH46: More 4A 32
Cobmoor Rd. ST7: Kids 3K 205
Coburg St. CH41: Birk 6C 34
Coburg Wharf L3: Liv 6H 35
COCK BANK 3B 218
Cock Brow SK14: Hyde 4D 28
Cockburn St. L8: Liv 1K 61
COCKER HILL 7B 4
Cocker Hill SK15: Stal 7B 4
Cockers La. SK15: Stal 2E 10
Cock Hall La. SK11: Lang, Sut E 2H 169
Cockhedge Grn. WA1: Warr 6G 41
WA2: Warr 6G 41
Cockhedge La. WA1: Warr 7F 41
Cockhedge Shop. Pk. WA1: Warr 7F 41
Cockhedge Way WA1: Warr 7F 41
Cockington Cl. CW9: N'ich 2F 163
Cocklade La. L24: Hale 7A 88
Cock La. CW5: B'hall 5K 209
CW9: Gt Bud 5F 115
Cock La. Ends WA8: Hal B 2B 88
Cockpit La. CW8: S'way 4E 160
Cocksfoot Dr. OL5: Moss 1F 5
Cocksheadhey Rd. SK10: Boll 2F 123
Cockshuts CW12: Cong 4F 183
Cocksmoss La. SK11: Mart 7D 168
Cockspur St. L3: Liv 2H 35
Cockspur St. W. L3: Liv 2H 35
COCKYARD 3D 217
Cocoa Yd. *CW5: Nant 2C 196*
(off Hospital St.)
CODDINGTON 2C 219
COEDPOETH 2A 218
Coe La. WA14: M'ton 6A 72
Cogshall La. CW9: And 1A 156
CW9: Comb, L Lei 3F 115
Cokers, The CH42: R Fer 5D 60
Colborne Av. SK5: Stoc 1J 25
SK6: Rom 2C 54
Colbourne Gro. SK14: Hat 7F 11
Colbourne Way SK14: Hat 7F 11
Colchester Cl. M23: Wyth 3E 48
Colchester Pl. SK4: Stoc 1K 51
Colchester Sq. CH4: Ches 6G 149
Coldfield Dr. M23: Wyth 6F 49
Coldmoss Dr. CW11: S'ach 5G 201
COLD MOSS HEATH 4G 201
Coldstream Cl. WA2: Warr 7D 16
Coldstream Dr. CH66: L Sut 3F 133
Colebrooke Cl. WA3: Birc 7B 18
Colebrook Rd. WA15: Timp 6A 48
Coleby Av. M22: Wyth 4B 76
Coleclough Pl. WA3: Cul 6F 7
Colehill Bank CW12: Cong 4G 183
Coleman Dr. CH49: Gre 2J 57
Colemere Cl. WA1: Padg 3A 42
Colemere Ct. CH65: Ell P 1D 134
Colemere Dr. CH61: Thin 7E 58
Colemore Av. M20: Manc 1F 51
Colenso Gro. SK4: Stoc 1K 51
Coleport Cl. SK8: Chea H 4J 77
Coleridge Cl. CH1: Blac 5H 145
CW11: Ett H 4A 200
SK5: Stoc 2H 25
Coleridge Dr. CH62: N Fer 6F 61
Coleridge Gro. WA8: Wid 4E 62
Coleridge Rd. SK5: Stoc 2H 25
Coleridge Way CW1: Crewe 1F 195
SK5: Stoc 2H 25
Cole St. CH43: Oxt 6B 34
Colin Rd. SK4: Stoc 7H 25
Coliseum Shop. & Leisure Pk.
CH65: Ell P 6F 135
Coliseum Way CH65: Ell P 7F 135
Collar Ho. Dr. SK10: Pres 5F 121
College Cl. CH43: Bid 6E 32
CH45: Wall 5E 12
SK2: Stoc 6E 52
SK9: Wilm 6G 97
WA1: Warr 7H 41
WA2: Fear 1B 42
College Ct. SK4: Stoc 1J 51
College Dr. CH63: Beb 6F 61
College Flds. CW2: Crewe 5A 194
WA8: Wid 7F 37
College Grn. CH4: Ches 4A 150
College Ho. SK4: Stoc 7E 24
WA14: Bow 4G 73
College La. CW6: Bun 4D 188
L1: Liv 3J 35
College Pl. WA2: Padg 2C 42
College Rd. ST7: Als 4C 202
Collegiate Rd. WA2: Warr 3F 41
Colley La. CW11: Bet H 4J 201
CW11: Blet, S'ach 4H 201
Colleys La. CW5: W'ston 6E 192
Collier Cl. SK14: Hat 2F 29
Collier's Row WA7: West 7E 88
Collier St. WA7: Run 3F 89
Collier Wlk. SK14: Hat 2F 29
Colliery Grn. Cl. CH64: L Nes 3C 130
Colliery Grn. Ct. CH64: L Nes 3C 130
Colliery Grn. Dr. CH64: L Nes 3C 130
Collinbrook Av. CW2: Crewe 5B 194
Colling Cl. M44: Irlam 2D 20
Collingham Grn. CH66: L Sut 3H 133
Collingham Rd. WA14: W Tim 3G 47
Collingham Way CW7: Wins 3E 178
Collingtree Av. CW7: Wins 1G 179
Collingwood Cl. SK10: Mac 2J 125
SK12: Poy 3F 101
Collingwood Rd. CH63: Beb 2B 86
M19: Manc 2C 24
Collin Rd. CH43: Bid 4H 33
COLLINS GREEN 2A 14 (1D 215)
Collins Grn. La. WA5: Col G 2B 14
Collinson Ct. WA6: Frod 7H 111
Collins St. CW2: Crewe 3A 194
Collin St. WA5: Warr 7C 40
Colmore Av. CH63: Spit 5K 85
Colne Rd. WA5: B'ood 5C 14
Colonial Rd. SK2: Stoc 6E 52
Colonnades, The L3: Liv 4G 35
Colorado Cl. WA5: Gt San 5A 40
Colquitt St. L1: Liv 4K 35
Colshaw Dr. SK9: Wilm 5A 98
Colshaw La. SK11: Sidd 4B 168
Colshaw Rd. M23: Wyth 7G 49
Colshaw Wlk. *SK9: Wilm 5A 98*
(off Howty Cl.)
Colson Ct. CH1: Ches 2B 212
Coltishall Ho. SK8: Chea 7J 51
Coltsfoot Cl. CH3: Hunt 6D 150
Coltsfoot Dr. WA14: B'ath 4F 47
Columbia La. CH43: Oxt 1A 60
Columbia Rd. CH43: Oxt 1A 60
Columbine Cl. CH3: Hunt 5D 150
WA8: Wid 1B 62
Columbine Wlk. *M31: Part 1H 45*
(off Central Rd.)
Columbus Dr. CH61: Pens 3G 83
Columbus Quay L3: Liv 2K 61
Column Rd. CH48: Cald, W Kir 3D 56
Colville Ct. WA2: Winw 1E 40
Colville Gro. M33: Sale 3J 47
WA15: Timp 6A 48
Colville Rd. CH44: Wall 7G 13
SK11: Mac 4G 125
Colwell Av. M32: S'ord 1G 23
Colwick Av. WA14: Alt 6J 47
Colwyn Av. M14: Manc 3B 24
Colwyn Cl. CH65: Ell P 5F 135
WA5: Call 2C 40
Colwyn Cres. SK5: Stoc 6J 25
Colwyn Rd. SK7: Bram 5C 78
SK8: Chea H 4G 77
Colwyn St. CH41: Birk 4K 33
Colyton Wlk. M22: Wyth 2B 76
COMBERBACH 3J 115 (3A 216)
Comberbach Dr. CW5: Stap 3E 196
Combermere Cl.
SK8: Chea H 1H 77
Combermere Pl.
CW1: Crewe 1C 194
(off Rigg St.)
Combermere St. L8: Liv 6K 35
SK16: Duk 1H 9
Comber Way WA16: Knut 5E 116
Comboy Dr. CW9: Rud 7H 157
COMBS 3D 217
Comely Av. CH44: Wall 7J 13
Comely Bank Rd. CH44: Wall 7K 13
Comer Ter. M33: Sale 7F 23
Commercial Av. SK8: Chea H 1B 98
Commercial Brow SK14: Hyde 6K 9
Commercial Rd. CH62: Brom 3E 86
SK7: H Gro 2H 79
SK10: Mac 4B 126
Commercial St. SK14: Hyde 7K 9
Common, The WA7: Halt 6C 90
Common Farm La. SK11: Snel 6A 166
Commonfield Rd. CH49: Woodc 4E 58
Commongate SK10: Mac 4B 126
Commonhall St.
CH1: Ches 5B 212 (2K 149)
Common La. CH3: Wave 2A 174
CW6: Clot, Dud 4C 174 & 4D 174
CW6: Kel 6B 172
CW9: Lac D 6J 159
M31: Carri 6E 20
SK11: Snel 6A 166
WA3: Cul 6D 6
WA4: Lwr S 6J 93
WA4: Warr 3J 67
WA6: Haps 7H 137
Common Rd. WA12: New W 1B 14
Commons, The CW11: S'ach 3F 201
COMMONSIDE
SK11 5D 126
WA6 3C 152 (3D 215)
Commonside WA6: Alv 6D 138
Commonside Bus. Pk.
WA4: H'ton 3C 92
Commons Mill CW11: S'ach 2F 201
Commonwealth Cl. CW7: Wins 6D 178
Community St. OL7: Ash L 1E 8
Commutation Row L3: Liv 2K 35
Company's Cl. WA7: West 1F 111
Compass Cl. WA7: Murd 2F 113
Compass Ct. CH45: Wall 3F 13
COMPSTALL 2H 55 (1D 217)
COMPSTALL BROW 2F 55
Compstall Mills Est.
SK6: Comp 2H 55
Compstall Rd. SK6: Comp, Rom 2C 54
SK6: Mar B 2G 55
Compton Cl. M41: Urm 2F 21
Compton Dr. M23: Wyth 3G 75
Compton Pl. CH4: Ches 5H 149
CH65: Ell P 3D 134
Compton Rd. CH41: Birk 3G 33
Compton St. SK15: Stal 1C 10
Comrie Wlk. M23: Wyth 7G 49
Comus St. L3: Liv 1J 35
Concert Sq. *L1: Liv 3J 35*
(off Concert St.)
Concert St. L1: Liv 3J 35
Concord Bus. Pk. M22: Wyth 4A 76
Concordia Av. CH49: Upt 7D 32
Concord Pl. WA2: Warr 2H 41
Concord Way SK16: Duk 2J 9
Condliffe Cl. CW11: S'ach 4G 201
Conduit St. OL6: Ash L 1H 9
Conery Cl. WA6: Hel 4C 138
Coney Gro. M23: Wyth 5G 49
WA7: B'vale 2D 112
Coneymead SK15: Stal 5B 4
Coney Wlk. CH49: Upt 6A 32
Congham Rd. SK3: Stoc 4A 52
CONGLETON 4G 183 (1C 221)
Congleton Bus. Cen.
CW12: Cong 3G 183
Congleton Bus. Pk. CW12: Cong 2D 182
Congleton Cl. SK9: Ald E 7F 119
Congleton Edge Rd.
CW12: Cong 7K 183
Congleton La. SK11: Chel 7D 166
SK11: Sidd 1C 168
Congleton Leisure Cen. 3G 183
Congleton Mus. *4G 183*
(off Market Sq.)
Congleton Retail Pk. CW12: Cong 2F 183

Countess Cl.—Cromwell Range

Countess Cl. SK11: Mac 5G 125
Countess Ct. CH1: Ches 5J 145
Countess Rd. M20: Manc 1D 50
SK11: Mac 5G 125
Countess St. OL6: Ash L 1J 9
SK2: Stoc 7E 52
Countess Way CH1: Ches 6J 145
Counting Ho. Rd. SK12: Dis 2H 103
County Av. OL6: Ash L 5A 4
County Sessions House 2J 35
(off William Brown St.)
County Ter. WA16: Knut 4D 116
Courier Row SK10: Boll 4C 122
Court, The CH63: Beb 2A 86
CH64: L Nes 2D 130
Courtenay Rd. CH47: Hoy 6B 30
Courteney Pl. WA14: Bow 4E 72
Courthill St. SK1: Stoc 4E 52
Court Ho., The CH65: Ell P 2E 134
Court La. CW8: Weav 4E 154
Courtney Av. CH44: Wall 1K 33
Courtney Grn. SK9: Wilm 4A 98
Courtney Rd. CH4: Ches 7F 149
CH42: R Fer 5F 61
Courts Vw. M33: Sale 6H 23
Court Yard, The CW12: Cong 3D 182
Courtyard, The CH2: Elt 5F 137
CH2: Upt 4C 146
CH64: W'ston 7E 106
CW8: Gor 5D 154
SK6: Bred 6F 27
(off Rodney Dr.)
SK14: H'rth 2J 11
Cousens Way CH1: Ches 6J 145
Cove, The WA15: Hale 2K 73
Covell Rd. SK12: Poy 1C 100
Covent Gdn. L2: Liv 3H 35
Covent Gdns. SK1: Stoc 7J 213 (3D 52)
Coventry Av. CH66: Gt Sut 1A 140
SK3: Stoc 5H 51
Coventry St. CH41: Birk 6C 34
Coverdale Av. L35: R'ill 1D 36
Coverdale Cl. WA5: Gt San 5H 39
Coverdale Fold CW11: Ett H 4B 200
Covert Cl. CW7: Wins 4C 178
Covert Ri. CH3: Tatt 3G 187
Covert Rd. M22: Shar 7A 50
Covertside CH48: W Kir 3E 56
Covington Pl. SK9: Wilm 1G 119
Cowan Way WA8: Wid 1F 63
Cowbrook La. SK11: Gaw 6F 129
Cowdell St. WA2: Warr 5F 41
Cowdrey Av. CH43: Bid 3F 33
Cowfields CW5: Nant 1C 196
Cowhey Cl. CH4: Ches 6J 149
Cow Hey La. WA7: Clif 2G 111
(not continuous)
Cow La. CH66: L Sut 2J 133
CW7: Wins 4F 179
M33: Sale 5K 23
SK2: Stoc 1H 79
SK7: Stoc 1H 79
SK9: Wilm 7K 97
SK10: Boll 4E 122
SK10: R'ow 7G 123
SK11: Mac 6A 126
WA6: Norl 5H 153
WA14: Dun M 7C 46
WA15: Ash 7K 73
Cowley Cl. CH49: Upt 7A 32
Cowley Way CW1: Crewe 5E 194
COWLISHAW BROW 6A 28
Cowlishaw Rd. SK6: Rom 6A 28
SK14: Hyde, Stoc 6A 28
Cowper Cl. CW2: Wis 6A 194
Cowthorne Dr. CH3: Wave 2A 174
COXBANK 3A 220
Coxton Rd. M22: Wyth 4A 76
Coylton Av. L35: R'ill 2D 36
Crab La. WA2: Fear 1A 42
Crabmill Dr. CW11: Elw 2C 200
Crabmill La. WA6: Norl 5F 153
Crabmill Rd. CW11: Most, Warm 2D 204
Crabtree Av. SK12: Dis 2H 103
WA15: H'rns 6D 74
Crab Tree Cl. L24: Hale 6B 88
Crabtree Cl. WA12: New W 1H 15
Crabtree Ct. SK12: Dis 1G 103
(off Buxton Old Rd.)
Crabtree Fold WA7: Nort 6E 90
CRABTREE GREEN 3B 218
Crabtree Gro. CW1: Crewe 7K 191
Crabtree La. WA13: Lymm 6C 70
WA16: H Leg 1F 95
Crabwall Pl. CH1: Blac 5G 145
CRACKLEY 2C 221
Craddock Ct. SY14: Mal 2H 207
(off Ryland Cl.)
Craddock Rd. M33: Sale 2C 48
Cradley WA8: Wid 3C 62
Cragside Way SK9: Wilm 1H 119
Craig Av. M41: Urm 1K 21
Craig Cl. SK4: Stoc 3K 51
SK11: Mac 7J 125
Craig Gdns. CH66: Ell P 1A 134
Craig Hall M44: Irlam 4C 20
Craighall Av. M19: Manc 3C 24
Craigleigh Gro. CH62: East 3A 108
Craigmore Av. M20: Manc 1K 49
Craig Rd. CW12: Cong 2H 183
SK4: Stoc 3H 51
SK11: Mac 7J 125
Craig Wlk. ST7: Als 7G 203
Craigweil Av. M20: Manc 1F 51
Craithie Rd. CH3: Ches 1D 150
Crampton Dr. WA15: H'rns 5C 74
Crampton La. M31: Carri 4G 21
CRANAGE 1G 181 (1B 220)
Cranage Av. SK9: Hand 1A 98
(off Spath La.)
Cranage Cl. WA7: Run 7K 89
Cranage Ct. CW12: Cong 3H 183
(off Brunswick St.)
Cranage La. CW9: N'ich 4J 157
Cranage Rd. CW2: Crewe 3A 194
M19: Manc 3E 24
Cranberry Cl. WA14: B'ath 4F 47
Cranberry Dr. M34: Den 7C 8
Cranberry La. ST7: Als 5A 202
CRANBERRY MOSS 6B 202
Cranberry Moss La.
ST7: Als 6B 202
Cranberry Rd. M31: Part 1H 45
Cranborne Av. WA4: Warr 4E 66
Cranborne Rd. CW1: Crewe 7J 191
Cranbourne Av. CH41: Birk 5K 33
CH46: More 5A 32
CH47: Meols 3F 31
SK8: Chea H 3K 77
Cranbourne Cl. WA15: Timp 6A 48
Cranbourne Ct. SK4: Stoc 7E 24
Cranbourne Rd. SK4: Stoc 7E 24
Crandon Dr. M20: Manc 4E 50
Crane Bank CH1: Ches 4A 212 (2J 149)
Cranebrook Cl. CW1: Crewe 5F 191
Cranesbill Cl. M22: Wyth 4J 75
Crane Wharf CH1: Ches 2J 149
Cranfield Dr. ST7: Als 6B 202
Cranford Av. M20: Manc 7A 24
M32: S'ord 1K 23
M33: Sale 5H 23
SK11: Mac 5C 126
WA16: Knut 4D 116
Cranford Cl. CH62: East 3A 108
Cranford Ct. CH4: Ches 6H 149
WA1: Wool 4E 42
Cranford Dr. M44: Irlam 1C 20
Cranford Gdns. SK6: Mar 4F 55
Cranford M. ST7: Als 6B 202
Cranford Rd. M41: Urm 1H 21
SK9: Wilm 5H 97
Cranford Sq. WA16: Knut 4D 116
Cranford St. CH44: Wall 2B 34
Cranham Rd. M22: Wyth 3G 75
CRANK 1D 215
Cranleigh Av. SK4: Stoc 7C 24
Cranleigh Cl. WA4: Stoc H 6F 67
Cranleigh Cres. CH1: Ches 6J 145
Cranleigh Dr. M33: Sale 3C 48
(Ashstead Rd.)
M33: Sale 6F 23
(Oaklands Dr.)
SK7: H Gro 5A 80
SK8: Chea 6H 51
Cranmere Av. M19: Manc 1F 25
Cranmere Cl. CW9: N'ich 2F 163
Cranmere Dr. M33: Sale 2H 47
Cranmer Rd. M20: Manc 1D 50
Cranshaw Av. WA9: Clo F 1K 37
Cranshaw La. WA8: Wid 1F 37
Cranston Dr. M20: Manc 4D 50
M33: Sale 1E 48
Cranston Gro. SK8: Gat 7B 50
Cranswick Grn. CH66: L Sut 3J 133
Crantock Dr. SK8: He Grn 5E 76
SK15: Stal 6E 4
Crantock St. M12: Manc 1E 24
Cranwell Av. WA3: Cul 6F 7
Cranwell Ct. M43: Droy 2A 8
(off Williamson La.)
Cranwell Dr. M19: Manc 7B 24
Cranwell Rd. CH49: Gre 2J 57
Cranworth St. SK15: Stal 1C 10
Craston Rd. M13: Manc 1B 24
Crauford Rd. CW12: Eat 5J 169
Craven Cl. CH41: Birk 6C 34
Craven Ct. WA2: Winw 7J 15
Craven Dr. WA14: B'ath 4G 47
Craven Rd. L35: R'ill 1C 36
SK5: Stoc 5J 25
WA14: B'ath 5G 47
(not continuous)
Craven St. CH41: Birk 6B 34
L3: Liv 2K 35
Craven Ter. M33: Sale 7H 23
Cravenwood OL6: Ash L 3A 4
Cravenwood Rd. SK5: Stoc 1H 25
CRAWFORD 1D 215
Crawford Av. WA8: Wid 4B 62
Crawford Cl. CH3: Hunt 6E 150
WA9: Clo F 1K 37
Crawford M. OL6: Ash L 1J 9
Crawford Pl. WA7: Run 1H 111
Crawford St. WA9: Clo F 1A 38
Crawford's Wlk. CH2: Ches 7C 146
Crawley Av. M22: Wyth 2K 75
WA2: Warr 1E 40
Crawley Gro. SK2: Stoc 6F 53
Crayfield Rd. M19: Manc 3E 24
Crayford Av. CW12: Cong 1J 183
Creden Av. M22: Wyth 2B 76
Crediton Cl. WA14: Alt 6F 47
Creek, The CH45: Wall 3E 12
Cresanne Cl. CW10: Mid 5D 180
Crescent, The CH2: Ches 6A 146
CH48: W Kir 3B 56
CH49: Gre 2A 58
CH60: Hes 1E 104
CH61: Pens 7C 58
CH63: H Beb 1J 85
CH65: Gt Sut 3B 134
CW5: Nant 1D 196
CW6: Utk 2B 176
CW8: H'ord 1K 161
CW8: Weav 4G 155
CW9: N'ich 7E 156
CW10: Mid 3B 180
CW12: Cong 4E 182
M19: Manc 2D 24
M41: Urm 1J 21
OL5: Moss 1C 4
SK3: Stoc 7D 52
SK6: Bred 7C 26
SK8: Chea 6F 51
SK10: Mac 3B 126
(not continuous)
SK10: Mot A 2B 120
SK15: Stal 4E 10
WA13: Lymm 3B 70
WA14: Alt 7E 46
WA15: Timp 5K 47
Crescent Cl. SK3: Stoc 7E 52
SK16: Duk 1H 9
Crescent Ct. M21: Chor H 2K 23
(off Alderfield Rd.)
M33: Sale 1B 48
Crescent Dr. WA6: Hel 5B 138
Crescent Gro. M19: Manc 2D 24
SK8: Chea 6E 50
Crescent Pk. SK4: Stoc 2A 52
Crescent Rd. CH44: Wall 7J 13
CH65: Ell P 2F 135
CW4: Cran 1F 181
CW12: Cong 4E 182
SK1: Stoc 1F 53
SK8: Chea 6E 50
SK9: Ald E 5G 119
SK16: Duk 1H 9
WA14: Alt 6E 46
WA15: Hale 3J 73
Crescent Row WA7: Run 4F 89
(off Hankey St.)
Crescent Vw. SK16: Duk 1H 9
(off Peel St.)
Crescent Way SK3: Stoc 7E 52
Cresgarth Ho. SK3: Stoc 1E 78
Cressbrook Rd. WA4: Stoc H 4G 67
Cressida Av. CH63: H Beb 6D 60
Cressingham Rd. CH45: N Bri 3H 13
M32: S'ord 2G 23
Cressington Av. CH42: Tran 4C 60
Cressington Gdns. CH65: Ell P 2E 134
Cresson Ct. CH43: Oxt 7J 33
CRESSWELL 3D 221
Cresswell Cl. WA5: Call 2B 40
Cresswellshawe Rd. ST7: Als 5E 202
Cresta Dr. WA7: West 1F 111
Crest Lodge SK7: Bram 3D 78
Crestwood Cl. CW2: Wis 7B 194
Crew Av. SK10: Mac 3B 126
Crewe Alexandra FC 4D 194
Crewe Bus. Pk. CW1: Crewe 4F 195
CREWE-BY-FARNDON 7D 186 (2C 219)
CREWE 2C 194 (2B 220)
Crewe Crematorium & Cemetery
CW1: Crewe 7H 191
Crewe Gates Farm Ind. Est.
CW1: Crewe 4F 195
Crewe Gates Ind. Est. CW1: Crewe 5G 195
CREWE GREEN 3H 195
Crewe Grn. CH49: Woodc 3D 58
Crewe Grn. Av. CW1: Hasl 2H 195
Crewe Grn. Rd. CW1: Crewe 3F 195
Crewe Hall Ent. Pk. CW1: Crewe 6J 195
Crewe La. CH3: Farn 6C 186
Crewe La. Sth. CH3: Cre F 7C 186
Crewe Rd. CW1: Crewe 4E 194
CW1: Crewe, Cre G, Hasl 3G 195
CW2: Shav 4C 198
CW2: Wis 1G 197
CW5: Hath, Walg 3G 211
CW5: Nant, W'ston, Wis 2D 196
CW11: S'ach, Whe, Wint
4C 204 & 7D 200
M23: Wyth 4E 48
ST7: Als 7A 202
ST7: Chu L 5G 203
Crewe Station (Rail) 4E 194
Crewe St. CH1: Ches 2E 212 (1B 150)
CW1: Crewe 2D 194
Crewe Swimming Pool 3B 194
Crewe Vagrants Sports Club 4H 197
Crewood Comn. Rd.
CW8: Crow, K'ley 1H 153
WA6: K'ley 1H 153
Crib La. CW6: Tarp 5F 175
Criccieth Ct. CH65: Ell P 6F 135
Criccieth Rd. SK3: Stoc 5J 51
Cricket St. M34: Den 6F 9
Cricklewood Rd. M22: Wyth 3J 75
Criftin Cl. CH66: Gt Sut 6J 133
CRIFTINS 3B 218
Crimes La. CW6: Bees 1A 188
Cringle Dr. SK8: Chea 1E 76
Cringle Hall Rd. M19: Manc 3C 24
Cringle Rd. M19: Manc 4E 24
Crisham Av. CW5: Aus 7C 196
Crispin Rd. M22: Wyth 5A 76
Critchley Cl. SK14: Hyde 2A 28
Criterion St. SK5: Stoc 1J 25
Croasdale Dr. WA7: Beec 2A 112
Crocus Av. CH41: Birk 5J 33
Crocus St. CW8: Barnt 2A 156
Croesmere Dr.
CH66: Gt Sut 6K 133
CROFT 4F 17 (1A 216)
Croft, The CH2: Ches 5A 146
CH49: Gre 3A 58
SK2: Stoc 6F 53
SK14: Mot 6H 11
WA7: Halt 5B 90
Croft Av. CH62: Brom 5C 86
Croft Av. E. CH62: Brom 4D 86
Croft Bank SK15: M'ook 5E 4
Croft Bus. Cen.
CH62: Brom 4E 86
Croft Bus. Pk. CH62: Brom 4E 86
Croft Cl. CH3: Row 2A 174
CH43: Noc 1H 59
CW6: Utk 2B 176
CW12: Cong 4H 183
WA15: H'rns 7C 74
Croft Cotts. CH66: Chil T 7B 108
(off School La.)
Croft Ct. CH65: Ell P 5G 135
WN7: Leigh 1C 6
Croft Dr. CH46: More 5B 32
CH48: Cald 7D 56
Croft Dr. E. CH48: Cald 6E 56
Croft Dr. W. CH48: Cald 6D 56
Croft Edge CH43: Oxt 2A 60
Croften Dr. CH64: L Nes 3C 130
Crofters, The CH49: Gre 1A 58
M33: Sale 1F 49
Crofters Cl. CH66: Gt Sut 7A 134
CW2: Wis 6B 194
WA16: Pick 1C 158
Crofters Ct. CW4: H Cha 3J 181
Crofters Grn. SK9: Wilm 1E 118
Crofters Heath CH66: Gt Sut 7A 134
Crofters Lea CW8: N'ich 6C 156
Crofters Way CH1: Sau 2A 144
Croft Gdns. WA4: Grap 6A 68
Croft Grn. CH62: Brom 3D 86
CROFT HEATH 3F 17
Croft Heath Gdns.
WA3: Croft 3F 17
Croft Ho. WA3: Croft 4F 17
Croftlands Rd. M22: Wyth 1A 76
Croft La. CH4: Dod 3C 184
CH62: Brom 5D 86
WA16: Knut 5F 117
Crofton Av. WA15: Timp 3A 48
Crofton Cl. WA4: App T 1C 94
Crofton Gdns. WA3: Cul 7E 6
Crofton Rd. CH42: Tran 2D 60
WA7: Run 5E 88
Croft Rd. M33: Sale 2D 48
SK8: Chea H 3K 77
SK9: Wilm 3D 118
Croft Row OL5: Moss 1E 4
Crofts, The CH3: Farn 6C 186
Crofts Bank Rd. M41: Urm 1C 22
Croftside WA1: Wool 5F 43
Croftside Way SK9: Wilm 1H 119
Croft St. SK14: Hyde 1H 27
SK15: Stal 7C 4
WA8: Wid 7G 63
Croftsway CH60: Hes 6F 83
Croft Technology Pk.
CH62: Brom 5F 87
Croft Trade Pk. CH62: Brom 4E 86
Croftwood Cl. CW7: Wins 4B 178
Cromar Rd. SK7: H Gro 2K 79
Cromarty Rd. CH44: Wall 7F 13
Crombie Av. M22: N'den 5K 49
Cromdale Av. SK7: H Gro 2K 79
Cromdale Way WA5: Gt San 6G 39
Cromer Dr. CH45: Wall 6G 13
CW1: Crewe 5G 191
Cromer Rd. CH47: Hoy 5B 30
M33: Sale 1C 48
SK8: Chea 6G 51
Cromer St. SK1: Stoc 2F 53
Cromley Dr. SK6: H Lan 7E 80
Cromley Rd. SK2: Stoc 2E 78
SK6: H Lan 6E 80
Crompton Cl. CW12: Cong 7J 169
SK6: Mar 5F 55
Crompton Dr. WA2: Winw 5K 15
Crompton Rd. M19: Manc 4D 24
SK11: Mac 4K 125
Crompton St. OL6: Ash L 5A 4
Crompton Way WA3: Low 2B 6
Cromwell Av. SK5: Den 1K 25
SK6: Mar 5D 54
SK8: Gat 6C 50
WA2: Warr 2A 40
WA5: Gt San, Old H, W'ook 2A 40
Cromwell Av. Sth.
WA5: Gt San 1A 66
Cromwell Ct. CW5: Nant 2C 196
M44: Irlam 4B 20
WA1: Warr 7E 40
(off Dixon St.)
Cromwell Dr. CW2: Shav 3C 198
Cromwell Gro. M19: Manc 2D 24
Cromwell Range M14: Manc 1A 24

Deanway—Dewsnap La.

Deanway M41: Urm 1G **21**
SK9: Wilm 5K **97**
Deanway Technology Cen.
SK9: Hand 3A **98**
Deanway Trad. Est.
SK9: Hand 3A **98**
Dearden St. SK15: Stal 7B **4**
Dearne Dr. M32: S'ord 1K **23**
Dearnford Av. CH62: Brom 1J **107**
Dearnford Cl. CH62: Brom 1J **107**
Debenham Rd. M32: S'ord 2F **23**
Debra Cl. CH66: Gt Sut 4J **133**
Debra Rd. CH66: Gt Sut 5J **133**
De Brook Cl. M41: Urm 2H **21**
Dee Av. WA15: Timp 7D **48**
Dee Banks
CH3: Ches, Gt Bou 3C **150**
Dee Cl. CW11: S'ach 1C **200**
Dee Cres. CH3: Farn 5B **186**
Dee Fords Av. CH3: Ches 2D **150**
Dee Hills Pk. CH3: Ches 2B **150**
Dee La. CH3: Ches 2B **150**
CH48: W Kir 3B **56**
LL13: Holt 7A **186**
Dee Mdws. LL13: Holt 7A **186**
Dee Pk. LL13: Holt 7A **186**
Dee Pk. Cl. CH60: Hes 1E **104**
Dee Pk. Rd. CH60: Hes 1E **104**
Deepcar St. M19: Manc 1D **24**
Deepdale WA8: Wid 2C **62**
Deepdale Cl. CH43: Bid 6F **33**
SK5: Stoc 2J **25**
WA5: Gt San 6H **39**
Deepdale Dr. L35: R'ill 1D **36**
Deeracre Av. SK2: Stoc 6G **53**
Dee Rd. CH2: Mic T 1J **147**
L35: R'ill 1B **36**
Deer Pk. Ct. WA7: Pal F 1A **112**
Deerwood Cl. CH66: L Sut 1K **133**
SK10: Mac 3G **125**
Deerwood Cres.
CH66: L Sut 1K **133**
Deerwood Vw. SK14: Hat 2F **29**
Dee Sailing Club 1A **82**
Dee Side LL13: Holt 7B **186**
Deeside CH60: Hes 6E **82**
CH65: Whit 5D **134**
Deeside Cvn. Site
CH1: Ches 1D **148**
Deeside Cl. CH43: Bid 6E **32**
CH65: Whit 6D **134**
Deeside Ct. CH3: Ches 2B **150**
CH64: Park 6E **104**
Deeside Cres. CH1: Sea 5A **144**
Deeside La. CH1: Sea 7A **144**
(not continuous)
Dee Sq. CW7: Wins 2H **179**
Dee Vw. CH3: Farn 5B **186**
Dee Vw. Ct. CH64: Nest 2C **130**
Dee Vw. Rd. CH60: Hes 6H **83**
Dee Way CW7: Wins 2H **179**
Deganwy Gro. SK5: Stoc 6J **25**
De Grouchy St. CH48: W Kir 2C **56**
Deirdre Av. WA8: Wid 4G **63**
De Lacy Row WA7: Cast 4C **90**
Delafield Av. M12: Manc 1D **24**
Delafield Cl. WA2: Fear 1K **41**
Delaford Cl. SK3: Stoc 1C **78**
Delahays Dr. WA15: Hale 3B **74**
Delahays Rd. WA15: Hale 3A **74**
Delaheyes Lodge WA15: Timp 7B **48**
Delaine Rd. M20: Manc 5A **24**
Delaisy Way CW7: Wins 3H **179**
DELAMERE 3G **173** (1D **219**)
Delamere Av. CH62: East 3K **107**
CH66: Gt Sut 3A **134**
M32: S'ord 1J **23**
(not continuous)
M33: Sale 1E **48**
WA8: Wid 4C **62**
WA9: Sut M 1G **37**
Delamere Cl. CH43: Bid 6E **32**
CH62: East 3K **107**
CW2: West 3K **199**
CW8: Barnt 2K **155**
CW11: S'ach 1D **200**
SK6: W'ley 6H **27**
SK7: H Gro 2A **80**
SK15: Carrb 3F **5**
Delamere Ct. *CW1: Crewe* *2C* ***194***
(off St Mary's St.)
ST7: Als 5A **202**
Delamere Dr. CH66: Gt Sut 4A **134**
SK10: Mac 2C **126**
Delamere Forest Pk. 7B **152**
Delamere Forest Touring Pk.
CW8: Dela 1F **173**
Delamere Grn. *CH66: Gt Sut* *4A* ***134***
(off Delamere Dr.)
Delamere Gro. *CH44: Wall* *2D* ***34***
(off Tudor Av.)
CW8: Dela 3G **173**
Delamere Ho. WA6: Frod 7J **111**
Delamere La. CH3: Ash H 4J **171**
Delamere Lodge *SK7: H Gro* *3H* ***79***
(off Chester Rd.)
DELAMERE PARK 1A **160**
Delamere Pk. Way E.
CW8: Cudd 1A **160**
Delamere Pk. Way W.
CW8: Cudd 2A **160**
Delamere Ri. CW7: Wins 3C **178**
Delamere Rd. CW5: Nant 3D **196**
CW12: Cong 3B **182**
M19: Manc 3E **24**
M34: Den 1A **26**
M41: Urm 1J **21**
SK2: Stoc 1F **79**
SK7: H Gro 2A **80**
SK8: Gat 7D **50**
SK9: Hand 2A **98**
WA6: K'ley, Norl 3C **152**
Delamere Station (Rail) 1G **173**
Delamere St. CH1: Ches 2B **212** (1K **149**)
CW1: Crewe 2C **194**
CW7: Wins 3B **178**
WA5: Warr 7C **40**
Delamer Rd.
WA14: Alt, Bow 4G **213** (2G **73**)
Delamore's Acre CH64: W'ston 7F **107**
Delaunays Rd. M33: Sale 7E **22**
Delavor Cl. CH60: Hes 6G **83**
Delavor Rd. CH60: Hes 6F **83**
Delenty Dr. WA3: Ris 7J **17**
Delery Dr. WA1: Padg 4J **41**
Delfur Rd. SK7: Bram 6D **78**
Delhi Rd. M44: Irlam 3C **20**
Dell, The CH3: Guil S 5J **147**
CH42: R Fer 4G **61**
CW6: Kel 4C **172**
CW8: Cudd 6K **153**
WA14: Hale 5J **73**
Dell Cl. CH63: Brom 1G **107**
Dell Ct. CH43: Pren 4J **59**
Dell Dr. WA2: Fear 2A **42**
Dell Gro. CH42: R Fer 5G **61**
Dell La. CH60: Hes 7K **83**
Dell Side SK6: Bred 1J **53**
Delmar Rd. WA16: Knut 4G **117**
Delphfield WA7: Nort 6F **91**
Delphfields Rd. WA4: App 6G **67**
Delph La. WA2: Warr 5C **16**
WA2: Winw 7J **15**
WA4: Dare 3J **91**
Delta Ct. CH4: Salt F 5C **148**
Delta Cres. WA5: W'ook 2A **40**
Delta Point M34: Aude 3D **8**
Delta Rd. M34: Aude 3D **8**
Delta Rd. E. CH42: R Fer 4G **61**
Delta Rd. W. CH42: R Fer 4G **61**
Delves Av. CH63: Spit 3K **85**
WA5: Warr 5D **40**
Delves Broughton Ct. CW1: Hasl 1K **195**
Delves Cl. CW2: Shav 3B **198**
Delves Rd. WA14: W Tim 3H **47**
Delves Wlk. CH3: Gt Bou 4E **150**
Delvine Dr. CH2: Upt 4A **146**
Delwood Gdns. M22: Wyth 1K **75**
Delyn Cl. CH42: R Fer 4D **60**
Demage Dr. CH66: Gt Sut 5K **133**
Demage La. CH1: Lea B 5B **140**
CH2: Upt 2A **146**
Demage La. Sth. CH2: Upt 3A **146**
De Massey Cl. SK6: W'ley 5G **27**
Demesne Cl. SK15: Stal 1D **10**
Demesne Cres. SK15: Stal 1D **10**
Demesne Dr. SK15: Stal 7D **4**
Demesne St. CH44: Wall 1D **34**
Demmings, The SK8: Chea 7H **51**
Demmings Ind. Est. SK8: Chea 7H **51**
Demmings Rd. SK8: Chea 7H **51**
Denbigh Cl. SK7: H Gro 5G **79**
WA6: Hel 7A **138**
Denbigh Ct. CH65: Ell P 5F **135**
WA7: Cast 4C **90**
Denbigh Cres. CW10: Mid 5C **180**
Denbigh Dr. CW7: Wins 5C **178**
Denbigh Gdns. CH65: Ell P 5E **134**
Denbigh Rd. CH44: Wall 1C **34**
M34: Den 2E **26**
Denbigh St. CH1: Ches 1A **212** (7J **145**)
OL5: Moss 1E **4**
SK4: Stoc 1B **52**
Denbury Av. WA4: Stoc H 3K **67**
Denbury Dr. WA14: Alt 7F **47**
Denbury Grn. SK7: H Gro 4E **78**
Denby La. SK4: Stoc 7G **25**
Denby Rd. SK16: Duk 3H **9**
Dene Brow M34: Den 3G **27**
Dene Ct. SK4: Stoc 2A **52**
Dene Dr. CW7: Wins 3E **178**
Denefield Cl. SK6: Mar B 3H **55**
Deneford Rd. M20: Manc 2C **50**
Dene Hollow SK5: Stoc 2K **25**
Dene Ho. SK4: Stoc 3G **51**
Denehurst Cl. WA5: Penk 1H **65**
Denehurst Pk. Way CW8: Cudd 1A **160**
Dene Pk. M20: Manc 2C **50**
Dene Rd. M20: Manc 1C **50**
Dene Rd. W. M20: Manc 1B **50**
Denes, The CW7: Wins 4E **178**
SK5: Stoc 2J **25**
Denesgate CW7: Wins 4E **178**
Deneshey Rd. CH47: Meols 4D **30**
Deneside Av. CW1: Crewe 7H **191**
Deneside Cres. SK7: H Gro 2K **79**
Denesway M33: Sale 1J **47**
(not continuous)
Deneway SK4: Stoc 2A **52**
SK6: H Lan 5F **81**
SK7: Bram 6A **78**
Deneway Cl. SK4: Stoc 2A **52**
Deneway M. SK4: Stoc 2A **52**
Denewood Ct. SK9: Wilm 1F **119**
Denford Pl. ST7: Chu L 3E **202**
Denhall Cl. CH2: Ches 5B **146**
Denhall La. CH64: Burt 6E **130**
Denham Av. WA5: Gt San 7K **39**
Denham Cl. CH43: Bid 5F **33**
Denham Dr. M44: Irlam 2D **20**
SK7: Bram 6B **78**
Denholm Rd. M20: Manc 4E **50**
Denise Av. WA5: Penk 7G **39**
Denison Rd. SK7: H Gro 5J **79**
Denison St. L3: Liv 1G **35**
Deniston Rd. SK4: Stoc 6E **24**
Denman Gro. *CH44: Wall* *2D* ***34***
(off Tudor Av.)
Denmark Rd. M33: Sale 5G **23**
Denmark St. WA14: Alt 3J **213** (1H **73**)
Dennett Cl. WA1: Wool 6E **42**
Denning Dr. CH61: Irby 6A **58**
Dennis Dr. CH4: Ches 5J **149**
Dennis Ho. SK4: Stoc 7E **24**
Dennison Rd. SK8: Chea H 5K **77**
Dennis Rd. WA8: Wid 6J **63**
Dennis Round Ct. ST7: Als 6D **202**
Denny Cl. CH49: Upt 1C **58**
Densham Av. WA2: Warr 3F **41**
Denshaw Av. M34: Den 5C **8**
Denshaw Cl. M19: Manc 1G **51**
Denson Rd. WA15: Timp 4B **48**
Denston Cl. CH43: Bid 5E **32**
CW2: Crewe 5B **194**
Denstone Av. M33: Sale 1J **47**
M41: Urm 1B **22**
Denstone Dr. CH4: Ches 7H **149**
Denstone Rd. M41: Urm 1B **22**
SK5: Stoc 2J **25**
Dent Cl. SK5: Stoc 5B **26**
Dentdale Dr. L5: Liv 1K **35**
Dentdale Wlk. M22: Wyth 5J **75**
Dentith Dr. CH1: Blac 5F **145**
DENTON 7E **8** (1D **217**)
Denton Bus. Pk. M34: Den 7C **8**
Denton Cl. CW7: Wins 3D **178**
Denton Ct. M34: Den 5D **8**
Denton Dr. CH45: Wall 5J **13**
CW9: N'ich 4H **157**
Denton Dr. Ind. Est. CW9: N'ich 4H **157**
Denton Ent. Cen. *M34: Den* *7E* ***8***
(off Pitt St.)
Denton Hall Farm Rd. M34: Den 1B **26**
Denton Rd. M34: Aude 5D **8**
Denton St Lawrence's Church *7E* ***8***
(off Town La.)
Denton Station (Rail) 6B **8**
Denton St. L8: Liv 1K **61**
WA8: Wid 4J **63**
Denton Swimming Pool 7D **8**
Denton Ter. M34: Aude 4D **8**
Denver Av. CW2: Crewe 3B **194**
Denver Dr. WA5: Gt San 5K **39**
WA15: Timp 6A **48**
Denver Rd. WA4: Westy 2A **68**
Denville Cres. M22: Wyth 2A **76**
Denwall Ho. *CH64: Nest* *7H* ***105***
(off Churchill Way)
Denyer Ter. *SK16: Duk* *1G* ***9***
(off Hill St.)
Denzell Gdns. 2E **72**
Depenbech Cl. SY14: Mal 2H **207**
Depleach Rd. SK8: Chea 7F **51**
Depmore La. WA6: New 1B **152**
Deptford Av. M23: Wyth 2G **75**
De Quincey Cl. WA14: W Tim 3H **47**
De Quincey Rd. WA14: W Tim 3H **47**
Deramore Cl. OL6: Ash L 6A **4**
Derby Cl. M44: Cad 6K **19**
Derby Ct. M33: Sale 1C **48**
Derby Dr. WA1: Warr 5J **41**
Derby Gro. M19: Manc 2E **24**
Derby Pl. CH2: Ches 7B **146**
Derby Range SK4: Stoc 7E **24**
Derby Rd. CH42: Tran 2C **60**
CH45: Wall 5G **13**
M14: Manc 4A **24**
M33: Sale 5D **22**
M41: Urm 1C **22**
SK4: Stoc 7F **25**
SK14: Hyde 6K **9**
WA4: Stoc H 5G **67**
WA8: Wid 2G **63**
Derby Row WA12: New W 3G **15**
Derbyshire Av. M32: S'ord 1F **23**
Derbyshire Cres. M32: S'ord 1G **23**
Derbyshire Grn. M32: S'ord 1J **23**
Derbyshire Gro. M32: S'ord 1G **23**
Derbyshire La. M32: S'ord 1H **23**
Derbyshire La. W. M32: S'ord 1F **23**
Derbyshire Rd. M31: Part 2F **45**
M33: Sale 7H **23**
SK12: Poy 1H **101**
Derbyshire Rd. Sth. M33: Sale 1C **48**
Derby Sq. L2: Liv 3H **35**
Derby St. CW1: Crewe 1B **194**
CW12: Cong 3F **183**
M34: Den 7C **8**
(not continuous)
OL5: Moss 1E **4**
SK3: Stoc 4B **52**
SK6: Mar 6F **55**
WA14: Alt 7J **47**
Derby Ter. M34: Aude 2C **8**
Derby Way SK6: Mar 6F **55**
Dereham Av. CH49: Upt 5D **32**
Dereham Way WA7: Nort 3F **91**
Derek Av. WA2: Warr 3H **41**
Dernford Av. M19: Manc 6C **24**
Derrington Av. CW2: Crewe 3C **194**
Derry Av. M22: Wyth 1A **76**
Derwen Rd. SK3: Stoc 5C **52**
Derwent Av. CW7: Wins 3J **179**
WA15: Timp 7D **48**
Derwent Cl. CH63: H Beb 1H **85**
CW4: H Cha 4G **181**
CW5: W'ston 1H **197**
L35: R'ill 1B **36**
M31: Part 7C **20**
M34: Den 1A **26**
SK11: Mac 6H **125**
ST7: Als 5B **202**
WA3: Cul 1B **18**
Derwent Dr. CH45: Wall 5G **13**
CH61: Pens 2H **83**
CH66: H'ton 5C **108**
CW12: Cong 5H **183**
M33: Sale 2A **48**
SK7: Bram 1F **99**
SK9: Hand 1K **97**
Derwent Rd. CH2: Ches 5C **146**
CH43: Oxt 1A **60**
CH47: Meols 4F **31**
CH63: H Beb 1H **85**
M41: Urm 1H **21**
SK6: H Lan 5E **80**
WA4: Warr 3E **66**
WA8: Wid 4C **62**
Derwent Ter. SK15: Stal 5B **4**
Derwent Way CH64: L Nes 1D **130**
SK9: Ald E 1B **166**
WN7: Leigh 1B **6**
Desford Cl. CH46: More 3J **31**
Desmond Cl. CH43: Bid 5F **33**
Desmond Rd. M22: Wyth 1A **76**
Desoto Rd. WA8: Wid 2D **88**
Desoto Rd. E. WA8: Wid 7F **63**
Desoto Rd. W. WA8: Wid 7F **63**
De Trafford M. *SK9: Wilm* *4A* ***98***
(off Colshaw Dr.)
De Traffords, The M44: Irlam 1E **20**
Deva Av. CH4: Salt 5E **148**
Deva Cl. SK7: H Gro 4H **79**
SK12: Poy 2A **100**
Deva Ct. CH2: Ches 1C **150**
Deva Hgts. CH3: Gt Bou 4C **150**
Deva La. CH2: Ches 4K **145**
Deva Link CH1: Ches 7H **145**
Devaney Wlk. M34: Den 2D **26**
Deva Rd. CH48: W Kir 3B **56**
CW2: Crewe 2H **193**
Deva Roman Experience 5B **212**
Deva Ter. CH3: Ches 2B **150**
Deveraux Dr. CH44: Wall 1A **34**
Deverill Rd. CH42: R Fer 4D **60**
Devisdale Ct. WA14: Alt 2F **73**
Devisdale Grange WA14: Bow 2F **73**
Devisdale Gro. CH43: Bid 5F **33**
Devisdale Rd. WA14: Alt 1F **73**
Devizes Dr. CH61: Irby 6A **58**
Devoke Rd. M22: Wyth 3H **75**
Devon Av. CH45: Wall 6J **13**
M19: Manc 3C **24**
Devon Cl. CW10: Mid 2D **180**
SK5: Stoc 7B **26**
SK10: Mac 2G **125**
Devon Dr. CH61: Pens 2G **83**
Devon Gdns. CH42: R Fer 4E **60**
Devon Pl. CW12: Cong 2G **183**
WA8: Wid 2G **63**
Devonport St. L8: Liv 7K **35**
Devon Rd. CH2: Ches 5C **146**
M31: Part 2G **45**
M41: Urm 2H **21**
M44: Cad 6A **20**
Devonshire Cl. CH43: Oxt 7A **34**
M41: Urm 1D **22**
Devonshire Ct. *M33: Sale* *1D* ***48***
(off Derbyshire Rd. Sth.)
SK2: Stoc 7E **52**
Devonshire Dr. SK9: Ald E 5G **119**
Devonshire Gdns. WA12: New W 1F **15**
DEVONSHIRE PARK 2B **60**
Devonshire Pk. Rd. SK2: Stoc 7E **52**
Devonshire Pl. CH4: Ches 4B **150**
CH43: Oxt 7K **33**
WA7: Run 4G **89**
Devonshire Rd. CH43: Oxt 7A **34**
CH44: Wall 7H **13**
(not continuous)
CH48: W Kir 4D **56**
CH49: Upt 7B **32**
CH61: Pens 2G **83**
SK4: Stoc 2K **51**
SK7: H Gro 5K **79**
WA1: Padg 4K **41**
WA14: Alt 6H **47**
Devon St. L3: Liv 2K **35**
Dewar Ct. WA7: Astm 3A **90**
Dewar St. WA3: Ris 6K **17**
Dewberry Cl. CH42: Tran 1C **60**
Dewes St. CW1: Crewe 1B **194**
Dewhurst Rd. WA3: Birc 1D **42**
De Wint Av. SK6: Mar B 4H **55**
Dewsnap Bri. SK16: Duk 4H **9**
Dewsnap Cl. SK16: Duk 4H **9**
Dewsnap La. SK14: Mot 4G **11**
SK16: Duk 4H **9**

Dewsnap Way—Dudleston

Dewsnap Way SK14: Hat 1F 29
(off Stockport Rd.)
Dexter St. L8: Liv 6K 35
Dexter Way CW10: Mid 2D 180
Dial Pk. Rd. SK2: Stoc 1H 79
Dial Rd. CH42: Tran 2C 60
SK2: Stoc 7G 53
WA15: H'rns 5C 74
Dialstone La. SK2: Stoc 5G 53
Dialstone Recreation Cen. 6H 53
Dial St. WA1: Warr 7G 41
Diamond St. SK2: Stoc 6E 52
Diamond Ter. SK6: Mar 1F 81
Diane Ho. L8: Liv 5K 35
(off Birley Ct.)
Dibbinsdale Local Nature Reserve 4C 86 & 6C 86
Dibbinsdale Rd. CH63: Brom 6B 86
Dibbins Grn. CH63: Brom 1G 107
Dibbins Hey CH63: Spit 4A 86
Dibbinview Gro. CH63: Spit 4B 86
Dibden Wlk. M23: Wyth 7G 49
Dickens Av. CH43: Pren 4J 59
Dickens Cl. CH43: Pren 4J 59
CW11: Ett H 3B 200
SK8: Chea H 1E 98
Dickens La. SK12: Poy 3C 100
Dickenson Rd. M14: Manc 1A 24
Dickenson St. L1: Liv 4J 35
WA2: Warr 5G 41
Dickens St. L8: Liv 6K 35
Dickinson Way ST7: Als 6B 202
Dicklow Cob SK11: L Wit 7K 167
Dickson Cl. WA8: Wid 5H 63
Dicksons Dr. CH2: Ches 5A 146
Dickson St. WA8: Wid 5G 63
(not continuous)
Didcot Rd. M22: Wyth 4J 75
DIDSBURY 1D 50 (1C 217)
Didsbury Pk. M20: Manc 2D 50
Didsbury Rd. SK4: Stoc 2F 51
Didsbury Sports Cen. & Swimming Pool 2D 50
Dierdens Ter. CW10: Mid 3C 180
Dierden St. CW7: Wins 3J 179
Digg La. CH46: More 3A 32
Diggle Wlk. SK15: Carrb 3F 5
(off Friezland Cl.)
Dig La. CW5: Wyb 4A 198
WA2: Fear 7G 17
WA6: Frod 1G 139
DILHORNE 3D 221
Dillors Cft. CW1: L'ton 4F 191
Dilworth Ct. SK2: Stoc 7J 53
Dimelow Ct. SY14: Mal 4G 207
Dinas Cl. CH1: Blac 7E 144
DINGLE 2B 214
Dingle, The CW1: Hasl 7A 204
CW8: Barnt 1A 156
(off Elmwood Rd.)
SK7: Bram 4A 78
SK14: Hyde 5K 27
WA13: Lymm 2A 70
Dingle Av. M34: Den 1G 27
SK9: Ald E 4C 118
WA12: New W 1C 14
Dingle Bank CH4: Ches 7A 212 (4K 149)
CW11: S'ach 3F 201
(off Dingle La.)
Dingle Bank Cl. WA13: Lymm 2A 70
Dingle Bank Rd. SK7: Bram 3B 78
Dinglebrook Gro. SK9: Wilm 5B 98
(off Malpas Cl.)
Dingle Cl. SK6: Rom 2D 54
SK10: Mac 1J 125
Dingle Gro. SK8: Gat 6B 50
Dingle Hollow SK6: Rom 2E 54
Dingle La. CW6: Kel 2D 172
CW7: Wins 3E 178
CW11: S'ach 3G 201
WA4: App 7K 67
Dingle Rd. CH42: Tran 1B 60
Dingle Wlk. CW7: Wins 3E 178
(in Winsford Cross Shop. Cen.)
Dingle Way CW8: Cudd 1B 160
Dingleway WA4: App 5H 67
Dinglewood SK7: Bram 4A 78
Dingwall Dr. CH49: Gre 2A 58
Dinmore Ct. SK2: Stoc 7H 53
(off Lisburne La.)
Dinmore Rd. CH44: Wall 7H 13
Dinmor Rd. M22: Wyth 4J 75
Dinnington Ct. WA8: Wid 2E 62
Dinsdale Rd. CH62: Brom 4E 86
Diploma Dr. CW10: Mid 2C 180
Dipper Dr. WA14: W Tim 3G 47
Discovery Pk. SK4: Stoc 5E 24
DISLEY 1G 103 (2D 217)
Disley Ho. SK3: Stoc 5C 52
(off James St.)
Disley Station (Rail) 1F 103
Disley Wlk. M34: Den 2F 27
Distaff Rd. SK12: Poy 2A 100
Ditchfield La. WA16: H Leg 2G 95
Ditchfield Pl. WA8: Wid 5B 62
Ditchfield Rd. WA5: Penk 2G 65
WA8: Wid 5A 62
DITTON 5C 62 (2C 215)
Ditton Ct. WA8: Hal B 1C 88
Ditton La. CH46: Leas 1A 32
Ditton Rd. WA8: Wid 7C 62
Ditton Wlk. M23: Wyth 6F 49
Dixon Cl. M33: Sale 2D 48
Dixon Ct. SK8: Chea 7F 51
SK11: Chel 6C 166
Dixon Dr. SK11: Chel 5B 166
Dixon Rd. CW12: Cong 1J 183
M34: Den 2G 27
Dixon St. M44: Irlam 3C 20
WA1: Warr 7E 40
Dobb Hedge Cl. WA15: H'rns 7C 74
Dobbinetts La. M23: Wyth 1D 74
WA15: Hale 1D 74
Dobb La. WA16: Mere 4K 95
Dobcross Cl. M13: Manc 1D 24
Dobell's Rd. CW9: N'ich 1E 162
(Boardmans Pl.)
CW9: N'ich 7E 156
(Lime Av.)
Dobers La. WA6: Frod, New 5J 139
DOBS HILL 1B 218
Dobson Ct. SY14: Mal 3H 207
(off High St.)
Dock Rd. CH41: Birk 2K 33
CW9: N'ich 6E 156
WA8: Wid 1F 89
(not continuous)
Dock Rd. Nth. CH62: P Sun 7H 61
Dock Rd. Sth. CH62: Brom 2D 86
Docks Link CH44: Wall 1J 33
Dock St. CH65: Ell P 1E 134
WA8: Wid 1G 89
Dock Yd. Rd. CH65: Ell P 2F 135
Dodd Av. CH49: Gre 2A 58
Dodd Dr. WA4: Westy 2B 68
Doddington Dr. CW11: S'ach 1G 201
Doddington Rd. CW2: Crewe 3A 194
Doddington Wlk. M34: Den 2E 26
Doddridge Rd. L8: Liv 7K 35
Dodd's La. CW12: Astb 7E 182
Doddswood Dr. CW12: Cong 2H 183
Dodge Fold SK2: Stoc 6J 53
Dodge Hill SK4: Stoc 4H 213 (2C 52)
Dodgsley Dr. WA6: K'ley 2D 152
DODLESTON 3D 184 (1B 218)
Dodleston Cl. CH43: Noc 1G 59
Dodleston La. CH4: Pul 6A 184
Doeford Cl. WA3: Cul 5D 6
DOE GREEN 2F 65
Doe's Mdw. Rd. CH63: Brom 7B 86
Dog La. CW4: H Cha 7K 181
CW5: Nant 1C 196
CW6: Kel 3A 172
SY14: Oldc, Thr 5J 207
Dogmore La. CW6: Rus 6J 177
Dolmans La. WA1: Warr 7F 41
(off Bridge St.)
DOLPHIN 3A 214
Dolphin Ct. CH4: Ches 4H 149
Dolphin Cres. CH66: Gt Sut 6A 134
Dombey Rd. SK12: Poy 4C 100
Dombey St. L8: Liv 6K 35
Domestic App. M90: Man A 6J 75
Dominic Cl. M23: Wyth 3E 48
Domino Ct. WA7: Man P 2D 90
Domville Cl. WA13: Lymm 2A 70
Domville Dr. CH49: Woodc 2D 58
Donagh Cl. SK10: Mac 2G 125
Donald Av. SK14: Hyde 2A 28
Dona St. SK1: Stoc 4E 52
(not continuous)
Doncaster Dr. CH49: Upt 6C 32
DONES GREEN 7A 114
Donkey La. SK9: Wilm 2F 119
Donne Av. CH63: Spit 3K 85
Donne Cl. CH63: Spit 3A 86
Donne Pl. CH1: Blac 4G 145
Donnington Av. SK8: Chea 6H 51
Donnington Cl. WN7: Leigh 1D 6
Donnington Way CH4: Salt 4G 149
Don Wlk. CH65: Ell P 1C 134
Dood's La. WA4: App 1A 94
Doodson Av. M44: Irlam 1D 20
Dooley La. SK6: Mar 5B 54
Dooley's Grig SK11: L Wit 6J 167
Dooley's La. SK9: Wilm 4D 96
Dorac Av. SK8: He Grn 6E 76
Dorans La. L2: Liv 3H 35
Dorchester Av. M34: Den 2E 26
Dorchester Cl. CH49: Upt 1C 58
SK9: Wilm 6A 98
WA15: Hale 2C 74
Dorchester Ct. M33: Sale 2B 48
SK8: Chea H 4K 77
Dorchester Dr. M23: Wyth 3E 48
Dorchester Pde. SK7: H Gro 4F 79
(off Jackson's La.)
Dorchester Pk. CH43: Noc 2G 59
WA7: Nort 3F 91
Dorchester Pk. Local Nature Reserve 3F 91
Dorchester Rd. CH4: Ches 6G 149
SK7: H Gro 4F 79
WA5: Gt San 7K 39
Dorchester Way CH43: Noc 2G 59
SK10: Mac 7K 121
WA5: B'ood 5C 14
Dorclyn Av. M41: Urm 1C 22
Doreen Av. CH46: More 4A 32
CW12: Cong 7K 183
Dorfield Cl. SK6: Bred 1J 53
Dorfold Cl. CW11: S'ach 2G 201
Dorfold Dr. CW5: Nant 2B 196
Dorfold Hall 7K 189
Dorfold St. CW1: Crewe 2C 194
Dorfold Way CH2: Upt 4B 146
Doric Av. SK6: Bred 1H 53
WA6: Frod 1J 139
Doric St. CH42: R Fer 3E 60
Dorin Ct. CH2: Upt 4A 146
Dorincourt CH43: Oxt 1K 59
Doris Rd. SK3: Stoc 4A 52
Dorking Cl. SK1: Stoc 5F 53
Dorland Gro. SK2: Stoc 5F 53
Dormer Cl. CH3: Row 2A 174
Dorney Cl. WA4: App 7J 67
Dornoch Ct. CW4: H Cha 5H 181
Dorothea St. WA2: Warr 5G 41
Dorothy Rd. SK7: H Gro 2K 79
Dorric Way CW1: Crewe 6H 191
Dorrington Cl. WA7: Murd 6F 91
Dorrington Rd. M33: Sale 7C 22
SK3: Stoc 5J 51
Dorris St. M19: Manc 3E 24
Dorrit Cl. SK12: Poy 4D 100
Dorrit St. L8: Liv 6K 35
Dorset Av. M34: Aude 2B 8
SK5: Stoc 6B 26
SK7: Bram 3B 78
SK8: Chea H 7A 52
Dorset Cl. CW12: Cong 2G 183
Dorset Dr. CH61: Pens 2G 83
Dorset Gdns. CH42: R Fer 4E 60
WA7: Pal F 1C 112
Dorset Pl. CH2: Ches 5D 146
Dorset Rd. CH2: Upt 3C 146
CH45: N Bri 4G 13
CH48: W Kir 2D 56
M19: Manc 2F 25
M44: Cad 6A 20
WA14: Alt 7F 47
Dorset St. M32: S'ord 2J 23
Dorset Wlk. SK10: Mac 2G 125
(off Kennedy Av.)
Dorset Way WA1: Wool 4B 42
Double Cop WN7: Leigh 1D 6
Dougals Way WN7: Leigh 1B 6
Doughton Grn. WA8: Wid 2E 62
Douglas Av. M32: S'ord 1J 23
Douglas Cl. CW8: H'ord 1B 162
WA8: Wid 2B 64
Douglas Dr. CH46: More 4A 32
Douglas Pl. CH4: Salt 5F 149
Douglas Rd. CH48: W Kir 2E 56
SK3: Stoc 1C 78
SK7: H Gro 2J 79
Douglas St. CH41: Birk 6D 34
SK14: Hyde 1K 27
Douglas Wlk. M33: Sale 6B 22
Doulton Cl. CH43: Bid 5E 32
CW7: Wins 1G 179
Doune Ct. CH65: Ell P 5F 135
Dounrey Cl. WA2: Fear 2A 42
Douthwaite Dr. SK6: Rom 3E 54
Dovebrook Cl. SK15: Carrb 2F 5
Dove Cl. CH2: Elt 4G 137
CH66: Ell P 1C 134
CW11: S'ach 1E 200
WA3: Birc 7A 18
WA6: Hel 3C 138
Dovecote Bus. & Technology Pk.
M33: Sale 7K 23
Dovecote Cl. CW2: Wis 6B 194
Dovecote Grn. WA5: W'ook 3J 39
Dovedale Av. CH62: East 2K 107
M41: Urm 1C 22
Dovedale Cl. CH43: Pren 3J 59
CW12: Cong 2J 183
SK6: H Lan 6E 80
WA2: Warr 1J 41
Dovedale Ct. WA8: Wid 2B 62
Dovedale Rd. CH45: Wall 4G 13
CH47: Hoy 4C 30
SK2: Stoc 5H 53
Dove Pl. CW7: Wins 2J 179
Dovepoint Rd. CH47: Meols 3F 31
Dover Cl. CH41: Birk 5C 34
WA7: Murd 1G 113
Dover Ct. CH65: Ell P 6F 135
Dovercourt Av. SK4: Stoc 1H 51
Dover Dr. CH65: Ell P 6F 135
CW7: Wins 5C 178
Dover Rd. CH4: Ches 5H 149
SK10: Mac 2C 126
WA4: Westy 2A 68
Dover St. SK5: Stoc 4H 25
WA7: Run 3H 89
Dovesmead Rd. CH60: Hes 7A 84
Dovestone Cres. SK16: Duk 3A 10
Doveston Gro. M33: Sale 5G 23
Doveston Rd. M33: Sale 5G 23
Doward St. WA8: Wid 3J 63
Dowland Cl. M23: Wyth 2F 49
DOWNALL GREEN 1D 215
Downes Cl. SK10: Mac 3H 125
Downes Grn. CH63: Spit 5A 86
Downes Way M22: Shar 6A 50
Downesway SK9: Ald E 6E 118
Downfields SK5: Stoc 2K 25
Downham Av. WA3: Cul 1A 18
Downham Chase WA15: Timp 6B 48
Downham Dr. CH60: Hes 6J 83
Downham Pl. CH1: Blac 6F 145
Downham Rd. CH42: Tran 2C 60
SK4: Stoc 6G 25
Downham Rd. Nth. CH61: Hes 4J 83
Downham Rd. Sth. CH60: Hes 6J 83
Downham Wlk. M23: Wyth 4E 48
Downing Cl. CH43: Oxt 2A 60
SK11: Sut E 2K 129
Downs, The CW8: Cudd 1A 160
SK8: Chea 2F 77
WA14: Alt 4G 213 (2G 73)
Downs Dr. WA14: Timp 4J 47
Downs End WA16: Knut 4G 117
Downsfield Rd. CH4: Ches 5G 149
Downside WA8: Wid 2B 62
Downs Rd. WA7: Run 5G 89
Downswood Ct. CH1: Ches 6K 145
Downswood Dr. CH1: Ches 6K 145
Dowson Rd. SK14: Hyde 4J 27
Dow St. SK14: Hyde 5J 9
Doyle Av. SK6: Bred 1H 53
Dragons Health Club
Chester 5K 149
Dragon Yd. WA8: Wid 1H 63
Drake Av. M22: Wyth 3H 75
M44: Cad 5B 20
Drake Cl. WA5: Old H 3B 40
Drake Ct. SK5: Stoc 7H 25
Drake Rd. CH46: Leas 7B 12
CH64: Nest 6H 105
WA14: B'ath 4F 47
Drakes Way SY14: Mal 1H 207
Draxford Ct. SK9: Wilm 1G 119
DRAYCOTT IN THE MOORS 3D 221
Drayford Cl. M23: Wyth 2F 49
Drayton Cl. CH61: Irby 1F 83
M33: Sale 2H 47
SK9: Wilm 5A 98
WA5: Gt San 6K 39
WA7: Run 5F 89
Drayton Cres. CW1: Crewe 1F 195
Drayton Dr. SK8: He Grn 6D 76
Drayton Gro. WA15: Timp 1A 74
Drayton Mnr. M20: Manc 4D 50
Drayton Rd. CH44: Wall 1C 34
Drenfell Rd. ST7: Sch G 1J 205
Drillfield Ct. CW9: N'ich 5F 157
Drillfield Rd. CW9: N'ich 5E 156
Drinkwater Gdns. L3: Liv 1K 35
Driscoll St. M13: Manc 1C 24
Drive, The CW4: H Cha 5J 181
M20: Manc 1E 50
M33: Sale 3J 47
SK5: Stoc 7A 26
SK6: Bred 1H 53
SK6: Mar 6E 54
SK8: Chea H 1A 78
SK10: Boll 4B 122
WA13: Lymm 4F 71
WA15: H'rns 5D 74
DriveTime (Golf Driving Range) 3E 66
Driveway L35: Whis 1A 36
Droitwich Av. CH49: Gre 1K 57
Dronfield Rd. M22: N'den 4K 49
Drovers La. WA6: Frod 4J 139
Drovers Way CW11: S'ach 4E 200
DROYLSDEN 1A 8 (1C 217)
Droylsden FC (Butchers Arms Ground) 1A 8
Droylsden Little Theatre 1A 8
(off Market St.)
Droylsden Rd. M34: Aude 1A 8
Druids Way CH49: Woodc 3D 58
Druitt Ct. CW1: Hasl 2K 195
Drumber, The CW7: Wins 3E 178
Drumble Fld. SK11: Chel 5C 166
Drummond Av. CH66: Gt Sut 4J 133
Drummond Ct. WA8: Wid 3K 63
Drummond Rd. CH47: Hoy 7B 30
Drummond Way SK10: Mac 3F 125
Druridge Dr. WA5: Penk 1H 65
DRURY 1A 218
Drury Cl. CW1: Crewe 2F 195
Drury La. CW1: Warm 1J 191
L2: Liv 3H 35
WA16: Knut 3E 116
Drury St. M19: Manc 2D 24
Dryden Av. SK8: Chea 6H 51
Dryden Cl. CH43: Bid 5J 33
CW2: Wis 5A 194
SK6: Mar 1F 81
SK16: Duk 3C 10
Dryden Pl. WA2: Warr 2G 41
Dryden Way M34: Den 3F 27
(off Spenser Av.)
Dryersfield CH3: Ches 3D 150
Dryfield Cl. CH49: Gre 1A 58
Dryhurst Dr. SK12: Dis 6K 81
Dryhurst La. SK12: Dis 1G 103
Dublin Cft. CH66: Gt Sut 7A 134
Dubthorn La. CW11: Bet H 4J 201
Duchess Pl. CH2: Ches 1B 212 (7K 145)
Duchy Rd. CW1: Crewe 6G 195
Duchy St. SK3: Stoc 5B 52
Duckinfield St. L3: Liv 3K 35
DUCKINGTON 2C 219
Duck La. CH3: Ash H 7H 171
Duck Pond La. CH42: Tran 3K 59
Duckworth Gro. WA2: Padg 3A 42
DUDDON 5C 174 (1D 219)
Duddon Cl. CH43: Oxt 2J 59
CW6: Dud 5C 174
CW9: N'ich 2D 162
DUDDON COMMON 4D 174
Duddon Rd. CW6: Clot, Dud 5C 174
DUDLESTON 3B 218

Eaton La.—Elm Beds Rd.

Eaton La. CW4: Goo 6G 165
CW6: Cote, Eat 7B 176
CW6: Eat 7F 177
CW6: R Hea 4K 175
CW9: Dave 4C 162
SK11: Mac 7A 126
Eaton M. CH4: Ches 4A 150
Eaton Pl. CW8: H'ord 2J 161
Eaton Rd. CH4: Ches, Ecc 7C 212 (4A 150)
CH43: Oxt 7A 34
CH48: W Kir 4B 56
CW6: Tarp 3J 175
M33: Sale 7F 23
ST7: Als 5D 202
WA14: Bow 4G 73
Eaton St. CH44: Wall 6H 13
CW2: Crewe 2C 194
L3: Liv 1H 35
WA7: Run 4G 89
Eaton Vw. CW9: Moult 6D 162
Eaton Way CW3: Audl 5C 210
EAVES BROW 4G 17
Eaves Brow Rd. WA3: Croft 4G 17
Ebbdale Cl. SK1: Stoc 4D 52
Ebenezer Pl. WA1: Warr 7E 40
Ebenezer St. CH42: R Fer 3F 61
Eberle St. L2: Liv 2H 35
EBNAL 1K 207 (3C 219)
Ebnal La. SY14: Mal 1K 207 & 2A 208
Ebnall Wlk. M14: Manc 4A 24
Ebony Cl. CH46: More 4J 31
Ebor Ho. M32: S'ord 2K 23
Ebor Rd. M22: Wyth 1A 76
Ebury Pl. CH4: Ches 7D 212 (4A 150)
ECCLES 1B 216
Eccles Bri. Rd. SK6: Mar 7F 55
Eccles Gro. WA9: Clo F 1A 38
Eccleshall Rd. CH62: P Sun 7H 61
ECCLESTON
CH4 2K 185 (1C 219)
WA10 1C 215
Eccleston Av. CH4: Ches 5A 150
CH62: Brom 5C 86
CH65: Ell P 3A 134
Eccleston Cl. CH43: Oxt 2J 59
WA3: Birc 6H 17
Eccleston Ct. *CW9: N'ich* *1D 162*
(off Harthill Cl.)
Eccleston Dr. WA7: Run 5J 89
Eccleston Rd. SK3: Stoc 1C 78
Eccleston Way *SK9: Hand* *2A 98*
(off Henbury Rd.)
Eccups La. SK9: Wilm 6D 96
Echo Arena 5H 35
Echo Cl. CH4: Salt 6F 149
Echo La. CH48: W Kir 4D 56
Eckersley Cl. M23: Wyth 6F 49
Ecton Av. SK10: Mac 5D 126
Ecton Cl. CW7: Wins 1H 179
Edale Av. M34: Aude 3C 8
M34: Den 3E 26
M41: Urm 2A 22
SK5: Stoc 2K 25
Edale Cl. CH62: East 2K 107
M44: Irlam 2D 20
SK7: H Gro 4J 79
SK8: He Grn 6F 77
WA14: Bow 4G 73
Edale Dr. CW6: Kel 3C 172
Edale Gro. M33: Sale 2J 47
OL6: Ash L 3B 4
Eddarbridge Est. WA8: Wid 1F 89
Eddisbury Cl. SK11: Mac 5C 126
Eddisbury Hill CW6: Kel 3F 173
CW8: Dela 3G 173
Eddisbury Hill Hill Fort 3F 173
Eddisbury Rd. CH44: Wall 6J 13
CH47: Hoy 1B 56
CH48: W Kir 1B 56
CH66: Whit 6B 134
Eddisbury Sq. WA6: Frod 7H 111
Eddisbury Ter. SK11: Mac 5C 126
Eddisbury Way CW9: N'ich 3D 162
Eddisford Dr. WA3: Cul 5D 6
Eddsibury Hill Pk. CW8: Dela 3G 173
Edelsten St. WA5: Warr 7D 40
Eden Av. CW7: Wins 2G 179
SK6: H Lan 6E 80
WA3: Cul 6J 7
Edenbridge Cl. CW2: West 5H 199
Edenbridge Gdns. WA4: App 3J 93
Edenbridge Rd. SK8: Chea H 1K 77
Eden Cl. CH66: Gt Sut 3J 133
L35: R'ill 2B 36
SK1: Stoc 4E 52
SK9: Wilm 2D 118
Eden Ct. M19: Manc 3D 24
Edendale WA8: Wid 3B 62
Edendale Dr. M22: Wyth 4K 75
Eden Dr. SK10: Mac 3C 126
Edenfield Cl. WA16: Mob 7B 102
Edenfield Ct. SK14: Hyde 2K 27
Edenfield Rd. WA16: Mob 7B 102
Edenhall Av. M19: Manc 3C 24
Edenhall Cl. CW4: H Cha 4G 181
Edenhurst Av. CH44: Wall 6J 13
Edenhurst Dr. WA15: Timp 7B 48
Edenhurst Rd. SK2: Stoc 6F 53
Eden Pk. Rd. SK8: Chea H 5G 77
Edenpark Rd. CH42: Tran 2B 60
Eden Pl. M33: Sale 6G 23
SK8: Chea 6F 51
Edensor Dr. WA15: Hale 2C 74
Edgar Cotts. CH4: Ches 7C 212
Edgar Ct. CH4: Ches 7C 212
CH41: Birk 5C 34
SK11: Mac *4K 125*
(off Bridge St.)
Edgar Pl. CH4: Ches 7C 212 (3A 150)
Edgars Dr. WA2: Fear 3A 42
Edgar St. L3: Liv 1J 35
Edgbaston Way
CH43: Bid 4F 33
Edgecote Cl. M22: Shar 6B 50
Edgecroft CH3: Tatt 3G 187
Edgedale Av. M19: Manc 6B 24
Edgefield Cl. CH43: Noc 1G 59
EDGE GREEN 2C 219
Edge Gro. CH2: Ches 1C 150
Edgehill Chase SK9: Wilm 7B 98
Edgehill Ct. M32: S'ord 2K 23
Edgehill Rd. CH46: More 4K 31
Edge La. M21: Chor H 2J 23
M32: S'ord 2J 23
SK14: Mot 6F 11
(not continuous)
EDGELEY
SK3 5A 52
SY13 3D 219
Edgeley Fold SK3: Stoc 5A 52
Edgeley Pk. 5C 52
Edgeley Rd. M41: Urm 3K 21
SK3: Stoc 5J 51
Edgemoor WA14: Bow 3E 72
Edgemoor Cl. CH43: Bid 5E 32
Edgemoor Dr. CH61: Irby 6K 57
Edgerley La. CH3: Chu 1E 186
Edge Vw. La. SK9: Ald E 5A 118
Edgeview Rd. CW12: Cong 7K 183
Edge Wlk. SK15: Stal 1C 10
Edgewater Pl. WA4: Westy 1B 68
Edgeway SK9: Wilm 2G 119
Edgewell La. CW6: Eat 6G 177
Edgewood Cl. WA8: Wid 5B 62
Edgewood Dr. CH62: Brom 2J 107
CW2: Wis 7A 194
Edgewood Rd. CH47: Meols 3E 30
CH49: Upt 6C 32
Edgeworth Dr. M14: Manc 4B 24
Edgeworth St. WA2: Warr 6E 40
Edinburgh Cl. M33: Sale 1H 47
SK8: Chea 6H 51
Edinburgh Ct. CH65: Ell P 5F 135
Edinburgh Dr. CH43: Pren 4K 59
SK6: W'ley 7H 27
SK10: Mac 3H 125
Edinburgh Pl. CW12: Cong 4H 183
Edinburgh Rd. CH45: Wall 6H 13
CW2: Wis 6J 193
CW12: Cong 4H 183
WA8: Wid 5A 62
Edinburgh Way CH4: Ches 3B 150
Edison Rd. WA7: Astm 3K 89
Edith Rd. CH44: Wall 1D 34
Edith St. WA7: Run 3F 89
Edith Ter. SK6: Comp 2H 55
Edleston Gro. *SK9: Wilm* *5B 98*
(off Picton Dr.)
Edleston Rd. CW2: Crewe 3D 194
Edmonton Ct. SK2: Stoc 1E 78
Edmonton Rd. SK2: Stoc 1E 78
Edmund Ct. SK4: Stoc 1C 52
Edmund St. L3: Liv 2H 35
Edmund Wright Way
CW5: Nant 2A 196
Edna St. CH2: Ches 7C 146
SK14: Hyde 2J 27
Edrich Av. CH43: Bid 4F 33
Edward Av. SK6: Bred 1J 53
Edward Ct. WA14: B'ath 5F 47
Edward Gdns. WA1: Wool 6F 43
Edward Pav. L3: Liv 4H 35
Edward Rd. CH47: Hoy 6D 30
WA5: Gt San 6F 39
Edwards Av. CW2: Shav 2C 198
Edwards Cl. CW2: Shav 2C 198
SK6: Mar 7E 54
Edwards Ct. M22: Wyth 2K 75
SK7: H Gro 5J 79
Edwards Rd. CH4: Ches 5H 149
Edward St. CH65: Ell P 1E 134
CW2: Crewe 4D 194
CW9: N'ich 5H 157
M33: Sale 7K 23
M34: Aude 3C 8
M34: Den 6E 8
M43: Droy 2A 8
SK1: Stoc 7J 213 (4D 52)
SK6: Mar B 3G 55
SK11: Mac 5J 125
SK14: Hyde 7H 9
(not continuous)
SK16: Duk 4H 9
WA8: Wid 4K 63
Edwards Way SK6: Mar 7E 54
ST7: Als 5F 203
WA8: Wid 5C 62
Edwin St. SK1: Stoc 4F 53
WA8: Wid 4J 63
Eeasbrook M41: Urm 2C 22
Egan Ct. *CH41: Birk* *5D 34*
(off Lord St.)
Egan Rd. CH43: Bid 4H 33
Egbert Rd. CH47: Meols 4D 30
Egdon Cl. WA8: Wid 3A 64
Egerton WA16: H Leg 1H 95
Egerton Av. CW8: H'ord 2K 161
WA1: Warr 5J 41
(not continuous)
WA13: Warb 4E 44
Egerton Ct. CH41: Birk 5D 34
M34: Den *6F 9*
(off Margaret Rd.)
SK3: Stoc 1E 78
Egerton Dr. CH2: Ches 5A 146
CH48: W Kir 3C 56
M33: Sale 6G 23
WA15: Hale 3A 74
Egerton Gdns. CH42: R Fer 4D 60
Egerton Gro. CH45: Wall 6H 13
Egerton Ho. SK4: Stoc 7D 24
WA7: Run 3H 89
Egerton Lodge *M34: Den* *6F 9*
(off Margaret Rd.)
Egerton M. M43: Droy 2A 8
WA4: Stoc H 4G 67
Egerton Moss WA15: Ash 7J 73
Egerton Pk. CH42: R Fer 4D 60
Egerton Pk. Arts College Sports Hall *6D 8*
(off Egerton St.)
Egerton Pk. Cl. CH42: R Fer 4D 60
Egerton Rd. CH1: Blac 5E 144
CH43: Clau 6K 33
CH62: N Fer 6G 61
M14: Manc 3A 24
SK3: Stoc 7E 52
SK9: Wilm 5J 97
WA13: Lymm 3J 69
WA15: Hale 2A 74
Egerton Rd. Nth. SK4: Stoc 6F 25
Egerton Rd. Sth. SK4: Stoc 6F 25
Egerton Sq. WA16: Knut 3E 116
Egerton St. CH1: Ches 2E 212 (1B 150)
CH45: N Bri 3H 13
CH65: Ell P 2E 134
CW12: Cong 4E 182
M34: Den 5C 8
M43: Droy 1A 8
WA1: Warr 7H 41
WA4: Stoc H 4G 67
WA7: Run 3F 89
Egerton Ter. M14: Manc 4A 24
Egerton Wlk. CH4: Dod 3D 184
Egerton Wharf CH41: Birk 4D 34
Eggbridge La. CH3: Wave 2A 174
Egmont St. OL5: Moss 1D 4
Egmont Ter. *SK15: Stal* *2C 10*
(off Spring Bank)
EGREMONT 6K 13 (1B 214)
Egremont Gro. SK3: Stoc 4K 51
Egremont Prom.
CH44: Wall 5K 13
CH45: Wall 5K 13
Egret Dr. M44: Irlam 1D 20
Egypt St. WA1: Warr 7E 40
WA8: Wid 6F 63
Elaine Cl. CH66: Gt Sut 4J 133
WA8: Wid 3J 63
Elaine Price Ct. WA7: Run 5F 89
Elaine St. WA1: Warr 5H 41
Elanor Rd. CW11: Elw 2B 200
Elbow St. M19: Manc 2D 24
Elbrus Dr. CH66: Ell P 1B 134
Elcho Ct. WA14: Bow 3F 73
Elcho Rd. WA14: Bow 2F 73
Elderberry Wlk. *M31: Part* *1G 45*
(off Wood La.)
Elderberry Way SK9: Wilm 6B 98
Elder Cl. SK2: Stoc 4H 53
Elder Ct. SK4: Stoc 1K 51
Eldercroft Rd.
WA15: Timp 7C 48
Elder Dr. CH4: Ches 6F 149
Elderfield Dr. SK6: Bred 7E 26
Elder Gro. CH48: W Kir 3C 56
Elder Ho. CH1: Ches 1F 149
Elderwood Rd. CH42: Tran 2D 60
Eldon Cl. M34: Aude 3D 8
Eldon Gro. *L3: Liv* *1J 35*
(off Limekiln La.)
Eldonian Way L3: Liv 1H 35
Eldon Pl. L3: Liv 1H 35
Eldon Rd. CH42: R Fer 3E 60
CH44: Wall 7H 13
M44: Irlam 1D 20
SK3: Stoc 5A 52
SK10: Mac 4G 125
Eldon St. L3: Liv 1H 35
WA1: Warr 7G 41
Eldon Ter. CH64: Nest 1C 130
Eldroth Av. M22: Wyth 2K 75
Eleanor Cl. CW1: Crewe 1K 193
Eleanor Pk. CH43: Bid 4F 33
Eleanor Rd. CH43: Bid 3G 33
CH46: More 3K 31
Eleanor St. CH65: Ell P 2E 134
WA8: Wid 6G 63
Electra Ho. CW1: Crewe 4G 195
Electra Way CW1: Crewe 4F 195
Electricity St. CW2: Crewe 3C 194
Elfet St. CH41: Birk 4J 33
Elf Mill Cl. SK3: Stoc 6C 52
Elf Mill Ter. SK3: Stoc 6C 52
Elgar Av. CH62: East 2K 107
Elgar Cl. CH65: Gt Sut 5B 134
Elgin Av. CW4: H Cha 5H 181
M20: Manc 1F 51
SK10: Mac 2H 125
WA4: Warr 3E 66
Elgin Cl. CH3: Ches 7D 146
Elgin Ct. L35: R'ill 2D 36
Elgin Dr. CH45: Wall 5J 13
M33: Sale 1E 48
Elgin Rd. SK16: Duk 4H 9
Elgin St. SK15: Stal 1C 10
Elgin Way CH41: Birk 5D 34
Elgol Cl. SK3: Stoc 7D 52
Eliot Cl. CH62: N Fer 6F 61
CW1: Crewe 2G 195
Elizabethan Way
CW9: Rud 7K 157
Elizabeth Av. M34: Den 5D 8
SK1: Stoc 4D 52
SK12: Dis 2G 103
SK15: Stal 7B 4
Elizabeth Cl. CW6: Kel 4C 172
CW11: Elw 2B 200
M32: S'ord 1J 23
Elizabeth Ct. M14: Manc 4A 24
SK4: Stoc 2A 52
WA8: Wid 6H 63
Elizabeth Cres. CH4: Ches 2B 150
Elizabeth Dr. WA1: Padg 4A 42
Elizabeth Gaskell Ct.
WA16: Knut 3D 116
Elizabeth Ho. SK4: Stoc 3K 51
SK11: Mac *5B 126*
(off Swettenham St.)
Elizabeth Rd. M31: Part 7C 20
Elizabeth St. CW1: Crewe 1B 194
CW12: Cong 4E 182
M34: Den 7C 8
SK11: Mac 5A 126
SK14: Hyde 7J 9
WA9: Clo F 1A 38
Elizabeth St. Ind. Est. *M34: Den* *7C 8*
(off Grey St.)
Elizabeth Ter. WA8: Wid 4D 62
Elkan Cl. WA8: Wid 2A 64
Elkan Rd. WA8: Wid 2K 63
Ella Gro. WA16: Knut 3F 117
Elland Dr. CH66: L Sut 3J 133
Ellaston Dr. M41: Urm 1C 22
Ellenbrook Rd. M22: Wyth 5K 75
Ellen's La. CH63: Beb 1B 86
Ellen St. M43: Droy 2A 8
SK4: Stoc 1B 52
WA5: Warr 5D 40
Elleray Pk. Rd. CH45: Wall 4G 13
Ellerby Cl. WA7: Murd 7G 91
Ellerman Rd. L3: Liv 2K 61
(not continuous)
Ellerton Av. CH66: L Sut 3J 133
Ellerton Cl. WA8: Wid 2D 62
Ellesmere Av. CH2: Ches 5A 146
SK6: Mar 6F 55
Ellesmere Cl. CW11: S'ach 1C 200
SK16: Duk 3K 9
Ellesmere Dr. SK8: Chea 7J 51
Ellesmere Gro. CH45: Wall 5H 13
Ellesmere Pl. *CW1: Crewe* *1C 194*
(off Rigg St.)
ELLESMERE PORT 3E 134 (3C 215)
Ellesmere Port Golf Cen. 1H 133
Ellesmere Port Stadium 5G 135
Ellesmere Port Station (Rail) 3E 134
Ellesmere Rd. CW9: N'ich 2F 163
SK3: Stoc 5J 51
WA3: Cul 6E 6
WA4: Stoc H, Walt 4F 67
WA14: Alt 6H 47
Ellesmere Rd. Nth. SK4: Stoc 6F 25
Ellesmere St. WA1: Warr 7G 41
(not continuous)
WA7: Run 4H 89
Ellesmere Ter. M14: Manc 4A 24
Ellesworth Cl. WA5: Old H 4A 40
Ellingham Way CW9: N'ich 3D 162
Ellington Dr. WA5: Gt San 7K 39
Elliot St. L1: Liv 3J 35
WA8: Wid 5H 63
Elliott Av. SK14: Hyde 5J 9
WA1: Warr 5J 41
Elliott Dr. M33: Sale 7D 22
Ellis La. WA6: Frod 6K 111
Ellison Cl. SK14: H'rth 2J 11
Ellison Ct. CH1: Ches 2C 212
Ellison Ho. *OL7: Ash L* *1F 9*
(off Park St.)
Ellison St. *WA1: Warr* *7G 41*
(off Ellesmere St.)
WA4: Stoc H 4H 67
Ellis St. CW1: Crewe 7G 191
SK14: Hyde 7A 10
WA8: Wid 6G 63
Ellon Av. L35: R'ill 2D 36
Ellwood Cl. L24: Hale 6B 88
Ellwood Grn. CW2: Hou 4E 198
Ellwood Rd. SK1: Stoc 3F 53
Elm Av. CH49: Upt 6A 32
WA8: Wid 3H 63
WA12: New W 1F 15
Elmbank Av. M20: Manc 1A 50
Elmbank Rd. CH62: N Fer 7G 61
Elmbank St. CH44: Wall 1B 34
Elm Beds Cvn. Pk. SK12: Poy 4H 101
Elm Beds Rd. SK12: Poy 4H 101

Elm Cl.—Ewart St.

Elm Cl. CH61: Pens 2J 83
CW2: Crewe 4J 193
CW6: Tarp 2J 175
M31: Part 1H 45
SK12: Poy 3E 100
SK14: Mot 6H 11
Elm Ct. CH63: H Beb 7C 60
CH65: Ell P 4H 135
CW1: Crewe 7J 191
SK1: Stoc 4F 53
Elm Cres. SK9: Ald E 5G 119
Elmdale Av. SK8: He Grn 3D 76
Elmdene Ct. CH49: Gre 3K 57
Elm Dr. CH49: Gre 2K 57
CW1: Crewe 7J 191
CW4: H Cha 3K 181
M32: S'ord 2G 23
SK10: Mac 2B 126
Elmfield Av. M22: N'den 4A 50
Elmfield Cl. SK9: Ald E 5G 119
Elmfield Ct. *SK3: Stoc 7D 52*
(off Elmfield Rd.)
Elmfield Dr. SK6: Mar 6E 54
Elmfield Ho. *SK3: Stoc 7D 52*
(off Plumley Cl.)
Elmfield Rd. M34: Aude 2B 8
SK3: Stoc 7D 52
SK9: Ald E 5G 119
Elmgate Gro.
M19: Manc 2D 24
Elm Grn. CH64: W'ston 7E 106
Elm Gro. CH4: Salt 6F 149
CH42: Tran 1C 60
CH47: Hoy 5D 30
CH66: Whit 7C 134
CW7: Wins 3H 179
M20: Manc 1D 50
M33: Sale 5G 23
M34: Den 5C 8
M41: Urm 1D 22
SK9: Ald E 5F 119
SK9: Hand 3K 97
(off Sagars Rd.)
SK14: Hyde 1A 28
ST7: Als 5F 203
WA1: Padd 5K 41
WA8: Wid 4H 63
Elm Ho. CH2: Ches 5J 145
Elmhurst Dr. M19: Manc 6C 24
Elmlea WA15: Alt 1K 73
Elmley Cl. SK2: Stoc 7A 54
Elmore Cl. CW4: H Cha 4H 181
WA7: Win H 5F 91
Elm Pk. Ct. M20: Manc 1D 50
Elm Pk. Rd. CH45: Wall 4G 13
Elmridge Dr. WA15: H'rns 5C 74
Elmridge Way CW8: Winn 4C 156
Elm Ri. SK10: Pres 5F 121
WA6: Frod 1J 139
Elm Rd. CH42: Tran 2C 60
(Derby Rd.)
CH42: Tran 3A 60
(Elm Rd. Nth.)
CH61: Irby 7C 58
CH63: H Beb 6E 60
CH64: W'ston 7E 106
CW8: Weav 6G 155
CW10: Mid 5D 180
CW12: Cong 3D 182
M20: Manc 1C 50
SK6: H Lan 6F 81
SK8: Gat 7C 50
WA2: Winw 7K 15
WA3: Rix 2C 44
WA5: Penk 1H 65
WA7: Run 6J 89
WA15: Hale 2J 73
Elm Rd. Nth. CH42: Tran 3A 60
Elm Rd. Sth. SK3: Stoc 5J 51
Elms, The OL5: Moss 1C 4
WA3: Low 3A 6
WA7: Run 5F 89
Elmsett Cl. WA5: Gt San 7G 39
Elmsleigh Rd. SK8: He Grn 3C 76
Elmsmere Rd. M20: Manc 1F 51
Elms Pk. CH61: Thin 1J 83
Elm Sq. CH4: Ches 5G 149
Elms Rd. SK4: Stoc 6E 24
SK15: Stal 6E 4
Elmstead Cres. CW1: Crewe 5E 190
Elmstead Rd. SK11: Chel 5C 166
Elmsted Cl. SK8: Chea H 2K 77
Elm St. CH41: Birk 6C 34
CH65: Ell P 1E 134
CW9: N'ich 4G 157
SK6: Bred 7E 26
Elmsway SK6: H Lan 7E 80
SK7: Bram 6A 78
SK10: Boll 3D 122
WA15: H'rns 5B 74
Elmswood Av. L35: R'ill 3D 36
Elmswood Dr. SK14: Hyde 7B 10
Elmswood Rd. CH42: Tran 1B 60
CH44: Wall 7K 13
Elmsworth Av. M19: Manc 2E 24
Elm Ter. CH47: Hoy 5D 30
CW1: Crewe 7K 191
Elm Tree Av. WA1: Padg 4K 41
WA13: Lymm 3K 69
Elm Tree Cl. SK15: Stal 2B 10
Elm Tree Ct. CH47: Hoy 4D 30
CW6: Eat 6G 177
Elm Tree Dr. M22: Wyth 2K 75
SK16: Duk 3A 10
Elmtree Dr. SK4: Stoc 2K 51
Elmtree Gro. CH43: Bid 4H 33
Elm Tree La. CW11: Elw 1B 200
Elm Tree Rd. CH1: Sau 3A 144
SK6: Bred 1G 53
WA13: Lymm 3K 69
Elmuir CH1: Blac 7F 145
Elmure Av. CH63: H Beb 1H 85
Elmwood M33: Sale 7B 22
WA7: Nort 5E 90
Elmwood Av. CH2: Ches 6C 146
WA1: Warr 5J 41
Elmwood Cl. ST7: Chu L 5H 203
Elmwood Ct. M32: S'ord 3H 23
SK10: Boll 6A 122
Elmwood Dr. CH61: Hes 4H 83
Elmwood Gro. CW7: Wins 4G 179
Elmwood Lodge M20: Manc 1C 50
Elmwood Pk. SK15: Stal 6E 4
Elmwood Rd. CW8: Barnt 1K 155
Elphins Dr. WA4: Warr 3G 67
Elsa Rd. M19: Manc 2F 25
Elsby Rd. ST7: Als 7G 203
Elsdon Rd. M13: Manc 1C 24
Elsinore Av. M44: Irlam 2C 20
Elson Dr. SK14: Hyde 4J 27
Elstree Av. CH3: Ches 7E 146
Elstree Ct. M41: Urm 1C 22
WA8: Wid 1K 63
Elswick Av. SK7: Bram 6C 78
Eltham Av. SK2: Stoc 7G 53
Eltham Cl. CH49: Woodc 3E 58
WA8: Wid 2A 64
Eltham Grn. CH49: Woodc 3E 58
Eltham St. M19: Manc 1D 24
Eltham Wlk. WA8: Wid 2A 64
ELTON
CH2 5F 137 (3C 215)
CW11 4A 200
Elton Av. M19: Manc 3D 24
Elton Cl. CH62: East 4K 107
SK9: Wilm 5B 98
WA3: Birc 7H 17
Elton Crossings Rd.
CW11: Elw, Ett H 3B 200
Elton Dr. CH63: Spit 4A 86
SK7: H Gro 5H 79
Elton Flashes (Nature Reserve) 5A 200
ELTON GREEN 6E 136 (3C 215)
Elton La.
CW11: Hasl, Wint 7A 200 & 4A 204
CW11: Wint 4B 204
WA6: Hel 4H 137
Elton Lordship La. WA6: Frod 2A 138
Elton Rd. CW11: Ett H 4A 200
M33: Sale 2J 47
Elverston St. M22: N'den 3A 50
Elvington Cl. CW12: Cong 4G 183
WA7: Sut W 4B 112
ELWORTH 2B 200 (1B 220)
Elworth Av. WA8: Wid 7G 37
Elworth Ct. *CW12: Cong 3H 183*
(off Herbert St.)
Elworth Rd. CW11: Elw 3B 200
Elworth St. CW11: S'ach 2E 200
Elworth Way *SK9: Hand 2A 98*
(off Delamere Rd.)
Elwyn Av. M22: N'den 5K 49
Elwyn Rd. CH47: Meols 3F 31
Ely Av. CH46: More 4K 31
Ely Cl. CH66: Gt Sut 1A 140
Ely Gdns. M41: Urm 1D 22
Ely Pk. WA7: Nort 4G 91
Embankment Bus. Pk., The
SK4: Stoc 3H 51
Embassy Cl. CH1: Blac 6D 144
Emberton Hall ST7: Als 5B 202
Emberton Pl. CW3: Audl 4C 210
Embleton Gro. WA7: Beec 2K 111
Emerald Dr. CW11: S'ach 1G 201
Emerald Rd. M22: Wyth 6B 76
Emerald St. M34: Den 7D 8
Emery Cl. SK4: Stoc 7D 24
WA14: Alt 5H 47
Emery Ct. SK4: Stoc 3H 51
Emily St. WA8: Wid 6G 63
Emily St. M19: Manc 2E 24
Emlyn Gro. SK8: Chea 6J 51
Emmett St. CW8: Barnt 2K 155
Empire Rd. SK16: Duk 4H 9
Empress Av. SK6: Mar 7F 55
Empress Dr. CW2: Crewe 3B 194
SK4: Stoc 7G 25
Empress Rd. CH44: Wall 7J 13
Emslie Ct. CH64: Park 1A 130
Emsworth Dr. M33: Sale 3C 48
Enderby Rd. CH1: Ches 2B 212 (1K 149)
Endfield Farm Cvn. Pk. WA16: H Leg 7F 71
ENDON 2D 221
Endon Av. SK10: Boll 4D 122
ENDON BANK 2D 221
Endsleigh Cl. CH2: Upt 2B 146
Endsleigh Gdns. CH2: Upt 2B 146
Enerby Cl. CH43: Bid 5F 33
Energis Fitness Club 5A 98
Enfield Av. M19: Manc 5D 24
Enfield Cl. CW2: Shav 4B 198
Enfield Pk. Rd. WA2: Fear 7E 16
Enfield Rd. CH65: Ell P 3D 134
Enfield St. SK14: Hyde 4K 27
Enfield Ter. CH43: Oxt 7A 34
Enford Av. M22: Wyth 3G 75
Englefield Av. CH4: Salt 5E 148
Englefield Cl. CW1: Crewe 5F 191
ENGLESEABROOK 2B 220
Englesea Gro. CW2: Crewe 5B 194
Ennerdale SK11: Mac 7G 125
Ennerdale Av. CH62: East 3A 108
WA2: Warr 1F 41
Ennerdale Cl. CW7: Wins 1E 178
SK9: Ald E 1B 166
Ennerdale Dr. CW12: Cong 4D 182
M33: Sale 6D 22
SK8: Gat 2D 76
WA6: Frod 7J 111
WA15: Timp 4A 48
Ennerdale Rd. CH2: Ches 5C 146
CH43: Pren 4H 59
CH45: Wall 3F 13
CW2: Crewe 3J 193
M31: Part 1G 45
M32: S'ord 1H 23
SK1: Stoc 5F 53
SK6: W'ley 7G 27
Ennerdale St. L3: Liv 1J 35
Ennerdale Ter. SK15: Stal 6B 4
Ennis Cl. L24: Hale 6A 88
M23: Wyth 7E 48
Ennisdale Dr. CH48: W Kir 2D 56
Enterprise Cen. Two *SK3: Stoc 3B 52*
(off Chester St.)
Enterprise Ct. CW11: Elw 2B 200
Enterprise Pk. CH65: Ell P 4G 135
Enterprise Way WA3: Low 3A 6
Enticott Rd. M44: Cad 6K 19
Enville Rd. WA14: Bow 2G 73
Enville St. M34: Aude 3E 8
WA4: Warr 1G 67
EPIC Leisure Cen. 4D 134
Epping Av. WA9: Sut M 1H 37
Epping Cl. L35: R'ill 2D 36
Epping Ct. CH60: Hes 5J 83
Epping Dr. M33: Sale 6B 22
WA1: Wool 4D 42
Epping Rd. M34: Den 1A 26
Epsom Av. M19: Manc 5C 24
M33: Sale 2G 47
SK9: Hand 2B 98
Epsom Cl. CH1: Ches 1J 149
SK7: H Gro 3K 79
Epsom Gdns. WA4: App 6J 67
Epsom Rd. CH46: Leas 1C 32
Epworth Cl. CH43: Clau 6K 33
WA5: B'ood 5C 14
Epworth Ct. SK4: Stoc 1K 51
Epworth Grange *CH43: Clau 6K 33*
(off Park Rd. W.)
Era St. M33: Sale 7G 23
ERBISTOCK 3B 218
Erfurt Av. CH63: Beb 2A 86
ERF Way CW10: Mid 4E 180
Erica Cl. SK5: Stoc 3K 25
Erica Ct. CH60: Hes 4G 83
Erica Dr. M19: Manc 7B 24
Eric Av. WA1: Padg 4J 41
Eric Bullows Cl. M22: Wyth 4J 75
Eric Dr. CW11: Elw 2B 200
Eric Fountain Rd. CH65: Ell P 4E 108
Eric Gro. CH44: Wall 7G 13
Eric Rd. CH44: Wall 7G 13
Eric St. WA8: Wid 3J 63
Erin Cl. L8: Liv 6K 35
Erindale Cres. WA6: Frod 2G 139
Erith Cl. SK5: Stoc 5A 26
Erlesdene WA14: Bow 2F 73
Erlesmere Av. M34: Den 6F 9
Ermine Rd. CH2: Ches 1E 212 (6B 146)
Erneley Cl. M12: Manc 1E 24
Ernest St. CW2: Crewe 4C 194
SK2: Stoc 6E 52
SK8: Chea 6E 50
Ernley Cl. CW5: Nant 1B 196
ERNOCROFT 2K 55
Ernocroft Rd. SK6: Mar B 3H 55
Erringdon Cl. SK2: Stoc 6H 53
Errington Av. CH65: Ell P 2E 134
Errol Av. M22: Wyth 1J 75
Errwood Cres. M19: Manc 3D 24
Errwood Pk. Works SK4: Stoc 5E 24
Errwood Rd. M19: Manc 6C 24
Erskine Rd. CH44: Wall 1B 34
M31: Part 2H 45
Erskine St. SK6: Comp 1H 55
Erwood St. WA2: Warr 6F 41
Eryngo St. SK1: Stoc 3E 52
ERYRYS 2A 218
Escolme Dr. CH49: Gre 2A 58
Esher Cl. CH43: Bid 5F 33
CH62: N Fer 5G 61
Esher Dr. M33: Sale 3C 48
Esher Rd. CH62: N Fer 5G 61
Eskdale CH65: Whit 5D 134
SK8: Gat 1E 76
Eskdale Av. CH46: More 3K 31
CH62: East 2K 107
SK6: W'ley 6G 27
SK7: Bram 1F 99
WA2: Warr 1G 41
(off Poplars Av.)
Eskdale Cl. CW7: Wins 2D 178
WA7: Beec 2K 111
Eskdale Dr. WA15: Timp 5C 48
Eskdale Ter. SK15: Stal 5B 4
Esk Rd. CW7: Wins 2H 179
Esplanade CH42: R Fer 3G 61
Esplanade, The CH62: N Fer 4G 61
Esporta Health & Fitness
Denton 7B 8
Essex Av. M20: Manc 1D 50
SK3: Stoc 4K 51
Essex Cl. CW12: Cong 1G 183
Essex Gdns. M44: Cad 7K 19
Essex Rd. CH2: Ches 5D 146
CH48: W Kir 2D 56
SK5: Stoc 6B 26
Essex Wlk. SK10: Mac 3G 125
Essington Wlk. M34: Den 2D 26
Esthers La. CW8: Weav 5G 155
Estonfield Dr. M41: Urm 1E 22
Etchells Rd. SK8: He Grn 4F 77
WA14: W Tim 4H 47
Etchells St. SK1: Stoc 6J 213 (3D 52)
Ethelbert Rd. CH47: Meols 4D 30
Ethelda Dr. CH2: Ches 5D 146
Ethel Rd. CH44: Wall 1C 34
Ethel Ter. M19: Manc 2D 24
Etherley Cl. M44: Irlam 1D 20
Etherow Av. SK6: Rom 2E 54
Etherow Brow SK14: B'tom 3J 29
Etherow Cl. CW11: S'ach 2C 200
Etherow Country Pk. 2J 55
Etherow Country Pk. Local Nature Reserve 1J 55
Etherow Country Pk. Vis. Cen. 2H 55
Etherow Ct. *SK14: Hyde 1K 27*
(off Ridling La.)
Etherow Gymnastics Cen. 3H 29
Etherow Ind. Est. SK13: Had 3J 11
(not continuous)
Etherow Way SK13: Had 2K 11
Ethos Ct. CH3: Ches 3E 212
Eton Ct. CW8: H'ord 1B 162
Eton Dr. CH63: Tho H 1J 105
SK8: Chea 3F 77
Eton Rd. CH65: Ell P 4F 135
Ettiley Av. CW11: Ett H 4A 200
ETTILEY HEATH 3B 200 (1B 220)
Ettrick Pk. CH3: Ches 1D 150
Euan Pl. *M33: Sale 7H 23*
(off Montague Rd.)
Euclid Av. WA4: Grap 3B 68
Eurolink WA9: St H 1F 37
Eurolink Bus. Pk. WA9: St H 1F 37
Europa Blvd. CH41: Birk 6D 34
WA5: W'ook 2A 40
Europa Bus. Pk. SK3: Stoc 6K 51
Europa Cen., The CH41: Birk 6D 34
Europa Pools 6C 34
Europa Sq. CH41: Birk 6D 34
Europa Way CH65: Ell P 2E 134
SK3: Stoc 6K 51
Eustace St. WA2: Warr 6E 40
Euston Gro. CH43: Oxt 7A 34
Evans Bus. Pk. CH65: Ell P 6G 109
Evans Cl. M20: Manc 1C 50
Evans Pl. WA4: Warr 2H 67
Evans Rd. CH47: Hoy 5C 30
Evans St. CW1: Crewe 7G 191
Eva Rd. SK3: Stoc 5J 51
Eva St. CW11: Elw 1B 200
Evelyn Rd. CH44: Wall 1B 34
Evelyn St. M14: Manc 3A 24
WA5: Warr 1B 66
Evenholme Flats WA14: Bow 3F 73
Evenwood Cl. WA7: Man P 2G 91
Everdon Cl. CW7: Wins 1G 179
Everest Cl. CH66: Gt Sut 5B 134
SK14: Hyde 6B 10
SK16: Duk 1G 9
Everest Rd. CH42: Tran 3C 60
SK14: Hyde 6B 10
Everglade Cl. SK11: Mac 7J 125
Evergreen Cl. CH49: Upt 6B 32
Evergreens, The *CW9: Los Gra 4C 158*
(off Langford Av.)
Evergreen Wlk. *M33: Sale 5B 22*
(off Epping Dr.)
Everite Rd. WA8: Wid 6B 62
Everite Rd. Ind. Est. WA8: Wid 6B 62
Everleigh Cl. CH43: Bid 5E 32
Eversleigh Dr. CH63: Beb 2A 86
Eversley WA8: Wid 3B 62
Eversley Cl. WA4: App 1J 93
WA6: Frod 2K 139
Eversley Ct. CH2: Ches 6K 145
M33: Sale 2B 48
Eversley Pk. CH2: Ches 6K 145
CH43: Oxt 2A 60
Eversley Rd. M20: Manc 1C 50
EVERTON 1B 214
Everton Brow L3: Liv 1K 35
Everton Rd. SK5: Stoc 1J 25
Everyman Theatre 4K 35
Evesham Av. M23: Wyth 5D 48
SK4: Stoc 1K 51
Evesham Cl. SK10: Mac 7B 122
WA4: Stoc H 5G 67
WN7: Leigh 1D 6
Evesham Dr. SK9: Wilm 4K 97
Evesham Gro. M33: Sale 7K 23
Evesham Rd. CH45: Wall 5F 13
SK8: Chea 1J 77
Eveside Cl. SK8: Chea H 1K 77
Ewart St. CH4: Salt F 4C 148

Ferndale—Flying Flds. Dr.

Ferndale SK9: Hand ... 3A 98
(off Station Rd.)
SK14: Hyde ... 4B 10
Ferndale Av. CH2: Elt ... 5E 136
CH44: Wall ... 7J 13
CH48: Fran ... 4J 57
SK2: Stoc ... 1F 79
Ferndale Cl. CW2: West ... 2H 199
CW11: S'ach ... 4G 201
WA1: Wool ... 5C 42
WA8: Bold H ... 5A 38
Ferndale Cres. SK11: Mac ... 5F 125
Ferndale Gdns. M19: Manc ... 5B 24
Ferndale Rd. CH47: Hoy ... 5C 30
M33: Sale ... 2B 48
Ferndown Av. SK7: H Gro ... 4G 79
Ferndown Dr. M44: Irlam ... 1D 20
Ferndown Rd. M23: Wyth ... 4D 48
Ferndown Way CW2: West ... 7J 199
Fern Gro. CH43: Noc ... 1G 59
Fernhill CH45: N Bri ... 3H 13
SK6: Mel ... 6H 55
Fernhill Rd. CH1: Blac ... 4F 145
Fernhill Wlk. WA9: Clo F ... 1J 37
Fern Ho. M23: Wyth ... 1G 75
Fernhurst WA7: Run ... 6K 89
Fernhurst Rd.
M20: Manc ... 6A 24
Fernie Cres. L8: Liv ... 7K 35
FERNILEE ... 3D 217
Fern Lea SK14: H'rth ... 1J 11
Fernlea SK4: Stoc ... 6F 25
SK8: He Grn ... 4D 76
WA15: Hale ... 4K 73
Fernlea Cl. SK13: Had ... 3K 11
Fernlea Ct. CH1: Sau ... 2A 144
Fern Lea Dr. SK11: Mac ... 4H 125
Fernleaf Cl. ST7: Rod H ... 1G 203
Fernlea M. CH43: Bid ... 4F 33
Fernlea Rd. CH60: Hes ... 6J 83
CW9: Mars ... 7H 115
Fernleigh CW8: N'ich ... 6B 156
Fernleigh Av. M19: Manc ... 2F 25
Fernleigh Cl. CW7: Wins ... 3B 178
CW10: Mid ... 6E 180
Fernley Av. M34: Den ... 1F 27
Fernley Rd. SK2: Stoc ... 6F 53
Fern Rd. CH65: Whit ... 6C 134
Ferns, The SK14: Hyde ... 5B 10
Ferns Cl. CH60: Hes ... 5E 82
Fernside Av. M20: Manc ... 6A 24
Ferns Rd. CH63: H Beb ... 1H 85
Fern Vw. WA15: Timp ... 7E 48
Fern Way CW8: Weav ... 4F 155
Fernway CW7: Wins ... 3J 179
Fernwood SK6: Mar B ... 5H 55
WA7: Nort ... 5D 90
Fernwood Av. M18: Manc ... 1G 25
Fernwood Gro. SK9: Wilm ... 6K 97
Ferny Brow Rd. CH49: Woodc ... 2E 58
Fernyess La. CH64: W'ston ... 2J 131
Ferries Cl. CH42: R Fer ... 5F 61
Ferrous Way M44: Irlam ... 5C 20
Ferryhill Rd. M44: Irlam ... 1D 20
Ferry La. CH1: Ches ... 3D 148
WA4: Thel ... 1E 68
Ferrymasters Way M44: Irlam ... 2D 20
Ferry Rd. CH62: East ... 2B 108
M44: Irlam ... 1D 20
(not continuous)
Ferryside CH44: Wall ... 2D 34
WA4: Thel ... 2C 68
Ferry Vw. Rd. CH44: Wall ... 2D 34
Ferryview Wlk. WA7: Cast ... 4B 90
Festival Av. CW3: Bue ... 6G 211
WA2: Warr ... 2H 41
Festival Cres. WA2: Warr ... 2H 41
Festival Dr. SK10: O Ald ... 5A 120
Festival Hill CW12: Cong ... 4H 183
Festival Rd. CH65: Ell P ... 3B 134
Festival Way WA7: Run ... 6J 89
Ffrancon Dr. CH63: H Beb ... 6E 60
FFRITH ... 2A 218
FIDDLER'S FERRY ... 4F 65
Fiddlers Ferry Rd. WA8: Wid ... 5J 63
Fiddler's Ferry Sailing Club ... 4G 65
Fiddlers La. CH1: Sau ... 1C 144
M44: Irlam ... 1E 20
Field Av. CW2: Crewe ... 5K 193
Field Bank Gro. M19: Manc ... 2F 25
Fieldbank Rd. SK11: Mac ... 4J 125
Field Cl. CH3: Tar ... 6B 170
CH62: N Fer ... 5G 61
CW8: N'ich ... 6B 156
SK6: Mar ... 7D 54
SK7: Bram ... 2G 99
SK10: Boll ... 4C 122
WA9: Clo F ... 1K 37
FIELDEN PARK ... 1B 50
Fieldfare CW7: Wins ... 4H 179
Fieldfare Cl. WA3: Birc ... 7A 18
Fieldgate WA8: Wid ... 6B 62
Fieldhead M. SK9: Wilm ... 6B 98
Fieldhead Rd. SK9: Wilm ... 6B 98
Field Hey La. CH64: W'ston ... 6G 107
(not continuous)
Fieldhouse La. SK6: Mar ... 6G 55
Fieldhouse Row WA7: Run ... 7K 89
Fielding Av. SK12: Poy ... 4D 100
Fielding Ind. Est. M34: Den ... 1B 26
Fieldings Wharf M43: Droy ... 2A 8
(off Market St.)
Field La. CH3: Tar ... 6B 170
CH3: Tatt ... 3H 187
CW2: Crewe ... 4H 193
WA4: App ... 7G 67
Field Pl. M20: Manc ... 1D 50
(off Crossway)
Field Rd. CH45: N Bri ... 4H 13
M33: Sale ... 5D 22
WA9: Clo F ... 1K 37
Fields, The CW5: W'ston ... 2H 197
SK6: Rom ... 3A 54
Fields Cl. ST7: Als ... 5F 203
Fields Cres. SK14: H'rth ... 1J 11
Fields Dr. CW11: S'ach ... 4E 200
Fieldsend Cl. SK15: Stal ... 2E 10
Fieldsend Dr. WN7: Leigh ... 2C 6
Fields Farm Cl. SK14: Hat ... 1E 28
Fields Farm Rd. SK14: Hat ... 2D 28
Fields Farm Wlk. SK14: Hat ... 1E 28
(off Fields Farm Rd.)
Fields Gro. SK14: H'rth ... 2J 11
Fieldside CW6: Dud ... 5C 174
Field Side Cl. WA16: Mob ... 6B 102
Fieldside Cl. CW4: Goo ... 6J 165
SK7: Bram ... 2G 99
Fieldside Rd. CH42: R Fer ... 3D 60
Fields Rd. CW1: Hasl ... 2K 195
CW12: Cong ... 6G 183
ST7: Als ... 5E 202
Field St. L3: Liv ... 1K 35
(not continuous)
SK6: Bred ... 1K 53
SK14: Hyde ... 5J 9
Fields Vw. Cl. CW5: Wyb ... 7B 198
Fieldsway WA7: West ... 1G 111
Field Va. Dr. SK5: Stoc ... 2K 25
Fieldvale Rd. M33: Sale ... 3J 47
Field Vw. Dr. SK11: Mac ... 7B 126
Fieldview Dr. WA2: Warr ... 3G 41
Field Wlk. M31: Part ... 1G 45
WA15: Hale ... 2B 74
Field Way ST7: Als ... 5F 203
Fieldway CH1: Sau ... 1B 144
CH2: Ches ... 6B 146
CH45: Wall ... 6G 13
CH47: Meols ... 5G 31
CH60: Hes ... 5A 84
CH63: H Beb ... 5C 60
CH66: L Sut ... 1H 133
CW8: Weav ... 4F 155
WA6: Frod ... 1J 139
WA8: Wid ... 3A 64
Fieldway Ct. CH41: Birk ... 4B 34
Fife Rd. WA1: Warr ... 5J 41
Fifth Av. CH43: Bid ... 5E 32
SK16: Duk ... 2F 9
WA7: Pal F ... 7B 90
Fildes Cl. WA5: Gt San ... 7A 40
Filey Rd. M14: Manc ... 3A 24
SK2: Stoc ... 5G 53
Filkin's La. CH3: Ches ... 2D 150
Filleigh WA14: Bow ... 3E 72
Fillmore Gro. WA8: Wid ... 2F 63
Finchale Dr. WA15: Hale ... 4B 74
Finch Cl. WA9: Clo F ... 1K 37
Finch Ct. CH41: Birk ... 5C 34
Finchdale Gdns. WA3: Low ... 2B 6
Finchdean Cl. CH49: Gre ... 1K 57
Finchett Ct. CH1: Ches ... 7J 145
(off Whipcord La.)
Finchett Dr. CH1: Ches ... 7J 145
Finchley Rd. WA15: Hale ... 4K 213 (2J 73)
Finch Pl. L3: Liv ... 2K 35
Finchwood Rd. M22: Shar ... 7A 50
Findlay Cl. WA12: New W ... 1E 14
(not continuous)
Findley Dr. CH46: Leas ... 1C 32
Findon Rd. M23: Wyth ... 6G 49
Finger Ho. La. WA8: Bold H ... 3K 37
Finger Post La. WA6: Norl ... 6G 153
Finghall Rd. M41: Urm ... 1A 22
Finland Rd. SK3: Stoc ... 5B 52
Finlan Rd. WA8: Wid ... 6F 63
Finlay Av. WA5: Penk ... 2G 65
Finlow Hill La. SK10: N Ald, O Ald ... 5A 120
Finney, The CH48: Cald ... 7E 56
Finney Cl. SK9: Wilm ... 4K 97
Finney Dr. SK9: Wilm ... 4K 97
FINNEY GREEN ... 5A 98
Finney La. SK8: He Grn ... 5C 76
Finney's La. CW10: Mid ... 2B 180
Finningley Ct. WA2: Padg ... 3J 41
Finny Bank Rd. M33: Sale ... 5F 23
Finsbury Cl. WA5: Gt San ... 1A 66
Finsbury Pk. WA8: Wid ... 7J 37
Finsbury Rd. SK5: Stoc ... 3H 25
Finsbury Wlk. CW7: Wins ... 3B 178
Finsbury Way SK9: Hand ... 4B 98
Finstall Rd. CH63: Spit ... 4K 85
Fir Av. SK7: Bram ... 5C 78
Firbank CH2: Elt ... 5G 137
Firbank Cl. WA7: Win H ... 5F 91
Firbank Rd. M23: Wyth ... 7G 49
Firbeck Cl. CW12: Cong ... 3B 182
Firbeck Gdns. CW2: Crewe ... 2H 193
Firbrook Ct. CH43: Bid ... 3F 33
Fir Cl. CW6: Tarp ... 2J 175
SK7: H Gro ... 2J 79
SK12: Poy ... 3D 100
Fir Ct. SK10: Mac ... 3G 125
Fircroft Ct. SK3: Stoc ... 1D 78
Firdale Rd. CW8: N'ich ... 6B 156
Firdene Cres. CH43: Noc ... 1H 59
Firecrest Ct. WA1: Warr ... 2E 66
Firemans Sq. CH1: Ches ... 3B 212
Firethorn Av. M19: Manc ... 5C 24
Firethorn Dr. SK14: Hyde ... 1B 28
Firethorn Wlk. M33: Sale ... 6B 22
(off Lavender Cl.)
Fir Gro. CW8: Weav ... 5H 155
M19: Manc ... 2D 24
SK11: Mac ... 7K 125
WA1: Padd ... 5K 41
Fir La. CW8: S'way ... 4D 160
Firman Cl. WA5: Gt San ... 4K 39
Fir Rd. M34: Den ... 7F 9
SK6: Mar ... 7E 54
SK7: Bram ... 4C 78
Firs, The CH43: Bid ... 4H 33
CH65: Ell P ... 6F 135
SK9: Wilm ... 2F 119
WA14: Bow ... 3F 73
Firs Av. CH63: Beb ... 3K 85
Firsby Av. SK6: Bred ... 7E 26
Firsby St. M19: Manc ... 2D 24
(off Barlow Rd.)
Firs Cl. SK8: Gat ... 2C 76
Firs Gro. SK8: Gat ... 1C 76
Firshaw Rd. CH47: Meols ... 3D 30
Firs La. WA4: App ... 1F 93
Firs Rd. M33: Sale ... 7C 22
(not continuous)
SK8: Gat ... 2C 76
First Av. CH43: Bid ... 6F 33
CW1: Crewe ... 4E 194
CW11: S'ach ... 4E 200
L35: R'ill ... 1B 36
SK12: Poy ... 5C 100
SK15: Carrb ... 4F 5
First Dig La. CW5: Stap ... 7F 197
Fir St. M44: Cad ... 5K 19
SK4: Stoc ... 5G 213 (2C 52)
WA8: Wid ... 3J 63
First Wood St. CW5: Nant ... 2B 196
Firsway M33: Sale ... 1G 47
Firswood Dr. SK14: Hyde ... 7B 10
Firswood Mt. SK8: Gat ... 1C 76
Firth Blvd. WA2: Warr ... 5G 41
Firth Cl. CW11: S'ach ... 2F 201
Firth Flds. CW9: Dave ... 4E 162
Firthfields Cl. CW9: Dave ... 4E 162
Fir Tree Av. CH4: Ches ... 6J 149
WA16: Knut ... 5G 117
Firtree Av. M33: Sale ... 7B 22
WA1: Padg ... 4A 42
Fir Tree Cl. CW8: Barnt ... 1A 156
SK16: Duk ... 2A 10
WA4: Stre ... 5H 93
Firtree Cl. CW7: Wins ... 3J 179
Fir Tree Cres. SK16: Duk ... 2A 10
Fir Tree Dr. SK14: Hyde ... 5K 9
Firtree Gro. CH66: Whit ... 1C 140
Fir Tree La. CH3: Lit ... 2H 151
SK16: Duk ... 3A 10
WA5: B'ood ... 4D 14
Firvale Av. SK8: He Grn ... 4D 76
Fir Way CH60: Hes ... 2E 104
Firwood Av. M41: Urm ... 1F 23
(not continuous)
Firwood Cl. SK2: Stoc ... 4G 53
Firwood Wlk. CW2: Crewe ... 6C 194
Fisher Av. WA2: Warr ... 3F 41
Fisherfield Dr. WA3: Birc ... 5B 18
Fishermans Cl. CW11: Wint ... 6C 204
Fishermore Rd. M41: Urm ... 1H 21
Fisher Rd. CH1: Blac ... 6F 145
Fishers Grn. CW6: Utk ... 4B 176
Fishers La. CH61: Pens ... 2G 83
CW5: Burl ... 5F 189
Fisher St. L8: Liv ... 6J 35
WA7: Run ... 3H 89
Fishpool Rd. CW6: Cote ... 6J 173
CW8: Dela ... 6J 173
Fistral Av. SK8: He Grn ... 5E 76
Fistral Cres. SK15: Stal ... 6E 4
Fit City
Cadishead ... 6A 20
Irlam ... 2D 20
Fitness First
Bromborough ... 3E 86
Crewe ... 2J 193
Runcorn ... 7A 90
Fitness Studio, The
Macclesfield ... 5B 126
(off Brook St.)
Fitton's Cl. CW5: Sou ... 4K 209
Fitton St. CW9: Los Gra ... 5C 158
Fitz Cl. SK10: Mac ... 1A 126
Fitz Cres. SK10: Mac ... 1A 126
Fitzgerald Ct. M34: Den ... 3F 27
Fitzherbert St. WA2: Warr ... 5F 41
Fitzroy St. M43: Droy ... 2A 8
OL7: Ash L ... 2E 8
SK15: M'ook ... 5E 4
Fitzwalter Rd. WA1: Wool ... 5D 42
Fitzwilliam Av. SK11: Sut E ... 2K 129
Fitzwilliam Wlk. WA7: Cast ... 4C 90
Five Ashes Cotts. SK10: Ker ... 6E 122
Five Ashes Rd. CH4: Ches ... 6H 149
FIVECROSSES ... 3K 139
Fiveways Pde. SK7: H Gro ... 5J 79
Fiveways Pk. CH64: Nest ... 4J 105
Flacca Ct. CH3: Tatt ... 2H 187
Flagcroft Dr. M23: Wyth ... 7H 49
Flaggwood Av. SK6: Mar ... 5D 54
Flag La. CH64: L Nes ... 1D 130
CW1: Crewe ... 2C 194
CW2: Crewe ... 3C 194
Flag La. Nth. CH2: Upt ... 2B 146
Flag La. Sth. CH2: Upt ... 2B 146
Flail Cl. CH49: Gre ... 1K 57
Flambards CH49: Woodc ... 2E 58
Flamstead Av. M23: Wyth ... 6E 48
Flander Cl. WA8: Wid ... 3C 62
FLASH ... 1D 221
Flash SK15: Carrb ... 2G 5
(off Carisbrook Rd.)
Flash, The CW12: Astb ... 7G 183
Flashes La. CH64: Ness ... 3F 131
Flash La. CW9: Ant ... 5D 94
SK10: Boll ... 4K 121
Flat La. CW6: Kel ... 4B 172
CW11: S'ach ... 3F 201
(not continuous)
Flatt La. CH43: Oxt ... 2J 59
CH65: Ell P ... 3D 134
Flavian Cl. CW10: Mid ... 2C 180
Flavian Ct. WA7: Cast ... 5A 90
Flaxcroft Rd. M22: Wyth ... 2H 75
Flaxfield Av. SK15: Stal ... 7E 4
Flaxhill CH46: More ... 3A 32
Flaxley Cl. WA3: Birc ... 6B 18
Flaxmere Dr. CH3: Gt Bou ... 3E 150
Flaxwood Wlk. M22: Wyth ... 2H 75
Flaxyards CW6: Eat ... 7F 177
Flaybrick Cl. CH43: Bid ... 4H 33
Flea La. CW10: Mid ... 4C 180
(off Long La.)
Fleck La. CH48: Cald, W Kir ... 4E 56
Fleetcroft Rd. CH49: Woodc ... 3D 58
Fleet St. CH65: Ell P ... 3C 134
L1: Liv ... 3J 35
OL6: Ash L ... 1F 9
(not continuous)
SK14: Hyde ... 6K 9
Fleetwood Cl. WA5: Gt San ... 1K 65
Fleetwood Wlk. WA7: Murd ... 7E 90
Fleming Dr. WA2: Winw ... 5K 15
Fleming Rd. M22: Wyth ... 3K 75
Fleming St. CH65: Ell P ... 2E 134
Fleming Way CH46: Leas ... 2D 32
Flemish Rd. M34: Den ... 1G 27
Flers Av. WA4: Warr ... 2G 67
Fletcher Av. CH42: R Fer ... 3D 60
Fletcher Cl. CH49: Woodc ... 2D 58
Fletcher Ct. WA16: Knut ... 4C 116
Fletcher Dr. SK12: Dis ... 7F 81
WA14: Bow ... 4G 73
Fletcher Gro. CW9: Rud ... 7H 157
Fletcher Moss Botanical Gdns. ... 3D 50
Fletcher's Bldgs. CH1: Ches ... 5C 212
Fletchers La. WA13: Lymm ... 1B 70
Fletchers Row WA7: Halt ... 5B 90
(off Spark La.)
Fletcher St. CW1: Crewe ... 1B 194
SK1: Stoc ... 6J 213 (3D 52)
WA4: Warr ... 2F 67
Fletsand Rd. SK9: Wilm ... 1H 119
FLINT ... 3A 214
Flint Cl. CH64: Nest ... 2C 130
SK7: H Gro ... 4G 79
Flint Ct. CH65: Ell P ... 6F 135
Flint Dr. CH64: Nest ... 1C 130
Flint Gro. M44: Cad ... 5K 19
Flint Mdw. CH64: Nest ... 1C 130
FLINT MOUNTAIN ... 3A 214
Flint Rd. CH4: Salt F ... 2A 148
Flint St. L1: Liv ... 5J 35
M43: Droy ... 1A 8
SK3: Stoc ... 4C 52
SK10: Mac ... 4B 126
FLIXTON ... 2J 21 (1B 216)
Flixton Dr. CW2: Crewe ... 4A 194
Flixton Pk. & Gardens ... 2J 21
Flixton Rd. M31: Carri ... 3H 21
M41: Urm ... 2J 21
(not continuous)
Flixton Station (Rail) ... 2J 21
Floatshall Rd. M23: Wyth ... 6F 49
Floats Rd. M23: Wyth ... 6E 48
FLOOKERSBROOK ... 1E 212 (6B 146)
Floral Pavilion Theatre ... 2J 13
Florence Av. CH60: Hes ... 5H 83
Florence Ct. SK3: Stoc ... 6K 51
Florence Pk. Ct. M20: Manc ... 1E 50
Florence Rd. CH44: Wall ... 1D 34
Florence St. CH41: Birk ... 6C 34
M33: Sale ... 5G 23
M43: Droy ... 2A 8
SK4: Stoc ... 4H 213 (2C 52)
WA4: Warr ... 2H 67
Florence Way SK14: H'rth ... 2J 11
Florida Cl. WA5: Gt San ... 5A 40
Florist St. SK3: Stoc ... 5C 52
Flour Mill Way CW1: Crewe ... 3G 195
Flowerscroft CW5: Nant ... 3E 196
Flowers La. CW1: Bra G, L'ton ... 3D 190
Flower St. CW8: N'ich ... 6C 156
FLOWERY FIELD ... 5J 9
Flowery Fld. SK2: Stoc ... 1E 78
Flowery Fld. Grn. SK14: Hyde ... 6H 9
Flowery Fld. Ind. Pk. SK14: Hyde ... 5J 9
Flowery Field Station (Rail) ... 5J 9
Floyd Dr. WA2: Warr ... 3F 41
Fluin La. WA6: Frod ... 6J 111
Flying Flds. Dr. SK11: Mac ... 7H 125

Froncysyllte—Gilderdale Cl.

FRONCYSYLLTE 3A 218
FRON ISAF 3A 218
Front St. CW11: S'ach 3G 201
Frost Dr. CH61: Irby 7K 57
Frosts M. CH65: Ell P 2D 134
Fryer Rd. CW9: Los Gra 4C 158
Fryer St. WA7: Run 3G 89
Fuchsia Cl. CH66: Gt Sut 7B 134
Fuchsia Wlk. CH49: Gre 3K 57
Fulbeck WA8: Wid 3C 62
Fulbeck Cl. CW2: Wis 6B 194
Fulbrook Cl. CH63: Spit 4K 85
Fulbrook Dr. SK8: Chea H 7J 77
Fulbrook Rd. CH63: Spit 4K 85
FULFORD 3D 221
Fulford Pk. CH46: More 4B 32
Fuller Dr. CW2: Wis 6A 194
FULLER'S MOOR 2C 219
Fullerton Rd. CW8: H'ord 1J 161
SK4: Stoc 2K 51
Fulmar Cl. SK12: Poy 2K 99
Fulmar Dr. M33: Sale 2G 47
SK2: Stoc 7K 53
Fulmards Cl. SK9: Wilm 7K 97
Fulshaw Av. SK9: Wilm 1F 119
Fulshaw Ct. SK9: Wilm 2F 119
FULSHAW PARK 1E 118
Fulshaw Pk. SK9: Wilm 3F 119
Fulshaw Pk. Sth.
SK9: Wilm 3E 118
Fulstone M. SK2: Stoc 6F 53
Fulton Av. CH48: W Kir 2E 56
Fulton Cl. WA4: Westy 1B 68
Fulton Gro. CW9: Dave 4E 162
Fulwood Gdns. CH66: L Sut 2J 133
Fulwood M. CH66: L Sut 2J 133
Fulwood Rd. CH66: L Sut 2J 133
Funsters 3C 194
Furber St. CW1: Crewe 1C 194
Furlong Rd. M22: Wyth 2H 75
Furnace St. SK14: Hyde 6H 9
SK16: Duk 1G 9
Furne Rd. CH1: Blac 6F 145
Furness Cl. CH49: Upt 6B 32
CW4: H Cha 4G 181
CW7: Wins 4C 178
SK12: Poy 2B 100
Furness Ct. WA7: Nort 2H 91
Furness Fld. SK14: Hyde 5B 28
Furness Gro. SK4: Stoc 3K 51
Furness Rd. M14: Manc 2A 24
M41: Urm 1C 22
SK8: Chea H 7A 78
FURNESS VALE 2D 217
Furnival Cl. M34: Den 1K 25
Furnival St. CW2: Crewe 4C 194
CW11: S'ach 2F 201
SK5: Stoc 1J 25
Furrocks Cl. CH64: Ness 3D 130
Furrocks La. CH64: Ness 3D 130
Furrocks Way CH64: Ness 3D 130
Furrows, The CH66: Gt Sut 1A 140
Further La. SK14: Hat 7F 11
Furze Wlk. M31: Part 1J 45
Furze Way CH46: More 3B 32
FX Leisure
Congleton 2E 182
Lowton 3A 6
Stalybridge 2D 10
Fylde Av. SK8: He Grn 5E 76
Fylde Ct. *M32: S'ord* 3H 23
(off Highfield Rd.)
Fylde Rd. SK4: Stoc 2J 51
Fytton Cl. SK11: Gaw 4B 128

G

Gable Av. SK9: Wilm 7H 97
Gable Ct. *CW5: Nant* 1C 196
(off Lady Helen Wlk.)
M34: Den 7E 8
Gables, The M33: Sale 1B 48
(Brooklands Rd.)
M33: Sale 6H 23
(Irlam Rd.)
ST7: Als 5D 202
Gables Cl. WA2: Fear 1K 41
Gable St. WA12: New W 1D 14
Gabriel Bank CW8: Crow 2H 153
Gabriel Cl. CH46: More 4C 32
Gadbrook Bus. Cen. CW9: Rud 1J 163
Gadbrook Pk. CW9: Rud 1J 163
Gadbrook Rd. CW9: Rud 7J 157
Gaddum Rd. M20: Manc 1E 50
WA14: Bow 4E 72
Gail Av. SK4: Stoc 2B 52
Gail Cl. SK9: Ald E 5G 119
Gainford Av. SK8: Gat 1D 76
Gainford Cl. WA8: Wid 2C 62
Gainford Rd. SK5: Stoc 2J 25
Gainsboro Rd. M34: Aude 1C 8
Gainsborough Av. M20: Manc 5A 24
SK6: Mar B 4H 55
Gainsborough Cl. SK9: Wilm 6A 98
Gainsborough Ct. WA8: Wid 4B 62
Gainsborough Dr. SK8: Chea 6H 51
Gainsborough Ho. M33: Sale 1K 47
Gainsborough Rd. CH45: Wall 7E 12
CH49: Upt 6B 32
CW2: Crewe 3A 194
WA4: Warr 3E 66
Gainsborough Wlk. M34: Den 2D 26
(not continuous)
SK14: Hyde 5K 9
Gairloch Av. M32: S'ord 1G 23
Gairloch Cl. WA2: Fear 7E 16
Gair Rd. SK5: Stoc 7J 25
Gair St. SK14: Hyde 6J 9
Gaisgill Ct. WA8: Wid 4C 62
Gala Bingo
Bromborough 3E 86
Stockport 6K 213 (3E 52)
Warrington 7F 41
Widnes 5H 63
Wythenshawe 3K 75
Gala Leo Casino 5J 35
Galbraith Cl. CW12: Cong 4E 182
Galbraith Rd. M20: Manc 1E 50
Gale Av. WA5: Warr 3D 40
Galion Way WA8: Wid 1F 63
Gallagher Ind. Est. CH44: Wall 2A 34
Gallopers La. CH61: Thin 7F 59
Galloway Cl. CW4: H Cha 5J 181
CW10: Mid 2E 180
Galloway Grn. CW12: Cong 1G 183
Gallowsclough La. CW8: Oak 7G 153
WA6: Norl 7G 153
Gallowsclough Rd. SK15: Mat 4F 11
Galston Av. L35: R'ill 2D 36
Galton St. L3: Liv 1G 35
Galtres Ct. CH63: H Beb 5D 60
Galtres Pk. CH63: H Beb 5D 60
Galway Av. WA8: Wid 2E 62
Galway Gro. CW2: Shav 3B 198
Galway Wlk. M23: Wyth 3F 75
Gambier Ter. L1: Liv 5K 35
GAMESLEY 1D 217
Game St. CW11: Whe 6E 200
Games Wlk. M22: Wyth 4H 75
Gamlin St. CH41: Birk 4J 33
Gamul Ct. CH3: Tar 7C 170
Gamul Pl. CH1: Ches 6C 212 (3A 150)
Gamul Ter. *CH1: Ches* 6C 212
(off Lwr. Bridge St.)
Ganney's Mdw. Rd. CH49: Woodc 3F 59
Ganton Cl. WA8: Wid 1H 63
Garden Av. M32: S'ord 1J 23
GARDEN CITY 1B 218
Garden Cl. SK10: Mac 3B 126
Garden Ct. CH1: Ches 3B 212 (1K 149)
CH42: Tran 4B 60
Gardeners Way OL7: Ash L 1C 8
Gardenfold Way M43: Droy 1A 8
Garden Hey Rd. CH46: More 5J 31
CH47: Meols 4D 30
Garden La. CH1: Ches 1A 212 (7J 145)
CH46: More 3B 32
L5: Liv 1K 35
WA14: Alt 1J 213 (7H 47)
Garden Rd. WA16: Knut 2D 116
Gardens, The CW11: S'ach 3F 201
LL13: Holt 6B 186
ST7: Chu L 5K 203
Gardenside CH46: Leas 7B 12
Gardens Rd. CH63: Beb 1B 86
Garden St. CW12: Cong 3E 182
M34: Aude 4E 8
SK2: Stoc 7G 53
SK10: Boll 3C 122
SK10: Mac 3B 126
SK14: B'tom 3H 29
(off Gorsey Brow)
SK14: Hyde 6K 9
Garden Ter. CH1: Ches 2A 212 (1K 149)
CH3: Ches 1C 150
SK6: Mar 4H 81
Garden Vs. SK8: He Grn 6D 76
Garden Wlk. M31: Part 1G 45
M34: Den 7F 9
Gardner Grange SK5: Stoc 7B 26
Gardner's Row L3: Liv 1J 35
Garfield Av. M19: Manc 2E 24
Garfield St. SK1: Stoc 2E 52
Garfield Ter. CH49: Upt 7D 32
Garfit St. CW10: Mid 2D 180
Garland Rd. M22: Wyth 2A 76
Garlick St. SK14: Hyde 7A 10
Garner Av. WA15: Timp 3A 48
Garner Cl. WA14: Bow 3H 73
Garners La. SK3: Stoc 7B 52
Garner St. WA2: Warr 5G 41
Garnett Av. WA4: Westy 1A 68
Garnett Cl. CW5: Stap 3D 196
Garnett's La. WA8: Hal B 2A 88
Garnett St. SK1: Stoc 7J 213 (3D 52)
Garrett Fld. WA3: Ris 6J 17
Garrett Wlk. SK3: Stoc 4A 52
Garrick Av. CH46: More 4K 31
Garrick Cl. WA14: Alt 6H 47
Garrick Rd. CH43: Pren 5J 59
Garrigill Ct. WA8: Wid 7H 37
Garron Wlk. M22: Wyth 3G 75
Garsdale Av. L35: R'ill 2D 36
Garsdale Cl. WA5: Gt San 5H 39
Garsden Wlk. M23: Wyth 1F 75
Garside St. M34: Den 1E 26
SK14: Hyde 2K 27
GARSTON 2C 215
Garston Cl. SK4: Stoc 1A 52
GARSWOOD 1D 215
Garswood Cl. CH46: Leas 1B 32
GARTH 3A 218
Garth, The CH43: Oxt 7H 33
Garth Av. WA15: Timp 6J 47
Garth Blvd. CH63: H Beb 5D 60
Garth Dr. CH2: Ches 5K 145
Garth Hgts. SK9: Wilm 7K 97
Garthland Rd. SK7: H Gro 2K 79
Garthorp Rd. M23: Wyth 3E 48
Garth Rd. CH65: Ell P 3H 135
M22: Wyth 1K 75
SK2: Stoc 5G 53
SK6: Mar 6G 55
Gartons La. WA9: Clo F, Sut M 1J 37
Gartside St. OL7: Ash L 1D 8
Garven Pl. WA1: Warr 7E 40
Garwood Cl. WA5: W'ook 3A 40
Gascoyne St. L3: Liv 1H 35
Gaskell Av. WA4: Westy 2A 68
WA16: Knut 3D 116
Gaskell Rd. WA14: Alt 6H 47
Gaskell St. SK16: Duk 2G 9
WA4: Stoc H 4G 67
Gas Rd. SK11: Mac 4A 126
Gas St. SK4: Stoc 6G 213 (3C 52)
SK14: H'rth 2J 11
Gatcombe M. SK9: Wilm 1F 119
Gatcombe Sq. *M14: Manc* 1A 24
(off Rusholme Gro.)
GATEACRE 2C 215
Gateacre Ct. CH66: Ell P 7G 109
Gateacre Wlk. M23: Wyth 4E 48
Gate Cen., The SK6: Bred 5D 26
Gatefield St. CW1: Crewe 2C 194
Gateley Cl. WA4: Thel 2E 68
GATESHEATH 1C 219
Gatesheath Dr. CH2: Upt 3B 146
Gate St. SK16: Duk 4F 9
Gatewarth Ind. Est. WA5: Warr 2B 66
Gatewarth St. WA5: Warr 2B 66
Gateway CW1: Crewe 4F 195
Gateway Pk. CH62: Brom 5E 86
Gateway Theatre 4B 212 (2K 149)
Gateway Trade Pk. WA2: Warr 4E 40
Gathill Cl. SK8: Chea H 4H 77
Gathurst Ct. WA8: Wid 5D 62
GATLEY 7D 50 (2C 217)
Gatley Ct. M22: N'den 5A 50
Gatley Grn. SK8: Gat 7C 50
Gatley Rd. M33: Sale 1E 48
SK8: Chea, Gat 7D 50
Gatley Station (Rail) 6D 50
Gatling Av. M12: Manc 1E 24
Gatwick Av. M23: Wyth 6H 49
Gauntlet Birds of Prey Eagle and Vulture Pk.
7H 95
Gaunts Way WA7: Pal F 1A 112
Gautby Rd. CH41: Birk 3H 33
Gavin Rd. WA8: Wid 6B 62
Gaw End La. SK11: L Grn 3G 129
Gawer Ct. *CH1: Ches* 6K 145
(off Gawer Pk.)
Gawer Pk. CH1: Ches 6K 145
GAWSWORTH 4C 128 (1C 221)
Gawsworth Av. CW2: Crewe 3K 193
M20: Manc 3E 50
Gawsworth Cl. CH43: Oxt 2J 59
CW4: H Cha 4H 181
CW9: N'ich 2F 163
SK3: Stoc 7B 52
SK7: Bram 1H 99
SK12: Poy 4E 100
ST7: Als 6D 202
WA15: Timp 6D 48
Gawsworth Ct. WA3: Ris 6A 18
Gawsworth Dr. CW11: S'ach 2G 201
Gawsworth Hall 5C 128
Gawsworth M. SK8: Gat 7D 50
Gawsworth Pl. M22: Wyth 4B 76
Gawsworth Rd. CH66: Gt Sut 3A 134
M33: Sale 3E 48
SK11: Gaw, Mac 3B 128
Gawsworth Way M34: Den 2F 27
SK9: Hand 2B 98
Gawthorne Cl. SK7: H Gro 3G 79
Gaybeech Cl. CH43: Bid 4E 32
Gaydon Rd. M33: Sale 7C 22
Gayhurst Av. WA2: Fear 2K 41
Gaymoore Cl. CH2: Ches 1B 212
GAYTON 7K 83 (2A 214)
Gayton Av. CH45: N Bri 3H 13
CH63: H Beb 5B 60
Gayton Cl. CH2: Ches 5B 146
Gayton Farm Rd. CH60: Hes 2D 104
Gayton La. CH60: Hes 1E 104
Gayton Mill Cl. CH60: Hes 7K 83
Gayton Parkway CH60: Hes 2F 105
Gayton Rd. CH60: Hes 1C 104
Gayton Sands Nature Reserve 5C 104
Gaytree Ct. CH43: Bid 5F 33
Gaywood Cl. CH43: Bid 5F 33
Geddington Rd. WA14: W Tim 4G 47
GEE CROSS 4K 27 (1D 217)
Gee Cross Fold SK14: Hyde 4K 27
Gee's Ct. CH3: Ches 2C 150
Gee St. SK3: Stoc 5B 52
Gelling St. L8: Liv 7K 35
Gemini Bus. Pk. WA5: W'ook 1A 40
(not continuous)
Gemmull Cl. CW3: Audl 5B 210
General St. WA1: Warr 7G 41
Genesis Cen., The WA3: Ris 6K 17
Geneva Rd. CH44: Wall 2C 34
CW7: Wins 4D 178
SK7: Bram 2B 78
George VI Av. CW10: Mid 6D 180
George VI Cl. CW10: Mid 6D 180
George Bates Cl. ST7: Als 6D 202
George Cl. WA6: Hel 6A 138
George Ct. *SK16: Duk* 1G 9
(off Hill St.)
George Kenyon M. CH4: Salt 5F 149
George La. SK6: Bred 7F 27
George Mann Cl. M22: Wyth 4J 75
George Richards Way
WA14: B'ath 5F 47
George Rd. CH47: Hoy 6D 30
WA5: Gt San 1A 66
George's Cl. SK12: Poy 3D 100
George's Ct. *SK11: Mac* 4K 125
(off Chestergate)
Georges Cres. WA4: Grap 3B 68
George's Dock Gates L3: Liv 3G 35
Georges Dockway L3: Liv 3G 35
George's Rd. M33: Sale 1B 48
SK4: Stoc 5F 213 (3B 52)
George's Rd. E. SK12: Poy 3D 100
George's Rd. W. SK12: Poy 3C 100
George St. CH1: Ches 3B 212 (1K 149)
CH41: Birk 5D 34
CH65: Ell P 1E 134
CW7: Wins 3F 179
CW8: Barnt 2A 156
CW11: Elw 1C 200
L3: Liv 2H 35
M34: Den 7F 9
M41: Urm 1D 22
SK1: Stoc 3E 52
SK6: Comp 2H 55
SK9: Ald E 6F 119
SK11: Mac 5A 126
SK15: Stal 7B 4
WA14: Alt 3H 213 (1H 73)
WA16: Knut 3E 116
George St. E. SK1: Stoc 4F 53
George St. W. SK1: Stoc 4F 53
SK11: Mac 4K 125
George's Wlk. *CW11: S'ach* 3F 201
(off High St.)
Georgia Av. CH62: Brom 3E 86
Georgia Pl. WA5: Gt San 5A 40
Gerald Rd. CH43: Oxt 1K 59
Gerard Av. CH45: Wall 4G 13
Gerard Dr. CW5: Nant 3A 196
Gerard Rd. CH45: Wall 5F 13
CH48: W Kir 2C 56
Gerard St. L3: Liv 2K 35
Germans Bldgs. SK2: Stoc 6E 52
Gerosa Av. WA2: Winw 3A 16
Gerrard Av. CH66: Gt Sut 4J 133
WA5: Warr 5D 40
WA15: Timp 4A 48
Gerrard Cl. OL7: Ash L 1E 8
Gerrard Dr. CW8: Weav 4G 155
Gerrard Rd. WA3: Croft 4F 17
Gerrards, The SK14: Hyde 4J 27
Gerrards Av. CH3: Ches 2D 150
Gerrards Cl. M44: Irlam 1D 20
Gerrards Gdns. SK14: Hyde 4K 27
Gerrards Hollow SK14: Hyde 4J 27
Gerrard St. SK15: Stal 1C 10
WA8: Wid 5H 63
Gerrardswood SK14: Hyde 4J 27
Gertrude St. CH41: Birk 6E 34
Giantswood La.
CW12: Cong, Hul W 1E 182
Gibb Hill CW9: Ant, Comb 2J 115
Gibb La. SK6: Mel 1K 81
Gibble Gabble *SK14: B'tom* 3H 29
(off King St.)
Gibbon Av. M22: Wyth 3K 75
Gibbon Dr. CW9: Los Gra 4C 158
Gibbs Ct. CH61: Irby 7C 58
Gib La. M23: Wyth 5H 49
Gib La. Cotts. *M23: Wyth* 5J 49
(off Gib La.)
Gibraltar La. M34: Den 3G 27
Gibraltar Row L3: Liv 2G 35
Gibsmere Cl. WA15: Timp 6D 48
Gibson Cl. CH61: Pens 3H 83
CW5: Nant 1B 196
Gibson Ct. CH65: Ell P 7K 109
Gibson Cres. CW11: Elw 3B 200
Gibsons Rd. SK4: Stoc 7E 24
Gibson St. WA1: Warr 7G 41
WA4: Stoc H 4H 67
Gibson Ter. *CH44: Wall* 6K 13
(off Royden Av.)
OL7: Ash L 2F 9
Gibson Way WA14: B'ath 4G 47
Gibwood Rd. M22: N'den 4J 49
Giffard Wlk. SK7: Bram 3E 78
Gigg La. WA4: Moo 1K 91
Gig La. WA1: Wool 4D 42
WA4: Thel 2E 68
Gilbert Bank SK6: Bred 7G 27
Gilbert Cl. CH63: Spit 4K 85
Gilbert Ct. WA3: Cul 7F 7
Gilbert Dr. WA4: Westy 1B 68
Gilbert Ho. WA7: Run 3E 88
Gilbert Rd. WA15: Hale 4J 73
Gilbert St. L1: Liv 4J 35
Gilchrist Av. SK11: Mac 5F 125
Gilchrist Rd. M44: Irlam 5B 20
Gildarts Gdns. L3: Liv 1H 35
Gildart St. L3: Liv 2K 35
Gilderdale Cl. WA3: Birc 6C 18

Gorstage—Greenbank Gdns.

GORSTAGE 7F 155
Gorstage La. CW8: Gor 5F 155
GORSTELLA 1C 184 (1B 218)
Gorstons La. CH64: L Nes 2E 130
Gorston Wlk. M22: Wyth 5J 75
GORTON 1C 217
Gorton Cres. M34: Den 1B 26
Gorton Rd. SK5: Stoc 1J 25
Gorton St. OL7: Ash L 1E 8
Gosford St. L8: Liv 1K 61
Gosforth Ct. WA7: Pal F 7A 90
Gosforth Pl. CH2: Ches 7C 146
Gosforth Wlk. M23: Wyth 3F 49
Gosling Cl. WA4: H'ton 4E 92
Gosling Rd. WA3: Croft 4G 17
Gosling Way CW12: Cong 3C 182
Gosport Cl. WA2: Padg 3J 41
Goss St. CH1: Ches 4B 212 (2K 149)
Gotham Rd. CH63: Spit 4A 86
Gotherage Cl. SK6: Rom 2E 54
Gotherage La. SK6: Rom 3E 54
Gothic Cl. SK6: Rom 2F 55
Gothic St. CH42: R Fer 3E 60
Gough Av. WA2: Warr 2E 40
Gough's La. WA16: Knut 7F 117
Gough St. SK3: Stoc 7F 213 (3B 52)
Goulden St. CW1: Crewe 1A 194
WA5: Warr 6C 40
Goulders Ct. WA7: B'vale 2D 112
Gould St. M34: Den 7D 8
Gourham Dr. SK8: Chea H 3H 77
Gourleys La. CH48: W Kir 4E 56
Govan St. M22: N'den 3A 50
Government Rd. CH47: Hoy 5C 30
Gower Av. SK7: H Gro 2G 79
Gower Ct. SK14: Hyde 3K 27
Gowerdale Rd. SK5: Stoc 6B 26
Gower Hey Gdns. SK14: Hyde 2K 27
Gower Rd. SK4: Stoc 7G 25
SK14: Hyde 2J 27
Gower St. L3: Liv 4H 35
Gowy Cl. CW11: S'ach 1C 200
SK9: Wilm 5B 98
ST7: Als 6A 202
Gowy Ct. CH66: Ell P 7F 109
CW6: Calv 4K 189
Gowy Cres. CH3: Tar 6B 170
Gowy Rd. CH2: Mic T 1J 147
Gowy Wlk. CW7: Wins 1H 179
Goyt Av. SK6: Mar 1F 81
Goyt Cres. SK1: Stoc 1F 53
SK6: Bred 1K 53
Goyt Mill SK6: Mar 1F 81
Goyt Rd. SK1: Stoc 1F 53
SK6: Mar 1F 81
SK12: Dis 2G 103
Goyt Valley SK6: Bred, Rom 2J 53
Goyt Valley Rd. SK6: Bred 1K 53
Goyt Valley Wlk. SK6: Bred 1K 53
Goyt Vw. SK6: Rom 2K 53
Grace Av. WA2: Warr 4F 41
Grace Cl. CH45: Wall 6H 13
CW1: Hasl 2J 195
Grace Ho. *WA8: Wid 4H 63*
(off Frederick St.)
Grace Rd. CH65: Ell P 2D 134
Gradwell St. L1: Liv 3J 35
SK3: Stoc 4B 52
Grafton Cres. L8: Liv 6K 35
Grafton Dr. CH49: Upt 1D 58
Grafton Gro. L8: Liv 1K 61
Grafton M. CH2: Ches 1C 212 (7A 146)
Grafton Rd. CH45: N Bri 4H 13
CH65: Ell P 1E 134
Graftons, The WA14: Alt 3H 213
Grafton St. CH43: Oxt 7A 34
L8: Liv 2K 61
(Beresford Rd.)
L8: Liv 6J 35
(Parliament St., not continuous)
SK4: Stoc 1C 52
SK14: Hyde 7J 9
SK15: M'ook 6E 4
WA5: Warr 6C 40
WA14: Alt 3J 213 (1H 73)
Grafton Wlk. CH48: W Kir 3D 56
Graham Av. CH66: Gt Sut 3K 133
Graham Cl. WA8: Wid 4C 62
Graham Cres. M44: Cad 7K 19
Graham Dr. SK12: Dis 6J 81
Graham Rd. CH1: Blac 6F 145
CH48: W Kir 2B 56
SK1: Stoc 4F 53
WA8: Wid 5C 62
Graham St. OL7: Ash L 1E 8
GRAIANRHYD 2A 218
GRAIG-FECHAN 2A 218
Grainger Av. CH43: Pren 3J 59
CH48: W Kir 1C 56
Grainger's Rd. CW9: N'ich 1E 162
Grain Ind. Est. L8: Liv 1K 61
Gralam Cl. M33: Sale 3E 48
Grammar School Ct. *WA4: Warr 2K 67*
(off Grammer School Rd.)
Grammar School La. CH48: W Kir 4E 56
Grammar School Rd. WA4: Warr 2K 67
WA13: Lymm 3B 70
Grampian Av. CH46: More 4C 32
Grampian Way CH46: More 4B 32
CH62: East 2K 107
CH64: L Nes 3C 130
CW7: Wins 5B 178
Granada Rd. M34: Den 1J 25
Granary M. SK12: Poy 3D 100
Granary Mill WA4: Pre H 1H 113
Granary Way L3: Liv 6J 35
M33: Sale 2K 47
Granary Wharf *CH3: Ches 1B 150*
(off Steam Mill St.)
Granby Cl. WA7: B'vale 2E 112
Granby Cres. CH63: Spit 4A 86
Granby Rd. M32: S'ord 2J 23
SK2: Stoc 7F 53
SK8: Chea H 5K 77
WA4: Walt 5F 67
WA15: Timp 3B 48
Grand Central *L3: Liv 3K 35*
(off Hilbre St.)
Grand Central Pools 7H 213 (3C 52)
Grand Central Sq.
SK1: Stoc 7H 213 (3C 52)
Grandford La. CW5: Ast 7H 209
Grand Junc. Retail Pk.
CW1: Crewe 2D 194
Grand Junc. Way CW1: Crewe 2E 194
Granford Cl. WA14: Alt 5H 47
GRANGE
CH48 3E 56 (2A 214)
WA1 3D 42
Grange, The CH42: R Fer 4E 60
CH44: Wall 7J 13
CW8: H'ord 1A 162
CW12: Cong 6K 183
SK3: Stoc 5A 52
(off Edgeley Rd.)
SK11: Mac 6H 125
SK14: Hyde 2A 28
Grange Av. CH45: Wall 5H 13
CW8: Barnt 2K 155
M19: Manc 3C 24
M32: S'ord 1J 23
M34: Den 1G 27
M41: Urm 1H 21
SK4: Stoc 6G 25
SK8: Chea H 2H 77
WA4: Westy 1J 67
WA15: Hale 3A 74
WA15: Timp 5B 48
Grangebrook Dr. CW7: Wins 1D 178
Grange Cl. CW1: Crewe 3E 194
CW2: West 3K 199
CW11: S'ach 2D 200
SK14: Hyde 2A 28
Grange Ct. CH43: Oxt 2K 59
CW7: Wins 3C 178
WA14: Bow 4G 73
Grange Cres. CH66: H'ton 6B 108
M41: Urm 2B 22
Grange Cross Cl. CH48: W Kir 4F 57
Grange Cross Hey CH48: W Kir 4F 57
Grange Cross La. CH48: W Kir 4F 57
Grange Dr. CH60: Hes 4H 83
CH63: Tho H 7E 84
CW8: H'ord 7K 155
WA5: Penk 1J 65
WA8: Wid 4D 62
Grange Employment Cen.
WA1: Wool 3E 42
Grange Farm Cl. WA5: Gt San 6B 40
Grange Farm Cres. CH48: W Kir 2F 57
Grange Grn. Mnr. WA4: H Wal 6C 66
Grangelands SK10: Mac 2G 125
Grange La. CW7: Wins 1C 178
CW8: Gor 6D 154
(not continuous)
CW8: W'ate 7J 161
M20: Manc 2D 50
SY14: Tils 7D 206
Grange Lea CW10: Mid 3B 180
Grangemoor WA7: Run 7K 89
Grange Mt. CH43: Oxt 7B 34
CH48: W Kir 3E 56
CH60: Hes 5H 83
Grange Old Rd. CH48: W Kir 3D 56
Grange Pk. Av. OL6: Ash L 3A 4
SK8: Chea 7F 51
SK9: Wilm 6H 97
WA7: Run 4J 89
Grange Pk. Rd. SK8: Chea 7F 51
Grange Pl. CH41: Birk 6B 34
M44: Cad 6A 20
Grange Pct. CH41: Birk 6D 34
Grange Rd. CH2: Ches 6A 146
CH3: Ash H 5J 171
CH3: Ches 1F 151
CH41: Birk 6C 34
(not continuous)
CH48: W Kir 3B 56
CH60: Hes 4H 83
CH65: Ell P 3E 134
CW8: Barnt 2K 155
CW8: Cudd 4C 160
CW9: Rud 7J 157
M33: Sale 7E 22
M41: Urm 2B 22
SK7: Bram 2D 78
SK11: Mac 6K 125
WA7: Run 4J 89
WA14: Bow 4G 73
WA15: Timp 5B 48
Grange Rd. E. CH41: Birk 6D 34
Grange Rd. Nth. SK14: Hyde 1A 28
WA7: Run 4J 89
Grange Rd. Sth. SK14: Hyde 2A 28
Grange Road Sports Cen. 7A 34
Grange Rd. W. CH3: Ches 1F 151
CH41: Birk 6A 34
CH43: Oxt 6A 34
Grangeside CH2: Upt 3A 146
Grangethorpe Dr. M19: Manc 4B 24
Grangethorpe Rd. M14: Manc 1A 24
M41: Urm 2B 22
Grange Vw. CH43: Oxt 7B 34
Grange Wlk. CH48: W Kir 4E 56
Grange Way CW11: S'ach 2D 200
Grangeway SK9: Hand 2K 97
WA7: Run 6J 89
Grangeway Ct. WA7: Run 6J 89
Grange Wood CH48: W Kir 4E 56
Grangewood Dr. SK11: Chel 5B 166
Granston Cl. WA5: Call 2C 40
Grant Cl. WA5: Old H 3B 40
Grantham Av. WA1: Warr 5J 41
WA4: Walt 5F 67
Grantham Cl. CH61: Pens 2G 83
CW9: N'ich 6H 157
Grantham Ct. *M34: Den 2E 26*
(off Stockport Rd.)
Grantham Rd. SK4: Stoc 2A 52
Grant Rd. CH46: Leas 1E 32
Granville Cl. CH45: Wall 5E 12
Granville Ct. CH45: Wall 5E 12
Granville Dr. CH66: L Sut 1H 133
Granville Gdns. M20: Manc 2C 50
Granville Rd. CH1: Ches 7J 145
CW9: N'ich 1F 163
M14: Manc 3A 24
M34: Aude 1A 8
M41: Urm 1D 22
SK8: Chea H 7K 51
SK9: Wilm 2E 118
WA15: Timp 6C 48
Granville Sq. CW7: Wins 4E 178
Granville St. CW7: Wins 4F 179
OL6: Ash L 1J 9
WA1: Warr 6H 41
WA7: Run 3G 89
Grapes St. SK11: Mac 5A 126
Graphite Way SK13: Had 2K 11
GRAPPENHALL 3B 68 (2A 216)
Grappenhall La. WA4: App T, Grap 2B 94
Grappenhall Rd. CH65: Gt Sut 4B 134
WA4: Stoc H 4H 67
Grappenhall Way CH43: Bid 5F 33
Grasmere SK11: Mac 6G 125
Grasmere Av. CH43: Noc 7F 33
CW2: Crewe 1K 193
CW12: Cong 4B 182
M41: Urm 2H 21
SK4: Stoc 5H 25
WA2: Warr 1H 41
Grasmere Cl. CW7: Wins 2E 178
SK15: Stal 5B 4
Grasmere Ct. *CH41: Birk 7B 34*
(off Penrith St.)
Grasmere Cres. SK6: H Lan 4E 80
SK7: Bram 5C 78
Grasmere Dr. CH45: Wall 5H 13
CW4: H Cha 4G 181
WA7: Beec 2A 112
Grasmere Rd. CH2: Ches 5C 146
CH64: Nest 2C 130
CH65: Ell P 6E 134
M31: Part 1G 45
M32: S'ord 1J 23
M33: Sale 2C 48
SK8: Gat 2D 76
SK9: Ald E 6F 119
WA6: Frod 7J 111
WA13: Lymm 1B 70
WA15: Timp 6C 48
Grasmere St. M12: Manc 1E 24
Grason Av. SK9: Wilm 5K 97
Grasscroft SK5: Stoc 5B 26
Grasscroft Rd. SK15: Stal 1B 10
GRASSENDALE 2B 214
Grassfield Way WA16: Knut 5E 116
Grassholme Dr. SK2: Stoc 6A 54
Grass Mead M34: Den 3F 27
Grassmoor Cl. CH62: Brom 6E 86
Grasswood Rd. CH49: Woodc 3E 58
Grassy La. WA6: Frod 1D 138
Grasville Rd. CH42: Tran 2D 60
Gratrix La. M33: Sale 1F 49
Gratrix Rd. CH62: Brom 6D 86
GRATTON 2D 221
GRAVEL 3H 179
Gravel Bank Rd. SK6: W'ley 5G 27
Gravel La. SK9: Wilm 3D 118
Grave Oak La. WN7: Leigh 1G 7
Gray Cl. SK14: Mot 7G 11
Graylag Cl. WA7: Beec 2B 112
Graylands Rd. CH62: P Sun 7H 61
Graymarsh Dr. SK12: Poy 4D 100
Graysands Rd. WA15: Hale 2K 73
Gray's Cl. ST7: Sch G 5F 205
Grayson M. *CH41: Birk 5E 34*
(off John St.)
Grayson St. L1: Liv 4J 35
Grayston Ct. SK6: Mar 5G 55
Grazing Dr. M44: Irlam 1E 20
GREASBY 2A 58 (2A 214)
Greasby Dr. CH66: Gt Sut 4A 134
Greasby Hill Rd. CH48: W Kir 4D 56
Greasby Rd. CH44: Wall 7G 13
CH49: Gre 2K 57
Great Ashfield WA8: Wid 2D 62
GREAT BARROW 3A 170 (1C 219)
GREAT BOUGHTON 4E 150
GREAT BUDWORTH 5H 115 (3A 216)
Gt. Charlotte St. L1: Liv 3J 35
(not continuous)
GREAT CROSBY 1B 214
Gt. Crosshall St. L3: Liv 2H 35
Gt. Egerton St. SK1: Stoc 5G 213 (2C 52)
SK4: Stoc 6G 213 (3C 52)
Greatfield Rd. M22: Wyth 2H 75
Gt. George Pl. L1: Liv 5K 35
Gt. George Sq. L1: Liv 4K 35
Gt. George St. L1: Liv 4K 35
Gt. Homer St. Shop. Cen. L5: Liv 1K 35
Gt. Howard St. L3: Liv 1G 35
Gt. King St. SK11: Mac 4K 125
GREAT MEOLS 3F 31
Gt. Moor St. SK2: Stoc 7F 53
Gt. Nelson St. L3: Liv 1K 35
Gt. Newton St. L3: Liv 2K 35
Gt. Norbury St. SK14: Hyde 7H 9
Great Oak Dr. WA15: Alt 2K 213 (1J 73)
Great Oak Sq. WA16: Mob 6B 102
Gt. Orford St. L3: Liv 3K 35
Gt. Portwood St. SK1: Stoc 5K 213 (2D 52)
Gt. Queen St. SK11: Mac 4K 125
Gt. Richmond St. L3: Liv 1K 35
Great Riding WA7: Nort 7E 90
GREAT SANKEY 6H 39 (2D 215)
Great Sankey Leisure Cen. 4F 39
GREAT SUTTON 4K 133 (3B 214)
Great Underbank
SK1: Stoc 6H 213 (3D 52)
Gt. Western Ho. CH41: Birk 5E 34
Great Wood Local Nature Reserve 3F 29
Greave SK6: Rom 7J 27
GREAVEFOLD 7J 27
Greave Fold SK6: Rom 7H 27
Greave Rd. SK1: Stoc 4G 53
Greaves La. SY14: Thr 6H 207
Greaves La. E. SY14: Thr 6H 207
Greaves Rd. SK9: Wilm 7E 96
Greaves St. L8: Liv 7K 35
Grebe Cl. SK12: Poy 2A 100
WA16: Knut 2F 117
Grebe Wlk. SK2: Stoc 1A 80
Gredle Cl. M41: Urm 1E 22
Greeba Av. WA4: Warr 2F 67
Greeba Rd. M23: Wyth 6E 48
Greek St. L3: Liv 2K 35
SK3: Stoc 4C 52
WA7: Run 3F 89
GREEN, THE 6B 192
Green, The CH48: Cald 6E 56
CH62: Brom 1D 86
CH63: Raby 3B 106
CH64: L Nes 2D 130
CH64: Nest 7G 105
CH64: W'ston 7E 106
CH65: Whit 6D 134
CW8: H'ord 1A 162
CW10: Mid 6D 180
CW12: Cong 4E 182
M31: Part 7C 20
SK4: Stoc 1A 52
SK6: Mar 2G 81
SK8: Chea H 5H 77
SK9: Hand 3B 98
SK14: Hyde 4B 10
SK15: M'ook 5F 5
ST7: Chu L 4H 203
WA7: Halt 5B 90
WA15: Timp 5B 48
(off Whitley Gdns.)
Greenacre SK8: He Grn 6E 76
Greenacre Cl. WA16: Knut 5F 117
Greenacre Dr. CH63: Brom 7C 86
Greenacre Rd. CH4: Ches 7G 149
Greenacres CW1: Crewe 7H 191
CW6: Dud 5B 174
CW11: S'ach 2E 200
WA6: Frod 2J 139
Greenacres, The WA13: Lymm 1C 70
Greenacres Cvn. Pk. WA6: Haps 7H 137
Greenacres Cl. CH43: Bid 4F 33
WN7: Leigh 2B 6
Greenacres Ct. CH2: Upt 1C 146
CH43: Bid 4F 33
Greenacres Dr. M19: Manc 7B 24
Greenacres Rd. CW12: Cong 4B 182
Greenall Av. WA5: Penk 1F 65
Greenall Rd. CW9: N'ich 5G 157
Greenalls Av. WA4: Warr 4F 67
Green & Slater Homes SK4: Stoc 1J 51
Green Av. CW6: Alp 2J 189
CW8: Barnt 2K 155
CW9: Dave 3D 162
Green Bank CH4: Ches 6B 150
CH63: Brim 4E 84
SK4: Stoc 4G 25
Greenbank CH2: Ince 3E 136
Greenbank Av. CH45: N Bri 4H 13
CH66: L Sut 1J 133
SK4: Stoc 2G 51
SK8: Gat 7C 50
Greenbank Cl. CW5: W'ston 1H 197
Greenbank Cres. SK6: Mar 7F 55
Greenbank Dr. CH61: Pens 3H 83
SK10: Boll 3D 122
Greenbank Gdns.
WA4: Stoc H 3K 67

Greenbank Ho.—Grosvenor Ct.

Greenbank Ho. *WA14: Bow* 2H 73
(off Albert Sq.)
Greenbank La. CW8: H'ord, N'ich 7B 156
Greenbank Pk. CW11: Whe 7E 200
Greenbank Rd. CH2: Ches 6D 146
CH42: Tran 2B 60
CH48: W Kir 1C 56
M33: Sale 6D 22
SK6: Mar B 3H 55
SK8: Gat 6C 50
WA4: Stoc H 3K 67
GREENBANK STATION (RAIL) 7C 156
Greenbank St. WA4: Warr 4G 67
Greenbank Ter. SK4: Stoc 4H 213
Greenbeech Cl. SK6: Mar 5E 54
Greenbooth Cl. SK16: Duk 3A 10
Greenbridge Cl. WA7: Cast 4C 90
Greenbridge Rd. WA7: Win H 4D 90
Greenbrow Rd. M23: Wyth 7G 49
(not continuous)
Green Cl. SK8: Gat 6C 50
Green Coppice WA7: Nort 6E 90
Green Ct. WN7: Leigh 1B 6
Green Courts WA14: Bow 2F 73
Greencourts Bus. Pk. M22: Wyth 5C 76
Green Cft. SK6: Rom 1D 54
Greencroft Rd. CH44: Wall 1B 34
Greendale Dr. CW10: Mid 5B 180
Greendale Gdns. CW1: Crewe 7K 191
Greendale Gro. M34: Den 3G 27
Greendale La. SK10: Pres 3E 120
Greendale Rd. CH62: P Sun 7F 61
Green Dr. M19: Manc 2C 24
SK9: Wilm 4A 98
ST7: Als 5E 202
WA15: Timp 5A 48
GREEN END 6C 24
Green End M34: Den 3G 27
Green End Rd. M19: Manc 6B 24
GREENFIELD 3A 214
Greenfield Av. M41: Urm 1C 22
Greenfield Cl. SK3: Stoc 6C 52
WA15: Timp 6C 48
Greenfield Ct. CW12: Cong 3D 182
Greenfield Cres. CH2: Ches 5E 146
CH3: Wave 1B 174
Greenfield Farm Ind. Est.
CW12: Cong 3D 182
Greenfield Gdns. CH2: Elt 5F 137
Greenfield La. CH2: Ches 5E 146
CH60: Hes 4E 82
WA6: Frod 6H 111
Greenfield Rd. CH3: Chri, Wave 1B 174
CH66: L Sut 1H 133
CW12: Cong 3D 182
SK10: Boll 4D 122
GREENFIELDS 4F 33
Greenfields CH2: Upt 1C 146
CW7: Wins 3J 179
Greenfields Av. CH62: Brom 7C 86
CW2: Shav 3B 198
WA4: App 5H 67
Greenfields Cl. CH64: L Nes 3D 130
WA1: Wool 5C 42
Greenfields Cres. CH62: Brom 7C 86
Greenfields Cft. CH64: L Nes 3C 130
Greenfields Dr. CH64: L Nes 4C 130
ST7: Als 6F 203
Greenfields La. CH3: Row 6J 151
SY14: Mal 2H 207
Greenfields Lodge CH3: Gt Bar 2A 170
Greenfield St. M34: Aude 3C 8
SK14: Hyde 1J 27
Greenfield Ter. M41: Urm 1H 21
Greenfield Way CH44: Wall 7H 13
CW8: Cudd 2D 160
Greenfinch Gdns. WA14: W Tim 3F 47
Green Fold Way WN7: Leigh 1H 7
Greenford Cl. SK8: Chea H 1K 77
Green Gables Cl. SK8: He Grn 4D 76
Green Ga. WA15: H'rns 7D 74
Greengate SK14: Hyde 3J 27
Greengate Rd. M34: Den 6F 9
ST7: Chu L 4G 203
Greengates *SK10: Mac* *2F 125*
(off Priory La.)
Greengates Cres. CH64: L Nes 3C 130
Greenhalgh St. SK4: Stoc 4H 213 (2C 52)
Green Hall M. SK9: Wilm 1G 119
Greenham Rd. M23: Wyth 2F 49
Green Haven CH43: Noc 7G 33
Greenhaven Ct. CW5: Hath 1G 211
Greenhay La. CH3: L Bar 7K 143
Greenhead Fold SK6: Rom 3A 54
Greenheath Way CH46: Leas 1C 32
Greenheys M43: Droy 1A 8
Greenheys Rd. CH44: Wall 1A 34
CH61: Irby 1E 82
Greenhill Av. M33: Sale 5F 23
Greenhill La.
WA4: L Whi .... 2A 114 & 3A 114
Green Hill Pl. SK3: Stoc 5B 52
Green Hill Rd. SK14: Hyde 7A 10
Greenhill Rd. WA15: Timp 6C 48
Greenhills Cl. SK11: Mac 5B 126
Green Hill St. SK3: Stoc 5B 52
Green Hill Ter. SK3: Stoc 5B 52
Greenhill Wlk. SK12: Dis 1G 103
Green Hollow Fold SK15: Carrb 4E 4
Greenhouse Farm Rd. WA7: Pal F 1D 112
Greenhow Av. CH48: W Kir 2C 56
Greenhythe Rd. SK8: He Grn 7E 76
Greening Rd. M19: Manc 1E 24
Greenings Ct. WA2: Warr 6G 41
Green Jones Brow
WA5: B'ood 5C 14
Green Lake La. CH3: Ald 6G 185
Greenland Cl. CW6: Tarp 3J 175
Greenlands CH3: Tatt 1H 187
Greenlands Cl.
SK8: Chea H 5G 77
Greenland St. L1: Liv 5J 35
Green La. CH1: Sau 3D 144
CH2: Pict 1E 146
CH3: Ches 1E 150
CH3: Guil S 7F 147
CH4: Ches 6F 149
CH41: Tran 1D 60
CH45: Wall 6B 12
(not continuous)
CH62: East 6F 87
CH63: Beb 1K 85
CH65: Ell P 4E 134
CH66: Gt Sut 4J 133
(not continuous)
CW3: Audl 7B 210
CW5: Edle 3A 196
CW5: W'ston 2H 197
CW6: Kel 4B 172
CW9: Dave 3E 162
CW9: Winc 1K 157
CW11: Most, Warm 3E 204
L3: Liv 3K 35
M33: Sale 5D 22
M44: Cad 6B 20
SK4: Stoc 1K 51
SK6: Rom 3B 54
SK7: H Gro 2H 79
SK9: Ald E 7E 118
SK9: Wilm 7J 97
SK10: Boll 2E 122
SK12: Dis 2F 103
SK12: Poy 2H 101
SK13: Had 3K 11
SK14: H'rth 1J 11
SK14: Hyde 1B 28
(Alvon Ct.)
SK14: Hyde 1B 28
(Crossbridge Rd.)
WA1: Padg 4A 42
WA2: Winw 4K 15
WA3: Low 1A 6
WA4: App, App T 1K 93
WA5: B'ood 4B 14
WA8: Wid 4E 62
WA15: Timp 2B 74
(not continuous)
WA16: Knut 2B 116
WA16: O Peo 2K 165
Green La. Cl. WA2: Winw 4K 15
Green La. Ind. Est. SK4: Stoc 2B 52
Green La. Nth. WA15: Timp 7B 48
GREEN LANE STATION (RAIL) 1E 60
Greenlaw Cl. CW9: N'ich 1F 163
Green Lawn CH42: R Fer 4E 60
Green Lawn Gro. CH42: R Fer 4E 60
Green Lawns Dr. CH66: Gt Sut 1B 140
Greenlea Av. M18: Manc 1G 25
Greenlea Cl. CH63: Beb 7E 60
CH65: Whit 6D 134
Greenleas Cl. CH45: Wall 5D 12
Greenleas Rd. CH45: Wall 5D 12
Green Mdws. SK6: Mar 5F 55
SK11: Mac 6G 125
Green Mdws. Dr. SK6: Mar 4F 55
Green Mdws. Wlk. M22: Wyth 4A 76
Green Mt. CH49: Upt 7D 32
Greenoak Dr. M33: Sale 3C 48
Greenoaks Farm Ind. Est.
WA8: Wid 4J 63
Green Oaks Path WA8: Wid 5K 63
Green Oaks Shop. Cen.
WA8: Wid 4H 63
Greenoaks Shop. Cen. WA8: Wid 5H 63
(not continuous)
Green Oaks Way WA8: Wid 5H 63
Greenock M. WA8: Wid 2E 62
Greenock St. L3: Liv 1G 35
Greenore Dr. L24: Hale 6A 88
Green Pk. CW8: Weav 6H 155
Greenpark Rd. M22: N'den 3K 49
Green Pastures SK4: Stoc 3F 51
Green Rd. M31: Part 1G 45
Greens Health & Fitness
Liverpool 2K 61
Greenside SK4: Stoc 3J 51
Greenside Av. WA6: Frod 1K 139
Greenside Cl. SK16: Duk 2B 10
Greenside Ct. CW9: Lac D 7H 159
Greenside Dr. CW9: Los Grn 7C 158
M44: Irlam 2C 20
WA14: Hale 4J 73
Greenside La. M43: Droy 1A 8
Greenside Pl. M34: Den 3F 27
Greenside Shop. Cen. M43: Droy 1A 8
Greenside Trad. Cen. M43: Droy 1A 8
Greenside Vw. SK14: Hyde 5B 10
Green St. CW11: S'ach 2F 201
LL13: Holt 6B 186
M14: Manc 4A 24
M32: S'ord 3H 23
SK3: Stoc 6D 52
SK9: Ald E 6F 119
SK10: Mac 5B 126
Green St. SK14: Hyde 2K 27
WA5: Warr 7C 40
(not continuous)
WA16: Knut 3E 116
Greensway CH4: Ches 4H 149
Greenthorne Av. SK4: Stoc 4G 25
Green Tree Gdns. SK6: Rom 2B 54
Greenvale Ct. SK8: Chea 6E 50
Greenvale Dr. SK8: Chea 6E 50
Green Vw. WA13: Lymm 7D 44
Greenview Dr. M20: Manc 4E 50
Green Villa Pk. SK9: Wilm 3D 118
Greenville Cl. CH63: Beb 1K 85
Greenville Rd. CH63: Beb 1K 85
Green Wlk. CW8: Cudd 2E 160
M31: Part 1G 45
M32: S'ord 1G 23
SK8: Gat 6C 50
SK14: Mot 1G 29
WA14: Bow 2E 72
WA15: Timp 5K 47
Greenwater Mdw. SK14: H'rth 2J 11
Green Way CH1: Sau 1B 144
SK14: Mot 1G 29
Greenway CH3: Farn 6C 186
CH49: Gre 1B 58
CH61: Pens 2G 83
CH62: Brom 3D 86
CH64: Park 5E 104
CW1: Crewe 7J 191
CW12: Cong 3D 182
M22: N'den 4A 50
SK6: Rom 3E 54
SK7: Bram 7B 78
SK9: Wilm 1G 119
SK14: Hyde 2J 27
ST7: Als 4C 202
SY14: Tils 6B 206
WA1: Padd 5K 41
WA4: App 5H 67
WA5: Gt San 5G 39
WA14: Alt 7E 46
Greenway Av. M19: Manc 3E 24
Greenway Cl. M33: Sale 1J 47
ST7: Rod H 1G 203
WA6: Hel 5B 138
Greenway Dr. CW9: N'ich 6H 157
Greenway Rd. CH42: Tran 2C 60
SK8: He Grn 6E 76
WA7: Run 5F 89
WA8: Wid 3H 63
WA15: Timp 4K 47
Greenways Ct. CH62: Brom 1H 107
Greenway St. CH4: Ches 7C 212 (3A 150)
Greenway Wlk. CW9: N'ich 6H 157
Greenwich Av. WA8: Wid 1K 63
Greenwood, The CW6: Tarp 5J 175
Greenwood Av. CH4: Ches 4A 150
CW12: Cong 3H 183
SK2: Stoc 6G 53
Greenwood Cl. CW8: Weav 4G 155
WA15: Timp 7D 48
Greenwood Ct. WA3: Ris 1A 18
(Cedar Ct.)
WA3: Ris 3K 17
(Warrington Rd.)
WA9: Clo F 1J 37
Greenwood Cres. WA2: Warr 2H 41
Green Wood Dr. WA7: Man P 2H 91
Greenwood Dr. SK9: Wilm 6A 98
WA12: New W 1G 15
Greenwood Gdns. SK6: Bred 1K 53
Greenwood La. CH44: Wall 6J 13
Greenwood Rd. CH47: Meols 4F 31
CH49: Woodc 2D 58
M22: Wyth 2H 75
WA13: Lymm 3A 70
Greenwood St. WA14: Alt 2H 213 (1H 73)
Greenwood Ter. WA16: Mob 6B 102
Greetham St. L1: Liv 4J 35
Greg Av. SK10: Boll 4B 122
Gregg M. SK9: Wilm 4J 97
Gregory Av. SK6: Rom 3C 54
Gregory Cl. WA5: Old H 5A 40
Gregory Row *WA3: Low* *1A 6*
(off Sandy La.)
Gregory St. SK14: Hyde 5K 9
Gregory Way SK5: Stoc 5J 25
Gregson Ct. CH45: N Bri 3J 13
Gregson Rd. SK5: Stoc 5H 25
WA8: Wid 4J 63
Greg St. SK5: Stoc 6H 25
Greg St. Ind. Est. SK4: Stoc 6H 25
Grendale Av. SK1: Stoc 3F 53
SK7: H Gro 4J 79
Grenfell Cl. CH64: Park 6F 105
Grenfell Ct. CH64: Park 7F 105
Grenfell Pk. CH64: Park 6F 105
Grenfell Rd. M20: Manc 1C 50
Grenfell St. WA8: Wid 5H 63
Grennan, The CH45: N Bri 3H 13
Grennan Ct. *CH45: N Bri* *3H 13*
(off The Grennan)
Grenville Cl. CW1: Hasl 1J 195
Grenville Cres. CH63: Brom 7C 86
Grenville Dr. CH61: Pens 3G 83
Grenville Rd. CH42: Tran 2E 60
CH64: Nest 6H 105
SK7: H Gro 2G 79
Grenville St. SK3: Stoc 4B 52
SK15: M'ook 5E 4
SK16: Duk 2H 9
Grenville St. Sth. L1: Liv 4J 35
Grenville Ter. OL6: Ash L 1J 9
Grenville Way CH42: Tran 2E 60
GRESFORD 2B 218
Gresford Av. CH2: Ches 7B 146
CH43: Pren 3K 59
CH48: W Kir 2D 56
Gresford Cl. WA5: Call 2C 40
Gresham St. M34: Den 6E 8
Gresham Wlk. *SK4: Stoc* *1C 52*
(off Hesketh St.)
Gresham Way M33: Sale 3A 48
Gresty Av. M22: Wyth 4B 76
Gresty Bldgs. *CW5: Nant* *1C 196*
(off Cowfields)
Gresty Grn. Rd. CW2: Shav 6D 194
Gresty La. CW2: Shav 1A 198
Gresty Rd. CW2: Crewe 4D 194
Gresty Side CW5: Nant 2A 196
Gresty Ter. CW1: Crewe 3E 194
Greswell St. M34: Den 6E 8
Greta Av. SK8: He Grn 7E 76
Greville Dr. CW7: Wins 3H 179
Grey Cl. SK6: Bred 7F 27
Grey Friars CH1: Ches 5A 212 (2K 149)
Greyfriars Cl. WA2: Fear 2A 42
Greyfriars Rd. M22: Wyth 3H 75
Greyhound Pk. Rd. CH1: Ches 1G 149
Greyhound Retail Pk. CH1: Ches 7G 145
Greyhound Rd. SK10: O Ald 6C 120
Greylands Cl. M33: Sale 7E 22
Greylands Rd. M20: Manc 4E 50
Greymist Av. WA1: Wool 5C 42
Grey Rd. WA14: Alt 1F 213 (7F 47)
Greys Ct. WA1: Wool 3C 42
Greystoke Av. M19: Manc 2F 25
M33: Sale 1B 48
WA15: Timp 6D 48
Greystoke Cl. CH49: Upt 1C 58
Greystoke Dr. SK9: Ald E 5F 119
Greystoke Rd. SK10: Mac 2C 126
Greystoke St. SK1: Stoc 3E 52
Greystone Pk. CW1: Crewe 2D 194
Greystone Rd. WA5: Penk 1H 65
Greystones CH66: Gt Sut 4K 133
Greystones Rd. CH3: Gt Bou 2F 151
Greystone Wlk. SK4: Stoc 4G 25
Grey St. L8: Liv 6K 35
M34: Den 7C 8
SK15: Stal 1D 10
WA1: Warr 6G 41
Grice St. WA4: Stoc H 4G 67
Griffin Av. CH46: More 4B 32
Griffin Cl. CH1: Blac 4G 145
Griffin Gro. M19: Manc 3D 24
Griffin La. SK8: He Grn 6F 77
Griffin M. WA8: Wid 2H 63
Griffin Trust (Mus.) 5D 108
Griffiths Av. WA3: Ris 6K 17
Griffiths Cl. CH49: Gre 2K 57
Griffiths Dr. CW9: Rud 7J 157
Griffiths Rd.
CW9: Los Gra, Los Grn, Rud 6K 157
Griffiths St. L1: Liv 4K 35
WA4: Westy 1K 67
Grig Pl. ST7: Als 4D 202
Grimsditch La. WA4: L Whi, Nor B 1A 114
Grimshaw Av. SK10: Boll 4D 122
Grimshaw Cl. SK6: Bred 7F 27
Grimshaw La. SK10: Boll 4C 122
Grimshaw St. SK1: Stoc 3E 52
Grimstead Cl. M23: Wyth 6E 48
Grindleton Av. M22: Wyth 2K 75
Grindley Bank CH2: Mic T 2J 147
GRINDLEY BROOK 3D 219
Grindley Gdns. CH65: Ell P 6E 134
Grinton Av. M13: Manc 1B 24
Grisedale Av. WA2: Warr 1F 41
Grisedale Cl. WA7: Beec 2A 112
Grisedale Rd. CH62: Brom 6F 87
Grisedale Way SK11: Mac 7H 125
Gritley Wlk. M22: Wyth 4J 75
Gritstone Dr. SK10: Mac 3H 125
Grizedale WA8: Wid 3B 62
Grizedale Cl. CW2: Crewe 4H 193
SK15: Carrb 2G 5
Grizedale Rd. SK6: W'ley 7G 27
Groarke Dr. WA5: Penk 7F 39
Groby Ct. WA14: Alt 3G 213 (1G 73)
Groby Pl. WA14: Alt 1G 213 (7G 47)
Groby Rd. CW1: Crewe 3J 191
M34: Aude 3D 8
WA14: Alt 3F 213 (1F 73)
Groby Rd. Nth. M34: Aude 2C 8
Groby St. SK15: Stal 1D 10
Grocott's Row CW5: Nant 2C 196
Grosvenor Av. CH48: W Kir 3C 56
CW8: H'ord 2K 161
ST7: Als 4E 202
WA1: Warr 5J 41
Grosvenor Cen. SK11: Mac 4A 126
Grosvenor Cl. SK9: Wilm 3F 119
ST7: Als 4E 202
WA5: Gt San 7A 40
Grosvenor Ct. CH1: Ches 4E 212 (2B 150)
CH43: Oxt 7A 34
CH47: Hoy 6C 30
CW1: Crewe 1B 194
CW7: Wins 5D 178
M33: Sale 6E 22
OL7: Ash L 1F 9
SK8: Chea 6F 51

Grosvenor Cres.—Halstone Av.

Grosvenor Cres. SK14: Hyde 2H 27
Grosvenor Dr. CH45: N Bri 3H 13
SK12: Poy 3B 100
Grosvenor Gdns. M22: Shar 6A 50
SK15: Stal 1B 10
WA12: New W 1F 15
Grosvenor Grange WA1: Wool 3B 42
Grosvenor Ho. *M33: Sale 7E 22*
(off Grosvenor Sq.)
OL7: Ash L 1F 9
(off Park St.)
Grosvenor Ho. Sq. SK15: Stal 1B 10
Grosvenor Ind. Est.
OL7: Ash L 1F 9
Grosvenor Lodge *SK7: H Gro 4F 79*
(off Dorchester Rd.)
Grosvenor Mus. 6B 212 (3K 149)
Grosvenor Pk. Rd.
CH1: Ches 4E 212 (2B 150)
Grosvenor Pk. Ter.
CH1: Ches 5E 212 (2B 150)
Grosvenor Pl. CH1: Ches 6C 212 (3A 150)
CH43: Oxt 7K 33
OL7: Ash L 1F 9
Grosvenor Rd.
CH1: Ches 7A 212 (4K 149)
CH3: Tar 4C 170
CH4: Ches 7A 212 (4K 149)
CH43: Oxt 6K 33
CH45: N Bri 3H 13
CH47: Hoy 6C 30
CW12: Cong 3C 182
M33: Sale 6E 22
M41: Urm 1B 22
SK4: Stoc 1J 51
(not continuous)
SK6: Mar 5F 55
SK8: Chea H 1A 78
SK14: Hyde 2J 27
WA8: Wid 1H 63
WA14: Alt 1K 213 (7J 47)
Grosvenor Sq. M33: Sale 7F 23
SK15: Stal 1B 10
(off Grosvenor St.)
Grosvenor St. CH1: Ches 6B 212 (3K 149)
CH44: Wall 6H 13
CW1: Crewe 1B 194
CW7: Wins 4F 179
L3: Liv 1J 35
M32: S'ord 1J 23
M34: Den 6C 8
OL7: Ash L 1E 8
(not continuous)
SK3: Stoc 4D 52
SK7: H Gro 2H 79
SK10: Mac 4K 125
SK15: Stal 1B 10
WA7: Run 3H 89
Grosvenor Wharf Rd. CH65: Ell P 1F 135
Grotto La. WA16: O Peo 3G 165
Grounds St. WA2: Warr 5F 41
Grove, The CH43: Oxt 2A 60
CH44: Wall 1B 34
CH63: Beb 1A 86
CW6: Tarp 2H 175
CW9: Dave 4F 163
M20: Manc 3D 50
M33: Sale 1B 48
M41: Urm 2J 21
SK2: Stoc 5C 52
SK8: Chea H 7J 77
SK13: Had 3K 11
ST7: Chu L 5H 203
WA5: Penk 1H 65
WA13: Lymm 2A 70
WA14: Alt 7H 47
WA16: Knut 1G 117
Grove Arc. SK9: Wilm 7J 97
Grove Av. CH3: Ches 7E 146
CH60: Hes 5H 83
CW9: Los Gra 4C 158
SK9: Wilm 7H 97
ST7: Chu L 5H 203
WA13: Lymm 2J 69
Grove Bank WA6: Hel 4C 138
Grove Cl. CW7: Wins 4C 178
Grove Ct. M33: Sale 7J 23
SK7: H Gro 2J 79
ST7: Als 5F 203
Grovedale Dr. CH46: More 3D 32
Grove Gdns. CH3: Lit 1H 151
Grove Ho. SK4: Stoc 3G 51
Groveland Av. CH45: Wall 5D 12
CH47: Hoy 5C 30
Groveland Rd. CH45: Wall 5D 12
Grove La. M20: Manc 1D 50
SK8: Chea H 7J 77
WA15: Hale 2A 74
WA15: Timp 5K 47
Grovemount CW9: Dave 4E 162
Grove Pk. 1D 98
Grove Pk. M33: Sale 7E 22
WA16: Knut 4E 116
Grove Pk. Av. ST7: Chu L 5H 203
Grove Pl. CH47: Hoy 5C 30
Grove Ri. WA13: Lymm 2A 70
Grove Rd. CH1: Mol 4A 140
CH42: R Fer 3E 60
CH45: Wall 5E 12
CH47: Hoy 5C 30
SK15: M'ook 5E 4
WA15: Hale 2J 73
Groves, The CH1: Ches 6C 212 (3A 150)
CH43: Oxt 7A 34
CH66: Whit 1C 140
Groveside CH48: W Kir 3B 56
Grove Sq. CH62: N Fer 6F 61
Grove St. CH62: N Fer 6G 61
SK7: H Gro 2J 79
SK9: Wilm 7J 97
SK16: Duk 1J 9
WA4: Warr 2G 67
WA7: Run 3F 89
Grove Ter. CH47: Hoy 5C 30
WA6: Hel 4C 138
Grove Way SK9: Wilm 7J 97
Grovewood Ct. CH43: Oxt 2A 60
Grovewood M. SK11: Mac 6K 125
Grub La. CW6: Kel 3B 172
Grundey St. SK7: H Gro 3J 79
Grundy Cl. WA8: Wid 2F 63
Grundy St. SK4: Stoc 2G 51
Guardian Ct. CH48: W Kir 4C 56
M33: Sale 6F 23
Guardian Lodge SK8: Gat 7C 50
Guardian M. M23: Wyth 3C 48
Guardian St. WA5: Warr 6D 40
Guardian St. Ind. Est.
WA5: Warr 6D 40
Guernsey Cl. CW10: Mid 2D 180
CW12: Cong 5J 183
M19: Manc 5D 24
WA4: App 5H 67
Guernsey Dr. CH65: Ell P 7E 134
Guernsey Rd. WA8: Wid 2A 64
Guest Slack WA6: K'ley 2C 152
Guest St. WA8: Wid 6G 63
Guffitts Cl. CH47: Meols 3F 31
Guffitt's Rake CH47: Meols 3F 31
GUIDE BRIDGE 2E 8
Guide Bridge Station (Rail) 2E 8
Guide Bridge Theatre 2D 8
Guide Bri. Trad. Est.
OL7: Ash L 2D 8
Guide La. M34: Aude 2E 8
Guilden Grn. CH3: Guil S 6H 147
GUILDEN SUTTON 5J 147 (1C 219)
Guilden Sutton La. CH3: Guil S 6F 147
(not continuous)
Guildford Av. SK8: Chea H 7J 77
Guildford Cl. CH4: Ches 5G 149
SK1: Stoc 5F 53
WA2: Padg 3A 42
Guildford Rd. M19: Manc 1E 24
SK16: Duk 3B 10
Guildford St. CH44: Wall 7K 13
OL5: Moss 1E 4
Guillemot Cl. CW1: Crewe 1F 195
Guinea Gap CH44: Wall 1D 34
Guinea Gap Baths & Recreation Cen.
. . . . 1D 34
Gullane Cl. SK10: Mac 7J 121
Gull Cl. SK12: Poy 3A 100
Gullet, The CW5: Nant 2C 196
Gulliver's World Theme Pk. 3C 40
Gulls Way CH60: Hes 6F 83
Gunco La. SK10: Pres 3K 121
SK11: Mac 6B 126
Gunn Gro. CH64: Nest 7J 105
Gun Rd. SK13: Chis 7J 29
GURNETT 1K 129
Gutterscroft CW1: Hasl 1K 195
Gutticar Rd. WA8: Wid 4B 62
Guy Cl. CH41: Tran 1D 60
Guy La. CH3: Wave 2B 174
Guywood Cotts. SK6: Rom 1C 54
Guywood La. SK6: Rom 1C 54
Gwenbury Av. SK1: Stoc 3F 53
Gwendoline Cl. CH61: Thin 1J 83
GWERNAFFIELD 1A 218
GWERNYMYNYDD 1A 218
GWERSYLLT 2B 218
Gwladys St. SK15: Carrb 3F 5
Gwyneth Morley Ct.
SK9: Hand 3A 98
GWYNFRYN 2A 218
GYFELIA 3B 218
Gylden Cl. SK14: Hyde 4C 10
Gypsy La. CH1: Mol 7B 140
SK2: Stoc 6G 53
(not continuous)
Gypsy Wlk. SK2: Stoc 6G 53
Gyte's La. M19: Manc 1F 25

H

Hackberry Cl. WA14: B'ath 4F 47
Hacked Way La. SK11: Mac F 6H 127
Hackins Hey L2: Liv 2H 35
Haddon Cl. CW2: Wis 7B 194
CW4: H Cha 4H 181
SK6: H Lan 7E 80
SK9: Ald E 5E 118
SK11: Mac 7J 125
Haddon Dr. CH61: Pens 2H 83
WA8: Wid 1B 62
Haddon Gro. M33: Sale 1A 48
SK5: Stoc 4H 25
WA15: Timp 5K 47
Haddon Ho. *CH64: Nest 7H 105*
(off Churchill Way)
Haddon La. CH64: Ness 4F 131
(not continuous)
Haddon Rd. CH42: R Fer 3F 61
SK7: H Gro 4J 79
SK8: He Grn 6E 76
Haddon Way M34: Den 2F 27
HADFIELD 1D 217
Hadfield Av. CH47: Hoy 5D 30
Hadfield Cl. WA8: Wid 4A 64
Hadfield Cres. OL6: Ash L 4A 4
Hadfield Rd. SK13: Had 3K 11
Hadfields Av. SK14: H'rth 2J 11
Hadfield St. CW9: N'ich 4G 157
SK16: Duk 3F 9
Hadfield Ter. OL6: Ash L 4A 4
Hadleigh Cl. WA5: Gt San 7F 39
Hadleigh Gro. WA7: Cast 4B 90
Hadley Av. CH62: Brom 5C 86
M13: Manc 1B 24
Hadley Cl. SK8: Chea H 4H 77
Hadley Dr. CW2: West 3K 199
Hadlow Grn. SK5: Stoc 5A 26
Hadlow La. CH64: W'ston 1K 131
Hadlow Rd. CH64: W'ston 3K 131
Hadlow Road Station Mus. 1A 132
Hadlow Ter. CH64: W'ston 1K 131
Hadrian Dr. CH1: Blac 4F 145
Hadrian Way CW8: S'way 4E 160
CW10: Mid 2C 180
Hadwens Bldgs. *L3: Liv 2H 35*
(off Pall Mall)
Hafod Cl. CH1: Blac 7E 144
Hagg Bank La. SK12: Dis 6K 81
HAGUE, THE 1K 29
Hague Pl. SK15: Stal 7B 4
Hague Rd. SK14: B'tom 3J 29
Haig Av. CH46: More 4C 32
M44: Cad 7K 19
WA5: Gt San 1J 65
Haig Ct. WA16: Knut 1G 117
Haigh Av. SK4: Stoc 6H 25
Haigh Lawn WA14: Alt 2F 73
Haigh Pk. SK4: Stoc 6H 25
Haigh St. L3: Liv 1K 35
(not continuous)
Haighton Ct. CW5: Nant 1C 196
Haig Rd. M32: S'ord 1J 23
WA8: Wid 4G 63
WA16: Knut 2G 117
Halcyon Rd. CH41: Birk 1B 60
Haldane Av. CH41: Birk 5J 33
Haldon Rd. M20: Manc 6A 24
HALE
L24 . . . . 7A 88 (2C 215)
WA15 . . . . 3J 73 (2B 216)
Hale Av. SK12: Poy 4C 100
HALE BANK 1B 88 (2C 215)
Halebank Rd. WA8: Hal B 1A 88
Hale Bank Ter. WA8: Hal B 2A 88
HALEBARNS 5C 74 (2B 216)
Hale Ct. WA8: Hal B 2A 88
WA14: Alt 3H 73
Hale Ga. Rd. WA8: Hal B 3A 88
Hale Grn. Ct. WA15: Hale 2A 74
Hale Gro. WA5: Gt San 6J 39
Hale Low Rd. WA15: Hale 2K 73
Hale M. WA8: Wid 6C 62
HALE MOSS 2K 73
Hale Rd. CH45: Wall 5J 13
L24: Hale 7A 88
SK4: Stoc 1A 52
WA8: Hal B, Wid 2B 88
WA8: Wid 6C 62
WA14: Alt 2H 73
WA15: Hale 2H 73
Hale Rd. Ind. Est. WA8: Hal B 1B 88
Halesden Rd. SK4: Stoc 6G 25
Hale Station (Rail) 3H 73
Hale St. L2: Liv 2H 35
WA2: Warr 5F 41
Hale Top M22: Wyth 3K 75
Hale Vw. WA7: Run 6E 88
WA14: Alt 3H 73
(off Ashley Rd.)
Hale Vw. Rd. WA6: Hel 4C 138
Hale Wlk. SK8: Chea 1J 77
HALEWOOD 2C 215
Haley Cl. SK5: Stoc 3J 25
Haley Rd. Nth. WA5: B'ood 5B 14
Haley Rd. Sth. WA5: B'ood 6B 14
Half Acre La. WA4: Thel 2E 68
Halfacre Rd. M22: Wyth 1J 75
Half Moon La. SK2: Stoc 6H 53
Half St. SK11: Mac 6A 126
Half-Tide Wharf L3: Liv 5H 35
Halifax Cl. WA2: Warr 2H 41
Halkett Cl. CH4: Salt 6F 149
HALKYN 3A 214
Halkyn Rd. CH2: Ches 1E 212 (7B 146)
Hallacres La. SK8: Chea H 5G 77
Hallam Mill *SK2: Stoc 6E 52*
(off Hallam St.)
Hallams Dr. CW5: Stap 3F 197
Hallams Pas. SK2: Stoc 6E 52
Hallam St. SK2: Stoc 6E 52
Hallas Gro. M23: Wyth 3H 49
Hallastone Rd. WA6: Hel 4B 138
Hall Av. M14: Manc 1A 24
M33: Sale 5D 22
SK15: Hey 4D 4
WA8: Wid 4A 62
WA15: Timp 5K 47
Halla Way WA4: Warr 2J 67
Hall Bank WA16: Mob 6D 102
Hall Bank Nth. *WA16: Mob 6D 102*
(off Hall Bank)
Hall Bank Sth. *WA16: Mob 6D 102*
(off Hall Bank)
Hallbottom St. SK14: Hyde 5A 10
Hall Cl. SK10: Mac 7A 122
SK14: Mot 5H 11
Hallcroft M31: Part 7C 20
Hallcroft Pl. WA4: Grap 3A 68
Hall Dr. CH49: Gre 2K 57
CW5: W'ston 1G 197
CW9: Mars 7H 115
SK14: Mot 5H 11
ST7: Als 6D 202
WA4: App 7H 67
Hallefield Cres. SK11: Mac 5B 126
Hallefield Dr. SK11: Mac 5B 126
Hallefield Rd. SK11: Mac 5B 126
Hall Farm Av. M41: Urm 1A 22
Hall Farm Cl. SK7: H Gro 2A 80
Hallfield Dr. CH2: Elt 5F 137
Hallfield Pk. CH66: Gt Sut 4K 133
Hallfields Rd. CH3: Tar 6B 170
WA2: Warr 4H 41
Hallgate Dr. SK8: He Grn 3C 76
Hallgate Rd. SK1: Stoc 4F 53
HALL GREEN
ST7 . . . . 3H 205 (2C 221)
SY14 . . . . 3C 219
Hall Grn. Cl. SK16: Duk 1H 9
Hall Grn. Rd. SK16: Duk 1H 9
Hall Gro. M14: Manc 1A 24
SK8: Chea 6E 50
SK10: Mac 7A 122
Hall Hill SK10: Boll 4B 122
Halliday Cl. WA3: Birc 1F 43
Halliwell Jones Stadium 6E 40
Halliwell's Brow WA16: H Leg 4G 95
Hall La. CW1: Warm 2K 191
CW3: Hank 1D 210
CW6: Kel 2C 172
CW6: Utk 4C 176
CW7: Darn 7D 178
CW9: Ant, L Lei . . . . . . 7E 114 & 1F 115
CW9: Los Gra, Winc 1K 157
CW11: Warm . . . . 2K 191 & 4A 200
L35: Cron, R'ill 4C 36
M23: Wyth 6H 49
M31: Part 7C 20
SK6: W'ley 5G 27
SK11: Sut E 1K 129
WA4: Dare 4A 92
WA4: Grap 5B 68
WA4: Lwr S, Stre 6H 93
WA5: B'ood 4D 14
WA8: Cron 4C 36
WA9: Bold 1B 38
WA16: Mob 6D 102
Hall La., The CW6: Rus 6H 177
Hall Mdw. SK8: Chea H 4G 77
Hall Moss La. SK7: Bram 1E 98
Hall Nook WA5: Penk 1H 65
Hall O'Shaw St. CW1: Crewe 2E 194
Hallows Av. WA2: Warr 3H 41
Hallows Cl. CW6: Kel 4B 172
Hallows Dr. CW6: Kel 4B 172
HALLOWSGATE 4B 172 (1D 219)
Hallowsgate Ct. CW6: Kel 4B 172
Hall Pool Dr. SK2: Stoc 5J 53
Hall Rd. M14: Manc 1A 24
SK7: Bram 4B 78
SK9: Hand 3B 98
SK9: Wilm 7H 97
WA1: Wool 5C 42
WA14: Bow 4G 73
Hallsgreen La. CH2: Wim T 2D 142
Hallshaw Av. CW1: Crewe 1E 194
Hallside Pk. WA16: Knut 5G 117
Halls Pl. CW9: N'ich 6E 156
Halls Rd. ST7: Mow C 5G 205
Hall St. OL6: Ash L 1K 9
SK1: Stoc 3E 52
SK8: Chea 6F 51
SK10: Mac 4K 125
SK14: Hyde 7G 9
WA1: Warr 7G 41
WA9: Clo F 1K 37
Hallsville Rd. M19: Manc 2F 25
Hall Ter. SK11: Lang 1G 169
WA5: Gt San 5G 39
Hall Vw. Cl. CW8: Gor 6D 154
Hallville Rd. CH44: Wall 1B 34
Hallwood Cl. WA7: Run 1H 111
Hallwood Ct. CH64: Nest 1C 130
Hallwood Dr. CH66: Leds 4D 132
Hallwood Link Rd. WA7: Pal F 1B 112
HALLWOOD PARK 1A 112
Hallwood Pk. Av. WA7: Pal F 1A 112
Hallwood Rd. M23: Wyth 6G 49
SK9: Hand 3A 98
Hallwood Wlk. CH65: Ell P 1D 134
Hallworth Av. M34: Aude 1A 8
Hallworthy Cl. WN7: Leigh 1B 6
HALMER END 3C 221
Halsall Av. WA2: Warr 4H 41
Halsall Cl. WA7: B'vale 2E 112
Halsall Grn. CH63: Spit 5B 86
Halsbury Rd. CH45: Wall 5H 13
Halstead Dr. M44: Irlam 2E 20
Halstead Gro. SK8: Gat 1B 76
Halstead Rd. CH44: Wall 1B 34
Halstone Av. SK9: Wilm 3D 118

Hazelwood Dr.—Hesketh Rd.

Hazelwood Dr. M34: Aude 4E 8
Hazelwood M. WA4: Grap 4C 68
Hazelwood Rd. CW8: Barnt 1A 156
M22: Wyth 5K 75
SK2: Stoc 1E 78
SK7: H Gro 3J 79
SK9: Wilm 6K 97
WA15: Hale 3J 73
Hazlehurst Rd. WA6: Frod 3J 139
Hazlemere Av. SK11: Mac 6H 125
HAZLES 3D 221
Headingley Rd. M14: Manc 4A 24
Headington Rd. CH49: Upt 7A 32
Headland Cl. CH48: W Kir 5C 56
Headlands, The CH3: Ches 4E 212
Headlands Rd. SK7: Bram 4D 78
Head St. L8: Liv 6K 35
Headworth Cl. CW9: N'ich 2E 162
Heald Cl. WA14: Bow 3G 73
Heald Dr. WA14: Bow 3G 73
HEALD GREEN 5D 76 (2C 217)
Heald Grn. Ho. M22: Wyth 5C 76
Heald Green Station (Rail) 5C 76
Heald Gro. SK8: He Grn 4C 76
Heald Rd. WA14: Bow 3G 73
Heald St. WA12: New W 1C 14
Healdwood Rd. SK6: W'ley, Rom 7H 27
Healey Cl. CW1: Crewe 5F 191
M23: Wyth 2F 49
Heanor Av. M34: Den 3F 27
Heapriding Bus. Pk. SK3: Stoc 3B 52
Heaps Farm Ct. SK15: Stal 2E 10
Heapy St. SK11: Mac 6B 126
Hearts Health Club
Wallasey 7G 13
(off Wallasey Rd.)
Heath, The WA7: West 7G 89
Heath Av. CH65: Whit 7C 134
CW11: S'ach 3J 201
M41: Urm 1D 22
ST7: Rod H 1F 203
Heath Bank CH3: Guil S 5G 147
Heathbank Av. CH44: Wall 1K 33
CH61: Irby 6K 57
Heathbank Cotts. CW5: Nant 1D 196
(off Birchin La.)
Heathbank Rd. CH42: Tran 2C 60
SK3: Stoc 5K 51
SK8: Chea H 6H 77
Heathbrook CW9: Rud 6J 157
Heath Cl. CH3: Gt Bou 3E 150
CH3: Tar 7B 170
CH48: W Kir 5C 56
CW11: S'ach 3H 201
Heathcote Av. SK4: Stoc 1A 52
Heathcote Cl. CH2: Ches 7K 145
Heathcote Gdns. CH63: Beb 1K 85
CW9: Rud 6J 157
SK6: Rom 3E 54
Heath Ct. CH66: L Sut 1H 133
ST7: Chu L 3G 203
Heath Cres. SK2: Stoc 7D 52
Heathdale CH63: Beb 3K 85
Heath Dr. CH3: Tar 7B 170
CH49: Upt 7D 32
CH60: Hes 5H 83
WA7: West 7G 89
WA16: Knut 3D 116
Heath End Rd. ST7: Als 3C 202
Heather Av. M44: Cad 5A 20
Heather Bank CH63: H Beb 7C 60
Heather Brow CH43: Clau 5J 33
SK15: Stal 3F 11
Heather Cl. CH66: Gt Sut 5A 134
SK11: L Grn 2G 129
WA3: Birc 6J 17
WA7: Beec 3A 112
Heather Ct. CH3: Gt Bou 3D 150
SK4: Stoc 6G 25
WA14: Bow 2F 73
Heatherdale Cl. CH42: Tran 1B 60
Heather Dene CH62: Brom 3D 86
Heatherdene Rd. CH48: W Kir 2C 56
Heatherfield Ct. CH42: Tran 1B 60
(off Victoria Flds.)
SK9: Wilm 6B 98
Heathergate Pl. CW2: Wis 6B 194
Heather Gro. M43: Droy 2A 8
SK14: H'rth 1J 11
Heather Lea M34: Den 1F 27
Heatherleigh CH48: Cald 7E 56
Heather Rd. CH60: Hes 5J 83
CH63: H Beb 2H 85
WA14: Hale 4J 73
WA15: Hale 4J 73
Heathers, The SK2: Stoc 1F 79
Heatherside SK5: Stoc 2K 25
SK15: Stal 7E 4
ST7: Mow C 7G 205
Heatherside Av. OL5: Moss 1F 5
Heather Wlk. M31: Part 1G 45
(off Gorse Sq.)
Heather Way SK6: Mar 6E 54
Heatherway M33: Sale 6C 22
Heatherways CW6: Tarp 1H 175
Heath Farm La. M31: Part 1J 45
Heathfield CH62: Brom 4D 86
SK9: Wilm 2F 119
Heathfield Av. CW1: Crewe 2B 194
M34: Den 1C 26
SK4: Stoc 6F 25
SK8: Gat 7D 50
Heathfield Cl. CW5: Nant 1D 196
CW12: Cong 3B 182
M33: Sale 7K 23
Heathfield Ct. CH65: Ell P 3D 134
Heathfield Ho. CH61: Thin 7D 58
Heathfield Pk. WA4: Grap 3A 68
WA8: Wid 2D 62
Heathfield Rd. CH43: Oxt 1B 60
CH63: Beb 1K 85
CH65: Ell P 3D 134
CW3: Audl 4C 210
SK2: Stoc 6D 52
Heathfields Cl. CH2: Ches 7A 146
Heathfield Sq. WA16: Knut 3D 116
Heathfield St. L1: Liv 3K 35
(not continuous)
Heathgate Cotts. SK9: Ald E 1C 166
Heath Grn. CW6: Tarp, Utk 1H 175
(not continuous)
Heath Gro. CH66: L Sut 1H 133
Heathland Rd. WA9: Clo F 1J 37
Heathlands, The CH46: Leas 1B 32
Heathlands Ho. WA16: Knut 3D 116
Heathlands Rd. CH66: L Sut 2H 133
Heathland Ter. SK3: Stoc 5C 52
Heath La. CH2: L Sta 2F 141
CH2: Stoak 2H 141
CH3: Ches, Gt Bou 3D 150
CH3: Gt Bar 2B 170
CH64: W'ston 6H 107
CH66: Chil T, L Sut 1D 132
CW8: L Lei 7A 114
CW9: Bud H, Gt Bud 4G 115
WA3: Croft 1F 17
WA16: All, Lwr P 3D 164
WA16: H Leg 7K 69
Heathmoor Rd. CH46: More 3A 32
Heath Pk. Gro. WA7: Run 6F 89
Heath Rd. CH2: Upt 3A 146
CH63: Beb, H Beb 1J 85
CW8: Weav 4H 155
CW11: S'ach 3H 201
CW12: Cong 4C 182
SK2: Stoc 6D 52
SK10: Boll 5B 122
WA5: Penk 7H 39
WA7: Run 6G 89
WA8: Wid 3D 62
WA14: Hale 3H 73
WA15: Timp 4K 47
Heath Rd. Cres. WA7: Run 6H 89
Heath Rd. Sth. WA7: Run, West 2F 111
Heathside CH60: Hes 5E 82
CW5: Nant 1D 196
Heathside Pk. Rd. SK3: Stoc 4H 51
Heathside Rd. M20: Manc 6A 24
SK3: Stoc 5J 51
Heath St. CW1: Crewe 2D 194
WA4: Stoc H 5G 67
Heath Ter. CH2: Upt 2B 146
Heath Vw. CW1: Hasl 3K 195
ST7: Als 4F 203
WA14: Alt 2H 73
(off Tipping St.)
Heathview Cl. WA8: Hal B 1A 88
Heathview Rd. WA8: Hal B 2A 88
Heath Way CW6: Tarp 4J 175
Heathway CH60: Hes 7K 83
Heathwood ST7: Rod H 2F 203
Heathwood Dr. ST7: Als 4C 202
Heathwood Gro. WA1: Padd 5B 42
Heathwood Rd. M19: Manc 7B 24
HEATLEY 6E 44 (2B 216)
Heatley Cl. CH43: Bid 5F 33
M34: Den 1A 26
WA13: Lymm 1C 70
Heatley La. CW5: B'hall 7K 209
Heatley Way SK9: Hand 2A 98
(off Delamere Rd.)
HEATON 1D 221
Heaton Av. SK7: Bram 2B 78
HEATON CHAPEL 6F 25
Heaton Chapel Station (Rail) 6F 25
Heaton Cl. CW10: Mid 6C 180
SK4: Stoc 1J 51
Heaton Ct. M33: Sale 7H 23
SK4: Stoc 7E 24
WA3: Ris 5A 18
Heaton Gdns. SK4: Stoc 7F 25
Heaton La. SK4: Stoc 6F 213 (3B 52)
HEATON MERSEY 2G 51
Heaton Mersey Ind. Est. SK4: Stoc 3G 51
HEATON MOOR 7E 24 (1C 217)
Heaton Moor Rd. SK4: Stoc 1K 51
HEATON NORRIS 5F 213 (2B 52)
Heaton Rd. SK4: Stoc 1A 52
Heaton Sq. CW7: Wins 4E 178
Heatons Sports Club 1K 51
Heaton St. M34: Den 7C 8
Heaton Towers SK4: Stoc 2C 52
(off Wilkinson Rd.)
Heaton Way CW2: West 3K 199
HEAVILEY 6E 52
Heaviley Gro. SK2: Stoc 6E 52
Heaward Cl. CW2: Shav 3B 198
Hebden Av. SK6: Bred 7F 27
WA3: Cul 5H 7
HEBDEN GREEN 5A 178 (1A 220)
Heber's Cl. SY14: Mal 1J 207
Heber Wlk. CW9: N'ich 5F 157
Hector Rd. M13: Manc 1C 24
Heddon Cl. SK4: Stoc 1G 51
Hedge Hey WA7: Cast 5C 90
Hedgelands Wlk. M33: Sale 6B 22
(off Epping Dr.)
Hedge Row SK10: R'ow 2G 123
Hedgerow Dr. CW9: Winc 2H 157
Hedge Rows, The SK14: Hyde 7B 10
Hedingham Cl. SK10: Mac 4G 125
Hefferston Grange Dr. CW8: Gor 6D 154
Hefferston Ri. CW8: Gor 6D 154
Heights, The WA6: Hel 4C 138
Heightside WA15: Timp 7B 48
(off Edenhurst Dr.)
Helena Cl. WA16: Knut 3G 117
Helena St. CH41: Birk 7D 34
Helen Ho. L8: Liv 5K 35
(off Birley Ct.)
Hellath Wen CW5: Nant 5C 196
Hellyar-Brook Rd. ST7: Als 5C 202
Helmdon Cl. CW7: Wins 1G 179
Helmingham Grn. CH41: Tran 1D 60
Helmsdale Cl. CW1: Crewe 7G 191
Helmsdale La. WA5: Gt San 6A 40
Helmsley Cl. WA5: Warr 5C 40
HELSBY 4B 138 (3C 215)
Helsby Av. CH62: East 4A 108
HELSBY MARSH 3B 138
Helsby Pk. Homes WA6: Frod 3E 138
Helsby Rd. M33: Sale 2E 48
WA6: Alv 7C 138
Helsby Sports & Social Club 7A 138
Helsby Station (Rail) 4B 138
Helsby St. WA1: Warr 6H 41
Helsby Way SK9: Hand 2A 98
Helston Cl. M44: Irlam 1E 20
SK7: Bram 6D 78
SK14: Hat 2E 28
WA5: Penk 7G 39
WA7: B'vale 2D 112
Helston Gro. SK8: He Grn 5E 76
Helston Wlk. SK14: Hat 2E 28
Helton Cl. CH43: Noc 2H 59
CW4: H Cha 4G 181
HELYGAIN 3A 214
Hembury Av. M19: Manc 5C 24
Hemingford Cl. CH66: Gt Sut 5K 133
Hemingford St. CH41: Birk 6C 34
Hemlegh Va. WA6: Hel 6B 138
Hemming St. CW8: Winn 4C 156
Hemmingsway L35: R'ill 1A 36
Hemmons Rd. M12: Manc 1E 24
Hempcroft Rd. WA15: Timp 7C 48
Hempshaw Bus. Cen. SK1: Stoc 5F 53
Hempshaw La. SK1: Stoc 5D 52
SK2: Stoc 4E 52
Hemswell Cl. CW7: Wins 4F 179
Hemsworth Av. CH66: L Sut 3J 133
Hemsworth Rd. M18: Manc 1G 25
HENBURY 4D 124 (3C 217)
Henbury Cl. CW10: Mid 5C 180
Henbury Dr. SK6: W'ley 5G 27
Henbury Gdns. WA4: App 3J 93
Henbury La. SK8: Chea H 7H 77
Henbury Pl. WA7: Run 1H 111
Henbury Ri. SK11: Henb 4D 124
Henbury Rd. SK9: Hand 2A 98
Henbury St. SK2: Stoc 1G 79
Henderson Cl. CH49: Upt 6A 32
WA5: Gt San 6F 39
Henderson Rd. WA8: Wid 5F 63
Henderson St. M19: Manc 3E 24
SK11: Mac 5K 125
Hendham Cl. SK7: H Gro 3E 78
Hendham Dr. WA14: Alt 7F 47
Hendon Cl. CW1: Crewe 1F 195
Hendon Dr. SK3: Stoc 5J 51
Hendon Wlk. CH49: Gre 2K 57
Henfield Wlk. M22: Wyth 2J 75
(off Cornfield Dr.)
HENHULL 7A 192
Henley Av. M44: Irlam 5B 20
SK8: Chea H 3G 77
Henley Cl. CH63: Spit 4A 86
CH64: Nest 2C 130
SK10: Mac 7J 121
WA4: App 7J 67
Henley Ct. WA7: Run 4K 89
Henley Dr. CW7: Wins 3G 179
WA15: Timp 5K 47
Henley Grange SK8: Chea 7E 50
Henley Pl. M19: Manc 5D 24
Henley Rd. CH4: Ches 5G 149
CH64: Nest 2C 130
CW2: West 6H 199
Henrietta St. CW12: Cong 3E 182
Henry Edward St. L3: Liv 1J 35
Henry Pl. CH1: Ches 2C 212 (1A 150)
Henry Sq. OL6: Ash L 1F 9
(off Stamford St. W.)
Henry St. CH41: Birk 6D 34
CW1: Crewe 1D 194
CW1: Hasl 2K 195
CW6: Tarp 2H 175
L1: Liv 4J 35
M34: Den 3G 27
M43: Droy 1A 8
SK1: Stoc 4F 53
SK14: Hyde 1J 27
WA1: Warr 7E 40
WA8: Wid 4J 63
WA13: Lymm 2A 70
Henry Wood Ct. CH4: Salt 5F 149
Henshall Av. WA4: Westy 1K 67
Henshall Dr. CW11: S'ach 1G 201
Henshall Hall Dr. CW12: Cong 5K 183
Henshall La. WA14: Dun M 6K 45
Henshall Rd. SK10: Boll 4B 122
Henshall St. CH1: Ches 1A 212 (7K 145)
Henshalls Way CW5: Nant 3B 196
Henshaw St. M32: S'ord 1J 23
Henson Gro. WA15: Timp 1A 74
Henthorne Rd. CH62: N Fer 5G 61
Henthorne St. CH43: Oxt 7B 34
Henwood Rd. M20: Manc 6A 24
Hepherd St. WA5: Warr 1B 66
Hepley Rd. SK12: Poy 3F 101
Hepple Cl. SK4: Stoc 1H 51
Hepworth St. SK14: Hyde 4K 27
Herald Dr. CW1: Crewe 3E 194
Heralds Cl. WA8: Wid 5B 62
Heralds Grn. WA5: W'ook 2J 39
Herberts La. CH60: Hes 6H 83
Herbert St. CW1: Crewe 1F 195
CW9: Los Gra 5C 158
CW12: Cong 3H 183
M32: S'ord 1J 23
M34: Den 6F 9
SK3: Stoc 5B 52
WA5: B'ood 5B 14
Herbert Swindells Cl.
CW2: Crewe 5D 194
Herculaneum Rd. L8: Liv 1K 61
Herdman St. CW2: Crewe 4D 194
Hereford Av. CH49: Upt 6B 32
CH66: Gt Sut 1A 140
Hereford Cl. SK10: Mac 3G 125
WA1: Wool 5D 42
Hereford Dr. SK9: Hand 3B 98
Hereford Gro. M41: Urm 1B 22
Hereford Pl. CH1: Blac 5H 145
Hereford Rd. SK5: Stoc 6B 26
SK8: Chea 1J 77
Hereford St. M33: Sale 7G 23
(not continuous)
Hereford Wlk. M34: Den 2E 26
(off Norwich Av.)
SK6: Rom 3A 54
Hereford Way CW10: Mid 2E 180
SK15: Stal 3E 10
Hereward Rd. CH3: Ches 2E 150
Heristone Av. M34: Den 7E 8
Heritage Ct. CH1: Ches 6C 212 (2A 150)
Heritage Gdns. M20: Manc 2D 50
SK4: Stoc 7F 25
(off Heaton Moor Rd.)
Heritage Wharf OL7: Ash L 1F 9
(off Portland Pl.)
Herle Dr. M22: Wyth 4J 75
Hermitage, The CH60: Hes 7H 83
(off School Hill)
Hermitage Av. SK6: Rom 2F 55
Hermitage Ct. CH1: Sau 2B 144
CW4: H Cha 4K 181
WA15: Hale 2A 74
(off Bancroft Rd.)
Hermitage Dr. CW4: H Cha 3K 181
Hermitage Gdns. SK6: Rom 2F 55
HERMITAGE GREEN 3A 16
Hermitage Grn. La. WA2: Winw 2J 15
Hermitage La.
CW4: Cran, H Cha 7G 165 & 1J 181
Hermitage Rd. CH1: Sau 2B 144
WA15: Hale 2K 73
Heron Av. SK16: Duk 3K 9
Heron Bus. Pk. WA8: Wid 5K 63
Heron Cl. CH3: Farn 6C 186
CW7: Wins 7E 178
WA7: Nort 6F 91
WA16: Knut 2F 117
Heron Ct. CH64: Park 1A 130
SK3: Stoc 5C 52
(off Lomas St.)
Heron Cres. CW1: Crewe 1F 195
Heron Dr. M34: Aude 1B 8
SK12: Poy 3K 99
Heronpark Way CH63: Spit 4B 86
Heron Pl. CH2: Ches 1C 212 (7A 146)
Heron Rd. CH47: Meols 5G 31
CH48: W Kir 5G 31
Herons Reach WA3: G'ury 4J 7
Heron St. SK3: Stoc 4B 52
Herons Way CH4: Ches 1G 185
WA7: Nort 2H 91
Herrick Cl. CW2: Wis 6A 194
Herriots Bus. Pk. SK16: Duk 3F 9
Herrod Av. SK4: Stoc 6H 25
Hertford Cl. CW12: Cong 2G 183
WA1: Wool 5E 42
Hertford Dr. CH45: Wall 5J 13
Hertford Gro. M44: Cad 5K 19
Hertford Ind. Est.
OL7: Ash L 1F 9
Hertford St. OL7: Ash L 1F 9
Hesketh Av. CH42: R Fer 4C 60
M20: Manc 1C 50
Hesketh Cl. WA5: Penk 1H 65
Hesketh Cft. CW1: Crewe 5F 191
Hesketh Dr. CH60: Hes 5J 83
CW9: Los Gra 4C 158
Hesketh Mdw. La.
WA3: Low 2A 6
Hesketh Pl. SK7: H Gro 1H 79
(off Fenton Av.)
Hesketh Rd. L24: Hale 7B 88
M33: Sale 1K 47

Hesketh St.—Hill End La.

Hesketh St. SK4: Stoc 7H 25
(All Saints' Rd.)
SK4: Stoc 1C 52
(Old Rd.)
WA5: Warr 1B 66
Hesketh St. Nth. WA5: Warr 1B 66
Hesketh Wlk. CH62: Brom 3C 86
Hesketh Way CH62: Brom 3C 86
Heskin Cl. L35: R'ill 1B 36
Hesnall Cl. WA3: G'ury 2J 7
Hessle Dr. CH60: Hes 7H 83
Hesslewell Ct. CH60: Hes 5J 83
Heston Av. M13: Manc 1B 24
Heston Dr. M41: Urm 1B 22
HESWALL 6J 83 (2A 214)
Heswall Station (Rail) 6B 84
Heswall Av. CH63: H Beb 5B 60
WA3: Cul 7E 6
Heswall Dales Nature Reserve 5G 83
Heswall Mt. CH61: Thin 1J 83
Heswall Point CH60: Hes 6J 83
Heswall Rd. CH66: Gt Sut 4K 133
SK5: Stoc 2J 25
Hetton Av. M13: Manc 1B 24
Hewetson Cres. SK11: Mac 5F 125
Hewitt Av. M34: Den 1J 25
Hewitt Gro. CW9: Winc 2B 158
Hewitt's Pl. *L2: Liv* *2H 35*
(off Vernon St.)
Hewitt St. CH2: Ches 7C 146
CW2: Crewe 4D 194
CW9: N'ich 3J 157
WA4: Warr 1G 67
Hexham Cl. M33: Sale 1H 47
SK2: Stoc 7J 53
Hexham Ct. *CH1: Ches* *1J 149*
(off Sedgefield Rd.)
Hexham Way SK10: Mac 7K 121
Hexworth Wlk. SK7: Bram 3E 78
Heybridge La. SK10: Pres 4J 121
Heybrook Rd. M23: Wyth 7H 49
Heydon Cl. CW12: Cong 3E 182
Heyes Av. WA15: Timp 5B 48
Heyes Dr. CH45: Wall 7C 12
WA13: Lymm 3J 69
WA15: Timp 5B 48
Heyes Farm Rd. SK11: Mac 5F 125
Heyes Ho. SK11: Mac 4F 125
Heyes La. SK9: Ald E 5F 119
WA15: Timp 5B 48
Heyes Leigh WA15: Timp 5B 48
Heyes Mt. L35: R'ill 2C 36
Heyes Pk. CW8: H'ord 2J 161
Heyes Rd. WA8: Wid 5C 62
Heyes Ter. *WA15: Timp* *4B 48*
(off The Old Orchard)
Heyeswood La. CW8: H'ord 2K 161
Heyfield Pk. Rd. CH66: L Sut 1H 133
Heygarth Dr. CH49: Gre 1A 58
Heygarth Rd. CH62: East 2K 107
HEYHEADS 2F 5
Heyheads New Rd.
SK15: Carrb 2F 5
Heyland Rd. M23: Wyth 6G 49
Heylee *OL7: Ash L* *2E 8*
(off South St.)
Hey Lock Cl. WA12: New W 3F 15
Heyridge Dr. M22: N'den 3K 49
HEYROD 4D 4
Heyrod Fold SK15: Hey 4D 4
Heyrod Hall Est. SK15: Hey 5D 4
Heyrod St. SK15: Carrb 4E 4
Heys, The CH62: East 2A 108
SK5: Stoc 2K 25
WA7: Run 5A 90
Heys Av. CH62: Brom 6D 86
M23: Wyth 3G 49
SK6: Rom 1E 54
Heysbank Rd. SK12: Dis 2G 103
Heys Ct. SK3: Stoc 4K 51
Heyscroft Rd. M20: Manc 5A 24
SK4: Stoc 2J 51
Heys Farm Cotts. SK6: Rom 1E 54
Heysham Cl. WA7: Murd 1F 113
Heyshaw Wlk. M23: Wyth 3F 49
Heyshoot La. WA3: Cul, G'ury 5J 7
(not continuous)
Heyside Cl. SK15: Carrb 3F 5
Heys La. SK6: Rom 1E 54
Heysoms Av. CW8: N'ich 7C 156
Heysoms Cl. CW8: N'ich 7C 156
Heythrop Dr. CH60: Hes 6A 84
Heyville Rd. CH63: H Beb 7D 60
Heywood Blvd. CH61: Thin 7D 58
Heywood Cl. CH61: Thin 7D 58
SK9: Ald E 5G 119
WA12: New W 3F 15
Heywood Grn. *CW2: Crewe* *6C 194*
(off Brookhouse Dr.)
Heywood Gro. M33: Sale 5F 23
Heywood Rd. CH66: Gt Sut 3J 133
M33: Sale 1B 48
SK9: Ald E 5G 119
Heywoods, The CH2: Ches 6K 145
Heywoods Ridge CW3: Audl 7A 210
Heywood St. CW12: Cong 4E 182
Heyworth Av. SK6: Rom 1D 54
Hibbert Av. M34: Den 5D 8
SK14: Hyde 2K 27
Hibbert La. SK6: Mar 7F 55
Hibbert St. SK4: Stoc 6H 25
SK5: Stoc 6H 25
Hibbert St. SK22: N Mil 1K 103
WA8: Wid 5H 63
Hibel Rd. SK10: Mac 3A 126
Hickenfield Rd. SK14: Hyde 5A 10
Hicken Pl. SK14: Hyde 5A 10
Hickhurst La. CW6: Eat, Rus 6H 177
Hickmans Rd. CH41: Birk 3A 34
Hickmore Heys CH3: Guil S 6J 147
Hickory Cl. WA1: Wool 5E 42
Hickson St. CW8: Barnt 2A 156
Hickton Dr. WA14: Alt 6F 47
Hidcote Cl. CW2: Wis 6B 194
Hield Gro. CW9: Ast B 5J 115
Hield La. CW9: Ast B 6J 115
Higginbotham Grn. SK11: Mac 6B 126
Higginson Cl. CW12: Cong 5K 183
Higginson Rd. SK5: Stoc 4H 25
Highacre Rd. CH45: N Bri 6G 13
Higham Av. WA5: Warr 3D 40
Higham Cotts. SK14: Hyde 3C 28
Higham La. SK14: Hyde 3A 28
Higham Sq. L5: Liv 1K 35
Higham St. SK8: Chea H 4J 77
High Ash Gro. M34: Aude 3C 8
High Bank M34: Den 1A 26
WA14: Alt 1H 213 (7H 47)
WA15: Hale 3A 74
High Bank Av. SK15: Stal 3E 10
High Bank Cl. CH43: Noc 7G 33
M44: Cad 5A 20
Highbank Cl. CW8: Barnt 2A 156
Highbank Dr. M20: Manc 4D 50
High Bank Rd. SK14: Hyde 7A 10
Highbank Rd. CW8: N'ich 6C 156
WA6: K'ley 1D 152
High Bankside SK1: Stoc 6J 213 (3D 52)
High Bent Av. SK8: Chea H 7J 77
Highbury SK4: Stoc 2H 51
Highbury Av. M41: Urm 1H 21
M44: Irlam 2D 20
Highbury Rd. SK4: Stoc 5F 25
Highcliffe Av. CH1: Ches 6J 145
Highcrest Av. SK8: Gat 7B 50
Highcroft SK14: Hyde 4K 27
Highcroft, The CH63: Beb 1A 86
Highcroft Av. CH63: Beb 1A 86
CW12: Cong 4H 183
M20: Manc 1A 50
High Cft. Cl. SK16: Duk 2B 10
Highcroft Grn. CH63: Beb 1A 86
Highcroft Rd. SK6: Rom 1C 54
High Cross La. CH3: Clut 2B 206
Highdales Rd. M23: Wyth 7H 49
High Elm Dr. WA15: H'rns 5C 74
High Elm Rd. WA15: H'rns 5C 74
High Elms SK8: Chea H 1E 98
Higher Ashton WA8: Wid 2F 63
HIGHER BANKS 2K 81
Higher Barlow Row SK1: Stoc 4D 52
Higher Barn Rd. SK13: Had 3K 11
HIGHER BEBINGTON 6C 60
Higher Bebington Rd. CH63: H Beb 7C 60
Higher Bents La. SK6: Bred 1K 53
HIGHER BUNBURY 5D 188
HIGHER BURWARDSLEY 6J 187
Higher Bury St. SK4: Stoc 2B 52
HIGHER CHISWORTH 7J 29
HIGHER DINTING 1D 217
HIGHER DISLEY 2H 103
Higher Downs WA14: Alt 2G 73
WA16: Knut 3G 117
HIGHER END 1D 215
HIGHERFENCE 4D 126
Higher Fence Rd. SK10: Mac 3C 126
Higher Ferry La. CH1: Ches 3C 148
Higherfold Farm SK6: H Lan 4D 80
HIGHER GAMESLEY 3K 29
Higher Greenshall La. SK12: Dis 2J 103
Higher Henry St. SK14: Hyde 2J 27
Higher Heyes Dr. WA6: K'ley 3C 152
Higher Hillgate SK1: Stoc 4C 52
HIGHER HURDSFIELD 2E 126 (3D 217)
HIGHER HURST 3A 4
HIGHER HYDEGREEN 4G 5
HIGHER KINNERTON 1B 218
Higher Knutsford Rd. WA4: Stoc H 2K 67
Higher La. SK10: Ker 5E 122
WA4: Dutt 4K 113
WA13: Lymm 3A 70
HIGHER MARSTON 7H 115
Higher Mdws. M19: Manc 3F 25
HIGHER POYNTON 3H 101 (2D 217)
Higher Rd. M41: Urm 1C 22
HIGHER RUNCORN 5F 89
HIGHER SHOTTON 1B 218
HIGHER SHURLACH 1J 163 (3A 216)
Higher Tame St. SK15: Stal 7C 4
HIGHER WALTON 6C 66 (2D 215)
Higher Wharf St. OL7: Ash L 1G 9
HIGHER WHITLEY 2C 114 (3A 216)
HIGHER WINCHAM 2B 158 (3A 216)
HIGHER WYCH 3C 219
High Fld. WA14: L Bol 3K 71
Highfield CH2: Elt 4F 137
M20: Manc 2D 50
M33: Sale 1C 48
SK8: Chea 2E 76
SK10: Pres 6H 121
Highfield Av. CW3: Audl 5C 210
CW9: Los Gra 4C 158
M33: Sale 1C 48
SK6: Rom 2K 53
Highfield Av. WA4: App 2H 93
WA5: Gt San 7J 39
Highfield Cl. CH44: Wall 1K 33
CH64: Nest 7H 105
M32: S'ord 3H 23
SK3: Stoc 1D 78
SK14: Hyde 4A 10
Highfield Country Pk. 3F 25
Highfield Ct. SK14: Mot 6H 11
Highfield Cres. CH42: R Fer 4E 60
SK9: Wilm 5K 97
WA8: Wid 3G 63
Highfield Dr. CH49: Gre 1A 58
CW5: Nant 1D 196
OL5: Moss 1D 4
SK10: Mac 2H 125
WA13: Lymm 3J 69
Highfield Est. SK9: Wilm 5K 97
Highfield Gdns. CH43: Clau 6J 33
SK14: H'rth 2J 11
SK14: Hyde 7A 10
Highfield Glen OL6: Ash L 4A 4
Highfield Gro. CH42: R Fer 4E 60
Highfield Ho. SK3: Stoc 7D 52
Highfield La. WA2: Winw 3B 16
Highfield Mdw. *OL5: Moss* *1D 4*
(off Highfield Dr.)
Highfield Pk. SK4: Stoc 2H 51
Highfield Pk. Rd. SK6: Bred 7D 26
Highfield Parkway SK7: Bram 2G 99
Highfield Pl. CW8: N'ich 6D 156
Highfield Rd. CH1: Blac 5E 144
CH42: R Fer 3E 60
CH64: Nest 7H 105
CH65: Ell P 3E 134
CH66: L Sut 2H 133
CW8: N'ich 6E 156
CW12: Cong 5G 183
M19: Manc 2F 25
M32: S'ord 3H 23
SK6: Mar 6F 55
SK6: Mel 6H 55
SK7: Bram 2D 78
SK7: H Gro 3A 80
SK8: Chea H 4G 77
SK10: Boll 3D 122
SK11: Mac 5K 125
SK12: Poy 2K 99
WA8: Wid 4F 63
WA13: Lymm 2J 69
WA15: Hale 3A 74
WA15: Timp 7B 48
Highfield Rd. Nth. CH65: Ell P 2E 134
Highfields CH60: Hes 5H 83
Highfield Sth. CH42: R Fer 6E 60
Highfield St. L3: Liv 1H 35
(not continuous)
M34: Aude 4E 8
M34: Den 5D 8
SK3: Stoc 4A 52
SK16: Duk 1G 9
Highfield St. W. SK16: Duk 1G 9
Highgate Cen. SK6: Bred 1K 53
Highgate Cl. CH60: Hes 4H 83
CW1: Crewe 5F 191
WA7: Nort 5F 91
Highgate Rd. WA14: Alt 1F 73
High Gates M33: Sale 6K 23
High Gates Cl. WA5: Warr 5C 40
High Gates Lodge WA5: Warr 5C 40
Highgreen Rd. CH42: Tran 2B 60
Highgrove M33: Sale 3A 48
Highgrove M. SK9: Wilm 1F 119
High Gro. Rd. SK8: Chea 7E 50
Highland M. SK6: Rom 7H 27
Highlands, The CW6: Bun 6C 188
OL5: Moss 1C 4
Highlands Dr. SK2: Stoc 6K 53
Highlands Ho. *OL5: Moss* *1C 4*
(off Old Brow)
Highlands Rd. SK2: Stoc 6K 53
WA7: Run 5F 89
Highland Way WA16: Knut 6E 116
HIGH LANE 6E 80 (2D 217)
HIGHLANE 7A 128 (1C 221)
High La. SK6: W'ley 6G 27
High Lawn WA14: Bow 3G 73
High Lea SK8: Chea 7E 50
SK9: Ald E 6H 119
High Lee Ho. *M33: Sale* *6J 23*
(off Broad Rd.)
HIGH LEGH 2H 95 (2A 216)
High Legh Rd. WA13: Lymm 5E 70
High Lowe Av. CW12: Cong 2J 183
High Mdw. SK8: Chea H 5G 77
High Mdws. SK6: Rom 1C 54
High Mt. CH60: Hes 6H 83
Highnam Wlk. M22: Wyth 4G 75
Highpark Rd. CH42: Tran 2B 60
High Peak Rd. OL6: Ash L 3B 4
High St. CH3: Farn 5B 186
CH3: Tar 6B 170
CH3: Tatt 3G 187
CH4: Salt 5E 148
CH62: Brom 5E 86
CH64: Nest 7H 105
CW2: Crewe 3D 194
CW5: Nant 2C 196
(not continuous)
CW6: Clot 7E 174
CW6: Tarp 2H 175
CW7: Wins 3D 178
High St. CW8: Weav 4F 155
CW9: Gt Bud 6G 115
CW9: N'ich 5E 156
CW11: S'ach 3F 201
CW12: Cong 4F 183
L2: Liv 2H 35
L24: Hale 7A 88
M43: Droy 1A 8
SK1: Stoc 6J 213 (3D 52)
SK7: H Gro 3K 79
SK8: Chea 6F 51
SK10: Boll 3E 122
SK11: Mac 6A 126
(not continuous)
SK14: Hyde 7A 10
SK15: Stal 2K 9
ST7: Harr 7J 205
ST7: Mow C 5H 205
ST7: Roo 7G 205
SY14: Mal 3H 207
WA6: Frod 7H 111
WA6: Norl 5G 153
WA7: Run 4F 89
WA14: Alt 2H 213 (1H 73)
HIGHTOWN
CW12 5K 183 (1C 221)
L38 1A 214
Hightown CW1: Crewe 2C 194
CW10: Mid 3C 180
CW11: S'ach 3F 201
Hightree Dr. SK11: Henb 4C 124
High Vw. ST7: Mow C 7F 205
WA6: Hel 4C 138
High Warren Cl. WA4: App 1F 93
High Wood Fold SK6: Mar B 4J 55
Highwood Rd. WA4: App 6G 67
Higson Av. SK6: Rom 2K 53
Hilary Av. SK8: He Grn 5F 77
Hilary Cl. CH3: Gt Bou 2E 150
SK4: Stoc 2B 52
WA5: Gt San 6F 39
WA8: Wid 2A 64
Hilary Dr. CH49: Upt 6D 32
Hilary Mans. *CH44: Wall* *7G 13*
(off Colville Rd.)
Hilary Rd. M22: Wyth 4J 75
Hilbre Av. CH44: Wall 7G 13
CH60: Hes 1B 104
Hilbre Bank CW6: Alp 2J 189
Hilbre Ct. CH48: W Kir 4B 56
Hilbre Dr. CH65: Ell P 7E 134
Hilbre Rd. CH48: W Kir 4C 56
M19: Manc 3C 24
Hilbre St. CH41: Birk 4C 34
L3: Liv 3K 35
Hilbre Vw. CH48: W Kir 3D 56
Hilbre Way SK9: Hand 2B 98
Hilda Av. SK8: Chea 7G 51
Hilda Gro. SK5: Stoc 7J 25
Hilda Rd. SK14: Hyde 4J 27
Hilda St. SK5: Stoc 7J 25
Hilden Pl. WA2: Warr 3H 41
Hilden Rd. WA2: Padg 3J 41
Hilden Sq. WA1: Warr 7E 40
Hilditch Cl. M23: Wyth 6H 49
Hill, The CW11: Blet, S'ach 3G 201
WA16: Knut 5F 117
Hillam Cl. M41: Urm 2E 22
Hillam Rd. CH45: Wall 5D 12
Hillary Av. CW12: Cong 4J 183
Hillary Dr. CW3: Audl 5C 210
Hillary Rd. CH62: East 2J 107
SK14: Hyde 5B 10
Hill Bank Cl. SK15: Carrb 4E 4
Hill Bark Rd. CH48: Fran 3H 57
Hillberry Cres. WA4: Warr 2F 67
Hillbrook Grange SK7: Bram 7B 78
Hillbrook Rd. SK1: Stoc 4G 53
SK7: Bram 7B 78
Hillburn Dr. CH41: Birk 3H 33
Hillbury Rd. SK7: Bram 4D 78
Hill Carr WA14: Alt 1F 73
HILLCLIFFE 6G 67
Hill Cliffe Rd. WA4: Walt 4F 67
Hill Cl. CH64: Ness 3F 131
CW6: Bun 7C 188
Hill Ct. CH64: Ness 3F 131
Hill Ct. M. SK6: Rom 2B 54
Hillcourt Rd. SK6: H Lan 6E 80
SK6: Rom 7H 27
Hillcrest SK14: Hyde 4A 28
WA7: Run 5K 89
Hillcrest Av. CW4: H Cha 4H 181
SK4: Stoc 2J 51
Hillcrest Ct. CH44: Wall 1K 33
Hillcrest Dr. CH49: Gre 2K 57
CH66: L Sut 2G 133
M19: Manc 4F 25
M34: Den 2G 27
Hillcrest Rd. CH66: L Sut 2H 133
CW6: Kel 2D 172
SK2: Stoc 6G 53
SK7: Bram 4D 78
SK10: Boll 4C 122
SK11: Gaw 1E 128
Hill Cft. SK2: Stoc 6J 53
Hillcroft Rd. CH44: Wall 1B 34
WA14: Alt 7E 46
Hill Dr. SK9: Hand 3B 98
Hill End SK6: Rom 7J 27
Hillend SK14: Mot 2H 29
Hill End La. SK14: Mot 2G 29

Hillend Pl.—Holly Rd. Nth.

Hillend Pl. M23: Wyth 2G 49
Hillend Rd. M23: Wyth 2G 49
Hillesden Ri. CW12: Cong 4H 183
Hillfield WA6: Frod 1H 139
WA7: Nort 6F 91
Hillfield Dr. CH61: Hes 4H 83
Hillfield Gdns. CW5: Nant 3C 196
Hillfield Pl. CW5: Nant 3C 196
Hillfield Rd. CH66: L Sut 1K 133
Hillfields CW12: Cong 2F 183
Hillfields Cl. CW12: Cong 2F 183
Hillfield Vw. CW5: Nant 3C 196
Hillfoot Cl. CH43: Bid 4F 33
Hillfoot Cres. WA4: Stoc H 6F 67
Hillfoot La. WA6: New 1A 152
Hillgate Bus. Cen. *SK1: Stoc 4D 52*
(off Swallow St.)
Hill Gro. CH46: More 5B 32
Hilliards Ct. CH4: Ches 1G 185
Hillingdon Av. CH61: Hes 4H 83
Hillingdon Rd. M32: S'ord 2K 23
Hillington Rd. M33: Sale 7D 22
SK3: Stoc 4A 52
Hill Mt. SK16: Duk 2B 10
Hillock La. WA1: Wool 5B 42
Hill Ridge CH43: Noc 7G 33
Hill Ri. SK6: Rom 2B 54
WA14: Alt 7E 46
Hill Rd. CH3: Burw 6J 187
CH4: Ecc 2K 185
CH43: Clau 5H 33
CW6: Peck 6J 187
Hill Rd. Nth. WA6: Hel 5C 138
Hill Rd. Sth. WA6: Hel 5C 138
Hillsboro Av. WA6: Frod 1J 139
Hillsdown Way CH66: Gt Sut 6J 133
Hillside CW8: N'ich 6B 156
WA13: Lymm 4G 71
Hillside Av. SK14: Hyde 5A 28
SK15: Carrb 3G 5
WA7: Run 6E 88
WA12: New W 1C 14
Hillside Cl. CH41: Tran 1D 60
SK7: Bram 6E 78
SK12: Dis 1G 103
ST7: Mow C 5H 205
WA6: Hel 4D 138
Hillside Ct. CH41: Tran 1D 60
SK10: Mac 3D 126
(off Springhill)
Hillside Cres. OL6: Ash L 4A 4
Hillside Dr. CH66: Ell P 7F 109
CW1: Crewe 1E 194
SK10: Mac 3D 126
Hillside Gro. SK6: Mar B 3H 55
WA5: Penk 1H 65
Hillside La. CW9: Moult 7D 162
Hillside Rd. CH1: Blac 6F 145
CH41: Tran 1D 60
CH43: Bid 4G 33
CH44: Wall 7E 12
CH48: W Kir 3E 56
CH60: Hes 7J 83
CW6: Kel 4C 172
SK2: Stoc 5H 53
SK6: W'ley 6H 27
SK14: Hyde 6H 27
WA4: App 3G 93
WA6: Frod 1J 139
WA15: Hale 2A 74
WA16: Knut 3E 116
Hillside Vw. CH43: Oxt 2K 59
M34: Den 4F 27
Hill St. CW1: Crewe 2D 194
CW7: Wins 3G 179
CW11: Elw 2B 200
L8: Liv 6J 35
(not continuous)
OL7: Ash L 1F 9
SK6: Rom 2B 54
SK11: Mac 6A 126
SK14: Hyde 3A 28
SK16: Duk 1G 9
WA1: Warr 7F 41
WA7: Run 4G 89
WA14: B'ath 4G 47
Hill St. Bus. Cen. *L8: Liv 6J 35*
(off Hill St.)
HILL TOP 6K 97
Hill Top CW8: Barnt 2A 156
SK6: Rom 1B 54
WA15: Hale 5A 74
Hilltop WA7: Nort 7E 90
Hill Top Av. CW7: Wins 3D 178
SK8: Chea H 4K 77
SK9: Wilm 6J 97
Hill Top Ct. SK8: Chea H 4K 77
Hilltop Ct. M14: Manc 2A 24
Hill Top Dr. WA15: Hale 4A 74
Hilltop Dr. SK6: Mar 6C 54
Hill Top La. CH64: Ness 3F 131
Hilltop La. CH60: Hes 6K 83
Hilltop Pk. WA16: Pick 1B 158
Hill Top Rd. CW8: Act B 2C 154
WA1: Wool 4C 42
WA4: Pre H 1H 113
WA4: Stoc H 3K 67
WA13: Lymm 3J 69
Hilltop Rd. CH3: Guil S 5J 147
Hill Vw. SK10: Boll 4C 122
SK15: Stal 4E 10
WA8: Wid 7F 37
Hill Vw. Av. WA6: Hel 7A 138
Hillview Av. CH48: W Kir 2C 56
Hillview Cl. WA6: Frod 1J 139
Hillview Ct. CH43: Bid 3F 33
Hill Vw. Dr. CH49: Upt 6D 32
Hill Vw. Ri. CW8: Winn 4D 156
Hill Vw. Rd. M34: Den 2K 25
Hillview Rd. CH61: Irby 6K 57
Hillwood Cl. CH63: Spit 5A 86
Hilrose Av. M41: Urm 1E 22
Hilton Av. M41: Urm 1C 22
WA5: Gt San 7K 39
Hilton Cl. CH41: Birk 6B 34
CW10: Mid 4B 180
SK11: Mac 5G 125
Hilton Ct. SK3: Stoc 7G 213 (4C 52)
Hilton Dr. M44: Cad 6K 19
Hilton Gro. CH48: W Kir 2B 56
SK12: Poy 2C 100
Hilton Ho. SK1: Stoc 7J 213 (3D 52)
Hilton Rd. M22: Shar 7A 50
SK7: Bram 4D 78
SK12: Dis 6H 81
SK12: Poy 1H 101
(not continuous)
Hiltons Farm Cl. M34: Aude 4D 8
Hilton St. SK3: Stoc 7F 213 (4B 52)
SK14: Hyde 5A 10
Himalayan Birch Cl.
CH66: Ell P 2A 134
Hinchley Cl. CW8: H'ord 1K 161
Hinchley Ct. CW12: Cong 3C 182
HINDERTON 6A 106
Hinderton Cl. CH41: Birk 1D 60
Hinderton Dr. CH48: W Kir 4F 57
CH60: Hes 1C 104
Hinderton Grn. CH64: Nest 7J 105
Hinderton La. CH64: Nest 6K 105
Hinderton Rd. CH41: Birk 7D 34
CH64: Nest 7J 105
Hinde St. CW5: Nant 3B 196
Hind Heath La. CW11: Whe 5D 200
Hind Heath Rd. CW11: Whe 4C 200
Hindle Av. WA5: Warr 3D 40
Hindley Av. M22: Wyth 3H 75
Hindley Cl. OL7: Ash L 1E 8
Hindley Cres. CW8: Barnt 2K 155
HINDLEY GREEN 1A 216
Hindley St. OL7: Ash L 1E 8
(not continuous)
SK1: Stoc 4D 52
Hindsford Cl. M23: Wyth 3D 48
Hind St. CH41: Birk 7D 34
Hinson St. CH41: Birk 6D 34
Hinton Cres. WA4: App 5J 67
Hinton Gro. SK14: Hyde 3B 28
Hinton M. SK1: Stoc 3F 53
Hinton Rd. CW2: Crewe 6D 194
WA7: Run 5G 89
Hipley Cl. SK6: Bred 6F 27
Hirsch Cl. CW5: Nant 2E 196
Historic Warships Vis. Cen. 3B 34
Hitchen Cl. SK16: Duk 3A 10
Hitchen Dr. SK16: Duk 3A 10
Hitchens Cl. WA7: Murd 7F 91
Hitch Lowes SK11: Chel 5C 166
HMP Risley WA3: Ris 3K 17
HMP Styal SK9: Styal 4H 97
HM Young Offenders' Institution Thorn Cross
WA4: App T 2C 94
Hobart Cl. SK7: Bram 2J 99
Hobart Way CH1: Blac 6E 144
Hobb La. WA4: Dare, Moo 1A 92
Hobbs Cl. CW1: Hasl 2J 195
Hobby Ct. WA7: Pal F 1A 112
Hobcroft La. WA16: Mob 3A 102
Hob Hey La. WA3: Cul 6D 6
HOB HILL 5C 206
Hob Hill SK15: Stal 1A 10
Hobhouse Ct. CH43: Clau 6A 34
Hob La. CH2: Wim T 2E 142
CH3: Chu 2C 186
WA6: Dun H 2E 142
Hoblyn Rd. CH43: Bid 4H 33
Hobson Ct. M34: Aude 4D 8
Hobson Cres. M34: Aude 4D 8
Hobson Moor Rd.
SK14: Mot 4G 11
Hobson St. SK5: Stoc 1J 25
SK11: Mac 5A 126
Hockenhall All. L2: Liv 2H 35
Hockenhull Av. CH3: Tar 6B 170
Hockenhull Cl. CH63: Spit 4A 86
M22: Wyth 3A 76
Hockenhull Cres. CH3: Tar 6B 170
Hockenhull La. CH3: Tar 7A 170
Hocker La.
SK10: N Ald, O Ald 2J 167 & 7A 120
Hockerley Cl. M33: Sale 6C 22
HOCKLEY 3E 100
Hockley Cl. SK12: Poy 3F 101
Hockley Paddock SK12: Poy 3E 100
Hockley Rd. M23: Wyth 7F 49
SK12: Poy 3F 101
Hodder Bank SK2: Stoc 7J 53
HODGEFOLD 4G 29
Hodge Fold SK14: B'tom 3G 29
Hodge La. CW8: Gor, H'ord 7F 155
SK14: B'tom 4G 29
Hodgkin Cl. CW5: Nant 3D 196
Hodgkinson Av. WA5: Warr 3D 40
Hodgson Ct. M19: Manc 4C 24
Hodgson Dr. WA15: Timp 4A 48
Hodnett Av. M41: Urm 2H 21
Hodnet Wlk. M34: Den 2D 26
Hogarth Dr. CH43: Noc 2G 59
Hogarth Rd. SK6: Mar B 4H 55
Hoghton Rd. L24: Hale 6B 88
Hogshead La. CW8: Oak 6A 160
Holbeck WA7: Nort 7E 90
Holbein Cl. CH4: Ches 5A 150
Holbeton Cl. SK7: Bram 2D 78
Holborn Ct. WA8: Wid 2F 63
Holborn Hill CH41: Tran 1D 60
Holborn Sq. CH41: Tran 1D 60
Holborn Sq. Ind. Est. CH41: Tran 1D 60
Holbrook Cl. WA5: Gt San 6G 39
Holbury Cl. CW1: Crewe 5G 191
Holcombe Cl. CH49: Gre 1A 58
WA14: Alt 6F 47
Holcombe Dr. SK10: Mac 1J 125
Holcombe Gdns. M19: Manc 6B 24
Holcombe Rd. M14: Manc 4B 24
Holcombe Wlk. SK4: Stoc 4G 25
Holcot Ct. CW7: Wins 1H 179
Holcroft La. WA3: Cul 7H 7
Holcroft Moss Nature Reserve 4F 19
HOLEHOUSE 6K 29
Hole Ho. Fold SK6: Rom 2B 54
Hole Ho. La. CW8: L Lei 1H 155
Holehouse La. SK10: Adl, Boll 1J 121
SK11: Lang 1H 169
ST7: Sch G 2K 203
Hole La. WA16: All 4B 164
Holes La. WA1: Wool 4B 42
Holford Av. CW9: Los Gra 4C 158
WA5: Warr 4D 40
Holford Ct. M34: Den 7E 8
Holford Cres. WA16: Knut 4E 116
Holford Moss WA7: Nort 3F 91
Holford St. CW12: Cong 3F 183
Holgrave Cl. WA16: H Leg 2H 95
Holiday La. SK2: Stoc 6K 53
Holkam Cl. CW9: N'ich 1E 162
Holker Cl. SK12: Poy 2E 100
Holker Way *M34: Den 2F 27*
(off Two Trees La.)
Holkham, The CH3: Ches 2E 150
Holkham Cl. WA8: Wid 4F 63
Holland Av. SK15: Stal 7B 4
Holland Cl. CW11: S'ach 4G 201
SK12: Poy 3D 100
Holland Ct. SK1: Stoc 5E 52
Holland Gro. CH60: Hes 5H 83
Holland Pk. SK7: Bram 6B 78
Holland Rd. CH45: Wall 4J 13
SK7: Bram 6C 78
SK14: Hyde 5A 10
Hollands La. CW6: Kel 2B 172
Hollands Pl. SK11: Mac 5C 126
Hollands Rd. CW9: N'ich 6E 156
Holland St. CW1: Crewe 7G 191
M34: Den 6C 8
SK11: Mac 5K 125
WA5: Warr 7C 40
Holland St. E. M34: Den 6C 8
Holland St. W. M34: Den 6C 8
Holland Wlk. CW5: Nant 1B 196
Holley Ct. *L35: R'ill 1C 36*
(off Rainhill Rd.)
Hollies, The CW2: Shav 3B 198
CW9: Moult 6D 162
CW9: N'ich 7D 156
M20: Manc 1B 50
SK4: Stoc 1K 51
SK8: Gat 7D 50
WA7: Run 6K 89
Hollies Ct. M33: Sale 7G 23
Hollies Dr. SK6: Mar 7G 55
Hollies La. SK9: Wilm 7C 98
Hollin Bank SK4: Stoc 4G 25
Hollinney Rd. M22: Wyth 4B 76
HOLLINFARE 1D 44 (1A 216)
Hollingford Pl. WA16: Knut 5E 116
HOLLINGWORTH 2J 11 (1D 217)
Hollingworth Cl. *SK1: Stoc 4D 52*
(off Mottram Fold)
Hollingworth Dr. SK6: Mar 2F 81
Hollingworth Rd. SK6: Bred 7D 26
Hollinhey Ter. SK14: H'rth 5K 11
Hollin La. SK9: Styal 7B 76
SK11: Sut E 3K 129
Hollin Rd. SK10: Boll 4D 122
Hollins, The SK6: Mar 6F 55
Hollins Av. SK14: Hyde 4K 27
Hollinsclough Cl. M22: Shar 7A 50
Hollinscroft Av. WA15: Timp 7D 48
Hollins Dr. WA2: Winw 5K 15
HOLLINS GREEN 2C 44
Hollins Grn. Gdns. *SK6: Mar 6F 55*
(off Station Rd.)
Hollins Grn. Rd. SK6: Mar 6F 55
Hollins Gro. M33: Sale 7F 23
Hollinshead Cl. ST7: Sch G 1J 205
Hollins Hill CW6: Cote, Utk 1E 176
Hollins La. CW9: Ant 5E 94
OL5: Moss 1E 4
SK6: Mar 6F 55
SK6: Mar B 5H 55
SY13: Marb 6C 208
WA2: Winw 5H 15
Hollins Mt. SK6: Mar B 4H 55
Hollins Rd. SK11: Mac 6C 126
Hollins St. SK15: Stal 2A 10
Hollins Ter. SK6: Mar 6F 55
SK11: Mac 6C 126
Hollins Vw. SK11: Mac 6A 126
Hollins Wlk. M22: Wyth 3K 75
Hollins Way WA8: Hal B 1B 88
HOLLINWOOD
OL8 1D 217
SY13 3D 219
Hollinwood La. SK6: Mar 3H 81
(not continuous)
Hollinwood Rd. SK12: Dis 1G 103
Hollow, The ST7: Mow C 7F 205
Holloway WA7: Run 5F 89
Hollow Dr. WA4: Stoc H 4J 67
Hollow End SK5: Stoc 4A 26
Hollow End Towers SK5: Stoc 4A 26
Hollow La. WA6: K'ley, New 1A 152
WA16: Knut 4F 117
HOLLOWMOOR HEATH 2D 170
Hollowmoor Heath CH3: Gt Bar 2C 170
Hollow Oak La. CW8: Cudd 2A 160
Hollowood Rd. SY14: Mal 1H 207
Hollows, The SK8: He Grn 4E 76
Hollows Ct. *SK14: Hyde 1K 27*
(off Ridling La.)
Hollow Va. Dr. SK5: Stoc 2J 25
Holly Av. CH63: Beb 3K 85
M41: Urm 1A 22
SK8: Chea 7F 51
WA12: New W 1G 15
Holly Bank CW3: Audl 7A 210
OL6: Ash L 1J 9
SK14: H'rth 2J 11
WA6: Alv 6D 138
WA6: Frod 7J 111
WA13: Lymm 3K 69
Hollybank M33: Sale 1C 48
SK15: M'ook 5E 4
WA4: Moo 1J 91
Holly Bank Cvn. Pk. WA3: Rix 3C 44
Hollybank Cl. CW8: Winn 4C 156
Holly Bank Cotts. *M31: Part 7C 20*
(off Manchester Rd.)
SK6: W'ley 6G 27
(off High La.)
Holly Bank Ct. SK8: Chea H 4J 77
Hollybank Ct. CH41: Birk 7C 34
WA8: Wid 4F 63
Holly Bank Ri. SK16: Duk 2A 10
Holly Bank Rd. SK9: Wilm 5J 97
Hollybank Rd. CH41: Birk 7C 34
WA7: Halt 6B 90
Hollybrook Dene SK6: Rom 2E 54
Hollybush Cres. CW5: W'ston 2H 197
Holly Bush La. WA3: Rix 4J 43
Holly Cl. CH2: Mic T 2J 147
L24: Hale 6A 88
WA15: Timp 6A 48
Holly Ct. CW8: S'way 4D 160
CW10: Mid 2B 180
M44: Irlam 1E 20
SK3: Stoc 7C 52
SK14: Hyde 1B 28
WA6: Hel 3C 138
Hollycroft Av. M22: Wyth 6K 49
Holly Dr. CW7: Wins 4E 178
M33: Sale 7F 23
Holly Farm Ct. WA8: Wid 1F 63
Hollyfield Rd. CH65: Ell P 3D 134
Hollyfields CW11: Wint 5C 204
Hollygate, The *SK3: Stoc 7B 52*
(off Chestergate)
Holly Grange SK7: Bram 2D 78
WA14: Bow 3H 73
Holly Gro. CH42: Tran 1D 60
M33: Sale 7J 23
M34: Den 7F 9
SK15: Stal 2K 9
WA1: Padd 5A 42
Holly Heath Cl. CW11: S'ach 4G 201
Hollyhedge Av. M22: Wyth 7K 49
Hollyhedge Ct. M22: Shar 7A 50
Hollyhedge Ct. Rd. M22: Shar 7A 50
Hollyhedge La. WA4: H Wal 7B 66
Hollyhedge Rd. M22: Shar, Wyth 7J 49
M23: Wyth 7F 49
SK8: Gat 1A 76
Hollyhey Dr. M23: Wyth 3J 49
Holly Ho. Dr. M41: Urm 1J 21
Hollyhouse Dr. SK6: W'ley 6F 27
HOLLYHURST 3D 219
Hollyhurst Rd. SY13: H'rst, Marb 7D 208
Holly La. SK9: Styal 2F 97
ST7: Als 6F 203
ST7: Harr 7J 205
Holly Mt. CW2: Shav 2E 198
Hollymount Av. SK2: Stoc 7G 53
Hollymount Dr. SK2: Stoc 7G 53
Hollymount Gdns. SK2: Stoc 7H 53
Hollymount Rd. SK2: Stoc 7G 53
Holly Pl. CH46: More 5C 32
Holly Rd. CH4: Ches 6G 149
CH65: Ell P 3E 134
CW8: Weav 5F 155
SK4: Stoc 6F 25
SK6: H Lan 6F 81
SK7: Bram 1H 99
SK11: Mac 5J 125
SK12: Poy 3D 100
WA5: Penk 7G 39
WA13: Lymm 7D 44
Holly Rd. Nth. SK9: Wilm 1F 119

Holly Rd. Sth.—Huddersfield Rd.

Holly Rd. Sth. SK9: Wilm 2F 119
Holly St. SK1: Stoc 3E 52
Holly Ter. SY14: Tils 6C 206
WA5: Penk 1H 65
Hollythorn Av. SK8: Chea H 6K 77
Holly Tree Ct. *CH43: Oxt* *7K 33*
(off Beresford Rd.)
Holly Tree Dr. WA16: Lwr P 3B 164
Hollytree Rd. WA16: Plum 2H 159
Holly Va. Cotts. SK6: Mar B 4K 55
Holly Vw. M22: Shar 1A 76
Holly Wlk. CW8: N'ich 6B 156
M31: Part 1F 45
Hollyway M22: N'den 4A 50
Hollywood WA14: Bow 3H 73
Hollywood Towers
SK3: Stoc 7F 213 (4B 52)
Hollywood Way SK4: Stoc 3B 52
Holm Cotts. CH43: Oxt 3J 59
Holmcroft Rd. M18: Manc 1G 25
Holmdale Av. M19: Manc 6B 24
Holmdale Ct. M33: Sale 7H 23
Holm Dr. CH2: Elt 5G 137
Holmefield M33: Sale 7G 23
Holmefield Dr. SK8: Chea H 5K 77
Holme Rd. M20: Manc 1B 50
HOLMES CHAPEL 4J 181 (1B 220)
Holmes Chapel Bus. Cen.
CW4: H Cha 4K 181
Holmes Chapel Leisure Cen. 5G 181
Holmes Chapel Rd. CW9: Lac D 6H 159
CW10: Mid 3D 180
CW12: Cong, Som 2A 182
SK11: Chel 7D 166
SK11: L Wit 5H 167
WA16: All .... 6H 159 & 5A 164
WA16: Knut 7F 117
Holmes Chapel Station (Rail) 4K 181
Holmes Ct. CH42: Tran 2B 60
SK1: Stoc 7K 213
WA3: Birc 7H 17
Holmesfield Rd. WA1: Warr 7H 41
Holmes St. SK2: Stoc 5C 52
SK8: Chea 6G 51
Holme St. CH3: Tar 6A 170
SK14: Hyde 1J 27
Holmesville Av. CW12: Cong 4D 182
Holmes Way M34: Den 4E 26
Holmesway CH61: Pens 2H 83
Holmeswood Cl. SK9: Wilm 6K 97
Holmfield CH2: Elt 5F 137
CH43: Oxt 3J 59
Holmfield Av. WA7: Run 4J 89
Holmfield Cl. SK4: Stoc 1B 52
Holmfield Dr. CH66: Gt Sut 5K 133
Holm Hey Rd. CH43: Pren 3J 59
Holm Hill CH48: W Kir 4D 56
Holmlands Cres. CH43: Oxt 3H 59
Holmlands Dr. CH43: Oxt 3H 59
Holmlands Way CH43: Oxt 3J 59
Holm La. CH43: Oxt 3J 59
Holmlea Dr. CW1: Crewe 3F 195
Holmlee Way SK10: Pres 5E 120
Holm Oak Way CH66: Gt Sut 1B 140
Holmrook WA14: Alt 7F 47
Holmshaw La. CW1: Hasl, O'ger 7B 204
Holmside Cl. CH46: More 4C 32
Holmside Gdns. M19: Manc 7B 24
Holmside La. CH43: Oxt 3J 59
Holm Vw. Cl. CH43: Oxt 2K 59
Holmville Rd. CH63: H Beb 1J 85
Holmway CH63: H Beb 1K 85
Holmwood WA14: Bow 2E 72
Holmwood Av. CH61: Thin 1A 84
Holmwood Dr. CH61: Thin 1A 84
CH65: Whit 5D 134
Holmwood Gdns. CH48: W Kir 4F 57
Holset Dr. WA14: Alt 7F 47
Holset Wlk. SK7: H Gro 3E 78
HOLT
L35 .... 1A 36
LL13 .... 7A 186 (2C 219)
Holt Av. CH46: More 4B 32
Holt Castle (remains of) 7B 186
Holt Gdns. WA16: Mob 7A 96
Holt Hey CH64: Ness 3E 130
Holt Hill CH41: Birk 1D 60
Holt Hill Ter. CH42: Tran 7D 34
Holt La. WA7: Halt 6B 90
Holt Rd. CH41: Tran 1D 60
Holt's La. SK9: Styal 3G 97
(not continuous)
Holt St. CW1: Crewe 2B 194
M34: Aude 2D 8
SK1: Stoc 4D 52
WA14: B'ath 4G 47
Holtwood Wlk. SK5: Stoc 4B 26
Holwick Rd. M23: Wyth 2F 49
Holybourne Wlk. M23: Wyth 4D 48
Holy Cross Cl. L3: Liv 1J 35
Holyhead Cl. WA5: Call 1B 40
Holyoake Av. WA8: Wid 1G 63
Holyrood Dr. CW2: Wis 6J 193
Holyrood Way CH3: Ches 7E 146
HOLYWELL 3A 214
Holywell Cl. CH64: Park 6E 104
Holywell Dr. WA1: Warr 7G 41
Holywell La. CH3: Clut 1A 206
Homebeck Ho. SK8: Gat 7C 50
Home Cl. CH3: Chri 4H 151
Homecrofts CH64: L Nes 3C 130
Homedee Ho. CH1: Ches 2B 212
Home Farm WA16: Mere 5G 95
Home Farm Av. SK10: Mac 3G 125
SK14: Mot 2G 29
Home Farm Cl. CH49: Woodc 3F 59
Home Farm La. CW8: Cudd 6K 153
Home Farm Rd. CH49: Woodc 3E 58
Homelands Cl. M33: Sale 2K 47
Homelands Rd. M33: Sale 2K 47
Homelaurel Ho. M33: Sale 2B 48
Homelyme Ho. SK12: Poy 3E 100
Home Pk. CH1: Mol 1G 145
Homer Dr. SK6: Mar B 4H 55
HOMER GREEN 1B 214
Homeshire Ho. ST7: Als 6E 202
Homestead, The M33: Sale 6E 22
Homestead Cl. M31: Part 7D 20
Homestead Ct. *CW9: N'ich* *6J 157*
(off Middlewich Rd.)
Homestead Cres. M19: Manc 1F 51
Homestead M. CH48: W Kir 3C 56
Homestead Rd. SK12: Dis 1F 103
Homeway WA6: Hel 6B 138
Homewood Av. M22: N'den 3K 49
Homewood Cres. CW8: H'ord 1A 162
Homewood Rd. M22: N'den 3J 49
Hondslough La. WA6: Norl 5B 152
Honeycombe Cotts. *SK8: Chea* *7G 51*
(off Oak Rd.)
Honey Flds. CW6: Tarp 3H 175
Honeysuckle Av. WA5: Warr 1C 66
Honeysuckle Cl. CH66: Gt Sut 1B 140
M23: Wyth 3D 48
SK6: W'ley 6F 27
WA8: Wid 1H 63
Honeysuckle Dr. SK15: Stal 7C 4
Honeysuckle Wlk. M33: Sale 5C 22
Honford Ct. SK9: Hand 3A 98
Honford Rd. M22: Wyth 1J 75
Hong Kong Av. M90: Man A 5G 75
Honister Av. WA2: Warr 2G 41
Honister Gro. WA7: Beec 2A 112
Honiton Av. SK14: Hat 1D 28
Honiton Wlk. *SK14: Hat* *1E 28*
(off Honiton Av.)
Honiton Way CW10: Mid 2D 180
WA5: Penk 1G 65
WA14: Alt 6E 46
Honsham Wlk. M23: Wyth 3E 48
Hood La. WA5: Gt San 7A 40
Hood La. Nth. WA5: Gt San 6A 40
Hood Mnr. Cen. WA5: Gt San 6A 40
Hood Rd. WA8: Wid 4F 63
Hood St. CH44: Wall 1C 34
L1: Liv 2J 35
Hood Wlk. M34: Den 4F 27
Hooker St. CW8: N'ich 6D 156
Hook La. CW6: Dud 5A 174
Hookstone Dr. CH66: L Sut 2J 133
HOOLE 7C 146 (1C 219)
HOOLE BANK 3F 147
Hoole Bri. CH1: Ches 1E 212 (7B 146)
CH2: Ches 1E 212 (7B 146)
Hoole Cl. SK8: Chea 7J 51
Hoole Gdns. CH2: Ches 7E 146
Hoole Ho. CH2: Ches 6E 146
Hoole La. CH2: Ches 1C 150
Hoole Pk. CH2: Ches 7C 146
Hoole Rd. CH2: Ches 7B 146
CH49: Woodc 2E 58
HOOLE VILLAGE 4F 147
Hoole Way CH1: Ches 2D 212 (1A 150)
HOOLEY HILL 3E 8
Hooley Range SK4: Stoc 1K 51
Hoolpool La. WA6: Hel 3K 137
Hooper St. SK1: Stoc 7H 213 (3C 52)
Hoose Ct. CH47: Hoy 5D 30
HOOTON 6B 108 (3B 214)
Hooton Grn. CH66: H'ton 5B 108
Hooton Hey CH66: Gt Sut 3K 133
Hooton La. CH66: H'ton 6C 108
Hooton Pk. Airfield CH65: H'ton 4D 108
Hooton Pk. La. CH65: H'ton 5D 108
Hooton Rd. CH64: W'ston 7F 107
CH66: H'ton 7F 107
Hooton Station (Rail) 6J 107
Hooton Way CH66: H'ton 5A 108
SK9: Hand *1A 98*
(off Beeston Rd.)
Hooton Works Trad. Est.
CH66: H'ton 5K 107
HOPE 2B 218
Hope Av. SK9: Hand 3K 97
Hope Carr La. WN7: Leigh 1H 7
Hope Carr Nature Reserve 1F 7
Hope Carr Ter. WN7: Leigh 1G 7
Hope Cotts. *CH66: Chil T* *7B 108*
(off New Rd.)
Hope Cft. CH66: Gt Sut 6B 134
Hopedale Rd. SK5: Stoc 5J 25
Hope Farm Pct. CH66: Gt Sut 6B 134
Hope Farm Rd. CH66: Gt Sut 7A 134
Hopefield Rd. WA13: Lymm 1D 70
HOPE GREEN 5C 100 (2D 217)
Hope Grn. Way SK10: Adl 4C 100
Hope La. SK10: Adl 5C 100
WA3: G'ury 1K 7
Hope Pl. L1: Liv 4K 35
Hope Rd. M33: Sale 3G 49
Hopes Carr SK1: Stoc 7K 213 (3D 52)
Hope St. CH4: Salt 5G 149
CH41: Birk 5C 34
CH45: N Bri 3H 13
Hope St. CW2: Crewe 4D 194
CW8: N'ich 6D 156
CW11: S'ach 3F 201
L1: Liv 4K 35
M34: Aude 5D 8
SK4: Stoc 6F 213 (3B 52)
SK7: H Gro 2H 79
SK10: Mac 4B 126
SK16: Duk 2G 9
(not continuous)
Hope St. W. SK10: Mac 4K 125
Hope Ter. SK3: Stoc 4C 52
SK16: Duk *2G 9*
(off Hope St.)
Hope Way L8: Liv 4K 35
Hopfield Rd. CH46: More 4C 32
Hopkins Cl. CW12: Cong 3D 182
Hopkins Fld. WA14: Bow 4F 73
Hopkinson Av. M34: Den 5C 8
Hopkinson Ct. CH1: Ches 2J 149
Hopkins St. SK14: Hyde 6K 9
Hopley Ct. *CW2: Crewe* *4C 194*
(off Stalbridge Rd.)
Hopton Av. M22: Wyth 2A 76
Hopwood Cl. WA3: Low 2A 6
Hopwood St. WA1: Warr 6G 41
(not continuous)
Horace Black Gdns.
CH65: Ell P 2E 134
Horace Gro. SK4: Stoc 7H 25
Horace Lawton Ct.
CW12: Cong 3F 183
Horatio St. CH41: Birk 6C 34
Horbury Av. M18: Manc 1G 25
Horbury Gdns. CH66: L Sut 3J 133
Hornbeam Av. CH66: Gt Sut 7B 134
Hornbeam Cl. CH2: Ches 7E 146
CH46: More 4J 31
M33: Sale 6B 22
WA7: Win H 5E 90
WA15: Timp 7E 48
Hornbeam Dr. CW8: H'ord 2H 161
Hornbeam Rd. M19: Manc 1E 24
Hornby Av. CH62: Brom 5C 86
Hornby Ct. CH62: Brom 5D 86
Hornby Cres. WA9: Clo F 1K 37
Hornby Dr. CW5: Nant 2E 196
CW12: Cong 3C 182
Hornby La. WA2: Winw 5K 15
Hornby Rd. CH62: Brom 5C 86
Hornby St. CH41: Birk 6E 34
Horncastle Cl. WA3: Low 2A 6
Hornchurch Dr. WA5: Gt San 6K 39
Hornchurch Ho. SK2: Stoc 6E 52
Hornsea Rd. SK2: Stoc 7A 54
Hornsmill Way WA6: Hel 5A 138
Horrocks La. WA1: Warr 7F 41
Horrocks Rd. CH2: Upt 5B 146
HORSE BRIDGE 2D 221
Horseman Pl. CH44: Wall 2D 34
HORSEMAN'S GREEN 3C 219
Horsemarket St. WA1: Warr 7F 41
Horseshoe Cl. WA6: K'ley 1C 152
Horseshoe Cres. WA2: Warr 1J 41
Horseshoe Dr. SK11: Mac 5J 125
Horseshoe La. SK9: Ald E 5F 119
Horsfall Gro. L8: Liv 1K 61
Horsfall St. L8: Liv 1K 61
Horsfield Way SK6: Bred 5D 26
Horsham Av. SK7: H Gro 4G 79
Horsley La. CW6: Bees 3A 188
Horstead Wlk. *M19: Manc* *1D 24*
(off Deepcar St.)
Horstone Cres. CH66: Gt Sut 6B 134
Horstone Gdns. CH66: Gt Sut 6C 134
Horstone Rd. CH66: Gt Sut 6B 134
Horticultural Cen., The in Wythenshawe Pk.
.... 4F 49
HORTON 2D 221
HORTON GREEN 3C 219
Horton St. SK1: Stoc 5E 52
Horton Way CW5: Stap 3E 196
Hortree Rd. M32: S'ord 1K 23
HORWICH END 2D 217
Horwood Cres. M20: Manc 6A 24
Hoscar Ct. WA8: Wid 6D 62
Hoscar Dr. M19: Manc 4C 24
Hoscote Pk. CH48: W Kir 3B 56
Hose Side Rd. CH45: Wall 4G 13
Hospital Rd. M23: Wyth 7E 48
Hospital St. CW1: Crewe 7J 191
CW5: Nant 2C 196
Hospital Way WA7: Pal F 7B 90
Hotel Rd. M90: Man A 6J 75
Hotham St. L3: Liv 2K 35
Hothersall Cl. CW1: L'ton 4G 191
Hothersall Rd. SK5: Stoc 4J 25
Hothfield Rd. CH44: Wall 1C 34
HOUGH
CW2 .... 5E 198 (2B 220)
SK10 .... 6J 119 (3C 217)
Hough Cl. SK10: R'ow 6G 123
HOUGH GREEN 4A 62 (2C 215)
Hough Grn. CH4: Ches 4H 149
WA15: Ash 7J 73
Hough Grn. Rd. WA8: Wid 3A 62
Hough Green Station (Rail) 3B 62
Hough Hill Rd. SK15: Stal 1B 10
(not continuous)
Hough La.
CW9: And, Barnt, Comb
.... 1K 155 & 3F 115
Hough La. SK9: Ald E 6J 119
SK9: Wilm 6J 119
SK14: Hyde 5A 10
WA6: Norl 6G 153
Houghley Cl. SK10: Mac 2K 125
Hough's La. WA4: H Wal 1E 92
Houghton Av. WA2: Warr 6G 41
Houghton Cl. CH2: Ches 1C 150
CW9: N'ich 2E 162
WA8: Wid 3J 63
Houghton Cft. WA8: Cron 7C 36
HOUGHTON GREEN 7D 16
Houghton La. L1: Liv 3J 35
Houghton Rd. CH49: Woodc 1E 58
L24: Hale 6B 88
Houghton St. L1: Liv 3J 35
L35: R'ill 1C 36
WA2: Warr 5F 41
WA8: Wid 3K 63
WA12: New W 1E 14
Houghton Way *L1: Liv* *3J 35*
(off St John's Cen.)
Houldsworth Av. WA14: Timp 5J 47
Houldsworth Sq. SK5: Stoc 4H 25
Houldsworth St. SK5: Stoc 4H 25
Houndings La. CW11: S'ach 5E 200
Hourd Way CH66: Gt Sut 1A 140
House La. WA8: Wid 6F 63
Housesteads SK14: Hat 2E 28
Housesteads Dr. CH2: Ches 7C 146
Housman Cl. CH1: Blac 5H 145
Houston Gdns. WA5: Gt San 4J 39
Hove, The WA7: Murd 1F 113
(not continuous)
Hove Cl. CW1: Crewe 5G 191
Hove Dr. M14: Manc 4B 24
Hoviley SK14: Hyde 7K 9
Hovington Gdns. M19: Manc 5B 24
Hovis Mill SK11: Mac 5B 126
Howard Av. CH62: Brom 6E 86
SK4: Stoc 5F 25
SK8: Chea H 4J 77
WA13: Lymm 1D 70
Howard Cl. SK6: Rom 2A 54
Howard Ct. CH64: Nest 6J 105
WA7: Man P 2E 90
Howard Dr. WA15: Hale 4A 74
Howard La. M34: Den 6E 8
Howard Pl. *SK14: Hyde* *1J 27*
(off Rutherford Way)
Howard Rd. CH4: Salt 5E 148
M22: N'den 3K 49
WA3: Cul 1B 18
Howards Rd. CH61: Thin 7E 58
Howard St. CW1: Crewe 1F 195
M32: S'ord 1J 23
M34: Aude 4E 8
M34: Den 5D 8
SK1: Stoc 4J 213 (2D 52)
SK15: M'ook 5E 4
Howards Way CH64: L Nes 2E 130
Howarth Ct. SK2: Stoc 7F 53
WA7: Run 4H 89
Howarth Dr. M44: Irlam 2C 20
Howbeck Cl. CH43: Clau 6J 33
Howbeck Ct. CH43: Oxt 7J 33
Howbeck Cres. CW5: Wyb 7A 198
Howbeck Dr. CH43: Clau 6J 33
Howbeck Rd. CH43: Oxt 7J 33
Howbeck Wlk. *CW2: Crewe* *6D 194*
(off Davenport Av.)
Howden Cl. SK5: Stoc 1H 25
Howell Dr. CH49: Gre 3A 58
Howell Rd. CH62: N Fer 6F 61
Howells Av. CH66: Gt Sut 5J 133
M33: Sale 6G 23
Howe Rd. CH4: Ches 4J 149
Howe St. OL7: Ash L 2E 8
SK10: Mac 3C 126
Howey Hill CW12: Cong 5F 183
Howey La. CW12: Cong 4F 183
WA6: Frod 1G 139
Howey Ri. WA6: Frod 1G 139
Howgill Cl. CH66: L Sut 2F 133
HOWLEY 7G 41 (2A 216)
Howley Cl. M44: Irlam 2E 20
Howley La. WA1: Warr 7H 41
Howley Quay WA1: Warr 7H 41
Howley Quay Ind. Est. WA1: Warr 7H 41
Howson Rd. WA2: Warr 2G 41
Howson St. CH42: R Fer 3E 60
Howty Cl. SK9: Wilm 5A 98
Hoxton Cl. SK6: Bred 7F 27
HOYLAKE 5C 30 (2A 214)
Hoylake Cl. WA7: Murd 1E 112
(not continuous)
Hoylake Rd. CH41: Birk 2G 33
CH46: More 5J 31
M33: Sale 2F 49
SK3: Stoc 4J 51
Hoylake Station (Rail) 6C 30
Hoyle Rd. CH47: Hoy 4C 30
Hoyle St. WA5: Warr 5D 40
Hubert Dr. CW10: Mid 4C 180
Hubert Worthington Ho.
SK9: Ald E *6F 119*
(off George St.)
Hucclecote Av. M22: Wyth 3J 75
Hucklow Av. M23: Wyth 3G 75
Huddersfield Rd. OL5: Moss 1F 5
SK15: Carrb 4F 5
SK15: M'ook, Stal 7C 4

Huddleston Cl.—Jackson Cl.

Huddleston Cl. CH49: Woodc 2E 58
Hudson Cl. WA5: Old H 4B 40
Hudson Rd. CH46: Leas 7A 12
SK14: Hyde 4K 27
WA2: Padg 2J 41
Hughes Av. WA2: Warr 2H 41
Hughes Dr. CW2: Crewe 2K 193
Hughes La. CH43: Oxt 2A 60
Hughes Pl. WA2: Warr 2H 41
Hughes St. WA4: Warr 2G 67
Hughson St. L8: Liv 7K 35
Hugh St. CH4: Ches 4A 150
Hulley Pl. SK10: Mac 3C 126 (off Hurdsfield Rd.)
Hulley Rd. SK10: Mac 1B 126
Hully St. SK15: Stal 7A 4
HULME
M15 1C 217
ST3 3D 221
WA2 1F 41
Hulme Cl. CH62: Brom 2C 86
Hulme Dr. WA15: Timp 5C 48
Hulme Hall Av. SK8: Chea H 5J 77
Hulme Hall Cl. SK8: Chea H 4J 77
Hulme Hall Cres. SK8: Chea H 5J 77
Hulme Hall Rd. SK8: Chea H 3J 77
Hulme La. WA16: Lwr P 4K 159
Hulme Rd. M33: Sale 1D 48
M34: Den 7A 8
SK4: Stoc 5G 25
Hulme's La. M34: Den 3D 26
Hulme Sq. SK11: Mac 7A 126
Hulme St. CW1: Crewe 1K 193
SK1: Stoc 5F 53
Hulmeswood Ter. M34: Den 4F 27 (off Tennyson Av.)
HULME WALFIELD 1C 221
Hulme Wlk. CH62: Brom 2C 86
Hulmewood CH63: Beb 6F 61
Hulse La. CW9: Lac D 4G 159
Hulton Cl. CW12: Cong 5K 183
Hulton St. M34: Den 6D 8
Humber Cl. WA8: Wid 2B 64
Humber Rd. CH66: Gt Sut 6B 134
WA2: Warr 2J 41
Humber St. CH41: Birk 3J 33
Hume Ct. CH47: Meols 4D 30
Hume St. M19: Manc 3E 24
WA1: Warr 6H 41
Humphrey Cres. M41: Urm 1F 23
Humphrey La. M41: Urm 1F 23
Humphrey Pk. M41: Urm 1F 23
Humphrey Park Station (Rail) 1F 23
Humphrey Rd. SK7: Bram 2C 78
Humphrey's Cl. WA7: Murd 7F 91
Huncoat Av. SK4: Stoc 6G 25
Hungerford Av. CW1: Crewe 2E 194
Hungerford Pl. CW11: S'ach 4E 200
Hungerford Rd. CW1: Crewe 2E 194
Hungerford Ter. CW1: Crewe 2F 195
Hungerford Wlk. M23: Wyth 5D 48 (off Butcher La.)
Hunstanton Cl. CH49: Upt 5D 32
Hunsterson Rd. CW5: Hath, Huns 3H 211
Hunston Rd. M33: Sale 1K 47
Hunt Cl. WA5: Gt San 4K 39
Hunter Av. CW2: Shav 7D 194
WA2: Warr 1F 41
Hunters Cl. SK6: Bred 1K 53
SK9: Wilm 5C 98
Hunters Ct. SK15: Stal 3E 10
SK16: Duk 3A 10
WA6: Hel 4D 138
WA7: Pal F 1A 112
Hunter's Cres. CH3: Tar 7C 170
Hunter's Dr. CH3: Tar 7B 170
Huntersfield CW2: Shav 4B 198
CW8: N'ich 6C 156
Hunters Hill CW8: Weav 4F 155
WA6: K'ley 2D 152
Hunters La. CW8: H'ord 2H 161
Hunters Lodge SK9: Wilm 5C 98 (off Hunters Cl.)
Hunters M. M33: Sale 6F 23
SK9: Wilm 7K 97
Hunters Pool La. SK10: Pres 3D 120
Hunters Ri. CW7: Wins 3D 178
Hunter St. CH1: Ches 4B 212 (2K 149)
L3: Liv 2J 35
Hunters Vw. SK9: Hand 3K 97
Hunter's Wlk. CH1: Ches 4B 212 (2K 149)
Hunters Way CH64: Park 7F 105
Huntingdon Cl. CH46: More 4J 31
Huntingdon Cres. SK5: Stoc 6B 26
Huntingdon Way M34: Den 2E 26
Hunting Lodge M. CW8: Cudd 2D 160
HUNTINGTON 5D 150 (1C 219)
HUNTLEY 3D 221
Huntley Rd. SK3: Stoc 5K 51
Huntley St. WA5: Gt San 1A 66
Huntly Chase SK9: Wilm 7K 97
Hunt Rd. SK14: Hyde 5B 10
Huntsbank Bus. Pk. CW2: Wis 7J 193
Hunts Cl. CH3: Gt Bou 2E 150
HUNT'S CROSS 2C 215
Hunts Fld. Cl. WA13: Lymm 3K 69
Huntsham Cl. WA14: Alt 6F 47
Hunts La. CW8: Gor, S'way 3E 160
WA4: Stoc H 3K 67
Hunts Lock CW9: N'ich 7E 156
Huntsman Dr. M44: Irlam 4C 20
Huntspill Rd. WA14: W Tim 4G 47
Hurdlow Lea SK13: Gam 2K 29 (off Brassington Cres.)
Hurdlow M. SK13: Gam 2K 29
Hurdlow Way SK13: Gam 2K 29 (off Brassington Cres.)
HURDSFIELD 3C 126 (3D 217)
Hurdsfield Cl. CW10: Mid 5C 180
Hurdsfield Grn. SK10: Mac 2B 126 (off Brocklehurst Av.)
Hurdsfield Ind. Est. SK10: Mac 1B 126 (Charter Way)
SK10: Mac 2A 126 (The Silk Rd.)
Hurdsfield Rd. SK2: Stoc 1G 79
SK10: Mac 3B 126
Hurford Av. CH65: Gt Sut 4B 134
Hurlbote Cl. SK9: Hand 1A 98
Hurleston Bldgs. CW5: Nant 1C 196 (off Weaver Rd.)
Hurlestone Cl. CH2: Mic T 1J 147
Hurley Cl. WA5: Gt San 7A 40
Hurley Dr. SK8: Chea H 3G 77
Hurn Cl. CW1: Crewe 5G 191
Hurrell Rd. CH41: Birk 3G 33
HURST 1D 217
Hurst, The WA6: K'ley 1D 152
Hurst Av. M33: Sale 1G 47
SK8: Chea H 7A 78
Hurst Bank CH42: R Fer 5E 60
Hurstbank Av. M19: Manc 7A 24
Hurstbrook Dr. M32: S'ord 1E 22
Hurst Cl. CW6: Bun 6D 188
Hurst Ct. CW6: Bun 6D 188
M23: Wyth 1F 75
Hurstfield Ind. Est.
SK5: Stoc 5H 25
Hurstfold Av. M19: Manc 1F 51
HURST GREEN 3D 219
Hursthead Rd. SK8: Chea H 6K 77
Hurstheads La. SK6: Rom 3B 54
Hurst La. SK10: Boll 3D 122
WA3: G'ury 4H 7
Hurst Lea Ct. SK9: Ald E 5F 119
Hurstmead Ter. M20: Manc 2D 50 (off South Rd.)
Hurst Mill La. WA3: G'ury 2J 7
HURST NOOK 3A 4
Hurst St. L1: Liv 4J 35
SK5: Stoc 4H 25
WA8: Wid 2G 89
Hurstvale Av. SK8: He Grn 4D 76
Hurst Wlk. M22: Wyth 3G 75
Hurstwood CH3: Wave 3A 174
OL6: Ash L 3A 4
Hurstwood Gro. SK2: Stoc 6K 53
Huskisson St. L8: Liv 5K 35
Hutchins' Cl. CW10: Mid 6E 180
Hutchinson Cl. CH43: Bid 6E 32
Hutchinson St. WA8: Wid 7F 63
Hutton Cl. WA3: Cul 5E 6
Hutton Dr. CW12: Cong 4J 183
HUXLEY 1D 219
Huxley Cl. CH46: More 4J 31
SK7: Bram 6C 78
SK10: Mac 2J 125
Huxley Ct. CH66: Ell P 7G 109
Huxley Dr. SK7: Bram 6C 78
Huxley La. CW6: Tive 6F 175
Huxley St. CW8: N'ich 6D 156
WA14: B'ath 5H 47
Huxton Grn. SK7: H Gro 3E 78
HUYTON 1C 215
Hyacinth Cl. SK3: Stoc 7B 52
Hyacinth Gro. CH46: More 2D 32
Hyacinth Wlk. M31: Part 2G 45 (off Redbrook Rd.)
HYDE 1J 27 (1D 217)
Hydebank SK6: Rom 3D 54
Hyde Central Station (Rail) 1H 27
Hyde Cl. CH65: Gt Sut 4B 134
WA7: Beec 1K 111
Hyde Festival Theatre 1J 27
Hyde Fold Cl. M19: Manc 5C 24
Hyde Gro. M33: Sale 7G 23
Hyde Ho. SK4: Stoc 6F 25
Hyde Leisure Pool 1A 28
Hyde North Station (Rail) 5H 9
Hyde Point SK14: Hyde 6H 9
Hyde Rd. M34: Den 6E 8
SK6: W'ley 6F 27
SK14: Mot 7G 11
Hydes Ter. SK15: Stal 7C 4
Hyde St. SK16: Duk 2J 9
Hyde United FC 1A 28
Hyde Way SK14: Mot 7G 11
Hydrangea Cl. M33: Sale 6B 22
Hydro Av. CH48: W Kir 4C 56
Hyldavale Av. SK8: Gat 6D 50
Hylton Av. CH44: Wall 7G 13
Hylton Ct. CH65: Ell P 6G 135
Hylton Dr. SK8: Chea H 4A 78
Hyslop St. L8: Liv 6K 35
Hythe Av. CW1: Crewe 5G 191
Hythe Rd. SK3: Stoc 4K 51

I

Ibis Ct. WA1: Warr 2E 66
Idaho Wlk. WA5: Gt San 6A 40 (off Washington Dr.)
Iffley Cl. CH49: Upt 7A 32
IFTON HEATH 3B 218
IGHTFIELD 3D 219
Ikin Cl. CH43: Bid 3F 33
Ilchester Rd. CH41: Birk 3J 33
CH44: Wall 1C 34
Ilex Av. WA2: Winw 5A 16
Ilford Av. CH44: Wall 2A 34
Ilford Way WA16: Mob 6B 102
Ilfracombe Rd. SK2: Stoc 4H 53
Iliad St. L5: Liv 1K 35
Ilkeston Wlk. M34: Den 3F 27
Ilkley Cres. SK5: Stoc 3H 25
ILLIDGE GREEN 1B 220
Illingworth Av. SK15: Stal 1D 10
Ilsley Cl. CH49: Upt 1C 58
Imperial Av. CH1: Blac 6D 144
CH45: Wall 5J 13
Imperial Chambers L1: Liv 2H 35 (off Davies St.)
Imperial Ct. CW5: Nant 2D 196
L2: Liv 2H 35 (off Exchange St. E.)
Imperial M. CH65: Ell P 2D 134
CW2: Crewe 3D 194 (off Lord St.)
Imperial Ter. M33: Sale 5F 23 (off Woodfield Gro.)
INCE 2E 136 (3C 215)
Ince Av. CH62: East 4K 107
INCE BLUNDELL 1B 214
Ince Cl. CH43: Oxt 1J 59
SK4: Stoc 1C 52
Ince Dr. CH3: Farn 6C 186
Ince & Elton Station (Rail) 4F 137
Ince Gro. CH43: Oxt 1J 59
Ince La. CH2: Elt 4F 137
CH2: Wim T 2D 142
Ince Orchards CH2: Elt 4F 137
Ince St. SK4: Stoc 1C 52
Inchcape Rd. CH45: Wall 6D 12
Independent Ho. SK8: Chea 2E 76
Indiana Gro. WA5: Gt San 5J 39
Indigo Rd. CH65: Ell P 3H 135
Ingersley Ct. SK10: Boll 3E 122
Ingersley Rd. SK10: Boll 3E 122
INGERSLEY VALE 4F 123
Ingersley Va. SK10: Boll 3E 122
Ingestre Ct. CH43: Oxt 2K 59
Ingestre Rd. CH43: Oxt 2K 59
Ingham Av. WA12: New W 2F 15
Ingham Cl. CH3: Ches 2D 150
Ingham Rd. WA8: Wid 1F 63
WA14: W Tim 4H 47
Ingham's Rd. WA3: Croft 2F 17
Ingleborough Rd. CH42: Tran 3C 60
Ingleby Ct. M32: S'ord 2K 23
Ingleby Rd. CH44: Wall 1K 33
CH62: N Fer 5G 61
Ingle Dr. SK2: Stoc 5G 53
Inglefield Ct. CH42: R Fer 4F 61 (off The Hawthornes)
Inglegreen CH60: Hes 6K 83
Inglehead Cl. M34: Den 1F 27
Inglemere Rd. CH42: R Fer 3D 60
Ingle Nook Cl. M31: Carri 5J 21
Inglenook Rd. WA5: Penk 1H 65
Ingle Rd. SK8: Chea 6J 51
Inglesham Cl. M23: Wyth 6H 49
WN7: Leigh 1E 6
Ingleton Cl. CH49: Gre 1A 58
CW4: H Cha 4G 181
SK8: Chea 6E 50
Ingleton Gro. WA7: Beec 2K 111
Ingleton Rd. SK3: Stoc 5A 52
Inglewood WA14: Alt 2F 73
Inglewood Av. CH46: More 5A 32
CW10: Mid 7D 180
Inglewood Cl. M31: Part 7B 20
WA3: Birc 5C 18
Inglewood Hollow SK15: Stal 2D 10
Ingram Dr. SK4: Stoc 1G 51
Inkerman St. SK14: Hyde 6J 9
Inley Cl. CH63: Spit 4A 86
Inley Rd. CH63: Spit 4K 85
Inman Rd. CH49: Upt 6B 32
Inman St. M34: Den 7E 8
Inner Gosling Cl. WA4: H'ton 5D 92
Innes St. M12: Manc 1E 24
Innisfree Cl. CH66: Gt Sut 3J 133
Insall Rd. WA2: Padg 2K 41
Intake Cl. CH64: W'ston 7F 107
International App. M90: Man A 6J 75
International Bus. Cen. WA5: W'ook 2A 40
International Slavery Mus. 4H 35
Intone Fitness Cen. 6E 202
Inveresk Ct. CH43: Noc 6H 33
Inveresk Rd. SY14: Tils 6B 206
Inverness Rd. SK16: Duk 3H 9
Inward Way CH65: Ell P 1D 134
Iona Cres. WA8: Wid 6F 37
Ionic St. CH42: R Fer 3E 60
Ion Path CW7: Wins 3K 179
IPSTONES 3D 221
Ipswich Wlk. M34: Den 2F 27 (off Lancaster Rd.)
IRBY 7A 58 (2A 214)
Irby Av. CH44: Wall 7G 13
Irby Cl. CH66: Gt Sut 4A 134
IRBY HEATH 7K 57
IRBY HILL 5K 57
Irby Rd. CH61: Hes, Irby, Pens 1F 83
Irbyside Rd. CH48: Fran 4J 57
Irby Wlk. SK8: Chea 1J 77
Ireland Rd. L24: Hale 7B 88
Ireland St. WA2: Warr 4F 41
WA8: Wid 4K 63
Irene Av. SK14: Hyde 6K 9
Iris Av. CH41: Birk 4J 33
Iris Cl. WA8: Wid 3C 62
Iris Wlk. M31: Part 2H 45 (off Cross La. W.)
IRLAM 5B 20 (1B 216)
Irlam Ind. Est. M44: Irlam 4B 20
Irlam Locks Circ. M44: Irlam 2E 20
Irlam Rd. M33: Sale 6H 23
M41: Urm 2E 20
Irlam Station (Rail) 4B 20
Irlam Wharf Rd. M44: Irlam 4D 20
Ironbridge Dr. CW4: H Cha 5J 181
Ironbridge Vw. L8: Liv 1K 61
Irons La. CH3: Gt Bar 1C 170
Irvin Dr. M22: Wyth 5C 76
Irvine Rd. CH42: Tran 3C 60
Irvine Ter. CH62: N Fer 5H 61
Irving Cl. SK2: Stoc 2E 78
Irving's Cres. CH4: Salt 5F 149
Irwell Chambers L3: Liv 2H 35 (off Fazakerley St.)
Irwell Ho. M44: Irlam 2E 20
Irwell La. WA7: Run 3H 89
Irwell Ri. SK10: Boll 3C 122
Irwell Rd. WA4: Warr 3F 67
Irwell St. L3: Liv 3H 35
WA8: Wid 2G 89
Irwin Dr. SK9: Hand 1K 97
Irwin Pl. SK8: Chea H 2H 77
Irwin Rd. WA14: B'ath 4G 47
Irwin St. M34: Den 7D 8
Isabella Ct. CH4: Salt 5F 149
Isherwood Cl. WA2: Fear 1K 41
Isherwood Dr. SK6: Mar 6D 54
Isherwood Rd. M31: Carri 5J 21
Isis Cl. CW12: Cong 5H 183
Islay Cl. CH65: Ell P 7E 134
Islington L3: Liv 2K 35
Islington Grn. WA8: Wid 1K 63
Islington Rd. SK2: Stoc 1G 79
Islip Cl. CH61: Irby 6A 58
Ismay Dr. CH44: Wall 6K 13
Ivatt Dr. CW2: Crewe 5E 194
Ivatt Ho. CW1: Crewe 2B 194 (off Blount Cl.)
Iveagh Cl. WA7: Pal F 7C 90
Iver Cl. CH2: Upt 3B 146
WA8: Cron 6C 36
Iver Rd. CH2: Upt 3B 146
Ivor Rd. CH44: Wall 6J 13
Ivy Av. CH63: H Beb 1J 85
L35: Whis 1A 36
WA12: New W 1F 15
Ivy Bank OL5: Moss 1F 5
Ivychurch M. WA7: Run 4K 89
Ivy Cotts. M34: Den 4F 27
Ivy Ct. CH4: Pul 7B 184
Ivycroft SK13: Had 3K 11
Ivydale Rd. CH42: Tran 2D 60
Ivy Dr. CW8: S'way 4D 160
Ivy Farm Ct. L24: Hale 7A 88
Ivy Farm Dr. CH64: L Nes 2D 130
Ivy Farm Gdns. WA3: Cul 6D 6
Ivy Farm Rd. L35: R'ill 1B 36
Ivy Gdns. CW12: Cong 4E 182
Ivy Ho. SK9: Ald E 1E 166
SK11: Mac 5H 125
Ivy La. CH46: More 2B 32
SK11: Mac 6H 125
ST7: Als 7F 203
Ivylea Rd. M19: Manc 7B 24
Ivy Lodge Cl. SK15: M'ook 5F 5
Ivymeade Cl. SK11: Mac 5G 125
Ivy Meade Rd. SK11: Mac 6G 125
Ivy M. CH2: Ches 5D 146
Ivy Rd. SK11: Mac 6G 125
SK12: Poy 3D 100
WA1: Wool 5E 42
Ivy St. CH41: Birk 6E 34
WA7: Run 5G 89
Ivy Wlk. M31: Part 1F 45

J

Jack Brady Cl. M23: Wyth 1E 74
Jackies La. WA13: Lymm 1B 70
Jackie Stewart Bus. Cen. CW6: Oul 3F 177
Jackie Wood Grn. CH65: Ell P 2D 134
Jack La. CW2: West 1J 199
CW9: Bos, Dave, Moult 7F 163
CW10: Bos 7F 163
M41: Urm 3F 21 (Dunster Dr.)
M41: Urm 1D 22 (Falcon Av.)
M43: Droy 1B 8 (not continuous)
Jack Lane Nature Reserve 3F 21
Jack McBain Ct. L3: Liv 1H 35
Jackson Av. CW5: Nant 2D 196
SK16: Duk 2J 9
WA1: Padd 5K 41
WA3: Cul 7E 6
Jackson Cl. CH63: H Beb 5E 60
L35: R'ill 3D 36
WA15: Timp 5C 48

Kingsmead Rd. Nth.—Ladywood Rd.

Kingsmead Rd. Nth. CH43: Oxt 7J 33
Kingsmead Rd. Sth. CH43: Oxt 7J 33
Kingsmead Sq. CW9: N'ich 2D 162
Kingsmere Av. M19: Manc 2C 24
Kings M. CH66: L Sut 1J 133
WA4: Stoc H 5G 67
Kingsmill Av. M19: Manc 3E 24
KINGS MOSS 1D 215
Kings Mt. CH43: Oxt 1A 60
Kingsnorth L35: Whis 2A 36
Kings Pde. CH45: Wall, N Bri 3D 12
L3: Liv 5H 35
Kings Reach Bus. Pk. SK4: Stoc 3A 52
Kings Rd. CH63: H Beb 5C 60
CH66: L Sut 1J 133
M32: S'ord 2K 23
M33: Sale 7E 22
M34: Aude 5A 8
M44: Irlam 5B 20
OL6: Ash L 3A 4
SK6: Rom 1A 54
SK7: H Gro 2J 79
SK8: Chea H 2H 77
SK9: Wilm 6F 97
WA2: Fear 2A 42
Kings Sq. CH41: Birk 6E 34
Kings Ter. SK16: Duk 1G 9
(off Queen St.)
KINGSTON 7G 9
Kingston Arc. SK14: Hat 1F 29
Kingston Av. M20: Manc 3D 50
SK11: Mac 5C 126
WA5: Gt San 6G 39
Kingston Cl. CH46: More 4B 32
M33: Sale 1H 47
SK14: Hat 1F 29
WA7: Run 4A 90
Kingston Ct. CH1: Sau 1C 144
M20: Manc 3D 50
(off Kingston Rd.)
Kingston Dr. M33: Sale 6J 23
M41: Urm 3A 22
Kingston Gdns. SK14: Hyde 7G 9
Kingston Hill SK8: Chea 1F 77
Kingston Mill SK3: Stoc 7F 213 (3B 52)
Kingston Pl. SK8: Chea H 3G 77
Kingston Rd. M20: Manc 3D 50
SK9: Hand 2K 97
Kingston St. SK3: Stoc 7F 213 (3B 52)
King St. CH1: Ches 3B 212 (1K 149)
CH42: R Fer 4F 61
CH44: Wall 6K 13
CH65: Ell P 2E 134
CW8: H'ord 1A 162
CW9: Lac D, Rud, What 6K 157
CW10: Byl 1C 180
CW11: Elw 1C 200
CW12: Cong 2H 183
M32: S'ord 2J 23
M34: Aude 4E 8
M34: Den 7E 8
M43: Droy 2A 8
(not continuous)
OL5: Moss 1E 4
SK7: Woodf 5E 98
SK10: Mac 4B 126
SK14: B'tom 3H 29
SK14: H'rth 2J 11
SK14: Hyde 7J 9
SK15: Stal 7B 4
SK16: Duk 1G 9
WA7: Run 3G 89
WA12: New W 1E 14
WA16: Knut 3E 116
King St. E. SK1: Stoc 5J 213 (2D 52)
King St. Trad. Est. CW10: Mid 2D 180
King St. W. SK3: Stoc 6G 213 (3C 52)
Kings Vw. SK4: Stoc 3A 52
Kingsville Rd. CH63: H Beb 1J 85
Kings Wlk. CH42: R Fer 4F 61
CH48: W Kir 3D 56
M43: Droy 2A 8
(off King St.)
KINGSWAY 5G 63
Kingsway CH2: Ches 6C 146
CH45: Wall 5G 13
CH60: Hes 1F 105
CH63: H Beb 6C 60
CW2: Crewe 3B 194
CW7: Wins 3G 179
CW9: N'ich 5G 157
L3: Liv 1H 35
M19: Manc 6B 24
M20: Manc 4E 50
M32: S'ord 2H 23
SK6: Bred 1J 53
SK7: Bram 3D 78
SK8: Chea, He Grn 3F 77
SK8: Gat 6E 50
SK10: Boll 4B 122
SK16: Duk 3K 9
WA6: Frod 7H 111
WA8: Wid 6G 63
WA12: New W 1F 15
WA14: Alt 1J 213 (7H 47)
Kingsway Av. M19: Manc 2C 24
Kingsway Bldgs. M19: Manc 6B 24
Kingsway Ct. L3: Liv 1J 35
Kingsway Cres. M19: Manc 6B 24
Kingsway Ho. WA4: Westy 1K 67
(off Kingsway Sth.)
WA8: Wid 6G 63
Kingsway Leisure Cen. 5G 63
Kingsway Nth. WA1: Warr 6J 41
Kingsway Pk. L3: Liv 1J 35
Kingsway Sth. SK8: Chea H 6G 77
WA4: Westy 7J 41
Kingsway Tunnel App. CH44: Wall 1H 33
Kingsway W. CH2: Ches 6B 146
Kings Wharf CH41: Birk 3E 34
KINGSWOOD 2J 39
Kingswood Av. CH1: Sau 1D 144
CW2: West 4H 199
Kingswood Blvd. CH63: H Beb 5D 60
Kingswood Ct. SK9: Wilm 7J 97
(off Grove Av.)
Kingswood Cres. CW10: Mid 7E 180
Kingswood Gro. SK5: Stoc 2J 25
Kingswood La. CH1: Blac, Sau 1D 144
Kingswood Rd. CH44: Wall 6J 13
M14: Manc 3A 24
WA5: W'ook 2J 39
Kings Wood Wlk. CW6: Kel 3C 172
Kington Rd. CH48: W Kir 2B 56
Kinloch Cl. CW1: Crewe 7G 191
Kinloss Rd. CH49: Gre 2K 57
Kinmel Av. SK5: Stoc 7B 26
Kinmel Cl. CH41: Birk 5C 34
Kinmel Wlk. M23: Wyth 6F 49
Kinnaird Cres. SK1: Stoc 4F 53
Kinnaird Rd. CH45: Wall 5G 13
Kinnerley Rd. CH65: Whit 5C 134
Kinnerton Cl. CH4: Salt 6E 148
CH46: More 4J 31
Kinnerton Rd. CH4: Dod, Lwr K 1A 184
Kinnington Way CH1: Bac 2B 140
Kinnock Pk. WA5: B'ood 5B 14
Kinross Av. SK2: Stoc 2E 78
Kinross Cl. WA2: Fear 7E 16
Kinross Rd. CH45: Wall 5D 12
Kinsale Dr. WA3: Birc 7H 17
Kinsale Wlk. M23: Wyth 2F 75
Kinsey Av. M23: Wyth 5F 49
KINSEY HEATH 7D 210 (3A 220)
Kinsey Rd. CH65: Ell P 7F 135
Kinsey's La. CH2: Ince 2D 136
Kinsey St. CW12: Cong 4G 183
Kintore Av. SK7: H Gro 2K 79
Kintore Cl. CH63: East 3H 107
CW7: Wins 2H 179
Kintore Dr. WA5: Gt San 6F 39
Kintyre Cl. CH65: Ell P 7E 134
Kipling Av. CH42: R Fer 4E 60
M34: Den 4F 27
WA2: Warr 3G 41
Kipling Cl. SK2: Stoc 5K 53
Kipling Cres. WA8: Wid 5F 63
Kipling Gro. WA9: Sut M 1G 37
Kipling Rd. CH1: Blac 5G 145
Kipling Way CW1: Crewe 2F 195
Kirby Cl. CH2: Ches 5A 146
CH48: W Kir 4D 56
Kirby Mt. CH48: W Kir 5D 56
Kirby Pk. CH48: W Kir 4D 56
Kirby Pk. Mans. CH48: W Kir 4C 56
Kirkacre Av. WA12: New W 3F 15
KIRKBY 1C 215
Kirkby Av. M33: Sale 2C 48
Kirkby Dr. M33: Sale 2D 48
KIRKBY INDUSTRIAL ESTATE 1C 215
Kirkby Rd. WA3: Cul 7F 7
Kirkcaldy Av. WA5: Gt San 6F 39
Kirk Cotts. CH45: Wall 4H 13
KIRKDALE 1B 214
Kirket Cl. CH63: Beb 2A 86
Kirket La. CH63: Beb 2K 85
Kirkfell Dr. SK6: H Lan 5E 80
Kirkfield Gro. CH42: R Fer 4F 61
Kirkham Cl. M34: Den 7E 8
WA5: Gt San 1K 65
Kirkham Rd. SK8: He Grn 4E 76
WA8: Wid 3J 63
Kirkland Av. CH42: Tran 3C 60
Kirkland Rd. CH45: N Bri 3J 13
Kirklands M33: Sale 2A 48
Kirklands, The CH48: W Kir 4D 56
Kirkley St. SK14: Hyde 2J 27
Kirkman Fold L35: R'ill 1B 36
Kirkmount CH49: Upt 7D 32
Kirk Rd. M19: Manc 4E 24
Kirkstall Cl. SK10: Mac 2J 125
SK12: Poy 2B 100
Kirkstall Rd. M41: Urm 1D 22
Kirkstead Rd. SK8: Chea H 6A 78
Kirkstone Av. WA2: Warr 2G 41
Kirkstone Ct. CW12: Cong 5C 182
Kirkstone Cres. WA7: Beec 3C 112
Kirkstone Rd. SK14: Hyde 5H 9
Kirkwall Dr. WA5: Penk 2J 65
Kirkway CH45: Wall 4H 13
CH49: Gre 1B 58
CH49: Upt 7C 32
CH63: H Beb 6C 60
Kirkwood Cl. CH3: Ches 1D 150
Kiskhill La. SK10: R'ow 5H 123
Kitchener Av. M44: Cad 7K 19
Kitchen St. CH1: Ches 5A 212 (2J 149)
L1: Liv 5J 35
Kitfield Av. CW10: Mid 5C 180
Kittiwake Cl. SK2: Stoc 7K 53
KITT'S MOSS 7B 78
Kitt's Moss La. SK7: Bram 7B 78
Kitty Wheeldon Gdns. M33: Sale 6F 23
(off Ashton La.)
Knap, The CH60: Hes 1D 104
Knaresborough Cl. SK5: Stoc 2H 25
Knaresborough Rd. CH44: Wall 7F 13
Knebworth Ct. CW12: Cong 6K 183
KNENHALL 3D 221
Knight Rd. WA5: B'ood 5C 14
Knightsbridge SK1: Stoc 4J 213 (2D 52)
Knightsbridge Av. CW9: N'ich 3D 162
WA4: Grap 2C 68
Knightsbridge Cl. SK9: Wilm 5A 98
WA8: Wid 1K 63
Knightsbridge Ct.
CH1: Ches 5E 212 (2B 150)
CH43: Noc 2G 59
WA1: Warr 7E 40
(off Palmyra Sq. Nth.)
Knight's Cl. SK11: Mac 5B 126
Knights Grange Outdoor Complex 1C 178
Knights La. CW6: Utk 1D 176
Knights Mdw. CW7: Wins 1D 178
Knight St. L1: Liv 4K 35
M20: Manc 2D 50
OL7: Ash L 1E 8
SK11: Mac 5B 126
SK14: Hyde 2A 28
Knights Way CW2: Shav 4B 198
Knivton St. SK14: Hyde 7A 10
Knob Hall Gdns. M23: Wyth 2F 75
Knole Av. SK12: Poy 2E 100
Knoll, The CH43: Oxt 2K 59
OL5: Moss 1C 4
WA7: Pal F 7B 90
WA14: Alt 7F 47
KNOLLS GREEN 3C 217
KNOLTON 3B 218
Knott Fold SK14: Hyde 3J 27
Knott Hill Local Nature Reserve 2A 4
Knottingley Dr. CH66: Gt Sut 3J 133
Knott La. SK14: Hyde 3J 27
Knott's Ho's. WN7: Leigh 1C 6
KNOTTY ASH 1C 215
Knowe, The CH64: W'ston 7F 107
Knowe Av. M22: Wyth 4K 75
Knowl, The CH3: Chu 2C 186
Knowl Cl. M34: Den 1A 26
Knowle Cl. CH66: Gt Sut 5A 134
Knowle Grn. SK9: Hand 3K 97
Knowle Pk. SK9: Hand 3K 97
Knowle Rd. SK6: Mel 6J 55
Knowles St. CH41: Birk 5B 34
WA8: Wid 3J 63
Knowle Way SK14: Mot 1G 29
(off Chain Bar La.)
Knowl La. CH3: Chu 2B 186
Knowl St. SK15: Stal 7C 4
KNOWSLEY 1C 215
Knowsley Cl. CH42: R Fer 4F 61
Knowsley Ct. CH2: Ches 6C 146
CH42: R Fer 4F 61
Knowsley Cres. SK1: Stoc 4F 53
Knowsley Dr. WN7: Leigh 1D 6
Knowsley La. ST7: Chu L 4J 205
Knowsley Rd. CH2: Ches 6C 146
CH42: R Fer 4F 61
CH45: Wall 5G 13
L35: R'ill 2D 36
SK1: Stoc 4F 53
SK7: H Gro 5K 79
SK11: Mac 7K 125
Knowsley Ter. SK1: Stoc 4F 53
(off Knowsley Rd.)
Knox Cl. CH62: P Sun 7G 61
Knox St. CH41: Birk 6E 34
KNUTSFORD 3E 116 (3B 216)
Knutsford Av. M33: Sale 7K 23
SK4: Stoc 4G 25
Knutsford Bus. Pk. WA16: Knut 1H 117
Knutsford Dr. WA16: Knut, Mere 2E 116
Knutsford Grn. CH46: More 3C 32
Knutsford Heath Nature Reserve 3D 116
Knutsford Heritage Cen. 3E 116
(off King St.)
Knutsford Leisure Cen. 4D 116
Knutsford Moor Nature Reserve 2E 116
Knutsford Old Rd. ST7: Chu L 4G 203
WA4: Grap 3A 68
Knutsford Rd. CH46: More 3B 32
CW4: Cran, H Cha 7D 164 & 1F 181
CW9: Ant, Ast B, Bud H 5A 94
SK9: Ald E, Wilm 4D 118
SK11: Chel 5B 166
ST7: Chu L, Rod H 4G 203
WA4: Grap 3A 68
WA4: Warr 1F 67
WA16: Mob 2H 117
(Longridge)
WA16: Mob 5A 118
(Paddock Hill)
KNUTSFORD SERVICE AREA 4A 116
Knutsford Sports Club 2D 116
Knutsford Station (Rail) 4E 116
Knutsford Vw. WA15: H'rns 5C 74
Knutsford Wlk. SK11: Mac 5B 126
(off Bank St.)
Knutsford Way CH1: Ches 1G 149
KNYPERSLEY 2C 221
Knypersley Av. SK2: Stoc 5G 53
Kronsbec Av. CH66: L Sut 2K 133
Kyle Ct. SK7: H Gro 4K 79
Kylemore Cl. CH61: Pens 3G 83
Kylemore Dr. CH61: Pens 3G 83
Kylemore Rd. CH43: Oxt 1K 59
Kylemore Way CH61: Pens 3G 83
Kyle Rd. SK7: H Gro 4K 79
Kynaston Dr. CH4: Salt F 4D 148
Kynder St. M34: Den 7E 8

L

LA Bowl
Warrington 1E 40
Laburnum Av. CW2: Crewe 4K 193
CW5: Nant 2D 196
(off Crewe Rd.)
M34: Aude 1B 8
SK14: Hyde 3J 27
SK15: Stal 2A 10
SK16: Duk 2A 10
WA1: Wool 5C 42
Laburnum Cl. CW12: Cong 2B 182
WA15: Timp 7B 48
Laburnum Ct. WA13: Lymm 1D 70
Laburnum Cres. CW8: Barnt 2A 156
Laburnum Farm Cl.
CH64: Ness 3E 130
Laburnum Gro. CH4: Salt 5F 149
CH61: Irby 7A 58
CH66: Whit 1C 140
CW1: Crewe 7J 191
CW8: Weav 5G 155
WA7: Run 6H 89
Laburnum La. WA5: Gt San 6E 38
WA15: Hale 5J 73
Laburnum Rd. CH43: Oxt 1B 60
CH45: N Bri 4H 13
CW9: Dave 3E 162
CW9: Rud 7H 157
M44: Cad 6A 20
SK11: Mac 7B 126
Laburnum Wlk. M33: Sale 6B 22
(off Epping Dr.)
Laburnum Way LL13: Holt 6A 186
SK3: Stoc 4K 51
Lace St. L3: Liv 2J 35
Lacey Av. SK9: Wilm 5J 97
Lacey Cl. SK9: Wilm 5J 97
Lacey Ct. SK9: Wilm 5J 97
WA8: Wid 6H 63
LACEY GREEN 5J 97
Lacey Grn. SK9: Wilm 6J 97
Lacey Gro. SK9: Wilm 5K 97
Lacey St. WA8: Wid 6G 63
LACH DENNIS 6H 159 (3B 216)
LACHE 6G 149 (1B 218)
Lache Hall Cres. CH4: Ches 7G 149
Lache La. CH4: Bald, Ches, Marl 7G 149
Lache Pk. Av. CH4: Ches 5H 149
Lacy Ct. CW12: Cong 4H 183
Lacy Gro. M32: S'ord 2J 23
Lacy St. M32: S'ord 2J 23
SK1: Stoc 7J 213 (4D 52)
Ladies Mile WA16: Knut 3D 116
Ladies Wlk. CH64: Nest 7H 105
CW10: Mid 5B 180
WA2: Winw 5J 15
WA9: Bold 1C 38
Lady Acre Cl. WA13: Lymm 3K 69
LADYBARN 4A 24
Ladybarn Cres. M14: Manc 4A 24
SK7: Bram 7D 78
Ladybarn Ho. M14: Manc 2A 24
Ladybarn La. M14: Manc 3A 24
Ladybarn Mnr. SK7: Bram 5C 78
Ladybarn Rd. M14: Manc 3A 24
Ladybower SK8: Chea H 1A 78
Ladybower Cl. CH49: Upt 6B 32
Ladybridge Ri. SK8: Chea H 2A 78
Ladybridge Rd. SK8: Chea H 3K 77
Ladybrook Av. WA15: Timp 5B 48
Ladybrook Ct. SK8: Chea H 2K 77
(off Ladybridge Rd.)
Ladybrook Gro. SK9: Wilm 4A 98
Ladybrook Rd. SK7: Bram 4A 78
Lady Chapel Cl. L1: Liv 5K 35
Lady Chapel Sq. L1: Liv 5K 35
(off Lady Chapel Cl.)
Ladycroft Cl. WA1: Wool 5E 42
Ladyewood Rd. CH44: Wall 1B 34
Ladyfield CH43: Bid 5F 33
Ladyfield St. SK9: Wilm 7J 97
Ladyfield Ter. SK9: Wilm 7J 97
LADY GREEN 1B 214
Lady Helen Wlk. CW5: Nant 1C 196
Lady Kelvin Rd. WA14: Alt 6G 47
Lady La. WA3: Croft 2H 17
WA16: Mob 4D 102
Lady Lever Art Gallery 7G 61
Ladypool L24: Hale 7A 88
Lady Richeld Cl. WA7: Nort 3F 91
Ladys Cl. SK12: Poy 2D 100
Lady's Incline SK12: Poy 2D 100
Ladysmith, The OL6: Ash L 4A 4
Ladysmith Dr. OL6: Ash L 4A 4
Ladysmith Rd. M20: Manc 1E 50
OL6: Ash L 4A 4
SK15: Stal 5B 4
Ladysmith St. SK3: Stoc 5C 52
Ladythorn Av. SK6: Mar 7G 55
Ladythorn Cres. SK7: Bram 7D 78
Ladythorn Gro. SK7: Bram 7D 78
Ladythorn Rd. SK7: Bram 6C 78
Ladywell Cl. SK7: H Gro 3E 78
Ladywood Rd. WA5: Old H 3A 40

LA Fitness—Lawnswood Gro.

LA Fitness
Northwich 4F 157
Sale, Washway Rd. 6F 23
Sale, Whitehall Rd. 2B 48
Lagan Ho. CH46: Leas 1B 32
Lagan Wlk. M22: Wyth 3A 76
Lagos Gro. CW7: Wins 2F 179
Laidon Av. CW2: Wis 6A 194
Lainton Ct. SK3: Stoc 4A 52
Laira Ct. WA2: Warr 5G 41
Laira St. WA2: Warr 5G 41
Laird Cl. CH41: Birk 4J 33
Lairdside Technical Pk.
CH41: Tran 1E 60
Lairds Pl. L3: Liv 1J 35
Laird St. CH41: Birk 4J 33
Laithwaite Cl. WA9: Sut M 1H 37
Lake Ent. Pk. CH62: Brom 4E 86
Lake Ho. Cl. CW8: Weav 4G 155
Lakeland Cl. L1: Liv 4J 35
Lakelands Cl. SK10: Mac 4C 126
Lake La. WA4: H Whi 2E 114
Lakemoor Country Pk. 7B 200
Lake Pl. CH47: Hoy 5C 30
Lake Rd. CH47: Hoy 5C 30
M34: Den 6E 8
SK15: Stal 5A 4
Lakeside CH4: Ches 2G 185
(not continuous)
SK8: Chea 2E 76
Lakeside Bldg. SK8: Chea 2E 76
Lakeside Cvn. Pk. CW7: Wins 5G 179
Lakeside Cl. CH2: Upt 3C 146
WA8: Wid 6A 62
Lakeside Ct. CH45: N Bri 3J 13
Lakeside Dr. SK12: Poy 1D 100
WA1: Warr 2E 66
Lakeside Grn. SK2: Stoc 6G 53
Lakeside Rd. WA13: Lymm 4K 69
Lakeside Vw. CW5: Nant 4C 196
CW9: Moult 7E 162
Lakes Rd. SK6: Mar, Mar B 6G 55
SK16: Duk 2H 9
Lake St. SK2: Stoc 7F 53
Lakes Vw. SK15: Stal 5A 4
Lakeswood SK16: Duk 2G 9
Lake Vw. CW12: Cong 4D 182
ST7: Als 7D 202
Lakewood CH4: Ches 2G 185
Laleham Grn. SK7: Bram 2B 78
Laleston Cl. WA8: Wid 5E 62
Lamaload Rd. SK10: R'ow 7G 123
Lamb Cott. Cvn. Pk. CW8: W'ate 7F 161
Lambert Cres. CW5: Nant 1A 196
Lambert Dr. M33: Sale 5C 22
Lamberton Dr. M23: Wyth 6E 48
Lambert's La. CW12: Cong 5D 182
Lambert St. L3: Liv 2K 35
OL7: Ash L 1E 8
Lambert Way CW8: H'ord 2K 161
L3: Liv 2K 35
Lambeth Gro. SK6: W'ley 6F 27
Lambeth Rd. SK5: Stoc 4J 25
Lambourn Av. WA8: Cron 7C 36
Lambourn Cl. SK12: Poy 2C 100
Lambourn Dr. CW1: L'ton 4G 191
Lambourne Cl. CH66: Gt Sut 1B 140
M22: Wyth 5K 75
Lambourne Gro. CW10: Mid 3B 180
Lambs Fold SK4: Stoc 6G 25
Lambsickle Cl. WA7: West 1F 111
Lambsickle La. WA7: Run, West 1F 111
Lambs La. WA1: Padd 5A 42
WA1: Padd, Padg 4A 42
Lamb Wlk. *M34: Den 4F 27*
(off Wordsworth Rd.)
Lamerton Cl. WA5: Penk 1F 65
Lamerton Way SK9: Wilm 4B 98
Lampeter Cl. WA5: Call 2C 40
Lampits La. CH3: Gt Bar 2B 170
Lamport Cl. WA8: Wid 2A 64
Lamport St. L8: Liv 6K 35
Lampton Cl. WA14: Alt 5H 47
Lamsholme Cl. M19: Manc 1D 24
Lanark Av. M22: N'den 4K 49
Lanark Cl. SK7: H Gro 3A 80
Lanark Gdns. WA8: Wid 2E 62
Lanark Wlk. SK10: Mac 2G 125
LANCASHIRE HILL 1C 52
Lancashire Hill SK4: Stoc 4J 213 (1C 52)
SK5: Stoc 4J 213 (1C 52)
Lancashire Rd. M31: Part 2G 45
Lancaster Av. CH45: Wall 6H 13
SK15: Stal 6B 4
WA7: Run 6E 88
WA8: Wid 3A 62
Lancaster Cl. CH62: P Sun 7G 61
CW7: Wins 6E 178
SK6: Rom 3A 54
SK7: H Gro 5H 79
WA2: Padg 2K 41
Lancaster Ct. M19: Manc 3C 24
WA4: Stoc H 4J 67
(off Lime Tree Av.)
Lancaster Dr. CH3: Ches 1E 150
Lancaster Flds. CW1: Crewe 4F 195
Lancaster Gdns. CH65: Ell P 5F 135
Lancaster Ho. *SK3: Stoc 4C 52*
(off York St.)
Lancaster Rd. M20: Manc 1C 50
M34: Den 2E 26
M44: Cad 6K 19
Lancaster Rd. SK9: Wilm 5B 98
WA8: Wid 2G 63
Lancaster St. SK1: Stoc 2E 52
WA5: Warr 7C 40
Lanceley Ct. SY14: Mal 3H 207
Lancelot Rd. M22: Wyth 3B 76
Lancelots Hey *L3: Liv 2G 35*
(off Union St.)
Lancelyn Ct. CH63: Spit 3A 86
Lancelyn Dr. SK9: Wilm 6A 98
Lancelyn Pct. *CH63: Spit 3A 86*
(off Spital Rd.)
Lancelyn Ter. CH63: Beb 2K 85
Lancer Ct. WA7: Astm 3A 90
Lancers Cft. CH66: Gt Sut 7A 134
Lancing Av. M20: Manc 1F 51
WA2: Warr 7K 15
Lancing Rd. CH65: Ell P 4F 135
Landcross Rd. M14: Manc 2A 24
Landcut La. WA3: Birc 1D 42
Lander Cl. WA5: Old H 5B 40
LAND GATE 1D 215
LANDICAN 5F 59
Landican Cemetery & Crematorium
CH49: Woodc 4E 58
Landican La. CH49: Woodc 5F 59
CH63: Store 7H 59
Landican Rd. CH49: Woodc 6E 58
Landkey Cl. M23: Wyth 2F 49
Land La. SK9: Wilm 1H 119
(not continuous)
Landmark Ho. SK8: Chea H 3K 77
L & M Bus. Pk. WA14: Alt 6G 47
Landscape Dene WA6: Hel 4D 138
Landsdowne Ho. CH41: Birk 6E 34
Landseer Av. CH64: L Nes 1D 130
WA4: Warr 4F 67
Landseer Dr. SK6: Mar B 5H 55
SK10: Mac 4F 125
LAND SIDE 1F 7
Landside WN7: Leigh 1F 7
Landswood Pk. CW8: H'ord 2A 162
Lane End Rd. M19: Manc 7A 24
LANE ENDS
CW1 2J 191
SK6, Marple Bridge 3J 55
SK6, Romiley 1D 54
SK12 3H 103
Lane Ends SK6: Rom 1D 54
Lanegate SK14: Hyde 3J 27
LANE HEAD 1A 216
Laneside Dr. SK7: Bram 4E 78
Laneside Rd. M20: Manc 4E 50
Langcliffe Cl. WA3: Cul 7E 6
Langdale Av. CH61: Pens 2H 83
M19: Manc 3E 24
WA13: Lymm 1B 70
Langdale Cl. CW7: Wins 2E 178
M34: Den 2D 26
SK6: H Lan 5E 80
SK8: Gat 2E 76
SK11: Mac 7G 125
WA2: Warr 1J 41
WA8: Wid 5C 62
WA15: Timp 7J 47
Langdale Ct. CW12: Cong 5C 182
Langdale Rd. CH45: Wall 4F 13
CH63: Beb 2J 85
CW2: Crewe 4H 193
M31: Part 1G 45
M32: S'ord 1H 23
M33: Sale 3J 47
SK4: Stoc 5F 25
SK6: W'ley 6G 27
SK7: Bram 1F 99
WA7: Run 5H 89
Langdale Ter. *SK15: Stal 5B 4*
(off Springs La.)
Langdale Way WA6: Frod 6J 111
Langden Cl. WA3: Cul 6D 6
Langdon Ho. *CH4: Ches 4J 149*
(off Hough Grn.)
Langfield Cres. M43: Droy 1B 8
Langfield Gro. CH62: Brom 2J 107
Langford L24: Hale 6A 88
Langford Ct. CH3: Tar 6C 170
Langford Dr. M44: Irlam 2D 20
Langford Rd. CW9: Los Gra 4C 158
SK4: Stoc 7F 25
Langford St. M34: Den 7E 8
SK11: Mac 4K 125
Langford Way WA4: App T 2D 94
Langham Ct. M20: Manc 1B 50
Langham Gro. WA15: Timp 4B 48
Langham Rd. SK4: Stoc 3K 51
WA14: Bow 3F 73
Langland Cl. M19: Manc 2G 25
WA5: Call 2C 40
Lang La. CH48: W Kir 2C 56
Lang La. Sth. CH48: W Kir 2D 56
LANGLEY 1H 169 (3D 217)
Langley Av. SK7: H Gro 4F 79
WA12: New W 2F 15
Langley Beck WA8: Wid 1J 63
Langley Cl. CH63: Spit 4A 86
CW11: S'ach 1G 201
M41: Urm 1D 22
Langley Ct. CH65: Ell P 5G 135
Langley Dr. CW2: Crewe 4A 194
SK9: Hand 3B 98
SK11: Mac 1F 129
Langley Hall SK11: Lang 1G 169
Langley Hall Cl. SK11: Lang 1G 169
Langley Hall Cotts. SK11: Lang 1G 169
Langley Rd. CH63: Spit 4A 86
CW9: N'ich 7F 157
M14: Manc 2A 24
M33: Sale 1J 47
SK11: Lang 2F 169
Langley St. L8: Liv 6K 35
Langport Dr. CH3: Ches 1F 151
Langsdale St. L3: Liv 1K 35
(not continuous)
Langstone Av. CH49: Gre 2K 57
Langston Grn. SK7: H Gro 4E 78
Langthorne St. M19: Manc 3E 24
Langton Cl. WA8: Wid 2B 62
Langton Grn. WA1: Wool 5D 42
Langwell Cl. WA3: Birc 6B 18
Lanreath Cl. SK10: Mac 3E 124
Lansdale Gdns. M19: Manc 6B 24
Lansdown Cl. SK8: Chea H 6A 78
Lansdowne WA3: Cul 1K 17
WA6: Frod 2K 139
Lansdowne Av. M34: Aude 1B 8
SK6: Rom 2D 54
Lansdowne Cl. CH41: Birk 4K 33
Lansdowne Ct. CH43: Bid 4J 33
Lansdowne Gro. CH4: Ches 4H 149
Lansdowne Ho. *M20: Manc 2D 50*
(off Wilmslow Rd.)
Lansdowne Pl. CH43: Bid 4J 33
Lansdowne Rd. CH41: Birk 4J 33
CH43: Bid 4J 33
CH45: Wall 3F 13
CW1: Crewe 1F 195
M33: Sale 5F 23
M41: Urm 3H 21
WA14: Alt 6H 47
Lansdowne Rd. Nth.
M41: Urm 2H 21
Lansdowne St. SK10: Mac 3B 126
Lanyard Way CW11: Mal B 6G 201
Lanyork Rd. L3: Liv 1G 35
Lapwing Cen. 5B 26
Lapwing Cl. CW7: Wins 7D 178
SK15: Stal 5B 4
Lapwing Gro. WA7: Pal F 1C 112
Lapwing La. M34: Ash L 1C 8
SK5: Stoc 4A 26
SK11: L Wit 1A 168
WA4: Moo 6H 65
Lapwing Ri. CH60: Hes 1C 104
Lapworth Cl. CH46: More 4J 31
Larch Av. CW2: Bas 2F 199
M32: S'ord 2J 23
SK8: Chea H 4J 77
SK11: Mac 7H 125
WA5: Penk 7G 39
WA8: Wid 3H 63
WA12: New W 1F 15
Larch Cl. CW8: Weav 6G 155
M23: Wyth 4C 48
SK6: Mar 7E 54
SK12: Poy 3E 100
WA7: Run 7J 89
Larchdale Cl. CH66: Whit 1B 140
Larches, The OL5: Moss 1F 5
Larchfields CH1: Sau 2B 144
Larch Gro. CH43: Bid 4H 33
Larchlea WA15: Alt 1K 73
Larch Ri. SK10: Pres 5E 120
Larch Rd. CH42: Tran 7B 34
CW2: Crewe 4J 193
M31: Part 1G 45
M34: Den 7F 9
WA7: Run 7J 89
Larch Tree Cl. CW8: Barnt 1A 156
Larch Way CH4: Salt 5F 149
Larchway SK6: H Lan 6F 81
SK7: Bram 6A 78
Larchways WA4: App 1H 93
Larchwood SK8: Chea 6F 51
Larchwood Cl. CH61: Pens 3H 83
M33: Sale 7B 22
Larchwood Dr. CH63: H Beb 6E 60
SK9: Wilm 6B 98
Larcombe Av. CH49: Upt 7C 32
LARDEN GREEN 2D 219
Largs Wlk. M23: Wyth 6F 49
Larke Ri. M20: Manc 1B 50
Larkfield Av. WA1: Padd 5A 42
Lark Hall Cl. SK10: Mac 5D 126
Lark Hall Cres. SK10: Mac 5D 126
Larkhall Ri. M22: Shar 7A 50
Lark Hall Rd. SK10: Mac 5D 126
Lark Hall Yd. SK10: Mac 5D 126
Lark Hill SK3: Stoc 4A 52
Larkhill SK15: Stal 4B 4
Larkhill Av. CH49: Upt 5D 32
Larkhill Cl. WA15: Timp 6B 48
Lark Hill Rd. SK3: Stoc 4A 52
Larkhill Rd. SK8: Chea H 7A 52
Larkhill Way CH49: Upt 5D 32
Larkin Cl. CH62: N Fer 6F 61
Larkspur Cl. CH4: Ches 7G 149
CW5: Nant 6C 192
WA7: Beec 3B 112
Larkspur Gro. WA5: Warr 2B 66
Larkstoke Cl. WA4: App 7J 67
Larksway CH60: Hes 6K 83
Larkswood Dr. SK2: Stoc 7K 53
Larkwood Cl. SK15: Carrb 2F 5
Larkwood Way SK10: Boll 6B 122
Larne Av. M32: S'ord 1H 23
SK3: Stoc 5K 51
Larne Ct. WA8: Wid 3E 62
Larton Farm Cl. CH48: W Kir 3F 57
Larton Rd. CH48: W Kir 2F 57
Lartonwood CH48: W Kir 2F 57
Larwood Av. SK4: Stoc 3K 51
Laser Quest
Chester 5C 212
Warrington 6F 41
Laskey La. WA4: Thel 1F 69
Lassell Fold SK14: Hyde 4C 10
LATCHFORD 2H 67
Latchford High Level Bri.
WA4: Warr 3J 67
Latchford Rd. CH60: Hes 1E 104
Latchford St. WA4: Westy 2A 68
Latchmere Rd. M14: Manc 3A 24
LATELY COMMON 1J 7
Latham Av. WA6: Hel 7B 138
WA7: Run 5H 89
Latham Cl. SK6: Bred 6E 26
Latham Rd. CW11: S'ach 4E 200
Latham St. CW7: Wins 3D 178
Latham Way CH63: Spit 4B 86
Lathom Av. CH44: Wall 7H 13
WA2: Warr 4F 41
Lathom Gro. M33: Sale 1E 48
Lathom Rd. M20: Manc 4A 24
M44: Irlam 3C 20
Lathom Way SK10: Mac 2C 126
Latimer Cl. WA8: Wid 1J 63
Latimer Dr. CW2: Crewe 2A 194
Launceston Cl. CW7: Wins 5C 178
SK7: Bram 6D 78
WA7: B'vale 1E 112
Launceston Dr. WA5: Penk 2G 65
Laund, The CH45: Wall 6F 13
Laura St. CW2: Crewe 5D 194
Laureate Way M34: Den 4F 27
Laurel Av. CH60: Hes 5H 83
CH63: H Beb 2J 85
SK8: Chea 7F 51
WA1: Wool 5D 42
WA12: New W 1G 15
Laurel Bank CW7: Wins 4E 178
SK14: Hyde 3H 27
SK15: Stal 2C 10
WA4: Grap 4C 68
WA8: Wid 2G 63
Laurelbanks CH60: Hes 5G 83
Laurel Cl. CW8: Barnt 1K 155
CW10: Mid 2B 180
CW11: S'ach 4G 201
Laurel Ct. SK4: Stoc 7E 24
Laurel Dr. CH64: W'ston 6G 107
CH65: Whit 6D 134
CW2: Crewe 4K 193
WA15: Timp 1B 74
Laurel End La. SK4: Stoc 1J 51
Laurel Farm Ct. CH2: Elt 4F 137
Laurel Grn. M34: Den 1F 27
Laurel Gro. CH2: Ches 7D 146
Laurel Ho. SK4: Stoc 7E 24
Laurelhurst Av. CH61: Pens 2J 83
Laurel Pk. CW6: Dud 5B 174
Laurel Rd. CH42: Tran 1C 60
SK4: Stoc 7E 24
Laurels, The CH46: Leas 1B 32
OL5: Moss 1E 4
SK6: H Lan 5F 81
Laurel St. SK4: Stoc 5G 213 (2C 52)
Laurel Wlk. M31: Part 2G 45
Laurel Way SK7: Bram 5A 78
Laurelwood Dr. CH66: Gt Sut 1A 140
Laurence Deacon Ct. CH41: Birk 5C 34
Laureston Av. CW1: Crewe 2F 195
Laurieston Ct. SK8: Chea 7E 50
Lauriston Cl. M22: Shar 6A 50
Lauriston Gallery, The *6G 23*
(within Waterside Arts Cen.)
Lausanne Rd. SK7: Bram 2C 78
Lavender Cl. M23: Wyth 3E 48
M33: Sale 6B 22
WA7: Run 5J 89
Lavender Dr. CW9: Rud 7K 157
Lavender Gdns. WA5: Warr 1C 66
Lavenders Brow SK1: Stoc 6K 213 (3D 52)
Lavender Wlk. M31: Part 2G 45
Lavenham Cl. SK7: H Gro 4J 79
SK10: Mac 2K 125
Lavington Av. SK8: Chea 6J 51
LAVISTER 7A 184 (2B 218)
Lavister Av. M19: Manc 1F 51
Lavister Cl. CW9: N'ich 2E 162
Lavrock Bank L8: Liv 1K 61
Lawfield Ct. SK7: Bram 3B 78
Lawford Cl. CW1: Crewe 5E 190
Lawford Dr. CH60: Hes 6A 84
Lawn Av. WA1: Padg 4K 41
Lawn Dr. CH2: Upt 3A 146
WA15: Timp 6J 47
Lawnfold SK13: Had 3K 11
Lawnhurst Av. M23: Wyth 4F 49
Lawnhurst Trad. Est. SK3: Stoc 7K 51
Lawns, The CH43: Bid 5G 33
SK9: Wilm 3D 118
WA14: Bow 2G 73
Lawns Av. CH63: Rab M 1G 107
Lawnsdale CW8: Cudd 1A 160
Lawnside Cl. CH42: R Fer 4E 60
Lawnswood Gro. CH2: Elt 5F 137

Lawrence Av.—Lilybrook Dr.

Lawrence Av. CW9: Moult ... 6D **162**
CW10: Mid ... 3C **180**
Lawrence Av. E. CW10: Mid ... 3C **180**
Lawrence Cl. CW4: Cran ... 2G **181**
CW11: Elw ... 3B **200**
Lawrence Ct. CH42: R Fer ... 5F **61**
Lawrence Pl. SK12: Poy ... 4C **100**
Lawrence Rd. M41: Urm ... 1H **21**
SK7: H Gro ... 2J **79**
WA14: Alt ... 6G **47**
Lawrence St. CW1: Crewe ... 2C **194**
SK1: Stoc ... 7H **213** (3C **52**)
Laws Gdns. CH3: Gt Bou ... 3D **150**
Lawson Av. SK8: Gat ... 7D **50**
Lawson Cl. WA1: Wool ... 5E **42**
Lawson Dr. WA15: Timp ... 6A **48**
Lawson Gro. M33: Sale ... 5F **23**
Lawson Wlk. M34: Den ... 3E **26**
Law St. CH2: Ches ... 7C **146**
Lawton Av. SK7: Bram ... 5C **78**
Lawton Cl. SK6: Rom ... 3K **53**
WA3: Cul ... 7E **6**
Lawton Coppice ST7: Chu L ... 3H **205**
LAWTON-GATE ... 4H **203**
Lawtongate Est. ST7: Chu L ... 4H **203**
Lawton Hall Dr. ST7: Chu L ... 5K **203**
LAWTON HEATH ... 3F **203**
LAWTON HEATH END ... 3D **202**
Lawton Heath Rd. ST7: Chu L ... 3F **203**
Lawton Moor Rd. M23: Wyth ... 3G **49**
Lawton Rd. L35: R'ill ... 2D **36**
SK4: Stoc ... 7F **25**
ST7: Als, Chu L ... 5E **202**
Lawton St. CW2: Crewe ... 3C **194**
CW12: Cong ... 4G **183**
L1: Liv ... 3K **35**
SK14: Hyde ... 7K 9
(off Hopkins St.)
SK15: Stal ... 1C **10**
Lawton Way CW11: S'ach ... 1C **200**
Laxey Av. WA1: Wool ... 6D **42**
Laxey St. L8: Liv ... 6K **35**
Laxton Cl. CH66: Gt Sut ... 1B **140**
Laxton Way CW10: Mid ... 2C **180**
Laycock Av. SK15: M'ook ... 5F **5**
Laycock Dr. SK16: Duk ... 3B **10**
Laycock Way M34: Den ... 4E **26**
Layland Av. WA3: Cul ... 6E **6**
Layton Av. CH43: Pren ... 3J **59**
SK14: Hyde ... 7H **9**
Layton Cl. SK1: Stoc ... 4E **52**
WA3: Birc ... 1E **42**
Layton Dr. SK6: Rom ... 1C **54**
Lazonby Cl. CH43: Bid ... 4F **33**
Lea Av. CW1: Crewe ... 2F **195**
CW4: Goo ... 6G **165**
Lea Bank Cl. SK11: Mac ... 4H **125**
Leabank St. M19: Manc ... 2D **24**
Leaburn Dr. M19: Manc ... 7B **24**
LEA BY BACKFORD ... 6C **140**
Leach Way CH61: Irby ... 7K **57**
Lea Cl. CH43: Noc ... 1H **59**
CW11: S'ach ... 4G **201**
Lea Ct. SK4: Stoc ... 7E **24**
Leacroft Rd. WA3: Ris ... 5A **18**
Lea Cross Gro. WA8: Wid ... 2C **62**
Leadbeaters Cl. SK11: Mac ... 5C **126**
Leadbeaters Rd. SK11: Mac ... 5C **126**
Leader Williams Rd. M44: Irlam ... 2C **20**
Lea Dr. CW5: Nant ... 3A **196**
Leadsmithy St. CW10: Mid ... 3C **180**
Leadworks La. CH1: Ches ... 3E **212** (1B **150**)
Leaf Gro. CW7: Wins ... 3C **178**
Leafield Av. M20: Manc ... 7A **24**
Leafield Cl. CH61: Irby ... 7C **58**
Leafield Dr. SK8: Chea H ... 7H **77**
Leafield Rd. SK12: Dis ... 1F **103**
Leaf La. CW7: Wins ... 2H **179**
Leaford Av. M34: Den ... 6C **8**
Leaford Cl. M34: Den ... 6C **8**
Leaf St. SK5: Stoc ... 4H **25**
Leafy Way CW8: Weav ... 6G **155**
Leagate M41: Urm ... 2D **22**
Lea Grn. Bus. Pk. WA9: St H ... 1F **37**
Lea Grn. Ind. Est. WA9: St H ... 1G **37**
Lea Grn. Rd. WA9: St H ... 1F **37**
Lea Hall Pk. CH1: Lea B ... 6C **140**
Leahurst Cl. CH2: Ches ... 6C **146**
Leahurst, University of Liverpool Veterinary Field Station ... 7C **106**
Leaks Ter. *WA16: Knut ... 3E 116*
(off Red Cow Yd.)
Lea La. CH3: Ald ... 6J **185**
Leamington Av. WA12: New W ... 2F **15**
Leamington Cl. CH64: Nest ... 2C **130**
WA5: Gt San ... 4J **39**
Leamington Ct. SK5: Stoc ... 4H **25**
Leamington Rd. CW12: Cong ... 3B **182**
SK5: Stoc ... 4H **25**
(not continuous)
SK10: Mac ... 3G **125**
Leander Rd. CH45: Wall ... 6G **13**
Lear Dr. CW2: Wis ... 6K **193**
Lea Rd. CH44: Wall ... 6J **13**
SK4: Stoc ... 7E **24**
SK8: He Grn ... 4D **76**
Leas, The CH45: Wall ... 4E **12**
CH61: Thin ... 7E **58**
WA15: Hale ... 2B **74**
Leas Cl. CH66: Gt Sut ... 3J **133**
Leaside WA7: Run ... 5K **89**
Leaside Dr. M20: Manc ... 6A **24**
Leaside Rd. CH1: Blac ... 4F **145**
Leaside Way SK9: Wilm ... 1H **119**
LEASOWE ... 7B **12** (1A **214**)
Leasowe Av. CH45: Wall ... 5E **12**
Leasowe Gdns. CH46: Leas ... 1B **32**
Leasowe Lighthouse ... 1K **31**
Leasowe Recreation Cen. ... 1D **32**
Leasowe Rd. CH44: Wall ... 7A **12**
CH45: Wall ... 7A **12**
CH46: Leas ... 1A **32**
Leasoweside CH46: Leas ... 7A **12**
Leasowe (Park & Ride) ... 2D **32**
Leasowe Station (Rail) ... 2C **32**
Leas Pk. CH47: Hoy ... 1B **56**
Lea's Pas. CW10: Mid ... 3B **180**
Leatham Cl. WA3: Birc ... 1E **42**
Leather La. *L2: Liv ... 2H 35*
(off Tempest Hey)
Leaton Av. M23: Wyth ... 6G **49**
Lea Way ST7: Als ... 6E **202**
Leaway CH49: Gre ... 1A **58**
Leawood Cl. CW8: H'ord ... 7K **155**
Leawood Gro. CH46: More ... 4C **32**
Ledbury Cl. CH43: Oxt ... 3H **59**
Ledbury Dr. CW2: Wis ... 7A **194**
Ledge Ley SK8: Chea H ... 5G **77**
Ledley St. SK10: Boll ... 4C **122**
LEDSHAM ... 7F **133** (3B **214**)
Ledsham Cl. CH43: Noc ... 1H **59**
WA3: Birc ... 1C **42**
Ledsham Ct. CH66: L Sut ... 2J **133**
Ledsham Hall La.
CH66: Leds ... 3E **132**
Ledsham La. CH66: Leds ... 4E **132**
Ledsham Pk. Dr. CH66: L Sut ... 2G **133**
Ledsham Rd. CH66: L Sut ... 3F **133**
Ledsham Village CH66: Leds ... 7F **133**
Ledson Rd. M23: Wyth ... 7F **49**
Ledston Cl. WA7: Win H ... 5F **91**
Ledward La. WA14: Bow ... 3F **73**
Ledward St. CW7: Wins ... 2H **179**
Ledyard Cl. WA5: Old H ... 5B **40**
Lee Av. WA14: B'ath ... 5F **47**
Leebangs Rd. SK14: B'tom ... 3H **29**
Leece St. L1: Liv ... 4K **35**
Leech Av. OL6: Ash L ... 4A **4**
Leech Brook Av. M34: Aude ... 4D **8**
Leech Brook Cl. M34: Aude ... 4D **8**
Leech Rd. SY14: Mal ... 3H **207**
Leech St. SK14: Hyde ... 7A **10**
SK15: Stal ... 1B **10**
Lee Cl. L35: R'ill ... 3D **36**
M44: Irlam ... 2C **20**
WA16: Knut ... 4D **116**
Lee Ct. M22: N'den ... 4A **50**
WA2: Warr ... 2G **41**
Lee Cres. M32: S'ord ... 1K **23**
Lee Dale Cl. M34: Den ... 1F **27**
Leedale St. M12: Manc ... 1D **24**
Lee Dr. CW8: N'ich ... 7D **156**
Leeds St. L3: Liv ... 1G **35**
Leegate Cl. SK4: Stoc ... 7C **24**
Leegate Gdns. SK4: Stoc ... 7C **24**
Leegate Ho. SK4: Stoc ... 7D **24**
Leegate Rd. SK4: Stoc ... 7C **24**
(not continuous)
LEE HEAD ... 5K **29** (1D **217**)
Lee Head SK13: Char ... 6K **29**
LEEK ... 2D **221**
LEEKBROOK ... 2D **221**
Leek Old Rd. SK11: Sut E ... 5J **129**
Leek Rd. CW12: Cong ... 6H **183**
SK11: Sut E ... 5H **129**
Leen La. CH1: Ches ... 4C **212**
Lee Rd. CH47: Hoy ... 5D **30**
Lees, The WA5: Gt San ... 4J **39**
(not continuous)
Lees Av. CH42: R Fer ... 3E **60**
M34: Den ... 1D **26**
Lee's Ct. SK1: Stoc ... 7J **213** (3D **52**)
Lees Hall Ct. M14: Manc ... 3A **24**
Lees Hall Cres. M14: Manc ... 3A **24**
Leeside SK4: Stoc ... 3J **51**
Lees La. CH64: L Nes, Nest ... 2E **130**
CH65: Ell P ... 4F **135**
SK9: Wilm ... 7E **98**
SK10: Pres ... 7E **98**
Lees Pk. Av. M43: Droy ... 1B **8**
Lees Pk. Way M43: Droy ... 1B **8**
Lees Rd. SK7: Bram ... 1G **99**
Lees St. M43: Droy ... 1A **8**
SK15: Stal ... 7B **4**
Leestone Rd. M22: Shar ... 6A **50**
Lee St. CH1: Ches ... 1B **150**
SK1: Stoc ... 7J **213** (3D **52**)
Leesway Dr. M34: Den ... 1F **27**
LEESWOOD ... 1A **218**
Leeswood Rd. CH49: Woodc ... 2D **58**
Lee Va. Dr. SK13: Char ... 4K **29**
Leewood Ct. SK4: Stoc ... 1K **51**
LEFTWICH ... 1F **163** (3A **216**)
Legh Cl. SK12: Poy ... 2D **100**
Legh Ct. M33: Sale ... 1D **48**
WA16: Knut ... 2H 117
(off Montmorency Rd.)
Legh Dr. M34: Aude ... 1A **8**
SK6: W'ley ... 5G **27**
Legh Gdns. WA16: Knut ... 4F **117**
Legh Ho. WA16: Knut ... 4F **117**
Legh Rd. CH62: N Fer ... 6G **61**
M33: Sale ... 1E **48**
SK10: Adl ... 6G **103**
Legh Rd. SK10: Pres ... 3H **121**
SK12: Dis ... 7G **81**
WA16: Knut ... 4F **117**
Legh St. WA1: Warr ... 7E **40**
WA12: New W ... 1C **14**
(not continuous)
WA13: Lymm ... 2A 70
(off Bridgewater St.)
Legion La. CH62: Brom ... 5D **86**
Legwood Ct. M41: Urm ... 1B **22**
Leibig Ct. WA8: Wid ... 5H **63**
Leicester Av. M34: Den ... 2E **26**
ST7: Als ... 4D **202**
WA15: Timp ... 4A **48**
Leicester Rd. M33: Sale ... 6G **23**
WA15: Hale ... 3J **73**
Leicester St. CW9: N'ich ... 4E **156**
SK5: Stoc ... 1J **25**
WA5: Warr ... 7C **40**
(not continuous)
LEIGH ... 1A **216**
Leigh Av. SK6: Mar ... 7E **54**
WA8: Wid ... 4F **63**
WA16: Knut ... 2G **117**
Leigh Cotts. WA15: Timp ... 1C **74**
LEIGH END ... 2J **7**
Leigh Fold SK14: Hyde ... 5K **9**
Leigh Grn. Cl. WA8: Wid ... 5C **62**
Leigh La. CW8: L Lei ... 1F **155**
Leigh Pl. *L1: Liv ... 3J 35*
(off Leigh St.)
Leigh Rd. CH48: W Kir ... 2C **56**
CW12: Cong ... 1K **183**
SK9: Wilm ... 2C **118**
WA15: Hale ... 3J **73**
Leighs Brow CW8: Barnt ... 2J **155**
Leighstone Ct. CH2: Ches ... 1B **212** (7K **145**)
Leigh St. L1: Liv ... 3J **35**
(not continuous)
SK11: Mac ... 5B **126**
SK14: Hyde ... 1K **27**
LEIGHTON ... 5D **190**
Leighton Av. CH47: Meols ... 4F **31**
Leighton Chase CH64: Nest ... 6G **105**
Leighton Ct. CH64: Nest ... 7G **105**
Leighton Dr. SK6: Mar B ... 4J **55**
WN7: Leigh ... 1B **6**
Leighton Pk. CH64: Nest ... 7G **105**
Leighton Rd. CH41: Tran ... 1D **60**
CH64: Nest ... 4F **105**
Leightons, The CH64: Nest ... 7G **105**
Leighton St. CW1: Crewe ... 1B **194**
Leighton Vw. CW1: Crewe ... 5F **191**
Leigh Way CW8: Weav ... 4F **155**
Leinster Gdns. WA7: Run ... 3F **89**
Leinster St. WA7: Run ... 3F **89**
Leiston Cl. CH61: Irby ... 6B **58**
Leith Av. M33: Sale ... 7K **23**
Leith Rd. M33: Sale ... 7K **23**
Lenham Cl. SK5: Stoc ... 5A **26**
Lenham Towers SK5: Stoc ... 5A **26**
Lenham Wlk. M22: Wyth ... 5K **75**
Lennox Av. CH45: N Bri ... 4H **13**
Lennox La. CH43: Bid ... 3F **33**
Lennox St. M34: Aude ... 4D **8**
Lenthall Av. CW12: Cong ... 6H **183**
Lenton Gdns. M22: Shar ... 7A **50**
Leominster Dr. M22: Wyth ... 2A **76**
Leominster Rd. CH44: Wall ... 7H **13**
Leonard Ho. CH41: Birk ... 2E **34**
Leonard St. CH1: Ches ... 7J **145**
WA2: Warr ... 5G **41**
WA4: Stoc H ... 4H **67**
WA7: Wes P ... 7D **88**
Leon Cl. WA5: Gt San ... 5F **39**
Leopold St. CH44: Wall ... 1D **34**
Lerryn Dr. SK7: Bram ... 4B **78**
Lesley Rd. M32: S'ord ... 2F **23**
Leslie Av. CH49: Gre ... 2A **58**
Leslie Gro. WA15: Timp ... 6A **48**
Leslie Rd. CW7: Wins ... 5B **178**
Lessingham Rd. WA8: Wid ... 2F **63**
Lester Cl. ST7: Als ... 5E **202**
Lester Dr. CH61: Irby ... 6K **57**
Lesters La. CH4: Lwr K ... 1C **184**
Lester St. M32: S'ord ... 1J **23**
Lestock St. L8: Liv ... 5K **35**
Leven Av. CW7: Wins ... 2G **179**
Levens Cl. SK8: Gat ... 1D **76**
WA5: Warr ... 6D **40**
Levens Hey CH46: More ... 4A **32**
LEVENSHULME ... 2D **24** (1C **217**)
Levenshulme Station (Rail) ... 2D **24**
Levenshulme Swimming Pools ... 2E **24**
Levenshulme Ter. *M19: Manc ... 2D 24*
(off Stockport Rd.)
Levenshulme Trad. Est. M19: Manc ... 1F **25**
Levens Rd. SK7: H Gro ... 3G **79**
Levens Way WA8: Wid ... 5C **62**
Leven Wlk. CH66: Ell P ... 7H **109**
M23: Wyth ... 6G **49**
Lever Av. CH44: Wall ... 2D **34**
Lever C'way. CH63: H Beb, Store ... 1E **84**
Leverett Cl. WA14: Alt ... 7E **46**
Leverhulme Ct. CH63: Beb ... 2A **86**
Lever St. SK7: H Gro ... 3H **79**
WA9: Clo F ... 1K **37**
Lever Ter. *CH42: Tran ... 2D 60*
(off Summerford Cl.)
Levisham Gdns. WA5: Warr ... 5C **40**
Lewes Av. M34: Den ... 2E **26**
Lewin St. CW10: Mid ... 3C **180**
Lewis Av. WA5: Warr ... 2D **40**
Lewis Cl. CH65: Ell P ... 1E **140**
CW5: Nant ... 2E **196**
Lewis Cres. WA8: Wid ... 6G **63**
Lewis Gro. WA8: Wid ... 4D **62**
Lewisham Rd. CH62: P Sun ... 7H **61**
Lewis Rd. SK5: Stoc ... 2J **25**
Lewis St. CW2: Crewe ... 3B **194**
SK14: Hyde ... 7K **9**
Lexden St. WA5: Warr ... 6C **40**
Lexington Wlk. *WA5: Gt San ... 5A 40*
(off Boston Blvd.)
Leybourne Av. M19: Manc ... 1E **24**
Leybrook Rd. M22: Wyth ... 2J **75**
Leyburn Av. M32: S'ord ... 1H **23**
M41: Urm ... 2K **21**
Leyburne Rd. SK2: Stoc ... 6H **53**
Leyburn Gro. SK6: Rom ... 2C **54**
Leyburn Rd. CH45: Wall ... 5F **13**
Leycester Cl. WA16: Knut ... 5G **117**
Leycester Dr. WA16: Mob ... 3A **102**
Leycester Rd. WA16: Knut ... 6F **117**
LEYCETT ... 3B **220**
Leycett Dr. M23: Wyth ... 3G **49**
Ley Cl. WA9: Clo F ... 1J **37**
Leyden Wlk. M23: Wyth ... 1G **75**
Leyfield Av. SK6: Rom ... 2C **54**
Leyfield Ct. CH4: Ches ... 6G **149**
SK6: Rom ... 2C **54**
Ley Hey Av. SK6: Mar ... 5F **55**
Ley Hey Ct. SK6: Mar ... 5F **55**
LEY HEY PARK ... 5E **54**
Ley Hey Rd. SK6: Mar ... 5F **55**
Leyland Av. M20: Manc ... 1F **51**
SK8: Gat ... 6D **50**
Leyland Dr. CH4: Salt F ... 5C **148**
Leyland Gro. CW1: Hasl ... 2J **195**
Leylands La. SK14: B'tom ... 5F **29**
Leyland St. SK4: Stoc ... 6G **213** (3C **52**)
Leyland Wlk. CW7: Wins ... 6D **178**
Ley La. SK6: Mar B ... 3J **55**
Leys Rd. WA14: Timp ... 4J **47**
Leyton Cl. WA7: Run ... 1H **111**
Liberty Cl. WA5: Gt San ... 5A **40**
Libson Cl. WA2: Fear ... 1A **42**
Lichfield Av. SK5: Stoc ... 4H **25**
WA4: Grap ... 6A **68**
WA15: Hale ... 2C **74**
Lichfield Cl. WA16: Knut ... 3H **117**
Lichfield Ct. CW7: Wins ... 5E **178**
Lichfield Dr. CH66: Gt Sut ... 1A **140**
Lichfield Rd. CH1: Blac ... 5G **145**
Lichfield St. CH45: N Bri ... 4J **13**
CW10: Mid ... 2D **180**
Lichfield Wlk. SK6: Rom ... 3A **54**
Lickers La. L35: Whis ... 2A **36**
Liddell Ct. CH45: Wall ... 6D **12**
Lidgate Gro. M20: Manc ... 1C **50**
Lidgetts La. SK10: R'ow ... 7F **123**
Liege Ho. *CH49: Upt ... 6C 32*
(off Manorside Cl.)
Lifestyles Millennium ... *2J 35*
(off Victoria St.)
Lifestyles Pk. Road ... 7K **35**
Liffey Av. M22: Wyth ... 2A **76**
Liffey Ct. *L3: Liv ... 2K 35*
(off London Rd.)
Lift La. CW9: And ... 2C **156**
Light Alders La. SK12: Dis ... 6G **81**
Lightborne Rd. M33: Sale ... 7C **22**
Lightburn St. WA7: Run ... 5F **89**
Lightfoot Cl. CH60: Hes ... 7K **83**
Lightfoot La. CH60: Hes ... 7K **83**
CW6: Eat ... 5G **177**
Lightfoot St. CH2: Ches ... 7B **146**
Lighthorne Av. SK3: Stoc ... 5H **51**
Lighthorne Gro. SK3: Stoc ... 5H **51**
Lighthorne Rd. SK3: Stoc ... 5H **51**
Lighthouse Rd. CH47: Hoy ... 6C **30**
Lightley Cl. CW11: Whe ... 5E **200**
Lightley Ct. CW11: Whe ... 5E **200**
LIGHT OAKS ... 2D **221**
Light Oaks Rd. WA3: G'ury ... 4J **7**
LIGHTWOOD
ST3 ... 3D **221**
ST10 ... 3D **221**
LIGHTWOOD GREEN
CW3 ... 3A **220**
L31 ... 3B **218**
Lilac Av. SK14: Hyde ... 3J **27**
WA5: Gt San ... 7J **39**
WA8: Wid ... 3H **63**
WA16: Knut ... 4C **116**
Lilac Cl. CW6: W'gton ... 6D **172**
Lilac Ct. CW12: Cong ... 4G **183**
Lilac Cres. WA7: Run ... 6J **89**
Lilac Dr. CW8: N'ich ... 7C **156**
Lilac Gro. CH66: Whit ... 1C **140**
WA4: Stoc H ... 4J **67**
Lilac Rd. WA15: Hale ... 2A **74**
Lilac St. SK2: Stoc ... 6D **52**
Lilac Wlk. M31: Part ... 1G **45**
Lilford Av. WA5: Warr ... 4C **40**
Lilford Dr. WA5: Gt San ... 6H **39**
Lilford Sq. SK11: Mac ... 7A **126**
Lilford St. WA5: Warr ... 5D **40**
(not continuous)
Lillian Gro. SK5: Stoc ... 3J **25**
Lillie Cl. CH43: Bid ... 4F **33**
Lillyfield CH60: Hes ... 1C **104**
Lilly St. SK14: Hyde ... 3A **28**
Lilybrook Dr. WA16: Knut ... 4F **117**

Lwr. Market St.—Magdalen Ct.

Lwr. Market St. SK14: B'tom 3H 29
Lwr. Meadow Dr. CW12: Cong 3E 182
Lwr. Meadow Rd. SK9: Hand 2B 98
Lwr. Mersey St. CH65: Ell P 1E 134
Lwr. Moat Cl. SK4: Stoc 1C 52
Lower Moss Wood (Nature Reserve) 1G 165
LOWER MOUNTAIN 2B 218
Lwr. New Hall Pl. L3: Liv 2G 35
(off Union St.)
Lwr. Park Cres. SK12: Poy 7G 79
Lwr. Park Rd. CH4: Ches 6E 212 (2B 150)
M14: Manc 1A 24
SK12: Poy 1A 100
Lwr. Park St. CW12: Cong 3G 183
LOWER PEOVER 1C 164 (3B 216)
Lwr. Rake La. WA6: Hel 4B 138
Lower Rd. CH62: P Sun 7G 61
Lwr. Robin Hood La.
WA6: Hel 5B 138
LOWER ROE CROSS 5G 11
LOWER STRETTON 6J 93
Lwr. Strines Rd. SK6: Mar 7G 55
LOWER TEAN 3D 221
Lwr. Thingwall La. CH61: Thin 7F 59
LOWER THREAPWOOD 7H 207
LOWER WALTON 5F 67 (2A 216)
Lwr. Wash La. WA4: Westy 2J 67
Lwr. Wharf St. OL6: Ash L 1G 9
LOWER WHITLEY 4B 114 (3A 216)
LOWER WITHINGTON 7K 167 (1C 221)
LOWER WYCH 3C 219
Lowes, The WA14: Bow 4F 73
Lowes La. SK11: Gaw 4C 128
Lowe St. M34: Den 7G 9
SK1: Stoc 7J 213 (3D 52)
SK11: Mac 5A 126
Loweswater Cl. WA2: Warr 1F 41
Loweswater Rd. SK8: Gat 2D 76
Loweswater Ter. SK15: Stal 5B 4
(off Ullswater Ter.)
Lowfield Av. OL6: Ash L 4A 4
Lowfield Gdns. WA3: G'ury 3J 7
Lowfield Gro. SK2: Stoc 5D 52
Lowfield Rd. SK2: Stoc 6C 52
SK3: Stoc 6C 52
Lowfields Av. CH62: East 4J 107
Lowfields Cl. CH62: East 4K 107
Low Hill WA6: Dun H 4H 143
Lowick Cl. SK7: H Gro 3H 79
Lowick Grn. SK6: W'ley 6E 26
Lowland Rd. SK2: Stoc 1F 79
Lowlands Rd. WA7: Run 4F 89
Lowland Way WA16: Knut 6E 116
Low Lea Rd. SK6: Mar B 5H 55
LOW LEIGHTON 2D 217
Lowndes Cl. SK2: Stoc 6F 53
Lowndes La. SK2: Stoc 5F 53
Lownorth Rd. M22: Wyth 5A 76
Lowry, The M14: Manc 3A 24
Lowry Bank CH44: Wall 1D 34
Lowry Cl. WA5: Gt San 6B 40
Lowry Ct. SK14: Mot 6H 11
Lowry Dr. SK6: Mar B 4H 55
Lowry Gro. SK14: Mot 7G 11
Lowside Av. SK6: W'ley 6H 27
Low St. ST7: Rod H 1F 203
Lowther Av. WA3: Cul 6F 7
WA15: Timp 6A 48
Lowther Dr. L35: R'ill 1B 36
Lowther Gdns. M41: Urm 1G 21
Lowther St. SK10: Boll 3E 122
LOWTON 1A 216
Lowton Bus. Pk. WA3: Low 2A 6
LOWTON COMMON 1A 6 (1A 216)
Lowton Rd. M33: Sale 2H 47
LOWTON ST MARY'S 3A 6
Lowton St Mary's By-Pass
WN7: Leigh 3C 6
Low Wood Cl. SK7: Bram 4A 78
Low Wood Gro. CH61: Barns 2A 84
Lowwood Gro. CH41: Birk 7C 34
Low Wood Rd. M34: Den 6A 8
Lowwood Rd. CH41: Birk 7C 34
Loxdale Dr. CH65: Gt Sut 5B 134
Loxley Cl. SK11: Mac 5J 125
WA5: Gt San 4J 39
Loyola Hey L35: R'ill 4E 36
Lucerne Cl. CH3: Hunt 5E 150
Lucerne Rd. CH44: Wall 2C 34
SK7: Bram 2C 78
Lucy St. SK3: Stoc 4C 52
Ludford Gro. M33: Sale 2K 47
Ludford St. CW1: Crewe 1C 194
Ludlow Av. CW1: Crewe 3E 194
Ludlow Cl. CW7: Wins 5C 178
SK10: Mac 2B 126
WA1: Padg 3B 42
Ludlow Ct. CH48: W Kir 4C 56
Ludlow Cres. WA7: Run 6H 89
Ludlow Dr. CH48: W Kir 4C 56
CH65: Ell P 5G 135
Ludlow Gro. CH62: Brom 5D 86
Ludlow Rd. CH1: Blac 5H 145
SK2: Stoc 4G 53
Ludlow Towers SK5: Stoc 4B 26
Ludwell Cl. CH4: Ches 5J 149
Lugano Rd. SK7: Bram 2C 78
LUGSDALE 6J 63
Lugsdale Rd. WA8: Wid 6G 63
Luke Fold SK15: Stal 2F 11
Luke Rd. M43: Droy 1A 8
Luke St. CH44: Wall 2D 34
L8: Liv 6K 35
Lullington Cl. M22: Wyth 4J 75
Lulworth Av. M41: Urm 1J 21
Lulworth Cl. CW7: Wins 5C 178
Lulworth Gdns. M23: Wyth 4F 49
Lumb Brook M. WA4: Stoc H 4J 67
Lumb Brook Rd. WA4: App, App T 6K 67
Lumbbrook Rd. WA4: App 4J 67
Lumb Cl. SK7: Bram 7C 78
Lumber La. WA5: B'ood 3B 14
Lumb Ho. SK7: Bram 7C 78
Lumb La. M34: Aude 1B 8
(not continuous)
SK7: Bram 7C 78
Lumina CH62: Brom 4E 86
Lumley Pl. CH1: Ches 5D 212 (2A 150)
Lumley Rd. CH2: Ches 6K 145
CH44: Wall 1C 34
SK11: Mac 5G 125
Lumley Wlk. L24: Hale 7B 88
Lumn Hollow SK14: Hyde 1K 27
(not continuous)
Lumn Rd. SK14: Hyde 1K 27
Lumpy St. CW12: Cong 3E 182
Lundy Dr. CH65: Ell P 1E 140
Lune Cl. CW12: Cong 5H 183
Lunedale Grn. SK2: Stoc 6J 53
Lune Wlk. M43: Droy 2A 8
(off Ellen St.)
Lune Way SK5: Stoc 6J 25
WA8: Wid 4C 62
LUNT 1B 214
Lunt Av. CW2: Crewe 4B 194
LUNT MOSS 1F 205
LUNTS HEATH 1H 63
Lunt's Heath Rd. WA8: Wid 7G 37
Lunts Moss ST7: Sch G 3K 203
Lupin Dr. CH3: Hunt 5E 150
Lupton St. M34: Den 6E 8
Lupus Way CH66: Gt Sut 5B 134
Lurgan Av. M33: Sale 1C 48
Lutener Av. WA14: W Tim 4G 47
Luton Dr. M23: Wyth 1G 75
Luton Rd. CH65: Ell P 3B 134
SK5: Stoc 3J 25
Luton St. WA8: Wid 6G 63
Lutyens Cl. SK10: Mac 4G 125
Luxor Gro. M34: Den 1J 25
LUZLEY 2C 4
Luzley Rd. OL5: Moss 1C 4
OL6: Ash L 4C 4
SK15: Stal 6C 4
Lycett Rd. CH44: Wall 6E 12
Lyceum Cl. CW1: Crewe 5F 191
Lyceum Pl. L1: Liv 3J 35
(off Ranelagh St.)
Lyceum Theatre
Crewe 2D 194
Lyceum Way CW1: Crewe 5F 191
Lychgate WA4: H Wal 6D 66
Lychgate M. SK4: Stoc 2G 51
Lychwood SK6: Mar 6F 55
Lycroft Cl. WA7: Run 1H 111
Lydbrook Cl. CH42: R Fer 2E 60
Lydbury Cl. WA5: Call 2B 40
Lydden Rd. CH65: Ell P 1D 134
Lydgate Cl. CW2: Wis 6K 193
M34: Den 2G 27
SK15: Carrb 3F 5
Lydgate Rd. M33: Sale 2C 48
Lydia Ann St. L1: Liv 4J 35
Lydiate, The CH60: Hes 7H 83
Lydiate La. CH64: W'ston 7D 106
WA7: Wes P 7D 88
Lydiat La. SK9: Ald E 7F 119
Lydney Av. SK8: He Grn 6E 76
Lydney Rd. M41: Urm 1G 21
Lydstep Ct. WA5: Call 2C 40
Lydyett La. CW8: Barnt 2A 156
CW9: And 2A 156
Lymcote Dr. CW8: H'ord 2K 161
Lyme Av. SK9: Wilm 5J 97
SK11: Mac 7A 126
Lyme Ct. SK7: H Gro 2H 79
SK14: Hyde 7K 9
Lymefield Ct. SK2: Stoc 5H 53
Lymefield Gro. SK2: Stoc 6F 53
Lymefield Ter. SK14: B'tom 3J 29
Lymefield Vis. Cen. 3J 29
LYME GREEN 3H 129
Lyme Grn. Bus. Pk. SK11: L Grn 2G 129
Lyme Grn. Pk. SK11: L Grn 3H 129
Lyme Gro. M33: Sale 1C 48
SK2: Stoc 5D 52
SK6: Mar 7F 55
SK6: Rom 2D 54
WA13: Lymm 3J 69
WA14: Alt 3G 213 (1G 73)
Lyme Ho. SK4: Stoc 3G 51
Lyme Lea Cl. SK8: Chea H 5K 77
Lyme Pk. Country Pk. 7G 81
Lyme Pl. SK16: Duk 2G 9
Lyme Rd. SK7: H Gro 4J 79
SK12: Dis 6G 81
SK12: Poy 3H 101
Lymes, The WA14: Bow 4G 73
Lyme St. SK4: Stoc 2G 51
SK7: H Gro 2H 79
WA1: Warr 7F 41
Lyme Ter. SK16: Duk 1G 9
Lyme Tree Ct. WA8: Cron 6C 36
Lyme Vw. SK11: L Grn 3H 129
Lyme Vw. Ct. SK6: Rom 2D 54
Lymewood Dr. SK9: Wilm 6B 98
SK12: Dis 7H 81
Lymington Dr. M23: Wyth 3D 48
Lymington Rd. CH44: Wall 7F 13
LYMM 2K 69 (2A 216)
Lymm Bri. WA13: Lymm 2A 70
Lymm Cl. SK3: Stoc 6B 52
Lymm Hall WA13: Lymm 2A 70
Lymmhay La. WA13: Lymm 1A 70
Lymmington Av.
WA13: Lymm 2J 69
Lymm Leisure Cen. 3D 70
Lymm Quay WA13: Lymm 2A 70
Lymm Rd. CH43: Bid 5G 33
WA4: Thel 2E 68
WA13: Lymm 4G 71
WA14: L Bol 4G 71
Lymm Wlk. SK8: Chea 1J 77
Lynalls Cl. CW12: Cong 3B 182
Lynas St. CH41: Birk 4C 34
Lynbrook Rd. CW1: Crewe 2F 195
Lyncastle Rd. WA4: App T 3C 94
Lyncastle Way WA4: App T 2D 94
Lyncombe Cl. SK8: Chea H 7K 77
Lyncroft Cl. CW1: Crewe 3F 195
Lyncroft Rd. CH44: Wall 2B 34
Lyndale WA7: Run 6J 89
Lyndale Av. CH62: East 3K 107
SK5: Stoc 1J 25
WA2: Fear 2K 41
WA2: Warr 4H 41
Lyndale Ct. CW7: Wins 1H 179
Lyndene Gdns. SK8: Gat 6D 50
Lyndene Rd. M22: Wyth 7K 49
Lyndhurst Av. CH61: Pens 3J 83
M33: Sale 1K 47
M34: Den 7D 8
SK6: Bred 7E 26
SK7: H Gro 4G 79
Lyndhurst Cl. CH61: Thin 1J 83
SK9: Wilm 2C 118
Lyndhurst Dr. WA15: Hale 3A 74
Lyndhurst Rd. CH45: Wall 5F 13
CH47: Meols 3F 31
CH61: Irby 1E 82
M32: S'ord 1G 23
SK5: Stoc 1H 25
Lyndhurst Vw. SK16: Duk 1H 9
Lyndon Gro. WA7: Run 6H 89
Lyndon Rd. M44: Irlam 2C 20
Lyneal Av. CH66: Gt Sut 5J 133
Lyne Edge Cres. SK16: Duk 3A 10
Lyne Edge Rd. SK16: Duk 3B 10
Lyneham L35: Whis 2A 36
Lyne Vw. SK14: Hyde 4A 10
Lyngard Cl. SK9: Wilm 5B 98
Lyngarth Ho. WA14: Alt 6J 47
(off Grosvenor Rd.)
Lyngate Cl. SK1: Stoc 4E 52
Lynham Av. WA5: Gt San 7K 39
Lynmouth Av. M41: Urm 3A 22
SK5: Stoc 4H 25
Lynn Av. M33: Sale 5H 23
Lynnbank CH43: Oxt 1A 60
Lynn Cl. WA7: Run 7J 89
Lynndene CH66: L Sut 1K 133
Lynnfield Ho. WA14: Alt 7H 47
Lynn Gro. SK11: Mac 6K 125
Lynnwood Rd. M19: Manc 2F 51
Lynside Wlk. M22: Wyth 6K 75
Lynthorpe Av. M44: Cad 5A 20
Lynton Av. M41: Urm 1F 21
M44: Cad 5B 20
SK14: Hat 1D 28
Lynton Cl. CH4: Ches 5G 149
CH60: Hes 1E 104
WA5: Penk 1G 65
WA16: Knut 4G 117
Lynton Ct. SK9: Ald E 5F 119
Lynton Cres. WA8: Wid 3E 62
Lynton Dr. CH63: Beb 3A 86
M19: Manc 4C 24
SK6: H Lan 5E 80
Lynton Gdns. WA4: App 2H 93
Lynton Gro. CW1: Hasl 1K 195
WA15: Timp 7K 47
Lynton La. SK9: Ald E 5F 119
Lynton M. SK9: Ald E 5F 119
Lynton Pk. Rd. SK8: Chea H 5H 77
Lynton Pl. ST7: Als 5E 202
Lynton Rd. CH45: Wall 5E 12
SK4: Stoc 6F 25
SK8: Gat 7E 50
Lyntonvale Av. SK8: Gat 6D 50
Lynton Wlk. SK14: Hat 1D 28
Lynton Way CW2: Wis 6A 194
Lynwood SK9: Wilm 1F 119
WA15: Hale 5A 74
Lynwood Av. CH44: Wall 1K 33
WA4: App 6G 67
Lynwood Dr. CH61: Irby 7B 58
Lynwood Gro. M33: Sale 6H 23
M34: Aude 1B 8
SK4: Stoc 5F 25
Lynwood Rd. CH1: Blac 5G 145
Lyon Ct. WA4: Warr 2K 67
Lyon Ind. Est. WA14: B'ath 5F 47
Lyon Rd. WA14: B'ath 5G 47
Lyons Cl. CH46: More 3B 32
Lyon's Fold M33: Sale 5G 23
Lyons La. WA4: App 7H 67
(not continuous)
Lyons Rd. CH46: More 3B 32
WA5: Penk 1H 65
Lyon St. CH1: Ches 2D 212 (1A 150)
CW1: Crewe 2D 194
SK11: Mac 5K 125
WA4: Warr 2K 67
Lyon Way SK5: Stoc 5H 25
Lysander Dr. WA2: Padg 2J 41
Lyster Cl. WA3: Birc 1F 43
Lytham Cl. OL6: Ash L 3A 4
WA5: Gt San 2J 65
Lytham Ct. OL6: Ash L 3A 4
Lytham Dr. CW7: Wins 2D 178
SK7: Bram 6E 78
Lytham Rd. M14: Manc 2B 24
M19: Manc 2B 24
M41: Urm 1F 21
SK8: He Grn 4D 76
WA8: Wid 3H 63
Lytham St. SK3: Stoc 6D 52
Lytherton Av. M44: Cad 7A 20
Lythgoes La. WA2: Warr 6F 41
(not continuous)
Lyth St. M14: Manc 4A 24
Lytton Av. CH42: R Fer 4E 60

M

Mabfield Rd. M14: Manc 2A 24
Mabledon Cl. SK8: He Grn 5F 77
Mablins La. CW1: Crewe 5G 191
Mabs Ct. OL6: Ash L 1J 9
McAllester Lodge CH43: Oxt 1J 59
(off Bidston Rd.)
Macalpine Cl. CH49: Upt 6D 32
Macauley Cl. SK16: Duk 3B 10
Macauley Rd. SK5: Stoc 2G 25
Macauley Way M34: Den 3F 27
McCarthy Cl. WA3: Birc 1G 43
McClellan Pl. WA8: Wid 4H 63
MACCLESFIELD 5A 126 (3D 217)
Macclesfield Crematorium
SK10: Mac 3J 125
MACCLESFIELD FOREST 3D 217
Macclesfield Leisure Cen. 3F 125
Macclesfield Rd. CW4: H Cha 4J 181
CW12: Cong 1G 183
SK7: H Gro 6K 79
SK9: Ald E 6F 119
SK9: Wilm 7K 97
SK10: O Ald . . . . 6F 119 & 5A 120
SK10: Pres 1G 125
SK10: R'ow 5J 123
Macclesfield Silk Mus. & Heritage Cen. 5A 126
Macclesfield Station (Rail) 4A 126
Macclesfield Town FC 1H 129
Macclesfield West Pk. Mus. 3K 125
Macdermott Rd. WA8: Wid 1F 89
Macdona Dr. CH48: W Kir 5C 56
Macdonald Dr. CH49: Gre 2A 58
Macdonald Rd. CH46: More 4K 31
M44: Irlam 4B 20
McGarva Way CH65: Ell P 4E 134
McGill Ct. CH41: Birk 5C 34
(off Cathcart St.)
McGough Cl. WA9: Sut M 1G 37
McKeagney Gdns. WA8: Wid 6D 62
McKee Av. WA2: Warr 2F 41
Mackenzie Ind. Pk. SK3: Stoc 6K 51
Mackenzie Rd. CH46: Leas 1E 32
McKinley St. WA5: Gt San 5J 39
McKinley Way WA8: Wid 2F 63
McLaren St. CW1: Crewe 6G 191
Macnair Ct. SK6: Mar 7G 55
Macnair M. SK6: Mar 7G 55
McNeill Av. CW1: Crewe 1K 193
Macon Ct. CW1: Crewe 3E 194
Macon Ind. Pk. CW1: Crewe 3E 194
Macon Way CW1: Crewe 3E 194
Maddock Rd. CH44: Wall 6K 13
Maddocks Cl. CH3: Farn 5B 186
Maddocks Hill WA6: Norl 6G 153
Maddock St. CH41: Birk 4B 34
Madeleine McKenna Ct. WA8: Wid 2B 62
MADELEY 3B 220
Madeley Cl. CH48: W Kir 4C 56
WA14: Hale 5J 73
Madeley Dr. CH48: W Kir 4C 56
MADELEY HEATH 3B 220
Madeley St. CW2: Crewe 5C 194
Madison Av. M34: Aude 2B 8
SK8: Chea H 3J 77
Madison Sq. L1: Liv 4K 35
Madras Rd. SK3: Stoc 5A 52
Madron Av. SK10: Mac 3E 124
Maelor Cl. CH63: Brom 1H 107
MAER 3B 220
MAES-GLAS 3A 214
MAESHAFN 1A 218
Maes-y-Coed CH4: Salt 5F 149
Magazine Av. CH45: N Bri 4H 13
Magazine Brow CH45: N Bri 4J 13
Magazine La. CH45: N Bri 4H 13
Magazine Rd. CH62: Brom 3D 86
Magazines Prom. CH45: N Bri 3J 13
Magazine Wlk. CH62: Brom 3D 86
Magdala Pl. CW9: N'ich 5H 157
Magdalen Ct. CW2: Crewe 5A 194

Magda Rd.—Maple Pl.

Magda Rd. SK2: Stoc 7G **53**
Magecroft CW1: L'ton 4G **191**
Magenta Av. M44: Irlam 5B **20**
Maggoty La. SK11: Gaw 4B **128**
MAGHULL 1B **214**
Mag La. WA13: Lymm 7B **70**
WA16: H Leg, Lymm 7B **70**
Magnolia Cl. CH66: Gt Sut 7B **134**
M31: Part 2G 45
(off Redbrook Rd.)
M33: Sale 6B **22**
WA1: Wool 5E **42**
Magnolia Ct. *M33: Sale 5B 22*
(off Magnolia Cl.)
Magnolia Dr. WA7: Beec 3B **112**
Magnolia Ri. SK10: Pres 5F **121**
Magnolia Wlk. CH49: Gre 3K **57**
Mahogany Wlk. *M33: Sale 6B 22*
(off Epping Dr.)
Mahood St. SK3: Stoc 5B **52**
Maida St. M12: Manc 1E **24**
Maiden Gdns. CH65: Ell P 5F **135**
Maidenhills CW10: Mid 4D **180**
Maidford Cl. M32: S'ord 1K **23**
Maidstone Cl. SK10: Mac 2J **125**
Maidstone Rd. SK4: Stoc 1F **51**
Maidstone Wlk. *M34: Den 2F 27*
(off Worcester Av.)
Maidwell Cl. CW7: Wins 1H **179**
Main Av. M19: Manc 4C **24**
Main Dr. WA14: Bow, Dun M 2B **72**
Main La. WA3: Croft 6A **6**
Main Rd. CH4: H Kin, Lwr K 1A **184**
CH62: P Sun 2B **86**
CW1: Crewe, Warm 2J **191**
CW2: Shav 4A **198**
CW2: West 7J **195**
CW4: Goo 7G **165**
CW5: Worl 6C **192**
CW5: Wyb 6A **198**
CW9: Moult 6D **162**
SK11: Lang 1H **169**
Main St. CH3: Gt Bar 3B **170**
SK14: Hyde 6J **9**
WA6: Frod 7G **111**
WA7: Halt 5B **90**
Mainwaring Cl. CW5: Stap 3E **196**
Mainwaring Dr. CH4: Salt F 4D **148**
SK9: Wilm 6A **98**
Mainwaring Rd. CH44: Wall 1C **34**
CH62: Brom 6D **86**
WA16: O Peo 3G **165**
Mainwaring Ter. M23: Wyth 2G **49**
Mainwood Rd. WA15: Timp 7C **48**
Mairesfield Av. WA4: Grap 3B **68**
Maisemore Flds. WA8: Wid 2E **62**
Maismore Rd. M22: Wyth 4G **75**
Maisterson Ct. CW5: Nant 2C **196**
Maitland Rd. CH45: N Bri 3J **13**
Maitland St. SK1: Stoc 5F **53**
Maitland Way CH1: Blac 6E **144**
Maitland-Wood Cl. CW9: N'ich 6J **157**
Maizefield Cl. M33: Sale 1F **49**
Major Cross St. WA8: Wid 6G **63**
Makepeace Cl. CH3: Ches 7F **147**
Malaga Av. M90: Man A 6H **75**
Malahide Ct. WA8: Wid 3E **62**
Malakoff St. SK15: Stal 2K **9**
Malam Dr. CW9: Rud 7J **157**
Malbank CW5: Nant 1C **196**
Malbank Rd. CW2: Crewe 2H **193**
Malbern Ind. Est. M34: Den 6C **8**
Malcolm Av. WA2: Warr 3H **41**
Malcolm Cres. CH63: Brom 1H **107**
Malcolm St. WA7: Run 4H **89**
Malden Gro. M23: Wyth 5G **49**
Maldon Cl. SK2: Stoc 6A **54**
Maldwyn Rd. CH44: Wall 6H **13**
Malgam Dr. M20: Manc 4D **50**
Malham Cl. WA5: Gt San 4G **39**
Malham Ct. SK2: Stoc 6H **53**
Malhamdale Av. L35: R'ill 2D **36**
Malhamdale Rd. CW12: Cong 1J **183**
Malin Cl. L24: Hale 6A **88**
Maliston Rd. WA5: Gt San 7K **39**
MALKIN'S BANK 6G **201**
Mall, The M33: Sale 7G **23**
SK14: Hyde 1J **27**
SK15: Stal 4F **11**
WA1: Warr 7F 41
(off Golden Sq. Shop. Cen.)
Mallaby St. CH41: Birk 4K **33**
Mallaig Cl. CW4: H Cha 6J **181**
Mallard Cl. SK2: Stoc 7A **54**
SK16: Duk 3K **9**
WA2: Warr 1H **41**
WA7: Beec 2B **112**
WA16: Knut 3F **117**
Mallard Ct. CW1: Crewe 4G **195**
SK8: He Grn 5E **76**
Mallard Cres. SK12: Poy 2K **99**
Mallard Grn. WA14: B'ath 4F **47**
Mallard La. WA3: Birc 1F **43**
Mallards, The SK11: Mac 4J **125**
Mallards Reach SK6: Rom 2B **54**
Mallard Way CH46: More 2H **13**
CW1: Crewe 4G **195**
CW7: Wins 6E **178**
Malley Gdns. OL5: Moss 1E **4**
Mall Grosvenor Shop. Cen.
CH1: Ches 5C **212** (2A **150**)
Malling Rd. M23: Wyth 1G **75**
Mallory Cl. WA16: Mob 1K **117**
Mallory Ct. CW12: Cong 3B **182**
WA14: Bow 2G **73**
Mallory Rd. CH42: Tran 3C **60**
CH65: Whit 4C **134**
SK14: Hyde 5B **10**
Mallory Wlk. CH4: Dod 3D **184**
M23: Wyth 4D **48**
Mallow Cl. CH3: Hunt 5D **150**
Mallowdale Cl. CH62: East 2A **108**
Mallowdale Rd. SK2: Stoc 7J **53**
Mallow Wlk. *M31: Part 2H 45*
(off Broom Rd.)
Malmesbury Cl. CH49: Gre 1K **57**
CW10: Mid 3B **180**
SK12: Poy 2C **100**
Malmesbury Pk. WA7: Nort 3F **91**
Malmesbury Rd. SK8: Chea H 7K **77**
Malory Cl. CW1: Crewe 1F **195**
MALPAS 3H **207** (3C **219**)
Malpas & District Sports Club 3G **207**
Malpas Av. CH43: Pren 3K **59**
Malpas Cl. CW9: N'ich 6H **157**
SK8: Chea 1J **77**
SK9: Wilm 5A **98**
Malpas Dr. CH63: H Beb 6D **60**
WA5: Gt San 7A **40**
WA14: Timp 4J **47**
Malpas Gro. CH45: Wall 5G **13**
Malpas Rd. CH45: Wall 5F **13**
CH65: Gt Sut 4B **134**
CW9: N'ich 5G **157**
WA7: Run 7H **89**
Malpas Way WA5: Gt San 1A **66**
Malsham Rd. M23: Wyth 2F **49**
Malta Rd. CH2: Most 1J **145**
Maltby Rd. M23: Wyth 6F **49**
Malt Kiln Rd. WA16: Plum 1H **159**
Malt Kiln Way CW11: S'ach 2F **201**
Maltmans Rd. WA13: Lymm 2K **69**
Malton Cl. WA8: Cron 7C **36**
Malton Dr. SK7: H Gro 6H **79**
WA14: Alt 6E **46**
Malton Rd. SK4: Stoc 7D **24**
Malt St. WA16: Knut 3E **116**
Malvern Av. CH65: Ell P 5E **134**
M41: Urm 1A **22**
M43: Droy 1B **8**
SK8: Gat 7B **50**
Malvern Cl. CW2: Shav 3B **198**
CW12: Cong 3B **182**
SK4: Stoc 1B **52**
WA5: Gt San 4J **39**
Malvern Dr. SK10: Mac 7B **122**
WA14: Alt 7F **47**
Malvern Gro. CH42: Tran 3C **60**
Malvern Rd. CH1: Blac 5H **145**
CH45: Wall 6D **12**
WA16: Knut 5D **116**
Malvern Way CW7: Wins 5C **178**
Malwood St. L8: Liv 1K **61**
MANCHESTER 1C **217**
Manchester Airport Aviation Viewing Pk. 1B **96**
Manchester Airport Eastern Link Rd.
SK7: Bram 2F **99**
SK8: Chea H 7G **77**
SK9: Hand 7G **77**
Manchester Airport Station (Rail) 6H **75**
Manchester Bus. Pk. M22: Wyth 5K **75**
MANCHESTER INTERNATIONAL AIRPORT 6H **75** (2C **217**)
Manchester Intl. Bus. Cen.
M22: Wyth 6C **76**
Manchester Metropolitan University
Alsager Campus 4B **202**
Didsbury Campus 2D **50**
Hollings Campus 1A **24**
Manchester Metropolitan University Cheshire
Crewe Campus 3F **195**
Manchester New Rd. M31: Part 1H **45**
Manchester Old Rd. M31: Carri 5G **21**
Manchester Rd.
CW9: Los Gra, N'ich 4G **157**
CW12: Eat 6F **169**
M31: Carri, Part 7C **20**
M34: Aude 3A **8**
M34: Den 6A **8**
M43: Droy 1A **8**
OL5: Moss 3D **4**
OL7: Ash L 1E **8**
SK4: Stoc 6F **25**
SK8: Chea 4F **51**
SK9: Wilm 7J **97**
SK10: Boll, Mac 5K **121**
SK13: Tint 1K **11**
SK14: H'rth 1K **11**
SK14: Hyde 7G **9**
WA1: Padd, Warr, Wool, Rix 6G **41**
WA3: Rix, Wool 5G **43**
WA14: Alt, B'ath, Timp 6H **47**
WA16: Knut, Mere 7J **95** & 1C **116**
Manchester Rd. Nth. M34: Den 6B **8**
Manchester Rd. Sth. M34: Den 7B **8**
Manchester Row WA12: New W 3G **15**
Manchester Rugby Club 1D **98**
MANCOT 1B **218**
Mancroft Cl. WA1: Wool 5E **42**
Mancunian Rd. M34: Den 3F **27**
Mandalay Gdns. SK6: Mar 5D **54**
Mandarin Ct. WA1: Warr 2E **66**
Mandarin Grn. WA14: B'ath 4F **47**
Mandeville St. M19: Manc 3E **24**
Manesty's La. L1: Liv 3J **35**
Manhattan Gdns. WA5: Gt San 4K **39**
Manifold Cl. CW11: S'ach 1C **200**
Manifold Dr. SK6: H Lan 7F **81**
MANLEY 2J **171** (3D **215**)
Manley Cl. CH43: Oxt 2J **59**
CW4: H Cha 4G **181**
CW9: Ant 6B **94**
CW9: N'ich 1F **163**
MANLEY COMMON 2K **171**
Manley Gdns. WA5: Warr 7D **40**
Manley Gro. SK7: Bram 7C **78**
SK14: Mot 7G **11**
Manley La.
WA6: Dun H, Manl 4J **143** & 1F **171**
WA6: Manl 2G **171**
Manley Quarry WA6: Manl 1F **171**
Manley Rd. M33: Sale 3J **47**
SK11: Gaw 7H **125**
WA6: Alv, Frod 7H **139** & 1J **171**
WA6: Alv, Manl 7D **138**
Manley Vw. CH2: Elt 5G **137**
Manley Way SK14: Mot 7H **11**
Manna Dr. CH2: Elt 5G **137**
Manners La. CH60: Hes 1B **104**
Mannings La. CH2: Hoo V 4E **146**
Mannings La. Sth. CH2: Ches 5D **146**
Manning St. CW2: Crewe 5D **194**
Mannington Cl. CH47: Meols 4F **31**
Mann Island L3: Liv 3G **35**
Mann St. L8: Liv 6K **35**
Manora Rd. CW9: N'ich 5F **157**
Manor Av. CW2: Crewe 5A **194**
CW4: Goo 6K **165**
CW9: Mars 7H **115**
L35: R'ill 2C **36**
M33: Sale 6C **22**
M41: Urm 2C **22**
Manor Cl. CH3: Gt Bar 2B **170**
CH64: Park 1A **130**
CW12: Cong 5J **183**
M34: Den 1G **27**
SK8: Chea H 5A **78**
SK9: Wilm 6F **97**
WA1: Wool 5D **42**
WA13: Lymm 3A **70**
Manor Ct. *CH48: W Kir 2B 56*
(off Bridge Rd.)
CH49: Gre 2K **57**
CH61: Irby 7A **58**
CW2: Crewe 5B **194**
CW5: Nant 1C 196
(off Cowfields)
M32: S'ord 2G **23**
M33: Sale 7C **22**
SK1: Stoc 3E 52
(off Hall St.)
Manor Cres. CW10: Mid 5C **180**
SK10: Mac 1A **126**
WA16: Knut 3F **117**
Manor Dr. CH3: Gt Bou 2E **150**
CH49: Upt 5C **32**
CW8: Barnt 3A **156**
CW9: N'ich 6H **157**
Mnr. Farm Cl. CH2: Mic T 2J **147**
Mnr. Farm Ct. WA6: Frod 6J **111**
Mnr. Farm Courtyard WA4: Moo 1K **91**
Mnr. Farm Cres. CH1: Cap 7H **133**
Mnr. Farm M. WA7: Man P 2F **91**
Mnr. Farm Rd. WA7: Man P 2E **90**
Manor Fell WA7: Pal F 7D **90**
Manorfield Cl. CH1: Cap 7G **133**
Manor Flds. CW10: Mid 5C **180**
Manor Gdns. *CW5: Nant 1C 196*
(off Manor Rd.)
SK9: Wilm 7A **98**
MANOR GREEN 5F **33**
Manor Gro. CW8: N'ich 7B **156**
Manor Hill CH43: Clau, Oxt 6K **33**
Mnr. Hill Rd. SK6: Mar 5F **55**
Manor Ho. CH62: Brom 6D **86**
CH66: Gt Sut 6K 133
(off Kelmscott Cl.)
Manor Ho., The CH49: Upt 5C **32**
Manorial Rd. CH64: Park 7F **105**
Manorial Rd. Sth. CH64: Park 7F **105**
Manor Ind. Est. M32: S'ord 3H **23**
WA4: Westy 1J **67**
Manor La. CH42: R Fer 3F **61**
CH45: Wall 6J **13**
CH66: Gt Sut 5K **133**
CW4: H Cha 5K **181**
CW9: What 3J **163**
CW10: Mid 4C **180**
WA16: Oll 7J **117**
Manor Lodge SK8: Chea H 4A **78**
Manor M. CH45: Wall 6J **13**
MANOR PARK
CW10 5B **180**
WA7 2E **90**
Manor Pk. CH3: Gt Bar 2B **170**
M41: Urm 2C **22**
Manor Pk. Av. WA7: Man P 2E **90**
Manor Pk. Bus. Pk. WA7: Man P 2D **90**
Manor Pk. Cl. CH61: Thin 7D **58**
Manor Pk. Ct. WA7: Man P 2E **90**
Manor Pk. Dr. CH66: Gt Sut 6K **133**
Manor Pk. Nth. WA16: Knut 3G **117**
Manor Pk. Sth. WA16: Knut 4F **117**
Manor Pl. CH62: Brom 1D **86**
WA8: Wid 4B **62**
Manor Rd. CH4: Ches 6J **149**
CH44: Wall 6H **13**
CH45: Wall 6H **13**
CH47: Hoy 4D **30**
CH61: Irby 7A **58**
CH62: East 1J **107**
CH63: Tho H 5D **84**
CW5: Nant 1C **196**
CW8: Cudd 4C **160**
CW11: S'ach 3H **201**
M19: Manc 1E **24**
M32: S'ord 2G **23**
M33: Sale 6G **23**
M34: Aude 3A **8**
M34: Den 1G **27**
SK5: Stoc 6A **26**
SK6: Mar 5F **55**
SK6: W'ley 6G **27**
SK7: Bram 4A **78**
SK8: Chea H 4A **78**
SK9: Wilm 6F **97**
SK14: Hyde 5A **10**
ST7: Mow C 5H **205**
WA6: Frod 6J **111**
WA7: Run 4K **89**
WA8: Wid 4B **62**
WA13: Lymm 3A **70**
(not continuous)
WA15: Alt 3K **213** (1J **73**)
Manor Rd. Nth.
CW5: Nant 7C **192**
Manor Road Station (Rail) 5D **30**
Manorside Cl. CH49: Upt 6C **32**
Manor Sq. CW7: Wins 4B **178**
Manor St. CW8: N'ich 7C **156**
M34: Aude 3E **8**
Manor Ter. SK11: Lang 2G **169**
Manor Vw. SK6: W'ley 6G **27**
Manor Wlk. *M34: Aude 3E 8*
(off Mt. Pleasant St.)
Manor Way CH43: Bid 5F **33**
CW2: Crewe 5B **194**
CW11: S'ach 3J **201**
Manse, The OL5: Moss 1D **4**
Manse Fld. Rd.
WA6: K'ley 2C **152**
Mansell Cl. WA8: Wid 7J **37**
Mansfield Av. M34: Den 6C **8**
Mansfield Cl. M34: Den 5C **8**
OL7: Ash L 1E **8**
WA3: Birc 7B **18**
Mansfield Cres. M34: Den 6C **8**
Mansfield Rd.
CH65: Whit 6C **134**
M41: Urm 2A **22**
OL5: Moss 1F **5**
SK14: Hyde 2K **27**
Mansfield St. L3: Liv 1K **35**
OL7: Ash L 2D **8**
Mansfield Vw. OL5: Moss 1F **5**
Mansion Dr. WA16: Knut 3F **117**
Mansion Ho., The
WA14: Alt 5H **47**
Manston Dr. SK8: Chea H 3J **77**
Manston Lodge SK2: Stoc 7F **53**
Manston Rd. WA5: Penk 2H **65**
Manton Av. M34: Den 1K **25**
Manton Ho. SK5: Stoc 7A **26**
Manvers St. SK5: Stoc 1C **52**
Manville Rd. CH45: N Bri 4H **13**
Manway Bus. Pk.
WA14: Timp 4J **47**
Manx Rd. WA4: Warr 2F **67**
Maori Dr. WA6: Frod 7G **111**
Maple Av. CH66: L Sut 2J **133**
M32: S'ord 2J **23**
M34: Aude 1A **8**
M34: Den 7D **8**
SK6: Mar 1F **81**
SK8: Chea H 3H **77**
SK11: Mac 7A **126**
SK12: Dis 1K **103**
SK12: Poy 3E **100**
SK15: Stal 2A **10**
ST7: Als 7F **203**
WA3: Low 3A **6**
WA7: Run 6J **89**
WA7: Sut W 3C **112**
WA8: Wid 4H **63**
WA12: New W 1G **15**
Maple Bank WA14: Bow 2F **73**
Maple Cl. CW4: H Cha 3K **181**
CW11: S'ach 3G **201**
CW12: Cong 2B **182**
M33: Sale 7B **22**
SK2: Stoc 6F **53**
Maple Ct. SK4: Stoc 7F **25**
Maple Cres. WA5: Penk 1H **65**
Maplecroft SK1: Stoc 4F **53**
Maple Dr. WA15: Timp 7E **48**
Maple Gro. CH2: Ches 6E **146**
CH4: Salt 6E **148**
CH62: Brom 6C **86**
CH66: Whit 7C **134**
CW1: Crewe 6K **191**
CW7: Wins 3H **179**
CW8: Barnt 1A **156**
CW8: N'ich 6B **156**
WA4: Warr 2H **67**
Maple Ho. SK14: Hyde 3A **28**
Maple La. CW8: Cudd 4C **160**
Maple Pl. ST7: Rod H 2G **203**

A-Z Cheshire Atlas 277

Maryland Cl.—Melford Dr.

Maryland Cl. WA5: Gt San 5A 40
Maryland La. CH46: More 3A 32
Maryland St. L1: Liv 4K 35
Marylon Dr. M22: N'den 4A 50
Marymount Cl. CH44: Wall 1A 34
Maryport Dr. WA15: Timp 5D 48
Marys Ga. CW2: Wis 6J 193
Mary St. CW1: Crewe 1E 194
M34: Den 6F 9
M43: Droy 1A 8
SK1: Stoc 5K 213 (2E 52)
SK8: Chea 6F 51
SK14: Hyde 7H 9
SK16: Duk 1G 9
WA8: Wid 6K 63
WA9: Clo F 1A 38
Maryville Cl. CH65: Ell P 2E 134
Maryville Wlk. CH65: Ell P 2E 134
Marzhan Way WA8: Wid 4J 63
Masefield Av. WA8: Wid 5F 63
Masefield Cl. CH62: N Fer 6F 61
SK16: Duk 3C 10
Masefield Dr. CH1: Blac 4F 145
CW1: Crewe 2F 195
SK4: Stoc 2J 51
WA2: Winw 6K 15
Masefield Gro. SK5: Stoc 2H 25
Masefield Way CW11: Ett H 4B 200
Maskery Pl. CW12: Cong 3F 183
Mason Av. WA1: Padg 4J 41
WA8: Wid 1G 63
Mason Cl. CH66: Gt Sut 6K 133
Masonic Pl. CH1: Ches 4D 212
Masons La. SK10: Mac 3C 126
Mason's Row CW6: Calv 4K 189
Mason St. CH1: Ches 2B 212 (1K 149)
CH45: N Bri 3H 13
OL7: Ash L 1E 8
WA1: Warr 7G 41
WA7: Run 3J 89
Massey Av. CW7: Wins 3G 179
CW8: H'ord 2K 161
WA5: Warr 2D 40
WA13: Lymm 3G 69
Massey Brook La. WA13: Lymm 3G 69
Massey Cl. CW5: Stap 3E 196
Masseyfield Rd. WA7: B'vale 2C 112
Massey Pk. CH45: Wall 6G 13
Massey Rd. M33: Sale 7K 23
WA15: Alt 3K 213 (1J 73)
Massey St. CH41: Birk 4C 34
SK1: Stoc 7J 213 (3D 52)
SK9: Ald E 6F 119
Massey Wlk. M22: Wyth 4B 76
Massie St. SK8: Chea 6F 51
Masters Ct. WA16: Knut 4D 116
Mather Av. WA7: Wes P 7D 88
Mather Cl. CW10: Mid 4C 180
Mather Ct. CH43: Oxt 7A 34
Mather Dr. CW9: Comb 3H 115
CW9: N'ich 6J 157
Mather Rd. CH43: Oxt 7A 34
Mathers Cl. WA2: Fear 7F 17
Mathew St. L2: Liv 3H 35
Mathew Street Gallery 3J 35
Mathieson Rd. WA8: Wid 1E 88
MATLEY 4E 10
Matley Cl. SK14: Hyde 5C 10
Matley Ct. SK14: Mot 4F 11
Matley Grn. SK5: Stoc 5B 26
Matley La. SK14: Hyde 5C 10
SK15: Mat 5C 10
Matley Pk. La. SK15: Stal 4E 10
Matlock Av. M34: Den 3F 27
M41: Urm 3A 22
OL6: Ash L 3A 4
Matlock Cl. M33: Sale 7H 23
WA5: Gt San 3J 39
Matlock Dr. SK7: H Gro 5J 79
Matlock M. *WA14: Alt 7J 47*
(off Renshaw St.)
Matlock Rd. M32: S'ord 1G 23
SK5: Stoc 2K 25
SK8: He Grn 6E 76
Matson Wlk. M22: Wyth 3G 75
Matterdale Cl. WA6: Frod 1K 139
Matterdale Ter. *SK15: Stal 5B 4*
(off Ullswater Ter.)
Matterhorn Rd. CH66: Ell P 1B 134
Matthew Cl. CH2: Ches 1C 150
CH44: Wall 2D 34
Matthews La. M12: Manc 4A 24
M18: Manc 1F 25
M19: Manc 1D 24
Matthews Pl. CW12: Cong 4J 183
Matthews St. WA1: Warr 5H 41
Matthew St. CH44: Wall 2D 34
Matthews Way CW3: Audl 6B 210
Matty's La. WA6: Frod 1G 139
Mauldeth Cl. SK4: Stoc 1J 51
Mauldeth Ct. SK4: Stoc 1J 51
Mauldeth Rd. M14: Manc 4A 24
M19: Manc 5B 24
M19: Manc, Stoc 7C 24
M20: Manc 4A 24
SK4: Stoc 2H 51
Mauldeth Road Station (Rail) 5B 24
Maurice Cl. SK16: Duk 2K 9
Maurice Jones Ct. CH46: More 3B 32
Maveen Ct. SK2: Stoc 1E 78
Maveen Gro. SK2: Stoc 1E 78
Mavis Dr. CH49: Woodc 2D 58
Mavor Ct. CW1: Crewe 2C 194
Mawdsley Av. WA1: Wool 5E 42
Mawdsley Cl. ST7: Als 6A 202
MAW GREEN 6K 191 (2B 220)
Maw Grn. Cl. CW1: Crewe 6K 191
Maw Grn. Rd. CW1: Crewe 6K 191
Maw La. CW1: Crewe, Hasl 6A 204
Mawson Cl. WA5: Old H 4B 40
Maxfield Cl. SK11: Mac 4G 125
Maxwell Av. SK2: Stoc 7G 53
Maxwell Cl. CH49: Upt 6D 32
CH65: Whit 6C 134
Maxwell Ct. CH42: Tran 2B 60
Maxwell Rd. CW12: Cong 6J 183
Maxwell St. CW2: Crewe 3C 194
WA3: Ris 5K 17
Mayall St. OL5: Moss 1D 4
May Av. CH44: Wall 2C 34
SK4: Stoc 2A 52
SK8: Chea H 7K 77
Maybank Rd. CH42: Tran 1C 60
Mayberry Gro. WA2: Padg 3C 42
Maycroft SK5: Stoc 5A 26
Maycroft Av. M20: Manc 6A 24
Maydews Pas. *SK11: Mac 5A 126*
(off Brook St.)
Maydor Av. CH4: Salt F 4D 148
May Dr. M19: Manc 5C 24
Mayer Av. CH63: Beb 2K 85
Mayer St. SK2: Stoc 5G 53
Mayes Ct. *M14: Manc 4A 24*
(off Sheringham Rd.)
Mayew Rd. CH61: Irby 7C 58
Mayfair Av. M41: Urm 1A 22
Mayfair Cl. SK12: Poy 2D 100
SK16: Duk 2A 10
WA5: Gt San 5F 39
Mayfair Ct. *CH43: Oxt 2A 60*
(off The Grove)
M14: Manc 3A 24
WA15: Timp 5B 48
Mayfair Dr. CW1: Crewe 1F 195
CW9: N'ich 3D 162
M33: Sale 2J 47
M44: Irlam 1D 20
Mayfair Gro. WA8: Wid 4D 62
Mayfair Pk. M20: Manc 1B 50
Mayfair Rd. M22: Wyth 2A 76
Mayfield Av. M32: S'ord 2G 23
M33: Sale 7K 23
M34: Den 4F 27
SK5: Stoc 6J 25
SK11: Mac 7K 125
WA8: Wid 4B 62
Mayfield Cl. CW4: H Cha 4K 181
WA15: Timp 6B 48
Mayfield Ct. WA8: Wid 3G 63
WA15: Timp 6B 48
Mayfield Dr. CH62: East 1C 108
CW7: Wins 1G 179
CW8: Cudd 2D 160
WN7: Leigh 2C 6
Mayfield Gdns. CH64: Nest 6H 105
Mayfield Gro. CW8: Cudd 2D 160
SK5: Stoc 6J 25
SK9: Wilm 2D 118
Mayfield M. CW1: Crewe 7E 190
Mayfield Rd. CH1: Blac 5E 144
CH45: Wall 6F 13
CH63: Beb 3A 86
CW9: N'ich 5H 157
SK6: Mar B 3H 55
SK7: Bram 2H 99
WA4: Grap 3A 68
WA15: Timp 6B 48
WA16: Mob 1K 117
Mayfields CH66: Ell P 1B 134
Mayfields Ho. *CH62: N Fer 6G 61*
(off Mayfields Nth.)
Mayfields Nth. CH62: N Fer 6G 61
Mayfields Sth. CH62: N Fer 6G 61
Mayfield St. M34: Aude 5D 8
Mayfield Ter. SK11: Mac 7K 125
Mayfield Vw. WA13: Lymm 3A 70
Mayflower Rd. CW5: Nant 4C 196
Mayford Rd. M19: Manc 1D 24
May Gro. M19: Manc 3E 24
Mayhurst Av. M21: Chor H 1K 49
Maynard Rd. WA14: W Tim 4G 47
Mayorlowe Av. SK5: Stoc 7B 26
Mayor's Rd. WA15: Alt 3K 213 (1J 73)
Maypole Cl. M31: Carri 5G 21
Maypool Dr. SK5: Stoc 5J 25
May Rd. CH60: Hes 6H 83
SK8: Chea H 7K 77
May St. L3: Liv 3K 35
Maythorn Av. WA3: Croft 4F 17
Maytree Av. CH3: Ches 1E 150
May Wlk. M31: Part 1G 45
Maywood SK9: Wilm 3D 118
Maywood Av. M20: Manc 4D 50
Mazenod Ct. *L3: Liv 1J 35*
(off Addison Way)
Mead Av. ST7: Sch G 1H 205
Mead Cl. WA16: Knut 4D 116
Meade, The SK9: Wilm 6K 97
Meade Cl. L35: R'ill 3D 36
M41: Urm 1B 22
Meadfoot Rd. CH46: More 3A 32
Meadow, The CH49: Woodc 2E 58
(not continuous)
CW4: Goo 7H 165
Meadow Av. CW2: West 2H 199
CW4: Goo 6G 165
CW12: Cong 5E 182
WA4: Warr 3E 66
WA9: Clo F 1K 37
WA15: Hale 2B 74
MEADOWBANK 1A 220
Meadow Bank CW6: Kel 4C 172
SK4: Stoc 2K 51
SK6: Bred 1K 53
WA15: Timp 5A 48
Meadowbank SK14: H'rth 1J 11
Meadowbank Cvn. Pk.
WA4: Moo 7A 66
Meadow Bank Ct. M32: S'ord 2G 23
Meadowbank Dr. CH66: L Sut 2G 133
Meadowbank Gdns. WA3: G'ury 3J 7
Meadowbrook Rd. CH46: More 5A 32
Meadowbrook Way SK8: Chea H 1K 77
Meadow Brow SK9: Ald E 5F 119
Meadow Cl. CH3: Farn 6C 186
CH3: Tar 6B 170
CH64: Nest 2C 130
CH64: W'ston 7E 106
CW2: Shav 2D 198
CW4: Goo 6J 165
CW7: Wins 1D 178
CW8: Cudd 2D 160
M32: S'ord 2K 23
M34: Den 4F 27
SK6: H Lan 5F 81
SK6: W'ley 6F 27
SK9: Wilm 3D 118
WA6: Hel 5B 138
WA8: Wid 2D 62
WA15: Hale 2B 74
WN7: Leigh 1E 6
Meadow Cotts. *CW12: Cong 3F 183*
(off Stonehouse Grn.)
Meadow Ct. CH1: Mol 1G 145
SY14: No H 3B 208
WA15: Hale 2C 74
Meadow Cres. CH49: Woodc 3D 58
Meadow Cft. CH64: W'ston 7D 106
SK7: H Gro 1J 79
ST7: Als 7F 203
Meadowcroft CH1: Sau 1C 144
CH60: Hes 5A 84
SK14: Mot 6H 11
Meadowcroft Cl. WA7: Cast 6C 90
Meadowcroft Rd. CH47: Meols 3F 31
Meadowcroft Way WN7: Leigh 1H 7
Meadow Dr. CW2: Wis 7K 193
CW8: Barnt 2K 155
SK10: Pres 4J 121
WA16: Knut 5D 116
Meadowfield CW6: Tarp 3H 175
Meadowfield Cl. CH42: R Fer 3E 60
Meadowfield Ct. SK14: Hyde 6J 9
Meadow Fld. Rd. CH4: Ches 6H 149
Meadow Ga. CW9: Winc 2B 158
Meadowgate CH48: Cald 7E 56
M41: Urm 2C 22
Meadowgate Cl. CW11: Ett H 4B 200
Meadow Gro. CW9: N'ich 1F 163
Meadow Home Pk. CW7: Wins 7C 162
Meadow Ind. Est. SK1: Stoc 1D 52
Meadow La. CH3: Hunt 6D 150
CH42: R Fer 3E 60
CH64: W'ston 6D 106
CH65: Ell P 2E 134
CW9: Comb 3H 115
CW9: Moult 7E 162
M34: Den 3F 27
SK12: Dis 1G 103
SK16: Duk 2J 9
WA2: Fear 2A 42
WA14: Dun M 1J 71
Meadow La. Ind. Pk.
CH65: Ell P 3F 135
Meadow La. Works CH65: Ell P 2F 135
Meadow Mill SK1: Stoc 1D 52
Meadow Pk. CH42: R Fer 3E 60
Meadow Ri. CH3: Clut 1B 206
CW7: Wins 3B 178
Meadow Rd. CH48: W Kir 2G 57
CW8: Weav 5H 155
M41: Urm 2C 22
Meadow Row WA7: Cast 5C 90
Meadows, The CH3: Ash H 7G 171
CH41: Birk 5C 34
(off Conway St.)
CH62: Brom 7D 86
CH64: L Nes 2D 130
CW12: Cong 3F 183
L35: R'ill 1C 36
M44: Cad 5B 20
SK6: Bred 7G 27
SK13: Had 3K 11
Meadows Cl. SK7: H Gro 2J 79
Meadows Ga. CW8: Crow 2J 153
Meadowside CH46: Leas 7B 12
CW8: N'ich 6C 156
SK7: Bram 3A 78
SK10: Adl 6G 101
SK12: Dis 1H 103
WA6: Frod 7G 111
Meadowside Av. M22: Wyth 1K 75
M44: Irlam 1D 20
Meadowside La. ST7: Sch G 5F 205
Meadowside M. CH1: Ches 6J 145
Meadowside Rd. CH62: Brom 7D 86
Meadows La. CH1: Sau 2B 144
CH4: Ches 7E 212 (4B 150)
Meadows Pl. CH4: Ches 3B 150
Meadows Rd. M33: Sale 5H 23
SK4: Stoc 4F 25
(not continuous)
SK8: Chea H 5H 77
SK8: He Grn 4D 76
Meadow St. CH45: N Bri 3G 13
CW9: N'ich 4F 157
SK2: Stoc 7G 53
SK14: Hyde 2K 27
Meadow Style Pk. ST8: Mow C 6K 205
Meadowsway CH2: Upt 2A 146
Meadowsweet Rd. WA16: Mob 2K 117
Meadowvale Cl. CW5: Nant 7C 192
Meadow Vw. CH2: Elt 5E 136
CW10: Mid 2B 180
WA13: Lymm 1K 69
Meadow Vw. Dr. WA6: Frod 1G 139
Meadow Wlk. CH61: Pens 3G 83
M31: Part 1G 45
SK6: Bred 1K 53
WA7: Pal F 7B 90
(off Halton Lea Shop. Cen.)
Meadow Way SK9: Wilm 3D 118
SK10: Mac 2B 126
ST7: Chu L 4H 203
WA15: Hale 2B 74
Mead Rd. WA1: Padg 4A 42
Meadscroft Dr. SK9: Ald E 6E 118
Meads Rd. ST7: Als 5E 202
Mead Way M34: Den 3E 26
Meadway CH45: Wall 6G 13
CH49: Upt 6E 32
CH60: Hes 1C 104
CH62: Spit 4C 86
CH66: L Sut 1H 133
M33: Sale 1J 47
SK6: H Lan 5F 81
SK7: Bram 1H 99
SK10: Pres 6H 121
SK12: Poy 1A 100
SK15: Stal 4F 11
SK16: Duk 3K 9
WA7: Run 5A 90
WA8: Wid 4A 62
Meadway Cl. M33: Sale 2J 47
Meadway Ct. SK7: Bram 1H 99
Meadway Rd. SK8: Chea H 2K 77
Meakin Cl. CW12: Cong 5K 183
Mealhouse Brow
SK1: Stoc 6J 213
Mealor's Weint CH64: Park 6E 104
Meal St. SK4: Stoc 1C 52
Mecca Bingo
Birkenhead 6C 34
Chester 3D 212 (1A 150)
Ellesmere Port 4D 134
Sale 7F 23
Meddings Cl. SK9: Ald E 7F 119
Meddowcroft Rd. CH45: Wall 5F 13
Medina Av. CW7: Wins 2G 179
Medina Cl. SK8: Chea H 1K 77
Medlar Cl. CH4: Ches 6G 149
Medlock Ct. CH43: Oxt 7K 33
Medlock Pl. M43: Droy 1A 8
Medlock St. M43: Droy 1A 8
Medway Cl. SK9: Wilm 4A 98
WA2: Warr 2J 41
WN7: Leigh 2C 6
Medway Cres. WA14: Alt 6G 47
Medway Rd. CH42: R Fer 3F 61
WA3: Cul 1B 18
Meeanee Dr. CW5: Nant 3A 196
MEERBROOK 1D 221
Meerbrook Rd. SK3: Stoc 4J 51
Mee St. SK11: Mac 7B 126
Meeting Ho. La.
WA6: Frod, New . . . . . 6K 139 & 1A 152
Meeting La. WA5: Penk 7F 39
Megabowl
Stockport 7H 213 (4C 52)
Meg La. SK10: Mac 4F 125
SK11: Sut E 3H 169
Megs La. CW9: Ant 6A 94
MEIR 3D 221
MEIR HEATH 3D 221
Melandra Castle Rd.
SK13: Gam 1K 29
Melandra Cres. SK14: Hat 1F 29
Melanie Dr. SK5: Stoc 3J 25
Melbecks Wlk. M23: Wyth 2F 49
Melbourne Av. M32: S'ord 1J 23
M90: Man A 5G 75
Melbourne Gro. CW1: Hasl 1J 195
Melbourne Rd. CH1: Blac 6D 144
SK7: Bram 7C 78
Melbourne St. CH45: N Bri 3G 13
M34: Den 1D 26
SK5: Stoc 3J 25
SK15: Stal 7B 4
Melbury Av. M20: Manc 7A 24
Melbury Ct. WA3: Ris 5A 18
Melbury Rd. SK8: Chea H 7K 77
Melchett Cres. CW9: Rud 6J 157
Meldon Rd. M13: Manc 1B 24
Melford Cl. CW2: Wis 6C 194
Melford Ct. WA1: Wool 4D 42
Melford Dr. CH43: Pren 4H 59
SK10: Mac 2K 125
WA7: Run 5J 89

Melford Rd.—Millennium Ct.

Melford Rd. SK7: H Gro 4K 79
Melfort Av. M32: S'ord 2K 23
Meliden Cres. M22: Wyth 2A 76
Meliden Gro. WA6: Hel 7B 138
Melkridge Cl. CH2: Ches 7D 146
Melksham Cl. SK11: Mac 5H 125
Melksham Dr. CH61: Irby 6A 58
Melland Rd. M18: Manc 1F 25
Melland Sports Cen. 1F 25
Meller Rd. M13: Manc 1C 24
MELLING 1B 214
Melling Av. SK4: Stoc 5H 25
Melling Cl. WN7: Leigh 1F 7
Melling Ct. CH45: N Bri 4J 13
MELLING MOUNT 1C 215
Melling Rd. CH45: N Bri 4J 13
Mellington Av. M20: Manc 4D 50
Mellock Cl. CH64: L Nes 2D 130
Mellock La. CH64: L Nes 1D 130
Melloncroft Dr. CH48: Cald 5C 56
Melloncroft Dr. W.
CH48: Cald 6D 56
MELLOR 6K 55 (2D 217)
Mellor Cl. OL6: Ash L 7A 4
WA7: Win H 6F 91
Mellor Ct. SK2: Stoc 5J 53
Mellor Cres. WA16: Knut 4C 116
Mellor Rd. CH42: Tran 3B 60
OL6: Ash L 5A 4
SK8: Chea H 4K 77
Mellors Bank ST7: Mow C 6H 205
Mellor Sports Club 6K 55
Mellor St. CW1: Crewe 1D 194
Mellor Vw. SK12: Dis 1G 103
Melrose CH46: More 3D 32
Melrose Av. CH3: Ches 1D 150
CH47: Hoy 5C 30
M20: Manc 1E 50
M33: Sale 7G 23
SK3: Stoc 5H 51
WA4: App 5H 67
WA5: B'ood 4C 14
Melrose Cres. SK3: Stoc 1B 78
SK12: Poy 1J 101
WA15: Hale 4B 74
Melrose Dr. CH66: Gt Sut 1B 140
CW1: Crewe 5G 191
Melrose Gdns. CH43: Pren 5J 59
Melsomby Rd. M23: Wyth 2G 49
Meltham Cl. SK4: Stoc 3G 51
Meltham Rd. SK4: Stoc 3G 51
Melton Av. M34: Den 1K 25
M41: Urm 1F 21
WA4: Walt 5F 67
Melton Cl. CH49: Upt 7B 32
CW12: Cong 3B 182
Melton Dr. CW12: Cong 3B 182
Melton Rd. WA7: Run 1J 111
Melton St. SK5: Stoc 7J 25
Melverley Dr. CH1: Blac 6D 144
Melville CH62: N Fer 4G 61
Melville Av. CH42: R Fer 4F 61
Melville Cl. WA2: Warr 5F 41
WA8: Wid 4K 63
Melville Rd. CH63: H Beb 1J 85
M32: S'ord 1G 23
M44: Cad 6K 19
Melvin Av. M22: Wyth 1A 76
Melyncourt Dr. SK14: Hat 7F 11
Menai Gro. SK8: Chea 6J 51
Menai Rd. SK3: Stoc 6C 52
Menai St. CH41: Birk 6B 34
Mendell Cl. CH62: Brom 6E 86
Mendip Av. M22: Wyth 1B 76
WA2: Warr 1F 41
Mendip Cl. CH42: Tran 4B 60
CH66: Gt Sut 5A 134
CW7: Wins 4C 178
SK4: Stoc 1C 52
SK8: He Grn 6D 76
Mendip Ct. SK4: Stoc 1C 52
Mendip Rd. CH42: Tran 4B 60
Menhuin Ho. CH2: Ches 5A 146
Menin Av. WA4: Warr 2G 67
Menlo Av. CH61: Irby 7C 58
Menlo Cl. CH43: Oxt 1H 59
Menlow Cl. WA4: Grap 4C 68
Mentmore Gdns. WA4: App 1K 93
Mentone Cres. M22: Wyth 1A 76
Mentone Rd. SK4: Stoc 1K 51
Mentor St. M13: Manc 1C 24
MEOLS 4F 31 (2A 214)
Meols Cl. CH66: Gt Sut 4A 134
L24: Hale 6B 88
Meols Ct. CH47: Hoy 6B 30
Meols Dr. CH47: Hoy 2B 56
CH48: W Kir 2B 56
Meols Pde. CH47: Meols 4D 30
Meols Station (Rail) 4F 31
Mercer Cl. SY14: Mal 3H 207
Mercer Rd. CH43: Bid 4H 33
Mercer St. M19: Manc 2E 24
WA5: B'ood 5B 14
Mercer Wlk. *CH65: Ell P 4E 134*
(off The Port Arcades)
Mercer Way CH4: Ches 5G 149
CW5: Nant 7C 192
Merchants Ct. CW1: Crewe 6H 191
L1: Liv 3H 35
Mercian Cl. CW2: Shav 3B 198
Mercian Way SK3: Stoc 5B 52
Mercia Sq. CH1: Ches 4C 212
Mercury Ct. CH1: Ches 1F 149
L3: Liv 2H 35
MERE 5G 95 (2B 216)
Mere, The OL6: Ash L 3A 4
SK8: Chea H 1J 77
Mere Av. CH63: Rab M 1G 107
Mere Bank CW9: Dave 6F 163
Merebank CH43: Oxt 1H 59
Merebank Rd. CW2: Crewe 5B 194
Merebrook Cl. SK11: Mac 4G 125
Merebrook Rd. SK11: Mac 4G 125
Mere Brook Wlk. CW2: Crewe 6C 194
Mere Cl. CH66: Gt Sut 6K 133
CW1: Hasl 2K 195
M33: Sale 1F 49
M34: Den 1A 26
WA16: Pick 1C 158
Mere Ct. CW2: West 2H 199
CW7: Wins 4F 179
SK11: Chel 5B 166
ST7: Als 5E 202
WA16: Knut 3E 116
Mere Cres. CW8: Oak 4J 173
Merecroft CH3: Ches 2D 150
Merecroft Av. CH44: Wall 2B 34
Meredith Av. WA4: Grap 3B 68
Meredith St. CW1: Crewe 1C 194
M14: Manc 4A 24
Mere Dr. M20: Manc 1D 50
Mere Farm Gro. CH43: Oxt 1J 59
Mere Farm Rd. CH43: Oxt 1H 59
Merefield Rd. WA15: Timp 7C 48
Mere Hall WA16: Mere 5F 95
Merehaven Cl. WA16: Pick 1B 158
MERE HEATH 6F 163 (3A 216)
Mereheath CH46: Leas 1B 32
Mereheath Dr. WA16: Mere 6K 95
Mereheath Gdns. *CH46: Leas 1B 32*
(off Mereheath)
Mereheath La.
WA16: Mere 6J 95 & 1C 116
Mereheath Pk. WA16: Knut 2D 116
Mere Ho. SK4: Stoc 3G 51
Mereland Av. M20: Manc 1E 50
Mere La. CH45: Wall 4E 12
CH60: Hes 4G 83
CW8: Cudd, S'way 4D 160
WA16: Pick 1B 158
Mere Pk. Rd. CH49: Gre 2K 57
Merepool Cl. SK6: Mar 5C 54
Mere Rd. CW2: West 2H 199
CW9: Mars 7H 115
WA2: Fear 2A 42
Mere's Edge Bus. Pk. WA6: Hel 6A 138
Mere Side SK15: Stal 5A 4
(not continuous)
Mereside Av. CW12: Cong 4D 182
Mereside Cl. SK8: Chea H 1H 77
SK10: Mac 3H 125
Mereside Rd. WA16: Mere 4J 95
Mere St. CW1: Hasl 2K 195
Merevale Cl. WA7: Beec 1A 112
Mere Vw. WA6: Hel 6A 138
Mere Vw. Cvn. Pk. WA16: Pick 1B 158
Mere Vw. Gdns. WA4: App 1J 93
Merewood Av. M22: Wyth 6K 49
Merewood Cl. WA2: Warr 1H 41
Mereworth CH48: Cald 7E 56
Mereworth Dr. CW9: N'ich 1E 162
Meriden Av. CH63: Spit 5A 86
Meridian Pl. M20: Manc 1C 50
Meriton Rd. SK9: Hand 2K 97
Merlewood Av. M19: Manc 4F 25
M34: Aude 1A 8
Merlin Av. CH49: Upt 6A 32
WA16: Knut 2F 117
Merlin Cl. CH49: Upt 6A 32
CW7: Wins 4H 179
SK2: Stoc 6A 54
WA7: Cast 5C 90
Merlin Ct. CW1: Crewe 5F 191
Merlin Ho. M19: Manc 7A 24
Merlin Rd. CH42: Tran 2B 60
Merlin Way CW1: Crewe 5F 191
Merlyn Av. M20: Manc 1E 50
M33: Sale 5H 23
M34: Den 1D 26
Merrick Av. M22: Wyth 1A 76
Merrick Cl. WA2: Warr 1J 41
Merridale, The WA15: Hale 5A 74
Merriden Rd. SK10: Mac 2J 125
Merrill's Av. CW2: Crewe 1J 193
Merrills La. CH49: Upt 7D 32
Merriman Av. WA16: Knut 2G 117
Merritt Av. CH41: Birk 4A 34
Merrivale Rd. CW2: Wis 6A 194
Merrybent Cl. SK2: Stoc 7H 53
Merrydale Cl. SK10: Mac 3G 125
Merryman's La. SK9: Ald E 1C 166
Mersey Bank Av. M21: Chor H 1K 49
Merseybank Ho. *CH62: N Fer 5G 61*
(off New Ferry Rd.)
Mersey Bank Lodge SK13: Had 2K 11
Mersey Bank Rd. SK13: Had 3K 11
Merseybank Rd. CH62: N Fer 5G 61
Mersey Ct. *CH44: Wall 2D 34*
(off Ferryside)
M33: Sale 6K 23
Mersey Cres. M20: Manc 1K 49
Mersey Dr. M31: Part 7D 20
Mersey La. Sth. CH42: R Fer 3F 61
Mersey Mdws. M20: Manc 1B 50
Mersey Pl. *CW7: Wins 3J 179*
(off Trent Av.)
Mersey Rd. CH42: R Fer 3F 61
M20: Manc 1B 50
M33: Sale 5G 23
SK4: Stoc 2H 51
WA7: Run 3G 89
WA8: Wid 2G 89
Merseyside Maritime Mus. 4H 35
Mersey Sq. SK1: Stoc 6H 213 (3C 52)
(not continuous)
Mersey St. CH44: Wall 2D 34
SK1: Stoc 2E 52
WA1: Warr 1F 67
Mersey Ter. *CH65: Ell P 1E 134*
(off Lwr. Mersey St.)
Merseyton Rd. CH65: Ell P 7J 109
Merseyton Rd. Workshops
CH65: Ell P 1E 134
(off Merseyton Rd.)
Mersey Tunnel - Toll L3: Liv 1E 34
(not continuous)
Mersey Valley Vis. Cen. 6K 23
Mersey Vw. *CH41: Tran 1D 60*
(off Marquis St.)
CH63: H Beb 7C 60
M41: Urm 3H 21
WA7: Wes P 7D 88
Mersey Vw. Cotts.
WA7: West 1F 111
Mersey Vw. Rd. WA8: Hal B 2B 88
Mersey Wlk. CH42: Tran 2D 60
WA4: Westy 7K 41
Merseyway SK1: Stoc 6H 213 (3C 52)
Mersham Ct. WA8: Wid 1F 63
Merston Dr. M20: Manc 4E 50
Merton Av. SK6: Bred 7F 27
SK7: H Gro 5K 79
Merton Cl. CH64: Nest 3C 130
Merton Dr. CH4: Ches 7G 149
CH49: Woodc 2D 58
Merton Gro. WA15: Timp 6B 48
Merton Pl. CH43: Oxt 6B 34
Merton Rd. CH45: Wall 6G 13
CH65: H'ton 4C 108
CH66: Gt Sut 5B 134
M33: Sale 6F 23
SK3: Stoc 4K 51
SK12: Poy 2A 100
Mertoun Rd. WA4: Walt 4F 67
Mervyn Rd. CW8: Weav 4H 155
Merwell Rd. M41: Urm 2H 21
Merwood Av. SK8: He Grn 5F 77
Mesham Cl. CH49: Upt 7B 32
Meshaw Cl. M23: Wyth 2E 48
Metcalfe Ct. *SK6: Rom 2B 54*
(off Metcalfe Dr.)
Metcalfe Dr. SK6: Rom 2B 54
Meteor Cres. WA2: Warr 1H 41
Methuen St. CH41: Birk 4K 33
M12: Manc 1E 24
Met Quarter, The L1: Liv 3J 35
Mevagissey Rd.
WA7: B'vale 2E 112
Mews, The CW4: H Cha 4J 181
CW6: Tarp 4H 175
CW8: Barnt 3A 156
M33: Sale 1C 48
SK8: Gat 7D 50
WA5: B'ood 5B 14
Mews Ct. CH64: W'ston 7E 106
Meyer St. SK3: Stoc 6D 52
Meynell Cl. CW2: Wis 5A 194
Meynell Pl. CH1: Blac 5H 145
Meyrick Ct. WA12: New W 1D 14
Miami Cl. WA5: Gt San 5K 39
Micawber Rd. SK12: Poy 4D 100
Michael Ct. M19: Manc 2F 51
Michael Dragonette Ct. L3: Liv 1H 35
Michaels Hey Pde. M23: Wyth 4C 48
Michigan Pl. WA5: Gt San 5A 40
Micklegate CH2: Mic T 2H 147
WA7: Murd 7F 91
Micklehead Bus. Village
WA9: St H 1G 37
MICKLEHEAD GREEN 1G 37
Micklehead Grn. WA9: St H 1F 37
MICKLEHURST 1E 4
Micklehurst Av. M20: Manc 1A 50
Micklehurst Grn. SK2: Stoc 7J 53
Micklehurst Rd. OL5: Moss 1E 4
MICKLE TRAFFORD 2H 147 (1C 219)
Micklewright Av. CW1: Crewe 1D 194
Mickley Hall La. CW5: B'hall 5K 209
Midbrook Wlk. *M22: Wyth 3H 75*
(off Plowden Rd.)
Middlecroft CH3: Guil S 5H 147
Middlefields SK8: Chea H 1K 77
Middle Hillgate SK1: Stoc 7K 213 (3D 52)
Middlehills SK11: Mac 6D 126
Middlehurst Av. CW8: Weav 5H 155
Middlehurst Rd. WA4: Grap 3A 68
Middle La. CH3: Ald 6G 185
CW12: Cong 2K 183
M31: Part 2F 45
WA6: K'ley 1A 152
Middlesex Rd. SK5: Stoc 5A 26
Middleton Rd. SK5: Stoc 1J 25
Middle Wlk. WA6: Frod 1H 139
WA16: Knut 3F 117
MIDDLEWICH 4C 180 (1B 220)
Middlewich Leisure Cen. 4C 180
Middlewich Rd.
CW1: Bra G, Crewe, L'ton, W'ood
2H 193
CW2: Crewe, Nant, Wis, W'ood
2H 193
CW4: Cran 1F 181
CW4: H Cha 4F 181
CW5: Nant, W'ston, Wis 7C 192
CW6: Kel 5F 173
CW7: Wins 3K 179
CW8: Dela 5F 173
CW9: N'ich 5G 157
CW10: Stan 2A 180
CW11: S'ach 2C 200
WA16: All, Lwr P
3B 164, 1C 164 & 5A 164
Middlewich St. CW1: Crewe 6J 191
MIDDLEWOOD 1H 101
Middlewood Dr. SK4: Stoc 3J 51
Middlewood Rd. SK6: H Lan 6D 80
SK12: Poy 6B 80
Middlewood Station (Rail) 7D 80
Middlewood Vw. SK6: H Lan 5D 80
Midghall St. L3: Liv 1H 35
Midhurst Cl. SK8: Chea H 5H 77
Midland Cotts. SK7: H Gro 4C 80
Midland Rd. SK5: Stoc 1J 25
SK7: Bram 1C 78
Midland St. CH43: Oxt 7B 34
WA8: Wid 4H 63
Midland Ter. *WA14: Alt 3H 73*
(off Ashley Rd.)
Midland Wlk. SK7: Bram 2C 78
(not continuous)
Midland Way WA1: Warr 7E 40
WA2: Warr 7E 40
Midlothian Ho. CH1: Ches 3E 212
Midpoint 18 Motorway Ind. Est.
CW10: Mid 3E 180
MID REDDISH 3J 25
MIDWAY 4C 100
Midway SK8: Chea H 1E 98
Midway Dr. SK12: Poy 4C 100
Midway St. M12: Manc 1D 24
Midwood St. WA8: Wid 5H 63
Milborne Cl. CH2: Upt 5B 146
Milburn Av. M23: Wyth 2H 49
Mildenhall Cl. WA5: Gt San 6K 39
MILE END 6F 53
Mile End La. SK2: Stoc 7F 53
Miles Cl. CH49: Gre 3K 57
WA3: Birc 1F 43
MILES GREEN 2C 221
Miles La. CH49: Gre 3K 57
Miles St. SK14: Hyde 1A 28
Milford Dr. M19: Manc 4E 24
Milford Gdns. WA4: App 2H 93
Milford Gro. SK2: Stoc 5G 53
Military Mus. 6B 212 (3K 149)
Milk St. CW12: Cong 3F 183
SK14: Hyde 1J 27
Mill, The SK15: Stal 1B 10
Millar Cres. WA8: Wid 6G 63
Mill Av. WA5: Gt San 5G 39
Mill Bank CH64: Ness 3E 130
Millbank WA13: Lymm 2A 70
Millbank Cl. SK11: Chel 5C 166
Millbank Cotts. WA6: Frod 7G 111
Millbank Ct. WA6: Frod 7G 111
Millbank Dr. SK10: Mac 2G 125
Mill Bank Rd. CH44: Wall 1K 33
Millbeck Cl. CW2: West 2H 199
Mill Bri. Cl. CW1: Crewe 3F 195
MILLBROOK 5E 4 (1D 217)
Millbrook SK14: H'rth 1J 11
Millbrook Av. M34: Den 2C 26
Millbrook Cl. CW7: Wins 4A 178
WA3: G'ury 5J 7
Millbrook Ct. CW10: Mid 3D 180
Millbrook End CH3: Tatt 2G 187
Millbrook Fold SK7: H Gro 5K 79
Millbrook Gro. *SK9: Wilm 5A 98*
(off Bankside Cl.)
Mill Brook Ind. Est. M23: Wyth 6E 48
Millbrook Rd. CH41: Birk 2A 34
M23: Wyth 2G 75
Millbrook St. SK1: Stoc 4D 52
Millbrook Towers SK1: Stoc 4D 52
MILL BROW 4K 55
Mill Brow CH63: H Beb 7C 60
SK6: Mar B 4K 55
SK14: B'tom 3H 29
WA8: Wid 3J 63
Mill Brow Rd. SK6: Mar B 4K 55
Millbuck Pk. CW11: Ett H 4A 200
Millbuck Way CW11: Ett H 3B 200
(not continuous)
Millbutt Cl. CH63: H Beb 7C 60
Mill Cl. CH2: Upt 4A 146
CH42: Tran 1C 60
WA2: Fear 1J 41
WA16: Knut 1H 117
Mill Ct. CH65: Ell P 2B 134
M41: Urm 1D 22
Mill Cft. CH64: Nest 6H 105
Millcroft CW11: Whe 5C 204
Millcroft Pk. CH49: Gre 2J 57
Mill Cross *CH3: Wave 2B 174*
(off Eggbridge La.)
Milldale Rd. WN7: Leigh 1B 6
Millennium Bus. Pk. WA3: Birc 2D 42
Millennium Ct. CH64: Nest 6H 105

Millennium Ga.—Moorcroft Ct.

Millennium Ga. CW1: Crewe 4F 195
Millennium Ho. M34: Den 1B 26
Millennium Wlk.
WA5: Gt San 5K 39
(off Arizona Cres.)
Miller Hey OL5: Moss 2E 4
Millers Cl. CH3: Wave 3A 174
CH46: More 5J 31
M33: Sale 1G 49
Millers Ct. SK10: Mac 4K 125
SK15: Stal 2A 10
Millersdale WA9: Clo F 1J 37
Millersdale Cl. CH62: East 2A 108
Millersdale Gro. WA7: Beec 1K 111
Millers La. WA13: Lymm 7D 44
Millers Mdw. SK10: R'ow 6G 123
Miller St. WA4: Warr 1G 67
Millers Way CH46: More 4K 31
Millers Wharf SK15: Stal 7C 4
ST7: Rod H 2G 203
Milley La. WA16: Pick 1E 158
Mill Farm Cl. WA2: Warr 1J 41
Mill Farm Est. CW5: Wren 3K 209
Millfield CH64: Nest 6H 105
Mill Fld. Cl. CH3: Farn 5C 186
Millfield Cl. CH63: H Beb 1H 85
Millfield Ct. WA15: Hale 3J 73
Millfield La. CW6: Tarp 2H 175
Millfield Rd. WA8: Wid 3J 63
Mill Flds. CW12: Cong 3F 183
Millfields CW5: Nant 2B 196
Millfield Ter. CH66: L Sut 1J 133
Millford Av. M41: Urm 1H 21
(not continuous)
Millford Gdns. M41: Urm 1H 21
Millgate CW8: Cudd 2C 160
SK1: Stoc 5J 213 (2D 52)
Millgate La. M20: Manc 3D 50
(Kingston Rd.)
M20: Manc 4C 50
(Parrs Wood Rd.)
Mill Grn. CH64: W'ston 7E 106
CW12: Cong 3F 183
SK11: Mac 6B 126
(off Cross St.)
Mill Grn. La. WA8: Wid 7K 37
Mill Hey L35: R'ill 3E 36
Mill Hey Rd. CH48: Cald 7E 56
Mill Hill CH43: Oxt 2K 59
Mill Hill Av. SK12: Poy 6H 79
Mill Hill Dr. CW11: S'ach 4E 200
Mill Hill Gro. SK14: Mot 1G 29
Mill Hill Hollow SK12: Poy 6H 79
Mill Hill La. CW11: S'ach 4E 200
Mill Hill Rd. CH61: Irby 5K 57
Mill Hill Way SK14: Mot 1G 29
(off Chain Bar La.)
Mill Ho. Av. WA4: Stoc H 4H 67
Millhouse Av. M23: Wyth 1G 75
Millhouse Cl. CH46: More 3J 31
Mill Ho. La. WA3: Birc, Croft 5F 17
Millhouse La. CH46: More 3J 31
Milliner Ct. SK2: Stoc 5H 53
Millingfield, The CW4: H Cha 5J 181
MILLINGTON 7K 71
Millington Cl. CH43: Pren 4H 59
WA7: Sut W 3B 112
WA8: Wid 5F 63
Millington Gdns. WA13: Lymm 7E 44
Millington Hall La.
WA14: M'ton 7K 71
Millington La. CW8: Gor 7D 154
WA14: M'ton 7K 71
Mill La. CH2: Upt 5K 145
CH3: Ald 7G 185
CH3: Gt Bar 3B 170
CH3: Tar S 5C 170
CH44: Wall 1K 33
CH49: Gre 2K 57
CH60: Hes 6K 83
CH64: Burt 7G 131
CH64: Ness 3E 130
CH64: W'ston 6D 106
CH66: Ell P, Gt Sut 4K 133
CW2: West 1G 199
CW3: Audl 7A 210
(Holly Bank)
CW3: Audl 5C 210
(Salford)
CW4: Goo 4J 165
CW4: H Cha 5K 181 & 7K 181
CW6: Cote 2E 176
CW6: Dud 4A 174
CW6: L Bud 2H 177
CW6: Rus 7H 177
CW6: Wee C 6B 172
CW7: Wins 7K 161
CW8: Cudd 1C 160
CW8: W'ate 7K 161
CW10: Mid 3C 180
(Kinderton St.)
CW10: Mid 3B 180
(Tewkesbury Cl.)
CW11: Hass, Whe, Mal B 7E 200
(not continuous)
CW11: Most 1A 200
L3: Liv 2J 35
L35: R'ill 2C 36
M22: N'den 3A 50
M34: Den 2G 27
SK5: Stoc 2J 25
SK6: Rom 5A 54
Mill La. SK6: W'ley 5F 27
(Botany Rd.)
SK6: W'ley 5F 27
(Wood Cotts., not continuous)
SK7: H Gro 5K 79
SK8: Chea 6F 51
SK8: Chea H 2K 77
SK9: Ald E 2B 166
SK10: Adl 5F 103
SK10: Boll 3F 123
SK10: Mot A, Pres 7F 99
SK11: Mac 5A 126
SK11: Snel 2K 165
SK14: Hyde 2G 27
ST7: Sch G 1K 205
WA2: Warr 7D 16
WA2: Winw 6H 15
WA4: H Wal 6C 66
WA4: Stoc H 4H 67
(not continuous)
WA5: Warr 7C 40
WA6: Frod 5A 112
WA6: K'ley 1E 152
WA8: Cron 7D 36
WA8: Wid, Bold H 7K 37
WA12: New W 1H 15
WA13: Lymm 6E 44
WA15: Ash 2A 96
WA16: Mob 6C 102
Mill La. Ind. Est. CH2: L Sta 7H 135
Millmead ST7: Rod H 2G 203
Mill Mdw. WA12: New W 1H 15
Millom Av. L35: R'ill 1B 36
M23: Wyth 3H 49
Millom Ct. WA15: Timp 6D 48
Millom Pl. SK8: Gat 2D 76
Mill Pk. Dr. CH62: East 4K 107
Mill Pool Cl. SK6: W'ley 6G 27
Millport Cl. WA2: Fear 2A 42
Millrace Dr. CW2: Wis 6B 194
Mill Ri. WA6: Hel 4C 138
Mill Rd. CH61: Thin 7D 58
CH62: Brom 3D 86
CH63: H Beb 6C 60
SK9: Wilm 7J 97
SK11: Mac 6A 126
Mill Row CW11: S'ach 3G 201
Millstone Cl. SK12: Poy 1E 100
Millstone Ct. SK6: Bred 1A 54
Millstone La. CW5: Nant 1D 196
Millstone Pas. SK11: Mac 6B 126
Millstream Cl. CW4: Goo 6J 165
Mill St. CH4: Ches 7D 212 (3A 150)
CH42: Tran 1C 60
CH64: Nest 7G 105
CW2: Crewe 3D 194
CW5: Nant 2C 196
CW12: Cong 3F 183
(Cross St.)
CW12: Cong 2H 183
(Havannah St.)
L8: Liv 6K 35
OL5: Moss 1D 4
SK6: W'ley 6F 27
SK7: H Gro 2H 79
SK9: Wilm 7J 97
SK11: Mac 4A 126
SK14: Hyde 5K 9
SK15: Stal 1D 10
WA14: Alt 1K 213 (7J 47)
Mill St. Mall SK11: Mac 4A 126
(off Grosvenor Cen.)
Mills Way CW1: L'ton 4G 191
Millthwaite Ct. CH44: Wall 7F 13
Millthwaite Rd. CH44: Wall 7F 13
Mill Vw. L8: Liv 7K 35
Mill Vw. Dr. CH63: H Beb 7B 60
Millwain Ho. SK4: Stoc 7D 24
Mill Way CW5: Nant 5D 196
Millway CH3: Wave 2B 174
WA15: H'rns 6C 74
Mill Wharf CH3: Wave 2B 174
Millwood CH63: H Beb 7C 60
WA7: Nort 5E 90
Millwood Cl. SK8: Chea H 5G 77
Millwood Dr. CW8: H'ord 2H 161
Millwood Ter. SK14: Hyde 1J 27
Millwood Vw. SK15: Stal 7C 4
Mill Yd. CH61: Thin 7E 58
Milman Way CH49: Upt 1C 58
Milne Cl. CW2: Wis 5K 193
SK16: Duk 2H 9
Milner Av. WA14: B'ath 5F 47
Milner Cop CH60: Hes 6J 83
Milner Rd. CH60: Hes 6J 83
CW8: N'ich 7B 156
Milner St. CH41: Birk 4K 33
WA5: Warr 7D 40
Milnes Av. WN7: Leigh 1F 7
Milnthorpe Rd.
WA5: B'ood 5B 14
MILTON 2D 221
Milton Av. L35: Whis 1A 36
M44: Irlam 5B 20
SK15: M'ook 5F 5
WA8: Wid 5F 63
Milton Cl. CH65: Ell P 4F 135
CW9: Winc 2C 158
CW10: Mid 7D 180
SK6: Mar 1F 81
SK16: Duk 3C 10
(not continuous)
Milton Ct. M19: Manc 7B 24
SK7: Bram 7C 78
Milton Cres. CH60: Hes 5J 83
SK8: Chea 7E 50
Milton Dr. CW2: Wis 6K 193
M33: Sale 5F 23
SK12: Poy 2C 100
WA15: Timp 3A 48
MILTON GREEN 2C 219
Milton Grn. CH61: Thin 7E 58
Milton Gro. M33: Sale 5F 23
WA4: Warr 2H 67
WA6: Hel 7A 138
Milton M. ST7: Als 6E 202
(off Crewe Rd.)
Milton Pavement CH41: Birk 6C 34
Milton Rd. CH1: Blac 4G 145
CH42: Tran 1B 60
CH44: Wall 2C 34
CH48: W Kir 2B 56
CH65: Ell P 4F 135
M32: S'ord 1K 23
M34: Aude 1C 8
SK7: Bram 6C 78
WA8: Wid 5F 63
Milton Rd. E. CH42: Tran 1C 60
Milton Rough CW8: Act B 3B 154
Milton St. CH1: Ches 3D 212 (1A 150)
SK14: Hyde 6J 9
WA8: Wid 1G 89
WA9: Sut M 2G 37
Milton Way CW11: Ett H 3B 200
Milvain Dr. WA2: Warr 3G 41
Milverton Av. SK14: Hat 2D 28
Milverton Dr. SK7: Bram 1E 98
Milverton Wlk. SK14: Hat 1D 28
Milwain Dr. SK4: Stoc 5F 25
Milwain Rd. M19: Manc 3C 24
M32: S'ord 2H 23
Mimosa Cl. CH2: Elt 4G 137
Minden Cl. M20: Manc 1E 50
Minehead Av. M41: Urm 3A 22
MINERA 2A 218
Miners Way WA8: Wid 6G 63
Minerva Av. CH1: Ches 1F 149
Minerva Cl. WA4: Warr 3H 67
Minerva Ct. CH1: Ches 1F 149
Minerva Rd. OL6: Ash L 1H 9
Minor Av. SK11: L Grn 3H 129
Minshull New Rd. CW1: Crewe 7E 190
Minshull St. WA16: Knut 3E 116
MINSHULL VERNON 1D 190
Minsmere Walks SK2: Stoc 7K 53
Minstead Cl. SK14: Hyde 2B 28
Minstead Wlk. M22: Wyth 3H 75
Minster Cl. CW7: Wins 7E 178
SK16: Duk 4J 9
Minster Ct. CW2: Wis 6J 193
WA7: Run 6E 88
Minster Dr. SK8: Chea 7J 51
WA14: Bow 5E 72
Minton Cl. CW12: Cong 5K 183
Minton Way WA8: Wid 7H 37
Miranda Av. CH63: H Beb 6D 60
Mirfield Av. SK4: Stoc 2K 51
Miriam Pl. CH41: Birk 4J 33
Mirion St. CW1: Crewe 2D 194
Missouri Dr. WA5: Gt San 5J 39
Misterton Wlk. M23: Wyth 5E 48
(off Sandy La.)
Misty Cl. WA8: Wid 3C 62
Mitchell Av. WA5: B'ood 6B 14
Mitchell Cl. SK8: Gat 6B 50
Mitchell Gdns. M22: Shar 7A 50
Mitchell Ho. SK8: Gat 6B 50
(off Mitchell Cl.)
Mitchell Pl. L1: Liv 3J 35
Mitchell St. WA4: Stoc H 5G 67
Mitford Cl. M14: Manc 4A 24
Mitford Rd. M14: Manc 4A 24
Mitford St. M32: S'ord 2H 23
Mithril Cl. WA8: Wid 2A 64
Mitton Cl. WA3: Cul 5E 6
MIXON 2D 221
Moadlock SK6: Rom 7H 27
Moat Av. M22: Wyth 7J 49
Moat Gdns. M22: Wyth 1J 75
Moat Ho. Dr. CW2: Crewe 4A 194
Moat La. WA3: Rix 2A 44
Moat, The (Nature Reserve) 2A 200
Moat Rd. M22: Wyth 1J 75
Moat Wlk. SK5: Stoc 4B 26
MOBBERLEY
ST10 3D 221
WA16 6B 102 (3B 216)
Mobberley Cl. M19: Manc 7B 24
WA4: Thel 2D 68
Mobberley Ct. CH63: Spit 3A 86
Mobberley Rd. SK9: Wilm 6C 96
WA14: Ash 1A 102
WA16: Knut 3F 117
WA16: Mob 1A 102
Mobberley Station (Rail) 3A 102
Mobberley Way CH63: Spit 3A 86
MOBLAKE 6F 211
Mockbeggar Dr. CH45: Wall 4D 12
Mockbeggar Wharf CH45: Wall 4E 12
Modbury Cl. SK7: H Gro 4E 78
MODDERSHALL 3D 221
Model Cotts. CW4: Cran 1G 181
Moelfre Dr. SK8: Chea H 6A 78
Moelwyn Dr. CH66: Ell P 1B 134
Moggie La. SK10: Adl 5E 100
Moira Sephton Ct. CH43: Noc 1G 59
(off Sandalwood Dr.)
Moison Ho. SK2: Stoc 6E 52
(off Canada St.)
MOLD 1A 218
Mollets Wood M34: Den 5F 9
MOLLINGTON 7B 140 (3B 214)
Mollington Ct. CH1: Mol 1F 145
Mollington Grange Bus. Pk.
CH1: Mol 3G 145
Mollington Link CH41: Birk 7D 34
Mollington Rd. CH44: Wall 1B 34
M22: Wyth 5A 76
Mollington St. CH41: Birk 7D 34
Molly Potts Cl. WA16: Knut 5F 117
Molyneux Av. WA5: Warr 4D 40
Molyneux Cl. CH49: Upt 7C 32
Molyneux Dr. CH45: N Bri 3H 13
Molyneux Rd. M19: Manc 2F 25
Mona Av. SK8: He Grn 4F 77
Monaco Dr. M22: N'den 2K 49
Monarch Cl. CW2: Crewe 2K 193
M44: Irlam 5B 20
Monarch Dr. CW9: N'ich 1D 162
Monarchs Quay L3: Liv 5H 35
Mona St. CH41: Birk 5J 33
SK14: Hyde 1K 27
Mona Way M44: Irlam 3E 20
Monck Dr. CW5: Nant 1B 196
Mond Rd. WA8: Wid 5G 63
Mond St. CW8: Barnt 3A 156
Money Ash Rd. WA15: Alt 2H 73
Monfa Av. SK2: Stoc 1E 78
Monica Dr. WA8: Wid 7G 37
Monica Gro. M19: Manc 3C 24
Monk Rd. CH44: Wall 7H 13
Monksdale Av. M41: Urm 1A 22
Monks Ferry CH41: Birk 6E 34
Monks Gro. CH65: Ell P 2D 134
MONK'S HEATH 3C 217
Monks La. CW1: Crewe 7E 190
CW3: Audl, Hank 2E 210
CW5: Act 6H 189
CW5: Nant 2C 196
(off Dysart Bldgs.)
Monks Orchard CW5: Nant 2D 196
Monks Pl. WA2: Warr 5G 41
Monks St. WA5: Warr 6C 40
Monk St. CH41: Birk 6E 34
(off Cross St.)
CW1: Crewe 1A 194
Monks Way CH48: W Kir 3C 56
CH63: Beb 2K 85
CW8: H'ord 2A 162
WA7: Pre B 2G 113
Monkswood Cl. WA5: Call 2C 40
Monmouth Av. M33: Sale 6E 22
Monmouth Cl. WA1: Wool 5E 42
Monmouth Rd. CH44: Wall 7F 13
SK8: Chea H 4K 77
Monroe Cl. WA1: Wool 5B 42
Monro St. L8: Liv 1K 61
Monsal Av. SK2: Stoc 5H 53
Monsall Cl. SK11: Mac 5C 126
Monsall Dr. SK11: Mac 5C 126
Montague Ct. M33: Sale 7H 23
(off Montague Rd.)
Montague Ho. SK3: Stoc 7F 213
Montague Rd. M33: Sale 7G 23
WA8: Wid 7A 62
Montague Way SK15: Stal 7B 4
Montagu Rd. SK2: Stoc 5H 53
Montagu St. SK6: Comp 2H 55
Montana Cl. WA5: Gt San 5A 40
Montclare Cres. WA4: Stoc H 4J 67
Montcliffe Cl. WA3: Birc 6H 17
Montgomery Cl. WA5: Gt San 4J 39
WA16: Knut 1G 117
Montgomery Hill CH48: Cald, Fran 5G 57
Montgomery Rd. M13: Manc 1C 24
WA8: Wid 5D 62
Montgomery Way CW7: Wins 5C 178
Montmorency Rd. WA16: Knut 2H 117
Monton Rd. SK5: Stoc 7B 26
Montpelier Av. WA7: West 1F 111
Montpellier Ct. CH45: N Bri 3G 13
(off Montpellier Cres.)
Montpellier Cres. CH45: N Bri 3G 13
Montpellier Ho. CH45: N Bri 3G 13
Montpellior Rd. M22: Wyth 3K 75
Montreal St. M19: Manc 2E 24
Montrose Av. CH44: Wall 3D 34
M32: S'ord 1G 23
SK2: Stoc 2E 78
SK16: Duk 3H 9
Montrose Cl. CW2: Shav 4B 198
SK10: Mac 3H 125
WA2: Fear 7E 16
Montrose Ct. CH4: Ches 4G 149
CH47: Hoy 6C 30
CW4: H Cha 5H 181
Montrose Cres. M19: Manc 2C 24
Monument Pl. L3: Liv 2K 35
Moody St. CW12: Cong 4F 183
Moon Gro. M14: Manc 1A 24
Moorby Av. M19: Manc 7B 24
Moorcot Ct. M23: Wyth 4F 49
Moor Cres. CH4: Lwr K 1A 184
Moorcroft WA16: Plum 2H 159
Moorcroft Av. CH3: Gt Bou 2E 150
Moorcroft Ct. CH3: Gt Bou 2E 150

Moorcroft Cres.—Mottram Cl.

Moorcroft Cres. CH3: Guil S 6F **147**
Moorcroft Dr. M19: Manc 7C **24**
Moorcroft M. CH4: Salt 5E **148**
Moorcroft Rd. CH45: Wall 6D **12**
M23: Wyth 3F **49**
Moorcroft Sq. SK14: Hyde 4K **9**
Moorcroft St. M43: Droy 2A **8**
Moorcroft Wlk. M19: Manc 7B **24**
Moordale Rd. WA16: Knut 3F **117**
Moorditch La. WA6: Frod 6F **111**
MOORE . . . . .1K **91 (2D 215)**
Moore Av. CH42: R Fer 3D **60**
WA4: Thel .2D **68**
Moore Cl. WA8: Wid 3K **63**
Moor Edge Rd. OL5: Moss 1G **5**
Moore Gro. WA13: Lymm 7D **44**
Moore La. WA4: Moo 6K **65**
Moore Nature Reserve 5K **65**
Moor End M22: N'den 4K **49**
Moore Wlk. *M34: Den 4F 27*
(off Wordsworth Rd.)
Mooreway L35: R'ill 3E **36**
Moorfield Av. M20: Manc 4A **24**
M34: Den 2F **27**
SK15: Stal .3E **10**
Moorfield Cl. M44: Irlam 1E **20**
Moorfield Cres. WA3: Low 3A **6**
Moorfield Dr. CH64: Park 5F **105**
SK9: Wilm 2D **118**
SK14: Hyde 5A **10**
Moorfield Gro. M33: Sale 1D **48**
SK4: Stoc .7E **24**
Moorfield Hgts. SK15: Carrb 2F **5**
Moorfield Pde. M44: Irlam 1E **20**
Moorfield Rd. M44: Irlam 1E **20**
WA8: Wid .1K **63**
Moorfields CW5: W'ston 1J **197**
L2: Liv 2H **35**
Moorfields Av. CH43: Noc 1G **59**
Moorfields Station (Rail) 2H **35**
Moorfield St. SK14: H'rth 2J **11**
Moorfield Ter. SK14: H'rth 2J **11**
SK15: Carrb 2F **5**
MOORGATE 3F **5**
Moorgate Cotts. SK15: Carrb 2G **5**
Moorgate Dr. SK15: Carrb 3F **5**
Moorgate M. SK15: Carrb 2F **5**
Moorgate Rd. SK15: Carrb 2F **5**
Moorhill Rd. SK11: Mac 1G **129**
Moorhouse Av. ST7: Als 5E **202**
Moorhouse Cl. CH2: Ches 5A **146**
Mooring Cl. WA7: Murd 1F **113**
Moorings, The CH3: Chri 4H **151**
CH41: Birk 7C **34**
CH60: Hes 6E **82**
CW10: Mid 3C **180**
CW12: Cong 5G **183**
SK12: Dis 1H **103**
Moorings Cl. CH64: Park 6E **104**
Moorland Av. M33: Sale 1C **48**
Moorland Cl. CH60: Hes 7J **83**
Moorland Dr. SK8: Chea H 5H **77**
WA7: Murd 7G **91**
Moorland Fold SK15: Stal 3F **11**
Moorland Pk. CH60: Hes 7J **83**
Moorland Rd. CH42: Tran 2D **60**
CH66: Ell P 7F **109**
M20: Manc 1D **50**
SK2: Stoc .1E **78**
SK15: Carrb 4F **5**
ST7: Mow C 5H **205**
Moorlands Av. CW8: Cudd 2D **160**
M41: Urm .1A **22**
Moorlands Cl. SK10: Mac 1K **125**
Moorlands Cres. OL5: Moss 1E **4**
Moorlands Dr. CW5: Wyb 6A **198**
(not continuous)
Moorlands Pk. CW8: Cudd 2D **160**
Moor La. CH3: Row 2A **174**
CH4: H Kin 4A **184**
CH4: Lwr K, H Kin 1A **184**
CH60: Hes 6H **83**
M23: Wyth 2G **49**
M41: Urm .1K **21**
SK7: Woodf 3G **99**
SK9: Wilm 2B **118**
WA6: Frod 7H **111**
WA6: Haps 6J **137**
WA8: Wid .6F **63**
(not continuous)
Moor La. Bus. Cen.
WA8: Wid .6G **63**
Moor La. Sth. WA8: Wid 6F **63**
Moor Lodge SK4: Stoc 7E **24**
Moor Nook M33: Sale 1D **48**
Moor Pk. Rd. M20: Manc 4E **50**
Moor-Park Way CW9: N'ich 2E **162**
Moor Pl. L3: Liv 2K **35**
Moor Platt *M33: Sale 1D 48*
(off Derbyshire Rd. Sth.)
Moor Rd. M23: Wyth 3E **48**
Moorsbrook Gro. *SK9: Wilm 5B 98*
(off Lyngard Cl.)
Moorsfield Av. CW3: Audl 6B **210**
MOORSIDE .1A **130**
Moorside WA4: Westy 1J **67**
WA16: Knut 3E **116**
Moorside Av. CH64: Park 7F **105**
Moorside Ct. *M33: Sale 7G 23*
(off Sibson Rd.)
M34: Den 6E **8**
WA8: Wid .6F **63**
Moorside Ho. *WA15: Timp 5C 48*
(off Oakleigh Ct.)
Moorside La. CH64: Park 1A **130**
M34: Den 6F **9**
(not continuous)
Moorside Rd. M41: Urm 1H **21**
OL5: Moss .1F **5**
SK4: Stoc .2J **51**
Moorside St. M43: Droy 1A **8**
Moors La. CW7: Darn, Wins 7D **178**
Moorson Av. ST7: Sch G 1J **205**
Moor St. CW12: Cong 4G **183**
L2: Liv 3H **35**
Moorton Av. M19: Manc 4C **24**
Moorton Pk. M19: Manc 4C **24**
Moor Top Pl. SK4: Stoc 1K **51**
Moorview Gdns. ST7: Harr 7J **205**
Moorway CH60: Hes 6K **83**
SK9: Wilm 2D **118**
Moorwood Dr. M33: Sale 1J **47**
Moran Cl. SK9: Wilm 4B **98**
Moran Cres. SK11: Mac 5J **125**
Moran Dr. WA5: Gt San 6J **39**
Moran Rd. SK11: Mac 5J **125**
Morar Rd. SK16: Duk 3J **9**
Moravian Cl. SK16: Duk 1H **9**
Moray Ct. CH1: Ches 4B **212**
Morcott La. L24: Hale 6A **88**
Morecroft Rd. CH42: R Fer 4F **61**
Morello Dr. CH63: Spit 4B **86**
Moresby Cl. WA7: Murd 7G **91**
Moresby Dr. M20: Manc 4D **50**
MORETON . . . . .4B **32 (1A 214)**
Moreton Av. M32: S'ord 1J **23**
M33: Sale .1J **47**
SK7: Bram 1H **99**
Moreton Cl. CW11: S'ach 2G **201**
SK16: Duk .4J **9**
MORETON COMMON 1A **32**
Moreton Dr. CW4: H Cha 4H **181**
SK9: Hand 3B **98**
SK12: Poy 2E **100**
ST7: Als .6D **202**
WN7: Leigh 1E **6**
Moreton Golf Cen. 2A **32**
Moreton Gro. CH45: Wall 5E **12**
Moreton Ho. *WA14: Alt 1F 73*
(off Groby Rd.)
Moreton La. SK2: Stoc 5G **53**
Moreton Pl. ST7: Sch G 2H **205**
Moreton Rd. CH49: Upt 5C **32**
CW2: Crewe 4K **193**
Moreton's Meade CW8: Weav 6H **155**
Moreton Station (Rail) 2B **32**
Moreton St. CW8: Winn 4C **156**
Moreton Ter. WA6: Frod 7G **111**
Moreton Wlk. SK2: Stoc 5G **53**
Moreville Cl. CW9: N'ich 2D **162**
Morgan Av. WA2: Warr 2G **41**
Morgan Cl. CH1: Blac 4G **145**
CW2: Crewe 2A **194**
Morgan Pl. SK5: Stoc 7J **25**
Morgans Way WA3: Low 2A **6**
Morgan Wlk. *CW5: Nant 1B 196*
(off Fairfax Dr.)
Morland Av. CH62: Brom 1J **107**
CH64: L Nes 1D **130**
MORLEY . . . . .4D **96 (2C 217)**
Morley Av. CH41: Birk 4A **34**
Morley Cl. CH2: Mic T 2J **147**
Morley Dr. CW12: Cong 5J **183**
MORLEY GREEN 5D **96**
Morley Grn. Rd. SK9: Wilm 5D **96**
Morley La. CH3: L Bar 5G **143**
Morley Rd. CH44: Wall 1K **33**
WA4: Warr 4E **66**
WA7: Run .5G **89**
Morley St. WA1: Warr 6G **41**
Mornant Av. CW8: H'ord 2J **161**
Morningside WA14: Alt 7F **47**
Morningside Dr. M20: Manc 4E **50**
Mornington Av. CH65: Ell P 3E **134**
SK8: Chea 1F **77**
Mornington Cl. CW11: Elw 2B **200**
Mornington Rd. CH45: N Bri 5H **13**
M33: Sale .6J **23**
SK8: Chea 1F **77**
Mornington St. L8: Liv 7K **35**
Morpeth Cl. CH46: More 4J **31**
Morpeth Rd. CH47: Hoy 7B **30**
Morpeth Wharf CH41: Birk 4D **34**
Morphany La. WA4: Dare 7C **92**
Morrell Rd. M22: N'den 4K **49**
Morreys La. CW6: Kel 2E **172**
MORRIDGE SIDE 2D **221**
MORRIDGE TOP 1D **221**
Morris Av. WA4: Westy 1K **67**
Morris Ct. CH43: Oxt 7J **33**
Morris Dr. CW8: Weav 4G **155**
Morris Gro. M41: Urm 3H **21**
Morrison Cl. WA5: Gt San 7J **39**
Morrison M. WA8: Wid 3D **62**
Morris Pk. CW8: H'ord 2A **162**
Mortar Mill Quay CH41: Birk 3C **34**
Mort Av. WA4: Westy 1A **68**
Mortimer Av. WA2: Warr 4F **41**
Mortimer Dr. CW11: S'ach 4G **201**
Mortimer St. CH41: Birk 6E **34**
Mortlake Cl. WA8: Wid 2C **62**
Mortlake Cres. CH3: Ches 2D **150**
Morton Av. WA6: Hel 7B **138**
Morton Cl. WA5: Old H 4A **40**
Morton Dr. SK11: Sut E 2K **129**
Morton Rd. CH1: Blac 6F **145**
WA7: Nort 6F **91**
Morton St. SK4: Stoc 7H **25**
Morton Ter. *M34: Den 2F 27*
(off Tatton Rd.)
SK6: W'ley 6G **27**
Mortuary Rd. CH45: Wall 5H **13**
Morval Cres. WA7: Run 5K **89**
Morven Av. SK7: H Gro 2K **79**
Morven Cl. WA2: Warr 1J **41**
Morven Dr. M23: Wyth 7G **49**
Moschatel Wlk. M31: Part 1H **45**
Moscow Rd. SK3: Stoc 5B **52**
Moscow Rd. E. SK3: Stoc 5B **52**
Mosedale Cl. M23: Wyth 6E **48**
Mosedale Gro. WA7: Beec 2A **112**
Mosedale Rd. CH62: Brom 4E **86**
Moseldene Rd. SK2: Stoc 7H **53**
Moseley Av. CH45: Wall 7G **13**
WA4: Westy 1A **68**
Moseley Ct. M19: Manc 2C **24**
SK8: Chea H 2H **77**
Moseley Grange
SK8: Chea H 2H **77**
Moseley Rd. CH63: Spit 5A **86**
M14: Manc 3A **24**
M19: Manc 3C **24**
SK8: Chea H 2H **77**
Moseley St. SK3: Stoc 4C **52**
Moses Ct. CH1: Ches 3E **212**
Mosley Cl. WA15: Timp 5K **47**
Mosley Rd. WA15: Timp 6B **48**
MOSS 2B **218**
Moss, The CW9: Comb 3J **115**
Mossack Av. M22: Wyth 4K **75**
MOSS BANK
WA5 . . . . .6K **63**
WA11 . . . . .1D **215**
Moss Bank CH1: Ches 6K **145**
CW7: Wins 3C **178**
CW8: Winn 5C **156**
SK7: Bram 1F **99**
Moss Bank Av. M43: Droy 1B **8**
Mossbank Cl. SK13: Had 3K **11**
Moss Bank Rd. WA8: Wid 6K **63**
Moss Bower Rd. SK11: Mac 1G **129**
Mossbray Av. M19: Manc 7A **24**
Moss Bri. CW11: Most 2A **200**
MOSSBROW . . . . .5F **45 (2B 216)**
Moss Brow SK10: Boll 4B **122**
Moss Chase SK11: Mac 1G **129**
Moss Cl. CH64: W'ston 7F **107**
WA4: Stoc H 3J **67**
Moss Cft. CW1: Crewe 5F **191**
Moss Cft. Cl. M41: Urm 1H **21**
Mossdale Cl. CW2: Crewe 2J **193**
WA5: Gt San 5J **39**
Mossdale Dr. L35: R'ill 1D **36**
Mossdale Rd. M23: Wyth 3F **49**
M33: Sale .3J **47**
Mossdene Rd. CH44: Wall 7F **13**
Moss Dr. CW10: Mid 6D **180**
WA6: Manl 2H **171**
Moss Farm Leisure Complex 5C **156**
Mossfield Cl. SK4: Stoc 2K **51**
Mossfield Rd. WA15: Timp 6D **48**
Moss Flds. ST7: Als 6B **202**
Mossfields CW1: L'ton 4F **191**
Mossford Av. CW1: Crewe 6G **191**
MOSSGATE .3D **221**
Moss Ga. WA3: Birc 5B **18**
Moss Grn. M31: Carri 3D **21**
Moss Gro. CH4: Salt 5F **149**
CH42: Tran 3A **60**
WA13: Lymm 1D **70**
Mossgrove Rd. WA15: Timp 5K **47**
Moss Hall La. CW6: Rus 5J **177**
Mosshall La. WA4: Lwr S 5K **93**
Moss Hey Dr. M23: Wyth 3H **49**
Moss Ind. Est. WN7: Leigh 1B **6**
Mosslands Cl. CH66: Gt Sut 6A **134**
Mosslands Dr. CH44: Wall 6E **12**
CH45: Wall 6E **12**
MOSS LANE . . . . .1H **129 (3D 217)**
Moss La. CH42: Tran 3A **60**
CW1: Bra G, L'ton, Min V 3D **190**
CW1: Warm 2H **191**
CW5: Wyb 6A **198**
CW6: Tarp 1G **175**
CW7: Wins 3K **179**
CW8: Cudd 3C **160**
CW8: Winn 6C **156**
(not continuous)
CW9: Los Grn . . . . . . .4G **159** & 3F **159**
CW9: Mars, Winc 1A **158**
CW11: Elw 2A **200**
CW12: Eat 7G **169**
M31: Part, Warb 1H **45**
M33: Sale .1H **47**
(Edinburgh Cl.)
M33: Sale .1F **47**
(Moss Rd.)
M44: Cad .6A **20**
SK7: Bram 1F **99**
SK9: Ald E 6G **119**
SK9: Styal 1E **96**
SK10: Boll 3B **122**
SK10: Mot A 1B **120**
SK11: L Wit, Sidd 2A **168**
SK11: Mac 7J **125**
SK14: B'tom 3G **29**
Moss La. ST7: Sch G 4H **205**
WA1: Wool 4E **42**
WA3: G'ury 5K **7**
(not continuous)
WA3: Rix .6F **19**
WA4: Moo 6J **65**
WA6: Manl 2H **171**
WA6: Norl 6J **153**
WA13: Warb 3G **45**
WA14: Alt 2J **213** (1H **73**)
WA15: Alt, Hale 2J **213** (1H **73**)
WA15: Timp 5K **47**
WA16: H Leg 7G **71**
WA16: Mere, O Tab . . . . .1A **116** & 7H **95**
Moss La. Bus. Cen. CW11: Ett H 3B **200**
Moss Lane Ground 2K **73**
Moss La. Ind. Est. CW11: Elw 2B **200**
MOSSLEY
CW12 . . . . .6J **183 (1C 221)**
OL4 . . . . .1D **217**
Mossley Av. CH62: Brom 6D **86**
MOSSLEY BROW 1D **4**
Mossley Ct. CW12: Cong 6H **183**
MOSSLEY CROSS 1C **4**
Mossley Gth. Cl. CW12: Cong 5J **183**
MOSSLEY HILL 2B **214**
Mossley Industrial Heritage Cen. 1D **4**
Mossley Rd. CH42: Tran 2D **60**
OL6: Ash L 5A **4**
Mossley Station (Rail) 1D **4**
Moss Lodge La. OL7: Ash L 1C **8**
Moss Mnr. M33: Sale 1J **47**
Mossmere Rd. SK8: Chea H 1J **77**
MOSS NOOK .6B **76**
Moss Nook Ind. Area M22: Wyth 5B **76**
Moss Pk. Rd. M32: S'ord 1F **23**
Moss Rd. CW8: Winn 4C **156**
CW12: Astb, Cong 7G **183**
M32: S'ord 1H **23**
M33: Sale .7A **22**
M44: Cad .1J **19**
SK9: Ald E 5G **119**
WA4: Westy 2A **68**
Moss Rose SK9: Ald E 5G **119**
Moss Rose Ground 1H **129**
MOSS SIDE
L39 . . . . .1B **214**
M14 . . . . .1C **217**
WA4 . . . . .6H **65**
Moss Side La. WA3: Rix 1A **44**
WA4: Moo 6G **65**
Moss Side Rd. M44: Cad 5A **20**
Moss Sq. CW1: Crewe 2D **194**
SK11: Mac 1H **129**
Moss St. CW8: Weav 4G **155**
M34: Aude .1A **8**
SK14: H'rth 2J **11**
WA8: Wid .6K **63**
Moss St. W. OL7: Ash L 1E **8**
Moss Ter. CW8: Winn 4B **156**
SK9: Wilm 6C **98**
SK11: Gaw 7H **125**
Mossvale CH66: L Sut 7E **108**
Moss Va. Rd. M41: Urm 1D **22**
(not continuous)
Moss Vw. Rd. M31: Part 1J **45**
SK11: Gaw 1E **128**
Moss Way M33: Sale 7D **22**
OL7: Ash L 1D **8**
ST7: Als .6B **202**
Mossways Cvn. Pk. SK9: Wilm 7D **96**
MOSSWAYS PARK 7D **96**
Mosswood Pk. M20: Manc 4D **50**
Mosswood Rd. SK9: Wilm 5B **98**
Mossy Bank Rd. CH44: Wall 7K **13**
MOSTON 1K **145**
Moston Community Nature Reserve
. . . . .2K **145**
Moston Ct. *CW12: Cong 3H 183*
(off Brunswick St.)
MOSTON GREEN 1B **220**
Moston Gro. WA13: Lymm 2K **69**
Moston Rd. CH2: Most, Upt 1K **145**
CW11: Ett H 4A **200**
Moston St. SK5: Stoc 4J **25**
Moston Way CH66: Gt Sut 5B **134**
MOSTYN 2A **214**
Mostyn Av. CH48: W Kir 4C **56**
CH60: Hes 6E **82**
M14: Manc 3B **24**
SK8: Chea H 4G **77**
Mostyn Gdns. CH64: Park 6E **104**
Mostyn Pl. CH1: Blac 4F **145**
MOSTYN QUAY 2A **214**
Mostyn Rd. SK7: H Gro 4F **79**
Mostyn Sq. CH64: Park 6E **104**
Mostyn St. CH44: Wall 1A **34**
SK15: Duk, Stal 2A **10**
SK16: Duk 2A **10**
Motcombe Farm Rd.
SK8: He Grn 4D **76**
Motcombe Gro. SK8: He Grn 2C **76**
Motcombe Rd. SK8: He Grn 3C **76**
Mote Hill Ct. WA1: Warr 6H **41**
Motherwell Av. M19: Manc 2D **24**
Motherwell Cl. WA8: Wid 2E **62**
Mottershead Cl. WA8: Wid 5G **63**
Mottershead Rd. M22: Wyth 1J **75**
WA8: Wid .5G **63**
Mottram Cl. CW10: Mid 5B **180**
SK8: Chea 7J **51**
WA4: Grap 2B **68**

Nevin Rd.—Norbury

Nevin Rd. CH1: Blac 7E 144
Nevis Dr. CW2: Crewe 3H 193
New Acre Ct. SK6: Rom 2B 54
(off Metcalfe Dr.)
New Acres Cl. CH43: Bid 4F 33
New Albert Ter. WA7: Run 3H 89
(off Fredric Pl.)
Newall Av. CW11: S'ach 4E 200
Newall Cl. CH3: Tatt 3H 187
Newall Cres. CW7: Wins 3H 179
NEWALL GREEN 1G 75
Newall Rd. M23: Wyth 2F 75
Newark Cl. CH43: Noc 1F 59
Newark Rd. SK5: Stoc 6J 25
Newarth Dr. WA13: Lymm 3C 70
New Bank Pl. WA8: Wid 4B 62
New Bank Rd. WA8: Wid 4B 62
New Barnet WA8: Wid 2F 63
New Beech Rd. SK4: Stoc 2G 51
New Belvedere Cl. M32: S'ord 1J 23
Newberry Gro. SK3: Stoc 7B 52
Newbiggin Way SK10: Mac 4K 125
(off Longacre St.)
New Bird St. L1: Liv 5J 35
Newbold Cl. SK16: Duk 2H 9
Newbold Ct. CW12: Cong 3H 183
(off Herbert St.)
Newbold Cres. CH48: W Kir 2F 57
Newbold Way CW5: Nant 4C 196
Newborough Cl. WA5: Call 2B 40
Newboult Rd. SK8: Chea 6G 51
Newbourne Cl. SK7: H Gro 2H 79
NEWBRIDGE 3A 218
New Bri. WA1: Warr 1F 67
WA4: Warr 1F 67
Newbridge Cl. CH49: Woodc 1E 58
WA5: Call 2A 40
WA7: B'vale 1E 112
New Bri. Ct. CH65: Ell P 4H 135
New Bri. La. SK1: Stoc 6K 213 (3D 52)
Newbridge Rd. CH2: L Sta 5H 135
CH65: Ell P 4H 135
Newbridge Vw. OL5: Moss 1E 4
NEW BRIGHTON
CH7 1A 218
CH44 2H 13 (1B 214)
New Brighton Cotts. SK11: Lang 2G 169
New Brighton Station (Rail) 3G 13
Newbrook Av. M21: Chor H 1K 49
NEW BROUGHTON 2B 218
Newburgh Cl. WA7: Win H 5F 91
Newburn CH43: Oxt 7A 34
Newburns La. CH43: Oxt 2A 60
Newbury Av. CW1: Crewe 6H 191
CW7: Wins 4B 178
M33: Sale 7B 22
Newbury Cl. SK8: Chea H 7J 77
WA8: Wid 2G 63
Newbury Ct. WA15: Timp 5K 47
(off Tulip Dr.)
Newbury Rd. CH4: Ches 5G 149
SK8: He Grn 6D 76
Newbury Way CH46: Leas 1C 32
Newby Av. L35: R'ill 1A 36
Newby Ct. CW12: Cong 5C 182
Newby Dr. M33: Sale 1E 48
SK8: Gat 6C 50
WA14: Alt 6H 47
Newby Rd. SK4: Stoc 2A 52
SK7: H Gro 3G 79
Newby Rd. Ind. Est. SK7: H Gro 3G 79
Newcastle Rd.
CW2: Chor, Hou, Shav 4C 198
CW5: Blak, Stap, W'ston 3F 197
CW11: Bet 5K 201
CW12: Astb, Cong, More 7B 182
Newcastle St. CW1: Crewe 1A 194
NEWCASTLE-UNDER-LYME 3C 221
Newcastle Wlk. M34: Den 2F 27
(off Trowbridge Rd.)
New Century Ho. M34: Den 7B 8
NEWCHAPEL 2C 221
New Chester Rd. CH41: Birk, Tran 7E 34
CH42: R Fer, Tran 7E 34
CH62: Brom, East, N Fer, P Sun 5G 61
CH66: H'ton 5B 108
Newchurch La. WA3: Cul 1A 18
Newcombe Av. WA2: Warr 4J 41
Newcombe Ct. M33: Sale 7E 22
(off Beech Gro.)
New Copper Moss WA15: Alt 1K 73
New Crane Bank
CH1: Ches 4A 212 (2J 149)
New Crane St. CH1: Ches 1J 149
Newcroft CH1: Sau 1C 144
Newcroft Cres. M41: Urm 2E 22
Newcroft Dr. M41: Urm 2F 23
SK3: Stoc 6B 52
Newcroft Rd. M41: Urm 2E 22
New Cut Ind. Est. WA1: Wool 5C 42
New Cut La. WA1: Wool 5B 42
Newdale Rd. M12: Manc 1E 24
Newdales Cl. CH43: Bid 4F 33
Newdigate St. CW1: Crewe 1C 194
(not continuous)
Newell Rd. CH44: Wall 6H 13
New Extension Quay CH65: Ell P 7J 109
New Farm Ct. CH3: Gt Bar 3B 170
NEW FERRY 6G 61 (2B 214)
New Ferry By-Pass
CH62: N Fer, P Sun 5G 61
New Ferry Rd. CH62: N Fer 6G 61
Newfield Ct. WA13: Lymm 7C 44
Newfield Dr. CW1: Crewe 1E 194
Newfield Rd. WA13: Lymm 2K 69
Newfield St. CW11: S'ach 2F 201
Newfield Ter. WA6: Hel 6B 138
New Forest Rd. M23: Wyth 4C 48
Newgate SK9: Wilm 7D 96
Newgate Rd. M33: Sale 3F 47
Newgate Row CH1: Ches 4C 212 (2A 150)
Newgate St. CH1: Ches 5C 212 (2A 150)
Newgate Wlk.
CH1: Ches 5C 212 (2A 150)
New Grosvenor Rd. CH65: Ell P 1D 134
NEWHALL 3A 220
New Hall Av. SK8: He Grn 6D 76
Newhall Ct. CH2: Upt 4B 146
Newhall Dr. M23: Wyth 2G 49
New Hall La. CH47: Hoy 6C 30
WA3: Cul, Ris 2K 17
(not continuous)
Newhall La. CH2: Upt 4B 146
New Hall Mnr. CH64: Nest 1H 105
New Hall Pl. L3: Liv 2G 35
New Hall Rd. M33: Sale 7K 23
Newhall Rd. CH2: Upt 4B 146
SK5: Stoc 1K 25
New Hall St. SK10: Mac 3K 125
Newhall St. L1: Liv 5J 35
Newham Cl. SK11: Sut E 2K 129
New Hampshire Cl. WA5: Gt San 5K 39
Newhaven Cl. SK8: Chea H 3A 78
Newhaven Ct. CW5: Nant 2D 196
Newhaven Rd. CH45: N Bri 4J 13
WA2: Warr 7A 16
New Henderson St. L8: Liv 6K 35
Newhey Av. M22: Wyth 7K 49
New Heyes CH64: Nest 6H 105
New Hey La. CH64: W'ston 1K 131
New Hey Rd. CH49: Woodc 1E 58
SK8: Chea 6G 51
Newhey Rd. M22: Wyth 1K 75
Newholme Ct. M32: S'ord 1K 23
Newhope Rd. CH41: Birk 5B 34
New Houses La. CH64: L Nes 4C 130
Newington L1: Liv 3K 35
Newington Ct. WA14: Bow 2G 73
Newington Way WA8: Wid 2F 63
New Inn La. CW11: Bet 7K 201
New Islington L3: Liv 2K 35
New King St. CW10: Mid 2C 180
Newland Cl. WA8: Wid 2C 62
Newland Dr. CH44: Wall 7G 13
Newland M. WA3: Cul 5E 6
Newlands Av. M44: Irlam 1D 20
SK7: Bram 5D 78
SK8: Chea H 6J 77
Newlands Cl. SK8: Chea H 6J 77
WA6: Frod 2J 139
Newlands Dr. M20: Manc 4E 50
SK9: Wilm 2D 118
Newlands Rd. CH63: Beb 2B 86
M23: Wyth 4F 49
SK8: Chea 6F 51
SK10: Mac 5F 125
WA4: Stoc H 3K 67
Newland Way CW5: Stap 3F 197
New La. CH3: Chu 1C 186
CH3: Hart 7G 187
CW7: Darn 7G 179
WA3: Croft 4F 17
WA4: App T 1B 94
NEW LANE END 1F 17 (1A 216)
New La. End WA3: Croft 1F 17
New Lawns SK5: Stoc 2K 25
Newling St. CH41: Birk 5B 34
Newlyn Av. CW12: Cong 6H 183
SK10: Mac 3E 124
SK15: Stal 6E 4
Newlyn Ct. CH47: Meols 3F 31
SK7: H Gro 4H 79
WA7: B'vale 1D 112
Newlyn Dr. M33: Sale 3C 48
SK6: Bred 1A 54
Newlyn Gdns. WA5: Penk 2F 65
Newlyn Rd. CH47: Meols 3F 31
Newman Cl. CW12: Cong 3D 182
New Mnr. Rd. WA4: Pre H 1K 113
New Mansion Ho. SK1: Stoc 5D 52
(off Wellington Rd. Sth.)
Newman's La. CW5: Stap 7H 197
Newman St. SK14: Hyde 7K 9
WA4: Westy 1K 67
Newmarket Cl. M33: Sale 2F 47
SK10: Mac 7K 121
New Mkt. Hall WA7: Run 3G 89
(off Granville St.)
New Mkt. Wlk. WA1: Warr 7F 41
NEW MILLS
M90 2A 102
SK22 2D 217
New Mills Newtown Station (Rail) 1K 103
New Mills Rd. SK13: Chis 7J 29
Newmoore La. WA7: Nort 3G 91
New Moor La. SK7: H Gro 2H 79
New Moss Rd. M44: Cad 5A 20
Newnham Dr. CH65: Ell P 4E 134
New Palace Amusement Pk. 2H 13
NEW PALE 1K 171
New Pale Rd.
WA6: K'ood, Man C 7H 139 & 2K 171
New Platt La. CW4: Cran 7C 164
(not continuous)
Newport Av. CH45: Wall 4D 12
SK5: Stoc 4H 25
Newport Cl. CH43: Noc 1F 59
Newport Rd. M34: Den 3G 27
New Quay L3: Liv 2G 35
Newquay Av. SK5: Stoc 4H 25
Newquay Cl. WA7: B'vale 1D 112
Newquay Ct. CW12: Cong 6G 183
Newquay Dr. SK7: Bram 6D 78
SK10: Mac 4E 124
New Quay Ter. L3: Liv 2G 35
(off New Quay)
New Ridd Ri. SK14: Hyde 3J 27
New Rd. CH66: Chil T 7B 108
CW5: Wren 4G 209
CW6: Dud 5C 174
CW7: Wins 2F 179
CW9: And 2B 156
SK10: Pres 4H 121
WA4: Warr 1F 67
(not continuous)
WA13: Lymm 2A 70
New Rd. Bus. Cen.
CW7: Wins 2F 179
Newry Ct. CH2: Ches 6A 146
Newry Pk. CH2: Ches 6A 146
Newry Pk. E. CH2: Ches 6A 146
NEWSBANK 1C 221
New School La.
CH66: Chil T 7C 108
Newsham Cl. WA8: Wid 1B 62
Newsham Rd. SK3: Stoc 6C 52
Newsholme Cl. WA3: Cul 7F 7
Newstead Av. M20: Manc 6A 24
Newstead Cl. SK12: Poy 1C 100
Newstead Gro. SK6: Bred 1K 53
Newstead Rd. WA8: Wid 7A 62
Newstead Ter. WA15: Timp 5K 47
New St. CH44: Wall 2D 34
CH64: L Nes 3C 130
CW1: Hasl 1J 195
CW11: Elw 2B 200
CW12: Cong 4G 183
M43: Droy 2A 8
SK9: Wilm 2D 118
SK14: B'tom 3H 29
SK15: Stal 2B 10
WA7: Run 4G 89
WA8: Wid 5H 63
WA14: Alt 4G 213 (1G 73)
New St. Cotts. CW12: Hav 7J 169
NEWSTREET LANE 3A 220
New Ter. SK9: Wilm 6J 97
SK14: Hyde 2K 27
(Ashley M.)
SK14: Hyde 5A 10
(Hamel St.)
NEWTON
CH2 5C 146 (1C 219)
CH3 1K 187 (2D 219)
CH48 3F 57 (2A 214)
SK14 6A 10 (1D 217)
WA6 6K 139
Newton Av. WA3: Ris 6K 17
Newton Bank CW10: Mid 3B 180
WA4: Dare 6K 91
Newton Bus. Pk.
SK14: Hyde 5B 10
Newton Ct. CH42: R Fer 4F 61
(off New Chester Rd.)
SK14: Hyde 5J 9
(off Markham St.)
SK15: Stal 7A 4
(off Newton St.)
Newton Cross La. CH48: W Kir 3F 57
Newton Dr. CH48: W Kir 3F 57
Newton for Hyde Station (Rail) 6A 10
Newton Gdns. WA3: Low 2A 6
Newton Grn. SK14: Hyde 5A 10
Newton Gro. WA2: Fear 1K 41
Newton Hall 6H 9
Newton Hall Ct. CH2: Ches 5C 146
SK14: Hyde 5H 9
Newton Hall Dr. CH2: Ches 5C 146
Newton Hall M. CW10: Mid 4C 180
Newton Hall Rd. SK14: Hyde 5H 9
NEWTON HEATH 1C 217
Newton Heath CW10: Mid 3B 180
Newton Hollow WA6: Frod 7J 139
Newton Hollows CH2: Ches 6C 146
Newton Ho. CH2: Ches 5C 146
NEWTONIA 4B 180
Newton La. CH2: Ches 5B 146
WA4: Dare, L Whi 6K 91
(not continuous)
NEWTON-LE-WILLOWS 1E 14 (1D 215)
Newton Moor Ind. Est. SK14: Hyde 5K 9
Newton Pk. Dr. WA12: New W 1J 15
Newton Pk. Rd. CH48: W Kir 3F 57
Newton Pk. Vw. CH2: Ches 6A 146
Newton Pl. CW12: Cong 4H 183
Newton Rd. CH44: Wall 7G 13
CH47: Hoy 5D 30
CH65: Ell P 3E 134
M41: Urm 1B 22
SK9: Wilm 5H 97
WA2: Winw 2J 15
WA3: Low 3A 6
WA14: Alt 5J 47
Newtons Cres. CW11: Wint 6B 204
Newtons Gro. CW11: Wint 6B 204
Newtons La. CW11: Wint 6B 204
Newton St. CH41: Birk 5C 34
CW1: Crewe 1C 194
M32: S'ord 2J 23
SK3: Stoc 4C 52
SK11: Mac 5K 125
SK14: Hyde 7J 9
SK15: Stal 7A 4
Newton Ter. SK16: Duk 1G 9
(off Queen St.)
Newton Way CH49: Upt 7C 32
L3: Liv 3K 35
NEWTON WOOD 4H 9
Newton Wood Rd.
SK16: Duk 4G 9
New Tower Ct. CH45: N Bri 3J 13
NEWTOWN
SK11 1D 221
SK12, High Peak 1K 103 (2D 217)
SK12, Stockport 3F 101
WA6 6K 111
Newtown CH64: L Nes 2D 130
Newtown Av. M34: Den 1F 27
Newtown Cl. CH1: Ches 2D 212 (1A 150)
Newville Dr. M20: Manc 6A 24
New Warrington Rd.
CW9: Mars, N'ich, Winc 4G 157
New Way Bus. Cen.
CH44: Wall 2C 34
New William Cl. M31: Part 7C 20
(off Moss La.)
New Zealand Rd. SK1: Stoc 3E 52
Niagara St. SK2: Stoc 6E 52
Nicholas Av. CW9: Rud 7H 157
Nicholas Ct. CH1: Ches 5A 212 (2K 149)
Nicholas Rd. CW8: Weav 4G 155
WA8: Wid 5C 62
Nicholas St. CH1: Ches 5B 212 (2K 149)
L3: Liv 1J 35
Nicholas St. M. CH1: Ches 5A 212 (2K 149)
Nicholls Dr. CH61: Pens 2H 83
Nicholls St. WA4: Grap 3B 68
Nicholson Av. SK10: Mac 3B 126
Nicholson Cl. SK10: Mac 3B 126
Nicholson Rd. SK14: Hyde 5H 9
Nicholson Sq. SK16: Duk 2G 9
Nicholson St. SK4: Stoc 2C 52
WA1: Warr 7D 40
Nickleby Rd. SK12: Poy 3C 100
Nickleford Hall Dr. WA8: Wid 6F 37
Nickolson Cl. CH2: Mic T 2J 147
Nico Ditch M18: Manc 1F 25
Nicola Ct. CH45: Wall 5J 13
Nicol Av. WA3: Wool 4F 43
Nidderdale Av. L35: R'ill 1D 36
Nidderdale Cl. CW12: Cong 1J 183
Niddries La. CW9: Moult 7D 162
Nield Ct. CH2: Upt 3A 146
Nield Rd. M34: Den 7E 8
Nields Brow WA14: Bow 3G 73
Nields Way SK6: Mel 1K 81
Nigel Gresley Cl. CW1: Crewe 2G 195
Nigel Rd. CH60: Hes 6A 84
Nigel Wlk. WA7: Cast 4C 90
Nightingale Cl. CH3: Farn 6C 186
CW10: Mid 6D 180
SK9: Wilm 5J 97
WA3: Birc 7A 18
WA7: Beec 2B 112
Nightingale Ct. CW7: Wins 6E 178
Nightingale Dr. M34: Aude 1B 8
Nightingale Gdns. M23: Wyth 3G 49
Nightingale Way ST7: Als 6C 202
Nile St. CW2: Crewe 4C 194
OL7: Ash L 2E 8
Ninfield Rd. M23: Wyth 1H 75
Nisbet Av. M22: Wyth 2A 76
Nixon Dr. CW7: Wins 2B 178
Nixon Rd. CW8: Cudd 3C 160
Nixons Row CW5: Nant 2A 196
Nixon St. CW1: Crewe 1K 193
SK3: Stoc 4C 52
SK11: Mac 4J 125
Noahs Ark La. WA16: Mob 6A 118
Noble Cl. WA3: Birc 1E 42
NOCTORUM 1G 59
Noctorum Av. CH43: Noc 7F 33
Noctorum Dell CH43: Noc 1G 59
Noctorum La.
CH43: Noc, Oxt 6G 33
Noctorum Rd. CH43: Noc 7G 33
Noctorum Way CH43: Noc 1G 59
Noel Dr. M33: Sale 7J 23
No Limits Fitness Cen. 1F 81
NO MAN'S HEATH 3B 208 (3D 219)
Nook, The CH2: Ches 6B 146
CH3: Guil S 6F 147
CH4: Salt 5F 149
CH43: Oxt 6A 34
CH48: Fran 3J 57
CW3: Hank 1E 210
M41: Urm 2C 22
SK7: Bram 1G 99
Nook La. CW9: Ant 4D 94
WA2: Fear 2B 42
WA4: Westy 2A 68
Noon Ct. WA12: New W 2E 14
Nora St. WA1: Warr 7G 41
Norbreck Av. CW2: Crewe 4B 194
SK8: Chea 6J 51
Norbreck Cl. WA5: Gt San 1J 65
Norburn Rd. M13: Manc 1C 24
NORBURY 3D 219

Oakfield Ct.—Old Pewterspear La.

Oakfield Ct. WA15: Timp 6K 47
Oakfield Dr. CH2: Upt 2B 146
WA8: Wid 5A 62
Oakfield Ho. WA15: Alt 2K 213
Oakfield M. M33: Sale 7F 23
SK3: Stoc 7D 52
Oakfield Ri. CW4: H Cha 4H 181
Oakfield Rd. CH1: Blac 6D 144
CH62: Brom 6C 86
CH66: Chil T 7K 107
M20: Manc 1C 50
SK3: Stoc 7D 52
SK9: Ald E 4G 119
SK12: Poy 2E 100
SK14: Hyde 5K 9
WA15: Alt 1K 213 (7J 47)
WA16: Plum 2H 159
Oakfield St. WA15: Alt 1K 213 (7J 47)
Oakfield Ter.
CH66: Chil T 7K 107
Oakfield Trad. Est.
WA15: Alt 1K 213 (7J 47)
Oak Fold SK10: Ker 5D 122
Oak Gdns. WA5: Penk 1F 65
OAKGROVE 6H 129 (1D 221)
Oak Gro. CH4: Salt 6E 148
CH65: Whit 5C 134
CW5: Nant 4C 196
M41: Urm 1D 22
SK8: Chea 7G 51
SK12: Poy 2C 100
Oakham Dr. CH46: More 3J 31
Oakham Rd. M34: Den 2F 27
Oakham St. L8: Liv 6J 35
OAKHANGER 2B 220
Oakhill Cl. SK10: Mac 7J 121
Oak Ho. CH2: Ches 5K 145
M14: Manc 2A 24
Oakhouse La. CW7: Wins 4C 178
(not continuous)
Oakhurst Chase SK9: Ald E 5F 119
Oakhurst Dr. CW2: Wis 7B 194
SK3: Stoc 7K 51
Oakland Av. CW1: Hasl 2J 195
M19: Manc 7B 24
SK2: Stoc 6G 53
Oakland Ct. SK12: Poy 2C 100
Oakland Dr. CH49: Upt 6D 32
Oakland Gdns. WA1: Warr 5J 41
Oaklands CH3: Guil S 5H 147
CH62: Brom 1J 107
L35: R'ill 1C 36
Oaklands Av. CH3: Tatt 2H 187
SK6: Mar B 4J 55
SK8: Chea H 3J 77
Oaklands Bus. Cen.
CH66: H'ton 5K 107
Oaklands Cl. SK9: Wilm 5B 98
Oaklands Ct. CW2: West 4K 199
(off Golden Hill)
WA9: Clo F 1J 37
Oaklands Cres. CH3: Tatt 2H 187
Oaklands Dene SK14: Hyde 1B 28
Oaklands Dr. CH61: Hes 5J 83
CH63: Beb 7F 61
M33: Sale 6F 23
SK7: H Gro 4J 79
WA13: Lymm 3K 69
Oaklands Ho. M14: Manc 2A 24
Oaklands Rd. SK14: Hyde 1B 28
WA3: Low 3A 6
WA16: Oll 7K 117
Oaklands Ter. CH61: Hes 4J 83
Oakland St. WA1: Warr 5J 41
WA8: Wid 2G 89
Oakland Va. CH45: N Bri 3J 13
Oak La. CH2: Hoo V 4F 147
CW8: Cudd 4C 160
SK9: Wilm 1E 118
SK10: Ker 6D 122
SK11: Mart 6D 168
Oak Lea Av. SK9: Wilm 2F 119
Oaklea Av. CH2: Ches 6C 146
Oakleaf M. CH43: Noc 7G 33
Oaklea Rd. CH61: Irby 7C 58
M33: Sale 6D 22
Oakleigh SK3: Stoc 1D 78
SK4: Stoc 1K 51
(off Heaton Moor Rd.)
WA16: Knut 6G 117
Oakleigh Av. M19: Manc 4C 24
WA15: Timp 5A 48
Oakleigh Ct. CW12: Cong 3B 182
WA15: Timp 5C 48
Oakleigh Gro. CH63: Beb 7E 60
Oakleigh Ho. M33: Sale 1J 47
SK10: Boll 3E 122
(off Hamson Dr.)
Oakleigh M. M33: Sale 1J 47
Oakleigh Ri. CW8: Winn 4D 156
Oakleigh Rd. SK8: Chea H 5G 77
Oakley Cl. CW11: S'ach 1E 200
Oakley Ct. CH65: Ell P 4E 134
Oakley St. CW1: Crewe 1C 194
Oakley Vs. SK4: Stoc 1K 51
Oak Lodge SK7: Bram 6D 78
Oak Mdw. CW8: Weav 6H 155
Oak Mdws. Ct. L35: R'ill 3E 36
OAKMERE 3K 173 (1D 219)
Oakmere Cl. CH46: Leas 1B 32
CW11: S'ach 2D 200
M22: Wyth 1K 75
Oakmere Dr. CH3: Gt Bou 3E 150
CH49: Gre 1K 57
CH66: Gt Sut 7B 134
WA5: Penk 2H 65
Oakmere Hall CW8: Oak 5B 160
Oakmere Pl. CW1: Crewe 1B 194
(off Rigg St.)
Oakmere Rd. CW7: Wins 2A 178
SK8: Chea H 1H 77
SK9: Hand 1A 98
Oakmere St. WA7: Run 4G 89
Oak M. SK9: Wilm 5K 97
Oakmoore WA7: Nort 2H 91
Oakmoor Rd. M23: Wyth 6G 49
Oakridge Cl. CH62: Spit 4C 86
Oakridge Rd. CH62: Spit 4C 86
Oak Rd. CH4: Ches 5G 149
CH63: H Beb 6E 60
CH66: H'ton 6K 107
M31: Part 2F 45
M33: Sale 7J 23
SK8: Chea 6G 51
SK10: Mot A, Pres 2C 120
SK11: Chel 5C 166
WA5: Penk 2H 65
WA13: Lymm 2J 69
WA15: Hale 2J 73
WA16: Mob 2A 118
Oaks, The CH62: Brom 6C 86
CW4: Goo 7H 165
SK8: He Grn 3C 76
SK14: Hyde 7B 10
WA8: Wid 1K 63
(off Hampton Ct. Way)
Oaks Bus. Pk., The
M23: Wyth 4E 48
Oaks Cl. WA9: Clo F 1K 37
Oaks Dr. CH2: Upt 3A 146
Oakside Cl. SK8: Chea 6G 51
Oaks La. CH61: Pens 2J 83
Oaks Pl. WA8: Wid 6G 63
Oakston Av. L35: R'ill 2D 36
Oak St. CH65: Ell P 1E 134
CW2: Crewe 3D 194
CW9: N'ich 4F 157
CW11: Elw 1B 200
M34: Aude 4E 8
SK3: Stoc 4K 51
SK7: H Gro 2H 79
SK14: Hyde 6K 9
ST7: Rod H 1F 203
WA3: Croft 4F 17
Oaksway CH60: Hes 1E 104
Oak Tree Cl. CW1: Crewe 1F 195
CW8: Barnt 1A 156
SK2: Stoc 4H 53
SK14: Hyde 1B 28
Oaktree Cl. CW6: Tarp 2J 175
Oaktree Cotts. SK8: Chea H 2H 77
Oak Tree Ct. SK8: Chea 7G 51
Oaktree Ct. CH2: Ches 7D 146
Oaktree Ct. Bus. Cen. CH64: Ness 2H 131
Oak Tree Cres. SK15: Stal 2B 10
Oak Tree Dr. CW1: Crewe 1F 195
SK16: Duk 3A 10
Oak Tree Ga. CW3: Audl 6B 210
Oaktree Pl. CH42: R Fer 2E 60
Oak Vw. SK11: Mart 6D 168
WA16: Knut 4G 117
Oak Vs. SK15: Carrb 2G 5
Oak Wlk. M34: Aude 4D 8
Oakway M20: Manc 4E 50
Oakways WA4: App 1H 93
Oak Wharf M. WA4: App 5G 67
OAKWOOD 1F 43
Oakwood M33: Sale 7B 22
Oakwood Av. M34: Aude 3D 8
SK8: Gat 7C 50
SK9: Wilm 1D 118
WA1: Warr 5H 41
Oakwood Cl. CH66: Gt Sut 7K 133
CW8: Barnt 3K 155
Oakwood Ct. WA14: Bow 5F 73
Oakwood Cres. CW2: Crewe 2J 193
CW11: S'ach 3J 201
Oakwood Dr. CH43: Bid 4H 33
SK10: Pres 5K 121
WN7: Leigh 1E 6
Oakwood Ga. WA3: Birc 7J 17
Oakwood Ho. CW8: Barnt 3K 155
(off Blackcroft Av.)
Oakwood La. CW8: Barnt 3K 155
CW11: Most 1A 200
WA14: Bow 4E 72
Oakwood Pk. CH43: Bid 4H 33
CH62: Brom 2J 107
Oakwood Rd. SK6: Rom 2C 54
SK12: Dis 1G 103
ST7: Rod H 1G 203
Oakworth Cl. CW12: Cong 2A 182
Oakworth Dr. CH62: N Fer 6H 61
Oarside Dr. CH45: Wall 5G 13
Oathills SY14: Mal 1H 207
Oathills Cl. CW6: Tarp 3J 175
Oathills Dr. CW6: Tarp 3J 175
Oathills Lea CW6: Tarp 3J 175
Oatlands SK9: Ald E 7G 119
Oatlands, The CH48: W Kir 4D 56
Oatlands Rd. M22: Wyth 4J 75
Oat Mkt. CW5: Nant 2C 196
Oat St. SK1: Stoc 5E 52
Oban Cres. SK3: Stoc 1B 78
Oban Dr. CH60: Hes 6J 83
M33: Sale 1E 48
Oban Gro. WA2: Fear 1A 42
Obelisk Way CW12: Cong 3E 182
Observatory Rd. CH43: Bid 4H 33
Occleston Cl. M33: Sale 3E 48
OCCLESTONE GREEN 1A 220
Occupiers La. SK7: H Gro 4A 80
Ocean Pk. CH44: Wall 3C 34
Ocean St. WA14: B'ath 6F 47
Ocean St. Trad. Est.
WA14: B'ath 6F 47
O'Connell Rd. L3: Liv 1J 35
Oddfellows Pas. CW10: Mid 3B 180
(off Chester Rd.)
Odeon Cinema
Bromborough 3E 86
Liverpool 2K 35
Warrington 3K 39
Odessa Wlk. WA5: Gt San 6K 39
Odyssey Cen. CH41: Birk 4B 34
Offal Pit La. WA6: Frod 1A 152
OFFERTON 7J 53 (2D 217)
Offerton Dr. SK2: Stoc 6H 53
Offerton Fold SK2: Stoc 5G 53
OFFERTON GREEN 6A 54
Offerton Grn. SK2: Stoc 6K 53
Offerton Ind. Est. SK2: Stoc 5G 53
Offerton La. SK2: Stoc 4F 53
Offerton Rd. SK2: H Gro, Stoc 2A 80
SK7: H Gro 2A 80
Offerton St. SK1: Stoc 2F 53
Off Grove Rd. SK15: M'ook 5E 4
Offley Av. CW11: S'ach 2F 201
Offley Rd. CW11: S'ach 2F 201
Off Lyons La. WA4: App 1J 93
Off Ridge Hill La. SK15: Stal 7A 4
(off Ridge Hill La.)
Off Stamford St. SK15: M'ook 5E 4
(off Stamford St.)
Off Vaudrey La. M34: Den 1F 27
Ogden Ct. SK14: Hyde 1K 27
(off Frank St.)
Ogden Gdns. SK16: Duk 2K 9
Ogden Gro. SK8: Gat 1B 76
Ogden Rd. SK7: Bram 1F 99
Ogden Sq. SK16: Duk 2G 9
Ogden St. M20: Manc 1D 50
SK14: B'tom 3J 29
Ohio Gro. WA5: Gt San 6A 40
Oil Sites Rd. CH65: Ell P 1F 135
Oil St. L3: Liv 1G 35
Okehampton Cres. M33: Sale 6C 22
Okell St. WA7: Run 4G 89
Old Albert Ter. WA7: Run 3H 89
(off Thomas St.)
Old Alder La. WA5: B'ood 5G 15
Old Applecroft CW11: Ett H 4A 200
Old Bank Cl. SK6: Bred 1A 54
Old Barn La. CH64: W'ston 7E 106
Old Barn Rd. CH44: Wall 1K 33
Old Bidston Rd. CH41: Birk 4A 34
Oldbrook Fold WA15: Timp 1B 74
Old Brow OL5: Moss 1D 4
(Mayall St.)
OL5: Moss 1D 4
(Vale Side)
Old Brow Ct. OL5: Moss 1D 4
Old Butt La. ST7: Talk 7K 203
OLDCASTLE HEATH 3C 219
Oldcastle La. SY14: Thr 5H 207
Old Chapel St. SK3: Stoc 5A 52
Old Cherry La. WA13: Lymm 7G 69
Old Chester Rd. CH41: Tran 1D 60
CH42: R Fer, Tran 2D 60
CH63: Beb, H Beb 4E 60
CH66: Gt Sut 3K 133
WA4: Dare 5K 91
WA4: H Wal 6D 66
WA6: Hel 5B 138
Old Church Cl. CH65: Ell P 1E 134
Old Church M. SK16: Duk 2K 9
Old Church Yd. L2: Liv 3G 35
Old Clatterbridge Rd.
CH63: Spit 4J 85
Old Coach Rd. CW6: Kel 3C 172
WA7: Run 3F 89
Old Court Ho. Rd.
CH62: Brom 1D 86
Old Court St. SK14: Hyde 1J 27
Old Courtyard, The
M22: Shar 7A 50
Oldcroft M. SK1: Stoc 5F 53
Old Cryers La. CH2: Elt 6E 136
Old Dairy M. SK14: Hyde 5H 9
Old Farm Cl. CH64: W'ston 7F 107
SK10: Mac 2H 125
Old Farm Dr. SK2: Stoc 6K 53
Old Farm M. SK8: Chea H 6A 78
OLDFIELD BROW 6E 46
Oldfield Cl. CH60: Hes 4G 83
Oldfield Cres. CH4: Ches 6G 149
Oldfield Dr. CH3: Ches 1F 151
CH60: Hes 4F 83
WA15: Timp 6K 47
WA16: Mob 6B 102
Oldfield Gdns. CH60: Hes 5F 83
Oldfield Gro. M33: Sale 6H 23
Oldfield La. CH48: W Kir 1H 57
WA14: Dun M 1C 72
Oldfield M. CH3: Ches 1F 151
WA14: Alt 1F 213 (7G 47)
Oldfield Rd. CH45: Wall 5F 13
CH60: Hes 4F 83
CH65: Ell P 3D 134
CW11: Whe 5D 200
M33: Sale 6H 23
WA13: Lymm 1H 69
WA14: Alt 1F 213 (7E 46)
Oldfield Way CH60: Hes 4F 83
Old Fold SK7: H Gro 1H 79
Old Garden, The WA15: Timp 5B 48
Old Gardens St. SK1: Stoc 7K 213 (4D 52)
Oldgate WA8: Wid 6C 62
Oldgate Cl. CW10: Mid 5B 180
OLD GLOSSOP 1D 217
Old Gorse Cl. CW2: Crewe 3J 193
Old Gorsey La. CH44: Wall 2A 34
Old Greasby Rd. CH49: Upt 7C 32
OLD HALL 4A 40
Old Hall Cl. SK14: Mot 5H 11
WA4: H Wal 5E 66
Old Hall Ct. CH3: Ash H 7H 171
M33: Sale 7K 23
SY14: Mal 3H 207
Old Hall Cres. SK9: Hand 3B 98
Old Hall Dr. CH65: Whit 4D 134
SK2: Stoc 6J 53
Old Hall Gdns. CH2: Ches 7B 146
CW11: S'ach 3F 201
Old Hall La. CH2: Elt 6E 136
M13: Manc 1B 24
M14: Manc 2A 24
M19: Manc 1B 24
SK6: Mel 7H 55
SK7: Woodf 5G 99
SK14: Mot 5H 11
Old Hall Pk. CH3: Guil S 5J 147
Old Hall Pl. CH1: Ches 5B 212 (2K 149)
Old Hall Rd. CH62: Brom 5E 86
CW9: N'ich 1F 163
M33: Sale 7K 23
SK8: Gat 6C 50
WA5: Old H 4B 40
Old Hall St. L3: Liv 2G 35
SK10: Mac 3A 126
SK16: Duk 3F 9
Oldhall St. SY14: Mal 3H 207
Oldham Av. SK1: Stoc 3F 53
Oldham Dr. SK6: Bred 7F 27
Oldham Pl. L1: Liv 3K 35
Oldhams Hill CW8: N'ich 4E 156
Oldhams Ri. SK10: Mac 7A 122
Oldham St. L1: Liv 4K 35
M34: Den 1B 26
M43: Droy 1A 8
SK5: Stoc 4H 25
SK10: Boll 3E 122
SK14: Hyde 1J 27
WA4: Warr 2G 67
Old Haymarket L1: Liv 2J 35
(not continuous)
Old Heyes Rd. WA15: Timp 4B 48
Old Hey Wlk. WA12: New W 2F 15
Oldknow Rd. SK6: Mar 6G 55
Old La. CH3: Ash H 4K 171
CH4: Pou, Pul 7B 184
CH60: Hes 6B 84
CW8: Act B 3B 154
CW9: Ant 7B 94
CW9: What 4J 163
L35: R'ill 1B 36
WA8: Wid 6D 62
Old Leeds St. L3: Liv 2G 35
Old Liverpool Rd. WA5: Warr 1B 66
Old Man of Mow, The 4H 205
Old Market Pl. WA1: Warr 7F 41
(off Horsemarket St.)
WA14: Alt 1J 213 (7H 47)
WA16: Knut 3E 116
Old Maryland La. CH46: More 3B 32
Old Meadow SK11: Mac 4K 125
Old Meadow Dr. M34: Den 5E 8
Old Meadow La. WA15: Hale 2B 74
Old Meadow Rd. CH61: Pens 2G 83
Old Middlewich Rd. CW11: S'ach 3F 201
(off Hightown)
Old Mill, The CH66: L Sut 1J 133
(off Station Rd.)
Old Mill Cl. CH60: Hes 7K 83
WA13: Lymm 6E 44
Old Mill Ct. CH2: Upt 4A 146
Old Mill La. SK7: H Gro 5A 80
SK11: Mac 6B 126
WA4: H Whi 4D 114
Old Mill Pl. CH3: Tatt 3H 187
Old Mill Rd. CW11: S'ach 3F 201
Oldmoor Rd. SK6: Bred 6D 26
Old Moss La. WA3: G'ury 4K 7
Old Newcastle Rd. CW5: W'ston 3H 197
Old Oak Dr. M34: Den 7F 9
Old Oak St. M20: Manc 1D 50
Old Orchard SK9: Wilm 7H 97
Old Orchard, The CW8: Cudd 2C 160
CW9: Ant 6B 94
WA15: Timp 4B 48
Old Orchard Pl. CW1: Crewe 1B 194
(off West St.)
Old Paddock, The CW4: Goo 7K 165
Old Pale Hgts. CW6: Kel 3F 173
Old Park Rd. CW1: Crewe 7K 195
Old Pasture Cl. SK2: Stoc 5J 53
Old Pearl La. CH3: Ches 2E 150
Old Pewterspear La. WA4: App 3H 93

Old Port Sq.—Owley Wood Rd.

Old Port Sq. CH1: Ches 1J 149
Old Post Office Pl. L1: Liv 3J 35
(off School La.)
Old Post Office Yd. CH1: Ches 4C 212
Old Pump La. CH49: Gre 2K 57
Old Quay Cl. CH64: Park 1A 130
Old Quay La. CH64: Park 1B 130
Old Quays, The WA4: Westy 2J 67
Old Quay St. WA7: Run 3H 89
Old Rectory Gdns. SK8: Chea 6F 51
Old Ribbon Mill, The SK11: Mac 6A 126
(off Pitt St.)
Old River Cl. M44: Irlam 1D 20
Old Rd. CW9: And 2C 156
OL6: Ash L 4A 4
SK4: Stoc 1C 52
SK8: Chea 6H 51
SK9: Hand 3A 98
SK9: Wilm 6J 97
SK14: Hyde 5J 9
SK14: Mot 4G 11
SK15: Stal 2D 10
SK16: Duk 1H 9
(not continuous)
WA4: Warr 1F 67
Old Ropery L2: Liv 3H 35
(off Drury La.)
Old School Cl. CH3: Farn 5B 186
CH64: L Nes 3D 130
CW8: Barnt 3A 156
Old School Ho., The CH43: Oxt 7K 33
(off Beresford Rd.)
Old School Ho. La. WA2: Winw 4K 15
Old School La. SK8: Chea H 5J 77
Old School M. SK16: Duk 2K 9
(off Vicarage Dr.)
Old School Way CH41: Birk 5H 33
Old Sealand Rd. CH1: Sea 4A 144
Old Seals Way CH1: Ches 7H 145
Old Smithy La. WA13: Lymm 3J 69
Old Stables, The M34: Aude 4E 8
Old Stack Yd. CH3: Gt Bar 2B 170
Old St. SK14: B'tom 3H 29
SK15: Stal 7B 4
OLD SWAN 1B 214
Old Tannery, The SK14: Hyde 3A 28
OLD TRAFFORD 1C 217
Old Upton La. WA8: Wid 1E 62
Old Vicarage Gdn. CW3: Audl 5B 210
Old Vicarage La. CW8: H'ord 1B 162
Old Vicarage Rd. CH64: W'ston 7F 107
Old Wargrave Rd. WA12: New W 1E 14
Old Warrington Rd.
CW9: Mars, N'ich 4F 157
Old Well Wlk. M33: Sale 2G 47
Old Welsh Rd. CH66: L Sut 3F 133
Old Woman's La. CH3: Chri 4G 151
Old Wood Rd. CH61: Pens 2H 83
Oldwood Rd. M23: Wyth 2G 75
Old Wool La. SK8: Chea H 7H 51
(not continuous)
Old Wrexham Rd. CH4: Ches 4K 149
O'Leary St. WA2: Warr 5G 41
Oleo Ter. M44: Irlam 1F 21
Olinda St. CH62: N Fer 6G 61
Olive Cres. CH41: Tran 1D 60
Olive Dr. CH64: Nest 7H 105
Olive Mt. CH41: Tran 1D 60
Oliver Cl. SK10: Boll 4C 122
Oliver Ho. CH66: Gt Sut 4K 133
(off Oliver La.)
Oliver La. CH41: Birk 6D 34
CH66: Gt Sut 4K 133
Olive Rd. CH64: Nest 7H 105
WA15: Timp 4A 48
Oliver St. CH41: Birk 6C 34
SK1: Stoc 4D 52
WA2: Warr 6F 41
Oliver St. E. CH41: Birk 6D 34
Olive Shapley Av. M20: Manc 1D 50
Olive Ter. SK14: B'tom 3H 29
Olive Wlk. M33: Sale 5B 22
(off Epping Dr.)
Olivia Cl. CH43: Noc 1F 59
Olivia Gro. M14: Manc 1A 24
Olivia M. CH43: Noc 1F 59
Olivier Ho. WA14: Alt 3J 213
Ollerbarrow Rd. WA15: Hale 3J 73
Ollershaw La.
CW9: Mars 7J 115 & 2G 157
OLLERTON 7K 117 (3B 216)
Ollerton Av. M33: Sale 5C 22
Ollerton Cl. CH43: Noc 1F 59
M22: N'den 3A 50
WA4: Grap 2B 68
Ollerton Pk. WA5: B'ood 4B 14
Ollerton Rd. SK9: Hand 1A 98
Ollier Av. M12: Manc 1D 24
Ollier St. WA8: Wid 6G 63
Olney Av. M22: Wyth 6K 49
Olwen Cres. SK5: Stoc 3J 25
Olympia Ct. M44: Irlam 1D 20
Olympia Pl. WA5: Gt San 5K 39
Olympic Ho. M90: Man A 6J 75
Olympic Way WA2: Birc 2C 42
Omega Blvd. WA5: Gt San 3F 39
Omega Circ. M44: Irlam 5C 20
Omega Dr. M44: Irlam 5C 20
Omer Av. M13: Manc 1C 24
Omer Dr. M19: Manc 4B 24
ONECOTE 2D 221
One Oak Ct. SK7: Bram 3A 78
One Oak La. SK9: Wilm 7C 98
One Park W. L1: Liv 3H 35
ONNELEY 3B 220
Onslow Rd. CH1: Blac 6E 144
CH45: N Bri 3H 13
CH62: N Fer 5G 61
SK3: Stoc 4A 52
ONSTON 4B 154
Onston La. CW8: Crow 4B 154
Onward St. SK14: Hyde 1J 27
Opal Ct. L3: Liv 2K 35
(off London Rd.)
M14: Manc 3A 24
Opal St. M19: Manc 3E 24
Open Eye Gallery 3J 35
(off Wood St.)
Openshaw La. M44: Cad 5B 20
(off Prospect Av.)
Orange Gro. WA2: Warr 2J 41
Orbital 24 M34: Den 7C 8
Orbital Way M34: Den 7C 8
Orchard, The CH3: Gt Bou 3D 150
CH45: Wall 4G 13
SK9: Ald E 7G 119
WA6: Hel 6B 138
Orchard Av. CW8: Act B 1B 154
M31: Part 7C 20
WA13: Lymm 2B 70
Orchard Brow WA3: Rix 2C 44
Orchard Cl. CH2: Ches 5A 146
CH66: Gt Sut 7B 134
CW4: Goo 6J 165
CW6: Bun 6D 188
CW7: Wins 5E 178
CW8: Barnt 2A 156
CW8: Weav 4G 155
CW9: Winc 1C 158
CW10: Mid 5D 180
SK8: Chea H 6A 78
SK9: Wilm 2E 118
SK11: Mac 6J 125
SK12: Poy 3D 100
WA6: Frod 2G 139
Orchard Cotts. CW6: Tarp 3J 175
Orchard Ct. CH3: Ches 2D 150
CH41: Tran 2E 60
CW1: Hasl 1K 195
SK2: Stoc 6H 53
ST7: Als 5F 203
WA3: Croft 3F 17
WA6: Frod 7G 111
WA15: Timp 5B 48
Orchard Cres. CW5: Nant 4C 196
SK10: N Ald 1G 167
Orchard Cft. CH3: Guil S 5H 147
Orchard Dene CW8: Cudd 1A 160
L35: R'ill 1C 36
Orchard Dr. CH64: L Nes 3C 130
CW8: L Lei 1G 155
SK9: Hand 4B 98
WA15: Hale 2A 74
Orchard Gdns. CW6: Tarp 4J 175
CW8: Weav 4E 154
SK8: Gat 6B 50
Orchard Ga. WA6: K'ley 1F 153
Orchard Grange CH46: More 5K 31
Orchard Grn. SK9: Ald E 6G 119
Orchard Gro. CH3: Farn 6C 186
Orchard Haven CH66: Gt Sut 7A 134
Orchard La. CH66: Chil T 7B 108
Orchard Pk. Cvn. Pk. CH2: Elt 4F 137
Orchard Pk. La. CH2: Elt 4F 137
Orchard Pl. M33: Sale 6G 23
SK12: Poy 2C 100
WA6: Hel 4C 138
WA15: Timp 5B 48
Orchard Ri. CW9: Moult 6D 162
SK14: Hyde 4A 28
Orchard Rd. CH46: More 3B 32
CH65: Whit 6C 134
SK6: Comp 2H 55
WA13: Lymm 7D 44
WA15: Alt 1K 213 (7J 47)
Orchard Rd. E. M22: N'den 2K 49
Orchard Rd. W. M22: N'den 2K 49
Orchards, The CH4: Salt 5E 148
CW2: Shav 3C 198
LL13: Holt 7A 186
(off Redwood Cl.)
SK3: Stoc 1D 78
WA16: Pick 1B 158
Orchard St.
CH1: Ches 2A 212 (1J 149)
CW1: Crewe 1C 194
CW5: W'ston 1H 197
CW9: N'ich 5G 157
SK1: Stoc 7K 213 (3D 52)
SK14: Hyde 1K 27
WA1: Warr 7G 41
WA2: Fear 2A 42
WA4: Stoc H 5G 67
Orchard Va. SK3: Stoc 6A 52
Orchard Wlk. CH64: Nest 7H 105
WA7: Pal F 7B 90
(off Halton Lea Shop. Cen.)
Orchard Way CH63: H Beb 7C 60
CW6: Kel 3C 172
CW12: Cong 3C 182
WA8: Wid 2A 62
Orchid Cl. CH3: Hunt 5E 150
M44: Irlam 3B 20
Orchil Cl. CH66: L Sut 2G 133
Ordnance Av. WA3: Birc 7K 17
Ordsall Cl. CW11: Whe 6D 200
ORFORD 2H 41 (1A 216)
Orford Av. SK12: Dis 1G 103
WA2: Warr 5G 41
Orford Cl. L24: Hale 6B 88
SK6: H Lan 6E 80
Orford Ct. WN7: Leigh 1H 7
Orford Grn. WA2: Warr 3H 41
Orford La. WA2: Warr 6F 41
Orford Pk. WN7: Leigh 1H 7
Orford Rd. WA1: Warr 4H 41
WA2: Warr 4H 41
Orford St. WA1: Warr 7F 41
Organ Way SK14: H'rth 2J 11
Oriel Cl. L2: Liv 3H 35
(off Water St.)
SK2: Stoc 6F 53
Oriel Ct. CH42: Tran 4A 60
M33: Sale 6G 23
Oriel Rd. CH42: Tran 2D 60
M20: Manc 1C 50
Oriel St. L3: Liv 1H 35
Oriole Ho. M19: Manc 1F 51
Orion Blvd. WA5: Gt San 3G 39
Orion Bus. Pk. SK3: Stoc 7A 52
Orion Way CW1: Crewe 4H 195
Orkney Cl. CH65: Ell P 7E 134
M23: Wyth 1G 75
WA8: Wid 2A 64
Orlando Cl. CH43: Noc 1F 59
Orlando Dr. WA5: Gt San 5A 40
Orme Cl. M41: Urm 1E 22
SK10: Mac 1A 126
SK10: Pres 3H 121
Orme Cres. SK10: Mac 1A 126
Ormerod Cl. CW11: S'ach 4G 201
SK6: Rom 3K 53
Ormerod Cl. CH63: Beb 1A 86
Ormesby Gro. CH63: Rab M 1G 107
Ormeston Lodge M41: Urm 2C 22
Orme St. SK9: Ald E 6F 119
Ormiston Rd. CH45: N Bri 4H 13
Ormond Cl. WA8: Wid 3C 62
Ormonde Rd. CH2: Ches 6K 145
Ormonde St. CH1: Ches 2E 212 (1B 150)
Ormond M. CH43: Noc 1F 59
Ormond St. CH45: Wall 6H 13
L3: Liv 2H 35
Ormond Way CH43: Noc 1F 59
Ormsby Cl. SK3: Stoc 1C 78
Orms Gill Pl. SK2: Stoc 6J 53
Ormskirk Rd. SK5: Stoc 5J 25
Orphanage St. SK4: Stoc 1C 52
ORRELL 1B 214
Orrell Cl. WA5: Gt San 6J 39
Orrell Rd. CH45: N Bri 4J 13
Orret's Mdw. Rd. CH49: Woodc 2E 58
Orrishmere Rd. SK8: Chea H 2H 77
Orrysdale Rd. CH48: W Kir 2B 56
Orston Cres. CH63: Spit 4A 86
Ortega Cl. CH62: N Fer 6H 61
Orthes Gro. SK4: Stoc 6G 25
Orthes St. L3: Liv 3K 35
Orton Av. M23: Wyth 3G 49
Orton Cl. CW7: Wins 1H 179
Orton Rd. M23: Wyth 3G 49
Orville Dr. M19: Manc 4C 24
Orwell Av. M22: Wyth 6K 49
Orwell Cl. SK9: Wilm 4A 98
WA9: Sut M 1G 37
Osborne Av. CH45: N Bri 4H 13
WA2: Warr 3H 41
Osborne Cl. CW11: Ett H 4B 200
SK9: Wilm 1J 119
Osborne Ct. CH43: Oxt 6A 34
(off Osborne Rd.)
CH62: P Sun 7G 61
Osborne Gro. CH45: N Bri 5H 13
CW2: Shav 3B 198
SK8: He Grn 2C 76
Osborne Rd. CH43: Oxt 7A 34
CH45: N Bri 4J 13
M19: Manc 2C 24
M34: Den 6E 8
SK2: Stoc 5D 52
SK14: Hyde 2K 27
WA4: Walt 4F 67
WA15: Alt 1K 213 (7J 47)
Osborne St. M20: Manc 1C 50
SK6: Bred 1H 53
Osborne Ter. M33: Sale 7G 23
Osborne Va. CH45: N Bri 4H 13
Osbourne Cl. CH62: Brom 7E 86
Osbourne Pl. WA14: Alt 3H 213
OSCROFT 5E 170 (1D 219)
Oscroft Wlk. M14: Manc 4A 24
(off Lyth St.)
Osier Cl. CH2: Elt 5G 137
Osmaston Rd. CH42: Tran 3K 59
Osprey Av. CW7: Wins 7D 178
Osprey Cl. CW10: Mid 7D 180
SK16: Duk 3K 9
WA2: Warr 1J 41
WA7: Beec 2B 112
Osprey Dr. M44: Irlam 1D 20
SK9: Wilm 6K 97
Ossett Cl. CH43: Noc 1F 59
WA7: Nort 6F 91
Ossington Wlk. M23: Wyth 2G 49
Ossmere Cl. CW11: S'ach 1D 200
Ostler's La. WA16: Mob 7A 96
Oswald St. SK5: Stoc 1J 25
Oteley Av. CH62: Brom 6D 86
Otley Gro. SK3: Stoc 1B 78
Ottawa Cl. M23: Wyth 1F 75
Otterburn Cl. CH46: More 4J 31
Otterburn Pl. SK2: Stoc 6J 53
Otterburn St. WA7: Nort 3G 91
Otters Bank CW7: Wins 3B 178
Ottersbank M. CW8: Dela 7J 173
OTTERSPOOL 2B 214
Otterspool Rd. SK6: Rom 3B 54
OUGHTRINGTON 1D 70 (2A 216)
Oughtrington Cres. WA13: Lymm 1D 70
Oughtrington La. WA13: Lymm 3C 70
Oughtrington Vw. WA13: Lymm 1D 70
OULTON 2F 177
Oulton Av. CH2: Upt 3B 146
M33: Sale 6K 23
Oulton Cl. CH43: Oxt 2H 59
Oulton Ct. WA4: Grap 3B 68
Oulton Dr. CW12: Cong 3B 182
Oulton Mill La. CW6: Cote 5B 176
Oulton Pk. Motor Racing Circuit 3F 177
Oulton Pl. CH1: Ches 2C 212 (1A 150)
Oulton Way CH43: Oxt 3H 59
Oundle Rd. CH46: More 3B 32
Ousel Nest CW8: Cudd 2A 160
Out La. CH3: Burw 5J 187
Outline Fitness & Leisure Cen. 6H 213
Outram Cl. SK6: Mar 1F 81
Outram Rd. SK16: Duk 4G 9
Outwood Dr. SK8: He Grn 5C 76
Outwood La. M90: Man A 5J 75
Outwood La. W. M90: Man A 5H 75
Outwood Rd. SK8: He Grn 5D 76
Oval, The 6E 60
Oval, The CH45: Wall 5F 13
CH65: Ell P 5E 134
SK8: He Grn 5D 76
Oval Dr. SK16: Duk 3G 9
Oval Vw. SK6: W'ley 6G 27
Ovenhouse La. SK10: Boll 5B 122
OVER 5C 178 (1A 220)
Over Ashberry WA14: W Tim 3F 47
Overchurch Rd. CH49: Upt 6B 32
Overdale SK6: Mar 6F 55
WA14: Alt 7F 47
Overdale Av. CH61: Barns 1B 84
Overdale Cres. M41: Urm 1J 21
Overdale La. CW8: Oak 5A 160
Overdale Rd. CH64: W'ston 6F 107
M22: Wyth 7K 49
SK6: Rom 3K 53
SK12: Dis 1J 103
Overdene Rd. CW7: Wins 4E 178
Overfields WA16: Knut 2H 117
Overgreen Gro. CH46: More 3A 32
Over Hall Dr. CW7: Wins 5D 178
Overhill Dr. SK9: Wilm 7B 98
Overhill La. SK9: Wilm 7B 98
Overhill Rd. SK9: Wilm 7A 98
OVER KNUTSFORD 4F 117
Overlea Dr. M19: Manc 6B 24
Overleigh Ct. CH4: Ches 4A 150
Overleigh Dr. CH4: Ecc 2J 185
Overleigh Rd.
CH4: Ches 7C 212 (4K 149)
Overleigh Ter.
CH4: Ches 7B 212 (4K 149)
Overmarsh CH64: Ness 4E 130
OVER PEOVER 3H 165 (3B 216)
Over Pl. WA16: Knut 5G 117
OVERPOOL 2A 134 (3B 214)
Overpool Gdns. CH66: Gt Sut 5B 134
Overpool Rd.
CH66: Ell P, Gt Sut, Whit 2A 134
(not continuous)
Overpool Station (Rail) 2A 134
Over Sq. CW7: Wins 4C 178
Overstrand CH48: W Kir 3B 56
OVERTON
LL13 3B 218
WA6 1J 139 (3D 215)
Overton Av. M22: Wyth 7K 49
Overton Cl. CH43: Oxt 2J 59
CW10: Mid 4B 180
CW12: Cong 3E 182
Overton Cres. M33: Sale 2H 47
SK7: H Gro 1J 79
Overton Dr. WA6: Frod 2J 139
OVERTON HEATH 1F 207
Overton Heath La. SY14: O Hea 1F 207
Overton Rd. CH44: Wall 7H 13
M22: Wyth 7K 49
Overton Way CH43: Oxt 2J 59
SK9: Hand 1A 98
Overway CW7: Wins 3F 179
Overwood Av. CH1: Mol 1F 145
Overwood La. CH1: Blac 6D 144
CH1: Mol 1E 144
Overwood Rd. M22: N'den 4K 49
Ovington Cl. WA7: Sut W 4B 112
Owen Cl. CH1: Blac 4F 145
Owen Rd. L35: R'ill 2C 36
Owens Corner WA4: App 3H 93
Owens Farm Dr. SK2: Stoc 5J 53
Owens Pk. M14: Manc 2A 24
Owen St. CW2: Crewe 4C 194
CW9: N'ich 5G 157
SK3: Stoc 7F 213 (3B 52)
WA2: Warr 5E 40
Owley Wood Rd. CW8: Weav 4H 155

Owlsfield—Park Rd.

Owlsfield WA12: New W 1H **15**
OWRYTN 3B 218
Oxborough Cl. WA8: Wid 1F **63**
Oxbridge Cl. M33: Sale 1H **47**
Oxenham Rd. WA2: Warr 1F **41**
Oxenhurst Grn. SK2: Stoc 7J **53**
Oxford Av. M33: Sale 7C **22**
Oxford Cl. CH66: Gt Sut 1A **140**
Oxford Ct. WA1: Warr 6H **41**
Oxford Dr. CH63: Tho H 1J **105**
SK6: W'ley 7H **27**
Oxford Gro. M44: Cad 5K **19**
Oxford Pk. Community Sports Cen. 2E 8
Oxford Rd. CH4: Ches 5G **149**
CH44: Wall 7J **13**
SK11: Mac 6J **125**
SK14: Hyde 3K **27**
SK16: Duk 2J **9**
WA7: Run 5G **89**
WA14: Alt 4H **213** (2H **73**)
Oxford St. *CH65: Ell P 2E **134***
(off Worcester St.)
CW1: Crewe 1B **194**
L7: Liv 3K **35**
OL7: Ash L 2E **8**
SK15: M'ook 5E **4**
SK15: Stal 1D **10**
WA4: Warr 1G **67**
WA8: Wid 5H **63**
Oxford St. E. OL7: Ash L 2E **8**
Oxford St. W. OL7: Ash L 2E **8**
Oxford Wlk. *M34: Den 2F **27***
(off Worcester Av.)
Oxford Way SK4: Stoc 1B **52**
Oxheys WA7: Nort 6E **90**
Oxheys La. CW6: Rus 7J **177**
Oxley Av. CH46: Leas 1E **32**
Oxmead Cl. WA2: Padg 3B **42**
Oxmoor Cl. WA7: B'vale 2C **112**
Oxmoor Local Nature Reserve 1F 91
Oxney Cl. SK11: Mac 4G **125**
OXTON 1J 59 (2A 214)
Oxton Av. M22: Wyth 1J **75**
Oxton Cl. WA8: Wid 1C **62**
Oxton Ct. CH43: Oxt 1A **60**
Oxton Grn. CH66: Gt Sut 4K **133**
Oxton Rd. CH41: Birk 7B **34**
CH44: Wall 1A **34**

P

Pacific Rd. CH41: Birk 5E **34**
WA14: B'ath 6E **46**
PACKMOOR 2C 221
Packsaddle Pk. SK10: Pres 6F **121**
Padarn Cl. CH4: Salt 6E **148**
Padbury Cl. *M41: Urm 1G **21***
(off Cheriton Rd.)
Padden Brook SK6: Rom 2B **54**
Padden Brook M. SK6: Rom 2B **54**
PADDINGTON 4K 41 (2A 216)
Paddington Bank
WA1: Warr 6K **41**
Paddock, The CH2: Elt 5E **136**
CH4: Ches 4J **149**
CH46: More 5K **31**
CH49: Upt 7E **32**
CH60: Hes 6A **84**
CH66: Gt Sut 5K **133**
CW5: W'ston 3H **197**
CW6: Tarp 3J **175**
CW8: H'ord 3B **162**
CW11: Ha Grn 7K **201**
CW11: S'ach 2F **201**
SK7: Bram 4B **78**
SK8: Chea 7G **51**
SK9: Hand 2A **98**
SK13: Had 2K **11**
SK14: H'rth 2K **11**
WA6: Hel 6C **138**
WA13: Lymm 2E **70**
WA15: Timp 1B **74**
Paddock Brow SK10: Pres 6H **121**
Paddock Chase SK12: Poy 7K **79**
Paddock Dr. CH64: Park 5G **105**
Paddock Gro. WA9: Clo F 1K **37**
PADDOCKHILL 4A 118
Paddock Hill WA16: Mob 5A **118**
Paddock La. CW3: Audl 6D **210**
WA13: Warb 4D **44**
WA14: Dun M 7J **45**
Paddock Ri. WA7: Beec 3A **112**
Paddock Rd. CH4: Ecc 3K **185**
SK14: Hyde 3J **27**
Paddock Row CH1: Ches 5C **212** (2A **150**)
Paddocks, The SK3: Stoc 1E **78**
SK10: Pres 6H **121**
Paddocks Grn. CW12: Cong 6H **183**
Paddock Vw. CW10: Mid 2C **180**
Paddock Wlk. CW8: Cudd 1A **160**
PADESWOOD 1A 218
PADGATE 3A 42
Padgate Bus. Cen.
WA1: Padg 4B **42**
Padgate La. WA1: Padg, Warr 5H **41**
(not continuous)
Padgate Station (Rail) 3A 42
Padgbury Cl. CW12: Cong 5C **182**
Padgbury La. CW12: Cong 4B **182**
Padmore Cl. CW1: Crewe 6F **191**
Padston Dr. ST7: Als 6C **202**
Padstow Cl. CW1: Crewe 5H **191**
SK10: Mac 4F **125**
SK14: Hat 7E **10**
WA5: Penk 2G **65**
Padstow Dr. SK7: Bram 6D **78**
Padstow Rd. CH49: Gre 2K **57**
Padstow Sq. WA7: B'vale 2D **112**
Padstow Wlk. SK14: Hat 7E **10**
Padworth Pl. CW1: L'ton 4G **191**
Padworth Wlk. M23: Wyth 4D **48**
Page Gro. CW2: Shav 4B **198**
Page La. WA8: Wid 4J **63**
Page Wlk. L3: Liv 1K **35**
(not continuous)
Pagewood Cl. CH43: Noc 1F **59**
Paignton Av. M19: Manc 3C **24**
SK14: Hat 1D **28**
Paignton Cl. WA5: Penk 1G **65**
Paignton Dr. M33: Sale 6C **22**
Paignton Gro. SK5: Stoc 4H **25**
Paignton Rd. CH45: Wall 5F **13**
Paignton Wlk. SK14: Hat 1D **28**
Pailin Dr. M43: Droy 1B **8**
Painswick Rd. CH66: Gt Sut 6A **134**
M22: Wyth 4H **75**
Paisley Av. CH62: East 3K **107**
Paisley St. L3: Liv 1G **35**
PALACE FIELDS 1C 112
Palacefields Av. WA7: Pal F 1B **112**
Palacefields Local Cen.
WA7: Pal F 1C **112**
Palace Hey CH64: Ness 3E **130**
Palace Rd. M33: Sale 6F **23**
OL6: Ash L 4A **4**
Palatine Cl. CH1: Blac 4E **144**
M44: Irlam 2C **20**
Palatine Ct. M34: Den 5D **8**
Palatine Ho. *SK3: Stoc 4C **52***
(off Old Chapel St.)
Palatine Ind. Est. WA4: Warr 2G **67**
Palatine M. M34: Den 6D **8**
Palatine Rd. CH44: Wall 2C **34**
CH62: Brom 5C **86**
M20: Manc 1C **50**
M22: N'den 3J **49**
Palatine St. M34: Den 5D **8**
(not continuous)
Palermo Cl. CH44: Wall 2C **34**
Palgrave Cl. CH1: Blac 5H **145**
Palin Dr. WA5: Gt San 6H **39**
Palliser Cl. WA3: Birc 1G **43**
Pall Mall CW5: Nant 2C **196**
L3: Liv 1H **35**
Palma Av. M90: Man A 5G **75**
Palmarsh Rd. WA8: Hal B 1B **88**
Palm Cl. M33: Sale 6B **22**
Palmer Av. SK8: Chea 6H **51**
Palmer Cl. CH43: Noc 2G **59**
CW9: N'ich 1E **162**
Palmer Cres. WA5: Old H 4B **40**
Palmer Rd. CW11: S'ach 3G **201**
Palmerston Cl. CH1: Ches 6J **145**
CW1: Hasl 1J **195**
M34: Den 7A **8**
Palmerston Rd. CH44: Wall 7F **13**
M34: Den 7A **8**
SK2: Stoc 2E **78**
SK11: Mac 5H **125**
Palmerston St. CH42: R Fer 3E **60**
SK10: Boll 3D **122**
Palmer St. M33: Sale 7F **23**
SK16: Duk 1G **9**
Palmer Vs. CH42: R Fer 4D **60**
Palm Gro. CH43: Oxt 6A **34**
CH66: Whit 7C **134**
Palm Hill CH43: Oxt 1A **60**
Palm St. M13: Manc 1C **24**
Palmwood Av. L35: R'ill 2D **36**
Palmwood Cl. CH43: Pren 4H **59**
Palmyra Ho. WA1: Warr 7E **40**
Palmyra Sq. Nth. WA1: Warr 7E **40**
Palmyra Sq. Sth. WA1: Warr 7E **40**
Paltridge Way CH61: Pens 2H **83**
Panfield Rd. M22: Wyth 1J **75**
Pangbourne Av. M41: Urm 1D **22**
Pangbourne Cl. SK3: Stoc 6A **52**
WA4: App 7J **67**
PANT 3B 218
PANTASAPH 3A 214
Panton Pl. CH2: Ches 7C **146**
Panton Rd. CH2: Ches 7C **146**
PANT Y WACCO 3A 214
Parade, The CH1: Blac 5F **145**
CH64: Park 5E **104**
SK6: Rom 3A **54**
SK9: Ald E 6F **119**
Parade Rd. M90: Man A 6J **75**
Paradise CH4: Ches 7D **212** (3A **150**)
Paradise Mill (Mus.) 5A 126
Paradise St. L1: Liv 4J **35**
M34: Aude 3E **8**
SK11: Mac 5K **125**
Paragon Cl. WA8: Wid 7H **37**
Parbold Ct. WA8: Wid 5D **62**
Parbutts La. SY14: Mal 3H **207**
Parish Cl. ST7: Als 5C **202**
Park, The CH3: Chri 3H **151**
WA5: Penk 2F **65**
Park & Ride
Boughton Heath 3F 151
Leasowe 2D 32
Sealand Road 1E 148
Park & Ride
Upton (The Zoo) 1A 146
Wrexham Road 2F 185
Park Av. CH1: Sau 1B **144**
CH3: Tatt 2H **187**
CH4: Salt 5F **149**
CH44: Wall 1C **34**
CW7: Wins 1H **179**
CW8: Weav 4G **155**
L35: R'ill 1C **36**
M19: Manc 2D **24**
M33: Sale 5F **23**
M41: Urm 1B **22**
SK3: Stoc 5H **51**
SK6: Rom 2C **54**
SK7: Bram 1G **99**
SK8: Chea H 4H **77**
SK9: Wilm 6K **97**
SK12: Poy 2D **100**
SK14: Hyde 6J **9**
WA4: Warr 2H **67**
WA8: Wid 3H **63**
WA14: Timp 4J **47**
WA15: Hale 4K **73**
Park Av. Nth. WA12: New W 1F **15**
Park Av. Sth. WA12: New W 1F **15**
Park Bank CW12: Cong 4H **183**
Park Blvd. WA1: Warr 1F **67**
Parkbridge Rd. CH42: Tran 2B **60**
Park Brook Rd. SK11: Mac 5H **125**
Parkbrook Rd. M23: Wyth 5H **49**
Park Bungs. SK6: Mar 7F **55**
Parkbury Ct. CH43: Oxt 2K **59**
Park Cl. CH3: Tar 6B **170**
CH41: Birk 6B **34**
SK15: Stal 6A **4**
WA14: Timp 4K **47**
Park Ct. CH1: Ches 4E **212**
CH48: W Kir 3B **56**
M22: Wyth 2K **75**
M33: Sale 6F **23**
WA1: Warr 7D **40**
WA6: Frod 7H **111**
WA7: Run 6G **89**
Park Ct. M. SK8: Chea 1G **77**
Park Cres. CW8: Cudd 2C **160**
M14: Manc 1A **24**
SK9: Wilm 5J **97**
WA4: App 7H **67**
Parkdale CH48: Cald 7E **56**
Parkdale Av. M34: Aude 3C **8**
Parkdale Ind. Est. WA1: Warr 1G **67**
Parkdale Rd. WA1: Padd 5A **42**
Park Dr. CH2: Ches 6D **146**
CH41: Birk 5K **33**
(not continuous)
CH43: Clau 5K **33**
CH65: Whit 5D **134**
CW2: Wis 5K **193**
SK4: Stoc 2K **51**
SK9: Wilm 5J **97**
SK14: Hyde 6J **9**
WA15: Hale 3K **73**
WA15: Timp 5A **48**
Park Dr. Gdns. CW2: Wis 6K **193**
Park Dr. Sth. CH2: Ches 6D **146**
Parkend Rd. CH42: Tran 2B **60**
M23: Wyth 1G **75**
Parker Av. CW8: H'ord 7K **155**
Parker Dr. CH3: Farn 6B **186**
Parker Dr. Sth. CH3: Farn 6C **186**
Parkers Bldgs. CH1: Ches 3E **212** (2B **150**)
Parkers Ct. WA7: Pal F 1A **112**
Parker's Rd. CW1: Crewe, L'ton 5F **191**
Parker St. L1: Liv 3J **35**
SK11: Mac 5B **126**
(not continuous)
WA1: Warr 1E **66**
WA7: Run 3H **89**
Parker's Yd. CH1: Ches 6C **212**
Parker Way CW12: Cong 3C **182**
Park Est. CW2: Shav 2D **198**
Parkett Heyes Rd. SK11: Mac 5F **125**
Parkfield CW1: L'ton 5F **191**
M43: Droy 1A **8**
Parkfield Av. CH41: Birk 6C **34**
M41: Urm 2A **22**
SK6: Mar 6F **55**
WA4: Westy 1A **68**
Parkfield Ct. WA14: Alt 3G **213** (1G **73**)
Parkfield Dr. CH44: Wall 7H **13**
CH65: Whit 6C **134**
CW5: Nant 3C **196**
WA6: Hel 5B **138**
Parkfield Pl. CH41: Birk 6C **34**
Parkfield Rd. CH63: Beb 3A **86**
CW9: N'ich 5G **157**
SK8: Chea H 4H **77**
WA14: Alt 3F **213** (1G **73**)
WA16: Knut 5F **117**
Parkfield Rd. Sth. M20: Manc 1C **50**
Parkfields SK15: Stal 6E **4**
Parkfields La. WA2: Fear 2K **41**
PARKGATE 6F 105 (3A 214)
Parkgate WA16: Knut 2G **117**
Parkgate Av. WA16: O Peo 3G **165**
Park Ga. Cl. SK6: Bred 6D **26**
Parkgate Ct. CH1: Ches 6J **145**
Parkgate Dr. SK2: Stoc 1F **79**
Parkgate Ho. *CH64: Park 5E **104***
(off Greenway)
Parkgate Ho. Ct. CH64: Park 6E **104**
Parkgate La. CH64: Nest 2H **105**
WA16: Knut 2G **117**
Parkgate Rd.
CH1: Ches, Mol 1A **212** (2F **145**)
CH1: Sau 1D **144**
CH1: Woodb 5B **132**
CH64: Nest 7G **105**
CH66: Leds 5B **132**
SK11: Mac 1G **129**
WA4: Stoc H 4H **67**
WA14: W Tim 4G **47**
Park Gates Av. SK8: Chea H 4A **78**
Park Gates Dr. SK8: Chea H 4A **78**
Parkgate Trad. Est. WA16: Knut 1G **117**
Parkgate Way *SK9: Hand 2A **98***
(off Davenham Rd.)
WA7: Murd 7E **90**
Park Grn. SK11: Mac 5A **126**
(not continuous)
Park Gro. CH41: Birk 7C **34**
M19: Manc 1D **24**
SK4: Stoc 7E **24**
SK11: Mac 6K **125**
PARK HILL 1C 215
Parkhill Ct. WA16: Knut 4F **117**
Park Hill Rd. WA15: Hale 4A **74**
Parkhill Rd. CH42: Tran 2B **60**
Park Ho. *M23: Wyth 5C **48***
(off Bridge Rd.)
Park Ho. Dr. CW11: S'ach 1G **201**
SK10: Pres 3H **121**
Park Ho. La. SK10: Pres 3H **121**
Park Ho. M. CW11: S'ach 1H **201**
Parkhurst Rd. CH42: Tran 3B **60**
Parkin Cl. SK16: Duk 2H **9**
Parkland Cl. WA4: App T 2B **94**
Parkland Ct. CH43: Bid 4F **33**
*CH49: Woodc 3D **58***
(off Childwall Grn.)
Parkland Dr. CH2: Elt 5E **136**
Parklands CH66: L Sut 3J **133**
CW10: Mid 5B **180**
*M33: Sale 6H **23***
(off Charlton Dr.)
SK6: Rom 1E **54**
SK7: Bram 4C **78**
SK9: Wilm 7K **97**
WA8: Wid 2C **62**
WA14: Alt 1F **73**
Parklands, The CW12: Cong 4J **183**
SK4: Stoc 7H **25**
Parklands Dr. CH2: Elt 5G **137**
CH60: Hes 1E **104**
CW2: West 4K **199**
M33: Sale 2H **47**
Parklands Gdns. CH66: L Sut 2K **133**
Parklands Rd. M23: Wyth 5F **49**
Parklands Sports Cen. 2J 75
Parklands Vw. CH66: L Sut 2K **133**
Parklands Way SK12: Poy 2D **100**
Parkland Vw. CW5: Nant 3B **196**
Park La. CH3: Lit 7J **147**
CH47: Meols 3G **31**
CW5: Hath 1G **211**
CW8: H'ord 2A **162**
CW9: Ast B, Pick 5J **115**
CW9: Moult 7E **162**
CW11: S'ach 3D **200**
CW12: Cong 4G **183**
L1: Liv 4J **35**
SK1: Stoc 4F **53**
SK11: Mac 6J **125**
(not continuous)
SK12: Poy 2D **100**
SK16: Duk 2H **9**
WA4: App, H Wal 1C **92**
WA6: Frod 7H **111**
WA13: Warb 3E **44**
WA14: L Bol 3K **71**
WA15: Hale 4A **74**
WA16: Pick 5J **115** & 1B **158**
Park La. Cvn. Site CH47: Meols 2H **31**
Parklea CH66: L Sut 2K **133**
Parkleigh CW12: Cong 4H **183**
Park Lodge M19: Manc 2D **24**
Park Lodge Cl. SK8: Chea 1G **77**
Park Mills Cl. CW5: W'ston 2H **197**
Park Mt. SK8: Gat 7C **50**
SK11: Mac 6H **125**
Park Mt. Cl. SK11: Mac 6H **125**
Park Mt. Dr. SK11: Mac 6H **125**
Park Pde. OL6: Ash L 1F **9**
Park Pde. Ind. Est. OL6: Ash L 1F **9**
Park Pl. L8: Liv 6K **35**
SK4: Stoc 2H **51**
Park Range M14: Manc 1A **24**
Park Ri. SK6: Rom 1C **54**
SK15: Stal 6A **4**
Park Rd. CH2: Tho M 7C **136**
CH42: Tran 2D **60**
CH44: Wall 1B **34**
CH47: Meols 3F **31**
CH48: W Kir 3B **56**
CH60: Hes 5K **83**
CH62: East 1A **108**
CH62: P Sun 1B **86**
CH64: W'ston 7G **107**
CH65: Ell P 4E **134**
(not continuous)
CW1: Hasl 1K **195**
CW5: Nant 4C **196**
CW5: W'ston 1G **197**

Park Rd.—Penketh Ct.

Park Rd. CW6: L Bud .2G 177
CW6: Oul .6D 176
CW6: Tarp .2H 175
CW8: Winn .4C 156
CW10: Mid .3C 180
CW12: Cong .3G 183
L8: Liv .6K 35
M31: Part .1J 45
M32: S'ord .1H 23
M33: Sale .5F 23
M34: Aude .2C 8
M34: Den .7D 8
SK4: Stoc .6E 24
SK6: Rom .1C 54
SK8: Chea .6G 51
SK8: Chea H .4A 78
SK8: Gat .6B 50
SK9: Wilm .7G 97
SK12: Dis .7F 81
SK14: Hyde .6J 9
SK16: Duk .1H 9
WA2: Warr .3H 41
WA5: Gt San .5E 38
WA7: Run .6F 89
WA8: Wid .4H 63
WA13: Lymm .5F 71
WA13: Warb .4D 44
(not continuous)
WA14: Bow .2E 72
WA14: Timp .4J 47
WA15: Hale .4J 73
WA15: Timp .4J 47
Park Rd. E. CH41: Birk .6B 34
Park Rd. Nth. CH41: Birk .5K 33
M41: Urm .1B 22
Park Rd. Sth. CH43: Clau .6A 34
M41: Urm .1B 22
WA12: New W .1F 15
Park Rd. W. CH4: Ches .4H 149
CH43: Clau .5K 33
Park Row SK4: Stoc .3G 51
Parkside CH44: Wall .1B 34
Parkside Av. WA9: Sut M .1H 37
Parkside Cl. CH63: Beb .7F 61
CH64: Park .7G 105
SK6: H Lan .5D 80
Parkside Ct. WA8: Wid .3G 63
Parkside La. SK6: Mel .6J 55
Parkside Rd. CH42: Tran .2D 60
CH63: Beb .7F 61
M33: Sale .1D 48
WA2: Winw .1A 16
Parkside Wlk. SK7: Bram .2C 78
(not continuous)
Park Sq. OL6: Ash L .5A 4
Parkstone Dr. CW1: Crewe .5G 191
Parkstone Rd. CH42: Tran .2B 60
M44: Irlam .1D 20
Park St. CH1: Ches .5D 212 (2A 150)
CH41: Birk .6C 34
(not continuous)
CH44: Wall .7J 13
CH64: Nest .7H 105
CW8: N'ich .6D 156
CW12: Cong .4G 183
(Kinsey St.)
CW12: Cong .4G 183
(Moor St.)
L8: Liv .7K 35
(not continuous)
M34: Den .7C 8
OL5: Moss .1D 4
OL6: Ash L .1F 9
OL7: Ash L .1F 9
SK1: Stoc .5J 213 (2D 52)
SK6: Bred .1K 53
SK10: Boll .3E 122
SK11: Mac .5A 126
SK15: Stal .1C 10
Parksway WA1: Wool .5D 42
Park Ter. OL5: Moss .1D 4
Park Va. CH64: Nest .1D 130
Parkvale Av.
CH43: Pren .5H 59
Park Va. Rd. SK11: Mac .6K 125
Park Vw. CH62: Brom .6C 86
CW1: Hasl .2K 195
CW3: Hank .1E 210
CW5: Nant .1D 196
CW12: Cong .3G 183
M14: Manc .4B 24
M34: Aude .2C 8
OL6: Ash L .5A 4
SK1: Stoc .5F 53
SK3: Stoc .5H 51
SK6: Bred .1G 53
SK7: H Gro .5B 80
SK8: Gat .6C 50
WA2: Warr .1J 41
WA14: L Bol .2K 71
Parkview Cl. CH41: Birk .5B 34
Park Vw. Ct.
M21: Chor H .2K 23
SK6: Rom .2C 54
Parkview Ct. CH60: Hes .6H 83
M32: S'ord .2K 23
Parkview Pk.
WA13: Lymm .4F 71
Parkville Rd.
M20: Manc .6A 24
Park Wlk. CH2: Ches .6A 146
Park Way CH1: Sau .1B 144
Parkway CH45: Wall .4E 12
CH47: Meols .4F 31
CH61: Irby .6C 58
CW4: H Cha .4J 181
M34: Den .7B 8
SK3: Stoc .5H 51
SK7: Bram .3C 78
SK9: Wilm .1G 119
Parkway Cl. CH61: Irby .6C 58
Park W. CH1: Ches .1F 149
CH60: Hes .7F 83
Parkwood Cl. CH62: Brom .5E 86
WA13: Lymm .3K 69
Parkwood Rd. M23: Wyth .5J 49
Parliament Cl. L1: Liv .5K 35
Parliament St. CW8: N'ich .6C 156
L8: Liv .5J 35
Parliament Way CH66: Gt Sut .1B 140
Parlington Cl. WA8: Wid .6C 62
Parndon Dr. SK2: Stoc .5G 53
Parnell Av. M22: N'den .4K 49
Parnell Rd. CH63: Spit .4A 86
Parnell Sq. CW12: Cong .4J 183
PARR .1D 215
Parr Gro. CH49: Gre .1K 57
Parrs Ct. M44: Irlam .1C 20
Parrs Mt. M. SK4: Stoc .2H 51
Parr's Rd. CH43: Oxt .2A 60
Parr St. L1: Liv .4J 35
SK11: Mac .5K 125
WA1: Warr .1G 67
(not continuous)
WA8: Wid .4J 63
Parrs Wood Av. M20: Manc .2E 50
Parrs Wood Ct. M20: Manc .3E 50
Parrs Wood Entertainment Cen. .3F 51
Parrs Wood La. M20: Manc .3E 50
Parrs Wood Rd. M20: Manc .4D 50
Parrs Wood Sports Cen. .3F 51
Parrs Wood Vw. WA4: Grap .4A 68
Parry Dr. WA4: Thel .2E 68
Parry Mead SK6: Bred .7F 27
Parry's La. WA7: Run .5G 89
Parry St. CH44: Wall .2C 34
Parsonage Ct. SK4: Stoc .7E 24
Parsonage Gdns. SK6: Mar .1G 81
Parsonage Grn. SK9: Wilm .7J 97
(off Alderley Rd.)
Parsonage Rd. M20: Manc .4A 24
M41: Urm .2H 21
(not continuous)
SK4: Stoc .7E 24
WA8: Wid .2F 89
Parsonage St. SK4: Stoc .5G 213 (2C 52)
SK11: Mac .5A 126
SK14: Hyde .1J 27
Parsonage Way SK8: Chea .7K 51
WA5: Gt San .7J 39
Parsons La. CH2: Ches .3J 145
Parson St. CW12: Cong .4E 182
PARTINGTON .1J 45 (1B 216)
Partington Leisure Cen. .2H 45
Partington Pl. M33: Sale .6G 23
(off School Rd.)
Partington Shop. Cen. M31: Part .1H 45
Partington Sq. WA7: Nort .2H 91
Partridge Av. M23: Wyth .6H 49
Partridge Cl. CW7: Wins .7E 178
CW12: Cong .5G 183
WA3: Birc .7K 17
Partridge Ct. SK2: Stoc .7F 53
Partridge Way CW9: Winc .2B 158
Parvey La. SK11: Sut E .4J 129
Pascal St. M19: Manc .3D 24
Paston Rd. M22: Shar .5K 49
Pasture Av. CH46: More .2B 32
Pasture Cl. CW6: Kel .4B 172
SK10: Mac .1K 125
WA9: Clo F .1J 37
Pasture Cres. CH46: More .3B 32
Pasture Dr. WA3: Croft .4F 17
Pasturefield Cl. M33: Sale .1F 49
Pasture Fld. Rd. M22: Wyth .4B 76
Pasturegreen Way M44: Irlam .1E 20
Pasture La. WA2: Padg .3B 42
Pasture Rd. CH46: More .1A 32
Pastures, The CH48: W Kir .3G 57
Pastures Dr. CW2: West .3K 199
Patch Cft. Rd. M22: Wyth .4B 76
Patch La. SK7: Bram .1G 99
(not continuous)
Paterson St. CH41: Birk .6B 34
Patmos La. WA16: Lwr P .4K 159
Paton Cl. CH48: W Kir .2E 56
Patricia Av. CH41: Birk .3J 33
Patrivale Cl. WA1: Padd .6K 41
Patten La. WA1: Warr .7F 41
(off Barbauld St.)
Patten St. CH41: Birk .4A 34
Patterdale SK8: Chea .7E 50
Patterdale Av. WA2: Warr .2G 41
Patterdale Cl. CW2: Crewe .3H 193
SK15: Stal .6B 4
Patterdale Rd. CH63: Beb .3K 85
M22: N'den .4A 50
M31: Part .1G 45
SK1: Stoc .5F 53
SK6: W'ley .7G 27
Patterdale Wlk. WA15: Timp .7D 48
(off Bowness Rd.)
Pattern Ho. SK15: Stal .7B 4
Patterson Cl. WA3: Birc .1E 42
Patterson St. M34: Den .6E 8
Patting Cl. M44: Irlam .1F 21
Patton Dr. WA5: Gt San .6K 39
Paul Cl. WA5: Gt San .6F 39
Paul Ct. SK1: Stoc .3E 52
(off Hall St.)
Paulden Av. M23: Wyth .6H 49
Paulden Rd. CW9: Los Gra .5C 158
Paulhan Rd. M20: Manc .7A 24
Paul Orr Ct. L3: Liv .1H 35
Paulsfield Dr. CH46: More .5B 32
Paul St. L3: Liv .1H 35
WA2: Warr .6E 40
Pavement La. WA16: Mob .1J 117
Pavilion Ct. WA12: New W .1D 14
Pavilions, The CH4: Ches .1G 185
CH43: Oxt .1K 59
CW9: Dave .4D 162
SK8: Chea .1F 77
Pavilion Way CW12: Cong .3E 182
SK10: Mac .3G 125
Paxford Pl. SK9: Wilm .2F 119
Payne Cl. WA5: Gt San .6B 40
Paythorne Cl. WA3: Cul .7F 7
Paythorne Grn. SK2: Stoc .7J 53
Peace Dr. WA5: Gt San .7B 40
Peacefield SK6: Mar .7E 54
Peaceville Rd. M19: Manc .2C 24
Peach Fld. CH3: Gt Bou .4E 150
Peach La. CW5: Nant .5E 192
Peach Tree Cl. L24: Hale .6B 88
Peacock Av. CW7: Wins .6D 178
WA1: Warr .6J 41
Peacock Cl. SK13: Had .3K 11
Peacock Dr. SK8: He Grn .7D 76
Peacock La. WA16: H Leg .7E 70
Peacock Way SK9: Hand .1A 98
(off Pickmere Rd.)
Peak Bank SK6: Rom .2A 54
Peakdale Av. SK8: He Grn .4D 76
Peakdale Rd. SK6: Mar .1G 81
Peak St. SK1: Stoc .3E 52
Peak Vw. SK13: Had .3K 11
Pearle St. SK10: Mac .3A 126
Pearl La. CH3: Ches .1E 150
CH3: Lit .2F 151
Pearl St. M34: Den .7D 8
SK7: H Gro .1J 79
SK10: Pres .4H 121
Pearl Way SK14: Mot .7H 11
Pear Mill Ind. Est. SK6: Bred .2G 53
Pearn Av. M19: Manc .6C 24
Pearn Rd. M19: Manc .6C 24
Pearson Av. WA4: Warr .3H 67
Pearson Cl. M31: Part .1J 45
Pearson Rd. CH42: Tran .7D 34
Pearson St. SK5: Stoc .1D 52
SK11: Mac .5B 126
SK16: Duk .4H 9
Peart Av. SK6: W'ley .5H 27
Pear Tree Av. CW1: Crewe .6G 191
WA7: Run .7J 89
Pear Tree Bank CW12: Cong .4G 183
Pear Tree Cl. CH60: Hes .5A 84
CW7: Wins .5E 178
CW8: Weav .4F 155
L24: Hale .7B 88
SK6: Mar B .4H 55
SK13: Had .3K 11
WA6: Frod .6K 111
Peartree Cl. CW11: S'ach .3J 201
Peartree Cres. WA12: New W .1F 15
Pear Tree Dr. CW9: Winc .1B 158
SK15: Stal .7C 4
Pear Tree Farm Cotts. CW9: Bil G .2K 163
Pear Tree Fld. CW5: Nant .3E 196
Pear Tree La. CW8: Act B .1B 154
Pear Tree Pl. WA4: Warr .1G 67
Pear Tree Wlk. M33: Sale .6B 22
(off Mountain Ash Cl.)
Peartree Wlk. M22: Wyth .1H 75
Pear Tree Way CH2: Ches .5C 146
Peartree Way CH66: Gt Sut .7A 134
Peart St. M34: Den .7D 8
Pearwood Cl. CW6: Tarp .3J 175
Peaslake Cl. SK6: Rom .2D 54
Peasley Cl. WA2: Padg .3B 42
PEASLEY CROSS .1D 215
Pebble Cl. SK15: Stal .5B 4
Peckfield Cl. WA7: B'vale .2C 112
PECKFORTON .2D 219
Peckforton Castle .3A 188
Peckforton Cl. CW11: S'ach .2C 200
SK8: Gat .7C 50
Peckforton Dr. CH66: Gt Sut .5A 134
WA7: Sut W .3B 112
Peckforton Gap CW6: Peck .7K 187
Peckforton Hall La. CW6: Spur .7A 188
Peckforton Rd. CW6: Bees .3B 188
Peckforton Wlk. SK9: Wilm .5B 98
(off Colshaw Dr.)
Peckforton Way CH2: Upt .4B 146
CW8: N'ich .6D 156
(off Beeston St.)
Peckmill Cl. SK9: Wilm .4B 98
Pedley Hill SK10: Adl .7E 100
SK10: R'ow .7H 123
Pedley St. CW2: Crewe .4D 194
Peebles Cl. CH66: L Sut .2F 133
CW4: H Cha .5H 181
Peel Av. CH42: Tran .2E 60
WA14: Hale .3H 73
Peel Cen., The SK1: Stoc .4K 213 (2E 52)
Peel Cl. WA1: Wool .6D 42
Peel Ct. SK2: Stoc .6E 52
(off Peel St.)
Peel Cres. CH3: Ash H .7G 171
Peel Dr. CW12: Astb .7D 182
M33: Sale .7K 23
Peelgate Dr. SK8: He Grn .3C 76
PEEL HALL .3B 76
Peel Hall La. CH3: Ash H .7G 171
Peel Hall Rd. M22: Wyth .2A 76
Peel Ho. La. WA8: Wid .2H 63
Peel La. CW12: Astb .6D 182
Peel Moat Ct. SK4: Stoc .6F 25
Peel Moat Rd. SK4: Stoc .6E 24
Peel Moat Sports and Target Fitness Cen. .6E 24
Peel Rd. WA15: Hale .2J 73
Peel Sq. CW1: Crewe .1B 194
(off Cornwall Gro.)
Peel St. CW1: Crewe .1B 194
M34: Aude .4D 8
M34: Den .6D 8
SK2: Stoc .6D 52
SK11: Mac .6A 126
SK14: Hyde .2K 27
SK15: Stal .1A 10
SK16: Duk .1H 9
WA7: Run .3F 89
Peel Ter. CH1: Ches .2E 212 (1B 150)
SK16: Duk .1G 9
(off Queen St.)
Peerglow Pk. Est. WA14: Timp .4J 47
Peerswood Ct. CH64: L Nes .3C 130
Peewit Cl. CW7: Wins .7E 178
Pegasus Ct. M33: Sale .6J 23
(off Broad Rd.)
Peggie's La. SK10: W Grn .1A 122
Pelham Cl. CW1: Hasl .1K 195
Pelham Rd. CH44: Wall .1K 33
WA4: Thel .2C 68
Pelham St. OL7: Ash L .2D 8
Pelican Cl. CW1: Crewe .1G 195
Pelwood Cl. CH49: Woodc .2E 58
Pemberton Cl. CH64: W'ston .7F 107
Pemberton Rd. CH1: Ches .3B 212 (1K 149)
CH49: Woodc .2E 58
Pembridge Ct. CH65: Ell P .5G 135
Pembridge Gdns. CH65: Ell P .5G 135
(off Rochester Dr.)
Pembroke Av. CH46: More .5B 32
M33: Sale .6E 22
Pembroke Cl. CH4: Ches .5B 150
Pembroke Ct. CH41: Tran .1E 60
SK6: Rom .2K 53
SK7: H Gro .3J 79
WA7: Man P .1E 90
Pembroke Dr. CH65: Whit .5C 134
Pembroke Gdns. L3: Liv .2K 35
WA4: App .2H 93
Pembroke Gro. M44: Cad .5K 19
Pembroke Ho. SK3: Stoc .4C 52
(off York St.)
Pembroke Pl. L3: Liv .2K 35
Pembroke Rd. SK11: Mac .5G 125
Pembroke St. L3: Liv .2K 35
Pembroke Way CW7: Wins .5C 178
M34: Den .2F 27
(off Worcester Av.)
Pembry Cl. SK5: Stoc .6A 26
Pembury Cl. M22: Wyth .2J 75
Penare WA7: B'vale .2E 112
Penarth Rd. M22: N'den .4K 49
Penbrook Cl. CW2: Crewe .3H 193
Pencarrow Cl. M20: Manc .1B 50
Penda Way CW11: S'ach .3F 201
(off Market Sq.)
Pendeen Cl. M22: Wyth .4A 76
Pendennis Ct. WA7: Cast .4B 90
Pendennis Rd. CH44: Wall .1B 34
SK4: Stoc .1A 52
Pendine Cl. WA5: Call .2A 40
PENDLEBURY .1B 216
Pendlebury Gdns. SK11: L Grn .3H 129
Pendlebury Rd. SK8: Gat .6C 50
Pendlebury St. WA4: Westy .2A 68
WA9: Clo F .1J 37
Pendlebury Towers SK5: Stoc .1D 52
Pendle Cl. CH49: Upt .6B 32
CH66: L Sut .2F 133
CW1: Crewe .1G 195
Pendle Gdns. WA3: Cul .1K 17
Pendle Ho. M34: Den .1E 26
Pendle Rd. M34: Den .1E 26
PENDLETON .1C 217
Pendle Wlk. SK5: Stoc .6K 25
Penfold Cl. CH1: Cap .7H 133
Penfold Hey CH2: Upt .3A 146
Penfolds WA7: Run .5K 89
Penfold Way CH4: Dod .3D 184
Pengham Wlk. M23: Wyth .3G 49
Pengwern Ter. CH45: Wall .4J 13
(off Holland Rd.)
Penhale M. SK7: Bram .6D 78
Peninsula Cl. CH45: Wall .3E 12
Peninsula Ho. WA2: Warr .5G 41
Penistone Dr. CH66: L Sut .3H 133
PENKETH .1G 65 (2D 215)
Penketh Av. WA5: Warr .4D 40
Penketh Bus. Pk. WA5: Gt San .1K 65
Penketh Ct. WA5: Penk .1F 65
WA7: Run .4H 89

Penketh Parish Swimming Pool—Pingard's La.

Penketh Parish Swimming Pool 1G 65
Penketh Rd. WA5: Gt San 1J 65
Penketh's La. WA7: Run 3G 89
Penkett Ct. CH45: Wall 5J 13
Penkett Gdns. CH45: Wall 5J 13
Penkett Gro. CH45: Wall 5J 13
Penkett Rd. CH45: Wall 5H 13
Penkford La. WA5: Col G 2A 14
Penkmans La. WA6: Frod 2J 139
PENLEY 3C 219
Penlington Ct. CW5: Nant 1D 196
Penmark Cl. WA5: Call 2A 40
Penmere Gro. M33: Sale 3J 47
Penmon Cl. CH1: Blac 7E 144
Penmon Dr. CH61: Pens 3H 83
Penmoor Chase SK7: H Gro 4F 79
Pennant Cl. WA3: Birc 1G 43
Penn Gdns. CH65: Ell P 3D 134
Penn Grn. SK8: Chea H 4K 77
Penn Ho. Cl. SK7: Bram 5C 78
Pennine Ct. SK10: Mac 2B 126
SK15: Stal 6E 4
Pennine Dr. OL6: Ash L 5A 4
WA14: Alt 7F 47
Pennine Gro. OL6: Ash L 3A 4
Pennine Rd. CH42: Tran 4B 60
CH44: Wall 7F 13
SK6: W'ley 5H 27
SK7: H Gro 4F 79
WA2: Warr 2J 41
Pennine Ter. SK16: Duk 1H 9
(off Peel St.)
Pennine Vw. M34: Aude 5D 8
SK15: Hey 5D 4
Pennine Wlk. CH66: L Sut 2H 133
Pennine Way CW7: Wins 4C 178
PENNINGTON 1A 216
Pennington Cl. WA6: Frod 5K 111
Pennington Ct. WN7: Leigh 1B 6
Pennington Dr. WA12: New W 1H 15
Pennington Flash Country Pk. 1B 6
Pennington Grn. CH66: Gt Sut 5J 133
Pennington La. WA9: Col G, St H 1A 14
Penningtons La. SK11: Gaw 7F 125
Pennington St. M12: Manc 1D 24
Penn La. WA7: Run 4F 89
Penny Bri. La. M41: Urm 2K 21
(not continuous)
Penny Brook Fold SK7: H Gro 2K 79
Penny La. SK5: Stoc 2D 52
SK10: R'ow 1G 127
WA5: Col G 3A 14
WA8: Cron 5A 36
Pennymoor Dr. CW10: Mid 1C 180
WA14: Alt 6F 47
Pennys La.
CW9: Lac D, Rud 6K 157 & 6F 159
(not continuous)
Pennystone Cl. CH49: Upt 6A 32
Penrhos Av. SK8: Gat 7B 50
Penrhos Rd. CH47: Hoy 6B 30
Penrhyd Rd. CH61: Irby 1F 83
Penrhyn Av. CH61: Thin 7D 58
SK8: Chea H 4G 77
Penrhyn Cres. SK7: H Gro 5G 79
WA7: Run 7H 89
Penrhyn Rd. CW8: Winn 5C 156
SK3: Stoc 4K 51
Penrith Av. M33: Sale 2C 48
SK5: Stoc 2J 25
SK11: Mac 7G 125
WA2: Warr 2G 41
Penrith Cl. M31: Part 7B 20
WA6: Frod 6K 111
Penrith Ct. CW12: Cong 4C 182
Penrith St. CH41: Birk 7B 34
Penrose Gdns. WA5: Penk 2F 65
Penroy Av. M20: Manc 1K 49
Penry Av. M44: Cad 5B 20
Penryn Av. M33: Sale 3C 48
Penryn Cl. WA5: Penk 2G 65
Pensall Dr. CH61: Hes 4H 83
Pensarn Av. M14: Manc 3B 24
Pensarn Gdns. WA5: Call 2B 40
Pensarn Gro. SK5: Stoc 7J 25
PENSBY 2J 83 (2A 214)
Pensby Av. CH2: Ches 5A 146
Pensby Cl. CH61: Thin 1J 83
Pensby Dr. CH66: Gt Sut 4K 133
Pensby Hall La. CH61: Hes 4H 83
Pensby Rd. CH60: Hes 5J 83
CH61: Hes, Irby, Pens 6H 83
Pensby St. CH41: Birk 4B 34
Pensford Rd. M23: Wyth 2F 75
Penshaw Ct. WA7: Pal F 7A 90
Penshurst Rd. SK5: Stoc 5A 26
Penshurst Wlk. M34: Den 2F 27
(off Two Trees La.)
Pentland Av. WA2: Warr 1F 41
Pentland Cl. CH3: Ches 1D 150
CW7: Wins 4C 178
SK7: H Gro 4F 79
Pentland Pl. WA2: Warr 1F 41
Pentland Way SK14: Hyde 4C 10
PENTRE 3A 218
PENTRE-CELYN 2A 218
Pentre Cl. CH3: Ash H 7H 171
PENTRE HALKYN 3A 214
Pentre La. CH3: Ash H 7H 171
Pentwyn Gro. M23: Wyth 5H 49
PEN-Y-BRYN 3A 218
PENYCAE 3A 218
PENYFFORDD 1B 218
PENYMYNYDD 1B 218
PEN-Y-STRYT 2A 218
Penzance Cl. SK10: Mac 4F 125
Peover Av. M33: Sale 7K 23
PEOVER HEATH 4J 165 (3B 216)
Peover La. SK11: Chel, Snel 7C 166
Peover Rd. SK9: Hand 1B 98
Peover St. L3: Liv 1J 35
Peover Wlk. SK8: Chea 7J 51
Pepler Av. M23: Wyth 2H 49
Peploe Wlk. M23: Wyth 3D 48
Pepper Cl. M22: Wyth 6K 49
Pepper Ct. SK9: Wilm 1F 119
Pepper Rd. SK7: H Gro 3F 79
Pepper Row CH1: Ches 5C 212
Peppers, The WA13: Lymm 2B 70
Pepper St. CH1: Ches 5C 212 (2A 150)
CH3: Chri 3G 151
CW5: Nant 2C 196
CW10: Mid 3C 180
L24: Hale 7A 88
SK11: Chel, Snel 1K 165
SK11: Henb 4C 124
WA4: App T 3A 94
WA13: Lymm 2A 70
WA16: Mob 2A 102
Percival Cl. CH2: Most 2K 145
Percival Ct. WA7: Run 5D 88
Percival La. WA7: Run 5D 88
Percival Rd. CH2: Most 1K 145
CH65: Ell P 2D 134
M43: Droy 1A 8
Percival St. WA1: Warr 7G 41
Percy James Cl. ST7: Als 5F 203
Percy Rd. CH4: Ches 7D 212 (4A 150)
CH44: Wall 2D 34
M34: Den 1D 26
Percy St. CW9: N'ich 5F 157
L8: Liv 5K 35
SK1: Stoc 5J 213 (2D 52)
SK15: Stal 1C 10
WA5: Warr 7C 40
(not continuous)
Percyvale St. SK10: Mac 4B 126
Peregrine Cl. CW7: Wins 7E 178
Peregrine Rd. SK2: Stoc 1K 79
Perimeter Rd. WA6: Hel 3G 137
Perrin Av. WA7: Run 6E 88
Perrin Rd. CH45: Wall 6E 12
Perrins Rd. WA5: B'ood 5C 14
Perrin St. SK14: Hyde 1J 27
Perry Av. SK14: Hyde 6B 10
Perry Flds. CW1: L'ton 4G 191
Perry Rd. WA15: Timp 6B 48
Perry St. L8: Liv 6J 35
WA7: Run 4H 89
Pershore Ho. CH42: Tran 4A 60
Perth Cl. CW4: H Cha 5H 181
SK7: Bram 1H 99
WA2: Fear 7E 16
Peterborough Cl. CH66: Gt Sut 2B 140
Peter Ct. M33: Sale 2H 125
Peter Destapleigh Way
CW5: Nant, Stap 4D 196
Peter Ellson Cl. CW2: Crewe 5D 194
Peterhouse Gdns. SK6: W'ley 7H 27
Peterhouse Rd. SK11: Sut E 2K 129
Peter Moss Way M19: Manc 2F 25
Peter Pl. CW1: Crewe 1B 194
Peter Price's La. CH63: H Beb 2J 85
Petersburg Rd. SK3: Stoc 6A 52
Peters Cl. SK10: Pres 4H 121
Peters Ct. WA15: Timp 7D 48
Petersfield Dr. M23: Wyth 5D 48
Petersfield Gdns. WA3: Cul 6E 6
Petersfield Way CW2: West 3K 199
Petersgate WA7: Murd 7F 91
Petersham Dr. WA4: App 1J 93
Peter's La. L1: Liv 3J 35
Peterstone Cl. WA5: Call 1B 40
Peter St. CH44: Wall 2D 34
CW9: N'ich 4G 157
L1: Liv 2J 35
M34: Den 7F 9
SK1: Stoc 2E 52
SK7: H Gro 2H 79
(not continuous)
SK11: Mac 6K 125
WA14: Alt 4H 213 (2H 73)
Peter St. W. SK11: Mac 5K 125
Peterswood Cl. M22: Wyth 2H 75
Peterwood CH42: R Fer 4F 61
Peter Wood Gdns. M32: S'ord 2F 23
Petham Ct. WA8: Wid 1E 62
Petheridge Dr. M22: Wyth 4H 75
PETRE BANK 2F 101
Petrel Av. SK12: Poy 2A 100
Petrel Cl. CW7: Wins 7E 178
SK3: Stoc 6B 52
Petrel Ho. M19: Manc 7A 24
Pettypool Activity Cen. 5E 160
Petunia Gro. SK11: Mac 7J 125
Petworth Av. WA2: Warr 1F 41
Petworth Cl. CW2: Wis 6B 194
M22: Shar 7A 50
Pevensey Dr. WA16: Knut 5E 116
Peveril Cl. WA4: App 5H 67
Peveril Dr. SK7: H Gro 5K 79
Peveril Gdns. SK12: Dis 1K 103
Peveril M. SK12: Dis 1K 103
Peveril Rd. WA14: B'ath 5G 47
Peveril Ter. SK14: Hyde 3A 28
Peveril Wlk. SK11: Mac 5G 125
Pewsey Rd. M22: Wyth 2B 76
PEWTERSPEAR 2K 93
Pewterspear Grn. District Distributor Rd.
WA4: App 2J 93
Pewterspear Grn. Rd. WA4: App 3H 93
Pewterspear La. WA4: App 2H 93
Pex Hill Country Pk. 6E 36
Pex Hill Ct. WA8: Wid 7E 36
Pexhill Ct. SK4: Stoc 2J 51
Pexhill Dr. SK10: Mac 5F 125
Pexhill Rd. SK10: Mac 7C 124
SK11: Gaw, Henb 7C 124
SK11: Sidd 2E 168
Pheasant Cl. WA3: Birc 7A 18
Pheasant Dr. CW9: Winc 2B 158
Pheasant Fld. L24: Hale 6A 88
Pheasant Ri. WA14: Bow 4H 73
Pheasant Wlk. WA16: H Leg 2G 95
Pheasant Way CW7: Wins 7E 178
Philharmonic Ct. L8: Liv 4K 35
(off Catharine St.)
Philharmonic Hall 4K 35
Philip Av. M34: Den 5D 8
Philip Dr. M33: Sale 2B 48
Philip Godlee Lodge M20: Manc 2D 50
Philip Leverhume Lodge
CH62: P Sun 7G 61
Philip Rd. WA8: Wid 5B 62
Philips La. CH66: Gt Sut 4J 133
Phillips Dr. WA5: Gt San 6G 39
Phillips Rd. CH1: Blac 7E 144
Phillips St. L3: Liv 1H 35
Phillip St. CH2: Ches 7B 146
Phillips Way CH60: Hes 6G 83
Phillip Way SK14: Hat 2F 29
Phipps' La. WA5: B'ood 3B 14
Phoenix Av. WA5: Warr 2D 40
Phoenix Ct. SK4: Stoc 6H 25
Phoenix Leisure Pk. 2C 194
Phoenix Pl. WA5: Gt San 5J 39
Phythian Cres. WA5: Penk 1H 65
Piccadilly SK1: Stoc 6J 213 (3D 52)
Pichael Nook WA4: Westy 1A 68
Pickenham Cl. SK11: Mac 6G 125
Pickerill Rd. CH49: Gre 2A 58
Pickering Cl. M41: Urm 1A 22
WA15: Timp 5A 48
Pickering Cres. WA4: Thel 2D 68
Pickering M. CH2: Ches 7B 146
(off Pickering St.)
Pickering Rd. CH45: N Bri 3H 13
Pickerings Cl. WA7: Run 1J 111
Pickerings Pasture Local Nature Reserve
3B 88
Pickerings Pasture Vis. Cen. 2B 88
Pickerings Rd. WA8: Hal B 1B 88
Pickering St. CH2: Ches 7B 146
Pickering Way CW5: Stap 3D 196
Pickford Ct. SK16: Duk 2H 9
Pickford La. SK16: Duk 2H 9
Pickford M. SK16: Duk 2H 9
(off Pickford La.)
Pickford's Brow SK1: Stoc 6J 213
Pickford St. SK11: Mac 5A 126
PICKMERE 1B 158 (3A 216)
Pickmere Cl. CW11: S'ach 2D 200
M33: Sale 2F 49
M43: Droy 1A 8
SK3: Stoc 6A 52
Pickmere Ct. CW1: Crewe 1C 194
Pickmere Dr. CH3: Gt Bou 3E 150
CH62: East 4A 108
(not continuous)
WA7: B'vale 2E 112
Pickmere Gdns. SK8: Chea H 7H 51
Pickmere La. CW9: Winc 1B 158
WA16: Pick 1B 158
Pickmere Rd. SK9: Hand 1A 98
Pickmere St. WA5: Warr 7C 40
Pickmere Ter. SK16: Duk 1G 9
Pickop St. L3: Liv 2H 35
Pickwick Cl. CW11: S'ach 1G 201
Pickwick Rd. SK12: Poy 3C 100
Pickwick St. L8: Liv 6K 35
Picow Farm Rd. WA7: Run, Wes P 5E 88
Picow St. WA7: Run 5F 89
PICTON 6B 142 (3C 215)
Picton Av. WA7: Run 5H 89
Picton Cl. CH43: Oxt 1J 59
CH62: East 4J 107
CW9: N'ich 2E 162
WA3: Birc 7H 17
Picton Dr. CW7: Wins 2C 178
SK9: Wilm 5B 98
Picton Gorse La. CH2: Hoo V, Pict 3E 146
Picton Hall
Liverpool 2J 35
(off Cuerden St.)
Picton La.
CH2: Mic T, Pict, Stoak, Wer 2J 141
Picton Sq. CW4: H Cha 4J 181
Picton Valley CH2: Pict 6A 142
Pierce St. SK11: Mac 4K 125
Pierpoint La. CH1: Ches 5B 212 (2K 149)
Pierpoint St. WA5: Warr 5D 40
Pigot Pl. WA4: Westy 7K 41
Pike, The CW5: Nant 4C 196
Pike La. WA6: K'ley 1B 152 & 1C 152
Pikemere Rd. ST7: Als 4C 202
Pikenall La. CW8: Act B, Crow 1K 153
Pike Rd. SK10: R'ow 4K 123
Pikes Hey Rd. CH48: Cald 6G 57
Pike St. WA4: Stoc H 4G 67
Pilgrim Cl. WA2: Winw 5K 15
Pilgrim St. CH41: Birk 6E 34
L1: Liv 4K 35
Pilgrims Way WA7: Nort 3F 91
Pilling St. M34: Den 7E 8
Pillmoss La. WA4: H'ton 5E 92
Pillory St. CW5: Nant 2C 196
Pimlico Rd. WA7: Run 4E 88
Pimlott Gro. SK14: Hyde 5J 9
Pimmcroft Way M33: Sale 1F 49
Pinders Farm Dr. WA1: Warr 7G 41
Pineacre Cl. WA14: W Tim 3F 47
Pineapple Pk. CW7: Wins 2J 179
Pineapple St. SK7: H Gro 3J 79
Pine Av. CH63: Beb 3K 85
WA8: Wid 3H 63
WA12: New W 1F 15
Pine Cl. M34: Aude 4D 8
SK6: Mar 1E 80
SK10: Mac 3C 126
Pine Ct. CH41: Birk 6C 34
SK7: Bram 3B 78
ST7: Als 5F 203
Pinedale Cl. CH43: Noc 1G 59
CH66: Whit 1C 140
Pine Gdns. CH2: Upt 4K 145
Pine Gro. CH2: Ches 6E 146
CH66: Whit 7C 134
CW7: Wins 3H 179
CW11: S'ach 3G 201
M33: Sale 5C 22
M34: Den 7F 9
SK16: Duk 2A 10
WA1: Padd 5A 42
Pine Hey CH64: Nest 6G 105
Pine Ho. CH1: Ches 5J 145
Pinehurst SK10: Pres 5F 121
Pinelea WA15: Alt 1K 73
Pinellas WA7: Run 3H 89
Pine Lodge SK7: Bram 6D 78
Pine M. L1: Liv 5K 35
Pineridge Cl. CH62: Spit 3C 86
Pine Rd. CH60: Hes 5A 84
M20: Manc 1C 50
SK7: Bram 5D 78
SK10: Mac 3C 126
SK12: Poy 3E 100
SK15: Stal 2K 9
WA7: Run 7J 89
Pines, The CH63: Spit 3B 86
M33: Sale 2B 48
WA8: Wid 1K 63
(off Hampton Ct. Way)
Pine St. SK6: W'ley 6G 27
SK14: Hyde 5J 9
Pine Tree Av. CH43: Noc 1F 59
Pine Tree Cl. CW8: Barnt 1A 156
Pinetree Cl. CH46: More 4C 32
CW7: Wins 3H 179
Pinetree Ct. CH44: Wall 6F 13
Pinetree Dr. CH48: W Kir 4E 56
Pinetree Gro. CH46: More 4C 32
Pine Trees WA16: Mob 2A 102
Pine Vw. Dr. CH61: Hes 4H 83
Pine Wlk. CW5: Nant 3D 196
M31: Part 1G 45
(off Wood La.)
Pine Walks CH42: Tran 4A 60
CH48: W Kir 4E 56
Pinewalks Ridge CH42: Tran 5B 60
Pine Way CH60: Hes 4G 83
Pineways WA4: App 1H 93
Pinewood M33: Sale 7C 22
WA14: Bow 3E 72
Pinewood Av. WA1: Warr 5J 41
Pinewood Cl. CH2: Elt 5G 137
SK4: Stoc 1J 51
SK16: Duk 1H 9
Pinewood Ct. CW2: Wis 7B 194
M33: Sale 6J 23
SK9: Wilm 5B 98
(off Brackenwood M.)
WA14: Hale 4J 73
Pinewood Dr. CH60: Hes 6K 83
Pinewood Rd. CW7: Wins 3C 178
SK9: Wilm 6B 98
WA5: B'ood 4C 14
Pinewoods, The SK6: W'ley 6G 27
Pinfold SK13: Had 3K 11
Pinfold, The LL13: Holt 7A 186
Pinfold Cl. WA15: H'rns 6D 74
Pinfold Ct. CH4: Ches 5B 150
CH48: W Kir 1B 56
M32: S'ord 2H 23
(off Barton Rd.)
Pinfold Dr. SK8: Chea H 4J 77
Pinfold La. CH4: Ches 5A 150
CH48: W Kir 1B 56
CW6: Alp 1J 189
CW6: L Bud 2G 177
CW10: Mid 3B 180
(off Newton Bank)
M90: Man A 7F 75
SK6: Rom 7J 27
WA16: M'all 2A 166
WA16: Plum 2K 159
Pinfold St. SK11: Mac 4K 125
Pinfold Way CW8: Weav 4G 155
Pingard's La. CW8: Crow 3J 153

Pingate Dr.—Poulton Royd Dr.

Pingate Dr. SK8: Chea H 7J 77
Pingate La. SK8: Chea H 7J 77
Pingate La. Sth. SK8: Chea H 7J 77
Pingot, The M44: Irlam 1E 20
Pingot Av. M23: Wyth 3H 49
Pingot Cft. CH3: Gt Bou 4E 150
Pingot La. SK14: B'tom 2J 29
WA6: Manl 1J 171
Pink Bank La. M12: Manc 1E 24
(not continuous)
Pinmill Brow WA6: Frod 1H 139
Pinmill Cl. WA6: Frod 1H 139
Pinner Fold SK15: Stal 6E 4
Pinner Pl. M19: Manc 5D 24
Pinners Brow WA2: Warr 6F 41
Pinners Brow Retail Pk.
WA2: Warr 6F 41
Pinners Fold WA7: Nort 5D 90
Pinnington La. M32: S'ord 1J 23
PINSLEY GREEN 3D 219
Pinsley Vw. CW5: Wren 2H 209
Pintail Av. SK3: Stoc 6B 52
Pintail Pl. CW7: Wins 6E 178
Pioneer Ct. OL7: Ash L 1F 9
(off Victoria St.)
Pioneer Pk. CH65: Ell P 7G 109
PIPE GATE 3B 220
Piperhill Av. M22: N'den 2K 49
Pipers, The CH60: Hes 5F 83
PIPERS ASH 6E 146
Pipers Ash CW7: Wins 3B 178
Piper's Cl. CH60: Hes 6F 83
Pipers Ct. CH2: Ches 6E 146
M44: Irlam 1F 21
Piper's End CH60: Hes 6F 83
Pipers La. CH2: Ches 6E 146
CH60: Hes 4E 82
(not continuous)
CH64: Pud 7A 132
Pipistrelle Ri. CH43: Noc 1G 59
Pipit Cl. M34: Aude 1B 8
Pipit La. WA3: Birc 1E 42
Pippin Cl. CW10: Mid 5C 180
Pippits Row WA7: Beec 3A 112
Pirie Cl. CW12: Cong 2J 183
Pirie Rd. CW12: Cong 1J 183
Pitch Cl. CH49: Gre 1A 58
Pitchcombe Rd. M22: Wyth 3H 75
Pitfield Cotts. SK14: Hyde 7H 9
Pitfield Gdns. M23: Wyth 5F 49
Pit La. CW2: Hou 5E 198
WA8: Wid 1G 63
Pitt La. SK11: L Wit 6K 167
Pittsburgh Ct. WA5: Gt San 6B 40
Pitts Cl. CH3: Tar 6C 170
Pitts Heath La. WA7: Nort 3F 91
Pitt St. L1: Liv 4J 35
M34: Den 7E 8
SK3: Stoc 4B 52
SK11: Mac 6A 126
SK14: Hyde 7J 9
WA5: Warr 6D 40
WA8: Wid 1G 89
Pitville Ter. WA8: Wid 6C 62
Place Rd. WA14: Alt 6G 47
Plain Pitt St. SK14: Hyde 5H 9
(not continuous)
Plaistow Ct. WA7: Pal F 7A 90
Plane Tree Cl. SK6: Mar 7D 54
Plane Tree Dr. CW1: Crewe 7K 191
Plane Tree Rd. CH63: H Beb 2J 85
Planetree Rd. M31: Part 1F 45
WA15: Hale 3A 74
Planetree Wlk. M23: Wyth 4C 48
Planet Way M34: Aude 5D 8
Planewood Gdns. WA3: Low 3A 6
Plantagenet Cl. CW7: Wins 6E 178
Plantation Bus. Pk. CH62: Brom 4F 87
Plantation Cl. WA7: Cast 5C 90
Plantation Ct. CH62: Brom 4F 87
Plantation Dr. CH66: Ell P 1A 134
Plantation Ind. Est. OL6: Ash L 1J 9
Plantation Rd. CH62: Brom 5F 87
Plantation St. OL6: Ash L 1J 9
Plant Cl. M33: Sale 6F 23
Planters, The CH49: Gre 1K 57
Plant La. CW11: Most 3A 200
Plant St. CW11: S'ach 2E 200
Plas Dinas CH1: Blac 7E 144
Plasman Ind. Cen. M19: Manc 2F 25
Plas Newton La. CH2: Ches 5B 146
Platt Av. CW11: S'ach 2E 200
PLATT BRIDGE 1A 216
Platt Ct. M14: Manc 1A 24
Platt Fields Pk. 1A 24
Platt Gro. CH42: R Fer 5F 61
Platt Hall (The Gallery of Costume) 1A 24
PLATT LANE 3D 219
Platt La. M14: Manc 1A 24
Platts Dr. M44: Irlam 1D 20
Platts La. CH3: Tar 7B 170
CW6: Dud 4A 174
Platt St. SK8: Chea 6G 51
SK16: Duk 3F 9
Platt Wlk. M34: Den 2D 26
Plaza Blvd. L8: Liv 6J 35
Pleachway SK4: Stoc 2H 51
Pleasant Hill St. L8: Liv 6J 35
Pleasant St. CH45: N Bri 4H 13
CW8: N'ich 6D 156
L3: Liv 3K 35
SK10: Mac 3C 126
Pleasant Ter. SK16: Duk 1H 9
(off Peel St.)
Pleasant Vw. SK6: Comp 1H 55
SK10: Mac 4D 124
Pleasant Way SK8: Chea H 7A 78
Pleasington Cl. CH43: Noc 1H 59
Pleasington Dr. CH43: Noc 1H 59
Pleck Rd. CH65: Whit 6C 134
PLEMSTALL 1K 147
Plemstall Cl. CH2: Mic T 2J 147
Plemstall La. CH2: Mic T 1J 147
Plemstall Way CH2: Mic T 1J 147
Plemston Ct. CH66: Ell P 7G 109
Plex, The ST7: Als 5E 202
Plinston Av. WA4: Westy 1K 67
Plough Cl. M41: Urm 1F 21
Plough Cft. ST7: Als 6B 202
Plough La. CH3: Chri, Wave 4H 151
Ploughmans Cl. CH66: Gt Sut 1A 140
Ploughmans Way CH66: Gt Sut 1A 140
SK10: Mac 1J 125
Plough St. SK16: Duk 2J 9
Plover Av. CW7: Wins 7E 178
Plover Cl. CH3: Farn 6C 186
SK10: Mac 7J 121
Plover Dr. WA7: Nort 6F 91
WA14: B'ath 4F 47
Plovers La. WA6: Hel 3C 138
Plowden Rd. M22: Wyth 3H 75
Plowley Cl. M20: Manc 2D 50
Plucksbridge Rd. SK6: Mar 2H 81
Plumbs Fold CW8: Barnt 3K 155
Plumer St. CH41: Birk 4K 33
PLUMLEY 2H 159 (3B 216)
Plumley Cl. CH3: Ches 2F 151
M33: Sale 1F 49
SK3: Stoc 7D 52
SK11: Mac 5B 126
Plumley Gdns. WA8: Wid 3A 62
Plumley Lime Beds Nature Reserve 2F 159
Plumley Moor Rd.
WA16: Lwr P, Plum 1G 159 & 1B 164
Plumley Rd. SK9: Hand 1A 98
Plumley Station (Rail) 2J 159
Plumpstons La. WA6: Frod 6H 111
Plumpton M. WA8: Wid 4J 63
Plum Ter. CH1: Ches 2A 212 (1K 149)
Plumtre Av. WA5: Warr 4D 40
PLUNGEBROOK 2E 126
Plymouth Cl. WA7: Murd 1G 113
Plymouth Dr. SK7: Bram 6C 78
Plymouth Gro. SK3: Stoc 5K 51
Plymouth Rd. M33: Sale 6C 22
Plymyard Av. CH62: Brom, East 1J 107
Plymyard Cl. CH62: Brom 2J 107
Plymyard Copse CH62: Brom 2J 107
Plymyard Ct. CH62: Brom 1H 107
Poachers La. WA4: Westy 2K 67
Pochard Av. CW7: Wins 6E 178
Pochard Dr. SK12: Poy 2K 99
WA14: B'ath 5F 47
Pochard Ri. WA7: Nort 6F 91
Pochin Way CW10: Mid 3E 180
Pocket Nook La. WA3: Low 2A 6
Pocklington Ct. WA2: Padg 3K 41
Pocklington Dr. M23: Wyth 5F 49
Podsmead Rd. M22: Wyth 3H 75
Poets Cnr. CH62: P Sun 1B 86
Points Ho. CW1: Crewe 1A 194
(off Dale Way)
Poise Brook Dr. SK2: Stoc 7K 53
Poise Brook Rd. SK2: Stoc 7K 53
Poise Cl. SK7: H Gro 2A 80
Poland St. M34: Aude 2D 8
Polden Cl. CH66: L Sut 2G 133
Poleacre Dr. WA8: Wid 3D 62
Poleacre La. SK6: W'ley 5H 27
Pole La. CW9: Ant 1K 115 & 7D 94
Police St. WA14: Alt 1J 213 (7H 47)
Pollard Av. WA6: Frod 1K 139
Pollard Dr. CW5: Stap 3F 197
Pollard Sq. M31: Part 1J 45
Pollen Cl. M33: Sale 2D 48
Pollen Rd. WA14: Alt 6G 47
Polletts Av. SK5: Stoc 5B 26
POLL HILL 4H 83
Poll Hill Rd. CH60: Hes 5H 83
Pollit Cft. SK6: Rom 3K 53
Pollitt Cres. WA9: Clo F 1J 37
Pollitt Sq. CH62: N Fer 5H 61
Pollitt St. WA9: Clo F 1J 37
Polperro Cl. SK10: Mac 3E 124
WA5: Penk 2G 65
Polperro Wlk. SK14: Hat 7E 10
Polruan Wlk. SK14: Hat 7F 11
Pomona St. L3: Liv 3K 35
Pond St. WA3: Low 2A 6
Pond Vw. Cl. CH60: Hes 6A 84
Ponsonby Rd. CH45: Wall 6E 12
M32: S'ord 1J 23
PONTBLYDDYN 1A 218
PONTFADOG 3A 218
PONT-FAEN 3A 218
PONTYBODKIN 2A 218
Pool Bank CH62: P Sun 6G 61
Pool Bank Bus. Pk. CH3: Tar 5C 170
Poolbank Rd. CH62: N Fer 6G 61
Poolcroft M33: Sale 1F 49
Poole Av. WA2: Warr 2F 41
Poole Cl. SK7: Bram 4B 78
Poole Cres. WA2: Warr 2F 41
Poole Hall Ind. Est.
CH65: Ell P 7H 109
(not continuous)
Poole Hall La. CH66: Ell P 7F 109
Poole Hall Rd. CH65: Ell P 7G 109
Poole Hill Rd.
CW5: Henh, Poole 4A 192 & 4K 189
POOLEND 2D 221
Pool End Cl. SK10: Mac 7A 122
Pool End Rd. SK10: Mac 7A 122
Poole Old Hall La.
CW5: Poole, Worl 2A 192
Poole Rd. CH44: Wall 6K 13
Poole St. CW7: Wins 3F 179
POOLFOLD 2C 221
Pool Hollow WA7: Run 5H 89
Pool Ho. Rd. SK12: Poy 1H 101
Pool La. CH2: Ince 4D 136
CH2: Tho M 6C 136
CH3: Tar S 4C 170
CH49: Woodc 3D 58
CH62: Brom 1C 86
CW8: S'way 4E 160
CW11: Wint 6C 204
WA4: Walt 4E 66
WA7: Run 3H 89
WA13: Lymm 1H 69
Pool Mdws. Rd. CW1: Hasl 2H 195
Pool Rd. WA3: Rix 1C 44
Poolside ST7: Sch G 2H 203
Poolside Ct. ST7: Als 5F 203
Poolside Rd. WA7: Run 5H 89
Pools Platt La. CW9: Ant 4E 94
Pool St. CH41: Birk 5C 34
SK11: Mac 6B 126
WA8: Wid 6H 63
Pooltown Rd. CH65: Ell P 2B 134
Pool Vw. CW11: Wint 6C 204
Poolwood Rd. CH49: Woodc 1E 58
Poor's Wood Nature Reserve 3C 162
Pope Way M34: Den 4F 27
(off Kipling Av.)
POPLAR 2000 SERVICE AREA 7H 69
Poplar Av. CH49: Upt 7C 32
CW9: Moult 6E 162
M19: Manc 4E 24
SK9: Wilm 2E 118
WA3: Cul 7F 7
WA5: Penk 1G 65
WA7: Run 7J 89
WA12: New W 1G 15
WA14: Alt 6J 47
Poplar Cl. CH65: Whit 4D 134
CW7: Wins 4C 178
CW8: Cudd 3C 160
CW12: Cong 2C 182
SK8: Gat 7D 50
WA7: Run 7J 89
Poplar Ct. CW5: Nant 3E 196
M34: Aude 4E 8
SK3: Stoc 7D 52
(off Garners La.)
Poplar Dr. CH63: Beb 2B 86
CW10: Mid 5D 180
ST7: Als 7F 203
Poplar Farm Cl. CH46: More 6K 31
Poplar Gro. CH2: Elt 5E 136
CH42: Tran 1C 60
(off Ash Rd.)
CW1: Crewe 1E 194
M33: Sale 1B 48
M41: Urm 1D 22
M44: Cad 5A 20
SK2: Stoc 1G 79
SK10: Boll 3D 122
Poplar Hall La. CH2: Chor B 2E 140
Poplar Ho. CH1: Ches 1G 149
Poplar Rd. CH4: Ches 6G 149
CH43: Oxt 1A 60
CW8: Weav 5G 155
M19: Manc 1F 51
M32: S'ord 3H 23
SK11: Mac 6A 126
SK16: Duk 3A 10
Poplar Row CH2: Elt 5F 137
Poplars, The CW2: Wis 7K 193
WA13: Lymm 1K 69
WA14: Alt 2H 213 (1G 73)
WN7: Leigh 2C 6
Poplars Av. WA2: Warr 7K 15
(not continuous)
Poplars Pl. WA2: Warr 2H 41
(off Hughes Av.)
Poplars Rd. SK15: Stal 6E 4
Poplar St. M34: Aude 3E 8
SK4: Stoc 2G 51
Poplar Ter. CH45: N Bri 4H 13
Poplar Vw. WA4: Moo 7J 65
Poplar Wlk. M31: Part 1F 45
(off Long Wlk.)
M34: Aude 4E 8
(off Poplar St.)
Poplar Way SK6: H Lan 6G 81
Poplar Weint CH64: Nest 7H 105
Poppies, The CW9: Moult 6E 162
Poppy Cl. CH46: More 2D 32
CW2: West 2J 199
M23: Wyth 3E 48
Poppyfields ST7: Als 6C 202
WA5: Warr 2B 66
Porlock Av. M34: Aude 2B 8
SK14: Hat 1D 28
Porlock Cl. CH60: Hes 1E 104
SK1: Stoc 4G 53
WA5: Penk 1G 65
Porlock Rd. M23: Wyth 6H 49
M41: Urm 3K 21
Porlock Wlk. SK14: Hat 1D 28
Portal Bus. Pk. CW6: Eat 7F 177
Portal Gro. M34: Den 2G 27
Portal M. CH61: Pens 3H 83
Portal Rd. CH61: Pens 3H 83
Port Arcades, The CH65: Ell P 3E 134
Portbury Cl. CH62: P Sun 7H 61
Portbury Wlk. CH62: P Sun 7G 61
Portbury Way CH62: P Sun 7H 61
Port C'way. CH62: Brom 2C 86
Porter Cl. L35: R'ill 3D 36
Porter Dr. CW9: N'ich 7H 157
Porters Cft. CH3: Guil S 5J 147
Porter St. L3: Liv 1G 35
WA7: Run 4J 89
Porter Way CW9: N'ich 7H 157
Portford Cl. SK10: Mac 3G 125
Porthcawl Cl. WA8: Wid 2C 62
Porthleven Dr. M23: Wyth 6E 48
Porthleven Rd. WA7: B'vale 2D 112
Porthtowan Wlk. SK14: Hat 7F 11
(off Underwood Rd.)
Portia Av. CH63: H Beb 6D 60
Portland, The M14: Manc 3A 24
Portland Basin Mus. 1F 9
Portland Chambers SK15: Stal 7C 4
(off Portland Pl.)
Portland Cl. SK7: H Gro 4F 79
Portland Ct. CH45: N Bri 2G 13
M20: Manc 1D 50
Portland Dr. CW7: Wins 4C 178
ST7: Sch G 2H 205
Portland Ga. CH62: P Sun 7H 61
(off Portbury Cl.)
Portland Gro. CW1: Hasl 1J 195
SK4: Stoc 7E 24
Portland Ho. SK6: Mar 7E 54
Portland Pl. OL7: Ash L 1F 9
SK15: Stal 7C 4
WA6: Hel 4C 138
Portland Rd. WA5: Gt San 5J 39
WA14: Bow 2G 73
Portland St. CH41: Birk 4K 33
CH45: N Bri 2G 13
WA7: Run 3F 89
Portland St. Sth. OL7: Ash L 1F 9
Portland Wlk. SK11: Mac 5G 125
Portloe Rd. SK8: He Grn 6D 76
Portman Pl. CW7: Wins 4B 178
(off Brockwell Cl.)
Portmarnock Cl. SK10: Mac 1J 125
Porto Hey Rd. CH61: Irby 1F 83
Portola Cl. WA4: Grap 3C 68
Porton Wlk. M22: Wyth 4H 75
Portrea Cl. SK3: Stoc 7C 52
Portree Av. CH63: East 2J 107
Portree Dr. CW4: H Cha 5H 181
Portrush Cl. SK10: Mac 7K 121
WA8: Wid 2E 62
Portrush Rd. M22: Wyth 3A 76
Portside WA7: Pre B 7G 91
Portside Bus. Pk. CH65: Ell P 7J 109
Portside Ind. Est. CH65: Ell P 7K 109
Portside Nth. CH65: Ell P 7J 109
Portside Sth. CH65: Ell P 7K 109
Portslade Wlk. M23: Wyth 7F 49
Portsmouth Pl. WA7: Murd 1G 113
Port St. SK1: Stoc 5G 213 (3C 52)
SK14: Hyde 1J 27
(off Market St.)
PORT SUNLIGHT 1B 86 (2B 214)
Port Sunlight Driving Range 1C 86
Port Sunlight Station (Rail) 1B 86
Portugal St. OL7: Ash L 1E 8
Portville Rd. M19: Manc 1D 24
Portway M22: Wyth 3H 75
PORTWOOD 1F 53
Portwood Ind. Est. SK1: Stoc 2F 53
Portwood Pl. SK1: Stoc 2D 52
Posnett St. SK3: Stoc 4A 52
Postles Pl. CW9: N'ich 7E 156
Post Office La. CH2: Tho M 7C 136
WA6: Norl 6E 152
WA7: Wes P 7D 88
Post Office Pl. CW9: N'ich 4F 157
Post Office St. WA14: Alt 1J 213 (7H 47)
Potter Cl. CW5: W'ston 3H 197
POTTERIES, THE 3C 221
Potters Barn, The 1B 202
Potter's La. WA8: Hal B 2A 88
Pottinger St. OL7: Ash L 1E 8
Pott La. SK11: Mac 6C 126
POTT SHRIGLEY 1F 123 (3D 217)
Pott St. WA14: Alt 2H 213 (1H 73)
POULTON
CH4 7E 184
CH44 1A 34
CH63 5A 86
Poulton Bri. Rd. CH41: Birk 2J 33
Poulton Cres. WA1: Wool 4C 42
Poulton Dr. WA8: Wid 6D 62
Poulton Grn. Cl. CH63: Spit 5K 85
Poulton Hall Rd. CH44: Wall 1K 33
CH63: Rab M 7A 86
Poulton Rd. CH44: Wall 1K 33
CH63: Spit 3A 86
Poulton Royd Dr. CH63: Spit 4K 85

Poulton Va.—Quarrybank Workshops

Poulton Va. CH44: Wall 2K 33
Pound Rd. CH66: L Sut 1J 133
Poundswick La. M22: Wyth 2J 75
Povey Rd. WA2: Warr 3G 41
Powder Mill Cl. M44: Irlam 2E 20
Powder Mill Rd. WA4: Westy 2A 68
Powell Av. SK14: Hyde 7K 9
WA3: Ris 7K 17
Powell's Orchard CH4: Ches 4K 149
Powell St. WA4: Warr 2K 67
Powerhouse Health & Fitness Cen. 7J 9
(off Borough Arc.)
Powerleague Soccer Cen.
Stockport 3K 51
Power Rd. CH42: R Fer 5F 61
CH62: Brom 5F 87
Powicke Dr. SK6: Rom 3K 53
Powis Rd. M41: Urm 2F 21
Pownall Av. SK7: Bram 6D 78
Pownall Ct. SK9: Wilm 6F 97
POWNALL GREEN 6C 78
POWNALL PARK 6G 97
Pownall Pl. *SK7: Bram* *6C 78*
(off Bramhall La. Sth.)
Pownall Rd. SK8: Chea H 4J 77
SK9: Wilm 6G 97
WA14: Alt 2H 73
Pownall Sq. L3: Liv 2H 35
SK11: Mac 4K 125
Pownall St. L1: Liv 4H 35
SK7: H Gro 2H 79
SK10: Mac 3A 126
Powys Ct. CH1: Ches 3A 212 (1K 149)
Powys St. *WA5: Warr* *7D 40*
(off Old Liverpool Rd.)
Poynings Dr. M22: Wyth 4J 75
POYNTON 2C 100 (2D 217)
Poynton Cl. WA4: Grap 2B 68
Poynton Ind. Est. SK12: Poy 5D 100
Poynton Leisure Cen. 4E 100
Poynton Sports Club 2D 100
Poynton Station (Rail) 2B 100
Poynton St. SK10: Mac 4K 125
Pratchitts Row CW5: Nant 2C 196
Precinct, The CH62: Brom 5D 86
CW2: Crewe 4K 193
SK2: Stoc 6H 53
SK3: Stoc 5B 52
SK8: Chea H 3K 77
SK14: H'rth 2J 11
Preece Cl. SK14: Hyde 6B 10
WA8: Wid 2D 62
Preece Ct. CW1: Crewe 1B 194
Preesall Av. SK8: He Grn 5D 76
PREES HIGHER HEATH 3D 219
Premier Pk. CW7: Wins 1J 179
Prentice Rd. CH42: R Fer 4D 60
PRENTON 5J 59 (2B 214)
Prenton Dell Av. CH43: Pren 5K 59
Prenton Dell Rd. CH43: Pren 4H 59
Prenton Farm Rd. CH43: Pren 5K 59
Prenton Hall Rd. CH43: Pren 4J 59
Prenton La. CH42: Tran 4A 60
Prenton Pk. 3B 60
Prenton Pk. Rd. CH42: Tran 2B 60
Prenton Pl. CH4: Ches 7E 212 (4B 150)
Prenton Rd. E. CH42: Tran 3B 60
Prenton Rd. W. CH42: Tran 3B 60
Prenton Village Rd. CH43: Pren 4J 59
Prenton Way CH43: Pren 4H 59
Prenton Way Bus. Units CH43: Pren . . . 4G 59
Prentonwood Ct. CH42: Tran 4B 60
PRESCOT 1C 215
Prescot Rd. WA8: Wid 2D 62
WA15: Hale 3K 73
Prescot St. CH2: Ches 7C 146
CH45: N Bri 3G 13
Prescott Rd. SK9: Wilm 5J 97
Prescott St. WA4: Warr 2J 67
Prescott Wlk. M34: Den 2G 27
Prestage St. M12: Manc 1E 24
PRESTBURY 5H 121 (3D 217)
Prestbury Av. CH43: Oxt 3H 59
WA15: Alt 6J 47
Prestbury Cl. CH43: Oxt 3H 59
CW9: N'ich 2E 162
SK2: Stoc 1H 79
WA8: Wid 5E 62
Prestbury Dr. SK6: Bred 1J 53
WA4: Thel 1D 68
Prestbury La. SK10: Pres 4H 121
Prestbury Link Rd. SK9: Wilm 2H 119
Prestbury Pk. SK10: Pres 5F 121
Prestbury Rd. SK9: Wilm 2J 119
SK10: Mac 1G 125
SK10: O Ald 5A 120
(not continuous)
Prestbury Station (Rail) 4H 121
Preston Av. M44: Irlam 4C 20
PRESTON BROOK 1H 113 (3D 215)
PRESTON ON THE HILL 1J 113 (2D 215)
Preston Rd. M19: Manc 3D 24
Preston St. L1: Liv 2J 35
WA9: Sut M 2G 37
Preston St. W. SK11: Mac 6J 125
PRESTWICH 1C 217
Prestwich Av. WA3: Cul 7E 6
Prestwich Cl. SK2: Stoc 5F 53
Prestwick Cl. *CW7: Wins* *2D 178*
(off Gleneagles Dr.)
SK10: Mac 6K 121
WA8: Wid 2F 63
Prestwood Ct. WA3: Ris 4B 18
Pretoria St. CH4: Ches 7D 212 (4A 150)
Price Av. CW11: S'ach 4E 200
Price Dr. CW11: S'ach 4E 200
Price's La. CH43: Oxt 1A 60
Price St. CH41: Birk 4A 34
L1: Liv 4H 35
SK16: Duk 2H 9
Price St. Bus. Cen. CH41: Birk 4B 34
Pride Cl. WA12: New W 1H 15
Pridmouth Rd. M20: Manc 5A 24
Priest Av. SK8: Gat 1C 76
Priestfield Rd. CH65: Ell P 3D 134
Priest La. SK10: Mot A 2B 120
Priestley Bus. Cen. WA5: Warr 7D 40
Priestley Ct. *CW5: Nant* *2C 196*
(off Hospital St.)
WA4: Warr *3G 67*
(off Eplhins Dr.)
Priestley St. WA5: Warr 7D 40
Priestnall Ct. *SK4: Stoc* *1H 51*
(off Priestnall Rd.)
Priestnall Recreation Cen. 1H 51
Priestnall Rd. SK4: Stoc 1H 51
Priestner Dr. WA6: Hel 4B 138
Priestway La. CH64: Burt 7J 131
Priesty Ct. CW12: Cong 4F 183
Priesty Flds. CW12: Cong 4F 183
Primary Cl. M44: Cad 6A 20
Primitive St. ST7: Mow C 5G 205
Primrose Av. CW1: Hasl 1J 195
M41: Urm 1C 22
SK6: Mar 6E 54
SK11: Mac 7J 125
SK14: Hyde 4J 27
Primrose Bank WA14: Bow 4G 73
Primrose Chase CW4: Goo 7H 165
Primrose Cl. CH3: Hunt 5D 150
WA2: Warr 2H 41
WA7: Cast 6C 90
WA8: Wid 4E 62
Primrose Cotts. *WA14: Bow* *4G 73*
(off Brickkiln Row)
Primrose Ct. *CH45: N Bri* *3H 13*
(off Egerton St.)
Primrose Cres. SK14: Hyde 3J 27
Primrose Gro. CH44: Wall 2D 34
PRIMROSE HILL 7K 69
Primrose Hill CH62: P Sun 7F 61
CW2: Crewe 1J 193
CW6: Kel 2D 172
CW8: Cudd 2C 160
L3: Liv 2J 35
Primrose Hill Cotts. *OL5: Moss* *1F 5*
(off Micklehurst Rd.)
Primrose La. WA6: Alv, Hel 7A 138
Primrose M. WA6: Alv 7D 138
Primrose Rd. CH41: Birk 5J 33
Primrose Ter. SK15: Stal 7C 4
PRIMROSE VALE 2H 183
Primrose Wlk. SK6: Mar 6E 54
Prince Albert Av. *M19: Manc* *1D 24*
(off Belvoir Av.)
Prince Albert M. *L1: Liv* *5K 35*
(off Up. Frederick St.)
Prince Albert St. CW1: Crewe 2D 194
Prince Edward Av. M34: Den 1E 26
Prince Edward St. CH41: Birk 5B 34
CW5: Nant 1C 196
Prince Edwin St. L5: Liv 1K 35
Prince Henry Sq. WA1: Warr 7F 41
Prince Rd. SK12: Poy 1H 101
Prince Rupert's Tower 1K 35
Princes Av. CH1: Ches 1B 150
CH48: W Kir 3C 56
CH62: East 1K 107
CW9: N'ich 5G 157
M20: Manc 1E 50
M44: Irlam 1E 20
SK6: Bred 1A 54
Princes Blvd. CH63: H Beb 5C 60
Prince's Cl. WA7: Cast 5B 90
Princes Ct. CW5: Nant 7C 192
Princes Dr. M33: Sale 1D 48
SK6: Mar 5E 54
Princes Gdns. L3: Liv 1H 35
Prince's Incline SK12: Poy 2D 100
Princes Pde. L3: Liv 2G 35
Princes Pk. CW8: Barnt 3K 155
Princes Pavement
CH41: Birk 6D 34
Princes Pl. WA8: Wid 4E 62
Princes Rd. CH65: Ell P 2B 134
M33: Sale 1C 48
SK4: Stoc 7D 24
SK6: Bred 1A 54
WA14: Alt 6H 47
Princess Av. M34: Den 7D 8
SK8: Chea H 2J 77
WA1: Padg 4A 42
WA1: Warr 6K 41
WA5: Gt San 5G 39
Princess Cl. CW2: Wis 6K 193
OL5: Moss 1F 5
SK16: Duk 2J 9
Princess Cres. CW10: Mid 6D 180
WA1: Warr 6K 41
Princess Dr. CW2: Wis 6K 193
CW5: Nant 1E 196
CW11: S'ach 1E 200
SK10: Boll 5B 122
Princess Gro. CW2: Wis 6K 193
Princess Parkway M22: N'den 4J 49
M23: Wyth 4J 49
Princess Rd. CH45: N Bri 4H 13
M20: Manc 1K 49
M21: Chor H 1K 49
M41: Urm 1A 22
SK9: Wilm 2E 118
WA13: Lymm 2J 69
WA16: All 5C 164
Princess St. CH1: Ches 4B 212 (2K 149)
CW1: Crewe 7H 191
CW7: Wins 3H 179
CW9: N'ich 3K 157
CW12: Cong 3F 183
SK10: Boll 4C 122
SK14: Hyde 1K 27
WA5: Warr 1B 66
WA7: Run 3G 89
WA14: B'ath 4G 47
WA16: Knut 3E 116
Princess Ter. CH43: Oxt 7B 34
Princes St. L2: Liv 2H 35
SK1: Stoc 6H 213 (3C 52)
WA8: Wid 5G 63
WA12: New W 1E 14
Princes Wlk. SK7: Bram 6E 78
Princes Way SK11: Mac 4F 125
Princesway CH45: Wall 5G 13
Princes Wood Rd. SK12: Poy 1H 101
Princeton Ct. WA5: Gt San 6B 40
Princeway WA6: Frod 7H 111
Prince William St. L8: Liv 6K 35
Prinknash Rd. M22: Wyth 3K 75
Printers Brow SK14: H'rth 2K 11
Printers Cl. M19: Manc 2F 51
SK4: Stoc 2F 51
Printers Dr. SK15: Carrb 3H 5
Printers Fold SK14: H'rth 2J 11
Printers Pk. SK14: H'rth 2K 11
Printworks La. M19: Manc 2F 25
Printworks Rd. SK15: Hey 6C 4
Prior Cl. CW2: Wis 5K 193
Priorsfield CH46: More 4B 32
Priory, The CH64: Nest 6G 105
L35: R'ill 1C 36
WA2: Winw 4K 15
Priory Av. CW9: N'ich 2E 162
Priory Cl. CH1: Ches 6K 145
CH63: Beb 3A 86
CW1: Crewe 5F 191
CW7: Wins 1D 178
CW12: Cong 7K 183
M33: Sale 5J 23
SK16: Duk 4J 9
WA7: Halt 5C 90
Priory Ct. SK5: Stoc 3H 25
WA7: Pre B 2G 113
WA14: Bow *4G 73*
(off Priory St.)
Priory Dr. SK10: Mac 2F 125
Priory Gdns. M20: Manc 1D 50
Priory La. SK5: Stoc 3H 25
SK10: Mac 2F 125
Priory M. CH41: Birk 6E 34
Priory Pl. CH1: Ches 4D 212 (2A 150)
Priory Rd. CH44: Wall 1D 34
CH48: W Kir 3D 56
M33: Sale 6H 23
SK8: Chea 7J 51
SK9: Wilm 6F 97
WA7: Win H 4E 90
WA14: Bow 5F 73
Priory St. CH41: Birk 6E 34
CW9: N'ich 5F 157
WA4: Warr 2F 67
WA14: Bow 5G 73
Priory Way CW8: H'ord 2A 162
Priory Wharf CH41: Birk 6E 34
Priscilla St. CW1: Crewe 2E 194
Pritchard Dr. CW9: Dave 4D 162
Pritchard St. M32: S'ord 1J 23
Pritt St. L3: Liv 1K 35
Private Dr. CH61: Barns 1B 84
Private Wlk. CH3: Ches 3D 150
Probert Cl. CW2: Crewe 2A 194
Probyn Rd. CH45: Wall 6E 12
Procter Rd. CH42: R Fer 4F 61
Proctor Rd. CH47: Hoy 6D 30
Proctors Cl. WA8: Wid 3J 63
Proctors La. CW11: Ett H 4B 200
Proffits La. WA6: Hel 3D 138
Progress Av. M34: Aude 4E 8
Progressive Bus. Pk.
M34: Aude 2D 8
Progress Pl. *L1: Liv* *2H 35*
(off Stanley St.)
Progress Way M34: Den 1B 26
Promenade, The WA4: Moo 6K 65
Promenade Cvn. Pk. WA4: Moo 6J 65
Promised Land La. CH3: Row 6H 151
Prophet Wlk. L8: Liv 7K 35
Prospect Av. M44: Cad 5B 20
Prospect Dr. CW9: Dave 4D 162
WA15: H'rns 6D 74
Prospect La. SK9: Ald E 5A 118
WA3: Rix 1J 43
Prospect Rd. CH42: Tran 4A 60
M44: Cad 5B 20
OL6: Ash L 4A 4
SK16: Duk 1J 9
Prospect Row WA7: West 7F 89
Prospect St. CW12: Cong 4E 182
Prospect Va. CH45: Wall 6F 13
SK8: He Grn 4D 76
Prosperity Way CW10: Mid 3D 180
Prosser Rd. CH2: Most 1J 145
Protector Way M44: Irlam 3C 20
Proudman Dr. CH43: Bid 5F 33
Provan Way CH1: Blac 5E 144
Provender Cl. WA14: B'ath 4H 47
Providence Cres. L8: Liv 6K 35
Providence St. M34: Aude 3E 8
Provident Av. M19: Manc 2F 25
Provident Way WA15: Timp 5A 48
Prubella Av. M34: Den 5D 8
Prunus Rd. CW1: Crewe 7J 191
Prussia St. L3: Liv 2H 35
(not continuous)
Pryors, The CH3: Tar 5C 170
Ptarmigan Pl. CW7: Wins 7E 178
Public Hall St. WA7: Run 3G 89
PUDDINGLAKE 1B 220
Pudding La. CW6: Tive 5F 175
SK14: Hat 7D 10
(not continuous)
PUDDINGTON 3B 214
Puddington La. CH64: Burt 7H 131
CH64: Pud 7B 132
Pudsey St. L1: Liv 2K 35
Puffin Av. SK12: Poy 2A 100
Puffin Cl. CH65: Ell P 1E 140
Puffingate Cl. SK15: Carrb 2F 5
PULFORD 7B 184 (2B 218)
Pulford App. CH4: Pou, Pul 7B 184
Pulford Av. CH43: Pren 3K 59
Pulford Cl. CW9: N'ich 2D 162
WA7: Beec 1A 112
Pulford Ct. CH4: Pul 7B 184
Pulford La. CH4: Dod 3D 184
Pulford Rd. CH1: Blac 5F 145
CH63: Beb 1K 85
CH65: Gt Sut 4B 134
CW7: Wins 3D 178
M33: Sale 2C 48
Pullman Cl. CH60: Hes 6B 84
M19: Manc 3E 24
Pullman Dr. CW9: N'ich 5H 157
M32: S'ord 1E 22
Pumpfields Rd. L3: Liv 1H 35
Pump La. CH3: Chu 2C 186
CH49: Gre 7J 31
WA7: Halt 6B 90
Pumptree M. SK11: Mac 5F 125
Purbeck Cl. M22: Wyth 4J 75
Purbeck Dr. CH61: Irby 6A 58
Purdy Cl. WA5: Old H 3B 40
Purley Av. M23: Wyth 3H 49
Purley Dr. M44: Cad 6K 19
Putney Ct. WA7: Pal F 7A 90
Puzzletree Ct. SK2: Stoc 5G 53
Pyecroft Cl. WA5: Gt San 6F 39
Pyecroft Rd. WA5: Gt San 6F 39
Pyecroft St. CH4: Ches 4A 150
Pye Rd. CH60: Hes 6H 83
Pymgate Dr. SK8: He Grn 3C 76
Pymgate La. SK8: He Grn 3C 76
Pym's La. CW1: Crewe, W'ood 7C 190
Pyramid & Parr Hall Theatre 1E 66
Pyramids Shop. Cen., The
CH41: Birk 6C 34
Pyrus Av. CW1: Crewe 7K 191
Pyrus Gro. WA6: Hel 4C 138
Pytcheley Hollow WA6: Norl 5G 153
Pytha Fold Rd. M20: Manc 6A 24

Q

Quad, The CH1: Ches 1F 149
Quadrant, The CH1: Ches 1E 148
CH47: Hoy 6C 30
SK1: Stoc 3F 53
SK6: Rom 2A 54
WA3: Ris *5K 17*
(off Faraday St.)
Quadrant Cl. WA7: Murd 1F 113
Quail Cl. WA2: Warr 1H 41
Quail Dr. M44: Irlam 1D 20
Quaintways CW8: H'ord 2B 162
Quaker La. CH60: Hes 5G 83
Quakers All. *L2: Liv* *2H 35*
(off Tempest Hey)
Quakers Coppice 4G 195
Quakers Coppice CW1: Crewe 4G 195
Quakers Way LL13: Holt 6B 186
Quantock Cl. CH66: L Sut 2G 133
CW7: Wins 5B 178
SK4: Stoc 2C 52
Quantum Marshfield Bank Pk.
CW2: Crewe 2H 193
Quarry Av. CH3: Farn 6C 186
CH63: Beb 2K 85
QUARRYBANK 1B 176
Quarry Bank CH41: Birk 7C 34
CW6: Utk 2B 176
Quarry Bank Flats *CH41: Birk* *7C 34*
(off Quarry Bank)
Quarry Bank Mill 3F 97
Quarry Bank Ri. CW7: Wins 4C 178
Quarry Bank Rd. SK9: Styal 3F 97
Quarrybank St. CH41: Birk 7B 34
CH43: Birk 7B 34
Quarrybank Workshops *CH41: Birk* *7B 34*
(off Quarrybank St.)

Quarry Cl.—Ravenoak Pk. Rd.

Quarry Cl. CH4: Ches 4K 149
CH61: Hes 4H 83
WA7: Run 5K 89
Quarry Clough SK15: Stal 2E 10
Quarry Ct. CH3: Farn 6C 186
WA8: Wid 4C 62
Quarry Hgts. SK15: Stal 2A 10
Quarry Hill CH3: Farn 6C 186
Quarry La. CH3: Chri 4G 151
CH3: Wave 4A 174
CH61: Thin 7D 58
CW6: Kel 4C 172
WA4: App 7H 67
WA6: Manl 1F 171
Quarrymans Vw. WA15: Timp 6B 48
Quarry Pk. *L35: R'ill 3D 36*
(off Lincoln Way)
Quarry Ri. SK6: Rom 1B 54
SK15: Stal 2A 10
Quarry Rd. CH64: Nest 6A 106
SK6: Rom 2B 54
Quarry Rd. E. CH60: Hes 5G 83
CH61: Hes 5G 83
CH63: Beb 2A 86
Quarry Rd. W. CH60: Hes 5G 83
Quarry St. SK6: W'ley 6G 27
SK15: Stal 1A 10
Quarter, The CH1: Ches 2D 212
Quay, The WA6: Frod 5K 111
Quay Bus. Cen. WA2: Winw 7J 15
Quay Cen., The WA2: Winw 7J 15
Quay Ct. *M44: Irlam 2E 20*
(off Bankquay Ct.)
Quay Fold WA5: Warr 7D 40
Quay Pl. WA7: Pre B 7G 91
Quay Side WA6: Frod 5K 111
Quayside CH64: L Nes 3B 130
CH65: Ell P 1F 135
(off Grosvenor Wharf Rd.)
CW12: Cong 5G 183
Quayside M. WA13: Lymm 2B 70
Quayside Way SK11: Mac 5B 126
Queastybirch La. WA4: H'ton 5E 92
Quebec Quay L3: Liv 6H 35
Quebec Rd. WA2: Warr 5H 41
Quebec St. M34: Den 6D 8
Queen Anne Ct. SK9: Wilm 1H 119
Queen Anne Pde. *L3: Liv 2G 35*
(off Old Hall St.)
Queen Annes Ct. SK11: Mac 6J 125
Queen Anne St. L3: Liv 1K 35
Queen Av. *L2: Liv 3H 35*
(off Sweeting St.)
Queenhill Dr. SK14: Hyde 5A 10
Queenhill Rd. M22: N'den 3A 50
Queen Mary's Dr.
CH62: P Sun 7G 61
Queens Av. CH1: Ches 1B 150
CH47: Meols 4E 30
CH65: Whit 5C 134
SK6: Bred 1A 54
SK10: Mac 2B 126
WA1: Warr 5J 41
WA3: G'ury 3J 7
WA8: Wid 5B 62
Queensberry St. L8: Liv 7K 35
Queensbury CH48: W Kir 2E 56
Queensbury Av. CH62: Brom 5E 86
Queensbury Cl. SK9: Wilm 6A 98
Queensbury Way WA8: Wid 2D 62
Queens Cl. SK4: Stoc 2J 51
SK10: Boll 5B 122
SK10: Mac 2B 126
SK14: Hyde 4K 27
WA7: Run 5F 89
Queens Ct. CH47: Hoy 5C 30
M41: Urm 1G 21
SK4: Stoc 2J 51
SK6: Mar 6G 55
SK9: Wilm 1F 119
(off Queens Rd.)
Queenscourt CH4: Ches 3B 150
Queens Cres. CH2: Upt 3B 146
CW1: Bra G 3D 190
WA1: Padg 4A 42
Queens Dock Commercial Cen.
L1: Liv 5J 35
Queens Dr. CH4: Ches 3B 150
CH43: Pren 4K 59
CH60: Hes 6G 83
CW5: Nant 2B 196
CW10: Mid 5D 180
CW11: S'ach 1E 200
SK4: Stoc 2J 51
SK8: Chea H 2J 77
SK14: Hyde 4A 28
WA4: Grap 3A 68
WA6: Hel 5B 138
QUEENSFERRY 1B 218
Queens Gdns. CH65: Ell P 3D 134
SK8: Chea 6G 51
Queensgate CH1: Ches 6K 145
CW8: N'ich 6D 156
SK7: Bram 1H 99
Queens Pde. CW7: Wins 3E 178
QUEEN'S PARK 7D 212 (3A 150)
Queens Pk. Dr. CW2: Crewe 2K 193
Queens Pk. Gdns.
CW2: Crewe 2J 193
Queen's Pk. Ho. CH4: Ches 7D 212
Queen's Pk. Rd.
CH4: Ches 7D 212 (3A 150)
Queens Pk. Vw.
CH4: Ches 7D 212 (3A 150)
Queens Pl. CH1: Ches 3D 212 (1A 150)
Queen Sq. L1: Liv 2J 35
Queens Rd. CH1: Ches 1B 150
CH3: Ches 1E 150
CH42: R Fer 4F 61
CH44: Wall 7K 13
CH47: Hoy 5B 30
CH66: L Sut 1J 133
M33: Sale 6E 22
M41: Urm 2C 22
SK6: Bred 1A 54
SK7: H Gro 2J 79
SK8: Chea H 1H 77
(not continuous)
SK9: Wilm 1F 119
WA7: Run 5F 89
WA15: Hale 2J 73
Queens Ter. SK9: Hand 2A 98
SK16: Duk 1G 9
Queen St. CH1: Ches 3D 212 (1A 150)
CH41: Tran 1D 60
CH45: Wall 6H 13
CH65: Ell P 1E 134
CW1: Crewe 2E 194
CW2: Shav 3C 198
CW5: Nant 2C 196
(off Hospital St.)
CW6: Bun 6C 188
CW9: N'ich 5E 156
CW10: Mid 3C 180
CW12: Cong 4E 182
(Booth St.)
CW12: Cong 2H 183
(Havannah St.)
M34: Aude 4E 8
M34: Den 6D 8
OL5: Moss 1D 4
SK6: Mar 6G 55
SK8: Chea 6H 51
SK10: Boll 3E 122
SK10: Mac 4B 126
SK14: Hyde 2K 27
SK15: Stal 7B 4
SK16: Duk 1G 9
WA7: Run 3G 89
WA12: New W 1E 14
WA16: Knut 3D 116
Queen St. Mills OL5: Moss 1E 4
Queens Wlk. *L1: Liv 5K 35*
(off Lady Chapel Cl.)
M43: Droy 1A 8
Queensway CH2: Ches 5C 146
CH41: Birk 4F 35
CH45: Wall 5G 13
CH60: Hes 1F 105
CW1: Crewe 2C 194
CW7: Wins 4E 178
M19: Manc 2F 51
M31: Part 7C 20
M44: Irlam 1C 20
OL5: Moss 1E 4
SK8: He Grn 5D 76
SK12: Poy 3C 100
SK16: Duk 3A 10
ST7: Als 4C 202
WA6: Frod 7H 111
WA7: Run 3F 89
WA8: Wid 7F 63
WA16: Knut 2C 116
Queensway Trad. Est. WA8: Wid 1G 89
Queens Wharf L3: Liv 5H 35
Queenswood Av. CH63: H Beb 5D 60
Queen Victoria St. SK11: Mac 4A 126
Quickwood *M34: Den 6F 9*
(off Herbert Sth.)
Quigley St. CH41: Tran 1E 60
Quill Ct. *M44: Irlam 5B 20*
(off Magenta Av.)
Quillet, The CH64: Nest 1D 130
Quinesway CH49: Upt 7C 32
Quinn St. WA8: Wid 6H 63
Quinta Rd. CW12: Cong 3C 182
QUOISLEY 6A 208

R

Rabbit La. SK14: Mot 4H 11
RABY 3B 106 (3B 214)
Raby Av. CH63: Rab M 1G 107
Raby Cl. CH60: Hes 7H 83
CH63: Rab M 7A 86
WA8: Wid 3A 64
Raby Ct. CH65: Ell P 5F 135
Raby Dell CH63: Rab M 1G 107
Raby Dr. CH46: More 5A 32
CH63: Rab M 7A 86
Raby Gdns. CH64: Nest 7H 105
Raby Gro. CH63: H Beb 5C 60
Raby Hall Rd. CH63: Brom, Rab M 2D 106
RABY MERE 7A 86
Raby Mere Rd. CH63: Raby, Rab M 3B 106
(not continuous)
Raby Pk. Cl. CH64: Nest 7H 105
Raby Pk. Rd. CH64: Nest 7H 105
Raby Rd. CH63: Raby 4A 106
CH63: Tho H 1A 106
CH64: Nest 7H 105
Race, The SK9: Hand 4A 98
Racecourse Pk. SK9: Wilm 1E 118
Racecourse Rd. SK9: Wilm 7F 97
Racefield Cl. WA13: Lymm 2B 70
Racefield Rd. WA14: Alt 2F 213 (1G 73)
WA16: Knut 4D 116
Rackhouse Rd. M23: Wyth 3H 49
Radbroke Cl. CW11: S'ach 1H 201
Radcliffe Av. WA3: Cul 7E 6
Radcliffe Cl. CH3: Tar 5C 170
Radcliffe Rd. CW7: Wins 6C 178
CW11: Whe 6D 200
SK11: Sut E 6H 129
Raddel La. WA4: H Whi 2B 114
Raddle Wharf CH65: Ell P 1E 134
Raddon Pl. WA4: Westy 2J 67
Radford Av. CH63: Spit 4B 86
Radford Cl. SK2: Stoc 5H 53
WA8: Wid 6C 62
Radford Dr. *M44: Irlam 1D 20*
(off Wentworth Av.)
Radford Ho. SK2: Stoc 5J 53
Radlet Dr. WA15: Timp 4A 48
Radlett Cl. WA5: Penk 2G 65
Radley Cl. M33: Sale 1H 47
Radley Dr. CH63: Tho H 1J 105
Radley La. WA2: Warr 7C 16
Radley Rd. CH44: Wall 6F 13
Radleys Ct. *L8: Liv 6K 35*
(off Up. Warwick St.)
RADNOR 1B 182
Radnor Av. CH60: Hes 5H 83
M34: Den 7A 8
Radnor Cl. CW11: S'ach 2C 200
CW12: Cong 3D 182
Radnor Dr. CH4: Ches 6H 149
CH45: Wall 5J 13
WA8: Wid 3D 62
Radnor Ho. *SK3: Stoc 4C 52*
(off Moseley St.)
Radnormere Dr. SK8: Chea H 1H 77
Radnor Pk. Trad. Est. CW12: Cong 2C 182
Radnor Pl. CH43: Oxt 6B 34
Radnor St. M32: S'ord 1J 23
WA5: Warr 6C 40
Radstock Rd. CH44: Wall 6E 12
M32: S'ord 1H 23
RADWAY GREEN 7A 202 (2B 220)
Radway Grn. CH66: Gt Sut 3A 134
Radway Grn. Rd. CW1: R Grn 7A 202
Radway Green Sports and Social Club 5F 203
Raeburn Av. CH48: W Kir 2D 56
CH62: East 1J 107
CH64: L Nes 1D 130
Raeburn Dr. SK6: Mar B 4H 55
Rae St. SK3: Stoc 4A 52
Raffles Rd. CH42: Tran 7B 34
Raffles St. L1: Liv 5K 35
Raglan Ct. WA3: Ris 5A 18
Raglan Dr. WA14: Timp 4J 47
Raglan Rd. M32: S'ord 1G 23
M33: Sale 1K 47
SK10: Mac 2C 126
Raglan St. SK14: Hyde 1H 27
Ragley Cl. SK12: Poy 2E 100
Raikes Cl. WA5: Gt San 6A 40
Railbrook Ct. CW2: Crewe 4D 194
Rail Ho. CW2: Crewe 4D 194
Railton Av. CW1: Crewe 6F 191
L35: R'ill 2D 36
Railton Cl. L35: R'ill 3D 36
Railway Age, The 3D 194
Railway Bank *SK14: Hyde 1H 27*
(off Bowling Grn. St.)
Railway Cotts. CH66: H'ton 6J 107
CW12: Cong 5J 183
SK6: Bred 7E 26
(off Kennett Dr.)
Railway Rd. CH42: R Fer 3E 60
(not continuous)
M41: Urm 1C 22
SK1: Stoc 7H 213 (4C 52)
SK6: Mar 6D 54
Railway St. CW2: Crewe 4D 194
SK4: Stoc 5G 213 (2C 52)
SK14: Hyde 1J 27
SK16: Duk 1G 9
WA12: New W 1E 14
WA14: Alt 3H 213 (1H 73)
Railway Ter. SK12: Dis 1G 103
Railway Vw. CW1: Crewe 2E 194
SK5: Stoc 1H 25
RAINBOW 6H 123
Rainbow Cl. WA8: Wid 2C 62
Rainbow St. CW1: Crewe 2D 194
Raincliff Av. M13: Manc 1C 24
Raines Cl. CH49: Gre 1B 58
RAINFORD 1C 215
Rainford Av. WA15: Timp 6A 48
Rainford Gdns. L2: Liv 3J 35
RAINFORD JUNCTION 1C 215
Rainford Sq. *L2: Liv 3J 35*
(off Mathew St.)
Rainford Trials Exhibition 1C 36
Rainham Way SK5: Stoc 5A 26
RAINHILL 1C 36 (1C 215)
Rainhill Rd. L35: R'ill 1C 36
Rainhill Station (Rail) 1C 36
RAINHILL STOOPS 3E 36
RAINOW 3G 123 (3D 217)
Rainow Cl. CW10: Mid 5B 180
Rainow Dr. SK12: Poy 4F 101
RAINOWLOW 4H 123
Rainow Rd. SK3: Stoc 6A 52
SK10: Mac 2D 126
Rainow Vw. SK10: Boll 2F 123
Rainow Way *SK9: Wilm 5B 98*
(off Malpas Cl.)
Rajar Wlk. WA16: Mob 6B 102
Rake, The CH62: Brom 6C 86
CH64: Burt 7H 131
Rake Cl. CH49: Upt 1D 58
Rake Hey CH46: More 4J 31
Rake Hey Cl. CH46: More 4K 31
Rake La. CH2: Chor B, Crou 3F 141
CH3: Chri 3K 151
CH4: Ecc 4F 185
CH45: N Bri, Wall 4H 13
CH49: Upt 1D 58
WA6: Dun H 2F 143
WA6: Hel 4C 138
(Hawkstone Gro.)
WA6: Hel 2K 137
(Lordship La.)
Rake M. CH49: Upt 1D 58
Rakersfield Ct. CH45: N Bri 3J 13
Rakersfield Rd. CH45: N Bri 3J 13
RAKEWAY 3D 221
Rake Way CH1: Sau 2B 144
Raleigh Cl. WA5: Old H 3B 40
Raleigh Rd. CH46: Leas 7A 12
CH64: Nest 6J 105
Raleigh St. M32: S'ord 1J 23
SK5: Stoc 7H 25
Ralph Av. SK14: Hyde 4K 27
Ralphs La. SK16: Duk 3H 9
Rambaldi Sq. *WA8: Wid 4H 63*
(off Cross St.)
Ramillies Av. SK8: Chea H 4K 77
Ramp Rd. E. M90: Man A 6J 75
Ramp Rd. Sth. *M90: Man A 6J 75*
(off Outwood La.)
Ramp Rd. W. M90: Man A 6H 75
Ramsay Cl. WA3: Birc 1E 42
Ramsbottom St. CW1: Crewe 1B 194
(not continuous)
Ramsbrook La. L24: Hale 6A 88
Ramsdale Rd. SK7: Bram 5C 78
Ramsden Ct. CH4: Ches 7G 149
Ramsey Av. M19: Manc 2G 25
Ramsey Cl. WA8: Wid 2A 64
Ramsey Ct. CH48: W Kir 5C 56
Ramsey Rd. CH65: Ell P 7E 134
Ramsgate Rd. SK5: Stoc 4J 25
Ramsgill Cl. M23: Wyth 3F 49
Randal St. SK14: Hyde 7K 9
Randle Bennett Cl. CW11: Elw 2C 200
Randle Cl. CH63: Spit 4A 86
Randle Mdw. CH66: Gt Sut 6B 134
Randle Mdw. Ct. *CH66: Gt Sut 6B 134*
(off Randle Mdw.)
Randle M. WA8: Wid 4H 63
Randle's Vw. CW12: Cong 6K 183
Randolph Pl. SK3: Stoc 5C 52
Randolph St. M19: Manc 1E 24
Ranelagh Pl. L3: Liv 3K 35
Ranelagh St. L1: Liv 3J 35
Ranford Rd. M19: Manc 3D 24
Range Ct. SK10: Mac 3B 126
Range Dr. SK6: W'ley 5H 27
Range Hall Ct. *SK1: Stoc 3E 52*
(off Hall St.)
Rangemoor Cl. WA3: Birc 5B 18
Rangemore Av. M22: N'den 4A 50
Range Rd. SK3: Stoc 6C 52
SK15: Duk, Stal 2C 10
Rankin St. CH44: Wall 2K 33
Rankin Way CH62: Brom 5E 86
Rannoch Cl. CH66: Gt Sut 5B 134
Ranulph Ct. WA6: Frod 1J 139
Ranwonath Ct. CH2: Ches 1C 212 (7A 146)
Ranworth Av. SK4: Stoc 2H 51
Ranworth Rd. WA5: Gt San 6G 39
Rappart Rd. CH44: Wall 1C 34
Rappax Rd. WA15: Hale 5A 74
Rassbottom Brow SK15: Stal 7A 4
Rassbottom Ind. Est. SK15: Stal 7A 4
Rassbottom St. SK15: Stal 7A 4
Ratcliffe Av. M44: Irlam 1D 20
Ratcliffe Pl. L35: R'ill 1B 36
Ratcliffe St. M19: Manc 2E 24
SK1: Stoc 4D 52
Ratcliffe Ter. OL5: Moss 1D 4
Ratcliffe Towers SK1: Stoc 4D 52
Rathbone Pk. CW6: Tarp 2J 175
Rathlin Cl. WA8: Wid 2A 64
Rathmell Cl. WA3: Cul 7E 6
Rathmell Rd. M23: Wyth 2F 49
Rathmore Cl. CH43: Oxt 2K 59
Rathmore Dr. CH43: Oxt 1K 59
Rathmore Rd. CH43: Oxt 1K 59
Rathvale Dr. M22: Wyth 5J 75
Raveley Av. M14: Manc 3A 24
Raven Cl. CW11: S'ach 1E 200
Ravendale Cl. CH43: Noc 1G 59
CW7: Wins 3F 179
Ravenfield Dr. WA8: Wid 2C 62
Ravenhead Cl. M14: Manc 3A 24
Ravenhead Sq. SK15: Carrb 4F 5
Ravenhill Cres. CH46: Leas 1C 32
Ravenhoe La. SK10: R'ow 7G 123
Ravenhurst Ct. WA3: Ris 6A 18
Ravenna Av. M23: Wyth 5D 48
Ravenoak Av. M19: Manc 3F 25
Ravenoak Pk. Rd. SK8: Chea H 5K 77

Ravenoak Rd.—Richmond Av.

Ravenoak Rd. SK2: Stoc 1E 78
SK8: Chea H 5K 77
Raven Rd. WA15: Timp 3B 48
Ravenscar Cres. M22: Wyth 5K 75
Ravenscourt *WA13: Lymm 2B 70*
(off Pepper St.)
Ravenscroft CW4: H Cha 4G 181
Ravenscroft Cl. CW10: Mid 2B 180
CW11: S'ach 2G 201
Ravenscroft Rd. CH43: Oxt 7B 34
CW2: Crewe 3J 193
Ravensdale Cl. WA2: Warr 1H 41
Ravensfield CW8: Cudd 2A 160
SK16: Duk 3A 10
Ravensfield Ind. Est. SK16: Duk 1F 9
Ravensfield Way SK16: Duk 2G 9
Ravensholme Ct. CH3: Tatt 2G 187
Ravensholme La. CH3: Tatt 2G 187
Ravens La. CW5: Act, Burl, Rav 7H 189
RAVENSMOOR 2A 220
Ravenstone Cl. CH49: Upt 5C 32
Ravenstone Dr. M33: Sale 6K 23
Ravenswood CW8: H'ord 2A 162
M20: Manc 1B 50
Ravenswood Av. CH42: R Fer 5E 60
SK4: Stoc 3J 51
Ravenswood Ct. SK3: Stoc 1D 78
Ravenswood Dr. SK8: Chea H 5K 77
Ravenswood Rd. CH61: Hes 4J 83
SK9: Wilm 3D 118
Raven Ter. *SK16: Duk 1H 9*
(off Peel St.)
Ravenwood Dr. M34: Aude 4D 8
WA15: H'rns 6C 74
Rawcliffe Cl. WA8: Wid 1F 63
Rawcliffe Rd. CH42: Tran 7C 34
Rawdon Cl. M19: Manc 2E 24
WA7: Pal F 7C 90
Rawlings Cl. WA3: Birc 1F 43
Rawpool Gdns. M23: Wyth 5G 49
Rawson Rd. CH1: Blac 7F 145
Rawsthorne Av. M18: Manc 1G 25
Ray Av. CW5: Nant 7D 192
Rayleigh Av. CW9: Dave 6F 163
Rayleigh Cl. SK10: Mac 3F 125
Raymond Av. WA4: Stoc H 4H 67
Raymond Rd. CH44: Wall 1B 34
M23: Wyth 2H 49
Raymond St. CH1: Ches 3A 212 (1K 149)
Raymond Way CH64: L Nes 1E 130
Rayner La. OL7: Ash L 1C 8
Rayners Cl. SK15: Stal 1A 10
Rayner St. SK1: Stoc 4F 53
Raynham Av. M20: Manc 1D 50
Rays Brow CW8: Barnt 3A 156
Reach, The L3: Liv 1J 35
Reade Av. M41: Urm 2H 21
Reade Cl. CH63: Spit 5A 86
Reade Ho. *M41: Urm 2J 21*
(off Flixton Rd.)
Readesdale Av. CW2: Crewe 4K 193
Reade's La. CW12: Cong 6K 183
Reading Dr. M33: Sale 7C 22
Reading Wlk. M34: Den 2E 26
Read St. SK14: Hyde 7H 9
Read St. W. SK14: Hyde 7H 9
Rean Mdw. CH3: Tatt 2H 187
Reaper Cl. WA5: Gt San 6B 40
REASEHEATH 4A 192 (2A 220)
Reay Ct. CH44: Wall 1D 34
Reay St. WA8: Wid 3J 63
Recorder's Steps CH1: Ches 6C 212
Rectory Cl. CH3: Farn 6B 186
CH42: Tran 1C 60
CH60: Hes 7H 83
CW2: Wis 6J 193
CW5: Nant 2C 196
M34: Den 1F 27
WA2: Winw 5A 16
Rectory Ct. SK6: Mar 7F 55
Rectory Flds. SK1: Stoc 3E 52
Rectory Gdns. WA13: Lymm 2A 70
Rectory Grn. SK1: Stoc 6K 213 (3E 52)
Rectory La. CH1: Cap 7F 133
CH60: Hes 7G 83
WA2: Winw 5K 15
WA13: Lymm 3A 70
Rectory Rd. CH48: W Kir 4C 56
Redacre SK12: Poy 7K 79
Redacre Cl. WA4: Dutt 4J 113
RED BANK 2H 15
Red Bank WA12: New W 2H 15
Red Bank Av. WA12: New W 2J 15
Redbarn Cl. SK6: Bred 7E 26
Redbourne Dr. CW2: West 6K 199
WA8: Wid 1B 62
Redbrick Ct. OL7: Ash L 1F 9
REDBROOK 3D 219
Redbrook Cl. CH62: Brom 1J 107
Redbrook Gro. *SK9: Wilm 5A 98*
(off Colshaw Dr.)
Redbrook Rd. M31: Part 2G 45
WA15: Timp 6D 48
Redbrook Way SK10: Adl 6G 103
Redbrow Hollow SK6: Comp 2G 55
Red Brow La. WA4: Dare 6G 91
WA7: Murd 6G 91
Redburn Rd. M23: Wyth 5H 49
Redcap Cl. CH45: Wall 3E 12
Redcar Cl. SK7: H Gro 4A 80
Redcar Dr. CH62: East 2J 107
Redcar Rd. CH45: Wall 5D 12
Redcote Ct. CH48: W Kir 4B 56
Red Cow Ct. *CW10: Mid 3C 180*
(off Wheelock St.)
Red Cow Yd. WA16: Knut 3E 116
Redcroft CH49: Gre 2K 57
Redcroft Gdns. M19: Manc 7B 24
Redcroft Rd. M33: Sale 5D 22
Red Cross St. L1: Liv 3H 35
REDDISH
SK5 4J 25 (1C 217)
WA13 7C 44
Reddish Cres. WA13: Lymm 1B 70
REDDISH GREEN 4G 25
Reddish La. WA13: Lymm 1A 70
(not continuous)
Reddish Leisure Cen. 4H 25
Reddish North Station (Rail) 1J 25
Reddish Rd. SK5: Stoc 4J 25
(not continuous)
Reddish South Station (Rail) 4J 25
REDDISH VALE 4K 25
Reddish Vale Country Pk. 4A 26
Reddish Vale Farm 4K 25
Reddish Vale Nature Reserve 3A 26
Reddish Va. Rd. SK5: Stoc 4J 25
Reddish Vale Sports Cen. (NW Regional Basketball Cen.) 3K 25
Reddish Vale Vis. Cen. 4A 26
Redditch Cl. CH49: Gre 1K 57
Reddy La. WA14: L Bol, M'ton 6J 71
(not continuous)
Redesdale Cl. WA2: Warr 2J 41
Redesmere Cl. CW9: N'ich 1F 163
CW11: S'ach 2D 200
M43: Droy 1A 8
SK10: Mac 3H 125
WA15: Timp 6D 48
Redesmere Dr. SK8: Chea H 1H 77
SK9: Ald E 6E 118
Redesmere La. SK11: Sidd 1E 168
Redesmere Pk. M41: Urm 3A 22
Redesmere Rd. SK9: Hand 1A 98
Redfern Av. CW12: Cong 2H 183
M33: Sale 1E 48
Redfern Ho. SK6: Rom 2A 54
Redfield Cl. CH44: Wall 7K 13
Redford Cl. CH49: Gre 1K 57
Redford Dr. SK7: Bram 3E 78
Red Gables WA4: App T 3B 94
Redgate CW8: N'ich 6C 156
SK14: Hyde 3J 27
Redgrave Ho. WA14: Alt 3J 213
Redgrave Wlk. M19: Manc 2F 25
Redhill Dr. SK6: Bred 1H 53
Redhill Gro. WA5: Gt San 6K 39
Red Hill Rd. CH63: Store 1F 85
Redhill Rd. CH4: Ches 5G 149
CW6: Kel 3B 172
Redhills M. CH65: Ell P 2D 134
Redhillswood Cl. CH65: Ell P 1D 134
Red Ho. SK10: Mac 3B 126
Redhouse Bank CH48: W Kir 2B 56
Redhouse Farm Maize Maze 5B 46
Red Ho. La. WA14: Dun M 4A 46
Redhouse La. CH48: W Kir 2B 56
SK6: Bred 7E 26
SK12: Dis 1H 103
Redland Av. SK5: Stoc 6J 25
Redland Cl. CH4: Ches 4H 149
Red La. CW11: Most 3A 200
SK12: Dis 2F 103
WA4: App 5F 67
WA4: L Whi 6B 114
WA6: Frod 7J 111
Red Lion La. CH66: L Sut 1J 133
CW5: Nant 2B 196
Redmere Dr. CH60: Hes 6B 84
Redmere Gro. M14: Manc 3A 24
Redmire M. SK16: Duk 3A 10
Redmond Cl. M34: Aude 3D 8
Redmont St. CH41: Tran 1D 60
Redmoor La. SK12: Dis 3K 103
SK22: Dis 3K 103
SK22: N Mil 1K 103
Redmoor Mill SK22: N Mil 1K 103
Red Pike CH66: L Sut 7E 108
Redpoll La. WA3: Birc 7K 17
Red Rocks Marsh Nature Reserve 1A 56
Red Rose Cres. M19: Manc 4F 25
Red Rose Gdns. M33: Sale 5G 23
Red Row SK7: H Gro 5B 80
Redruth Av. SK10: Mac 3F 125
Redruth Cl. WA7: B'vale 1E 112
Redshank Av. CW7: Wins 7D 178
Redshank Dr. SK10: Mac 7J 121
Redshank La. WA3: Birc 7A 18
Redshaw Cl. CW10: Mid 6C 180
M14: Manc 2A 24
Redstone Cl. CH47: Meols 4E 30
Redstone Dr. CH60: Hes 5E 82
CW7: Wins 3B 178
Red Stone Hill WA6: Hel 4B 138
Redstone Pk. CH45: Wall 3F 13
Redstone Ri. CH43: Noc 6G 33
Redstone Rd. M19: Manc 1F 51
RED STREET 2C 221
Redtail Cl. WA7: Run 3F 89
Redvale Dr. M19: Manc 4C 24
Redvales Ct. WA3: Birc 7H 17
Redvers Av. CH66: H'ton 5B 108
Redway SK10: Ker 4E 122
Redwood M33: Sale 7B 22
Redwood Cl. CH4: Salt 5F 149
CH43: Oxt 3J 59
CW8: Barnt 1A 156
LL13: Holt 7A 186
SK3: Stoc 4K 51
WA1: Wool 6E 42
Redwood Ct. SK10: Boll 6B 122
Redwood Dr. CH2: Elt 4G 137
CH66: Gt Sut 7B 134
CW1: Crewe 7E 190
M34: Aude 4D 8
SK6: Bred 1K 53
Redwood Ho. M22: N'den 3A 50
Reece Cl. CH2: Mic T 2H 147
Reece Ct. SK16: Duk 2J 9
Reed Bed Nature Reserve 4K 115
Reed La. CW9: Ant 5A 94
Reeds Av. E. CH46: Leas 1C 32
Reeds Av. W. CH46: Leas 1C 32
Reedshaw Bank SK2: Stoc 7H 53
Reeds La. CH46: Leas, More 1C 32
Reedsmere Cl. WA4: Stoc H 3J 67
Reedsmere Wlk. CW9: Comb 2J 115
Reedville CH43: Oxt 7A 34
Reedville Gro. CH46: Leas 2C 32
Reedville Rd. CH63: Beb 1K 85
Reeman Cl. SK6: Bred 7F 27
Reeman Ct. SK9: Wilm 4J 97
Rees Cres. CW4: H Cha 3J 181
Reeve Cl. SK2: Stoc 7K 53
Reeves Rd. CH3: Gt Bou 3E 150
Reeve St. WA3: Low 2B 6
Reevey Av. SK7: H Gro 3G 79
Regal Cinema
Northwich 5E 156
Regal Cl. CH66: Gt Sut 5A 134
CW9: N'ich 2D 162
Regal Cres. WA8: Wid 5B 62
Regency Ct. CH2: Mic T 2H 147
CH42: R Fer 4F 61
(off Rock La. W.)
CW7: Wins 5D 178
(off Blenheim Gdns.)
CW10: Mid 3D 180
M33: Sale 7E 22
SK2: Stoc 6E 52
SK8: Chea H 3J 77
SK15: Stal 7B 4
(off Waterloo Rd.)
WA15: Hale 2C 74
Regency Gdns. SK8: Chea H 5G 77
SK14: Hyde 6A 10
Regency Pk. SK9: Wilm 2E 118
WA8: Wid 2E 62
Regency Sq. WA5: Warr 5D 40
Regency Wlk. CW10: Mid 2D 180
Regency Way CW9: N'ich 2D 162
Regent Av. SK11: Mac 6J 125
WA1: Padg 4A 42
Regent Bank SK9: Wilm 2E 118
Regent Cinema
Marple 6F 55
Regent Cl. CW2: Shav 4B 198
SK7: Bram 2G 99
SK8: Chea H 1A 78
SK9: Wilm 2E 118
Regent Ct. SK4: Stoc 6F 25
WA14: Alt 2H 213 (1H 73)
WA15: H'rns 5C 74
(off Dial Rd.)
Regent Dr. M34: Den 2C 26
OL5: Moss 2E 4
Regent Fold OL5: Moss 2E 4
Regent Ho. SK4: Stoc 6G 213
Regent Rd. CH45: Wall 5D 12
SK2: Stoc 6E 52
WA8: Wid 4H 63
WA14: Alt 2G 213 (1G 73)
Regents, The SK9: Wilm 6K 97
Regents Cl. CH3: Ches 1E 150
CH61: Thin 7E 58
Regents Ga. CW5: Nant 2E 196
Regent St. CH65: Ell P 3B 134
CW9: Moult 6E 162
L3: Liv 1G 35
WA1: Warr 7E 40
WA7: Run 3G 89
WA12: New W 1D 14
WA16: Knut 3E 116
Regents Way CH63: H Beb 5C 60
CW7: Wins 4B 178
(off Berkeley Ri.)
Regina Av. SK15: Stal 7B 4
Registry Cl. CW9: N'ich 2D 162
Reid Av. WA5: Warr 4D 40
Reid Cl. M34: Den 3F 27
Reid Ct. CH66: L Sut 1J 133
Reid St. CW1: Crewe 7H 191
Reigate Rd. M41: Urm 3H 21
Reins Cft. CH64: Nest 6H 105
Rembury Pl. WA4: Dutt 4H 113
Remer St. CW1: Crewe 6J 191
Rena Cl. SK4: Stoc 1B 52
Rena Ct. SK4: Stoc 1B 52
Renaissance Ct. CW1: Crewe 3G 195
Renaissance Way CW1: Crewe 2G 195
Rendel Cl. M32: S'ord 1J 23
WA12: New W 1G 15
Rendelsham Cl. CH49: Upt 7B 32
Rendel St. CH41: Birk 5C 34
Rendlesham Cl. WA3: Birc 5C 18
Renfrew Av. CH62: East 2K 107
Renfrew Cl. SK10: Mac 2G 125
Rennie Cl. M32: S'ord 1K 23
Renown Cl. WA3: Ris 7J 17
Renshaw St. CW9: N'ich 3J 157
L1: Liv 3K 35
WA14: Alt 7J 47
Renshierds Pl. WA16: H Leg 1H 95
Renton Av. WA7: Run 4K 89
Renton Rd. M22: Wyth 1K 75
M32: S'ord 1K 23
Renwick Av. L35: R'ill 1A 36
Repton Av. M34: Den 1K 25
M41: Urm 1G 21
SK14: Hyde 7K 9
Repton Cl. M33: Sale 1H 47
WA16: H Leg 2H 95
Repton Dr. CW1: Hasl 1K 195
Repton Rd. CH65: Ell P 4F 135
Reservoir Rd. CH42: Tran 4A 60
SK3: Stoc 5B 52
Reservoir Rd. Nth. CH42: Tran 3A 60
Reservoir Ter. *CH3: Ches 1C 150*
(off Spital Wlk.)
Rest Hill Rd. CH63: Store 1F 85
Retreat, The CW1: Crewe 7H 191
SK6: Rom 3C 54
Reuben St. SK4: Stoc 7H 25
Revesby Cl. WA8: Wid 3D 62
Reveton Grn. SK7: Bram 3E 78
Rex Bldgs. SK9: Wilm 1G 119
Rexcine Way SK14: Hyde 5B 10
Reynard St. SK14: Hyde 7J 9
Reynell Rd. M13: Manc 1C 24
Reyner St. OL6: Ash L 1K 9
Reynolds Av. WA3: Ris 6K 17
Reynolds Dr. SK6: Mar B 4H 55
Reynolds La. CW11: Blet, S'ach 3J 201
CW11: S'ach 2J 201
Reynolds M. SK9: Wilm 6B 98
Reynolds St. WA4: Westy 2J 67
Reynold St. SK14: Hyde 1J 27
RHEWL 3A 218
RHEWL-MOSTYN 3A 214
RHIWABON 3B 218
Rhode Ho's. SK6: Mar 2F 81
Rhoden St. CW1: Crewe 1G 195
Rhodes Cl. CW1: Hasl 2K 195
Rhodes St. SK14: Hyde 7H 9
WA2: Warr 5G 41
Rhodes St. Nth. SK14: Hyde 7H 9
Rhodesway CH60: Hes 7K 83
Rhona Cl. CH63: East 3H 107
Rhona Dr. WA5: Gt San 6G 39
Rhone Cl. CH3: Gt Bou 4D 150
Rhos Av. M14: Manc 3B 24
SK8: Chea H 4H 77
Rhos Dr. SK7: H Gro 4H 79
RHOSESMOR 1A 218
RHOSLLANERCHRUGOG 3A 218
RHOSTYLLEN 3B 218
RHUDDALL HEATH 4J 175 (1D 219)
Rhuddlan Ct. CH4: Salt 5F 149
CH65: Ell P 6F 135
Rhuddlan Rd. CH1: Blac 6E 144
Rhum Cl. CH65: Ell P 7E 134
RHYDTALOG 2A 218
RHYDYMWYN 1A 218
Rhyl St. L8: Liv 7K 35
WA8: Wid 6F 63
Ribble Av. CW7: Wins 3J 179
L35: R'ill 1C 36
Ribble Cl. WA3: Cul 1A 18
WA8: Wid 2B 64
Ribble Pl. CW7: Wins 3J 179
Ribblesdale CH65: Whit 5D 134
Ribblesdale Av. CW12: Cong 1J 183
Ribblesdale Rd. CH62: East 2A 108
Ribble St. CH41: Birk 3J 33
Ribble Wlk. *M43: Droy 2A 8*
(off Ellen St.)
Ribchester Gdns. WA3: Cul 7G 7
Rice Hey Rd. CH44: Wall 6J 13
Rice La. CH44: Wall 6J 13
(not continuous)
Rice St. L1: Liv 4K 35
Richard Allen Way *L5: Liv 1K 35*
(off Netherfield Rd. Sth.)
Richard Chubb Dr. CH44: Wall 5K 13
Richard Cl. WA7: Cast 5C 90
Richard Moon St. CW1: Crewe 2B 194
Richard Reynolds Ct.
M44: Cad 5B 20
(off Dean Rd.)
Richards Cl. M34: Aude 3D 8
Richards Cft. CH3: Gt Bou 4D 150
Richards Gro. CW12: Cong 3C 182
Richardson Cl. CW2: Shav 2D 198
CW11: Elw 3B 200
Richardson Rd.
CH42: R Fer 4D 60
Richardson St. SK1: Stoc 5E 52
WA2: Warr 4G 41
Richard St. CW1: Crewe 2B 194
CW9: N'ich 6H 157
SK1: Stoc 1D 52
Richbell Cl. M44: Irlam 4B 20
Richmond Av. M41: Urm 1D 22
SK9: Hand 1A 98
WA4: Grap 2C 68
WA4: Westy 1K 67
WA7: Run 4A 90

Richmond Cl.—Rocksavage Way

Richmond Cl. CH63: Beb 7F 61
CW2: West 6K 199
CW11: Elw 2C 200
M33: Sale 1F 49
OL5: Moss 1F 5
SK15: Stal 1B 10
SK16: Duk 4J 9
WA3: Cul 6D 6
WA13: Lymm 1D 70
Richmond Ct. CH3: Ches 1C 150
CH65: Ell P 5F 135
CW8: H'ord 1B 162
M34: Aude 4D 8
SK2: Stoc 7H 53
WA4: Westy 2A 68
WA8: Wid 1K 63
WA14: Bow 3F 73
Richmond Cres. CH3: Ches 2F 151
OL5: Moss 1F 5
Richmond Dr. CW9: N'ich 2F 163
WA13: Lymm 1D 70
Richmond Gdns. WA12: New W 1F 15
Richmond Grn. SK7: Bram 7D 78
WA14: Bow 3F 73
Richmond Gro. SK8: Chea H 3H 77
Richmond Hill SK11: Mac 6B 126
SK14: Hyde 2A 28
WA14: Bow 3F 73
WA16: Knut 4F 117
Richmond Hill Rd. SK8: Chea 7E 50
Richmond Ho. *SK15: Stal* 1B 10
(off Grosvenor St.)
Richmond M. CH2: Ches 1C 150
Richmond Pk. M14: Manc 2A 24
Richmond Pl. SK11: Mac 6B 126
Richmond Rd. CH63: Beb 7E 60
CW1: Crewe 2E 194
M14: Manc 3A 24
SK4: Stoc 2H 51
SK6: Rom 1C 54
SK16: Duk 4J 9
WA14: Alt 1H 213 (7H 47)
WA14: Bow 3F 73
Richmond Row L3: Liv 1K 35
Richmond St. CH45: N Bri 2H 13
L1: Liv 3J 35
M34: Aude 4D 8
OL6: Ash L 1F 9
SK14: Hyde 1K 27
SK15: Stal 7C 4
WA4: Westy 2A 68
WA8: Wid 4J 63
Richmond Ter. SK6: Mar 4H 81
Richmond Vw. *OL5: Moss* 1F 5
(off Bk. Micklehurst Rd.)
Richmond Village CW5: Nant 2E 196
Richmond Way CH61: Hes 4H 83
CH61: Thin 6D 58
Rich Vw. CH43: Oxt 2A 60
Rickaby Cl. CH63: Brom 6C 86
Ricroft Rd. SK6: Comp 1H 55
Ridding Av. M22: Wyth 2A 76
Ridding Cl. SK2: Stoc 6H 53
Ridding La. WA7: B'vale 2D 112
Riddings, The CH65: Whit 4D 134
Riddings Ct. CW8: H'ord 2A 162
WA15: Timp 4K 47
Riddings La. CW5: Wyb 7A 198
CW8: H'ord 2K 161
Riddings Rd. WA15: Hale 4K 73
WA15: Timp 4K 47
Ridge, The CH60: Hes 4F 83
CW8: Dela 3G 173
SK6: Mar 2G 81
Ridge Av. SK6: Mar 1G 81
WA15: H'rns 7C 74
Ridgebourne Cl. WA5: Call 2B 40
Ridge Cl. SK6: Rom 2E 54
Ridge Cres. SK6: Mar 2G 81
Ridgedale Cen. SK6: Mar 6F 55
Ridge-End SK6: Mar 3H 81
Ridge End Fold SK6: Mar 4G 81
Ridgefield Rd. CH61: Pens 1H 83
RIDGE HILL 6B 4
Ridge Hill SK11: Sut E 2F 169
Ridge Hill La. SK15: Stal 7A 4
Ridgemere Rd. CH61: Pens 1H 83
Ridgemont Av. SK4: Stoc 2K 51
Ridgemont Wlk. M23: Wyth 2F 49
Ridge Pk. SK7: Bram 7B 78
Ridge Rd. SK6: Mar 1G 81
Ridges La. CH3: Row, Sai, Wave 7F 151
Ridge Vw. SK11: Mac 7K 125
Ridgeview Rd. CH43: Noc 7G 33
RIDGEWAY 2C 221
Ridgeway SK9: Wilm 7C 98
Ridgeway, The CH3: Tar 5C 170
CH47: Meols 5F 31
CH60: Hes 7K 83
CH63: H Beb 5C 60
SK12: Dis 6J 81
WA6: Frod 5E 138
WA7: Murd 1F 113
WA8: Cron 6C 36
Ridgeway Cl. CH66: Gt Sut 6J 133
Ridgeway, The (Country Holiday Pk.)
WA6: Frod 6G 139
Ridgeway Rd. WA15: Timp 7C 48
Ridgewood Dr. CH61: Pens 2G 83
Ridgmont Rd. SK7: Bram 1H 99
RIDGWARDINE 3A 220
Ridgway, The SK6: Rom 3A 54
Ridgway Gdns. WA13: Lymm 2K 69
Ridgway St. CW1: Crewe 1D 194
WA2: Warr 5H 41
Riding Cl. M33: Sale 7K 23
WA9: Clo F 1J 37
Ridings, The CH1: Sau 1B 144
CH43: Noc 7G 33
SK9: Wilm 3C 118
Ridings Hey CH43: Noc 1G 59
Ridings Rd. SK13: Had 2K 11
Ridley Cl. CW2: Hou 5E 198
Ridley Dr. WA5: Gt San 1A 66
WA14: Timp 3J 47
Ridley Gro. CH48: W Kir 2B 56
M33: Sale 1F 49
Ridley Rd. SK10: Boll 3B 122
Ridley St. CH43: Oxt 7B 34
Ridling La. SK14: Hyde 1K 27
Ridsdale WA8: Wid 5C 62
Rifle Rd. M33: Sale 6K 23
Riga Rd. M14: Manc 2A 24
Rigby Av. CW1: Crewe 6F 191
Rigby Dr. CH49: Gre 3A 58
Rigby's Row CW5: Nant 2C 196
Rigby St. L3: Liv 2G 35
WA14: Alt 4J 213 (2H 73)
Rigg St. CW1: Crewe 1B 194
Riley Bank M. WA6: Frod 7H 139
Riley Cl. CW11: Ett H 4C 200
M33: Sale 3F 47
Riley Dr. WA7: Run 6G 89
Rileys La. WA16: Pick 1B 158
Rileywood Cl. SK6: Rom 3K 53
Rilshaw La. CW7: Wins 4G 179
Rilston Av. WA3: Cul 7D 6
Rimington Cl. WA3: Cul 7E 6
Rimmer St. L3: Liv 2K 35
Rimsdale Cl. CW2: Wis 7A 194
SK8: Gat 2C 76
Ringmer Dr. M22: Wyth 4J 75
Ringmore Rd. SK7: Bram 3E 78
Ring O'Bells La. SK12: Dis 1G 103
Ring Rd. CH1: Bac 2B 140
CH3: Ches, Gt Bou 6E 146
Ringstead Cl. SK9: Wilm 5A 98
Ringstead Dr. SK9: Wilm 5A 98
RINGWAY 7F 75
Ringway CH3: Wave 2B 174
CH64: Nest 6J 105
CH66: Gt Sut 4A 134
Ringway Cl. SK10: Mac 7J 121
Ringway Gro. M33: Sale 2E 48
Ringway M. M22: Shar 7A 50
Ringway Rd. M22: Wyth 6J 75
M90: Man A 6J 75
WA7: Run 4K 89
Ringway Rd. W. M22: Man A 5J 75
M90: Man A 5J 75
Ringways CH62: Brom 3D 86
Ringway Trad. Est. M22: Wyth 5A 76
Ringwood CH43: Oxt 2K 59
Ringwood Av. M12: Manc 1E 24
M34: Aude 1B 8
SK7: H Gro 4F 79
SK14: Hyde 2B 28
Ringwood Cl. WA3: Birc 6C 18
Rink St. M14: Manc 4A 24
Ripley Av. SK2: Stoc 1F 79
SK8: Chea H 1E 98
Ripley Cl. SK7: H Gro 5J 79
Ripley St. WA5: Warr 5C 40
Ripley Way M34: Den 3E 26
Ripon Av. CH66: L Sut 3J 133
Ripon Cl. SK1: Stoc 4D 52
SK10: Mac 1K 125
WA15: Hale 4C 74
Ripon Cres. M32: S'ord 1E 22
Ripon Dr. CW2: Wis 6A 194
Ripon Gro. M33: Sale 5E 22
Ripon Rd. CH45: Wall 5E 12
M32: S'ord 1E 22
Ripon Row WA7: Run 1K 111
Ripon St. CH41: Tran 1D 60
Ripon Wlk. SK6: Rom 3A 54
Rippleton Rd. M22: Wyth 1A 76
Riseley's Pas. *SK10: Mac* 4A 126
(off King Edward St.)
Riseley St. SK10: Mac 4K 125
Rishworth Cl. SK2: Stoc 7H 53
Rising Sun Cl. SK11: Gaw 7H 125
Rising Sun Rd. SK11: Gaw 1E 128
RISLEY 5K 17 (1A 216)
Risley Employment Area WA3: Ris 4A 18
Risley Moss Local Nature Reserve 7B 18
Risley Moss Vis. Cen. 6B 18
Risley Rd. WA3: Ris 6A 18
Rissington Av. M23: Wyth 6H 49
Ritherup La. L35: R'ill 1C 36
Rivacre Brow CH66: Ell P 1A 134
Rivacre Bus. Cen. CH66: Ell P 3A 134
Rivacre Pk. 6D 108
Rivacre Rd. CH62: East 3B 108
CH66: Ell P 1A 134
CH66: Ell P, H'ton 3B 108
Rivacre Valley Country Pk. 7F 109
Riva La. CH60: Hes 4G 83
Riva Rd. M19: Manc 2F 51
Riveacre Rd. CH65: H'ton 3B 108
Rivenmill Cl. WA8: Wid 7J 37
Riverbank Cl. CH60: Hes 1C 104
CW5: Nant 6C 192
SK10: Boll 3C 122
Riverbank Rd. CH60: Hes 1B 104
CH62: Brom 2E 86
Riverbank Wlk. M20: Manc 1K 49
Riverbend Technology Cen.
M44: Irlam 5D 20
Riverbrook Rd. WA14: W Tim 3F 47
Riverdane Rd. CW12: Cong 2G 183
River Gro. CH62: N Fer 5G 61
River Ho. *M43: Droy* 1A 8
(off Medlock St.)
River La. CH3: Farn 5B 186
CH4: Ches 7B 212 (4K 149)
CH4: Salt 4E 148
M31: Part 7C 20
M34: Den 7G 9
Rivermead Av. WA15: H'rns 6C 74
Rivermead Cl. M34: Den 4F 27
Rivermead Rd. M34: Den 3F 27
Riverpark Gdns. *L8: Liv* 6K 35
(off Hyslop St.)
River Rd. WA4: Warr 2F 67
(not continuous)
Riversdale WA1: Wool 5F 43
WA6: Frod 6J 111
Riversdale Rd. CH44: Wall 7K 13
CH48: W Kir 3B 56
SK8: Chea 6E 50
WA7: Halt 5A 90
Riversdale Vw. SK6: W'ley 6F 27
Rivershill M33: Sale 5F 23
Rivershill Gdns. WA15: H'rns 7C 74
Riverside CH4: Salt 4D 148
CH48: W Kir 5C 56
CH62: P Sun 1B 86
CW5: Nant 2B 196
CW9: N'ich 1G 163
SK16: Duk 1H 9
Riverside Av. M21: Chor H 1K 49
M44: Irlam 2E 20
Riverside Bowl 2H 13
Riverside Bus. Pk. SK9: Wilm 7K 97
Riverside Cl. WA1: Warr 1G 67
Riverside Ct. CH3: Gt Bou 4C 150
CH62: N Fer 4G 61
M20: Manc 1B 50
SK6: Mar B 4G 55
SK11: Lang 1H 169
Riverside Cres. CW4: H Cha 3J 181
Riverside Dr. L3: Liv 2K 61
M41: Urm 3A 22
SK10: Pres 6H 121
Riverside Gro. CW2: Crewe 3H 193
Riverside Ho. CH41: Birk 3E 34
Riverside Ind. Est. CH4: Salt 4F 149
Riverside Pk. CW8: N'ich 7D 156
Riverside Pk. Cvn. Site M22: N'den 3A 50
Riverside Retail Pk. WA1: Warr 1G 67
Riverside Trad. Est. CW8: N'ich 6E 156
WA5: Penk 4F 65
Riverside Wlk. CH64: L Nes 3B 130
L3: Liv 4G 35
(not continuous)
Riversmead CH3: Hunt 6D 150
Riverstone Dr. M23: Wyth 5D 48
River St. CW12: Cong 3F 183
SK1: Stoc 1F 53
SK9: Wilm 6J 97
SK11: Mac 6B 126
Riverton Rd. M20: Manc 4D 50
River Vw. *CH41: Tran* 1D 60
(off Marquis St.)
CH62: N Fer 5H 61
CW7: Wins 3F 179
SK5: Stoc 4K 25
Riverview SK4: Stoc 4H 51
Riverview Gdns. CH42: R Fer 3E 60
River Vw. Res. Cvn. Pk.
WA8: Wid 5J 63
Riverview Rd. CH44: Wall 1D 34
CH62: Brom 3F 87
CH64: L Nes 3D 130
River Wlk. *WA7: Pal F* 7B 90
(off Halton Lea Shop. Cen.)
Riverwood Rd. CH62: Brom 5F 87
Riviera Dr. CH42: R Fer 4C 60
Rivington Av. CH43: Noc 1H 59
Rivington Ct. WA1: Wool 4E 42
Rivington Gro. M34: Aude 2B 8
M44: Cad 5A 20
Rivington Rd. CH44: Wall 1C 34
CH65: Ell P 3E 134
WA7: Pre B 4H 113
WA15: Hale 3K 73
RIXTON 2B 44
Rixton Av. WA5: Warr 4D 40
Rixton Claypits Local Nature Reserve 2B 44
Rixtonleys Dr. M44: Irlam 3E 20
Rixton Pk. Homes WA3: Rix 2B 44
Roaches Way SK11: Mac 7J 125
Roachill Cl. WA14: Alt 7F 47
Road Beta CW10: Mid 4D 180
Road Five CW7: Wins 2K 179
Road Four CW7: Wins 2J 179
Road One CW1: Crewe 6K 195
CW7: Wins 1J 179
Roadside CH3: Chri 3G 151
Road Three CW7: Wins 3K 179
Road Two CW1: Crewe 6J 195
CW7: Wins 2J 179
Roan Ct. SK11: Mac 5C 126
Roan Ho. Way SK11: Mac 5C 126
Roan M. SK11: Mac 5B 126
Roan Way SK9: Ald E 7G 119
Roaring Ga. La. WA15: Hale, Ring 2E 74
Robert Bolt Theatre, The 6G 23
(within Waterside Arts Cen.)
Robert Dr. CH49: Gre 2B 58
Robert Lawrence Ct. M41: Urm 2K 21
Robert Moffat WA16: H Leg 1H 95
Robert Owen Gdns. M22: N'den 4K 49
Robert Salt Ct. WA14: Alt 6J 47
Roberts Ct. WA7: Pal F 1B 112
Robertscroft Cl. M22: Wyth 1J 75
Roberts Dr. CW9: Rud 7J 157
Roberts Fold WA3: Birc 7J 17
Robertson St. L8: Liv 7K 35
Roberts Rd. CW9: Los Gra 5C 158
Roberts St. L3: Liv 1G 35
Robert's Ter. CH1: Ches 2J 149
Robert St. CH41: Birk 5C 34
CW8: N'ich 7D 156
M33: Sale 7K 23
SK14: Hyde 7H 9
SK16: Duk 2G 9
WA5: Warr 6D 40
WA7: Run 4J 89
WA8: Wid 4H 63
Robeson Way M22: Shar 6A 50
Robin Cl. CW11: S'ach 1E 200
SK11: Chel 5C 166
WA7: Murd 7F 91
Robin Cres. SK11: L Grn 3H 129
Robin Cft. SK6: Bred 1H 53
Robin Hood Av. SK11: Mac 7K 125
Robin Hood La. WA6: Hel 7B 138
Robin La. SK11: Chel 5C 166
SK11: L Grn 3H 129
Robin Rd. WA14: W Tim 3G 47
Robinsbay Rd. M22: Wyth 5A 76
Robins Cl. SK7: Bram 6C 78
SK10: R'ow 6H 123
Robins Cft. CH66: Gt Sut 6B 134
Robins La. SK7: Bram 6B 78
WA3: Cul 1J 17
Robinson Cl. CH3: Gt Bar 1C 170
Robinson Pk. *SK15: Stal* 1K 9
(off Robinson St.)
Robinson Rd. CH65: Ell P 4G 135
Robinsons Cft. CH3: Gt Bou 4E 150
Robinson St. SK3: Stoc 5B 52
SK14: Hyde 7A 10
SK15: Stal 2K 9
Robins Way SK10: Boll 4D 122
Robinsway WA14: Bow 4G 73
Robinswood Rd. M22: Wyth 3K 75
Robin Way CH49: Woodc 3E 58
Robson Gro. WA1: Warr 6H 41
Robson St. WA1: Warr 6H 41
Roby Cl. L35: R'ill 1C 36
Roby Gro. WA5: Gt San 6J 39
Roche Gdns. SK8: Chea H 7K 77
Rochester Cl. SK16: Duk 3B 10
WA5: Gt San 7A 40
Rochester Cres. CW1: Crewe 7K 191
Rochester Dr. CH65: Ell P 6F 135
WA14: Timp 3J 47
Rochester Gro. SK7: H Gro 2J 79
Rochester Rd. CH42: R Fer 3F 61
Rochford Ho. *M34: Aude* 4D 8
(off Denton Rd.)
Rock, The WA6: Hel 6B 138
Rock Av. CH60: Hes 5H 83
Rock Bank CH49: Upt 7D 32
Rock Bank Ri. SK10: Boll 2D 122
Rock Cl. CH42: R Fer 3E 60
Rock Dr. WA6: Frod 6J 111
Rockfarm Cl. CH64: L Nes 2E 130
Rockfarm Dr. CH64: L Nes 2E 130
Rockfarm Gro. CH64: L Nes 2E 130
ROCK FERRY 3E 60 (2B 214)
Rock Ferry By-Pass CH42: R Fer 2F 61
Rock Ferry Station (Rail) 3E 60
Rockfield Cl. WA8: Wid 3D 62
Rockfield Dr. WA6: Hel 6C 138
Rockfield M. WA4: Grap 3K 67
Rockford Gdns. WA5: Gt San 4J 39
Rockford Lodge WA16: Knut 4G 117
Rock Gdns. SK14: Hyde 4K 27
Rockingham Cl. WA3: Birc 5D 18
Rockland Rd. CH45: Wall 4F 13
Rocklands, The CH43: Noc 6G 33
Rocklands Av. CH63: Beb 6F 61
Rocklands La. CH63: Tho H 6G 85
Rock La. CH2: Ches 1B 212 (7K 145)
CH3: Durw 5J 187
WA8: Wid 1F 63
Rock La. E. CH42: R Fer 4F 61
(not continuous)
Rock La. W. CH42: R Fer 4E 60
Rocklee Gdns. CH64: L Nes 2E 130
Rocklis Grange *CH64: Nest* 7H 105
(off Tannery La.)
Rocklynes SK6: Rom 2B 54
Rock Pk. CH42: R Fer 3F 61
(not continuous)
Rock Pk. Rd. CH42: R Fer 4G 61
Rockpoint Av. CH45: N Bri 4J 13
Rock Retail Pk. CH41: Birk 7D 34
Rock Rd. M41: Urm 1E 22
WA4: Westy 1J 67
ROCKSAVAGE 2J 111
Rocksavage Expressway WA7: Clif 2K 111
Rocksavage Way WA7: Run 2G 111

Rockside—Rowan Gro.

Rockside ST7: Mow C 6G 205
Rock St. SK14: Hyde 4K 27
Rock Ter. OL5: Moss 3D 4
SK16: Duk 1H 9
Rockville St. CH42: R Fer 3E 60
Rockwood Av. CW2: Crewe 3A 194
Rockwood Cl. CW2: Crewe 3A 194
Rockybank Rd. CH42: Tran 2C 60
Rocky La. CH3: Tatt 4G 187
CH60: Hes 6H 83
Rocky La. Sth. CH60: Hes 6J 83
Rococo Sq. CH45: N Bri 2J 13
Rodborough Gdns. M23: Wyth 2F 75
Rodborough Rd. M23: Wyth 2F 75
Roddy La. WA6: K'ley 1E 152
Rode, The ST7: Als 5E 202
Rode Ct. CW12: Cong 3H 183
Rode Hall & Gardens 2J 203
RODEHEATH 1C 221
RODE HEATH 2G 203 (2C 221)
Rodeheath Cl. SK9: Wilm 7A 98
Rode Ho. Cl. ST7: Rod H 2G 203
Rodepool Cl. SK9: Wilm 4A 98
Roderick St. L3: Liv 1K 35
Rode St. CW6: Tarp 1F 175
Rodgers Cl. WA6: Frod 6H 111
Rodmill Dr. SK8: Gat 1C 76
Rodney Dr. SK6: Bred 6F 27
Rodney St. CH41: Birk 7C 34
L1: Liv 4K 35
SK11: Mac 5A 126
Roe All. *L1: Liv* *3J 35*
(off Wood St.)
Roebourne Ri. CH1: Blac 6E 144
Roebuck Gdns. M33: Sale 7F 23
Roebuck La. M33: Sale 7F 23
Roebuck M. M33: Sale 1B 48
Roebuck St. CW1: Crewe 1C 194
Roeburn Way WA5: Penk 2F 65
ROE CROSS 4G 11
Roe Cross Grn. SK14: Mot 5G 11
Roe Cross Ind. Pk. SK14: Mot 5H 11
Roe Cross Rd. SK14: Mot 4G 11
Roedean Gdns. M41: Urm 1F 21
Roedean Wlk. CW1: Crewe 7J 191
Roehampton Dr. WA7: Pal F 7A 90
Roehurst La. CW7: Wins 2E 178
Roehurst Way CW7: Wins 2E 178
Roemarsh Ct. WA7: Pal F 1A 112
Roe St. CW12: Cong 4G 183
L1: Liv 3J 35
SK11: Mac 5K 125
Roewood La. SK10: Mac 3D 126
(Clarendon Dr.)
SK10: Mac 4E 126
(Ecton Av.)
Roften Works Ind. Est. CH66: H'ton 6J 107
Rogate Dr. M23: Wyth 7G 49
Roger Cl. SK6: Rom 3K 53
Roger Hay SK8: Chea H 2K 77
Rogerson Cl. WA15: Timp 5C 48
Rokeby Av. M32: S'ord 2J 23
Rokeby Cl. L3: Liv 1K 35
Rokeby Ct. WA7: Man P 1F 91
Rokeby St. L3: Liv 1K 35
Roker Av. CH44: Wall 1K 33
M13: Manc 1C 24
Roker Pk. Av. M34: Aude 3C 8
Roklis Bldg. *CH44: Wall* *7K 13*
(off Liscard Rd.)
Roklis Ct. CH49: Upt 1D 58
Roland Av. CH63: H Beb 7C 60
WA7: Run 5F 89
Roland Rd. SK5: Stoc 4J 25
Rolands Wlk. WA7: Cast 5B 90
Rolleston Dr. CH45: Wall 4F 13
CH63: Beb 2A 86
Rolleston St. WA2: Warr 6E 40
Rollins La. SK6: Mar B 3G 55
Rolls Av. CW1: Crewe 6E 190
Rolt Cres. CW10: Mid 4B 180
Roman Amphitheatre
Chester 5D 212 (2A 150)
Romana Sq. WA14: Timp 4J 47
Roman Cl. WA7: Cast 4A 90
WA12: New W 1F 15
Roman Ct. CH64: L Nes 1D 130
Roman Dr. CH1: Blac 4E 144
Romanes St. CW8: N'ich 6D 156
Roman Lakes Leisure Pk. 1H 81
Roman Rd. CH43: Pren 5K 59
CH47: Meols 3E 30
CH63: Store 5K 59
SK4: Stoc 4H 213 (2C 52)
WA4: Stoc H 4G 67
Roman Way CW11: S'ach 2C 200
Romford Av. M34: Den 6F 9
Romford Rd. M33: Sale 5D 22
ROMILEY 2C 54 (1D 217)
Romiley Pools & Target Fitness Cen. 2B 54
Romiley Pct. SK6: Rom 2C 54
Romiley Rd. CH66: Ell P 2A 134
Romiley Station (Rail) 2C 54
Romiley St. SK1: Stoc 2F 53
Romney Cl. CH64: L Nes 1C 130
WA8: Wid 3A 64
Romney Cft. CH64: L Nes 1D 130
Romney Towers SK5: Stoc 5A 26
Romney Way CH64: L Nes 1D 130
SK5: Stoc 5A 26
Romsdal Vs. SK6: Rom 2B 54
Romsey Dr. SK8: Chea H 7A 78
Romsey Gdns. M23: Wyth 6G 49
Rona Av. CH65: Ell P 7E 134
Ronald Dr. WA2: Fear 2B 42
Ronaldshay WA8: Wid 3A 64
Ronaldsway CH49: Upt 6C 32
CH60: Hes 1C 104
Ronan Rd. WA8: Wid 1E 88
Rone Cl. CH46: More 4A 32
Rood Hill CW12: Cong 3F 183
Rood La. CW12: Cong 3F 183
Rookery Cl. CW5: Nant 2D 196
CW6: Kel 4B 172
CW11: Ett H 4A 200
SK15: Stal 3F 11
Rookery Ct. CW11: Ett H 4A 200
Rookery Dr. CH3: Tatt 2H 187
CW5: Nant 3C 196
Rookery Farm Rd. CW6: Til 1F 189
Rookery Gdns. CW9: Dave 3D 162
Rookerypool Cl. SK9: Wilm 4A 98
Rookery Ri. CW7: Wins 4H 179
Rookery Rd. SY14: Tils 6B 206
Rookfield M33: Sale 6H 23
Rookfield Av. M33: Sale 6H 23
Rook St. CW2: Crewe 4C 194
Rooks Way CH60: Hes 6G 83
Rookwood Av. M23: Wyth 5F 49
Rookwood Hill SK7: Bram 4C 78
Roome St. WA2: Warr 5G 41
Rooth St. SK4: Stoc 2B 52
Rope Bank Av. CW2: Wis 7A 194
Rope La. CW2: Shav, Wis 7K 193
Rope Race (Indoor Climbing) *1F 81*
(within Goyt Mill)
Rope Wlk. CW12: Cong 3F 183
Ropewalk, The CH64: Park 6F 105
Ropewalks Sq. *L1: Liv* *4K 35*
(off Wood St.)
Ropeworks, The *CH1: Ches* *1J 149*
(off Whipcord La.)
Rosalind Av. CH63: H Beb 6D 60
Rosam Ct. WA7: Pal F 1A 112
Rosclare Dr. CH45: Wall 5F 13
Roscoe Av. WA2: Warr 4H 41
WA12: New W 1H 15
Roscoe Cres. WA7: Wes P 7E 88
Roscoe La. L1: Liv 4K 35
Roscoe Pl. L1: Liv 4K 35
Roscoe Rd. M44: Irlam 2B 20
Roscoe St. L1: Liv 4K 35
SK3: Stoc 4B 52
Roscommon Way WA8: Wid 2E 62
Roscote, The CH60: Hes 7H 83
Roscote Cl. CH60: Hes 7H 83
Roseacre CH48: W Kir 2B 56
Roseacre Dr. SK8: He Grn 4E 76
Roseate Ct. CH45: Wall 3E 12
Rose Av. M44: Irlam 2C 20
Rose Bank SK10: Boll 4C 122
WA13: Lymm 2A 70
Rose Bank Cl. SK14: H'rth 2J 11
Rosebank Cl. CW7: Wins 4G 179
Rosebank Rd. M44: Cad 7K 19
Rosebank Wlk. CW8: Barnt 1K 155
Roseberry St. SK2: Stoc 1H 79
Roseberry Way CW1: Hasl 2J 195
Rosebery Av. CH44: Wall 7J 13
Rosebery Gro. CH42: Tran 3A 60
Rosebrae Ct. CH41: Birk 5F 35
CH60: Hes 5J 83
Rose Cl. CH1: Blac 7E 144
WA7: Murd 2F 113
Rose Cotts. *M14: Manc* *3A 24*
(off Ladybarn La.)
Rose Ct. CH41: Birk 6C 34
Rose Cres. M44: Irlam 2C 20
WA8: Wid 6F 63
Rosecroft CH62: Brom 1H 107
Rosecroft Cl. SK3: Stoc 1C 78
Rosecroft Ct. CH47: Hoy 6B 30
Rosedale Av. WA1: Wool 5C 42
Rosedale Ct. M34: Den 7D 8
Rosedale Rd. CH42: Tran 2D 60
SK4: Stoc 6G 25
Rosedale Way SK16: Duk 4H 9
Rosedene Cl. CH2: Upt 2B 146
Rose Farm Ct. CW9: Winc 1K 157
Rosefield Av. CH63: H Beb 6D 60
Rosefield Cl. SK3: Stoc 7C 52
Rosefinch Rd. WA14: W Tim 3G 47
Rose Gdns. CH64: L Nes 2D 130
Rosegarth Av. M20: Manc 1K 49
Rosehay Av. M34: Den 1E 26
ROSEHILL 3G 73
Rose Hill L3: Liv 1J 35
M34: Den 7C 8
SK15: Stal 2A 10
Rose Hill Cl. OL6: Ash L 4A 4
Rose Hill Cres. OL6: Ash L 4A 4
Rose Hill Marple Station (Rail) 6D 54
Rose Hill Rd. OL6: Ash L 4A 4
Rosehill Rd. CW2: Crewe 5B 194
Roselands Av. M33: Sale 2K 47
Roselands Ct. CH42: R Fer 4D 60
LL12: Ross 7A 184
Rose La. SK6: Mar 6E 54
Rose Lea Cl. WA8: Wid 1G 63
Roselee Ct. CH42: R Fer 4F 61
Rose Leigh *M41: Urm* *1C 22*
(off Crofts Bank Rd.)
Roseleigh Av. M19: Manc 4C 24
Rosemary Av. WA4: Stoc H 3J 67
WA7: Beec 3B 112
Rosemary Cl. CH43: Bid 4H 33
WA5: Gt San 6A 40
Rosemary Dr. SK14: Hyde 4J 27
Rosemary La. SK1: Stoc 7K 213 (3E 52)
Rosemary Row CH3: Tatt 3G 187
Rosemary Wlk. *M31: Part* *2H 45*
(off Broom Rd.)
Rosemead Av. CH61: Pens 2H 83
Rosemead Ct. SK5: Stoc 5J 25
Rosemere Dr. CH1: Bac 2B 140
Rosemoor Gdns. WA4: App 1K 93
Rose Mt. CH43: Oxt 2A 60
WA2: Winw 3A 16
Rosemount *CW10: Mid* *3C 180*
(off Lewin St.)
SK14: Hyde 5J 9
Rosemount Cl. CH43: Oxt 2K 59
Rosemount Cres. SK14: Hyde 5H 9
Rose Mt. Dr. CH45: Wall 5G 13
Rosemount Pk. CH43: Oxt 1K 59
Roseneath SK7: Bram 4B 78
Roseneath Av. M19: Manc 2F 25
Roseneath Rd. M41: Urm 1B 22
Rose Pl. CH42: Tran 1C 60
L3: Liv 1J 35
(not continuous)
Rose St. L1: Liv 3J 35
SK5: Stoc 1D 52
WA8: Wid 6F 63
Rose Ter. CW1: Crewe 1C 194
SK15: Stal 1B 10
Rose Tree Mdw. CW9: Los Gra 5C 158
Rose Va. SK8: He Grn 4D 76
Rosevale Av. M19: Manc 6B 24
Rose Vw. Av. WA8: Wid 3G 63
Roseville Dr. CW12: Cong 6K 183
Roseville M. M33: Sale 7G 23
Rose Wlk. M31: Part 1G 45
SK6: Mar 6E 54
Roseway SK7: Bram 3D 78
SK11: Mac 7A 126
Rose Wharf SK11: Mac 5C 126
Rosewood M34: Den 7C 8
SK14: H'rth 2J 11
Rosewood Av. CH2: Ches 5A 146
SK4: Stoc 3J 51
WA1: Warr 5J 41
WA6: Frod 1K 139
Rosewood Cl. CW1: Crewe 7K 191
SK16: Duk 4J 9
WA8: Wid 5B 62
Rosewood Dr. CH46: More 4J 31
CW7: Wins 3B 178
Rosewood Farm Ct. WA8: Wid 7E 36
Rosewood Gdns. *M33: Sale* *1F 49*
(off Hart Av.)
SK8: Gat 6B 50
Rosewood Gro. CH1: Sau 1C 144
Rosewood Wlk. M23: Wyth 4C 48
Rosgill Cl. SK4: Stoc 2G 51
Roslin Ct. CH43: Oxt 1A 60
Roslin Rd. CH43: Oxt 1A 60
CH61: Irby 7A 58
Roslyn Av. M41: Urm 2H 21
Roslyn Rd. SK3: Stoc 7C 52
Roslyn St. CH42: Tran 2E 60
Rossall Av. M32: S'ord 1H 23
Rossall Cl. L24: Hale 6B 88
Rossall Ct. CH46: Leas 2C 32
SK7: Bram 7C 78
Rossall Dr. SK7: Bram 7C 78
Rossall Gro. CH66: L Sut 2K 133
Rossall Rd. CH46: More 3C 32
WA5: Gt San 1K 65
WA8: Wid 3K 63
Ross Av. CH46: Leas 7C 12
M19: Manc 2C 24
SK3: Stoc 7C 52
Rossbank Rd. CH65: Ell P 1C 134
Rosscliffe Rd. CH65: Ell P 1C 134
Ross Cl. WA5: Old H 5B 40
Ross Dr. CH66: Gt Sut 3J 133
Rossenclough Cl. SK9: Wilm 5K 97
Rossendale Cl. CH43: Noc 1G 59
Rossendale Dr. WA3: Birc 5B 18
Rossendale Rd. SK8: He Grn 5E 76
ROSSETT 2B 218
Rossett Av. M22: Wyth 5K 75
WA15: Timp 4A 48
Rossett Bus. Village LL12: Burt 7A 184
Rossett Cl. CW9: N'ich 2D 162
WA5: Call 2C 40
Rossetti Wlk. *M34: Den* *4F 27*
(off Wordsworth Rd.)
Rossfield Rd. CH65: Ell P 1C 134
Ross Gro. M41: Urm 1B 22
Rossington Pk. SK13: Had 1K 11
Rossington Pl. SK13: Had 2K 11
Rossiter Dr. CH43: Bid 6F 33
Rosslare Rd. M22: Wyth 3A 76
Ross Lave La. M34: Den 3A 26
SK5: Den 3A 26
Rosslave Wlk. SK5: Stoc 4B 26
Rosslyn Cres. CH46: More 4B 32
Rosslyn Dr. CH46: More 4B 32
Rosslyn Gro. WA15: Timp 6A 48
Rosslyn La. CW8: Cudd 3D 160
Rosslyn Pk. CH46: More 5B 32
Rosslyn Rd. CH3: Ches 7E 146
SK8: He Grn 4F 77
Rossmill La. WA15: H'rns 6B 74
Rossmore Bus. Pk. CH65: Ell P 1D 134
Rossmore Bus. Village CH65: Ell P 1D 134
Rossmore Ct. CH66: Ell P 2A 134
Rossmore Gdns. CH66: L Sut 2K 133
Rossmore Ind. Est. CH65: Ell P 1C 134
(not continuous)
Rossmore Rd. E. CH65: Ell P 1B 134
Rossmore Rd. W.
CH66: Ell P, L Sut 1K 133
Rossmore Trad. Est. CH65: Ell P 2C 134
Rossmount Rd. CH65: Ell P 2C 134
Ross Rd. CH65: Ell P 2C 134
Ross St. WA8: Wid 4H 63
Ross Twr. Ct. CH45: N Bri 3J 13
Rossview Ct. CH42: R Fer 3G 61
Rosswood Rd. CH65: Ell P 2C 134
ROSTHERNE 2B 216
Rostherne Av. CH44: Wall 1K 33
CH66: Gt Sut 4A 134
SK6: H Lan 5E 80
Rostherne Cl. WA5: Warr 1B 66
Rostherne Ct. WA14: Alt 2H 73
Rostherne Cres. WA8: Wid 3D 62
Rostherne Dr. WA16: Mere 5K 95
Rostherne Mere 7C 72
Rostherne Rd. M33: Sale 1F 49
SK3: Stoc 7C 52
SK9: Wilm 3E 118
Rostherne St. WA14: Alt 2H 73
Rostherne Way CW11: S'ach 2D 200
Rosthernmere Rd. SK8: Chea H 1H 77
Rostrevor Rd. SK3: Stoc 7C 52
(not continuous)
Rostron Brow SK1: Stoc 6J 213
Rostron St. M19: Manc 2E 24
Rosyth Cl. WA2: Fear 1K 41
Rothay Dr. SK5: Stoc 3J 25
WA5: Penk 2F 65
Rothbury Cl. CH46: More 4K 31
WA7: Beec 1A 112
Rothbury Ct. WA9: Sut M 2H 37
Rotherby Rd. M22: Shar 7A 50
Rotherdale Av. WA15: Timp 7D 48
Rother Dr. CH65: Ell P 1C 134
Rother Dr. Bus. Pk. CH65: Ell P 1C 134
Rotherhead Dr. SK11: Mac 7J 125
Rothermere Wlk. *M23: Wyth* *5E 48*
(off Sandy La.)
Rotherwood CH43: Noc 7G 33
Rotherwood Av. M32: S'ord 1K 23
Rotherwood Cl. CH63: H Beb 7C 60
Rotherwood Rd. SK9: Wilm 1B 118
Rothesay Av. SK16: Duk 3H 9
Rothesay Cl. WA7: Cast 4B 90
Rothesay Ct. CH63: Beb 2K 85
Rothesay Cres. M33: Sale 2G 47
Rothesay Dr. CH62: East 3K 107
Rothesay Gdns. CH43: Pren 4J 59
Rothesay Rd. CH4: Ches 4H 149
Rothiemay Rd. M41: Urm 2H 21
Rothley Av. M22: Wyth 7K 49
Rothsay Cl. L5: Liv 1K 35
Rottingdene Dr. M22: Wyth 4J 75
ROUGH CLOSE 3D 221
ROUGHCOTE 3D 221
Roughdale Av. WA9: Sut M 1H 37
Roughey Gdns. M22: Wyth 1K 75
Rough Heys La. SK11: Henb 4B 124
Roughlea Av. WA3: Cul 6D 6
Roughley Av. WA5: Warr 1B 66
Roughley Ho. *CH41: Birk* *5E 34*
(off Bridge St.)
ROUGHWOOD 1B 202
Roughwood La.
CW11: Hass, Ha Grn 7K 201
ST7: Chu L 1B 202
Roundabout, The WA8: Cron 6D 36
Roundcroft SK6: Rom 1E 54
Round Gdns. SK10: Boll 2D 122
Round Hey OL5: Moss 1D 4
Roundhey SK8: He Grn 5D 76
Round Hill Mdw. CH3: Gt Bou 4E 150
Round Mdw. SK10: R'ow 6G 123
ROUNDTHORN 6E 48
Round Thorn WA3: Croft 3F 17
Roundthorn Ind. Est. M23: Wyth 6E 48
(not continuous)
Roundthorn Rd. M23: Wyth 6F 49
Roundway SK7: Bram 7B 78
Roundwood Rd. M22: N'den 5K 49
Roundy La. SK10: Adl 6K 103
Routledge St. WA8: Wid 4H 63
Row, The CH47: Hoy 5C 30
Rowan Av. M33: Sale 2C 48
WA3: Low 4A 6
Rowan Cl. CW7: Wins 1E 178
CW8: Dela 3G 173
CW10: Mid 6E 180
CW11: S'ach 2D 200
ST7: Als 6E 202
ST7: Chu L 3D 202
WA5: Gt San 6H 39
WA7: Run 7J 89
Rowan Ct. CH49: Gre 3J 57
CH63: H Beb 7C 60
M14: Manc 4A 24
SK14: Hyde *2K 27*
(off Stockport Rd.)
Rowan Cres. SK16: Duk 3A 10
Rowan Dr. SK8: Chea H 5A 78
Rowan Gro. CH63: H Beb 2J 85

Rowan Lodge—Saffron Wlk.

Rowan Lodge SK7: Bram . . . 6D 78
Rowan Pk. CH3: Chri . . . 4H 151
Rowan Pl. CH2: Ches . . . 6E 146
Rowan Ri. CW8: Barnt . . . 2K 155
Rowan Rd. CW8: Weav . . . 5G 155
Rowans, The CW9: N'ich . . . 7D 156
OL5: Moss . . . 1E 4
WA8: Wid . . . 1K 63
(off Hampton Ct. Way)
Rowans Cl. CW1: Crewe . . . 6E 190
SK15: Stal . . . 6D 4
Rowanside SK10: Pres . . . 5F 121
Rowanside Dr. SK9: Wilm . . . 6B 98
Rowan St. SK14: Hyde . . . 2A 28
Rowanswood Dr. SK14: Hyde . . . 7B 10
Rowan Tree Cl. CH49: Gre . . . 2J 57
Rowan Tree Dr. M33: Sale . . . 3B 48
Rowan Tree Rd. WA16: Mob . . . 2A 118
Rowan Wlk. M31: Part . . . 2G 45
SK13: Had . . . 3K 11
Rowan Way SK10: Mac . . . 3B 126
ROWARTH . . . 2D 217
Rowarth Av. M34: Den . . . 3F 27
Rowarth Rd. M23: Wyth . . . 3F 75
Rowbotham St. SK14: Hyde . . . 3K 27
Rowcliffe Av. CH4: Ches . . . 7H 149
Rowcon Cl. M34: Aude . . . 5D 8
(not continuous)
Rowdell Wlk. M23: Wyth . . . 2H 49
Rowe Grn. M34: Den . . . 7E 8
Rowena Ct. CH2: Ches . . . 7C 146
Rowfield Dr. M23: Wyth . . . 2F 75
Rowland Av. M41: Urm . . . 1D 22
Rowland Cl. WA2: Fear . . . 1A 42
Rowlands Hgts. CH1: Ches . . . 2E 212
Rowlands Vw. CW6: Utk . . . 2B 176
Rowlandsway M22: Wyth . . . 3K 75
Rowley Dr. SK7: H Gro . . . 5J 79
Rowley Way WA16: Knut . . . 6F 117
ROW-OF-TREES . . . 4C 118
Rowood Av. SK5: Stoc . . . 1J 25
Rowsley Gro. SK5: Stoc . . . 4H 25
Rowsley Rd. M32: S'ord . . . 1F 23
Rowson Ct. *CH45: N Bri . . . 3H 13*
(off Pickering Rd.)
M33: Sale . . . 7J 23
(off Oak Rd.)
Rowson Dr. M44: Cad . . . 5A 20
Rowson St. CH45: N Bri . . . 2H 13
Rowthorn Cl. WA8: Wid . . . 5E 62
ROWTON . . . 6J 151 (1C 219)
Rowton Bri. Rd. CH3: Chri . . . 4H 151
Rowton Cl. CH43: Oxt . . . 2J 59
CW9: N'ich . . . 2E 162
Rowton La. CH3: Row . . . 5H 151
Rowton Rd. CW2: Crewe . . . 2H 193
Roxborough Cl. WA5: B'ood . . . 5D 14
Roxburgh Av. CH42: Tran . . . 3C 60
Roxburgh Cl. SK10: Mac . . . 3H 125
Roxburgh Rd. CH66: L Sut . . . 2F 133
Roxby Way WA16: Knut . . . 6E 116
Roxholme Wlk. M22: Wyth . . . 5J 75
Roxton Rd. SK4: Stoc . . . 5F 25
Royal, The CH47: Hoy . . . 6A 30
Royal Arc. *CW1: Crewe . . . 2C 194*
(off Tower Way)
Royal Av. M41: Urm . . . 1C 22
WA8: Wid . . . 5B 62
Royal Ct. *CH42: R Fer . . . 4F 61*
(off Rock La. W.)
CW9: Rud . . . 1J 163
SK11: Mac . . . 5B 126
Royal Court Theatre . . . 3J 35
Royal Cres. SK8: Chea . . . 3E 76
Royal Gdns. CW9: Dave . . . 3D 162
WA14: Bow . . . 3D 72
Royal George St. SK3: Stoc . . . 4C 52
Royal La. CW6: Eat . . . 6G 177
Royal Liverpool Golf Course . . . 7A 30
Royal London Bus. Pk.
WA5: W'ook . . . 1C 40
Royal Mail St. L3: Liv . . . 3K 35
Royal Mdws. SK10: Mac . . . 3H 125
Royal M. CW9: Rud . . . 1J 163
ROYAL OAK . . . 1C 215
Royal Oak Ind. Est. *SK1: Stoc . . . 5D 52*
(off Cooper St.)
Royal Oak Rd. M23: Wyth . . . 5F 49
(not continuous)
Royal Oak Yd. SK1: Stoc . . . 6J 213
Royal Pl. WA8: Wid . . . 5B 62
Royal Quay L3: Liv . . . 4H 35
Royal Rd. SK12: Dis . . . 2G 103
ROYAL'S GREEN . . . 3A 220
Royal Shop. Arc. CH64: Nest . . . 1C 130
Royal Standard Way CH42: Tran . . . 2E 60
Royalthorn Av. M22: Wyth . . . 6K 49
Royalthorn Dr. M22: Wyth . . . 6J 49
Royalthorn Rd. M22: Wyth . . . 6J 49
Royce Av. WA15: Alt . . . 7J 47
Royce Cl. CW1: Crewe . . . 6F 191
Royce Ct. WA16: Knut . . . 3E 116
Royden Av. CH44: Wall . . . 6K 13
M44: Irlam . . . 3C 20
WA7: Run . . . 6F 89
Royden Rd. CH49: Upt . . . 6B 32
(not continuous)
Royden Way L3: Liv . . . 2K 61
Royds Cl. CW8: H'ord . . . 1A 162
Roylance Dr. CW10: Mid . . . 4C 180
Royle Cl. SK2: Stoc . . . 7E 52
Royleen Dr. WA6: Frod . . . 2K 139
Royle Grn. Rd. M22: N'den . . . 4A 50
Royle Higginson Ct. M41: Urm . . . 2B 22
Royle Pk. CW12: Cong . . . 3F 183
Royles Cotts. M33: Sale . . . 1B 48
Royles Pl. CW8: N'ich . . . 7C 156
Royles Sq. *SK9: Ald E . . . 6F 119*
(off South St.)
Royle St. CW7: Wins . . . 3F 179
CW9: N'ich . . . 5G 157
CW12: Cong . . . 3F 183
M14: Manc . . . 4A 24
M34: Den . . . 5E 8
SK1: Stoc . . . 5D 52
Royley Carr Flats *SK6: Bred . . . 1K 53*
(off Field St.)
Royon Dr. SK3: Stoc . . . 5K 51
Royston Av. CH44: Wall . . . 7K 13
WA1: Padd . . . 5A 42
Royston Cl. CH66: Gt Sut . . . 5B 134
Royton Av. M33: Sale . . . 2E 48
Rozel Cres. WA5: Gt San . . . 1K 65
RUABON . . . 3B 218
Ruabon Rd. M20: Manc . . . 2E 50
Rubbing Stone CH48: Cald . . . 7E 56
Rubens Cl. SK6: Mar B . . . 4J 55
Rubin Dr. CW1: Crewe . . . 6E 190
Ruby St. M34: Den . . . 1D 26
Ruddpark Rd. M22: Wyth . . . 4K 75
Rudd St. CH47: Hoy . . . 5C 30
Rudgrave M. CH44: Wall . . . 6K 13
Rudgrave Pl. CH44: Wall . . . 6K 13
Rudgrave Sq. CH44: Wall . . . 6K 13
RUDHEATH . . . 7J 157 (3A 216)
Rudheath Cl. CW2: Crewe . . . 1H 193
Rudheath La. WA7: Nort . . . 3F 91
Rudheath Leisure Cen. . . . 6J 157
Rudheath Way CW9: Rud . . . 1J 163
Rudloe Ct. WA2: Padg . . . 3K 41
Rudman St. OL7: Ash L . . . 1F 9
Rudstone Cl. CH66: L Sut . . . 3H 133
RUDYARD . . . 2D 221
Rudyard Cl. SK11: Mac . . . 6J 125
Rudyard Gro. M33: Sale . . . 2J 47
SK4: Stoc . . . 5G 25
Rue De Bohars CW6: Tarp . . . 4J 175
Rufford Av. SK14: Hyde . . . 1A 28
Rufford Cl. CW2: Wis . . . 6B 194
WA8: Wid . . . 3C 62
Rufford Ct. WA1: Wool . . . 4E 42
Rufford Rd. CH44: Wall . . . 1B 34
Rufus Ct. CH1: Ches . . . 3B 212 (1K 149)
Rufus Ct. Row CH1: Ches . . . 3B 212
Rufus St. M14: Manc . . . 4B 24
Rugby Cl. SK10: Mac . . . 7B 122
Rugby Dr. M33: Sale . . . 2A 48
SK10: Mac . . . 1B 126
Rugby Ho. SK10: Mac . . . 1A 126
Rugby Pk. SK4: Stoc . . . 3G 51
Rugby Rd. CH44: Wall . . . 6F 13
CH65: Ell P . . . 5E 134
Rugby Wlk. CH65: Ell P . . . 5F 135
Ruislip Ct. WA2: Padg . . . 3K 41
Rullerton Rd. CH44: Wall . . . 7G 13
RULOE . . . 5K 153
Rumford Pl. L3: Liv . . . 2H 35
Rumford St. L2: Liv . . . 2H 35
RUNCORN . . . 3G 89 (2D 215)
Runcorn Dock Rd. WA7: Run . . . 4E 88
Runcorn East Station (Rail) . . . 7F 91
Runcorn Hill Local Nature Reserve . . . 6F 89
Runcorn Hill Vis. Cen. . . . 6F 89
Runcorn Rd.
CW8: Barnt, L Lei . . . 7A 114 & 1H 155
WA4: Dare, H Wal, Moo . . . 2H 91
Runcorn Ski & Snowboard Cen. . . . 7D 90
Runcorn Spur Rd. WA7: Run . . . 4H 89
Runcorn Station (Rail) . . . 4F 89
Runcorn Swimming Pool . . . 3H 89
Rundle St. CH41: Birk . . . 4K 33
Runger La. M90: Man A . . . 6F 75
Runnell, The CH64: Nest . . . 4G 105
Runnymead Wlk. *WA8: Wid . . . 3J 63*
(off William St.)
Runnymede WA1: Wool . . . 5D 42
Runnymede Cl. SK3: Stoc . . . 5A 52
Runnymede Ct. SK3: Stoc . . . 6A 52
WA8: Wid . . . 4J 63
(off William St.)
Runnymede Gdns. *WA8: Wid . . . 4J 63*
(off Cliffe St.)
Rupert Row WA7: Cast . . . 6C 90
Rupert St. SK5: Stoc . . . 4H 25
Rupert Ter. SK5: Stoc . . . 4H 25
Ruscoe Av. CW11: S'ach . . . 3C 200
Ruscolm Cl. WA5: Gt San . . . 5F 39
Rushall Wlk. M23: Wyth . . . 3F 75
Rushden Rd. M19: Manc . . . 1E 24
Rushes Mdw. WA13: Lymm . . . 7D 44
Rushey Av. M22: Wyth . . . 6J 49
Rushey Cl. WA15: H'rns . . . 6D 74
Rushey Rd. M22: Wyth . . . 7J 49
Rushfield Cres. WA7: B'vale . . . 2D 112
Rushfield Dr. M13: Manc . . . 1C 24
Rushfield Rd. CH4: Ches . . . 6J 149
SK8: Chea H . . . 7J 77
Rushford Av. M19: Manc . . . 1D 24
Rushford Ct. *M19: Manc . . . 1D 24*
(off Rushford Av.)
RUSHFORD PARK . . . 1D 24
Rushford St. M12: Manc . . . 1D 24
Rush Gdns. WA13: Lymm . . . 1C 70
RUSHGREEN . . . 1C 70
Rushgreen Cl. CH43: Bid . . . 5F 33
Rushgreen Rd. WA13: Lymm . . . 1B 70
Rushmere Av. M19: Manc . . . 2E 24
Rushmere Cl. SK10: W Grn . . . 1C 122
Rushmere La. CH3: Ald . . . 6G 185
Rushmoor Cl. M44: Irlam . . . 1D 20
Rushmore Dr. WA8: Wid . . . 2F 63
Rushmore Gro. WA1: Padd . . . 5A 42
RUSHOLME . . . 1C 217
Rusholme Gdns. *M14: Manc . . . 1A 24*
(off Wilmslow Rd.)
Rusholme Gro. M14: Manc . . . 1A 24
Rushside Rd. SK8: Chea H . . . 7H 77
Rush St. SK16: Duk . . . 2A 10
RUSHTON . . . 4J 177 (1D 219)
Rushton Cl. CW9: N'ich . . . 6H 157
SK6: Mar . . . 7G 55
WA5: B'ood . . . 4C 14
WA8: Wid . . . 2F 63
Rushton Dr. CH2: Upt . . . 3B 146
CW2: Hou . . . 5E 198
CW10: Mid . . . 5C 180
SK6: Mar . . . 1F 81
SK6: Rom . . . 1C 54
SK7: Bram . . . 3B 78
Rushton Fold SK10: Mot A . . . 1B 120
Rushton Gdns. SK7: Bram . . . 2B 78
Rushton La. CW6: Oul . . . 7D 176 & 3F 177
Rushton Rd. SK3: Stoc . . . 5K 51
SK8: Chea H . . . 7J 77
Rushtons, The CH66: L Sut . . . 1J 133
RUSHTON SPENCER . . . 1D 221
Rushton St. M20: Manc . . . 2D 50
Rushworth Ct. SK4: Stoc . . . 6F 25
Rushycroft SK14: Mot . . . 6H 11
Rushyfield Cres. SK6: Rom . . . 1D 54
Ruskin Av. CH42: R Fer . . . 4E 60
CH44: Wall . . . 1K 33
M34: Aude . . . 3B 8
M34: Den . . . 2C 26
WA2: Warr . . . 2G 41
Ruskin Ct. WA16: Knut . . . 3E 116
Ruskin Dr. CH65: Ell P . . . 5F 135
M33: Sale . . . 7B 22
Ruskin Gdns. SK6: Bred . . . 1A 54
Ruskin Gro. SK6: Bred . . . 1A 54
Ruskin Rd. CW2: Crewe . . . 3C 194
CW12: Cong . . . 4E 182
SK5: Stoc . . . 2H 25
Ruskin Way CH43: Noc . . . 2G 59
WA16: Knut . . . 2E 116
Rusland Av. CH61: Pens . . . 2H 83
Rusland Ct. M33: Sale . . . 6F 23
SK2: Stoc . . . 5F 53
(off Sylvester Av.)
Rusland Wlk. M22: Wyth . . . 3J 75
Russell Av. M33: Sale . . . 6J 23
SK6: H Lan . . . 6E 80
ST7: Als . . . 4E 202
Russell Cl. CW12: Cong . . . 6H 183
Russell Ct. WA8: Wid . . . 1H 63
Russell Dr. CW1: Hasl . . . 1J 195
M44: Irlam . . . 1D 20
Russell Fox Ct. *SK5: Stoc . . . 4H 25*
(off Broadstone Rd.)
Russell Gdns. SK4: Stoc . . . 3K 51
Russell Pl. M33: Sale . . . 6G 23
Russell Rd. CH42: R Fer . . . 2E 60
(not continuous)
CH44: Wall . . . 6E 12
CW7: Wins . . . 4D 178
M31: Part . . . 1J 45
WA7: Run . . . 5E 88
Russell St. CH3: Ches . . . 3E 212 (1B 150)
CH41: Birk . . . 5D 34
L3: Liv . . . 3K 35
SK2: Stoc . . . 6E 52
SK6: Comp . . . 1H 55
SK14: Hyde . . . 7J 9
SK16: Duk . . . 2H 9
Russet Cl. CW10: Mid . . . 2B 180
Russet Rd. CW8: Weav . . . 5G 155
Russet Way SK9: Ald E . . . 4D 118
Rutherford Cl. SK14: Hyde . . . 1H 27
Rutherford Dr. WA16: Knut . . . 6G 117
Rutherford Way SK14: Hyde . . . 1J 27
Ruthin Av. SK8: Chea H . . . 3G 77
Ruthin Cl. WA5: Call . . . 1C 40
Ruthin Ct. CH65: Ell P . . . 5F 135
Ruthin Wlk. WA6: Hel . . . 7A 138
Rutland Av. M34: Den . . . 1F 27
M41: Urm . . . 1D 22
WA4: Walt . . . 5F 67
Rutland Cl. CW11: Ett H . . . 4A 200
CW12: Cong . . . 2G 183
OL6: Ash L . . . 1J 9
SK8: Gat . . . 6D 50
Rutland Ct. SK2: Stoc . . . 7E 52
Rutland Cres. SK5: Stoc . . . 6C 26
Rutland Dr. CW8: Weav . . . 4F 155
CW10: Mid . . . 5C 180
Rutland La. M33: Sale . . . 7K 23
(not continuous)
Rutland Pl. CH2: Ches . . . 5D 146
Rutland Rd. M31: Part . . . 2G 45
M44: Cad . . . 6A 20
SK7: H Gro . . . 5J 79
SK11: Mac . . . 1G 129
WA14: Alt . . . 6H 47
Rutland St. OL6: Ash L . . . 1J 9
SK14: Hyde . . . 5J 9
WA7: Run . . . 4F 89
Rutter Av. WA5: Warr . . . 2D 40
Rutter's La. SK7: H Gro . . . 3G 79
Rutter St. L8: Liv . . . 7K 35
Ryburn Cl. CW2: West . . . 4H 199
Ryburn Rd. SK11: Mac . . . 7H 125
Rycroft Rd. CH44: Wall . . . 1B 34
CH47: Meols . . . 4F 31
Rydal Av. CH43: Noc . . . 7F 33
M33: Sale . . . 6E 22
M41: Urm . . . 3K 21
SK6: H Lan . . . 5E 80
SK7: H Gro . . . 2G 79
SK14: Hyde . . . 1F 9
WA4: Warr . . . 3E 66
Rydal Bank CH44: Wall . . . 7J 13
CH63: Beb . . . 6F 61
Rydal Cl. CH61: Pens . . . 2H 83
CH64: L Nes . . . 2D 130
CH65: Ell P . . . 6E 134
CW4: H Cha . . . 5H 181
CW7: Wins . . . 1E 178
M34: Den . . . 1A 26
SK8: Gat . . . 1D 76
Rydal Ct. CW12: Cong . . . 4C 182
Rydal Dr. WA15: H'rns . . . 5D 74
Rydal Gro. CH4: Ches . . . 5H 149
WA6: Hel . . . 7B 138
WA7: Run . . . 6H 89
Rydal Mt. CW1: L'ton . . . 4G 191
SK5: Stoc . . . 1J 25
SK9: Ald E . . . 4D 118
Rydal Pl. SK11: Mac . . . 6H 125
Rydal St. WA12: New W . . . 1F 15
Rydal Wlk. SK15: Stal . . . 6B 4
Rydal Way ST7: Als . . . 4D 202
WA8: Wid . . . 4C 62
Ryde Av. M34: Den . . . 3G 27
SK4: Stoc . . . 2K 51
Ryde Cl. CW1: Crewe . . . 5G 191
Ryder Av. WA14: Alt . . . 5J 47
RYDER BROW . . . 1F 25
Ryder Cl. L35: R'ill . . . 1A 36
Ryder Rd. WA1: Wool . . . 4C 42
WA8: Wid . . . 1H 63
Ryders St. CW8: N'ich . . . 5D 156
Ryebank Av. CW1: Crewe . . . 6G 191
Ryebank Way SK10: Mac . . . 1K 125
Ryeburn Av. M22: Wyth . . . 2K 75
Rye Cl. ST7: Als . . . 6C 202
WA9: Clo F . . . 1J 37
Ryecroft CH2: Elt . . . 5F 137
Ryecroft Bus. Cen. *OL7: Ash L . . . 1E 8*
(off Ryecroft St.)
Ryecroft Cl. CW10: Mid . . . 5B 180
RYECROFT GATE . . . 1D 221
Ryecroft Gro. M23: Wyth . . . 5G 49
Ryecroft Ho. *OL7: Ash L . . . 1F 9*
(off Park St.)
Ryecroft La. CH3: Tar . . . 5A 174
M34: Aude . . . 3D 8
WA16: Mob . . . 1J 117
Ryecroft Pk. Sports Club . . . 4H 77
Ryecroft Rd. CH60: Hes . . . 7A 84
M32: S'ord . . . 2H 23
Ryecroft St. OL7: Ash L . . . 1E 8
Ryecroft Vw. M34: Aude . . . 2B 8
Ryedale Cl. SK4: Stoc . . . 1K 51
Ryedale Way CW12: Cong . . . 6K 183
Ryefield OL7: Ash L . . . 1E 8
Ryefield Cl. WA15: Timp . . . 7C 48
Ryefield Rd. M33: Sale . . . 2G 47
Ryfields Village WA2: Warr . . . 4H 41
Ryland Cl. SK5: Stoc . . . 2J 25
Ryland Pk. CH61: Thin . . . 1J 83
Rylands Cl. SY14: Mal . . . 2H 207
Rylands Dr. WA2: Warr . . . 5G 41
Rylands Hey CH49: Gre . . . 1A 58
Rylands St. WA1: Warr . . . 7F 41
WA8: Wid . . . 5H 63
Rylatt Ct. *M33: Sale . . . 6E 22*
(off Ashton La.)
Ryles Cl. SK11: Mac . . . 7K 125
Ryles Cres. SK11: Mac . . . 7K 125
Ryles Ho. SK11: Mac . . . 7K 125
Ryle's Pk. Rd. SK11: Mac . . . 7K 125
Ryle St. SK11: Mac . . . 6A 126
Ryleys Gdns. *L2: Liv . . . 2H 35*
(off Tempest Hey)
Ryleys La. SK9: Ald E . . . 6E 118
Rylstone Av. M21: Chor H . . . 1K 49

S

Sabre Cl. WA7: Murd . . . 7F 91
Sack St. SK14: Hyde . . . 5J 9
Saddleback Dr. SK10: Pres . . . 4G 121
Saddlers Ri. WA7: Nort . . . 6E 90
Saddler's Way SK11: Mac . . . 5H 127
Saddlery Way CH1: Ches . . . 2J 149
Saddlestone Gro. L8: Liv . . . 7K 35
Saddlewood Av. M19: Manc . . . 2F 51
Sadler Cl. CW7: Wins . . . 3E 178
Sadler Rd. CW7: Wins . . . 3E 178
Sadler's Cl. CW4: H Cha . . . 4H 181
Sadlers La. CW6: Cote . . . 4B 176
Sadler St. WA8: Wid . . . 4J 63
Sadlers Wells CW6: Bun . . . 6C 188
Saffron Cl. WA2: Padg . . . 3B 42
Saffron Wlk. M22: Wyth . . . 5K 75
M31: Part . . . 2H 45
(off Cross La. W.)

Sagars Rd.—St Paul's Cl.

Sagars Rd. SK9: Styal 2J **97**
Sage Cl. WA2: Padg 2C **42**
SAIGHTON 1C **219**
Saighton La. CH3: Sai, Wave 4A **174**
St Agnes Rd. M13: Manc 1C **24**
St Agnes St. SK5: Stoc 1J **25**
St Aidans Ct. CH43: Clau 6J **33**
WA9: Clo F 1A **38**
St Aidans Dr. WA8: Wid 6F **37**
St Aidan's Ter. CH43: Clau 6J **33**
St Alban Rd. WA5: Penk 7G **39**
St Alban's Av. SK4: Stoc 6F **25**
St Alban's Cres. WA14: W Tim 4G **47**
St Albans Dr. CW5: Nant 4D **196**
St Albans Rd. CH43: Clau 5K **33**
CH44: Wall 7H **13**
St Aldates SK6: Rom 2K **53**
St Ambrose Ct. *WA4: Warr 3F 67*
(off Boswell Av.)
St Ambrose Rd. WA8: Wid 4J **63**
St Ambrose Way *L5: Liv 1K 35*
(off Everton Brow)
St Andrew's Av. CW2: Crewe 5C **194**
WA15: Timp 5J **47**
St Andrews Cl. CW9: Rud 6K **157**
M33: Sale 3G **47**
SK4: Stoc 7E **24**
SK6: Rom 3B **54**
SK13: Had 3K **11**
WA2: Fear 7F **17**
St Andrews Ct. CH43: Noc 6G **33**
CH65: Ell P 6G **135**
CW2: Crewe 5C 194
(off St Andrew's Av.)
SK1: Stoc 3E **52**
SK11: Mac 5J 125
(off Brough St. W.)
SK13: Had 3K **11**
WA15: Hale 2K **73**
St Andrews Dr. CW4: H Cha 5H **181**
St Andrews Gdns. L3: Liv 2K **35**
ST7: Als 7F **203**
St Andrews Rd. CH43: Oxt 6A **34**
CH63: Beb 2A **86**
CH65: Ell P 5F **135**
M32: S'ord 1G **23**
SK4: Stoc 7E **24**
SK8: He Grn 4E **76**
SK11: Mac 5J **125**
St Andrew St. L3: Liv 3K **35**
St Andrews Wlk. CH2: Mic T 1J **147**
St Annes CH1: Ches 2C **212** (1A **150**)
St Annes Av. CW10: Mid 4C **180**
WA4: Grap 3B **68**
St Anne's Av. E. WA4: Grap 3B **68**
St Annes Cl. CH41: Birk 5C **34**
St Annes Ct. *L3: Liv 1K 35*
(off St Anne St.)
M33: Sale 7H **23**
M34: Aude 4D **8**
St Anne's Dr. M34: Den 6F **9**
St Annes Gro. CH41: Birk 4B **34**
St Anne's La. CW5: Nant 2B **196**
St Annes Pl. CH2: Ches 2B **212**
CH41: Birk 4B **34**
St Annes Rd. M34: Aude 4E **8**
M34: Den 5E **8**
WA8: Wid 3H **63**
St Annes St. *SK14: B'tom 3H 29*
(off Lwr. Market St.)
St Annes Ter. CH41: Birk 4B **34**
St Anne St. CH1: Ches 2C **212** (1A **150**)
(not continuous)
CH41: Birk 4B **34**
(not continuous)
L3: Liv 1K **35**
St Annes Way CH41: Birk 5C **34**
St Ann Pl. L35: R'ill 1C **36**
St Anns Pde. SK9: Wilm 7J **97**
St Anns Rd. CW10: Mid 3B **180**
SK7: H Gro 3G **79**
St Ann's Rd. Nth. SK8: He Grn 4E **76**
St Ann's Rd. Sth. SK8: He Grn 4E **76**
St Ann's Sq. SK8: He Grn 5E **76**
St Ann's St. M33: Sale 1F **49**
St Ann's Wlk. *CW10: Mid 3C 180*
(off Beech St.)
St Anthony Pl. WA2: Winw 5A **16**
St Asaph Dr. WA5: Call 1B **40**
St Asaph Rd. CH66: Gt Sut 1A **140**
St Augustine's Av. WA4: Westy 1K **67**
St Augustines Dr. *CW2: West 4K 199*
(off Abbey Pk. Way)
St Augustine's Rd. SK3: Stoc 4K **51**
St Austell Av. SK10: Mac 3E **124**
St Austell Cl. CH46: More 3J **31**
WA5: Penk 2G **65**
WA7: B'vale 1D **112**
St Austell Dr. SK8: He Grn 5D **76**
St Austins La. WA1: Warr 1F **67**
St Barnabas Ct. SK11: Mac 6A **126**
St Barnabas Pl. WA5: Warr 6C **40**
St Bartholomew Rd. L3: Liv 1J **35**
St Bede's Av. CW8: Weav 4G **155**
St Bedes Vw. WA8: Wid 4G **63**
St Bees Cl. SK8: Gat 2D **76**
St Benedict's Cl. WA2: Warr 5F **41**
St Brannocks Rd. SK8: Chea H 6K **77**
St Brides Cl. WA5: Penk 2G **65**
St Bride's Rd. CH44: Wall 6K **13**
St Bridgets Cl. WA2: Fear 1K **41**
WA8: Wid 1G **89**
St Bridgets Ct. CH4: Ches 5J **149**
St Bridget's La. CH48: W Kir 4C **56**
St Catherine Dr. CW8: H'ord 2J **161**
St Catherines Gdns. CH42: Tran 1C **60**
St Chads Av. SK6: Rom 2C **54**
St Chads Cl. CW5: Wyb 7A **198**
St Chad's Flds. CW7: Wins 7D **178**
St Chads Gro. SK6: Rom 2C **54**
St Chads Hamlet CH1: Blac 6G **145**
St Chads Rd. CH1: Blac 6G **145**
M20: Manc 4A **24**
St Charles Cl. SK13: Had 2K **11**
St Christophers Cl. CH2: Upt 2A **146**
St Christopher's Dr. SK6: Rom 2A **54**
St Christophers Ho. *SK1: Stoc 5D 52*
(off Wellington Rd. Sth.)
St Clair St. CW2: Crewe 5D **194**
St Clement Cl. *M41: Urm 2C 22*
(off Manor Av.)
St Clements Ct. CW2: West 6H **199**
M44: Irlam 1E **20**
SK11: Mac 6A 126
(off Hobson St.)
St Clements Fold M41: Urm 1D **22**
St Columba's Cl. CH44: Wall 6K **13**
St David Rd. CH43: Clau 6K **33**
CH62: East 1B **108**
St Davids Av. SK6: Rom 2B **54**
St Davids Cl. L35: R'ill 1C **36**
M33: Sale 1A **48**
St Davids Dr. C66: Gt Sut 1B **140**
WA5: Call 2C **40**
St Davids La. CH43: Noc 7G **33**
St David's Retail Pk. CH4: Salt 4E **148**
St Davids Rd. SK7: H Gro 4G **79**
SK8: Chea 7J **51**
St David's Ter. CH4: Salt F 4D **148**
St David's Wlk. M32: S'ord 1F **23**
St Edmunds Ho. CH65: Ell P 4G **135**
St Edmund's Rd. CH63: Beb 1K **85**
St Edwards Cl. CH41: Birk 4A **34**
SK11: Mac 6A **126**
St Edwards M. *CH41: Birk 4A 34*
(off Old Bidston Rd.)
St Elisabeth's Way SK5: Stoc 4H **25**
St Elizabeth Pk. M34: Den 7C **8**
St Elmo Av. SK2: Stoc 5H **53**
St Elmo Pk. SK12: Poy 2H **101**
St Elmo Rd. CH44: Wall 6K **13**
St Elphins Cl. WA1: Warr 7G **41**
St Gabriels Ct. ST7: Als 6D **202**
St George's CH1: Ches 2D **212** (1A **150**)
St Georges Av. CH42: Tran 3C **60**
CH66: Gt Sut 1B **140**
WA15: Timp 5A **48**
St Georges Cl. WA4: App 3J **93**
WA16: Knut 5G **117**
St Georges Ct. *CW2: West 4K 199*
(off Abbey Pk. Way)
M32: S'ord 2H **23**
SK14: Hyde 1K **27**
WA8: Wid 5D **62**
WA14: B'ath 5F **47**
St George's Cres. CH3: Wave 2A **174**
CH4: Ches 6E **212** (3B **150**)
WA15: Timp 4A **48**
St Georges Dr. SK14: Hyde 2J **27**
St George's Gdns. M34: Den 2F **27**
St George's Gro. CH46: More 4A **32**
St George's Ho. *SK15: Stal 7B 4*
(off Cambridge St.)
St George's Mt. CH45: N Bri 3H **13**
St George's Pk. CH45: N Bri 3H **13**
St George's Pl. L1: Liv 2J **35**
SK11: Mac 6A **126**
St Georges Rd. CH45: Wall 5E **12**
CW7: Wins 4D **178**
M14: Manc 4B **24**
M31: Carri 5G **21**
M32: S'ord 1H **23**
St George's St. SK11: Mac 6A **126**
SK15: Stal 6A **4**
St George's Way CH63: Tho H 1K **105**
CW9: N'ich 1E **162**
L1: Liv 3J 35
(off St John's Cen.)
St Giles *CH3: Ches 2C 150*
(off Sandy La.)
St Giles Dr. SK14: Hyde 1A **28**
ST HELENS 1C **215**
St Helens Cl. CH43: Clau 6A **34**
WA3: Rix 1D **44**
St Helens Linkway L35: R'ill 3F **37**
WA9: St H 1F **37**
St Helens Rd. CW9: N'ich 5F **157**
WN7: Leigh 2B **6**
St Helier Sq. M19: Manc 6C **24**
SK4: Manc 6C **24**
St Hilary Brow CH44: Wall 7F **13**
St Hilary Dr. CH45: Wall 6F **13**
St Hilarys Pk. SK9: Ald E 6F **119**
St Hilda's Cl. M22: N'den 3A **50**
St Hilda's Dr. WA6: Frod 6J **111**
St Hilda's Rd. M22: N'den 3K **49**
M34: Aude 4D **8**
St Hilda's Vw. M34: Aude 5D **8**
St Hugh's Cl. CH43: Clau 6A **34**
WA14: Timp 4J **47**
St Ives Av. SK8: Chea 6J **51**
St Ives Cl. SK10: Mac 3F **125**
St Ives Ct. CH43: Clau 5K **33**
St Ives Cres. M33: Sale 3A **48**
St Ives Rd. CH43: Clau 6K **33**
St James Av. CH2: Upt 3C **146**
CW12: Cong 4E **182**
SK11: Gaw 3B **128**
St James Cl. CH49: Gre 1A **58**
CW3: Audl 5C **210**
WA6: Frod 6H **111**
St James Ct.
CH45: N Bri 3H 13
(off Victoria Rd.)
CW12: Cong 4E **182**
M20: Manc 1D 50
(off Moorland Rd.)
M20: Manc 3D **50**
(Millgate La.)
SK8: Chea H 7H **77**
SK14: Hat 1E **28**
WA4: Warr 1F **67**
WA15: Alt 2K **213** (1J **73**)
St James Dr. M33: Sale 1A **48**
SK9: Wilm 1F **119**
St James Gro. WA14: Timp 3K **47**
St James Ho. SK4: Stoc 1B **52**
St James Lodge *SK3: Stoc 1E 78*
(off The Crescent)
St James Mt. L35: R'ill 2C **36**
St James Pl. L8: Liv 5K **35**
St James Rd. CH41: Birk 4J **33**
CH45: N Bri 3H **13**
L1: Liv 5K **35**
L35: R'ill 2C **36**
SK4: Stoc 6E **24**
St James St. CH1: Ches 2D **212** (1A **150**)
L1: Liv 5J **35**
St James Ter. *CW7: Wins 4B 178*
(off Cavendish Cl.)
St James Wlk. *CW8: N'ich 6D 156*
(off Beeston St.)
St James Way CW8: H'ord 1B **162**
SK8: Chea H 7H **77**
St John Av. WA4: Warr 3F **67**
St John's Av. CW9: Los Gra 4B **158**
WA16: Knut 4D **116**
St Johns Brow WA7: Run 3H **89**
St John's Cen. L1: Liv 3J **35**
St Johns Cl. CH47: Meols 4E **30**
CW9: Rud 6K **157**
SK6: Rom 2B **54**
SK16: Duk 2K **9**
St Johns Ct. CH1: Ches 4D **212**
CW7: Wins 3C **178**
SK14: Hyde 7A **10**
WA1: Warr 5K 41
(off Grantham Av.)
WA14: Bow 2H **73**
WA16: Knut 3G 117
(off Churchfields)
St Johns Dr. CW7: Wins 4B **178**
SK14: Hyde 7A **10**
St Johns Ho. CH65: Ell P 3G **135**
St John's La. L1: Liv 2J **35**
St John's Pavement CH41: Birk 6C **34**
St John's Pl. SK4: Stoc 2G **51**
St John's Rear Rd.
CH4: Ches 6E **212** (3B **150**)
St Johns Rd. CH4: Ches 6E **212** (3B **150**)
CH45: Wall 6E **12**
CH62: East 2B **108**
CW12: Cong 2H **183**
M34: Den 5E **8**
SK4: Stoc 2G **51**
SK7: H Gro 4F **79**
SK9: Wilm 4D **118**
SK11: Mac 5K **125**
WA14: Alt 4G **213** (2G **73**)
WA16: Knut 4D **116**
St John's Sq. CH41: Birk 6C **34**
L1: Liv 3J 35
(off St John's Cen.)
St Johns Ter. CH1: Ches 2A **212**
St John St. CH1: Ches 4D **212** (2A **150**)
CH41: Birk 6C **34**
M44: Irlam 1D **20**
SK16: Duk 2K **9**
(not continuous)
WA7: Run 3H **89**
St Johns Vs. WA8: Wid 3D **62**
St Johns Wlk. *SK3: Stoc 4K 51*
(off Oak St.)
St John's Way CW8: S'way 4D **160**
CW11: S'ach 3J **201**
L1: Liv 3J 35
(off St John's Cen.)
St Joseph's Cl. WA5: Penk 7G **39**
St Josephs Cres. L3: Liv 1K **35**
St Josephs Way CW5: Nant 2E **196**
St Katherines Way WA1: Warr 7H **41**
St Kilda Cl. CH65: Ell P 7E **134**
St Kilda's Rd. CH46: More 5B **32**
St Laurence Cl. CH41: Birk 5C **34**
St Laurence Dr. CH41: Birk 5C **34**
St Lawrence Cl. CW5: Nant 1D **196**
M34: Den 1E **26**
St Lawrence Rd. M34: Den 7E **8**
WA6: Frod 1H **139**
St Leonard's Ct. M33: Sale 7E **22**
St Leonards Dr. WA15: Timp 6K **47**
St Leonards Rd. SK4: Stoc 6G **25**
St Lesmo Ct. SK3: Stoc 5A **52**
St Lesmo Rd. SK3: Stoc 4K **51**
St Lucia Rd. CH44: Wall 6K **13**
St Lukes Cl. CW4: H Cha 4K **181**
St Lukes Cres. SK16: Duk 2H **9**
WA8: Wid 1H **63**
St Luke's Ho. SK10: Mac 4G **125**
St Lukes Pl. L1: Liv 4K **35**
St Luke's Way WA6: Frod 6H **111**
St Margaret's Av. M19: Manc 5C **24**
WA2: Warr 3H **41**
St Margarets Cl. WA14: Alt 2F **213** (1G **73**)
St Margaret's Rd. CH47: Hoy 6B **30**
SK8: Chea 6J **51**
WA14: Alt 3F **213** (1G **73**)
St Mark's Av. WA14: Alt 7E **46**
St Marks Ct. CH43: Oxt 7A **34**
M22: Wyth 3J 75
(off Stoneacre Rd.)
SK16: Duk 1G **9**
St Marks Cres. CH66: Gt Sut 1B **140**
St Mark's Rd. CH4: Ches 5G **149**
St Marks St. M19: Manc 2F **25**
SK6: Bred 7F **27**
SK16: Duk 1G **9**
ST MARTIN'S 3B **218**
St Martin's Av. SK4: Stoc 2A **52**
St Martin's Cl. SK14: Hyde 1B **28**
St Martins Dr. CH66: Gt Sut 6K **133**
St Martin's La. WA7: Murd 7F **91**
St Martins Rd. M33: Sale 5C **22**
SK6: Mar 6G **55**
St Martin's Way CH1: Ches 3A **212** (1K **149**)
St Mary's Av. CH44: Wall 7H **13**
CW8: Weav 4G **155**
M34: Den 3F **27**
St Mary's Cl. L24: Hale 6A **88**
St Marys' Cl. SK1: Stoc 6K **213** (3E **52**)
St Mary's Cl. ST7: Als 4D **202**
WA4: App 7G **67**
St Marys Ct. CH49: Upt 1D **58**
CW5: Act 6K **189**
CW12: Cong 4C **182**
M19: Manc 2D 24
(off Elbow St.)
WA3: Low 1B **6**
St Mary's Dr. CW8: W'ate 6J **161**
SK5: Stoc 5J **25**
SK8: Chea 6H **51**
St Mary's Ga. CH41: Birk 6E **34**
SK1: Stoc 6K **213** (2D **52**)
St Mary's Grn. WA1: Warr 7G **41**
St Mary's Hill CH1: Ches 6C **212** (3A **150**)
St Marys Ind. Pk. SK14: Hyde 4B **10**
St Marys Rd. CH4: Dod 3D **184**
CW5: Nant 7C **192**
M33: Sale 6E **22**
SK12: Dis 2G **103**
SK14: Hyde 5K **9**
WA5: Gt San, Penk 7H **39**
WA7: Halt 5B **90**
WA8: Wid 2G **89**
WA14: Bow 3F **73**
(not continuous)
St Mary's St. CH44: Wall 7H **13**
CW1: Crewe 2C **194**
WA4: Warr 1G **67**
St Mary's Vw. *SK14: Hyde 5A 10*
(off Bradley Grn. Rd.)
St Marys Way SK1: Stoc 2E **52**
St Matthews Cl. CW1: Hasl 2K **195**
WA4: App 6H **67**
St Matthews Ct. M32: S'ord 2H **23**
St Matthew's Rd. SK3: Stoc 4B **52**
St Matthew's Ter. SK3: Stoc 4B **52**
St Mawes Cl. WA8: Wid 3E **62**
St Mawes Ct. SK10: Mac 3F **125**
St Mawgan Ct. WA2: Padg 2K **41**
St Michael's Av. SK7: Bram 6C **78**
St Michael's Cl. CW8: L Lei 1G **155**
WA8: Wid 6C **62**
St Michaels Ct. M33: Sale 5D **22**
St Michael's Gro. CH46: More 4A **32**
St Michael's Ind. Est. WA8: Wid 6C **62**
St Michaels Pk. CH62: P Sun 7G **61**
St Michaels Rd. SK14: Hyde 1B **28**
WA8: Wid 6C **62**
WA9: St H 1G **37**
St Michael's Row
CH1: Ches 5C **212** (2A **150**)
St Michael's Sq. CH1: Ches 5C **212**
St Michaels Ter. *SK10: Mac 4A 126*
(off Churchside)
St Michael's Vw. *CW1: Crewe 1B 194*
(off Rigg St.)
WA8: Wid 6D **62**
St Michael's Way CW10: Mid 3C **180**
St Monica's Cl. WA4: App 6J **67**
St Nicholas Pl. L3: Liv 3G **35**
(not continuous)
St Nicholas Rd. CH45: Wall 6D **12**
WA3: Low 1A **6**
St Olave St. CH1: Ches 6C **212** (3A **150**)
St Oswald's CH1: Ches 2C **212** (1A **150**)
St Oswald's Av. CH43: Bid 3F **33**
St Oswalds Cl. SY14: Mal 3H **207**
WA2: Winw 5A **16**
St Oswald's M. CH43: Bid 3F **33**
St Oswalds Rd. M19: Manc 1E **24**
St Oswald's Way
CH1: Ches 2B **212** (1K **149**)
St Patricks Cl. WA8: Wid 1G **89**
St Paul's Av. CH44: Wall 2D **34**
St Paul's Cl. CH42: R Fer 3D **60**
CW1: Crewe 2C **194**
SK15: Stal 7D **4**

Sankey Valley Pk.—Shady Oak Rd.

Sankey Valley Pk. 1C 40
Sankey Way WA5: Gt San 7J 39
Santa Rose Blvd.
WA5: Gt San 5J 39
Santon Av. M14: Manc 3B 24
Sapling Gro. M33: Sale 2H 47
Sapling La. CW6: Eat, Tarp 1K 175
Sargent Rd. SK6: Bred 2H 53
Sark Av. CH65: Ell P 7D 134
Sark Ho. CH2: Ches 6E 146
Sarl Williams Ct.
CH1: Ches 2B 212 (1K 149)
Sarn Av. M22: Wyth 1K 75
Sarn Bank Rd. SY14: Thr 7H 207
Sarn Rd. SY14: Thr 5G 207
Sarra La. CH3: Burw 6H 187
Sarus Ct. WA7: Man P 2D 90
SAUGHALL 1B 144 (1B 218)
Saughall Cl. CW9: N'ich 2D 162
Saughall Hey CH1: Sau 1B 144
SAUGHALL MASSIE 6K 31
Saughall Massie La. CH49: Upt 7B 32
Saughall Massie Rd. CH48: W Kir 2E 56
CH49: Gre, Upt 2E 56
Saughall Rd. CH1: Blac 5E 144
CH1: Blac, Ches 5F 145
CH46: More 5K 31
CH49: Upt 6K 31
Saundersfoot Cl. WA5: Call 2C 40
Saunders Honda Stadium 2F 149
Saunders St. CW1: Crewe 2B 194
Saunton Cl. CW7: Wins 2B 178
Savannah Pl. WA5: Gt San 5A 40
SAVERLEY GREEN 3D 221
Savernake Rd. SK6: W'ley 6H 27
Saville Av. WA5: Warr 5D 40
Saville Ri. CW7: Wins 3F 179
Saville Rd. SK8: Gat 6D 50
Saville St. SK11: Mac 6B 126
Savoy Cinema
Stockport 1K 51
Savoy Rd. CW1: Crewe 6G 195
Sawley Cl. WA3: Cul 1A 18
WA7: Murd 7G 91
Sawley Dr. SK8: Chea H 7K 77
Sawpit St. WA13: Warb 5J 45
WA14: Dun M 5J 45
Sawyer Brow SK14: Hyde 6A 10
Saxbrook Wlk. M22: Wyth 2B 76
Saxfield Dr. M23: Wyth 6J 49
Saxholme Wlk. M22: Wyth 3J 75
Saxon Av. SK16: Duk 2H 9
Saxon Cl. WA4: App 1F 93
Saxon Ct. M33: Sale 1B 48
Saxon Crossway CW7: Wins 3C 178
Saxon Dr. M34: Aude 3D 8
Saxon Rd. CH46: More 3C 32
CH47: Meols 4D 30
WA7: Run 4J 89
Saxons La. *CW8: N'ich 6C 156*
(off Heysoms La.)
CW8: N'ich 7D 156
(Alfred St.)
Saxon St. M34: Den 7E 8
M43: Droy 1A 8
Saxon Ter. WA8: Wid 4H 63
Saxon Way CH1: Blac 4E 144
CH66: Gt Sut 1B 140
CW11: S'ach 3G 201
(off Palmer Rd.)
Saxthorpe Cl. M33: Sale 6C 22
Sayce St. WA8: Wid 4H 63
Scafell Av. WA2: Warr 1G 41
Scafell Cl. CH62: East 4J 107
CH66: Ell P 1B 134
SK6: H Lan 5E 80
Scaife Rd. CW5: Nant 1D 196
Scalby Wlk. M22: Wyth 4K 75
Scargill Cl. M14: Manc 3A 24
Scarisbrick Av. M20: Manc 1F 51
Scarisbrick Rd. M19: Manc 3C 24
Scar La. SY14: Tils 7E 206
Schofield Rd. M43: Droy 1A 8
SCHOLAR GREEN 2H 205 (2C 221)
Scholars Cl. CH4: Salt 5F 149
SK10: Mac 4E 124
Scholars' Ct. *CH64: Nest 7H 105*
(off Cross St.)
Scholars Grn. La. WA13: Lymm 2B 70
Scholfield Av. M41: Urm 2E 22
School Av. CH64: L Nes 2D 130
M32: S'ord 1K 23
School Bank WA6: Norl 5H 153
School Brow SK6: Rom 2A 54
WA1: Warr 7G 41
School Cl. CH46: More 3C 32
SK12: Poy 3E 100
SY13: Marb 6C 208
WA16: Knut 4C 116
School Ct. SK3: Stoc 6D 52
School Cres. CW1: Crewe 2E 194
SK15: Stal 6A 4
School Dr. CW8: Barnt 2K 155
SK16: Duk 4K 9
WA13: Lymm 7E 44
School Fld. Cl. CW3: Bue 6H 211
Schoolfield Cl. CH49: Woodc 3E 58
Schoolfield Rd. CH49: Woodc 3E 58
Schoolfold La. SK10: Adl 7F 101
SCHOOL GREEN 7D 178 (1A 220)
School Grn. CH3: Clut 2A 206
School Gro. M20: Manc 5A 24
School Hill CH60: Hes 7H 83
School La. CH2: Elt 5E 136
CH2: Mic T 2H 147
CH3: Ald 6G 185
CH3: Burw 6H 187
CH3: Guil S 5H 147
CH43: Bid 3F 33
CH44: Wall 6E 12
CH45: Wall 7E 12
CH47: Hoy 5C 30
(not continuous)
CH47: Meols 3E 30
CH61: Thur 7J 57
CH62: N Fer 6G 61
CH63: H Beb 7C 60
CH64: L Nes 2D 130
CH64: Nest 5A 106
CH64: Park 6E 104
CH66: Chil T 6A 108
CW3: Audl 5C 210
CW5: Nant 1C 196
CW6: Bun 5B 188
CW8: H'ord 1A 162
CW8: S'way 4D 160
CW9: Ant 7A 94
CW9: Gt Bud 5H 115
CW9: Los Gra 5C 158
CW9: Moult 6D 162
CW11: Elw 2B 200
CW11: S'ach 3J 201
CW11: Warm 3C 204
CW12: Astb 6D 182
CW12: Eat 5F 169
L1: Liv 3J 35
L35: R'ill 3E 36
(not continuous)
M19: Manc 2F 51
M20: Manc 1D 50
M31: Carri 5H 21
M44: Cad 6A 20
M44: Irlam 1C 20
SK4: Stoc 6F 25
SK6: Comp 7C 28
SK8: Chea H 5H 77
(not continuous)
SK10: O Ald 5A 120
SK11: Henb 6A 124
SK11: Mart 6D 168
SK12: Poy 2E 100
SK14: Hyde 4K 27
SK15: Carrb 2F 5
SY13: Marb, Nor 6C 208
WA3: Ris 6D 18
WA3: Rix 2C 44
WA4: H Whi 1C 114
WA6: Frod 1J 139
WA6: Manl 1J 171
WA6: Norl 7E 152
WA7: Halt 6B 90
WA8: Bold H 5A 38
WA14: Dun M 5B 46
WA16: Oll 1G 165 & 7K 117
(not continuous)
School M. SK7: Bram 6C 78
School Rd. CH65: Ell P 3D 134
CW7: Wins 2H 179
CW9: Rud 1J 163
M32: S'ord 1H 23
M33: Sale 6G 23
(not continuous)
SK9: Hand 2A 98
WA2: Warr 3G 41
WA15: Hale 2K 73
School Rd. Nth. CW9: Rud 7K 157
(not continuous)
School Rd. Sth. CW9: Rud 7J 157
Schools Hill SK8: Chea 2F 77
School St. CH2: Ches 7B 146
CW1: Hasl 1K 195
SK7: H Gro 3J 79
WA4: Warr 1F 67
School St. Ind. Est. SK7: H Gro 3J 79
School Vw. *SK11: Sut E 3K 129*
(off Hollin La.)
School Way CW9: N'ich 5F 157
WA8: Wid 2K 63
School Yd. SK4: Stoc 2G 51
Schooner Cl. WA7: Murd 1F 113
Schubert Cl. CH66: Gt Sut 4A 134
Science Pk. Nth. WA3: Birc 5J 17
Science Pk. Sth. WA3: Ris 6J 17
Scilly Cl. CH65: Ell P 7E 134
Scoresby Rd. CH46: Leas 1E 32
Scotch Hall La.
CW9: Ant 4E 114, 1F 115 & 6A 94
SCOT HAY 3C 221
Scotia Av. CH62: N Fer 6H 61
Scotland Rd. L3: Liv 1J 35
WA1: Warr 7F 41
Scott Av. CW1: Crewe 2F 195
L35: Whis 1A 36
WA8: Wid 5F 63
WA9: Sut M 1G 37
Scott Cl. CW11: Elw 3B 200
SK5: Stoc 7J 25
SK10: Mac 5D 126
ST7: Rod H 1F 203
Scott Dr. SK6: Mar B 4J 55
WA15: Alt 1K 73
Scott Ga. M34: Aude 3D 8
Scotthope Cl. SK11: Mac 6G 125
Scotton Av. CH66: L Sut 3H 133
Scott Rd. M34: Den 2D 26
SK10: Pres 4H 121
Scotts Pl. CH41: Birk 5J 33
Scotts Quays CH41: Birk 3D 34
Scott St. CH45: Wall 6H 13
WA2: Warr 6F 41
Scott Wlk. WA12: New W 2F 15
SCOUT 2D 4
Scout Dr. M23: Wyth 1F 75
Scroggins La. M31: Part 7C 20
Scythes, The CH49: Gre 1K 57
Scythia Cl. CH62: N Fer 5H 61
Sea Bank CW10: Mid 3D 180
Seabank Av. CH44: Wall 6J 13
Seabank Ct. CH48: W Kir 4B 56
Seabank Rd. CH44: Wall 3H 13
CH45: N Bri, Wall 3H 13
CH60: Hes 1B 104
SEABRIDGE 3C 221
Seabury St. WA4: Westy 2A 68
SEACOMBE 3C 34 (1B 214)
Seacombe Dr. CH66: Gt Sut 5A 134
Seacombe Gro. SK3: Stoc 4K 51
Seacombe Prom. CH44: Wall 7K 13
(not continuous)
Seacombe Vw. CH44: Wall 2D 34
Sea Ct. CH45: Wall 4F 13
Seafield Av. CH60: Hes 1B 104
Seafield Dr. CH45: Wall 4G 13
Seafield Rd. CH62: N Fer 5G 61
Seaford Cl. WA7: Win H 5F 91
Seaford Pl. WA2: Warr 7K 15
SEAFORTH 1B 214
Seaforth Dr. CH46: More 5B 32
Seagrave Cl. CW9: N'ich 1E 162
Seagull Cl. CW1: Crewe 1F 195
Seahill Rd. CH1: Sau, Sea 3A 144
SEALAND 4A 144 (1B 218)
Sealand Cl. M33: Sale 2E 48
WA2: Padg 4J 41
Sealand Ind. Est. CH1: Ches 1G 149
Sealand Rd. CH1: Ches, Sea 4A 144
M23: Wyth 2F 49
Sealand Road (Park & Ride) 1E 148
Sealand Way *SK9: Hand 2A 98*
(off Henbury Rd.)
Sea La. WA7: Run 4K 89
Seale Av. M34: Aude 3C 8
Seal Rd. SK7: Bram 5D 78
Sealy Cl. CH63: Spit 5A 86
Seamons Dr. WA14: Alt 6F 47
Seamons Rd. WA14: Alt, Dun M 6E 46
Seamons Wlk. *WA14: Alt 7F 47*
(off Seamons Rd.)
Sea Rd. CH45: Wall 3F 13
Seathwaite Cl. WA7: Beec 2A 112
Seaton Cl. CW1: Crewe 5G 191
SK7: H Gro 4H 79
Seaton Pk. WA7: Nort 3G 91
Seaton Rd. CH42: Tran 1B 60
CH45: Wall 5G 13
Seattle Cl. WA5: Gt San 5K 39
Sea Vw. CH47: Hoy 5C 30
CH64: L Nes 4C 130
Seaview Av. CH45: Wall 6G 13
CH61: Irby 7A 58
CH62: East 1C 108
Seaview La. CH61: Irby 7A 58
Seaview Rd. CH45: Wall 5G 13
Seaville St. CH1: Ches 1B 150
Seawood Gro. CH46: More 5A 32
Sebastian Cl. SK6: Mar B 5H 55
Secker Av. WA4: Warr 3H 67
Secker Cres. WA4: Warr 3H 67
Second Av. CH43: Bid 6E 32
CW1: Crewe 5F 195
CW11: S'ach 4E 200
L35: R'ill 1B 36
SK12: Poy 5C 100
SK15: Carrb 4F 5
WA7: Pal F 6B 90
Second Dig La. CW5: Stap 7G 197
Second Wood St. CW5: Nant 2D 196
Sedbergh Cl. CW4: H Cha 4G 181
Sedbergh Gro. WA7: Beec 2A 112
Sedbergh Rd. CH44: Wall 6F 13
Sedburgh Cl. M33: Sale 2H 47
Sedbury Cl. M23: Wyth 3F 49
Seddon Rd. WA14: Hale 3H 73
Seddon St. CW10: Mid 2C 180
L1: Liv 4J 35
M12: Manc 1E 24
Sedge Cl. SK5: Stoc 3K 25
Sedgefield Cl. CH46: More 4D 32
SK10: Mac 7K 121
Sedgefield Rd. CH1: Ches 1J 149
CH46: More 4D 32
Sedgefield Wlk. M23: Wyth 2F 49
Sedgeford Cl. SK9: Wilm 5K 97
Sedgemere Av. CW1: Crewe 5F 191
Sedgemoor Cl. SK8: Chea H 3K 77
Sedgewick Cres. WA5: B'ood 5B 14
Sedum Cl. CH3: Hunt 5D 150
Seeley Av. CH41: Birk 5K 33
Seel St. L1: Liv 3J 35
OL5: Moss 1C 4
SEFTON 1B 214
Sefton Av. CW12: Cong 5J 183
WA8: Wid 2G 63
Sefton Cres. M33: Sale 5G 23
Sefton Dr. SK9: Wilm 4K 97
SEFTON PARK 2B 214
Sefton Rd. CH2: Ches 6D 146
CH42: R Fer 4F 61
CH45: N Bri 4H 13
CH62: N Fer 5F 61
M33: Sale 6G 23
Sefton St. L8: Liv 6J 35
Seiont Ho. L8: Liv 7K 35
Selborne L35: Whis 2A 36
Selbourne Cl.
CH49: Woodc 2F 59
SK5: Stoc 1H 25
Selby Cl. M32: S'ord 1F 23
SK12: Poy 1C 100
WA7: Nort 2G 91
Selby Gdns.
SK8: Chea H 7A 78
Selby Grn. CH66: L Sut 3H 133
Selby Rd. M32: S'ord 1F 23
Selby St. CH45: Wall 6H 13
SK4: Stoc 7G 25
WA5: Warr 7C 40
(not continuous)
Selkirk Av. CH62: East 3K 107
WA4: Westy 2A 68
Selkirk Cl. CH66: L Sut 3F 133
SK10: Mac 2G 125
Selkirk Dr. CH4: Ches 4H 149
CW4: H Cha 5H 181
Selkirk Rd. CH4: Ches 4H 149
Seller St. CH1: Ches 3E 212 (1B 150)
Selsdon Cl. CH4: Ches 4K 149
Selsey Av. M33: Sale 1K 47
SK3: Stoc 5H 51
Selsey Cl. CW1: Crewe 5G 191
Selsey Dr. M20: Manc 4E 50
Selside Wlk. *M14: Manc 3A 24*
(off Boland Dr.)
Selstead Rd. M22: Wyth 4J 75
Selston Cl. CH63: Spit 4A 86
Selworth Av. M33: Sale 7K 23
Selworth Cl. WA15: Timp 6J 47
Selworthy Dr. CW1: Crewe 6G 191
WA4: Thel 2D 68
Selwyn Cl. WA8: Wid 2A 64
Selwyn Dr. SK8: Chea H 6A 78
SK11: Sut E 2K 129
Semper Cl. CW12: Cong 2J 183
Seneschal Ct. WA7: Pal F 1A 112
Senior Av. M14: Manc 4B 24
Senna La. CW9: Ant, Comb 1F 115
Sennen Cl. WA7: B'vale 2D 112
Sens Cl. CH1: Ches 4A 212 (2K 149)
Sepal Cl. SK5: Stoc 2K 25
Sephton Av. WA3: Cul 7E 6
Serin Cl. SK2: Stoc 7K 53
Serpentine, The CH4: Ches 4J 149
Serpentine Rd. CH44: Wall 6J 13
Service St. SK3: Stoc 4K 51
Servite Cl. CH65: Ell P 2B 134
Servite Pl. CH64: Nest 1C 130
Set St. SK15: Stal 1A 10
Seven Acres La. CH61: Thin 7D 58
Sevenoaks Av. SK4: Stoc 6D 24
Sevenoaks Cl. SK10: Mac 2J 125
Sevenoaks Rd. SK8: Gat 6D 50
Seven Row CH64: L Nes 3C 130
Seven Sisters La. WA16: Oll 7J 117
Seven Stiles Dr. SK6: Mar 5E 54
Severn Cl. CW12: Cong 5H 183
SK10: Mac 2G 125
WA2: Warr 2J 41
WA8: Wid 2B 64
WA14: Alt 6G 47
Severn Dr. SK7: Bram 7A 78
Severn Rd. L35: R'ill 1B 36
WA3: Cul 1A 18
Severn St. CH41: Birk 3K 33
Severnvale CH65: Whit 5D 134
Severn Wlk. CW7: Wins 2H 179
Severn Way SK5: Stoc 6K 25
Sewell St. WA7: Run 4H 89
Sextant Cl. WA7: Murd 2F 113
Seymour Chase WA16: Knut 5F 117
Seymour Ct. CH42: Tran 1D 60
SK4: Stoc 2G 51
WA7: Man P 3E 90
Seymour Dr. CH66: Ell P 2A 134
WA1: Padd, Padg 5A 42
Seymour Gro. M33: Sale 7G 23
SK6: Mar 6E 54
WA15: Timp 7A 48
Seymour Pl. E. CH45: N Bri 3J 13
Seymour Pl. W. CH45: N Bri 3H 13
Seymour Rd. SK2: Stoc 7F 53
SK8: Chea H 5J 77
Seymour St. CH42: Tran 1D 60
CH45: N Bri 3H 13
L3: Liv 2K 35
M34: Den 7C 8
Seymour Ter. *L3: Liv 2K 35*
(off Seymour St.)
Shackleton Cl. WA5: Old H 4A 40
Shackleton Rd. CH46: Leas 7B 12
Shade Ter. SK6: H Lan 6F 81
Shadewood Cres. WA4: Grap 3B 68
Shadewood Rd. SK11: Mac 6H 125
Shadowbrook Av. M23: Wyth 1G 75
Shadowmoss Rd. M22: Wyth 6A 76
Shady Brook La. CW8: Weav 4F 155
Shady Gro. ST7: Als 5E 202
Shady La. M23: Wyth 5D 48
Shady Oak Rd. SK2: Stoc 6K 53

South Pde.—Stamford St.

South Pde. CH48: W Kir 3B 56
CH64: Park 7F 105
SK7: Bram 3D 78
WA7: Wes P 7D 88
South Pk. Bus. Cen.
SK11: Mac 6A 126
South Pk. Ct. *CH44: Wall* *1D 34*
(off Demesne St.)
South Pk. Dr. SK12: Poy 2D 100
South Pk. Rd. SK8: Gat 6D 50
SK11: Mac 5K 125
Sth. Pier Rd. CH65: Ell P 1F 135
Southpoint SK4: Stoc 2J 51
Southpool Cl. SK7: Bram 3E 78
South Quay L3: Liv 5H 35
SOUTH REDDISH 5J 25
South Ridge M34: Den 5E 8
Southridge Rd.
CH61: Pens 1J 83
South Rd. CH42: Tran 2B 60
CH48: W Kir 4B 56
CH65: Ell P 3H 135
(Bridges Rd.)
CH65: Ell P 5E 134
(Malvern Av.)
CH65: H'ton 4D 108
M20: Manc 2D 50
WA7: Wes P 7D 88
WA14: Bow 3G 73
(not continuous)
WA14: Hale 5H 73
South Side SK14: Hyde 2A 28
Southside SK6: Bred 5D 26
South St. CH3: Ches 2D 150
CW2: Crewe 4D 194
CW12: Cong 3F 183
OL7: Ash L 2D 8
SK9: Ald E 6F 119
ST7: Mow C 6F 205
WA8: Wid 5H 63
South Ter. SK9: Ald E 7F 119
South Va. Cres. WA15: Timp 7K 47
South Vw. CH4: Ches 7D 212 (4A 150)
CH62: Brom 1D 86
SK5: Stoc 1J 25
SK6: W'ley 5H 27
SK11: L Wit 7K 167
SK15: Carrb 3G 5
SK16: Duk 1H 9
South Vw. Av. SK11: Gaw 3B 128
South Vw. Cotts. ST7: Chu L 4G 203
South Vw. Gdns. SK8: Chea 2E 76
South Vw. Rd. CH1: Ches 3A 212 (1J 149)
South Vw. Ter. WA5: Cuer 2C 64
South Vs. CH45: N Bri 4H 13
South Wlk. SK15: Stal 1B 10
Southwark Dr. SK16: Duk 4J 9
Southwark Pl. CW7: Wins 4B 178
South Way CH1: Blac 6F 145
Southway *CW10: Mid* *3C 180*
(off St Ann's Rd.)
M43: Droy 2A 8
WA7: Pal F 7B 90
(not continuous)
WA8: Wid 5D 62
WA14: Alt 6J 47
Southway Av. WA4: App 6H 67
Southwell Cl. SK6: Rom 3A 54
Southwell Cl. M32: S'ord 2H 23
Southwell Pl. L8: Liv 7K 35
Southwell St. L8: Liv 7K 35
South W. Av. SK10: Boll 4C 122
Southwick Rd. CH42: Tran 2D 60
M23: Wyth 2G 49
Sth. Wirral Retail Pk. CH62: Brom 3D 86
Southwold Cl. M19: Manc 2F 25
Southwold Cres. WA5: Gt San 6F 39
Southwood Av. WA7: Win H 4E 90
Southwood Rd. CH62: Brom 5F 87
SK2: Stoc 1F 79
Southworth Av. WA5: Warr 4D 40
Southworth La. WA2: Winw 4C 16
WA3: Croft 4C 16
Southyard St. M19: Manc 3E 24
Sovereign Cl. CW9: Rud 7K 157
WA7: Murd 7F 91
Sovereign Ct. WA3: Birc 7H 17
Sovereign Ho. SK8: Chea 6H 51
Sovereign Way CH1: Ches 1F 149
CH41: Birk 3C 34
SOWCAR 3F 123
Sowcar Way SK10: Boll 3F 123
Spa Cl. SK5: Stoc 3H 25
Spalding Dr. M23: Wyth 3G 75
Sparkford Av. M23: Wyth 3D 40
Spark Hall Cl. WA4: Stre 4J 93
Spark La. WA7: Halt 5B 90
Spark Rd. M23: Wyth 5F 49
Sparks Cl. CH3: Gt Bou 4E 150
Sparks La. CH61: Thin 7D 58
Sparling St. L1: Liv 5J 35
(not continuous)
Sparrow Cl. SK5: Stoc 1H 25
Sparrowfield Cl. SK15: Carrb 2F 5
Sparrowhawk Cl. WA7: Pal F 7C 90
Sparrow La. WA16: Knut 4F 117
Sparth Ct. SK4: Stoc 1B 52
Sparthfield Rd. SK4: Stoc 1B 52
Sparth Hall SK4: Stoc 1B 52
Sparth La. SK4: Stoc 1B 52
Spathfield Ct. SK4: Stoc 1B 52
Spath Holme M20: Manc 1C 50
Spath La. SK8: Chea H 2B 98
(not continuous)
SK9: Hand 1A 98
Spath La. E. SK8: Chea H 1E 98
Spath Rd. M20: Manc 1B 50
Spath Wlk. SK8: Chea H 1E 98
Speakman St. WA7: Run 3F 89
Spectrum Bus. Pk. SK3: Stoc 6K 51
Spectrum Way SK3: Stoc 6A 52
Speedkarting 1D 66
Speed's Way CH3: Farn 5B 186
Speedwell SK13: Tint 1K 11
Speedwell Cl. CH3: Hunt 6E 150
CH60: Hes 6A 84
SK13: Tint 1K 11
Speedwell Dr. CH60: Hes 6A 84
Speedwell Rd. CH41: Birk 5J 33
SPEKE 2C 215
Speke Rd. WA8: Wid 6A 62
Speke Wlk. M34: Den 2D 26
Spellow Pl. *L3: Liv* *2G 35*
(off Union St.)
Spencer Av. CH46: More 3D 32
SK14: Hyde 5J 9
Spencer Brook SK10: Pres 5G 121
Spencer Cl. CW2: Wis 6A 194
ST7: Als 5A 202
Spencer M. SK10: Pres 5G 121
Spencer St. CW8: Barnt 2A 156
CW8: N'ich 6D 156
SK5: Stoc 3J 25
SK16: Duk 2H 9
Spenders La. WA7: Ast 6F 113
Spenlow Cl. SK12: Poy 5D 100
Spennithorne Rd. M41: Urm 1A 22
Spennymoor Ct. WA7: Pal F 7A 90
Spenser Av. CH42: R Fer 4E 60
M34: Den 3F 27
Spenser Cl. WA8: Wid 4F 63
Spenser Rd. CH64: Nest 6H 105
Spey Cl. CW7: Wins 2G 179
CW10: Mid 1D 180
WA14: Alt 6G 47
Spey Ho. SK5: Stoc 1J 25
Spike Island Vis. Cen. 1G 89
Spindle Av. SK15: Stal 6D 4
Spindles, The OL5: Moss 1E 4
Spindle St. CW12: Cong 3G 183
Spindle Whorl CW10: Mid 3C 180
Spindlewood Cl. SK15: Stal 7E 4
Spindrift Ct. CH48: W Kir 4B 56
Spink La. WA16: Pick 1C 158
Spinnaker Cl. WA7: Murd 1F 113
Spinner Cres. CW9: Comb 3J 115
Spinners La. SK12: Poy 2B 100
Spinners Pl. WA1: Warr 6G 41
Spinners Way SK10: Boll 4C 122
Spinney, The CH48: W Kir 3F 57
CH49: Upt 6D 32
CH60: Hes 2F 105
CH63: Spit 3B 86
CH64: Park 6G 105
CW5: W'ston 1H 197
CW8: Cudd 1A 160
CW11: S'ach 3G 201
M41: Urm 1K 21
SK8: Chea 2G 77
SK12: Poy 2B 100
ST7: Chu L 4H 205
WA6: Norl 6F 153
Spinney Av. CW4: Goo 6K 165
WA8: Wid 4A 62
Spinney Cl. CW7: Wins 4H 179
SK9: Hand 3K 97
WA9: Clo F 1J 37
Spinney Dr. CH66: Gt Sut 6K 133
CW2: West 2H 199
M33: Sale 1H 47
Spinney End CH3: Tatt 3G 187
Spinney Gdns. WA4: App T 2B 94
Spinney Gro. M34: Den 5E 8
Spinney La. WA16: Knut 2C 116
Spinney Mead SK10: Mac 3B 126
Spinney Rd. M23: Wyth 5H 49
Spinney Wlk. WA7: Cast 5C 90
Spires Gdns. WA2: Winw 4K 15
Spirewood Gdns. SK6: Rom 3A 54
SPITAL 3B 86 (2B 214)
Spital Heyes CH63: Spit 3B 86
Spital Rd. CH62: Brom, Spit 3A 86
CH63: Spit 3A 86
Spital Station (Rail) 3B 86
Spital Wlk. CH3: Ches 1C 150
Spode Grn. La. WA14: L Bol 4A 72
Sportaid Health & Fitness Club *4A 126*
(off Sunderland St.)
Spout Brook Rd. SK15: Hey 4C 4
Spout Grn. *SK14: Mot* *5H 11*
(off Old Rd.)
Spout La. WA16: Mob 6C 102
Spragg St. CW12: Cong 3G 183
Sprainger St. L3: Liv 1G 35
Spring Av. CH66: L Sut 2J 133
SK14: Hyde 3A 28
Spring Bank SK15: Stal 1C 10
ST7: Sch G 1K 205
WA14: Bow 2H 73
Springbank SK10: Boll 4B 122
Spring Bank Av. M34: Aude 3C 8
Springbank Cl. SK6: W'ley 5H 27
WA7: Run 1H 111
Springbank Ct. SK6: W'ley 6G 27
Springbank Cres. CW7: Wins 4D 178
Springbank Gdns. WA13: Lymm 7D 44
Spring Bank La. SK15: Hey 4D 4
Springbank La. SK10: Adl 5K 103
Springbank Pl. SK1: Stoc 7H 213 (4C 52)
Springbank Rd. SK6: W'ley 5H 27
Spring Bank Ter. M34: Aude 3B 8
Springbourne WA6: Frod 2K 139
Springburn Gdns. WA1: Wool 5F 43
Spring Cl. ST7: Rod H 1F 203
Spring Ct. WA7: Run 4H 89
Spring Ct. M. SK14: H'rth 5K 11
Springcroft CH64: Park 6F 105
Springdale Cl. CH46: More 3D 32
Springdale Gdns. M20: Manc 1C 50
Springe La. CW5: B'ley, Burl 7F 189
Spring Farm Bus. Cen. CW1: Min V 2F 191
Springfield L3: Liv 1K 35
(not continuous)
M41: Urm 1B 22
SK13: Char 5K 29
Springfield Av. CH48: W Kir 2F 57
SK5: Stoc 4H 25
SK6: Mar 6F 55
SK7: H Gro 2H 79
SY14: Mal 3H 207
WA1: Padg 4K 41
WA4: Grap 2B 68
WA6: Hel 5B 138
WA13: Lymm 7D 44
Springfield Cl. CH49: Woodc 3F 59
SK13: Had 3K 11
Springfield Cres. CW8: Barnt 2J 155
Springfield Dr. CH2: Ches 6B 146
CW2: Wis 7K 193
CW12: Cong 3F 183
SK9: Wilm 2C 118
Springfield La. M44: Irlam 1C 20
Springfield Rd. M33: Sale 7G 23
SK8: Gat 1D 76
SK11: Mac 4G 125
SY14: Mal 3H 207
WA8: Wid 5A 62
WA14: Alt 1J 213 (7H 47)
WA16: Mob 1K 117
Springfields CH2: Mic T 2H 147
CW8: Cudd 2A 160
SK10: Pres 4H 121
WA6: Hel 5B 138
WA16: Knut 2G 117
Springfield St. M34: Aude 4E 8
WA1: Warr 7E 40
Spring Gdns. CH66: L Sut 2J 133
CW1: Crewe 1E 194
CW5: Nant 2D 196
SK1: Stoc 7K 213 (3E 52)
SK7: H Gro 2H 79
SK10: Mac 3A 126
SK14: Hyde 6J 9
WA15: Timp 7C 48
Spring Hill CW6: Tarp 4H 175
Springhill SK10: Mac 3D 126
Springhill Av. CH62: Brom 1J 107
Springholm Dr. WA4: App 3H 93
Spring La. WA3: Croft 5G 17
WA13: Lymm 2G 71
Spring Mdw. CW8: Winn 4D 156
Springmeadow SK13: Char 4K 29
Spring Rd. SK3: Stoc 4A 52
SK12: Poy 4E 100
WA14: Hale 3H 73
Springs, The WA14: Bow 3F 73
(not continuous)
Springside SK4: Stoc 4G 25
Springs La. SK15: Stal 6A 4
Springs Ri. SK15: Stal 6A 4
(not continuous)
Spring St. CH42: Tran 2E 60
M12: Manc 1D 24
SK9: Wilm 7H 97
SK14: B'tom 2H 29
SK14: H'rth 5K 11
SK15: Stal 7B 4
WA8: Wid 7G 63
Spring Va. CH45: Wall 4E 12
SK7: H Gro 3J 79
Springvale Bus. Cen. CW11: Ett H 3B 200
Springvale Cl. CW11: Ett H 3B 200
Springvale Ind. Est. CW11: Ett H 3B 200
Springwater Dr. CW2: West 5J 199
Springwell Cl. CW2: Wis 6C 194
Springwell Gdns. SK14: Hat 2F 29
Springwell Way SK14: Hat 2F 29
Springwood Av. WA16: Knut 2G 117
Springwood Cl. CH1: Blac 6D 144
SK10: Boll 6A 122
Springwood Ct. SK10: Boll 6A 122
Springwood Cres. SK6: Rom 2E 54
Springwood La. SK6: Rom 2F 55
Springwood Way CH62: N Fer 5F 61
SK10: Boll 6A 122
SPROSTON GREEN 1B 220
Sproston Way CW9: N'ich 2D 162
Spruce Av. CW8: S'way 3E 160
Spruce Cl. CH42: Tran 1C 60
WA1: Wool 5E 42
Spruce Gro. ST7: Rod H 2G 203
Spruce Lodge SK8: Chea 6F 51
Spruce Wlk. M33: Sale 5B 22
Spuley La. SK10: Boll, P Shr 2G 123
Spunhill Av. CH66: Gt Sut 5J 133
Spurling Rd. WA5: B'ood 5C 14
Spurston Cl. WA16: H Leg 2H 95
SPURSTOW 7B 188 (2D 219)
Spurstow Cl. CH43: Oxt 2J 59
Spurstow M. SK8: Chea H 5K 77
Square, The CH1: Ches 3E 212 (1B 150)
CH2: Ince 3E 136
CH3: Chri 3H 151
CW3: Audl 5B 210
CW4: H Cha 4J 181
SK4: Stoc 1A 52
SK14: Hyde 1J 27
SK16: Duk 3A 10
WA13: Lymm 2A 70
WA15: H'rns 5C 74
Square Fold M43: Droy 1A 8
Square St. SK11: Mac 6B 126
Squibb Dr. CH46: Leas 2D 32
Squires Av. WA8: Wid 4F 63
Squirrel Cl. CW8: N'ich 6B 156
Squirrel Dr. WA14: B'ath 4G 47
Squirrels Chase SK10: Pres 6G 121
Squirrel's Jump SK9: Ald E 6G 119
Stable Cl. CH49: Gre 1A 58
Stablefold OL5: Moss 1D 4
Stable La. CH3: Mould 3J 171
CW6: Cote 4A 176
Stable M. CW8: S'way 5D 160
Stablings, The SK9: Wilm 2F 119
Stackfield, The CH48: W Kir 2G 57
Stadium Ind. Est., The CH1: Ches 7H 145
Stadium Rd. CH62: Brom 3E 86
Stadium Way CH1: Ches 1H 149
Stadmorslow La. ST7: Harr 7K 205
Staffin Av. CH65: Ell P 1D 140
Stafford Cl. SK10: Mac 2G 125
Stafford Gdns. CH65: Ell P 3D 134
Stafford Rd. WA4: Warr 3G 67
Stafford St. CW1: Crewe 1C 194
CW3: Audl 5C 210
L3: Liv 2K 35
Stafford Wlk. *M34: Den* *2F 27*
(off Lancaster Rd.)
SK10: Mac *2G 125*
(off Wiltshire Wlk.)
Stage La. WA13: Lymm 1D 70
Stag Ind. Est. WA14: B'ath 6F 47
Stainburne Rd. SK2: Stoc 6G 53
Staines Cl. WA4: App 1J 93
Stainforth Cl. WA3: Cul 6D 6
Stainmoor Ct. SK2: Stoc 6H 53
Stainmore Cl. WA3: Birc 5C 18
Staithes Rd. M22: Wyth 5K 75
Stakes, The CH46: Leas 1B 32
Stalbridge Dr. WA7: Nort 2H 91
Stalbridge Rd. CW2: Crewe 4C 194
Staley Cl. SK15: Stal 7D 4
Staley Farm Cl. SK15: Stal 5E 4
Staley Hall Cres. SK15: Stal 6D 4
Staley Hall Rd. SK15: Stal 6D 4
Staley Rd. OL5: Moss 1E 4
(not continuous)
Stallard Way CW10: Mid 4C 180
Stalmine Av. SK8: He Grn 5D 76
STALYBRIDGE 1C 10 (1D 217)
Stalybridge Celtic FC 2D 10
Stalybridge Country Pk. 2H 5
Stalybridge Rd. SK14: Mot 6H 11
Stalybridge Station (Rail) 7A 4
Stalyhill Dr. SK15: Stal 3F 11
Staly Ind. Est. SK15: Stal 7C 4
Stamford Av. CW2: Crewe 3C 194
SK15: Stal 1K 9
WA14: Alt 7E 46
STAMFORD BRIDGE 1C 219
Stamford Brook Rd.
WA14: W Tim 4G 47
Stamford Cl. SK11: Mac 1G 129
SK15: Stal 1K 9
Stamford Ct. CH3: Ches 1F 151
SK11: Mac *1G 129*
(off Stamford Rd.)
Stamford Dr. SK15: Stal 1K 9
Stamford Grange WA14: Alt 2H 213 (1G 73)
Stamford Gro. SK15: Stal 7A 4
Stamford La. CH3: Cot E 1K 151 & 3K 151
Stamford New Rd.
WA14: Alt 3J 213 (1H 73)
Stamford Pk. 7A 4
Stamford Pk. Rd.
WA15: Alt, Hale 4K 213 (2J 73)
Stamford Pl. M33: Sale 7H 23
SK9: Wilm *7J 97*
(off Manchester Rd.)
Stamford Rd. CH1: Blac 4F 145
M13: Manc 1B 24
M31: Carri 5G 21
M34: Aude 3C 8
M41: Urm 1A 22
OL5: Moss 1D 4
SK9: Ald E 6G 119
SK9: Wilm 5H 97
SK11: Mac 1G 129
WA14: Bow 3F 73
WA14: L Bol 3K 71
Stamford Sq. WA14: Alt 2J 213
Stamford St. CH65: Ell P 3C 134
M33: Sale 5F 23
OL5: Moss 1C 4
SK15: M'ook 5E 4
SK15: Stal 1K 9
(not continuous)
WA14: Alt 1J 213 (7H 47)

Tavistock Rd.—Thrapston Av.

Tavistock Rd. CH45: Wall 5E **12**
M33: Sale 6C **22**
WA5: Penk 1G **65**
Tavlin Av. WA5: Warr 3D **40**
Tawny Ct. WA7: Pal F 7A **90**
Tawton Av. SK14: Hat 7F **11**
TAXAL 2D **217**
Taxmere Cl. CW11: S'ach 2D **200**
Tayfield Rd. M22: Wyth 3J **75**
Tayleur Ter.
WA12: New W 1G **15**
Taylor Bus. Pk. WA3: Ris 1A **18**
Taylor Dr. CW5: Nant 2A **196**
Taylor La. M34: Den 6C **8**
Taylor Rd. WA14: Alt 7E **46**
Taylor's La. WA5: Cuer 3C **64**
Taylor Sq. *SK11: Mac 6K **125***
(off Slater St.)
Taylors Row WA7: Run 4J **89**
Taylor St. CH41: Birk 5D **34**
M34: Den 6E **8**
SK14: H'rth 2J **11**
SK14: Hyde 7A **10**
SK15: Stal 1C **10**
WA4: Warr 4E **66**
WA8: Wid 4J **63**
Taylor Ter. *SK16: Duk 1G **9***
(off Hill St.)
Teal Av. SK12: Poy 2K **99**
WA16: Knut 3F **117**
Tealby Cl. CW9: N'ich 5G **157**
Teal Cl. CW7: Wins 7E **178**
SK2: Stoc 7K **53**
WA2: Warr 1J **41**
WA14: B'ath 4F **47**
Teal Gro. WA3: Birc 1F **43**
Teals Way CH60: Hes 6F **83**
Tebay Rd. CH62: East 6E **86**
Tedder Dr. M22: Wyth 6B **76**
Tedder Sq. WA8: Wid 5D **62**
Teddington Cl. WA4: App 1J **93**
Teehey Cl. CH63: H Beb 7C **60**
Teehey Gdns. CH63: H Beb 7C **60**
Teehey La. CH63: H Beb 7C **60**
Tees Ct. CH65: Ell P 1C **134**
Teesdale Cl. SK2: Stoc 6J **53**
WA5: Gt San 5H **39**
Teesdale Rd. CH63: Beb 2J **85**
Tees St. CH41: Birk 3J **33**
Tegg's Nose Country Pk. 7G **127**
Teggsnose La. SK11: Mac 6F **127**
Tegid Way CH4: Salt 6E **148**
Tegsnose Mt. SK11: Lang 1H **169**
Telegraph La. CH45: Wall 6C **12**
Telegraph Rd. CH48: Cald 6G **57**
CH60: Hes 6G **57**
CH61: Thur 6G **57**
Telfer Av. M13: Manc 1B **24**
Telfer Ct. CW10: Mid 6E **180**
Telfer Rd. M13: Manc 1B **24**
Telford Cl. CH43: Oxt 1A **60**
CW12: Cong 5J **183**
M34: Aude 3D **8**
SK10: Mac 3D **126**
WA4: Westy 2B **68**
WA8: Wid 1D **62**
Telford Ct. CH1: Dun 3A **140**
Telford Gdns. CW11: Whe 6D **200**
Telford Pl. CW5: Nant 2A **196**
Telford Rd. CH65: Ell P 4G **135**
SK6: Mar 1G **81**
Telford's Quay CH65: Ell P 1F **135**
Telford Way CH4: Salt 5G **149**
CW3: Audl 6B **210**
CW10: Mid 3E **180**
Telham Wlk. M23: Wyth 7G **49**
Temperance Sq. SK14: Mot 6H **11**
Temperance St. SK14: B'tom 3H **29**
Temperance Ter. *SK6: Mar 6F **55***
(off Hollins La.)
Tempest Hey L2: Liv 2H **35**
Tempest Rd. SK9: Ald E 6H **119**
Templar Ct. SK10: Mac 3J **125**
Temple Chambers CH1: Ches 3C **212**
Temple Ct. L2: Liv 3H **35**
WA3: Ris 5K **17**
Temple La. L2: Liv 2H **35**
Templemore Rd. CH43: Oxt 1K **59**
Temple Rd. CH42: Tran 3B **60**
M33: Sale 7J **23**
Temple St. L2: Liv 2H **35**
Templeton Dr. WA2: Fear 1A **42**
WA14: Alt 6F **47**
Tenbury Cl. WA5: Gt San 4J **39**
Tenby Cl. WA5: Call 2D **40**
Tenby Dr. CH46: More 4C **32**
SK8: Chea H 4K **77**
WA7: Run 4K **89**
Tenby Rd. SK3: Stoc 5K **51**
SK11: Mac 6G **125**
Tenchersfield CW5: Nant 3E **196**
Tenement La. SK7: Bram 2A **78**
Tennyson Av. CH42: R Fer 4E **60**
CW1: Crewe 2F **195**
M34: Den 4F **27**
SK16: Duk 3B **10**
Tennyson Cl. CW2: Wis 5A **194**
CW9: N'ich 7H **157**
SK4: Stoc 2K **51**
SK11: Mac 5F **125**
ST7: Rod H 1F **203**
Tennyson Dr. WA2: Warr 2G **41**
Tennyson Rd. CH65: Whit 4C **134**
SK5: Stoc 2G **25**
SK8: Chea 6H **51**
WA8: Wid 4G **63**
Tennyson St. WA9: Sut M 2G **37**
Tennyson Wlk. CH1: Blac 5H **145**
Tenpin
Chester 7G **145**
East Didsbury 3F **51**
Ellesmere Port 7F **135**
Tensing Cl. WA5: Gt San 4K **39**
Tensing Fold SK16: Duk 1G **9**
Tenter Brow SK15: Stal 7A **4**
Tenterden Wlk. *M22: Wyth 2J **75***
(off Poundswick La.)
Terence Av. WA1: Padd 6K **41**
Terminal Rd. E. M90: Man A 6H **75**
Terminal Rd. Nth.
M90: Man A 6H **75**
Terminus Rd. CH62: Brom 3D **86**
Tern Cl. SK16: Duk 3K **9**
WA8: Wid 1H **63**
WA14: B'ath 4F **47**
Tern Dr. SK12: Poy 2A **100**
Tern Way CH46: More 3J **31**
Terrace Rd. WA8: Wid 1G **89**
Tetbury Rd. M22: Wyth 4H **75**
Tetbury St. CH41: Birk 7B **34**
CH43: Birk 7B **34**
Tetchill Cl. CH66: Gt Sut 6K **133**
WA7: Nort 6F **91**
Tetlow Fold SK14: Hyde 7C **10**
Tetlow St. SK14: Hyde 5K **9**
Tetton Ct. CW12: Cong 3H **183**
Tetton La. CW10: Most 1D **204**
CW11: Most 1D **204**
Tewkesbury Av. WA15: Hale 2C **74**
Tewkesbury Cl. CH2: Upt 3C **146**
CH66: Gt Sut 1A **140**
CW10: Mid 3B **180**
SK8: Chea H 7K **77**
SK12: Poy 1C **100**
Tewkesbury Dr. SK10: Mac 7B **122**
Tewkesbury Rd. SK3: Stoc 6K **51**
Texas St. OL6: Ash L 1H **9**
Textilis Ho. SK1: Stoc 7H **213**
Teynham Wlk. *M22: Wyth 4J **75***
(off Selstead Rd.)
Thackeray Dr. CH3: Ches 7F **147**
Thackeray Towers CH1: Ches 2E **212**
Thackery Ct. CW11: Ett H 3B **200**
Thames Av. WN7: Leigh 1F **7**
Thames Cl. CW12: Cong 5H **183**
WA2: Warr 2H **41**
Thamesdale CH65: Whit 5C **134**
Thames Gdns. CH65: Whit 5C **134**
Thames Pl. *CW7: Wins 3J **179***
(off Trent Av.)
Thames Rd. WA3: Cul 1A **18**
Thames Side CH65: Whit 5D **134**
Thames Trad. Cen. M44: Irlam 4C **20**
Thankerton Av. M34: Aude 1C **8**
Thatcher Cl. WA14: Bow 5G **73**
Thatchers Mt. WA5: Col G 2A **14**
THATTO HEATH 1D **215**
Thaxted Dr. SK2: Stoc 7A **54**
Thaxted Wlk. M22: Wyth 5J **75**
The . . . .
Names prefixed with 'The' for example 'The Acorn Ho.' are indexed under the main name such as 'Acorn Ho., The'
Theatre Ct. CW9: N'ich 5E **156**
Theatre Royal 1J **27**
THELWALL 2D **68** (2A **216**)
Thelwall Cl. WA15: Alt 6J **47**
Thelwall La. WA4: Warr, Westy 2K **67**
Thelwall New Rd. WA4: Grap, Thel 2A **68**
Thelwall New Rd. Ind. Est.
WA4: Thel 1C **68**
Thelwall Rd. CH66: Gt Sut 4A **134**
M33: Sale 1E **48**
Theobald Rd. WA14: Bow 4H **73**
Thermal Rd. CH62: Brom 2D **86**
Thermopylae Pas. CH43: Noc 6G **33**
Thetford Cl. SK10: Mac 1K **125**
Thetford Rd. WA5: Gt San 6G **39**
Thewlis St. WA5: Warr 7C **40**
THINGWALL 1K **83** (2A **214**)
Thingwall Dr. CH61: Irby 7D **58**
Thingwall Grange CH61: Thin 7E **58**
Thingwall Recreation Cen. 7E **58**
Thingwall Rd. CH61: Irby 7A **58**
Thingwall Rd. E. CH61: Thin 6D **58**
Third Av. CH43: Bid 6E **32**
CW1: Crewe 5F **195**
CW11: S'ach 4E **200**
SK12: Poy 5C **100**
SK15: Carrb 3F **5**
WA7: Pal F 6B **90**
Thirlby Dr. M22: Wyth 4K **75**
Thirlmere SK11: Mac 7G **125**
Thirlmere Av. CH43: Noc 6F **33**
WA2: Warr 1G **41**
Thirlmere Cl. CW4: H Cha 6G **181**
CW7: Wins 1G **179**
SK9: Ald E 6E **118**
*SK15: Stal 5B **4***
(off Springs La.)
WA6: Frod 7K **111**
Thirlmere Ct. CW12: Cong 4C **182**
Thirlmere Dr. CH45: Wall 6H **13**
WA13: Lymm 2B **70**
Thirlmere Rd. CH2: Ches 5D **146**
CH64: Nest 2C **130**
CH65: Whit 6D **134**
CW2: Crewe 5K **193**
M22: Wyth 3H **75**
M31: Part 7B **20**
SK1: Stoc 5F **53**
Thirlmere Way WA8: Wid 5C **62**
Thirsk Av. M33: Sale 1G **47**
Thirsk Cl. WA7: Run 1J **111**
Thirsk Way SK10: Mac 1K **125**
Thistle Cl. SK15: Stal 3F **11**
WA16: Pick 1B **158**
Thistle Ho., The *SK15: M'ook 5E **4***
(off Bramble Ct.)
Thistle Sq. M31: Part 2G **45**
Thistleton Av. CH41: Birk 4J **33**
Thistleton Cl. SK11: Mac 6A **126**
Thistle Wlk. *M31: Part 2G **45***
(off Thistle Sq.)
Thistlewood Dr. SK9: Wilm 7A **98**
Thistley Flds. SK14: Hyde 3H **27**
Thomas Av. CW5: Stap 4E **196**
Thomas Brassey Cl. CH2: Ches 7B **146**
Thomas Cl. CH1: Blac 4G **145**
CH2: Mic T 2J **147**
CH65: Whit 6D **134**
M34: Den 6F **9**
ST7: Als 5F **203**
Thomas Ct. CH43: Oxt 7B **34**
WA7: Pal F 7B **90**
Thomas Gibbon Cl. *M32: S'ord 2H **23***
(off Mitford St.)
Thomas Hodges Ct. CW4: H Cha 4K **181**
Thomas Jones Way WA7: Run 4G **89**
Thomason's Bri. La. WA4: H Wal 7C **66**
Thomas Row *CW5: Nant 1C **196***
(off Dog La.)
Thomas St. CH41: Birk 7D **34**
CW1: Crewe 1D **194**
CW12: Cong 3G **183**
M32: S'ord 1K **23**
SK1: Stoc 5D **52**
SK6: Bred 1A **54**
SK6: Comp 2H **55**
WA7: Run 3H **89**
WA8: Wid 6G **63**
WA15: Alt 2K **213** (1J **73**)
Thomas St. W. SK1: Stoc 5D **52**
Thompson Av. WA3: Cul 7E **6**
Thompson Cl. M34: Den 7B **8**
WA12: New W 2F **15**
Thompson Ct. M34: Den 7A **8**
*SK15: Stal 7A **4***
(off Thompson Fold)
Thompson Fold SK15: Stal 7A **4**
Thompson Rd. M34: Den 7A **8**
Thompson St. CH41: Tran 1D **60**
WA3: Ris 6K **17**
Thomson Gdns. CW12: Cong 3C **182**
Thomson St. SK3: Stoc 4C **52**
Thorburn Cl. CH62: N Fer 5G **61**
Thorburn Ct. CH62: N Fer 4G **61**
Thorburn Cres. CH62: N Fer 5G **61**
Thorburn Rd. CH62: N Fer 5G **61**
Thoresway Rd. M13: Manc 1B **24**
SK9: Wilm 2E **118**
Thorlby Rd. WA3: Cul 7F **7**
Thorley Dr. M41: Urm 1C **22**
WA15: Timp 7B **48**
Thorley Gro. CW2: Crewe 5A **194**
Thorley La. M90: Man A 4F **75**
WA15: Ring 4E **74**
WA15: Timp 6B **48**
Thorley M. SK7: Bram 6D **78**
Thorley Rd. WA15: Timp 7C **48**
Thorn Bank SK15: Carrb 2G **5**
Thorn Bank Lodge SK4: Stoc 7E **24**
Thornberry Cl. CH1: Sau 2C **144**
Thornbrook Way CW11: Ett H 4B **200**
Thornbury Av. SK14: Hat 7F **11**
Thornbury Cl. SK8: Chea H 4A **78**
Thornby Wlk. M23: Wyth 7G **49**
THORNCLIFFE
SK14 . . . . 4K **11**
ST13 . . . . 2D **221**
Thorncliffe Av. SK16: Duk 3H **9**
Thorncliffe Gro. M19: Manc 2F **25**
Thorncliffe Rd. CH44: Wall 1K **33**
SK13: Had 3K **11**
Thorncliffe Va. SK14: H'rth 4K **11**
Thorncliffe Wood SK14: H'rth 5K **11**
Thorn Cl. WA5: Penk 2H **65**
WA7: Run 7J **89**
Thorn Cl. *SK15: Stal 7B **4***
(off Waterloo Rd.)
Thorncroft Dr. CH61: Barns 2K **83**
Thorndale Ct. *WA15: Timp 7A **48***
(off Stockport Rd.)
Thorndale Gro. WA15: Timp 7A **48**
Thorn Dr. M22: Wyth 5C **76**
Thorndyke Cl. L35: R'ill 3E **36**
Thorne Av. M41: Urm 1K **21**
Thorne Cl. SK10: Pres 6H **121**
Thornedge WA15: Timp 4K **47**
Thorne Dr. CH66: L Sut 3H **133**
Thorne Ho. M14: Manc 1A **24**
Thorne La. CH44: Wall 6F **13**
Thorneside M34: Den 5E **8**
(not continuous)
Thorness Cl. CH49: Gre 3K **57**
Thorneycroft Cl. WA15: Timp 7B **48**
Thorneycroft Dr. WA1: Warr 6G **41**
Thorneycroft Rd. WA15: Timp 7B **48**
Thorneycroft St. CH41: Birk 4K **33**
Thorney Dr. SK8: Chea H 7A **78**
Thorneyholme Dr. WA16: Knut 4F **117**
Thornfield Ct. *SK4: Stoc 1J **51***
(off Thornfield Rd.)
Thornfield Gro. SK8: Chea H 3J **77**
Thornfield Hey CH63: Spit 4A **86**
SK9: Wilm 6B **98**
Thornfield Ho. SK8: Chea H 3J **77**
Thornfield Rd. M19: Manc 6B **24**
SK4: Stoc 1J **51**
Thornfields CW1: L'ton 4G **191**
Thorn Gro. M14: Manc 3A **24**
M33: Sale 7G **23**
SK8: Chea H 7J **77**
WA15: Hale 2J **73**
Thorngrove Av. M23: Wyth 5D **48**
Thorngrove Dr. SK9: Wilm 1H **119**
Thorngrove Hill SK9: Wilm 1H **119**
Thorngrove Ho. M23: Wyth 5D **48**
Thorngrove Rd. SK9: Wilm 1H **119**
Thornham Cl. CH49: Upt 5D **32**
Thornham Rd. M33: Sale 2J **47**
Thornhill Cl. M34: Den 1K **25**
Thornhill Rd. M43: Droy 1A **8**
SK4: Stoc 2H **51**
Thornholme Rd. SK6: Mar 1F **81**
Thorn Ho. *SK15: Stal 7B **4***
(off Waterloo Rd.)
Thorn La. CW8: H'ord 1B **162**
Thornlea WA15: Alt 1K **73**
Thornleigh Av. CH62: East 4A **108**
Thornleigh Dr. CH66: Ell P 2A **134**
Thornley Cl. WA13: Lymm 2J **69**
Thornley Cres. SK6: Bred 7F **27**
Thornley La. Nth. M34: Stoc 1J **25**
Thornley La. Sth. M34: Den, Stoc 1J **25**
SK5: Stoc 1J **25**
Thornley Ri. M34: Aude 3C **8**
Thornley Rd. CH46: More 5K **31**
WA13: Lymm 2J **69**
Thornleys Rd. M34: Den 6F **9**
Thornley St. SK14: Hyde 2K **27**
Thornridge CH46: More 4D **32**
Thorn Rd. SK7: Bram 1G **99**
WA1: Padd 4A **42**
WA7: Run 7J **89**
Thorns Dr. CH49: Gre 3K **57**
THORNSETT 2D **217**
Thornsgreen Rd. M22: Wyth 5K **75**
THORNTON 1B **214**
Thornton WA8: Wid 5E **62**
Thornton Av. CH63: H Beb 5C **60**
M34: Aude 2B **8**
M41: Urm 1K **21**
SK11: Mac 7H **125**
Thornton Bank CW6: Alp 2J **189**
Thornton Cl. CW7: Wins 1H **179**
WA3: Low 1A **6**
WN7: Leigh 1F **7**
Thornton Comn. Rd.
CH63: Rab M, Tho H 7F **85**
Thornton Cres. CH60: Hes 1E **104**
Thorntondale Dr. WA5: Gt San 5G **39**
Thornton Dr. CH2: Ches 5A **146**
CW2: Wis 7A **194**
SK9: Hand 3A **98**
Thornton Ga. SK8: Gat 6C **50**
Thornton Grn. La. CH2: Tho M 6C **136**
Thornton Gro. CH63: H Beb 5C **60**
THORNTON HOUGH 1K **105** (2B **214**)
THORNTON-LE-MOORS 6C **136** (3C **215**)
Thornton M. CH66: Chil T 7C **108**
Thornton Pl. SK4: Stoc 7E **24**
Thornton Rd. CH45: Wall 5G **13**
CH63: H Beb 5C **60**
CH65: Ell P 4F **135**
SK8: He Grn 4E **76**
WA5: Gt San 1K **65**
Thornton Sq. SK11: Mac 7H **125**
Thornton St. CH41: Birk 4K **33**
Thorn Tree Cl. L24: Hale 7B **88**
Thorn Tree Dr. CW1: L'ton 4F **191**
Thorntree Grn. WA4: App T 1B **94**
Thorn Wlk. M31: Part 2G **45**
Thornway SK6: H Lan 6F **81**
SK7: Bram 5A **78**
SK10: Boll 4D **122**
Thornwythe Gro. CH66: Gt Sut 4A **134**
Thornycroft CW7: Wins 3B **178**
Thornycroft Cl. SK11: Gaw 4C **128**
Thornycroft St. SK11: Mac 5B **126**
Thorold Gro. M33: Sale 7K **23**
Thorpe Bank CH42: R Fer 5E **60**
Thorpe Cl. CW1: Crewe 5E **190**
M34: Den 6E **8**
WA15: Timp 5C **48**
Thorpe Gro. SK4: Stoc 5G **25**
Thorpe Hall Gro. SK14: Hyde 4A **10**
Thorpe La. M34: Den 5E **8**
Thorp St. SK10: Mac 4A **126**
Thorsby Av. SK14: Hyde 1A **28**
Thorsby Rd. WA15: Timp 7J **47**
Thorsby Way *M34: Den 2F **27***
(off Tatton Rd.)
Thorstone Dr. CH61: Irby 6K **57**
Thorsway CH42: R Fer 3E **60**
CH48: Cald 5E **56**
Thowler La. WA14: M'ton 7H **71**
Thrapston Av. M34: Aude 1C **8**

Threaphurst La.—Treborth Rd.

Threaphurst La. SK7: H Gro 5C 80
THREAPWOOD
ST10 . . . . . 3D 221
SY14 . . . . . 6H 207 (3C 219)
Threapwood Rd. M22: Wyth 4A 76
Three Acres Dr. SK5: Stoc 6H 25
Three Acres La. SK8: Chea H 6G 77
Three Counties Rd. OL5: Moss 1E 4
Three Flds. Cl. CW12: Cong 3C 182
Three La. Ends M34: Den 1E 26
THREE LANES END 7J 31
Three Old Arches CH1: Ches 5C 212
Threeways CW8: Cudd 2A 160
Thresher Av. CH49: Gre 1K 57
Thresher Cl. M33: Sale 1F 49
(off Windmill Rd.)
Threshfield Dr. WA15: Timp 5B 48
Throstle Bank St. SK14: Hyde 6H 9
Throstle Gro. SK6: Mar 7D 54
Thrush Way CW7: Wins 1G 179
Thurcaston Rd. WA14: W Tim 3G 47
Thurleigh Rd. M20: Manc 1D 50
Thurlestone Dr. SK7: H Gro 3F 79
Thurlestone Rd. WA14: Alt 6F 47
THURLWOOD 1G 203
Thursby Rd. CH62: Brom 4E 86
Thursfield Ct. CH1: Ches 2J 149
(off New Crane St.)
THURSTASTON 1D 82 (2A 214)
Thurstaston Common Local Nature Reserve 5H 57
Thurstaston Rd. CH60: Hes 5G 83
CH61: Irby, Thur 1D 82
Thurston Cl. WA5: Gt San 6B 40
Thurston Grn. SK9: Ald E 6F 119
Thurston Rd. CH4: Salt 6F 149
Thynne St. WA1: Warr 1E 66
Tibb's Cross La. WA8: Bold H 4K 37
Tib St. M34: Den 1E 26
Tickford Bank WA8: Wid 3E 62
Tidal La. WA1: Padg 4K 41
Tideswell Cl. SK8: He Grn 5F 77
Tideswell Rd. SK7: H Gro 5J 79
Tideswell Way M34: Den 3F 27
Tideway CH45: Wall 3E 12
Tidnock Av. CW12: Cong 1G 183
Tiffield Ct. CW7: Wins 1H 179
Tilbey Dr. WA6: Frod 7G 111
Tilbury Pl. WA7: Murd 1G 113
Tilby Cl. M41: Urm 1H 21
Tildsley Cres. WA7: West 1F 111
Tillard Av. SK3: Stoc 4K 51
Tilley St. WA1: Warr 7G 41
Tillhey Rd. M22: Wyth 3K 75
Tillotson Cl. L8: Liv 7K 35
Tilman Cl. WA5: Gt San 4J 39
Tilney Av. M32: S'ord 2K 23
Tilson Rd. M23: Wyth 7E 48
TILSTOCK 3D 219
Tilstock Av. CH62: N Fer 5G 61
Tilstock Cres. CH43: Pren 4J 59
Tilstock Wlk. M23: Wyth 4E 48
TILSTON 6B 206 (2C 219)
Tilston Av. WA4: Westy 1A 68
Tilstone Cl. CW2: Hou 5E 198
CW9: N'ich 1F 163
TILSTONE FEARNALL 6K 175 (1D 219)
Tilston Rd. CH45: Wall 5G 13
SY14: Kidn, Mal 1G 207
Tilston Wlk. SK9: Wilm 5B 98
Timberfields Rd. CH1: Sau 2B 144
Timber La. CW9: N'ich 4E 156
TIMBERSBROOK 1C 221
Timbersbrook Gro. SK9: Wilm 4A 98
(off Colshaw Dr.)
Timberscombe Gdns. WA1: Wool 6E 42
Timber St. SK10: Mac 3C 126
Timbrell Av. CW1: Crewe 7E 190
Timmis Cl. WA2: Fear 1A 42
Timmis Cres. WA8: Wid 4G 63
TIMPERLEY 5K 47 (2B 216)
Timperley Av. WA4: Westy 1A 68
Timperley Ct. WA8: Wid 5H 63
(off Alfred Cl.)
Timperley Cricket, Hockey, Tennis & Lacrosse Club 7K 47
Timperley La. WN7: Leigh 1H 7
Timperley Station (Metro) 4K 47
Timpson Rd. M23: Wyth 5E 48
Tinas Way CH49: Upt 7D 32
Tindall St. SK5: Stoc 1J 25
Tinkersfield CW5: Stap 3E 196
Tinker's Pas. SK14: Hyde 1K 27
(off Lumn Rd.)
Tinker St. SK14: Hyde 7J 9
Tinkwood La. SY14: Thr 5J 207
Tinsley St. WA4: Westy 2K 67
Tintagel Cl. SK10: Mac 4F 125
WA7: B'vale 1E 112
Tintagel Ct. SK15: Stal 7A 4
Tintagel Wlk. SK14: Hat 7F 11
Tintern Av. CH2: Upt 4C 146
M41: Urm 3K 21
Tintern Cl. SK12: Poy 1C 100
WA5: Call 2C 40
Tintern Dr. CH46: More 4B 32
WA15: Hale 3C 74
Tintern Gro. SK1: Stoc 3F 53
Tintern Rd. SK8: Chea H 7K 77
TINTWISTLE 1D 217
Tipperary St. SK15: Carrb 4F 5
Tipping Brow WA16: Mob 6D 102
Tipping St. WA14: Alt 2H 73
Tipton Cl. SK8: Chea H 1K 77
Tipton Dr. M23: Wyth 2H 49
Tiree Cl. SK7: H Gro 4K 79
Tirley La. CW6: Utk, W'gton 1B 176
TIRNEWYDD 3A 214
Tirza Av. M19: Manc 3C 24
Titchfield St. L3: Liv 1J 35
Tithebarn Cl. CH60: Hes 7H 83
Tithe Barn Ct. SK4: Stoc 7C 24
Tithebarn Dr. CH64: Park 5E 104
Tithe Barn Rd. SK4: Stoc 7C 24
Tithebarn Rd. WA15: H'rns 5C 74
Tithebarn St. L2: Liv 2H 35
Tithings, The WA7: Run 5A 90
TITTENSOR 3C 221
TIVERTON 7H 175 (1D 219)
Tiverton Av. CH44: Wall 7G 13
M33: Sale 1K 47
Tiverton Cl. CH2: Ches 5B 146
CW11: S'ach 2G 201
WA8: Wid 2C 62
Tiverton Ct. CW9: N'ich 1D 162
(off Blakemere Dr.)
Tiverton Dr. M33: Sale 1K 47
SK9: Wilm 5A 98
Tiverton Sq. WA5: Penk 1G 65
Tiviot Dale SK1: Stoc 5J 213 (2D 52)
Tiviot Way SK5: Stoc 1D 52
Tobermory Rd. SK8: He Grn 4E 76
Tobin St. CH44: Wall 7K 13
Toft Cl. CH4: Ches 6F 149
WA8: Wid 4F 63
Toft Rd. WA16: Knut 4E 116
Toft Way SK9: Hand 2B 98
Toftwood Av. L35: R'ill 3D 36
Toftwood Gdns. L35: R'ill 3D 36
Toleman Av. CH63: Beb 1A 86
Tolland La. WA15: Hale 5K 73
Tollard Cl. SK8: Chea H 7K 77
Toll Bar Av. SK11: Mac 5C 126
Toll Bar Pl. WA2: Warr 7K 15
(off Poplars Av.)
Toll Bar Rd. CH3: Gt Bou 2F 151
SK11: Mac 4G 125
WA2: Warr 1E 40
Toll Bar St. SK1: Stoc 7K 213 (4D 52)
Tollemache Cl. SK14: Mot 5H 11
Tollemache Dr. CW1: Crewe 5F 191
Tollemache Rd. CH41: Birk 5J 33
CH43: Bid 4J 33
CH43: Clau 5J 33
SK14: Mot 5H 11
Tollemache St. CH45: N Bri 3J 13
Tollemache Ter. CH2: Ches 1C 150
Tollgate Dr. CW3: Audl 5B 210
Tollitt St. CW1: Crewe 2C 194
Tomcroft La. M34: Den 1C 26
Tomkinson Cl. CW1: Crewe 6E 190
Tomkinson St. CH2: Ches 7B 146
Tom La. WA14: Rost 7C 72
Tomlinson Av. WA2: Warr 4H 41
Tomlins Ter. CH1: Blac 5F 145
(off Burton Rd.)
Tom Mann Cl. L3: Liv 2J 35
Tommy's La. CW1: Crewe 4E 194
CW12: Cong 2H 183
Tom Pendry Sq. SK15: Stal 1B 10
(off Melbourne St.)
Tom Shepley St. SK14: Hyde 1K 27
Tomwood Ri. SK13: Char 5K 29
Tonbridge Cl. SK10: Mac 2J 125
Tonbridge Rd. M19: Manc 3E 24
SK5: Stoc 3J 25
Tonge Grn. SK15: Mat 4F 11
Toogood Ct. CH2: Mic T 2J 147
Topcroft Cl. M22: N'den 4A 50
Topfield Rd. M22: Wyth 1J 75
Topgate Cl. CH60: Hes 6K 83
Top Pk. Cl. WA13: Warb 3G 45
Topping Ct. WA3: Birc 7H 17
Toppings, The SK6: Bred 1A 54
Top Rd. WA6: Frod 3K 139
WA6: K'ley 2C 152
Top Sandy La. WA2: Warr 1F 41
Top Station Rd. ST7: Mow C 5G 205
Torbay Dr. SK2: Stoc 5F 53
Torbay Rd. M41: Urm 2D 22
Torbrook Gro. SK9: Wilm 4A 98
(off Bosley Cl.)
TORKINGTON 3J 79
Torkington Ho. SK7: H Gro 3K 79
Torkington La. SK6: H Gro 2D 80
Torkington Mnr. SK7: H Gro 2B 80
Torkington Rd. SK7: H Gro 3J 79
SK8: Gat 7D 50
SK9: Wilm 1H 119
Torkington St. SK3: Stoc 5B 52
Toronto Av. M90: Man A 6H 75
Toronto Rd. SK2: Stoc 6E 52
Toronto St. CH44: Wall 1D 34
Torquay Gro. SK2: Stoc 1F 79
Torr Dr. CH62: East 7G 87
Torridon Gro. CH66: Gt Sut 5B 134
Torridon Wlk. M22: Wyth 5J 75
Torrin Cl. SK3: Stoc 7D 52
Torrington Dr. CH61: Thin 7E 58
SK14: Hat 1E 28
Torrington Gdns. CH61: Thin 6E 58
Torrington Rd. CH44: Wall 7G 13
Torr Ri. CW6: Tarp 3J 175
Torr Rd. SK11: Mac 1G 129
Torrs Riverside Pk., The 1K 103
Torver Wlk. M22: Wyth 4H 75
Torwood CH43: Noc 5G 33
Total Fitness
Altrincham 3H 213
Chester 6K 145
Prenton 5G 59
Warrington 4E 40
Wilmslow 2C 98
Totland Cl. WA5: Gt San 5E 38
Totland Gro. CH2: Ches 6B 146
Totnes Av. SK7: Bram 3E 78
Totnes Rd. M33: Sale 6C 22
Totridge Cl. SK2: Stoc 7H 53
Tottenham Dr. M23: Wyth 5D 48
Tourist Info. Cen.
Altrincham 2J 213 (1H 73)
Bredbury 1A 54
Brinnington 6B 26
Cheadle Hulme 3J 77
Chester 4B 212 (2K 149)
Congleton 4G 183
Knutsford 4E 116
Liverpool, Salthouse Quay 4H 35
Liverpool, Williamson St. 3J 35
Macclesfield 4A 126
Manchester International Airport, Terminal 1 . . . . . 6H 75
Manchester International Airport, Terminal 2 . . . . . 5G 75
Nantwich 2C 196
Poynton 2D 100
Runcorn, Church St. 3G 89
Runcorn Town Hall 5H 89
Stockport, Chestergate 6H 213 (3D 52)
Stockport, Market Pl. 5J 213 (2D 52)
Warrington 7E 40
Wilmslow 1G 119
Tourney Grn. WA5: W'ook 2J 39
Tours Av. M23: Wyth 2G 49
Tower Gdns. L3: Liv 3G 35
Towergate CH1: Ches 4A 212
TOWER HILL
L33 . . . . . 1C 215
SK11 . . . . . 7G 123
Tower Hill CH42: Tran 2C 60
SK10: R'ow 7G 123
Tower Hill Ct. CW12: Cong 3D 182
Tower Hill Rd. ST7: Mow C 4J 205
ST8: Bro L, Mow C 4J 205
Tower Ho., The SK11: Mac 4K 125
(off Bridge St.)
Tower La. CW8: Weav 4E 154
WA7: Nort 7E 90
WA13: Lymm 3B 70
Tower Prom. CH45: N Bri 2J 13
Tower Quays CH41: Birk 4D 34
Tower Rd. CH1: Ches 3A 212 (1J 149)
CH41: Birk 4D 34
CH42: Tran 4A 60
(Reservoir Rd.)
CH42: Tran 2C 60
(Tower Hill)
Tower Rd. Nth. CH60: Hes 4G 83
Tower Rd. Sth. CH60: Hes 5H 83
Towers, The CH42: Tran 3D 60
SK10: Mac 4G 125
Towers Bus. Pk. M20: Manc 3E 50
Towers Cl. CW2: Wis 7A 194
SK12: Poy 1E 100
Towers Ct. WA5: Warr 5C 40
Towers La. WA6: Alv, Hel 7A 138
Towers Rd. SK12: Poy 6K 79
Tower St. L3: Liv 7J 35
SK14: Hyde 2J 27
SK16: Duk 1J 9
Tower Way CW1: Crewe 2C 194
Tower Wharf CH1: Ches 3A 212 (1K 149)
CH41: Birk 4D 34
Townbridge Ct. CW8: N'ich 5D 156
Towncroft M34: Den 6F 9
Towneley Ct. WA8: Wid 4G 63
TOWN END 6C 36 (2C 215)
Townend St. SK14: Hyde 1K 27
Town Farm La. WA6: Norl 5F 153
Townfield M41: Urm 2A 22
Townfield Av. CH3: Farn 5B 186
Townfield Cen. CH43: Oxt 2H 59
Townfield Cl. CH43: Oxt 2H 59
Townfield Ct. CW8: Barnt 2A 156
Townfield Gdns. CH63: H Beb 6E 60
WA14: Alt 1H 213 (7H 47)
Townfield La. CH1: Mol 5A 140
CH3: Farn 5A 186
CH3: Tar 6A 170
CH43: Oxt 2H 59
CH63: Beb 6E 60
CH63: Beb, H Beb 6E 60
CW6: Tive 6H 175
CW8: Barnt 1K 155
WA2: Winw 6K 15
WA6: Frod 1J 139
WA13: Warb 4D 44
Townfield Rd. CH48: W Kir 3C 56
WA7: Win H 4E 90
WA14: Alt 1H 213 (7H 47)
WA16: Mob 6B 102
TOWN FIELDS 5D 178
Town Flds. CH45: Wall 5E 12
Townfields CW11: S'ach 4E 200
WA16: Knut 3G 117
Townfields Cotts. CW7: Wins 5E 178
(off Grosvenor Ct.)
Townfields Cres. CW7: Wins 5E 178
Townfields Dr. CW7: Wins 6D 178
Townfields Gdns. CW7: Wins 5E 178
Townfields Rd. CW7: Wins 5E 178
Townfield Vw. WA7: Win H 4E 90
Townfield Way CH44: Wall 7H 13
Town Fold SK6: Mar B 5H 55
Town Ga. Dr. M41: Urm 1F 21
Town Hall Dr. WA7: Run 5H 89
Town Hill WA1: Warr 7F 41
Town La. CH63: H Beb 7C 60
CH64: L Nes 2D 130
L24: Hale 7A 88
M34: Den 1C 26
SK13: Char 5K 29
SK16: Duk 2H 9
WA16: Mob 1K 117
Town La. Ct. M34: Den 1D 26
Townley Ct. CH47: Hoy 5C 30
(off Seaview)
Townley Fold SK14: Hyde 4C 10
Townley Mill SK11: Mac 5A 126
(off Townley Pl.)
Townley Pl. SK11: Mac 5A 126
Townley St. SK11: Mac 5A 126
Townley Ter. SK6: Mar 6G 55
(off Canal St.)
Town Mdw. La. CH46: More 4J 31
Town Rd. CH42: Tran 2C 60
Townscliffe La. SK6: Mar B 5H 55
Towns Cft. Lodge M33: Sale 5D 22
(off Green La.)
Townsend Farm La. WA14: Dun M 3A 46
Townsend La. ST7: Sch G 1H 203
Townsend Rd. CW12: Cong 4G 183
Townsend St. CH41: Birk 3H 33
Towns Fld. Dr. CW6: L Bud 2H 177
TOWNS GATE 1F 21
Townsgate Way M44: Irlam 2E 20
Townshend Av. CH61: Irby 1F 83
Townshend Rd. CW9: Los Gra 4C 158
Township Cl. CH3: Clut 2A 206
Townson Dr. WN7: Leigh 1F 7
Town Sq. CW9: N'ich 5E 156
M33: Sale 7G 23
WA7: Pal F 7B 90
(off Halton Lea Shop. Cen.)
Town St. SK6: Mar B 5H 55
Towns Vw. SK15: Stal 1C 10
Town Vw. CH43: Oxt 7B 34
Town Vw. M. CH43: Oxt 7B 34
Town Wlk. WA7: Pal F 7B 90
(off Halton Lea Shop. Cen.)
Town Well WA6: K'ley 1D 152
TOXTETH 6K 35 (2B 214)
Toxteth St. L8: Liv 7K 35
(not continuous)
Trackside Bus. Pk. CW11: Ett H 3A 200
Tracy Dr. WA12: New W 1H 15
Tradewind Sq. L1: Liv 4K 35
(off Kent St.)
TRAFALGAR 2A 86
Trafalgar Av. CH44: Wall 6K 13
M34: Aude 3B 8
SK12: Poy 3F 101
Trafalgar Cl. CW9: N'ich 3D 162
SK12: Poy 3F 101
Trafalgar Ct. WA8: Wid 7G 63
Trafalgar Dr. CH63: Beb 2A 86
Trafalgar Ho. M34: Aude 3B 8
(off Audenshaw Rd.)
WA14: Alt 6H 47
Trafalgar Rd. CH44: Wall 6J 13
M33: Sale 5H 23
Trafalgar Sq. OL5: Moss 1C 4
(off Wyre St.)
OL7: Ash L 1E 8
(not continuous)
Trafalgar St. OL7: Ash L 2E 8
Trafford Av. M41: Urm 1D 22
WA5: Warr 5C 40
Trafford Cres. WA7: Run 1J 111
Trafford Dr. WA15: Timp 4B 48
Trafford Gro. M32: S'ord 2J 23
TRAFFORD PARK 1B 216
Trafford Pl. SK9: Wilm 1J 119
Trafford Rd. SK9: Ald E 6F 119
SK9: Wilm 5J 97
Trafford St. CH1: Ches 1C 212 (7A 146)
Trafford Water Sports Cen. 5K 23
Tragan Cl. SK2: Stoc 6H 53
Tragan Dr. SK2: Stoc 6H 53
WA5: Penk 2F 65
Tramore Wlk. M22: Wyth 3K 75
Tramway Rd. M44: Irlam 4C 20
Tramway St. CH1: Ches 2E 212 (1B 150)
Tranby Cl. M22: Wyth 1B 76
TRANMERE 2D 60 (2B 214)
Tranmere Dr. SK9: Hand 3B 98
Tranmere Recreation Cen. 3B 60
Tranmere Rd. SK3: Stoc 4K 51
Tranmere Rovers FC 3B 60
Trap St. SK11: L Wit 7K 167
Travis Brow SK4: Stoc 6F 213 (3B 52)
Travis St. SK14: Hyde 1K 27
WA8: Wid 5H 63
Trawden Grn. SK2: Stoc 1H 79
Treacle Brow SK14: Hyde 3A 28
(off Mottram Old Rd.)
Treborth Rd. CH1: Blac 7E 144

Warway—Wellington Mans.

Warway SY14: T Grn 7J **207**
Warwick Av. M34: Den 2E **26**
WA5: Gt San 5F **39**
WA5: Warr 5D **40**
WA12: New W 1G **15**
Warwick Cl. CH43: Oxt 7B **34**
CH64: Nest 3C **130**
SK4: Stoc 7G **25**
SK8: Chea H 1J **77**
SK11: Mac 6G **125**
SK16: Duk 4H **9**
WA16: Knut 4G **117**
Warwick Ct. CH65: Ell P 6G **135**
M34: Den 3F 27
(off Wordsworth Rd.)
SK4: Stoc 7G **25**
Warwick Dr. CH45: Wall 5J **13**
CH48: W Kir 5D **56**
M33: Sale 7J **23**
SK7: H Gro 5H **79**
WA15: Hale 4J **73**
Warwick Ga. CW5: Ast 7G **209**
Warwick Gro. M34: Aude 2B **8**
WA7: Cast 5B **90**
Warwick Ho. *M19: Manc 1D 24*
(off Central Av.)
M33: Sale 7J 23
(off Temple Rd.)
Warwick Mall SK8: Chea 6F **51**
Warwick M. SK11: Mac 6G **125**
Warwick Pl. CW7: Wins 6D **178**
Warwick Rd. CH1: Blac 5G **145**
CH49: Upt 7B **32**
M44: Cad 6A **20**
SK4: Stoc 1A **52**
SK6: Rom 2E **54**
SK11: Mac 6F **125**
WA15: Hale 4J **73**
Warwick St. L8: Liv 6K **35**
Warwick Ter. *SK16: Duk 1G 9*
(off Hill St.)
Warwick Wlk. *SK11: Mac 6G 125*
(off Warwick Rd.)
Wasdale Dr. SK8: Gat 2D **76**
Wasdale Gro. CW1: L'ton 4G **191**
Wasdale Ter. SK15: Stal 5B **4**
Washbrook Av. CH43: Bid 4F **33**
Washbrook Dr. M32: S'ord 2G **23**
WASH END 2B **6**
Wash End WA3: Low 2B **6**
WASHERWALL 3D **221**
Washford Dr. M23: Wyth 4D **48**
Washington Cl. SK8: Chea H 5H **77**
WA8: Wid 2F **63**
Washington Dr.
WA5: Gt San 5A **40**
Wash La. WA4: Warr 3J **67**
WA16: All 4B **164**
WASHPOOL 6J **123**
Washway Rd. M33: Sale 3J **47**
Wasley Cl. WA2: Fear 1A **42**
Wastdale Ct. CH46: More 3K **31**
Wastdale Dr. CH46: More 3K **31**
Wastdale M. CH46: More 3K **31**
Wastdale Rd. M23: Wyth 1F **75**
Waste La. CW6: Kel 3D **172**
CW8: Cudd 3B **160**
CW8: Oak 4J **173**
Watchgate SK7: H Gro 3G **79**
Watch La. CW11: Most 3A **200**
(not continuous)
Watchlane Flash (Nature Reserve) 3A **200**
Waterbank Row CW9: N'ich 6E **156**
Waterbridge Ct. WA4: App 5H **67**
WA13: Lymm 2H **69**
Water Bus. Pk. CH65: Ell P 1F **135**
Waterfield Cl. CH63: H Beb 1H **85**
Waterfoot Cotts. *SK14: Mot 6H 11*
(off Rushycroft)
Waterford Av. M20: Manc 1K **49**
SK6: Rom 2F **55**
Waterford Dr. CH64: L Nes 1E **130**
Waterford Pl. SK8: He Grn 5D **76**
Waterford Rd. CH43: Oxt 7J **33**
Waterford Way WA7: Murd 1E **112**
(not continuous)
Waterfront WA4: Pre H 1H **113**
Waterfront Bus. Area L8: Liv 5K **35**
Waterfront Bus. Area Parliament St. Nth.
L1: Liv 5K 35
(off New Bird St.)
L1: Liv 5J 35
(off Simpson St.)
Waterfront Bus. Area Parliament St. Sth.
L8: Liv 6K 35
(off Stanhope St.)
Waterfront Dr. WA4: Westy 2B **68**
Watergate M34: Aude 2B **8**
Water Ga. Rd. CH1: Ches 3A **212**
Watergate Row Nth.
CH1: Ches 4B **212** (2K **149**)
Watergate Row Sth.
CH1: Ches 5B **212** (2K **149**)
Watergate Sq. CH1: Ches 5A **212** (2K **149**)
Watergate St. CH1: Ches 5A **212** (2K **149**)
Water Gro. Rd. SK16: Duk 3A **10**
Waterhouse Av. SK10: Boll 3C **122**
Waterhouse Way SK5: Stoc 4H **25**
Water La. SK9: Wilm 7H **97**
SK13: Had 2J **11**
SK14: H'rth 2J **11**
Water-Lode CW5: Nant 1A **196**
WATERLOO
L21 1B **214**
WA6 3A **152**
Waterloo Cen. WA8: Wid 7G **63**
Waterloo Cl. CH65: Ell P 3E **134**
Waterloo Cotts. SK6: Rom 2E **54**
WA6: K'ood 3A **152**
Waterloo Ct. CH63: Beb 7F **61**
SK15: Stal 7A 4
(off Hully St.)
Waterloo Dock L3: Liv 1G **35**
Waterloo Ind. Est.
SK1: Stoc 7K **213** (3D **52**)
Waterloo La. WA6: Frod, K'ood 7J **139**
WA6: K'ood, New 4A **152**
Waterloo Pl. CH41: Birk 7D **34**
SK1: Stoc 7K 213
(off Watson Sq.)
Waterloo Quay L3: Liv 1G **35**
Waterloo Rd. CH2: Ches 6K **145**
CH45: N Bri 2H **13**
CW1: Hasl 2K **195**
CW8: N'ich 6D **156**
L3: Liv 1G **35**
SK1: Stoc 7K **213** (3D **52**)
SK6: Rom 2E **54**
SK7: Bram 4D **78**
SK12: Poy 4F **101**
SK15: Stal 7B **4**
WA7: Run 4F **89**
WA8: Wid 1G **89**
Waterloo St. W. SK11: Mac 4K **125**
Watermead M33: Sale 3A **48**
Watermead Cl. SK3: Stoc 1C **78**
Watermead Dr. WA7: Pre B 2H **113**
Watermeetings La. SK6: Rom 2E **54**
Watermill Dr. SK11: Mac 5C **126**
Waterpark Cl. CH43: Pren 4J **59**
Waterpark Ho. *CH42: Tran 3A 60*
(off Storeton Rd.)
Waterpark Rd. CH42: Tran 3K **59**
CH43: Pren 4J **59**
Water Rd. SK15: Stal 7A **4**
Waters Edge CH1: Ches 3A **212** (1J **149**)
CW9: And 2C **156**
SK6: Mar B 4G **55**
Watersedge WA6: Frod 5K **111**
Watersedge Apartments
CH45: N Bri 2J 13
(off Tower Prom.)
Watersedge Cl. SK8: Chea H 2K **77**
Waters Edge M. CW10: Mid 4C **180**
Watersfield Cl. SK8: Chea H 5H **77**
Waters Grn. SK11: Mac 4A **126**
Waterside M33: Sale 6H **23**
SK6: Mar 1F **81**
SK11: Mac 5B **126**
SK14: Hat 2E **28**
WA4: App 5H **67**
Waterside Arts Cen. 6G **23**
Waterside Av. SK6: Mar 7F **55**
Waterside Cl. SK14: Hat 1E **28**
Waterside Cotts. CW5: Wren 1H **209**
Waterside Ct. M41: Urm 1G **21**
WA7: Run 3E **88**
Waterside Dr. WA6: Frod 5J **111**
Waterside La. WA8: Hal B 1C **88**
Waterside M. CW11: Whe 6E **200**
Waterside Plaza *M33: Sale 6G 23*
(off Tatton Rd.)
Waterside Rd. SK12: Dis 6K **81**
Waterside Vw. CH1: Ches 3C **212** (1A **150**)
CW9: Rud 6K **157**
Waterside Wlk. SK14: Hat 1D **28**
Waterside Way CW10: Mid 2B **180**
Waters Reach SK6: H Lan 2C **200**
SK12: Poy 1E **100**
Waters Reams CH3: Gt Bou 3E **150**
Waters Rd. CH65: Ell P 1F **135**
Water St. CH41: Birk 6E **34**
CH44: Wall 7K **13**
CH62: P Sun 1C **86**
CW9: N'ich 6E **156**
L2: Liv 3H **35**
L3: Liv 3G **35**
M34: Aude 3E **8**
M34: Den 6B **8**
SK1: Stoc 2D **52**
SK10: Boll 3D **122**
SK11: Mac 5K **125**
SK14: Hyde 7J **9**
SK15: Stal 7B **4**
WA7: Run 3G **89**
WA8: Wid 7G **63**
Water Tower 3A **212** (1K **149**)
Water Twr. Rd. CH64: Nest 6H **105**
Water Twr. St. CH1: Ches 3B **212** (1K **149**)
Watertower Vw. CW2: Ches 1C **150**
Waterway CH3: Wave 2B **174**
Waterways WA5: Gt San 6B **40**
Waterworks La. CH66: H'ton 6K **107**
WA2: Winw 5A **16**
Watery La. CW12: Astb 7C **182**
WA2: Winw 5H **15**
WA6: Frod 2K **139** & 3K **139**
Watford Rd. M19: Manc 5D **24**
Watkin Av. SK13: Had 3K **11**
Watkins Av. WA12: New W 1C **14**
Watkinson St. L1: Liv 5J **35**
Watkinson Way WA8: Wid 4F **37**
Watkin St. SK14: Hyde 5B **10**
WA2: Warr 5F **41**
Watling Ct. CH3: Ches 1F **151**
CW8: S'way 4E **160**
Watling Cres. CH4: Ches 4A **150**
Watling Dr. CW6: Kel 4F **173**
Watling Ga. WA14: Timp 3J **47**
Watling St. CW9: N'ich 5E **156**
Watmough St. L5: Liv 1K **35**
Watson Ct. *CH41: Birk 5E 34*
(off Argyle St.)
Watsons M. SK9: Wilm 7J **97**
Watson Sq. SK1: Stoc 7K **213** (3D **52**)
Watson St. CH41: Birk 5C **34**
M34: Den 7G **9**
Watton Cl. WA4: Thel 2C **68**
Watts St. M19: Manc 3E **24**
Wavell Av. WA8: Wid 5C **62**
Wavell Rd. M22: Wyth 3K **75**
Waveney Dr. SK9: Wilm 4A **98**
WA14: Alt 6G **47**
Waveney Rd. M22: Wyth 1A **76**
Waverley Av. M32: S'ord 1K **23**
WA4: App 5H **67**
Waverley Cl. SK10: Mac 5D **126**
Waverley Ct. CW2: Crewe 4D **194**
Waverley Dr. SK8: Chea H 7K **77**
Waverley Gro. CH42: Tran 3B **60**
Waverley Rd. CH47: Hoy 5D **30**
M33: Sale 5H **23**
SK3: Stoc 5A **52**
SK14: Hyde 3J **27**
Waverley Ter. CH2: Ches 6B **146**
WAVERTON 2A **174** (1C **219**)
Waverton Av. CH43: Oxt 3H **59**
SK4: Stoc 4G **25**
Waverton Bus. Pk. CH3: Wave 7J **151**
Waverton Cl. CW2: Hou 5E **198**
CW9: N'ich 2D **162**
Waverton Mill Quays CH3: Wave 2B **174**
Waverton Pk. *CH3: Wave 2B 174*
(off Guy La.)
Waverton Rd. CH66: Gt Sut 3A **134**
WAVERTREE 2B **214**
Wavertree Av. ST7: Sch G 1H **205**
WA8: Wid 5F **63**
Wavertree Ct. CH66: Ell P 1B **134**
Wavertree Dr. CW10: Mid 5B **180**
Wavertree Rd. CH1: Blac 5D **144**
Waybutt La. CW2: Balt, Chor 6H **199**
Wayfarers Ct. WA16: Pick 1B **158**
Wayfarers Dr. WA12: New W 1H **15**
Wayford Cl. WA6: Frod 6H **111**
Wayford M. WA6: Frod 6H **111**
Wayland Rd. Sth. M18: Manc 1G **25**
Waymark Gdns. WA9: Sut M 1H **37**
WAYS GREEN 4F **179**
Way's Grn. CW7: Wins 4F **179**
Wayside ST7: Als 7G **203**
Wayside Cl. WA13: Lymm 3K **69**
Wayside Ct. CH2: Mic T 2J **147**
Wayside Dr. SK12: Poy 2B **100**
Wayside Gdns. SK7: H Gro 3A **80**
Wayside Rd. SK10: Mac 4C **126**
Waystead Cl. CW9: N'ich 2E **162**
Waywell Cl. WA2: Fear 1K **41**
Weald Dr. CH66: L Sut 2G **133**
Wealstone Ct. CH2: Ches 5B **146**
Wealstone La. CH2: Upt 4A **146**
Weaste La. WA4: Thel 4D **68**
Weates Cl. WA8: Wid 2A **64**
Weatherley Dr. SK6: Mar 6D **54**
Weatherstones Bus. Cen.
CH64: Nest 7B **106**
Weatherstones Cotts. CH64: Nest 7C **106**
Weaver Av. L35: R'ill 1B **36**
Weaver Bank CW5: Nant 2B **196**
Weaver Cl. CW11: S'ach 2C **200**
ST7: Als 6B **202**
WA14: Bow 4G **73**
Weaver Ct. *CW9: N'ich 5E 156*
(off London Rd.)
Weaver Cres. WA6: Frod 6K **111**
Weaver Grange CW9: Moult 6D **162**
Weaver Gro. CH2: Mic T 1J **147**
Weaver Hall La. CW7: Darn 7H **179**
WEAVERHAM 5G **155** (3A **216**)
Weaverham Cl. M13: Manc 1C **24**
Weaverham Leisure & Community Cen. 5G **155**
Weaverham Rd.
CW8: Cudd, Gor, S'way 4D **160**
Weaverham Wlk. *M33: Sale 1E 48*
(off Mottram Rd.)
Weaverham Way SK9: Hand 2B **98**
Weaver La. WA6: Frod 5H **111**
Weaver Pk. Ind. Est. WA6: Frod 5K **111**
Weaver Parkway Country Pk. 7C **162**
Weaver Rd. CH65: Ell P 5E **134**
CW5: Nant 1C **196**
CW8: N'ich 6D **156**
CW9: Moult 7D **162**
WA3: Cul 1B **18**
WA6: Frod 6K **111**
WA7: West 1G **111**
Weaver Sailing Club 5K **111**
Weavers Ct. SK11: Mac 5K **125**
SK14: Mot 6H **11**
Weavers Fold WA1: Warr 6G **41**
Weaverside CW5: Nant 5C **196**
Weaverside Av. WA7: Sut W 3B **112**
Weavers La. SK7: Bram 7B **78**
Weaver St. CH1: Ches 5B **212** (2K **149**)
CW7: Wins 4F **179**
Weaver Valley Rd. CW7: Wins 1G **179**
Weaver Vw. CW3: Audl 6A **210**
CW8: N'ich 6E **156**
CW8: Weav 4G **155**
Weaver Way CW9: N'ich 5E **156**
Webb Dr. WA5: B'ood 5C **14**
Webb Gro. SK14: Hat 2F **29**
Webb La. SK1: Stoc 3E **52**
Webb's Ct. CW9: N'ich 6E **156**
Webb's La. CW10: Mid 2C **180**
Webb Wlk. SK14: Hat 2G **29**
Webster Av. CH44: Wall 6K **13**
Websters Holt CH49: Upt 6C **32**
Websters La. CH66: Gt Sut 6B **134**
Webster St. L3: Liv 2J **35**
Weddell Cl. WA5: Old H 5B **40**
Wedgwood Dr. WA8: Wid 1H **63**
Wednesbury Dr. WA5: Gt San 6H **39**
Wedneshough Grn. SK14: H'rth 5K **11**
WEETWOOD COMMON 7A **172**
Weighbridge Ct. M44: Irlam 1F **21**
Weint, The WA3: Rix 1D **44**
Weir La. WA1: Wool 6E **42**
WA4: Warr 1H **67**
Weir St. CW9: N'ich 6E **156**
WA4: Warr 4E **66**
Welbeck Av. WA12: New W 1G **15**
Welbeck Cl. CW10: Mid 3B **180**
Welbeck Rd. SK5: Stoc 2J **25**
SK14: Hyde 1A **28**
Welbeck St. Sth. OL6: Ash L 1F **9**
(not continuous)
OL7: Ash L 1F **9**
Welburn Av. M22: Wyth 2A **76**
Welbury Rd. M23: Wyth 3F **49**
Welch Rd. SK14: Hyde 6A **10**
Welcomb Cl. SK6: Bred 7E **26**
Welcroft St. SK1: Stoc 7K **213** (4D **52**)
Weldon Cres. SK3: Stoc 1C **78**
Weldon Rd. WA14: Alt 6G **47**
Weld Rd. M20: Manc 4A **24**
Welford Av. CH43: Pren 3J **59**
Welford Cl. SK9: Wilm 6B **98**
Welford Grn. SK5: Stoc 6J **25**
Welkin Rd. SK6: Bred 1G **53**
Welkin Rd. Ind. Est. SK6: Bred 1G **53**
Wellacre Av. M41: Urm 1G **21**
Welland Cl. CW11: Ett H 4A **200**
Welland Rd. CH63: H Beb 1H **85**
SK9: Chea, Wilm 4A **98**
Welland St. SK5: Stoc 2J **25**
Well Av. SY14: Mal 3H **207**
Well Bank CW11: S'ach 3F **201**
WA16: O Peo 3H **165**
Wellbank SK15: Stal 2E **10**
Wellbrae Cl. CH49: Upt 7A **32**
Wellbridge Rd. SK16: Duk 4G **9**
Wellbrook Cl. WA7: B'vale 2E **112**
Well Cl. CH64: Ness 4E **130**
Wellcroft Cl. CW2: Wis 7B **194**
Wellcroft Gdns. WA13: Lymm 3C **70**
Welldale M. M33: Sale 6K **23**
Weller Av. SK12: Poy 4C **100**
Weller Cl. SK12: Poy 4C **100**
Wellesbourne Cl. CH64: Nest 2B **130**
SK10: Mac 3G **125**
Wellesbourne Dr. M23: Wyth 5F **49**
Wellesley Av. CH65: Ell P 3E **134**
CW1: Hasl 2J **195**
Wellesley Gro. CH63: Beb 7F **61**
Wellesley Rd. CH44: Wall 7H **13**
(not continuous)
Wellesley Wlk. *CH65: Ell P 3E 134*
(off Wellesley Av.)
Welles St. CW11: S'ach 2F **201**
Well Farm Cl. SY14: Mal 3H **207**
WA1: Wool 4D **42**
Wellfield CW7: Wins 2H **179**
SK6: Rom 7H **27**
WA7: Pre B 2G **113**
WA8: Wid 2G **63**
Wellfield Cl. WA16: Pick 1C **158**
Wellfield Gdns. WA15: Hale 2C **74**
Wellfield La. WA15: Hale, Timp 1C **74**
Wellfield Rd. M23: Wyth 5G **49**
SK2: Stoc 6G **53**
WA3: Cul 6E **6**
Wellfield St. WA5: Warr 6C **40**
(not continuous)
Wellgate Av. M19: Manc 3E **24**
WELL GREEN 2C **74**
Wellgreen Cl. WA15: Hale 2C **74**
Well Grn. Lodge *WA15: Hale 2C 74*
(off Wellfield La.)
Wellingford Av. WA8: Hal B 1B **88**
Wellington Cen. OL6: Ash L 1J **9**
Wellington Cl. CH63: Beb 7F **61**
CH65: Ell P 3E **134**
CW12: Cong 2F **183**
M33: Sale 5H **23**
WA2: Padg 2K **41**
WA12: New W 1D **14**
WA16: Knut 1G **117**
Wellington Ct. *CH65: Ell P 3E 134*
(off Arthur Av.)
Wellington Gdns. WA12: New W 1D **14**
Wellington Ga. L24: Hale 6A **88**
Wellington Gro. SK2: Stoc 5D **52**
Wellington Ho. *M32: S'ord 2H 23*
(off Sandy La.)
Wellington Mans. *CH45: N Bri 2G 13*
(off Atherton St.)

Wellington Mill—Weston Dr.

Wellington Mill SK3: Stoc 7H 213
Wellington Pde. *SK16: Duk* *1G 9*
(off Queen St.)
Wellington Pl. CH1: Ches 2D 212
WA14: Alt 4H 213 (1H 73)
Wellington Rd. CH43: Oxt 7K 33
CH45: N Bri 2G 13
CH63: Beb 7F 61
CH65: Ell P 4D 134
(not continuous)
CW5: Nant 3C 196
L8: Liv 1K 61
M14: Manc 3A 24
SK7: H Gro 5B 80
SK10: Boll 4C 122
WA15: Timp 6J 47
Wellington Rd. Nth. CH65: Ell P 3E 134
SK4: Stoc 4F 213 (4E 24)
Wellington Rd. Sth.
SK1: Stoc 7H 213 (3C 52)
SK2: Stoc 3C 52
SK3: Stoc 7H 213 (3C 52)
Wellington St. CW8: N'ich 6D 156
L3: Liv 1J 35
M32: S'ord 2H 23
M34: Aude 4E 8
SK1: Stoc 7H 213 (3C 52)
SK7: H Gro 2K 79
SK11: Mac 5A 126
SK14: Hyde 7H 9
WA1: Warr 7G 41
WA7: Run 3G 89
WA8: Wid 7G 63
WA12: New W 1D 14
Wellington St. Ind. Est. *WA8: Wid* *7G 63*
(off Wellington St.)
Wellington St. Workshops
WA1: Warr *7G 41*
(off Wellington St.)
Wellington Ter. CH41: Birk 7C 34
SK16: Duk *1G 9*
(off Queen St.)
Well La. CH1: Mol 1G 145
CH2: Ches 5B 146
CH3: Mould 3H 171
CH42: R Fer, Tran 2C 60
CH49: Gre 2K 57
CH60: Hes 1D 104
CH63: H Beb 7C 60
CH64: Ness 3D 130
CW6: L Bud 2H 177
CW8: Weav 3F 155
CW9: Ant 6A 94
SK10: Pres 2K 121
SK10: R'ow 2E 126
ST7: Als 6D 202
WA4: Lwr S 6J 93
WA5: Penk 2G 65
(not continuous)
WA6: K'ley 1D 152
WA6: Manl 3H 171
Well Mead SK6: Bred 1J 53
Well Mdw. SK14: Hyde 6J 9
Well Mdw. Ct. *SK14: Hyde* *6J 9*
(off Well Mdw.)
Well Row SK14: B'tom 3H 29
Wells Av. CW1: Hasl 1K 195
Wells Cl. CH2: Mic T 2J 147
CH66: Gt Sut 1A 140
SK8: He Grn 6E 76
WA1: Wool 4B 42
Wells Ct. SK16: Duk 4H 9
Wells Dr. SK4: Stoc 2G 51
SK16: Duk 4H 9
WELLS GREEN .... **7A 194 (2A 220)**
Well St. CW7: Wins 3D 178
ST7: Mow C 5H 205
SY14: Mal 3H 207
Wellswood Dr. CW2: Wis 7K 193
Wellswood Rd. CH66: Ell P 1A 134
Wellwood Cl. CH65: Ell P 1D 134
Welman Way WA15: Alt 1K 73
Welsby Cl. WA2: Fear 1K 41
Welshampton Cl.
CH66: Gt Sut 6K 133
Welsh La. CW7: Wins 6E 178
Welshman's La. CW5: Henh, Nant 7A 192
Welshpool Cl. M23: Wyth 2H 49
WA5: Call 1B 40
Welshpool Way M34: Den 2F 27
Welsh Rd. CH1: Woodb 7D 132
CH4: Bald, Dod 1C 184
CH66: Leds, L Sut, Chil T 7D 132
Welsh Row CW5: Nant 1A 196
SK10. N Ald 2F 167
ST7: Mow C 5J 205
Welton Av. CH49: Upt 7C 32
M20: Manc 2E 50
Welton Cl. SK9: Wilm 3E 118
Welton Dr. SK9: Wilm 3D 118
Welton Gro. SK9: Wilm 3D 118
Welton Rd. CH62: Brom 4D 86
Welwyn Cl. WA4: Thel 2C 68
Wembley Cl. SK3: Stoc 7B 52
Wembley Rd. M18: Manc 1F 25
Wembury Wlk. *SK14: Hat* *7F 11*
(off Cambourne Rd.)
Wemyss Av. SK5: Stoc 2J 25
Wemyss Rd. CH1: Blac 6E 144
Wendlebury Cl. WN7: Leigh 1E 6
Wendon Rd. M23: Wyth 7H 49
Wendover Cl. CH43: Noc 1G 59
Wendover Rd. M23: Wyth 3D 48
M41: Urm 1B 22
Wenger Rd. WA8: Wid 7H 37
Wenlock Cl. SK2: Stoc 6A 54
SK10: Mac 2J 125
WA1: Padg 4A 42
Wenlock Gdns. CH66: Gt Sut 6B 134
Wenlock La. CH66: Gt Sut 6B 134
Wenlock Rd. M33: Sale 2A 48
WA7: Beec 3C 112
WN7: Leigh 1E 6
Wenlock Way CH4: Salt 5G 149
Wensleydale Av. CH62: East 2K 107
CW12: Cong 1J 183
L35: R'ill 1D 36
SK8: Chea 6E 50
Wensleydale Cl. M23: Wyth 2F 75
WA5: Gt San 4H 39
Wensley Dr. SK7: H Gro 6H 79
Wensley Rd. SK5: Stoc 7J 25
SK8: Chea 6E 50
Wentworth Av. CH45: N Bri 4H 13
M41: Urm 2A 22
M44: Irlam 1D 20
SK11: Mac 6G 125
WA1: Wool 5B 42
WA15: Timp 6A 48
Wentworth Cl. CH43: Noc 1G 59
CW9: Rud 6K 157
SK6: Mar 4F 55
WA8: Wid 7G 37
Wentworth Dr. CH63: Brom 2H 107
M33: Sale 6E 22
SK7: Bram 6E 78
Wentworth Gro. CW7: Wins 1B 178
Wentworth Rd. SK5: Stoc 2J 25
Wentworth Wlk. SK14: Hyde 5A 10
Werburgh Cl. WA13: Warb 4E 44
Wernbrook Cl. CH43: Noc 1G 59
Werneth Av. SK14: Hyde 3A 28
Werneth Cl. M34: Den 1E 26
SK7: H Gro 1J 79
Werneth Ct. *SK14: Hyde* *2K 27*
(off Stockport Rd.)
Werneth Hollow SK6: W'ley 5G 27
Werneth Low Country Pk. **3C 28**
Werneth Low Rd. SK6: Rom 7J 27
SK14: Hyde 7J 27
Werneth Recreation Cen. **2K 53**
Werneth Ri. SK14: Hyde 4A 28
Werneth Rd. SK6: W'ley 6G 27
SK14: Hyde 1A 28
Werneth St. M34: Aude 5E 8
SK1: Stoc 2F 53
Werneth Vw. SK7: H Gro 5B 80
Werneth Wlk. *M34: Den* *1E 26*
(off Werneth Cl.)
WERRINGTON **3D 221**
WERVIN .... **5J 141 (3C 215)**
Wervin Cl. CH43: Oxt 3H 59
Wervin Mobile Home Pk.
CH2: Wer 5J 141
Wervin Rd.
CH2: Crou, Stoak, Upt, Wer 4J 141
CH43: Oxt 3H 59
Wesley Av. CH44: Wall 6J 13
CW11: S'ach 3F 201
ST7: Als 5E 202
Wesley Cl. CH64: Park 7G 105
CW5: Nant 2C 196
Wesley Ct. CW7: Wins 3G 179
CW12: Cong 4F 183
SK4: Stoc 2H 51
Wesley Gro. CH44: Wall 1D 34
Wesley Mt. *SK4: Stoc* *2C 52*
(off Dodge Hill)
Wesley Pl. CW2: Crewe 4D 194
CW9: N'ich 5F 157
Wesley Sq. M41: Urm 1K 21
Wesley St. SK1: Stoc 7K 213 (3D 52)
SK7: H Gro 2J 79
Wessenden Bank E. SK2: Stoc 7H 53
Wessenden Bank W. SK2: Stoc 7H 53
Wessex Cl. CW2: Shav 4C 198
WA1: Wool 5E 42
Wessex Dr. CW9: Rud 7H 157
Westage Gdns. M23: Wyth 5G 49
Westage La.
CW9: Ast B, Bud H, Gt Bud 5G 115
W. Alfred Ct. *CH43: Oxt* *7B 34*
(off Alfred Rd.)
West Av. CW1: Crewe 2B 194
CW2: West 2H 199
CW9: Rud 7J 157
CW10: Mid 2C 180
M19: Manc 4C 24
SK8: He Grn 4E 76
SK15: Stal 7B 4
ST7: Talk 7K 203
WA2: Warr 4F 41
WA4: Stoc H 4G 67
WA14: Alt 7E 46
WEST BANK .... **2G 89 (2D 215)**
West Bank CH1: Ches 6K 145
SK9: Ald E 7F 119
Westbank Av. CH45: N Bri 4J 13
W. Bank Dock Est. WA8: Wid 1E 88
W. Bank Rd. SK10: Mac 3J 125
Westbank Rd. CH42: Tran 2B 60
M20: Manc 6A 24
W. Bank St. WA8: Wid 1G 89
W. Bond St. SK11: Mac 5K 125
Westbourne Av. CH48: W Kir 3C 56
CW1: Crewe 7F 191
Westbourne Dr. SK9: Wilm 6A 98
Westbourne Gro. CH48: W Kir 3C 56
M33: Sale 7F 23
SK5: Stoc 3J 25
Westbourne M. CW12: Cong 4D 182
Westbourne Pk. M41: Urm 1C 22
Westbourne Rd. CH1: Ches 6H 145
CH43: Oxt 7B 34
CH44: Wall 7F 13
CH48: W Kir 3B 56
M14: Manc 3A 24
M34: Den 1D 26
M41: Urm 1C 22
WA4: Stoc H 6F 67
Westbridge M. WA1: Padd 5K 41
WESTBROOK **2K 39**
Westbrook Av. WA4: Warr 3H 67
Westbrook Cen. WA5: W'ook 3K 39
Westbrook Cres.
WA5: Gt San, W'ook 2K 39
(not continuous)
Westbrook Dr. SK10: Mac 3K 125
Westbrook Rd. CH46: More 5K 31
WA6: K'ley 1C 152
Westbrook Way WA5: W'ook 3J 39
W. Brow Gdns. CH43: Bid 4F 33
Westbury Av. M33: Sale 3G 47
Westbury Cl. CW2: Wis 6C 194
CW10: Mid 4C 180
WA1: Padg 4A 42
Westbury Ct. SK11: Mac 4H 125
Westbury Dr. SK6: Mar 6E 54
SK11: Mac 5H 125
Westbury St. CH41: Tran 1D 60
SK14: Hyde 5H 9
Westbury St. Ind. Est. SK14: Hyde 5H 9
Westbury Way CH4: Ches 5G 149
Westby Cl. SK7: Bram 6E 78
West Cheshire Sailing Club **4D 12**
Westcliffe Ct. WA8: Wid 1H 63
Westcliff Gdns. WA4: App 3J 93
West Cl. CH43: Noc 7G 33
SK10: Boll 4C 122
Westcott Way CH43: Noc 1G 59
Westcourt Rd. M33: Sale 5E 22
Westcroft Rd. M19: Manc 7A 24
M20: Manc 7A 24
Westdale Gdns. M19: Manc 6D 24
Westdale Rd. CH42: R Fer 3D 60
WA1: Padd 5A 42
Westdean Cres. M19: Manc 6C 24
WEST DERBY **1B 214**
W. Downs Rd. SK8: Chea H 2H 77
West Dr. CH49: Upt 7D 32
CH60: Hes 7J 83
CH64: Nest 2B 130
CW7: Wins 2H 179
SK8: Gat 1C 76
SK13: Tint 1K 11
WA5: Gt San 1K 65
W. Dudley St. CW7: Wins 3G 179
West End CH3: Ash H 7G 171
SK14: B'tom 3G 29
West End Av. SK8: Gat 6C 50
West End Cotts. CW12: Cong 4E 182
Westenra Av. CH65: Ell P 2B 134
Westerham Cl. SK10: Mac 2J 125
Westerhope Way WA8: Wid 2F 63
Western App. CH2: Ches 6B 146
Western Approaches Mus.
Underground Wartime Mus. **2H 35**
Western Av. CH1: Blac 7D 144
CH62: Brom 3D 86
CW5: Nant 4C 196
SK11: Mac 7J 125
(not continuous)
Western Av. Shop. Mall *CH1: Blac* *6E 144*
(off Western Av.)
Western Circ. M19: Manc 5C 24
Western Ct. CH2: Ches 6B 146
Western Dr. SK11: Mac 7K 125
Western Pk. CW11: Whe 5C 204
Western Rd. M41: Urm 2H 21
Westfield WA14: Alt 4F 213 (2G 73)
Westfield Cl. CH4: Ches 4J 149
CW7: Wins 7D 178
Westfield Cres. WA7: Run 5E 88
Westfield Dr. CW2: Wis 6J 193
SK6: W'ley 6H 27
WA16: Knut 4C 116
Westfield Gro. CW8: Barnt 1J 155
M34: Aude 5D 8
Westfield M. WA7: Run 5F 89
Westfield Rd. CH44: Wall 3C 34
CW9: N'ich 6G 157
SK8: Chea H 5H 77
ST7: Mow C 5G 205
WA7: Run 5E 88
Westfields WA15: Hale 5K 73
Westfields Av. SK10: Mac 3J 125
W. Float Ind. Est. CH41: Birk 2A 34
Westford Rd. WA4: Warr 4E 66
Westford Villa SK8: Chea 7E 50
Westgate M33: Sale 7F 23
M41: Urm 2A 22
SK9: Wilm 2F 119
WA8: Wid 6B 62
WA15: Hale 3J 73
Westgate Av. CW7: Wins 3B 178
Westgate Pk. CW2: Hou 5E 198
West Ga. Rd. M90: Man A 7F 75
Westgate Rd. CH62: P Sun 2B 86
Westgate St. OL7: Ash L 1F 9
West Gro. CH60: Hes 6H 83
M33: Sale 1B 48
OL5: Moss 1D 4
ST7: Als 5F 203
W. Hall Ct. WA16: H Leg 1H 95
Westhay Cres. WA3: Birc 6B 18
WEST HEATH **4D 182**
W. Heath Gro. WA13: Lymm 1J 69
W. Heath Shop. Cen. CW12: Cong 3C 182
West Heaton Bowling & Tennis Club **7D 24**
W. Hill Cl. SK15: Stal 7A 4
Westholm Av. SK4: Stoc 4E 24
Westholme Cl. CW2: Crewe 6C 194
CW12: Cong 3D 182
Westholme Ct. *SK9: Ald E* *5F 119*
(off Horseshoe La.)
Westhouse Cl. CH63: Brom 2H 107
West Ho. Ct. SK10: Mac 3F 125
West Hyde WA13: Lymm 2J 69
WEST KIRBY .... **3B 56 (2A 214)**
West Kirby Concourse (Leisure Cen.) **3B 56**
W. Kirby Rd. CH46: More 6K 31
West Kirby Station (Rail) **3B 56**
West Knowe CH43: Oxt 1J 59
Westland Av. SK1: Stoc 3F 53
Westland Dr. WA2: Padg 3J 41
Westlands, The CW12: Cong 4E 182
Westlands Cl. CH64: Nest 6J 105
Westlands Rd. CW10: Mid 3B 180
West La. CW8: Cudd 3C 160
WA7: Pal F 7A 90
WA13: Lymm 6E 70
WA16: H Leg, Lymm 2G 95
West Lea M34: Den 7F 9
Westlea Dr. M18: Manc 1G 25
WESTLEIGH **1A 216**
Westleigh SK4: Stoc 7D 24
W. Lodge Dr. CH48: W Kir 2B 56
W. Lorne St. CH1: Ches 2A 212 (1K 149)
Westmead Dr. WA15: Timp 5B 48
West Mdw. SK5: Stoc 2K 25
Westmere Cl. CW2: West 2H 199
Westmere Dr. CW1: Crewe 4F 195
Westminster Av. CH4: Ches 5J 149
SK5: Stoc 4H 25
Westminster Bri. CH65: Ell P 3E 134
Westminster Cl. CW8: H'ord 1B 162
CW10: Mid 3B 180
M33: Sale 1H 47
SK6: Mar 5D 54
WA4: Grap 3C 68
WA8: Wid 5B 62
Westminster Ct. *CH2: Ches* *1C 150*
(off Westminster Rd.)
CH43: Oxt 7J 33
Westminster Dr. CH62: Brom 7D 86
SK8: Chea H 7K 77
SK9: Wilm 3F 119
Westminster Grn.
CH4: Ches 7C 212 (4A 150)
Westminster Gro. CH65: Ell P 2E 134
CW7: Wins *4B 178*
(off St Johns Dr.)
Westminster Ind. Pk. CH65: Ell P 2B 134
Westminster Pl. *WA1: Warr* *7F 41*
(off Winwick St.)
Westminster Retail Pk. CH65: Ell P 2F 135
Westminster Rd. CH2: Ches 7C 146
CH44: Wall 7H 13
CH65: Ell P 2E 134
SK10: Mac 2J 125
WA15: Hale 2A 74
Westminster St. CW2: Crewe 3C 194
M19: Manc 2E 24
Westminster Ter.
CH4: Ches 7B 212 (4K 149)
Westminster Way SK16: Duk 4H 9
Westmoor Gables SK4: Stoc 7D 24
Westmoreland Cl. WA14: Bow 5F 73
Westmoreland Rd. CH45: N Bri 4J 13
Westmorland Av. SK16: Duk 2K 9
WA8: Wid 4H 63
Westmorland Cl. SK5: Stoc 5B 26
SK10: Mac 2G 125
Westmorland Dr. L3: Liv 1H 35
SK5: Stoc 5A 26
Westmorland Rd. M20: Manc 2C 50
M31: Part 2G 45
M33: Sale 2C 40
M41: Urm 2B 22
Westmorland Ter. CW4: H Cha 4H 181
W. Oak Pl. SK8: Chea H 4J 77
WESTON
CW2 .... **2H 199 (2B 220)**
SK11 .... **5G 125 (3D 217)**
WA7 .... **1F 111 (2D 215)**
Weston Av. M41: Urm 2A 22
Weston Cen. CW1: Crewe 4E 194
Weston Cl. CW9: N'ich 1E 162
CW10: Mid 5C 180
Weston Ct. CW2: Shav 2C 198
M14: Manc 1A 24
WA7: West 7F 89
WESTON COYNEY **3D 221**
Weston Cres. WA7: West 1F 111
Weston Dr. M34: Den 7F 9
SK8: Chea H 1B 78

A-Z Cheshire Atlas 313

Weston Gro.—Whitnall St.

Weston Gro. CH2: Upt 4B 146
M22: N'den 4A 50
SK4: Stoc 5F 25
Weston La. CW2: Bas, Shav 2D 198
WESTON POINT 7D 88
Weston Point Docks WA7: Wes P 7D 88
Weston Point Expressway
WA7: Run, West 5E 88
Weston Rd. CW1: Crewe 4E 194
CW2: West 6G 195
(not continuous)
M44: Irlam 1D 20
SK9: Wilm 1J 119
WA7: Run, West 6E 88
Weston Sq. SK11: Mac 5G 125
Weston St. SK5: Stoc 7H 25
Weston Vw. WA7: Clif 3K 111
West Over SK6: Rom 4A 54
Westover Rd. WA1: Padg 5K 41
West Pde. M33: Sale 1G 47
West Pk. SK14: Hyde 4K 27
West Pk. Av. M34: Den 1G 27
SK12: Poy 2K 99
West Pk. Dr. CH66: Gt Sut 1B 140
West Pk. Gdns. CH43: Bid 4F 33
West Pk. Rd. SK1: Stoc 2F 53
SK7: Bram 3B 78
West Pl. M19: Manc 4C 24
W. Point Lodge *M19: Manc 3C 24*
(off Slade La.)
W. Quay Rd. WA2: Winw 1D 40
Westray Rd. M13: Manc 1B 24
Westrees CW8: Cudd 1A 160
West Rd. CH43: Noc 7G 33
CH65: Ell P 5E 134
CH65: Ell P, H'ton 4D 108
CW8: Weav 4E 154
CW12: Cong 3D 182
WA7: Wes P 7D 88
WA14: Bow 3G 73
Westry Cl. CH46: More 4J 31
West St. CH2: Ches 1E 212 (7B 146)
CH45: Wall 6H 13
CW1: Crewe 1A 194
CW1: Hasl 1J 195
CW2: Crewe 2J 193
(not continuous)
CW10: Mid 3C 180
CW12: Cong 3E 182
SK3: Stoc 3B 52
SK9: Ald E 6F 119
SK11: Mac 4J 125
SK14: Hyde 5J 9
SK15: Stal 7A 4
SK16: Duk 1G 9
ST7: Mow C 6F 205
WA2: Warr 5F 41
WEST TIMPERLEY 4G 47
West Twr. M. SK6: Mar 1G 81
West Va. CH64: Nest 2C 130
West Va. Rd. WA15: Timp 6K 47
West Vw. CH41: Tran 1E 60
CH66: Chil T 7B 108
(off Orchard La.)
CW1: Bra G 3D 190
CW1: Crewe 7G 191
CW9: N'ich 5G 157
M34: Aude 3D 8
WA2: Padg 3A 42
Westview Cl. CH43: Noc 1G 59
West Vw. Rd. M22: N'den 4A 50
WA6: Norl 5H 153
Westville Dr. CW12: Cong 4C 182
Westville Gdns. M19: Manc 6B 24
Westward Ho CH48: Cald 7E 56
Westward Rd. CH3: Ches 3D 150
SK9: Wilm 1E 118
West Way CW4: H Cha 4H 181
CW11: Whe 5D 200
Westway CH43: Noc 1G 59
CH46: More 3B 32
CH49: Gre 1A 58
CH60: Hes 1C 104
CW2: Shav 2D 198
M43: Droy 3A 8
WA7: Pal F 7A 90
Westway Sq. CH46: More 3B 32
Westwood WA7: Win H 5E 90
WA14: Alt 1F 73
Westwood Av. M41: Urm 2E 22
SK14: Hyde 7C 10
WA15: Timp 5K 47
Westwood Cl. CW2: West 6H 199
Westwood Ct. CH43: Oxt 7J 33
CH64: Nest 5H 105
Westwood Dr. M33: Sale 2B 48
Westwood Gro. CH44: Wall 7G 13
Westwood Rd. CH43: Bid 6F 33
M32: S'ord 1G 23
SK2: Stoc 1F 79
SK8: He Grn 5D 76
Westwood Trad. Est. SK6: Mar 7D 54
WESTY 1K 67
Westy La. WA4: Westy 1J 67
Wet Ga. La. WA13: Lymm 1E 70
Wetherall St. M19: Manc 2E 24
Wetheral Rd. SK10: Mac 2J 125
Wetherby Av. CH45: Wall 6E 12
Wetherby Cl. CH1: Ches 1J 149
Wetherby Dr. SK7: H Gro 3A 80
Wetherby Way CH66: L Sut 2H 133
Wethersfield Rd. CH43: Noc 2H 59
WETLEY ROCKS 3D 221
Wetreins La. CH3: Cre F 7D 186
Wetstone La. CH48: W Kir 4D 56
WETTENHALL 1A 220
Wettenhall Rd. CW5: Poole, Rea 2A 192
Wetton La. CW8: Act B 1B 154
Wetton Way SK11: Sut E 3H 169
Wexford Av. L24: Hale 6A 88
Wexford Cl. CH43: Oxt 1H 59
Wexford Rd. CH43: Oxt 1J 59
Wexford Wlk. M22: Wyth 3A 76
Weybourne Cl. CH4: Ches 6F 149
CH49: Upt 5D 32
Weybourne Dr. SK6: Bred 7E 26
Weybridge Cl. WA4: App 6J 67
Weybridge Dr. SK10: Mac 1J 125
Weybrook Rd. M19: Manc 4E 24
Weycroft M. CW1: Crewe 1C 194
Weygates Dr. WA15: H'rns 6C 74
Weyhill Rd. M23: Wyth 7G 49
Weymoor Cl. CH63: Spit 4K 85
Weymouth Cl. WA7: Murd 1G 113
Weymouth Rd. OL6: Ash L 3A 4
WA5: B'ood 5C 14
Whaddon Dr. CH4: Ches 7G 149
WHALEY BRIDGE 2D 217
Whaley La. CH61: Irby 7C 58
Whalley Av. M19: Manc 1E 24
M33: Sale 6H 23
WA3: G'ury 3J 7
Whalley Cl. WA15: Timp 4K 47
Whalley Dr. CW6: Rus 6H 177
Whalley Gro. WA8: Wid 2K 63
Whalley Hayes SK10: Mac 4K 125
Whalley Rd. CH42: Tran 7C 34
CW9: N'ich 5F 157
SK2: Stoc 5G 53
WA15: Hale 3A 74
Whalley St. WA1: Warr 6G 41
Wharburton Cl. CW8: S'way 4C 160
Wharf, The *CH1: Ches 1J 149*
(off New Crane St.)
CW1: Crewe 2D 194
WA7: Pre B 1H 113
Wharf Cl. *WA14: Alt 5H 47*
(off Bridgewater Rd.)
Wharf Cotts. OL5: Moss 1E 4
Wharfdale Av. CW1: L'ton 4G 191
Wharfdale Cl. WA5: Gt San 5J 39
Wharfdale Rd. CW12: Cong 1J 183
Wharfe Cl. CW12: Cong 5H 183
Wharfedale WA7: Pal F 1D 112
Wharfedale Av. CH42: Tran 3A 60
Wharfedale Dr. CH62: East 2A 108
L35: R'ill 1D 36
Wharfedale Rd. CH45: Wall 5F 13
SK5: Stoc 3H 25
Wharfe La. CH65: Ell P 1C 134
Wharf Ind. Est. WA1: Warr 1G 67
Wharf Mill CW12: Cong 5H 183
Wharford La. WA7: Nort 3G 91
Wharf Rd. M33: Sale 5H 23
WA12: New W 1B 14
WA14: Alt 5H 47
Wharfside Ct. WA4: App 4J 67
Wharf St. CH62: P Sun 1B 86
SK4: Stoc 1C 52
SK16: Duk 1G 9
WA1: Warr 1F 67
Warncliffe Cl. SK13: Had 3K 11
WHARTON 2G 179 (1A 220)
Wharton Bri. CW7: Wins 1H 179
Wharton Cl. CH49: Upt 6A 32
Wharton Ct. CH3: Ches 1C 150
Wharton (Donefields) Ind. Est.
CW7: Wins 1H 179
Wharton Gdns. CW7: Wins 1H 179
Wharton Hall CW7: Wins 1H 179
Wharton Pk. Rd. CW7: Wins 2G 179
Wharton Retail Pk. CW7: Wins 1G 179
Wharton Rd. CW7: Wins 3G 179
WHATCROFT 6K 163
Whatcroft Cl. WA7: Run 1K 111
Whatcroft Hall La. CW9: What 6K 163
Wheatcroft SK3: Stoc 7D 52
SK13: Had 3K 11
Wheatcroft Cl. WA5: Gt San 6A 40
Wheatfield SK15: Stal 3F 11
Wheatfield Cl. CH46: More 5C 32
CH66: Gt Sut 5J 133
CW8: Barnt 2K 155
SK6: Bred 7F 27
SK10: Mac 1K 125
Wheatfield Rd. WA8: Cron 7C 36
Wheatland Bus. Pk. CH44: Wall 2C 34
Wheatland Cl. WA9: Clo F 1J 37
Wheatland La. CH44: Wall 1C 34
Wheatland Rd. CH60: Hes 7A 84
Wheatlands WA7: Run 5A 90
Wheatley Rd. CW1: Crewe 7K 191
Wheat Moss SK11: Chel 5C 166
Wheatsheaf La. CW9: Ant 7A 94
Wheelman Rd. CW1: Crewe 6F 191
WHEELOCK 6D 200 (2B 220)
Wheelock Cl. CW9: N'ich 7E 156
SK9: Wilm 5A 98
ST7: Als 6B 202
Wheelock Dr. CW7: Wins 3J 179
WHEELOCK HEATH 5C 204 (2B 220)
Wheelock St. CW10: Mid 3C 180
Wheelwright Cl. SK6: Mar 4F 55
Wheldon Cl. CH2: Upt 2B 146
Wheldon Rd. WA8: Wid 6A 62
Wheldrake Cl. CH66: L Sut 3H 133
Whelmar Est. SK8: Chea H 1K 77
WHELSTON 3A 214
Whernside WA8: Wid 2C 62
Whernside Cl. SK4: Stoc 1C 52
Whetstone Ct. *CH41: Birk 7C 34*
(off Whetstone La.)
Whetstone Hey CH66: Gt Sut 3K 133
Whetstone La. CH41: Birk 7C 34
Whickham Cl. WA8: Wid 2F 63
Whimberry Dr. SK15: Carrb 4E 4
Whimberry Way M20: Manc 5A 24
Whimbrel Cl. WA7: Beec 2B 112
Whimbrel Rd. SK2: Stoc 7A 54
Whinberry Rd. WA14: B'ath 5F 47
Whinchat Cl. SK2: Stoc 1A 80
Whinchat Dr. WA3: Birc 1F 43
Whinfell Gro. WA7: Beec 2A 112
Whinmoor Cl. CH43: Noc 6G 33
Whipcord La. CH1: Ches 2A 212 (7J 145)
Whirley Cl. CW10: Mid 5C 180
SK4: Stoc 6G 25
WHIRLEY GROVE 1E 124
Whirley La. SK10: Henb 4A 124
Whirley Rd. SK10: Henb, Mac 2C 124
Whirlow Rd. CW2: Wis 7B 194
WHISTERFIELD 1A 168 (3C 217)
Whisterfield La. SK11: Sidd 1A 168
WHISTON
OL3 3D 221
WA5 1C 215
Whiston Cl. CW7: Wins 1G 179
SK11: Mac 1F 129
WA16: H Leg 2H 95
WHISTON EAVES 3D 221
Whiston M. SK11: Lang 1G 169
Whiston St. SK11: Mac 5K 125
Whitbarrow Rd. WA13: Lymm 1J 69
Whitburn Av. M13: Manc 1B 24
Whitburn Rd. M23: Wyth 1G 75
WHITBY 4C 134 (3B 214)
Whitby Av. CH2: Ches 5A 146
CH45: Wall 6E 12
M14: Manc 3B 24
M41: Urm 1D 22
WA2: Warr 2H 41
Whitby Cl. CW1: Crewe 5G 191
SK8: Chea 6E 50
SK12: Poy 2B 100
WHITBYHEATH 6C 134 (3B 214)
Whitby Rd. CH1: Bac 1C 140
CH65: Ell P, Whit 4D 134
(not continuous)
M14: Manc 3A 24
WA7: Run 5G 89
Whitby's La. CW7: Wins 3C 178
WHITCHURCH 3D 219
Whitchurch Cl. WA1: Padg 4A 42
Whitchurch Rd. CH3: Brox 1E 206
CH3: Chri, Gt Bou, Row, Wave 2E 150
CH3: Row, Wave 5J 151
CW3: Audl 6A 210
CW5: Ast, B'hall, Sou 7G 209
Whitchurch Way WA7: Run 1K 111
White Av. CW2: Crewe 2K 193
Whitebank Av. SK5: Stoc 7B 26
Whitebarn Rd. SK9: Ald E 7G 119
Whitebeam Av. CH66: Gt Sut 7B 134
Whitebeam Cl. WA7: Win H 5E 90
WA15: Timp 7E 48
Whitebeam Row *CW8: Weav 6H 155*
(off Walnut Av.)
Whitebeam Wlk. CH49: Gre 3J 57
M33: Sale 6C 22
(off Manor Av.)
White Bear Yd. *WA16: Knut 3E 116*
(off Canute Pl.)
Whitebrook Ct. M33: Sale 1B 48
White Broom WA13: Lymm 1D 70
Whitecarr La. M23: Wyth 2D 74
WA15: Hale 2D 74
Whitechapel L1: Liv 3J 35
Whitechapel St. M20: Manc 1D 50
White Clover Sq. WA13: Lymm 3C 70
Whitecroft Ct. SK10: Mac 2B 126
Whitecroft Gdns. M19: Manc 7B 24
Whitecroft Heath Rd. SK11: L Wit 1A 168
Whitecroft Rd. CH66: Gt Sut 6A 134
SK6: Stri 4J 81
Whitecroft Vs. M31: Part 2G 45
Whitecross Rd. WA5: Warr 7C 40
Whitefield SK4: Stoc 1B 52
WA13: Lymm 1C 70
Whitefield Av. WA12: New W 1J 15
Whitefield Cl. CH49: Woodc 2E 58
WA13: Lymm 7C 44
Whitefield Ct. WA3: Ris 1A 18
Whitefield Gro. WA13: Lymm 1C 70
Whitefield Rd. M33: Sale 6E 22
SK6: Bred 7D 26
WA4: Stoc H 5F 67
Whitefields CH2: Elt 5F 137
WHITEFIELDS CROSS 2B 64
White Friars CH1: Ches 5B 212 (2K 149)
Whitefriars Wlk. M22: Wyth 5K 75
WHITEGATE 7K 161 (1A 220)
Whitegate Av. WA3: Cul 1A 18
Whitegate Cl. CW10: Mid 6C 180
Whitegate Flds. LL13: Holt 6A 186
Whitegate La. CH3: Ash H 7G 171
Whitegate Pk. M41: Urm 1H 21
Whitegate Rd. CW7: Wins 1A 178
Whitegates SK8: Chea 7F 51
SK14: B'tom 2H 29
Whitegates Cl. CH64: W'ston 6D 106
WA15: Timp 7B 48
Whitegates Cres. CH64: W'ston 7D 106
Whitegates Rd. SK8: Chea 7F 51
Whitehall CW6: L Bud 1G 177
Whitehall Cl. CW8: Barnt 1K 155
SK9: Wilm 2F 119
Whitehall Dr. CW8: H'ord 2B 162
White Hall La. CW11: Warm 1D 204
Whitehall La. CW6: L Bud 1F 177
Whitehall Pl. WA6: Frod 7H 111
(not continuous)
Whitehall Rd. M20: Manc 1E 50
M33: Sale 2B 48
White Hart Gdns. CW8: H'ord 2J 161
White Hart La. CW2: Wis 6J 193
White Hart St. SK14: Hyde 6J 9
Whitehaven Gdns. M20: Manc 2C 50
Whitehaven Pl. SK14: Hyde 5H 9
Whitehaven Rd. SK7: Bram 1F 99
Whitehead St. M34: Aude 3D 8
Whiteheath Way CH46: Leas 1C 32
Whitehill Ind. Est. SK4: Stoc 5H 25
(not continuous)
Whitehill St. SK4: Stoc 7H 25
SK5: Stoc 7H 25
Whitehill St. W. SK4: Stoc 7G 25
Whiteholme Av. M21: Chor H 1K 49
White Horse All. *CW10: Mid 3C 180*
(off Lewin St.)
WHITEHOUGH 2D 217
WHITEHOUSE 3H 113
White House, The WA4: Warr 3G 67
White Ho. Dr. WA1: Wool 5E 42
Whitehouse Dr. M23: Wyth 7G 49
WA15: Hale 5B 74
Whitehouse Expressway
WA7: B'vale, Pal F 1A 112
Whitehouse Ind. Est. WA7: Pre B 3G 113
(not continuous)
Whitehouse La. CH60: Hes 5A 84
CH63: Brim 5A 84
CW5: Nant 1D 196
WA14: Dun M 5B 46
WA16: Plum 1G 159
Whitehurst Rd. SK4: Stoc 7C 24
Whitelake Av. M41: Urm 1J 21
Whitelands OL6: Ash L 1H 9
Whitelands Ind. Est. SK15: Stal 1K 9
Whitelands Mdw. CH49: Upt 7B 32
Whitelands Rd. OL6: Ash L 1H 9
White La. CH3: Chri 4G 151
Whitelea Dr. SK3: Stoc 7B 52
Whiteleggs La. WA13: Lymm 4D 70
WHITELEY GREEN 1B 122
Whiteley Pl. WA14: Alt 6H 47
White Lodge Cl. CH62: Brom 2J 107
White Lodge M. CW8: Cudd 3D 160
Whitelow Rd. SK4: Stoc 1J 51
Whitemere Ct. CH65: Ell P 1E 134
Whitemore Rd. CW10: Mid 6C 180
White Nancy Monument 4E 122
Whiteoak Cl. SK6: Mar 5E 54
Whiteoak Ct. M14: Manc 3A 24
Whiteoak Rd. M14: Manc 3A 24
White Pk. Cl. CW10: Mid 2D 180
Whitesands Rd. WA13: Lymm 1J 69
Whiteside Cl. CH49: Upt 1D 58
Whites La. CW2: West 1H 199
Whitesmead Cl. SK12: Dis 2G 103
Whites Mdw. CH3: Gt Bou 4D 150
Whitestar Ct. *M44: Irlam 1D 20*
(off Ferry Rd.)
White St. SK11: Mac 6A 126
WA1: Warr 7E 40
WA4: Stoc H 4G 67
WA8: Wid 1G 89
White Ter. SK14: Hyde 3H 27
Whitethorn Av. M19: Manc 4C 24
WA5: Gt San 7H 39
Whitethorn Cl. SK6: Mar 5E 54
Whitethroat Wlk. WA3: Birc 1F 43
Whitewell Cl. CW5: Nant 2D 196
Whitewell Dr. CH49: Upt 6C 32
Whitfield Av. WA1: Padd 5K 41
Whitfield Ct. CH42: Tran 1C 60
Whitfield Dr. SK11: Mac 7J 125
Whitfield La. CH60: Hes 4J 83
Whitfields, The SK10: Mac 3H 125
WHITFIELDS CROSS 2A 64
Whitfield St. CH42: Tran 1C 60
WHITFORD 3A 214
Whitford Rd. CH42: Tran 1B 60
Whitley Av. CW8: Barnt 2K 155
WA4: Westy 1A 68
Whitley Cl. CW10: Mid 5B 180
WA7: Run 6F 89
Whitley Dr. CH44: Wall 6K 13
CW8: H'ord 2K 161
Whitley Gdns. WA15: Timp 5B 48
Whitley Pl. WA15: Timp 5C 48
Whitley Rd. SK4: Stoc 1K 51
Whitley St. L3: Liv 1G 35
Whitlow Av. CW5: Nant 3D 196
WA14: B'ath 4F 47
Whitlow La. CW9: Moult 6E 162
Whitmoor Cl. L35: R'ill 3E 36
WHITMORE 3C 221
Whitnall St. SK14: Hyde 5J 9

Whitney Cft.—Windmill Hill Av. Nth.

Whitney Cft. SK10: Mac . . . 4D 126
Whitsand Rd. M22: Shar . . . 7A 50
Whitsbury Av. M18: Manc . . . 1G 25
Whitstable Pk. WA8: Wid . . . 1E 62
Whittaker Av. WA2: Warr . . . 2H 41
Whittaker Cl. CW1: Crewe . . . 6F 191
CW12: Cong . . . 1G 183
Whittington Gdns. CW9: Dave . . . 4E 162
Whittington St. OL7: Ash L . . . 1F 9
Whittle Av. WA5: Gt San . . . 4H 39
Whittle Hall La. WA5: Gt San . . . 6H 39
Whittles Av. M34: Den . . . 7F 9
Whittles Wlk. M34: Den . . . 1F 27
Whittlewood Cl. WA3: Birc . . . 6B 18
Whitton Dr. CH2: Upt . . . 5B 146
Whitwell Cl. WA5: Gt San . . . 5F 39
Whitworth Cl. WA3: Birc . . . 1E 42
Whitworth Ct. CW7: Man P . . . 2F 91
Whitworth La. M14: Manc . . . 2A 24
Wibbersley Pk. M41: Urm . . . 1J 21
Wickenby Dr. M33: Sale . . . 7F 23
Wicken St. SK2: Stoc . . . 5G 53
Wicker La. CH3: Guil S . . . 5J 147
WA15: H'rns . . . 5B 74
Wickham Cl. CH44: Wall . . . 2C 34
Wickham Ct. CW2: West . . . 4K 199
Wicklow Av. SK3: Stoc . . . 5K 51
Wicklow Cl. CH66: L Sut . . . 2G 133
Wicklow Dr. M22: Wyth . . . 3A 76
Wickstead Cl. CW5: Nant . . . 3E 196
Wicksten Dr. WA7: Run . . . 4J 89
Widdale Av. L35: R'ill . . . 1D 36
Widdale Cl. WA5: Gt San . . . 5H 39
Widgeon Cl. SK12: Poy . . . 2A 100
Widgeon Rd. WA14: B'ath . . . 4F 47
Widgeons Covert CH63: Tho H . . . 2J 105
WIDNES . . . 6G 63 (2D 215)
Widnes Crematorium WA8: Wid . . . 2G 63
Widnes Rd. WA5: Cuer, Penk . . . 3B 64
WA8: Wid . . . 6G 63
(not continuous)
Widnes Station (Rail) . . . 2G 63
Widnes Trade Pk. WA8: Wid . . . 6J 63
Widnes Vikings RLFC . . . 5F 63
Wiend, The CH2: Ches . . . 6A 146
CH42: R Fer . . . 4C 60
CH63: Beb . . . 1A 86
Wigg Island Community Pk. Local Nature Reserve . . . 3K 89
Wight Cl. CH65: Ell P . . . 7E 134
Wighurst Wlk. M22: Wyth . . . 4K 75
Wigmore Cl. WA3: Birc . . . 5B 18
Wigsey La. WA13: Warb . . . 5C 44
WIGSHAW . . . 1J 17
Wigshaw Cl. WN7: Leigh . . . 1F 7
Wigshaw La. WA3: Cul . . . 1H 17
Wigwam Cl. SK12: Poy . . . 2B 100
Wilbraham Cl. CH2: Mic T . . . 2J 147
CW5: Act . . . 6K 189
Wilbraham Rd. CW5: Act . . . 6K 189
CW8: Weav . . . 4H 155
CW12: Cong . . . 3H 183
M14: Manc . . . 2A 24
Wilbraham St. CH41: Birk . . . 6D 34
WA9: Clo F . . . 1A 38
Wilbrahams Way ST7: Als . . . 5E 202
Wilcote Cl. WA8: Wid . . . 1J 63
Wilcott Dr. M33: Sale . . . 6D 22
SK9: Wilm . . . 3E 118
Wilcott Rd. SK8: Gat . . . 7C 50
Wildbank Chase SK15: Stal . . . 3F 11
WILDBOARCLOUGH . . . 1D 221
Wildbrook Dr. CH41: Birk . . . 3G 33
Wild Clough SK14: Hyde . . . 2A 28
Wilderhope Cl. CW2: Wis . . . 7C 194
WILDERSPOOL . . . 3G 67 (2A 216)
Wilderspool C'way. WA4: Warr . . . 1F 67
Wilderspool Cres. WA4: Warr . . . 4F 67
Wilderspool Pk. WA4: Warr . . . 3G 67
Wilderswood Cl. M20: Manc . . . 6A 24
Wilde St. L3: Liv . . . 2K 35
Wilding Av. WA7: Run . . . 4H 89
Wildings Old La. WA3: Croft . . . 3F 17
Wilding St. CW1: Crewe . . . 2E 194
Wildmoor La. CH3: L Bar . . . 7G 143
Wildmoor Wood Cl. SK15: Carrb . . . 4E 4
Wild St. M34: Den . . . 7E 8
SK2: Stoc . . . 6E 52
SK6: Bred . . . 2K 53
SK7: H Gro . . . 3H 79
SK16: Duk . . . 2J 9
Wildwood Cl. SK2: Stoc . . . 7E 52
Wildwood Gro. WA1: Padd . . . 5B 42
Wilford Av. M33: Sale . . . 2A 48
Wilfred Owen Dr. CH41: Birk . . . 5H 33
Wilkes Av. CH46: Leas . . . 1E 32
WILKESLEY . . . 3A 220
Wilkin Cft. SK8: Chea H . . . 4G 77
Wilkins La. SK9: Styal . . . 1F 97
Wilkinson Av. WA1: Padd . . . 6K 41
Wilkinson Cl. WA8: Wid . . . 1G 89
Wilkinson Ct. *CW7: Wins . . . 6C 178*
(off Wilkinson Way)
Wilkinson Rd. SK4: Stoc . . . 5G 213 (2C 52)
Wilkinson St. CH41: Birk . . . 7B 34
CH43: Birk . . . 7B 34
CH65: Ell P . . . 2D 134
M33: Sale . . . 7J 23
WA2: Warr . . . 5G 41
Wilkinson St. M. *CH65: Ell P . . . 2E 134*
(off Wilkinson St. Nth.)
Wilkinson St. Nth. CH65: Ell P . . . 2E 134
Wilkinson Way CW7: Wins . . . 5C 178
Wilks Av. M22: Wyth . . . 3B 76
Willan Rd. CH1: Blac . . . 6E 144
Willan St. CH43: Oxt . . . 1A 60
Willard St. SK7: H Gro . . . 2H 79
WILLASTON
CH64 . . . 7E 106 (3B 214)
CW5 . . . 1H 197 (2A 220)
Willaston Grn. M. CH64: W'ston . . . 7E 106
Willaston Hall Gdns. CW5: W'ston . . . 1G 197
Willaston Rd. CH46: More . . . 3A 32
CH63: Raby, Tho H . . . 7H 85
Willaston Way *SK9: Hand . . . 1A 98*
(off Sandiway Rd.)
Willdor Gro. SK3: Stoc . . . 6K 51
Willenhall Rd. M23: Wyth . . . 2J 49
Willerby Cl. SK10: Mac . . . 4K 125
William Beamont Way *WA1: Warr . . . 7E 40*
(off Ebenezer Pl.)
William Brown St. L3: Liv . . . 2J 35
(not continuous)
William Cl. M41: Urm . . . 2B 22
William Ct. CH64: Nest . . . 5J 105
William Foden Cl. CW11: Elw . . . 2B 200
William Ford Ho. SK14: Mot . . . 6H 11
William Henry St. L3: Liv . . . 1K 35
William Jessop Way L3: Liv . . . 2G 35
William Johnson Gdns. CH65: Ell P . . . 2D 134
William Penn Cl. WA5: Penk . . . 7G 39
Williams Cl. CH2: Ches . . . 6K 145
Williamson Art Gallery & Mus. . . . 7A 34
Williamson Av. SK6: Bred . . . 7F 27
Williamson Dr. CW5: Nant . . . 2A 196
Williamson La. M43: Droy . . . 2A 8
Williamson Sq. L1: Liv . . . 3J 35
Williamson St. L1: Liv . . . 3J 35
SK5: Stoc . . . 4J 25
William St. CH1: Ches . . . 3C 212 (1A 150)
CH2: Ches . . . 7C 146
CH41: Birk . . . 6D 34
CH44: Wall . . . 2D 34
CW7: Wins . . . 3F 179
CW9: N'ich . . . 5G 157
CW12: Cong . . . 2J 183
M20: Manc . . . 1D 50
OL7: Ash L . . . 1E 8
SK10: Mac . . . 4C 126
SK14: Hyde . . . 1J 27
WA8: Wid . . . 3J 63
Williams Way SK11: Henb . . . 4D 124
WA6: Frod . . . 7G 111
William Wlk. *WA14: Alt . . . 2H 73*
(off Yarwood St.)
William Way WN7: Leigh . . . 1B 6
Willington Av. CH62: East . . . 4K 107
WILLINGTON CORNER . . . 7D 172 (1D 219)
Willington La. CW6: Clot, W'gton . . . 6E 174
CW6: Kel . . . 4C 172
CW6: W'gton . . . 4C 172
(not continuous)
Willington Rd. CH3: Osc . . . 6A 172
CW6: Dud . . . 5C 174
CW6: Wee C, W'gton . . . 6A 172
Willis Rd. SK3: Stoc . . . 6C 52
Willis St. WA1: Warr . . . 6H 41
Williton Wlk. M22: Wyth . . . 2B 76
Willmer Cres. ST7: Mow C . . . 6F 205
Willmer Rd. CH42: Tran . . . 7B 34
WILLOUGHBRIDGE . . . 3B 220
Willoughby Av. M20: Manc . . . 1E 50
Willoughby Cl. M33: Sale . . . 6F 23
WA5: Old H . . . 3A 40
Willoughby Rd. CH44: Wall . . . 7F 13
Willow Av. M41: Urm . . . 1D 22
SK5: Stoc . . . 7J 25
SK8: Chea H . . . 3H 77
WA8: Wid . . . 3H 63
Willoway Rd. CH3: Ches . . . 1E 150
Willow Bank M14: Manc . . . 3A 24
SK8: Chea H . . . 7J 77
WA6: Alv . . . 6D 138
WA15: Timp . . . 6A 48
Willowbank CW5: Nant . . . 1D 196
Willow Bank Cl. SK2: Stoc . . . 5H 53
Willow Bank Ct. M20: Manc . . . 4D 50
Willowbank Dr. SK10: Boll . . . 3F 123
Willowbank Rd. CH42: Tran . . . 2C 60
CH62: N Fer . . . 7G 61
Willowbrook Gdns. M22: Wyth . . . 1J 75
Willowbrow Rd. CH63: Raby . . . 3B 106
Willow Cl. CH2: Upt . . . 2A 146
CW7: Wins . . . 1E 178
SK12: Poy . . . 3D 100
SK16: Duk . . . 3A 10
WA7: Run . . . 7H 89
WA13: Lymm . . . 1A 70
WA16: Mob . . . 2A 118
Willow Ct. CH63: H Beb . . . 7C 60
CW5: Nant . . . 7D 192
CW7: Wins . . . 2J 179
CW10: Mid . . . 2C 180
M14: Manc . . . 3A 24
M33: Sale . . . 6K 23
SK6: Mar . . . 7E 54
SK8: Gat . . . 6C 50
SK10: Mac . . . 1J 125
ST7: Als . . . 5F 203
WA2: Winw . . . 1D 40
Willow Cres. CH2: Ches . . . 6D 146
CW2: Crewe . . . 4K 193
WA1: Padg . . . 4B 42
WA4: Moo . . . 6J 65
Willowcroft Rd. CH44: Wall . . . 2B 34
Willowdale Av. SK8: He Grn . . . 3D 76
Willowdale Way CH66: Gt Sut . . . 7B 134
Willow Dr. CH1: Blac . . . 5E 144
CW6: Bun . . . 6C 188
CW11: S'ach . . . 2J 201
M33: Sale . . . 2J 47
SK9: Hand . . . 3A 98
WA4: Stoc H . . . 4J 67
Willow Fold M43: Droy . . . 2A 8
Willow Grn. CW8: Weav . . . 5G 155
WA16: Knut . . . 2D 116
Willow Grn. La. CW8: L Lei . . . 1D 154
Willow Gro. CH2: Ches . . . 6E 146
CH2: Elt . . . 5E 136
CH46: More . . . 5A 32
CH66: Whit . . . 7C 134
CW8: Barnt . . . 1A 156
M34: Den . . . 7D 8
SK6: Mar . . . 7F 55
Willow Hayes CH3: Ash H . . . 7H 171
Willowherb Cl. CH3: Hunt . . . 5D 150
Willow Ho. CH1: Ches . . . 1F 149
Willow La. CH63: Raby . . . 4C 106
CW4: Goo . . . 6H 165
WA4: App . . . 2H 93
Willow Lawn *SK8: Chea H . . . 2J 77*
(off Vaudrey Dr.)
Willow Lea CH1: Mol . . . 7B 140
CH43: Oxt . . . 1K 59
Willow Mead SK6: Rom . . . 1D 54
Willowmead Dr. SK10: Pres . . . 6H 121
Willow Moss Cl. CH46: More . . . 2D 32
Willow Pk. CH49: Gre . . . 1K 57
M14: Manc . . . 3A 24
SK2: Stoc . . . 5G 53
(off Wicken St.)
Willow Rd. CH4: Ches . . . 5G 149
M31: Part . . . 2G 45
SK6: H Lan . . . 6F 81
Willows, The CH45: Wall . . . 4E 12
CW8: N'ich . . . 7D 156
CW9: Winc . . . 2B 158
CW11: S'ach . . . 2F 201
M31: Part . . . 1H 45
M33: Sale . . . 2H 47
SK4: Stoc . . . 1J 51
WA5: Gt San . . . 7H 39
WA6: Frod . . . 7J 111
WA9: Clo F . . . 1J 37
Willows Cl. CW2: Wis . . . 6B 194
Willows End SK15: Stal . . . 6E 4
Willow Sq. *CW7: Wins . . . 2H 179*
(off Bradbury Rd.)
Willow St. CW12: Cong . . . 3G 183
Willow Tree Ct. M33: Sale . . . 1B 48
WA8: Wid . . . 3K 63
Willow Tree Gro. ST7: Rod H . . . 2G 203
Willow Tree M. SK8: He Grn . . . 5D 76
Willow Tree Rd. WA14: Alt . . . 3H 73
Willow Wlk. M43: Droy . . . 1B 8
Willow Way M20: Manc . . . 1E 50
SK7: Bram . . . 6A 78
SK10: Pres . . . 6H 121
Willow Wood Cl. OL6: Ash L . . . 6A 4
Wilmcote Gdns. SK6: Bred . . . 1K 53
Wilmere La. WA8: Wid . . . 7G 37
Wilmington Rd. M32: S'ord . . . 1G 23
Wilmot Av. WA5: Gt San . . . 6H 39
WILMSLOW . . . 7J 97 (2C 217)
Wilmslow Av. CH66: Gt Sut . . . 3A 134
Wilmslow By-Pass
SK9: Wilm . . . 3F 119
Wilmslow Ct. SK9: Hand . . . 3A 98
Wilmslow Cres. WA4: Thel . . . 1D 68
Wilmslow Dr. CH66: Gt Sut . . . 3A 134
Wilmslow Leisure Cen. . . . 7J 97
Wilmslow Old Rd. SK10: Mot A . . . 1B 120
WA15: Ring . . . 7F 75
WILMSLOW PARK . . . 6A 98
Wilmslow Pk. Nth. SK9: Wilm . . . 7K 97
Wilmslow Pk. Sth. SK9: Wilm . . . 7K 97
Wilmslow Rd. M14: Manc . . . 1A 24
M20: Manc . . . 1D 50
M90: Man A . . . 2A 96
SK7: Woodf . . . 6E 98
SK8: Chea . . . 2F 77
(Schools Hill)
SK8: Chea . . . 7F 51
(Warren Av.)
SK8: Chea, He Grn . . . 3F 77
SK9: Ald E . . . 5F 119
SK9: Hand . . . 1A 98
SK9: Styal . . . 7F 75
SK10: Mot A, Pres . . . 1C 120
(not continuous)
SK10: Pres . . . 7F 99
WA15: Ring . . . 7F 75
Wilmslow Station (Rail) . . . 7K 97
Wilmslow Wlk. SK11: Mac . . . 5B 126
Wilne Rd. CH45: Wall . . . 5G 13
Wilpshire Av. M12: Manc . . . 1E 24
Wilsbury Grange CW8: H'ord . . . 1K 161
Wilsden Rd. WA8: Wid . . . 4B 62
Wilson Av. CH44: Wall . . . 7K 13
Wilson Brook Ct. SK14: Hyde . . . 7K 9
Wilson Cl. WA4: Thel . . . 2D 68
WA8: Wid . . . 4K 63
Wilson Cres. CW9: Los Gra . . . 4D 158
Wilson Dr. CW9: Moult . . . 7E 162
Wilson La. WA3: Ris . . . 6K 17
Wilson Patten St. WA1: Warr . . . 1E 66
Wilson Rd. CH44: Wall . . . 7K 13
SK4: Stoc . . . 7E 24
Wilsons La. CH65: Whit . . . 5C 134
Wilson St. M33: Sale . . . 6G 23
SK14: Hyde . . . 1K 27
WA5: Warr . . . 5E 40
Wilstan Av. CH63: H Beb . . . 1H 85
Wilsthorpe Cl. M19: Manc . . . 5F 25
Wilton Av. SK8: He Grn . . . 6E 76
Wilton Cl. CW9: N'ich . . . 2D 162
Wilton Cres. SK9: Ald E . . . 5E 118
SK11: Mac . . . 6F 125
Wilton Dr. WA15: H'rns . . . 5C 74
Wilton Grange CH48: W Kir . . . 1B 56
Wilton La. WA3: Cul . . . 5A 6
Wilton Paddock M34: Den . . . 6A 8
Wilton Rd. CH42: R Fer . . . 4F 61
Wilton St. CH44: Wall . . . 7H 13
L3: Liv . . . 1K 35
(off Soho St.)
M34: Den . . . 6D 8
SK5: Stoc . . . 1J 25
Wiltshire Av. SK5: Stoc . . . 7B 26
Wiltshire Cl. SK10: Mac . . . 2F 125
WA1: Wool . . . 5D 42
Wiltshire Dr. CW12: Cong . . . 2G 183
Wiltshire Rd. M31: Part . . . 2G 45
Wiltshire Wlk. *SK10: Mac . . . 2G 125*
(off Wiltshire Cl.)
Wilwick La. SK11: Mac . . . 5G 125
Wimbledon Dr. SK3: Stoc . . . 5A 52
Wimbledon St. CH45: Wall . . . 6H 13
WIMBOLDS TRAFFORD . . . 4D 142
Wimborne Av. CH61: Thin . . . 1J 83
Wimborne Cl. SK8: Chea H . . . 1A 78
Wimborne Way CH61: Irby . . . 6A 58
Wimbrick Cl. CH46: More . . . 4C 32
Wimbrick Ct. CH46: More . . . 4C 32
Wimbrick Hey CH46: More . . . 4C 32
Winbolt St. SK2: Stoc . . . 1G 79
Wincanton Av. M23: Wyth . . . 4D 48
WINCHAM . . . 2J 157 (3A 216)
Wincham Av. CW9: Winc . . . 2J 157
Wincham Bus. Pk. CW9: Winc . . . 2J 157
Wincham La. CW9: Winc . . . 2J 157
Wincham Pk. . . . 3H 157
Wincham Rd. M33: Sale . . . 2J 47
Winchcombe Cl. WN7: Leigh . . . 1E 6
Winchester Av. CH65: Ell P . . . 4F 135
M34: Den . . . 2E 26
WA5: Gt San . . . 7A 40
Winchester Cl. CW2: Shav . . . 4B 198
SK9: Wilm . . . 2D 118
Winchester Ct. *CW2: West . . . 4K 199*
(off Abbey Pk. Way)
Winchester Dr. CH44: Wall . . . 7G 13
M33: Sale . . . 7C 22
SK4: Stoc . . . 2K 51
SK10: Mac . . . 4G 125
Winchester Pk. M20: Manc . . . 1B 50
Winchester Pl. WA8: Wid . . . 5C 62
Winchester Rd. M32: S'ord . . . 1C 22
M41: Urm . . . 1C 22
SK16: Duk . . . 3B 10
WA15: Hale . . . 4C 74
Winchester Sq. CH4: Ches . . . 6G 149
WINCLE . . . 1D 221
Wincle Av. SK12: Poy . . . 4F 101
Windermere Av. CH2: Ches . . . 4D 146
M33: Sale . . . 2D 48
M34: Den . . . 1K 25
WA2: Warr . . . 1G 41
WA8: Wid . . . 1H 63
Windermere Cl. CH64: L Nes . . . 1D 130
Windermere Ct. *CH41: Birk . . . 7B 34*
(off Penrith St.)
Windermere Dr. CW12: Cong . . . 4C 182
SK9: Ald E . . . 6E 118
Windermere Rd. CH43: Noc . . . 7F 33
CH65: Ell P . . . 6E 134
CW2: Crewe . . . 4J 193
CW7: Wins . . . 2D 178
M41: Urm . . . 2B 22
SK1: Stoc . . . 6F 53
SK6: H Lan . . . 5E 80
SK9: Hand . . . 2K 97
SK14: Hyde . . . 5H 9
SK15: Stal . . . 6B 4
SK16: Duk . . . 2H 9
Windermere St. WA8: Wid . . . 1H 63
Windfield Gdns. CH66: L Sut . . . 1K 133
Windfields Cl. SK8: Chea H . . . 2K 77
Windgate Ri. SK15: Carrb . . . 4E 4
Windings, The CW10: Mid . . . 2B 180
Windle Ct. SK2: Stoc . . . 7J 53
WA3: Birc . . . 7H 17
Windle Ct. Ind. Est. CH64: Nest . . . 5H 105
WINDLE HILL . . . 7B 106 (3B 214)
WINDLEHURST . . . 5D 80
Windlehurst Ct. SK6: H Lan . . . 6D 80
Windlehurst Hall SK6: H Lan . . . 4F 81
Windlehurst Old Rd. SK6: Mar . . . 3F 81
Windlehurst Rd. SK6: H Lan, Mar . . . 5D 80
Windmill Cl. CW3: Bue . . . 5G 211
M34: Den . . . 1A 26
WA4: App . . . 7G 67
Windmill Dr. CW3: Audl . . . 6B 210
Windmill Gdns. CH43: Bid . . . 4F 33
WINDMILL HILL . . . 4E 90
Windmill Hill Av. E.
WA7: Nort, Win H . . . 4F 91
Windmill Hill Av. Nth. WA7: Win H . . . 3F 91

Woodford Rd.—Wrengate Ho.

Woodford Rd. CH62: N Fer 5G 61
SK7: Bram, Woodf 1H 99
SK9: Wilm 6E 98
SK12: Poy 2K 99
Wood Gdns. SK9: Ald E 5G 119
Woodgate Av. ST7: Chu L 4H 203
Woodgate Cl. SK6: Bred 1K 53
Wood Grn. CH43: Bid 4F 33
Wood Gro. M34: Den 6E 8
SK6: W'ley 6F 27
Woodhall Av. CH4: Salt 5F 149
CH44: Wall 7K 13
Woodhall Cl. SK7: Woodf 3H 99
WA5: Gt San 4J 39
Woodhall Cres. SK5: Stoc 7K 25
Woodhall Rd. SK5: Stoc 7J 25
Woodham Cl. CW8: H'ord 1B 162
Woodham Gro. CH64: L Nes 3D 130
Woodham Rd. M23: Wyth 3F 49
Woodhatch Rd. WA7: B'vale 2D 112
Woodhead Dr. WA15: Hale 4K 73
Woodhead Rd. CH62: P Sun 7H 61
WA15: Hale 4K 73
Woodhead Row CH62: P Sun 1C 86
Woodhead St. CH62: N Fer 6G 61
Wood Heath Way
CH62: East 7G 87
WOODHEY 6D 60
Woodhey Ct. CH63: H Beb 5E 60
M33: Sale 3J 47
Wood Hey Gro. M34: Den 1F 27
Woodhey Gro. CH63: H Beb 6E 60
Woodhey Rd. CH63: H Beb 6E 60
Woodheys SK4: Stoc 1H 51
Woodheys Cotts. SK6: Mar B 7F 29
Woodheys Dr. M33: Sale 3H 47
Woodhouse Cl. WA3: Birc 1E 42
Woodhouse End Rd. SK11: Gaw 4C 128
Woodhouse La. M22: Wyth 1K 75
M33: Sale 3F 47
(not continuous)
M90: Man A 6K 75
SK11: Gaw 4B 128
WA14: Dun M 1K 71
(not continuous)
Woodhouse La. E. WA15: Timp 3A 48
Woodhouse La. Nth. M22: Wyth 5K 75
WOODHOUSE PARK 4H 75
Woodhouse Pk. Lifestyle Cen. 4H 75
Woodhouse Rd. M22: Wyth 5K 75
WA14: Dun M 1B 72
WOODHOUSES
M33 2G 47 (1B 216)
OL7 1D 217
WA6 3F 139 (3D 215)
Woodhouses La. WA6: Frod 3F 139
Woodhouses Pk. WA6: Frod 3F 139
Wooding Cl. M31: Part 7D 20
Woodin Rd. CH42: R Fer 5F 61
Woodkind Hey CH63: Spit 4A 86
Woodlake Av. M21: Chor H 1J 49
Woodlan Ct. CW6: Utk 3B 176
Woodland Av. CH47: Meols 3E 30
CW1: Crewe 3F 195
CW5: Nant 2D 196
SK7: H Gro 4J 79
WA8: Wid 4F 63
WA13: Lymm 3C 70
Woodland Bank CH2: Mic T 1J 147
Woodland Cl. SK11: Chel 5C 166
Woodland Ct. ST7: Als 4E 202
Woodland Dr. CH45: N Bri 4J 13
CH49: Woodc 2D 58
WA13: Lymm 3B 70
Woodland Gdns. CW1: Crewe 7J 191
Woodland Gro. CH42: R Fer 5E 60
Woodland Rd. CH42: R Fer 5E 60
CH48: W Kir 3F 57
CH49: Woodc 2D 58
CH65: Whit 6C 134
M19: Manc 3D 24
ST7: Rod H 1F 203
WOODLANDS
M41 2F 21
SK15 3E 10
Woodlands CW8: H'ord 1A 162
SK14: Hyde 1A 28
SK15: Stal 3D 10
Woodlands, The CH41: Birk 7C 34
CH49: Upt 6C 32
CW8: Winn 5D 156
CW9: Winc 1C 158
Woodlands Av. CH1: Ches 6J 145
CW12: Cong 2F 183
M32: S'ord 1J 23
M41: Urm 1F 21
M44: Irlam 1D 20
SK6: W'ley 6F 27
SK8: Chea H 3J 77
Woodlands Cvn. Pk. WA16: All 5C 164
Woodlands Cl. CH64: Park 7G 105
CW6: Cote 5B 176
SK8: Chea H 5J 77
SK13: Tint 1K 11
SK14: B'tom 2G 29
SK15: Stal 3E 10
Woodlands Ct. SK2: Stoc 4J 53
SK9: Ald E 7F 119
WA15: Timp 7J 47
(off Woodlands Parkway)
WA16: Knut 3F 117
Woodlands Cres. WA16: H Leg 2H 95
Woodlands Dr. CH2: Ches 6B 146
CH61: Barns 2A 84
CW2: West 4J 199
CW4: Goo 6J 165
M33: Sale 3C 48
SK2: Stoc 4G 53
SK6: W'ley 6F 27
WA4: Thel 2D 68
WA16: Knut 3F 117
Woodlands End SK11: Chel 5C 166
Woodlands Gro. CW8: Barnt 2J 155
SK14: B'tom 2G 29
Woodlands La. CH3: Ches 1D 150
CH48: W Kir 4E 56
WA15: Timp 7J 47
Woodlands Pk. SK14: Hyde 1B 28
Woodlands Pk. Rd. SK2: Stoc 4H 53
Woodlands Parkway
WA15: Timp 6J 47
Woodlands Rd. CH3: Hunt 5D 150
CH4: Ches 4H 149
CH61: Irby 1F 83
CH64: Park 7G 105
CW8: H'ord 1A 162
M33: Sale 6H 23
SK4: Stoc 2F 51
SK9: Hand 3B 98
SK9: Wilm 5G 97
SK11: Mac 6K 125
SK12: Dis 7G 81
SK15: Stal 3E 10
WA14: Alt 1J 213 (7H 47)
WA15: Alt 1J 213 (7H 47)
Woodlands Rd. E. CW8: H'ord 1B 162
Woodlands Way CW6: Tarp 1J 175
Woodland Ter. M31: Part 1G 45
Woodland Vw. CH66: Chil T 7C 108
SK14: Hyde 7A 10
Woodland Wlk. CH62: Brom 5C 86
WA7: Cast 5C 90
Wood La. CH45: Wall 5E 12
CH49: Gre 7A 32
CH64: Burt 6G 131
CH64: Park 5F 105
CH64: W'ston 6F 107
CW4: Goo 6G 165
CW6: Clot 4D 174 & 3A 176
CW8: Weav 5H 155
CW12: Cong 2K 183
M31: Part 1F 45
SK6: Mar 7D 54
WA4: App 5J 67
WA7: Murd 1E 112
WA7: Sut W 3B 112
WA15: Timp 7A 48
WA16: Mob 2B 102
Wood La. E. SK10: Adl 6G 101
WOOD LANE END 5G 101
Wood La. Nth. SK10: Adl 6G 101
Wood La. Sth. SK10: Adl 7F 101
Wood La. W. SK10: Adl 6E 100
Woodlark Cl. CW7: Wins 4H 179
Woodlea WA15: Alt 1K 73
Woodlea Av. CH2: Upt 3C 146
M19: Manc 5B 24
Woodlea Cl. CH62: Brom 2J 107
Woodlea Ct. CW8: N'ich 6C 156
Woodlea Dr. SK10: Boll 3B 122
Woodleigh WA14: Alt 7E 46
Woodleigh Ct. SK9: Ald E 5F 119
WOODLEY 6F 27 (1D 217)
Woodley Bank SK14: Hyde 5H 27
Woodley Cl. SK2: Stoc 5H 53
Woodley Fold WA5: Penk 2H 65
Woodley Pct. SK6: W'ley 6F 27
Woodley Station (Rail) 6G 27
Woodman St. SK1: Stoc 5H 213 (2C 52)
Wood Mt. WA15: Timp 7B 48
Woodmount Cl. SK6: Rom 2E 54
Woodnoth Dr. CW2: Shav 2C 198
Wood Orchard La. CW3: Audl 7C 210
Woodpecker Cl. CH49: Upt 7A 32
WA3: Birc 7A 18
Woodpecker Dr. CW9: N'ich 2E 162
Woodridge WA7: Win H 5E 90
Woodridings WA14: Bow 2F 73
Wood Rd. M33: Sale 3B 48
WA15: Timp 3B 48
(not continuous)
Woodrow Way M44: Irlam 4C 20
Woodroyd Cl. SK7: Bram 4B 78
Woodruffe Gdns. SK6: Rom 4A 54
Woodruff St. L8: Liv 1K 61
Woodruff Wlk. M31: Part 1H 45
Woods, The WA14: Alt 6J 47
Wood's Cl. WA16: Oll 7K 117
WOODSEATS 5H 29
Woodseats La. SK13: Char 4H 29
Woodseaves Cl. M44: Irlam 2E 20
WOODS END 1H 21
Woodsend Circ. M41: Urm 1G 21
(not continuous)
Woodsend Cres. Rd. M41: Urm 1G 21
Woodsend Rd. Sth. M41: Urm 1H 21
(not continuous)
Woods Gro. SK8: Chea H 6K 77
WOODSIDE 4K 171
Woodside CH65: Whit 6E 134
SK4: Stoc 3H 51
SK11: Sidd 1D 168
ST7: Chu L 4H 205
WA16: Knut 4F 117
Woodside Av. CH46: More 5A 32
CW2: Crewe 5K 193
M19: Manc 6C 24
ST7: Als 5F 203
WA6: Frod 1K 139
Woodside Bus. Pk. CH41: Birk 5E 34
Woodside Ct. CH1: Ches 6K 145
Woodside Dr. CW11: S'ach 3G 201
SK6: H Lan 6E 80
SK14: Hyde 2K 27
Woodside Ferry App. CH41: Birk 5E 34
Woodside Gdns. M31: Part 7C 20
(off Lock La.)
Woodside La. CW2: Crewe 5K 193
SK12: Poy 2D 100
WA13: Lymm 4D 70
Woodside M. SK7: Bram 3A 78
Woodside Rd. CH1: Blac 5D 144
CH61: Irby 7B 58
WA5: Gt San 5H 39
Woodside St. SK15: Carrb 3F 5
Woodside Tennis Club 7E 80
Woodside Ter. CW9: N'ich 2G 163
Woods La. CW8: Crow, Cudd 5K 153
SK8: Chea H 6K 77
WOODS MOOR 1F 79
Woodsmoor La. SK2: Stoc 1E 78
SK3: Stoc 1E 78
Woodsmoor Station (Rail) 1F 79
Woodsome Cl. CH65: Whit 7D 134
Woodsome Dr. CH65: Whit 7D 134
Woodsorrel Rd. CH41: Birk 5J 33
Woods Rd. M44: Irlam 3C 20
Woodstock Av. SK5: Stoc 6J 25
SK8: Chea H 6J 77
WA12: New W 1G 15
Woodstock Cl. SK10: Mac 2G 125
WN7: Leigh 1E 6
Woodstock Ct. SK9: Hand 1B 98
Woodstock Cres. SK6: W'ley 6F 27
Woodstock Dr. CW10: Mid 7E 180
Woodstock Gdns. WA4: App 7K 67
Woodstock Grn. SK5: Stoc 5K 25
Woodstock Gro. WA8: Wid 3D 62
Woodstock Rd. CH44: Wall 1K 33
SK6: W'ley 6F 27
WA14: B'ath 4G 47
Wood St. CH41: Birk 5C 34
CH47: Hoy 5C 30
CH62: P Sun 1B 86
CW2: Crewe 4D 194
CW12: Cong 3F 183
L1: Liv 3J 35
M34: Den 6E 8
SK3: Stoc 7F 213 (4B 52)
SK8: Chea 6F 51
SK11: Mac 5A 126
(not continuous)
SK14: H'rth 2J 11
SK14: Hyde 1K 27
SK15: Stal 7B 4
SK16: Duk 4H 9
ST7: Mow C 5G 205
WA1: Warr 6H 41
WA8: Wid 4J 63
WA14: Alt 2J 213 (1H 73)
Woodthorn Cl. WA4: Dare 2H 91
Woodthorpe Dr. SK8: Chea H 3J 77
Wood Top Cl. SK2: Stoc 5J 53
Woodvale WA14: Bow 3G 73
Woodvale Cl. CH43: Bid 4F 33
WA2: Padg 3J 41
Woodvale Ct. CH49: Woodc 4D 58
(off Childwall Grn.)
Woodvale Rd. CH66: L Sut 2K 133
WA16: Knut 5E 116
Wood Vw. M22: N'den 3K 49
Woodview Av. CH44: Wall 2D 34
M19: Manc 6C 24
Woodview Cres. WA8: Wid 5A 62
Woodview Rd. WA8: Wid 5A 62
Woodville Dr. M33: Sale 6F 23
SK6: Mar 7D 54
SK15: Stal 6E 4
Woodville Gro. SK5: Stoc 5J 25
Woodville Pl. WA8: Wid 4D 62
Woodville Rd. CH42: Tran 1B 60
M33: Sale 6F 23
WA14: Alt 3F 213 (1G 73)
Woodward Rd. CH42: R Fer 5F 61
Woodward St. CW8: Weav 4G 155
Woodward Wlk. CH3: Tar 5C 170
Woodway CH49: Gre 1A 58
Woodway Ct. CH62: Brom 4F 86
Woodwise La. M23: Wyth 3E 48
Woodyear Rd. CH62: Brom 7E 86
Woolacombe Cl. WA4: Warr 3H 67
Woolaston Dr. ST7: Als 6E 202
Woolden Rd. M44: Cad 4H 19
Wooler Cl. CH46: More 4K 31
Woollam Dr. CH66: L Sut 1K 133
Woolley Av. SK12: Poy 4C 100
WOOLLEY BRIDGE 3J 11
Woolley Bri. SK13: Had 3K 11
Woolley Bri. Rd. SK13: Had 3K 11
Woolley Cl. SK14: H'rth 3J 11
WA6: Frod 5K 111
Woolley La. SK14: H'rth 1J 11
(Meadowbank)
SK14: H'rth 6K 11
(Samuel St.)
Woolley Mill La. SK13: Tint 1J 11
Woolley Ter. SK16: Duk 1G 9
(off Queen St.)
Woolmer Cl. WA3: Birc 5C 18
WOOLSTON 5C 42 (1A 216)
Woolston Av. CW12: Cong 4H 183
Woolston Dr. CW2: Hou 5E 198
Woolston Grange Av. WA1: Wool 2C 42
WA2: Padg 2C 42
Woolston Hall WA1: Wool 5D 42
Woolston Leisure Cen. 5D 42
WOOLTON 2C 215
Woolton Ct. CH66: Ell P 7G 109
Woolton Hall M14: Manc 2A 24
WOORE 3B 220
Woore Rd. CW3: Audl, Bue 5C 210
Wootton St. SK14: Hyde 6J 9
Worcester Av. M23: Wyth 4F 49
M34: Den 2F 27
SK5: Stoc 6B 26
Worcester Cl. SK6: Rom 3A 54
WA5: Gt San 7A 40
Worcester Pl. CH1: Blac 6H 145
Worcester Rd. CH43: Bid 4G 33
M33: Sale 1H 47
SK8: Chea H 1J 77
Worcester St. CH65: Ell P 2E 134
Worcester Wlk. CH65: Ell P 2E 134
Wordsworth Av. CH42: R Fer 4E 60
WA4: Warr 2F 67
WA8: Wid 5F 63
WA9: Sut M 1G 37
Wordsworth Cl. CW2: Wis 5K 193
CW11: Ett H 3B 200
SK16: Duk 3B 10
Wordsworth Cres. CH1: Blac 5G 145
Wordsworth Dr. CW1: Crewe 2F 195
Wordsworth Ho. SK10: Mac 3G 125
(off Priory Ct.)
Wordsworth M. CH1: Blac 5H 145
Wordsworth Rd. M34: Den 4F 27
SK5: Stoc 2G 25
Wordsworth Sq. CH1: Blac 5G 145
Wordsworth Wlk. CH48: W Kir 5C 56
Wordsworth Way CH66: Gt Sut 7A 134
ST7: Als 5E 202
Works La. CW9: N'ich 3K 157
World Mus. Liverpool 2J 35
World Way M90: Man A 5H 75
WORLESTON 1D 192 (2A 220)
Worleston Cl. CW10: Mid 6C 180
Worrall St. CW12: Cong 3G 183
SK3: Stoc 5C 52
(not continuous)
Worsborough Av. WA5: Gt San 7K 39
Worsdell Cl. CW2: Crewe 6E 194
Worsdell Ho. CW1: Crewe 2C 194
(off Blount Cl.)
WORSLEY 1B 216
Worsley Av. CH1: Sau 2B 144
WA4: Westy 1K 67
Worsley Ct. M14: Manc 1A 24
Worsley Cres. SK2: Stoc 5G 53
Worsley Dr. CW12: Cong 5K 183
Worsley Gro. M19: Manc 2D 24
Worsley Rd. WA4: Walt 4F 67
Worsley St. WA5: Warr 5D 40
Worth Ct. SK12: Poy 4C 100
WORTHENBURY 3C 219
Worthing Cl. SK2: Stoc 6H 53
Worthing St. CW9: N'ich 5H 157
Worthington Av. M31: Part 1H 45
Worthington Cl. CW5: Nant 2E 196
SK11: Henb 4D 124
SK14: Hat 1F 29
WA7: Pal F 7C 90
Worthington Ct. CH2: Ches 6A 146
M33: Sale 7K 23
Worthington Rd. M33: Sale 7K 23
M34: Den 2G 27
Worthington St. SK15: Stal 1A 10
Worthington Way M34: Den 6D 8
Worth's La. M34: Den 4F 27
Wray Av. WA9: Clo F 1K 37
Wray Cl. M22: Wyth 1K 75
Wray Ct. WA9: Clo F 1K 37
Wray Gdns. M19: Manc 3F 25
Wrayton Lodge M33: Sale 1B 48
WRECSAM 2B 218
Wrekin Av. M23: Wyth 2G 75
Wrekin Way CH4: Ches 5G 149
WRENBURY 2H 209 (3D 219)
Wrenbury Cl. CH43: Oxt 3J 59
WA7: Sut W 3B 112
Wrenbury Cres. SK3: Stoc 6A 52
Wrenbury Dr. CW9: N'ich 1D 162
SK8: Chea 6G 51
Wrenbury Hall Dr. CW5: Wren 1K 209
WRENBURY HEATH 1K 209
Wrenbury Heath Rd.
CW5: Sou, Wren 4F 209
Wrenbury Ind. Est. CW5: Wren 4K 209
Wrenbury Rd. CW5: Ast, Wren 4K 209
SY13: Marb 6C 208
Wrenbury Station (Rail) 3K 209
Wrenbury Wlk. M33: Sale 1E 48
(off Mottram Rd.)
Wren Cl. M34: Aude 1B 8
SK2: Stoc 7K 53
SK10: Mac 3H 125
WA3: Birc 7A 18
WA7: Pal F 1C 112
Wrengate Ho. M20: Manc 1B 50

HOSPITALS, TREATMENT CENTRES, WALK-IN CENTRES and HOSPICES covered by this atlas.

N.B. Where it is not possible to name these facilities on the map,
the reference given is for the road in which they are situated.

ALEXANDRA BMI HOSPITAL, THE 6F **51**
Mill Lane
CHEADLE
SK8 2PX
Tel: 0161 4283656

ALTRINCHAM GENERAL HOSPITAL 2H **213** (1H **73**)
Market Street
ALTRINCHAM
WA14 1PE
Tel: 0161 9286111

ALTRINCHAM PRIORY HOSPITAL 5A **74**
Rappax Road
Hale
ALTRINCHAM
WA15 0NX
Tel: 0161 9040050

ARROWE PARK HOSPITAL 4D **58**
Arrowe Park Road
WIRRAL
CH49 5PE
Tel: 0151 6785111

ASHTON HOUSE HOSPITAL 1A **60**
26 Village Road
Oxton
PRENTON
CH43 5SR
Tel: 0151 6539660

BEECHWOOD CANCER CARE CENTRE 7B **52**
Chelford Grove
STOCKPORT
SK3 8LS
Tel: 0161 4760384

BOWMERE HOSPITAL 5J **145**
Countess of Chester Health Park
Liverpool Road
CHESTER
CH2 1BQ
Tel: 01244 364582

CASUALTY PLUS WALK-IN CENTRE (CHEADLE) 6F **51**
The Alexandra BMI Hospital
Mill Lane
CHEADLE
SK8 2PX
Tel: 0161 4282161

CHEADLE ROYAL HOSPITAL 3E **76**
100 Wilmslow Road
CHEADLE
SK8 3DG
Tel: 0161 4289511

CHERRY TREE HOSPITAL 7G **53**
Cherry Tree Lane
STOCKPORT
SK2 7PZ
Tel: 0161 4831010

CHESHIRE & MERSEYSIDE NHS TREATMENT CENTRE
....1B **112**
Earls Way
RUNCORN
WA7 2HH
Tel: 01928 574001

CHESHIRE SPIRE HOSPITAL 5H **93**
Fir Tree Close
Stretton
WARRINGTON
WA4 4LU
Tel: 0845 6022500

CLAIRE HOUSE CHILDREN'S HOSPICE 5H **85**
Clatterbridge Road
WIRRAL
CH63 4JD
Tel: 0151 3344626

CLATTERBRIDGE CENTRE FOR ONCOLOGY
....5H **85**
Clatterbridge Road
WIRRAL
CH63 4JY
Tel: 0151 3341155

CLATTERBRIDGE HOSPITAL 5H **85**
Clatterbridge Road
WIRRAL
CH63 4JY
Tel: 0151 3344000

CONGLETON WAR MEMORIAL HOSPITAL
....5H **183**
Canal Road
CONGLETON
CW12 3AR
Tel: 01260 294800

COUNTESS OF CHESTER HOSPITAL 4J **145**
The Countess of Chester Health Park
Liverpool Road
CHESTER
CH2 1UL
Tel: 01244 365000

EAST CHESHIRE HOSPICE 3G **125**
Millbank Drive
MACCLESFIELD
SK10 3DR
Tel: 01625 610364

ELLESMERE PORT HOSPITAL 6C **134**
114 Chester Rd.
Whitby
ELLESMERE PORT
CH65 6SG
Tel: 01244 365000

FRANCIS HOUSE CHILDREN'S HOSPICE 2E **50**
390 Parrswood Road
MANCHESTER
M20 5NA
Tel: 0161 4344118

GROSVENOR (CHESTER) NUFFIELD HOSPITAL
....5K **149**
Wrexham Road
CHESTER
CH4 7QP
Tel: 01244 680444

HALTON GENERAL HOSPITAL 1B **112**
Hospital Way
RUNCORN
WA7 2DA
Tel: 01928 714567

HALTON HAVEN HOSPICE 2E **112**
Barnfield Avenue.
Murdishaw
RUNCORN
WA7 6EP
Tel: 01928 712728

HOLLINS PARK HOSPITAL 5J **15**
Hollins Lane
WARRINGTON
WA2 8WA
Tel: 01925 664000

HOSPICE OF THE GOOD SHEPHERD 5D **140**
Gordon Lane
Backford
CHESTER
CH2 4DG
Tel: 01244 851091

HYDE DAY HOSPITAL 2A **28**
Grange Road South
HYDE
SK14 5NY
Tel: 0161 6043445

KNUTSFORD & DISTRICT COMMUNITY HOSPITAL
....4D **116**
Bexton Road
KNUTSFORD
WA16 0BT
Tel: 01565 757220

LEIGHTON HOSPITAL 4D **190**
Middlewich Road
CREWE
CW1 4QJ
Tel: 01270 255141

MACCLESFIELD DISTRICT GENERAL HOSPITAL 4J **125**
Victoria Road
MACCLESFIELD
SK10 3BL
Tel: 01625 421000

MEADOWS HOSPITAL, THE 5J **53**
Owens Farm Drive
STOCKPORT
SK2 5EQ
Tel: 0161 419 6000

MURRAYFIELD SPIRE HOSPITAL 1B **84**
Holmwood Drive
Heswall
WIRRAL
CH61 1AU
Tel: 0845 6002110

NEIL CLIFFE CANCER CARE CENTRE 1F **75**
Wythenshawe Hospital, Southmoor Road
MANCHESTER
M23 9LT
Tel: 0161 2912912

NEWTON COMMUNITY HOSPITAL 1E **14**
Bradlegh Road
NEWTON-LE-WILLOWS
WA12 8RB
Tel: 01925 222731

NHS WALK-IN CENTRE (BURNAGE) 5C **24**
within Burnage Health Care Centre
347 Burnage Lane
MANCHESTER
M19 1EW
Tel: 0161 443 0600

NHS WALK-IN CENTRE (LIVERPOOL CITY CENTRE)
....3J **35**
Unit 4, Charlotte Row
53 Great Charlotte Street
LIVERPOOL
L1 1HU
Tel: 0151 285 3535

NHS WALK-IN CENTRE (WIRRAL) 7H **13**
Victoria Central Hospital, Mill Lane
WALLASEY
CH44 5UF
Tel: 0151 678 5111

NHS WALK-IN CENTRE (WIRRAL ARROWE PARK) . . .4D **58**
Arrowe Park Hospital
Arrowe Park Road
WIRRAL
CH49 5PE
Tel: 0151 488 3706

NHS WALK-IN CENTRE (WYTHENSHAWE FORUM) 3J **75**
Forum Square
Civic Centre
Simonsway
Wythenshawe
MANCHESTER
M22 5RX
Tel: 0161 490 8082

REGENCY SPIRE HOSPITAL .4J **125**
West Street
MACCLESFIELD
SK11 8DW
Tel: 01625 501150

ST ANN'S HOSPICE (HEALD GREEN) 3E **76**
St Ann's Road North
Heald Green
CHEADLE
SK8 3SZ
Tel: 0161 4378136

ST CATHERINE'S HOSPITAL (BIRKENHEAD) 1C **60**
Church Road
BIRKENHEAD
CH42 0LQ
Tel: 0151 6787272

ST JOHN'S HOSPICE IN WIRRAL 5J **85**
Mount Road
Higher Bebington
WIRRAL
CH63 6JE
Tel: 0151 3342778

ST LUKE'S HOSPICE (CHESHIRE) 4F **179**
Grosvenor House, Queensway
WINSFORD
CW7 4AW
Tel: 01606 551246

ST ROCCO'S HOSPICE 5C **40**
Lockton Lane
WARRINGTON
WA5 0BW
Tel: 01925 575780

SOUTH CHESHIRE PRIVATE HOSPITAL 4D **190**
Leighton
CREWE
CW1 4QP
Tel: 01270 500411

STEPPING HILL HOSPITAL 1G **79**
Poplar Grove
STOCKPORT
SK2 7JE
Tel: 0161 4831010

TAMESIDE GENERAL HOSPITAL 5A **4**
Fountain Street
ASHTON-UNDER-LYNE
OL6 9RW
Tel: 0161 3316000

TARPORLEY WAR MEMORIAL HOSPITAL 2J **175**
14 Park Road
TARPORLEY
CW6 0AP
Tel: 01829 732436

VICTORIA CENTRAL HOSPITAL 7H **13**
Mill Lane
WALLASEY
CH44 5UF
Tel: 0151 6785111

VICTORIA INFIRMARY 5D **156**
Winnington Hill
NORTHWICH
CW8 1AW
Tel: 01606 564000

WARRINGTON HOSPITAL 6D **40**
Lovely Lane
WARRINGTON
WA5 1QG
Tel: 01925 635911

WILLOW WOOD HOSPICE 6A **4**
Willow Wood Close
ASHTON-UNDER-LYNE
OL6 6SL
Tel: 0161 3301100

WYTHENSHAWE HOSPITAL 1F **75**
Southmoor Road
Wythenshawe
MANCHESTER
M23 9LT
Tel: 0161 998 7070

The representation on the maps of a road, track or footpath is no evidence of the existence of a right of way.

The Grid on this map is the National Grid taken from Ordnance Survey® mapping with the permission of the Controller of Her Majesty's Stationery Office.

SAFETY CAMERA INFORMATION

Safety camera locations are publicised by the Safer Roads Partnership who operate them in order to encourage drivers to comply with speed limits at these sites. It is the driver's absolute responsibility to be aware of and to adhere to speed limits at all times.

By showing this safety camera information it is the intention of Geographers' A-Z Map Company Ltd., to encourage safe driving and greater awareness of speed limits and vehicle speed. Data accurate at time of printing.